P9-EMO-303

PAGE 54 — ON THE ROAD

YOUR COMPLETE DESTINATION GUIDE
In-depth reviews, detailed listings
and insider tips

PAGE 847 — SURVIVAL GUIDE

VITAL PRACTICAL INFORMATION TO
HELP YOU HAVE A SMOOTH TRIP

THIS EDITION WRITTEN AND RESEARCHED BY

John Noble,

Kate Armstrong, Ray Bartlett, Gregor Clark, John Hecht, Beth Kohn,
Tom Masters, Freda Moon, Brendan Sainsbury, Lucas Vidgen, Luke Waterson

welcome to
Mexico

An Outdoor Life

From the southern jungles to the smoking, snowcapped volcanoes and the cactus-dotted northern deserts, all surrounded by 10,000km of coast strung with sandy beaches and wildlife-rich lagoons, Mexico is an endless adventure for the senses. A climate that ranges from temperate to hot almost everywhere makes for a life spent largely in the open air. Take it easy by lying on a beach, dining alfresco or strolling the streets of some pretty town, or get out and snorkel warm Caribbean reefs, hike mountain cloud forests or take a boat in search of dolphins or whales.

Soul Food

Mexico is packed with history and culture. Its pre-Hispanic civilizations built some of the world's great archaeological monuments, from Teotihuacán's towering pyramids to the exquisitely decorated temples of the Maya. The Spanish colonial era left beautiful towns full of gorgeous, tree-shaded plazas and elaborately carved stone churches and mansions. Modern Mexico has seen a surge of great art from the likes of Diego Rivera and Frida Kahlo. Top-class museums and galleries around the country document Mexico's long and fascinating history and its endless creative verve. Popular culture is just as vibrant, from the underground dance clubs of Mexico City to the sentimental crooning of *ranchera* singers.

Jungles, deserts; teeming cities, one-street pueblos; fiesta fireworks, Frida's angst: Mexico conjures up so many contradictory images. One thing's for sure: no preconceptions will ever live up to the reality.

(left) Church in Mexico's northern deserts
(below) Colorful ceramic skulls

Travel for All

Travel in Mexico is what you make it and the country caters to all types of voyager. Stay in pampered resorts, budget beach huts or colonial mansions. Eat cutting-edge fusion food in chic gourmet restaurants or *abuela's* (grandmother's) recipes at a busy market *comedor* (food stall). Getting from A to B is easy thanks to comfortable buses that run almost anywhere and an extensive domestic flight network. Or try renting a car: Mexico has some excellent roads, and outside the cities traffic is mostly light.

Los Mexicanos

At the heart of your Mexican experience will be the Mexican people. A superdiverse crew from city hipsters to shy indigenous villagers, they're justly renowned for their love of color and frequent fiestas but are also philosophical folk, to whom timetables (while worthy of respect) are less important than *simpatía* (empathy). You will rarely find Mexicans less than courteous; they're often positively charming, and they know how to please their guests. They may despair of ever being well governed, but they are fiercely proud of Mexico, their one-of-a-kind homeland with all its variety, tight-knit family networks, beautiful-ugly cities, deep-rooted traditions, unique agave-based liquors and sensationally tasty, chili-laden food. It doesn't take long to understand why.

› Mexico

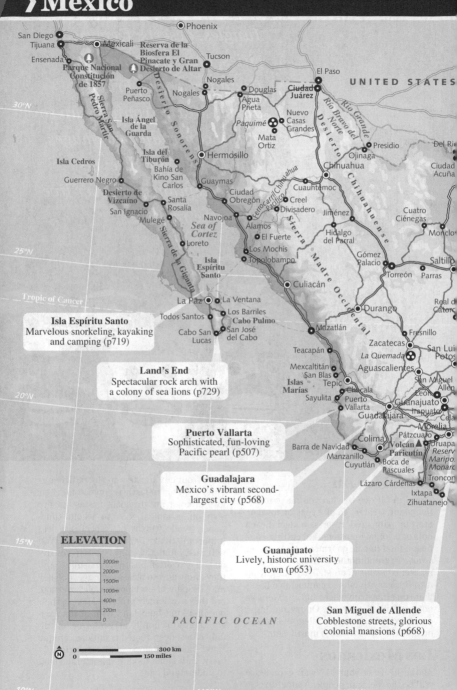

Phoenix

San Diego
Tijuana
Ensenada
Mexicali
Parque Nacional
Constitución
de 1857
Reserva de la
Biosfera El
Pinacate y Gran
Desierto de Altar
Tucson

Sierra San Pedro Mártir

Isla Ángel
de la
Guarda

Isla Cedros

Guerrero Negro

Desierto de
Vizcaíno

San Ignacio

Mulegé

Santa
Rosalía

Isla del
Tiburón

Bahía de
Kino San
Carlos

Sea of
Cortez

Loreto

Isla
Espíritu
Santo

La Paz
La Ventana

Los Barriles
Cabo Pulmo
San José
del Cabo

Todos Santos

Cabo San
Lucas

Puerto
Peñasco

Nogales

Nogales

Douglas
Agua
Prieta

Paquimé

Mata
Ortiz

Hermosillo

Guaymas

Ciudad
Obregón

Navojoa

Álamos

El Fuerte

Los Mochis

Topolobampo

Culiacán

Mazatlán

Teacapán

Mexcaltitán

San Blas

Islas
Marías

Sayulita

Chacala

Tepic

Puerto
Vallarta

Barra de Navidad

Colima

Manzanillo

Cuyutlán

Boca de
Pascuales

Lázaro Cárdenas

Ixtapa
Zihuatanejo

El Paso

UNITED STATES

Ciudad
Juárez

Nuevo
Casas
Grandes

Presidio

Ojinaga

Chihuahua

Del Río

Ciudad
Acuña

Ferrocarril Chihuahua Pacífico

Cuauhtémoc

Creel

Divisadero

Jiménez

Hidalgo
del Parral

Gómez
Palacio

Torreón

Cuatro
Ciénegas

Monclo

Saltillo

Parras

Durango

Real d
Cator

Mazatlán

Fresnillo

Zacatecas

San Lui
Potos

La Quemada

Aguascalientes

San Miguel
Allen

León

Guanajuato

Irapuato

Guadalajara

Morelia

Pátzcuaro

Volcán
Paricutín

Boca de
Pascuales

Uruapa
Reserv
Maripo
Monar

Troncon

Cela

Río Bravo del Norte

Rio Grande

Desierto de Chihuahua

Sierra Madre Occidental

Sierra de la Giganta

Desierto Sonorens

Isla Espíritu Santo
Marvelous snorkeling, kayaking
and camping (p719)

Land's End
Spectacular rock arch with
a colony of sea lions (p729)

Puerto Vallarta
Sophisticated, fun-loving
Pacific pearl (p507)

Guadalajara
Mexico's vibrant second-
largest city (p568)

Guanajuato
Lively, historic university
town (p653)

San Miguel de Allende
Cobblestone streets, glorious
colonial mansions (p668)

ELEVATION

3000m
2000m
1500m
1000m
400m
200m
0

PACIFIC OCEAN

Tropic of Cancer

30°N

25°N

20°N

15°N

10°N

115°W

110°W

105°W

0   300 km
0   150 miles

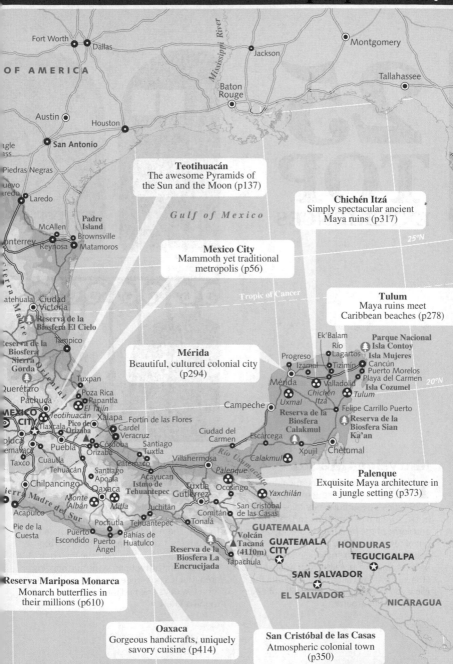

Teotihuacán
The awesome Pyramids of
the Sun and the Moon (p137)

Chichén Itzá
Simply spectacular ancient
Maya ruins (p317)

Mexico City
Mammoth yet traditional
metropolis (p56)

Tulum
Maya ruins meet
Caribbean beaches (p278)

Mérida
Beautiful, cultured colonial city
(p294)

Palenque
Exquisite Maya architecture in
a jungle setting (p373)

Reserva Mariposa Monarca
Monarch butterflies in
their millions (p610)

Oaxaca
Gorgeous handicrafts, uniquely
savory cuisine (p414)

San Cristóbal de las Casas
Atmospheric colonial town
(p350)

25 TOP EXPERIENCES

Marvelous Mérida

1 The cultural capital of the Yucatán Peninsula, this large but manageable city (p294) has a beautifully maintained colonial heart, a wealth of museums and galleries and some of the best food in the region. Just out of town are wildlife reserves, graceful haciendas (estates) and jungle-shrouded cenotes to swim in. A little further afield, the little-visited Maya sites along the Ruta Puuc allow you to step back in time without being jostled by tour groups.

Tulum

2 Take a world-famous Maya ruin, plonk it down beside the achingly white sands and turquoise-blue waters of the Caribbean and you've got the rightly popular Tulum (p278). There are accommodations here for all budgets, from beachside shacks to top-end resorts, plus some fantastic restaurants and so many attractions in the surrounding area that it's no wonder many people come for a few days and find themselves still here, months later.

Puerto Vallarta, Pacific Pearl

3 Tucked between jungle-clad mountains and North America's second-largest bay, Mexico's most appealing Pacific resort (p507) combines its dazzling setting with a fun-loving atmosphere that welcomes everyone from foodies and shopping devotees to outdoors enthusiasts and the international gay and lesbian community. Travel an hour out of town and you can be basking on a secluded beach, horseback riding in the Sierra Madre, whale-watching, diving or reeling in a giant fish worthy of a tall tale at happy hour.

Shopping for Artisan Crafts

4 Mexico's superbright, infinitely varied *artesanías* (handicrafts; see p824) are today's successors to the lavish costumes and beautiful ceramics of pre-Hispanic nobility, and to the everyday handcrafted clothes, baskets and pots of their humbler subjects. Everywhere you go – whether browsing city stores, wandering through markets or visiting artisans in their village workshops – the skill, creativity and color sense of potters, weavers, metalsmiths, carvers and leatherworkers delights the eye and tempts the pocket.

DAN GAIR / LONELY PLANET IMAGES©

5

6

Chichén Itzá

5 Sure, it's on every tour-bus itinerary and you're never going to have the place to yourself, but there's a reason why this Maya site (p317) was declared one of the new Seven Wonders of the World – it is simply spectacular. From the imposing, monolithic El Castillo pyramid (where the shadow of the plumed serpent god Kukulcán creeps down the staircase during the spring and autumn equinoxes) to the Sacred Cenote and curiously designed El Caracol, you don't have to be an archaeologist to have an amazing time here.

Isla Espíritu Santo

6 As if snorkeling with gentle whale sharks isn't enough, this unique Sea of Cortez island (p719) offers unparalleled diving, camping under a canopy of stunning stars, and kayaking along myriad azure bays with marvelous pastel cliffs. There's even a sea-lion colony. Espíritu Santo is spectacular in every way, thanks mainly to its unique geography. Pink sandstone here has been eroded by wind and waves into fingerlike protrusions, each harboring a beautiful cove.

Traditional Mexico City

7 To fully appreciate the quintessential Mexico City (p56) experience, you've got to embrace its time-honored traditions. You may find yourself on a gondola gliding through the ancient canals of Xochimilco, or knocking back tequilas in old cantinas once frequented by Mexican revolutionaries. Or perhaps it's the simple pleasure of munching on pre-Hispanic street eats (insects, anyone?). Never ones to shy away from a fiesta, *chilangos* celebrate their past with fervor – even the Lady of Guadalupe gets her very own late-night mariachi serenades in December.

The Pyramids of Teotihuacán

8 Once among Mesoamerica's greatest cities, Teotihuacán (p137), just an hour out of Mexico City, is a popular day trip from the capital. The awesomely massive Pirámide del Sol (Pyramid of the Sun) and Pirámide de la Luna (Pyramid of the Moon) dominate the remains of the metropolis. Even centuries after its collapse in the 8th century AD, Teotihuacán remained a pilgrimage site for Aztec royalty.

ALEX ADDLEM

ARIADNE VAN ZANDBERGEN/LONELY PLANET IMAGES©

RICHARD I'ANSON/LONELY PLANET IMAGES©

Relax on the Oaxaca Coast

9 After a few days on this 550km sequence of sandy Pacific beaches (p448), you'll be so relaxed you may not be able to leave. Head for the surf mecca and fishing port of Puerto Escondido, the low-key resort of Bahías de Huatulco, or the ultra-laid-back hangouts of Zipolite, San Agustinillo or Mazunte. Soak up the sun, eat good food, imbibe in easygoing beach bars, and when the mood takes you, have a surf or snorkel, or board a boat to sight turtles, dolphins, whales, crocs or birdlife.

Oaxaca City

10 This highly individual southern city (p414) basks in bright upland light and captivates the visitor with gorgeous handicrafts, frequent fiestas and handsome colonial architecture. A uniquely savory cuisine is served at restaurants and market stalls, and the finest mezcal is distilled in nearby villages. Within easy reach are the superb ancient Zapotec capital, Monte Albán, dozens of indigenous craft-making villages with busy weekly markets, and the cool, forested hills of the Sierra Norte, perfect for hikers, mountain bikers and horseback riders.

Mexican Art

11 If there's one art form that expresses Mexicans' emotions best, it's painting (p817). Mexican artistic creativity has ranged from vividly colorful pre-Hispanic murals and the revolutionary epics of Diego Rivera to the tortured canvases of Frida Kahlo and edgy contemporary installations. Every city worth its salt has art museums displaying the best from the past and commercial galleries showcasing the creative currents of the present.

JOHN ELK III/ALAMY©

Guanajuato

12 The glorious World Heritage–listed city of Guanajuato (p653) packs a huge amount into its narrow valley. This former mining town (now a colorful university city) is a feast of plazas, fun museums, opulent colonial mansions and pastel-hued houses. Snake your way along pedestrian alleyways, people-watch in the squares, mingle with marvelous mariachi groups, or party heartily at *estudiantinas* (traditional street parties) and in the many student bars. The underground tunnels – the town's major transport routes – make for a particularly quirky way to get around.

Guadalajara

13 Mexico's second-largest city (p568) manages to dazzle despite being more a collection of pueblos than a great metropolis. This charmer gets under your skin with colonial buildings, awesome public spaces and wonderful craft shopping in the arty suburbs of Tlaquepaque and Tonalá. The young and middle-class party all weekend in smart bars and heaving dance clubs, and there's nowhere better in western Mexico to eat out. Don't miss Jalisco's slow-burning capital.

Monarchs in Their Millions

14 Canopies of golden-orange butterflies cover the forests and hillsides in the Reserva Mariposa Monarca (Monarch Butterfly Reserve; p610), perhaps Mexico's most astonishing yearly natural phenomenon. It's the kind of annual event to plan your trip around – between November and March the migrant monarchs cover every surface, weighing down tree branches and changing the landscape into a permanent sunset as they winter far from the freezing Great Lakes during one of the planet's most spectacular migrations.

San Miguel de Allende

15 After a hard morning of hitting the shops, churches and galleries along the cobblestone colonial streets of San Miguel de Allende (p668), there's nothing better than enjoying a luxurious respite at one of the thermal pools outside town – one of the most relaxing experiences in the region. After your soak, head to the nearby Santuario de Atotonilco (p680), a fascinating magnet for Mexican pilgrims.

Pátzcuaro & the Purépecha

16 The mystical heart of the Purépecha people, stunning Lago de Pátzcuaro (p618) is one of Mexico's cultural highlights, surrounded by ancient communities living in colonial-era, terracotta-roofed villages. Pátzcuaro town (p612), perfectly preserved yet progressive, is a superb place to buy local arts and crafts. Book way ahead to come to the Pátzcuaro area during the Día de Muertos celebrations, as the events here are among the most colorful (and consequently popular) in the country.

WITOLD SKRYPCZAK/LONELY PLANET IMAGES©

DOUGLAS STEAKLEY/LONELY PLANET IMAGES©

Land's End, Baja California

17 Whether the beautiful rock formation El Arco (The Arch; p729) comes as one stop of a cruise itinerary or at the end of a 1700km road trip, Land's End is a spectacular sight. Pelicans dive into the blue-green water, beach-goers lounge on Lover's Beach, *pangas* (skiffs) toodle around the sea-lion colony, and when the sun sets behind the arch the scenery is just magic. It's as beautiful under the water as above – moray eels and a myriad of fish await those who don flippers and a mask.

Savor the Flavors

18 Mexican cuisine (p829) is like no other, and every part of Mexico has unique variations on that uniqueness, based on local ingredients and what's fresh at the market. For the tastiest travels, venture to try local dishes from restaurants and busy market and street stalls. You'll lose count of the delicious new tastes you encounter. When it's time for fine dining, seek out some of the legion of creative chefs who concoct amazing flavor combinations from traditional and innovative ingredients.

17

LEE FOSTER/LONELY PLANET IMAGES©

18

Peerless Palenque

19 Gather all your senses and dive headfirst into the ancient Maya world, where pyramids rise above jungle treetops and furtive monkeys shriek and catapult themselves through dense canopy. Wander the mazelike Palace, gazing up at its iconic tower. Scale the stone staircase of the Temple of the Inscriptions, the lavish mausoleum of Pakal (Palenque's mightiest ruler), and survey the sprawling ruins (p373) from this apex. Mind your vertigo on the descent.

The Riviera Maya

20 Stretching from the jet-setting, spring-breaking funfest of Cancún (p250) to the backwaters of the Sian Ka'an Biosphere Reserve (p285), the Riviera gets a bad rap for overdevelopment, mostly thanks to Cancún. Elsewhere, however, there are multiple opportunities to kick back without getting trampled, from little beachside fishing villages to cosmopolitan travelers' hot spots. And with water this blue, sand this white and jungle this lush, it's easy to overlook the excesses and let yourself be seduced by the dreamy tropical surrounds.

The Pacific Coastline

21 Running from the desert islands of Baja California to verdant coves backed by lush tropical mountains, and from untrammeled expanses of sand to mangrove-fringed lagoons teeming with birdlife, Mexico's Pacific coastline is stunning in its natural beauty. Punctuating this primordial grandeur are a series of lively resort towns – Mazatlán, Puerto Vallarta, Manzanillo, Ixtapa, Zihuatanejo and Acapulco – interspersed with world-class surf spots such as Barra de Nexpa, Boca de Pascuales, Troncones and Puerto Escondido.

Mexico's Last Train Journey

22 Mexico's national passenger train network is dead but the Ferrocarril Chihuahua Pacífico (Copper Canyon Railway; p754) remains alive and kicking as one of Latin America's best rail trips. Trains transport passengers from sea level at Los Mochis up to Chihuahua's high desert plains, via the sensational rocky landscapes of the Copper Canyon. Vistas from your window include alpine forests, subtropical valleys and glimpses of some of the world's deepest canyons. For optimal views, alight at a photogenic stop en route and linger – for an hour, or a week.

Veracruz, the Partying Port

23 Don't come to Veracruz (p195) with a traditional tourist tick list. This is a city for the hidden and the visceral. Spontaneity rules in the *zócalo,* an absorbing plaza that acts as a makeshift living room for the locals; on the breezy *malecón,* a seawalk for lovers, dreamers and alfresco entertainers; and in the 200-year-old Gran Café de la Parroquia, so steeped in tradition that it's become embedded in the city's identity. Slip under the radar and soak it all up.

Taxco, Silver City

24 Since silver deposits were discovered here in the 16th century, Taxco (p181) has ridden dramatic waves of boom and bust. Scattered down a precipitous hillside and surrounded by cliffs and mountains, its remarkably well-preserved colonial architecture and magnificent church, the baroque masterpiece Templo de Santa Prisca, make for one of the most beguiling scenes in central Mexico. While the silver mines have been depleted, the tradition continues, and Taxco remains home to hundreds of silver shops.

Magical San Cristóbal

25 Saunter the cobblestone streets of hill-ringed San Cristóbal de las Casas (p350), the high-altitude colonial city in the heart of indigenous Chiapas. A heady mix of modern and Maya, with cosmopolitan cafes and traditional culture, it's also a jumping-off point for Chiapas' natural attractions and fascinating Tzotzil and Tzeltal villages. Spend sunny days exploring its churches and markets or horseback riding through fragrant pine forest, and nippy evenings warmed by the fireplace of a cozy watering hole.

need to know

Currency
» Pesos (M$)

Language
» Spanish; also about 70 indigenous languages

When to Go

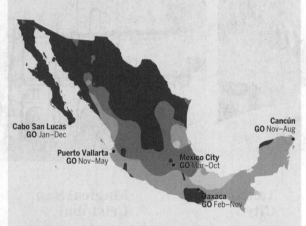

Cabo San Lucas
GO Jan–Dec

Puerto Vallarta
GO Nov–May

Cancún
GO Nov–Aug

Mexico City
GO Mar–Oct

Oaxaca
GO Feb–Nov

Desert or semi-desert, dry climate
Warm to hot summers, mild winters
Tropical climate, wet & dry season
Tropical climate, rain year-round

High Season
(Dec–Apr)

» December to April, the driest months over most of Mexico, bring winter escapees from colder countries.

» Christmas and Easter are Mexican holiday times, with transportation and coastal accommodations very busy.

Shoulder Season
(Jul & Aug)

» Holiday time for many Mexicans and foreigners. Hot almost everywhere, and very wet on the Pacific coast.

Low Season
(May, Jun, Sep–Nov)

» May & June see peak temperatures in many areas.

» September is the heart of the hurricane season, which may not bring hurricanes but does bring heavy rains on the Yucatán and Pacific coast.

Your Daily Budget

Budget less than
M$500

» Hostels and budget hotels: MS$150 to M$200 per person

» Save on meals by staying where you can cook

» Limited funds for activities or partying

» Travel by bus

Midrange
M$1000 –1500

» Doubles M$600 to M$1000 in comfortable hotels

» Good dinner with drinks: M$150 to M$250

» Afford some taxis, rental cars, activities, nightlife, shopping

Top end more than
M$2000

» Doubles from M$1200 in luxury hotels

» Enjoy plenty of fine meals, activities, outings and shopping

Money

» ATMs and money-changing offices widely available. Credit cards accepted in many midrange and top-end hotels.

Visas

» Every tourist must have a tourist permit. Some nationalities also need visas.

Cell Phones

» Many US and Canadian cellular carriers offer Mexico roaming deals. Mexican SIM cards can only be used in unlocked phones.

Transportation

» Good, inexpensive intercity bus services; extensive internal air network. Over 6000km of toll highways provide the best conditions for drivers.

Websites

» **Mexico Cooks!** (www.mexicocooks.typepad.com) Superb blog on Mexican life.

» **Lonely Planet** (www.lonelyplanet.com/mexico) Destination information, traveler forum and more.

» **Planeta.com** (www.planeta.com) Great articles, listings and links.

» **Mexconnect** (www.mexconnect.com) Goldmine on everything under the Mexican sun.

» **Lanic** (lanic.utexas.edu/la/mexico) Best broad collection of Mexico links.

» **México** (www.visitmexico.com) Official tourism site.

Exchange Rates

Australia	A$1	M$13.80
Canada	C$1	M$13.45
Euro zone	€1	M$18.10
Japan	¥100	M$17.85
New Zealand	NZ$1	M$10.50
UK	UK£1	M$21.60
USA	US$1	M$13.90

For current exchange rates, see www.xe.com.

Important Numbers

Country code	52
Emergency	066
International access code	00
National tourist assistance	078

Arriving in Mexico

» **Mexico City airport** (p128)
Authorized taxis, with ticket offices inside airport, cost M$194 to central areas
Metro (M$3) operates from 5am (6am Friday, 7am Saturday) to midnight; Terminal Aérea station is 200m from Terminal 1

» **Cancún airport** (p258)
ADO buses to downtown Cancún (M$45) and Playa del Carmen (M$150)
Airport shuttles M$150 per person to downtown; vans M$476/544 to downtown/hotel zone; taxi rates are similar

Safety & Security

Most of the Mexico news you hear back home is about drug-gang violence, in which some 50,000 Mexicans were killed between 2007 and 2011. On the ground in Mexico, you're highly unlikely to be aware of it. The great majority of the violence involves only the gangs and the Mexican security forces, and happens in a small number of places, chiefly in northern Mexico. Most of Mexico's most visited areas, such as the Yucatán Peninsula, have barely been touched by the violence. Tourists have very rarely been victims.

Before you go, read the Mexico information and warnings from sources such as the **US State Department** (travel.state.gov) and **UK Foreign Office** (www.fco.gov.uk). Keep your eye on the news, travel by day and on toll highways where possible, and don't wander into neighborhoods unfrequented by tourists after dark. See p856 for further information.

first time

Everyone needs a helping hand when they visit a country for the first time. There are phrases to learn, customs to get used to and etiquette to understand. The following section will help demystify Mexico so your first trip goes as smoothly as your fifth.

Language

The main language of Mexico is Spanish. Many Mexicans in the tourism industry, business or the arts also speak at least some (often good) English. In any accommodations catering to international travelers, you can expect to get by with English. Still, it's useful and polite to know at least a few words of Spanish. Mexicans appreciate being greeted with *'Buenos días'* or some other phrase in their own tongue, even if they then break into fluent English!

Booking Ahead

It's a good idea to reserve accommodations for your first night in Mexico, or if you're arriving somewhere at night, and for any lodgings during busy seasons (including Mexican holiday times).

It is often possible to reserve through hotel and hostel websites – best done a couple of days in advance. If you can't reserve online, you can do so by telephone: normally you'll just need to give your name and estimated time of arrival.

Hello.	Hola.
I would like to book ...	Quisiera reservar ...
a single/double room	una habitación sencilla/doble
in the name of	en nombre de
from ... to ... (date)	desde ... hasta ...
How much is it per night/person?	¿Cuánto cuesta por noche/persona?
Thank you very much.	Muchas gracias.

What to Wear

Casual and comfortable are the key words. In beach towns, shorts or shortish skirts are normal for many locals as well as visitors; sleeveless tops are fine, too. Take some long sleeves and long pants/skirts to protect against sun and mosquitoes, or for slightly less casual evening wear. In non–beach towns long pants, longish skirts and at least short sleeves are standard. Women will feel more comfortable with covered shoulders. Dress conservatively when visiting churches. You'll want at least a jumper or light jacket for cooler inland areas and air-conditioned buses or planes. A hat is essential; you can buy good, cheap ones in Mexico.

What to Pack

» Passport
» Credit or ATM card
» International electrical adaptor (for non–North Americans)
» Camera
» Cell phone and charger
» Swimming and beach gear
» Phrasebook
» Toiletries
» Small medical kit
» Flashlight (torch)
» Money belt
» Padlock
» Driver's license and other paperwork (if you're driving)
» Sun hat and shades
» Sunscreen
» Pocketknife

Checklist

» Check the validity of your passport

» Check the airline baggage restrictions

» Organize travel insurance (see p853)

» Make any necessary bookings (for accommodations, travel, sights)

» Inform your credit/ debit card company

» Check if you can use your cell phone (see p857)

» Get necessary immunizations well in advance (see p852)

» Check your government's Mexico travel information (see p857)

Etiquette

Mexicans are not huge sticklers for etiquette: their natural warmth takes precedence.

» Greetings

'Mucho gusto' (roughly 'A great pleasure') is a polite thing to say when you're introduced to someone. A handshake is the normal physical greeting; women may just touch each other on the right forearm. If it's a woman and a man, the woman offers her hand first. Male friends may perform an abrazo (a back-slapping hug); women and friends of opposite sexes usually kiss once on the cheek.

» Pleasing people

Mexicans love to hear that you're enjoying their country. As a rule, they are slow to criticize or argue, expressing disagreement more by nuance than by blunt contradiction.

» Visiting homes

An invitation to a Mexican home is an honor for an outsider; as a guest you will be treated very hospitably. Take a small gift if you can, such as flowers or something for the children.

Tipping

» Why?
Tourism and hospitality workers often depend on tips to supplement miserable wages.

» Restaurants
Tip around 15% unless service is included in the check.

» Hotels
It's nice to leave 5% to 10% of your room costs for the staff.

» Taxis
Drivers don't expect tips unless they provide some extra service.

» Porters
Airport and hotel porters get M$50 to M$100 depending on how much they carry.

» Attendants
Car-parking and gas-station attendants expect M$5 or M$10.

Money

Plan on making all cash purchases with pesos. Only a few businesses accept US dollars. It's easy to get pesos from ATMs using a major credit or debit card (Visa, Master-Card, American Express). For greatest security, use ATMs during daylight and use the ones *inside* banks or hotels. Take a small reserve of cash to exchange if ATMs prove unavailable or inconvenient. Change cash US dollars (and often Canadian dollars, euros or pounds sterling) at banks or *casas de cambio* (exchange offices). *Casas de cambio* are usually quicker than banks and may offer better rates. Use major credit and debit cards at many airlines, travel agencies, midrange or top-end hotels, restaurants and stores. Swipe devices are more common than 'chip and PIN' machines.

what's new

For this new edition of Mexico, our authors have hunted down the fresh, the transformed, the hot and the happening. These are some of our favorites. For up-to-the-minute recommendations, see lonelyplanet.com/mexico.

En Vía, Oaxaca

1 A great new nonprofit concept combining tourism with rural development, En Vía's tours take visitors into the homes and workshops of village women and your tour fee helps to provide them with microfinance loans to develop small businesses (p423).

Ensenada's Wine Route

2 Baja California's vineyards are at last coming into their own and producing some highly acclaimed wines. The Ruta del Vino is dotted with gourmet restaurants and boutique B&Bs, too (p699).

Sierra Gorda Ecotourism

3 Querétaro state's Sierra Gorda Biosphere Reserve has 12 community-run lodges from which you can explore this ultradiverse region's tropical and cloud forests, deserts, mountain villages and World Heritage–listed colonial missions (p690).

Parque de Aventuras Barrancas del Cobre

4 The Copper Canyon just got even more exciting: this canyon-rim adventure park features Latin America's longest zip-lines and a cable car, letting thrill-seekers soar across canyons more than 2000m deep (p760).

Museo Soumaya Plaza Carso, Mexico City

5 Testament to the vast fortune of Mexican Carlos Slim, the world's richest man, this beautiful new museum houses his extensive collection of art by Mexican and world greats (p79).

Boutique Hotel Quinta Chanabnal, Palenque

6 If the ancient Maya had branched off into building small boutique hotels, the results might have looked something like this (p380).

Mercado de Sabores Poblanos, Puebla

7 This huge and sparkling new food court with 130-odd vendors is the perfect place to try out Puebla's distinctive culinary specialties (p150).

Palacio de Hierro Museums, Orizaba

8 Orizaba's famous 'Iron Palace,' designed by Gustave Eiffel in the 1890s, has converted its interior into six different museums encapsulating everything from beer to soccer, and they're all free (p223).

Casa Rosa, Morelia

9 Morelia's most beloved lodgings have a new location and are better than ever, with fabulously Mexican decor and the same friendly-as-ever owners (p605).

Museo de Cacao, Ruta Puuc

10 Between the fascinating archaeological sites south of Mérida, take a whirlwind look at every aspect of the cocoa plant, sacred to the ancient Maya and still treasured today (p311).

Molika, Mazatlán

11 Exquisite sandwiches, salads and homemade breads, in a high-ceilinged old building redone with designer colors, make Molika the hottest new lunch and dinner hangout in Old Mazatlán (p491).

if you like...

Beach Resorts

If sand, sun, turquoise seas and an urban vibe in the background are your dream of Mexico, you can make it come true anywhere from the Pacific to the Caribbean.

Puerto Vallarta A sophisticated Pacific resort with dazzling beaches, stylish restaurants and hot nightlife that is also Mexico's gay beach capital (p507)

Playa del Carmen The hip resort of the Caribbean coast, with a European style of chic (p267)

Mazatlán Unique among Mexican resorts in that it combines an attractive old colonial center and cultural attractions with classic fun in the sun (p483)

Zihuatanejo This easygoing Pacific town has beautiful beaches and accommodations for all budgets and is still a fishing town (p539)

Cancún The mother of Mexican resorts, an unabashed party town for international tourists with a good Caribbean beach fronting 15km of resort hotels and condominiums (p250)

Getaway Beaches

With 10,000km of coast, Mexico still has hundreds of beaches where you don't need to do anything except enjoy the sea, sun and seafood.

Oaxaca coast International budget travelers make a beeline for the blissed-out beach villages of Zipolite (p463), Mazunte (p467) and San Agustinillo (p465)

Xcalak No cruise ships, no gas station, no bank, no grocery store and a wonderful barrier reef – the Caribbean coast as it once was (p288)

Playa Maruata Tranquil, low-budget Michoacán fishing village beloved by beach bums and sea turtles (p533)

Barra de Potosí Palm-fringed white sands, calm waters, a lagoon full of birds and a handful of guesthouses (p547)

Isla Holbox Swim with whale sharks off the endless beaches of this sandy-streeted island where the Caribbean meets the Gulf of Mexico (p264)

Luxury Spas & Hotels

Let yourself be pampered to your heart's content at these deluxe lodgings.

Mar de Jade, Chacala Idyllic Pacific miniresort with yoga classes, temascal (pre-Hispanic sauna) sessions, vegetarian-friendly food and regular meditation and wellness retreats (p504)

Hacienda de los Santos, Álamos A gorgeous, antique-decked hotel comprising five restored colonial homes, with three pools, three restaurants and 520 tequilas (p749)

Las Mañanitas, Cuernavaca The stunning Las Mañanitas boasts gardens decked with sculpture and strutting peacocks, and a top-class, French-accented restaurant (p176)

La Casa Que Canta, Zihuatanejo This superdeluxe clifftop hotel has exquisite decor, superb service, no TVs and no kids under 16 (p541)

Casa Oaxaca, Oaxaca City Boutique city hotel dedicated to art and handicrafts, with large rooms in stunning contemporary style and a beautiful colonial patio (p424)

Present Moment Retreat, Troncones This Pacific spa resort, with thatched-roof bungalows in beautiful gardens, offers yoga, meditation and massage (p536)

» Folk musicians, Oaxaca city (p414)

Pyramids & Temples

The cities and sacred precincts of Mexico's ancient civilizations awe and intrigue with their majesty and mystery.

Teotihuacán Mexico's biggest ancient city, with the massive Pyramids of the Sun and Moon and mural-decked palaces (p137)

Palenque Exquisite Maya temples backed by steamy, jungle-covered hills (p373)

Chichén Itzá A monument to ancient Mexico's obsession with time and death (p317)

Uxmal Large Maya site with a riot of carved-stone ornamentation (p306)

Yaxchilán Impressive temples in a wonderful setting deep in the Chiapas jungle, reached only by river (p384)

Monte Albán The ancient Zapotec capital sits on a peerless hilltop site outside Oaxaca (p436)

Tulum These late Maya temples and pyramids sit right on a beautifully rugged stretch of Caribbean coast (p278)

Calakmul High pyramids in a huge, remote Maya city, still largely hidden beneath a sea of rainforest (p335)

Historic Colonial Towns

Most of what's beautiful in urban Mexico owes itself to the 300-year period of Spanish rule, when towns were laid out with elegant, shady plazas and gorgeous stone palaces and churches.

Guanajuato The opulent mansions and narrow, winding streets of this lively university town and cultural center are squeezed into a picturesque, steep valley (p653)

San Miguel de Allende Charming, artsy town of cobblestone streets and lovely stone architecture, given an international dimension by its many foreign (mainly US) residents (p668)

Oaxaca Gorgeous southern city with an indigenous flavor and stunning art and artisanry (p414)

Zacatecas The magnificent cathedral of this city built on silver is the ultimate expression of colonial baroque (p628)

Mérida Beautiful plazas and palaces adorn the Yucatán Peninsula's cultural capital (p294)

Taxco The churches and mansions of this perfectly preserved silver town are scattered down a spectacularly steep hillside (p181)

Shopping

Mexico's star buys are the wonderful, colorful handicrafts – textiles, ceramics, masks, woodwork, metalwork, leatherwork, jewelry – made predominantly by indigenous people.

Oaxaca The city is full of markets and stores offering an array of the most inventive and colorful handicrafts (p432); also visit some of the villages where they are made (p435)

San Miguel de Allende A mind-boggling array of craft shops, selling folk art from all over Mexico (p678)

Guadalajara The artisans' suburbs of Tlaquepaque (upscale; p585) and Tonalá (down to earth; p573) are replete with classy ceramics, furniture, glassware and much more

Bázar Sábado This Saturday market in Mexico City has some of Mexico's best handcrafted jewelry, woodwork, ceramics and textiles (p120)

Indigenous village markets Weekly markets are bustling occasions to visit as much for the local atmosphere as to buy; some of the most fascinating happen in villages around Oaxaca (p439) and San Cristóbal de las Casas (p366)

If you like... scenic train rides, the Ferrocarril Chihuahua Pacífico (Copper Canyon Railway) climbs more than 2000m as it traverses the northwest's spectacular canyon country (p754)

Mexican Cuisine

Mexican food has as many variations as there are Mexican cooks. Any good eatery's offerings depends on what fresh ingredients are in season locally.

Mexico City The capital's fancy and humble eateries cook up an unrivaled range of fare from all around Mexico; it's also the epicenter of creative *nueva cocina mexicana* – Mexican *nouvelle cuisine* (p103)

Seafood Mexicans love their seafood and, naturally, it's most delicious on the coasts, from Baja California's beloved fish tacos to Veracruz' famed *huachinango a la veracruzana* (snapper in a tomato-based sauce)

Oaxaca Famed for its seven varieties of *mole* (type of chili sauce), a high point of Mexican culinary art (p428)

Cooking classes Prepare your own Mexican feasts under the guidance of an expert in Oaxaca (p423), Zihuatanejo (p545), Tepoztlán (p168) or Tlaxcala (p160)

Beef Northwest Mexico is ranching territory: carnivores will love its ubiquitous *carne asada* (marinated grilled beef), served in a taco or on a plate

Museums & Galleries

The great pride Mexicans take in their own culture is amply demonstrated by the country's marvelous museums and galleries.

Museo Nacional de Antropología, Mexico City The National Anthropology Museum is chock-full of stupendous relics of pre-Hispanic Mexico (p75)

Museo Frida Kahlo, Mexico City The poignant home of the haunted artist (p89)

Palacio Nacional, Mexico City Diego Rivera's famous Mexican history murals (p61)

Palacio de Bellas Artes, Mexico City Immense murals by Mexico's four greatest muralists (p69)

Instituto Cultural de Cabañas, Guadalajara José Clemente Orozco's masterly 1930s murals on the theme of freedom (p571)

Museo Rafael Coronel, Zacatecas Wonderful collection of Mexican folk art (p628)

Museo Nacional de la Muerte, Aguascalientes All things related to death, but far from macabre (p637)

Museo León Trotsky, Mexico City Russian revolutionary's last refuge (p89)

Live Music & Dance

The country abounds with spots to hear, and often dance to, real live musicians playing anything from salsa to ska.

Mexico City clubs The capital offers plenty of live music any night – for ska and punk head to Multiforo Alicia (p116); for salsa, to Mama Rumba (p117)

Ballet Folclórico de México A two-hour festive blur of costumes and dance from all over Mexico (p115)

Mariachis For a nice dose of trumpet-tooting sentimentality, head to Mexico City's Plaza Garibaldi (p116) or Guadalajara's El Parián (p584)

Guelaguetza Oaxaca's fantastically colorful July feast of folk dance (p433)

Casa de la Salsa Morelia's cavernous, feel-good salsa club (p608)

Veracruz Marimbas and mariachis compete noisily on the Zócalo nightly (p197)

La Mutualista Vintage Guadalajara salsa hall with a Cuban band (p584)

Puerto Escondido This Pacific town's international scene spawns gigs by all kinds of live bands (p456)

If you like... pre-Hispanic drinks
Quaff a mug of *pulque* (an alcoholic maguey-based beverage) at one of Mexico City's *pulquerías* such as Las Duelistas (p110)

If you like... pre-Hispanic food
Sample wild boar or grasshoppers at Restaurante Chon (p104)

Diving & Snorkeling

Mexico's Caribbean coast, with the world's second-largest barrier reef, is world-famous for its warm, translucent waters full of wonderful corals and tropical fish. The Pacific coast doesn't have quite the same visibility or diversity, but snorkeling and diving there can be great, with good prospects of seeing dolphins, turtles and whales.

Banco Chinchorro Off the southern end of the Caribbean coast, this is the northern hemisphere's largest coral atoll, with many wrecks (p288)

Isla Cozumel Surrounded by 65 reefs with stunning coral formations, Cozumel is one of the world's most popular diving destinations, with sites good for everyone from beginners to the experienced (p274)

Isla Mujeres This island off Cancún has some lovely dives with plenty of coral and some spectacular marine creatures (p260)

Bahías de Huatulco A string of beautiful Pacific bays with several coral plates and over 100 dive sites (p472)

Surfing

Countless spots along the Pacific coast are bombarded with superb waves from May to October/November. Beginners can learn the craft almost year-round.

Puerto Escondido The Mexican Pipeline can get up to 12m, the Punta Zicatela point break works almost daily, and there are beginners' waves, too – plus a great traveler scene (p449)

Boca de Pascuales Legendary, aggressive barrel swells, strictly for experienced surfers (p531)

Troncones Several world-class spots, with a long, strong left point break and some excellent beach breaks, too (p535)

Todos Santos San Pedrito beach has Hawaii-like tubes (p732)

Sayulita Dependable, medium-sized waves, good for practising or learning, and a mellow party vibe (p505)

Barra de Nexpa One of several spots with healthy waves along the little-touched Michoacán coast (p533)

Ensenada There's a wonderful point break at San Miguel (p701)

San Blas Good for intermediates and beginners, with many beach and point breaks, and one of the world's longest waves (p505)

Hiking, Mountain Biking & Horseback Riding

Mexico's rugged landscape naturally makes for some spectacular long or short excursions. Best seasons vary from place to place and a guide is advisable on some routes.

Copper Canyon The northwest's spectacular canyon country is great for exploring on foot, horse or mountain bike, for a few hours or a couple of weeks (p752)

Pueblos Mancomunados These small, isolated Oaxacan mountain villages are linked by a scenic trail network, with horses, mountain bikes and good rural lodgings available (p445)

Oaxaca Outstanding short- or long-distance rides with Horseback Mexico (p421) and, by bike, with Bicicletas Pedro Martínez (p435)

Volcanoes Dormant volcanoes that you can summit without technical climbing include Nevado de Toluca (p190), Paricutín (p624) and Nevado de Colima (p599)

Sierra de la Laguna Serious Baja hiking for hard-core wilderness junkies (p725)

DAN GAIR/LONELY PLANET IMAGES©

» Surfing the waves, Michoacán coast (p531)

Wildlife

Mexico's huge natural variety, from tropical rainforest to coastal lagoons, endows it with a vast range of accessible wildlife. Plan carefully: most of it is seasonal.

Whales From December/January to March, watch whales in Baja California's lagoons (p709), off Puerto Vallarta (p519) or along the Oaxaca coast (p448)

Butterflies The trees and earth of Michoacán's Reserva Mariposa Monarca turn bright orange when millions of huge monarch butterflies flutter in every winter (p610)

Sea turtles Mexican beaches are major sea-turtle breeding grounds – enjoy up-close turtle experiences at Cuyutlán (p530), Playa Escobilla (p458), Puerto Arista (p398), Tecolutla (p233) or Isla Mujeres (p261)

Whale sharks Swim with the world's biggest fish at Isla Holbox (p265) or Espíritu Santo (p719)

Howler monkeys Spot these eerily roaring primates in the jungle canopy at Palenque (p373), Yaxchilán (p384) or Laguna Miramar (p396)

Birds Mexico's forests and coastal lagoons thrill bird lovers – for bright pink clouds of flamingos head to Río Lagartos (p325) or Celestún (p313)

Kayaking & Rafting

There's plenty of adventure for paddlers along Mexico's coasts and rivers.

Sea of Cortez A long trip around the islands of the Bahía de Loreto National Marine Park from Loreto is a sea kayaker's dream (p715)

Pacific Coast Numerous spots along the Pacific coast will rent you a kayak or take you on a kayak tour of the coasts, lagoons or islands. Top locations include Puerto Vallarta (p510), Barra de Potosí (p547) and bird-thronged Laguna Manialtepec (p458)

Veracruz rafting Veracruz state, with rivers plunging down from the Sierra Madre Oriental, is Mexico's white-water rafting center. The main bases are Jalcomulco (p218) and Tlapacoyan (p234)

Oaxaca rafting Rivers near Bahías de Huatulco have waters suitable for everyone from beginners (including children) to experienced rafters (p473)

Reserva de la Biosfera Sian Ka'an Kayak is the choice way to explore this vast jungle-and-wetlands reserve on the Caribbean coast (p285)

Tequila & Mezcal

A growing number of bars around the country are geared to letting drinkers sip and savor top-quality varieties of these two iconic, closely related Mexican liquors.

La Botica The few branches of this quaint small chain are among Mexico City's most congenial mezcal bars (p112)

Los Amantes Oaxacan agave fields produce what's reckoned to be the best mezcal of all, and this quaint Oaxaca tasting room will serve you three good mezcals for a bargain M$100 (p430)

Atotonilco El Alto A highland Jalisco town producing what's considered the smoothest and sweetest tequila; free tours at Siete Leguas distillery (p592)

Tequila Express This train-tour-cum-party from Guadalajara visits the pretty Herradura tequila hacienda and throws in mariachi music, lunch and masses of tequila (p592)

Tequila The drink is named for this none-too-pretty Jalisco town where you can tour distilleries and visit the National Tequila Museum (p592)

month by month

January

It's warm to hot in coastal and lowland areas, cool in the highlands, and dry everywhere, attracting flocks of foreign tourists. The first week is Mexican holiday season, making transportation and coastal resorts busy.

Día de los Santos Reyes

January 6 (Three Kings' Day or Epiphany), rather than Christmas, is the day when Mexican children traditionally receive presents, commemorating the Three Kings' gifts for the baby Jesus. Mexicans eat *rosca de reyes*, a large oval sweetbread decorated with candied fruit.

Migratory Bird Season

January is the peak season for migratory birds along Mexico's Pacific coast. Lagoons and rivers at places such as Laguna Manialtepec (p458) and Lagunas de Chacahua (p459) are packed with fowl, and San Blas even holds an International Migratory Bird Festival (avessanblas.uan.mx; p500).

February

Temperatures are marginally higher than in January, but it remains dry, making this a great month to be in most of Mexico, though it can still be cold in the north and at high altitudes.

Whale-Watching Season

Magnificent gray whales calve in bays and lagoons around Baja California from mid-December to mid-April. Whales can also be spotted along the whole Pacific coast during this period. Best months for Baja whale-watching (p709) are February and March.

Día de la Candelaria

Candlemas (February 2), commemorating the infant Jesus' presentation in the temple, is widely celebrated. In Tlacotalpan several days of festivities (p236) feature bull-running in the streets and a flotilla of boats following an image of the Virgin down the Río Papaloapan.

Carnaval

A big bash preceding the 40-day penance of Lent, Carnaval happens during the week leading up to Ash Wednesday (February 13, 2013; March 5, 2014). It's wildest in Veracruz (p200) and Mazatlán (p488), with parades and masses of music, drink, dancing, fireworks and fun.

Monarch Butterfly Season

From about mid-November to March the forests of the Reserva Mariposa Monarca (Monarch Butterfly Reserve; p610) turn bright orange as millions of large monarch butterflies winter here. The best time to watch them is on a warm, sunny afternoon in February.

Sierra Norte Hiking

Cool, dry weather from January to March makes for the best hiking conditions among the forests, hills and remote villages of Oaxaca's beautiful Sierra Norte (p445), home to an excellent ecotourism program.

March

It's getting steadily warmer all over Mexico, but it's still dry, and the winter season for foreign tourism continues.

Vernal Equinox
Visitors mob ancient Chichén Itzá (p317) for the spring (March 20–21) and autumnal (September 21–22) equinoxes, when patterns of light and shadow resemble a serpent ascending or descending El Castillo pyramid. Almost the same effect happens every day for a week preceding and following each equinox.

⭐ Festival Internacional del Cine
Mexico's most important film festival (www.ficg.mx; p576) draws top international actors and directors to Guadalajara for 10 days each March, with more than 300 films screened to over 100,000 viewers.

Spring Break
US students get a week's break in late February or March (dates vary between colleges). Many head to Mexican resorts such as Cancún, Puerto Vallarta, Cabo San Lucas or Acapulco for days of over-the-top partying. Be in it, or steer clear!

April

Temperatures continue to increase but it stays dry. Semana Santa (Holy Week), which can be in March or April, is Mexico's major holiday week of the year, with tourist accommodations and transportation packed.

Semana Santa
Semana Santa (Holy Week) is the week from Palm Sunday to Easter Sunday (March 31, 2013; April 20, 2014). Good Friday sees solemn processions in many places, and enormous crowds attend a re-enactment of the Crucifixion in Iztapalapa, Mexico City (p97).

Feria de San Marcos
Millions of people attend the exhibitions, bullfights, cockfights, rodeos, concerts and other events of Mexico's biggest state fair, in the city of Aguascalientes (p640). It lasts about three weeks from mid-April, with the biggest parade on April 25.

May

Temperatures reach annual peaks in cities such as Mérida (average daily high 35°C), Guadalajara (31°C), Oaxaca (30°C) and Mexico City (26°C). It's low season for tourism, meaning low prices in many accommodations.

Feria de Morelia
This three-week fair (p604) sees regional dance performances, bullfights, agricultural and handicraft exhibitions, fireworks and plenty of partying in the Michoacán capital.

Feria de Corpus Christi
Papantla's big bash features spectacular *voladores* (fliers) performances and indigenous dances, plus *charreadas* (Mexican rodeos), parades and bullfights (p229).

June

The rainy season has started, bringing heavy downpours in the southeast, in some places along the Pacific coast and in the central highlands. Tourism remains at low levels, and so are accommodations prices.

🍴 Festival del Mole Poblano
Puebla celebrates its most famous contribution to Mexican cuisine, the chocolatey sauce called *mole poblano,* in early June (p149). This is also the month when *huitlacoche,* a black corn fungus considered a delicacy since Aztec times, comes into season in central Mexico.

🏃 Surf's Up
Countless spots along the Pacific coast, including Puerto Escondido with its legendary Mexican Pipeline (p449), are bombarded with superb waves from about May to November. June, July and August generally see the biggest waves. Beginners can learn the craft almost year-round at numerous spots.

July

It's still rainy in the southeast, central highlands and along the Pacific coast, but this is a summer holiday month for both foreigners and Mexicans, bringing busy times at many tourist destinations, and higher prices at some.

☆ Guelaguetza

Oaxaca is thronged for this fantastically colorful feast of regional dance (p433) on the first two Mondays after July 16, with plenty of other celebratory events accompanying it.

✸ Jornadas Villistas

The northern town of Hidalgo del Parral goes wild for the week leading up to the anniversary of Pancho Villa's assassination here (July 20). Horseback riders make a six-day marathon journey to Parral, and bikers arrive in their thousands (p777).

🏃 Swimming with Whale Sharks

Massive whale sharks congregate to feed on plankton off Isla Holbox between mid-May and mid-September. The best time to swim with these gentle giants is July (p265).

(Above) Traditional Día de Muertos decorations, Pátzcuaro (p612)
(Below) Street parade for Día de Nuestra Señora de Guadalupe, San Cristóbal de las Casas (p350)

August

The summer holiday season continues, as do the rains, although they're less intense in most areas. June to August are brutally hot in the north.

☆ Feria Internacional de la Guitarra

The town of Paracho, famed for making high-quality string instruments, holds this week-long international guitar fair, with music, dance and exhibitions, in early August (p624).

 Feria de Huamantla

Huamantla, east of Mexico City, lets rip over a few days and nights during its mid-August fair. On August 14 the streets are carpeted with flowers and colored sawdust; a few days later there's a Pamplona-esque running of the bulls (p164).

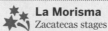 Festival del Chile en Nogada

In late August Puebla's restaurants celebrate a notable Puebla-invented dish, *chiles en nogada* – stuffed chilies with a creamy walnut sauce and pomegranate seeds. The green, white and red colors yield a patriotic flavor, being those of the Mexican flag. See p149.

La Morisma

Zacatecas stages a spectacular mock battle with over 2000 participants, commemorating the triumph of the Christians over the Moors in old Spain, usually on the last weekend of August (p632).

September

Summer holidays are over. It's the height of the hurricane season on the Yucatán Peninsula and Mexico's coasts. Hurricanes strike erratically, but it's a rainy month everywhere, and visibility for Caribbean divers is worse.

Día de la Independencia

On Independence Day (September 16), patriotic celebrations mark the anniversary of Miguel Hidalgo's 1810 call to rebellion

against Spain, the Grito de Dolores: on the 15th, the Grito is repeated from every Mexican town hall, followed by fireworks. The biggest celebrations are in Mexico City (p97).

October

It's still a low season for tourism, and hurricane season continues, but the rains have eased off except on the Yucatán Peninsula.

Fiestas de Octubre

Guadalajara's big bash (www.fiestasdeoctubre.com.mx; p576) fills the whole month with free entertainment, livestock shows, art exhibitions and sporting events. Thousands of passionate pilgrims crawl on their knees behind an image of the Virgin Mary carried to the city's Basílica de Zapopan.

Feria del Café y del Huipil

For several days around October 4, the remote mountain village Cuetzalan honors its patron saint (St Francis of Assisi), the coffee harvest and the *huipil* (indigenous women's tunic) with hearty drinking, indigenous dances and *voladores* performances (p165).

Festival Internacional Cervantino

Guanajuato's two-week arts festival (www.festivalcervantino.gob.mx; p660), dedicated to Spanish writer Miguel de Cervantes, is one of the biggest cultural happenings in Latin America, with performances by music, dance

and theater groups from around the world.

Copper Canyon

October, along with November and March, is one of the best months to visit northwest Mexico's spectacular canyon country (p752), with temperatures not too hot at the bottom of the canyons nor too cold at the top.

Fiesta de San Francisco

Between late September and late October 150,000 pilgrims fill the remote, half-abandoned northern town of Real de Catorce to pay homage to the figure of St Francis of Assisi in the town's church (p650).

November

Another quiet month on the tourism front. The weather is mostly dry and temperatures are subsiding. Snow tops the high peaks of the central volcanic belt.

Día de Muertos

(Day of the Dead; November 2) Cemeteries come alive as families decorate graves and commune with their dead, some holding all-night vigils. Special altars appear in homes and public buildings. Associated events may start days before, notably around Pátzcuaro (p615) and Oaxaca (p424). See also p816.

Fiestas de Noviembre

The Pacific coastal town of Puerto Escondido buzzes throughout November with concerts, a folk dance festival, sailfish and surfing competitions and plenty more (p452).

★ Feria de la Plata

Some of Mexico's best silverwork is on show during the week-long national silver fair in Taxco in late November or early December. *Charreadas*, concerts, dances and donkey races add to the fun (p184).

★ Feria del Aguacate

The city of Uruapan considers itself the world avocado capital, and this three-week celebration in November/December often includes attempts to make the world's biggest guacamole (p622).

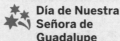

December

A dry month almost everywhere, and as cool as it gets. International winter tourism gets going, and the Christmas–New Year period is Mexican holiday time, with accommodations busy and prices often raised.

★ Día de Nuestra Señora de Guadalupe

Several days of festivities throughout Mexico lead up to the feast day of the Virgin who is the country's religious patron – Day of Our Lady of Guadalupe (December 12). Millions converge on Mexico City's Basílica de Guadalupe (p97).

★ Christmas

Christmas is traditionally celebrated with a feast in the early hours of December 25, after midnight Mass. Pre- or post-Christmas events in some towns include *pastorelas* (nativity plays), as in Tepotzotlán (p134) and Pátzcuaro (p616), and *posadas* (candlelit processions), as in Taxco (p184).

itineraries

Whether you've got six days or 60, these itineraries provide a starting point for the trip of a lifetime. Want more inspiration? Head online to lonelyplanet. com/thorntree to chat with other travelers.

Two to Three Weeks
Riviera Maya & Costa Maya Getaway

> Once you're over the beach and nightclubs of **Cancún**, slip across to more relaxed **Isla Mujeres** for some good snorkeling or diving. If you brought kids along, spend a day at one of the mainland 'eco-parks' such as **Selvática** with its 12 zip-lines. South along the Caribbean coast, spend some days at **Tulum**, which has one of Mexico's most perfect beaches and most spectacularly sited Maya ruins. Within day-trip reach are the jungle-surrounded Maya pyramids and temples of **Cobá** and the wild **Reserva de la Biosfera Sian Ka'an**. South of Tulum the coast takes the name Costa Maya – far less developed and touristed than the 'Riviera Maya' to the north. **Mahahual** remains a laid-back Caribbean village despite cruise-ship visits, with marvelous snorkeling and diving at the offshore coral atoll **Banco Chinchorro**. To really escape, head on to the tiny fishing town of **Xcalak**, another excellent diving and snorkeling base. Returning northward, wind up your trip with a stop at chic **Playa del Carmen**, a great base for superlative diving and snorkeling on **Isla Cozumel** and cenote (limestone sinkhole) diving or swimming at **Cristalino Cenote**.

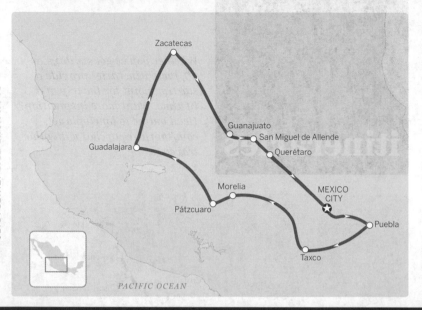

Two to Four Weeks
Colonial Towns & Cities of Mexico's Heartland

The nation's capital is ringed by a necklace of colonial cities that are blessed with gorgeous architecture of carved stone and colorful tiles, broad plazas, splashing fountains and lively, modern cultural scenes – Mexico's historic, architectural and artistic gems. To do justice to all these cities would easily occupy a month and might result in travel (and monument) fatigue, but you can get a very good taste of the region by selecting about five destinations for a shorter tour.

Mexico City itself has a large concentration of grand colonial architecture, starting with its central plaza, the Zócalo, and the cathedral and National Palace that flank it. The colonial center is interestingly spiced with plenty of more modern, and a bit of pre-Hispanic, architecture and art.

Head east for **Puebla**, which has the country's greatest concentration of restored colonial churches and mansions – many of the latter now housing interesting museums – and is still one of the most Spanish-influenced cities in Mexico. Southward, charming hillside **Taxco** harbors many silver workshops and other surprises in its lovely cobblestone alleyways.

Go west to Michoacán's lively capital **Morelia**, home to an imposing cathedral and many well-preserved buildings. **Pátzcuaro** is a handsome, low-rise, highland town where the indigenous Purépecha sell their wares around one of Mexico's loveliest central plazas. Further west, *muy mexicano* **Guadalajara**, Mexico's second-largest city, is perhaps less quaint than its neighbors but retains beautiful plazas and plenty of fine colonial architecture, not to mention fabulous shopping and nightlife.

To the north, trip up to prosperous **Zacatecas**, a stylish silver city with a stupendous baroque cathedral. Heading back toward Mexico City you reach El Bajío, the region famed as the Cuna de la Independencia (Cradle of Independence) for its vital role in the early-19th-century independence movement that put an end to Mexico's colonial era. Here, lively **Guanajuato** awaits in a ravine awash with quixotic *callejones* (alleys), a vibrant student life and historical reminders galore, while the festive and charming expat capital **San Miguel de Allende** is full of beautifully restored colonial buildings, including many homes. Before you hit Mexico City again, don't neglect handsome **Querétaro**, which has several fine museums and a very walkable historic center.

» (above) The legendary waves at
Puerto Escondido's Playa Zicatela
(p448)
» (left) The cobblestone streets of
colonial San Cristóbal de las Casas
(p350)

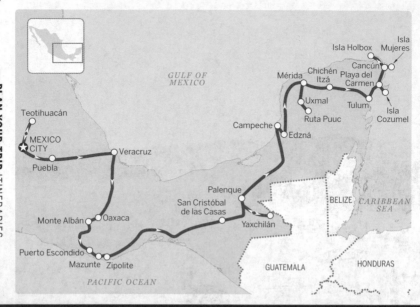

Six Weeks
Beaches, Cities & Temples of Mexico's South

This classic journey leads travelers south from Mexico's central heartland to its glorious Caribbean beaches, and gives as good a sampling of the country's highlights as you can get in a few weeks. Start by exploring **Mexico City**, a fascinating megalopolis that is key to any understanding of Mexico, the country. Take a side trip to **Teotihuacán**, capital of ancient Mexico's biggest empire, with its awesome pyramids. Then head east to colonial **Puebla** and the fun-loving, tropical port city of **Veracruz**, before crossing the mountains southward to **Oaxaca**. This lovely colonial city, with Mexico's finest handicrafts, sits at the heart of a beautiful region with a large indigenous population. Don't miss the ancient Zapotec capital, **Monte Albán**, just outside the city.

Cross the Sierra Madre del Sur to one of the sun-baked beach spots on the Oaxaca coast, such as **Puerto Escondido**, **Mazunte** or **Zipolite**. Continue east to **San Cristóbal de las Casas**, a beautiful, cool, highland town surrounded by intriguing indigenous villages. Move on through Chiapas to **Palenque**, perhaps the most stunning of all Maya cities, with its backdrop of emerald-green jungle, and **Yaxchilán**, another marvelous Maya city accessible only by river, echoing with the growls of howler monkeys deep in the Lacandón Jungle.

Head northeast to the Yucatán Peninsula, with a first stop at **Campeche**, an attractive mix of painstakingly restored colonial city and bustling modern town, and a side trip to the nearby Maya site of **Edzná**. Move on to colonial **Mérida**, the Yucatán's lively cultural capital and the base for visiting the superb Maya ruins of **Uxmal** and the **Ruta Puuc**. Next stop is **Chichén Itzá**, the Yucatán's most celebrated ancient Maya site. From here, head directly to **Tulum** on the Caribbean coast, a Maya site with a glorious beach nearby. Now make your way northward along the Riviera Maya to the hip beach town of **Playa del Carmen**, with a side trip to **Isla Cozumel** for world-class snorkeling and diving, before reaching Mexico's most popular and most unabashed coastal resort, **Cancún**. For final relaxation, head out to **Isla Mujeres** or low-key **Isla Holbox**. At Holbox, if it's between mid-May and mid-September, you can take a swim with some giant (and harmless) whale sharks.

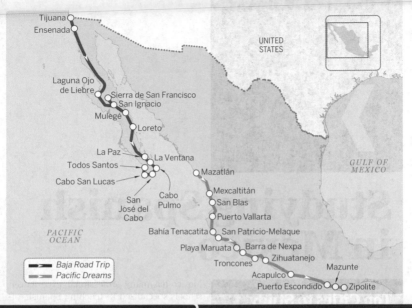

Baja Road Trip
Pacific Dreams

Three Weeks
Baja Road Trip

Four Weeks
Pacific Dreams

Over 1700km along the Carretera Transpeninsular (Hwy 1) from Tijuana to Los Cabos is a classic Mexican road trip, traversing deserts, beautiful remote coastlines and half a dozen all-different cities.

Get a feel for the border buzz of **Tijuana**, then savor the surf and wines of **Ensenada** before moving further south to watch the whales on **Laguna Ojo de Liebre** (January to March). Cross the Desierto de Vizcaíno to the leafy oasis of **San Ignacio**, and check out the ancient rock art of the **Sierra de San Francisco**. Follow this with some diving or kayaking in the Sea of Cortez off **Mulegé** or **Loreto**.

Further south, cosmopolitan **La Paz** provides access to brilliant beaches and the superb marine life of **La Ventana**. Try snorkeling or diving the coral reef off uncrowded **Cabo Pulmo** before landing at the foot of the peninsula and sampling tranquil **San José del Cabo** and the party scene of **Cabo San Lucas**. Slip away to artsy **Todos Santos** for a change of pace and some of Baja California's best surf.

Mexico's Pacific coast is a glittering sequence of pristine jungle-lined beaches, super surf, busy resorts and every grade of coastal dream in between.

Sip margaritas on the lively plaza in **Mazatlán**, a beach town with an artsy historic core, before visiting the ancient island of **Mexcaltitán** and the surf and wildlife-rich lagoons of laid-back **San Blas**. Then it's on to clubs, gourmet food, whale-watching and shopping in **Puerto Vallarta**.

Isolated beaches abound on the Costalegre, home to some luxurious resorts: spend a day (or more) on the beaches of palm-fringed **Bahía Tenacatita**. Moving on, don't miss the street tacos in **San Patricio-Melaque**. Hang out at tranquil **Playa Maruata**, the most beautiful beach in Michoacán, or rent a *cabaña* (cabin) at the quaint surfer haven of **Barra de Nexpa**. Surf, snorkel or take to horseback at **Troncones** before hiring a kayak at charming **Zihuatanejo**.

See the cliff divers and learn a little Mexican history in **Acapulco** before moving on to relaxed **Puerto Escondido**, with its A-grade surf and a lively little after-dark scene. To end your trip, lie back in a hammock at the low-budget paradise beaches of **Mazunte** or **Zipolite**.

Studying Spanish in Mexico

Top Cities to Study Spanish

Oaxaca Lovely southern city with several good language schools (p421).

Guanajuato Lively university town with popular language schools (p659).

Cuernavaca Mexico's highest concentration of language schools, attracting many US college students (p176).

Puebla Attractive colonial city (p145), with the prestigious Universidad de las Américas Puebla (www.udlap.mx) at nearby Cholula.

San Cristóbal de las Casas Charming highland town with several schools good for travelers (p356).

Mexico City Latin America's biggest university, UNAM, offers courses for foreigners (p95).

Guadalajara Mexico's second-largest city has university and private courses (p574).

Mérida Private-school and university courses in the Yucatán's cultural capital (p299).

Xalapa Courses at the Universidad Veracruzana in this urbane state capital (p210).

Mexico has many professional, experienced schools specialized in teaching Spanish, offering everything from short courses for travelers to longer courses for serious students of the language. Schools are often located in Mexico's most attractive and interesting cities, and present a great opportunity to get an inside experience of Mexican life. Extracurricular activities such as dance, cooking, music, excursions and volunteering are usually programmed into courses or available as optional extras. Many schools also offer specialist courses in fields like Spanish for medicine or social work, or Mexican indigenous languages, as well as cultural courses in history, arts, politics etc.

It's important to do your research to find schools that provide the kind of teaching and experience you want. Check out schools (many are recommended in this book) via their websites or reviews on the internet, by talking to people who have studied in Mexico, and by emailing schools with your questions. Here are key points to consider.

Schools

» Private school or university? Many Mexican universities have special departments providing tailor-made courses for foreigners (usually lasting between one month and one semester). Some universities also accept foreigners with good Spanish into their regular classes under semester-abroad, year-abroad or student-exchange arrangements. Time spent at a Mexican university can be a real cultural immersion experience.

Private schools typically offer shorter courses, from one week to three months. They may provide smaller class sizes and be more expensive. You'll be part of a mixed Mexican/foreign ambience, but these schools generally provide plenty of opportunities for local cultural contact.

» Traveler- or college student–oriented? Some courses are geared mainly to college students who want credits for their courses back home; many Mexican language schools and universities have close links with foreign (especially US) colleges. Some private schools focus more on classes for travelers or independent language students.

» Flexibility Some schools are particularly flexible, allowing you to start when you want, and study as much as you like, for as long as you want. Others have more fixed schedules, which you must fit in with. Most traveler-oriented schools allow you to start any Monday.

» Atmosphere Does the school seem friendly and welcoming? Is it well organized? Are the other students there to party or to learn?

Courses

» Intensive or relaxed? You could have up to 40 contact hours per week or as little as 10, or take just a handful of private classes. Schools offer many options.

» Short or long? Do you want just a one-week beginner's course, or a full year's study toward your degree back home – or something in between? Many schools recommend one month as a minimum to make significant progress.

» Conversation/grammar/textual study? Check out course content to see which aspects of language learning or skills it emphasizes.

RESOURCES

» Lonely Planet (www.lonelyplanet.com) The Thorn Tree message board has many reports and recommendations on schools.

» 123 TeachMe (www.123teachme.com) Listings of more than 100 language schools in Mexico.

The **National Registration Center for Study Abroad** (www.nrcsa.com), **AmeriSpan** (www.amerispan.com) and **Spanish Abroad** (www.spanishabroad.com) are among US-based organizations offering a range of study programs in Mexico.

VISAS

If your studies are for more than six months, you'll need a student visa. Contact your school and/or Mexican consulate about this.

» Class size Very variable. Generally, the smaller the class, the more it costs and the more teacher attention you'll get, but it may be a less social experience.

» Will they teach at my level? Most schools offer teaching at all levels, from beginner to advanced. You will usually take a test to determine your level when you arrive. Try to find out if the school really teaches each level separately or if it sometimes groups different levels together. There are several widely recognized systems to define levels of proficiency in a foreign language, most with five or six levels from beginner/elementary to advanced/fluent.

» Will I get a certificate/diploma/college credit? This varies from school to school and course to course. If you need credits for a college course back home, be sure to check that your college will approve a course for this purpose. Widely recognized general Spanish-language qualifications include Mexico's Examen de Posesión de la Lengua Española (EPLE) and Spain's Diplomas de Español como Lengua Extranjera (DELE).

Where to Live?

Most schools offer a choice of living options including homestays with local families, apartments, bed-and-breakfasts or their own student houses or rooms. Homestays are often the cheapest option (typically around US$150 per week for your own room in a family's home and two meals a day), and will give you a closer experience of Mexican life. An hour at the dinner table can develop your practical Spanish skills as much as a few hours in a classroom.

Costs

A typical rate for group classes in private schools is US$10 per hour. All up, 25 hours of classes per week, plus homestay accommodations and meals, averages around US$400. Courses at universities are often cheaper, though classes may be bigger. Some schools charge extra for enrollment/registration and/or materials.

Exploring Mexico's Ancient Ruins

Where

Most of Mexico's major pre-Hispanic sites are scattered around the center, south and southeast of the country, where the greatest ancient civilizations developed.

When

The ideal months to visit archaeological sites are outside the rainy season and avoiding the highest temperatures. For the main archaeological regions, this means:

Central Mexico August, October to April

Gulf coast November to April

Yucatán Peninsula November to April

Chiapas October to May

Oaxaca October to March

Most sites are open from 9am to 5pm. If they have a closing day, it is usually Monday. The best time of day to go is soon after opening time, when temperatures are lower and the main visitor crowds have not arrived yet.

Don't Miss

The top five sites that everyone should see if they can:

» Teotihuacán

» Palenque

» Chichén Itzá

» Uxmal

» Monte Albán

Mexico's ancient civilizations were the most sophisticated and formidable in North and Central America, and their cities and sacred precincts are a national treasure and a highlight of the country. Their tall pyramids, richly decorated temples and palaces, ritual ball-game courts and gruesome sacrificial sites have amazed outsiders since the Spaniards arrived on Mexican soil in 1519. Visiting them today is still very much a journey of discovery into an extraordinary past, and an experience not to be missed even if you have no prior knowledge of ancient Mexico.

Archaeologists have been uncovering ancient sites and making spectacular discoveries here since the 19th century. Many impressive sites have been restored and made accessible to visitors. Others have been explored in part, and thousands more remain untouched, beneath the earth or forests. Ancient Mexico may have had as many as 25 million people when the Spanish arrived, so there's still much to be discovered.

The most famous sites are often thronged with large numbers of visitors (arrive early). Others are hidden away on remote hilltops or shrouded in thick jungle, and can be the most exciting and rewarding to visit, for those with an adventurous spirit.

Mexico's Ancient Civilizations

The major civilizations were these (for more background, see p799):

» **Olmec** Mexico's 'mother culture' was centered on the Gulf coast, from about 1200 BC to 400 BC.

Mexico Ruins

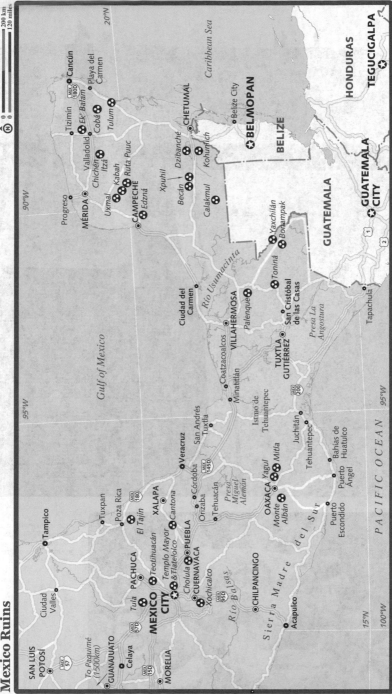

WITOLD SKRYPCZAK/LONELY PLANET IMAGES©

» (above) The world's third-largest
pyramid, Pirámide del Sol at
Teotihuacán (p139)
» (left) The feathered serpent deity on
the facade of Templo de Quetzalcóatl,
Teotihuacán (p139)

It's famed for the giant stone sculptures known as Olmec heads.

» **Teotihuacán** This city with its huge pyramids, 50km from Mexico City, flourished in the first seven centuries AD, and ruled the biggest of the ancient Mexican empires.

» **Maya** The Maya, in southeast Mexico and neighboring Guatemala and Belize, flowered most brilliantly in numerous city-states between AD 250 and AD 900. They're famed for their exquisitely beautiful temples and stone sculpture. Maya culture lives on today.

» **Toltec** A name for the culture of a number of central Mexican city-states, from around AD 750 to AD 1150. The warrior sculptures of Tula are the most celebrated monuments.

» **Aztec** With their capital at Tenochtitlán (now Mexico City) from AD 1325 to AD 1521, the Aztecs came to rule most of central Mexico from the Gulf coast to the Pacific. The best known Aztec site is the Templo Mayor in Mexico City.

Pre-Hispanic Numbers

Ancient Mexicans loved numbers. We've assembled some of our own:

» **8km** of tunnels dug by archaeologists beneath Cholula's Tepanapa Pyramid

» **70m** – the height of Teotihuacán's Pyramid of the Sun

» **100km** – the length of the *sacbé* (stone-paved avenue) from Cobá to Yaxuna

» **120 mural-covered walls** in Teotihuacán's Tetitla Palace

» **300 masks of Chac**, the rain god, at Kabah's Palace of Masks

» **6500 buildings** at Calakmul

» **15,000 ritual ball-game courts** found in Mexico (so far)

» **20,000 human hearts** ripped out for the rededication of Tenochtitlán's Templo Mayor in 1487

Resources

» **Instituto Nacional de Antropología e Historia** (INAH; www.inah.gob.mx) You can take virtual tours of a dozen archaeological sites and museums on the website of Mexico's National Institute of Anthropology and History, which administers 180 *zonas arqueológicas* (archaeological sites).

» **An Archaeological Guide to Central and Southern Mexico** Joyce Kelly's book was published in 2001 and is still the best of its kind, covering 70 sites.

» **Archaeology of Ancient Mexico and Central America: An Encyclopedia** A reference book by Susan Toby Evans and David L Webster, incorporating recent discoveries and scholarship.

» **Mesoweb** (www.mesoweb.com) A great, diverse resource on ancient Mexico, especially the Maya.

Site Practicalities

» Admission to archaeological sites costs from nothing up to M$166, depending on the site (only a couple of much-visited sites on the Yucatán Peninsula cost more than M$51).

» Go protected against the sun and, at jungle sites, against mosquitoes.

» Heavily visited sites have facilities such as cafes or restaurants, bookstores, souvenir stores, audio guides in various languages, and authorized (but not fixed-price) human guides.

» Little-visited sites may have no food or water available.

» Guided tours to many sites are available from nearby towns, but public transportation is usually available, too.

» Major sites are usually wheelchair accessible.

» Explanatory signs may be in Spanish only, or in Spanish and English, or in Spanish, English and a local indigenous language.

Top Sites & Museums

Some sites have their own museums, but there are also important city and regional museums which hold many of the most valuable and impressive pre-Hispanic artifacts and provide fascinating background on ancient Mexico.

» **Museo Nacional de Antropología, Mexico City** The superb National Museum of Anthropology (p75) has sections devoted to all the important ancient civilizations and includes such treasures as the famous Aztec sun stone and a replica of King Pakal's treasure-laden tomb from Palenque.

» **Museo de Antropología, Xalapa** Mainly devoted to Gulf coast cultures, this excellent museum (p208) contains seven Olmec heads and other masterly sculptures among its 29,000-piece collection.

» **Parque-Museo La Venta, Villahermosa** This outdoor museum-cum-zoo (p408) holds several Olmec heads and other fine sculptures from the site of La Venta, moved here in the 1950s when La Venta was under threat from petroleum exploration.

» **Museo de la Arquitectura Maya, Campeche** Excellent overview of the Maya sites in Campeche state and their varied architectural styles (p327).

PRE-HISPANIC SITES

	SITE	PERIOD	DESCRIPTION
CENTRAL MEXICO	Teotihuacán (p137)	AD 0-700	Mexico's biggest ancient city, capital of Teotihuacán empire
	Templo Mayor (p123)	AD 1375-1521	ceremonial center of the Aztec capital, Tenochtitlán
	Cholula (p155)	AD 0-1521	city & religious center
	Tula (p136)	AD 900-1150	major Toltec city
	Cantona (p164)	AD 600-1000	huge, well-preserved, little-visited city
	Tlatelolco (p92)	12th century AD-1521	site of main Aztec market & defeat of last Aztec emperor Cuauhtémoc
	Xochicalco (p179)	AD 600-1200	large, hilltop religious & commercial center
CHIAPAS	Palenque (p373)	100 BC-AD 740	beautiful major Maya city
	Yaxchilán (p384)	7th-9th century AD	Maya city
	Toniná (p371)	c AD 600-900	Maya temple complex
	Bonampak (p384)	8th century AD	Maya site
NORTHERN MEXICO	Paquimé (p775)	AD 900-1340	trading center linking central Mexico with northern desert cultures
OAXACA	Monte Albán (p436)	500 BC-AD 900	hilltop ceremonial center of Zapotec civilization
	Mitla (p441)	c AD 1300-1520	Zapotec religious center
	Yagul (p440)	AD 900-1400	Zapotec & Mixtec ceremonial center
VERACRUZ	El Tajín (p231)	AD 600-1200	town & ceremonial center of Classic Veracruz civilization
YUCATÁN PENINSULA	Chichén Itzá (p317)	2nd-14th century AD	large, well restored Maya/Toltec city
	Uxmal (p306)	AD 600-900	Maya city
	Tulum (p278)	c AD 1200-1600	late Maya town & ceremonial center
	Calakmul (p335)	approx 1st-9th century AD	huge, once very powerful Maya city, little restored
	Cobá (p283)	AD 600-1100	Maya city
	Kabah (p310)	AD 750-950	Maya city
	Ruta Puuc (p311)	AD 750-950	three Puuc Maya sites (Sayil, Xlapak, Labná)
	Edzná (p333)	600 BC-AD 1500	Maya city
	Becán (p336)	550 BC-AD 1000	large Maya site
	Xpujil (p337)	flourished 8th century AD	Maya settlement
	Ek' Balam (p324)	approx AD 600-800	Maya city
	Dzibanché (p338)	approx 200 BC-AD 1200	Maya city
	Kohunlich (p338)	AD 100-600	Maya city

HIGHLIGHTS	LOCATION/TRANSPORTATION
Pyramids of Sun and Moon, Calzada de los Muertos, palace murals	50km northeast of Mexico City; frequent buses
ceremonial pyramid	downtown Mexico City
world's widest pyramid	8km west of Puebla; frequent buses
stone pillars carved as warriors	80km north of Mexico City; 1km walk or taxi from Tula bus station
24 ball courts, unique street system	90km northeast of Puebla; taxi or *colectivo* from Oriental
Aztec temple-pyramid	northern Mexico City; trolleybus or metro
Pyramid of Quetzalcóatl	35km southwest of Cuernavaca; bus
exquisite temples with jungle backdrop	7km west of Palenque town; frequent combis
temples & other buildings in jungle setting	beside Río Usumacinta, 15km northwest of Frontera Corozal; van from Palenque to Frontera Corozal (170km), boat from Frontera Corozal to Yaxchilán
temples & pyramids on hillside	14km east of Ocosingo; combis from Ocosingo
superb, if weathered, frescoes	150km southeast of Palenque; van or bus to San Javier (140km), then taxi
adobe walls & buildings, clay macaw cages, rare geometric pottery	Casas Grandes village; buses from Nuevo Casas Grandes, 7km north
pyramids, observatory, panoramas	6km west of Oaxaca; bus
unique stone mosaics	46km southeast of Oaxaca; bus or *colectivo*
large ball court, rock 'fortress'	35km southeast of Oaxaca; bus or *colectivo*, then 1.5km walk
rare niched pyramids, 17 ball courts, *voladores'* (fliers') performances	6km west of Papantla; bus
El Castillo 'calendar temple,' Mexico's biggest ball court, El Caracol observatory, Platform of Skulls	117km east of Mérida, 2km east of Pisté village, 44km west of Valladolid; buses from Mérida, Pisté & Valladolid
pyramids, palaces, riotous sculpture featuring masks of rain god Chac	80km south of Mérida; buses from Mérida
temples & towers on superb Caribbean-side site	Tulum, 130km south of Cancún; taxi, walk or cycle from town
high pyramids with views over rainforest	60km south of Escárcega-Chetumal road; car, tour from Campeche or Chicanná, taxi from Xpujil
towering pyramids in jungle setting	Cobá village, 50km northwest of Tulum; buses from Tulum & Valladolid
Palace of Masks, with 300 Chac masks	104km south of Mérida; buses from Mérida & Uxmal
palaces with elaborate columns & sculpture, including Chac masks	113-122km south of Mérida; car, until excursion bus from Mérida is reinstated
five-story pyramid-palace, Temple of Masks	53km southeast of Campeche; buses & shuttle service from Campeche
towered temples	8km west of Xpujil; taxi or car
three-towered ancient 'skyscraper'	Xpujil town, 123km west of Chetumal; buses from Campeche & Chetumal
huge Acrópolis & high pyramid with unusual carving	23km north of Valladolid by taxi or *colectivo*
semiwild site with palaces & pyramids	85km west of Chetumal; car, or tour from Xpujil
Temple of the Masks	72km west of Chetumal; car, tour from Xpujil, or bus & 8.5km walk/hitchhike

Travel with Children

Best Regions for Kids

Yucatán Peninsula

Cancún, the Riviera Maya and nearby islands are geared to giving holidaymakers fun. The area is full of great beaches with every imaginable aquatic activity, hotels designed to make life easy, and attractions from jungle zip-lines to swimming in underwater rivers. Other parts of the peninsula are great if your kids will enjoy exploring Maya ruins.

Central Pacific Coast

The Pacific coast offers all conceivable types of fun in, on and under the ocean and lagoons, and a vast range of places to base yourself, from sophisticated Puerto Vallarta to easygoing Zihuatanejo and countless smaller spots where your time is just yours and your family's.

Mexico City

The capital keeps kids happy with a hands-on children's museum, a first-rate zoo, dedicated kids' entertainment, and parks and plazas full of space and fun.

Mexico for Kids

The sights, sounds and colors of Mexico excite and stimulate children just as they do adults.

Mexicans Love Children

Mexicans will give children a warm welcome almost everywhere. Any child whose hair is less than jet-black will be affectionately called 'güero' (blondie), and with a handful of exceptions, children are welcome at all accommodations and almost any cafe or restaurant.

Eating

Children may be less keen to experiment with new tastes than their parents are, but fortunately Mexico has plenty of eateries serving up familiar international fare. Italian restaurants are plentiful, food common in Western countries such as eggs, steaks, bread, rice and cheese is available everywhere, and fresh fruit is abundant. Simpler Mexican snacks like quesadillas, burritos and tacos – or steaming corn cobs straight from a street cart – are good ways of trying out local flavors. Restaurant staff are accustomed to children and can usually provide high chairs if needed, or make something that's not actually on the menu, if requested.

The spacious, open-air character of many Mexican eateries conveniently means that children aren't compelled to sit nicely at the table all the time.

Sleeping

Mexico has some excitingly different places to stay which will please most kids – anything beachside is a good start, and rustic *cabañas* (cabins) provide a sense of adventure (but choose one with good mosquito nets!). Many hotels have a rambling layout and a good amount of open-air space – courtyards, pool areas, gardens – allowing for some light exploring by kids. The most family-oriented hotels, with expansive grounds and facilities like shallow pools and playgrounds, tend to be found on the coasts.

Family rooms are widely available, and many hotels will put an extra bed or two in a room at little or no extra charge. However, baby cots may not be available in budget accommodations. You can find a room with air-conditioning almost anywhere, and most midrange and top-end hotels have wi-fi access and child-friendly channels on the TV for when your kids just need to flop down in front of something entertaining.

In this book the symbol 🖪 identifies particularly family-friendly places where you can stay and eat.

Getting Around

Watching scenery go by is not most kids' favorite pastime, so try to do your traveling between towns in smallish chunks of a few hours at most. Most Mexican buses show nonstop movies on video screens, which diverts most kids above toddler age, and most of the movies are pretty family-friendly. Children under 13 pay half-price on many long-distance buses, and if they're small enough to sit on your lap, they will usually go for free. If you're traveling with a baby or toddler, consider investing in deluxe buses for the extra space and comfort. Car rental is a practical alternative to buses: if you want a car with a child safety seat, the major international rental firms are the most reliable providers.

Of course, some forms of traveling are fun – there are boat trips of many kinds to be had, especially along the coasts, and bicycles, ATVs (all terain vehicles) and horses to be rented for outings. Several cities offer quickfire tours around their sights in motorized streetcars.

Health & Safety

Children are more easily affected than adults by heat, disrupted sleeping patterns and strange food. Be particularly careful that they don't drink tap water or consume any questionable food or beverage. Take care to avoid sunburn, cover them up against insect bites, and ensure you replace fluids if a child gets diarrhea.

Don't hesitate to go to a doctor if you think it may be necessary. In general, privately run hospitals and clinics in Mexico offer better facilities and care than public ones. Do make sure you have adequate travel insurance that will cover the cost of private medical care.

Child safety provisions in Mexico may be less effective than what you are accustomed to. Check out things like toddler pools, cribs, guardrails and even toys so that you're aware of any potential hazards.

Breast-feeding in public is rarely seen in Mexico.

Children's Highlights
On & in the Water

» **Learn to surf** Kids as young as five can take classes at many spots with gentler waves along the Pacific coast, including San Agustinillo's Coco Loco Surf Club.

» **Spot turtles, dolphins and whales** Boat trips are available at many places along the Pacific coast.

» **Snorkel in the Caribbean** Many beaches on the Caribbean coast and its offshore islands provide calm waters and colorful marine life for beginners.

» **Sail on a pirate ship** The *Marigalante*, a replica Spanish galleon, does pirate-themed daytime cruises from Puerto Vallarta.

» **Ride a gondola** Cruise ancient Aztec canals at Xochimilco, Mexico City.

» **Waterslide thrills** Mazatlán's MazAgua and Puerto Vallarta's Aquaventuras Park are two of the best water parks in the country, the latter with dolphin shows, too.

Multi-Adventure

» **Parque de Aventuras Barrancas del Cobre** The Copper Canyon Adventure Park's spine-tingling seven zip-lines carry you halfway to the canyon floor from its lip at 2400m. There's rappelling, climbing and a cable car, too.

» **Selvática** Award-winning 12-zip-line circuit through the jungle near Cancún, with its own cenote (limestone sinkhole) for swimming.

» **Río Secreto** Hike and swim through a 600m-long cavern near Playa del Carmen.

» (above) Children playing in the ancient island village of Mexcaltitán (p496)

» (left) The colonial-era Mina El Edén, Zacatecas, once among Mexico's richest mines (p629)

PLANNING

» When deciding your itinerary, bear in mind that few kids like traveling all the time; they're usually happier if they can settle into a place for a while, make friends and get on with some of the things they like doing back home.

» See a doctor about vaccinations at least one month – preferably two – before your trip.

» It's a good idea to book some accommodations for at least the first couple of nights, even if you plan to be flexible once you have arrived.

» Diapers (nappies) and sunscreen are widely available, but you may not easily find wet wipes, other creams, baby foods or familiar medicine outside larger cities and tourist towns. Bring what you need.

» Lonely Planet's *Travel with Children* has lots of practical advice on the subject, drawn from firsthand experience.

» **Boca del Puma** Zip-lining, horseback riding, wall climbing and a cenote to dip into, near Puerto Morelos.

» **Aktun Chen** Near Akumal, featuring a 600m-long cave, a 12m-deep cenote, 10 zip-lines and a small zoo.

Animals

» **Baja whale-watching** See massive gray whales and their calves off the coasts of Baja California (January to March) – usually requires several hours in a boat, so best for older kids.

» **Zoológico de Chapultepec** Mexico City's large zoo has a wide range of the world's creatures, including three pandas, in large enclosures.

» **La Ventanilla** Take a boat ride through a lagoon full of crocs and release baby turtles into the ocean at this Oaxaca ecotourism scheme.

» **El Refugio de Potosí, Barra de Potosí** Hold snakes and tarantulas and observe parrots, hummingbirds, armadillos and a jaguarundi (small wild feline).

» **Zoomat, Tuxtla Gutiérrez** Has 180 species, all from the state of Chiapas, including several types of big cat.

Museums, Mines & Ruins

» **Papalote Museo del Niño** There are two of these fun, hands-on, children's museums – one in Mexico City, one in Cuernavaca. Good for kids up to about 11.

» **Cobá** This jungle-surrounded ancient Maya site near Tulum has a zip-line as well as pyramids, and bicycles for cruising around its network of pathways.

» **Mina El Edén, Zacatecas** Take a miniature train into this colonial-era silver mine, then walk past old mineshafts and over subterranean pools.

Spectacles

» **Voladores (Fliers)** This indigenous Totonac rite involves men climbing up a 30m-high pole, then casting themselves off backward, attached only by ropes. Performed regularly at El Tajín and Papantla.

» **Folk dance** Highly colorful, entertaining shows are given regularly by the Ballet Folclórico de México in Mexico City and by several Guelaguetza groups in Oaxaca.

regions at a glance

Mexico City

Museums ✓✓✓
Architecture ✓✓✓
Food ✓✓

Museum Mecca

You name it, Mexico City probably has a museum for it: from cutting-edge contemporary art to peculiar collections of torture instruments and antique toys. And since many exhibitions are free on Sunday, cash-strapped art buffs have no excuse. Most people come to visit the world-class National Museum of Anthropology in Chapultepec park or Frida Kahlo's famed blue house in bohemian Coyoacán, but in a city with 100-plus museums, that's just getting started.

Architecture Overload

Few other places in the Western Hemisphere, if any, can boast an architectural offering of gleaming skyscrapers, colonial palaces and pre-Hispanic ruins. In the Centro Histórico, Mexico City's 34-block downtown area alone, we're talking about more than 1500 buildings that are classified as historic and artistic monuments. Over in the trendy Roma and Condesa neighborhoods, you'll be wining and dining in grandiose Porfiriato-era mansions and well-preserved art-deco edifices.

Focus on Food

Regional Mexican cuisine gets top billing in the capital. As expected in such a culinary melting pot, everyone here debates over where you can find, say, the best Guerrero-style green *pozole* (soup) or the most exquisite Oaxacan *mole* (sauce). Street eats are fiendishly addictive, and if you feel like splurging there's no shortage of gourmet restaurants crafting refined versions of traditional fare.

Around Mexico City

Food ✓✓✓
Ruins ✓✓
Small-Town Escapes ✓✓✓

Regional Specialties

An incredible variety of indigenous ingredients and imported culinary influences combine to create complex regional cuisines. Many towns, even small *pueblitos*, have their own specialty, such as the pasties from the mining villages above Pachuca or Puebla's famed *mole poblano*.

Ancient Architecture

Some of Mexico's most awe-inspiring ruins stand within a few hours of the capital. Teotihuacán, with its stunning Pyramids of the Sun and Moon, is the most famous. But fascinating sites such as Cacaxtla, Xochitécatl, Xochicalco and Cantona can be explored in virtual solitude.

Pueblos Mágicos

With their leafy plazas, traditional crafts and gorgeous colonial edifices, remarkably well-preserved 'magical towns' such as Cuetzalan, Real del Monte, Malinalco and Valle de Bravo provide a perfect escape from the thick air and crowds of the capital.

Veracruz

Archaeological Sites ✓✓✓
Ecotourism ✓
Food ✓✓

Ancient Cultures

Many distinct pre-Hispanic cultures graced Mexico's Gulf coast, and all have left a weighty legacy. Examine the Classic Veracruz ruins of El Tajín with its curious 'niche' pyramid; the magnificence of Totonac Zempoala, where Cortés forged an alliance against the Aztecs; and the ancient Olmec settlement of Tres Zapotes.

Going Green

A geographic anomaly of rugged volcanoes and unsullied rainforest, the Los Tuxtlas region is working hard to promote Mexico's green credentials with rustic accommodations, isolated hiking opportunities and a nascent tourist infrastructure.

Fish, Glorious Fish

Thanks to the state's 690km-long coastline, fish headlines most Veracruz menus, in particular the spicy mélange known as *huachinango a la veracruzana*. Lining up behind it are the distinctive *moles* of Xico and the gourmet coffee of Coatepec.

p194

Yucatán Peninsula

Diving & Snorkeling ✓✓
Maya Ruins ✓✓
Beaches ✓✓✓

Into the Blue

With hundreds of kilometers of Caribbean coastline bounded by the world's second-largest barrier reef, the Yucatán is a magnet for divers and snorkelers. Banco Chinchorro is the superstar and the underwater sculpture garden off Cancún provides another unique experience.

Oldies but Goodies

From world-famous sites to smaller, equally worthy ones, the Yucatán is dotted with pyramids, platforms and temples – many of which are surprisingly easy to reach and have a resonating atmosphere even the loudest tour groups can't diminish.

A Day at the Beach

Finding the right beach for you is simply a matter of hopping a bus (or boat). From the debauchery of Cancún to the lonely coastlines of the Costa Maya, the region's bleach-white sand and beautiful warm water must not be missed.

p247

Chiapas

Culture ✓✓✓
Activities ✓✓✓
Nature ✓✓✓

Temples & Tradition

The world of the Maya lives on everywhere you turn here, from the preserved stone temples of Classic Maya civilization to the persistence of dramatic pre-Hispanic religious rituals and the intricate handwoven textiles and clothing still worn by many.

In Motion

Whether you're rappelling down into an endless jungle sinkhole, bouncing over a stretch of white water in a rubber raft or summiting a 4000m volcano, Chiapas has a multitude of ways to churn up your adrenaline.

Birds & Beasts

Nesting turtles, roaring monkeys and flashes of rainbow plumage are standard fare in the jungles and mist-shrouded mountains and on the sandy beaches of this biodiverse region that's full of rare and endangered wildlife.

p339

Oaxaca

Culture ✓✓✓
Beaches ✓✓✓
Crafts ✓✓

Cultural Hub
Oaxaca state is a hub of culture in so many senses: from the vibrant arts scene and beautiful colonial buildings of Oaxaca city to the unique festivals, crafts and costumes of the Zapotecs and other indigenous peoples. It all wraps up in a unique and proud Oaxacan regional identity.

Beach Life
With 550km of sandy Pacific strands and wildlife-rich lagoons, Oaxaca's coastline has it all – the pumping surf of Puerto Escondido, the blissed-out traveler scene of Zipolite and Mazunte, and the resort attractions of low-key Bahías de Huatulco.

Arts & Crafts
Oaxaca's folk-art scene is the richest in Mexico, inspired chiefly by the large indigenous populace. Browsing the stores and markets of Oaxaca city and visiting village workshops, you'll be amazed by the colorful creativity of Oaxacan weavers, potters and woodcarvers.

p411

Central Pacific Coast

Beaches ✓✓✓
Food ✓✓✓
Outdoor Activities ✓✓✓

Surf & Sand
Conjure up the beach of your dreams and you'll find it here, whether your idea of paradise involves wiggling your toes in the sand with margarita in hand, or chasing perfect waves along an endless ultramarine horizon.

Seafood Heaven
Sidle up to a beachside table at sunset, grab a cold beer and a wedge of fresh-cut lime, and settle into a plateful of *pescado zarandeado* (charbroiled fish stuffed with veggies and spices), *tiritas* (citrus-and-chili-marinated raw fish slivers) or shrimp and red snapper cooked a dozen different ways.

Natural Highs
Kayak across a lagoon at dawn, ride horses into the Sierra Madre, swim among flitting butterflies in a boulder-strewn river, watch pelicans and whales parade through the waves or scan the nighttime sands for nesting mama turtles.

p481

Western Central Highlands

Food ✓✓✓
Scenery ✓✓
Culture ✓✓

Culinary Feast
There's nowhere better to get a taste of Mexico's amazingly diverse culinary culture: delicious *sopitas* in Colima, pre-Hispanic ingredients brought to life as *alta cocina* (haute cuisine) in Morelia, and Guadalajara's diverse array of contemporary Mexican gourmet restaurants. You'll eat outstanding food here.

Dramatic Scenery
Tiny Colima state packs more of a scenic punch than almost anywhere in the region, with its dramatic twin volcanoes. For more glorious scenery don't miss the modern marvel, Volcán Paricutín, in Michoacán.

Cultural Offerings
The western central highlands groan with indigenous culture, most notably that of the thriving Purépecha people whose arts and crafts are sold around Pátzcuaro. You'll find superb art galleries and history museums in Guadalajara and Morelia, and great shopping for arts and crafts in Tlaquepaque.

p565

Northern Central Highlands

Museums ✓✓
Food ✓✓
Towns & Cities ✓✓

Baja California

Water Sports ✓✓✓
Wine Regions ✓✓✓
Scenery ✓✓✓

Copper Canyon & Northern Mexico

Outdoor Adventures ✓✓✓
Cultures ✓✓
Museums ✓

Monumental Museums

Home to fascinating indigenous cultures and most of the silver that brought fabulous opulence to colonial grandees, this region was also the birthplace of Mexican independence from Spain. Some of the country's best museums highlight everything from indigenous artisanry and historical heroes to contemporary art.

Street & Table Food

The region's cities all have their own takes on classic Mexican bites, whether a trusty tortilla or a 'traditional' taco. Celebrated chefs, especially in San Miguel de Allende and San Luis Potosí, now offer cutting-edge, contemporary and international cuisine.

Pedestrian Paradise

Cobblestone colonial-era streets make for fascinating exploration on foot. Towns here are made for getting lost in – up narrow *callejones* (alleys) or down steep steps. Without doubt, you'll eventually end up on a pretty, laurel-tree-filled plaza.

p626

Surfing & Diving

Baja is a paradise for surfers of all levels, with beach, point, and reef breaks up and down the Pacific coastline. Divers can do a two-tank dive in the Pacific and be at the natural aquarium of the Sea of Cortez in time for a night dive.

Ruta del Vino

Valle de Guadalupe is producing probably the best wines in Mexico and this 'Napa Sur' is poised to garner international acclaim. Its Wine Route makes for a great day (or two) out.

Majestic Mountains, Tropical Paradise

Where else in the world is desert just steps away from turquoise lagoons? At every corner are vistas that seem pulled from the pages of a vacation calendar.

p691

Great Outdoors

The north is all about topographical overload. An idyllic coastline, vast deserts and dramatic canyons with climates from alpine to subtropical all contribute to a wealth of wildlife and tantalizing hiking and bicycling routes.

Singular Cultures

This region offers great encounters with indigenous peoples. The mysterious Tarahumara inhabit the Copper Canyon, and the Pacific coast is home to the Seri with their distinctive handicrafts. Chihuahua state is the center of Mexico's largest group of Mennonites, who produce delectable foodstuffs.

Museum Scene

Cracking museums give the north real cultural clout. Sample Hermosillo's impressive MUSAS art museum, or Chihuahua's many museums reflecting its role in Mexican history. Monterrey and Saltillo boast must-see museums on the steel industry, deserts and birds.

p735

> **Every listing is recommended by our authors, and their favorite places are listed first**

> **Look out for these icons:**

 Our author's top recommendation   A green or sustainable option   No payment required

See the Index for a full list of destinations covered in this book.

On the Road

Mexico City

📞 55 / POP 20 MILLION / ELEV 2240M

Best Places to Eat

» Pujol (p107)
» El Hidalguense (p106)
» Contramar (p106)
» Corazón de Maguey (p109)
» Hostería de Santo Domingo (p103)

Best Places to Stay

» Red Tree House (p100)
» Villa Condesa (p101)
» Chalet del Carmen (p102)
» Hotel Catedral (p97)
» Mexico City Hostel (p98)

Why Go?

Much-maligned Mexico City is cleaning up its act these days. Revamped public spaces are springing back to life, the culinary scene is exploding and a cultural renaissance is blooming. But here's the kicker: by somehow managing to distance itself from the drug war, the nation's capital has emerged as a 'safe haven' of sorts.

Remember that Mexico City is, and has ever been, the sun in the Mexican solar system. A stroll through the buzzing downtown area reveals the city's storied history, from its pre-Hispanic underpinnings and colonial-era splendor to its unabashed contemporary edge. Organized chaos rules in this high-octane megalopolis, yet rest assured that the city offers plenty of escape valves in the way of old-school cantinas, intriguing museums, dramatic murals and boating excursions along ancient canals. With all that and so much more going on here, you just might be swayed to scrap those beach plans.

When to Go

Mexico City

Late Mar–Apr Vacationing *chilangos* clear out for the Easter holiday, leaving the city remarkably calm.

May The Centro's streets become lively stages for cultural events during the Festival de México.

Nov Rainy season ends and the month begins with colorful Day of the Dead festivities.

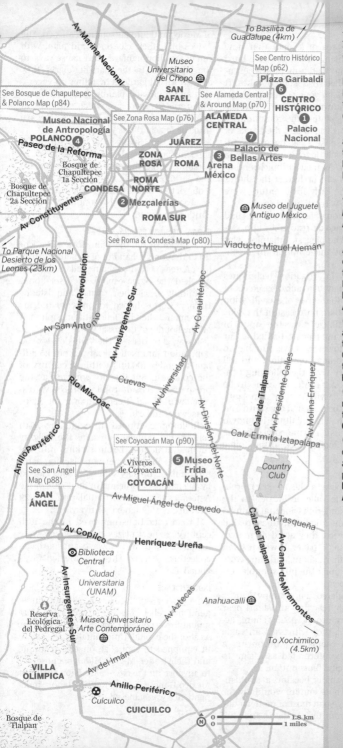

To Basílica de
Guadalupe (4km)

Av Marina Nacional

See Bosque de Chapultepec
& Polanco Map (p84)

Museo
Universitario
del Chopo

See Centro Histórico
Map (p62)

Plaza Garibaldi

SAN
RAFAEL

Museo Nacional
de Antropología
POLANCO ④
Paseo de la Reforma

See Zona Rosa Map (p76)

See Alameda Central
& Around Map (p70)

ALAMEDA
CENTRAL

CENTRO
HISTÓRICO

⑥

Palacio
Nacional

①

JUÁREZ

ZONA
ROSA

ROMA

Palacio de
Bellas Artes

⑦

Bosque de
Chapultepec
1a Sección

CONDESA

ROMA
NORTE

Arena
México

③

Bosque de
Chapultepec
2a Sección

Av Constituyentes

② Mezcalerías

ROMA SUR

Museo del Juguete
Antiguo México

To Parque Nacional
Desierto de los
Leones (23km)

See Roma & Condesa Map (p80)

Viaducto Miguel Alemán

Av Revolución

Av San Antonio

Av Insurgentes Sur

Av Cuauhtémoc

Cuevas

Río Mixcoac

Av Universidad

Av División del Norte

Calz de Tlalpan

Av Presidente Calles

Av Molina Enríquez

Calz Ermita Iztapalapa

See Coyoacán Map (p90)

Anillo Periférico

See San Ángel
Map (p88)

SAN
ÁNGEL

Viveros
de Coyoacán

⑤ Museo
Frida
Kahlo

COYOACÁN

Country
Club

Av Miguel Ángel de Quevedo

Av Tasqueña

Av Copilco

Henríquez Ureña

Calz de Tlalpan

Av Canal de Miramontes

Biblioteca
Central

Ciudad
Universitaria
(UNAM)

Av Insurgentes Sur

Av Aztecas

Anahuacalli

Reserva
Ecológica
del Pedregal

Museo Universitario
Arte Contemporáneo

To Xochimilco
(4.5km)

VILLA
OLÍMPICA

Av del Imán

Anillo Periférico

Cuicuilco

CUICUILCO

Bosque de
Tlalpan

N   0   1.8 km
    0   1 miles

Mexico City Highlights

① Study Diego Rivera's tableau of Mexican history at the **Palacio Nacional** (p61)

② Sip some smoky agave-based drinks at the **mezcalerías** (see boxed text, p112) in Roma and Condesa

③ Cheer on the 'good guys' at the *lucha libre* bouts of **Arena México** (p118)

④ Gaze upon the Aztec sun stone and other superb relics from Mexico's pre-Hispanic past at the **Museo Nacional de Antropología** (p75)

⑤ Share Frida's pain at her blue birthplace, the Casa Azul in Coyoacán, now home to the **Museo Frida Kahlo** (p89)

⑥ Sing along to mariachi ballads in the soulful **Plaza Garibaldi** (p66)

⑦ Feast your eyes on the colorful murals and folkloric dance performances at the **Palacio de Bellas Artes** (p69)

History

Driving over the sea of asphalt that now overlays this highland basin, you'd be hard pressed to imagine that, a mere five centuries ago, it was filled by a chain of lakes. It would further stretch your powers to think that today's downtown was on an islet crisscrossed by canals, or that the communities who inhabited this island and the banks of Lago de Texcoco spoke a patchwork of languages that had as little to do with Spanish as Malay or Urdu. As their chronicles related, the Spaniards who arrived at the shores of that lake in the early 16th century were just as amazed to witness such a scene.

A loose federation of farming villages had evolved around Lago de Texcoco by approximately 200 BC. The biggest, Cuicuilco, was destroyed by a volcanic eruption three centuries later.

Breakthroughs in irrigation techniques and the development of a maize-based economy contributed to the rise of a civilization at Teotihuacán, 40km northeast of the lake. For centuries Teotihuacán was the capital of an empire whose influence extended as far as Guatemala. However, it was unable to sustain its burgeoning population, and fell in the 8th century. Over the following centuries power in central Mexico came to be divided between varying locally important cities, including Xochicalco to the south and Tula to the north. Their culture is known as Toltec (Artificers), a name coined by the later Aztecs, who looked back to the Toltec rulers with awe.

AZTEC MEXICO CITY

The Aztecs, or Mexica (meh-*shee*-kah), probably arrived in the Valle de México in the 13th century. A wandering tribe that claimed to have come from Aztlán, a mythical region in northwest Mexico, they acted as mercenary fighters for the Tepanecas, who resided on the lake's southern shore, and they were allowed to settle upon the inhospitable terrain of Chapultepec.

The tribe wandered the swampy fringes of the lake, finally reaching an island near the western shore around 1325. There, according to legend, they witnessed an eagle standing atop a cactus and devouring a snake, which they interpreted as a sign to stop and build a city, Tenochtitlán.

Tenochtitlán rapidly became a sophisticated city-state whose empire would, by the early 16th century, span most of modern-day central Mexico from the Pacific to the Gulf of Mexico and into far southern Mexico. The Aztecs built their city on a grid plan, with canals as thoroughfares and causeways to the lakeshore. In the marshier parts, they created raised gardens by piling up vegetation and mud, and planting willows. These *chinampas* (versions of which still exist at Xochimilco in southern Mexico City) gave three or four harvests yearly.

When the Spanish arrived in 1519, Tenochtitlán's population was 200,000 to 300,000, while the entire Valle de México had perhaps 1.5 million inhabitants, making it one of the world's densest urban areas. For an account of the Spanish conquest of Tenochtitlán, see p806.

CAPITAL OF NUEVA ESPAÑA

So assiduously did the Spanish raze Tenochtitlán that only a handful of structures from the Aztec period remain today. Having wrecked the Aztec capital, they set about rebuilding it as their own. Conquistador Hernán Cortés hoped to preserve the arrangement whereby Tenochtitlán siphoned off the bounty of its vassal states.

Ravaged by disease, the Valle de México's population shrank drastically – from 1.5 million to under 100,000 within a century of the conquest. But the city emerged as the prosperous, elegant capital of Nueva España, with broad streets laid over the Aztec causeways and canals.

Building continued through the 17th century but problems arose as the weighty colonial structures began sinking into the squishy lakebed. Furthermore, lacking natural drainage, the city suffered floods caused by the partial destruction in the 1520s of the Aztecs' canals. One torrential rain in 1629 left the city submerged for five years!

Urban conditions improved in the 18th century as new plazas and avenues were installed, along with sewage and garbage-collection systems. This was Mexico City's gilded age.

INDEPENDENCE

On October 30, 1810, some 80,000 independence rebels, fresh from victory at Guanajuato, overpowered Spanish loyalist forces west of the capital. Unfortunately, they were ill equipped to capitalize on this triumph, and their leader, Miguel Hidalgo, chose not to advance on the city – a decision that cost Mexico 11 more years of fighting before independence was achieved.

HAVE YOUR SAY

Found a fantastic restaurant that you're longing to share with the world? Disagree with our recommendations? Or just want to talk about your most recent trip?

Whatever your reason, head to lonelyplanet.com, where you can post a review, ask or answer a question on the Thorntree forum, comment on a blog, or share your photos and tips on Groups. Or you can simply spend time chatting with like-minded travelers. So go on, have your say.

Following the reform laws established by President Benito Juárez in 1859, monasteries and churches were appropriated by the government, then sold off, subdivided and put to other uses. During his brief reign (1864–67), Emperor Maximilian laid out the Calzada del Emperador (today's Paseo de la Reforma) to connect Bosque de Chapultepec with the center.

Mexico City entered the modern age under the despotic Porfirio Díaz, who ruled Mexico for most of the years between 1876 and 1911. Díaz ushered in a construction boom, building Parisian-style mansions and theaters, while the city's wealthier residents escaped the center for newly minted neighborhoods toward the west.

MODERN MEGALOPOLIS

After Díaz fell in 1911, the Mexican Revolution (see p810) brought war, hunger and disease to the streets of Mexico City. Following the Great Depression, a drive to industrialize attracted more money and people.

Mexico City continued to mushroom in the 1970s, as the rural poor sought economic refuge in its thriving industries, and the population surged from 8.7 to 14.5 million. Unable to contain the new arrivals, Mexico City spread beyond the bounds of the Distrito Federal (DF) and into the adjacent state of México. The result of such unbridled growth was some of the world's worst traffic and pollution.

For seven decades, the federal government ruled the DF directly, with presidents appointing 'regents' to head notoriously corrupt administrations. Finally, in 1997, the DF gained political autonomy. In 2000 Andrés Manuel López Obrador, of the left-leaning

PRD (Party of the Democratic Revolution), was elected mayor. *Capitalinos* (capitel-city residents) approved of 'Amlo.' His initiatives included an ambitious makeover of the Centro Histórico and the construction of an overpass for the city's ring road.

While López Obrador was narrowly defeated in the presidential election of 2006 (an outcome he fiercely contested), his former police chief Marcelo Ebrard won a sweeping victory in Mexico City, consolidating the PRD's grip on the city government. The PRD passed a flood of progressive initiatives, including same-sex marriage and the legalization of abortion and euthanasia.

◉ Sights

You could spend months exploring all the museums, monuments, plazas, colonial buildings, monasteries, murals, galleries, archaeological finds, shrines and religious relics this encyclopedia of a city has to offer.

The Distrito Federal comprises 16 *delegaciones* (boroughs), which are in turn subdivided into some 1800 *colonias* (neighborhoods). Though this vast urban expanse appears daunting, the main areas of interest to visitors are fairly well defined and easy to traverse.

Note that some major streets, like Avenida Insurgentes, keep the same name for many kilometers, but the names (and numbering) of many lesser streets switch every few blocks.

Often the easiest way to find an address is by asking for the nearest metro station. Or if you know the name of the *colonia*, you can locate streets at www.guiaroji.com.mx, in Spanish.

Besides their regular names, many major streets are termed Eje (axis). The Eje system establishes a grid of priority roads across the city.

CENTRO HISTÓRICO

Packed with magnificent buildings and absorbing museums, the 34-block area defined as the Centro Histórico is the obvious place to start your explorations. More than 1500 of its buildings are classified as historic or artistic monuments and it is on the Unesco World Heritage list. It also vibrates with modern-day street life and nightlife, and is a convenient area to stay.

Since 2000, money has been poured into upgrading the image and infrastructure of the Centro. Streets have been repaved, buildings refurbished, lighting and traffic flow

MEXICO CITY IN...

Two Days

Day one dawns and you find yourself standing in the Zócalo, once the center of the Aztec universe. Explore the pre-Hispanic ruins at the **Templo Mayor**, then admire Diego Rivera's ambitious cinematic murals at the **Palacio Nacional**. Next, head south to **Xochimilco** and hire a *trajinera* (gondola) for a cruise along ancient canals. Day two, delve into Mexico's past at the **Museo Nacional de Antropología** and **Castillo de Chapultepec**. Come nightfall, indulge in tequila tasting with the mariachis at **Plaza Garibaldi**.

Four Days

With a couple more days, head out to the pyramids at **Teotihuacán**. In the evening plug into the lively nightlife scene in **Roma** or **Condesa**. Greet the new day with a stroll around the **Alameda Central**, making time to acquaint yourself with the **Palacio de Bellas Artes** and the recently minted **Plaza Juárez**, then do some *artesanías* (handicrafts) shopping at **La Ciudadela**.

One Week

Get to know the southern districts: visit the **Museo Frida Kahlo** in Coyoacán and do dinner and mezcal sampling at **Corazón de Maguey** on the delightful Jardín Centenario; or shop for quality crafts at San Ángel's **Bazar Sábado** market. Reserve Wednesday or Sunday evening for the **Ballet Folclórico**.

---

improved and security bolstered. New museums, restaurants and clubs have moved into the renovated structures, and festivals and cultural events are staged in the plazas, spurring a real downtown revival.

Zócalo
PLAZA

The heart of Mexico City is the Plaza de la Constitución, though residents began calling it the Zócalo (Map p62), meaning 'base,' in the 19th century when plans for a major monument to independence went unrealized, leaving only the pedestal. Measuring 220m from north to south, and 240m from east to west, it's one of the world's largest city squares.

The ceremonial center of Aztec Tenochtitlán, known as the Teocalli, lay immediately northeast of the Zócalo. In the 1520s Cortés paved the plaza with stones from the ruins of the complex. In the 18th century, the Zócalo was given over to a maze of market stalls until it was dismantled by Santa Anna, who placed the unfinished monument in its center.

Today, the Zócalo is home to the powers that be. On its east side is the Palacio Nacional (the presidential palace), on the north the Catedral Metropolitana, and on the south the city government offices. Jewelry shops and extravagant hotels line the arcade known as the Portal de Mercaderes on the plaza's west side.

As you emerge from metro Zócalo onto the vast central plaza, you may hear the booming of drums from the direction of the cathedral – the Aztec dancers are doing their thing. Wearing snakeskin loincloths, elaborately feathered headdresses and shell ankle bracelets, they move in a circle and chant in Náhuatl in what appears to be a display of pre-Hispanic aerobics. At the center, engulfed in a cloud of fragrant copal smoke, drummers bàng on the congalike *huehuetl* (indigenous drum) and the barrel-shaped, slitted *teponaztli*.

Variously known as Danzantes Aztecas, Danza Chichimeca or Concheros, the dancers perform their ritual daily near the Templo Mayor. It is meant to evoke the Aztec *mitote*, a frenzied ceremony performed by preconquest Mexicans at harvest times. Yet scant evidence exists that the dancers' moves bear any resemblance to those of their forebears.

The square has variously served as a forum for mass protests, free concerts, a human chessboard, a gallery of spooky Day of the Dead altars and an ice-skating rink. It's even been a canvas for photo artist Spencer Tunick, who filled the square with 18,000 nude Mexicans in May 2007 (a record for

Tunick, who has staged similar photo shoots in cities around the world).

The huge Mexican flag flying in the middle of the Zócalo is ceremonially raised at 8am by soldiers of the Mexican army, then lowered at 6pm.

TOP CHOICE Palacio Nacional   HISTORIC BUILDING

(National Palace; Map p62; www.palacionacional. gob.mx, in Spanish; Plaza de la Constitución; admission free; ◷9am-5pm; MZócalo) Home to the offices of the president of Mexico, the Federal Treasury and dramatic murals by Diego Rivera, this palace fills the entire east side of the Zócalo.

The first palace on this spot was built by Aztec emperor Moctezuma II in the early 16th century. Cortés destroyed the palace in 1521, rebuilding it as a fortress with three interior courtyards. In 1562 the crown purchased the building from Cortés' family to house the viceroys of Nueva España, a function it served until Mexican independence.

As you face the palace, high above the center door hangs the **Campana de Dolores**, the bell rung in the town of Dolores Hidalgo by Padre Miguel Hidalgo in 1810 at the start of the War of Independence. From the balcony underneath it, the president delivers the *grito* (shout) – *¡Viva México!* – on September 15 to commemorate independence.

Inside you'll see **Diego Rivera murals** along the main staircase (painted between 1929 and 1935) that depict Mexican civilization from the arrival of Quetzalcóatl (the Aztec plumed serpent god) to the postrevolutionary period. The nine murals covering the north and east walls of the first level above the patio chronicle indigenous life before the Spanish conquest.

The visitors' entrance is on Calle Moneda.

Templo Mayor   RUIN

(Map p62; www.templomayor.inah.gob.mx, in Spanish; Seminario 8; admission M$57; ◷9am-5pm Tue-Sun; MZócalo) Before the Spaniards demolished it, the Teocalli of Tenochtitlán covered the site where the cathedral now stands and the blocks to its north and east. It wasn't until 1978, after electricity workers happened on an eight-ton stone-disc carving of the Aztec goddess Coyolxauhqui, that the decision was taken to demolish colonial buildings and excavate the Templo Mayor. The temple is thought to be on the exact spot where the Aztecs saw their symbolic eagle, perching on a cactus with a snake in its beak – the symbol of Mexico today. In Aztec belief this was, literally, the center of the universe.

Like other sacred buildings in Tenochtitlán, the temple was enlarged several times, with each rebuilding accompanied by the sacrifice of captured warriors. What we see today are sections of the temple's different phases. At the center is a platform dating from about 1400; on its southern half, a sacrificial stone stands in front of a shrine to Huizilopochtli, the Aztec war god. On the northern half is a *chac-mool* (a Maya reclining figure) before a shrine to the water god, Tláloc. By the time the Spanish arrived, a 40m-high double pyramid towered above this spot, with steep twin stairways climbing to shrines of the two gods.

The entrance to the temple site and museum is east of the cathedral, across the hectic **Plaza del Templo Mayor**. Authorized tour guides (with Sectur ID) offer their services by the entrance. Alternatively, rent an audio guide – available in English (M$80) – inside the museum.

The onsite **Museo del Templo Mayor** (included in the site's admission price) houses a model of Tenochtitlán and artifacts from the site, and gives a good overview of Aztec civilization. Pride of place is given to the great wheel-like stone of Coyolxauhqui (She of Bells on her Cheek), best viewed from the top-floor vantage point. She is shown decapitated, the result of her murder by Huizilopochtli, her brother, who also killed his 400 brothers en route to becoming top god.

Ongoing excavation continues to turn up major pieces. Just west of the temple, a monolithic stone carved with the image of Tlaltecuhtli, the goddess of earth fertility, was unearthed in October 2006. Archaeologists say this might mark the tomb of Ahuízotl, the Aztec emperor who immediately preceded Moctezuma II.

Another key finding was made in 2011 when a ceremonial platform dating from 1469 was uncovered. Based on historical documents, archaeologists believe the 15m structure was used to cremate Aztec rulers. Now more than ever, researchers feel they are inching closer to the first discovery of an Aztec emperor's tomb.

Catedral Metropolitana   CATHEDRAL

(Metropolitan Cathedral; Map p62; Zócalo; admission free; ◷8am-8pm; MZócalo) Mexico City's most iconic structure, this cathedral is a monumental edifice: 109m long, 59m wide

MEXICO CITY SIGHTS

Centro Histórico

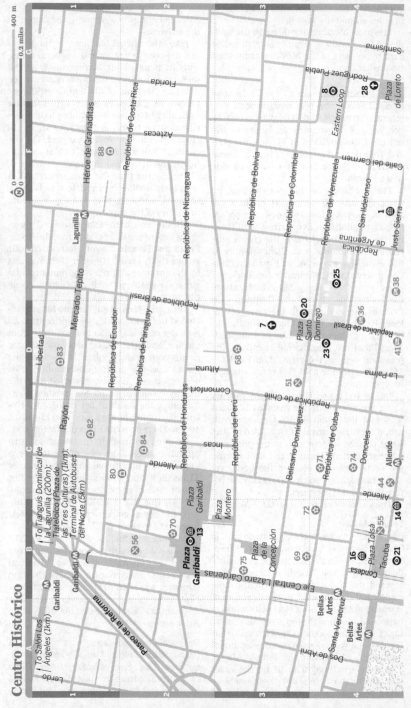

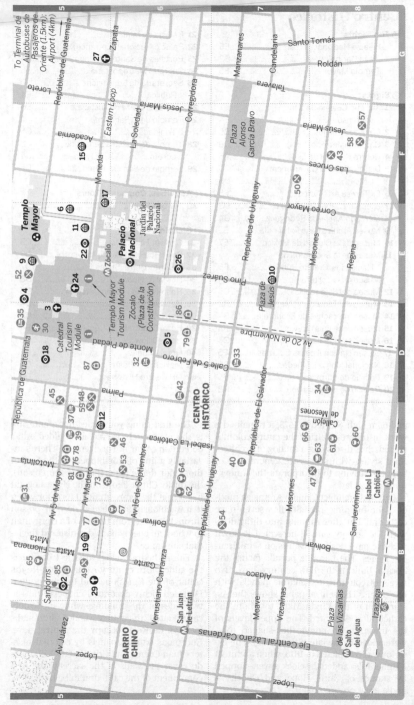

Centro Histórico

Top Sights

Palacio Nacional	E6
Plaza Garibaldi	B2
Templo Mayor	E5

Sights

1	Antiguo Colegio de San Ildefonso	E4
2	Casa de Azulejos	B5
3	Catedral Metropolitana	D5
4	Centro Cultural de España	E5
5	Distrito Federal Government Offices	D6
6	Ex Teresa Arte Actual	E5
7	Iglesia de Santo Domingo	D3
8	Mercado Abelardo Rodríguez	G4
9	Museo Archivo de la Fotografía	E5
10	Museo de la Ciudad de México	E7
11	Museo de la Secretaría de Hacienda y Crédito Público	E5
	Museo de la Tortura	(see 21)
12	Museo del Estanquillo	C5
13	Museo del Tequila y el Mezcal	B2
14	Museo Interactivo de Economia	B4
15	Museo José Luis Cuevas	F5
16	Museo Nacional de Arte	B4
17	Museo Nacional de las Culturas	F5
18	Nacional Monte de Piedad	D5
19	Palacio de Iturbide	B5
20	Palacio de la Inquisición	D3
21	Palacio de Minería	B4
22	Palacio Nacional (Entrance)	E5
23	Portales de Santo Domingo	D4
24	Sagrario Metropolitano	E5
25	Secretaría de Educación Pública	E4
26	Suprema Corte de Justicia	E6
27	Templo de la Santísima Trinidad	G5
28	Templo de Nuestra Senora de Loreto	G4
29	Templo de San Francisco	B5

Activities, Courses & Tours

30	Turibús Stop	D5

Sleeping

31	Chillout Flat	C5
32	Gran Hotel Ciudad de México	D6
33	Hampton Inn & Suites	D7
34	Hostal Regina	D8
35	Hostel Mundo Joven Catedral	D5
36	Hotel Azores	D4
37	Hotel Canadá	C5
38	Hotel Catedral	E4
39	Hotel Gillow	C5
40	Hotel Isabel	C7
41	Mexico City Hostel	D4
42	NH Centro Histórico	D6

and 65m high. Started in 1573, it remained a work in progress during the entire colonial period, thus displaying a catalog of architectural styles, with successive generations of builders striving to incorporate the innovations of the day.

Original architect Claudio Arciniega modeled the building after Seville's seven-nave cathedral, but after running into difficulties with the spongy subsoil he scaled it down to a five-nave design of vaults on semicircular arches. The baroque portals facing the Zócalo, built in the 17th century, have two levels of columns and marble panels with bas-reliefs. The central panel shows the Assumption of the Virgin Mary, to whom the cathedral is dedicated. The upper levels of the towers, with unique bell-shaped tops, were added in the late 18th century. The exterior was completed in 1813, when architect Manuel Tolsá added the clock tower – topped by statues of Faith, Hope and Charity – and a great central dome.

The first thing you notice upon entering is the elaborately carved and gilded Altar de Perdón (Altar of Forgiveness). There's invariably a line of worshippers at the foot of the Señor del Veneno (Lord of the Poison), the dusky Christ figure on the right. Legend has it that the figure attained its color when it miraculously absorbed a dose of poison through its feet from the lips of a clergyman to whom an enemy had administered the lethal substance.

The cathedral's chief artistic treasure is the gilded 18th-century **Altar de los Reyes** (Altar of the Kings), behind the main altar. Fourteen richly decorated chapels line the two sides of the building, while intricately carved late-17th-century wooden choir stalls by Juan de Rojas occupy the central nave. Enormous painted panels by colonial masters Juan Correa and Cristóbal de Villalpando cover the walls of the sacristy, the first component of the cathedral to be built.

Visitors may wander freely, though they're asked not to do so during Mass. A M$10 donation is requested to enter the **sacristy** or **choir**, where docents provide commentary, and you can climb the **bell tower** (admission M$15; ☻10:30am-6pm). Mexico City's archbishop conducts Mass at noon on Sundays.

Adjoining the east side of the cathedral is the 18th-century **Sagrario Metropolitano** (☻8am-7:30pm). Originally built to house the archives and vestments of the archbishop, it is now the city's main parish church. Its front entrance and mirror-image eastern portal are superb examples of the ultradecorative Churrigueresque style.

Around the Cathedral   NEIGHBORHOOD

FREE **Centro Cultural de España** (Spanish Cultural Center; Map p62; www.ccemx.org, in Spanish; República de Guatemala 18; ☻10am-9pm Tue-Sat, to 4pm Sun; MZócalo), around the back of the cathedral, has a variety of cutting-edge exhibitions going on. The splendidly restored building, which conquistador Hernán Cortés once awarded to his butler, has a rooftop terrace for tapas-munching and there's live music Wednesday to Saturday from 10pm.

FREE **Museo Archivo de la Fotografía** (Photographic Archive Museum; Map p62; www.cultura.df.gob.mx/index.php/maf, in Spanish; República de Guatemala 34; ☻10am-6pm Tue-Sun; MZócalo) draws from a century's worth of images taken for the *Gaceta oficial del Distrito Federal* (the DF public record) to preserve the memory of its streets, plazas, buildings and people.

Facing the cathedral's west side is Mexico's national pawnshop, the **Nacional Monte de Piedad** (Map p62; www.montepiedad.com.mx; Monte de Piedad 7; ☻8:30am-6pm Mon-Fri, to 1pm Sat; MZócalo), founded in 1774 by silver magnate Pedro Romero de Terreros. People pawn their jewelry and other possessions in the central hall for loans at 4% interest; unclaimed items are sold in shops off the central passageway. A store inside sells outstanding handicrafts from Oaxaca.

✪ Plaza Garibaldi PLAZA

Every night the city's mariachi bands gather to belt out heartfelt ballads in this festive square. Wearing silver-studded outfits, they toot their trumpets and tune their guitars until approached by someone who'll pay for a song (about M$100). Also roaming Garibaldi are white-clad *son jarocho* groups, hailing from Veracruz, and *norteño* combos, who bang out northern-style folk tunes.

The notoriously seedy Garibaldi recently underwent a makeover that included heightened security, but it's still rough around the edges. The latest addition to the plaza is the **Museo del Tequila y el Mezcal** (Map p62; www.mutemgaribaldi.mx; Plaza Garibaldi; admission incl tasting M$50; ☉11am-7pm Mon, Wed & Sun, to 10pm Thu-Sat; Ⓜ Garibaldi), with exhibits explaining the origins and production process of Mexico's two most popular distilled agave drinks. The tour ends with a tasting on a stylish terrace bar overlooking the plaza. An onsite store sells some decent, albeit overpriced, tequilas and mezcals.

Calle Moneda STREET

Flanked by magnificent *tezontle* (red volcanic rock) buildings, Calle Moneda, north of the Palacio Nacional, is an unlikely stage for the never-ending cat-and-mouse antics between *ambulantes* (mobile street vendors) and the city's antipiracy police squads.

FREE Museo de la Secretaría de Hacienda y Crédito Público (Museum of the Finance Secretariat; Map p62; www.shcp.gob.mx /difusion_cultural/museo_arte,in Spanish; Moneda 4; ☉10am-5pm Tue-Sun; Ⓜ Zócalo) shows off its

vast collection of Mexican art, much of it contributed by painters and sculptors in lieu of paying taxes. This former colonial archbishop's palace also hosts a full program of cultural events (many free), from puppet shows to chamber-music recitals. The museum was being renovated at the time of research.

FREE Ex Teresa Arte Actual (Map p62; www.exteresa.bellasartes.gob.mx, in Spanish; Primo Verdad 8; ☉10am-6pm; Ⓜ Zócalo), around the

corner from the museum, is a teetering former 17th-century convent, converted into a museum. Built atop a sloshy lake bed, Mexico City is sinking fast, as evidenced by the museum's notably lopsided floor.

FREE Museo Nacional de las Culturas (National Museum of Cultures; Map p62; Moneda 13; ☉10am-5pm Tue-Sun; Ⓜ Zócalo), constructed in

1567 as the colonial mint, exhibits art, dress and handicrafts of the world's cultures.

A block further east, then a few steps north, a former convent houses the **Museo José Luis Cuevas** (Map p62; www.museojose luiscuevas.com.mx, in Spanish; Academia 13; admission M$20, Sun free; ☉10am-5:30pm Tue-Sun; Ⓜ Zócalo). The museum showcases the works of artist Cuevas, a leader of the 1950s Ruptura movement, which broke with the politicized art of the postrevolutionary regime. Cuevas' *La giganta,* an 8m-tall bronze female figure with some male features, dominates the central patio.

Two blocks further east, the **Templo de la Santísima Trinidad** (Map p62; cnr Santísima & Zapata) sports a hyper-baroque facade with cherubs and apostles set into the finely filigreed stonework.

Plaza Santo Domingo PLAZA

Smaller and less hectic than the nearby Zócalo, this plaza has long served as a base for scribes and printers. Descendants of the scribes who did the paperwork for merchants using the customs building (now the Education Ministry) across the square, they work on the west side beneath the **Portales de Santo Domingo** (Map p62), aka Portales de Evangelistas.

To the north stands the maroon stone **Iglesia de Santo Domingo** (Map p62), a beautiful baroque church dating from 1736. The three-tiered facade merits a close look: statues of St Francis and St Augustine stand in the niches alongside the doorway. The middle panel shows St Dominic de Guzmán receiving a staff and the Epistles from St Peter and St Paul, respectively. At the top is a bas-relief of the Assumption of the Virgin Mary.

East of the church, the 18th-century **Palacio de la Inquisición** (Map p62) was headquarters of the Holy Inquisition in Mexico until Spain decreed its closure in 1812. Its official shield shows up at the top of the facade.

Murals NOTABLE BUILDING

In the 1920s the postrevolution Minister of Education, José Vasconcelos, commissioned talented young artists – among them Diego Rivera, David Alfaro Siqueiros and José Clemente Orozco – to decorate numerous public buildings with dramatic, large-scale murals conveying a new sense of Mexico's past and future.

WANT MORE?

For in-depth information, reviews and recommendations at your fingertips, head to the Apple App Store to purchase Lonely Planet's *Mexico City Guide* iPhone app.

Alternatively, head to **Lonely Planet** (www.lonelyplanet.com/mexico-city) for planning advice, author recommendations, traveler reviews and insider tips.

FREE **Secretaría de Educación Pública** (Secretariat of Education; Map p62; República de Brasil 31; ⊗9am-6pm Mon-Fri; MZócalo) is housed in one such building, a former monastery. The two front courtyards (on the opposite side of the building from the entrance off Plaza Santo Domingo) are lined with 120 fresco panels painted by Diego Rivera in the 1920s. Together they form a tableau of 'the very life of the people,' in the artist's words. Each courtyard is thematically distinct: the one on the east end deals with labor, industry and agriculture, while the interior one depicts traditions and festivals. On the latter's top level is a series on proletarian and agrarian revolution, underneath a continuous red banner emblazoned with a Mexican *corrido* (folk song). The likeness of Frida Kahlo appears in the first panel as an arsenal worker.

A block back toward the Zócalo, then east, is the **Antiguo Colegio de San Ildefonso** (Map p62; www.sanildefonso.org.mx, in Spanish; Justo Sierra 16; admission M$45, Tue free; ⊗10am-5:30pm Tue-Sun; MZócalo). Built in the 16th century as a Jesuit college, it later became a prestigious teacher-training institute. In the 1920s, Rivera, Orozco, Siqueiros and others were brought in to do murals. Most of the work on the main patio is by Orozco; look for his portrait of Cortés and La Malinche underneath the staircase. The amphitheater, off the lobby, holds Rivera's first mural, *La creación,* undertaken upon his return from Europe in 1923. Mural tours (in Spanish) are given at noon and 4:30pm. Nowadays, the San Ildefonso hosts outstanding temporary exhibitions.

More Orozco murals are inside the **Suprema Corte de Justicia** (Supreme Court; Map p62; Pino Suárez 2; admission free, ID required; ⊗9am-5pm Mon-Fri; MZócalo), south of the Zócalo. In 1940 the artist painted four panels around the first level of the central stairway, two of which deal with the theme of justice. A more contemporary take on the same subject, *Los siete crímenes mayores* (The Seven Worst Crimes), by Rafael Cauduro, unfolds over the three levels of the building's southwest stairwell. Executed in his hyper-realist style, the series catalogs the horrors of state-sponsored crimes against the populace, including the ever-relevant torture-induced confession. On the southeast corner of the building's interior, Ángel Ismael Ramos Huitrón's *En búsqueda de la justicia* (In Search of Justice) reflects on the Mexican people's constant struggle to obtain justice, as does the social-realism work *La justicia* (Justice), by Japanese-Mexican artist Luis Nishizawa, on the northwest stairwell. At the northeast end, Leopoldo Flores Valdes' *Todo movimento social es justicia* (All Social Movements Are Just) depicts scenes involving freedom fighters such as Miguel Hidalgo and Emiliano Zapata. Free audio guides in English are available at the entrance.

The **Mercado Abelardo Rodríguez** (Map p62; cnr República de Venezuela & Rodríguez Puebla; ⊗8am-6pm; MZócalo), northeast of the Zócalo, became a canvas for a group of young international artists under the tutelage of Diego Rivera in the 1930s. Some of the most exuberant works, created by the American Greenwood sisters, cover the stairwell leading up to the community center, at the market's northeast corner. On the 1st floor, *Historia de México,* by Japanese artist Isama Noguchi, is a dynamic three-dimensional mural sculpted of cement and plaster that symbolizes the struggle against fascism. Other murals inside the market's entry corridors are paeans to rural laborers and their traditions, though some are fading from neglect.

A block south, the **Templo de Nuestra Señora de Loreto** (Map p62; San Ildefonso 80; MZócalo) has a remarkable dome. Ringed at the base by stained-glass images, the dome crowns an unusual four-lobed cross with semicircular chapels in the lobes. After the 1985 earthquake the building was raided of its treasures, and the murals that covered the underside of the cupola were allowed to deteriorate.

Plaza Tolsá   PLAZA

Several blocks west of the Zócalo is this handsome square, named after the illustrious late-18th-century sculptor and architect who completed the Catedral Metropolitana.

Manuel Tolsá also created the bronze equestrian statue of the Spanish king Carlos IV (who reigned from 1788 to 1808), which is the plaza's centerpiece. It originally stood in the Zócalo, then on Paseo de la Reforma, before being moved here in 1979.

King Carlos rides in front of the **Museo Nacional de Arte** (National Art Museum; Map p62; www.munal.com.mx, in Spanish; Tacuba 8; admission M$33, Sun free; ☺10am-5:30pm Tue-Sun; ⓂBellas Artes). Built around 1900 in the style of an Italian Renaissance palace, it holds collections representing every school of Mexican art until the early 20th century. A highlight is the work of José María Velasco, depicting the Valle de México in the late 19th century.

Opposite is the **Palacio de Minería** (Palace of Mining; Map p62; www.palaciomineria.unam.mx; Tacuba 5; admission M$25; ☺tours 11am & 1pm Sat & Sun; ⓂBellas Artes), where mining engineers were trained in the 19th century. Today it houses a branch of the national university's engineering department. A neoclassical masterpiece, the palace was designed by Tolsá and built between 1797 and 1813. Visits are by guided tour only. The palace contains a small **museum** (admission M$10; ☺10am-6pm Wed-Sun) on Tolsá's life and work. Also in the building is the **Museo de la Tortura** (Museum of Torture; admission M$40; ☺10am-6pm), with European torture instruments from the 14th to 19th centuries on display, including a metal-spiked interrogation chair and the menacing skull splitter.

One block east of the plaza, the former hospital of the Bethlehemites (the only religious order to be established in the Americas) has since 2006 been the home of the **Museo Interactivo de Economía** (Interactive Museum of Economics; Map p62; www.mide.org.mx, in Spanish; Tacuba 17; adult/child M$55/45; ☺9am-6pm Tue-Sun; ⓂAllende). A slew of hands-on exhibits is aimed at breaking down economic concepts. For coin connoisseurs, the highlight is the Banco de México's numismatic collection.

Avenida Madero   STREET

This stately avenue west of the Zócalo boasts a veritable catalog of architectural styles.

FREE **Museo del Estanquillo** (Map p62; www.museodelestanquillo.com, in Spanish; Isabel La Católica 26; ☺10am-6pm Wed-Mon; ⓂAllende), housed in a gorgeous neoclassical building two blocks from the square, contains the vast pop-culture collection amassed over the decades by DF essayist and pack rat Carlos Monsivais. The museum illustrates various phases in the capital's development by means of the numerous photos, paintings and movie posters from the collection.

FREE **Palacio de Iturbide** (Map p62; Av Madero 17; ☺10am-7pm; ⓂAllende), with its late-18th-century baroque facade, is a few blocks westward. Built for colonial nobility, in 1821 it became the residence of General Agustín Iturbide, a hero of the struggle for independence who was proclaimed emperor here in 1822. (He abdicated less than a year later, after General Santa Anna announced the birth of a republic.) Now known as the Museo Palacio Cultural Banamex, it hosts exhibits drawn from the bank's vast Mexican art collection.

Half a block past the pedestrian corridor Gante stands the amazing **Casa de Azulejos** (House of Tiles; Map p62; www.sanborns.com.mx/sanborns/azulejos.asp, in Spanish; Av Madero 4; ☺7am-1am; ⓂAllende). Dating from 1596, it was built for the Condes (Counts) del Valle de Orizaba. Most of the tiles that adorn the outside walls were produced in China and shipped to Mexico on the Manila *naos* (Spanish galleons used until the early 19th century). The building now houses a Sanborns restaurant in a covered courtyard around a Moorish fountain. The staircase has a 1925 mural by Orozco.

Across the way, the **Templo de San Francisco** (Map p62; Av Madero 7) is a remnant of the vast Franciscan monastery erected in the early 16th century over the site of Moctezuma's private zoo. In its heyday it extended two blocks south and east. The monastic complex was divvied up under the postindependence reform laws; in 1949, it was returned to the Franciscan order in a deplorable state and subsequently restored. The elaborately carved doorway is a shining example of 18th-century baroque.

Rising alongside the monastery, the **Torre Latinoamericana** (Latin American Tower; Map p70; www.torrelatino.com; Eje Central Lázaro Cárdenas 2; adult/child M$60/50; ☺9am-10pm; ⓂBellas Artes) was Latin America's tallest building when constructed in 1956. Thanks to the deep-seated pylons that anchor the building, it has withstood several major earthquakes. If you want to learn more about the construction of the tower and downtown's centuries-long development, a museum on the 38th floor houses a permanent photography exhibition. Up above, views from the 41st-floor lounge bar and the 44th-floor observation deck are spectacular, smog permitting.

Museo de la Ciudad de México   MUSEUM
(Museum of Mexico City; Map p62; www.cultura.df.gob.mx/index.php/recintos/museos/mcm, in Spanish; Pino Suárez 30; admission M$23; ☺10am-6pm Tue-Sun; ⓂPino Suárez) Formerly a palace of the Counts of Santiago de Calimaya, this 18th-century baroque edifice now houses a museum with temporary exhibits focusing on city history and culture. Upstairs is the former studio of Joaquín Clausell, considered Mexico's foremost impressionist. The artist used the four walls of the windowless room as an ongoing sketchbook during the three decades that he worked here until his death in 1935.

ALAMEDA CENTRAL & AROUND
Emblematic of the downtown renaissance, the green rectangle immediately northwest of the Centro Histórico holds a vital place in Mexico City's cultural life. Surrounded by historically significant buildings, the Alameda Central has been the focus of ambitious redevelopment over the past decade. In particular, the high-rise towers on the Plaza Juárez have transformed the zone south of the park, much of which was destroyed in the 1985 earthquake. Metro stations Bellas Artes and Hidalgo are located on the Alameda's east and west sides, respectively. The north–south Eje Central Lázaro Cárdenas passes just east of the park.

Palacio de Bellas Artes   ARTS CENTER
(Palace of Fine Arts; Map p70; www.palacio.bellasartes.gob.mx, in Spanish; cnr Av Juárez & Eje Central Lázaro Cárdenas; admission M$39, Sun free; ☺10am-6pm Tue-Sun; ⓂBellas Artes) Dominating the east end of the Alameda is this splendid white-marble palace, a concert hall and arts center commissioned by President Porfirio Díaz. Construction began in 1905 under Italian architect Adamo Boari, who favored neoclassical and art nouveau styles. Complications arose as the heavy marble shell sank into the spongy subsoil, and then the Mexican Revolution intervened. Architect Federico Mariscal eventually finished the interior in the 1930s, utilizing the more modern art deco style.

Immense murals dominate the upper floors. On the 2nd floor are two early-1950s works by Rufino Tamayo: *México de hoy* (Mexico Today) and *Nacimiento de la na-*

cionalidad (Birth of Nationality), a symbolic depiction of the creation of the *mestizo* (mixed ancestry) identity.

At the west end of the 3rd floor is Diego Rivera's famous *El hombre en el cruce de caminos* (Man at the Crossroads), originally commissioned for New York's Rockefeller Center. The Rockefellers had the original destroyed because of its anticapitalist themes, but Rivera recreated it here in 1934.

On the north side are David Alfaro Siqueiros' three-part *La nueva democracia* (New Democracy) and Rivera's four-part *Carnaval de la vida mexicana* (Carnival of Mexican Life); to the east is José Clemente Orozco's *La katharsis* (Catharsis), depicting the conflict between humankind's 'social' and 'natural' aspects.

The 4th-floor **Museo Nacional de Arquitectura** (admission M$22, Sun free; ☺10am-5:30pm Tue-Sun) features changing exhibits on contemporary architecture.

The recently renovated **Bellas Artes theater** (only available for viewing at performances) is itself a masterpiece, with a stained-glass curtain depicting the Valle de México. Based on a design by Mexican painter Gerardo Murillo (aka Dr Atl), it was assembled by New York jeweler Tiffany & Co from almost a million pieces of colored glass.

In addition, the palace stages outstanding temporary art exhibitions and the Ballet Folclórico de México (see p115).

Museo Mural Diego Rivera   MUSEUM
(Diego Rivera Mural Museum; Map p70; www.museomuraldiegorivera.bellasartes.gob.mx, in Spanish; cnr Balderas & Colón; admission M$17, Sun free; ☺10am-6pm Tue-Sun; ⓂHidalgo) Among Diego Rivera's most famous works is *Sueño de una tarde dominical en la alameda central* (Dream of a Sunday Afternoon in the Alameda Central), painted in 1947. In the 15m-long mural the artist imagined many of the figures who walked in the city from colonial times onward, among them Cortés, Juárez, Porfirio Díaz and Francisco Madero. All are grouped around a *Catrina* (skeleton in prerevolutionary women's garb). Rivera himself, as a pug-faced child, and Frida Kahlo stand beside the skeleton. Charts identify all the characters. The Museo Mural Diego Rivera was built in 1986 to house the mural, after its original location, the Hotel del Prado, was wrecked by the 1985 earthquake.

Alameda Central & Around

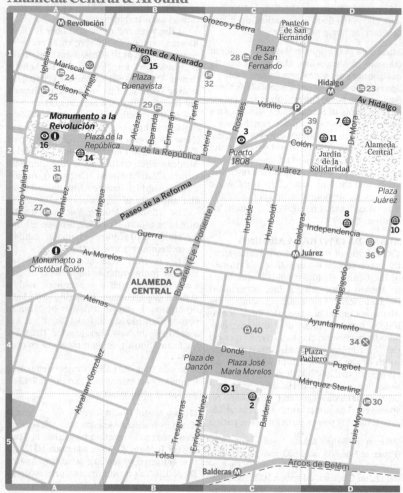

Alameda Central

PARK

Created in the late 1500s by mandate of then-viceroy Luis de Velasco, the Alameda (Map p70) took its name from the *álamos* (poplars) planted over its rectangular expanse. By the late 19th century the park was graced with European-style statuary and lit by gas lamps. It became the place to be seen for the city's elite. Today the Alameda is a popular refuge, particularly on Sunday when families stroll its pathways and gather for open-air concerts.

Plaza Juárez

PLAZA

Representing the new face of the zone, this modern plaza is opposite the Alameda's **Hemiciclo a Juárez** (Map p70), a marble monument to postindependence president Benito Juárez, and behind the fully restored **Templo de Corpus Christi**, which now holds the DF's archives. The plaza's centerpiece is a pair of Tetris-block towers by leading Mexican architect Ricardo Legorreta: the 24-story **Foreign Relations Secretariat** and the 23-story **Tribunales** (Courts) building front a set of 1034 reddish pyramids in a

caust. Audio guides in English are available (M$70).

La Ciudadela — PLAZA

The formidable compound now known as 'The Citadel' started off as a tobacco factory in the late 18th century, though it's best known as the scene of the Decena Trágica (Tragic Ten Days), the coup that brought down the Madero government in 1913. Today it is home to the **Biblioteca de México José Vasconcelos** (National Library; Map p70; www.bibliotecademexico.gob.mx, in Spanish; Plaza de la Ciudadela 4; ☉8:30am-7:30pm; Ⓜ Balderas), with holdings of over 300,000 volumes and an extensive map collection. The central halls are given over to art exhibits.

FREE **Centro de la Imagen** (Map p70; http://centrodelaimagen.conaculta.gob.mx, in Spanish; Plaza de la Ciudadela 2; ☉11am-6pm Tue-Sun; Ⓜ Balderas), the city's photography museum, is at the Calle Balderas entrance. This innovatively designed space stages compelling exhibitions, often focusing on documentary views of Mexican life.

Across the plaza, inside the **Centro de Artesanías La Ciudadela** (Map p70; cnr Balderas & Dondé; ☉10am-6pm; Ⓜ Balderas), vendors offer a wide array of crafts from around Mexico, including black pottery from Oaxaca, guitars from Michoacán and silver jewelry from Taxco.

Museo de Arte Popular — MUSEUM

(Museum of Popular Art; Map p70; www.map.df.gob.mx; Revillagigedo 11; admission M$40, Sun free; ☉10am-5:30pm Tue & Thu-Sun, to 8:30pm Wed; Ⓜ Juárez) Opened in 2006, this museum is a major showcase for Mexico's folk arts and traditions. Contemporary crafts from all over Mexico are thematically displayed, including carnival masks from Chiapas, *alebrijes* (fanciful animal figures) from Oaxaca and trees of life from Puebla. The museum occupies the former fire department headquarters, itself an outstanding example of 1920s art deco by architect Vicente Mendiola. The ground-level shop sells quality handicrafts.

Palacio Postal — HISTORIC BUILDING

(Map p70; www.palaciopostal.gob.mx, in Spanish; Tacuba 1; Ⓜ Bellas Artes) More than just Mexico City's central post office, this early-20th-century palace is an Italianate confection designed by the Palacio de Bellas Artes' original architect, Adamo Boari. The beige stone facade features baroque columns and

broad pool, a collaboration between Legorreta and Spanish artist Vicente Rojo.

The newest addition to the plaza is the **Museo Memoria y Tolerancia** (Museum of Memory & Tolerance; Map p70; www.myt.org.mx, in Spanish; Plaza Juárez 12; admission M$55; ☉9am-6pm Tue-Fri, 10am-7pm Sat & Sun; Ⓜ Bellas Artes), a mazelike museum of 55 halls dedicated to preserving the memory of genocide victims throughout the world. The multimedia exhibit chronicles crimes committed against humanity in Cambodia, Guatemala, Sudan, Rwanda and the former Yugoslavia, and those that occurred during the Holo-

Alameda Central & Around

Top Sights
Monumento a la Revolución.................A2
Palacio de Bellas Artes.........................F2

Sights
1 Biblioteca de México José Vasconcelos.....................................C4
Centro de Artesanías La Ciudadela...............................(see 40)
2 Centro de la Imagen...........................C5
3 El Caballito...C2
4 Foreign Relations Secretariat (SRE)...E3
5 Hemiciclo a Juárez...............................E2
6 Iglesia de la Santa Veracuz....................E2
7 Laboratorio de Arte Alameda...............D2
8 Museo de Arte Popular.........................D3
9 Museo Franz Mayer...............................E1
10 Museo Memoria y Tolerancia..............D3
11 Museo Mural Diego Rivera...................D2
12 Museo Nacional de Arquitectura.................................F2
13 Museo Nacional de la Estampa............E1
14 Museo Nacional de la Revolución...A2
15 Museo Nacional de San Carlos.............B1
16 Observation Deck................................A2
17 Palacio Postal.......................................F2
Postal Museum.............................(see 17)
18 Templo de Corpus Christi.....................E2
19 Torre Latinoamericana.........................F3
20 Tribunales (Courts) Building.................E3

Activities, Courses & Tours
21 Tranvía Tour Stop..................................F2
22 Turibús Stop..E2

Sleeping
23 Boutique Hotel de Cortés......................D1
24 Casa de los Amigos...............................A1
25 Hotel Edison..A1
26 Hotel Marlowe.......................................E3
27 Hotel Mayaland......................................A3
28 Hotel Mónaco...C1
29 Hotel New York.....................................B2
30 Hotel San Diego....................................D5
31 Palace Hotel..A2
32 Ramada Reforma...................................C1

Eating
33 Churrería El Moro..................................F4
Cloister Café.................................(see 9)
34 El Cuadrilátero......................................D4
35 Mi Fonda..E4

Drinking
36 Bósforo..D3
37 Café La Habana......................................B3
38 Las Duelistas...E4

Entertainment
39 Cinemex Real..D2

Shopping
40 Centro de Artesanías La Ciudadela..C4
41 Gandhi Bellas Artes...............................F3
42 La Europea..E4
43 Mercado San Juan..................................E4
44 Plaza de la Computación y Electrónica..F4

carved filigree around the windows; inside, the bronze railings on the monumental staircase were cast in Florence.

FREE **Postal museum** (10am-6pm Mon-Fri, to 4pm Sat & Sun), on the 1st floor, is where philatelists can ogle the first stamp ever issued in Mexico.

Plaza de Santa Veracruz PLAZA

The sunken square north of the Alameda across Avenida Hidalgo is named for the slanting structure on the right, the **Iglesia de la Santa Veracruz**. Elaborately carved pillars flank the doorway of the 18th-century church.

On the opposite side of the plaza, the **Museo Franz Mayer** (Map p70; www.franzmayer.org.mx, in Spanish; Av Hidalgo 45; admission M$45, Tue free; 10am-5pm Tue-Sun; M Bellas Artes) is housed in the old hospice of the San Juan de Dios order, which under the brief reign of Maximilian became a halfway house for prostitutes. The museum is the fruit of the efforts of Franz Mayer, born in Mannheim, Germany, in 1882. Prospering as a financier in his adopted Mexico, Mayer amassed the collection of Mexican silver, textiles, ceramics and furniture now on display. The exhibit halls open onto a sumptuous colonial patio, where you can grab a bite at the excellent Cloister Café.

Adjacent to the museum, across an alley, the **Museo Nacional de la Estampa** (Map p70; www.museonacionaldelaestampa.bellasartes.

gob.mx, in Spanish; Av Hidalgo 39; admission M$11, Sun free; ☉10am-5:45pm Tue-Sun) is devoted to the graphic arts, with thematic exhibits from its collection of more than 12,000 prints.

Laboratorio de Arte Alameda MUSEUM
(Alameda Art Laboratory; Map p70; www.artealameda.bellasartes.gob.mx, in Spanish; Dr Mora 7; admission M$15, Sun free; ☉9am-5pm Tue-Sun; MHidalgo) As is often the case with museums in the Centro Histórico, the 17th-century former convent building that contains the Laboratorio de Arte Alameda is at least as interesting as its contents. Here you can catch installations by leading experimental artists from Mexico and abroad, with an emphasis on electronic and interactive media.

PLAZA DE LA REPÚBLICA & AROUND
This recently revamped plaza, west of Alameda Central, is dominated by the copper-domed Monumento a la Revolución. The grand art deco building northeast of the plaza is the Frontón de México, a now-defunct jai-alai (a game like squash) arena.

Monumento a la Revolución MONUMENT
Begun in the 1900s under Porfirio Díaz, this monument (Map p70) was originally meant to be a legislative chamber. But construction (not to mention Díaz' presidency) was interrupted by the Revolution. Though they considered demolishing it, the new regime chose instead to modify the structure and give it a new role. Unveiled in 1938, it contains the tombs of the revolutionary and postrevolutionary heroes Pancho Villa, Francisco Madero, Venustiano Carranza, Plutarco Elías Calles and Lázaro Cárdenas.

The plaza and the monument got a major makeover in 2010 to commemorate Mexico's centennial anniversary of the Revolution. From dusk to 10pm color-changing lights highlight the new-look square's geyserlike fountains and the monument's renovated architectural features.

The star attraction is the 65m-high **Observation Deck** (Map p70; www.mrm.mx; Plaza de la República; admission M$40, Wed free; ☉10am-6pm Tue-Thu, to 10pm Fri & Sat, to 8pm Sun; ▯Plaza de la República), reachable by a glass elevator. The vertigo-inducing lift opens to a spiraling staircase that ascends to a wide terrace with a panoramic view of the city.

Underlying the plaza, the renovated **Museo Nacional de la Revolución** (National Museum of the Revolution; Map p70; admission M$23, Sun free; ☉9am-5pm Tue-Sun) covers a 63-year period, from the implementation of the constitution guaranteeing human rights in 1857 to the installation of the postrevolutionary government in 1920. Explanatory text is untranslated.

Museo Universitario del Chopo MUSEUM
(Map p57; www.chopo.unam.mx, in Spanish; Enrique González Martínez 10; admission M$30, Tue free; ☉10am-7pm Tue-Sun; ▯Revolución) Seven blocks northwest of Plaza de la República rise the prominent spires of this revamped university-run museum. Forged of iron in Dusseldorf around the turn of the 20th century, parts of the old building were brought over in pieces and assembled in Mexico City to serve as a pavilion for trade fairs. Much thought goes into the Chopo's organization; ramps are used as showroom floors, and high ceilings permit larger-than-life exhibits showcasing contemporary art from Mexico and abroad. The museum also hosts contemporary dance performances and film screenings.

Museo Nacional de San Carlos MUSEUM
(Map p70; www.mnsancarlos.com, in Spanish; Puente de Alvarado 50; admission M$28, Sun free; ☉10am-6pm Wed-Mon; MRevolución) This museum exhibits a formidable collection of European art from the 14th century to early 20th century, including works by Rubens and Goya. The unusual rotunda structure was designed by Manuel Tolsá in the late 18th century.

PASEO DE LA REFORMA
Mexico City's grandest thoroughfare traces a bold southwestern path from Tlatelolco to Bosque de Chapultepec, skirting the Alameda Central and Zona Rosa. Emperor Maximilian of Hapsburg laid out the boulevard to connect his castle on Chapultepec Hill with the old city center. After his execution, it was given its current name to commemorate the reform laws instituted by President Benito Juárez. Under the López Obrador administration, the avenue was smartly refurbished and its broad, statue-studded medians became a stage for book fairs and art exhibits. It is currently undergoing aggressive development, with office towers and new hotels springing up along its length.

Paseo de la Reforma links a series of monumental *glorietas* (traffic circles). A couple of blocks west of the Alameda Central is **El Caballito** (Map p70), a bright-yellow representation of a horse's head by the sculptor Sebastián. It commemorates another equestrian sculpture that stood here for 127 years and today fronts the Museo Nacional de Arte (p68). A few blocks southwest is the **Monumento a Cristóbal Colón** (Map p70), an 1877 statue of Columbus gesturing toward the horizon.

Reforma's busy intersection with Avenida Insurgentes is marked by the **Monumento a Cuauhtémoc** (Map p76), memorializing the last Aztec emperor. Two blocks northwest is the **Jardín del Arte** (Map p76), site of a lively Sunday art market (p120).

The **Centro Bursátil** (Map p76), an angular tower and mirror-ball ensemble housing the nation's stock exchange (Bolsa), marks the northeast corner of the Zona Rosa. Continuing west past the US embassy, you reach the symbol of Mexico City, the **Monumento a la Independencia** (Map p76; ⊘10am-noon Sat & Sun for visits inside; Ⓜ Insurgentes). Known as 'El Ángel,' this gilded Winged Victory on a 45m pillar was sculpted for the independence centennial of 1910. Inside the monument are the remains of Miguel Hidalgo, José María Morelos, Ignacio Allende and nine other notables.

At Reforma's intersection with Sevilla is the monument commonly known as **La Diana Cazadora** (Diana the Huntress; Map p76), a 1942 bronze sculpture actually meant to represent the Archer of the North Star. The League of Decency under the Ávila Camacho administration had the sculptor add a loincloth to the buxom babe, and it wasn't removed until 1966.

A 2003 addition to the Mexico City skyline, the **Torre Mayor** (Map p76; Paseo de la Reforma 505; Ⓜ Chapultepec) stands like a sentinel before the gate to Bosque de Chapultepec. The earthquake-resistant structure, which soars 225m above the capital, is anchored below by 98 seismic-shock absorbers. Unfortunately, the building's observation deck was shut down.

Metro Hidalgo accesses Paseo de la Reforma on the Alameda end, while the Insurgentes and Sevilla stations provide the best approach from the Zona Rosa. On the Insurgentes metrobús route, the 'Reforma' and 'Hamburgo' stops lie north and south of the avenue respectively. Along Reforma itself, any westbound 'Metro Auditorio' bus goes through the Bosque de Chapultepec, while 'Metro Chapultepec' buses terminate at the east end of the park. In the opposite direction, 'Metro Hidalgo' and 'La Villa' buses head up Reforma to the Alameda Central and beyond.

ZONA ROSA

Wedged between Paseo de la Reforma and Avenida Chapultepec, the 'Pink Zone' was developed as an international playground and shopping district during the 1950s, when it enjoyed a cosmopolitan panache. Since then, however, the Zona Rosa has been in gradual decline and has lost ground to more fashionable neighborhoods, such as Condesa and Roma, arriving at its current condition as a hodgepodge of touristy boutiques, strip clubs, discos and fast-food franchises. People-watching from its sidewalk cafes reveals a higher degree of diversity than elsewhere: it's one of the city's premier gay and lesbian districts and an expat magnet, with a significant Korean population. The Ebrard administration renovated the Calle Génova corridor in an attempt to put the zone back in the pink.

CONDESA

Colonia Condesa's architecture, palm-lined esplanades and parks echo its origins as a haven for a newly emerging elite in the early 20th century. Only recently has 'La Condesa' earned its reputation as a trendy area of informal restaurants, hip boutiques and hot nightspots. Fortunately, much of the neighborhood's old flavor remains, especially for those willing to wander outside the valet-parking zones. Stroll the pedestrian medians along Ámsterdam, Avenida Tamaulipas or Avenida Mazatlán to admire art deco and California colonial-style buildings. The focus is the peaceful **Parque México** (Map p80), the oval shape of which reflects its earlier use as a horse-racing track. Two blocks northwest is **Parque España** (Map p80), with a children's fun fair.

ROMA

Northeast of Condesa, Roma is a bohemian enclave inhabited by artists and writers. This is where Beat writers William S Burroughs and Jack Kerouac naturally gravitated during their 1950s sojourn in Mexico City. Built at the turn of the 20th century, the neighborhood is a showcase for Parisian-influenced architecture, which was favored by the Porfirio Díaz regime. Some of the most outstanding examples stand along Colima and Tabasco. When in Roma, linger in the cafes and check out a few art galleries. A stroll down Orizaba passes two lovely plazas – Río de Janeiro, with a statue of David, and Luis Cabrera, which has dancing fountains. On weekends inspect the antique market along Álvaro Obregón, the main thoroughfare.

Galleries

Small, independent art galleries are scattered around Roma – see www.arte-mexico. com for maps.

FREE Centro de Cultura
Casa Lamm   CULTURAL BUILDING
(Map p80; www.galeriacasalamm.com.mx, in Spanish; Álvaro Obregón 99; ⊘10am-6pm; 🚇Álvaro Obregón) This cultural complex contains a gallery for contemporary Mexican painting and photography as well as an excellent art library.

Galería Nina Menocal   GALLERY
(Map p80; www.ninamenocal.com; Zacatecas 93; ⊘10am-6pm Mon-Fri, to 2pm Sat; 🚇Álvaro Obregón) Highlights emerging Cuban and Latin American artists.

MUCA Roma   MUSEUM
(Map p80; www.mucaroma.unam.mx, in Spanish; Tonalá 51; ⊘10am-6pm Tue-Sun; 🚇Durango) Sponsored by Universidad Nacional Autónoma de México (UNAM), this museum exhibits Mexican and international contemporary art.

BOSQUE DE CHAPULTEPEC

Chapultepec – Náhuatl for 'Hill of Grasshoppers' – served as a refuge for the wandering Aztecs before becoming a summer residence for their noble class. It was the nearest freshwater supply for Tenochtitlán; in the 15th century Nezahualcóyotl, ruler of nearby Texcoco, oversaw the construction of an aqueduct to channel its waters over Lago de Texcoco to the pre-Hispanic capital.

Today Mexico City's largest park, the Bosque de Chapultepec covers more than 4 sq km, with lakes, a zoo and several excellent museums. It also remains an abode of Mexico's high and mighty, containing the current presidential residence, **Los Pinos** (Map p84), and a former imperial palace, the Castillo de Chapultepec.

Sunday is the park's big day, as vendors line the main paths and throngs of families come to picnic, navigate the lake on rowboats and crowd into the museums. Most of the major attractions are in or near the eastern **1a Sección** (1st Section; Map p84; ⊘5am-5pm Tue-Sun), while a large amusement park and children's museum dominate the **2a Sección** (2nd Section; Map p84; ⊘24hr).

A pair of bronze lions overlooks the main gate at Paseo de la Reforma and Lieja. At the time of writing, a 104m-high monument, dubbed 'Estela de Luz' (Pillar of Light), was being built here to belatedly commemorate Mexico's bicentennial anniversary in 2010. Because of the delays in construction, locals jokingly refer to the tower as the 'tricentennial monument.'

Other access points are opposite the Museo Nacional de Antropología and by metro Chapultepec. The fence along Paseo de la Reforma serves as the **Galería Abierta de las Rejas de Chapultepec**, an outdoor photo gallery extending from the zoo entrance to the Rufino Tamayo museum.

Chapultepec metro station is at the east end of the Bosque de Chapultepec, near the Monumento a los Niños Héroes and Castillo de Chapultepec. Auditorio metro station is on the north side of the park, 500m west of the Museo Nacional de Antropología. 'Auditorio' buses pass along the length of Paseo de la Reforma.

To get to the 2a Sección and La Feria amusement park from metro Chapultepec find the 'Paradero' exit and catch a 'Feria' bus at the top of the stairs. These depart continuously and travel nonstop to the 2a Sección, dropping off riders at the Papalote Museo del Niño and La Feria.

Museo Nacional de Antropología   MUSEUM
(National Museum of Anthropology; Map p84; www.mna.inah.gob.mx, in Spanish; cnr Paseo de la Reforma & Calz Gandhi; admission M$51, audio guides M$75; ⊘9am-7pm Tue-Sun; 🚇Auditorio) This world-class museum stands in an extension of the Bosque de Chapultepec. Its long, rectangular courtyard is surrounded on three sides by two-level display halls. The 12 ground-floor *salas* (halls) are dedicated to pre-Hispanic Mexico, while upper-level *salas* show how Mexico's indigenous descendants live today, with the contemporary cultures located directly above their ancestral civilizations.

Everything is superbly displayed, with much explanatory text translated into English. Audio guides in English are available at the entrance. The vast museum offers more than most people can absorb in a single visit. Here's a brief guide to the ground-floor halls, proceeding counterclockwise around the courtyard.

Culturas Indígenas de México Currently serves as a space for temporary exhibitions.

Introducción a la Antropología Introduces visitors to the field of anthropology.

Zona Rosa

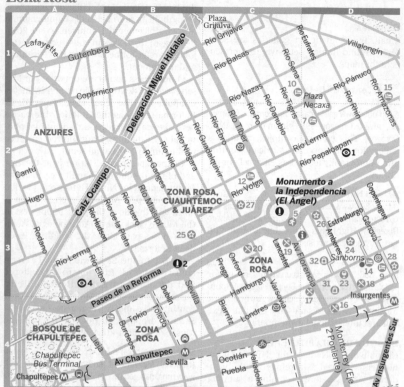

Poblamiento de América Demonstrates how the hemisphere's earliest settlers got here and survived and prospered in their new environment.

Preclásico en el Altiplano Central Focuses on the pre-Classic period, treated here as running from approximately 2300 BC to AD 100, and the transition from a nomadic hunting life to a more settled farming life in Mexico's central highlands.

Teotihuacán Displays models and objects from the Americas' first great and powerful state.

Los Toltecas y su Época Covers cultures of central Mexico between about AD 650 and 1250; on display is one of the four basalt warrior columns from Tula's Temple of Tlahuizcalpantecuhtli.

Mexica Devoted to the Mexica, aka Aztecs. Come here to see the famous sun stone, unearthed beneath the Zócalo in

1790, and other magnificent sculptures from the pantheon of Aztec deities.

Culturas de Oaxaca Displays the fine legacy of Oaxaca's Zapotec and Mixtec civilizations.

Culturas de la Costa del Golfo Spotlights the important civilizations along the Gulf of Mexico including the Olmec, Totonac and Huastec. Stone carvings include two Olmec heads weighing in at almost 20 tons.

Maya Exhibits findings from southeast Mexico, Guatemala, Belize and Honduras. A full-scale replica of the tomb of King Pakal, discovered deep in the Templo de las Inscripciones at Palenque, is simply breathtaking.

Culturas del Occidente Profiles cultures of western Mexico.

Culturas del Norte Covers the Casas Grandes (Paquimé) site and other cultures

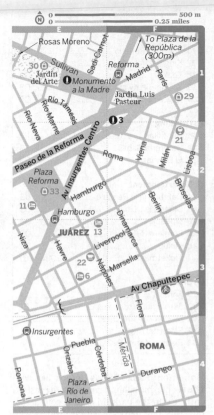

Map p84; www.mnh.inah.gob.mx, in Spanish; adult/child under 13yr M$51/free; ⊘9am-5pm Tue-Sun; ⓂChapultepec).

Historical exhibits chronicle the period from the rise of colonial Nueva España to the Mexican Revolution. In addition to displaying such iconic objects as the sword wielded by José María Morelos in the Siege of Cuautla and the Virgin of Guadalupe banner borne by Miguel Hidalgo in his march for independence, the museum features a number of dramatic interpretations of Mexican history by leading muralists including Juan O'Gorman's panoramic *Retablo de la independencia* (Panel of Independence).

The east end of the castle preserves the palace occupied by Maximilian and Carlota, with sumptuously furnished salons opening onto an exterior deck that affords sweeping city views. On the upper floor, Porfirio Díaz' opulent rooms surround a patio where a tower marks the top of Chapultepec Hill, 45m above street level.

To reach the castle, follow the road that curves up the hill behind the Monumento a los Niños Héroes. Alternatively, a trainlike vehicle (M$13 round trip) runs up every 15 minutes while the castle is open.

Back at ground level, follow the south side of the hill's base to find the formidable **Tribuna Monumental de las Águilas** (Map p84), dedicated to Mexico's WWII veterans. On the left side of the monument, enter the **Audiorama** (Map p84), a pebbly garden with body-contoured benches where you can enjoy opera or classical music.

Museo de Arte Moderno   MUSEUM
(Museum of Modern Art; Map p84; www.mam.org.mx, in Spanish; cnr Paseo de la Reforma & Calz Gandhi; admission M$22, Sun free; ⊘10:15am-5:20pm Tue-Sun; ⓂChapultepec) This museum exhibits its work by noteworthy 20th-century and contemporary Mexican artists, including canvasses by Dr Atl, Rivera, Siqueiros, Orozco, Tamayo, O'Gorman and Frida Kahlo's *Las dos Fridas,* possibly her best-known painting.

Museo Rufino Tamayo   MUSEUM
(Map p84; www.museotamayo.org; cnr Paseo de la Reforma & Calz Gandhi; admission M$15, Sun free; ⊘10am-6pm Tue-Sun; ⓂAuditorio) This is a multilevel structure built to house international modern art donated by Oaxaca-born painter Rufino Tamayo to the people of Mexico. The museum exhibits cutting-edge works from around the globe, which

from northern Mexico, and traces their links with indigenous groups of the US southwest.

In a clearing about 100m in front of the museum's entrance, indigenous Totonac people perform their spectacular *voladores* rite – 'flying' from a 20m-high pole – every 30 minutes.

Castillo de Chapultepec   HISTORIC BUILDING
A visible reminder of Mexico's bygone aristocracy, the 'castle' that stands atop Chapultepec Hill was begun in 1785 but not completed until after independence, when it became the national military academy. When Emperor Maximilian and Empress Carlota arrived in 1864, they refurbished it as their residence. It then sheltered Mexico's presidents until 1939 when President Lázaro Cárdenas converted it into the **Museo Nacional de Historia** (National History Museum;

Zona Rosa

are thematically arranged with shows from the Tamayo collection. At our last visit the Tamayo was undergoing renovation.

FREE **Zoológico de Chapultepec** ZOO
(Map p84; www.chapultepec.df.gob.mx, in Spanish; ⊘9am-4pm Tue-Sun; MAuditorio) Home to a wide range of the world's creatures in large open-air enclosures, the Chapultepec zoo was the first place outside China where pandas were born in captivity. The zoo has three of these rare bears, descendants of the original pair donated by the People's Republic in 1975. Endangered Mexican species include the Mexican grey wolf and the hairless *xoloitzcuintle,* the only surviving dog breed from pre-Hispanic times.

Jardín Botánico GARDENS
(Botanical Garden; Map p84; admission free; ⊘10am-4pm Tue-Sun; MChapultepec) Highlighting Mexico's plant diversity, the 4-hectare complex is divided into sections that reflect the country's varied climatic zones. The garden also features a greenhouse full of rare orchids.

Monumento a Los Niños Héroes MONUMENT
The six marble columns marking the eastern entrance to the park (Map p84) commemorate the 'boy heroes,' six brave cadets who perished in battle. On September 13, 1847, some 8000 US troops stormed Chapultepec Castle, which then housed the national military academy. Mexican General Santa Anna retreated before the onslaught, but the youths, aged 13 to 20, chose to defend the castle. Legend has it that one of them, Juan Escutia, wrapped himself in a Mexican flag and leapt to his death rather than surrender.

Segunda (2a) Sección PARK
The 2nd Section of the Bosque de Chapultepec lies west of the Periférico. In addition to family attractions, there is a pair of upscale lake-view restaurants on the Lago Mayor and Lago Menor.

Kids will enjoy **La Feria** (Map p84; www. feriachapultepec.com.mx, in Spanish; passes M$90-180; ⊘11am-6pm Tue-Fri, 10am-7pm Sat, 10am-8pm Sun; MConstituyentes), an old-fashioned amusement park with some hair-raising rides. An all-access 'Platino' passport is good for everything, including the rollercoasters.

Your children won't want to leave **Papalote Museo del Niño** (Map p84; www.papalote. org.mx, in Spanish; admission M$120; ⊙9am-6pm Mon-Wed & Fri, 9am-11pm Thu, 10am-7pm Sat & Sun; MConstituyentes). At this innovative, hands-on museum, kids can put together a radio program, lie on a bed of nails, join an archaeological dig and try out all manner of technological gadgets and games. Little ones also get a kick out of the planetarium.

About 200m west of the Papalote, turn right to reach the **Fuente de Tlaloc** (Map p84), an oval pool inhabited by a huge mosaic-skinned sculpture of the rain god by Diego Rivera. There's more Rivera art inside the recently renovated Chapultepec waterworks building, behind the fountain. The artist painted a series of murals entitled **El Agua, El Origen de la Vida** (Water, Origin of Life; Map p84; admission M$21.50; ⊙10am-5pm Tue-Sun) for the inauguration of the project, constructed in the 1940s to channel the waters of the Río Lerma into giant cisterns to supply the city. Experimenting with waterproof paints, Rivera covered the collection tank and part of the pipeline with images of amphibious beings.

To the north is the beautiful **Fuente de Xochipilli** (Map p84), dedicated to the Aztec 'flower prince,' with terraced fountains around a pyramid in the *talud-tablero* style typical of Teotihuacán.

POLANCO

The affluent neighborhood of Polanco, north of Bosque de Chapultepec, arose in the 1940s as a residential alternative for a burgeoning middle class anxious to escape the overcrowded Centro. Metro Polanco is in the center of the neighborhood while metro Auditorio is on its southern edge.

Polanco is known as a Jewish enclave, though the Jewish community has largely migrated further west to Lomas de Chapultepec. Today the area is known for its exclusive hotels, fine restaurants and designer stores along Avenida Presidente Masaryk. Some of the city's most prestigious museums and art galleries are here or in nearby Bosque de Chapultepec.

FREE **Museo Soumaya Plaza Carso** MUSEUM (www.museosoumaya.org, in Spanish; Blvd Cervantes 303; ⊙10:30am-6:30pm) Plated with 16,000 aluminum hexagons, this dreamlike six-story museum holds an impressive collection of sculptures by Frenchman Auguste Rodin and Catalan surrealist Salvador Dalí.

Property of Mexican tycoon Carlos Slim (the world's richest man) and named after his late wife, the recently built Soumaya also houses paintings by French impressionists (Renoir and Monet) and 20th-century Mexican artists (Siqueiros and Rivera), and the list goes on. To get here take an 'Ejército Defensa' bus from metro Chapultepec to the corner of Avenida Ejército Nacional and Avenida Ferrocarril de Cuernavaca, then walk one block north.

FREE **Galería López Quiroga** GALLERY (Map p84; www.lopezquiroga.com, in Spanish; Aristóteles 169; ⊙10am-7pm Mon-Fri, to 2pm Sat; MPolanco) Specializes in sculptures, paintings and photography by contemporary Latin American and Mexican artists, including works of Francisco Toledo, Rufino Tamayo and José Luis Cuevas.

XOCHIMILCO & AROUND

Almost at the southern edge of the DF, a network of canals flanked by gardens is a vivid reminder of the city's pre-Hispanic legacy. Remnants of the *chinampas* where the indigenous inhabitants grew their food, these 'floating gardens' are still in use today. Gliding along the canals in a fancifully decorated *trajinera* is an alternately tranquil and festive experience. As if that weren't reason enough for an excursion, Xochimilco (off Map p57) also boasts several visitor-friendly *pulquerías* (*pulque* sellers) and one of the city's best art museums.

To reach Xochimilco, take the metro to the Tasqueña station. Then follow the signs inside the station to the transfer point for the Tren Ligero (M$3), a light-rail system that extends to neighborhoods not reachable by metro. Xochimilco is the last stop. Upon exiting the station, turn left (north) and follow Avenida Morelos to the market, Jardín Juárez and church. If you don't feel like walking, bicycle taxis (M$30) will shuttle you to the *embarcaderos* (boat landings).

Canals HISTORIC SITE
Xochimilco, Náhuatl for 'Place where Flowers Grow,' was an early target of Aztec hegemony, probably due to its inhabitants' farming skills. The Xochimilcas piled up vegetation and mud in the shallow waters of Lake Xochimilco, a southern offshoot of Lago de Texcoco, to make fertile gardens called *chinampas,* which later became an economic base of the Aztec empire. As the *chinampas* proliferated, much of the lake

Roma & Condesa

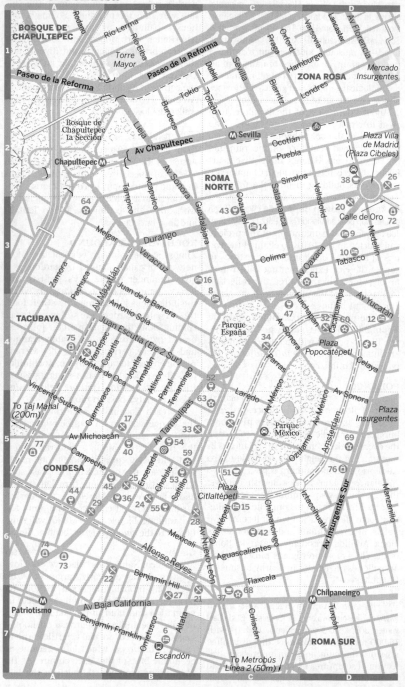

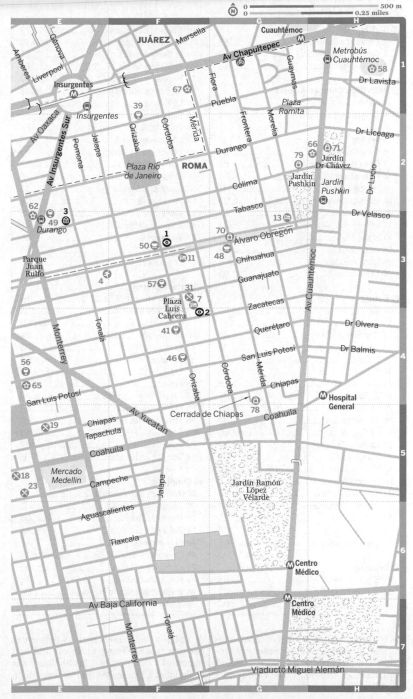

Roma & Condesa

was transformed into a series of canals. Approximately 180km of these waterways remain today and provide a favorite weekend destination for *chilangos*. The *chinampas* are still under cultivation, mainly for garden plants and flowers such as poinsettias and marigolds. Owing to its cultural and historical significance, Xochimilco was designated a Unesco World Heritage site in 1987.

On weekends a fiesta atmosphere takes over as the waterways become jammed with boats carrying groups of families and friends. Local vendors and musicians hover alongside the partygoers serving food and drink. (Midweek, the mood is far mellower.)

Hundreds of colorful *trajineras* await passengers at the village's nine *embarcaderos*. Nearest to the center are Salitre and San Cristóbal, both 400m east of the plaza, and Fernando Celada, 400m west of the plaza on Avenida Guadalupe Ramírez. Boats seat 14 to 20 persons; official cruise prices (M$200 per hour) are posted. On Saturday and Sunday and holidays, 60-person *lanchas colectivos* (boat taxis) run between the Salitre, Caltongo and Nativitas *embarcaderos*, charging M$25 per passenger for a one-way trip.

Though the canals are definitely the main attraction, Xochimilco has plenty to see. East of Jardín Juárez (Xochimilco Centro's main square) is the 16th-century **Parroquia de San Bernardino de Siena**, with elaborate gold-painted *retablos* (altarpieces) and a tree-studded atrium. South of the plaza, the bustling **Mercado de Xochimilco** covers two vast buildings: the one nearer the Jardín Juárez has fresh produce and an eating 'annex' for *tamales* and various prepared food; the other sells flowers, *chapulines* (grasshoppers), sweets and excellent *barbacoa* (savory barbecued mutton).

Museo Dolores Olmedo Patiño   MUSEUM
(www.museodoloresolmedo.org.mx; Av México 5843; admission M$55, Tue free; ☺10am-6pm Tue-Sun; ⎇La Noria) Possibly the most important Diego Rivera collection of all belongs to this museum, ensconced in a peaceful 17th-century hacienda 2km west of central Xochimilco.

Dolores Olmedo Patiño, who resided here until her death in 2002, was a socialite and a patron of Rivera. The museum's 144 Rivera works – including oils, watercolors and lithographs from various periods – are displayed alongside pre-Hispanic figurines and folk art. Another room is reserved for Frida Kahlo's paintings. Outside the exhibit halls in the estate's gardens, you'll see peacocks and *xoloitzcuintles,* a pre-Hispanic hairless dog breed.

To get here take the Tren Ligero from metro Tasqueña to La Noria station. Leaving the station, turn left at the top of the steps and descend to the street. Upon reaching an intersection with a footbridge, take a sharp left, almost doubling back on your path, onto Antiguo Camino a Xochimilco. The museum is 300m down this street.

SAN ÁNGEL

Settled by the Dominican order soon after the Spanish conquest, San Ángel, 12km southwest of the center, maintains its colonial splendor despite being engulfed by the metropolis. It's often associated with the big Saturday crafts market held alongside the Plaza San Jacinto. Though the main approach via Avenida Insurgentes is typically chaotic, wander westward to experience the old village's cobblestoned soul; it's a tranquil enclave of colonial mansions with massive wooden doors, potted geraniums behind window grills and bougainvillea spilling over stone walls.

The La Bombilla station of the Avenida Insurgentes metrobús is about 500m east of the Plaza San Jacinto. Otherwise, catch a bus from metro Miguel Ángel de Quevedo, 1km east, or metro Barranca del Muerto, 1.5km north along Avenida Revolución.

Plaza San Jacinto   PLAZA
Every Saturday the Bazar Sábado (p120) brings masses of color and crowds of people to this square, 500m west of Avenida Insurgentes.

FREE **Museo Casa del Risco** (Map p88; www.isidrofabela.com, in Spanish; Plaza San Jacinto 15; ☺10am-5pm Tue-Sun; ⎇La Bombilla) is midway along the plaza's north side – look for the elaborate fountain inside the courtyard. The fountain is a mad mosaic of Talavera tile and Chinese porcelain. Upstairs is a treasure trove of Mexican baroque and medieval European paintings.

About 50m west of the plaza is the 16th-century **Iglesia de San Jacinto** (Map p88) and its peaceful gardens.

**Museo Casa Estudio
Diego Rivera y Frida Kahlo**   MUSEUM
(Diego Rivera & Frida Kahlo Studio Museum; Map p88; www.estudiodiegorivera.bellasartes.gob.mx, in Spanish; Diego Rivera 2, cnr Av Altavista; admission M$11, Sun free; ☺10am-6pm Tue-Sun) If you saw the movie *Frida,* you'll recognize this museum, 1km northwest of Plaza San Jacinto. Designed by their friend, architect and painter Juan O'Gorman, the innovative abode was the home of the artistic couple from 1934 to 1940, with a separate house for each of them. Rivera's house preserves his upstairs studio, while Frida's (the blue one)

Bosque de Chapultepec & Polanco

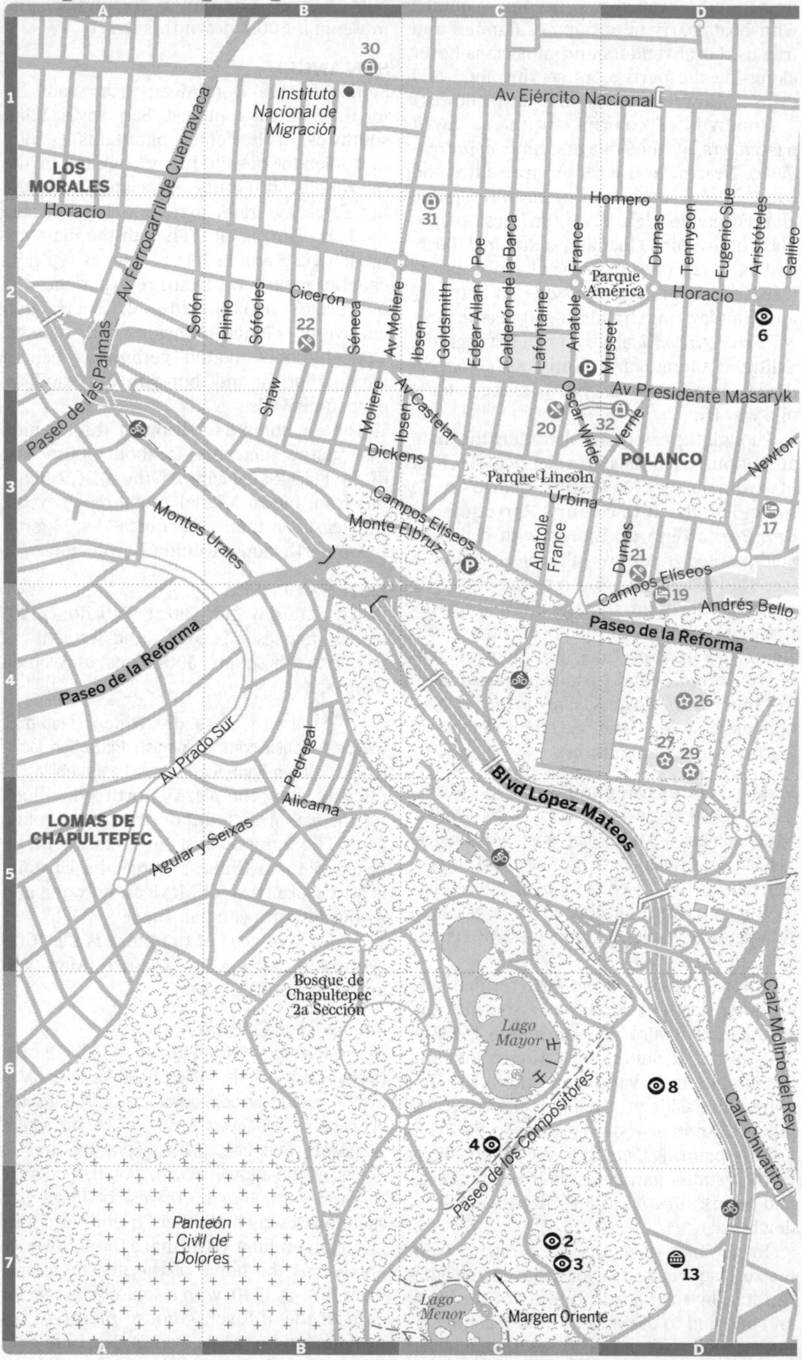

LOS MORALES

Horacio

Instituto Nacional de Migración

30

Av Ejército Nacional

31

Homero

Horacio

Av Ferrocarril de Cuernavaca

Solón

Plinio

Sófocles

Cicerón

22

Séneca

Av Molière

Ibsen

Goldsmith

Edgar Allan

Poe

Calderón de la Barca

Lafontaine

Anatole

France

Dumas

Tennyson

Eugenio Sue

Aristóteles

Galileo

Parque América

Horacio

6

Shaw

Molière

Ibsen

Av Castelar

Dickens

Av Presidente Masaryk

20

32

Verne

Oscar Wilde

Musset

POLANCO

Newton

Paseo de las Palmas

Montes Urales

Campos Elíseos

Monte Elbruz

Parque Lincoln

Urbina

Anatole France

Dumas

21

17

Campos Elíseos

19

Andrés Bello

Paseo de la Reforma

Paseo de la Reforma

LOMAS DE CHAPULTEPEC

Av Prado Sur

Pedregal

Alicama

Aguilar y Seixas

Blvd López Mateos

26

27

29

Bosque de Chapultepec 2a Sección

Lago Mayor

Paseo de los Compositores

8

Calz Molino del Rey

Calz Chivatito

4

Panteón Civil de Dolores

2

3

13

Lago Menor

Margen Oriente

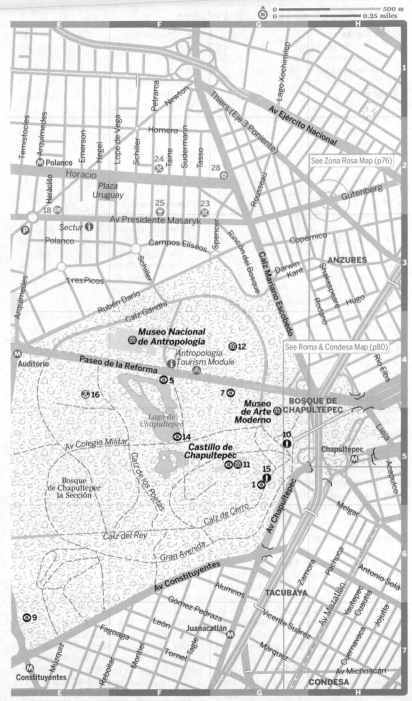

0 500 m
0 0.25 miles

E F G H

Av Ejército Nacional

See Zona Rosa Map (p76)

Lago Xochimilco

Thiers (Eje 3 Poniente)

Petrarca
Newton
Homero
Schiller
Taine
Sudermann
Tasso

24
28

Temístocles
Arquímedes
Emerson
Hegel
Lope de Vega

Ⓜ **Polanco**

Herádito
Horacio

Plaza
Uruguay

18

Av Presidente Masaryk

25
23

Gutenberg

Spencer
Rincón del Bosque

Calz Mariano Escobedo

Ressosa

Copérnico

ANZURES

Sectur ℹ

Polanco

Campos Elíseos

Ⓟ

Schiller

Darwin
Kant

Shakespeare

Hugo

Arquímedes

Tres Picos

Rubén Darío

Calz Gandhi

**Museo Nacional
de Antropología**

12

Rodano

See Roma & Condesa Map (p80)

Río Elba

Ⓜ
Auditorio

Paseo de la Reforma

Antropología
Tourism Module

5

16

7

**Museo
de Arte
Moderno**

**BOSQUE DE
CHAPULTEPEC**

10

Llela

Lago de
Chapultepec

14

**Castillo de
Chapultepec**

11

15

1

Chapultepec
Ⓜ

Acapulco

Av Colegio Militar

Calz de los Poetas

Bosque
de Chapultepec
la Sección

Melgar

Av Chapultepec

Calz de Cerro

Calz del Rey

Gran Avenida

Av Constituyentes

Alumnos

TACUBAYA

Zamora
Pachuca

Antonio Solá

9

Gómez Pedraza

León

Juanacatlán

Ⓜ

Vicente Suárez

Av Mazatlán

Yautepec
Cuautla

Jojutla

Fagoaga

Múzquiz
Rebollar
Montiel
Tornel
Tagle

Márquez

Cuernavaca

Ⓜ
Constituyentes

Av Michoacán

CONDESA

E F G H

Bosque de Chapultepec & Polanco

has changing exhibits from the memorabilia archives.

The closest bus stop is metrobús La Bombilla. Then it's a 2km walk or taxi ride.

Across the street is the San Ángel Inn (p108). Now housing a prestigious restaurant, the former *pulque* (low-alcohol brew) hacienda is historically significant as the place where Pancho Villa and Emiliano Zapata agreed to divide control of the country in 1914.

Museo de El Carmen   MUSEUM
(Map p88; www.museodeelcarmen.org, in Spanish; Av Revolución 4; admission M$41, Sun free; ⊙10am-5pm Tue-Sun; ⌕La Bombilla) A storehouse of magnificent sacred art, this museum occupies a former school run by the Carmelite order. The collection includes eight oils by Mexican master Cristóbal de Villalpando; however, the big draw is the collection of a dozen mummies in the crypt. Thought to be the bodies of 17th-century benefactors of the order, they were uncovered during the revolution by Zapatistas looking for buried treasure.

Museo de Arte Carrillo Gil   MUSEUM
(Map p88; www.museodeartecarrillogil.com, in Spanish; Av Revolución 1608; admission M$15, Sun free; ⊙10am-6pm Tue-Sun; ⌕Altavista) One of the city's first contemporary art spaces, this museum was founded by Yucatecan businessman Álvaro Carrillo Gil to store a large collection that he had amassed over many years. Unfortunately, he died several months after the 1974 inauguration. Long ramps in the center of the remodeled building lead up to cutting-edge temporary exhibits and some of the lesser-known works by Diego Rivera, José Clemente Orozco and David Alfaro Siqueiros.

Jardín de la Bombilla   PARK
In this tropically abundant park spreading east of Avenida Insurgentes, paths encircle the **Monumento a Álvaro Obregón** (Map p88), a monolithic shrine to the postrevolutionary Mexican president. The monument was built to house the revolutionary general's arm, lost in the 1915 Battle of Celaya, but the limb was cremated in 1989. 'La Bombilla' was the name of the restaurant where

Obregón was assassinated in 1928. The killer, José de León Toral, was involved in the Cristero rebellion against the government's anti-Church policies.

In July the park explodes with color as the main venue for **Feria de las Flores**, a major flower festival.

CIUDAD UNIVERSITARIA

Two kilometers south of San Ángel, the **Ciudad Universitaria** (University City; off Map p88; www.unam.mx; ☐Centro Cultural Universitario) is the main campus of the Universidad Nacional Autónoma de México (UNAM). With about 316,000 students and 36,000 teachers, it is Latin America's largest university. Five former Mexican presidents are among its alumni, as is Carlos Slim, ranked the world's richest man in 2011.

Founded in 1551 as the Royal and Papal University of Mexico, UNAM is the second-oldest university in the Americas. It occupied various buildings in the center of town until the campus was transferred to its current location in the 1950s. Although it is a public university open to all, UNAM remains 'autonomous,' meaning the government may not interfere in its academic policies. It is Mexico's leading research institute and has long been a center of political dissent.

An architectural showpiece, UNAM was placed on Unesco's list of World Heritage sites in 2007. Most of the faculty buildings are scattered at the north end. As you enter from Avenida Insurgentes, it's easy to spot the **Biblioteca Central** (Central Library), 10 stories high and covered with mosaics by Juan O'Gorman. The south wall, with two prominent zodiac wheels, covers colonial times, while the north wall deals with Aztec culture. **La Rectoría**, the administration building at the west end of the vast central lawn, has a vivid, three-dimensional Siqueiros mosaic on its south wall, showing students urged on by the people.

Across Avenida Insurgentes stands the Estadio Olímpico (p118), built of volcanic stone for the 1968 Olympics. With seating for 72,000, it's home to UNAM's Pumas soccer club, which competes in the national league's Primera División. Over the main entrance is Diego Rivera's dramatic sculpted mural on the theme of sports in Mexican history.

East of the university's main esplanade, the **Facultad de Medicina** (Faculty of Medicine) features an intriguing mosaic mural by Francisco Eppens on the theme of Mexico's *mestizaje* (blending of indigenous and European races).

A second section of the campus, about 2km south, contains the Centro Cultural Universitario (p115), with five theaters, two cinemas as well as the **Museo Universitario Arte Contemporáneo** (MUAC; Map p57; www.muac.unam.mx; admission Thu-Sat M$40, Wed & Sun M$20; ⊙10am-6pm Wed, Fri & Sun, noon-8pm Thu & Sat; ☐Centro Cultural Universitario). Designed by veteran architect Teodoro González de León, this striking new museum houses avant-garde temporary exhibitions consisting mostly of paintings, sculptures and multimedia art from Mexico and abroad.

Need a break? Hit the cultural center's delightful Azul y Oro restaurant (p109).

Just north of the cultural complex is the **Museo Universitario de Ciencias** (Universum; www.universum.unam.mx, in Spanish; adult/child M$69/59; ⊙9am-5pm Mon-Fri, 10am-5pm Sat & Sun), a science museum with a planetarium and kids' activities.

Nearby you'll also find the university sculpture garden, with a trail leading through volcanic fields past a dozen or so innovative pieces. The most formidable work is an enormous ring of concrete blocks by sculptor Mathias Goeritz.

To get to University City, take Línea 1 of the metrobús to the Centro Cultural Universitario (CCU) station. Or go to metro Universidad and hop on the 'Pumabús,' a free on-campus bus service. The Pumabús has limited service on weekends and holidays.

COYOACÁN

Coyoacán ('Place of Coyotes' in the Náhuatl language), about 10km south of downtown, was Cortés' base after the fall of Tenochtitlán. Only in recent decades has urban sprawl overtaken the outlying village. Coyoacán retains its restful identity, with narrow colonial-era streets, cafes and a lively atmosphere. Once home to Leon Trotsky and Frida Kahlo (whose houses are now fascinating museums), it has a decidedly countercultural vibe, most evident on weekends, when assorted musicians, mimes and crafts markets draw large but relaxed crowds to Coyoacán's central plazas.

The nearest metro stations to central Coyoacán, 1.5km to 2km away, are Viveros, Coyoacán and General Anaya. If you don't fancy a walk, get off at Viveros station, walk south to Avenida Progreso and catch an eastbound 'Metro Gral Anaya' pesero

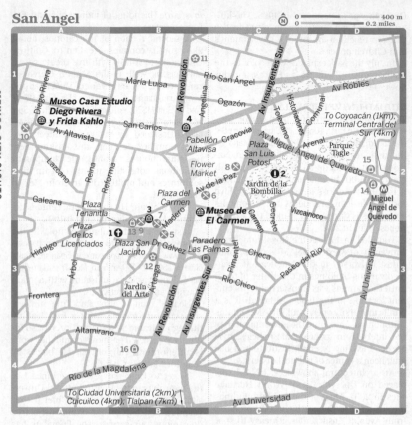

San Ángel

◉ **Top Sights**

Museo Casa Estudio Diego Rivera
y Frida Kahlo.................................A1
Museo de El Carmen B2

◉ **Sights**

1 Iglesia de San Jacinto............................B3
2 Monumento a Álvaro Obregón.............C2
3 Museo Casa del Risco B2
4 Museo de Arte Carrillo Gil....................B2

⊗ **Eating**

5 Barbacoa de Santiago...........................B3
6 Cluny...B2
7 Fonda San Ángel.....................................B3
8 Montejo C2
9 Saks..B3

10 San Ángel Inn...A2
Taberna del Léon..........................(see 16)

◎ **Drinking**

La Camelia.....................................(see 7)

✪ **Entertainment**

11 Centro Cultural Helénico......................B1
12 El Breve Espacio B3
Mamá Rumba.................................(see 16)

🔒 **Shopping**

13 Bazar Sábado...B3
14 Gandhi...D2
15 Gandhi...D2
16 Plaza Loreto...B4

(Mexico City name for a *colectivo*) to the market. Returning, 'Metro Viveros' peseros go west on Malintzin; 'Metro Coyoacán' and 'Metro Gral Anaya' peseros depart from the west side of Plaza Hidalgo.

San Ángel–bound peseros and buses head west on Avenida Miguel Ángel de Quevedo, five blocks south of Plaza Hidalgo.

Museo Frida Kahlo   MUSEUM
(Map p90; www.museofridakahlo.org.mx; Londres 247; admission M$75; ☺10am-6pm Tue-Sun; MCoyoacán) Renowned Mexican artist Frida Kahlo was born in, and lived and died in, the 'Blue House,' now a museum. Almost every visitor to Mexico City makes a pilgrimage here to gain a deeper understanding of the painter (and maybe to pick up a Frida handbag).

Built by her father Guillermo three years before Frida's birth, the house is littered with mementos and personal belongings that evoke her long, often tempestuous relationship with husband Diego Rivera and the leftist intellectual circle they often entertained there. Kitchen implements, jewelry, outfits, photos and other objects from the artist's everyday life are interspersed with art, as well as a variety of pre-Hispanic pieces and Mexican crafts. The collection was greatly expanded in 2007 upon the discovery of a cache of previously unseen items that had been stashed in the attic.

Kahlo's art expresses the anguish of her existence as well as her flirtation with socialist icons: portraits of Lenin and Mao hang around her bed, and in the upstairs studio an unfinished portrait of Stalin stands before a poignantly positioned wheelchair. In another painting, *Retrato de la familia* (Family Portrait), the artist's Hungarian-Oaxacan roots are fancifully entangled.

Plaza Hidalgo & Jardín Centenario   PLAZA
The focus of Coyoacán life, and the scene of most of the weekend fun, is its central plaza – actually two adjacent plazas: the **Jardín Centenario**, with the village's iconic coyotes frolicking in its central fountain; and the larger, cobblestoned **Plaza Hidalgo**, with a statue of the eponymous independence hero.

The **Casa de Cortés** (Map p90; Jardín Hidalgo 1; ☺8am-8pm; MViveros), on the north side of Plaza Hidalgo, is where conquistador Cortés established Mexico's first municipal seat during the siege of Tenochtitlán, and later had the defeated emperor Cuauhtémoc tortured to make him divulge the location of Aztec treasure (the scene is depicted on a mural inside the chapel). Contrary to popular thought, Cortés never actually resided here. The building now houses Coyoacán's delegation offices.

The **Parroquia de San Juan Bautista** (Map p90) and its adjacent ex-monastery dominate the east side of Plaza Hidalgo. First erected in 1592 by the Franciscans, the single-nave church has a lavishly ornamented interior, with painted scenes all over the vaulted ceiling. Be sure to inspect the cloister, featuring Tuscan columns and a checkerboard of carved relief panels in the corner of the ceilings.

Half a block east, the **Museo Nacional de Culturas Populares** (Map p90; www.culturas populareseindigenas.gob.mx, in Spanish; Av Hidalgo 289; admission M$11, Sun free; ☺10am-6pm Tue-Thu, to 8pm Fri-Sun; MViveros) stages innovative exhibitions on folk traditions, indigenous crafts and celebrations in its various courtyards and galleries.

Anahuacalli   MUSEUM
(Diego Rivera Anahuacalli Museum; Map p57; www. museoanahuacalli.org.mx; Calle Museo 150; admission adult/child M$35/15; ☺11am-4:30pm Wed-Sun) Designed by Diego Rivera to house his collection of pre-Hispanic art, this museum, 3.5km south of Coyoacán, is a templelike structure of dark volcanic stone. The 'House of Anáhuac' (Aztec name for the Valle de México) also contains one of Rivera's studios and some of his work, including a study for 'Man at the Crossroads,' the mural that was commissioned for the Rockefeller Center in 1934. In November, elaborate Day of the Dead offerings pay homage to the painter.

Visits are by guided tour only and a M$75 entry fee includes admission to the nearby Museo Frida Kahlo.

To get to Anahuacalli, take the Tren Ligero (from metro Tasqueña) to the Xotepingo station. Exit on the west side and walk 200m to División del Norte; cross and continue 600m along Calle Museo.

Museo León Trotsky   MUSEUM
(Map p90; www.museocasadeleontrotsky.blogspot. com, in Spanish; Av Río Churubusco 410; admission M$40; ☺10am-5pm Tue-Sun; MCoyoacán) Having come second to Stalin in the power struggle in the Soviet Union, Trotsky was expelled in 1929 and condemned to death in absentia. In 1937 he found refuge in Mexico. At first Trotsky and his wife, Natalia, lived in Frida Kahlo's Blue House, but after falling

Coyoacán

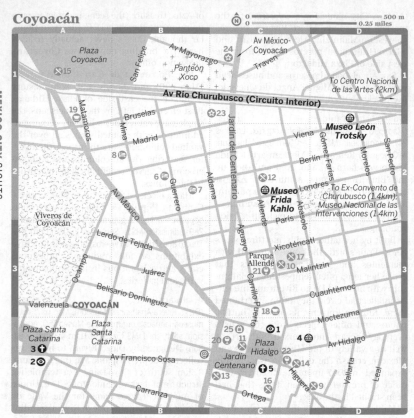

out with Kahlo and Rivera they moved a few streets northeast.

The Trotsky home, now a museum, remains much as it was on the day when a Stalin agent, a Catalan named Ramón Mercader, caught up with the revolutionary and smashed an ice pick into his skull. Memorabilia and biographical notes are displayed in buildings off the patio, where a tomb engraved with a hammer and sickle contains the Trotskys' ashes.

The entrance is at the rear of the old residence, facing Circuito Interior.

Ex-Convento de Churubusco   HISTORIC BUILDING

Scene of a historic military defeat, the 17th-century former Monastery of Churubusco (off Map p90) stands within peaceful wooded grounds, 1.5km east of Plaza Hidalgo. On August 20, 1847, Mexican troops defended the monastery against US forces advancing from Veracruz in a dispute over the US an-

nexation of Texas. The Mexicans fought until they ran out of ammunition and were beaten only after hand-to-hand fighting.

The US invasion was but one example in a long history of foreign intervention in Mexico, as compellingly demonstrated by the **Museo Nacional de las Intervenciones** (National Interventions Museum; off Map p90; cnr Calle 20 de Agosto & General Anaya; admission M$41, Sun free; 9am-6pm Tue-Sun; M General Anaya), inside the former *convento*. Displays include an American map showing operations in 1847 and the plot by US ambassador Henry Lane Wilson to bring down the Madero government in 1913.

The superbly restored exhibit rooms, bordered by original frescoes, surround a small cloister where numbered stations provided instructions for meditating monks. Leaving the museum, wander amid the monastery's old orchard, which now holds wonderful gardens.

Coyoacán

MEXICO CITY SIGHTS

To reach Churubusco, catch an eastbound 'Metro General Anaya' bus from Carrillo Puerto, off Plaza Hidalgo. Otherwise, walk 500m west from the General Anaya metro station.

Viveros de Coyoacán   PARK
(Map p90; admission free; ☉6am-6pm; Ⓜ Viveros) A pleasant approach to Coyoacán's central plazas is via the Viveros de Coyoacán, the principal nurseries for Mexico City's parks and gardens. The 390-sq-km swath of greenery, 1km west of central Coyoacán, is popular with joggers and great for a stroll, but watch out for belligerent squirrels! From metro Viveros, walk south (right, as you face the fence) along Avenida Universidad and take the first left, Avenida Progreso.

A block south of Viveros is the quaint **Plaza Santa Catarina**, with the modest, mustard-colored church that gives the square its name. Across the street, the **Centro Cultural Jesús Reyes Heroles** (Map p90; Francisco Sosa 202; ☉8am-8pm; Ⓜ Viveros) is a colonial estate hosting book presentations, dance classes and other activities. Take a wander round the grounds, where yuccas and jacarandas spring from carefully tended gardens. The 700m walk east along Avenida Francisco Sosa to Jardín Centenario passes some fine colonial buildings, several of which house cafes.

CUICUILCO
One of the oldest significant remnants of pre-Hispanic settlement within the DF, **Cuicuilco** (Map p57; Av Insurgentes Sur s/n; admission free; ☉9am-5pm; ⬛ Villa Olímpica) echoes a civilization that stood on the shores of Lago de Xochimilco as far back as 800 BC. In its heyday in the 2nd century BC, the 'place of singing and dancing' counted as many as 40,000 inhabitants; at that time, the Teotihuacán civilization was only just beginning to rise to importance. The site was abandoned a couple of centuries later, however, after an eruption of the nearby Xitle volcano covered most of the community in lava.

The principal structure is a huge circular platform of four levels, faced with volcanic stone blocks, that probably functioned as a ceremonial center. Set amid a park studded with cacti and shade trees, the platform can be easily scaled for views of the southern districts, including the formidable Xitle. The site has a small museum.

TLALPAN
Tlalpan today is 'what Coyoacán used to be' – an outlying village with a bohemian atmosphere coupled with some impressive

colonial architecture. The municipal seat of Mexico City's largest *delegación,* Tlalpan sits at the foot of the southern Ajusco range and enjoys a cooler, moister climate. There are some fine restaurants along the arcades of the cute plaza and a 141-year-old cantina nearby, called **La Jalisciense** (Plaza de la Constitución 7; ⊘noon-1:30am Mon-Sat).

FREE **Museo de Historia de Tlalpán** (Plaza de la Constitución 10; ⊘10am-6pm Tue-Sun), half a block from the plaza, hosts compelling historical exhibits in naturally lit galleries off the courtyard.

There's a sublime simplicity about the **Capilla de las Capuchinas Sacramentarias** (Av Hidalgo 43; admission M$60; ⊘9:30am-noon Mon-Fri), the chapel of a convent for Capuchin nuns designed by modernist architect Luis Barragán in 1952. The austere altar, free of the usual iconography, consists only of a trio of gold panels. In the morning, light streams through the stained-glass window by Mathias Goeritz.

To get here take the Línea 1 metrobús to Fuentes Brotantes and walk four blocks east to Tlalpan's main square.

TLATELOLCO & GUADALUPE

FREE **Plaza de las Tres Culturas** HISTORIC SITE (Plaza of the Three Cultures; off Map p62; www.tlatelolco-inah.gob.mx, in Spanish; cnr Eje Central Lázaro Cárdenas & Flores Magón; ⊘8am-5:30pm; ⓂTlatelolco) So named because it symbolizes the fusion of pre-Hispanic and Spanish roots into the Mexican *mestizo* identity, this plaza displays the architectural legacy of three cultural facets: the Aztec pyramids of **Tlatelolco**, the 17th-century Spanish Templo de Santiago and the modern tower that now houses the Centro Cultural Universitario.

Recent archaeological finds have altered long-held views about Tlatelolco's history. According to the conventional version, Tlatelolco was founded by an Aztec faction in the 14th century on a separate island in Lago de Texcoco and later conquered by the Aztecs of Tenochtitlán. But a pyramid excavated on the site in late 2007 actually predates the establishment of Tenochtitlán by as much as 200 years. All agree, however, that Tlatelolco was the scene of the largest public market in the Valle de México, connected by a causeway to Tenochtitlán's ceremonial center.

During the siege of the Aztec capital, Cortés defeated Tlatelolco's defenders, led by Cuauhtémoc. An inscription about the battle in the plaza translates as 'This was neither victory nor defeat. It was the sad birth of the *mestizo* people that is Mexico today.'

You can view the remains of Tlatelolco's main pyramid-temple and other Aztec buildings from a walkway around them. Tlatelolco's main temple was constructed in stages, with each of seven temples superimposed atop its predecessor. The double pyramid on view, one of the earliest stages, has twin staircases that supposedly ascended to temples dedicated to Tláloc and Huitzilopochtli. Numerous calendar glyphs are carved into the outer walls.

Recognizing the significance of the site, the Spanish erected the **Templo de Santiago** here in 1609, using stones from the Aztec structures as building materials. Just inside the main doors of this church is the **baptismal font of Juan Diego** (see p93).

Tlatelolco is also a symbol of modern troubles. On October 2, 1968, hundreds of student protesters were massacred here by government troops on the eve of the Mexico City Olympic Games. The weeks before the Olympics had been marked by a wave of protests against political corruption and authoritarianism, and president Gustavo Díaz Ordaz, anxious to present an image of stability to the world, was employing heavy-handed tactics to stop the unrest.

On that October day, helicopters hovered over the Plaza de las Tres Culturas and a massive police contingent cordoned off the protest zone. Suddenly shots rang out, apparently from the balcony that served as a speakers' platform. Police then opened fire on the demonstrators and mayhem ensued. A government-authorized account reported 20 protesters killed, although the real number is acknowledged to be closer to 400.

The generally accepted theory, though there are many, is that the government staged the massacre, planting snipers on the balcony. To this day the incident still generates a massive protest march from Tlatelolco to the Zócalo on October 2.

The **Centro Cultural Universitario Tlatelolco** (www.tlatelolco.unam.mx, in Spanish; Flores Magón 1; admission M$20; ⊘10am-6pm Tue-Sun; ⓂTlatelolco) commemorates and documents the events that occurred. A component of the UNAM, it contains two interesting permanent exhibits. The **Colección Andrés Blaisten** comprises the largest privately owned collection of Mexican 20th-century art, with paintings, prints and

FRIDA & DIEGO

A century after Frida Kahlo's birth, and over 50 years after Diego Rivera's death, the pair's fame and recognition are stronger than ever. In 2007 a retrospective of Kahlo's work at the Palacio de Bellas Artes attracted more than 440,000 visitors. Though attendance at the Rivera survey that followed was not so phenomenal, the show reminded visitors that the prolific muralist had been an international star in his own lifetime. Their memory is inseparably linked, and both artists were frequent subjects in each other's work.

Rivera first met Kahlo, 21 years his junior, while painting at the Escuela Nacional Preparatoria, where she was a student in the early 1920s. Rivera was already at the forefront of Mexican art; his commission at the school was the first of many semipropaganda murals on public buildings that he was to execute over three decades. He had already fathered children by two Russian women in Europe, and in 1922 he married Lupe Marín in Mexico. She bore him two more children before their marriage broke up in 1928.

Kahlo was born in Coyoacán in 1907 to a Hungarian-Jewish father and Oaxacan mother. She contracted polio at age six, leaving her right leg permanently thinner than her left. In 1925 she was horribly injured in a trolley accident that broke her right leg, collarbone, pelvis and ribs. She made a miraculous recovery but suffered much pain thereafter. It was during convalescence that she began painting. Pain – physical and emotional – was to be a dominating theme of her art.

Kahlo and Rivera both moved in left-wing artistic circles, and they met again in 1928; they married the following year. The liaison, described as 'a union between an elephant and a dove,' was always a passionate love-hate affair. Rivera wrote: 'If I ever loved a woman, the more I loved her, the more I wanted to hurt her. Frida was only the most obvious victim of this disgusting trait.'

In 1934, after a spell in the US, the pair moved into a new home in San Ángel, now the Museo Casa Estudio Diego Rivera y Frida Kahlo (p83), with separate houses linked by an aerial walkway. After Kahlo discovered that Rivera had had an affair with her sister, Cristina, she divorced him in 1939, but they remarried the following year. She moved back into her childhood home, the Casa Azul in Coyoacán, and he stayed at San Ángel – a state of affairs that endured for the rest of their lives, and their relationship endured, too.

Despite the worldwide wave of Fridamania that followed the hit biopic *Frida* in 2002, Kahlo had only one exhibition in Mexico in her lifetime, in 1953. She arrived at the opening on a stretcher. Rivera said of the exhibition: 'Anyone who attended it could not but marvel at her great talent.' She died at the Blue House the following year. Rivera called it 'the most tragic day of my life... Too late I realized that the most wonderful part of my life had been my love for Frida.'

sculptures by both obscure and famed artists such as María Izquierdo and Juan Soriano. The **Memorial del 68** chronicles the tragedy.

Along Eje Central Lázaro Cárdenas, northbound 'Central Autobuses del Norte' trolleybuses pass right by the Plaza de las Tres Culturas.

Basílica de Guadalupe HISTORIC SITE
In December 1531, the story goes, an indigenous Christian convert named Juan Diego stood on Cerro del Tepeyac (Tepeyac Hill), site of an old Aztec shrine, and beheld a beautiful lady dressed in a blue mantle trimmed with gold. She sent him to tell the bishop, Juan de Zumárraga, that he had seen the Virgin Mary, and that she wanted a shrine built in her honor. But the bishop didn't believe him. Returning to the hill, Juan Diego had the vision several more times. After her fourth appearance, the lady's image was miraculously emblazoned on his cloak, causing the church to finally accept his story, and a cult developed around the site.

Over the centuries Nuestra Señora de Guadalupe came to receive credit for all manner of miracles, hugely aiding the acceptance of Catholicism by Mexicans. Despite the protests of some clergy, who saw the cult as a form of idolatry (with the Virgin as a Christianized version of the Aztec goddess Tonantzin), in 1737 the Virgin was officially declared the patron of Mexico. Two

WORTH A TRIP

PARQUE NACIONAL DESIERTO DE LOS LEONES

Cool, fragrant pine and oak forests dominate this 20-sq-km **national park** (☉6am-5pm) in the hills surrounding the Valle de México. Some 23km southwest of Mexico City and 800m higher, it makes for a fine escape from the carbon monoxide and concrete.

The name derives from the **Ex-Convento del Santo Desierto de Nuestra Señora del Carmen** (Camino al Desierto de los Leones; admission M$10.50; ☉10am-5pm Tue-Sun), the 17th-century former Carmelite monastery within the park. The Carmelites called their isolated monasteries 'deserts' to commemorate Elijah, who lived as a recluse in the desert near Mt Carmel. The 'Leones' in the name may stem from the presence of wild cats in the area, but more likely it refers to José and Manuel de León, who once administered the monastery's finances.

The restored monastery has exhibition halls and a restaurant. Tours in Spanish are run by guides (garbed in cassock and sandals) who lead you through expansive gardens around the buildings and the patios within, as well as some underground passageways.

The rest of the park has extensive walking trails. (Robberies have been reported, so stick to the main paths.)

Ruta (route) 43 buses depart to the former *convento* from metro Viveros at 7am Monday to Friday, and from Paradero Las Palmas in San Ángel (Map p88) at noon and 3pm (also Monday to Friday). On Saturday and Sunday there are hourly departures from Paradero Las Palmas from 9am to 3pm. Be sure to ask the driver if the bus arrives as far as the *ex-convento* (some stop short in a mountain town called Santa Rosa).

centuries later she was named celestial patron of Latin America and empress of the Americas, and in 2002 Juan Diego was canonized by Pope John Paul II. Today the Virgin's shrines around the Cerro del Tepeyac are the most revered in Mexico, attracting thousands of pilgrims daily and hundreds of thousands on the days leading up to her feast day, December 12. Some pilgrims travel the last meters to the shrine on their knees.

Around 1700, to accommodate the faithful flock, the four-towered Basílica de Guadalupe was erected at the site of an earlier shrine. But by the 1970s, the old yellow-domed building proved inadequate to the task, so the new **Basílica de Nuestra Señora de Guadalupe** (off Map p57; www.virgendeguadalupe.org.mx, in Spanish; Plaza de las Américas 1; Ⓜ La Villa–Basilica) was built next door. Designed by Pedro Ramírez Vázquez, it is a vast, round, open-plan structure with a capacity for over 40,000 people. The image of the Virgin hangs above and behind the basilica's main altar, with moving walkways to bring visitors as close as possible.

The rear of the Antigua Basílica is now the **Museo de la Basílica de Guadalupe** (www.mubagua.org.mx, in Spanish; admission M$5; ☉10am-5:30pm Tue-Sun), with a fine collection of colonial art interpreting the miraculous vision.

Stairs behind the Antigua Basílica climb about 100m to the hilltop **Capilla del Cerrito** (Hill Chapel), where Juan Diego had his vision, then lead down the east side of the hill to the Parque de la Ofrenda, with gardens and waterfalls around a sculpted scene of the apparition. Continue on down to the baroque **Templo del Pocito**, a circular structure with a trio of tiled cupolas, built in 1787 to commemorate the miraculous appearance of a spring where the Virgen de Guadalupe had stood. From there the route leads back to the main plaza, re-entering it beside the 17th-century **Antigua Parroquia de Indios** (Parish of Indians).

To reach the Basílica de Guadalupe, take the metro to La Villa–Basílica station, then walk two blocks north along Calzada de Guadalupe. Or you can take any 'Metro Hidalgo–La Villa' bus heading northeast on Paseo de la Reforma. To return downtown, walk to Calzada de los Misterios, a block west of Calzada de Guadalupe, and catch a southbound 'Metro Hidalgo' or 'Metro Chapultepec' bus.

🏃 Activities

Bicycling

On Sunday morning Paseo de la Reforma is closed to auto traffic from Bosque de Chapultepec to the Alameda Central, and you can join the legions of *chilangos* who happily skate or cycle down the avenue.

For a more ambitious trek, the urban cycling group **Bicitekas** (http://bicitekas.org, in Spanish) organizes rides departing from the Monumento a la Independencia (Map p76) at 9:30pm every Wednesday. Groups of more than 100 cyclists ride to destinations like Coyoacán, Xochimilco and Ciudad Satélite. Participants must be sufficiently robust to handle treks of up to 40km. Helmets and rear lights are required.

For information on renting bicycles and around-town routes, see p129.

Kayaking

Ecotourism center Michmani (p102) rents kayaks for M$100 per hour, making for a great opportunity to take in some of the quieter parts of the Xochimilco canals and do some bird-watching while you're at it. You'll spot ducks, egrets and herons, among many other migratory and endemic species, and you can also visit the many nurseries along the shores of the waterways.

Ice-Skating

As part of Mayor Marcelo Ebrard's campaign to bring fun recreational activities to the city's poorer inhabitants, a huge ice-skating rink is installed in the Zócalo during the Christmas holiday season. Ice skates are available for loan free of charge, if you don't mind waiting up to an hour.

Gyms

Some top-end hotels, especially those with spas, have day rates available for nonguests. Otherwise, there are several city gyms where you can use the equipment and take classes inexpensively.

Centro Qi GYM
(Map p80; www.centroqi.mx, in Spanish; Amsterdam 317, Condesa; per day M$222; ☉6am-11pm Mon-Thu, 6am-10pm Fri, 8am-6pm Sat, 9am-4pm Sun; ⓐSonora) Stylish Condesa gym with climbing wall and yoga classes.

Caba's Gym GYM
(Map p80; Álvaro Obregón 160, Roma; per day M$40; ☉6am-10pm Mon-Fri, 8am-2pm Sat; ⓐÁlvaro Obregón) Small gym with good-value daily rates.

Jogging

One popular place for a morning run is the path that skirts the oval Parque México (p74). Runners also use the broad and narrow paths crisscrossing the gardens of Viveros de Coyoacán (p91). Bosque de Chapultepec (p75), of course, offers many kilometers of tree-shaded trails.

Courses

Eat Mexico COOKING COURSE
(☎cell phone 55-35042135; www.eatmexico.com; cooking class per person US$140, tours US$85-145) Local food expert Lesley Tellez and chef Ruth Alegria have teamed up to offer Mexican cooking classes for small or large groups. Eat Mexico also does interesting street food, market and *mezcalería* (mezcal bar) tours led by bilingual guides.

Centro de Enseñanza Para Extranjeros LANGUAGE COURSE
(Foreigners' Teaching Center; ☎5622-2470; www.cepe.unam.mx; Universidad 3002, Ciudad Universitaria; six-week course US$430; ⓜCopilco) The national university (p87) offers six-week intensive classes, meeting for three hours from Monday through Friday. Students who already speak Spanish may take content courses on Mexican art and culture.

Quirky Mexico City

Anyone who's spent time in Mexico will understand why French poet André Breton called it 'the surrealist country par excellence.' Something strange lurks beneath the surface of everyday life.

Museo del Juguete Antiguo México MUSEUM
(Antique Toy Museum; Map p57; www.museodeljugueteantiguomexico.blogspot.com, in Spanish; Dr Olvera 15, cnr Eje Central Lázaro Cárdenas; admission M$50; ☉9am-6pm Mon-Fri, 9am-4pm Sat, 10am-4pm Sun; ⓜObrera) Mexican-born Japanese collector Roberto Shimizu has amassed more than a million toys in his lifetime, and this museum showcases about 40,000 pieces, ranging from life-size robots to tiny action figures. Shimizu himself designed many of the funky display cases from recycled objects.

Isla de las Muñecas BOAT TOUR
For a truly surreal experience, head for Xochimilco and hire a gondola to the Island of the Dolls, where hundreds of creepy, decomposed dolls hang from trees. An island resident fished the playthings from the canals to mollify the spirit of a girl who had drowned nearby. The best departure point for the four-hour round trip is the Embarcadero Cuemanco (see p102).

MEXICO CITY FOR CHILDREN

As with elsewhere in Mexico, kids take center stage in the capital. Many theaters, including the Centro Cultural del Bosque (p115), stage children's plays and puppet shows on weekends and during school holidays. Cartoons are a staple at cinemas around town, though keep in mind that children's films are often dubbed in Spanish.

Museums frequently organize hands-on activities for kids. The Museo Nacional de Arte (p68) offers children's art workshops on Saturday and Sunday from 11am to 2pm.

Mexico City's numerous parks and plazas are usually buzzing with kids' voices. Bosque de Chapultepec is the obvious destination, and then there are the Papalote Museo del Niño (p79), La Feria (p78) and the Chapultepec zoo (p78), not to mention several lakes with rowboat rentals. Also consider Condesa's Parque México (p74), where kids can rent bikes, and Sunday is family activities day. Plaza Hidalgo (p89) in Coyoacán is another fun-filled spot with balloons, street mimes and cotton candy.

In Xochimilco (p102) kids find the sensation of riding the gondolas through the canals as magical as any theme park. Also in this part of town is the Museo Dolores Olmedo Patiño (p83), where peacocks and pre-Hispanic dogs occupy the gardens, and children's shows are performed in the patio on Saturday and Sunday at 1pm. The museum also has workshops for children.

Another great option is the Museo del Juguete Antiguo México (p95), a fascinating toy museum with more than 40,000 collectibles on display.

Patrick Miller   DANCING
(Map p80; www.patrickmiller.com.mx, in Spanish; Mérida 17; ☉10:30pm-4am Fri; Ⓜ Insurgentes) People-watching doesn't get any better than at this throbbing disco, founded by Mexico City DJ Patrick Miller. With a clientele ranging from black-clad '80s throwbacks to cross-dressers, the fun begins when dance circles open and regulars pull off moves that would make John Travolta proud.

La Faena   CANTINA
(Map p62; Venustiano Carranza 49B; ☉11am-midnight; Ⓜ San Juan de Letrán) This forgotten relic of a bar doubles as a bullfighting museum, with matadors in sequined outfits glaring intently from dusty cases, and bucolic canvases of grazing bulls.

Mercado de Sonora   MARKET
(cnr Fray Servando & Rosales; Ⓜ Merced) This place has all the ingredients for Mexican witchcraft. Aisles are crammed with stalls hawking potions, amulets, voodoo dolls and other esoterica. This is also the place for a *limpia* (spiritual cleansing), a ritual involving clouds of incense and a herbal brushing. Sadly, some vendors at the market trade illegally in endangered animals. The market is two blocks south of metro Merced, in Colonia Merced Balbuena.

Santa Muerte Altar   SHRINE
(Alfarería, north of Mineros; Ⓜ Tepito) Garbed in a sequined white gown, wearing a wig of dark tresses and clutching a scythe in her bony hand, the Saint Death figure bears an eerie resemblance to Mrs Bates from the film *Psycho*. The Santa Muerte is the object of a fast-growing cult in Mexico, particularly in crime-ridden Tepito, where many of her followers have lost faith in Catholicism. Enter the notoriously dangerous Tepito 'hood at your own risk. It's three blocks north of metro Tepito.

☞ Tours

Turibús Circuito Turístico   BUS TOUR
(Map p62, Map p70 & Map p76; www.turibus.com.mx; adult/child 4-12yrs M$125/65; ☉9am-9pm) The total *recorrido* (route) lasts about three hours, but you can get off and back on the red double-decker bus at any designated stop. Buses pass every 30 minutes, stopping on the west side of the cathedral, among other places. Fares are slightly higher on weekends.

Tranvía   TOUR
(Map p70; ☏5491-1615; adult/child M$50/30, cantina tour M$150; ☉11am-5pm; Ⓜ Bellas Artes) A motorized version of a vintage streetcar runs a 45-minute circuit of the Centro Histórico, with guides relating fascinating bits of lore (in Spanish) along the way. On Thursday night at 8pm there's a special cantina tour (reservation required). Tours depart from Avenida Juárez by Bellas Artes.

Mexico Soul & Essence CULINARY EXPERIENCE
(☎5564-8457; www.mexicosoulandessence.com, www.ruthincondechi.com; tours US$175-225) Customized culinary/cultural excursions by Ruth Alegría, one of the city's foremost food experts. She can arrange dining outings, market tours and/or specialized excursions such as the vanilla route in Veracruz.

Journeys Beyond the Surface TOUR
(☎cell phone 55-17452380; www.travelmexicocity.com.mx; tours M$1700-2500) Personalized walking tours on aspects of the DF experience, with an off-the-beaten-track attitude. Cultural excursions consist of graffiti and street art, cooking tours, and trips to Oaxaca if you're itching to get out of the city.

✯ Festivals & Events

Mexico City celebrates some unique local events in addition to all the major nationwide festivals (see p28), which often take on a special flavor in the capital.

Semana Santa RELIGIOUS
The most evocative events of Holy Week (late March or April) are in the Iztapalapa district, 9km southeast of the Zócalo, where a gruesomely realistic Passion Play is enacted on Good Friday.

Festival de México MUSIC
In May, the Centro Histórico's plazas and theaters become venues for a slew of international artists and performers (www.festival.org.mx, in Spanish).

Foundation of Tenochtitlán DANCE
Held on August 13 to celebrate the foundation of the Mexican capital, this is a major summit for Concheros (Aztec dancers) on Plaza de las Tres Culturas (p92) in Tlatelolco.

Grito de la Independencia FIREWORKS
On September 15, the eve of Independence Day, thousands gather in the Zócalo to hear the Mexican president's version of the Grito de Dolores (Cry of Dolores) – Hidalgo's famous call to rebellion against the Spanish in 1810 – from the central balcony of the Palacio Nacional at 11pm. Afterwards, there's a fireworks display.

Día de Muertos TRADITIONAL
In the lead-up to Day of the Dead (November 2), elaborate *ofrendas* (altars) show up everywhere. Some of the best are at Anahuacalli (p89), the Museo Dolores Olmedo Patiño (p83), the Zócalo, and at San Andres

Mixquic, in the extreme southeast of the Distrito Federal.

Fiesta de Santa Cecilia MUSIC
The patron saint of musicians is honored with special fervor at Plaza Garibaldi (p66) on November 22.

Día de Nuestra Señora de Guadalupe RELIGIOUS
At the Basílica de Guadalupe (p93), the Day of Our Lady of Guadalupe caps 10 days of festivities that honor Mexico's religious patron. The numbers of pilgrims reach millions by December 12, when groups of indigenous dancers perform nonstop on the basilica's broad plaza.

🛏 Sleeping

As a frequent destination for both Mexican and foreign visitors, the DF overflows with lodging options – everything from no-frills guesthouses to top-flight hotels. Some of the most reasonable places are in the Centro Histórico, while more luxurious accommodations, including branches of some major international chains, are concentrated in Polanco and the Zona Rosa. In the trendy Roma and Condesa neighborhoods, the offerings range from hostels to chic boutique hotels. Midrange lodgings, most featuring restaurants and bars, abound in the Alameda and Plaza de la República areas, though they tend to trade character for neutral modern comfort. (Note that places with the word *garage* on the sign generally cater to short-term trysting guests.)

CENTRO HISTÓRICO
For nonbusiness travelers, the historic center is the obvious place to stay. Ongoing renovations of its infrastructure and preservation of its numerous historic edifices have boosted the zone's appeal, and it remains one of the more affordable areas.

TOP CHOICE **Hotel Catedral** HOTEL $$
(Map p62; ☎5518-5232; www.hotelcatedral.com; Donceles 95; s/d from M$590/680; P🐕@🛜; MZócalo) Near 'one of the most busiest touristic areas,' as the website points out, this comfortable lodging has clearly considered its prime location. Request a remodeled room (the firm mattresses and new dark wood furnishings are well worth the additional M$60). For impressive cityscape views, grab a drink on the rooftop terrace.

Chillout Flat
GUESTHOUSE $$

(Map p62; ☑5948-7048; www.chilloutflat.com. mx; Bolívar 8; s/d incl breakfast from M$720/840; ⊛@☎; MAllende) Chill with other guests in a friendly downtown apartment-turned-guesthouse consisting of five colorful rooms with hardwood floors. Street-facing rooms recently got double-pane windows for noise reduction. Reservations a must.

Mexico City Hostel
HOSTEL $

(Map p62; ☑5512-3666; www.mexicocityhostel. com; República de Brasil 8; dm incl breakfast from M$170, s/d M$350/400; ⊛@☎; MZócalo) Steps from the Zócalo, this colonial structure has been artfully restored, with original wood beams and stone walls as a backdrop for modern, energy-efficient facilities. Spacious dorms have three or four sturdy bunk beds on terra-cotta floors. Immaculate bathrooms trimmed with *azulejo* (painted ceramic tiles) amply serve around 100 occupants.

Hotel Isabel
HOTEL $

(Map p62; ☑5518-1213; www.hotel-isabel.com.mx; Isabel La Católica 63; s/d M$270/420, without bathroom M$210/310; ⊛@☎; MIsabel La Católica) Just a few blocks from the Zócalo, the Isabel is a longtime budget-traveler's favorite, offering large, well-scrubbed rooms with old but sturdy furniture, high ceilings and great balconies, plus a hostel-like social scene.

Hostal Regina
HOSTEL $

(Map p62; ☑5709-4192; www.hostalcentrohistorico regina.com; Calle 5 de Febrero 53; dm M$190, r without bathroom M$450; ⊛@☎; MIsabel La Católica) Off the lively Regina corridor, this 18th-century historic building was recently transformed into a happening hostel with new bunks, contemporary bathroom fixtures and a steady dose of rooftop parties.

Hampton Inn & Suites
HOTEL $$$

(Map p62; ☑8000-5000; www.hamptonmexico city.com; Calle 5 de Febrero 24; r incl breakfast from M$1244, ste from M$1747; ⊛❋@☎; MZócalo) This well-preserved historic gem has undergone an impressive makeover and it's only two blocks from all the action in the Zócalo. Well-appointed rooms with contemporary furnishings surround a six-story atrium with a stained-glass ceiling.

Hotel Gillow
HOTEL $$

(Map p62; ☑5510-0791; www.hotelgillow.com; Isabel La Católica 17; s/d M$660/720; P⊛@☎; MAllende) In this historic building with old-fashioned service, the recently revamped rooms are done up with faux wood floors and flat-screen TVs. For views, request an Avenida 5 de Mayo or Isabel La Católica unit.

Gran Hotel Ciudad de México
HOTEL $$$

(Map p62; ☑1083-7700; www.granhoteldelaciudad demexico.com.mx, in Spanish; Av 16 de Septiembre 82; r/ste incl breakfast from M$2282/3254; P⊛❋@☎; MZócalo) The Gran Hotel flaunts the French art nouveau style of the prerevolutionary era. Crowned by a stained-glass canopy crafted by Tiffany in 1908, the atrium is a fin de siècle fantasy of curved balconies, wrought-iron elevators and chirping birds in giant cages. Rooms do not disappoint in comparison.

NH Centro Histórico
HOTEL $$$

(Map p62; ☑5130-1850; www.nh-hotels.com; Palma 42; r/ste from M$1720/2120; P⊛❋@☎; MZócalo) Riding the downtown development wave, Spanish chain NH planted a branch in the center. Lounges and rooms get a Euro-minimalist treatment, and spacious suites occupy the curved corners of the aerodynamically designed 1940s structure.

Hotel Azores
HOTEL $

(Map p62; ☑5521-5220; www.hotelazores.com, in Spanish; República de Brasil 25; s/d M$320/400; P⊛@☎; MZócalo) Near the cheerful Plaza Santo Domingo, rooms off the Azores' bright interior courtyards are neither large nor luxurious, but they're quite a bargain and all are in excellent shape.

Hostel Mundo Joven Catedral
HOSTEL $

(Map p62; ☑5518-1726; www.mundojovenhostels. com/hcatedral.php; República de Guatemala 4; dm from M$200, d M$468; ⊛@☎; MZócalo) Backpacker central, this HI affiliate is abuzz with a global rainbow of young travelers. Dorms are tidy and guests relish the rooftop bar, yet it's not the quietest of hostels.

Hotel Canadá
HOTEL $$

(Map p62; ☑5518-2106; www.hotelcanada.com. mx; Av 5 de Mayo 47; s/d incl breakfast M$450/570; P⊛☎; MAllende) This long-standing hotel has redone its smallish rooms, adding new carpets, peach-toned headboards and sepia photos of old Mexico. Affable staff cater to a primarily business clientele.

ALAMEDA CENTRAL & AROUND
Like the Centro Histórico, this section is undergoing major renovations, though pockets of neglect are reminders of the 1985 earthquake that devastated the zone. By day the

neighborhood bustles with shoppers, but after dark it quietens down considerably.

Boutique Hotel de Cortés   BOUTIQUE HOTEL $$$

(Map p70; ☑5518-2181; www.boutiquehoteldecortes.com; Av Hidalgo 85; r incl breakfast M$2400, ste from M$3500; ⊜✴⬤; ⓂHidalgo) Formerly a hospice for Augustinian pilgrims, this boutique hotel offers tasteful rooms and suites encircling a lovely 17th-century baroque patio. Adding an artistic touch, the modern rooms feature floral-patterned carved headboards and furnishings. The smart rooftop lounge bar overlooks the Alameda.

Hotel Marlowe   HOTEL $$

(Map p70; ☑5521-9540; www.hotelmarlowe.com.mx; Independencia 17; s/d/tr M$570/710/880; ᴘ⊜✴@⬤; ⓂSan Juan de Letrán) The remodeled Marlowe stands across from Chinatown's pagoda gate. Above a bright, airy lobby are spacious rooms with good carpets, colorful bedspreads, soothing art and inset lighting. Fitness freaks will appreciate the gym with a view.

Hotel Mónaco   HOTEL $$

(Map p70; ☑5566-8333; www.hotel-monaco.com.mx; Guerrero 12; r M$550; ᴘ⊜✴@⬤; ⓂHidalgo) Opposite Plaza de San Fernando, this refurbished older hotel is poised between rundown Colonia Guerrero and the Reforma corridor. Old-school bellboys proudly escort you down hallways with piped-in Muzak to your neatly furnished room.

Hotel San Diego   HOTEL $

(Map p70; ☑5510-3523; www.hotelsandiego.com.mx, in Spanish; Luis Moya 98; s/d M$350/450; ᴘ⊜@⬤; ⓂBalderas) This generic option two blocks east of La Ciudadela should appeal to peso-pinchers. Above the lobby's imitation leather sofas are decently sized rooms with furniture of a recent vintage and tiled bathrooms.

PLAZA DE LA REPÚBLICA & AROUND

Further away from the Zócalo, the area around the Monumento a la Revolución is awash with hotels, with a number of dives interspersed amid the business-class establishments. Unaffected by the wave of development sweeping the Centro and Reforma corridor, the semiresidential zone offers glimpses of neighborhood life.

Ramada Reforma   HOTEL $$

(Map p70; ☑5097-0277; www.ramadareforma.com, in Spanish; Puente de Alvarado 22; s/d from M$825/950; ᴘ⊜✴@⬤✉; ⓂHidalgo) Choose from refurbished 'standard' digs in this hotel's older section or pricier 'superior' rooms in the new wing. A heated indoor pool awaits on the top floor. Just 1½ blocks from Reforma.

✎ Casa de los Amigos   HOSTEL $

(Map p70; ☑5705-0521; www.casadelosamigos.org, in Spanish; Mariscal 132; dm M$100, r without bathroom M$140; ⊜@⬤; ⓂRevolución) The Quaker-run Casa is primarily a residence for NGO workers, researchers and others seeking social change, but it welcomes walk-in travelers. Vegetarian breakfast (M$25) is served and there's a two-night minimum stay. Additionally, guests can take (free) weekly Spanish and yoga classes.

Hotel Edison   HOTEL $

(Map p70; ☑5566-0933; Edison 106; s/d M$279/329; ᴘ⊜@⬤; ⓂRevolución) Beyond the bunkerlike exterior, accommodations face a rectangular garden surrounded by pre-Hispanic motifs. Although they come with faded wallpaper and dated fixtures, some rooms are enormous, with large marble washbasins and closets.

Hotel New York   HOTEL $$

(Map p70; ☑5566-9700; Edison 45; s/d incl breakfast M$560/610; ᴘ⊜⬤; ⓂRevolución) A few blocks northeast of Plaza de la República, this is a relatively stylish option in a zone crammed with cut-rate hotels. Rates include wireless internet – that is, if the signal reaches your room.

ZONA ROSA & AROUND

Foreign businesspeople and tourists check in at the glitzy hotels in this international commerce and nightlife area. Less-expensive establishments dot the quieter streets of Colonia Cuauhtémoc, north of Reforma, and Juárez, east of Insurgentes.

Casa González   GUESTHOUSE $$

(Map p76; ☑5514-3302; www.hotelcasagonzalez.com; Río Sena 69; s/d/tr/ste incl breakfast from M$480/660/960/1170; ᴘ⊜@⬤; ⓂInsurgentes) A family-run operation for nearly a century, the Casa is a perennial hit with travelers seeking peace and quiet. Set around several flower-filled patios and semiprivate terraces, it's extraordinarily *tranquilo*. Original portraits and landscapes decorate the rooms, apparently done by a guest in lieu of payment.

Hotel María Cristina
HOTEL $$

(Map p76; ☏5703-1212; www.hotelmariacristina .com.mx; Río Lerma 31; s/d/ste from M$770/ 860/1110; ❉❖✳@❖; ❖Reforma) Dating from the 1930s, this facsimile of an Andalucian estate makes an appealing retreat, particularly the adjacent bar with patio seating. Though lacking the lobby's colonial splendor, rooms are generally bright and comfortable.

Hotel Cityexpress
BUSINESS HOTEL $$

(Map p76; ☏1102-0280; www.cityexpress.com. mx; Havre 21; s/d incl breakfast M$1005/1088; ❉❖✳@❖; ❖Hamburgo) The Cityexpress emphasizes comfort and functionality, but decor outshines the neutral-modern favored by most hotels in this price category. It has captivating views of the nearby towers springing up in this transitional zone.

Palace Hotel
HOTEL $$

(Map p70; ☏5566-2400; www.palace-hotel.com. mx; Ramírez 7; s/d M$430/650; ❉❖@❖; ❖Plaza de la República) Run by gregarious Asturians, the Palace has large, neatly maintained rooms, some with broad balconies giving terrific views down palm-lined Ramírez to the domed monument. Cash-paying guests get substantial discounts.

Hotel del Principado
HOTEL $$

(Map p76; ☏5233-2944; www.hoteldelprincipado. com.mx; Londres 42; s/d incl breakfast M$710/920; ❉❖@❖; ❖Insurgentes) Conveniently poised between the Zona Rosa and Colonia Roma, this friendly little place makes a nice cocoon. The carpet has been replaced with faux wood floors and the keys have been updated to cards.

Hotel Bristol
HOTEL $$

(Map p76; ☏5533-6060; www.hotelbristol.com. mx; Plaza Necaxa 17; s/d M$811/931; ❉❖✳❖; ❖Insurgentes) A good-value option in the pleasant and central Cuauhtémoc neighborhood, the Hotel Bristol caters primarily to business travelers, offering quality carpet, soothing colors and also an above-average restaurant.

Hotel Mayaland
HOTEL $$

(Map p70; ☏5566-6066; www.hotelmayaland.com. mx; Antonio Caso 23; s/d M$520/690; ❉❖@❖; ❖Plaza de la República) This business-oriented hotel on a sterile street has well-maintained facilities with a semi-Maya motif. Typically neutral rooms feature textured pink walls, flowery canvases and inset lighting.

Hotel del Ángel
HOTEL $$

(Map p76; ☏5533-1032; www.hoteldelangel.mx, in Spanish; Río Lerma 154; r M$1050; ❉❖✳❖; ❖Insurgentes) Nearby construction has blocked views of the iconic monument this establishment is named after, but rather than brood, the hotel has jazzed up some of the rooms by adding postmodern furniture and fixtures.

Four Seasons Hotel
BUSINESS HOTEL $$$

(Map p76; ☏5230-1818; www.fourseasons.com/ mexico; Paseo de la Reforma 500; r from US$500; ❉❖✳@❖✳❖; ❖Sevilla) One of the city's most elegant lodgings, the Four Seasons was designed to resemble a French-Mexican late-19th-century structure, with aristocratically furnished rooms facing a beautifully landscaped central courtyard.

6M9 Guest House
GUESTHOUSE $$$

(Map p76; ☏5208-8347; www.6m9guesthouse.com. mx; Marsella 69; s/d incl breakfast from US$85/95; ❖❖✳; ❖Hamburgo) Exclusively serving a gay male clientele, the 6M9 occupies a Porfiriato-era building within walking distance of Pink Zone bars. The fun-filled facilities include a small pool, steam room and complimentary bar. Reservations online only.

Hostal Boutique La Tercia
HOSTEL $

(Map p76; ☏5533-7848; www.hostalboutiquelater cia.com.mx, in Spanish; Génova 75; dm/s/d M$160/ 450/600; ❖❖; ❖Insurgentes) The self-proclaimed 'boutique hostal' label seems a bit much given the generally austere makeup of this place, but it's spotless and in the heart of the bustling Pink Zone, an area not known for its budget accommodations.

Hotel Geneve
HOTEL $$$

(Map p76; ☏5080-0800; www.hotelgeneve.com. mx; Londres 130; r from M$2200; ❉❖✳@❖; ❖Insurgentes) This Zona Rosa institution strives to maintain a belle époque ambience despite the globalized mishmash around it. Rooms get the colonial treatment, with handsome carved-wood headboards and colonial-style dressers and nightstands.

CONDESA

Thanks to the recent appearance of several attractive lodgings, this neighborhood south of Bosque de Chapultepec can make an excellent base, with plenty of after-hours restaurants and cafes.

⌅TOP CHOICE Red Tree House
B&B $$$

(Map p80; ☏5584-3829; www.theredtreehouse. com; Culiacán 6; s/d/ste incl breakfast from US$101/

119/196; ⊖ ⑤; ⓂChilpancingo) Just off the delightful Plaza Citlaltépetl, the area's first B&B has all the comforts of home, if your home happens to be decorated with exquisite taste. Each of the 17 bedrooms and suites is uniquely furnished, and the roomy penthouse has a private patio. Downstairs, guests have the run of a cozy living room with fireplace, and a lovely rear garden, the domain of friendly pooch Abril.

Villa Condesa
BOUTIQUE HOTEL $$$
(Map p80; ⚑5211-4892; www.villacondesa.com.mx; Colima 428; r incl breakfast from US$118; ⊖ ⑤; ⓂChapultepec) You can say *adiós* to hectic Mexico City from the moment you set foot in the Villa's leafy lobby. The 14 rooms in this striking historic building combine classic touches (each has a piece of antique furniture) with the modern trappings of a first-rate hotel. Reservations required; children under 12 not allowed.

Casa Comtesse
B&B $$
(Map p80; ⚑5277-5418; www.casacomtesse.com; Benjamín Franklin 197; r incl breakfast from M$800; Ⓟ⊖@⑤; ⓂEscandón) Run by an amiable French transplant, this 1940s historic building houses eight rooms done up in tasteful contemporary style. Downstairs, guests mingle over breakfast in a parquet-floored dining area. The Casa arranges tours to the Teotihuacán ruins.

Condesa df
BOUTIQUE HOTEL $$$
(Map p80; ⚑5241-2600; www.condesadf.com, in Spanish; Veracruz 102; r incl breakfast from M$3146; ⊖❋@⑤; ⓂChapultepec) Setting Condesa hipness standards since its 2005 opening, this is where Paris Hilton and U2 stayed during their visits. Rooms in the remodeled 1920s building encircle an atrium/bar that draws scenemakers nightly.

Hotel Roosevelt
HOTEL $$
(Map p80; ⚑5208-6813; www.hotelroosevelt.com.mx; Insurgentes Sur 287, cnr Av Yucatán; s/d M$550/770; Ⓟ⊖⑤; ⓀÁlvaro Obregón) On the eastern edge of Condesa and within easy reach of the Cuban club district, this friendly if functional hotel should appeal to nocturnally inclined travelers.

ROMA
A slew of galleries, sidewalk cafes and bars lie within walking distance of most of the following places, and with party-central Colonia Condesa conveniently nearby, you'll find more than enough late-night distractions.

Casa de la Condesa
SUITES $$$
(Map p80; ⚑5574-3186; www.extendedstaymexico.com; Plaza Luis Cabrera 16; ste from M$1209; ⊖❋⑤; ⓀÁlvaro Obregón) Right on the delightful Plaza Luis Cabrera, the Casa makes a tranquil base for visitors on an extended stay, offering 'suites' that are essentially studio apartments with kitchens. See the website for weekly rates.

La Casona
BOUTIQUE HOTEL $$$
(Map p80; ⚑5286-3001; www.hotellacasona.com.mx; Durango 280; r incl breakfast M$2100; ⊖❋⑤; ⓂSevilla) This stately mansion was restored to its early-20th-century splendor to become one of the capital's most distinctive boutique hotels. Each of the 29 rooms is uniquely appointed to bring out its original charm.

Hotel Milán
HOTEL $$
(Map p80; ⚑5584-0222; www.hotelmilan.com.mx, in Spanish; Álvaro Obregón 94; s/d M$465/495; Ⓟ⊖❋@⑤; ⓀÁlvaro Obregón) Sitting on the main corridor of bohemian Roma, the Milán has gone modern with minimalist decor and contemporary art in its new-look lobby. In keeping with the makeover, upgraded rooms feature remodeled bathrooms.

Hotel Stanza
HOTEL $$
(Map p80; ⚑5208-0052; www.stanzahotel.com, in Spanish; Álvaro Obregón 13; r/ste M$820/1300; Ⓟ⊖❋@⑤; ⓀJardín Pushkin) A business travelers' hotel on the east end of Álvaro Obregón, the Stanza makes a cushy, relatively inexpensive launching pad or re-entry chamber. Nearby bars and restaurants are hopping on weekends.

Hostal 333
HOSTEL $
(Map p80; ⚑5207-4842; www.hostal333.com; Colima 333; dm incl breakfast US$12.50; r US$36; ⊖@⑤; ⓀDurango) Roma's latest hipster hostel, the 333 offers standard-issue dorm rooms, or you can opt for private digs with bathroom. Guests revel in fiestas, barbecues and occasional gigs on a pleasant rooftop patio flanked by potted plants.

Hostel Home
HOSTEL $
(Map p80; ⚑5511-1683; www.hostelhome.com.mx; Tabasco 303; dm incl breakfast M$150; ⊖@⑤; ⓀDurango) Housed in a fine Porfiriato-era building and managed by easygoing staff, this 20-bed hostel is on the narrow tree-lined Calle Tabasco, a gateway to the Roma neighborhood.

POLANCO

North of Bosque de Chapultepec, Polanco has excellent business and boutique hotel accommodations.

Casa Castelar
SUITES **$$$**

(Map p84; ☎5281-4990; www.casacastelar.com, in Spanish; Av Castelar 34; ste incl breakfast from US$133; ⊜🖥; MAuditorio) An affordable option by Polanco standards, the large suites here give you plenty of bang for your buck. The Castelar has no common areas, but breakfast is served at your door.

Hábita Hotel
BOUTIQUE HOTEL **$$$**

(Map p84; ☎5282-3100; www.hotelhabita.com; Av Presidente Masaryk 201; s/d M$3328/4420; P⊜❄🖥🏊; MPolanco) Architect Enrique Norten turned a functional apartment building into a smart boutique hotel. Decor in the 36 rooms is boldly minimalist, and the rooftop bar, Área (p113), is a hot nightspot.

W Mexico City Hotel
HOTEL **$$$**

(Map p84; ☎9138-1800; www.whotels.com; Campos Elíseos 252; r from M$4500; P⊜❄@🖥; MAuditorio) One of the four sentinels opposite the Auditorio Nacional, this 25-floor business hotel is determined to break away from the stodginess of its neighbors. Minimalist rooms include silken hammocks hanging in the shower area.

XOCHIMILCO

There's no better way to appreciate the natural wonders of Xochimilco's canals than camping in the middle of it all.

Michmani
CAMPGROUND **$**

(www.xochimilco.df.gob.mx/turismo/michmani_precios.html, in Spanish; Embarcadero Cuemanco, off Anillo Periférico Sur; campsites per person incl tent M$120, cabins M$650) Ecotourism center Michmani arranges stays at **La Llorona Cihuacoatl** (reservations ☎5489-7773) campground, which sits on a peaceful off-grid *chinampa* (garden). The center rents tents, but you'll have to bring a sleeping bag, or you can stay in a tiny rustic cabin with two beds. Also available are barbecue grills and temascals (steam baths; M$200) for groups of 10 or more.

To get here, go to metro General Anaya and exit the station on the east side of Calzada de Tlalpan, then walk 50m north to catch a 'Tláhuac Paradero' pesero. Get off at the Embarcadero Cuemanco entrance and walk about 1km to Michmani, just beyond the *embarcadero*. From there a boat will take you to La Llorona.

COYOACÁN & CIUDAD UNIVERSITARIA

The southern community has two hostels and several appealing guesthouses. Check with the Coyoacán tourist office (p124) about short-term homestays.

Chalet del Carmen
TOP CHOICE
GUESTHOUSE **$$**

(Map p90; ☎5554-9572; www.chaletdelcarmen.com; Guerrero 94; s/d/ste from M$599/989/1269; ⊜🖥; MCoyoacán) Run by a friendly Coyoacán native and his Swiss wife, this ecofriendly house strikes a warm blend of Mexican and European aesthetics. On offer are five rooms and two suites with antique furnishings and brilliant natural lighting. Reservations a must.

La Casita del Patio Verde
B&B **$$$**

(☎cell phone 55-27186793; www.bbmexicocity.com; Callejón de la Escondida 41; r incl breakfast from US$88, ste US$165; ⊜@🖥; MViveros) Tucked away on a cobblestoned street, the tranquil Casita has three rustic-chic guestrooms and, of course, its namesake verdant garden. The *cabaña* (cabin) room, off the garden, comfortably sleeps four. Reservations are required. From metro Viveros, go south on Avenida Universidad, turn left on Avenida Francisco Sosa, go right on Zaragoza, then head left on Dulce Oliva to reach nearby Callejón de la Escondida.

Hostal Cuija Coyoacán
HOSTEL **$**

(Map p90; ☎5659-9310; www.hostalcuijacoyoacan.com; Berlín 268; dm M$200, r from M$650; ⊜@🖥; MCoyoacán) The new kid on the Coyoacán block, this lizard-themed HI hostel comes as clean as they get and is just a short walk from all the action.

Hostal Frida
GUESTHOUSE **$$**

(Map p90; ☎5659-7005; www.hostalfridabyb.com.mx; Mina 54; r M$700; ⊜🖥; MCoyoacán) Don't let the 'hostal' tag fool you: this family-run place has well-appointed accommodations more along the lines of a guesthouse. Each of the five wood-floored doubles occupies its own level in adjacent structures, and most include kitchens.

El Cenote Azul
HOSTEL **$**

(☎5554-8730; www.elcenoteazul.com; Alfonso Pruneda 24; dm M$150; ⊜🖥; MCopilco) This laid-back hostel near the UNAM campus has six neatly kept four- or two-bed rooms sharing three Talavera-tiled bathrooms. The downstairs cafe is a hangout for university students. See the website for directions.

AIRPORT

Hotel Aeropuerto   HOTEL $$
(☎5785-5318; www.hotelaeropuerto.com.mx; Blvd Puerto Aéreo 380; s/d M$590/730; P😊🛜; MTerminal Aérea) Although there are three upscale hotels linked to the terminals, this affordable hotel across the street serves just fine for weary travelers. Not as bleakly functional as the aluminum facade portends, the only nonchain in the zone has helpful reception staff and neutral modern rooms, some overlooking the airport runway through soundproof windows. Turn left outside the domestic terminal; beyond the metro, take a left onto Blvd Puerto Aéreo and cross via the pedestrian bridge.

🍴 Eating

The capital offers eateries for all tastes and budgets, from soulful taco stalls to exclusive restaurants. In recent years, the city has emerged as a major destination for culinary travelers, as Mexican chefs win the sort of praise formerly reserved for their counterparts in New York and Paris. Most of the hottest venues for contemporary cuisine show up in Polanco and Condesa.

Budget eaters will find literally thousands of restaurants and holes in the wall serving *comida corrida* (set lunch) for as little as M$40. Market buildings are good places to look for these, while *tianguis* (indigenous people's street markets) customarily have an eating area offering tacos and quesadillas.

Certain items can be found all over town. In the evening, vendors roam the streets on bicycles selling hot *tamales,* their arrival heralded by nasal-toned recordings through cheap speakers. You'll know the *camote* (sweet potato) man is coming by the shrill steam whistle emitted from his cart, heard for blocks around.

CENTRO HISTÓRICO

The historic center is a great place to enjoy traditional Mexican dishes in elegant surroundings at places like El Cardenal and Café de Tacuba. Many venues open only for breakfast and lunch.

El Cardenal   MEXICAN $$$
(Map p62; www.restauranteelcardenal.com; Palma 23; dishes M$125-178; ⊗8am-6:30pm Mon-Sat, 9am-6:30pm Sun; P😊; MZócalo) Possibly the finest place in town for a traditional meal, El Cardenal occupies three floors of a Parisian-style mansion with a pianist sweetly playing in the background. Breakfast is a must, served with a tray of just-baked sweet rolls and a pitcher of frothy, semisweet chocolate. For lunch, go for the oven-roasted veal breast or *escamoles* (ant larvae, a much-coveted specialty).

Hostería de Santo Domingo   MEXICAN $$
(Map p62; www.hosteriadesantodomingo.com.mx, in Spanish; Belisario Domínguez 72; dishes M$80-140, chile en nogada for 2 people M$195; ⊗9am-10:30pm Mon-Sat, to 9pm Sun; P😊; MAllende) Whipping up classic Mexican fare since 1860, this hugely popular restaurant has a festive atmosphere, enhanced by chamber music. You can experiment with other dishes, but the real draws are the enormous *chiles en nogada* (chilies stuffed with ground meat, fruit and topped with walnut sauce). The Hostería is the city's oldest restaurant and some even say it's haunted.

Café de Tacuba   MEXICAN $$
(Map p62; www.cafedetacuba.com.mx, in Spanish; Tacuba 28; mains M$80-140, 4-course lunches M$200; ⊗8am-11:30pm; 😊; MAllende) Before the band (see p819) there was the restaurant. Way before. A fantasy of colored tiles, brass lamps and oil paintings, this mainstay has served *antojitos* (tortilla-based snacks such as tacos and *gorditas* – corn tortilla-based pockets stuffed with cheese, meat and other fillings) since 1912.

Los Cocuyos   TAQUERÍA $
(Map p62; Bolívar 54; tacos M$10; ⊗11am-6am; MSan Juan de Letrán) *Suadero* (beef) tacos abound in the capital, but this place reigns supreme. The bubbling vat of meats ain't a pretty sight, but the tacos taste oh-so-good. Try the artery-choking *Campechano,* a beef-and-sausage-combo taco.

El Huequito   TAQUERÍA $
(Map p62; www.elhuequito.com.mx, in Spanish; Gante 1; taco al pastor M$11; ⊗9am-11pm Sun-Thu, to 1:30am Fri & Sat; 😊; MZócalo) These old pros have been churning out delectable *tacos al pastor* (marinated, spit-roasted pork) since 1959. Something to wet your whistle? Go for the *misil* (missile), a three-liter beer tower.

Taquería Los Paisas   TAQUERÍA $
(Map p62; Jesús María 131; tacos M$14; ⊗9am-midnight; MPino Suárez) This corner taco stand southeast of the Zócalo offers over-

stuffed steak, sausage and *pastor* (spit-roasted pork) tacos or *Campechano* tacos. Help yourself from the heaping trays of garnishes.

La Casa de las Sirenas
MEXICAN $$$

(Map p62; www.lacasadelassirenas.com.mx, in Spanish; República de Guatemala 32; mains M$200-240; ⊘11am-11pm Mon-Sat, to 6pm Sun; ⊝; ⓂZócalo) Housed in a 17th-century relic, Sirenas has a top-floor terrace that looks toward the Zócalo via the Plaza del Templo Mayor. It's an ideal perch to enjoy regional dishes prepared with contemporary flair, such as chicken bathed in pumpkin-seed *mole* (a type of chili sauce).

La Casa del Pavo
SANDWICHES $

(Map p62; Motolinía 40; tortas M$24; ⊘8am-9pm; ⊝; ⓂAllende) What to order is no great secret at the house that *pavo* (turkey) built.

Al Andalus
MIDDLE EASTERN $$

(Map p62; www.restaurantesalandalus.com.mx, in Spanish; Mesones 171; dishes M$125-155; ⊘8am-6pm; ⊝; ⓂPino Suárez) In a superb colonial mansion in the Merced market district, Al Andalus caters to the capital's substantial Lebanese community with old standbys like shawarma, kebabs and falafel.

Los Girasoles
MEXICAN $$$

(Map p62; www.restaurantelosgirasoles.com; Plaza Tolsá; mains M$160-194; ⊘1pm-midnight Tue-Sat, to 9pm Sun & Mon; Ⓟ⊝; ⓂAllende) This fine restaurant overlooking the grand Plaza Tolsá boasts an encyclopedic range of Mexican fare, from pre-Hispanic ant larvae and grasshoppers to contemporary dishes such as red snapper encrusted with *huanzontle* flowers.

Helus
MIDDLE EASTERN $

(Map p62; www.productoshelus.com.mx, in Spanish; República de El Salvador 157; turnovers M$18, pastries M$12-22; ⊘9:30am-7pm Mon-Fri, to 5pm Sat; ⊝⚑; ⓂPino Suarez) Lebanese pastries, *empanadas* (turnovers) and various vegetarian goodies are prepared by a distant relative of Mexican billionaire Carlos Slim.

Café El Popular
CAFE $

(Map p62; Av 5 de Mayo 52; dishes M$57-77; ⊘24hr; ⊝; ⓂAllende) So popular was this tiny round-the-clock cafe that another more amply proportioned branch was opened next door. Fresh pastries, *café con leche* (coffee with milk) and good combination breakfasts are the main attractions.

Vegetariano Madero
VEGETARIAN $

(Map p62; www.losvegetarianos.com.mx, in Spanish; Av Madero 56; set lunches M$68; ⊘8am-8pm; ⊝⚑; ⓂAllende) Despite the austere entrance, there's a lively restaurant upstairs where a pianist plinks out old favorites. The meatless menu includes a range of tasty variations on Mexican standards, and there are vegan options as well.

Restaurante Chon
MEXICAN $$

(Map p62; mains M$80-165; ⊘1-6:30pm Mon-Sat; ⊝; ⓂPino Suárez) Pre-Hispanic fare is the specialty of this cantina-style restaurant. Sample *maguey* (agave) worms, grasshoppers, wild boar and other delicacies.

Casino Español
SPANISH $$

(Map p62; Isabel La Católica 29; 4-course lunches M$120; ⊘11am-6pm Mon-Fri; ⊝; ⓂAllende) The old Spanish social center, housed in a fabulous Porfiriato-era building, has a popular cantina-style eatery downstairs, where the courses keep coming, and an elegant restaurant upstairs, with classic Spanish fare such as *paella valenciana* (paella Valencia-style).

Mercado San Camilito
MARKET $

(Map p62; Plaza Garibaldi; pozoles M$60; ⊘24hr; ⊝; ⓂGaribaldi) This block-long building contains more than 70 kitchens serving Jalisco-style *pozole,* a broth brimming with hominy kernels and pork, served with garnishes such as radish and oregano. (Specify *maciza* if pig noses and ears fail to excite you.)

ALAMEDA CENTRAL & AROUND

Though places on the immediate perimeter of the Alameda cater to an upscale clientele, head down Luis Moya or along Ayuntamiento, south of the Alameda, for pockets of the neighborhood's rustic heritage in the form of *torta* (sandwich) stands and chicken-soup vendors. Mexico City's modest Chinatown (Barrio Chino) covers a single paper-lantern-strung block of Calle Dolores, one block south of the park, but its mediocre restaurants are best avoided.

Churrería El Moro
DESSERTS $

(Map p70; Eje Central Lázaro Cárdenas 42; hot chocolate with 4 churros M$60; ⊘24hr; ⊝; ⓂSan Juan de Letrán) A fine respite from the Eje Central crowds, El Moro manufactures long, slender deep-fried *churros* (doughnut-like fritters), just made to be dipped in thick hot chocolate.

Mi Fonda SPANISH $

(Map p70; López 101; paellas M$50; ⏱11:30am-5pm Tue-Sun; ✆; MSan Juan de Letrán) Working-class *chilangos* line up for their share of *paella valenciana*, made fresh daily and patiently ladled out by women in white bonnets. Jesús from Cantabria oversees the proceedings.

El Cuadrilátero SANDWICHES $

(Map p70; Luis Moya 73; tortas M$57-76; ⏱7am-8pm Mon-Sat; ✆; MJuárez) Owned by wrestler Super Astro, this *torta* joint features a shrine to *lucha libre* (Mexican wrestling) masks. The mother of all *tortas,* the 1.3kg cholesterol-packed Torta Gladiador, is free if you can gobble it in 15 minutes.

ZONA ROSA & AROUND
While the Zona Rosa is packed with places to eat and drink, with few exceptions the area is dominated by uninspiring 'international' fare and fast-food franchises. Notably outside this stream are the numerous restaurants catering to the neighborhood's growing Korean community.

Tezka INTERNATIONAL $$$

(Map p76; www.tezka.com.mx, in Spanish; Amberes 78; dishes M$180-295, tasting menu M$480; ⏱1-5pm & 8-11pm Mon-Fri, 1-6pm Sat, 1-5pm Sun; P✆; MInsurgentes) Specializing in contemporary Basque cuisine, Tezka ranks among Mexico City's finest restaurants. The regularly changing menu features elaborately prepared dishes such as rack of lamb, or you can dabble in the four-course tasting menu (two appetizers, a main dish and dessert).

Fonda El Refugio MEXICAN $$$

(Map p76; Liverpool 166; dishes M$150-210; ⏱1-11pm; P✆; MInsurgentes) Amid a collection of colorful pots and whimsical ceramic ornaments, the family-run *fonda* (inn) serves Mexican favorites such as *mole poblano* (chicken drenched in a chocolate-based sauce) and *chiles rellenos* (chillies stuffed with ground beef).

King Falafel MIDDLE EASTERN $

(Map p76; Londres 178; falafels M$55, salads M$55-62; ⏱10am-7pm Mon-Sat; ✆✍; MInsurgentes) Run by an English-speaking Syrian Jew, this small eatery has a vegetarian-friendly menu of falafel in pita bread, mixed salads, tabouleh and fresh hummus.

Young Bin Kwan ASIAN $$

(Map p76; Av Florencia 15; bulgogis M$150; ⏱11am-11pm; P✆; MInsurgentes) Enormous portions of *bulgogi* (marinated beef grilled at your ta-

ble) are complemented by a fabulous array of side dishes (sesame leaves, bean sprouts, kimchi etc) at this large Korean dining hall.

Yug Vegetariano VEGETARIAN $$

(Map p76; www.lovegetariano.com; Varsovia 3; buffet lunches M$89, dishes M$50-87; ⏱7am-9pm Mon-Fri, 8:30am-8pm Sat & Sun; ✆✍; MSevilla) The menu is gastro-heaven for vegetarians and vast enough for most carnivorous folk to find something they fancy. Choose from specialties such as squash-flower crepes, or go the buffet route.

CONDESA
La Condesa has become the hub of the eating-out scene, and dozens of informal bistros and cafes – many with sidewalk tables – compete for space along several key streets. The neighborhood's culinary heart is at the convergence of Michoacán, Vicente Suárez and Tamaulipas; other good restaurants and cafes ring Parque México.

Lampuga SEAFOOD $$$

(Map p80; www.lampuga.com.mx, in Spanish; Ometusco 1, cnr Av Nuevo León; mains M$148-196; ⏱2pm-midnight Mon-Sat, to 6pm Sun; ✆; MChilpancingo) Fresh seafood is the focus of this French bistro-style restaurant. Tuna *tostadas* (baked or fried tostilla) make great starters, as does the smoked marlin carpaccio; for a main course, have the catch of the day grilled over coals.

El Califa TAQUERÍA $

(Map p80; www.elcalifa.com.mx, in Spanish; Altata 22, cnr Alfonso Reyes; tacos M$24-47; ⏱12:30pm-6am; P✆; MChilpancingo) This popular *taquería (taco stall)* puts its own spin on the classic snack, grilling slices of beef and tossing them on handmade tortillas. Tables are set with a palette of savory salsas in sturdy clay bowls.

Pablo El Erizo SEAFOOD $$$

(Map p80; www.pabloelarizo.com, in Spanish; Montes de Oca 6; mains M$130-200; ⏱1-11pm Mon-Sat, to 6pm Sun; ✆; MCampeche) Using fresh ingredients from Ensenada, this bistro has a knack for preparing regional dishes such as Baja-style shrimp tacos and *tostadas* topped with pistachio-crusted seared tuna and crispy onions.

La Rambla STEAKHOUSE $$

(Map p80; Ometusco s/n, btwn Av Baja California & Benjamín Hill; mains M$70-129; ⏱1:30-9:30pm Mon-Thu, 1:30-11:30pm Fri & Sat, 2-7:30pm Sun; ✆✍; MEscandón) Owned by a Montevideo native, this intimate Uruguayan steakhouse grills tender cuts such as *milanesa de res* (breaded steak) and it does vegetarian pizzas for nonmeat eaters, all at very reasonable prices.

El Tizoncito
TAQUERÍA **$**

(Map p80; www.eltizoncito.com.mx, in Spanish; Av Tamaulipas 122, cnr Campeche; tacos from M$10.50; ☺noon-3:30am Sun-Thu, to 4:30am Fri & Sat; ☺; Ⓜ Patriotismo) Since this place claims to have invented *taco al pastor* (ie cooked on a spit), half the fun is watching the grillmen deftly put them together. If there are no seats, try the bigger location two blocks east on Campeche.

Rojo Bistrot
FRENCH **$$$**

(Map p80; www.rojobistrot.com, in Spanish; Ámsterdam 71; mains M$150-185; ☺2-11pm Mon-Thu, to midnight Fri & Sat, to 5pm Sun; ☺; 🚇 Sonora) On a leafy corner near Parque México, this eatery is popular as much for its vibrant social scene as for the French-inspired cuisine. Regulars praise the *risotto negro* with calamari in white wine sauce.

Taquería Hola
TAQUERÍA **$**

(Map p80; Ámsterdam 135, cnr Av Michoacán; tacos M$15; ☺9am-9pm Mon-Sat, to 3pm Sun; ☺; 🚇 Campeche) Mid-morning, local snackers crowd this friendly hole in the wall for a stand-up chomp. Choose from a remarkable array of taco fillings, all temptingly displayed in clay dishes.

Orígenes Orgánicos
ORGANIC **$$**

(Map p80; www.origenesorganicos.com, in Spanish; Plaza Popocatépetl 41A; salads M$70, 3-course lunches M$136; ☺8:30am-9:30pm Mon-Fri, to 6:30pm Sat & Sun; ☺🖫; 🚇 Sonora) More than just a place to buy soy milk and certified organic produce, this store/cafe facing one of Condesa's loveliest plazas prepares tasty meals with an emphasis on fresh, seasonal, organic ingredients.

Taj Mahal
INDIAN **$$**

(off Map p80; www.tajmahalenmexico.com, in Spanish; Francisco Márquez 134; mains M$120-170; ☺2-10pm Sun-Thu, to midnight Fri & Sat; ☺🖫; Ⓜ Juancatlán) A hard-working Bangladeshi man who used to roam the Condesa selling clothes out of a suitcase now has his own restaurant specializing in Indian cuisine. Vegetarians will find many options here, including garlic naan, vegetable biryani and flavored yogurt drinks.

Café La Gloria
FRENCH **$$**

(Map p80; Vicente Suárez 41; dishes M$95-150; ☺1pm-midnight Mon-Thu, 1pm-2am Fri, 10am-midnight Sat & Sun; Ⓟ☺; Ⓜ Patriotismo) A hip bistro in the heart of the zone, La Gloria remains a popular meeting place thanks to the generous salads, zesty pastas and the quirky art on display.

El Diez
ARGENTINE **$$**

(Map p80; www.eldiez.com.mx, in Spanish; Benjamín Hill 187; steaks M$136-148, pizzas from M$86; ☺1pm-midnight Sun-Thu, to 1am Fri & Sat; Ⓟ☺; Ⓜ Patriotismo) This unpretentious steak place is popular for its quality Argentine cuts, served on a cutting board with dressed salad. Those with less carnivorous appetites can order pizza by the square meter.

La Capital
MEXICAN **$$$**

(Map p80; Av Nuevo León 137; mains M$155-180; ☺1pm-1am Mon-Wed, to 2am Thu-Sat, to 6pm Sun; Ⓟ☺; Ⓜ Chilpancingo) Riding the latest 'cantina chic' (oxymoron?) wave, the Capital does traditional Mexican fare with a gourmet twist. Try the chili-encrusted tuna or the duck enchiladas.

Nevería Roxy
ICE CREAM **$**

(Map p80; www.neveriaroxy.com.mx, in Spanish; Av Mazatlán 80, cnr Montes de Oca; scoops M$15, banana splits M$55; ☺11am-8pm; ☺; Ⓜ Chapultepec) The old-fashioned Roxy makes its own ice cream and sherbet onsite, including such tropical flavors as *zapote* (sapodilla) and guava. Another branch is at Avenida Tamaulipas 161, at Alfonso Reyes.

ROMA

🄳 TOP CHOICE El Hidalguense
MEXICAN **$**

(Map p80; Campeche 155; order of 3 tacos M$72; ☺7am-6pm Fri-Sun; ☺; 🚇 Campeche) Slow-cooked over aged oak wood in an underground pit, the Hidalgo-style *barbacoa* at this family-run eatery is off-the-charts delectable. Get things started with a rich consommé or *queso asado* (grilled cheese with herbs), then move on to the tacos. Top it off on a warm and fuzzy note by sampling the flavored *pulques*.

Contramar
SEAFOOD **$$$**

(Map p80; ☏5514-9217; www.contramar.com.mx, in Spanish; Durango 200; mains M$160-218; ☺1:30-6:30pm Sun-Thu, 1-8pm Fri & Sat; Ⓟ☺; 🚇 Durango) Fresh seafood is the star attraction at this stylish dining hall with a seaside ambience. The specialty is tuna fillet Contramar-style –

AROUND MEXICO IN A DAY

The capital has long attracted opportunity-seekers from all over the republic. Fortunately, these folks from Mérida, Chiapas, Jalisco and Guerrero strive to keep their traditions alive, first and foremost in the kitchen.

Con Sabor a Tixtla (Map p80; Chiapas 173; tacos M$15-20, mains M$67-79; ⊘1-6pm Mon & Tue, 10am-6pm Wed-Sun; ☺✐; ▣Sonora) The home-cooked goodness of retired school teacher Enedina Bello González draws on two generations of family recipes from Tixtla, Guerrero. Specialties in this colorful Roma eatery include *mole verde* (green mole sauce) tacos and Tixtla-style stuffed chilies.

La Polar (www.lapolar.com.mx; Guillermo Prieto 129, San Rafael; birrias M$103; ⊘7am-2am; ▣☺; ▧San Cosme) Run by a family from Ocotlán, Jalisco, this boisterous beer hall has essentially one item on the menu: *birria,* a spiced goat stew. Spirits are raised further by mariachis and *norteño* combos who work the half-dozen salons here.

Coox Hanal (Map p62; 2nd fl, Isabel La Católica 83; dishes M$48-68; ⊘10:30am-6:30pm; ☺; ▧Isabel La Católica) Started in 1953 by boxer Raúl Salazar from Mérida, this establishment prepares top-notch Yucatecan fare such as *poc chuc* (grilled pork marinated in orange juice) and *cochinita pibil* (pit-cooked pork). And then there's the obligatory four-alarm *habanero* salsa.

Los Tolucos (Hernández y Dávalos 40, cnr Bolívar; pozoles M$56; ⊘10am-9pm; ☺; ▧Lázaro Cárdenas) Voted the best *pozole* (pork and hominy broth) in a Mexico City radio station contest, the Guerrero-style green *pozole* here has been drawing people from far and wide for more than four decades. It's three blocks east of metro Lázaro Cárdenas in Colonia Algarín.

Tamales Chiapanecos María Geraldine (Map p90; Plaza Hidalgo; tamales M$30; ⊘10am-10pm Sat & Sun; ▧Viveros) At the passageway next to the San Juan Bautista church, look for these incredible *tamales* by Chiapas native doña María Geraldine. Wrapped in banana leaves, they're stuffed with ingredients like olives, prunes and almonds and laced with sublime salsas.

---

split, swabbed with red chili and parsley sauces, and grilled to perfection. Also a standout is the tuna *tostada,* topped with crispy onions.

Ciénega   COLOMBIAN $$
(Map p80; Coahuila 200; dishes M$100-130; ⊘10am-7pm; ☺; ▣Campeche) The folksy background music of accordion-driven *vallenatos* (folk music) sets the tone at this popular Colombian comfort-food restaurant. Colombian expats go straight for the *sancocho* and *ajiaco* dishes, hearty stews just like mom used to make.

Il Postino   ITALIAN $$
(Map p80; Plaza Villa de Madrid 6; dishes M$120-160; ⊘1:30pm-midnight Mon-Sat, to 6pm Sun; ▣☺; ▣Durango) Run by a pair of chefs from Rome and Milan, this Italian restaurant features terrace dining along Plaza Villa de Madrid. You might start off with an octopus carpaccio, followed by sea bass wrapped in calzone.

Non Solo Panino   SANDWICHES $
(Map p80; http://nonsolo.mx; Plaza Luis Cabrera 10; sandwiches M$55-80; ⊘1pm-12:30am Mon-Wed, to 1am Thu-Sat; ☺; ▣Álvaro Obregón) The dancing fountains make a lovely backdrop for Italian sandwiches with fillings such as mozzarella, pesto and smoked salmon stuffed into fresh-baked baguettes.

POLANCO & BOSQUE DE CHAPULTEPEC

Polanco is home to the signature restaurants of several of Mexico City's internationally hot chefs. Other places listed here present excellent regional cuisine from the Mexican coast.

TOP
CHOICE **Pujol**   MEXICAN $$$
(Map p84; ✆5545-4111; Petrarca 254; dishes M$298-395; menú degustación from M$965; ⊘1:30-4pm & 7-11pm Mon-Sat; ▣☺; ▧Polanco) Arguably Mexico's best haute cuisine restaurant, Pujol offers a contemporary take on classic Mexican dishes in a smartly

minimalist setting. Famed chef Enrique Olvera regularly reinvents the menu, which includes the *menú degustación*, a multiple-course tasting extravaganza. Make reservations well ahead of time.

Izote
MEXICAN $$$
(Map p84; ☎5280-1671; www.izote.com.mx, in Spanish; Av Presidente Masaryk 513; dishes M$275-344; ◷1-11pm Mon-Sat, to 6pm Sun; Ⓟ🖘; Ⓜ Polanco) Patricia Quintana is the celebrated owner of this fashionable upbeat restaurant with an innovative menu. Simple yet superbly presented dishes include *tamales* filled with *huitlacoche* (corn fungus) and duck enchiladas in *mole*.

Dulce Patria
MEXICAN $$$
(Map p84; ☎3300-3999; www.dulcepatriamexico.com, in Spanish; Anatole France 100; mains $287-359; ◷1:30-11pm Mon-Sat, to 5pm Sun; 🖘; Ⓜ Polanco) After a brief sabbatical, cookbook author Martha Ortiz has returned to the Mexico City culinary scene with this new gourmet restaurant. Reinvented traditional Mexican dishes such as *mole* enchiladas stuffed with plantain are deftly plated and wonderfully delicious.

El Bajío
MEXICAN $$
(Map p84; http://carnitaselbajio.com.mx, in Spanish; Dumas 7; dishes M$80-122; 🖘; Ⓜ Auditorio) Owner Carmen 'Titita' Ramírez has built a reputation for producing down-home Veracruz-style food and regional dishes from all over Mexico. Meaty meals such as *barbacoa* and *carnitas* (deep-fried pork) are El Bajío's signature fare.

Los Arcos
SEAFOOD $$$
(Map p84; www.restaurantelosarcos.com.mx; Tasso 330; mains M$143-169; ◷11am-8pm Sun-Wed, to 11pm Thu-Sat; 🖘; Ⓜ Polanco) Specializing in Pacific coast fare, this Mexican chain restaurant is definitely worth its salt. Try the *pescado a las brasas* (charbroiled whole fish sold by the kilo), and order a side dish of refried beans for good measure.

SAN ÁNGEL

Taberna del León
MEXICAN $$$
(Map p88; Plaza Loreto 173; dishes M$258-330; ◷2-11pm Mon-Thu, 2pm-midnight Sat, noon-6pm Sun; Ⓟ🖘; Ⓟ Doctor Gálvez) Chef Monica Patiño is one of the new breed of female stars stirring up traditional cuisine in innovative ways. Seafood is the specialty here, with the likes of Baja California stone crab and corn blini with Norwegian salmon.

Montejo
YUCATECAN $$
(Map p88; Av de la Paz 16; mains M$95-170; ◷1pm-midnight; 🖘; Ⓟ La Bombilla) Along a cobbled street lined with restaurants, this inconspicuous Yucatecan establishment whips up favorites like *sopa de lima* (lemon soup), *cochinita pibil* (marinated pork) and *papadzules* (tacos with hard-boiled eggs in pumpkin-seed sauce).

San Ángel Inn
MEXICAN $$$
(Map p88; www.sanangelinn.com; Diego Rivera 50; mains M$160-270; ◷1pm-1am Mon-Sat, to 10pm Sun; Ⓟ🖘) Classic Mexican meals are served in the various elegant dining rooms of this historic estate next to the Museo Casa Estudio Diego Rivera y Frida Kahlo (p83). Even if you don't splurge for dinner, have one of the renowned margaritas in the garden.

Saks
MEXICAN $$
(Map p88; www.saks.com.mx; Plaza San Jacinto 9; dishes M$127-178; ◷7:30am-6pm Sun & Mon, to midnight Tue-Fri, to 11pm Sat; Ⓟ🖘🖉; Ⓟ La Bombilla) Hang out on Saks' sunbathed terrace, which has live music, and choose from meatless specialties such as *poblano* (from Puebla) chilies stuffed with trufflelike corn fungus and Camembert soufflé.

Cluny
FRENCH $$
(Map p88; www.cluny.com.mx, in Spanish; Av de la Paz 57; dishes M$127-195; ◷12:30pm-midnight Mon-Sat, to 11pm Sun; Ⓟ🖘; Ⓟ La Bombilla) For unpretentious French cuisine, this bistro located in a shopping center hits the spot. Quiche, salads, crepes, decadently delicious desserts and generous portions are the order of the day.

Barbacoa de Santiago
MEXICAN $
(Map p88; Plaza San Jacinto 23; tacos M$18-22; ◷9am-7pm Sun-Fri, 8:30am-7:30pm Sat; Ⓟ La Bombilla) A quick and affordable *taquería* off the plaza, this place is famous for its *barbacoa* and *carnitas* tacos served on freshly made tortillas.

Fonda San Ángel
MEXICAN $$
(Map p88; www.fondasanangel.com.mx, in Spanish; Plaza San Jacinto 3; dishes M$115-155, brunches M$160; ◷8am-midnight Mon-Thu, to 1am Fri & Sat, 9am-7pm Sun; Ⓟ🖘; Ⓟ La Bombilla) On weekends, this attractive restaurant by the plaza does an abundant brunch buffet with all kinds of egg dishes, pastries and freshly squeezed juices, plus great quesadillas.

COYOACÁN

TOP CHOICE **Corazón de Maguey**   MEXICAN $$
(Map p90; www.losdanzantes.com/category/cora
zon, in Spanish; Jardín Centenario 9A; mains M$89-
149; ⊗1pm-1am; ⊜; ⓂViveros) Adorned with
old glass jugs used for transporting mez-
cal, this attractive restaurant does Oaxacan
fare like gut-busting *tlayudas* (large tortil-
las folded over ingredients such as squash
blossom) and elaborate dishes such as beef
tongue in red *mole*.

Supertacos Chupacabras   TAQUERÍA $
(Map p90; cnr Av Río Churubusco & Av México;
tacos M$10; ⊗24hr; ⓂCoyoacán) Named after
the mythical 'goat sucker' (something like
Bigfoot), this famous street stall slings beef
and sausage tacos (with 'a secret ingredi-
ent of 127 spices'). Avail yourself of the fried
onions, *nopales* (cactus paddles) and other
tasty toppings.

Los Danzantes   MEXICAN $$$
(Map p90; www.losdanzantes.com, in Spanish;
Jardín Centenario 12; dishes M$138-195; ⊗1:30-
midnight Mon-Fri, 9am-2am Sat & Sun; ⊜;
ⓂViveros) Los Danzantes puts a contemporary spin on Mexican cuisine with dishes
like *huitlacoche* raviolis in *poblana* sauce
and organic chicken in black *mole*. You'll
also find mezcal from its own distillery.

Mercado de Antojitos   MARKET $
(Map p90; Higuera, cnr Plaza Hidalgo & Caballo
Calco; pozoles M$50; ⊜; ⓂViveros) Near Coy-
oacán's main plaza, this busy spot has all
kinds of snacks, including deep-fried quesadillas, *pozole* and *esquites* (boiled corn ker-
nels served with a dollop of mayo). Look for
the 'Pozole Estilo Michoacán.'

Tostadas Coyoacán   MEXICAN $
(Map p90; Allende; tostadas M$20-30; ⊗11am-
6pm; ⊜; ⓂViveros) At this place inside Coyoacán's main market, between Malintzin
and Xicoténcatl, the *tostadas* are piled high
with things such as ceviche, marinated octopus and shredded chicken.

El Jardín del Pulpo   SEAFOOD $$$
(Map p90; www.eljardindelpulpo.com; cnr Allende
& Malintzin; dishes M$150-170; ⊗11am-6pm; ⊜;
ⓂViveros) Visitors descend on the communal
tables at this market-corner place to devour
shrimp tacos, fried whole fish, oyster cock-
tails and the namesake *pulpo en su tinta*
(octopus cooked in its own ink).

Churrería de Coyoacán   DESSERTS $
(Map p90; Allende 38; bag of 4 churros M$15;
ⓂViveros) Here are Coyoacán's best deep-
fried snacks. Get in line for a bag – cream-
filled or straight up – then stroll over to Café
El Jarocho (p113) for coffee.

El Caracol de Oro   INTERNATIONAL $
(Map p90; Higuera B22; dishes M$60-85; ⊗10am-
midnight Mon-Sat, to 10pm Sun; ⊜; ⓂViveros) Coy-
oacán's alternative set occupies the jazzily
painted tables here, munching on nouveau
natural fare such as chicken topped with
apple curry and goat cheese, and cheese-
stuffed chilies bathed in mango sauce.

Entrevero   INTERNATIONAL $$$
(Map p90; Jardín Centenario 14C; pizzas M$130-
160, dishes M$160-220; ⊗1-11:30pm Sun-Thu, to
12:30am Fri & Sat; ⊜; ⓂViveros) Another nice
plaza-side spot that is known for its grilled
meats, served Uruguayan-style. Nonmeat
options include tuna steaks, a grilled vegetable platter and thin-crust pizzas.

El Mesón de los Leones   MEXICAN $
(Map p90; Allende 161; dishes M$55-85; ⊗11am-
6pm Sun-Fri; ⊜; ⓂViveros) This longtime
family-run restaurant satisfies diners with
its unwaveringly authentic menu and genial
atmosphere. Dig into specialties like *carne
asada estilo de León* – roasted meat with
mole sauce accompanied by guacamole and
beans.

El Kiosko de Coyoacán   ICE CREAM $
(Map p90; Plaza Hidalgo 6; per scoop M$20; ⊗8am-
10pm Mon-Thu, to 11pm Fri-Sun; ⊜; ⓂViveros) This
obligatory weekend stop has homemade ice
cream and ice lollies in flavors ranging from
mango with chili to passion fruit.

OTHER NEIGHBORHOODS

Fonda Margarita   MEXICAN $
(Adolfo Prieto 1364; mains half-portions M$27-37,
full portions M$41-48; ⊗5:30am-11:30am Mon-Sat;
⊜; 🚇Parque Hundido) Possibly the capital's
premier hangover-recovery spot, this humble eatery under a tin roof whips up batches
of comfort food such as pork in *salsa verde*
and *frijoles con huevo* (beans with egg). The
fonda is beside Plaza Tlacoquemécatl, six
blocks east of Avenida Insurgentes.

Azul y Oro   MEXICAN $$
(Centro Cultural Universitario; mains M$95-148;
⊗10am-6pm Mon & Tue, 10am-8pm Wed-Fri,
10am-8pm Sat, 9am-7pm Sun; ⊜; 🚇Centro Cultur-
al Universitario) Chef Ricardo Muñoz searches
high and low within Mexico for traditional

recipes that he reinvents to perfection. Fruits of his research include duck-filled pastries topped with *mole negro* and *sopa de tortilla* (tortilla soup). See p87 for directions to Centro Cultural Universitario.

La Voragine ITALIAN **$$**
(Madero 117, Colonia Tlalpan; mains M$65-120; ⏲1pm-2am Tue-Sat, to midnight Sun; 🚭🍷; Fuentes Brotantes) Run by a jovial couple from New York and DF, this muraled pizzeria/bar prepares savory pizzas, manicotti and flambéed mushrooms in white-wine sauce. It's a half-block north of Tlalpan's main square.

Drinking

Cafes, bars and cantinas are all key social venues on the capital's landscape. The traditional watering holes are, of course, cantinas – no-nonsense places with simple tables, long polished bars and serious waiters in formal white jackets. A humbler kind of drinking establishment rooted in ancient Mexican tradition, *pulquerías* serve *pulque* (a pre-Hispanic alcoholic beverage). These places are lately experiencing a resurgence, with young *chilangos* rediscovering the joys of sharing a pitcher of the milky quaff. Another drink that is being 'taken back' by Mexican youth is mezcal, the rustic mother of tequila. Mexico City has banned smoking in bars, though many establishments provide open-air smoking areas.

CENTRO HISTÓRICO

Hostería La Bota BAR
(Map p62; http://hosterialabota.blogspot.com, in Spanish; San Jerónimo 40; ⏲1pm-midnight Sun-Tue, to 2am Wed-Sat; MIsabel La Católica) *Cerveza* (beer), mezcal and tapas are served amid a profusion of warped bullfighting bric-a-brac and mismatched furniture. A portion of your bar tab sponsors local art projects.

Las Duelistas PULQUERÍA
(Map p70; Aranda 28; ⏲10am-9pm Mon-Sat; MSalto del Agua) Now graffitied with pre-Hispanic psychedelia, this classic *pulquería* has been rediscovered by young artists and musicians. Despite the new look, the *pulque* is still dispensed straight from the barrel in a variety of flavors.

La Ópera Bar BAR
(Map p62; www.barlaopera.com, in Spanish; Av 5 de Mayo 10; ⏲1pm-midnight Mon-Sat, to 6pm Sun; MAllende) With booths of dark walnut and an ornate tin ceiling (said to have been punctured by Pancho Villa's bullet), this late-19th-century watering hole remains a bastion of tradition.

Salón Corona BAR
(Map p62; www.saloncorona.com.mx, in Spanish; Bolívar 24; ⏲10am-midnight Sun-Thu, to 2am Fri & Sat; MAllende) Amiable staff serve up *tarros* (mugs) of light or dark *cerveza de barril* (draft beer) in this boisterous beer hall, where you can also get a taste of soccer-mad Mexico.

La Risa PULQUERÍA
(Map p62; Mesones 71; ⏲11am-8:30pm Mon-Sat; MIsabel La Católica) University students squeeze into this intimate watering hole that has been pouring *pulque* since 1900. At M$15 a pop you can well afford to treat a struggling college kid to a mug.

Bar Mancera BAR
(Map p62; Venustiano Carranza 49; ⏲1-9pm Mon-Wed, to 3am Thu-Sat; MSan Juan de Letrán) This atmospheric gentlemen's salon seems preserved in amber, with ornate carved paneling and well-used domino tables. Lately it's been adopted by young clubbers, who set up turntables Thursday to Saturday from around 9pm.

Café Jakemir CAFE
(Map p62; Isabel La Católica 88; ⏲8am-9pm Mon-Sat; MIsabel La Católica) Run by a family of Lebanese coffee traders from Orizaba, this old distribution outlet, now transformed into a popular cafe, has excellent cappuccinos.

ZONA ROSA & AROUND

The Pink Zone, the capital's international party center, boasts the highest concentration of bars and clubs in town, and prices at the numerous venues along Londres and Florencia reflect its tourist orientation. Amberes has become the hub of Zona Rosa's gay and lesbian bar scene.

Café La Habana CAFE
(Map p70; http://cafelahabana.blogspot.com, in Spanish; Av Morelos 62; ⏲7am-1am Mon-Sat, 8am-10:30pm Sun; MJuárez) This grand coffeehouse is a traditional haunt for writers and journalists, who linger for hours over a *café americano*. Legend has it that Fidel and Che plotted strategy here prior to the Cuban revolution.

El Bandazo BAR
(Map p76; Londres 148; ⏲8pm-3am Fri & Sat; MInsurgentes) At this slice of northern Mexico

in the DF, you can knock back beers with urban cowboy types while listening to rambunctious brass-band music from Sinaloa and Durango. Bands take the stage at midnight and the dancing that ensues is a show in and of itself.

Bar Milán
BAR

(Map p76; Milán 18; ⊗9pm-3am Thu-Sat; ⊒Reforma) On a quiet backstreet, this cavelike hangout overflows most weekends with a mixed-nationality crowd. Purchase *milagros* (drink tickets), then make your way over to the cactus-trimmed bar.

Cafetería Gabi's
CAFE

(Map p76; Nápoles 55, cnr Liverpool; ⊗7:30am-10pm; ⊒Hamburgo) Cluttered with caffeine-related paraphernalia, this family-run coffeehouse buzzes with conversation as occupants of neighboring offices pour in for a rich *café con leche* and a crispy *banderilla* (sticklike glazed pastry).

CONDESA
Condesa's bar scene continues to thrive, and new places are popping up (and shutting down) all the time. The following are relatively well established and filled beyond capacity Thursday through Saturday evenings. The confluence of Avenidas Tamaulipas and Nuevo León has emerged as a major bar zone, earning it a reputation as a haven for *fresas* (literally 'strawberries,' a derogatory term for upper-class youth).

Pata Negra
BAR

(Map p80; www.patanegra.com.mx, in Spanish; Av Tamaulipas 30; ⊗1:30pm-2am; ⊒Campeche) Nominally a tapas bar, this oblong salon draws a friendly mix of 20-something *chilangos* and expats. There's live music on Saturday, and if you're lucky you'll get to hear a Veracruz-style *son jarocho* band.

Black Horse
PUB

(Map p80; www.caballonegro.com; Mexicali 85; ⊗6pm-2am Tue-Sat; ⓜPatriotismo) Besides the screening of soccer matches and pouring draft beer, this British pub boasts an international social scene and has excellent funk, jazz and indie-rock bands playing the back room.

El Centenario
CANTINA

(Map p80; Vicente Suárez 42; ⊗noon-1am Mon-Sat; ⓜPatriotismo) Laden with bullfighting memorabilia, this cantina is an enclave of tradition amid the larely modish restaurant zone.

T-Gallery
BAR

(Map p80; Saltillo 39; ⊗5pm-1am Mon-Wed, to 2am Thu-Sat; ⓜPatriotismo) A low-key crowd kicks back with cocktails in the various salons of this lovely old Condesa home, each appointed with a splendid array of kitschy sofas, coffee tables and mirrors. Jazz, blues and Cuban combos jam downstairs.

Salón Malafama
BAR

(Map p80; http://salonmalafama.com.mx; Av Michoacán 78; table per hr M$80; ⊗5pm-midnight Sun & Mon, 10am-1am Tue-Thu, 1pm-2:30am Fri & Sat; ⊛; ⊒Campeche) This sleek billiard hall doubles as a bar and it's also known as a gallery of photo art. The well-maintained tables are frequented by both pool sharks and novices.

Condesa df
BAR

(Map p80; www.condesadf.com, in Spanish; Veracruz 102; ⊗1pm-2am Mon-Sat, to midnight Sun; ⓜChapultepec) The bar of the fashionable Condesa df has become an essential stop on the Condesa circuit. Up on the roof, guests lounge on big-wheel wicker sofas and enjoy views of verdant Parque España across the way.

Pastelería Maque
CAFE

(Map p80; Ozulama 4; ⊒Campeche) Condesa sophisticates gather in the mornings and evenings at this Parisian-style cafe-bakery near Parque México. Waiters bring around trays of freshly baked croissants and *conchas* (round pastries sprinkled with sugar).

Rexo
COCKTAIL BAR

(Map p80; Saltillo 1; ⊗1:30pm-2am; ⓜCampeche) A minimalist, triple-deck supper club, the perennially popular Rexo really packs them in toward the weekend. The revelry converges on the bar at the bottom, which serves *mezcaltinis* and other unusual cocktails.

Hookah Lounge
BAR

(Map p80; Campeche 284; ⊗4pm-2am Mon-Thu, 3pm-2am Fri & Sat; ⓜChilpancingo) The fun revolves around the water pipes (from M$130). A bewildering array of tobacco flavors is available. Wednesday to Saturday nights, DJs produce an eclectic mix of electronica and Arabic rhythms.

Café Bola de Oro
CAFE

(Map p80; www.boladeoro.com.mx, in Spanish; Av Nuevo León 192B; ⊗7am-10pm Mon-Fri, 9am-7pm Sat; ⓜChilpancingo) This outlying branch of the Xalapa coffee purveyor is a good place to score a bag of Coatepec beans or simply enjoy a cup of Veracruz' fine, full-bodied blends.

MEZCAL RENAISSANCE

Mezcal, known erroneously as 'that drink with the worm in it,' is finally getting the respect it deserves. (The worm was a marketing gimmick for gullible North American consumers.) Many think of it as a rustic relative to the more refined tequila, when, in fact, tequila is just one form of mezcal derived from a particular plant that grows in the state of Jalisco, the blue agave. But mezcals are produced from many varieties of agave (or maguey) throughout Mexico, including the states of Durango, Zacatecas, Michoacán, Guerrero and, most famously, Oaxaca. Many small-scale mezcal makers still produce the drink in limited, handcrafted batches.

Straight up, mezcal is typically served with slices of orange, and orangey salt blended with chili and – old myths die hard – a powder made from maguey worms. And like a fine single-malt scotch, it's meant to be savored slowly rather than knocked back.

A number of venues around Mexico City now serve mezcal to the new breed of discerning aficionados.

La Clandestina (Map p80; Álvaro Obregón 298, Colonia Roma; ⊘6pm-2am Tue-Sat; ⊜; ◪Álvaro Obregón) Fashioned after a rural mom-and-pop shop, the tiny Clandestina has a detailed menu describing the elaboration process of the mezcals dispensed from jugs on high shelves. In true clandestine fashion, there's no sign outside, so look for the 'Casa Rey' frameshop sign left behind by the previous tenants.

Fly Mezcalina (Map p80; Orizaba 145, Colonia Roma; ⊘2pm-midnight Mon-Wed, 2pm-2am Thu & Fri, 6pm-2am Sat; ◪Álvaro Obregón) An elegantly furnished space in a Porfiriato-era residence, the Fly organizes tastings on Tuesdays at 9pm. Mezcal fans can appreciate the subtle gradations in flavor based on where the beverage is distilled.

Bósforo (Map p70; http://es-la.facebook.com/bosfor0; Luis Moya 31, cnr Independencia, Colonia Centro; ⊘4pm-2am Tue-Sat; Ⓜ Juárez) Blink your eyes and you just might walk past the friendliest neighborhood *mezcalería* in town. Behind the Bósforo's nondescript curtain await top-notch mezcals, obscure world-music tunes and surprisingly good bar grub.

Al Andar (Map p62; www.myspace.com/al_andar; Regina 27, Colonia Centro; ⊘11am-1:30am; Ⓜ Isabel La Católica) Most of the late-night action at this tiny downtown bar spills out onto a convivial pedestrian thoroughfare. Choose from 25 varieties of top-notch mezcal while munching on *chapulines* (grasshoppers) and orange slices.

La Botica (Map p80; www.labotica.com.mx, in Spanish; Alfonso Reyes 120, Colonia Condesa; ⊘5pm-midnight Mon-Wed, to 2am Thu-Sat; Ⓜ Patriotismo) Like an old apothecary, La Botica dispenses its elixirs from squat bottles lined up on the shelf. A good mezcal to start off with is *cuishi,* distilled from a wild maguey in Oaxaca. La Botica has other branches with similar hours at Campeche 396 in Condesa and Orizaba 161 in Colonia Roma.

ROMA

TOP CHOICE **Los Insurgentes** PULQUERÍA
(Map p80; www.lapulqueria.org, in Spanish; Av Insurgentes Sur 226; ⊘1pm-12:30am Mon-Wed, to 2:30am Thu-Sat; ◪Durango) Standing at the center of a booming *pulque* revival, this three-story Porfiriato-era house may not please the purists, but unlike in traditional *pulquerías,* here you get live music, DJ sets and other alcoholic drinks not called *pulque.*

Cantina Covadonga CANTINA
(Map p80; Puebla 121; ⊘1pm-1:30am Mon-Wed, to 3am Thu & Fri; Ⓜ Insurgentes) Echoing with the sounds of clacking dominoes, the old Asturian social hall is a traditionally male enclave, though hipsters of both sexes have increasingly moved in on this hallowed ground.

La Bodeguita del Medio BAR
(Map p80; www.labodeguitadelmedio.com.mx, in Spanish; Cozumel 37; ⊘1:30pm-2am Thu-Sat, to 1am Sun-Wed; Ⓜ Sevilla) The walls are scribbled with verses and messages at this animated branch of the famous Havana joint. Have a mojito (a Cuban concoction of rum and mint leaves), and enjoy the excellent *son cubano* combos that perform here.

Travazares Taberna
TAVERNA

(Map p80; Orizaba 127; ⊙7:30am-1:30am; ▣Álvaro Obregón) The downstairs adjunct of a cultural center, this popular Roma hangout strikes a suitably bohemian tone. Choose the candlelit salon of your liking to chat it up over wine or beer.

Los Bisquets Obregón
CAFE

(Map p80; www.lbbo.com.mx, in Spanish; Álvaro Obregón 60; ⊙7am-midnight; ▣Álvaro Obregón) *Chilangos* flock here for the *pan chino* (Chinese pastries) and *café con leche*, dispensed from two pitchers, Veracruz-style.

Café Villa de Madrid
CAFE

(Map p80; Plaza Villa de Madrid 13; ⊙7am-9pm Mon-Fri, 1-5pm Sat; ▣Durango) With just a few sidewalk tables at the top of Plaza Villa de Madrid, this longtime storefront operation roasts beans from the family *finca* (farm) in Chiapas. They also roll their own cigars.

Maison de Thé Caravanserai
TEAHOUSE

(Map p80; www.caravanserai.com.mx, in Spanish; Orizaba 101; ⊙10am-10pm Mon-Fri, noon-10pm Sat & Sun; ▣Álvaro Obregón) This French-style tearoom has more than 170 blends categorized by their intended use or effects. Visitors relax on comfortable sofas to enjoy their chosen brews, which are ceremoniously served on silver trays.

Tiki Bar
THEME BAR

(Map p80; www.tiki.com.mx, in Spanish; Querétaro 227; ⊙7:30pm-midnight Wed, to 2am Thu-Sat; ▣Sonora) Amid the salsa dance clubs, this South Pacific–themed bar spreads on the kitsch with bamboo-fringed walls and teak floors. The wacky cocktails such as *chocotikis*, *mojotikis* and various other rum creations are the real draw.

POLANCO

Though not as cutting-edge as Condesa, this well-heeled neighborhood gets quite lively after dark.

Área
COCKTAIL BAR

(Map p84; www.hotelhabita.com; Av Presidente Masaryk 201; ⊙7pm-2am Wed-Sat; ▣Polanco) Atop of the Hábita Hotel, this open-air roof lounge does a brisk trade in exotic martinis, with sweeping city views as a backdrop and videos projected on the wall of a nearby building.

Big Red
BAR

(Map p84; Av Presidente Masaryk 101; ⊙noon-10pm Mon, noon-midnight Tue, 11am-2am Wed-Sat; ▣Po-

lanco) A volume dealer, with drinks priced by the ounce (M$20 for Bacardi or Centenario tequila), plus whatever mixer you choose. Thus the place attracts a broader cross section of the populace than the usual Polanco *antro* (bar).

XOCHIMILCO

Pulquería El Templo de Diana
PULQUERÍA

(Madero 17, cnr Calle 5 de Mayo; ⊙10am-9pm; ▣Xochimilco) This classic *pulquería*, a block east of the main market, has a cheerful sawdust-on-the-floor vibe, with a mixed-age crowd enjoying giant mugs of the *maguey*-based beverage behind the swinging doors. Even a few females may pop in. Delivered fresh daily from Hidalgo state, *pulque* is expertly blended with flavorings like coffee, prickly pear and pine nut.

Pulquería La Botijona
PULQUERÍA

(Av Morelos 109; ⊙9am-9:30pm; ▣Xochimilco) Possibly the cleanest *pulque* dispenser in town, this institutional green hall near the train station is a friendly family-run establishment, with big plastic pails of the traditional quaff lining the shelves.

SAN ÁNGEL

La Camelia
BAR

(Map p88; Madero 3; ⊙karaoke 9pm-3am Fri & Sat; ▣La Bombilla) This restaurant-cantina has been drawing Mexican celebrities since 1931, as evidenced by the stars' photos on the walls. On Friday and Saturday karaoke nights, it's your time to shine with a rendition of, say, Michael Jackson or Madonna. Liquid courage comes in the form of tequila or *cerveza mexicana*.

COYOACÁN

TOP CHOICE **La Bipo**
BAR

(Map p90; www.facebook.com/labipo.coyoacan; Malintzin 155; ⊙1pm-12:30am Mon-Wed, to 2am Thu-Sat, to 11pm Sun; ▣Viveros) Part-owned by Mexican heartthrob Diego Luna (of *Y tu mamá también* movie fame), this popular cantina plays up the kitschier elements of Mexican popular culture, with wall panels fashioned from plastic crates and sliced tin buckets as light shades. Got the munchies? Try the revamped versions of classic Mexican snacks.

Café El Jarocho
CAFE

(Map p90; www.cafeeljarocho.com.mx, in Spanish; Cuauhtémoc 134; ⊙6am-1am; ▣Coyoacán) This immensely popular joint churns out cappuccinos for long lines of java hounds. As there's no seating inside, people have their coffee standing in the street or sitting on curbside benches. Another **branch** (Map p90; Av México 173D) is near Viveros park.

El Hijo del Cuervo
BAR

(Map p90; www.elhijodelcuervo.com.mx, in Spanish; Jardín Centenario 17; ⊙4pm-midnight Mon-Wed, 1pm-2am Thu-Sat, 1pm-midnight Sun; Ⓜ Viveros) A Coyoacán institution, this stone-walled hall on the Jardín Centenario is a thinking person's drinking person's habitat. Assorted musical ensembles perform on Tuesday, Wednesday and Thursday nights.

La Guadalupana
CANTINA

(Map p90; Higuera 2; ⊙noon-12:30am Mon-Sat; Ⓜ Viveros) Serving drinks for more than seven decades, this rustic tavern breathes tradition, down to the blasé waiters in white coats. There are *botanas* (snacks) and *tortas* as well as heartier fare.

☆ Entertainment

There's so much going on in Mexico City on any given evening, it's hard to keep track. *Tiempo Libre,* the city's comprehensive what's-on magazine, helps you sort it all out. Published on Thursdays, it covers live music, theater, movies, dance, art and nightlife. Other useful guides include the monthlies *Donde Ir* (www.dondeir.com) and *Chilango* (www.chilango.com, in Spanish), the latter with a *Time Out* supplement. *Primera Fila,* a Friday section of the *Reforma* newspaper, has lots of entertainment listings, too.

Ticketmaster (☑5325-9000; www.ticketmaster.com.mx, in Spanish) sells tickets for all the major venues via internet, phone or at any of the following booking services: **Auditorio Nacional** (Map p84; ☑9138-1350; Paseo de la Reforma 50; ⊙10am-7pm Mon-Sat, 11am-6pm Sun; Ⓜ Auditorio); **Liverpool** Centro (Map p62; Venustiano Carranza 92; ⊙11am-7pm; Ⓜ Zócalo), Polanco (Map p84; Mariano Escobedo 425; ⊙11am-7pm; Ⓜ Polanco); or **Mixup** Centro (Map p62; Av Madero 51; ⊙10am-9pm Mon-Sat, 11am-8pm Sun; Ⓜ Zócalo); Zona Rosa (Map p76; Génova 76; ⊙10am-8pm; Ⓜ Insurgentes).

Nightclubs

The capital's thriving club scene has become an obligatory stop on the international DJ circuit. To find out what's going on, pick up flyers at Condesa's Malafama billiard hall (p111).

(p111)

⌖ Centro Cultural de España
LIVE MUSIC

(Map p62; www.ccemx.org, in Spanish; República de Guatemala 18, Colonia Centro; admission free; ⊙10pm-2am Wed-Sat; Ⓜ Zócalo) Young hipsters pack the terrace of this place each weekend for its excellent DJ and live-music sessions. Located directly behind the cathedral, the rebuilt colonial structure is usually quaking by midnight.

El Under
MUSIC

(Map p80; www.theunder.org, in Spanish; Monterrey 80, Colonia Roma; ⊙8pm-5am Fri & Sat; Ⓠ Durango) At this underground scene favorite, black-clad youth dance to the likes of Morrissey and Bauhaus on the old house's lower level, while upstairs local bands grind out everything from garage punk to rockabilly and death metal.

Fever
CLUB

(Map p80; www.fever.com.mx, in Spanish; Av Nuevo León 67, Colonia Condesa; ⊙10pm-2am Wed-Sat; Ⓠ Sonora) The pretty people come out to strut their stuff on an illuminated tempered-glass dance floor at this flashy two-story nightclub. International DJs mix it up with house, disco beats and the occasional funkytown sounds.

Cinemas

Mexico City is a banquet for moviegoers. Almost everything is screened here and ticket prices are around M$50, with many places offering discounts on Wednesdays. Except for children's fare, movies are in original languages with Spanish subtitles. *El Universal* and *La Jornada* have daily listings.

Cinépolis Diana
CINEMA

(Map p76; www.cinepolis.com.mx, in Spanish; Paseo de la Reforma 423, Colonia Cuauhtémoc; Ⓜ Sevilla) The program includes commercial releases and international film festival titles.

Cinemex Real
CINEMA

(Map p70; www.cinemex.com, in Spanish; Colón 17, Colonia Centro; Ⓜ Hidalgo) This cinema screens mostly Hollywood movies and the occasional Mexican hit.

Cineteca Nacional
CINEMA

(Map p90; www.cinetecanacional.net, in Spanish; Av México-Coyoacán 389, Colonia Xoco; Ⓜ Coyoacán) Thematically focused film series are shown on nine screens, with at least one for Mexican cinema. It hosts the Muestra Internacional de Cine, an international film festival, in November. At the time of research, the Cineteca was undergoing renovation.

Lumiere Reforma
CINEMA

(Map p76; www.cinemaslumiere.com, in Spanish; Río Guadalquivir 104, Colonia Cuauhtémoc; Ⓜ Sevilla) Primarily arthouse flicks.

Cine Lido
CINEMA

(Map p80; www.cinelido.com.mx, in Spanish; Av Tamaulipas 202, Colonia Condesa; Ⓜ Patriotismo) Single-screen theater with Mexican cinema or foreign fare inside cultural center Bella Época (p119).

Filmoteca de la UNAM
CINEMA

(www.filmoteca.unam.mx, in Spanish; Av Insurgentes Sur 3000; tickets M$30; 🚇 Centro Cultural Universitario) Two cinemas at the Centro Cultural Universitario screen films from a collection of more than 43,000 titles. See p87 for directions for getting to the Centro Cultural Universitario.

Dance, Classical Music & Theater

Orchestral music, opera, ballet, contemporary dance and theater are all abundantly represented in the capital's numerous theaters. Museums, too, serve as (often free) performance venues, including the **Museo de la Secretaría de Hacienda y Crédito Público** (p66) and the **Museo de la Ciudad de México** (p69). The national arts council (Conaculta) provides a rundown of events on its Spanish-language website (www.cnca. gob.mx) and in Friday's *La Jornada*.

If your Spanish is up to it, you might like to sample Mexico City's lively theater scene. The website **MejorTeatro** (www.mejorteatro. com.mx, in Spanish) covers the major venues. Performances are generally Thursday to Sunday evenings with weekend matinees.

Palacio de Bellas Artes
PERFORMING ARTS

(Map p70; www.bellasartes.gob.mx; Av Hidalgo 1, Colonia Centro; ⊗ box office 11am-7pm; Ⓜ Bellas Artes) The Orquesta Sinfónica Nacional and prestigious opera companies perform in Bellas Artes' ornate theater, while chamber groups appear in the recital halls. The venue is most famous, though, for the **Ballet Folclórico de México** (www.balletamalia.com; ⊗ performances 8:30pm Wed, 9:30am & 8:30pm Sun), a two-hour festive blur of costumes, music and dance from all over Mexico. Tickets are usually available on the day of the show at the Palacio, or from Ticketmaster.

Centro Cultural Universitario
PERFORMING ARTS

(www.cultura.unam.mx, in Spanish; Av Insurgentes Sur 3000; 🚇 Centro Cultural Universitario) Ensconced in the woodsy southern section of the national university campus, Centro Cultural Universitario comprises five theaters, including the Sala Nezahualcóyotl, home of the UNAM Philharmonic; the Teatro Alarcón, a drama stage; and the Sala Miguel Covarrubias, a contemporary dance venue. See p87 for directions.

Centro Nacional de las Artes
PERFORMING ARTS

(CNA; www.cenart.gob.mx, in Spanish; Av Río Churubusco 79, Colonia Country Club; Ⓜ General Anaya) A sprawling art institute near Coyoacán that has many free events across the artistic spectrum, including contemporary dance and classical concerts. To get here, exit metro General Anaya (Línea 2) on the east side of Calzada de Tlalpan, then walk north to the corner and turn right.

Centro Cultural del Bosque
PERFORMING ARTS

(Map p84; www.ccb.bellasartes.gob.mx, in Spanish; cnr Paseo de la Reforma & Campo Marte, Colonia Chapultepec Polanco; ⊗ box office noon-3pm & 5-7pm Mon-Fri & prior to events; Ⓜ Auditorio) Behind the Auditorio Nacional, the Centro Cultural del Bosque features six theaters, including the Teatro de la Danza, dedicated to modern dance. On Saturday and Sunday afternoons, children's plays and puppet shows are staged.

Foro Shakespeare
THEATER

(Map p80; www.foroshakespeare.com, in Spanish; Zamora 7, Colonia Condesa; Ⓜ Chapultepec) A small independent theater with an eclectic program.

Centro Cultural Helénico
THEATER

(Map p88; www.helenico.gob.mx, in Spanish; Guadalupe Inn, Av Revolución 1500, Colonia Guadalupe Inn; 🚇 Altavista) This complex includes a 450-seat theater for major productions and a smaller cabaret-style venue.

Live Music

Mexico City's eclectic music offering rocks. On any given night, you can hear traditional Mexican, Cuban, jazz, electronica, garage punk and so on. Music sounds off everywhere: in concert halls, bars, museums and on public transportation, and free gigs often take place at the Zócalo and the Monumento a la Revolución. The 'Conciertos' sections of

Tiempo Libre (www.tiempolibre.com.mx) and Ticketmaster (www.ticketmaster.com.mx) include show listings. Roma, Condesa and the Centro have the highest concentration of venues.

CONCERTS

José Cuervo Salón CONCERT VENUE
(☏5255-5322; www.ticketmaster.com.mx/jose-cuervo-salon-boletos-mexico/venue/163961; Andrómaco 17, cnr Moliere, Colonia Ampliación Granada) A warehouse-sized venue for touring rock, world-music and salsa stars. With excellent sound, a wall-length bar and a dance floor for thousands, this is one of Mexico's most cutting-edge clubs. It's best reached by taxi.

El Plaza Condesa CONCERT VENUE
(Map p80; ☏5256-5381; http://elplaza.mx, in Spanish; Juan Escutia 4, Colonia Condesa; 🚇Campeche) The new spot on the Condesa nightlife scene, this former movie theater now raises the curtain for pop and rock groups from Mexico and abroad.

Auditorio Nacional CONCERT VENUE
(Map p84; ☏9138-1350; www.auditorio.com.mx, in Spanish; Paseo de la Reforma 50, Colonia Chapultepec Polanco; 🚇Auditorio) Major gigs by Mexican and visiting rock and pop artists take the stage at the 10,000-seat Auditorio Nacional. The adjoining Lunario del Auditorio (www.lunario.com.mx, in Spanish) is a large club mostly for jazz and folk acts.

Teatro de la Ciudad CONCERT VENUE
(Map p62; ☏5130-5740, ext 2020; www.cultura.df.gob.mx/index.php/recintos/teatros/tcm, in Spanish; Donceles 36, Colonia Centro; 🚇Allende) Built in 1918, this lavishly restored 1300-seat hall gets some of the more interesting touring groups in music, dance and theater.

MARIACHIS
The thriving music scene at Plaza Garibaldi (p66) gets going by about 8pm and stays busy until 3am.

TOP CHOICE El Tenampa MARIACHIS
(Map p62; www.salontenampa.com; Plaza Garibaldi 12; ⊙1pm-3am; 🚇Garibaldi) Graced with murals of the giants of Mexican song and enlivened by its own songsters, El Tenampa is a festive cantina on the north side of the plaza; a visit here is obligatory.

ROCK
The street market Tianguis Cultural del Chopo (p120) has a stage at its north end

every Saturday afternoon for young and hungry alternative, metal and punk bands.

El Imperial Club CONCERT VENUE
(Map p80; http://elimperial.tv, in Spanish; Álvaro Obregón 293, Colonia Roma; ⊙10pm-3am Tue-Sat; 🚇Sevilla) Mexican indie bands and the occasional imported act perform in this ornate two-story house with antique furnishings and cool vintage touches throughout.

Multiforo Alicia CONCERT VENUE
(Map p80; www.multiforoalicia.blogspot.com, in Spanish; Av Cuauhtémoc 91A, Colonia Roma; 🚇Jardín Pushkin) Behind the graffiti-scrawled facade is Mexico City's premier indie-rock club. A suitably dark, seatless space, the Alicia stages up-and-coming punk, surf and ska bands, who hawk their music at the store downstairs. See the website for show times.

Pasagüero CONCERT VENUE
(Map p62; ☏5512-6624; www.myspace.com/pasaguero; Motolinía 33, Colonia Centro; ⊙10pm-3:30am Thu-Sat; 🚇Allende) Some visionary developers took a historic building and transformed its stonewalled ground level into a space for various cultural happenings, especially rock and electronica gigs.

JAZZ & BLUES

Zinco Jazz Club JAZZ
(Map p62; www.zincojazz.com, in Spanish; Motolinía 20, Colonia Centro; ⊙9pm-2am Wed-Sat; 🚇Allende) A vital component in the Centro's rebirth, Zinco is a subterranean supper club featuring local jazz and funk outfits as well as touring artists. The intimate basement room fills up fast when big-name acts take the stage.

Ruta 61 BLUES
(Map p80; www.ruta61.com.mx, in Spanish; Av Baja California 281, Colonia Condesa; ⊙music from 10pm Wed-Sat; 🚇Chilpancingo) This split-level venue stages electric blues artists in the Buddy Guy/Howlin' Wolf mold. About once a month there's a direct-from-Chicago act, though you're more likely to see a local cover band.

LATIN DANCE
The city's many aficionados have a circuit of clubs and *salones de baile* (dance halls) to choose from. At the clubs listed here, it's customary to go in a group and share a bottle of rum or tequila (from around M$600, including mixers).

You might learn a few great steps at the **Plaza de Danzón** (Map p70), northwest of

La Ciudadela near metro Balderas. Couples crowd the plaza every Saturday afternoon to do the *danzón,* an elegant and complicated Cuban step that infiltrated Mexico in the 19th century. Lessons in *danzón* and other steps are given from around 3:30pm to 5:30pm.

Cuban dance clubs abound in Roma, particularly near the intersection of Avenida Insurgentes and Medellín.

Mama Rumba   DANCING
(Map p80; www.mamarumba.com.mx, in Spanish; Querétaro 230, cnr Medellín, Colonia Roma; ☺9pm-3am Thu-Sat; ☐Sonora) Managed by a Havana native, Mama Rumba features contemporary salsa, with music by the house big band. Dance instructors will get you started Wednesday and Thursday at 9pm and Saturday at 8pm. Mama Rumba has a larger branch in San Ángel at Plaza Loreto (p120).

Salón Los Ángeles   DANCING
(off Map p62; Lerdo 206, Colonia Guerrero; ☺6-11pm Tue & Sun; ⓂTlatelolco) Fans of Cuban music shouldn't miss the outstanding orchestras, nor the graceful dancers who fill the vast floor of this atmospheric ballroom, particularly on Tuesday evenings, when an older crowd comes for *danzón.* It's located in the rough Colonia Guerrero, so take a taxi.

CABARET

La Perla   CABARET
(Map p62; www.cabaret-laperla.com, in Spanish; República de Cuba 44, Colonia Centro; ☺shows 11pm & 1am Fri & Sat; ⓂBellas Artes) Once a red-light venue, this cabaret has been reborn in the age of irony as a cradle of kitsch, with hilarious drag shows featuring traditional Mexican songstresses. Tickets go fast.

El Bataclán   CABARET
(Map p80; www.labodega.com.mx, in Spanish; Popocatépetl 25, cnr Amsterdam; ☺9pm-1am Wed-Sat; ☐Álvaro Obregón) A theater within a club (La Bodega), this intimate cabaret showcases some of Mexico's more offbeat performers, with frequent appearances by wonderfully surreal Astrid Hadad. Afterwards, catch top-notch Cuban *son* combos.

Bar El Vicio   CABARET
(Map p90; www.lasreinaschulas.com, in Spanish; Madrid 13, Colonia del Carmen; ☺9:30pm-midnight Mon-Thu, 10:30pm-3am Fri & Sat, 7pm-midnight Sun; ⓂCoyoacán) With liberal doses of politically and sexually irreverent comedy and a genre-bending musical program, this alternative cabaret is appropriately located in Frida Kahlo's old stomping grounds.

TROVA & TRADITIONAL

Cafebrería El Péndulo   LIVE MUSIC
(Map p80; www.pendulo.com, in Spanish; Av Nuevo León 115, Colonia Condesa; ☐Campeche) Leading Mexican singer-songwriters play at this cafe-bookstore and at a second branch in Zona Rosa (Map p76; Hamburgo 126, Colonia Juárez; ⓂInsurgentes).

El Balcón Huasteco   LIVE MUSIC
(www.elbalconhuasteco.com, in Spanish; Sor Juana Inés de la Cruz 248, Colonia Agricultura; ☺from 6pm Fri & Sat; ⓂNormal) This center for the preservation of the Huastec culture of Hidalgo and Veracruz stages performances by fiery trios and prepares snacks hailing from the region. Should you feel inspired, music and dance classes are offered here. It's two blocks north of metro Normal.

El Breve Espacio   LIVE MUSIC
(Map p88; www.elbreveespacio.mx, in Spanish; Frontera 4, Colonia San Ángel; ☺2-10pm Mon-Wed, to 2am Thu-Sat; ☐La Bombilla) Folk singers in the Silvio Rodríguez mold take the stage at this temple of *trova* (troubadour-type folk music) near San Ángel's Plaza San Jacinto.

Sports

Most of the daily newspapers have a generous sports section where you can find out who is kicking which ball where. True enthusiasts should look for *La Afición* (www.laaficion.com, in Spanish), a daily devoted to sports.

Corridas de toros (bullfights) take place on Sunday from 4pm at the **Monumental Plaza México** (www.lamexico.com, in Spanish; Augusto Rodin 241, Colonia Noche Buena; ☐Ciudad de los Deportes), one of the largest bullrings in the world, a few blocks west of Avenida Insurgentes.

SOCCER

The capital stages two or three *fútbol* (soccer) matches in the national Primera División almost every weekend of the year. Mexico City has three teams: América, nicknamed Las Águilas (the Eagles), Las Pumas of UNAM, and Cruz Azul. There are two seasons: January to June and August to December, each ending in eight-team playoffs and a two-leg final to decide the champion.

The biggest match of all is El Clásico, between América and Guadalajara, which fills the Estadio Azteca with 100,000 flag-waving fans. Get tickets in advance for this one.

GAY & LESBIAN MEXICO CITY

Now that the Distrito Federal (DF) assembly has approved a same-sex marriage law, Mexico City is seen as a bastion of tolerance in an otherwise conservative country. The long-time heart of gay life is the Zona Rosa – in particular Calle Amberes. Yet many night owls prefer the downtown scene along República de Cuba. Free magazines *Homópolis* and *Ser Gay*, both in Spanish and available in some clubs, have useful information.

Marrakech Salón (Map p62; República de Cuba 18, Colonia Centro; ☉6pm-3am Fri & Sat; Ⓜ︎Allende) Typical sights and sounds at this retro bar include bare-chested bartenders, bar-top dancing and festive music ranging from 1980s pop to hip-shaking *cumbias* (dance music from Colombia). It gets crowded and steamy, but no one seems to mind.

Lipstick (Map p76; Amberes 1, Zona Rosa; ☉10pm-3am Thu-Sat; Ⓜ︎Insurgentes) Far less asphyxiating and more upscale than the other bars along this raucous gay strip, Lipstick does DJ nights in a gorgeous two-story house with a terrace and smoking area overlooking the tree-lined Paseo de la Reforma.

Wawis (Map p62; cnr Eje Central Lázaro Cárdenas & República de Perú, Colonia Centro; ☉9pm-5am Fri-Sun; Ⓜ︎Garibaldi) Up above a seedy street scene, this mixed gay disco provides plenty of elbow room to get your salsa, *cumbia* and reggaeton grooves on. Wawis is good-humoredly named after a Mexican slang term meaning 'fellatio.'

Bar Oasis (Map p62; República de Cuba 2G, Colonia Centro; ☉3pm-1am Sun-Thu, 3pm-3am Fri & Sat; Ⓜ︎Bellas Artes) This packed disco cuts across socioeconomic lines, with both working-class regulars and businessmen dancing against a Day-Glo cityscape. Stick around past midnight for shows featuring lip-synching trannies.

Tom's Leather Bar (Map p80; www.toms-mexico.com, in Spanish; Av Insurgentes Sur 357, Colonia Condesa; ☉9pm-3am Tue-Sun; Ⓜ︎Sonora) For those who dare to get medieval, Tom's provides the props, with heraldic shields, crossed swords and candelabras highlighting a decidedly decadent decor. When the fat lady sings, the show's about to begin.

Tickets (M$95 to M$600 for regular season games) are usually available at the gate, or from Ticketmaster. There are several stadiums that host games.

Estadio Azteca STADIUM
(www.esmas.com/estadioazteca, in Spanish; Calz de Tlalpan 3665; Ⓡ︎Estadio Azteca) The country's biggest stadium (capacity 105,000) is home to the América club. Games are played on weekend afternoons; check the website for kickoff times. Take the Tren Ligero from metro Tasqueña to the Estadio Azteca station.

Estadio Olímpico STADIUM
(www.clubpumasunam.com, in Spanish; Av Insurgentes Sur 3000, Ciudad Universitaria; Ⓡ︎CU) Home of the Pumas. To get here, go right after exiting metrobús station CU and look for the bus stop for free university transportation (called the Pumabús). 'Ruta 6' goes to Estadio Olímpico.

Estadio Azul STADIUM
(www.cruz-azul.com.mx, in Spanish; Indiana 255, Colonia Nápoles; Ⓡ︎Ciudad de los Deportes) The stadium is next door to the Plaza México bullring.

BASEBALL

Mexico City has one team in the Liga Mexicana de Béisbol, the **Diablos Rojos** (www.diablos.com.mx, in Spanish). During the regular season (March to July) they play every other week at the **Foro Sol** (cnr Av Río Churubusco & Viaducto Río de la Piedad; Ⓜ︎Ciudad Deportiva). From the metro, it is a five-minute walk over to the ballpark. See the website for game times.

LUCHA LIBRE (MEXICAN WRESTLING)

Mexico City's two wrestling venues, the 17,000-seat **Arena México** (Map p80; www.arenamexico.com.mx, in Spanish; Dr Lavista 197, Colonia Doctores; ☉7:30pm Tue & 8:30pm Fri; Ⓡ︎Cuauhtémoc) and the smaller **Arena Coliseo** (Map p62; República de Perú 77; ☉5pm Sun, except 3rd Sun of the month; Ⓜ︎Lagunilla) are taken over by a circus atmosphere each week, with flamboyant *luchadores* (wrestlers) like Místico and Último Guerrero going at each other in teams or one-on-one. There are three or four bouts, building up to the most formidable match-ups.

Shopping

Shopping can be a real joy here, with *artesanías* (handicrafts) vendors, quirky shops and street markets competing for your disposable income.

Bookstores

Rare-book aficionados can dig up some gems in the used bookstores along Donceles in the Centro. Books in English can be found in top-end hotels, major museums and the following bookstores.

CENTRO HISTÓRICO

American Bookstore   BOOKS
(Map p62; Bolívar 23; ☺10am-7pm Mon-Fri, to 5:30pm Sat; ⓜAllende) Has novels and books on Mexico in English, plus Lonely Planet guides.

Gandhi   BOOKS
(www.gandhi.com.mx, in Spanish; ☺10am-9pm Mon-Sat, 11am-8pm Sun) Av Madero (Map p62; Av Madero 32; ⓜZócalo); Bellas Artes (Map p70; Juárez 4; ⓜBellas Artes); San Ángel (Map p88; Av Miguel Ángel de Quevedo 121; ⓜMiguel Ángel de Quevedo) Citywide chain with a voluminous range of texts on Mexico and Mexico City. There are two outlets on the same block in San Ángel.

Librería Madero   BOOKS
(Map p62; www.libreriafimadero.com, in Spanish; Av Madero 12; ☺10am-6:30pm Mon-Fri, to 2pm Sat; ⓜAllende) Mexican history, art and architecture, including many secondhand titles.

OTHER AREAS

Bella Época   BOOKS
(Map p80; Av Tamaulipas 202, cnr Benjamín Hill, Colonia Condesa; ⓜPatriotismo) One of the largest bookstores in Latin America; shelves books, CDs and DVDs inside an impressive art deco–style cultural center.

Under the Volcano Books   BOOKS
(Map p80; www.underthevolcanobooks.com; Cerrada de Chiapas 40C, Colonia Roma; ☺2-8pm Sun & Wed, to 10pm Thu-Sat; ⓜHospital General) Deals in buying and selling used English-language titles; an excellent selection and very good prices.

Markets

Mexico City's markets are worth visiting not just for their varied contents but also for a glimpse of the frenetic business conducted within. Besides the major ones listed here,

neighborhood markets (indicated by 'Mi Mercado' signs) also make for an interesting wander.

Centro de Artesanías
La Ciudadela   HANDICRAFTS
(Map p70; cnr Balderas & Dondé, Colonia Centro; ☺10am-6pm; ⓜBalderas) A favorite destination for good stuff from all over Mexico. Worth seeking out are Oaxaca *alebrijes* (whimsical painted animals), guitars from Paracho, and Huichol beadwork. Prices are generally fair, even before you bargain.

Tianguis Dominical de la Lagunilla   MARKET
(off Map p62; cnr Gónzalez Bocanegra & Paseo de la Reforma, Colonia Centro; ☺Sun; ⓜGaribaldi) At this collector's oasis you can hunt for antiques, old souvenirs and bric-a-brac; books and magazines are alongside La Lagunilla building.

Mercado Insurgentes   ARTS & CRAFTS
(Map p76; cnr Londres & Av Florencia, Zona Rosa; ☺10am-7:30pm Mon-Sat, to 4pm Sun; ⓜInsurgentes) Packed with crafts – silver, pottery, leather, carved wooden figures – but you'll need to bargain to get sensible prices.

Mercado San Juan   MARKET
(Map p70; Pugibet 21, Colonia Centro; ☺8am-5:30pm; ⓜSan Juan de Letrán) Specializes in gourmet food items such as *huitlacoche* (corn fungus) and rare fruit. Local chefs and foodies come here to score ingredients not available elsewhere in the city.

Mercado de Jamaica   MARKET
(cnr Guillermo Prieto & Congreso de la Unión, Colonia Jamaica; ☺8am-7pm; ⓜJamaica) Huge, colorful flower market, featuring both baroque floral arrangements and exotic blooms. It's one block south of metro Jamaica.

La Lagunilla   MARKET
(Map p62; cnr Rayón & Allende, Colonia Centro; ☺9am-8pm Mon-Sat, 10am-7pm Sun; ⓜGaribaldi) This enormous complex comprises three buildings: building No 1 contains clothes and fabrics, No 2 has food and No 3 sells furniture.

STREET MARKETS

In most neighborhoods you'll find a *tianguis* (indigenous people's market; from the Náhuatl *tianquiztli*) at least once a week selling everything from fresh produce to clothing and antiques. *Tianguis* generally set up by 10am and break down around about 5pm.

Tianguis Cultural del Chopo   MUSIC
(Juan Nepomuceno, Colonia Buenavista; ⊘10am-4pm Sat; ⓂBuenavista) Gathering place for the city's various youth subcultures, with most of the vendor stalls devoted to music CDs. At the far end is a concert stage for young-and-hungry bands. The main entrance is one block east of metro Buenavista.

Bazar Sábado   ARTS & CRAFTS
(Map p88; Plaza San Jacinto 11, San Ángel; ⊘10am-5:30pm Sat; 🚋La Bombilla) The Saturday bazaar showcases some of Mexico's best handcrafted jewelry, woodwork, ceramics and textiles. Artists and artisans also display their work in Plaza San Jacinto itself and in adjacent Plaza Tenanitla.

Bazar Artesanal de Coyoacán   HANDICRAFTS
(Map p90; Plaza Hidalgo, Coyoacán; ⊘9am-11pm Fri-Sun; ⓂViveros) Has handmade hippie jewelry and indigenous crafts, jugglers, fortune-tellers and incense.

Bazar de la Roma   ANTIQUES
(Map p80; Jardín Dr Chávez, Colonia Doctores; ⊘Sat & Sun; 🚋Jardín Pushkin) East of Avenida Cuauhtémoc, this market has used and antique items, large and small: books, beer trays, posters and furniture. A similar antiques and art market (see Map p80) runs along Álvaro Obregón on the same days.

Bazar de Oro   MARKET
(Map p80; Calle de Oro, Colonia Roma; ⊘Wed, Sat & Sun; 🚋Durango) This upscale street market between Avenida Insurgentes and Plaza Villa de Madrid has clothing, gifts and an excellent eating section.

Plaza del Ángel   ANTIQUES
(Map p76; www.antiguedadesplazadelangel.com. mx; Londres btwn Amberes & Av Florencia, Zona Rosa; ⊘Sat & Sun; ⓂInsurgentes) Flea market within a mall of high-end antique shops selling silver jewelry, paintings, ornaments and furniture.

Tepito   MARKET
(Map p62; Héroe de Granaditas, Colonia Tepito; ⊘Wed-Mon; ⓂLagunilla) The mother of all street markets: a maze of semipermanent stalls spreading east and north from La Lagunilla, with miles of clothes, pirated CDs and DVDs and electronics. Also known as the Thieves' Market for its black-market goods and pickpockets. Enter crime-ridden Tepito at your own risk.

Jardín del Arte   ARTS & CRAFTS
(Map p76; btwn Sullivan & Villalongín, Colonia San Rafael; ⊘Sun; 🚋Reforma) This place has paintings by local artists, plus art supplies and some food.

Shops

Chilangos increasingly shop in modern malls with designer-clothing stores, cosmeticians and Starbucks franchises, and more of these shrines to consumerism are popping up all the time. Among the more pleasant are **Plaza Loreto** (Map p88; cnr Av Revolución & Río de la Magdalena; ⊘11am-8pm; 🚋Dr Gálvez) in San Ángel; the open-air **Antara** (Map p84; www.antara.com.mx, in Spanish; Av Ejército Nacional 843B; ⊘11am-8pm; ⓂPolanco) in Polanco, and **Plaza Reforma 222** (Map p76; Paseo de la Reforma 222; ⊘11am-9pm; ⓂInsurgentes) at the east end of the Zona Rosa.

CENTRO HISTÓRICO

Mexico City's smartest department-store chains, **El Palacio de Hierro** (Map p62; www.palaciodehierro.com.mx, in Spanish; Av 20 de Noviembre 3; ⊘11am-8:30pm Mon-Fri, to 9pm Sat, to 7:30pm Sun; ⓂZócalo) and **Liverpool** (Map p62; www.liverpool.com.mx, in Spanish; Venustiano Carranza 92; ⊘11am-8:30pm Mon-Fri, to 9pm Sat, to 7:30pm Sun; ⓂZócalo) both maintain their original 1930s stores downtown.

The streets around the Zócalo are lined with stores that specialize in everyday goods; you'll find plenty of shops selling similar items along the same street. To the west, photography supplies and used books show up on Donceles. Jewelry and gold outlets, as well as numismatics shops, are found along Palma, while opticians are east of the square on Avenida Madero. To the south, shoes are available on Avenida 20 de Noviembre, and music instruments are along Bolívar. To the north, you'll find costume jewelry on República de Colombia and República de Venezuela.

Hundreds of computer stores huddle in the **Plaza de la Computación y Electrónica** (Map p70; Eje Central Lázaro Cárdenas; ⓂSan Juan de Letrán), south of Uruguay.

Mumedi   GIFTS
(Mexican Design Museum; Map p62; www.mumedi. org; Av Madero 74; ⊘11am-9pm Mon, 8am-9pm Tue-Sun; ⓂZócalo) This museum gift shop has pop culture knick-knacks, handbags and jewelry crafted by local designers.

La Europea   DRINK
(Map p70; www.laeuropea.com.mx, in Spanish; Ayuntamiento 21; MSan Juan de Letrán) Get reasonably priced tequila, mezcal and wine here.

Dulcería de Celaya   FOOD
(Map p62; www.dulceriadecelaya.com, in Spanish; Av 5 de Mayo 39; ⊘10:30am-7:30pm; MAllende) Candy store operating since 1874 with candied fruits and coconut-stuffed lemons; worth a look just for the ornate building.

Galería Eugenio   HANDICRAFTS
(Map p62; Allende 84; ⊘11am-6pm Mon-Sat; MGaribaldi) Sells more than 5000 masks from all over the country; it's in the Lagunilla market area.

ZONA ROSA

TOP⧸CHOICE **Fonart**   HANDICRAFTS
Mixcoac (Patriotismo 691; ⊘10am-8pm Mon-Fri, 10am-7pm Sat, 11am-5pm Sun; MMixcoac); Reforma (Map p76; www.fonart.gob.mx; Paseo de la Reforma 116; ⊘10am-7pm Mon-Fri, to 4pm Sat & Sun; ⊠Reforma) This government-run crafts store sells quality wares from around Mexico, from Olinalá lacquered boxes to Teotitlán del Valle blankets, as well as pottery and glassware. Prices are fixed.

CONDESA & ROMA

Condesa presents an enticing array of trendy boutiques, quirky shops and gourmet food stores scattered around the neighborhood. In Roma, much of the retail activity is along central Álvaro Obregón.

El Hijo del Santo   GIFTS
(Map p80; www.elhijodelsanto.com.mx/coffeeshop, in Spanish; Av Tamaulipas 219; ⊘10am-9pm Mon-Sat; MPatriotismo) Owned by wrestler El Hijo del Santo, this specialty store sells (you guessed it) all things Santo. Among the offerings are kitschy portraits, hipster handbags and the ever-popular Santo mask.

Vértigo   ARTS & CRAFTS
(Map p80; www.vertigogaleria.com, in Spanish; Colima 23; ⊘noon-8pm Mon-Fri, to 7pm Sat, to 6pm Sun; ⊠Jardín Pushkin) The store at this funky art gallery sells silkscreens, graphic T-shirts and etchings made by popular Argentine illustrator Jorge Alderete. In addition to 'low brow' art shows, Vértigo stages the occasional acoustic music gig.

NaCo Miscelánea   CLOTHING
(Map p80; www.chidochido.com, in Spanish; Yautepec 126B; ⊘11am-7pm Mon-Sat; MPatriotismo) This cheeky little streetwear store in the heart of Condesa carries the NaCo line of T-shirts, emblazoned with edgy or graphic messages relating to Mexican pop culture.

La Naval   DRINK
(Map p80; www.lanaval.com.mx, in Spanish; Av Insurgentes Sur 373; ⊠Campeche) Name your poison: this gourmet store stocks a tantalizing selection of mezcals, tequilas and Cuban cigars.

POLANCO

Polanco's Avenida Presidente Masaryk, aka the Rodeo Drive of Mexico, is lined with designer stores and other high-end establishments.

🍃**Green Corner**   FOOD
Condesa (Map p80; Av Mazatlán 81; ✍; MJuanacatlán); Polanco (Map p84; Homero 1210; www.greencorner.org, in Spanish; ⊘8am-10pm; ✍; MPolanco) A rare find in the DF, this organic-food store purchases items from small producers throughout Mexico. Both branches sell organic fruit, vegetables and cheese; the Condesa store has a vegetarian-friendly restaurant.

Pasaje Polanco   SHOPPING CENTER
(Map p84; Av Presidente Masaryk 360; ⊘11am-8pm; MPolanco) A classy complex flanked by sophisticated boutiques and specialty stores.

ℹ Information

Dangers & Annoyances

Mexico City is generally portrayed as extremely crime-ridden, so first-time visitors are often surprised at how safe it feels. While crime rates remain significant – 48 muggings, two homicides and five taxi holdups a day in 2010 – a few precautions greatly reduce any dangers (see also p856).

Robberies happen most often in areas frequented by foreigners, including Plaza Garibaldi and the Zona Rosa. Be on your guard at the airport and bus stations. Crowded metro cars and buses are favorite haunts of pickpockets; keep a close eye on your wallet and avoid carrying ATM cards or large amounts of cash. In case of robbery, don't resist – hand over your valuables rather than risk injury or death.

Statistically, traffic takes more lives in the capital than street crime. Always look both ways when crossing streets, as some one-way streets have bus lanes running counter to the traffic flow, and traffic on some divided streets runs in just one direction. Never assume that a green light means it's safe to cross, as cars may turn into your path; cross with other pedestrians.

Although not as prevalent as in the 1990s, taxi assaults still occur. Many victims have hailed a cab on the street and been robbed by armed accomplices of the driver. Taxis parked in front of nightclubs or restaurants should be avoided unless authorized by the management. Rather than hailing cabs, phone a radio *sitio* (taxi service). See p130 for recommended companies.

Emergency

The Policía Turística, recognizable by their blue-and-gray uniforms, patrol Paseo de la Reforma and the Centro Histórico, some zipping around on Segways. They are supposed to be able to speak English. Mobile units of the PGJDF (Federal District Attorney General's Office) assist crime victims on the spot; call ☎061.

Agencia del Ministerio Público (☎5345-5382; Amberes 54; Ⓜ Insurgentes) Report crimes and get legal assistance.

Cruz Roja (Red Cross; ☎065, 5395-1111)

Fire (☎068)

Immigration

Instituto Nacional de Migración (☎2581-0100; www.inm.gob.mx; Av Ejército Nacional 862, Polanco; ⊘9am-1pm Mon-Fri) You'll need to come here if you want to extend a tourist permit, replace a lost one, or deal with other nonstandard immigration procedures. Take the 'Ejército Defensa' bus from metro Chapultepec.

Internet Access

Public internet services are easily located. Rates range from M$10 to M$30 per hour. Additionally, many cafes offer wireless internet.

CENTRO HISTÓRICO

Copy Land (Gante 12; ⊘9am-7pm Mon-Fri, 10am-2pm Sat; Ⓜ Allende)

Esperanto (Independencia 66; ⊘8am-10pm Mon-Sat, 9am-8pm Sun; Ⓜ Juárez)

ZONA ROSA

Plenty of cybercafes occupy the Insurgentes roundabout.

Conecte Café (Génova 71; cnr Londres; ⊘8:30am-1am Mon-Fri, 10am-2am Sat, 10am-1am Sun; Ⓜ Insurgentes) Offers all of the usual sevices of an internet cafe.

CONDESA & ROMA

Tecno Informática (Vicente Suárez 25; ⊘8am-10pm Mon-Sat; Ⓜ Patriotismo)

COYOACÁN

Papelería Fiscal (Jardín Centenario 4; ⊘7am-10pm Mon-Sat, 9am-9pm Sun; Ⓜ Viveros) Coffee shop with internet cafe upstairs.

Internet Resources

The following sites compile oodles of information on the capital.

Artes Visuales (www.artesvisuales.com.mx, in Spanish) Covers DF galleries and museums.

Consejo Nacional Para la Cultura y las Artes (www.conaculta.gob.mx/cultura, in Spanish) Online arts and culture magazine that lists goings-on about town.

Secretaría de Cultura del Distrito Federal (www.cultura.df.gob.mx, in Spanish) Festivals and museum events.

Secretaría de Turismo (www.mexicocity.gob. mx) City tourism office's listings and practical information.

Sistema de Transporte Colectivo (www. metro.df.gob.mx, in Spanish) All about the Mexico City metro.

Laundry

Lavanderías charge M$50 to M$90 for a 3kg load – slightly less if you do it yourself.

Lavandería Automática Edison (Edison 91; ⊘10am-7pm Mon-Fri, to 6pm Sat; Ⓜ Revolución) Near Plaza de la República.

Lavandería Lavamextil (Río Pánuco 122, cnr Río Tiber; ⊘9am-7pm Mon-Fri, to 3pm Sat; Ⓜ Insurgentes)

Maps

Mexico City tourist modules hand out color maps with enlargements of the Centro Histórico, Coyoacán and San Ángel. If you need more detail, pick up a Guía Roji foldout map of Mexico City (M$70), or a Guía Roji *Ciudad de México* street atlas (M$249), updated annually, with a comprehensive index. Find them at Sanborns stores and larger newsstands.

Inegi (www.inegi.gob.mx, in Spanish) Centro (Balderas 71; ⊘9am-4pm Mon-Fri; Ⓜ Juárez), Colonia Mixcoac (Patriotismo 711; ⊘9am-4pm Mon-Fri; Ⓜ Mixcoac) Mexico's national geographical institute publishes topographical maps covering the whole country (subject to availability). Headquarters are in Colonia Mixcoac.

Media

English-language daily the *News* (www.thenews. com.mx), sold at Sanborns stores and some newsstands, has news plus some local cultural coverage. *Inside México* (www.insidemex.com) is a free monthly in English that covers expat life in Mexico; pick up a copy at cafes and hotels around town.

Tiempo Libre (www.tiempolibre.com.mx), the city's Spanish-language what's-on weekly, comes out on Thursdays and is sold at newsstands everywhere.

Recommended Spanish-language newspapers include *La Jornada*, which has excellent cultural coverage, *El Universal* and *Reforma*, the latter available at convenience stores and some metro stations.

English-language newspapers and magazines are sold at Sanborns stores and at **La Torre de Papel** (www.torredepapel.com, in Spanish; Filomena Mata 6A, Colonia Centro; ⊘8am-6pm Mon-Fri, 9am-3pm Sat; MAllende), which also stocks newspapers from around Mexico.

Medical Services

For recommendation of a doctor, dentist or hospital, call your embassy or **Sectur** (⊅078), the tourism ministry. A list of area hospitals and English-speaking physicians (with their credentials) is on the **US embassy website** (http://mexico.usembassy.gov/eng/eacs_doctors.html). A private doctor's consultation generally costs between M$500 and M$1200.

Hospital ABC (American British Cowdray Hospital; ⊅5230-8000, emergency 5230-8161; www.abchospital.com; Sur 136 No 116, Colonia Las Américas; MObservatorio) English-speaking staff, great hospital.

Hospital Ángeles Clínica Londres (⊅5229-8400, emergency 5229-8445; www.hospital angelesclinicalondres.com, in Spanish; Durango 50, Colonia Roma; MCuauhtémoc)

The pharmacies in **Sanborns** (www.sanborns.com.mx) stores are among the most reliable, as are the following places.

Farmacia París (www.farmaciaparis.com, in Spanish; República de El Salvador 97, Colonia Centro; MIsabel La Católica)

Farmacias del Ahorro (www.fahorro.com.mx, in Spanish; Yucatán 40, Colonia Roma; ⊘24hr; ⊞Álvaro Obregón)

Médicor (www.medicor.com.mx, in Spanish; Independencia 66, Colonia Centro; ⊘9am-6pm Mon-Sat, to 7pm Sun; MJuárez) For homeopathic remedies.

Money

Most banks and *casas de cambio* (exchange offices) change cash and traveler's checks, but some handle only euros and US or Canadian dollars. Rates vary, so check a few places. The greatest concentration of ATMs, banks and *casas de cambio* is on Paseo de la Reforma between the Monumento a Cristóbal Colón and the Monumento a la Independencia.

Cambios Centro Histórico (Av Madero 13; ⊘9:30am-6:30pm Mon-Sat, 10am-6pm Sun; MBellas Artes)

Centro de Cambios y Divisas (www.ccd.com.mx, in Spanish; Paseo de la Reforma 87F; ⊘8:30am-7:30pm Mon-Fri, 9am-5pm Sat, 9:30am-2:30pm Sun; ⊞Reforma)

Post

The stamp windows, marked *estampillas*, at **Palacio Postal** (www.palaciopostal.gob.mx, in Spanish; Tacuba 1; MBellas Artes) stay open beyond normal post-office hours (until 8pm Monday to Friday, and to 4pm on Saturday and Sunday). Even if you don't need stamps, check out the sumptuous interior (see p71).

Other branches, scattered around town, are generally open from 9am to 4pm Monday to Friday and 9am to 1pm Saturday.

Cuauhtémoc (Río Tiber 87; MInsurgentes)

Plaza de la República (Arriaga 11; MRevolución)

Zona Rosa (Londres 208; MSevilla)

Telephone & Fax

There are thousands of Telmex card phones scattered around town. Pick up cards at shops or newsstands bearing the blue-and-yellow 'Ladatel' sign.

Some *papelerías* (stationery stores), copy shops and internet cafes offer fax service; look for *fax público* signs. Sending one page to the US or Canada costs about M$10; receiving a fax costs M$5.

Toilets

Use of the bathroom is free at all Sanborns stores. Most market buildings have public toilets; just look for the 'WC' signs. Hygiene standards vary at these latter facilities, and a fee of M$3 to M$5 is usually charged. Toilet paper is dispensed by an attendant on request.

Tourist Information

The national tourism ministry, **Sectur** (⊅078; Av Presidente Masaryk 172; ⊘8am-6pm Mon-Fri, 10am-3pm Sat; MPolanco), hands out brochures on the entire country, though you're better off at the tourism modules for up-to-date information about the capital.

The Mexico City Tourism Ministry has modules in key areas, including the airport and bus stations. They can answer your queries and distribute a map and practical guide. Most staff members speak English.

These offices are open from 9am to 6pm daily, unless otherwise noted.

Antropología (Paseo de la Reforma; MAuditorio) At the entry to the Museo Nacional de Antropología.

Basílica de Guadalupe (Plaza de las Américas 1; MLa Villa-Basilica)

Bellas Artes (cnr Juárez & Peralta; MBellas Artes)

Catedral (MZócalo) West of the Catedral Metropolitana.

Del Ángel (cnr Paseo de la Reforma & Av Florencia; MInsurgentes) On the Zona Rosa side of Monumento a la Independencia.

Templo Mayor (MZócalo) East of the Catedral Metropolitana.

Xochimilco (ℝXochimilco) At the Nativitas boat landing.

Additionally, these city *delegaciones* (urban governmental subdivisions) operate tourist information offices.

Coyoacán (www.coyoacan.df.gob.mx, in Spanish; Jardín Hidalgo 1; ⊗8am-8pm; MViveros) Inside the Casa de Cortés.

Xochimilco (www.xochimilco.df.gob.mx/turismo, in Spanish; Pino 36; ⊗9am-9pm Mon-Fri, 8am-7pm Sat & Sun; ℝXochimilco) Just off the Jardín Juárez.

Travel Agencies

A number of midrange and top-end hotels have an *agencia de viajes* onsite or can recommend one nearby.

Mundo Joven (www.mundojoven.com, in Spanish; ⊗10am-7pm Mon-Fri, to 2pm Sat) Airport (Sala E2, international arrivals); Polanco (Eugenio Sue 342, cnr Homero; MPolanco); Zócalo (República de Guatemala 4; MZócalo) Specializes in travel for students and teachers, with reasonable airfares from Mexico City. Issues ISIC, ITIC, IYTC and HI cards.

Turismo Zócalo (www.turismozocalo.com, in Spanish; 2nd fl, Palma 34, Centro; MZócalo) Inside the Gran Plaza Ciudad de México mall; also functions as a Boletotal outlet.

❶ Getting There & Away

Air

Aeropuerto Internacional Benito Juárez (✆2482-2424; www.aicm.com.mx; Capitán Carlos León s/n, Colonia Peñón de los Baños; MTerminal Aérea), 6km east of the Zócalo, is Mexico City's only passenger airport. A new terminal has expanded the airport's capacity. Located 3km from the main terminal, Terminal 2 is connected by monorail, which departs every 10 minutes. Carriers operating out of the new terminal include Aeromar, Aeroméxico, Copa Airlines, Delta and Lan. All other airlines depart from Terminal 1. See p861 for information on international and domestic airlines serving Mexico.

Both terminals have *casas de cambio* (money exchange offices) and peso-dispensing ATMs. Car-rental agencies and luggage lockers are in Salas A and E2 of Terminal 1.

Direct buses to Cuernavaca, Querétaro, Toluca, Puebla and Córdoba depart from platforms adjacent to Sala E and from Terminal 2. Ticket counters in Terminal 1 are on the upper level, off the food court. A pedestrian bridge off Sala B leads to an ADO bus terminal with service to Acapulco and Veracruz.

Some 30 different airlines provide international service to Mexico City. You can fly direct from more than 30 cities in the USA and Canada, half a dozen each in Europe, South America and Central America/Caribbean, as well as from Tokyo. Seven different airlines connect the capital to about 50 cities within Mexico. See p861 and p864 for further information on international and domestic flights.

Bus

Mexico City has four long-distance bus terminals serving the four compass points: Terminal Norte (north), Terminal Oriente (called TAPO, east), Terminal Poniente (Observatorio, west) and Terminal Sur (south). All terminals have baggage-check services or lockers, as well as tourist information modules, newsstands, card phones, internet, ATMs and snack bars. For directions to the bus stations, see p128.

There are also buses to nearby cities from the airport (see the table, p126, and above).

For trips of up to five hours, it usually suffices to go to the bus station, buy your ticket and go. For longer trips, many buses leave in the evening and may well sell out, so buy your ticket beforehand.

You can purchase advance tickets at **Boletotal** (✆5133-5133, 800-009-90-90; http://boletotal.mx), a booking agency for more than a dozen bus lines out of all four stations. (A 10% surcharge is added to the cost of the ticket up to a maximum of M$50.) Outlets are generally open from 10am to 6:30pm Monday to Friday, and mornings only on Saturday. Ticketbus also offers purchase by phone with Visa or MasterCard.

Buenavista (Buenavista 9, cnr Orozco y Berra; MRevolución)

Centro Histórico (Isabel La Católica 83E, cnr Regina; MIsabel La Católica)

Condesa (cnr Aguascalientes & Av Insurgentes Sur; MChilpancingo)

Polanco (cnr Av Presidente Masaryk & Hegel; MPolanco)

Roma Norte (Mérida 156, cnr Zacatecas; MHospital General)

Zócalo (Turismo Zócalo, Palma 34; MZócalo)

LINES

Check schedules by visiting the bus lines' websites. See the table on p126 for a list of daily services from Mexico City. More information can be found in other town and city sections of this book. It's all subject to change, of course.

ADO Group (www.ado.com.mx, in Spanish) Includes ADO Platino (deluxe), ADO GL (executive), OCC (1st class), ADO (1st class) and AU (2nd class).

Autobuses Teotihuacanos (✆5587-0501) Second class.

Autovías (www.hdp.com.mx, in Spanish) First class.

Estrella Blanca Group (www.estrellablanca. com.mx, in Spanish) Operates Futura and Elite (1st class).

Estrella de Oro (www.estrelladeoro.com.mx, in Spanish) Executive and 1st class.

Estrella Roja (www.estrellaroja.com.mx) First class.

ETN (www.etn.com.mx, in Spanish) Includes ETN (deluxe) and Turistar (executive and deluxe).

Ómnibus de México (www.odm.com.mx, in Spanish) First class.

Primera Plus (www.primeraplus.com.mx) Deluxe and 1st class.

Pullman de Morelos (www.pullman.com.mx) Executive, deluxe and 1st class.

TERMINALS

The largest of the four bus terminals, **Terminal de Autobuses del Norte** (www.centraldelnorte. com.mx, in Spanish; Eje Central Lázaro Cárdenas 4907, Colonia Magdalena de las Salinas; Ⓜ Autobuses del Norte) serves points north, including cities on the US border, plus some points west (Guadalajara, Puerto Vallarta), east (Puebla) and south (Acapulco, Oaxaca). Deluxe and 1st-class counters are mostly in the southern half of the terminal. Luggage-storage services and ATMs are in the central passageway.

Terminal de Autobuses de Pasajeros de Oriente (TAPO; Calz Zaragoza 200, Colonia Diez de Mayo; Ⓜ San Lázaro) serves points east and southeast, including Puebla, Veracruz, Yucatán, Oaxaca and Chiapas. Bus-line counters are arranged around a rotunda with a restaurant, internet terminals and an ATM at the center. There's a left-luggage service in Tunnel 1.

Central de Autobuses del Poniente (Observatorio; Sur 122, Colonia Real del Monte; Ⓜ Observatorio) is the point for buses heading to Michoacán and shuttle services running to nearby Toluca. In addition, ETN offers service to Guadalajara.

Terminal Central del Sur (Av Tasqueña 1320, Colonia Campestre Churubusco; Ⓜ Tasqueña) serves Tepoztlán, Cuernavaca, Taxco, Acapulco and other southern destinations, as well as Oaxaca, Huatulco and Ixtapa-Zihuatanejo. Estrella de Oro (Taxco) and Pullman de Morelos (Cuernavaca) counters are on the right side of the terminal, while Futura (Acapulco) and OCC (Tepoztlán) are on the left. In Sala 2, you'll find a left-luggage service and an ATM.

Car & Motorcycle

RENTAL

Car-rental companies have offices at the airport, at bus stations and in the Zona Rosa area of the city. Rates generally start at about M$750 per day, but you can often do better by booking on-line. You can find a list of rental agencies online at www.mexicocity.gob.mx.

Avis (www.avis.com; Paseo de la Reforma 308; Ⓜ Insurgentes)

Thrifty (www.thrifty.com; Paseo de la Reforma 322; Ⓜ Insurgentes)

ROADSIDE ASSISTANCE

The *Ángeles Verdes* (Green Angels) can provide assistance between 8am and 6pm. Just phone ☏ 078 and tell them your location. For more information on the *Ángeles Verdes*, see boxed text, p867.

ROUTES IN & OUT OF THE CITY

Whichever way you come in, once you're past the last *caseta* (toll booth) you enter a no-man's-land of poorly marked lanes and chaotic traffic. These *casetas* are also the points from which 'Hoy No Circula' rules take effect (see p130).

EAST From Puebla, the highway eventually feeds traffic left into Calzada Zaragoza. Stay on Zaragoza for about 10km, then move left and follow signs for Río de la Piedad (aka Viaducto Miguel Alemán), exiting left after the metro crosses the highway. From the Viaducto, exits access all the key areas. Get off at Viaducto Tlalpan to reach the Zócalo, and Avenida Monterrey to Roma and the Zona Rosa.

Coming out of the airport, keep left to head south along Blvd Puerto Aéreo. After you cross Zaragoza, watch for signs to Río de la Piedad and Viaducto Alemán.

Heading for Puebla, Oaxaca or Veracruz, take the Viaducto Alemán east. This is most conveniently accessed off Avenida Cuauhtémoc (Eje 1 Poniente). Immediately after crossing over the Viaducto – by the Liverpool department store – turn left for the access ramp. Take the Viaducto to Calzada Zaragoza, then follow the signs for Oaxaca until you join the Puebla highway.

NORTH From Querétaro, the last toll booth as you approach the city is at Tepotzotlán. Continue south, following signs for Ciudad Satélite and Toreo. Move into the lateral road (running parallel to the main road) at the first signs indicating the 'Río San Joaquín' exit, which appears just north of the giant dome of the Toreo arena. Take this exit; the ramp curves left over the Periférico. Keep right as you go over, then follow signs for 'Circuito Interior.' After passing the Corona factory, take the Thiers exit. Keep left, following signs for Reforma, and you'll end up on Río Misisipi, which intersects Reforma at the Diana roundabout. Turn left on Reforma to get to the Centro Histórico, or continue straight ahead for Roma.

Leaving the city, the simplest option is to take Reforma to the west end of Bosque de Chapultepec, then a right exit to pick up the Periférico northbound.

BUSES FROM MEXICO CITY

DESTINATION	TERMINAL IN MEXICO CITY	BUS COMPANY	FARE (M$)	DURATION	FREQUENCY (DAILY)
Acapulco	Sur	Estrella de Oro, Futura	449-555	5hr	hourly
	Norte	Futura	415	5hr	hourly
Bahías de Huatulco	Sur	OCC, Turistar	748-1020	14-15hr	3
	Norte	OCC	728	16hr	4:45pm
Campeche	Oriente (TAPO)	ADO, ADO GL	1118-1342	16-18hr	6
	Norte	ADO	1130	17-18hr	2
Cancún	Oriente (TAPO)	ADO, ADO GL	1520-1720	24-27hr	5
Chetumal	Oriente (TAPO)	ADO	1206-1254	20hr	2
Chihuahua	Norte	Ómnibus de México	1295	20hr	12
Cuernavaca	Sur	Pullman de Morelos	86	1¼hr	frequent
Guadalajara	Norte	ETN, Primera Plus	543-650	7hr	frequent
	Poniente	ETN	650	7hr	5
Guanajuato	Norte	ETN, Primera Plus	381-455	5hr	22
Matamoros	Norte	ETN, Futura	910-1185	12-14hr	3
Mazatlán	Norte	Elite, Turistar	965-1130	13-15½hr	hourly
Mérida	Oriente (TAPO)	ADO, ADO GL	1262-1560	19½-20hr	6
Monterrey	Norte	ETN, Futura	810-1055	12-12½hr	15
Morelia	Poniente	ETN	370	4½hr	frequent
Nuevo Laredo	Norte	Futura, Turistar	995-1295	15-15½hr	7
Oaxaca	Oriente (TAPO)	ADO, ADO GL, ADO Platino	434-770	6-6½hr	hourly
	Sur	ADO GL, OCC	458-532	6½hr	7
Palenque	Oriente (TAPO)	ADO	846	13hr	6:10pm
Papantla	Norte	ADO	242	5½-6hr	5
Pátzcuaro	Norte	Autovías, Primera Plus	374	5hr	11
	Poniente	Autovías	370	5hr	18
Puebla	Airport	Estrella Roja	200	2hr	11
	Oriente (TAPO)	ADO, ADO GL, AU	110-148	2hr	frequent
Puerto Escondido	Sur	OCC, Turistar	760-975	14hr	4

DESTINATION	TERMINAL IN MEXICO CITY	BUS COMPANY	FARE (M$)	DURATION	FREQUENCY (DAILY)
Puerto Vallarta	Norte	ETN, Futura	954-1135	12-12½hr	6
Querétaro	Norte	ETN, Primera Plus	197-235	2¾-3hr	frequent
	Airport	Primera Plus	269	3hr	hourly
	Poniente	Primera Plus	197	3hr	17
San Cristóbal de las Casas	Oriente (TAPO)	ADO GL, OCC	944-1130	12½-14hr	6
	Norte	OCC	970	13-13½hr	4
San Luis Potosí	Norte	ETN, Primera Plus	380-445	5hr	hourly
San Miguel de Allende	Norte	ETN, Primera Plus	288-345	4hr	9
Tapachula	Oriente (TAPO)	ADO GL, ADO Platino, OCC	996-1440	16½-18hr	9
Taxco	Sur	Estrella Blanca, Estrella de Oro	159	3hr	10
Teotihuacán	Norte	Autobuses Teotihuacán	36	1hr	hourly 6am-6pm
Tepoztlán	Sur	OCC	94	1¼hr	frequent
Tijuana	Norte	Elite	1764	41hr	12
Toluca	Airport	TMT Caminante	135	1¾hr	hourly
	Poniente	ETN, Flecha Roja	42-58	1hr	frequent
Tuxtla Gutiérrez	Oriente (TAPO)	ADO, ADO GL, ADO Platino, OCC	882-1310	11½-13hr	12
Uruapan	Poniente	Autovías, ETN	431-520	6hr	22
Veracruz	Oriente (TAPO)	ADO, ADO GL, ADO Platino	378-634	5½hr	frequent
	Sur	ADO GL	452	5½hr	3
Villahermosa	Oriente (TAPO)	ADO, ADO GL, ADO Platino, AU	628-1256	10-13¼hr	24
Xalapa	Oriente (TAPO)	ADO, ADO GL, ADO Platino, AU	230-466	4½-5hr	frequent
Zacatecas	Norte	Ómnibus de México	540	7hr	14
Zihuatanejo	Sur	Estrella de Oro, Futura	630-699	9hr	5
	Poniente	Autovías	480	9hr	4

Coming from Pachuca, Hidalgo and northern Veracruz, the highway feeds into Avenida Insurgentes. Follow the signs for the Centro Histórico and Zona Rosa. Leaving the city, take Insurgentes north (also the route to Teotihuacán).

SOUTH After the last *caseta* on the autopista from Cuernavaca, continue straight, taking a right exit for Calzada Tlalpan (some signs are hidden behind trees). Calzada Tlalpan eventually feeds into Avenida 20 de Noviembre, which ends at the Zócalo. Leaving town, turn right (south) at the Zócalo onto Pino Suárez, which becomes Calzada Tlalpan. About 20km south, signs indicate a left exit for the *cuota* (toll highway) to Cuernavaca.

WEST Coming from Toluca, about 4km past the high-rises of Santa Fe, keep left and follow signs for Paseo de la Reforma. Go straight down Reforma, past the Fuente de Petróleos and Bosque de Chapultepec to reach downtown. Heading west out of the city, take Paseo de la Reforma, which feeds right into the *cuota* (toll highway) to Toluca.

ⓘ Getting Around

Mexico City has an inexpensive, easy-to-use metro and an equally cheap and practical bus system plying all the main routes. Taxis are plentiful, but some are potentially hazardous (see p121).

To/From the Airport

The metro is convenient for getting to the airport, though hauling luggage amid rush-hour crowds can be a Herculean task. Authorized taxis provide a painless, relatively inexpensive alternative.

METRO The airport metro station is Terminal Aérea, on Línea 5 (yellow). It's 200m from terminal 1: leave by the exit at the end of Sala A (domestic arrivals) and continue past the taxi stand to the station.

To the city center, follow signs for 'Dirección Politécnico'; at La Raza (seven stops away) change for Línea 3 (green) toward 'Dirección Universidad.' Metro Hidalgo, at the west end of the Alameda, is three stops south; it's also a transfer point for Línea 2 (blue) to the Zócalo.

To get to the Zona Rosa from the airport, take Línea 5 to 'Pantitlán,' the end of the line. Change for Línea 1 (pink) and get off at metro Insurgentes.

There is no convenient metro link to Terminal 2, but red buses at the entrance of Terminal 2 go to metro Hangares (Línea 5).

TAXI Safe and reliable 'Transporte Terrestre' taxis, recognizable by their yellow doors and airplane logos, are controlled by a fixed-price ticket system.

Purchase taxi tickets from booths labeled 'Sitio 300,' located in Sala E1 (international arrivals), on your left as you exit customs, and by the Sala A (domestic arrivals) exit. Fares are determined by zones (shown on a map next to the booth). A ride to the Zócalo or Zona Rosa is M$194, and to the Condesa it's M$226. One ticket is valid for up to four passengers.

Taxi stands for the Sitio 300 taxis are outside Sala A and at the far end of the international terminal (Terminal 1). Porters may offer to take your ticket and luggage the few steps to the taxi, but hold on to the ticket and hand it to the driver. Drivers won't expect a tip for the ride, but will always welcome one.

To reserve a Transporte Terrestre taxi to the airport, call ☑5571-9344.

To/From the Bus Terminals

The metro is the fastest and cheapest way to or from any bus terminal, but it's tricky to maneuver through crowded stations and cars. Taxis are an easier option: all terminals have ticket booths for secure *taxis autorizados,* with fares set by zone (M$20 surcharge from 10pm to 6am). An agent at the exit will assign you a cab.

TERMINAL NORTE Metro Línea 5 (yellow) stops at Autobuses del Norte, just outside the terminal. To the center, follow signs for 'Dirección Pantitlán,' then change at La Raza for Línea 3 (green) toward 'Dirección Universidad.' (The La Raza connection is a six-minute hike through a 'Tunnel of Science.')

The taxi kiosk is in the central passageway; a cab for up to four people to the Alameda or Zócalo costs M$85.

TERMINAL ORIENTE (TAPO) This bus terminal is next door to metro station San Lázaro. To the center or Zona Rosa, take Línea 1 (pink) toward 'Dirección Observatorio.'

The authorized taxi booth is at the top (metro) end of the main passageway from the rotunda. The fare to the Zócalo is M$60; to the Zona Rosa it's M$70.

TERMINAL PONIENTE Observatorio metro station, the eastern terminus of Línea 1 (pink), is a couple of minutes' walk across a busy street (the pedestrian bridge has been closed until further notice). A taxi ticket to Colonia Roma costs M$70; to the Zócalo it's M$98.

TERMINAL SUR Terminal Sur is a two-minute walk from metro Tasqueña, the southern terminus of Línea 2, which stops at the Zócalo. For the Zona Rosa, transfer at Pino Suárez and take Línea 1 to Insurgentes (Dirección Observatorio). Going to the terminal, take the 'Autobuses del Sur' exit, which leads upstairs to a footbridge. Descend the last staircase on the left, then walk through a street market to reach the building.

Authorized taxis from Terminal Sur cost M$95 to the Zona Rosa or Centro Histórico. Ticket booths are by the main exit and in Sala 3.

Bicycle

Bicycles can be a viable way to get around town and are often preferable to overcrowded, recklessly driven buses. Although careless drivers and potholes can make DF cycling an extreme sport, if you stay alert and keep off the major thoroughfares, it's manageable. The city government has encouraged bicycle use and it's definitely catching on.

Bikes are loaned free from a module on the west side of the Catedral Metropolitana from 10:30am to 6pm Monday to Saturday, and 9:30am to 4:30pm on Sunday. Leave a passport or driver's license for three hours of riding time. You'll also find modules at Plaza Villa de Madrid in Roma, and several along Paseo de la Reforma, near the Monumento a la Independencia and Auditorio Nacional.

The *ciclovía* is an extensive bike trail that follows the old bed of the Cuernavaca railroad as far as the Morelos border. It extends from Avenida Ejército Nacional in Polanco through the Bosque de Chapultepec, skirting the Periférico freeway from La Feria to Avenida San Antonio, with several steep bridges passing over the freeways.

Another path follows Avenida Chapultepec along a protected median from Bosque de Chapultepec to the Centro Histórico, though a detour through the streets of Colonia Roma is ignored by motorists. A third route runs along Paseo de la Reforma from the Auditorio Nacional to the Museo Rufino Tamayo.

Bus, Pesero & Trolleybus

Mexico City's thousands of buses and peseros (also called microbuses or combis) operate from around 5am till 10pm daily; electric trolleybuses generally run until midnight. Only a few routes run all night, notably those along Paseo de la Reforma. The metrobús passes along Avenida Insurgentes until midnight. This means you'll get anywhere by bus and/or metro during the day but will probably have to take a few taxis after hours.

Peseros are gray-and-green minibuses operated by private firms. They follow fixed routes, often starting or ending at metro stations, and will stop at virtually any street corner. Route information is randomly displayed on cards attached to the windshield. Fares are M$3 for trips of up to 5km, and M$3.50 for 5km to 12km. Add 20% to all fares between 11pm and 6am. Municipally operated trolleybuses and full-sized cream-and-orange buses (labeled 'RTP') only pick up at bus stops; fares are M$2 (M$4 for the express) regardless of distance traveled. Privately run green-and-yellow buses charge M$4 to M$5.

A recently installed alternative to peseros, Línea 1 of the metrobús (see www.metrobus.df.gob.mx for routes) plies a dedicated lane along Avenida Insurgentes from metro Indios Verdes in the northern DF down to the southern end of Tlalpan. Línea 2, which connects with Línea 1 at the Nuevo León station, runs west to east along Eje 4 Sur from metro Tacubaya to metro Tepalcates. Línea 3 operates on a north–south route from the Tenayuca station to Ethiopia, where you can transfer to Línea 2.

These 18m-long wheelchair-accessible Volvo vehicles stop at metro-style stations in the middle of the street, spaced at three- to four-block intervals. Access is by prepaid card, issued by machines at the entrance to the platforms, and rides cost M$5. Rechargeable cards (M$10) are placed on a sensor device for entry. The metrobús generally runs from 5am to midnight Monday to Friday, and 5am to 11:30pm on Saturday and Sunday.

Pesero routes ply practically every street that crisscrosses the Centro Histórico grid, while trolleybuses follow a number of the key *ejes* (priority roads) throughout the rest of the city.

Here are some useful routes:

Autobuses del Sur & Autobuses del Norte (trolleybus) Eje Central Lázaro Cárdenas between north and south bus terminals (stops at Plaza de las Tres Culturas, Plaza Garibaldi, Bellas Artes/Alameda, metro Hidalgo).

Metro Hidalgo–La Villa (bus) Paseo de la Reforma between Auditorio Nacional or metro Chapultepec and Basílica de Guadalupe (stops at Zona Rosa, Avenida Insurgentes, Alameda/metro Hidalgo, Plaza Garibaldi, Plaza de las Tres Culturas).

Metro Sevilla–P Masaryk (pesero) Between Colonia Roma and Polanco via Álvaro Obregón and Avenida Presidente Masaryk (stops at metro Niños Héroes, Avenida Insurgentes, metro Sevilla, Leibnitz).

Metro Tacubaya–Balderas–Escandón (pesero) Between Centro Histórico and Condesa, westbound via Puebla, eastbound via Durango (stops at Plaza San Juan, metro Balderas, metro Insurgentes, Parque España, Avenida Michoacán).

Car & Motorcycle

Touring Mexico City by car is strongly discouraged, unless you have a healthy reserve of patience. Even more than elsewhere in the country, traffic rules are seen as suggested behavior. Red lights may be run at will, no-turn signs are ignored and signals are seldom used. On occasion you may be hit with a questionable traffic fine. Nevertheless, you may want to rent a car here for travel outside the city. Avoid parking on the street; most midrange and top-end hotels have guest garages.

DRIVING RESTRICTIONS To help combat pollution, Mexico City operates its 'Hoy No Circula' (Don't Drive Today) program, banning many vehicles from being driven in the city between 5am and 10pm on one day each week. Additionally, vehicles of nine years and older are prohibited from operating one Saturday a month. Exempted from the restriction are cars with a *calcomanía de verificación* (emissions verification sticker), obtained under the city's vehicle-pollution assessment system.

For vehicles without the sticker (including foreign-registered ones), the last digit of the license-plate number determines the day when they cannot circulate. See the Locatel website (www.locatel.df.gob.mx, in Spanish) for restrictions.

DAY	PROHIBITED LAST DIGITS
Monday	5, 6
Tuesday	7, 8
Wednesday	3, 4
Thursday	1, 2
Friday	9, 0

Metro

The metro system (www.metro.df.gob.mx, in Spanish) offers the quickest way to get around Mexico City. Ridden by about 4.2 million passengers on an average weekday, it has 175 stations and more than 200km of track on 11 lines. Trains arrive every two to three minutes during rush hours. At M$3 a ride, it's one of the world's cheapest subways.

All lines operate from 5am to midnight weekdays, 6am to midnight Saturday and 7am to midnight Sunday. Platforms and cars can become alarmingly packed during rush hours (roughly 7:30am to 10am and 3pm to 8pm). At these times the forward cars are reserved for women and children, and men may not proceed beyond the 'Sólo Mujeres y Niños' gate.

With such crowded conditions, it's not surprising that pickpocketing occurs, so watch your belongings.

The metro is easy to use. Lines are color-coded and each station is identified by a unique logo. Signs reading 'Dirección Pantitlán,' 'Dirección Universidad' and so on name the stations at the end of the lines. Check a map for the direction you want. Buy a *boleto* (ticket), or several, at the *taquilla* (ticket window), feed it into the turnstile, and you're on your way. When changing trains, look for 'Correspondencia' (Transfer) signs. Maps of the vicinity around each station are posted near the exits.

Taxi

Mexico City has several classes of taxi. Cheapest are the cruising red-and-gold street cabs, though they're not recommended due to the risk of assaults (see p121). If you must hail a cab off the street, check that it has actual taxi license plates: numbers are preceded with the letters A or B. Check that the number on them matches the number painted on the bodywork. Also look for the *carta de identificación* (called the *tarjetón*), a postcard-sized ID that should be displayed visibly inside the cab, and ensure that the driver matches the photo. If the cab you've hailed does not pass these tests, get another one.

In *libre* cabs (street cabs), fares are computed by *taxímetro* (meter), which should start at M$6 to M$7. The total cost of a 2km or 3km ride in moderate traffic – say, from the Zócalo to the Zona Rosa – should be M$30 to M$40. Between 11pm and 6am, add 20%.

Radio taxis, which come in many different colors, cost about two or three times as much as the others, but this extra cost adds an immeasurable degree of security. When you phone, the dispatcher will tell you the cab number and the type of car.

Some reliable radio-taxi firms, available 24 hours, are listed below. Maps in this chapter show the location of some key *sitios* (taxi services) for radio taxis.

Radio Maxi Seguridad (☎5768-8557, 5552-1376)

Sitio Parque México (☎5286-7129, 5286-7164)

Taxi-Mex (☎9171-8888)

Taxis Radio Unión (☎5514-8124)

Around Mexico City

Best Places to Eat

» El Mural de los Poblanos (p151)

» Restaurante y Cabañas San Diego (p144)

» La Sibarita (p169)

Best Places to Stay

» Casa Limón (p192)

» Hotel Hacienda de Cortés (p176)

» Posada del Tepozteco (p169)

Why Go?

With its daunting size and seemingly endless sprawl, the megalopolis of Mexico City might seem like a challenge to escape from, but even if you're in Mexico's capital for only a week, the ancient ruins, *pueblos mágicos* (magical villages) and stunning mountain landscape of the surrounding area should not be missed. Mexico City – like many capitals – has little in common with even its closest neighbors.

While many visitors to the region take a day trip to the awe-inspiring archaeological complex at Teotihuacán, the area offers much more – from the captivating colonial cities of Taxco, Puebla and Cuernavaca to the eccentric, small towns of Valle de Bravo and Tepoztlán. For those eager to taste some crisp, particulate-free mountain air, there are *pueblitos* (small towns) like Cuetzalan and Real del Monte, the volcanic giants such as Popocatépetl and Iztaccíhuatl, and the lesser-known ruins of Xochicalco and Cantona to visit.

When to Go
Puebla City

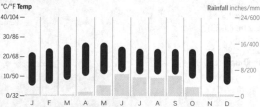

May–Oct During the rainy season afternoon showers wash the air clean and bring wild mushrooms to the forests.

Sep The weeks leading up to Independence Day are the time to taste the seasonal specialty *chiles en nogada*.

Nov–Apr The drier months are nominally cooler, making for pleasant daytime city exploration and casual hikes.

Around Mexico City Highlights

1 Enjoy a sunset drink on **Cuetzalan's** (p165) tiny *zócalo* amid the dramatic scenery of the Sierra Madre Oriental

2 Be blown away by the spectacular pyramids at **Teotihuacán** (p137) or discover some of central Mexico's most magnificent, lesser-known ancient sites at **Xochicalco** (p179) and **Cantona** (p164)

3 Wander the steep cobblestone streets of **Taxco** (p181) and scope out the city's famed silver shops

4 Have a close encounter with Mexico's New Age culture in **Tepoztlán** (p167) and **Malinalco** (p191)

5 Hang out lakeside at the gorgeous weekend getaway of **Valle de Bravo** (p190)

6 Visit the grand haciendas and rural *pulque* producers in the **Tlaxcalan countryside** (p164)

7 Climb volcanic peaks, like **La Malinche** (p163), **Nevado de Toluca** (p190) or **Iztaccíhuatl** (p157)

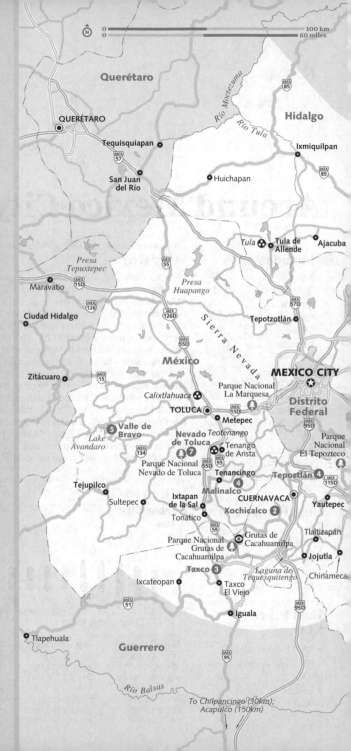

History

Long a cultural and economic crossroads, the region around present-day Mexico City has hosted a succession of important indigenous civilizations (notably the Teotihuacán, Toltec and Aztec). By the late 15th century, the Aztecs had managed to dominate all but one of central Mexico's states. Many archaeological sites and museums preserve remnants of pre-Hispanic history; Puebla's Museo Amparo (p147) provides an excellent overview of the region's history and cultures.

Postconquest, the Spanish transformed central Mexico, establishing ceramic industries at Puebla, mines at Taxco and Pachuca, and haciendas producing wheat, sugar and cattle throughout the region. The Catholic Church used the region as a base for its missionary activities, and left a series of imposing churches and fortified monasteries. Today, most towns retain a central plaza surrounded by colonial buildings.

❶ Getting There & Around

The cities, towns and (to a lesser extent) even the villages around Mexico City enjoy excellent bus links to both the capital and each other. Even the very smallest backwaters have daily services to Mexico City and to the closest transportation hub. While airports also serve Puebla, Toluca, Cuernavaca and Pachuca in the region, it's nearly always cheaper and easier to fly to Mexico City and travel onward from there. For all but the most obscure sights, traveling by bus is the easiest and most affordable option.

NORTH OF MEXICO CITY

The biggest attraction north of Mexico City is the extraordinary complex at Teotihuacán, once the largest metropolis in the Americas and one of Mexico's most spectacular pre-Hispanic sights. Farther north, the well-preserved stone statues at Tula also draw visitors.

Far less visited but equally impressive are Parque Nacional El Chico and the mining village of Mineral del Chico – the perfect escape from the big city, with stunning views, wide open spaces and friendly locals.

Pachuca, the fast-growing capital of dynamic Hidalgo state, has brightly painted houses, an attractive colonial center and a great line in Cornish pasties. From Pachuca, well-paved routes snake east and north to the Gulf coast, traversing some spectacular country as the fringes of the Sierra Madre Oriental mountain range tumble to the coastal plain.

Tepotzotlán

📞55 / POP 38,000 / ELEV 2300M

This *pueblo mágico* is an easy day trip from Mexico City, but feels far from the chaotic streets of the capital, despite the fact that urban sprawl creeps closer to Tepotzotlán's colonial center every year.

◉ Sights

Museo Nacional del Virreinato   MUSEUM
(National Museum of the Viceregal Period; 📞5876-0245; www.virreinato.inah.gob.mx; Plaza Hidalgo 99; admission M$49; ◷9am-6pm Tue-Sun) There's a very simple reason to visit this wonderful museum comprising the restored Jesuit **Iglesia de San Francisco Javier** and an adjacent **monastery**. Much of the folk art and fine art on display – silver chalices, pictures created from inlaid wood, porcelain, furniture and religious paintings and statues – comes from Mexico City cathedral's large collection, and the standard is very high.

Once a Jesuit college of indigenous languages, the complex dates from 1606. Additions were made over the following 150 years, creating a showcase for the developing architectural styles of New Spain.

Don't miss the **Capilla Doméstica**, with a Churrigueresque main altarpiece that boasts more mirrors than a carnival funhouse. The facade is a phantasmagoric array of carved saints, angels, plants and people, while the interior walls and the Camarín del Virgen adjacent to the altar are swathed with a circus of gilded ornamentation.

✯ Festivals & Events

Pastorelas (Nativity Plays)   RELIGIOUS
Tepotzotlán's highly regarded *pastorelas* (nativity plays) are performed inside the former monastery in the weeks leading up to Christmas. Tickets, which include Christmas dinner and piñata smashing, can be purchased at La Hostería del Convento de Tepotzotlán after November 1 (see p135) or via **Ticketmaster** (📞5325-9000; www.ticketmaster.com.mx).

🛏 Sleeping

Tepotzotlán is geared toward day trippers, but there are a couple of good-value hotels.

Hotel Posada San José HOTEL $
(☎5876-0520; Plaza Virreinal 13; r from M$300-400) Housed in a handsome colonial building on the south side of the *zócalo* (main plaza), this centrally located budget hotel has 12 small, spare rooms with tiled bathrooms. Some of the rooms – especially those overlooking the plaza and those near the hotel's water pump – are noisy.

Hotel Posada del Virrey HOTEL $
(☎5876-1864; Av Insurgentes 13; r with/without Jacuzzi M$500/350; P 📶) A short walk from the *zócalo,* this modern, motel-style posada (inn) is popular with weekenders. Rooms can be a bit dark but they're clean, quiet and have televisions.

Eating & Drinking

It's best to avoid the many almost indistinguishable, tourist-centric restaurants on the *zócalo,* where the food is mediocre and prices are high. Along with the restaurants listed below, a better option is to join the locals at the market behind the Palacio Municipal, where food stalls serve rich *pozole* (a thin stew of hominy, pork or chicken), *gorditas* (round masa cakes), and freshly squeezed juices all day long.

Taquería la Dueña TAQUERÍA $
(Plaza Virreinal 13; tacos M$10-35; ⏲1pm-1am Fri & Sat, 1pm-midnight Sun-Thu) Around the corner from Posada San José, this popular *taquería* (taco place) serves a delicious range of tacos and *asadas* (grilled meats) at market prices. The wafting smell of smoky, grilled cuts of beef – along with the hordes of happy carnivores – makes la Dueña hard to miss. The daily set menu (M$40) is a bargain.

La Hostería del Convento de Tepotzotlán MEXICAN $$
(www.hosteriadelconvento.com.mx; Plaza Virreinal 1; mains M$90-155; ⏲11am-8pm) Housed within the monastery's bougainvillea-walled courtyard, La Hostería serves traditional brunch and lunch fare – hearty soups, young chicken with *manzano* chilies, and *cecina adobada* (Oaxacan-style chili-marinated pork) – to an elite clientele. On Sunday, there's often live music.

Argento & Escarto PUB
(Plaza Virreinal 7; ⏲1pm-midnight Tue-Sun) This straight-forward snack bar is the place for casual sidewalk beer-drinking. *Chelas preparadas* (beer cocktails) come in two sizes: five liter or one liter. The music – remixes of Top 40 classics – is loud and the crowd is all ages, from college-aged kids snapping photos and chain-smoking cigarettes, to older couples mooning over bad wine.

Getting There & Around

Tepotzotlán is on the Mexico–Querétaro highway. From Mexico City's Terminal Norte, second-class Autotransportes Valle del Mezquital (AVM) buses (M$36, 40 minutes) stop at the new Tepotzotlán bus terminal every 20 minutes en route to Tula. First class *(directo)* buses stop every 40 minutes. From the station, catch a combi (M$7) or secure taxi (M$35) to the *zócalo.*

Tula

☎773 / POP 26,000 / ELEV 2060M

A major city of the ancient, central-Mexican culture widely known as Toltec, Tula is best known for its fearsome 4.5m-high stone warrior figures. Though less spectacular and far smaller than Teotihuacán, Tula is nonetheless fascinating and worth the effort of a day trip for those interested in ancient Mexican history. The modern town of Tula de Allende is surrounded by a Pemex refinery and an odoriferous petrochemical plant but the center, which has undergone improvements in recent years, is fine for an overnight stay.

History

Tula was an important city from about AD 900 to 1150, reaching a peak population of 35,000. Aztec annals tell of a king called Topiltzin – fair-skinned, black-bearded and long-haired – who founded a Toltec capital in the 10th century. There's debate, however, about whether Tula was this capital.

The Toltecs were empire-builders upon whom the Aztecs looked with awe, going so far as to claim them as royal ancestors. Topiltzin was supposedly a priest-king, dedicated to peaceful worship (the Toltecs sacrificed only animals) of the feathered serpent god Quetzalcóatl. Tula is known to have housed followers of the less-likable Tezcatlipoca (Smoking Mirror), god of warriors, witchcraft and life and death – worshiping Tezcatlipoca required human sacrifices. The story goes that Tezcatlipoca appeared in various guises in order to provoke Topiltzin. As a naked chili-seller, he aroused the lust of Topiltzin's daughter and eventually married her. As an old man, he persuaded the teetotaling Topiltzin to get drunk.

The humiliated leader eventually left for the Gulf coast, where he set sail eastward on a raft of snakes, promising one day to return and reclaim his throne. (This myth caused the Aztec emperor Moctezuma much consternation when Hernán Cortés appeared on the Gulf coast in 1519.) Tula was abandoned in the early 13th century, seemingly after a violent destruction by a neighboring indigenous group.

◉ Sights

Zona Arqueológica ARCHAEOLOGICAL SITE
(admission M$41, video use M$35; ⏰9am-5pm)
Two kilometers north of the center, the ruins of the main ceremonial center of Tula are perched on a hilltop, with views over rolling countryside (as well as the industrial sprawl nearby).

Throughout the site, explanatory signs are in English, Spanish and Náhuatl. Near the main museum and the entrance to the site, you'll find souvenir markets on the weekends. Both of the onsite museums are free with site admission. At the time of research, the site was undergoing excavation and was somewhat disheveled. If making a special trip, it may be worth calling ahead to check if the work is complete.

The main **site museum** displaying ceramics, metalwork, jewelry and large sculptures is near the main entrance, at the far side of the *zona* from downtown.

Ball Court
From the museum, the first large structure you'll reach is the **Juego de Pelota No 1** (Ball Court No 1). Archaeologists believe its walls were decorated with sculpted panels that were removed under Aztec rule.

Pirámide B
At the top of **Pirámide B**, also known as the Temple of Quetzalcóatl or Tlahuizcalpantecuhtli (the Morning Star), the remains of three columnar roof supports – which once depicted feathered serpents with their heads on the ground and their tails in the air – remain standing. The four basalt warrior telamones (male figures used as supporting columns) at the top, and the four pillars behind, supported the temple's roof. Wearing headdresses, breastplates shaped like butterflies and short skirts held in place by sun disks, the warriors hold spear-throwers in their right hands and knives and incense bags in their left. The telamon on the left side is a replica of the original, now in Mexico City's Museo Nacional de Antropología (p75). The columns behind the telamones

depict crocodile heads (which symbolize the Earth), warriors, symbols of warrior orders, weapons and Quetzalcóatl's head.

On the pyramid's north wall are some of the carvings that once surrounded the structure. These show the symbols of the warrior orders: jaguars, coyotes, eagles eating hearts, and what may be a human head in Quetzalcóatl's mouth.

Gran Vestíbulo
Now roofless, the **Gran Vestíbulo** (Great Vestibule) extends along the front of the pyramid, facing the plaza. The stone bench carved with warriors originally ran the length of the hall, possibly to seat priests and nobles observing ceremonies in the plaza.

Coatepantli
Near the north side of Pirámide B is the **Coatepantli** (Serpent Wall), which is 40m long, 2.25m high and carved with rows of geometric patterns and a row of snakes devouring human skeletons. Traces remain of the original bright colors with which most of Tula's structures were painted.

Palacio Quemado
Immediately west of Pirámide B, the **Palacio Quemado** (Burned Palace) is a series of halls and courtyards with more low benches and relief carvings, one depicting a procession of nobles. It was probably used for ceremonies or reunion meetings.

Sala de Orientación Guadalupe Mastache
On the far side of the plaza is a path leading to the **Sala de Orientación Guadalupe Mastache**, a small museum named after one of the archaeologists who pioneered excavations here. It includes large items taken from the site, including some huge caryatid feet and a visual representation of how the site might have looked in its prime.

Tula's fortress-like **cathedral**, just off the *zócalo*, was part of the 16th-century monastery of San José. Inside, its vault ribs are decorated in gold.

🛏 Sleeping

Hotel Casablanca HOTEL $
(☎732-11-86; www.casablancatula.com; Pasaje Hidalgo 11; s/d/tr M$350/400/450; ℗🐶) Contrary to what its name suggests, this comfortable business hotel is orange and far more practical than it is grand. Right in the heart of Tula, and located at the end of a

narrow pedestrian street, Casablanca offers 36 rooms, all with TV, a private bathroom and free wi-fi (the connection is best in the rooms closest to the lobby). Parking access is around back, via Avenida Zaragoza.

Hotel Real Catedral HOTEL $$
(✆732-08-13; www.tulaonline.com/hotelcatedral; Av Zaragoza 106; r M$699, ste M$825-1287; P❋❂) Directly off the plaza, the Real Catedral is tasteful and comfortable, with some luxurious perks (cable TV, a small gym, in-room coffeemakers, hairdryers and safes) for the price. Many of the inside rooms lack natural light, but the suites offer balconies and street views. There's also a great selection of black-and-white photos of Tula in the lobby. The price includes a continental breakfast.

Best Western Tula BUSINESS HOTEL $$
(✆732-45-75; www.bestwesterntula.com; Av Zaragoza s/n; r US$65; P❋❂) This business-friendly relative newcomer has 18 modern rooms on Tula's main street. Small and friendly enough not to feel like an anonymous chain hotel, this cozy Best Western is giving Real Catedral a run for its money. A price war between the two hotels means that prices at each are constantly in flux and often identical.

 Eating

Cocina Económica Las Cazuelas MEXICAN $
(Pasaje Hidalgo 129; menu del día M$35; ⊘7am-7:30pm Mon-Fri; to 7pm Sat, to 6pm Sun) Come here for an excellent *menu del día* (menu of the day) that includes your choice of soup, main plate – options include dishes like chicken in *adobo, chiles rellenos* (cheese-filled chiles) and *milanesa* (a thin cut of fried, breaded meat) – and *agua del día* (water flavored with fresh fruit). The upstairs balcony, away from the kitchen, is cooler than the steamy, main dining room. The house-made salsas – green and red – are tasty.

Mana VEGETARIAN $
(Pasaje Hidalgo 13; menu del día M$45; ⊘9am-5pm Sun-Fri; ❂) This simple vegetarian restaurant serves a generous *menu del día* that includes wholewheat bread, vegetable soup and a pitcher of natural fruit juice. There's also a selection of veggie burgers, taquitos, quesadillas, soups and salads. Everything's fresh, hearty and homemade.

❶ Getting There & Away

Tula's **bus depot** (Xicoténcatl 14) is a short walk from downtown. First-class Ovnibus (✆732-96-00; www.gvm.com.mx) buses travel to/from Mexico City's Terminal Norte (M$71, 1¾ hours, every 40 minutes) and to/from Pachuca (M$83, 1¾ hours, hourly). AVM runs 2nd-class buses to the same destinations every 15 minutes.

❶ Getting Around

If you arrive in Tula by bus, the easiest way to get around is on foot. To reach the *zócalo* from the station, turn right on Xicoténcatl, then immediately left on Rojo del Río and walk two blocks to Hidalgo. Take a right on Hidalgo, which dead-ends at Plaza de la Constitución, Tula's main square.

To reach the Zona Arqueológica continue across the plaza to Quetzalcóatl, an attractive, recently renovated pedestrian street that leads to a footbridge over the Tula river. Take the stairs up the hillside to the right, and continue along Toltan-Del Tesoro to the site's secondary entrance.

Unfortunately, the town's bus station lacks an *empaque* (baggage check), which is problematic for daytrippers traveling with luggage.

Teotihuacán
✆594 / ELEV 2300M

This complex of awesome pyramids set amid what was once Mesoamerica's greatest city is just 50km northeast of Mexico City and is among the world's most-touristed destinations. The sprawling site compares to the ruins of the Yucatán and Chiapas in terms of its significance and anyone lucky enough to come here will be inspired by the astonishing technological might of the Teotihuacán (teh-oh-tee-wah-*kahn*) civilization.

Set in a mountain-ringed offshoot of the Valle de México, Teotihuacán is known for its two massive pyramids, the Pirámide del Sol (Pyramid of the Sun) and the Pirámide de la Luna (Pyramid of the Moon), which dominate the remains of the metropolis. Teotihuacán was Mexico's biggest ancient city and the capital of what was probably Mexico's largest pre-Hispanic empire. (See p801 for an outline of its importance.) Exploring the site is fascinating, although rebuffing the indefatigable hawkers can be exhausting and crowds can be huge, especially in the middle of the day. As usual, going early pays off, especially as the midday sun can be intense.

Teotihuacán

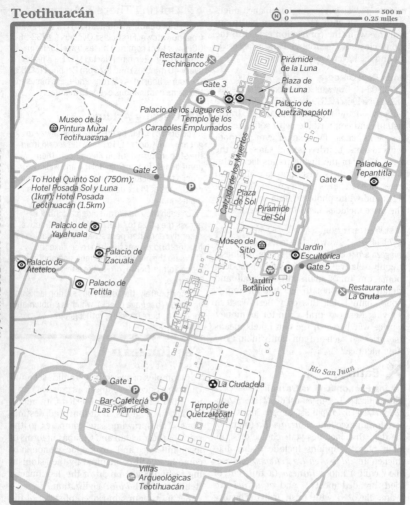

The city's grid plan was plotted in the early part of the 1st century AD, and the Pirámide del Sol was completed – over an earlier cave shrine – by AD 150. The rest of the city was developed between about AD 250 and 600. Social, environmental and economic factors hastened its decline and eventual collapse in the 8th century.

The city was divided into quarters by two great avenues that met near La Ciudadela (the Citadel). One of them, running roughly north–south, is the famous Calzada de los Muertos (Avenue of the Dead) – so called because the later Aztecs believed the great buildings lining it were vast tombs, built by giants for Teotihuacán's first rulers. The major structures are typified by a *talud-tablero* style, in which the rising portions of stepped, pyramid-like buildings consist of both sloping *(talud)* and upright *(tablero)* sections. They were often covered in lime and colorfully painted. Most of the city was made up of residential compounds, some of which contained elegant frescoes.

Centuries after its fall, Teotihuacán remained a pilgrimage site for Aztec royalty, who believed that all of the gods had sacrificed themselves here to start the sun moving at the beginning of the 'fifth world,' inhabited by the Aztecs. It remains an important pilgrimage site: thousands of New Age devotees flock here each year to celebrate the vernal equinox (between March 19 and March 21) and to soak up the mystical energies believed to converge here.

Though ancient Teotihuacán covered more than 20 sq km, most of what can be seen today lies along nearly 2km of the Calzada de los Muertos. Buses arrive at a traffic circle by the southwest entrance (Gate 1); four other entrances are reached by the ring road around the site. There are parking lots and ticket booths at each entrance. Your ticket allows you to re-enter via any of them on the same day. The site museum is just inside the main east entrance (Gate 5).

Crowds at the **ruins** (admission M$51; ☺7am-5pm) are thickest from 10am to 2pm, and it is busiest on Sunday, holidays and around the vernal equinox. Due to the heat and altitude, it's best to take it easy while exploring the expansive ruins. Bring a hat and water – most visitors walk several kilometers, and the midday sun can be brutal. Afternoon rain showers are common from June to September. There's a M$45 fee for the use of a video camera and parking costs an additional M$45.

⊙ Sights

Pirámide del Sol   PYRAMID

The world's third-largest pyramid, surpassed in size only by Egypt's Cheops and the pyramid of Cholula (p155), overshadows the east side of the Calzada de los Muertos. The base is 222m long on each side, and it's now just over 70m high. The pyramid was cobbled together around AD 100, from three million tons of stone, without the use of metal tools, pack animals or the wheel.

The Aztec belief that the structure was dedicated to the sun god was validated in 1971, when archaeologists uncovered a 100m-long underground tunnel leading from the pyramid's west flank to a cave directly beneath its center, where they found religious artifacts. It's thought that the sun was worshiped here before the pyramid was built and that the city's ancient inhabitants traced the origins of life to this grotto.

When Teotihuacán was at it's height, the pyramid's plaster was painted bright red, which must have been a radiant sight at sunset. Clamber up the pyramid's 248 steps –

yes, we counted – for an inspiring overview of the ancient city.

Pirámide de la Luna   PYRAMID

The Pyramid of the Moon, at the north end of the Calzada de los Muertos, is smaller than the Pirámide del Sol, but it's more gracefully proportioned – far more aesthetically pleasing and not nearly as hulkish. Completed around AD 300, its summit is nearly the same height as Pirámide del Sol because it's built on higher ground.

The **Plaza de la Luna**, located just in front of the pyramid, is a handsome arrangement of 12 temple platforms. Some experts attribute astronomical symbolism to the total number of 13 (made up of the 12 platforms plus the pyramid), a key number in the day-counting system of the Mesoamerican ritual calendar. The altar in the plaza's center is thought to have been the site of religious dancing.

Calzada de los Muertos   RUIN

Centuries ago, the Calzada de los Muertos must have seemed absolutely incomparable to its inhabitants, who were able to see its buildings at their best. Gate 1 brings you to the avenue in front of La Ciudadela. For 2km to the north, the avenue is flanked by former palaces of Teotihuacán's elite and other major structures, such as the Pirámide del Sol. The Pirámide de la Luna looms large at the northern end.

La Ciudadela   RUIN

The expansive, square complex called the Citadel is believed to have been the residence of the city's supreme ruler. Four wide walls, each 390m long and topped by 15 pyramids, enclose a huge open space, of which the main feature, to the east, is a pyramid called the **Templo de Quetzalcóatl**, which is believed to have been built around AD 250. The temple is flanked by two large complexes of rooms and patios, which may have been the city's administrative center.

The temple's most fascinating feature is a facade, which was revealed by excavating. The four surviving steps of this facade (there were originally seven) are adorned with striking carvings which were later covered (around AD 400) to obscure their spiritual significance. In the *tablero* panels, the sharp-fanged, feathered serpent deity, its head emerging from a necklace of 11 petals, alternates with a four-eyed, two-fanged creature identified either as the rain god Tláloc or the fire serpent, bearer of the sun on its daily journey across the sky. On the *talud* (the pyramid's slope) panels are side views of the plumed serpent.

Museo del Sitio
MUSEUM

(⊙9am-4:30pm) Further north along the Calzada de los Muertos toward the pyramids and across the river, there is a path to the right leading to the site museum, just south of the Pirámide del Sol. It's a refreshing stop midway through a site visit, and admission is included in the ticket. Nearby are the **Jardín Escultórica** (a lovely sculpture garden with Teotihuacán artifacts), a botanic garden, public toilets, a snack bar, picnic tables and a bookstore.

The museum is divided thematically, with explanations in English and Spanish. There are excellent displays of artifacts, fresco panels and an impressive large-scale model of the city set under a transparent walkway, from where the real Pirámide del Sol can be viewed through a wall-size window.

Palacio de Tepantitla
PALACE

This priest's residence, 500m northeast of the Pirámide del Sol, is home to Teotihuacán's most famous fresco, the worn **Paradise of Tláloc**. The mural flanks a doorway in a covered patio in the building's northeast corner. The rain god Tláloc, attended by priests, is shown on both sides. To the right of the door appears his paradise, a garden-like Eden with people, animals and fish swimming in a mountain-fed river. To the left of the door tiny human figures are engaged in a unique ball game. Frescoes in other rooms show priests with feather headdresses.

Palacio de Quetzalpapálotl
PALACE

Off the Plaza de la Luna's southwest corner is the Palace of the Quetzal Butterfly, thought to be the home of a high priest. A flight of steps leads up to a roofed portico with an abstract mural, and nearby a well-restored patio has columns carved with images of the quetzal bird or a hybrid quetzal butterfly.

The **Palacio de los Jaguares** (Jaguar Palace) and **Templo de los Caracoles Emplumados** (Temple of the Plumed Conch Shells) are behind and below the Palacio de Quetzalpapálotl. The lower walls of several chambers off the patio of the Jaguar Palace display parts of murals showing the jaguar god in feathered headdresses, blowing conch shells and apparently praying to the rain god Tláloc.

The **Templo de los Caracoles Emplumados**, entered from the Palacio de los Jaguares' patio, is a now-subterranean structure of the 2nd or 3rd century. Carvings on what was its facade show large shells – possibly used as musical instruments – decorated with feathers and four-petal flowers. The base on which the facade stands has a rainbow-colored mural of birds with water streaming from their beaks.

Museo de la Pintura Mural Teotihuacana
MUSEUM

(⊙9am-4:30pm) On the ring road near Gate 3, this impressive museum showcases murals from Teotihuacán, as well as reconstructions of murals you'll see at the ruins. Admission is included in the site ticket.

Palacio de Tetitla & Palacio de Atetelco
PALACE

Another group of palaces lies west of the site's main area, several hundred meters northwest of Gate 1. Many of the murals, discovered in the 1940s, are well preserved or restored, and perfectly intelligible. Inside the sprawling **Palacio de Tetitla**, no fewer than 120 walls are graced by murals with Tláloc, jaguars, serpents and eagles among the easiest figures to make out. Some 400m west is the **Palacio de Atetelco**, whose vivid jaguar or coyote murals – a mixture of originals and restorations – are in the Patio Blanco (White Patio) in the northwest corner.

About 100m further northeast are **Palacio de Zacuala** and **Palacio de Yayahuala**, a pair of enormous walled compounds that probably served as communal living quarters. Separated by the original alleyways, the two structures are made up of numerous rooms and patios but few entranceways.

🛏 Sleeping

The town of San Juan Teotihuacán, 2km from the archaeological zone, has a few good overnight options, which make sense if you want to start early at the site before the crowds arrive.

Hotel Posada Teotihuacán
HOTEL $

(☑956-04-60; Canteroco 5, San Juan Teotihuacán; s/d/tr M$299/399/499; ᴘ) The rooms at this centrally located, family-run, budget posada are smallish but clean and all have a TV and private bathroom.

Hotel Posada Sol y Luna
HOTEL $$

(☑956-23-68/71; www.posadasolyluna.com; Cantú 13, San Juan Teotihuacán; r from M$455; P🐾🛜) At the east end of town, en route to the pyramids, this well-run hotel has 16 fine but unexciting rooms, all with TV and bathroom. Junior suites have rather ancient Jacuzzis in them – not worth paying extra for unless you have rheumatism.

Hotel Quinto Sol
HOTEL $$$

(☑956-18-81; www.hotelquintosol.com.mx; Av Hidalgo 26, San Juan Teotihuacán; s/d/tr/q M$890/1100/1300/1400; P@🛜🏊) There's a reason the Quinto Sol is where most tourist groups stay when visiting the ruins at Teotihuacán. With its fine facilities – including a decent-size pool, large, well-appointed rooms, in-room security boxes and room service – this is one of the best-equipped hotels in town.

Villas Arqueológicas Teotihuacán
HOTEL $$$

(☑55-5836-9020; www.villasarqueologicas.com.mx; Periférico Sur s/n, Zona Arqueológica; r M$1107-1607; P@🛜🏊) Just south of the Zona Arqueológica, this elegant hotel has a small gym, heated outdoor pool, a lit tennis court, playground and a spa with temascal (a traditional Mexican sweat lodge). There's also a refined Mexican restaurant. Wi-fi signal is only accessible in the lobby.

✖ Eating

Eating near the ruins is usually a pricey and disappointing experience. You're much better off bringing a picnic, though there are a couple of adequate restaurants worth seeking out. The most convenient is on the 3rd floor of the old museum building near Gate 1, where the busy **Bar-Cafetería Las Pirámides** serves panoramic views of La Ciudadela.

TOP CHOICE **Restaurante Techinanco** MEXICAN $$

(Zona Arqueológica ring road; mains M$75-120; ⊙9am-6pm) A short walk from Gate 3, behind the Pirámide de la Luna, this homey restaurant serves excellent home cooking at comparatively reasonable prices. The small menu takes in local favorites from tacos *fritos* (fried tacos) to enchiladas, authentic homemade *moles* (chili-sauce dishes) and other traditional fare. Ask the ebullient owner, Emma (nicknamed Mayahuel), about her curative massage (from M$600); call 24 hours in advance to arrange a temas-cal (steam bath) for up to 10 people (around M$3000).

Restaurante La Gruta
MEXICAN $$$

(Zona Arqueológica ring road; www.lagruta.com.mx; mains M$182-269; ⊙10am-6pm) Set in a vast cave a short distance from Gate 5, this tourist-centric restaurant is unapologetically gimmicky. Yet the food, while pricey, is surprisingly good and there's a 40-minute folkloric dance show on Saturdays at 3:30pm and Sundays 3:30pm and 5:30pm. Reservations are a good idea.

ⓘ Information

There's an **information booth** (☑956-02-76; www.inah.gob.mx; ⊙7am-6pm) near the southwest entrance (Gate 1). Free Spanish-only site tours by authorized guides are available, with **reservations** (☑958-20-81).

Head to **Lonely Planet** (www.lonelyplanet.com/mexico/north-of-mexico-city/teotihuacan) for planning advice, author recommendations, traveler reviews and insider tips.

ⓘ Getting There & Away

During daylight hours, Autobuses México–San Juan Teotihuacán runs buses from Mexico City's Terminal Norte to the ruins (M$36, one hour) every hour from 7am to 6pm. When entering the Terminal Norte, turn left and walk to the second-to-last desk on the concourse. Make sure your bus is headed for 'Los Pirámides,' not the nearby town of San Juan Teotihuacán (unless you are heading to accommodations in San Juan). There have been recent reports from readers of armed robberies on these buses. Check with the US State Department (http://travel.state.gov) for current warnings.

At the ruins, buses arrive and depart from near Gate 1, also making stops at Gates 2 and 3. Return buses are more frequent after 1pm. The last bus back to Mexico City leaves at 6pm; some terminate at Indios Verdes metro station, but most continue to Terminal Norte.

ⓘ Getting Around

To reach the pyramids from San Juan Teotihuacán, take a taxi (M$30) or any combi (M$10) labeled 'San Martín' departing from Avenida Hidalgo, beside the central plaza. Combis returning to San Juan stop at Gates 1, 2 and 3.

Pachuca

☑771 / POP 260,000 / ELEV 2425M

The unassuming capital of Hidalgo state is scattered over steep, wide hills and crowned with a massive Mexican flag and towering statue of Christ. Its charming, brightly painted town center is visible for miles around, although growth in recent years has led to far-from-lovely urban sprawl developing beyond the candy-box houses of the old town.

Even so, Pachuca is an underappreciated provincial capital, an excellent staging post for trips north and east into the dramatic Sierra Madre Oriental, and an appealing place to spend a couple of days away from the tourist hustle.

Silver was unearthed nearby as early as 1534, and Real del Monte's mines still produce quite a respectable amount of ore. Pachuca was also the gateway through which *fútbol* (soccer) entered Mexico, introduced in the 19th century by miners from Cornwall, England. The Cornish population also gave the town its signature dish, meat pastries known as pasties (and recognizable to any Brit as a Cornish pasty, albeit with some typically Mexican fillings).

◉ Sights

The 40m-high **Reloj Monumental** (Clock Tower), built between 1904 and 1910 to commemorate the independence centennial, overshadows the north end of Pachuca's *zócalo*, Plaza de la Independencia, which is flanked by Avenida Matamoros on the east and Avenida Allende on the west. Guerrero runs parallel to Avenida Allende, 100m to the west. Some 700m to the south, Guerrero and Avenida Matamoros converge at the modern Plaza Juárez.

FREE **Cuartel del Arte**　　CULTURAL BUILDING
(cnr Hidalgo & Arista; ⊙10am-6pm Tue-Sun) This gorgeous, sprawling cultural center is an oasis of calm at Pachuca's bustling heart. Formerly the Convento de San Francisco, the complex includes three excellent museums, an art gallery, a theater, a library and several lovely plazas. It's worth looking into the impressive (and still functioning) Parroquia de San Francisco church as well. From Plaza de la Independencia, walk two blocks east to Miguel Hidalgo and about 650m south to the corner of Hidalgo and Arista.

One highlight is the excellent **Museo Nacional de la Fotografía**, which displays early imaging technology and stunning selections from the 1.5 million photos in the National Institute of Anthropology and History (INAH) archives. The images – some by Europeans and Americans, many more by pioneering Mexican photojournalists such as Nacho López and Agustín Victor Casasola – provide a fascinating glimpse of Mexico from 1873 to the present.

Museo de Minería　　MUSEUM
(☏715-09-76; www.distritominero.com.mx; Mina 110; adult/student M$20/15; ⊙10am-6pm Tue-Sun) Two blocks south and half a block east of the *zócalo*, Pachuca's mining museum provides a good overview of the industry that shaped the region. Headlamps, miners' shrines and old mining maps are on display, and photos depict conditions in the shafts from the early years to the present. There's a M$20 charge to use a camera and a M$50 charge for the use of a video camera. The museum also coordinates a '*ruta de turismo cultural minero*' (mining culture tourism route) in English, Spanish or French which visits several mining sites in the region.

⑂ Tours

Tranvía Turistico　　TRAM
(☏718-71-20; www.tranviaturisticopachuca.com; adult/child M$60/50; ⊙11am-6pm Wed-Fri, 10:30am-6:30pm Sat & Sun) Motor trolley tours depart hourly from the plaza's west side, traveling to 24 sites around the city, including the hilltop Cristo statue. The entire trip takes just over an hour.

🛏 Sleeping

Hotel de los Baños　　HOTEL **$**
(☏713-07-00; Av Matamoros 205; s M$260, d M$430-480, t/q M$490/545; P@🛜) With its beautifully tiled old-world lobby stuffed with antiques, the Baños is one of Pachuca's most charming budget hotels. While some of the 56 rooms have recently been renovated and others have antique fittings and lack natural light, all have cable TV, phones and clean bathrooms. Those with a preference should ask to see a couple of different room styles. Parking is an extra M$40. The hotel is located a block southeast of the *zócalo*.

Hotel Emily　　BUSINESS HOTEL **$$$**
(☏715-08-28, 800-501-63-39; www.hotelemily. com.mx; Plaza Independencia; r M$1251, ste M$1511; P🖨@🛜) On the south side of the *zócalo*, Emily has an excellent location, with balconies overlooking the Reloj Monumental. Rooms are modern and stylish, with flat-screen televisions, laundry service and gym access. The hotel restaurant has generic but surprisingly tasty food in a sterile setting.

✕ Eating

Pachuca's famous regional specialty *pastes* (pasties) are available all over town, including at the bus station. Baked in pizza ovens, they contain a variety of fillings – such as beans, pineapple and rice pudding – probably never imagined by the Cornish miners who brought this English culinary tradition to Mexico.

Mina La Blanca Restaurant Bar   MEXICAN $$
(www.restaurantlablanca.com.mx; Av Matamoros 201; mains M$55-165; ⊙8am-10pm) Pachuca's most famous restaurant, La Blanca has been serving traditional *hidalguense* food – including *pastes* and a mean *caldo de hongo* (mushroom soup) – since 1953. The walls, adorned with black-and-white photos and stained glass windows depicting industrial mining scenes, speak of Pachuca's history. This is also a great place to come for a low-key drink in the evening.

Mesón de los Ángeles   MEXICAN $
(Guerrero 723; comida corrida M$55; ⊙9am-8pm Mon-Sat) This homey hole-in-the-wall restaurant has vintage bullfighting posters plastered across its tiled blue-and-white interior and is perfect for a quick bite. From flavorful tacos to *mole verde* (pumpkin seed, walnut, almond, lettuce and tomatillo sauce), *picadillo* (ground beef) or *tinga* (tangy stew), everything here is home-style and authentic.

Aldamary Marisquería   SEAFOOD $$
(Blvd San Javier 100B; mains M$35-125; ⊙9am-7pm) Across the street from the main bus station, this bustling *marisquería* (seafood restaurant) serves amazingly fresh seafood – including shrimp empanadas, oyster cocktails, stuffed crab, *molcajetes* (ingredients cooked in a large, stone mortar), and eight kinds of soup, including a remarkable shrimp *caldo* (broth) – to a grateful local crowd. Despite its unlikely location in a provincial capital in the Hidalgo highlands, far from the nearest ocean, prices are surprisingly affordable.

Espresso Central   CAFE $
(Av Revolución 1008; snacks M$33-55; ⊙8am-midnight Mon-Sat; ☎) In a stylish, two-story shopping complex built of converted shipping containers, Espresso Central has something for everyone. In addition to quality espresso drinks, there are domestic microbrews and decent wine, chai and herbal teas and snacks, like crepes and waffles, sandwiches on bagels, ciabatta or pumpernickel.

At night, the cafe becomes a trendy night spot, where Pachuca's cool kids and suit-wearers hang out most nights of the week.

Eurobistrot   INTERNATIONAL $$$
(www.eurobistrot.com.mx; Av Revolución 805; mains M$94-205; ⊙2-11pm Mon-Sat, 2-6pm Sun; ☎) For something international, this upscale European-style bistro serves dishes ranging from fried calamari and Cobb salads to fish and chips and *medallón de res* (beef medallions) in mustard sauce. There's a decent wine list (though only two wines by the glass), jazz playing quietly in the background and an exciting dessert list, including a mean lemon meringue parfait.

❶ Information

ATMs are numerous around Plaza de la Independencia.
Internet (Technopolis; Allende 502; per hr M$5; ⊙9am-9pm Mon-Fri, 10am-9pm Sat & Sun)
Tourist Module (☎715-14-11; www.pachuca.gob.mx; Plaza de la Independencia; ⊙8:30am-4:30pm) Inside the clock tower; occasionally offers free city maps.

❶ Getting There & Away

Pachuca's **bus station** (☎713-34-71; Cam Cueso) is 20 minutes from downtown. There's an ADO 1st-class bus service to/from Mexico City's TAPO terminal (M$78, 1 hour 40 min, every half or one hour), Terminal Norte in Mexico City (M$78, 1½ hours, every 10 minutes), Poza Rica (M$174, five hours, two daily) and Puebla (M$134, two hours, three daily). Some routes have GL elite service with wi-fi. Buses also go frequently to and from Tula, Puebla and Querétaro.

Three scenic roads (Hwys 85, 105 and 130/132D) climb into the forested, often foggy, Sierra Madre Oriental.

❶ Getting Around

From the bus station, *colectivos* marked 'Centro' deposit passengers at Plaza de la Constitución (M$6), a short walk from the *zócalo;* in the reverse direction, hop on along Avenida Allende. By taxi the trip costs M$35.

Around Pachuca

PARQUE NACIONAL EL CHICO
☎771
You can take an easy and very lovely day trip or weekend retreat from Pachuca to the nearly 3000-hectare **El Chico National Park** (www.parqueelchico.gob.mx), which was

DON'T MISS

REAL DEL MONTE

This gorgeous mountain town is a tangle of houses, restaurants and pasty shops scattered across a pine tree-carpeted hillside. The air is thin here, so don't be surprised if you find yourself with a mild case of altitude sickness, but it's also clean and so crisp it seems colder than it likely is (bring a sweater, if not a coat).

Two kilometers past the Hwy 105 turnoff for Parque Nacional El Chico, Real del Monte (officially known as Mineral del Monte) was the scene of a miners' strike in 1776 (commemorated as the first strike in the Americas). Most of the town was settled in the 19th century, after a British company commandeered the mines. Cornish-style cottages line many of the steep, cobbled streets.

Hotel Paraíso Real Hospedaje-Cafetería (☎771-797-02-20; www.hotelparaisoreal. com; s/d Sun-Thu M$500/600, Fri & Sat M$600/700; P❂⚉) has a friendly, family-run vibe and clean, modern rooms with tiled floors, cable TV and room service. There's an eclectic mix of rooms; some have low ceilings, while others have Jacuzzis (an additional M$100), balconies and views over town. Another good option, just next door, is **Hotel Real del Monte** (☎771-715-56-54; www.hotelesecoturisticos.com.mx; r Sun-Thu M$600, Fri & Sat M$700; ⚉), a 15-room hotel run by the same high-standards company that operates the two main hotels in the nearby town of Mineral del Monte.

Second-class buses depart Pachuca's terminal for Real del Monte (M$9, 30 minutes, hourly). Combis (M$7.50, 30 minutes, every 30 minutes) leave from the northwest corner of Plaza de la Constitución, north of the *zócalo*.

established in 1898, and the charming old mining village **Mineral del Chico**, which is among the newest *pueblos mágicos*. The views are wonderful, the air is fresh and the mountains have some great hiking among spectacular rock formations and beautiful waterfalls.

◎ Sights

Colectivos marked 'Carboneras' (M$6) will drop you at the trailhead to the *mirador* (lookout) at **Peña del Cuervo**. From there, it's about a 25-minute walk.

Ask at the local hotels or the park's **visitors center** (Centro de Visitantes; Carretera Pachuca-Mineral del Chico Km 7.5), a 10-minute drive from the village, for details about possible guided outdoor activities.

⚏ Sleeping & Eating

Mineral del Chico is an established weekend getaway, but it can feel like a ghost town during the week, when visitors may be hard pressed to find an open place to eat after dark and even some hotels shutter their doors. However, the available hotels often lower their prices, and you'll have the trails and peaks almost entirely to yourself.

There are several **campgrounds** (campsites M$150, cabins M$400) with rudimentary facilities between Km 7 and Km 10 on Carretera Pachuca en route to Mineral del Chico.

TOP CHOICE **Restaurante y Cabañas San Diego** — CABAÑAS $$

(☎044-771-125-6173; Carretera Pachuca s/n; mains M$80-120) Set off from the highway beside a rushing creek on the way into town (look for signs at the turnoff to El Paraíso), San Diego is a true mountain escape. There's a new, modern restaurant beside the highway, but follow the stairs down the hill to the simple wood plank fish shack, where you can watch your meal – phenomenal fresh trout – being caught and prepared in one of nine ways. The *a la mexicana*, stuffed with Oaxacan cheese, onions, chilies and thick chunks of garlic is excellent. There are also two comfortable but rustic cabins available for rent, one smaller (up to four people, M$700) than the other (up to 10 people, M$1800).

Hotel El Paraíso — LODGE $$

(☎715-56-54; www.hotelesecoturisticos.com.mx; Carretera Pachuca s/n; r Sun-Thu M$850, Fri & Sat from M$950; P❂⚉) Nestled inside large, well-maintained grounds at the base of the mountain, with a fast-flowing stream running nearby, El Paraíso certainly has a location worthy of its name. The large, modern rooms lack individuality or charm, but they're very comfortable. The hotel also has the only internet in town, for those who demand a side of connectivity with their escapism. It's possible to pay extra for an all-inclusive experience.

Hospedaje El Chico
GUESTHOUSE $

(☑715-47-41; Corona del Rosal 1; r M$350-550) Just up from the church, this small, 10-room homestay is a decent budget option, with clean if unexciting rooms. If El Chico appears to be closed mid-week, ask next door at Casa Biseña. The same family owns both businesses.

❶ Getting There & Away

From Pachuca, blue-and-white *colectivos* to Mineral del Chico (M$11) depart every 20 minutes from 8am to 6pm from Calle Hidalgo, outside the Mercado Juárez on the corner of Avenida de la Raza.

There's no direct transit service from Real del Monte, but those wanting to avoid a trip back to Pachuca to transfer *colectivos* can hire a taxi for about M$150.

EAST OF MEXICO CITY

The views get seriously dramatic as you head east from the capital, the landscape peppered with the snow-capped, volcanic peaks of Popocatépetl, Iztaccíhuatl, La Malinche and Pico Orizaba – the country's highest summit. The rugged Cordillera Neovolcánica offers anything from invigorating alpine strolls to demanding technical climbs. Unpredictable Popocatépetl, however, remains off-limits due to volcanic activity.

The gorgeous colonial city of Puebla – Mexico's fifth-largest city – is the dominant regional center, a local transportation hub and a big tourist draw with its cathedral, rich culinary traditions, intriguing history and excellent museums. The surrounding state of Puebla is predominantly rural and home to approximately half a million indigenous people. This enduring presence provides the region with a rich handicraft legacy, with products including pottery, carved onyx and fine hand-woven and embroidered textiles.

Tlaxcala, the capital of the tiny state of the same name, has recently emerged as an attractive destination in its own right, with an exciting array of new restaurants, museums and boutique hotels. Far-flung Cuetzalan, meanwhile, is surrounded by lush, dramatic scenery and is among the most seemingly time-forgotten villages in the country.

Puebla

☑222 / POP 1.4 MILLION / ELEV 2160M

Once a bastion of conservatism, Catholicism and tradition, Puebla has come out of its colonial-era shell in recent years. The city retains a fantastically well-preserved center, a stunning cathedral and a wealth of beautiful churches, while younger *poblanos* (people from Puebla) are embracing the city's increasingly thriving art and nightlife scenes.

The city is well worth a visit, with 70 churches in the historic center alone, more than a thousand colonial buildings adorned with the *azulejos* (painted ceramic tiles) for which the city is famous, and a long culinary history that can be explored in any restaurant or food stall. For a city of its size, Puebla is far more relaxed and less gridlocked than you might expect.

History

Founded by Spanish settlers in 1531, as Ciudad de los Ángeles, with the aim of surpassing the nearby pre-Hispanic religious center of Cholula, the city became known as Puebla de los Ángeles ('La Angelópolis') eight years later, and quickly grew into an important Catholic center. Fine pottery had long been crafted from the local clay and after the colonists introduced new materials and techniques Puebla pottery evolved as both an art and an industry. By the late 18th century, the city had emerged as a major producer of glass and textiles. With 50,000 residents by 1811, Puebla remained Mexico's second-biggest city until Guadalajara overtook it in the late 19th century.

In 1862 General Ignacio de Zaragoza fortified the Cerro de Guadalupe against the French invaders and on May 5 that year his 2000 men defeated a frontal attack by 6000, many of whom were handicapped by diarrhea. This rare Mexican military success is the reason for annual (and increasingly corporate-sponsored and drunken) celebrations in the USA, where the holiday is far more significant than in Mexico and hundreds of streets are named 5 de Mayo. Few seem to remember that the following year the reinforced French took Puebla and occupied the city until 1867. *Touché!*

Modern Puebla is still centered around the city's Old Town, with the large, leafy *zócalo* and Mexico's tallest cathedral at its heart. The *centro histórico* is home to most of the attractions, hotels and restaurants of interest to international travelers, most of

Puebla

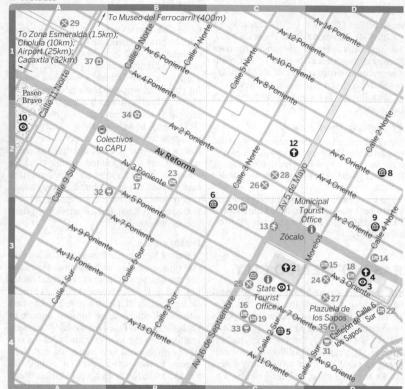

which are within a few blocks of the main plaza.

The Zona Esmeralda, 2km west of the *zócalo*, is a stretch of Avenida Juárez with chi-chi boutiques, upscale restaurants and trendy nightclubs.

◉ Sights

Zócalo   PLAZA
Puebla's central plaza was originally a marketplace where bullfights, theater and hangings occurred, before assuming its current arboretum-like appearance in 1854. The surrounding arcades date from the 16th century. The plaza fills with an entertaining mix of clowns, balloon hawkers and food vendors on weekend evenings.

Catedral   CATHEDRAL
(cnr Avs 3 Oriente & 16 de Septiembre) Puebla's impressive cathedral, which appears on Mexico's M$500 bill, occupies the entire block south of the *zócalo*. Its architecture is a blend of severe Herreresque-Renaissance and early baroque styles. Construction began in 1550, but most of it took place under Bishop Juan de Palafox in the 1640s. At 69m, the towers are Mexico's tallest. The dazzling interior, the frescoes and the elaborately decorated side chapels are awe-inspiring, and most have bilingual signs explaining their history and significance.

Plaza de Revolución   PLAZA
(Paseo Bravo, btw Reforma & 11 Poniente on Constitucion de 1917) This multi-block park, recently renovated and re-planted, is an attractive counter to the *centro histórico*'s *zocálo*. The park is festive and crowded in the afternoons, when kids in school uniforms, lunching office workers and rockers practicing guitar gather to eat, play and relax beneath trees from around the world – labeled with their species and origins.

Puebla

◎ Sights
Biblioteca Palafoxiana.................(see 1)
1 Casa de la Cultura..............................C3
2 Catedral..C3
3 Edificio Carolino................................D3
4 Iglesia de la Compañía.....................D3
5 Museo Amparo.................................. C4
6 Museo Bello..C3
7 Museo Casa del Alfeñique.................E3
8 Museo de la Revolución....................D2
9 Museo Poblano de Arte
   Virreinal...D3
10 Plaza de Revolución A2
11 Templo de San Francisco..................F3
12 Templo de Santo Domingo................C2

☉ Activities, Courses & Tours
13 Turibus..C3

☐ Sleeping
14 Casona de la China Poblana...............D3
15 El Hotel Boutique Puebla de
   Antaño...D3
16 El Sueño Hotel & Spa C4
17 Gran Hotel San Agustín B2
18 Hotel Colonial...................................D3
19 Hotel Mesón de San Sebastián......... C4
20 Hotel Provincia Express.....................C3
21 La Purificadora..................................F3
22 Mesón Sacristía de la
   Compañía.. D4
23 NH Puebla...B2

⊗ Eating
24 Amalfi Pizzeria D3
25 El Mural de los Poblanos....................C3
26 El Patio de las Ranas C2
   La Purificadora.......................... (see 21)
27 La Zanahoria...................................... D4
28 Las Ranas..C2
29 Mercado de Sabores.......................... A1
   Restaurante Sacristía ....(see 22)

⊖ Drinking
30 A Go Go E4
31 All Day Café D4
32 Barra Beer...B2
33 Utopia.. C4

⊕ Entertainment
34 Librería Cafetería Teorema...............B2

⌂ Shopping
35 Antiques Market D4
36 El Parián Crafts Market.......................E3
37 Talavera Uriarte A1

Museo Amparo   MUSEUM
(www.museoamparo.com; Calle 2 Sur 708; adult/student M$35/25, Mon free; ☺10am-6pm Wed-Mon) This superb private museum, housed in two linked 16th- and 17th-century colonial buildings, has recently undergone a massive, multi-million dollar renovation. Loaded with pre-Hispanic artifacts, displayed with explanatory information sheets in English and Spanish, the collection is staggering.

Notice the thematic continuity in Mexican design – the same motifs appear again and again on dozens of pieces. An example: the collection of pre-Hispanic cult skeleton heads are eerily similar to the candy skulls sold during Día de los Muertos.

Templo de Santo Domingo   CHURCH
(cnr Avs 5 de Mayo & 4 Poniente) This fine Dominican church features a stunning **Capilla del Rosario** (Rosary Chapel), south of the main altar, which is the main reason to come here. Built between 1650 and 1690, it's

heavy on gilded plaster and carved stone, with angels and cherubim seemingly materializing from behind every leaf. See if you can spot the heavenly orchestra.

Museo Poblano de Arte Virreinal MUSEUM
(Calle 4 Norte 203; adult/student M$30/25, Tue free; ⊘10am-4:30pm Tue-Sun) Opened in 1999, this top-notch museum is housed in the 16th-century Hospital de San Pedro. Galleries display excellent contemporary art and a fascinating permanent exhibit on the hospital's history.

Casa de la Cultura CULTURAL BUILDING
(Av 5 Oriente 5; ⊘10am-8pm) Occupying the entire block facing the south side of the cathedral, the former bishop's palace is a classic 17th-century brick-and-tile edifice, which now houses government offices, the Casa de la Cultura and the State Tourist Office. Inside are art galleries, a bookstore and cinema, and a congenial cafe out back in the courtyard.

Upstairs is the 1646 **Biblioteca Palafoxiana** (admission M$25, Tue free; ⊘10am-5pm Mon-Fri, to 4pm Sat & Sun), the first public library in the Americas. The library's gorgeous shelves – carved cedar and white pine – house thousands of rare books, including the 1493 *Nuremberg Chronicle* and one of the earliest New World dictionaries.

Iglesia de la Compañía CHURCH
(cnr Av Palafox y Mendoza & Calle 4 Sur) This Jesuit church with a 1767 Churrigueresque facade is also called Espíritu Santo. Beneath the altar is a tomb said to be that of a 17th-century Asian princess who was sold into slavery in Mexico and later freed. She was supposedly responsible for the colorful *china poblana* costume – a shawl, frilled blouse, embroidered skirt, and gold and silver adornments. This costume became a kind of 'peasant chic' in the 19th century. But *china* (*chee*-nah) also meant 'maidservant,' and the style may have evolved from Spanish peasant costumes.

Next door is the 16th-century **Edificio Carolino**, now the main building of Universidad Autónoma de Puebla.

Museo del Ferrocarril MUSEUM
(Calle 11 Norte 1005; www.museoferrocarriles. org.mx; admission M$11, Sun free; ⊘9am-5pm Tue-Sun) This excellent railway museum is housed in Puebla's former train station and the spacious grounds surrounding it, which are strewn with defunct Mexican rolling

stock. There are ancient steam-powered monsters through to relatively recent passenger carriages, and you can enter many of them. One carriage contains an excellent collection of photos of various derailments and other disasters that occurred during the 1920s and '30s.

Templo de San Francisco CHURCH
(Av 14 Oriente; ⊘8am-8pm) The north doorway of this church is a good example of 16th-century plateresque; the tower and fine brick-and-tile facade were added in the 18th century. In the north chapel is the mummified body of San Sebastián de Aparicio, a Spaniard who migrated to Mexico in 1533 and planned many of the country's roads before becoming a monk. Since he's now the patron saint of drivers, merchants and farm workers, his canonized corpse attracts a dutiful stream of thankful worshipers.

Museo de la Revolución MUSEUM
(Av 6 Oriente 206; adult/student M$30/25, Tue free; ⊘10am-5pm Tue-Sun) This pockmarked 19th-century house, which was closed at the time of research, was the scene of the first battle of the 1910 Revolution. Betrayed only two days before a planned uprising against the dictatorship of Porfirio Díaz, the Serdán family (Aquiles, Máximo, Carmen and Natalia) and 17 others fought 500 soldiers until only Aquiles, their leader, and Carmen were left alive. Aquiles, hidden under the floorboards, might have survived if the damp hadn't provoked a cough that gave him away. Both were subsequently killed. The house retains its bullet holes and some revolutionary memorabilia, including a room dedicated to female insurgents.

Museo Casa del Alfeñique MUSEUM
(Av 4 Oriente 416; adult/student M$30/25, Tue free; ⊘10am-5pm Tue-Sun) Another museum undergoing renovation at the time of research, this colonial house is an outstanding example of the over-the-top 18th-century decorative style *alfeñique,* characterized by elaborate stucco ornamentation and named after a candy made from sugar and egg whites. The 1st floor details the Spanish conquest, including indigenous accounts in the form of drawings and murals. The 2nd floor houses a large collection of historic and religious paintings, local furniture and household paraphernalia, although all labeling is in Spanish only.

FREE **Museo Bello** MUSEUM
(www.museobello.org; Av 3 Poniente 302; ⊙10am-4pm Tue-Sun) This house is filled with the diverse art and crafts collection of the 19th-century industrialist Bello family. There is exquisite French, English, Japanese and Chinese porcelain and a large collection of Puebla Talavera. The museum closes every January for maintenance.

⌲ Tours

Turibus BUS TOUR
(☏226-72-89; www.turibus.com.mx; adult/child M$150/80; departs 11:30am) Operated by ADO bus lines, this three-hour, double-decker bus tour gives an overview of Puebla's *centro histórico* and the nearby town of Cholula. Leaves from the west side of the *zócalo*.

✵✵ Festivals & Events

Feria de Puebla MUSIC
Starting in late April and ending in late May, this fair honors the state's achievements with cultural and music events.

Cinco de Mayo PARADE
The city's May 5 celebrations mark the day, 150 years ago, when the Mexican army defeated the French. There's typically a parade.

Festival del Mole Poblano FOOD
In early June the city celebrates its most famous contribution to the culinary arts: *mole poblano,* a thick sauce of chilis, fruits, nuts, spices and chocolate.

Festival del Chile en Nogada FOOD
Leaving no culinary stone unturned, in August the city's savvy restaurateurs promote the country's 'patriotic recipe' - a chili stuffed with picadillo and topped in a luscious walnut cream sauce.

Día de Muertos TRADITIONAL
Puebla has jumped on the bandwagon, with a four-day citywide cultural program starting in late October devoted to the Day of the Dead.

🛏 Sleeping

Puebla's hotel scene is crowded and competitive, with a huge range of accommodations options and new arrivals constantly stirring things up. In recent years quite a few boutique three- and four-star hotels aimed at discerning travelers have entered the market, and standards are high.

Many hotels in the city can be spotted some way off with illuminated 'H' signs over their entrance, although some of the newer generation are clearly seeking discretion and don't advertise quite so directly. It's worth searching online for special last-minute, seasonal and weekend package rates.

Most colonial buildings have two types of room – interior and exterior – with the former often lacking windows and the latter frequently having windows or balconies exposed to a noisy street. Hotels that lack on-site parking often have an arrangement with nearby garages.

Hotel Provincia Express BUSINESS HOTEL $$
(☏246-35-57; Av Reforma 141; s/d incl breakfast M$400/500; P@🛜) Tile fetishists on a budget, look no further! This wonderful place has one of the most stunning traditional interiors in Puebla and all at knock-down prices. Refitted in 2007 the rooms themselves are simple but modern and spotlessly clean, while the corridors and facade are visually exciting. Provincia Express's popularity, coupled with thin doors, means it can be noisy at night.

Hotel Colonial HOTEL $$
(☏246-46-12, 800-013-00-00; www.colonial.com.mx; Calle 4 Sur 105; s/d M$680/780; @🛜) Once part of a 17th-century Jesuit monastery and existing as a hotel in various forms since the mid-19th century, this hotel exudes heritage from its many gorgeously furnished rooms (half of the 67 rooms have retained colonial decor, and half are modern). There's a good restaurant, lobby wi-fi and a fantastic gilt-clad elevator complete with liveried porters. Noise from live music and the street can be a problem, but otherwise this is an excellent choice with an unbeatable vibe and location.

Hotel Mesón de San Sebastián BOUTIQUE HOTEL $$$
(☏242-65-23; www.mesonsansebastian.com; Av 9 Oriente 6; r incl breakfast M$950-1500; 🛜🛗) This elegant boutique hotel has a colorful courtyard, accommodating staff who speak English, and garners parental praise for being family-friendly (a rarity in the world of designer bed sheets and ruthlessly selected *objets d'art*). Each of the 17 rooms are individually decorated and named after a saint. The master suites are particularly stunning, but all rooms have TV, phone, minibar and antique furnishings.

El Sueño Hotel & Spa
BOUTIQUE HOTEL $$$

(☎232-64-23/89, 800-690-84-66; www.elsueno-hotel.com; Av 9 Oriente 12; ste incl breakfast M$1500-2500; P❋☎) An oasis of minimalist chic amid the colonial bustle of Puebla's old town, Sueño's 11 rooms are sleek, high-ceilinged and thematically decorated. Each is inspired by a different female Mexican artist. There's a hot tub and sauna, plasma TVs in the rooms and a martini bar in the lobby.

Mesón Sacristía de la Compañía
BOUTIQUE HOTEL $$$

(☎242-45-13; www.mexicoboutiquhotels.com/mesonsacristia; Calle 6 Sur 304; ste incl breakfast M$1600-2000; P☎) With eight rooms set around a bright, kitschy, pink courtyard, this small inn feels like the home of an eccentric grandmother. The junior suites are actually just standard rooms, while the two master suites are bigger and worthy of the title. The downstairs restaurant, which serves aromatic US-style breakfasts and refined *poblano* cuisine, gets rave reviews from guests.

NH Puebla
BUSINESS HOTEL $$

(☎309-19-19, 800-726-0528; www.nh-hotels.com; Calle 5 Sur 105; r US$87-US$111; P❋☎▨) Attracting both business travelers and pleasure seekers, NH offers a mix of style and service without being stuffy. The rooms are large and contemporary, with extremely comfortable beds, good views and access to the rooftop bar and a small pool and gym.

El Hotel Boutique Puebla de Antaño
BOUTIQUE HOTEL $$$

(☎246-24-03; www.hotelpuebladeantano.com; Av 3 Oriente 206; ste M$1750-2100; ☎▨) This new boutique hotel has marble washbasins, crown molding, in-room fireplaces and Jacuzzis, and vintage photographs on the walls. The ground floor is home to one of Puebla's more refined French-influenced restaurants, Casa de los Espejos, while the rooftop Las Chismes de Puebla bar is almost painfully chic (think summertime in the Hamptons).

Casona de la China Poblana
LUXURY HOTEL $$$

(☎242-56-21; www.casonadelachinapoblana.com; cnr Calle 4 Norte & Av Palafox y Mendoza; ste M$2242-3776; P) This elegant boutique hotel is stunning and knows it. Shamelessly dubbing itself Puebla's 'most exclusive hotel,' China Poblana has massive, gorgeous suites decorated in a mixture of styles, a lovely courtyard and the La Cocina de la China Poblana restaurant.

La Purificadora
BOUTIQUE HOTEL $$$

(☎309-19-20; www.lapurificadora.com; Callejón de la 10 Norte 802; r from US$180, ste US$295; P☎▨) From the trendy hotel company that runs Mexico City's chic Condesa df, Purificadora's stunning design has sharp, dramatic angles and a magnificent infinity pool on the roof. As its sister hotel did in the capital, La Purificadora has fast become the hip hangout of the *poblano* elite. Prices vary widely and rise Friday through Sunday, with frequent last-minute specials on the hotel's website.

Gran Hotel San Agustín
HOTEL $

(☎232-50-89; Av 3 Poniente 531; s/d/tr/q incl breakfast M$220/310/350/410; P) Probably the best bargain in town, this straightforward budget option is near the *centro histórico*, and has clean rooms, a plant-filled courtyard with a small fountain and a free breakfast. It's not the kind of place where you'll want to spend the day (the rooms are dark and unexciting), but it's a perfectly fine base for exploring the city on a budget.

🍴 Eating

Puebla's culinary heritage, of which *poblanos* are rightly proud, can be explored in a range of eateries throughout the city from humble street-side food stalls to elegant colonial-style restaurants. However, given the city's renown as a culinary center, it's surprising how few truly excellent high-end restaurants there are.

The 6570-sq-m $4.1 million **Mercado de Sabores Poblanos** (Av 4 Poniente btw 11 & 13 Norte) is a thrilling addition to Puebla's food scene. A sparkling new food court serves local specialties like *cemitas* (a style of sandwich unique to Puebla), *pipián verde* (green pumpkin-seed sauce), and *tacos árabes* (Arabic taco) from 130-odd vendors.

TOP CHOICE Las Ranas
TAQUERÍA $

(Av 2 Poniente 102; tacos & tortas M$6-13; ⊙noon-10pm) A true local institution, this is *the* place to try one of Puebla's great dishes: the *taco árabe*. At Las Ranas, you'll find unbelievably moist *al pastor* (shepherd-style) pork. Marinated and spit-grilled, then rolled in fresh, slightly charred Middle Eastern–style flat bread, these tacos are as simple as they are unforgettable. Both the main restaurant and its annex across the street **El Patio de**

PUEBLA'S UNFORGETTABLE SEASONAL TREATS

Justly famous for its incredible cuisine, Puebla also offers an array of seasonal, local delicacies that adventurous eaters should not miss.

» *Escamoles* (March-June) – Ant larvae, look like rice and are usually sautéed in butter.

» *Gusanos de maguey* (April-May) – Worms that inhabit the maguey plant, typically fried in a drunken chili and *pulque* (a low alcohol brew made from the maguey plant) sauce.

» *Huitlacoche* (June-October) – Inky-black corn fungus with an enchanting, earthy flavor. Sometimes spelt *cuitlacoche*.

» *Chiles en nogada* (July-September) – Green chilies stuffed with *picadillo* (a mix of ground meat and dried fruit), covered with a creamy walnut sauce and sprinkled with red pomegranate seeds.

» *Chapulines* (October-November) – Grasshoppers purged of digestive matter, then dried, smoked or fried in lime and chili powder.

las Ranas (Av 2 Poniente 205) are perpetually full but the food – especially at this price – is worth the wait.

El Mural de los Poblanos   MEXICAN $$
(☎242-05-03; www.elmuraldelospoblanos.com; Av 16 de Septiembre 506; mains M$75-175; ☺1-10pm Mon-Wed, 1-11pm Thu-Sat, 1-7pm Sun) Set back from the street in a gorgeous, plant-filled colonial courtyard, El Mural de los Poblanos serves excellent, traditional *poblano* dishes in an elegant setting. The house specialty is five kinds of *mole*. Other favorites include the smoky goat-cheese-stuffed ancho *chile relleno* (dried *poblano* chili) and the trilogy of *cemitas*. Reservations are a good idea on busy Friday and Saturday nights and holidays.

La Zanahoria   VEGETARIAN $
(Av 5 Oriente 206; mains M$20-60, set meals M$55; ☺☒) This (entirely meat-free) godsend for vegetarians is a great place for lunch, and is moments from the *zócalo* and the Museo Amparo. The restaurant is split into two –

the express service area (including a juice bar and a health food snack shop) in the front and the more relaxed service of the spacious interior colonial courtyard where everything from veggie *hamburguesas* to *nopales rellenos* (stuffed cactus paddles) are served. In addition to the extensive a la carte menu, there's a popular daily buffet (adult/child M$69/38 Monday to Friday, M$85/43 Saturday and Sunday).

Amalfi Pizzeria   PIZZERIA $$
(☎403-77-97; Av 3 Oriente 207B; pizzas M$100-155) It's easy to see why this excellent wood oven pizzeria – with dim lighting, terracotta walls and beamed ceilings – is a popular date spot. In addition to a wide selection of fine, thin-crust pies, there's decent wine and traditional Italian accompaniments, like caprese salads. Because the dining room is small, a reservation wouldn't hurt.

Restaurante Sacristía   MEXICAN $$
(☎242-45-13; Calle 6 Sur 304; mains M$95-142; ☺11am-11:30pm Mon-Sat, 11am-6pm Sun) Set in the delightful colonial patio of the boutique hotel Mesón Sacristía de la Compañía, this is an elegant place for a meal of authentic *mole* and creative twists on rich *poblano* cuisine, or a cocktail, or coffee and dessert in the intimate Confesionario bar. Live piano and violin soloists lend a romantic ambience, most nights from around 9pm. If you like what you taste, inquire about the small-group cooking classes.

La Purificadora   INTERNATIONAL $$$
(www.lapurificadora.com; Callejón de la 10 Norte 802, Paseo San Francisco, Barrio El Alto; mains M$115-235; ☐) The restaurant at La Purificadora, one of Puebla's newest and chicest boutique hotels, is set in a spare, loft-like space with unfinished walls and long, narrow wood-plank tables. The menu, meanwhile, tends toward the indulgent and elaborate, with dishes such as jumbo shrimp with chipotle hollandaise or a cassoulet of Mennonite asadero cheese, dehydrated tomato and confit of onion.

🍷 Drinking

During the day students pack the sidewalk tables along the pedestrian-only block of Avenida 3 Oriente, near the university. At night, mariachis lurk around Callejón de los Sapos – Calle 6 Sur between Avenidas 3 and 7 Oriente – but they're being crowded out by the bars on nearby Plazuela de los Sapos.

These rowdy watering holes are packed on weekend nights, when many of them become live-music venues.

All Day Café
CAFE

(Ave 7 Oriente; sandwiches M$40-55) This cafe-bar, a student hangout just off Plazuela de los Sapos, is housed in a bright courtyard and turns into a club in the evenings. It serves a range of sandwiches, salads, pastries, coffees and cocktails all day long (as the name suggests).

A Go Go
COCKTAIL BAR

(Av 3 Oriente 603) There's something incongruous about this hole-in-the-wall bar, with its pounding techno and stylish hordes of cocktail-slurping hipsters. But the cocktails here are creative, cheap and abundant while the bar's kitchen serves good-sized portions of surprisingly edible bar food late into the evening.

Barra Beer
SPORTS BAR

(Av 5 Poniente 705C) With its impressive beer list, this shrine to *las cervezas del mundo* (beers of the world) serves beers from far and wide, including 21 varieties of German beer, and brews from China, Spain, Belgium and Ireland. Unless you're desperate for your native brew, try something from the good list of artisanal Mexican beers.

Utopía
PUB

(Av 9 Oriente 1B; ☺7pm-2am Mon-Sat) This wonderful Belgian beer spot has an exceptional selection of both European and Mexican beers – along with beer soup, Belgian frites, bistro toasts and other classic pub food.

☆ Entertainment

Librería Cafetería Teorema
LIVE MUSIC

(☑298-00-28; Av 2 Poniente 703-3; cover M$10-30; ☺10am-2:30pm & 4:30pm-3am) This wonderful bookstore-cafe, the epicenter of Puebla's bohemian cultural life, fills with a mixed crowd of students and professors listening to different genres of live music from 9:30pm to 1am. Call for info on nightly events.

🔒 Shopping

West of the Museo de Arte Popular Poblano, several shops along Avenida 18 Poniente sell the colorful, hand-painted ceramics known as Talavera. Designs reveal Asian, Spanish-Arabic and Mexican indigenous influences. Bigger pieces are expensive, delicate and difficult to transport.

A number of shops along Avenida 6 Oriente, to the east of Avenida 5 de Mayo, sell traditional handmade Puebla sweets such as *camotes* (candied sweet potato sticks) and *jamoncillos* (bars of pumpkin seed paste).

Talavera Uriarte
CERAMICS

(Av 4 Poniente 911; www.uriartetalavera.com.mx; ☺9am-7pm Mon-Sat, 10am-5pm Sun) Unlike most of Puebla's Talavera shops, Uriarte still makes its pottery on-site. The showroom displays a gorgeous selection of high-quality, intricately-painted pieces. Founded in 1824, the company was recently purchased by a Canadian expat. Factory tours are offered 10am to 2pm Monday through Friday. The shop also hands out an excellent, very useful map of downtown Puebla.

El Parián Crafts Market
HANDICRAFTS

(Plaza Parián) Browse local Talavera, onyx and trees of life, as well as the types of leather, jewelry and textiles that you'll find in other cities. Some of the work is shoddy, but there's also some quality handiwork and prices are reasonable.

Plazuela de los Sapos
ANTIQUES

A wonderful array of quirky antique shops dominates Callejón de los Sapos, around the corner of Avenida 5 Oriente and Calle 6 Sur. Most shops open from 10am through to 7pm. On Sunday, there is a lively outdoor antiques market.

ℹ Information

Emergency
Cruz Roja (Red Cross; ☑235-86-31)
Fire (☑245-73-92)
Tourist Police (☑800-903-92-00)

Internet Access
There are several places to get online along Calle 2 Sur; most charge M$5 to M$10 per hour.

Medical Services
Hospital UPAEP (☑229-81-34; Av 5 Poniente 715)

Money
ATMs are plentiful throughout the city. Banks on the *zócalo* and Avenida Reforma have exchange and traveler's check facilities.

Post
Main Post Office (☑232-64-48; Av 16 de Septiembre s/n)

BUSES FROM PUEBLA

DESTINATION	FARE (M$)	DURATION	FREQUENCY (DAILY)
Cuetzalan	118	3hr	4
Mexico City (TAPO or Tasquena)	114-154	2-2½hr	50
Oaxaca	354	4¼hr	6
Veracruz	274	3½hr	28

Tourist Information

Municipal Tourist Office (Portal Hidalgo 14; ⊙9am-8pm Mon-Fri, to 3pm Sun)

State Tourist Office (⏺246-20-44; Av 5 Oriente 3; ⊙8am-8pm Mon-Sat, 9am-2pm Sun) In the Casa de Cultura building, facing the cathedral yard.

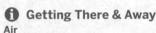 Getting There & Away

Air

Puebla's international airport **Aeropuerto Hermanos Serdán** (⏺232-00-32; www.aero puertopuebla.com) was in the midst of political turmoil at the time of research, with some services being canceled. Until management improves and airlines offer additional routes, the Toluca airport is likely a better option. There are, however, several domestic Volaris flights and a Continental flight to/from Houston. The airport is 22km west of Puebla off Hwy 190.

Bus

Puebla's full-service **Central de Autobuses de Puebla** (CAPU; www.capu.com.mx; ⏺249-72-11; Blvd Norte 4222) is 4km north of the *zócalo* and 1.5km off the autopista.

From Mexico City and towns to the west, most buses to and from Puebla use the capital's TAPO station, though some travel to Terminal Norte. The trip takes about two hours.

Both **ADO** (www.ado.com.mx) and **Estrella Roja** (ER; ⏺800-712-22-84; www.estrellaroja. com.mx) travel frequently between the two cities, operating both 1st-class and deluxe buses with wi-fi internet.

From CAPU, there are buses at least once a day to almost everywhere to the south and east.

Frequent 'Cholula' *colectivos* (M$6, 30 minutes) stop at the corner of Avenida 6 Poniente and Calle 13 Norte.

Car & Motorcycle

Puebla is 123km east of Mexico City by Hwy 150D. Traveling east of Puebla, 150D continues to Orizaba (negotiating a cloudy, winding 22km descent from the 2385m-high Cumbres de Maltrata en route), Córdoba and Veracruz.

❶ Getting Around

Most hotels and places of interest are within walking distance of Puebla's *zócalo*. At the CAPU bus station, buy a ticket at the kiosk for an **authorized taxi** (www.taxisautorizadoscapu. com; M$55) to the city center. Alternatively, follow signs for 'Autobuses Urbanos' and catch combi 40 to Avenida 16 de Septiembre, four blocks south of the *zócalo*. The ride takes 15 to 20 minutes.

From the city center to the bus station, catch any northbound 'CAPU' *colectivo* from Blvd 5 de Mayo at Avenida Palafox y Mendoza, three blocks east of the *zócalo*, or from the corner of Calle 9 Sur and Avenida Reforma. All city buses and *colectivos* cost M$5.50.

Call **Radio Taxi** (⏺243-70-59) for secure taxi service within the city – a good idea if you're traveling alone or going out at night.

Cholula

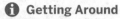
⏺222 / POP 88,000 / ELEV 2170M

Though it's almost a suburb of Puebla these days, Cholula is far different in its history and ambience. Owing to its large student population, the town has a surprisingly vibrant nightlife and some decent restaurants and accommodations options within a short walk of the huge *zócalo*.

Cholula is also home to the widest pyramid ever built – the Pirámide Tepanapa. Despite this claim to fame, the town's ruins are largely ignored because, unlike those of Teotihuacán or Tula, the pyramid has been so badly neglected over the centuries that it's virtually unrecognizable as a manmade structure.

History

Between around AD 1 and 600, Cholula grew into an important religious center, while powerful Teotihuacán flourished 100km to the northwest. Around AD 600, Cholula fell to the Olmeca-Xicallanca, who built nearby Cacaxtla. Some time between AD 900 and

1300 the Toltecs and/or Chichimecs took over and it later fell under Aztec dominance. There was also artistic influence from the Mixtecs to the south.

By 1519 Cholula's population had reached 100,000 and the Great Pyramid was already overgrown. Cortés, having befriended the neighboring Tlaxcalans, traveled here at the

Cholula

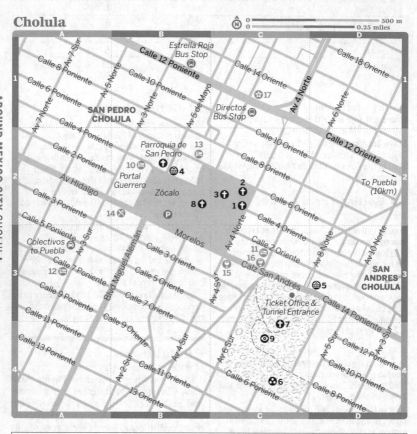

Cholula

Sights

1	Capilla de la Tercera Orden	C2
2	Capilla Real	C2
3	Ex-Convento de San Gabriel	C2
4	Museo de la Ciudad de Cholula	B2
5	Museo de Sitio de Cholula	D3
6	Patio de los Altares	C4
	Pirámide Tepanapa	(see 7)
7	Santuario de Nuestra Señora de los Remedios	C4
8	Templo de San Gabriel	B2
9	Zona Arqueológica	C4

Sleeping

10	Casa Calli	B2
11	Estrella de Belem	C3
12	Hotel La Quinta Luna	A3
13	Hotel Real de Naturales	B2

Eating

14	Güero's	B2

Drinking

15	Bar Reforma	C3
16	La Lunita	C3

Entertainment

17	Container City	C1

request of the Aztec ruler Moctezuma, but it was a trap and Aztec warriors had set an ambush. The Tlaxcalans tipped off Cortés about the plot and the Spanish struck first. Within a day they killed 6000 Cholulans before the city was looted by the Tlaxcalans. Cortés vowed to build a church here for every day of the year, or one on top of every pagan temple, depending on which legend you prefer. Today there are 39 churches – far from 365 but still plenty for a small town.

The Spanish developed nearby Puebla to overshadow the old pagan center and Cholula never regained its importance, especially after a severe plague in the 1540s decimated its indigenous population.

◎ Sights

Zona Arqueológica
PYRAMID

(☎235-97-20; admission M$41; ☺9am-6pm Tue-Sun) The **Pirámide Tepanapa**, located two blocks to the southeast of Cholola's central plaza, looks more like a hill than a pyramid and has a domed church on top so it's tough to miss. The town's big draw card is no letdown with miles of tunnels veining the inside of the structure. The Zona Arqueológica comprises the excavated areas around the pyramid and the tunnels underneath. The tunnels were closed and undergoing ongoing renovations at the time of research. While they are inaccessible, admission to the site is temporarily free.

Visitors normally enter via the tunnel on the north side, which takes you on a spooky route through the center of the pyramid. Several pyramids were built on top of each other during various reconstructions, and over 8km of tunnels have been dug beneath the pyramid by archaeologists to penetrate each stage. You can see earlier layers of the building from the access tunnel, which is a few hundred meters long.

The access tunnel emerges on the east side of the pyramid, from where you can follow a path around to the **Patio de los Altares** on the south side. Ringed by platforms and unique diagonal stairways, this plaza was the main approach to the pyramid. Three large stone slabs on its east, north and west sides are carved in the Veracruz interlocking scroll design. At its south end is an Aztec-style altar in a pit, dating from shortly before the Spanish conquest. On the mound's west side is a reconstructed section of the latest pyramid, with two earlier exposed layers.

The Pirámide Tepanapa is topped by the brightly decorated **Santuario de Nuestra Señora de los Remedios**. It's a classic symbol of conquest, though possibly an inadvertent one as the church may have been built before the Spanish realized the mound contained a pagan temple. You can climb to the church for free via a path starting near the northwest corner of the pyramid.

The small **Museo de Sitio de Cholula** (Calz San Andrés), across the road from the ticket office and down some steps, provides the best introduction to the site with a cutaway model of the pyramid mound showing the various superimposed structures. Admission is included in the site ticket.

Zócalo
PLAZA

The **Ex-Convento de San Gabriel**, facing the east side of Cholula's huge *zócalo* (also known as Plaza de la Concordia), includes a tiny but interesting **Franciscan library** and three fine churches, all of which will appeal to travelers interested in antique books and early religious and Franciscan history. On the left, as you face the ex-convent from the *zócalo*, is the Arabic-style **Capilla Real**, which has 49 domes and dates from 1540. In the middle is the 19th-century **Capilla de la Tercera Orden**, and on the right is the **Templo de San Gabriel**, founded in 1530 on the site of a pyramid.

The small but excellent **Museo de la Ciudad de Cholula** (☎261-90-53; cnr Av 5 de Mayo & Calle 4 Poniente; admission M$20, Sun free; ☺9am-3pm Thu-Tue) is housed in a fantastically restored colonial building on the *zócalo*. The collection includes ceramics and jewelry from the Pirámide Tepanapa, as well as later colonial paintings and sculptures. Most interestingly you can watch through a glass wall as museum employees painstakingly restore smashed ceramics and repair jewelry.

Festivals & Events

Festival de la Virgen de los Remedios
DANCE

Perhaps the most important Cholulan holiday of the year, this festival is celebrated the week of September 1. There are traditional dances daily atop the Great Pyramid. Cholula's regional feria is held during the following weeks.

Quetzalcóatl ritual
CULTURAL

On both the spring (late March) and fall (late September) equinoxes, this pre-Hispanic ritual is re-enacted with poetry, sacrificial dances, firework displays and music performed on traditional instruments at the pyramids.

Shrove Tuesday   HISTORICAL
Masked Carnaval dancers re-enact a battle between French and Mexican forces in Huejotzingo, 14km northwest of Cholula off Hwy 190.

🛏 Sleeping

With a clutch of good-value hotels and a couple of boutique favorites, Cholula makes an attractive alternative to staying in Puebla for those who prefer a laid-back pace.

TOP CHOICE Estrella de Belem   LUXURY HOTEL $$$
(261-19-25; www.estrelladebelem.com.mx; Calle 2 Oriente 410; r incl breakfast M$1888-2478; P❋ 🛜🗙) This beautiful recent addition to Cholula's hotel scene has just six rooms, each with gorgeous, thoughtful touches like radiant-heat floors, noise-blocking windows, bathtubs and LCD televisions. The master suites are especially luxurious, with fireplaces and Jacuzzis. Common areas include a lovely, grassy courtyard and a small, rooftop swimming pool that has views over the town. No children under 12.

Casa Calli   BOUTIQUE HOTEL $$
(261-56-07; www.hotelcasacalli.com; Portal Guerrero 11; r from M$450; P🛜🗙) Right on the *zócalo*, the hotel contains 40 stylishly minimalist rooms, an attractive pool and an Italian restaurant-bar in the lobby. Recently purchased by the same company that operates several of the trendiest hotels in the region – including La Purificadora in Puebla and Condesa df in the capital – Casa Calli has recently undergone a major facelift. Prices, however, remain reasonable and weekend spa packages are available (from M$1980).

Hotel La Quinta Luna   LUXURY HOTEL $$$
(247-89-15; www.laquintaluna.com; Av 3 Sur 702; r incl breakfast M$1650, ste incl breakfast M$1900-3200; P🛜) This rarefied hotel oozes colonial style and is popular with a wealthy weekender crowd. The six rooms occupy a thick-walled 17th-century mansion set around a charming garden and are a gorgeous mix of colonial antiques, plush bedding, wired amenities such as flat-screen TVs, DVD players and wi-fi, and contemporary art. Meetings with the featured artists are happily arranged. There's a great library and the excellent restaurant is open to nonguests who reserve.

Hotel Real de Naturales   BUSINESS HOTEL $$
(247-60-70, www.hotelrealdenaturales.com; Calle 6 Oriente 7; s/tr/q M$550/650/750, ste M$950-1100; P🛜🗙🛏) This new 45-room hotel was built in the colonial style to blend into the surrounding architectural landscape and it succeeds with its shady courtyards, tile baths, tasteful black and white photography and elegant archways. Its central location and many considered details make it an excellent bargain for the price.

🍴 Eating & Drinking

Güero's   MEXICAN $$
(Av Hidalgo 101; mains M$40-104; ⊙9am-11pm; 🛏) Decorated with antique photos of Cholula, this lively, family-friendly hangout has been a Cholula institution since 1955. Besides pizza, pasta and burgers, hearty Mexican choices include *pozole, cemitas* and quesadillas, all served with a delicious *salsa roja* (red sauce).

La Lunita   CANTINA
(www.lalunita.com; cnr Avs Morelos & 6 Norte 419) In the shadow of the pyramid, this raucous, family-run bar has been in business since 1939. Painted in bright colors and decorated with an assortment of old advertising posters and other knick-knacks, La Lunita looks a lot like the movie version of a Mexican cantina. But this isn't a tourist spot. It's popular with locals who come for its broad-ranging menu, live music and plentiful drinks.

Bar Reforma   CANTINA
(cnr Avs 4 Norte & Morelos; ⊙6pm-1am Mon-Sat) Attached to Hotel Reforma, Cholula's oldest drinking spot is a classic, smoky corner abode with swinging doors, specializing in iceless margaritas and freshly prepared sangrias. After 9pm it's popular with the university pre-clubbing crowd.

☆ Entertainment

East of the pyramid on Calle 14 Poniente, around the Avenida 5 de Mayo intersection, bars and discos compete for the short attention span of local students on Thursdays to Saturdays.

The new **Container City** (www.container city.com.mx; cnr 2 Norte & 12 Oriente) is hopping at night. A collection of trendy bars, restaurants, clubs and shops set in revamped and stacked former-shipping containers, this is the hangout of choice for Cholula's fashionistas and hipsters.

ℹ️ Getting There & Away

Frequent *colectivos* to Puebla (M$7, every 20 minutes) leave from the corner of Calle 5 Poniente and Calle 3 Sur, while larger *directos*, or buses (M$6, every 30 minutes), leave from the corner of Calle 2 Norte and Calle 12 Oriente. Buses and colectivos stop two or three blocks north of the *zócalo*.

Popocatépetl & Iztaccíhuatl

Mexico's second- and third-highest peaks, volcanoes Popocatépetl (po-po-ka-*teh*-pet-l; 5452m) and Iztaccíhuatl (iss-ta-*see*-wat-l; 5220m) form the eastern rim of the Valle de México, about 40km west of Puebla and 70km southeast of Mexico City. While the craterless Iztaccíhuatl is dormant, Popocatépetl (Náhuatl for 'Smoking Mountain,' also called Don Goyo and Popo) is very active and its summit has been off-limits for the last decade. Between 1994 and 2001, Popo's major bursts of activity triggered evacuations of 16 villages and warnings to the 30 million people who live within striking distance of the crater; a December 2005 explosion catapulted ash 5km into the sky.

Mexico's **Centro Nacional de Prevención de Desastres** (National Disaster Prevention Center; ☎24hr hotline 55-5205-1036; www.cenapred.gob.mx) monitors volcanic activity via variations in gas emissions and seismic intensity. Though almost entirely in Spanish, the website posts daily webcam photo captures and updates on conditions.

Historically, Popo has been relatively tranquil, with most activity occurring in the cooler winter months when ice expands and cracks the solidified lava around the crater rim. The last really big blast occurred over a thousand years ago, and volcanologists estimate that there's a 10% chance of one in the near future. At the time of writing, a crack team of scientists were continuing to observe Popo's increasingly predictable outbursts with great interest. The good news is that the fetching Iztaccíhuatl (White Woman), 20km north of Popo from summit to summit, remains open to climbers.

Hiking & Climbing

Izta's highest peak is **El Pecho** (5220m). All routes require a night on the mountain and there's a shelter hut between the staging point at La Joya, the main southern trailhead, and Las Rodillas, one of Itza's lesser peaks, that can be used during an ascent of El Pecho. On average, it takes at least five hours to reach the hut from La Joya, then another six hours from the hut to El Pecho, and six hours back to the base.

Before making the ascent, climbers must contact the **Parque Nacional Iztaccíhuatl-Popocatépetl** (☎597-978-38-29; http://iztapopo.conanp.gob.mx; Plaza de la Constitución 9B, Amecameca; ⊙9am-6pm Mon-Fri, to 3pm Sat), located on the southeast side of Amecameca's *zócalo*, to register. All visitors must pay the M$28 per day park entrance fee. The park's website also offers excellent maps and a handy downloadable English-language climbing guide.

About 24km up from Amecameca, there are lower-altitude trails through pine forests and grassy meadows near Paso de Cortés, the trailhead which leads to breathtaking glimpses of nearby peaks. La Joya is another 4km from Paso de Cortés. *Colectivos* departing from Amecameca's plaza for Paso de Cortés cost M$40. From the national park office, taxis will take groups to La Joya (40 minutes) for a negotiable M$350.

Basic shelter is available at the **Altzomoni Lodge** (beds per person M$28), roughly halfway between Paso de Cortés and La Joya. You must reserve in advance at the park office and bring bedding, warm clothes and drinking water.

Climate & Conditions

It can be windy and well below freezing any time of year on Izta's upper slopes, and it's nearly always below freezing near the summit at night. Ice and snow are fixtures here; the average snow line is 4200m. The ideal months for ascents are November to February, when there is hard snowpack for crampons. The rainy season (April to October) brings with it the threat of whiteouts, thunderstorms and avalanches.

Anyone can be affected by altitude problems including life-threatening altitude sickness. Even Paso de Cortés is at a level where you should know the symptoms (see p853).

Guides

Iztaccíhuatl should be attempted *only* by experienced climbers. Because of hidden crevices on the ice-covered upper slopes, a guide is advisable. Besides the following reader recommendation, the national park office may have suggestions.

Livingston Monteverde (www.tierradentro.com; climb@tierradentro.com), who is based in

Tlaxcala, is a founding member of the Mexican Mountain Guide Association, with 25 years of climbing experience. He speaks fluent English, basic French and some Hebrew and Italian.

Mario Andrade (☎55-1038-4008, 55-1826-2146; mountainup@hotmail.com) is an authorized, English-speaking guide, based in Mexico city, who has led many Izta climbs. His fee is US$350 for one person, less per person for groups. The cost includes round-trip transportation from Mexico City, lodging, mountain meals and rope usage.

Tlaxcala

📱 246 / POP 90,000 / ELEV 2250M

The capital of Mexico's smallest state is unhurried and unselfconscious, with a compact colonial downtown defined by grand government buildings, imposing churches and one of the country's more stunning central plazas. Despite its small stature, Tlaxcala is neither timid nor parochial. With a large student population, good restaurants and bars, and a handful of excellent museums, the city has a surprisingly vibrant cultural life. Because there's no single attraction that puts Tlaxcala on tourist itineraries it remains largely undiscovered – despite its location less than two hours from Mexico City.

Two large central plazas converge at the corner of Avenidas Independencia and Muñoz. The northern one, which is surrounded by colonial buildings, is the *zócalo* called Plaza de la Constitución. The southern square is Plaza Xicohténcatl. Traveling by bus you'll arrive a 10-minute walk from the *zócalo* at the city's hilltop station.

History

In the last centuries before the Spanish conquest, numerous small warrior kingdoms (*señoríos*) arose in and around Tlaxcala. Some of them formed a loose federation that

Tlaxcala

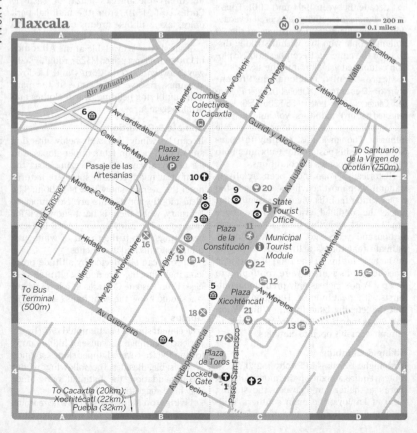

remained independent of the Aztec empire as it spread from the Valle de México in the 15th century. The most important kingdom seems to have been Tizatlán, now in ruins on the northeast edge of Tlaxcala.

When the Spanish arrived in 1519, the Tlaxcalans fought fiercely at first but ultimately became Cortés' staunchest allies against the Aztecs (with the exception of one chief, Xicoténcatl the Younger, who tried to rouse his people against the Spanish and is now a Mexican hero). In 1527 Tlaxcala became the seat of the first bishopric in Nueva España but a plague in the 1540s devastated the population and the town has played only a supporting role ever since.

◉ Sights

Museo de Arte de Tlaxcala   MUSEUM
(Plaza de la Constitución 21; adult/student/under 12 M$20/10/free, Sun free; ☺10am-6pm Tue-Sun) This fantastic contemporary art museum houses an excellent cache of early Frida Kahlo paintings which have recently been returned to the museum after several years on loan to other museums around the world. Both the museum's main building on the *zócalo* and the smaller **branch** (Guerrero 15; admission free) hold interesting temporary exhibits and a good permanent collection of modern Mexican art.

Plaza de la Constitución   PLAZA
It's easy to pass an afternoon reading or just people-watching in Tlaxcala's shady, spacious *zócalo* – especially now that the plaza offers free wi-fi access.

The 16th-century **Palacio Municipal**, a former grain storehouse, and the **Palacio de Gobierno** occupy most of its north side. Inside the latter there are vivid murals of Tlaxcala's history by Desiderio Hernández Xochitiotzin. The 16th-century building on the plaza's northwest side is the **Palacio de Justicia**, the former Capilla Real de Indios, built for the use of indigenous nobles. The handsome mortar bas-reliefs around its doorway include the seal of Castilla y León and a two-headed eagle, symbol of the Hapsburg monarchs who ruled Spain in the 16th and 17th centuries.

Off the northwest corner of the *zócalo* is the orange stucco and blue-tile **Parroquia de San José**. As elsewhere in the *centro histórico*, bilingual signs explain the significance of the church and its many fountains.

Museo Vivo de Artes y Tradiciones Populares   MUSEUM
(Blvd Sánchez 1; adult/student M$15/8; ☺10am-6pm Tue-Sun) This popular arts museum has displays on Tlaxcalan village life, weaving and *pulque*-making, sometimes with demonstrations. Artisans serve as guides to the over 3000 artifacts on display. The cafe and handicrafts next door at the **Casa de Artesanías** are also worth a look.

Museo de la Memoria   MUSEUM
(Av Independencia 3; adult/student M$10/5; ☺10am-5pm Tue-Sun) This modern history

Tlaxcala

museum looks at folklore through a multi-media lens and has well-presented exhibits on indigenous government, agriculture and contemporary festivals. Explanations are only in Spanish.

Santuario de la Virgen de Ocotlán CHURCH
One of Mexico's most spectacular churches is an important pilgrimage site for those who believe the Virgin appeared here in 1541 – her image stands on the main altar in memory of the apparition. The classic Churrigueresque facade features white stucco 'wedding cake' decorations contrasting with plain red tiles. During the 18th century, indigenous artisan Francisco Miguel spent 25 years decorating the altarpieces and the chapel beside the main altar.

Visible from most of the town, the hilltop church is 1km northeast of the *zócalo*. Walk north from the *zócalo* on Avenida Juárez/Avenida Independencía for three blocks, then turn right onto Zitlalpopocatl. Alternatively, 'Ocotlán' *colectivos* (M$6) travel along this same route.

Ex-Convento Franciscano de la Asunción HISTORIC BUILDING
This former monastery is up along a shaded path from the southeast corner of Plaza Xicohténcatl. Built between 1537 and 1540, it was one of Mexico's earliest monasteries and its church – the city's cathedral – has a beautiful Moorish-style wooden ceiling.

Just below the monastery, beside the 19th-century Plaza de Toros (bullring), is a **capilla abierta** (open chapel) with three unique Moorish-style arches. One of the entrances was locked at the time of research, but you can access the *capilla* from other entry points.

Museo Regional de Tlaxcala (adult M$41, under 13 & over 60 free; ⊙10am-6pm), housed within the monastery building, has a large collection of religious paintings and sculpture and some pre-Hispanic artifacts from nearby archaeological sites.

🍽 Courses

Estela Silva's Mexican Home Cooking School COOKING COURSE
(☑468-09-78; www.mexicanhomecooking.com) Learn to cook traditional *poblano* cuisine with Señora Estela Salas Silva, a Puebla native who teaches an intimate gastronomic course with her sous-chef husband Jon Jarvis, in the couple's Talavera-tiled kitchen in Tlacochcalco, 10km south of Tlaxcala. The

English-Spanish bilingual course includes all meals and drinks plus lodging in comfortable private rooms with fireplaces (transportation to/from the school can be arranged). The standard package is an all-inclusive, six-night/five-day course (US$1798) but one-day classes and shorter stays can be arranged.

👉 Tours

Tranvía El Tlaxcalteca BUS TOUR
(☑458-53-24; Plaza de la Constitución; adult/child M$50/35; ⊙every 2hr noon-6pm Wed-Sun) This motorized streetcar visits 33 downtown sights. No reservations necessary.

Festivals & Events

Virgen de Ocotlán RELIGIOUS
On the third Monday in May, the figure of the Virgen de Ocotlán is carried from its hilltop perch at Santuario de La Virgen de Ocotlán to neighboring churches, attracting equal numbers of onlookers and believers. Throughout the month, processions commemorating the miracle attract pilgrims from around the country.

Nacional de Danza Folklórica DANCE
This vibrant celebration brings dancers from around the country to Tlaxcala's Teatro Xicohténcatl during the last week of September.

Fiesta de Todos los Santos TRADITIONAL
Tlaxcala's Fiesta de Todos los Santos draws people from around the state between late October and mid-November, when *charrería* (horsemanship), bullfights and other rodeo-inspired pageantry take center stage. The festival kicks off with a *pamplonada* (running of the bulls) and includes Día de Muertos activities.

🛌 Sleeping

TOP CHOICE Posada La Casona de Cortés BOUTIQUE HOTEL $$
(☑462-20-42; lacasonadecortes.com.mx; Av Lardizábal 6; r from M$500-700, ste $M800; P🐾) Set around a lush courtyard garden with fruit trees and a fountain, this affordable boutique hotel seems almost too good to be true. The rooms, which have firm beds, tiled floors and high-pressure showers, are decorated with *artesanías* (handicrafts) from around the country. There's also an on-site restaurant and bar with a working 1950s jukebox and a roof deck with views of church steeples and volcanic peaks.

Hotel Posada San Francisco
LUXURY HOTEL $$$

(☎462-60-22; www.posadasanfrancisco.com; Plaza de la Constitución No 17; r M$1203-1339, ste M$2220;) The Posada San Francisco is the kind of place you'd expect to find a famous author swilling fine tequila – check out the stained-glass ceiling in the lobby, the bullfighter-themed bar, the large pool and the airy patio restaurant. While the common areas evoke the building's 17th-century grandeur, the rooms are modern. All have bathtubs – the rarest of luxuries at Mexican hotels – and air-conditioning.

Hotel Alifer
BUSINESS HOTEL $$

(☎462-30-62; www.hotelalifer.com.mx; Av Morelos No 11; r M$450-650; P🖥) One of the best budget options is the motel-style Hotel Alifer which is up a small hill from the *zócalo*. Some rooms are a bit dingy and dark (avoid bottom-floor rooms that face the echoing hallways and lack exterior windows) but upstairs rooms are clean and spacious with TV and phone. There's free wi-fi in the lobby.

Hostería de Xicohténcatl
GUESTHOUSE $$

(☎466-33-22; Portal Hildalgo 10; s/d/tr M$400/450/650, ste M$650-1200; P🖥) Half of the 16 rooms at this straightforward budget *hostería* are large, multiroom suites with kitchens, making it a bargain for families, groups or those in town for an extended stay. The *hostería* is clean, if a bit sterile, and the location – right on Plaza Xicohténcatl – is excellent. Wi-fi only reaches rooms closest to the lobby.

✘ Eating

For a small city, Tlaxcala has an impressive number – and diversity – of good restaurants. The eastern side of the *zócalo* is overrun by underwhelming sidewalk cafes but there are better options on the south side and on the nearby Plaza Xicohténcatl. Tlaxcala's market is one of the most pleasant around.

Desayunos Lupita
REGIONAL CUISINE $

(Muñoz Camargo 14; set breakfasts M$50; ⊗8:30am-4pm Mon-Fri, to 1:30pm Sat & Sun) This ultra-popular breakfast and lunch spot serves quintessential *tlaxcalteco* food, like *huaraches* (an oblong, fried corn base with a variety of toppings), tamales, atoles and quesadillas filled with everything from huitlacoche to squash flower. It's glorified street food, perfect for those with a taste for central Mexican specialities but squeamish about eating from carts and stalls. Set breakfasts include your choice of main dish, fresh-squeezed juice, fruit salad and *café de olla*.

Fonda del Convento
REGIONAL CUISINE $$

(Paseo de San Francisco 1; mains M$60-130; ⊗8am-8pm) This unassuming home-style restaurant has been a local favorite for four decades. The menu focuses on traditional Tlaxcalteca cuisine, including *guisanos* (maguey worms), *escamoles* (ant larvae), *mole poblano*, rabbit in *pulque* and a family-recipe *pipián* (green pumpkin seed sauce).

Vinos y Piedra
TAPAS $$

(Plaza de la Constitución 19; tapas M$35-160; ⊗9am-midnight Mon-Sat, to 9pm Sun) Vinos y Piedra has a true wine bar (complete with spittoons at each table), a basement wine cellar (visible through a section of see-through floor) and a selection of both domestic and imported *vinos*. This hangout for Tlaxcala's elite serves elegant tapas-style small plates with an emphasis on highfalutin' ingredients like Iberian ham, filet mignon, grapes rolled in blue cheese and pistachios. The sidewalk tables, protected beneath an arched awning, are great for an evening drink.

Tirol
MEXICAN $$

(Av Independencia 7A; breakfast M$40-75, mains M$50-230; ⊗8am-9pm Tue-Sun) Sleek and modern with stark white decor and attentive service, this excellent, upscale restaurant is popular for its four-course set menu (M$65 to M$120) at lunch and a swanky ambience after dark.

🍷 Drinking

Pulquería Tía Yola
PULQUE BAR

(Plaza Xicohténcatl 7; ⊗10am-9pm) Sip one of a dozen or so flavors of house-made *pulque* in a stone courtyard decorated with Day of the Dead figurines and bullfighting posters. The sidewalk tables along the plaza are a prime location for weekend people-watching.

Antiokía
CAFE

(Av Lardizábal 35; ⊗5:30-10pm Mon-Sat) There's no sign outside this romantic, hole-in-the-wall hangout but you'll know it by the smell – an irresistible mix of chocolate, freshly ground coffee and exotic teas. Mostly a cafe and dessert shop, Antiokía also serves savory fondues and paninis.

Revolución
SPORTS BAR

(Portal Hildalgo 9; ⊗noon-midnight Sun-Thu, to 2am Fri & Sat) Overlooking the *zócalo* this pleasantly rowdy 2nd-story sports bar has an expansive drink list, several large-screen TVs and stone walls decorated with musical instruments and sports equipment.

❶ Information

Several banks on Avenida Juárez, near the tourist office, exchange dollars and have ATMs. Internet cafes are plentiful, but there's also free wi-fi in and around the *zócalo*.

Farmacia Cristo Rey (Av Lardizábal 15; ⊗24hr) Around-the-clock pharmacy.

Hospital General (☑462-35-55; Corregidora s/n)

Police (☑464-52-57)

Post Office (cnr Avs Muñoz & Díaz)

SECTURE State Tourist Office (☑465-09-60; www.tlaxcala.gob.mx/turismo; cnr Avs Juárez & Lardizábal; ⊗9am-6pm Mon-Fri, 10am-6pm Sat) The English-speaking staff are eager to sing Tlaxcala's praises and equip travelers with good maps and a handful of brochures.

❶ Getting There & Away

Tlaxcala's recently renovated bus terminal sits on a hill 1km west of the central plaza. For Mexico City's TAPO terminal, **ATAH** (☑466-00-87) runs 1st-class buses (M$112, two hours) every 20 minutes. Frequent 2nd-class Flecha Azul buses rumble to Puebla (M$17). Taxis between the station and downtown cost M$30.

❶ Getting Around

Most *colectivos* (M$5) passing the bus terminal are heading into town, although it takes no time to walk. To reach the terminal from the center, catch a blue-and-white *colectivo* on the east side of Blvd Sánchez. Taxis between the terminal and the *zócalo* cost M$35.

Cacaxtla & Xochitécatl

These sister **sites** (admission M$45; ⊗9am-5:30pm), about 20km southwest of Tlaxcala and 32km northwest of Puebla, are among Mexico's most intriguing.

Cacaxtla (ca-*casht*-la) is one of Mexico's most impressive ancient ruins with its many high-quality, vividly painted depictions of daily life. Rather than being relegated to a museum collection, these works – including frescoes of a nearly life-size jaguar and eagle warriors engaged in battle – are on display within the site itself. Located atop a scrubby hill with wide views of the surrounding countryside, the ruins were discovered in 1975 when men from the nearby village of San Miguel del Milagro, looking for a reputedly valuable cache of relics, dug a tunnel and uncovered a mural.

The much older ruins at Xochitécatl (so-chi-*teh*-catl), 2km away and accessible from Cacaxtla on foot, include an exceptionally wide pyramid as well as a circular one. A German archaeologist led the first systematic exploration of the site in 1969, but it wasn't until 1994 that it was opened to the public.

History

Cacaxtla was the capital of a group of Olmeca-Xicallanca, or Putún Maya, who arrived in central Mexico as early as AD 450. After the decline of Cholula (which they probably helped bring about) in around AD 600, they became the chief power in southern Tlaxcala and the Puebla valley. Cacaxtla peaked from AD 650 to 950 and was abandoned by AD 1000 in the face of possibly Chichimec newcomers.

Two kilometers west of Cacaxtla and atop a higher hill, the ruins of Xochitécatl predate Christ by a millennium. Just who first occupied the spot is a matter of dispute but experts agree that, whereas Cacaxtla primarily served as living quarters for the ruling class, Xochitécatl was chiefly used for gory Quecholli ceremonies honoring Mixcoatl, god of the hunt. That isn't to say Cacaxtla didn't hold similar ceremonies – the discovery of the skeletal remains of hundreds of mutilated children attest to Cacaxtla's bloody past.

◉ Sights

Cacaxtla   ARCHAEOLOGICAL SITE
From the parking lot opposite the site entrance it's a 200m walk to the ticket office, museum and restaurant.

From the ticket office it's another 600m downhill to the main attraction – a natural platform, 200m long and 25m high, called the **Gran Basamento** (Great Base), now sheltered under an expansive metal roof. Here stood Cacaxtla's main civic and religious buildings and the residences of its ruling priestly classes. At the top of the entry stairs is the **Plaza Norte**. From here, the path winds clockwise around the ruins until you reach the **murals**, many of which clearly show Maya influence among the symbols from the Mexican highlands. This combination of styles in a mural is unique to Cacaxtla.

Before reaching the first mural you'll come to a small patio, of which the main feature is an **altar** fronted by a small square pit, in which numerous human remains were discovered. Just beyond the altar you'll find the **Templo de Venus** which contains two anthropomorphic sculptures – a man and a woman – in blue, wearing jaguar-skin skirts. The temple's name is attributed to the appearance of numerous half-stars around the female figure which are associated with Earth's sister planet, Venus.

On the opposite side of the path, away from the Plaza Norte, the **Templo Rojo** contains four murals, only one of which is currently visible. Its vivid imagery is dominated by a row of corn and cacao crops whose husks contain human heads.

Facing the north side of Plaza Norte is the long **Mural de la Batalla** (Battle Mural), dating from before AD 700. It shows two warrior groups, one wearing jaguar skins and the other bird feathers, engaged in ferocious battle. The Olmeca-Xicallanca (the jaguar warriors with round shields) are clearly repelling invading Huastecs (the bird warriors with jade ornaments and deformed skulls).

Beyond the Mural de la Batalla, turn left and climb the steps to see the second major **mural group**, behind a fence to your right. The two main murals (c AD 750) show a figure in a jaguar costume and a black-painted figure in a bird costume (believed to be the Olmeca-Xicallanca priest-governor) standing atop a plumed serpent.

Xochitécatl ARCHAEOLOGICAL SITE
Because of its outline and the materials used, archaeologists believe the circular **Pirámide de la Espiral** was built between 1000 and 800 BC. Its form and hilltop location suggest it may have been used as an astronomical observation post or as a temple to Ehécatl, the wind god. From here the path passes three other pyramids.

The **Basamento de los Volcanes**, which is all that remains of the first pyramid, is the base of the Pirámide de los Volcanoes and it's made of materials from two periods. Cut square stones were placed over the original stones, visible in some areas, and then stuccoed over. In an interesting twist, the colored stones used to build Tlaxcala's municipal palace appear to have come from this site. The **Pirámide de la Serpiente** gets its name from a large piece of carved stone with a snake head at one end. Its most impressive feature is the huge pot found at its

center, carved from a single boulder, which was hauled from another region. Researchers surmise it was used to hold water.

Experts speculate that rituals honoring the fertility god were held at the **Pirámide de las Flores**, due to the discovery of several sculptures and the remains of 30 sacrificed infants. Near the pyramid's base – Latin America's fourth widest – is a pool carved from a massive rock, where the infants were believed to have been washed before being killed.

☞ Tours

México Viejo TOUR
(🖉246-466-85-83; mexicoviejotours.com; Interior 2, Guridi y Alcocer 50, Tlaxcala; per person M$495; ⊘depart 10am, return 2:30pm) A guided tour of the history of the site, this is a good option for travelers with more money than time.

❶ Getting There & Away

Considering how close the archeological zone is to Mexico City, Tlaxcala and Puebla – it's roughly smack in the middle of the three cities – getting to and from Cacaxtla-Xochitécatl via public transit is inconvenient and time-consuming.

Cacaxtla is 1.5km uphill from a back road between San Martín Texmelucan (near Hwy 150D) and Hwy 119, the secondary road between Tlaxcala and Puebla. To reach the site from Tlaxcala, catch a 'San Miguel del Milagro' colectivo from the corner of Escalona and Sánchez Piedras, which will drop you off about 500m from Cacaxtla.

From Puebla, Flecha Azul buses go direct from the CAPU terminal to the town of Nativitas, about 3km east of Cacaxtla; from there, catch a 'Zona Arqueológica' colectivo to the site.

Between Cacaxtla and Xochitécatl, taxis (M$40) are available on weekends, or walk the 2km (about 25 minutes).

La Malinche

The long, sweeping slopes of this dormant 4460m volcano, named after Cortés' indigenous interpreter and lover, dominate the skyline northeast of Puebla.

The main route to the volcano is via Hwy 136; turn southwest at the 'Centro Vacacional Malintzi' sign. Before you reach the center, you must register at the entrance of the **Parque Nacional La Malintzi**. La Malinche, Mexico's fifth-tallest peak, is snowcapped only a few weeks each year, typically in May.

Centro Vacacional IMSS Malintzi (🖉55-5238-2701; centrosvacacionales.imss.gob.mx; campsites M$50, cabins up to 6 people M$630-940, up to 9 people M$1020; (P⚹), operated by the Mexican Social Security Institute, has 50 cabins, including rustic and 'luxury' options, at a frosty 3333m. This family-oriented resort has woodsy grounds and fine views of the peak. The remodeled cabins are basic but include TV, fireplace, hot water and kitchen with refrigerator. It gets crowded from Friday to Sunday but is quiet midweek. Those not staying can park here for M$30. Prices are about M$100 higher on weekends and holidays.

Beyond the vacation center, the road becomes impassable by car. It's about 1km by footpath to a ridge, from where it's an arduous five-hour round-trip hike to the top. Hikers should take precautions against altitude sickness (see p853).

Huamantla

📞247 / POP 52,000 / ELEV 2500M

Huamantla has invested greatly in its downtown in recent years, gussying up its colonial city center and renovating its charming *zócalo*. With La Malinche looming over town, this is a pleasant base camp for exploring the surrounding countryside, once you get past its sprawling suburbs.

Huamantla sees a few sleepless nights during its annual **feria** in August. The day before the Feast of the Assumption (August 15), locals blanket the town's streets with elaborate carpets of flowers and colored sawdust. The following Saturday, there's a Pamplona-esque running of the bulls, similar to that in Spain – but more dangerous since the uncastrated males charge from two directions. During the feria, rates double and rooms are reserved well in advance. If everything is full, seek out a room in Puebla or Tlaxcala.

◉ Sights

Museo de Títere   MUSEUM

(Parque Juárez 15; adult/student & senior/child M$20/10/5, Sun free; ⊙10am-5pm Tue-Sat, 10am-3pm Sun) The national puppet museum displays dolls and marionettes from all around the world in a fantastic new building on the *zócalo*. It's a fun stop for the young and young at heart.

⌸ Sleeping & Eating

TOP
CHOICE **Hacienda Soltepec**   HISTORIC HOTEL $$

(📞472-14-66; Carretera Huamantla-Puebla Km 3; r from M$670, ste from M$790; P🕸❄) Ten min-

utes outside of town, this gorgeous renovated hacienda rises like a castle above the Tlaxcalan countryside. A former movie set (María Félix stayed here for months while filming one of her classics), there are views of Malinche, horse stables, tennis courts and a fantastic in-house restaurant at this romantic time machine. The hacienda's owner leads a very fun *pulque* tour (no more than four people, M$400).

Hotel Centenario   HOTEL $$

(📞472-05-87; Juárez Norte 209; r M$300-600, ste M$700; P🅿@🛜) Just a short walk from the *zócalo*, Hotel Centenario has 33 bright pink rooms which are spacious, with new bathrooms and wi-fi access. The staff are helpful, and there's a good coffee shop in the lobby.

La Casa de los Magueyes   MEXICAN $$

(Reforma Sur 202; mains M$50-90) A wonderful home-style restaurant that serves regional dishes made with seasonal ingredients such as maguey buds and wild mushrooms.

❶ Getting There & Away

Oro and Suriano have frequent services from Puebla. ATAH runs buses from Tlaxcala's main station every seven minutes (M$24). The bus doesn't always stop at a station, so be sure to tell the driver that you're going to Huamantla Centro to avoid missing the town entirely.

Cantona

Given its isolation, a good distance from any town of significance, the vast and incredibly well-preserved Mesoamerican city of **Cantona** (admission M$41; ⊙9am-7pm) is virtually unknown to travelers. With 24 ball courts discovered, this is now believed to be the biggest single urban center in Mesoamerica, stretched over 12 sq km in an ethereal lavabed landscape dotted with cacti and yucca and enjoying incredible views of Pico de Orizaba to the south.

The site was inhabited from AD 600 to 1000 and is of interest for two main reasons: unlike most other Mesoamerican cities, no mortar was used to build it, meaning all the stones are simply held in place by their weight. It's also unique in its design sophistication – all parts of the city are linked by an extensive network of raised roads connecting some 3000 residences. There are several small pyramids and an elaborate **acropolis** at the city's center. With good information panels in English and a newly completed access road, Cantona is now being promoted as a tourist attraction, with a new site museum under construction at the time of research, although it's likely you'll be completely alone when you visit.

From Oriental, which is the nearest decent-sized town, Grupo Salazar covered pickup-truck *colectivos* leave every 20 minutes from the corner of Carretera Federal Puebla-Teziutlan and 8 Poniente for Cantona. The trucks have 'Tepeyahualco' (M$35, 45 minutes) on their windshield. Tell the driver your destination when you board.

Otherwise, taxis to the site are M$150 or more for a round-trip. If you have your own transportation, visiting Cantona makes for a good side trip en route to Cuetzalan.

Cuetzalan

📞233 / POP 6000 / ELEV 980M

One of the most exhilarating trips in the region, the gorgeous drive to Cuetzalan is an adventure in itself. Beyond the Zaragoza turnoff, the road becomes dramatic, snaking up hills and around hairpin bends, and offering breathtaking views. At the end of it all is the remote town of Cuetzalan (Place of the Quetzals). A striking village built on a precipitous slope, Cuetzalan is famed for its vibrant festivals and Sunday *tianguis* (a weekly street market) that attract scores of indigenous people in traditional dress. The humidity hovers around 90%, and on the clearest days you can see all the way from the hilltops to the Gulf coast, 70km away, as the quetzal flies.

◉ Sights & Activities

Town Center NEIGHBORHOOD
Three structures rise above Cuetzalan's skyline: the plaza's freestanding **clock tower**, the Gothic spire of the **Parroquia de San Francisco** and, to the west, the tower of the French Gothic **Santuario de Guadalupe**, with its highly unusual decorative rows of *los jarritos* (clay vases). The Casa de Cultura houses a small, underwhelming but free regional **museum** (Alvarado; ☉8am-7:30pm).

Las Brisas WATERFALL
About 5km northeast of town, there's a pair of lovely waterfalls called **Las Brisas** and **Cascada del Salto**. The natural swimming pools beneath the falls are enticing – bring your bathing kit. Rickshaw mototaxis will deposit you at the trailhead and await your return. The road to the falls was under construction at the time of research.

★★ Festivals & Events

Feria del Café y del Huipil TRADITIONAL
For several lively days around October 4, Cuetzalan celebrates both its patron saint, St Francis of Assisi, and the start of the coffee harvest with the Festival of Coffee and Huipiles, featuring hearty drinking, traditional quetzal dancing and airborne *voladores* (literally 'fliers'), the Totonac ritual in which men, suspended by their ankles, whirl around a tall pole.

The *voladores*, whose tradition was recognized as an Intangible Cultural Heritage by Unesco in 2009, perform for tourists (and tips) several times a day on weekends. It's a remarkable, not-to-miss performance.

🛏 Sleeping

Tosepan Kali LODGE $
(📞331-09-25; www.tosepankali.com; Km 1.5 de la Carretera Cuetzalan, San Miguel Tzinacapan; r from M$350) High on a steep hill midway between Cuetzalan and the nearby town of San Miguel Tzinacapan, Tosepan Kali looks like a tree house nestled into the area's dense foliage. Constructed largely of bamboo and stone, this sprawling ecohotel – its name means 'our house' in Náhuatl – is the work of a local indigenous cooperative. The location and craftsmanship are both beautiful, though the pricier cabins with views over the valley to Cuetzalan are especially appealing.

Hotel Posada Cuetzalan HOTEL $$
(📞331-01-54; www.posadacuetzalan.com; Zaragoza 12; s/d/tr/q M$585/830/985/1080; 🅿🛜🐾) This handsome hotel, 100m uphill from the *zócalo*, has three large courtyards full of chirping birds, a swimming pool, a good restaurant featuring local fruit liqueurs and 36 well-kept rooms with tropical colors, tiled floors, lots of lightly stained wood and cable TV. There's wi-fi in the front rooms near the office.

Hotel La Casa de la Piedra BOUTIQUE HOTEL $$$
(📞331-00-30; www.lacasadepiedra.com; García 11; r M$630-1200, ste M$1600; 🅿🐾) All 16 rooms in this renovated-yet-rustic former coffee-processing warehouse have picture windows and refinished wood floors. Upstairs, the two-level suites accommodate up to four people and offer expansive views of the valley; downstairs rooms have tiled

bathrooms, rough stone walls, and one or two beds.

Taselotzin LODGE $
(☑331-04-80; www.taselotzin.mex.tl; Yoloxóchitl, Barrio Zacatipan; dm/s/d/tr/q M$140/309/513/855, cabins for up to 10 people M$1400; [P][☎][♨]) Just outside Cuetzalan, this hostel is run by an association of Nahua craftswomen who campaign for fair trade. It's an excellent initiative, and the hotel offers traditional massages, fair-trade handicrafts, herbal medicines and a restaurant that serves traditional local dishes. It has 10 cozy private rooms, with good views amid peaceful gardens, plus two dorm-style cabins. Follow the right-hand fork past the turnoff to the Puebla road; watch for an inconspicuous sign on the right-hand side, about 300m downhill.

Posada Quinto Palermo HOTEL $$
(☑331-04-52; Calle 2 de Abril 2; s/d/tr M$526/750/990; ☎) This basic hotel has the best location in town and a roof deck overlooking the palm trees and steeples of Cuetzalan's gorgeous *zócalo*. The 15 rooms have almost comically bad color schemes and tacky art. Ask for a room facing the front of the hotel, which has windows onto the plaza. Parking (M$30) at a nearby lot can be arranged at check-in.

Posada Jaqueline GUESTHOUSE $
(☑331-03-54; Calle 2 de Abril 2; s/d M$100/150) Jaqueline's 20 basic but clean rooms, overlooking the uphill side of the *zócalo*, are one of Cuetzalan's best-value-in-town options. Some upstairs rooms share a balcony and have views over the town.

🍴 Eating & Drinking

Regional specialties, sold at many roadside stands, include fruit wines, smoked meats and herbal liqueurs.

Restaurante Yoloxóchitl MEXICAN $
(Calle 2 de Abril No 1; mains M$35-60; ☎) Beautifully decorated with plants, antiques, and ancient jukeboxes, Yoloxóchitl has views over the cathedral and a selection of salads, *antojitos* (tortilla-based snacks) and meat dishes, as well as wild mushrooms pickled in chipotle chili.

La Terraza SEAFOOD $$
(Hidalgo 33; mains M$60-100; ⊘9am-9pm) This family-run restaurant – with bright, lemon-lime-painted walls decorated with photos of the town's annual festivities – is extremely popular with locals for its large selection of breakfasts, *mariscos* (seafood), quesadillas, *platillos de la región,* and crawfish (in season).

Bar El Calate BAR
(Morelos 9B; shots from M$8) On the west side of the *zócalo*, this is *the* place to sip homemade hooch. There are 36 flavors, including liquors infused with coffee, limes, berries – you name it. Try the all-curing *yolixpán*, which is a local herbal liquor with an anis flavor.

🛍 Shopping

Centro de Desarrollo Artesanal Matachiuj ARTS & CRAFTS
(Hidalgo 917; ⊘9am-7pm Wed-Mon) This new fair-trade market has a range of quality weavings and other crafts that come with the benefit of meeting the producer, as many wares are made onsite by local artisans.

ℹ Information

On the east side of the *zócalo*, there's a semi-helpful **tourist office** (☑331-00-15; ⊘8am-4pm) with much-needed (although very unclear) town maps. Next door, Santander has an ATM.

ℹ Getting There & Away

From 6am to 6pm, Vía runs four buses a day between Puebla and Cuetzalan (M$154, four hours). It pays to check road conditions and buy your return bus tickets in advance during the rainy season. Primera Plus runs six buses a day, starting at 4am, between Cuetzalan and Mexico City's TAPO bus station (M$278, six hours). The last bus to TAPO leaves at 3:50pm. There are additional services on Sundays.

ℹ Getting Around

On the town's steep streets, three-wheeled mototaxis (from M$25 or about M$100 an hour) offer rides with a thrill. Covered pickup trucks provide transportation (M$6) to nearby *pueblitos*.

Yohualichán

About 8km northeast of Cuetzalan, the last 2km via a steep cobblestone road, this ceremonial **pre-Hispanic site** (admission M$31; ⊘9am-5:30pm) has niche pyramids similar to El Tajín's that are in varying states of ruin. The site is impressive and well worth a visit, not least for the great views from this side of the valley. The entrance is adjacent to Yohualichán's church and town plaza. To get here, ask at the tourist office for a *camión* (truck) passing by the pyramids.

SOUTH OF MEXICO CITY

A host of great destinations sit south of the Mexican capital, including mystical Tepoztlán, breathtaking Taxco and the superb complex of caves at Grutas de Cacahuamilpa. The main road south from Mexico City, Hwy 95D, climbs from the smog-choked Valle de México into refreshing pine forests above 3000m and then descends to Cuernavaca, 'the city of eternal spring,' a long-time popular escape from Mexico City and a home-away-from-home for many North Americans and Chilangos who own second houses here.

The state of Morelos, which encompasses Cuernavaca and Tepoztlán, is one of Mexico's smallest and most densely populated. Valleys at different elevations have a variety of microclimates, and many fruits, grains and vegetables have been cultivated here since pre-Hispanic times. The archaeological sites at Tepoztlán and Xochicalco show signs of the agricultural Tlahuica civilization and the Aztecs who subjugated them. During the colonial era, most of the region was controlled by a few families, including descendants of Cortés. You can visit their palaces and haciendas, along with 16th-century churches and monasteries. Unsurprisingly, the *campesinos* of Morelos were fervent supporters of the Mexican Revolution, and local lad Emiliano Zapata (see boxed text, p171) is the state's hero. Those with an interest should head to Cuautla for everything Emiliano.

The mountainous state of Guerrero boasts utter gems such as the silver mining tourist mecca Taxco, one of the best-preserved colonial towns in Mexico.

Tepoztlán

♪739 / POP 14,000 / ELEV 1700M

A weekend trip from the capital to Tepoztlán rarely disappoints. This beautifully situated small town with a well-preserved historic center surrounded by soaring jagged cliffs is just 80km south of Mexico City. As the birthplace of Quetzalcóatl, the omnipotent serpent god of the Aztecs over 1200 years ago (according to Mesoamerican legend),

Tepoztlán is a major Náhuatl center and a mecca for New Agers who believe the area has a creative energy.

This *pueblo mágico* boasts an impressive pyramid, a great crafts market and a host of charming restaurants and hotels. It also retains indigenous traditions, with some elders still speaking Náhuatl and younger generations learning it in school, making it a rarity among the towns ringing the Mexican capital.

Everything in Tepoztlán is easily accessible on foot, except the cliff-top Pirámide de Tepozteco, a 2.5km strenuous hike away. Street names change in the center of town; for example Avenida 5 de Mayo becomes Avenida Tepozteco north of the *zócalo*.

◉ Sights

Pirámide de Tepozteco   PYRAMID
(admission M$37; ⊙9am-5pm) The uncontested main sight in town is this 10m-high pyramid, although it's actually some 400m *above* the town, perched atop a sheer cliff at the end of a very steep path that begins at the end of Avenida Tepozteco. Built in honor of Tepoztécatl, the Aztec god of the harvest, fertility and *pulque*, the pyramid is more impressive for its location than for its actual size. Be warned that the path is exhausting. Heading off early is recommended to beat the heat, and the 2km walk is not recommended to anyone not physically fit. At the top, depending on haze levels, you may be rewarded with a panorama of the valley. Bring your own water, and good shoes are highly recommended. Video camera use is M$45.

Ex-Convento Domínico de la
Natividad   CHURCH
This monastery, situated east of the *zócalo,* and the attached church were built by Dominican priests between 1560 and 1588. The plateresque church facade has Dominican seals interspersed with indigenous symbols, floral designs and various figures, including the sun, moon and stars, animals, angels and the Virgin Mary. Upstairs, various cells house a bookstore, galleries and a **regional history museum**.

The monastery's arched entryway is adorned with an elaborate **seed mural** of pre-Hispanic history and symbolism. Every year during the first week of September local artists sow a new mural from 60 varieties of seeds.

Tepoztlán

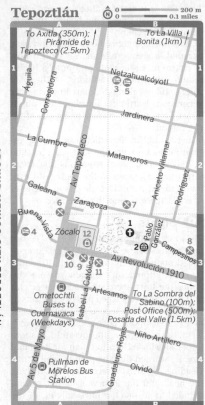

N 0 ———————— 200 m
   0 ———————— 0.1 miles

To Axitla (350m);
Pirámide de
Tepozteco (2.5km)

To La Villa
Bonita (1km)

Netzahualcóyotl

Aguila

Corregidora

Jardinera

La Cumbre

Av Tepozteco

Matamoros

Aniceto Villamar

Galeana

Zaragoza

Rodríguez

Buena Vista

Zócalo

Pablo González

Campesinos

Av Revolución 1910

Isabel La Católica

Artesanos

Ometochtli
Buses to
Cuernavaca
(Weekdays)

To La Sombra del
Sabino (100m);
Post Office (500m);
Posada del Valle (1.5km)

Niño Artillero

Av 5 de Mayo

Guadalupe Rojas

Pullman de
Morelos Bus
Station

Olvido

Tepoztlán

◉ Sights
1 Ex-Convento Dominico de la
   Natividad..B3
2 Museo Arqueológico Carlos
   Pellicer..B3

⊜ Sleeping
3 Hotel Posada Ali..................................B1
4 Posada del Tepozteco..........................A3
5 Posada Nican Mo Calli B1

✕ Eating
6 El Brujo...A2
7 El Ciruelo...B2
8 El Mango
   Biergarten-Restaurante....................B3
9 La Luna Mextli.....................................A3
   La Sibarita...................................(see 4)
10 Los Buenos Tiempos...........................A3
11 Tepoznieves A3

ⓐ Shopping
12 Market..A3

one of Mexico's most celebrated chefs. García's course earns rave reviews from students. The six guest rooms have French doors opening onto a gorgeous patio overlooking the Tepoztlán valley, with a swimming pool carved out of volcanic rock and a citrus orchard. There are a variety of packages; check the website for promotions.

Museo Arqueológico
Carlos Pellicer   MUSEUM
(Pablo González 2; admission M$10; ◷10am-6pm Tue-Sun) Behind the Dominican church, this archaeology museum has a small but interesting collection of pieces from around the country, donated by Tabascan poet Carlos Pellicer Cámara. The objects on display, a mix of human and animal figures, are lively and vibrant. The stone fragments depicting a pair of rabbits – the symbol for Ometochtli, the leader of the 400 rabbit gods of drunkenness – were discovered at the Tepozteco pyramid site.

◔ Courses

La Villa Bonita   COOKING COURSE
(☑777-169-72-32; Aniceto Villamar 150, Colonia Tierra Blanca; www.lavillabonita.com; 3-day, 4-night courses incl accommodations US$1250-1550) On a hillside above town, this 2009 cooking school is the project of Ana García,

✵ Festivals & Events

Tepoztlán is a hyper-festive place, with many Christian feasts superimposed on pagan celebrations. With eight *barrios* (neighborhoods) and an equal number of patron saints, there always seems to be some excuse for fireworks.

Carnaval   DANCE
During the five days preceding Ash Wednesday (46 days before Easter Sunday), Carnaval features the colorful dances of the Huehuenches and Chinelos with feather headdresses and beautifully embroidered costumes.

Fiesta del Templo   RELIGIOUS
On September 7, an all-night celebration goes off on Tepozteco hill near the pyramid, with copious consumption of *pulque* in honor of Tepoztécatl. The following day is the Fiesta del Templo, a Catholic celebration featuring theater performances in Náhuatl.

The holiday was first intended to coincide with – and perhaps supplant – the pagan festival, but the *pulque*-drinkers get a jump on it by starting the night before.

🛏 Sleeping

Tepoztlán has a range of good accommodations options, but as a small town with lots of visitors, it can sometimes be hard to find a room during festivals and on weekends. If you can't find a room, keep your eyes peeled for private homes offering weekend rooms, marked with *hospedaje económico* signs.

TOP CHOICE Posada del Tepozteco   LUXURY HOTEL $$$

(📞395-00-10; www.posadadeltepozteco.com; Paraíso 3; s/d M$2250/2700, ste M$3200-4700; P@🅰🏊) This gorgeous hotel was built as a hillside mansion in the 1930s. The 20 rooms are airy and individually decorated, and most have magnificent views over town. In the age of boutique luxury, some rooms may be underwhelming. The focus of this old-world hotel is its refined atmosphere, wonderful garden and pool. The guest book contains many famous names, including Angelina Jolie, who stayed in room 5 when she dropped by. The service is exceptional and rates are discounted up to 30% during the week.

Hotel Posada Ali   GUESTHOUSE $$

(📞395-19-71; Netzahualcóyotl 2C; s/d M$500/900; P🛜🏊) An excellent value, Ali is a friendly, family-run hotel with a mix of 20 comfortable rooms, from the small and dark (and quieter and more affordable) rooms on the lower floors to the larger rooms upstairs, with views of the mountains. There's a communal sitting room, *frontón* (jai alai) court and a small pool. The upstairs balcony with hammock chairs is a lovely place to sit and relax. Prices rise on weekends.

Posada Nican Mo Calli   HOTEL $$

(📞395-31-52; www.hotelnican.com; Netzahualcóyotl 4A; r M$800, ste M$1000-1800; P🅰🛜🏊) With brightly painted public areas, a heated pool, stylish rooms (some with balconies and great mountain views) and plenty of animals hanging around, Nican Mo Calli is just right for a romantic weekend away and one of the best options in town.

Posada del Valle   RESORT $$

(📞395-05-21; www.posadadelvalle.com.mx; Camino a Mextitla 5; r M$960; P🏊) Located east

of town, this hotel-spa has quiet, romantic rooms (no children under 16) and a good Argentine restaurant. Spa packages, which cost extra, include two nights' accommodations, breakfast, massages and a visit to the *temascal* (indigenous Mexican steam bath). It's 2km down Avenida Revolución 1910 – just follow the signs for the final 100m to the hotel.

🍴 Eating & Drinking

This small town is hopping on weekends, when cafes and bars fill up with enthusiastic visitors. Unfortunately for those visiting midweek, many of the best spots are only open Friday to Sunday.

TOP CHOICE La Sibarita   MEXICAN $$$

(📞395-00-10; www.posadadeltepozteco.com; Posada del Tepozteco; mains M$145-295; ⊗8am-10pm Sun-Thu, 8am-11pm Fri & Sat) High on a hill above town, the restaurant at Posada del Tepozteco has gorgeous views of the valley below. With surreal cliffs and a pyramid overhead, the restaurant's setting could scarcely be more striking. The menu features dishes like steak in *foie gras* sauce, chicken breast stuffed with goat cheese and Italian herbs, *róbalo* (snook) carpaccio in vinaigrette and rose-petal *nieve* (frozen dessert) – all paired with imported wines.

El Brujo   BAKERY $

(Av 5 de Mayo; breakfasts M$60-70; ⊗9am-9pm; 🅰) This wonderful new bakery-restaurant on the town's main drag is the best bet for a full breakfast (with excellent omelettes and Mexican standards like *chilaquiles* – strips of fried corn tortillas, bathed in sauce). It also has great espresso drinks or fantastic after-dinner desserts. Just looking at the cake case will likely start you salivating.

Los Buenos Tiempos   BAKERY $

(Av Revolución 1910 No 14B; pastries M$6-30) Head here for the best pastries around – the smell drifting over the *zócalo* alone will probably bring you on autopilot. There's also good coffee and a lively social scene, and it's a great place to buy a pastry breakfast to take up to the pyramid with you.

La Sombra del Sabino   CAFE $

(www.lasombradelsabino.com.mx; Av Revolución 1910 No 45; mains M$60-90; ⊗10am-7pm Wed-Sun; 🛜) This 'literary cafe' and bookstore serves coffee, tea, wine or beer and simple fare – pastries, sandwiches and salads – in a contemplative garden setting. La Sombra del Sabino also hosts readings and events and sells a small selection of English-language books.

El Mango
Biergarten-Restaurante   GERMAN $$
(www.elmango.org; Campesinos 7; mains M$60-145; ⊙2-9pm Fri-Sun) Craving goulash, spaetzle, bratwurst and hearty, freshly baked bread? This German-run beer garden, just down the hill from the *zócalo,* serves genuine German food in the heart of central Mexico. To wash it down, Mango's beer list includes both imported European beers and domestic, artisanal *cerveza.* There's live jazz and blues on weekends. See the website for event calendar.

Axitla   MEXICAN $$
(Av Tepozteco; breakfast M$40-110, mains M$75-150; ⊙10am-7pm Wed-Fri, from 9am Sat & Sun) This Swiss Family Robinson–style sprawling treehouse, just off the pathway to the archaeological site, is set amid thick forest. There's a good selection of breakfasts available (M$40 to M$100) and a wide-ranging Mexican and international menu, including chicken breast stuffed with *huitlacoche* in *chipotle* sauce, sweet and sour ribs, and quail.

La Luna Mextli   INTERNATIONAL $$$
(Av Revolución 1910 16; mains M$85-220; ⊙12pm-10pm) La Luna Mextli has its own in-house gallery and is stuffed with local art. The food here is also excellent, from Mexican standards to an entire list of Argentine steaks and *parrillada* (mixed grill).

El Ciruelo   INTERNATIONAL $$$
(www.elciruelo.com.mx; Zaragoza 17; mains M$115-235; ⊙1-6pm Mon-Thu, 1pm-11pm Fri & Sat, 1-7pm Sun) Set in a courtyard with views of the cliffs and pyramid, this longstanding favorite serves an impressive upscale menu of dishes from *camarones al curry* (curried shrimp) and *salmón chileno a la mantequilla* (Chilean salmon in butter sauce) to good pizzas, salads and international dishes, though prices seem a bit inflated.

A homegrown ice-cream emporium, **Tepoznieves** (Av Revolución 1910 s/n; scoops M$10-25) has several locations in this tiny town. Serving some 100 heavenly flavors, including exotics such as cactus and pineapple-chili, it's an obligatory stop.

🔒 Shopping

Tepoz has a fantastic, atmospheric daily **market** that convenes on the *zócalo.* It's at its fullest on Wednesday and Sunday. As well as the daily fruit, vegetable, clothing and crafts on sale, on Saturday and Sunday stalls around the *zócalo* sell a wide selection of handicrafts.

❶ Information

On the west side of the plaza, Bancomer and HSBC have ATMs. There are several internet cafes scattered around town.

❶ Getting There & Around

Pullman de Morelos/OCC (www.pullman.com.mx; Av 5 de Mayo 35) runs 1st-class buses to/from Mexico City's Terminal Sur (M$95, 1½ hours, hourly 5am to 8pm) and direct buses to/from Mexico City's airport ($145, 1½ hours, three daily).

Ometochtli direct buses run to Cuernavaca (M$18, 45 minutes) every 20 minutes, 6am to 10pm. They leave from the Ometochtli station, on the hill leading out of town on the Cuernavaca–Tepotzlán road (at the west end of 5 de Mayo).

ADO buses to Cuautla (M$20, 20 minutes) depart frequently from the Hwy 115D tollbooth just outside town.

Cuautla

🕾 735 / POP 150,000 / ELEV 1300M

Cuautla (*kwout-*la) has none of Tepoztlán's scenic beauty or the architectural merit of Cuernavaca, but it does have sulfur springs that have attracted people for centuries, as well as serious revolutionary credentials.

Cuautla was a base for one of Mexico's first leaders in the independence struggle, José María Morelos y Pavón, until he was forced to leave when the royalist army besieged the town in 1812. A century later it became a center of support for Emiliano Zapata's revolutionary army. However, if Mexican history and *balnearios* (bathing places) aren't your thing, there's absolutely nothing for you here – modern Cuautla is a perfectly pleasant town, but there's little to see and do aside from the above.

The two main plazas are Plaza Fuerte de Galeana, better known as the Alameda (a favorite haunt of mariachis-for-hire at weekends), and the *zócalo.*

¡QUE VIVA ZAPATA!

A peasant leader from Morelos state, Emiliano Zapata (1879–1919) was among the most radical of Mexico's revolutionaries, fighting for the return of hacienda land to the peasants with the cry '*¡Tierra y libertad!*' (Land and freedom!). The Zapatista movement was at odds with both the conservative supporters of the old regime and their liberal opponents. In November 1911 Zapata disseminated his *Plan de Ayala,* calling for restoration of all land to the peasants. After winning numerous battles against government troops in central Mexico (some in association with Pancho Villa), he was ambushed and killed in 1919. The following route traces some of Zapata's defining moments.

Ruta de Zapata

In Anenecuilco, 6km south of Cuautla, what's left of the adobe cottage where Zapata was born (on August 8, 1879) is now the **Museo de la Lucha para la Tierra** (Av Zapata; admission M$30; ☺10am-5pm).

About 20km south is the **Ex-Hacienda de San Juan Chinameca** (in the town of the same name), where in 1919 Zapata was lured into a fatal trap by Colonel Jesús Guajardo, following the orders of President Venustiano Carranza, who was eager to dispose of the rebel leader and consolidate the post-revolutionary government. Pretending to defect to the revolutionary forces, Guajardo set up a meeting with Zapata, who arrived at Chinameca accompanied by a guerrilla escort. Guajardo's men gunned down the general before he crossed the abandoned hacienda's threshold.

The hacienda has a small and, unfortunately, horribly maintained **museum** (Cárdenas; ☺9:30am-5pm) with a meager collection of photos and newspaper reproductions. But there's a statue of Zapata astride a rearing horse at the entrance, where you can still see the bullet holes where the revolutionary died and where old men gather to celebrate their fallen hero.

From Chinameca head 20km northwest to Tlaltizapán, the site of the excellent **Cuartel General de Zapata** (Guerrero 2; ☺10am-6pm Tue-Sun), the main barracks of the revolutionary forces. Here you can see Zapata's rifle (the trigger retains his fingerprints), the bed where he slept and the outfit he was wearing at the time of his death (riddled with bullet holes and stained with blood).

Though it's possible to do this route via *colectivo* (yellow 'Chinameca' combis traveling to Anenecuilco and Chinameca leave from the corner of Garduño and Matamoros in Cuautla every 10 minutes), it can be an all-day ordeal. The Morelos state tourism office in Cuernavaca arranges tours of the route.

◎ Sights

Ex-Convento de San Diego   HISTORIC BUILDING
In 1911 presidential candidate Francisco Madero embraced Emiliano Zapata at Cuautla's old **train station** (in the Ex-Convento de San Diego). Steam enthusiasts will want to come on Saturday, when Mexico's only steam-powered train fires up for short rides from 4pm to 9pm. The Ex-Convento is now home to the **Casa de Cultura** (☎352-52-21; Batalla 19 de Febrero s/n) and Cuautla's **tourist office** (☎352-52-21; ☺9am-8pm).

Museo Histórico del Oriente   MUSEUM
(Callejón del Castigo 3; admission M$31; ☺9am-5pm Tue-Sun) The former residence of José María Morelos houses the Museo Histórico del Oriente. Each room here covers a different historical period with displays of pre-Hispanic pottery, good maps and early photos of Cuautla and Zapata.

The iconic rebel's remains lie beneath the imposing **Zapata monument** in the middle of Plazuela Revolución del Sur.

🏃 Activities

Balnearios   SWIMMING
Cuautla's best-known *balneario* is the riverside **Agua Hedionda** (Stinky Water; ☎352-00-44; www.aguahedionda.mx; end of Av Progreso; adult/child M$50/30; ☺6:30am-5:30pm;). Waterfalls replenish two lake-sized pools with sulfur-scented tepid water. Take an 'Agua Hedionda' bus (M$6) from Plazuela Revolución del Sur. There's a two-for-the-price-of-one deal on Thursdays. Weekend prices rise by M$20.

Other *balnearios* worth visiting include **El Almeal** (Hernández; adult/child M$50/30, campsites per person M$60; ⊘9am-6pm; ☒) and the nicer **Los Limones** (Gabriel Teppa 14; adult/child M$55/40; ⊘8:30am-6pm; ☒). Both places are served by the same spring (no sulfur) and have extensive shaded picnic grounds. Prices are reduced to M$30 Monday to Friday.

🛏 Sleeping & Eating

Hotel Defensa del Agua   HOTEL $
(☑352-16-79; Defensa del Agua 34; s/tr/q M$150/370/450, d M$220-300; P☒) This modern, clean hotel is set out in a motel style with a small pool and spacious rooms with TV, phone and fan. There's a very handy Italian Coffee Company branch in the building for breakfast. Avoid rooms with windows facing the noisy street.

Hotel & Spa Villasor   RESORT $$
(☑352-65-21; www.hotelvillasor.com.mx; Av Progreso; s/d M$445/580, ste M$990; P☒☒) Out of town and located opposite the Agua Hedionda baths, this modern place has a large pool and comfortable rooms equipped with phone, fan and cable TV. With its own spa treatments, Villasor is the best option for relaxation, but it's not convenient for those without transportation.

Alameda   SANDWICHES $
(Los Bravos & Ferrara; breakfasts M$50-85; ⊘7:30am-7:30pm; ☑) Situated between the *zócalo* and Plaza Alameda, this bright, tropical-toned fast food diner serves excellent breakfasts, including large, tasty omelets and a dazzling array of freshly squeezed fruit juices. For lunch, it has a full range of hamburgers, *tortas* and sandwiches, including many vegetarian options.

Las Golondrinas   MEXICAN $$
(www.lasgolondrinas.com.mx; Catalán 19A; mains M$75-125; ⊘8am-11:30pm) Set in a 17th-century building filled with plants and koi ponds, Golondrinas offers an attractive atmosphere and excellent service. House specialties include a range of *molcajetes* (spicy stews cooked in a large stone mortar).

🛈 Getting There & Away

OCC (☑800-702-80-00; www.ado.com.mx) has 1st-class buses to Mexico City's Terminal Sur (M$106, every 15 minutes). Across the street, **Pullman de Morelos** (☑352-73-71; www.pullman.com.mx) travels to Tepoztlán (M$20, 20 minutes, every 20 minutes).

Cuernavaca
☑777 / POP 340,000 / ELEV 1480M

There's always been a formidable glamour surrounding Cuernavaca (kwehr-nah-*vah*-kah), the high-society capital of Morelos state. With its vast, gated haciendas and sprawling estates, it has in the past attracted everyone from the Shah of Iran to Charlie Mingus to its year-round warmth, clean air and attractive architecture.

Today this tradition continues, even though urban sprawl has put a decisive end to the clean air, and you're more likely to see vacationing North Americans and college students studying Spanish on month-long courses than meet international royalty and great artists in the street.

History

The first settlers to the valleys of modern Morelos are believed to have arrived in 1500 BC. In the centuries between 200 and 900 AD they organized a highly productive agricultural society and developed Xochicalco and other large constructions throughout the region. Later, the dominant Mexica (Aztecs) called them Tlahuica, which means 'people who work the land.' In 1379 a Mexica warlord conquered Cuauhnáhuac, subdued the Tlahuica and exacted an annual tribute that included 16,000 pieces of *amate* (bark paper) and 20,000 bushels of corn. The tributes payable by the subject states were set out in a register the Spanish later called the Códice Mendocino, in which Cuauhnáhuac was represented by a three-branch tree; this symbol now graces Cuernavaca's coat of arms.

The Mexica lord's successor married the daughter of the Cuauhnáhuac leader, and from this marriage was born Moctezuma I Ilhuicamina, the 15th-century Aztec king, who was a predecessor to Moctezuma II Xocoyotzin, encountered by Cortés. Under the Aztecs, the Tlahuica traded extensively and prospered. Their city was a learning and religious center, and archaeological remains suggest they had a considerable knowledge of astronomy.

When the Spanish arrived the Tlahuica were fiercely loyal to the Aztecs. In April 1521 they were finally overcome and Cortés torched the city. Soon the city became known as Cuernavaca, a more Spanish-friendly version of its original appellation.

In 1529 Cortés received his belated reward from the Spanish crown when he was named Marqués del Valle de Oaxaca, with an estate that covered 22 towns, including Cuernavaca, and 23,000 indigenous Mexicans. After he introduced sugar cane and new farming methods, Cuernavaca became a Spanish agricultural center, as it had been for the Aztecs. Cortés' descendants dominated the area for nearly 300 years.

With its salubrious climate, rural surroundings and colonial elite, Cuernavaca became a refuge for the rich and powerful in the 1700s and 1800s, including José de la Borda, the 18th-century Taxco silver magnate. Borda's lavish home was later a retreat for Emperor Maximilian and Empress Carlota. Cuernavaca has also attracted many artists and achieved literary fame as the setting for Malcolm Lowry's 1947 novel *Under the Volcano*.

Most important sites, bus terminals and budget-conscious hotels are near Cuernavaca's Plaza de Armas.

◉ Sights & Activities

Plaza de Armas & Jardín Juárez   PLAZA
Cuernavaca's *zócalo,* the Plaza de Armas, is flanked on the east by the Palacio de Cortés, on the west by the **Palacio de Gobierno** and on the northwest and south by restaurants and roving bands of mariachis. Although you can't enter the Palacio de Gobierno, it is a nice spot to contemplate some attractive architecture and enjoy the music. This *zócalo* is the only main plaza in Mexico without a church, chapel, convent or cathedral overlooking it.

Adjoining the northwest corner is the smaller **Jardín Juárez**, where the central gazebo (designed by tower specialist Gustave Eiffel) houses juice and sandwich stands, and hosts live band concerts on Thursday and Sunday evenings from 6pm. Roving vendors sell balloons, ice cream and corn on the cob under the trees, which fill up with legions of cacophonous grackles at dusk.

Palacio de Cortés   HISTORIC BUILDING
Cortés' imposing medieval-style fortress stands opposite the southeast end of the Plaza de Armas. Construction of this two-story, stone, fortress-style palace was accomplished between 1522 and 1532 and was built on the base of the city pyramid that Cortés destroyed after taking Cuauhnáhuac. The base is still visible from various points on the ground floor. Cortés resided here until he turned tail for Spain in 1541. The palace remained with Cortés' family for most of the next century but by the 18th century it was

being used as a prison. During the Porfirio Díaz era it became government offices.

Since 1974 the palace has housed the excellent **Museo Regional Cuauhnáhuac** (admission M$41; ⊘9am-6pm Tue-Sun), which has two floors of exhibits highlighting Mexican cultures and history. The last ticket is sold at 5:30pm. On the ground floor exhibits focus on pre-Hispanic cultures, including the local Tlahuica and their relationship with the Aztec empire. Most labeling is in Spanish only, with a few well-translated exceptions.

Upstairs covers events from the Spanish conquest to the present. On the balcony is a fascinating mural by Diego Rivera, commissioned in the mid-1920s by Dwight Morrow, the US ambassador to Mexico. Flowing from right to left, scenes from the Conquest through to the 1910 Revolution emphasize the cruelty, oppression and violence that have characterized Mexican history.

Recinto de la Catedral   CHURCH
Cuernavaca's cathedral stands in a large high-walled *recinto* (compound) – the entrance gate is on Hidalgo. Like the Palacio de Cortés, the cathedral was built in a grand fortress-like style, in an effort to impress, intimidate and defend against the natives. Franciscans started work on what was one of Mexico's earliest Christian missions in 1526, using indigenous labor and stones from the rubble of Cuauhnáhuac. The first structure was the **Capilla Abierta de San José**, an open chapel on the cathedral's west side.

The cathedral itself, the **Templo de la Asunción de María**, is plain and solid, with an unembellished facade. The side door, which faces north to the compound's entrance, shows a mixture of indigenous and European features – the skull and crossbones above it is a symbol of the Franciscan order. Inside are frescoes rediscovered early in the 20th century. Cuernavaca was a center for Franciscan missionary activities in Asia and the frescoes – said to show the persecution of Christian missionaries in Japan – were supposedly painted in the 17th century by a Japanese convert to Christianity.

The cathedral compound also holds two smaller churches. On the right as you enter is the **Templo de la Tercera Orden de San Francisco**. Its exterior was carved in 18th-century baroque style by indigenous artisans and its interior has ornate, gilded decorations. On the left as you enter is the

Cuernavaca

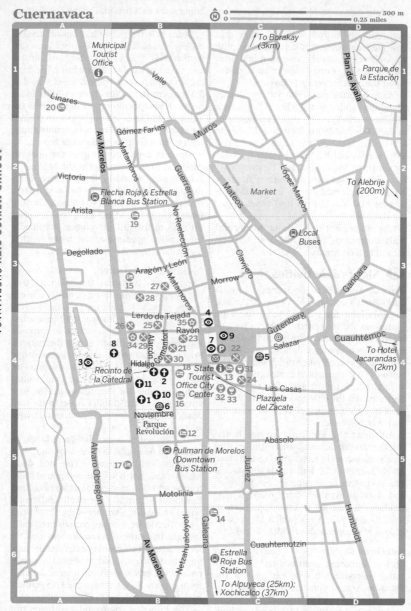

19th-century **Capilla del Carmen** where believers seek cures for illness.

Museo Robert Brady
MUSEUM

(www.bradymuseum.org; Netzahualcóyotl 4; admission M$35; ⊙10am-6pm Tue-Sun) Let's face it, who wouldn't want to be independently wealthy and spend their life traveling around the world collecting gorgeous little things for their lavish Mexican mansion? If that option isn't open to you, visit this museum – easily Cuernavaca's best – and live

Cuernavaca

time appreciating the exquisite taste of one man. Brady lived in Cuernavaca for 24 years after a spell in Venice, but his collections range from Papua New Guinea and India to Haiti and South America.

Originally part of the monastery within the Recinto de la Catedral, the house is a stunning testament to a man who knew what he liked. Every room, including the two gorgeous bathrooms and kitchen, is bedecked in paintings, carvings, textiles, antiques and folk arts from all corners of the earth. Among the treasures are works by well-known Mexican artists including Rivera, Tamayo, Kahlo and Covarrubias, as well as Brady's own paintings (check out his spot-on portrait of his friend Peggy Guggenheim). The gardens are lovely too, with a very tempting (but off-limits) swimming pool in one of them and a little cafe in the other.

Classic and contemporary films are shown in the museum's courtyard every Thursday at 5pm for a M$25 donation. Movies are in their original language with Spanish subtitles.

Jardín Borda GARDEN
(Av Morelos 271; adult/child M$30/15, Sun free; ⏰10am-5:30pm Tue-Sun) Beside the 1784 **Parroquia de Guadalupe**, this extravagant property, inspired by Versailles, was designed in 1783 for Manuel de la Borda as an addition to the stately residence built by his father José de la Borda. From 1866 Emperor Maximilian and Empress Carlota entertained their courtiers here and used the house as a summer residence.

The gardens are formally laid out on a series of terraces with paths, steps and fountains, and they originally featured a botanical collection with hundreds of varieties of ornamental plants and fruit trees. Because of a water shortage, the baroque-style fountains operate only on weekends.

Duck into the house to get an idea of how Mexico's 19th-century aristocracy lived. In typical colonial style, the buildings are arranged around courtyards. In one wing, the **Museo de Sitio** has exhibits on daily life during the empire period and original documents with the signatures of Morelos, Juárez and Maximilian.

Several romantic paintings in the **Sala Manuel M Ponce**, a recital hall near the entrance of the house, show scenes of the garden in Maximilian's time. One of the most famous paintings depicts Maximilian in the

vicariously. The one-time home of American artist and collector Robert Brady (1928–86), this museum which is housed in the **Casa de la Torre**, is a wonderful place to spend

garden with La India Bonita, the 'pretty Indian' who later became his lover.

Papalote Museo del Niño
MUSEUM

(Av Vicente Guerrero 205; admission M$120; ☉10am-8pm Fri-Wed, to 11pm Thu) Built as part of a land deal with the city, this excellent new children's museum has an odd location in a shopping center beside a Costco, about 4km north of downtown, but for travelers with children it's well worth seeking out. Geared towards education, technology and play, the museum includes a large Lego exhibit, musical elements and lots of bright colors. There's an IMAX in the same complex and discounts for families and groups.

 ## Courses

Cuernavaca is a well-established center for studying Spanish at all levels and has dozens of language schools. As such, standards are high, teaching is usually very thorough and prices competitive (generally M$2500 to M$5000 per week, plus fees and housing). The best schools offer small-group or individual instruction at all levels with four to five hours per day of intensive instruction plus a couple of hours' conversation practice. Classes begin each Monday, and most schools recommend a minimum enrollment of four weeks.

With so many teaching styles and options, prospective students should research the choices carefully. Contact the tourist office for an extensive list of schools.

Festivals & Events

Carnaval
CARNIVAL

Over the five days leading up to Ash Wednesday (falling on late February or early March), Cuernavaca's colorful Carnaval celebrations feature parades and art exhibits, plus street performances by Tepoztlán's Chinelo dancers.

Feria de la Primavera
CULTURAL

From late March to early April, the city's Spring Fair includes cultural and artistic events plus concerts and a beautiful exhibit of the city's spring flowers.

Sleeping

A steady stream of boutique hotels have opened in recent years and some of the best in the country are here, aimed squarely at weekend refugees from the capital. Budget hotels tend to be simple and spare, while midrange hotels are few and far between.

The town fills up with visitors from Mexico City at weekends and holidays, when prices rise significantly at many hotels.

TOP CHOICE Hotel Hacienda de Cortés
HISTORIC HOTEL $$$

(☎315-88-44, 800-220-76-97; www.hotelhacienda decortes.com; Plaza Kennedy 90; r from M$2350, ste $2937-6000; P ⊠) Built in the 16th century by Martín Cortés, who succeeded Hernán Cortés as Marqués del Valle de Oaxaca, this former sugar mill was renovated in 1980. It boasts 23 rooms of various levels of luxury, each with its own private garden and terrace. There's a swimming pool built around old stone columns and an excellent restaurant.

La Casa Azul
BOUTIQUE HOTEL $$$

(☎314-21-41, 314-36-34; www.hotelcasaazul.com. mx; Arista 17; r M$1350, ste M$1500-1800; P ⊛⊠) This 24-room boutique hotel is a short walk from the town center and has lots of charm. Originally part of the Guadalupe Convent, the hotel has soothing fountains, two pools and a great selection of local arts and crafts throughout. Prices go up at the weekend.

Las Mañanitas
LUXURY HOTEL $$$

(☎362-00-00; www.lasmananitas.com.mx; Linares 107; ste incl breakfast Sun-Thu M$2351-4828; P ⊛⊠) This utterly stunning place is where to head if you plan to impress someone. It's very much a destination hotel – you may not leave it for the whole weekend, after all – and so the fact that it's not in the exact center of town is irrelevant. The rooms are large and beautifully decorated yet understated, and many have large terraces overlooking the private gardens, stuffed full of peacocks and featuring a heated pool. Prices go up during the weekend.

Hostería del Sol
GUESTHOUSE $$

(☎318-32-41; Callejón de la Bolsa del Diablo; s/d with or without bathroom M$400/500; ⊠) This well-located charmer has reasonable prices and is spotlessly clean. Half of the hotel's six rooms share bathrooms, while all rooms are beautifully decorated in traditional blue and yellow tones. It's best to ring ahead, although at the time we visited staff didn't speak English. Rooms with windows facing Plazuela del Zacate can be noisy on weekends.

Hotel Juárez
HOTEL $

(☎314-02-19; Netzahualcóyotl 19; r M$350; P ⊠) The rooms at this basic and well-located hotel are large and airy but lack natural light. To compensate, a breezy terrace overlooks a grassy backyard, an attractive swimming pool and Cuernavaca's clay-tiled rooftops. It's nothing fancy but it's a good budget option.

Hotel Las Hortensas
HOTEL $

(☎318-52-65; www.hotelhortensias.com; Hidalgo 13; s M$240, d M$320-370) Cheap and central, Las Hortensas has small, sparse rooms, a lush garden and a friendly staff that seem to constantly be cleaning. Street-side rooms are noisy, so bring earplugs or ask for one of the darker interior rooms.

Hotel Colonial
HOTEL $

(☎318-64-14; Aragón y León 19; s/d/tr/q M$265/320/420/480; ⊗) While basic, this relaxed backpacker hotel is excellent value. There's a garden at its center, wi-fi and cable TV. The upstairs rooms with balconies and tall ceilings are best.

Hotel Antigua Posada
HOTEL $$

(☎310-21-79; www.hotelantiguaposada.com; Galeana 69; r incl breakfast M$935-1000, ste incl breakfast M$1100-1200; [P][⊗][☀]) This exclusive little hideaway is a short walk from the center of town and boasts just 11 rooms behind its unpromising exterior. But once inside there's a lovely courtyard and great service. The rooms are gorgeous, complete with wooden beams and rustic touches.

Casa Colonial
BOUTIQUE HOTEL $$$

(☎312-70-33, 800-623-08-43; www.casacolonial.com; Netzahualcóyotl 37; r M$1215, ste $1495-2525; [P][⊗][☀]) Set in a charming garden around a large pool, this 16-room, 19th-century mansion with beautifully furnished rooms has been lovingly restored and cleverly updated.

Hotel Jacarandas
RESORT $$$

(☎315-77-77; www.jacarandas.com.mx; Cuauhtémoc 133, Colonia Chapultepec; r from M$1450-5600; [P][⊗][☀]) This sprawling five-star retreat is designed as an escape from city life. Set in rambling grounds graced with lots of trees, lush gardens, a good restaurant and three pools of varying temperatures, this is an attractive – if pricey – weekend option. It's 2km east of the center.

Hotel Laam
BUSINESS HOTEL $$

(☎314-44-11; www.laamhotel.com; Av Morelos 239; ste M$900-1350; [P][⊗][☀]) With a slick, motel feel and comfortable, if sterile, rooms (some with huge terraces), this new-ish hotel is good value. Set back from the road, giving it distance from street noise, Hotel Laam comes with a tiled swimming pool and well-tended grounds.

Eating

Cuernavaca is a great food town which has a few excellent high-end restaurants and plenty of good cafes. There are, however, surprisingly few inticing midrange options.

TOP CHOICE Restaurante Hacienda de Cortés
INTERNATIONAL $$$

(☎315-88-44, 800-220-76-97; www.hotelhaciendadecortes.com; Plaza Kennedy 90; mains M$85-320; ⊗ 7am-12:30pm, 1:30-5pm, 7-11pm) Situated in the tranquil grounds of Hotel Hacienda de Cortés, this elegant but unpretentious hotel restaurant serves an excellent selection of salads and delicious international entrees, including a fantastic vegetarian lasagne, tuna in almond sauce with risotto, and well-prepared Angus steaks. The dining room is spectacular, with massive vines climbing the walls and wrought-iron chandeliers overhead.

L'arrosoir d' Arthur
FRENCH $$

(http://larrosoir.com.mx; Calle Juan Ruiz de Alarcón 13; menu of the day M$80-130; ⊗9am-midnight) As much a hangout and nightspot as a restaurant, this new French-owned restaurant in a loft space downtown has excellent, affordable French dishes (crepes, cassolette, chicken in mustard sauce), good cocktails and wines and live music, theater, dance and poetry events on weekends.

Iguana Green's
MEXICAN $

(Rayón 24; mains M$33-80; ⊗7am-11pm) With food this good and this cheap it would easy for Iguana to be just another anonymous *pozole* shop and still draw crowds, but the family that runs this friendly little restaurant takes obvious pride in creating a festive space – with crayon-colored chairs and tables and a mural along the wall.

Gaia Bistro-Wine Bar
MEXICAN $$$

(☎312-36-56; www.gaiarest.com.mx; Juárez 102; mains M$120-320; ⊗1-11pm Mon-Thu, to midnight Fri & Sat, to 6pm Sun) Once the mansion of the 'Mexican Charlie Chaplin,' actor Mario Moreno, this stylish restaurant has a very impressive international menu, with dishes like linguini with shrimp in cilantro sauce and a 'fish trilogy' served with tamarind and chili. Reserve a table with a view of the

Diego Rivera mosaic that adorns the bottom of the swimming pool.

El Barco
MEXICAN $

(Rayón 3; mains M$52-90; ⊙11am-11pm) This popular, no-nonsense joint specializes in Guerrero-style *pozole,* the all-curing Mexican version of matzo-ball soup. Heaping clay bowls are accompanied by fine oregano, mildly hot red chili, shredded lettuce, limes and chopped onions. Specify *pollo* (chicken) *maciza* unless you'd like your soup to include bits of fat, and *especial* if you enjoy avocado. For refreshment, there's ice-cold beer, pitchers of *agua de jamaica* (hibiscus water) and top-shelf tequilas.

La Comuna
CAFE $

(Morrow 6; mains M$30-55; ⊙9am-9pm Mon-Sat; 🛜) Decorated with fair-trade handicrafts and serving 'slow food' set meals – as well as excellent organic coffee and cheap beer – Comuna is the home of Cuerna's political left. There's a book exchange, art on the walls and regular lectures.

La India Bonita
MEXICAN $$

(Morrow 115; www.laindiabonita.com; mains M$75-190; ⊙8am-9:30pm) Set in a lush courtyard, Cuernavaca's oldest restaurant also has some of its best traditional Mexican food – from *brocheta al mezcal* (skewered meats marinated in *mezcal*) to *chile en nogada* (*poblano* pepper in walnut sauce) – with the occasional enticing twist. India Bonita operates a tasty bakery next door.

Restaurant Las Mañanitas
FRENCH $$$

(Linares 107; breakfasts M$105-285, mains M$260-500; ⊙8am-noon & 1-11pm) The restaurant and bar of Cuernavaca's most famous hotel Las Mañanitas is a luxurious splurge, open to all. The expansive menu has a heavy French accent, with dishes such as entrecote Bourguignon, and sumptuous desserts. Choose between tables inside the mansion or on the terrace where you can watch wildlife wander among fine modern sculptures in the garden. Reservations are recommended.

Casa Hidalgo
MEXICAN $$$

(Jardín de los Héroes 6; mains M$155-195) Directly opposite the Palacio de Cortés, with a great terrace and an even better upstairs balcony, this is one of Cuernavaca's most popular eateries and attracts a well-heeled crowd of local socialites and wealthy visitors. The menu is eclectic (try cold mango-agave soup with jicama or *tlaxcalteca* chicken breast stuffed

with cheese and roasted *poblano* pepper with three salsas: squash blossom, spinach and chipotle, for example).

Bon's Café
CAFE $

(Comonfort 6B; mains M$40-55; ⊙8am-10pm Mon-Thu, 8:30am-11pm Fri & Sat; 🛜) Head to this large, open cafe on a *callejón* (alley or very short street) for affordable, delicious breakfasts – including scrumptious bagel sandwiches, waffles and croissants – and a quiet place to read or use your laptop (wifi is free). Afternoon fare includes simple paninis and heaped salads.

Tamuz
INTERNATIONAL $$$

(www.tamuz.com.mx; Reforma N. 501; mains M$85-250; ⊙ 8am-6pm Tue-Wed, to 10pm Thu, to 11pm Fri & Sat, to 6pm Sun) With an Israeli chef and a menu that includes dishes like chicken marsala, Tel Aviv–style, pita with smoked salmon dip, and polenta, this restaurant, in one of the Cuernavaca's more posh neighborhoods, has a Los Angeles-esque design (modern, spare and characterless) with a lovely backyard.

Hare Krishna
VEGETARIAN $

(Rayón 24; comida corrida M$50; ⊙10am-6:30pm Mon-Sat; 🖉) Come early to this hole-in-the-wall vegetarian restaurant which serves delicious and generous set meals, meat-free hamburgers and house-baked whole wheat bread. The cafe's cook also offers vegetarian cooking classes.

Trattoria Marco Polo
PIZZERIA $$

(Hidalgo 30; pizzas M$66-142; ⊙1-10:30pm) Italian dishes – including a broad range of excellent, thin-crust pizza – and an attractive setting just across from the cathedral make this a decent option for reasonably priced international fare with a view.

Drinking

There's a buzzing nightlife in Cuernavaca, supported by a year-round student population that keeps places busy every night of the week. Plazuela del Zacate and the adjacent alley Las Casas have a good mix of rowdy and laid-back bars – all open around sunset and staying open until the last patron leaves. There are no cover charges and almost every downtown bar offers two-for-one drink specials most nights of the week.

El Kiosco
JUICE BAR

This gazebo in the center of the plaza, opposite Teatro Ocampo, serves fresh fruit

XOCHICALCO

Atop a desolate plateau with views for miles around, Xochicalco (admission M$51; ⊘9am-6pm, last ticket 5pm) is a relatively easy day trip from Cuernavaca that shouldn't be missed. Large enough to make the journey worthwhile, but not so well known as to be overrun with tourists, this exceptional site is one of the most impressive in the region.

A Unesco World Heritage site and one of central Mexico's most important archaeological sites, Xochicalco (so-chee-*cal*-co) is Náhuatl for 'place of the house of flowers.' The collection of white stone ruins, many still to be excavated, covers approximately 10 sq km. They represent the various cultures – Tlahuica, Toltec, Olmec, Zapotec, Mixtec and Aztec – for which Xochicalco was a commercial, cultural and religious center. When Teotihuacán began to weaken around AD 650 to 700, Xochicalco began to rise in importance, achieving its peak between AD 650 and 900, with far-reaching cultural and commercial relations. Around AD 650 Zapotec, Maya and Gulf coast spiritual leaders convened here to correlate their respective calendars. Xochicalco remained an important center until around 1200, when its excessive growth precipitated a demise similar to that of Teotihuacán.

The site's most famous monument is the **Pirámide de Quetzalcóatl**. Archaeologists have surmised from its well-preserved bas-reliefs that astronomer-priests met here at the beginning and end of each 52-year cycle of the pre-Hispanic calendar. Site signs are in English and Spanish, but information at the excellent, ecologically sensitive **museum**, situated 200m from the ruins, is in Spanish only.

From October through May, the site offers a nighttime **light show** (✆737-374-30-90 for reservations; xochicalco.mor@inah.gob.mx) on Friday and Saturday nights. It's quite a spectacle.

From Cuernavaca's market, buses with 'Xochi' on their windshield (M$13) depart every 30 minutes for the site entrance. On arrival, you'll need to walk to the museum to buy tickets. The last return bus leaves around 6pm. Alternatively, take a taxi (M$20) from the site to the nearby town of Alpuyeca, where there are frequent buses back to Cuernavaca.

smoothies made with a variety of exotic fruits, vegetables and nuts.

El Romántico   BAR
(Plazuela del Zacate) The walls of this small bar are adorned with black-and-white photographs of classic Mexican film stars, some rather seductively posed. The real appeal is cheap drinks and a jubilant crowd.

La Plazuela   DJ
(Las Casas) For those not into the guitar scene, this is the home of booming house and techno.

D'ubai   DJ
(Juárez 2) D'ubai has a balcony overlooking the Palacio de Cortés, and DJs and dancing on weekends.

☆ Entertainment

Hanging around the central plazas is a popular activity, especially on Sunday evenings, when open-air concerts are often staged. Jardín Borda (p175) hosts recitals many Thursday nights.

Nightclubs
The better discos impose a modest cover charge but women are usually let in for free. Some discos enforce dress codes and trendier places post style police at the door. Things really get going after 11pm. Some recommended venues include the following.

Alebrije   CLUB
(Plan de Ayala 405; www.elalebrijecuernavaca.com; ⊘10pm-late Fri & Sat) This is a massive space, heavy on flashing lights and techno.

Borakay   CLUB
(Av Teopanzolco 503; ⊘10pm-late Wed-Sat) Borakay is an upscale, indoor-outdoor club for Cuerna's hipster elite. Dress to impress.

Theaters
If your *español* is up to it, sample Cuernavaca's theater scene.

Cine Teatro Morelos   CINEMA
(✆318-10-50; Av Morelos 188; tickets from M$25) Morelos' state theater hosts quality film series, plays and dance performances. There's

BUSES FROM CUERNAVACA

DESTINATION	FARE (M$)	DURATION	FREQUENCY (DAILY)
Cuautla	50	1½hr	28
Mexico City	82-92	1½hr	40
Mexico City Airport	150	2hr	24
Taxco	71	1½hr	3
Tepoztlán	18	½hr	28

a full schedule posted out front and a bookstore and cafe inside.

Teatro Ocampo THEATER
(☑318-63-85; Jardín Juárez 2) Near Jardín Juárez, this theater stages contemporary plays. A calendar of cultural events is posted at its entrance.

Information

Emergency
Ambulance (☑311-85-02)
Cruz Roja (Red Cross; ☑315-35-05)
Fire (☑317-14-89)
Tourist Police (☑800-903-92-00)

Internet Access
There's also internet access at the Futura and Estrella Blanca bus station.
Cyber Gasso (per hr M$7; ⊗7:30am-9:30pm Mon-Sat, 9:30am-9:30pm Sun; ✺) Hidalgo (Hidalgo 40); Guternberg (Guternberg 198)

Laundry
Nueva Tintorería Francesa (Juárez 2; per kg M$15; ⊗9am-7pm Mon-Fri, to 2:30pm Sat)

Medical Services
Hospital Inovamed (☑311-24-82; Cuauhtémoc 305) In Colonia Lomas de la Selva, 1km north of town.

Post
Main post office (Plaza de Armas; ⊗8am-6pm Mon-Fri)

Tourist Information
There's an information booth in the cathedral and other kiosks around town, including at most bus stations. Ask for maps.
Municipal tourist office (☑329-44-04; www. cuernavaca.gob.mx/turismo; Av Morelos 278; ⊗9am-6pm) Also has a tourist police office.
State Tourist Office (www.morelosturistico. com; ⊗8am-6pm Mon-Fri) main branch (☑314-38-72/81, 800-987-82-24; Av Morelos Sur 187); city center (☑314-39-20; Hidalgo 5) This excellent tourist office has a wealth of brochures, maps and information.

Getting There & Away

Hwy 95D (the Mexico City–Acapulco toll road) skirts the city's east side. If you're driving from the north take the Cuernavaca exit and cross to Hwy 95 (where you'll see a statue of Zapata on horseback). Hwy 95 becomes Blvd Zapata, then Avenida Morelos as you descend south into town. From Avenida Matamoros (still traveling south) the Avenida Morelos is one way, northbound only. To reach the center, veer left down Matamoros.

Bus
Cuernavaca's main-line bus companies operate the following separate long-distance terminals.
Estrella de Oro (EDO; ☑312-30-55; www. estrelladeoro.com.mx; Av Morelos Sur 812)
Estrella Roja (ER; ☑318-59-34; www.estrella roja.com.mx; cnr Galeana & Cuauhtemotzin)
Flecha Roja & Estrella Blanca (FR & EB; ☑312-26-26; www.estrellablanca.com.mx; Av Morelos 503, btwn Arista & Victoria) Futura services leave from here as well.
Pullman de Morelos (PDM; ☑318-09-07; www.pullman.com.mx; cnr Calles Abasolo & Netzahualcóyotl)

See the table above for daily 1st-class and deluxe services from Cuernavaca.

Car & Motorcycle
Cuernavaca is 89km south of Mexico City, a 1½-hour drive on Hwy 95 or a one-hour trip via Hwy 95D. Both roads continue south to Acapulco – Hwy 95 detours through Taxco, Hwy 95D is more direct and much faster.

Getting Around
You can walk to most places of interest in central Cuernavaca. Local buses (M$6) advertise their destinations on their windshields. Many local buses, and those to nearby towns, leave from the southern corner of the city's labyrinthine market. Taxis to most places in town cost M$30.

To get to the Estrella de Oro bus terminal, 1km south (downhill) of the center, take a Ruta 20 bus down Galeana; in the other direction, catch any bus heading up Avenida Morelos. Ruta 17 buses head up Avenida Morelos and stop within one block of the Pullman de Morelos terminal at Casino de la Selva. All other depots are walking distance from the *zócalo*.

Taxco

📞 762 / POP 52,000 / ELEV 1800M

The first sight of Taxco (*tahss*-ko) across the steep valley as you approach it from the north is enough to take your breath away. Scattered down a precipitous hillside surrounded by dramatic mountains and cliffs, its perfectly preserved colonial architecture and the twin belfries of its baroque masterpiece, Templo de Santa Prisca, make for one of the most beguiling views anywhere in the central highlands.

Taxco, 160km southwest of Mexico City, has ridden waves of boom and bust associated with the fantastically wealthy silver deposits discovered here in the 16th century and then repeatedly until the early 20th century. With its silver now almost depleted, the town has fallen back on tourism to sustain it. As such, it's a rare example of preservation-centric development in Mexico. Unlike many colonial-era towns, Taxco has not been engulfed by industrial suburbs, and its status as a national historical monument means that even new buildings must conform to the old in scale, style and materials.

The downside of this embrace of the past is that the town sometimes feels like a museum piece that's given itself over to visitors, who flood Taxco during the weekend and during festivals. Despite this, Taxco is a striking small city and one of the best weekend trips from the capital.

History

Taxco was called Tlachco (Ball-Playing Place) by the Aztecs, who dominated the region from 1440 until the Spanish arrived. The colonial city was founded by Rodrigo de Castañeda in 1529, with a mandate from Hernán Cortés. Among the town's first Spanish residents were three miners – Juan de Cabra, Juan Salcedo and Diego de Nava – and the carpenter Pedro Muriel. In 1531, they established the first Spanish mine in North America.

The Spaniards came searching for tin, which they found in small quantities, but by 1534 they had discovered tremendous lodes of silver. That year the Hacienda El Chorrillo was built, complete with water wheel, smelter and aqueduct – the remains of the latter form the old arches (Los Arcos) over Hwy 95 at the north end of town.

The prospectors quickly depleted the first silver veins and fled Taxco. Further quantities of ore were not discovered until 1743. Don José de la Borda, who had arrived in 1716 from France at the age of 16 to work with his miner brother, accidentally unearthed one of the region's richest veins. According to the legend, Borda was riding near where the Templo de Santa Prisca now stands when his horse stumbled, dislodged a stone and exposed the precious metal.

Borda went on to make three fortunes and lose two. He introduced new techniques of draining and repairing mines, and he reportedly treated his indigenous workers better than most colonial mine owners. The Templo de Santa Prisca was the devout Borda's gift to Taxco. His success attracted more prospectors, and new silver veins were found and played out. With most of the silver gone, Taxco became a quiet town with a dwindling population and economy.

In 1929 a US architect and professor named William (Guillermo) Spratling arrived and, at the suggestion of the then US ambassador Dwight Morrow, set up a silver workshop as a way to rejuvenate the town. (Another version has it that Spratling was writing a book and resorted to the silver business because his publisher went bust. A third has it that Spratling had a notion to create jewelry that synthesized pre-Hispanic motifs with art deco modernism.) The workshop evolved into a factory, and Spratling's apprentices began establishing their own shops. Today, Taxco is home to hundreds of silver shops, many producing for export.

While one of the joys of Taxco is getting lost while aimlessly wandering the pretty streets, it's actually a very easy place to find your way around. The twin belfries of Santa Prisca make the best landmark, situated as they are on the *zócalo*, Plaza Borda. Nearly all of the town's streets are one way, with the main road Avenida de los Plateros being the only major two-way street. This is where both bus stations are located and is the road for entering and leaving the town. The basic *colectivo* route is a counterclockwise loop going north on Avenida de los Plateros and south through the center of town.

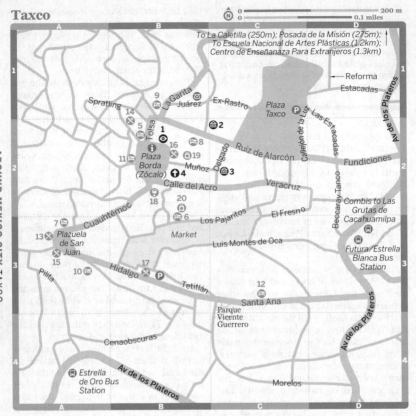

Taxco

◎ **Sights**

1 Casa Borda (Centro Cultural Taxco)	B2
2 Museo de Arte Virreinal (Casa Humboldt)	C2
3 Museo Guillermo Spratling	C2
4 Templo de Santa Prisca	B2

🛏 **Sleeping**

5 Hotel Agua Escondida	B2
6 Hotel Casa Arellano	B3
7 Hotel Casa Grande	A3
8 Hotel Emilia Castillo	B2
9 Hotel Mi Casita	B1
10 Hotel Santa Prisca	A3
11 Posada Los Balcones	B2
12 Pueblo Lindo	C3

🍴 **Eating**

13 Hostería Bar El Adobe	A3
La Concha Nostra	(see 7)
14 La Hacienda de Taxco	B2
15 La Hamburguesa	A3
16 Pozolería Tía Calla	B2
17 Restaurante Santa Fe	B3

🍷 **Drinking**

| 18 Bar Berta | B2 |

🛍 **Shopping**

19 EBA Elena Ballesteros	B2
20 Mercado de Artesanías Plata	B2
Patio de las Artesanías	(see 16)

◎ Sights & Activities

Templo de Santa Prisca   CHURCH

The icon of Taxco, Santa Prisca was a labor of love for town hero José de la Borda. The local Catholic hierarchy allowed the silver magnate to donate this church to Taxco on the condition that he mortgage his mansion and other assets to guarantee its completion. The project nearly bankrupted him but the risk was well worth it – the resulting building is one of Mexico's most beautiful and striking pieces of baroque architecture. It was designed by Spanish architects Juan Caballero and Diego Durán, and was constructed between 1751 and 1758.

Perhaps Santa Prisca's most striking feature (best viewed side-on) is the contrast between its belfries, with their elaborate Churrigueresque facade overlooking the Plaza Borda, and the far more simple, constrained and elegant nave. The rose-colored stone used on the facade is extraordinarily beautiful in the sunlight – look out for the oval bas-relief depiction of Christ's baptism above the doorway. Inside, the intricately sculpted, gold-covered altarpieces are equally fine Churrigueresque specimens.

Museo Guillermo Spratling   MUSEUM

(Delgado 1; admission M$31; ⊗9am-5pm Tue-Sat, to 3pm Sun) This very well laid-out three-story history and archaeology museum is off an alley behind Templo de Santa Prisca. It contains a small but excellent collection of pre-Hispanic jewelry, art, pottery and sculpture from US silversmith William Spratling's private collection. The phallic cult pieces are a particular eye-opener. On the basement floor there are examples of Spratling's designs using pre-Hispanic motifs. The top floor hosts occasional temporary exhibits.

Museo de Arte Virreinal   MUSEUM

(Ruiz de Alarcón 12; adult/student M$20/15; ⊗10am-6pm Tue-Sun) This charming, rather rag-tag religious art museum is housed in a wonderful old house that is often referred to as Casa Humboldt, even though the famous German explorer and naturalist Friedrich Heinrich Alexander von Humboldt slept here for only one night in 1803! The museum hosts a small but well-displayed collection of art, which is labeled in English and Spanish. The most interesting exhibit describes restoration work on Santa Prisca, during which some fabulous material (including tapestries, woodwork altarpieces and rich decorative fabrics) was discovered in the basement of the house, and

there is also an interesting display on the Manila Galleons, which pioneered trade between the Americas and the Far East.

FREE Casa Borda   CULTURAL BUILDING

(Centro Cultural Taxco, Plaza Borda; ⊗10am-6pm Tue-Sun) Built by José de la Borda in 1759, the Casa Borda serves as a cultural center hosting experimental theater and exhibiting contemporary sculpture, painting and photography by Guerrero artists. The building, however, is the main attraction. Due to the unevenness of the terrain, the rear window looks out on a precipitous four-story drop, even though the entrance is on the ground floor.

Teleférico   CABLE CAR

(one-way/round-trip adult M$45/65, child M$30/45; ⊗8am-7pm) From the north end of Taxco, near Los Arcos, a Swiss-made gondola ascends 173m to the Hotel Monte Taxco resort affording fantastic views of Taxco and the surrounding mountains. To find the entrance, walk uphill from the south side of Los Arcos and turn right through the Escuela Nacional de Artes Plásticas gate.

◈ Courses

Taxco is a popular place for foreigners to study.

Centro de Enseñanza
Para Extranjeros   LANGUAGE

(CEPE; ☎622-34-10; www.cepe.unam.mx; courses from M$2942 per month) This branch of Mexico City's Universidad Nacional Autónoma de México offers intensive Spanish-language courses in the atmospheric Ex-Hacienda El Chorrillo. Advanced students may take additional courses in Mexican art history, geography and literature.

Escuela Nacional de Artes Plásticas   ARTS

(☎622-36-90; www.enap.unam.mx) Next door, this school offers arts workshops in painting, sculpture and jewelry from US$1200 per course.

✯ Festivals & Events

Be sure to reserve your hotel in advance if your visit coincides with one of Taxco's annual festivals. Double-check exact dates of moveable feasts with the tourist office.

Fiestas de Santa Prisca
& San Sebastián   RELIGIOUS

Taxco's patron saints are honored on January 18 (Santa Prisca) and January 20 (San

Sebastián), when locals parade by the Templo de Santa Prisca for an annual blessing, their pets and farm animals in tow.

Jornadas Alarconianas   ARTS
This summertime cultural festival, honoring Taxco-born playwright Juan Ruiz de Alarcón, presents concerts and dance performances by internationally renowned performing artists.

Día del Jumil   FOOD
The Monday after the Day of the Dead (November 2), locals celebrate the *jumil* – the edible beetle said to represent the giving of life and energy to Taxco residents for another year. Many families camp on the Cerro de Huixteco (above town) over the preceding weekend, and townsfolk climb the hill to collect *jumiles* and share food and camaraderie.

Feria de la Plata   CRAFTS
The week-long national silver fair convenes in late November or early December. Craft competitions are held and some of Mexico's best silverwork is on display. Other festivities include rodeos, concerts, dances and burro races.

Las Posadas   CULTURAL
From December 16 to 24, nightly candlelit processions fill Taxco's streets with door-to-door singing. Children are dressed up to resemble biblical characters. At the end of the night, they attack piñatas.

🛏 Sleeping

Taxco has a wealth of hotels, from large four- and five-star resorts to charming family-run posadas. During holiday weekends, when the hordes arrive from Mexico City, it's a good idea to reserve ahead.

Earplugs are also a good idea. Owing to the innumerable Volkswagen taxis that serve as transportation in this, the steepest of hill towns, street noise is a problem nearly everywhere.

TOP CHOICE⟩ Hotel Mi Casita   INN $$
(☑627-17-77; www.hotelmicasita.com; Altos de Redondo 1; s/tr from M$500/750, d M$600-650, ste M$700-850; ❄@☎) With 12 beautifully and individually decorated rooms just moments from the *zócalo* and wraparound balconies with views over the cathedral, this elegant bed and breakfast is one of the best bets in town. A colonial home run by a family of jewelry designers, the comfortable rooms

feature original hand-painted bathroom tiles, and some have private terraces. Three rooms have rustic Talavera bathtubs, and all have fans and cable TV. Prices include breakfast.

Pueblo Lindo   HOTEL $$$
(☑622-34-81; www.pueblolindo.com.mx; Hidalgo 30; r & ste incl breakfast from US$94-126; P@ ☎⚟) This elegant new hotel – one of the first significant additions to the city's scene in recent years – manages to balance style and substance, embracing a Mexican-inspired aesthetic (bright colors, wooden furnishings) without being traditionalist. There are flatscreen TVs, wi-fi, a bar-lounge and excellent service. The rooftop pool has fantastic views, as do many of the rooms.

Hotel Casa Arellano   GUESTHOUSE $
(☑622-02-15; Los Pajaritos 23; dm M$140, s with/ without bathroom M$210/160, d M$320/280) Taxco's backpacker-friendly guesthouse has basic, clean rooms and three well-tended balconies of flowers, caged birds, and a variety of rooms and ample terraces for relaxing. Rooms can sleep up to five people (M$750).

Hotel Casa Grande   HOTEL $
(☑622-09-69; www.hotelcasagrande.com.mx; Plazuela de San Juan 7; s with/without bathroom M$250/170, d M$390/250, tr M$450/300; ☎) Its excellent location and superb terrace overlooking the square makes Casa Grande the most attractive budget option in town. But bring your earplugs as the music from the restaurant-bar La Concha Nostra goes late into the night.

Posada Los Balcones   HOTEL $
(☑622-02-50; Plazuela de los Gallos 5; s/d M$300/ 450) As its name suggests, many of the 15 rooms at this straightforward budget hotel have small balconies overlooking the boisterous street below. Just moments from Santa Prisca, Los Balcones is centrally located. Every room has its own bathroom and TV.

Hotel Santa Prisca   HOTEL $$
(☑622-00-80; Cenaobscuras 1; s/d/tr/ste M$350/ 500/550/800; P) The 31-room Santa Prisca has traditional Mexican decor and a welcoming courtyard garden. It has a great location too, right in the thick of things. Rooms are smallish, but most have breezy private balconies. All have two beds, and newer, sunnier rooms fetch a bit more. The parking lot is reached via a tunnel at the hotel's uphill end.

Hotel Emilia Castillo　　　　　INN $$
(☎622-67-17; www.hotelemiliacastillo.com; Ruiz de Alarcón 7; s/d/tr M$500/550/600) All 14 rooms are spotlessly clean and have beautiful tiled bathrooms. Owned by a family of famous silver workers, this intimate hotel has colonial charm and reasonable prices. Sadly, it's in an especially noisy location – ask for a room at the back but don't miss the views from the rooftop terrace.

Hotel Agua Escondida　　　BUSINESS HOTEL $
(☎622-07-36, 800-504-03-11; www.aguaescondida. com; Plaza Borda 4; s/d M$375/450; [P][@][🛜][🌊]) Facing the *zócalo,* Hotel Agua Escondida has two swimming pools and a cafe-bar on a high terrace with unmatchable views of Santa Prisca. The 60 comfortable rooms, popular with visiting silver importers, have Mexican furnishings, cable TV and phone. Rooms with balconies overlooking the street suffer from traffic noise. The hotel's exceedingly reasonable prices rise at the weekend.

Posada de la Misión　　　LUXURY HOTEL $$$
(☎622-00-63, 800-008-29-20; www.posadamisi on.com; Cerro de la Misión 32; r incl breakfast M$1000-3000; [P][🛜][🌊]) On a steep hill overlooking town, the rambling grounds of La Misión are a luxurious escape from Taxco's bustle. The rooms are large, bright and airy – and many have balconies with breathtaking views. There's also a gorgeous pool and Jacuzzi under a mosaic of Cuauhtémoc, and an excellent restaurant.

🍴 Eating & Drinking

Many of the best spots in town to grab a bite are also a good place to down a drink.

Pozolería Tía Calla　　　　MEXICAN $
(Plaza Borda 1; mains M$40-60; ⊘1-10pm Wed-Mon) There are no fine vistas or breezy *terrazas* (terraces) here – just authentic, no-nonsense *pozole,* served up in Auntie Calla's basement. Pick your poison: chicken or pork. Pork comes loaded with *chicharrón* (fried pork skin), avocado and all the fixings. No matter your meat choice, the broth is always pork-based. The beer steins are chilled and there's *fútbol* on the *tele*. What more could you ask for?

La Caletilla　　　　　　SEAFOOD $$
(Av de los Plateros 198; mains M$75-140; ⊘11am-6pm Thu-Tue) High in the mountains and far from the sea, Taxco's perhaps the last place you'd expect to find a great *marisquería.* But La Caletilla's small, fish-only menu is loved by locals who flock to its large tiled terrace for heaped portions of delicate ceviche, three kinds of seafood soup and well-prepared platters of shrimp and fish.

La Hacienda de Taxco　　　MEXICAN $$
(Plaza Borda 4; mains M$36-115; ⊘7:30am-10:30pm; [♿]) Offering an extensive menu of traditional Mexican dishes (including house-made jam in the morning and a 20-ingredient, house-made *mole* in the afternoon) La Hacienda also has considerate touches, like the option of egg-white-only breakfasts and child-sized portions.

Hostería Bar El Adobe　　　MEXICAN $$
(Plazuela de San Juan 13; mains M$45-150) This place doesn't share the captivating views of the tourist restaurants on the plaza, but the interior is charmingly decorated with black and white photos of everyone from Pancho Villa to Elvis. On weekends, there's *pozole* (M$65), live *trova* music on Saturday night and a buffet on Sunday (M$115).

Restaurante Santa Fe　　　MEXICAN $
(Hidalgo 2; mains M$55-90; ⊘8am-9pm) In business for over 50 years, Santa Fe is a favorite among locals for its fairly priced traditional fare like *conejo en chile ajo* (rabbit in garlic and chile). The walls are plastered with patron photos and some excellent black-and-white shots of ye olde Taxco. The three-course *menu del día* is a bargain at M$70.

La Concha Nostra　　　　ITALIAN $$
(Plazuela de San Juan 5; pizzas M$35-115; ⊘noon-midnight) On the 2nd floor of the Hotel Casa Grande, this popular pizza-and-pasta place serves food and drink until midnight. You can watch the action on Plazuela San Juan from the balcony. Live music shakes the house on weekend evenings.

Bar Berta　　　　　　　CANTINA
(Cuauhtémoc; ⊘11am-8pm) By rights Berta should be flooded with lost-looking tourists, but instead there's a clientele of local roughs knocking back stiff drinks and watching *fútbol*. There's a tiny upstairs terrace for people-watching over the *zócalo*. Try a Berta (tequila, honey, lime and mineral water), the house specialty.

La Hamburguesa　　　　BURGERS $
(Plazuela de San Juan 5; set breakfasts from M$30-50, burgers from M$18; ⊘8am-11pm Thu-Tue) For a quick, affordable meal try this popular diner on the west side of Plazuela San Juan. It serves five styles of set breakfasts in the

BUSES FROM TAXCO

DESTINATION	FARE (M$)	DURATION	FREQUENCY (DAILY)
Acapulco	237	4-5hr	7 EDO
Cuernavaca	75	1½hr	5 EDO
	71	1½hr	4 from Futura terminal
Mexico City (Terminal Sur)	175	3hr	4 EDO
	173	3hr	5 from Futura terminal

morning and burger-and-fries combos at lunch and dinner.

 Shopping

If you're looking for silver there are several shops in the **Patio de las Artesanías** (Plaza Borda) building. **EBA Elena Ballesteros** (www.ebaplata.com; Muñoz 4) has creative, well-crafted designs.

For quantity rather than quality, trawl the vast, poorly displayed masses of rings, chains and pendants at the **Mercado de Artesanías Plata** (⊘11am-8pm).

 Information

Several banks around the main plazas and bus stations have ATMs. There are card phones near Plaza Borda, and quieter ones in nicer hotel lobbies.

Cruz Roja (Red Cross; ☏065)
Hospital General (☏622-93-00)
Police (☏622-10-17)
Post Office (Palacio Municipal, Juárez 10)
Tourist Module (Plaza Borda) There's a tourism kiosk in the main plaza that mostly exists to hand out brochures and push tours.

 Getting There & Away

The shared Futura/Estrella Blanca terminal on Avenida de los Plateros offers luggage storage. The Estrella de Oro (EDO) terminal is at the south end of town.

For more frequent bus services to the coast, take a shared taxi ($24) from in front of the bus station to the nearby town of Iguala, about 30 minutes away.

 Getting Around

Apart from walking, combis (white Volkswagen minibuses) and taxis are the best way to navigate Taxco's steep and narrow cobbled streets.

Combis (M$4.50) are frequent and operate from 7am to 8pm. 'Zócalo' combis depart from Plaza Borda, travel down Cuauhtémoc to Plazuela de San Juan, then head down the hill on Hidalgo. They turn right at Morelos, left at Avenida de los Plateros, and go north until La Garita, where they turn left and return to the *zócalo*. 'Arcos/Zócalo' combis follow the same route except that they continue past La Garita to Los Arcos, where they do a U-turn and head back to La Garita. Combis marked 'PM' (for Pedro Martín) go to the southern end of town from Plaza Borda, past the Estrella de Oro bus station. Taxis cost M$20 to M$35 for trips around town.

Parque Nacional Grutas de Cacahuamilpa

One of central Mexico's most stunning natural sights, the **Cacahuamilpa caverns** (http://cacahuamilpa.conanp.gob.mx; admission M$40, mandatory tour guide M$22; ⊘10am-7pm) is a must-see for anyone visiting Taxco or Cuernavaca. The scale of the caves is hard to imagine, with vast chambers up to 82m high leading 1.2km beneath the mountainside, inside of which are mind-blowing stalactites and stalagmites.

Unfortunately, individual access to the (perfectly safe) pathway through the caves is not allowed. Instead, visitors are required to indulge guides who lead large group tours (departures each hour on the hour), with constant stops to point out shapes (Santa Claus, a kneeling child, a gorilla) in the rock. Thankfully, at the end of the one-hour tour, you can wander back to the entrance – if you're not afraid of the dark – at your own pace. Most guides do not speak English.

From the cave exit it's possible to follow a path 15 minutes to the fast-flowing **Río Dos Bocas**. There are spectacular views year-round and tranquil pools for swimming during the dry season. Bring bug spray.

Weekends are often very crowded, with long lines and large group tours – making mid-week a more pleasant time for a visit. There are restaurants, snacks and souvenir shops near the entrance. The last ticket is sold at 5pm.

❶ Getting There & Away

To reach the caves, take an Estrella Blanca 'Grutas' bus from the main Avenida de los Plateros bus terminal in Taxco (M$25). You'll be deposited at the crossroads where the road splits off to Cuernavaca. From there, walk 350m downhill to the park's visitor center.

WEST OF MEXICO CITY

The area to the west of Mexico City is dominated by the large industrial and administrative city of Toluca, the capital of the state of Mexico. While pleasant, Toluca has little to recommend it to travelers and most bypass it enroute to the area's two wonderful small-town, colonial gems: Malinalco, a sleepy and remote village with some fascinating pre-Hispanic ruins perched above it, and Valle de Bravo, a cosmopolitan getaway favored by Mexico's elite and located on the shores of a large, artificial reservoir a dramatic two-hour drive west of Toluca. The countryside surrounding Toluca itself is scenic with pine forests, rivers and a huge extinct volcano, Nevado de Toluca.

Toluca

🕿722 / POP 490,000 / ELEV 2660M

Like many colonial Mexican cities, Toluca's development has created a ring of urban sprawl around what remains a very picturesque old town. The traffic problems alone can be enough to dampen the city's appeal, however those who make time to visit will find Toluca a pleasant, if bustling, small city. It's an enjoyable place to spend a day or two exploring attractive plazas, lively shopping arcades, art galleries and museums.

Toluca was an indigenous settlement from at least the 13th century. The Spanish founded the modern city in the 16th century after defeating the resident Aztecs and Matlazincas, and it became part of Hernán Cortés' expansive domain, the Marquesado del Valle de Oaxaca. Since 1830 it's been the capital of Mexico state, which surrounds the Distrito Federal on three sides, like an upside-down U.

The main road from Mexico City becomes Paseo Tollocan on Toluca's eastern edge, before bearing southwest and becoming a ring road around the city center's southern edge. Toluca's bus station and the huge Mercado Juárez are 2km southeast of the center, off Paseo Tollocan.

The vast Plaza de los Mártires, with the cathedral and Palacio de Gobierno, marks the town center. Most of the action, however, is concentrated a block south in the pedestrian precinct. Shady Parque Alameda is three blocks west along Hidalgo.

◉ Sights

City Center   HISTORIC BUILDING
The 19th-century **Portal Madero**, running 250m along Avenida Hidalgo, is lively, as is the commercial arcade along the pedestrian street to the east, which attracts mariachis after 9pm. A block north, the large, open expanse of **Plaza de los Mártires** is surrounded by fine old government buildings; the 19th-century **cathedral** and the 18th-century **Templo de la Santa Veracruz** are on its south side.

On Plaza Garibay's north side is the 18th-century **Templo del Carmen**.

TOP CHOICE Cosmovitral Jardín Botánico   GARDENS
(Cosmic Stained-Glass Window Botanical Garden; cnr Juárez & Lerdo de Tejada; adult/child M$10/5; ☺9am-6pm Tue-Sun) At the northeast end of Plaza Garibay, the stunning and unique Cosmovitral Jardín Botánico was built in 1909 as a market. The building now houses 3500 sq meters of lovely gardens, lit through 48 stained-glass panels by the Tolucan artist Leopoldo Flores.

Centro Cultural Mexiquense   MUSEUM
(State of Mexico Cultural Center; Blvd Reyes Heroles 302; admission M$10, Sun free; ☺10am-3pm Tue-Fri, 10am-6pm Sat, 10am-3pm Sun) This large cultural center, 4.5km west of the city center, houses three good museums (which all keep the same hours). It's no must-see but still a worthwhile diversion for visitors interested in local arts and crafts, local archaeology and modern art.

To get here it's easiest to take one of the plentiful *colectivos* from outside the Mercado Juárez – just look for 'Centro Cultural' on its destination board. The circuitous ride takes 20 minutes. Get off by the large grass roundabout near the Monterrey University Toluca Campus, cross to the opposite side and the museum complex is through the gate and down the road. From downtown you can take a cab (M$40).

The **Museo de Culturas Populares** has a wonderfully varied collection of Mexico's traditional arts and crafts, with some astounding 'trees of life' from Metepec, whimsical Day of the Dead figures and a fine display of *charro* (cowboy) gear. There are also mosaics, traditional rugs, a loft and a gift shop.

The **Museo de Arte Moderno** traces the development of Mexican art from the late-19th-century Academia de San Carlos to the Nueva Plástica and includes paintings by Tamayo, Orozco and many others. There's an impressive spherical mural of people fighting against slavery, which makes up part of the building itself, as well as more recent exhibits with some challenging pieces of contemporary art.

The **Museo de Antropología e História** is the standout museum, and presents exhibits on the state's history from prehistoric times to the 20th century, with a good collection of pre-Hispanic artifacts. It also traces pre-Hispanic cultural influences up to the modern day in tools, clothing, textiles and religion. Sadly nearly all the labels are only in Spanish.

Museo Modelo de Ciencias e Industria   MUSEUM
(www.mumci.org; Av Hidalgo Oriente No 201; admission M$45; ☺10am-6pm Tue-Fri, to 8pm Sat & Sun) The recently opened Mueso Modelo de Ciencias e Industria is one of the odder museums you're likely to encounter in Mexico. Devoted to the corporate history of the Modelo beer company, the museum is a propaganda machine extolling the virtues of one of Mexico's most famous conglomerates. It is, however, good for a laugh. The best thing going for the complex, besides the attractive facade, is its **IMAX** (admission M$65; ☺last show 4:30pm) theater, which is incredibly well-priced.

Museo de Bellas Artes   MUSEUM
(Degollado 102; admission M$10; ☺10am-6pm Tue-Sat, to 3pm Sun) The ex-convent buildings adjacent to the Templo del Carmen, on the north side of Plaza Garibay, house Toluca's Museo de Bellas Artes, which exhibits paintings from the colonial period to the early 20th century.

Other Museums   MUSEUM
On Bravo, opposite the Palacio de Gobierno, are three museums (each named after the artist it showcases): one dedicated to landscape painter **José María Velasco** (Lerdo de Tejada 400; admission M$10; ☺10am-6pm Tue-Sat, to 3pm Sun), another to painter **Felipe Santiago Gutiérrez** (Bravo Norte 303; admission free; ☺10am-3pm Tue-Sun) and the last to multifaceted Mexican-Japanese artist **Luis Nishizawa** (Bravo Norte 305; adult/student M$10/5; ☺10am-6pm Tue-Sat, to 3pm Sun).

☞ Tours

Tranvía   TRAM
(☏330-50-54; www.tranviatoluca.com; adult/child M$40/30; departs hourly 11am-5pm) On Saturdays, Sundays and holidays, this motorized trolly leaves from the cathedral and visits two dozen sites in the city.

⊨ Sleeping

Hotel Colonial   INN $$
(☏215-97-00; Hidalgo Oriente 103; r from M$550; P🛈) The rooms overlooking the busy main road are the best, but also the loudest, at this well-run and excellent-value hotel. The impressive lobby and friendly staff are other good reasons to come here. Rates include free parking nearby in a lot on Juárez.

Fiesta Inn Toluca Centro   BUSINESS HOTEL $$$
(☏167-89-00; www.fiestainn.com; Allende Sur 124; r US$90-120; P@🛈) This modern, sleek 85-room Fiesta Inn (formerly the Gran Hotel) has airy, comfortable rooms, a small gym and a cafe-bar-restaurant in the lobby. There's a second Fiesta Inn near the airport.

✕ Eating & Drinking

Toluqueños take snacking and sweets very seriously and you can join them in the arcades around Plaza Fray Andrés de Castro. Other stalls sell candied fruit and *jamoncillos* (pumpkin-seed pastes), and *mostachones* (sweets made of burned milk). Most eateries in the center are open from around 8am to 9pm.

TOP CHOICE / **La Gloria Chocolatería y Pan 1876**   CAFE $
(Quintana Roo; snacks M$10-35; ☺11am-11pm) You feel lucky just to be here, and you'll almost certainly be the only foreign visitor when you come. This wonderful, friendly, family-run cafe serves a tempting menu of local cuisine, from *tacos al pastor* (spicy pork tacos) and delicious *sermones* (sandwiches) stuffed with oven-baked pork or shredded chicken bathed in *mole poblano*.

BUSES FROM TOLUCA

DESTINATION	FARE (M$)	DURATION	FREQUENCY (DAILY)
Cuernavaca	67	2hr	24
Mexico City (Poniente)	42-55	1 hr	40
Morelia	245	2hr	14
Taxco	91	3hr	7
Valle de Bravo	53	2hr	10
Zihuatenejo	400	9 hr	3

La Vaquita Negra del Portal   SANDWICHES $
(Portal Reforma 124B; sandwiches M$20-35;
☺9am-8:30pm) On the northwest corner of
the arcades, smoked hams and huge green-
and-red sausages hanging over the deli
counter signal first-rate *tortas*. Try a messy
toluqueña (red pork chorizo sausage, white
cheese, cream, tomato and *salsa verde*), and
don't forget to garnish your heaped sandwich with spicy pickled peppers and onions.

Hostería Las Ramblas   MEXICAN $$
(Calle 20 de Noviembre 107D; mains M$85-115;
☺9am-8pm) Located on a pedestrian mall,
this atmospheric restaurant feels like a
throwback to the 1950s, with white table-
cloths and retro decor. Attentive waiters
serve full breakfasts, including some excel-
lent vegetarian options like the *omelette
campesino* – panela cheese, *rajas (poblano
chili)* and zucchini – and a variety of lunch
and dinner entrees like *mole verde* and
conejo al ajillo (liberally garlicked rabbit).

🛍 Shopping

Casart   ARTS & CRAFTS
(Casa de Artesanía; Aldama 102; ☺10am-6pm Tue-
Sun) This new downtown location of Casart –
the state organization promoting local crafts –
is fantastic both for its beautiful home, set
around a courtyard, and its wonderful se-
lection of quality arts and crafts. Prices are
fixed and therefore higher than you might
be able to get haggling in markets for an
inferior product (for the best prices, go di-
rectly to the source).

❶ Information

There are banks with ATMs near Portal Madero.
Cruz Roja (Red Cross; ☎217-33-33)
City Tourist Office (☎384-11-00 ext 104; www.
toluca.gob.mx/turismo; Plaza Fray Andrés de
Castro, Edificio B, Local 6, Planta Baja)

State Tourist Office (☎212-59-98; www.
edomexico.gob.mx; turismo@edomex.gob.mx;
cnr Urawa & Paseo Tollocan) Inconveniently
located 2km southeast of the center, but with
English-speaking staff and good maps.
Tourist Information Kiosk (Palacio Municipal)
Helpful kiosk with free city map.

❶ Getting There & Away

The modern, efficient and low-stress **Aerop-
uerto Internacional de Toluca** (☎279-28-00;
www.am-ait.com) is an excellent alternative to
Mexico City's massive and intimidating airport.
Conveniently located off Hwy 15, about 10km
from downtown, the airport is adjacent to the
industrial zone and a group of business-friendly
chain hotels.

Toluca is the hub for domestic budget airline
Interjet (www.interjet.com.mx), which offers
flights all over Mexico.

Spirit Airlines (☎800-772-7117; www.spirit.
com), **Continental Express** (☎800-900-50-00,
in the US 800-523-3273; www.continental.com)
and **Volaris** (☎800-122-80-00; www.volaris.
com.mx) also offer international service. They
fly travelers between Toluca and several cities in
the United States, including Los Angeles, Chica-
go, Las Vegas, Houston, San Francisco, Seattle,
Newark, Miami, New York and Atlanta.

Europcar (www.europcar.com), **Dollar** (www.
dollar.com) and **Alamo** (www.alamo.com) all
have rental-car offices at Toluca International
Airport.

Toluca's **bus station** (Berriozábal 101) is 2km
southeast of the center. Ticket offices for many
destinations are on the platforms or at the gate
entrances, and it's fair to say it can be a confus-
ing place.

❶ Getting Around

'Centro' buses go from outside Toluca's bus
station to the town center along Lerdo de Tejada.
From Juárez in the center, 'Terminal' buses go to
the bus station (M$6). Taxis from the bus station
to the city center cost around M$30.

Nevado de Toluca

Among the highest peaks in the region, the long-extinct volcano Nevado de Toluca (also known as Xinantécatl) is Mexico's fourth-tallest peak. Nevado has two summits on the crater rim. The lower summit, Pico del Aguila (4620m), is closer to the parking area and is the more common day hike. The main or highest summit is called Pico del Fraile (4704m) and requires an additional three to four hours of hike time.

The earlier you reach the summit, the better the chance of clear views. The crater contains two lakes, El Sol and La Luna. The summit area can be snowy from November to March, and is sometimes good for cross-country skiing and the **Parque Nacional Nevado de Toluca** is closed during the heaviest snowfalls.

From the park entrance a road winds 3.5km up to the **main gate** (entrance per vehicle M$20; ☺8am-5pm); last entry is at 3pm. From there it's a 17km drive along an unsurfaced road up to the crater. Dress warmly – it gets chilly up top.

Just beyond the gate, **Posada Familiar** (campsite/dm M$75/150) offers basic lodging at a heavily used refuge with shared hot showers, a kitchen (without utensils) and a common area with a fireplace. Bring extra blankets. On Saturday and Sunday, food is served at stalls around Parque de los Venados and at the gate near the summit. Midweek, bring your own food and water.

From Toluca, taxis will take you to the trailhead for upwards of M$250, or there and back (including time for a look around) for a negotiable M$500. Be sure to hire a newer taxi; the road up is very rough and dusty. Most international car rental companies also have offices in Toluca.

Mario Andrade leads one-day **climbs** (☎55-1038-4008, 55-1826-2146; mountainup@hotmail.com; US$200 incl transportation, 1 meal & park entrance) and also guides climbers on Izta ascents.

Valle de Bravo

☏726 / POP 26,000 / ELEV 1800M

With one of the loveliest colonial centers in central Mexico, the *pueblo mágico* of Valle de Bravo is an utter charmer and a wonderful spot for an escape from Mexico City. A long, winding and occasionally stunning mountain road runs the 85km west from Toluca, taking you to the shores of Lake Avandaro – this is an artificial lake, the result of the construction of a hydroelectric station.

The setting here is reminiscent of the northern Italian lakes, with thickly wooded, mist-clad hills and red terracotta roofing used throughout the town. Valle, as it's known, is famous for being the weekend retreat of choice for the capital's well-connected upper classes. The views at the lakeside are stunning but the beguiling and largely intact colonial center is arguably the real draw here. Boating on the lake is very popular as well, as are hiking and camping in the hills around the town. Valle is set up well for visitors. There's a tourist-info kiosk on the wharf and essential services, including ATMs and internet cafes, are found around the main plaza, which is a 10-minute walk uphill from the waterfront.

In late October or early November, the week-long **Festival de las Almas**, an international arts and culture extravaganza, brings in music and dance troupes from all over Europe and Latin America.

🛏 Sleeping

For a small town, this popular weekend escape from Mexico City has a good selection of budget posadas and midrange hotels. The most affordable options are within two blocks of the bus station.

Posada Familiar Los Girasoles GUESTHOUSE $
(☎262-29-67; Plaza Independencia 1; s M$300, d M$400-500, tr M$500, q M$600-750) The nine-room Girasoles has an enviable location on the *zócalo*. It has spacious and spotlessly clean rooms, complete with rustic touches and a warm, family-run feeling. Expect to be asked where you're from and shown photos of former guests (all 'friends') who have stayed here.

Hotel Casanueva BOUTIQUE HOTEL $$$
(☎262-17-66; Villagrán 100; r from M$1200) Set on the *zócalo,* the Casanueva has individually designed rooms decorated with tasteful arts and crafts. The most stylish option downtown, the hotel's suite, which sleeps four, is especially lovely. Some rooms have private balconies over the square.

Rodavento RESORT $$$
(☎251-41-82; www.rodavento.com; Carretera Valle de Bravo-Los Saucos Km 3.5; ste from M$2500;

P✳✵) Set on a sprawling property outside of Valle, this rustic-luxe hotel distinguishes itself with its nature-centric design – using earth tones, traditional wood stoves, and sliding glass doors opening onto the forest, gardens and a private lake.

El Santuario
RESORT $$$

(🖉262-91-00; www.elsantuario.com; Carretera Colorines, San Gaspar; r from US$350; P✳✵) Twenty minutes outside town, this gorgeous hillside hotel has an infinity pool, fountains, an in-house spa and rooms with magnificent lake views. There's also a golf course, horse stables and a marina with sailboat rentals.

🗙 Eating & Drinking

There are scores of restaurants and cafes along the wharf and around the *zócalo*; many are only open from Friday to Sunday.

TOP CHOICE Ciento Once
INTERNATIONAL $$

(http://cientooncevalle.blogspot.com; Calzada de Santa María 111; tapas M$35-100) Visit the plant-filled back deck of this homey restaurant for house-made bread, a wide range of authentic tapas, a small selection of excellent entrees – including tuna steaks and *arrachera* (grilled beef) – and some quality wine, all house-made by a former anthropologist who recently relocated from Mexico City.

Los Helechos
MEXICAN $

(Joaquín Arcadio Pagaza; breakfast M$60; ☺8am-10pm; 🛜) The best option for breakfast and the first to open, Los Helechos offers excellent *chilaquiles* (strips of fried corn tortillas, bathed in sauce) or *huevos rancheros* (fried eggs served on a tortilla, with toppings and refried beans), with one of a dozen or so varieties of fresh fruit juice and a strong cup of *café americano*.

Restaurante Paraíso
FISH $$

(Fray Gregorio Jiménez de la Cuenca s/n; mains M$75-160; ☺8am-11pm) With fantastic lake views and a sprawling menu of seafood specialties, plus excellent and imaginatively prepared local trout, come early and watch the sunset from the rooftop patio.

ℹ Getting There & Away

Considering the hordes of tourists who descend on Valle each weekend, transportation options are relatively few. Most visitors are affluent Mexicans, who come by car.

Autobuses Mexico-Toluca-Zinacantepec y Ramales runs hourly 2nd-class *directos* from early morning to late afternoon between Mexico City's Terminal Poniente (M$113, three hours) and Valle de Bravo's small bus terminal on Calle 16 de Septiembre. For a scenic ride ask for the southern, 'Los Saucos' route, which travels along Hwy 134 and through a national park. If driving that's the route to take as well.

Malinalco

🖉714 / POP 8000 / ELEV 1740M

Set in a valley of dramatic cliffs and ancient ruins, this *pueblo mágico* is rapidly becoming the next Tepoztlán. Weekends now see crowds, but still far fewer than those that descend on more easily accessible weekend escapes. The drive to Malinalco is one of the most enjoyable to be had in the area, with dramatic scenery lining the road south of Toluca.

There are already a clutch of hippie stores, a handful of international restaurants and, it seems, a surprising number of boutique hotels (eight have opened in the last two years). The town is far from fully developed though – and it's almost unnervingly quiet mid-week, when it can still be a challenge to find a decent place to eat outside of the market.

The village itself has a charming colonial core set around a well-preserved convent and two central plazas which sit side by side. In the larger plaza, the **tourist module** (www.malinalco.net; ☺9am -6pm) offers limited help and there's an ATM on Hidalgo, on the convent's north side. **Cyber Malinalco** (Hidalgo 104; per hr M$10) offers reasonably priced internet access.

⊙ Sights

Aztec Temples
ARCHAEOLOGICAL SITE

A short but bracing hike up the mountainside above Malinalco takes you to one of the country's few reasonably well-preserved **temples** (admission M$41; ☺9am-6pm Tue-Sun), from where there are stunning views of the valley and beyond. From the main square follow signs to the *zona arqueológica,* which take you up the hillside on a well-maintained footpath with signs in Spanish, English and Náhuatl; the last ticket is sold at 5pm. The site itself is fascinating and includes *El Paraíso de los Guerreros* (a mural that once covered an entire wall) depicting fallen warriors becoming deities and living in paradise.

The Aztecs conquered the region in 1476 and were busy building a ritual center here when they were conquered by the Spanish. **El Cuauhcalli** (the Temple of the Eagle and Jaguar Knight, where sons of Aztec nobles were initiated into warrior orders) survived because it was hewn from the mountainside itself. The entrance is carved in the form of a fanged serpent.

Temple IV (located on the far side of the site) continues to baffle archaeologists. As the room is positioned to allow the first rays of sunlight to hit it at dawn, there has been speculation that this place was part of a Mexica sun cult, a solar calendar or a meeting place for nobles – or some combination of these.

Situated near the site entrance, the **Museo Universitario Dr Luis Mario Schneider** (admission M$10; ☺10am-4pm Tue-Sun) explores the region's history and archaeology in a beautiful modern museum space.

Augustinian Convent CHURCH
A well-restored 16th-century **convent** (admission free), fronted by a tranquil tree-lined yard, faces the central plaza. Impressive frescoes fashioned from herb- and flower-based paint adorn its cloister.

👉 Tours

Tour Gastronómico Prehispánico CULINARY EXPERIENCE
(☎55-55091411; aplegaspi@progidy.net.mx) This pre-Hispanic food tour includes a visit to the market, a cooking class using traditional utensils and methods, and a three-course meal.

🛏 Sleeping

While quite a few accomodations have opened in recent years, giving this small town an inordinate number of hotel rooms, reservations remain a good idea. Because Malinalco is geared toward weekend visitors, you'll have no trouble finding a room Sunday to Thursday nights – though some of the nicer hotels aren't open for walk-ins mid-week.

Casa Limón BOUTIQUE HOTEL **$$$**
(☎147-02-56; www.casalimon.com; Río Lerma 103; r/ste incl breakfast from M$2400/2800; P🖥❄) Surrounded by a stark high-desert landscape, this ultra-trendy boutique hotel is Malinalco's most famous attraction. With its slate pool and intriguing artworks, Limón draws hipsters from far and wide. The seductive indoor-outdoor bar and excellent restaurant complete the scene. Limón can

be fiendishly difficult to find in the poorly signposted backstreets but it's worth the effort. The hotel's **restaurant** (mains M$80-220; ☺1-10pm Thu-Sun) is an elegant indoor-and-outdoor tree house–like space (with a reed roof and surrounded by chirping crickets). Mains are classic international, from *coq au vin* to almond trout, and the wine list is superb.

Casa Mora BOUTIQUE HOTEL **$$$**
(☎147-05-72; www.casamora.net; Calle de la Cruz 18; ste incl breakfast M$2200-2400; P🖥❄) You'll feel more like a houseguest than a tourist at this beautifully appointed oasis. It's the pet project of a local artist who maintains five beautiful rooms, all of which enjoy an intimate and romantic atmosphere. Unfortunately, Mora's location makes getting to and fro without one's own transportation fairly inconvenient. Prices are lower mid-week.

Casa Navacoyan BOUTIQUE HOTEL **$$$**
(☎147-04-11; www.casanavacoyan.com; Prolangación Calle Pirul 62; ste incl breakfast from M$1500-2000; P🖥❄) This gorgeous, new hotel on the outskirts of town has just six rooms – each decorated in a sort of upscale, homestyle aesthetic, like staying at your wealthy aunt's house in the country. The immaculately groomed yard is the real attraction, with palm trees, a gorgeous pool and views of Malinalco's famed hills and cliffs.

El Asoleadero HOTEL **$$**
(☎147-01-84; cnr Aldama & Comercio; r M$450-500, with kitchen M$600-650; P🖥❄) Just uphill from Malinalco's main drag, El Asoleadero offers spacious and airy rooms with striking views of the *pueblito* (village) and surrounding cliffs. There are also lounge chairs and a small pool in the courtyard and cold beer for sale in the lobby.

Hotel Santa Mónica GUESTHOUSE **$**
(☎147-00-31; Hidalgo 109; r M$350; 🖥) Just a few steps from the *zócalo* and en route to the archaeological zone, this is one of the better budget options, with clean rooms (all with private bathroom and TV) scattered around a simple courtyard.

🍴 Eating & Drinking

Perhaps surprisingly for such a small town, Malinalco has a few very good restaurants. Unfortunately for those visiting midweek though, most of the better options are only open Friday through Sunday.

TOP CHOICE **Los Placeres** INTERNATIONAL $$

(Principal s/n; mains M$75-190; ⊘2-10pm Fri, 9am-11pm Sat, 9am-6pm Sun; 🛜🍴) This artsy restaurant on Malinalco's *zócalo* serves international fare (Nicoise salad or chicken curry), alongside creative takes on traditional Mexican dishes, like omelets with *poblano* sauce, trout with *ancho* chilies or fondue *al tequila*. There are elaborate murals, tile mosaic tabletops and the likes of Robert Johnson on the sound system.

El Puente de Má-Li INTERNATIONAL $$

(Hidalgo 22; mains M$80-130; ⊘1pm-6pm Tue-Thu, to 11pm Fri & Sat, 9am-6pm Sun) After the tiny bridge as you leave the *zócalo* for the ruins, this atmospheric restaurant is set around a colonial dining room and a great back garden where you can try a selection of *antojitos*, pastas, soups and steaks.

Koi ASIAN $$

(Morelos 18; mains M$55-150; ⊘2pm-midnight Fri & Sat, to 8pm Sun & Mon) With its artful, Asian-inspired touches and creative menu, Koi is an unexpected pleasure. Offerings include pad thai, fish tempura and asparagus teriyaki – all of which are tasty but scarcely resemble their Asian namesakes.

❶ Getting There & Away

Most public transportation to Malinalco goes via Tenancingo. **Águila** (📞800-224-84-52; www. autobusesaguila.com.mx), however, runs two buses each afternoon (4:20pm and 6:20pm) from Mexico City's Terminal Poniente (M$66, about 1½ hours) to Malinalco.

From Toluca, take an Águila bus to Tenancingo (M$19, one hour, every 10 to 20 minutes) and ask the driver to let you off at the *colectivo* to Malinalco. From Tenancingo it's also possible to hire a taxi to Malinalco for M$65.

Though the distances are short, traveling from Malinalco to Cuernavaca can take hours. It is, however, possible to hire a taxi (M$165, about one hour) and travel between the two towns via the incredibly scenic trip through Puente Caporal-Palpan-Miacatlán, to the town of Alpuyeca, near the Xochicalco ruins. From there, it's easy to flag one of the frequent buses traveling along Hwy 95, and continue either north (to Cuernavaca and Mexico City) or south (to Taxco and the coast).

Ixtapan de la Sal

📞721 / POP 18,000 / ELEV 1880M

Ixtapan is known throughout Mexico for its curative waters, which have attracted visitors since the town was founded centuries ago by indigenous travelers from the Pacific coast who were amazed to discover salt water inland, while on their way to Tenochtitlán. Despite its long history, there's not much to see here and the only reason to stop is to visit **Ixtapan Parque Acuático** (📞800-493-27-26; www.parqueixtapan.com; adult/child M$180/free; ⊘spa 8am-7pm, aquatic park 9am-6pm), a sprawling water park mixing curative thermal water pools with waterfalls, water slides, a wave pool and a miniature railway. There's a range of hotels in town.

Águila buses run from Toluca (M$41, one hour, every 20 minutes) and Taxco (M$51, 1¼ hours; every 45 minutes).

Veracruz

Includes »

Best Places to Eat

» Gran Café de La Parroquia (p203)

» Las Delicias Marinas (p208)

» Plaza Pardo (p230)

» La Fonda (p212)

Best Places to Stay

» Posada del Emperador (p222)

» Hotel Imperial (p201)

» Posada del Cafeto (p211)

» Casa Real del Café (p215)

Why Go?

Imagine a mini-version of Machu Picchu but without the tourists, a ballroom dance with a sexy Afro-Cuban twist, a mountain as fickle and majestic as Kilimanjaro and the world's first (unaccredited) bungee-jumpers. Unusual epiphanies are the norm on Mexico's central Gulf coast, a snapshot of a nation with its guard down where the runaway juggernaut called 'global homogenization' gets stopped in its tracks by a staunch population of culturally proud *jarochos* who have embellished their downtowns with pretty plazas rather than ugly shopping malls. Despite being only two flying hours out of Houston, Texas, Veracruz is serially overlooked by visitors from the English-speaking north who jet over it on their way to spring breaks in Cancún or Cozumel. As a result, nothing ever feels 'staged' here, allowing you to dive unmolested into a 3000-year-old culture, dodge beach crowds and argue about conflicting *mole* (a type of chili sauce) recipes with opinionated waiters in Spanish.

When to Go
Veracruz City

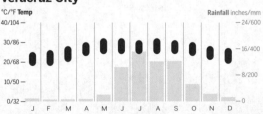

Oct Cheap prices, bearable temperatures and barely another tourist in sight.

Feb–Mar The Veracruz Carnaval kicks off the biggest party on Mexico's eastern coast.

Nov–Feb Peak tourist season for non-Mexicans with less rain and balmy temperatures.

History

The Olmecs, Mesoamerica's earliest known civilization, built their first great center around 1200 BC at San Lorenzo in southern Veracruz state. In 900 BC the city was violently destroyed, but Olmec culture lingered for several centuries at Tres Zapotes. During the Classic period (AD 250–900) the Gulf coast developed another distinctive culture, known as the Classic Veracruz civilization. Its most important center was El Tajín, which was at its peak between AD 600 and 900. In the post-Classic period the Totonacs established themselves in the region south of Tuxpan. North of Tuxpan, the Huastec civilization flourished from 800 to 1200. During this time, the warlike Toltecs also moved into the Gulf coast area. In the mid-15th century, the Aztecs overtook most of the Totonac and Huastec areas, exacting tributes of goods and sacrificial victims and subduing revolts.

When Hernán Cortés arrived in April 1519, he made Zempoala's Totonacs his first allies against the Aztecs by vowing to protect them against reprisals. Cortés set up his first settlement, Villa Rica de la Vera Cruz (Rich Town of the True Cross), and by 1523 all the Gulf coast was in Spanish hands. Forced slavery, newly introduced diseases and the ravages of war severely reduced indigenous populations.

Veracruz harbor became an essential trade and communications link with Spain and was vital for anyone trying to rule Mexico, but the climate, tropical diseases and pirate threats inhibited the growth of Spanish settlements.

Under dictator Porfirio Díaz, Mexico's first railway linked Veracruz to Mexico City in 1872, stimulating industrial development. In 1901 oil was discovered in the Tampico area, and by the 1920s the region was producing a quarter of the world's oil. In the 1980s the Gulf coast still held well over half of Mexico's reserves and refining capacity. Today, the region is not as large a player as it used to be, but is still a significant contributor to Mexico's oil economy.

Dangers & Annoyances

Mexico's infamous drug war migrated to Veracruz in early 2011 with nasty gang wars firing off in Veracruz City, Boca del Río and Xalapa. Yet, despite some understandably bad press, Veracruz – if you're not a journalist or a member of a drug cartel – is still relatively safe. At the time of writing no foreign tourists and few innocent Mexican bystanders had been directly affected by the violence.

Travelers should remain wary of petty theft in cheap hotel rooms and pickpocketing in crowded market areas, especially in big cities. Hurricanes threaten between June and November. Check out the US National Hurricane Center website (www.nhc.noaa.gov) for the latest. Mosquitoes in coastal regions carry dengue fever, especially in central and southeastern Veracruz.

Veracruz City

☑ 229 / POP 430,000

Veracruz, like all great port cities, is an unholy mélange of grime, romance and melted-down cultures. Conceived in 1519, this is Mexico's oldest European-founded settlement, but, usurped by subsequent inland cities, it's neither its most historic, nor most visually striking. Countless sackings by the French, Spanish and Americans have siphoned off the prettiest buildings, leaving a motley patchwork of working docks and questionable hybrid architecture punctuated by the odd stray colonial masterpiece. But Veracruz's beauty is in its grit rather than its grandiosity. A carefree spirit reigns in the *zócalo* (main square) most evenings where the primary preoccupation is who to cajole into a *danzón* (traditional couples dance). Well known for their warmth and animation, *jarochos* (people from Veracruz City and surrounding low-lying coastal areas) are lovers not fighters, a fact reflected in their musical dexterity which has a notable Afro-Cuban influence. Fear not: there are kid-friendly aquariums and interesting museums here, but Veracruz's best 'sights' are the less obvious things: its energetic plazas, its cafes full of chin-wagging locals and the unscripted encounters that await in its wild urban pastiche.

History

Hernán Cortés arrived at the site of present-day Veracruz on Good Friday April 21, 1519, and thus began his siege of Mexico. By 1521 he had crushed the Aztec empire.

Veracruz provided Mexico's main gateway to the outside world for 400 years. Invaders and pirates, incoming and outgoing rulers, settlers, silver and slaves – all came and went, making Veracruz a linchpin in Mexico's history. In 1569 English sailor Francis Drake survived a massive Spanish sea attack

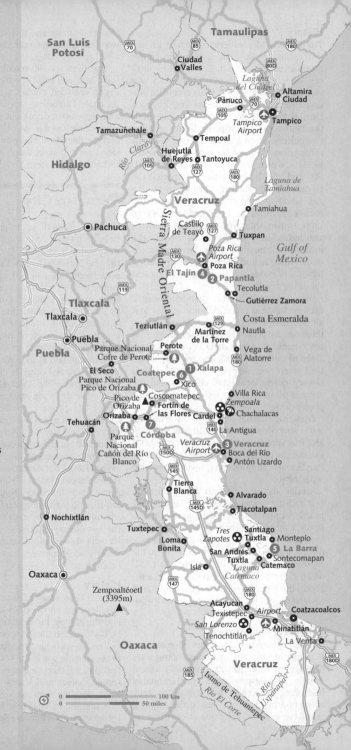

Veracruz Highlights

❶ Decipher a triumvirate of Mesoamerican cultures in Xalapa's architecturally magnificent **Museo de Antropología** (p208)

❷ Watch grown men fly at a one-of-a-kind **voladores ceremony** (boxed text, p230) in Papantla

❸ Plug into the urban energy of **Veracruz** (p195)

❹ Imagine past glories at the extensive ruins of **El Tajín** (p231)

❺ Take a boat across Laguna de Sontecomapan for fresh fish on the beach at **La Barra** (p243)

❻ Sip gourmet coffee in the cloud forest–encased town of **Coatepec** (p214)

❼ Become part of the cast in the 'outdoor stage' that is Córdoba's **Parque de 21 de Mayo** (p218)

here. In 1683 vicious Frenchman Laurent de Gaff, with 600 men, held the 5000 inhabitants of Veracruz captive, killing escapees, looting, drinking and raping. Soon after, they left much richer.

In 1838 General Antonio López de Santa Anna fled Veracruz in his underwear under bombardment from a French fleet in the Pastry War. But the general managed to respond heroically, expelling the invaders. When Winfield Scott's army attacked Veracruz during the Mexican-American War, more than 1000 Mexicans died before the city surrendered.

In 1861 Benito Juárez announced that Mexico couldn't pay its debts to Spain, France and Britain. The British and Spanish planned only to take over Veracruz's customhouse, but retreated on seeing that Frenchman Napoleon III sought to conquer Mexico. After Napoleon III's five-year intervention ended, Veracruz experienced revitalization. Mexico's first railway was built between Veracruz and Mexico City in 1872, and foreign investment poured into the city.

In 1914 US troops occupied Veracruz, halting a delivery of German arms to dictator, Victoriano Huerta. Later in the Revolution, Veracruz was briefly the capital of the reformist Constitutionalist faction led by Venustiano Carranza.

Today, Veracruz is an important deepwater port, handling exports, manufacturing and petrochemical industries. Tourism, particularly from the domestic sector, is another large income earner.

◉ Sights

TOP CHOICE Zócalo   PLAZA

A costumed señorita grabs you by the arm and shouts 'Baile!' (Dance!), two dozen shoeshiners sit hunched over their newspaper-reading clientele frantically polishing, and a three-piece marimba band launches into 'La Bamba' from underneath the colonial porches of the main plaza. Any exploration of Veracruz has to begin in its zócalo (also called the Plaza de Armas and Plaza Lerdo), the city's unofficial outdoor 'stage' where inspired organized events 'overlap' with the day-to-day improvisation of Mexican life. All cities have their plazas, but Veracruz's somehow seems busier and more ebullient than the rest. The handsome public space is framed on three sides by portales (arcades), the 17th-century Palacio Municipal and an 18th-century cathedral. The level of activity accelerates throughout the day until the evening, when the zócalo becomes thick with music, entertainers, merrymakers and bystanders.

Paseo del Malecón & Boulevard   STREET, LANDMARK

Veracruz's harbor is a busy oil port with rigs off the coast, but that somehow adds to the gritty romanticism of the waterfront walk on the malecón (harbor boardwalk), starting at the rows of vendor stalls at Plaza de las Artesanías, which sell a kaleidoscope of souvenirs. Here you'll pass the high-rise Pemex building, which is an early example of modern Mexican architecture and has some interesting murals.

Heading south, the malecón becomes a wide pedestrian walkway called the boulevard (pronounced 'boo-ley-bar'). Following the coast, it continues south roughly 8km, passing lighthouse piers, statues of famous government figures, and monuments to the city's defenders and sailors who died at sea. Two notable newcomers are the statue of the Spanish emigrant celebrating Veracruz's role as a disembarkation point for immigrants, and the statue of Alexander Von Humboldt, the German naturalist/explorer who visited the area in 1803–04 and collected important information about the flora and indigenous cultures. The malecón makes for a fabulous run.

Two blocks inland from the malecón is the 1998 Altar a la Patria, an obelisk marking the buried remains of those who defended Veracruz during its numerous conflicts.

FREE Museo Histórico Naval   MUSEUM

(Arista 418; ⊙9am-5pm Tue-Sun) Welcome to Mexico, land of the free museum; in this case, a multifarious, beautifully laid-out museum. Occupying a former naval academy, the Museo Histórico Naval offers gratis tuition in Mexico's maritime heritage with rooms full of weapons and model ships and exhibits on the US attacks on Veracruz in 1847 and 1914.

FREE Museo de la Ciudad de Veracruz   MUSEUM

(Veracruz City Museum; Av Zaragoza 39; ⊙10am-6pm Mon-Sat, to 3pm Sun) The displays at the Museo de la Ciudad de Veracruz do a good job of informing visitors of the city's history from the pre-Hispanic era, and also give a feel for the essence of this proud and lively city through explanations of its music, its diverse ethnic roots and its politics.

San Juan de Ulúa FORTRESS, MUSEUM
(www.sanjuandeulua.com.mx; admission M$48; ☺9am-4:30pm Tue-Sun) The city's colonial fortress has been almost swallowed up by the modern port and today you have to squint to pick it out amid the container ships and the cranes across the harbor. The fort was originally built on an island that's since been connected to the mainland by a causeway. The earliest fortifications date from 1565 and a young Francis Drake got his comeuppance here in a violent battle in 1569. During the colonial period the fort and island became the main entry point for Spanish newcomers to Mexico.

The central part of the fortress was a prison, and a notoriously inhumane one, during the Porfirio Díaz regime. Today, San Juan de Ulúa is an empty ruin of passageways, battlements, bridges and stairways undergoing lengthy renovations. Guided tours are available in Spanish and, sometimes, English. To get there, you can take a taxi (M$50) or, weather permitting, a lancha (boat taxi; M$25) from the malecón.

Baluarte de Santiago FORTRESS, MUSEUM
(Canal s/n; admission M$41; ☺10am-4:30pm Tue-Sat, to 5pm Sun) Until 1880 Veracruz was a walled city surrounded by mighty medieval defenses. The Baluarte de Santiago, the only surviving fort of nine, was built in 1526 beside what was then the waterfront. A small exhibit of pre-Hispanic gold jewelry inside is barely worth the entry fee. However, you can walk around the outside battlements for free.

Acuario de Veracruz AQUARIUM
(☑931-10-20; www.acuariodeveracruz.com; Blvd Camacho s/n; adult/child M$100/55, Tiburonería M$300/150; ☺10am-7pm Mon-Thu, to 7:30pm Fri-Sun) Veracruz's aquarium is allegedly the best of its kind in Latin America, though it still falls a long way short of similar establishments in the US and Europe. Situated 2km south of the center in a small generic mall on the waterfront, it centers on a large doughnut-shaped tank filled with sharks, rays and turtles that glide around visitors. Other tanks house freshwater and saltwater fish, reptiles and amphibians, river otters and even manatees; but, for a really dramatic encounter climb into the Tiburonería, a transparent safety cage that is lowered into a pool of feeding sharks.

Museo Cera MUSEUM
(Waxwork Museum; www.museodecera.com.mx/veracruz; Blvd Camacho s/n; adult/child M$60/35; ☺10am-7pm Mon-Thu, to 7:30pm Fri-Sun) Right next to the aquarium, the waxwork museum tries to snag the same customers (families primarily) by selling joint ticket packages. It's not quite Madame Tussaud's, but has collected 120-plus figures from a frankly un-scary Frankenstein to a rather plastic-looking Beatles.

FREE Fototeca ARTS CENTER
(Callejón El Portal de Miranda 9; ☺9am-3pm & 4-6pm Tue-Sun) On the southeast side of the zócalo, this small arts center has rotating photographic and video exhibitions. It's spread over three floors of a restored colonial building, though sometimes only the ground floor is operating.

Faro Carranza LANDMARK, LIGHTHOUSE
(Paseo del Malecón) Facing the waterfront on the malecón, Faro Carranza holds a lighthouse and navy offices guarded by a large statue of Venustiano Carranza. It was here that the 1917 Mexican Constitution was drafted. Every Monday morning the Mexican navy goes through an elaborate parade in front of the building.

Museo Agustín Lara MUSEUM
(Ruíz Cortines s/n; adult/student M$15/7.50; ☺10am-2:30pm & 4-6pm Tue-Fri, 10am-2:30pm Sat & Sun) A monument to one of Veracruz's most famous musical icons, this museum displays a range of Agustín Lara's personal belongings, furniture and memorabilia in the musician's old city residence. It is situated just off Blvd Camacho, 2km south of the Acuario de Veracruz and 4km from the city center.

Beaches & Lagoons BEACH, LAKE
Inseparable from the jarocho identity is the beach. You'll find pleasant stretches of them all the way down through Boca del Río. As a rule of thumb, the further from the oil rigs the better, but locals patronize them all.

Alternatively, you can find lanchas (M$120) by the aquarium that will take you to Cancuncito, a sandbar off the coast touted as the best beach in Veracruz, with light sand and clear water. Another part of the lancha beat is the Isla de Sacrificios. The island was once used for Totonac human sacrifice and later as a leprosy colony. It's now part of a protected nature and ma-

Veracruz

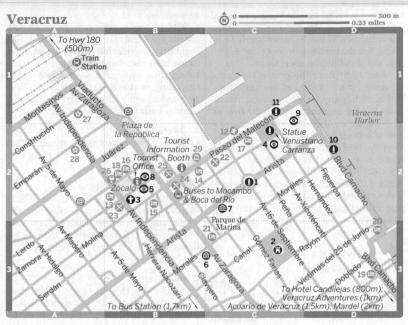

To Hwy 180 (500m)

Veracruz

⊙ Sights
1	Altar a la Patria	C2
2	Baluarte de Santiago	C3
3	Cathedral	B2
4	Faro Carranza	C2
5	Fototeca	B2
6	Museo de la Ciudad de Veracruz	C3
7	Museo Histórico Naval	C2
8	Palacio Municipal	B2
9	Pemex Building	C1
10	Statue of Alexander Von Humboldt	D2
11	Statue of the Spanish Emigrant	C1

⊕ Activities, Courses & Tours
	Amphibian	(see 16)
12	Harbor Tours	C2
	Tranvías Bus	(see 12)

🛏 Sleeping
13	Gran Hotel Diligencias	B2
14	Hawaii Hotel	B2
15	Hotel Casa Blanca	B2
16	Hotel Colonial	B2
17	Hotel Emporio	C2
18	Hotel Imperial	B2
19	Hotel Villa Rica	D3
20	Mar y Tierra	D3
21	Mesón del Mar	C3

✖ Eating
22	Gran Café de la Parroquia	C2
23	Gran Café del Portal	B2
	Los Canarios	(see 17)
24	Mariscos Tano	B2
25	Nieves de Malecón	B2

🍷 Drinking
	Bar El Estribo	(see 13)
26	Bar Prendes	B2

🎭 Entertainment
27	Las Barricas	A1
28	Teatro Principal Francisco Javier Clavijero	A2

🛍 Shopping
	Libros y Arte Fototeca	(see 5)
29	Mercado de Artesanías	B2

rine reserve called Parque Marino Nacional Sistema Arrecifal Veracruzano. Sometimes, when tourism is low, *lanchas* aren't to be found, but the harbor-tour boats (see following) will stop there on some tours.

Some 11km from the center, the gritty, off-shoot town of **Boca del Río** has a smattering of brightly colored seafood restaurants looking over the mouth of the river on Blvd Camacho. Also, *lanchas* offering **boat tours** to mangrove forests leave from here. Over the bridge, the coastal road continues about 8km further down the coast from Boca del Río to **Mandinga**, known for its seafood (especially *langostinos bicolores* – two-colored prawns), where you can also hire a boat (from the *zona de restaurantes*) to take you around mangrove lagoons rich with wildlife.

 ## Activities

Diving & Snorkeling

You wouldn't expect lucid diving right near such an oil-rigged city, but Veracruz has some good options (including at least one accessible wreck) on the reefs near the off-shore islands.

Veracruz Adventures DIVING, SNORKELING
(www.veracruzadventures.com; Blvd Camacho 681A; 1/2 immersions M$550/750) Of the various dive schools in the city, this is a good choice. It has quality equipment and arranges diving and snorkeling excursions from the Veracruz area. Guides speak English.

Courses

Language Immersion School LANGUAGE
(931-47-16; www.veracruzspanish.com; Alacio Pérez 61; 1st week per person incl homestay, classes & food M$8140, without bathroom M$7190) A North American–owned school, this laid-back outfit offers Spanish courses centered around learning about the city and its culture. There are also opportunities to travel around the state and take in some Mexican cooking classes. There's accommodations available onsite. There's no sign. Walk 200m north along the Blvd Camacho sea-drive from the Acuario de Veracruz, turn left and head half a block away inland.

Tours

Take a city tour, see surrounding sites or play around in nature while leaving logistics to a tour company.

Amphibian ADVENTURE
(931-09-97; www.amphibianveracruz.com; Hotel Colonial lobby, Lerdo 117; per person from M$400) In addition to offering activity-based tours, Amphibian also conducts diving and snorkeling trips, rafting trips to nearby rivers, rappelling, and sightseeing trips to places such as El Tajín and Roca Partida – a rocky outcrop jutting straight out of the ocean.

Aventura Extrema ADVENTURE
(980-84-57; www.aventuraextrema.com) Offers rappelling, horseback riding, rafting and hiking in the area.

Harbor Tours BOAT
(www.asdic.com.mx; adult/child M$80/50; 8am-9pm) Boats from the *malecón* offer 45-minute tours of the harbor. They leave when they're full (about every 30 minutes), so be prepared for a wait, particularly in the slow season.

Tranvías Bus BUS
(tours M$30-45) This open-air bus with trolleylike wooden trimmings gives one-hour city tours to the beat of tropical tunes. It's better at night when it's merrily lit up with colored lights. Departs Paseo del Malecón.

 ## Festivals & Events

Carnaval CARNIVAL
Veracruz erupts into a nine-day party before Ash Wednesday in February or March with flamboyant parades winding through the city daily, beginning with one devoted to the 'burning of bad humor' and ending with the 'funeral of Juan Carnaval.' Chuck in fireworks, dances, salsa and samba music, handicrafts, folklore shows and children's parades, and it adds up to one of Mexico's greatest fiestas. See the tourist office for a program of events.

Festival Internacional Afrocaribeño CULTURAL
This festival of Afro-Caribbean culture held in the last two weeks of July features academic and business forums and a trade show, but the main attractions are the dance and music performances (many of them free), film screenings and art expositions, with many nations from the Caribbean and Latin America participating.

Sleeping

Hotel prices vary greatly according to demand and can shift from day to day at busy times (mid-July to mid-September, Carnaval,

Semana Santa, Christmas and New Year), during which you should book in advance and know that prices may increase 10% to 40%. Ask about discounts.

It can be entertaining to stay near the *zócalo,* which is music-filled and near museums and the *malecón.* If nightlife is your thing, think about staying on Blvd Camacho.

TOP CHOICE Hotel Imperial HOTEL $$
(☎932-12-04; www.hotelimperialveracruz.com; Lerdo 153; s/d/ste M$600/700/900; ⊝❉🛜🌊) The languid Imperial right on the *zócalo* is heaven for lovers of warts-and-all Mexican reality. Sure, it's a little dark in the corridors, and the shadier corners might hide some forgotten mildew, but keep your eyes peeled for the details – the original stained-glass, hand-operated lift, for instance – and you'll find that this is a truly magnificent building. Large rooms mix handy modernities with an authentic aura of old-world seediness.

Hotel Emporio LUXURY HOTEL $$$
(☎932-00-20; www.hotelesemporio.com/veracruz; Paseo del Malecón 224; r from M$2350; 🅿⊝❉@🌊🐾) Veracruz's emblematic hotel is well worth splashing out on, especially if it's running an offer (as little as M$1200 in low season). As if the lavish interior (three pools, gym, cocktail bar and huge light-filled rooms) wasn't enough, there's also a dynamite location on the liveliest stretch of the *malecón,* expansive harbor views and the Gran Café de la Parroquia (p203) right next door. If none of this swings it for you, you're clearly in the wrong town. Try Cancún.

Nu Hotel HOTEL $$
(☎937-09-17; www.nuhotel.com.mx; Av La Fragua 1066; s/d M$450/500; 🅿❉🛜) Like a diamond in the rough, the new Nu has pitched itself amid the scruffy next-to-bus-station hovels and declared war. It's no contest really, especially at these prices. Savor the clean, minimalist-chic rooms; young, casual staff; and cool downstairs cafe. The only real drawback is the location, 3km south of the *zócalo,* which isn't really handy for anything – except the buses, of course.

Hotel Colonial HOTEL $$
(☎932-01-93; www.hcolonial.com.mx; Lerdo 117; r M$495-780; 🅿❉@🛜🌊) The confusingly sprawling Colonial nobly ages and becomes more and more dated while resting on its main laurel – a central *zócalo* location. Not surprisingly, the rooms can be noisy, but the

hotel has so many nooks and crannies that more tranquil escapes can easily be procured at the back. Rooms have a centrally controlled air-conditioning and sound system so you'd better like 1980s synth-pop and Barry Manilow.

Gran Hotel Diligencias HOTEL $$
(☎923-02-80, 800-505-55-95; www.granhoteldiligencias.com; Av Independencia 1115; r M$1150; 🅿⊝❉@🛜🌊) The fanciest option on the *zócalo* is not actually its most atmospheric (that would be the Imperial), but the Diligencias is a good central perch with huge rooms that deliver elegance, if not personality. You'll find a better atmosphere downstairs in the adjoining El Estribo Bar and Villa Rica restaurant. Discounts are advertised during the low season.

Hotel Candilejas HOTEL $$
(☎932-58-72; www.hotelcandilejas.com.mx; Barragán 35; s/d M$420/550; 🅿❉) It's all about modesty. Flanked bizarrely on two sides by the unsubtle Novo Mar hotel monolith, the Candilejas still manages to steal the show. Bank on friendly staff, tranquil communal areas and clean, journeyman rooms, many of which have precious balconies with *malecón* views.

Hotel Casa Blanca HOTEL $
(☎200-46-24; Trigueros 49; s/d M$250/400; ❉) The old colonial frontage hides a dustier interior, but despite its close-to-the-*zócalo* location, the Casa Blanca doesn't pretend to be posh – or expensive. Yesterday's bed sheets are hung up on the 1st-floor balconies to dry, intricate tile-work embellishes the stairway and a decent restaurant downstairs plays on a Spanish-Mexican theme.

Hotel Villa Rica HOTEL $
(☎932-48-54; Blvd Camacho 165; with fan M$150, with air-con M$250-400; ❉🛜) A friendly bunch runs this small seaside hotel with bare-bones rooms that are clean and breezy, some with tiny tiled ocean-view balconies.

Mar y Tierra HOTEL $$
(☎931-38-66; www.hotelmarytierra.com; Sainz de Baranda s/n; s M$450-685, d M$550-845; 🅿❉🛜🌊) Despite some piecemeal remodeling, the Mar y Tierra's general demeanor leaves you wondering if the designers got their tips from Fidel Castro's Cuba (think austere). Drab rooms aside, the hotel has a prime *malecón* location, plus a rooftop pool with fine vistas of the city and sea.

Mesón del Mar
BOUTIQUE HOTEL $$

(☎932-50-43; www.mesondelmar.com.mx; Morales 543; s/d M$500/600; 🅿🖨🛜📶) A colonial downtown place with clean, well cared for rooms with tall ceilings (some have cool lofts and balconies). Staff are friendly and, while the boutique moniker might be a little overstated to those used to European refinement, this is a well-priced central option which ably captures the essence of Veracruz.

Hawaii Hotel
HOTEL $$

(☎938-00-88; www.hawaiihotel.com.mx; Paseo del Malecón 458; s M$550-700, d M$600-800; 🅿🖨🛜📶) Who knows why it's called the Hawaii Hotel? The building shape is contemporary with gleaming light-colored marble and white decor inside. It's the best value on the *malecón,* and some rooms have marvelous views of it.

Hotel Bello
HOTEL $$

(☎922-48-28; www.hotelbello.com; Ruíz Cortines 258; r M$800-1100; 🅿🖨🛜@📶) Both the lobby and the rooms manage to be colorful and cheerful without being cheesy. Higher-floor double rooms have ample balconies equipped with wooden deck furniture and city or sea views. It's in a bar-and-restaurant district near the beach, 5km south of the *zócalo.* To get here, head 4km south from the city center on Blvd Camacho before turning right at the major junction with Ruíz Cortines. The hotel is 500m along on the left.

✖ Eating

Two main factors strongly influence Veracruz cooking: its location by the ocean and its role as a port. The first factor means there's an abundance of seafood. The second has made it a melting pot for various foreign cultures and dishes.

Using seafood and the pre-Hispanic diet of beans, corn and squash as a base, the local cuisine has absorbed Spanish and Afro-Caribbean influences over the last five centuries to create such genre-blending dishes as *huachinango a la veracruzana* (red snapper in a spicy tomato sauce), *arroz a la tumbada* (a kind of paella-like soup) and *pollo encacahuatado* (chicken in a peanut sauce). Excellent seafood can be procured anywhere, but the condensed strip of *palapas* (thatched-roof shelters) on the *malecón* just south of the aquarium has made it their (sometimes expensive) specialty. Not surprisingly, there's something delicious about eating seafood within sight and smell of the sea.

The *zócalo* cafes under the ever-lively, music-filled *portales* are popular spots for drinks and food. They all offer the same tasty, price-hiked varieties. Alternatively, you can join *jarochos* in the mazes of Mercado Hidalgo, where you can find nooks that serve cheap delectable local favorites like *cocteles de mariscos* (seafood cocktails), *mondongo* (prepared cow stomach) and delicious *moles.*

Los Canarios
SPANISH, MEXICAN $$

(Paseo del Malecón 224; meals M$70-150; 🖨📶) With large windows overlooking the *malecón,* it's hard to walk past this new place in the recently renovated Hotel Emporio and not get a guilty urge to slink inside to reacquaint yourself with à la mode Spanish cooking mixed, of course, with a few Mexican inflections. The paella's excellent, and the breaded chicken is unusually succulent. Fine service doesn't miss a beat.

Nieves de Malecón
ICE CREAM $

(Av Zaragoza 286; cups M$3-10; 🕙11am-7pm) *Jarochos* prefer sorbets *(nieves)* over ice cream and this is one of the town's sorbet favorites sandwiched between the *malecón* and the *zócalo.* Loquacious 'callers' stand outside drumming up business, competing with a rival place (with its own 'callers') directly across the street. Generous portions are laden with fresh fruit chunks – or you can opt for the Veracruz staple, vanilla.

Ninfas
MEXICAN, BREAKFAST $

(Av Xicoténcatl 1154; meals M$30-80; 🕙7am-11pm Tue-Sat, 7am-5pm Sun & Mon) Far from what passes for Veracruz's tourist track, this neighborhood restaurant is usually stuffed with locals enjoying the good food and amiable family who serve it. The homemade tortillas are memorably rustic; so is the huevos rancheros breakfast. Set menu is M$50.

Mariscos Tano
SEAFOOD $

(Molina 20; meals M$30-90; 🕙8am-10pm) A de facto rehearsal room for a trio of local *jarocho* musicians, Tano is an unintentionally retro seafood joint crammed with faded photos of the owner posing with Vegas girls and mustached *hombres* in kipper ties from c 1975. The food is economical and tasty, and the atmosphere kind of salt-of-the-sea Veracruz with a *son* soundtrack.

Villa Rica Mocambo
SEAFOOD $$$

(Calz Mocambo 527; mains M$150-280; 🕙noon-10pm) For those on short itineraries, there

DON'T MISS

GRAN CAFÉ DE LA PARROQUIA

To say that Veracruz's greatest 'sight' is a cafe might seem like a slur on this grizzled port city's reputation. But walk into the **Gran Café de la Parroquia** (www.laparroquia. com; Gómez Farías 34; mains M$40-120; ☺6am-midnight) – 203-years-old and counting – and the penny will quickly drop. Pulling in anything from 2000 to 4000 customers a day, every facet of Veracruz's diverse personality is on show inside the immense but un-showy interior – holding court, making noise and, more appropriately, tapping their spoons on their coffee glasses. The spoon-tapping – a Parroquia tradition that dates from the 1890s – is to attract the attention of the ultra-professional waiters who cruise like ballet dancers between the tables carrying two huge steaming jugs, one filled with coffee and the other with hot milk. The de rigueur drink in La Parroquia is *lechero*, a milky coffee brought to your table as an espresso measure in the bottom of a glass. Tap your spoon on the glass rim and – hey presto – a white-jacketed waiter quickly appears, extends his jug high in the air, and fills your three-quarters-empty glass with aerated milk employing all the precision of Tiger Woods putting a birdie.

The Parroquia has inspired some spin-offs in recent years, but none come close to matching the atmosphere and spirit of the original on Veracruz's Paseo del Malecón. Recommended menu items include quesadillas, fruit plates, spicy soups and possibly the best *tres leches* cake you'll ever taste.

---

aren't many reasons to make the pilgrimage to Boca del Río. But food – and this restaurant in particular – could swing it. Fish is the all-compassing ingredient, from charcoal-grilled octopus to stuffed sea bass, and the beachside service is attentive.

Gran Café del Portal CAFE, INTERNATIONAL **$$**
(Av Independencia 1187; snacks M$50-130; ☺7am-midnight) The slightly less-famous alternative to the Parroquia plays on its closer-to-the-*zócalo* location and continued uniqueness (there are no Xalapan or Cordobés offshoots of the Portal). Prices are a tad higher than its rival, but the deft aim of the coffee/milk-pouring waiters is equally precise.

Ulúa Fish SEAFOOD **$$$**
(☏922-72-64; www.uluafish.com; Ruíz Cortines 2; mains M$70-240; ☺7am-noon & 2-11pm Tue-Sun; ☻) This upscale cafe was opened by famous chef José Burela Picazzo, who also founded a cooking school in the city and has written a cookbook about the local specialties of Veracruz state. If you are in the mood to slam your credit card for excellent seafood, this is the place. To get here, head 4km south from the city center on Blvd Camacho before turning right at the major junction with Ruíz Cortines. The hotel is 300m along on the left.

Mardel ARGENTINE, BREAKFAST **$$$**
(☏937-56-42; www.mardelrestaurant.com; Blvd Camacho 2632; mains M$75-250; ☺7am-11pm Mon-Sat, to 7pm Sun) Opened in 2009 by an ex-Argentine soccer player (alas, not Messi), this upscale restaurant, literally over the water, specializes in Argentine favorites (steaks then!), but there are also Mexican and Spanish influences on the extensive menu. More recently Mardel has been opening at 7am to lure in early morning *malecón* strollers for a lavish breakfast.

 Drinking

The *portales* cafes are drinking strongholds. But head south on the *malecón* and you'll find plenty of other choices.

Bar Prendes BAR
(Lerdo; ☺9am-late) For a front-row seat for whatever's happening in the *zócalo* on any given night, look no further than Prendes with its trendy modern furniture occupying a prize slice of real estate under the *portales*. Beers come in long tubes with taps at the bottom for groups. Billy-no-mates can opt for a solitary bottle of Corona.

La Cava BAR
(Blvd Camacho btwn Uribe & Barragán; ☺5pm-close) Definitely a neighborhood favorite, this tiny bar illuminated with black lights seems to host lots of laughter and cocktail-induced intimacy.

Velitas BAR
(cnr Blvd Camacho & Militar; drinks M$15-50; ☺5pm-close) This popular little seaside *palapa* on Blvd Camacho could be romantic with its

DANZÓN DAYS

It's hard to wander far in Veracruz without stumbling into a plaza-full of romantic *jarochos* indulging in the city's favorite pastime, the *danzón*, an elegant tropical dance which melds influences of the French contradance with the rhythms of African slaves.

As with most Latin American dances, the *danzón* has its roots in Cuba where it was purportedly 'invented' in 1879 by popular band leader Miguel Failde who showcased his catchy dance composition *Las Alturas de Simpson* in the port city of Matanzas. Elegant and purely instrumental in its early days, the *danzón* required dancers to circulate in couples rather than groups, a move which scandalized white polite society of the era. By the time the dance arrived in Mexico, brought by Cuban immigrants in the 1890s, it had become more complex, expanding its peculiar syncopated rhythm, and adding other instruments such as the congas to form an *orquesta típica*.

Though the *danzón* faded in popularity in Cuba in the 1940s and '50s with the arrival of the *mambo* and the *chachachá*, in Mexico it continued to flourish. Indeed, since the 1990s the *danzón* has undergone a huge revival in Veracruz, particularly among mature citizens. The bastion of the dance is the *zócalo* on Friday and Saturday evenings.

tiki-torch ambience or just a laid-back place to grab a cocktail while checking out the ocean and the people strolling past on the boulevard. On weekends there's live music.

Bar El Estribo
BAR

(Av Independencia 1115; ☺9am-late) Because Gran Hotel Diligencia's bar is raised up above sidewalk level and fenced off, it's the only place on the *zócalo* where one can eat and drink outside without hawkers in your face selling their stock every 10 minutes. The Pepito sandwich is good, as are the drink and wine selections.

☆ Entertainment

Of course, there are always marimbas and mariachis on the *zócalo*. And the coastline boulevard is known as *la barra más grande del mundo,* the biggest bar in the world, *barra* referring to both the sandbar and the drinks bar. During holiday times, it's an outdoor party with live music and dancing in the streets. Many venues line Blvd Camacho.

Teatro Principal Francisco Javier Clavijero
THEATER

(Emparán 166) This theater has had a long history and many incarnations. It moved here in 1819 and adopted its current architectural style (French neoclassical with some tremendous mosaics) in 1902. The latest refurb was in 2011. Plays, musicals and classical concerts are performed here.

La Casona de la Condesa
CLUB

(www.casonadelacondesa.com; Blvd Camacho 1520; cover Fri & Sat M\$30-60; ☺10pm-5am Tue-Sun) The weird Jesus art is meant to be edgy but feels whacked out. La Casona attracts an older (ie not teenage) crowd and offers solid live music at night. It is situated close to the seafront, 5km south from the city center on Blvd Camacho.

Las Barricas
LIVE MUSIC, CLUB

(www.lasbarricascentro.com; Constitución 72; cover Fri & Sat & for live music; ☺1pm-late Mon-Sat) This *jarocho*-recommended live-music venue and club plays a variety of music: reggaeton, salsa, pop, rock etc. It's on the small side, so expect to be packed in with the raucous, jovial crowd, especially on weekends.

🔒 Shopping

Avenida Independencia is the city's main shopping thoroughfare. Souvenirs are best procured at the Mercado de Artesanías on the *malecón.* You can buy cheap bottles of vanilla here and good-quality coffee. Jewelry – especially silver – is also economical and sometimes engraved with interesting Aztec/Mayan motifs.

Mercado de Artesanías
MARKET, SOUVENIRS

(Paseo del Malecón) Souvenir city populates 30-plus tiny adjacent booths that line the stretch of the *malecón* closest to the *zócalo,* selling everything from T-shirts to vanilla.

Libros y Arte Fototeca
BOOKS

(Callejón El Portal de Miranda 9; ☺10am-7:45pm Mon-Sat, from 1pm Sun) Inside the Fototeca building on the corner of the *zócalo,* this place has good regional and international selections.

ℹ Information

Emergency
Ambulance, Fire & Police (☏066)

Internet Access
Internet (Lerdo 357; per 30min/1hr M$6/10; ☉9am-7:30pm)

Laundry
Lavandería Mar y Sol (Av Madero 616; wash & dry per load M$30; ☉8:30am-9pm Mon-Sat)

Left Luggage
There's a 24-hour facility in the 2nd-class terminal of the bus station.

Medical Services
Beneficencia Española (☏932-00-21; www.benever.com.mx; Av 16 de Septiembre 955) A hospital that can offer general medical services to visitors to Mexico.
Hospital Regional (☏932-36-90; Av 20 de Noviembre 1074)

Money
There's a cluster of banks with ATMs a block north of the *zócalo*.

Post
Post office (Plaza de la República 213) A five-minute walk north of the *zócalo*.

Telephone
Card phones proliferate around the *zócalo*.

Tourist Information
Tourist office (www.veratur.gob.mx; Palacio Municipal; ☉10am-6pm) Has mostly helpful staff and plenty of maps and brochures. There's another small **booth** (cnr Paseo del Malecón & Arista; ☉10am-6pm) at the far western end of the Mercado de Artesanías.

ℹ Getting There & Away

Air
Veracruz International Airport (Airport code: VER) is 18km southwest of the center, near Hwy 140. Frequent flights to Monterrey, Villahermosa, Mérida, Cancún and Mexico City are offered by **Aeroméxico** (www.aeromexico.com) and **MAYair** (www.mayair.com.mx) in addition to a handful of other national airlines.

Direct flights to/from Houston are offered by **Continental Airlines** (www.continental.com).

Bus
Veracruz is a major hub, with good services up and down the coast and inland along the Córdoba–Puebla–Mexico City corridor. Buses to and from Mexico City can be heavily booked at holiday times.

The **bus station** (Av Díaz Mirón btwn Collado & Orizaba) is 3km south of the *zócalo* and has ATMs. The 1st-class/deluxe area is in the part of the station closest to Orizaba. For more frequent and slightly cheaper and slower 2nd-class services, enter on the other side from Avenida Lafragua. There's a 24-hour luggage room here.

Daily 1st-class ADO departures include the ones listed in the following table.

Buses leaving Veracruz also go to Campeche, Cancún, Chetumal, Matamoros, Mérida, Nuevo Laredo and Salina Cruz.

VERACRUZ VERACRUZ CITY

BUSES FROM VERACRUZ

DESTINATION	FARE (M$)	DURATION	FREQUENCY (DAILY)
Acayucan	243	3hr	frequent
Catemaco	136	3½hr	8
Córdoba	116	1½hr	hourly
Mexico City (TAPO)	394	5½hr	frequent
Oaxaca	444	7½hr	2
Orizaba	132	2½hr	frequent
Papantla	192	4hr	7
Puebla	318	3½hr	12
San Andrés Tuxtla	130	3hr	14
Santiago Tuxtla	124	2½hr	14
Tampico	464	9½hr	5
Tuxpan	262	6hr	frequent
Villahermosa	445	7½hr	frequent
Xalapa	98	2hr	frequent

Car & Motorcycle

Many car-rental agencies have desks at the Veracruz airport. There are also some larger agencies scattered around town. Rates start at M$300 per day. Agencies include **Dollar** (📞935-88-08; Fiesta Inn, Blvd Camacho s/n).

❶ Getting Around

Veracruz airport is small, modern and well organized, with a cafe and several shops. There's no bus service to or from town; official taxis cost M$200 to the *zócalo*. You must buy a ticket upfront from a booth in the arrivals hall.

To get to downtown from the 1st-class bus station, take a bus marked 'Díaz Mirón y Madero' (M$6). It will head to Parque Zamora then up Avenida Madero. For the *zócalo*, get off on the corner of Avenida Madero and Lerdo and turn right. Returning to the bus stations, pick up the same bus going south on Avenida 5 de Mayo. Booths in the 1st- and 2nd-class stations sell taxi tickets to the center (*zócalo* area; M$30). In the tourist office, you can get a summary sheet of official taxi-ride costs, which is helpful for guarding against tourist price inflation.

Buses marked 'Mocambo-Boca del Río' (M$7.50 to Boca del Río) leave regularly from the corner of Avenida Zaragoza and Serdán, near the *zócalo*; they go via Parque Zamora and Blvd Camacho to Playa Mocambo (20 minutes) and on to Boca del Río (30 minutes). AU buses also go there from the 2nd-class station.

CENTRAL VERACRUZ

Curvy Hwy 180 follows the coast south past dark-sand beaches to Cardel, where Hwy 140 branches west to Xalapa, the state capital. Charming mountain towns sprinkle the inland volcanic ranges, which are laced with dramatic river gorges. From Veracruz, Hwy 150D heads southwest to Córdoba, Fortín de las Flores and Orizaba, on the edge of the Sierra Madre.

Central Coast

The beaches north of the city of Veracruz are a popular Mexican vacation spot, and the area also boasts the impressive Zempoala ruins.

ZEMPOALA
📞296 / POP 9500

The pre-Hispanic Totonac town of Zempoala (or Cempoala) stands 42km north of Veracruz and 4km west of Hwy 180 in modern Zempoala. The turnoff is by a Pemex station 7km north of Cardel. There's a *voladores* pole and performances are enacted sporadically – normally during Semana Santa and holidays. Zempoala is most easily reached through Cardel – take a bus marked 'Zempoala' (M$10) from next to Hotel Cardel, or a taxi (M$70).

History

Zempoala became a major Totonac center after about AD 1200 and fell to the Aztecs in the mid-15th century. The 30,000-person town had defensive walls, underground water and drainage pipes. As Hernán Cortés approached the town, one of his scouts reported that the buildings were made of silver – but it was only white paint shining in the sun.

Zempoala's chief – a corpulent fellow nicknamed by the Spanish *el cacique gordo* (the fat chief) – struck an alliance with Cortés for protection against the Aztecs. But his hospitality didn't stop the Spanish from smashing his gods' statues and lecturing his people on the virtues of Christianity. It was at Zempoala in 1520 that Cortés defeated the expedition sent by Cuba's Spanish governor to arrest him.

A smallpox epidemic in 1575–77 decimated Zempoala and most of the survivors moved to Xalapa. By the 17th century the town was abandoned. The present town dates from 1832. Townsfolk fled here in 1955 during category 5 Hurricane Janet, which caused further damage to the ruins.

◉ Sights

🏛 **Archaeological Site** ARCHAEOLOGICAL SITE (admission M$37; ⏰9am-6pm) The archaeological site is lush, with a lovely mountain backdrop. Though not as monumental as El Tajín, it's still astounding. Most of the buildings are faced with smooth, rounded, riverbed stones, but many were originally plastered and painted. A typical feature is battlementlike 'teeth' called *almenas*.

The **Templo Mayor** (Main Temple) uncovered in 1972 is an 11m-high pyramid with a wide staircase ascending to the remains of a shrine. When they first encountered Zempoala, Cortés and his men lodged in **Las Chimeneas**, whose hollow columns were thought to be chimneys – hence the name.

The circle of stones in the middle of the site is the **Circulo de los Guerreros** where lone captured soldiers battled against groups of local warriors. Few won.

There are two main structures on the west side. One is known as the **Templo del Sol** and has two stairways climbing its front side in typical Toltec-Aztec style. The sun god was called Tonatiun and sacrifices were offered to him here on the **Piedra de Sacrificios**. The 'fat chief,' officially known as Xicomacatl, sat facing the macabre spectacle on the appropriately large **altar**.

To its north, the second structure is the **Templo de la Luna**, with a structure similar to Aztec temples to the wind god, Ehecatl.

East of Las Chimeneas is **Las Caritas** (Little Heads), named for niches that once held several small pottery heads. Another large temple to the wind god, known as the **Templo Dios del Aire**, is in the town itself – go back south on the site entrance road, cross the main road in town and then go around the corner to the right. The ancient temple, with its characteristic circular shape, is beside an intersection.

The small site **museum** has some interesting clay figurines, polychrome plates and obsidian flints. It's best to check it out first. There are four Spanish-speaking guides at the site who give explanations for free (tips recommended). **Roberto del Moral Moreno** (📞cell phone 296-1053472) is the only one who knows some English. He charges approximately M$100.

🛈 Getting There & Away
The bus from Cardel (M$10) drops you right outside the site entrance.

CHACHALACAS
📞296 / POP 2000
The seaside town of Chachalacas guards giant sand dunes, unkempt rows of tasty snack-shacks and a tourist demographic that is 99% Mexican. If you're a foreigner trying to escape your countrymen, this is a good place to hide out. The small, elongated settlement hugs the beach 10km northeast of Cardel.

◉ Sights & Activities
Beach
BEACH, WALKING
The main 'sight' is the beach. The part nearest to town offers plenty of activities including wet bikes and banana boat rides (M$50 per person). A hike along the beach is highly recommended. Continue north for 3km and you'll encounter some gigantic **sand dunes** falling directly to the ocean. They make fine viewpoints if you've the energy to climb them. Alternatively, you can hire an ATV

(M$250 per hour) from the beach and motor up.

🛏 Sleeping & Eating
Campgrounds are advertised as you walk the beachside strip, where you'll find mostly budget to midrange hotels.

Punta Real
LUXURY HOTEL $$$
(📞962-58-93; www.puntareal.com.mx; cnr Sáenz de la Peña & Condor; r from M$1390; P☺✳☎✿⛷) Traditionally, the most upscale beach option isn't always the best, but it *is* in Chachalacas. Despite its 'small resort' status, the beachfront Punta Real has a tranquil Buddhist vibe with large but weirdly shaped rooms, lovely grounds and interesting freebies; count on apples and sachets of mosquito repellent. It plays strongly on its spa, but there's also a gym, various pools and mini-golf.

Hotel Gran Palmeiras
HOTEL $$
(📞962-54-65; Ribera del Río 39; d M$550; P✳⛷) Turn right at the entrance to the town and within 300m you're in the domain of the Palmeiras, a primarily Mexican enclave at the mouth of a river with giant king-sized beds filling otherwise simple rooms. There's a pool and a restaurant, but it's dead off season.

Hotel Spidi
HOTEL, CAMPGROUND $
(📞962-50-48; www.hotelspidi.com; cnr Espinosa & Azul; campsites per tent M$150, r from M$400; P✳☎⛷) The Spidi has a grass lot beside it for camping. Showers and bathrooms for campers are found inside the hotel. It's an extra M$40 per day for campers to use the pool.

Restaurante Marily
SEAFOOD $
(Paseo de las Aves 14; mains from M$35; ⏱8am-8pm) The usual stash of beachside *palapas* is brightened by the pink tones of Marily, with a huge selection of seafood, satisfying *plátanos con crema* (bananas with cream sauce) and quesadillas that are just asking to be washed down with a cold bottle of Corona beer.

🛈 Getting There & Away
People mostly travel to Chachalacas through the transportation hub Cardel, where there are regular buses and microbuses (M$14) that go to the beach from the 2nd-class bus station on the main plaza. Alternatively, a taxi from Cardel is M$70 to M$90.

LA ANTIGUA

296 / POP 990

The city of Veracruz' second incarnation (1525–99) reveals little of its past identity in a languid grid of sleepy, cobbled streets and moss-covered ruins. People still live here, but it's a backwater these days, albeit a pleasant one, and worth a detour on the basis of its historical significance and well-known fish restaurant, Las Delicias Marinas.

A Spanish settlement was established here in 1525, and it's rumored that this is where conquistador Cortés moored his boats to a **Ceiba tree**. The tree – gnarly and gigantic – is still standing. The eye-catching ruined building half-strangled by tree roots and vines is a 16th-century **custom house**, sometimes erroneously called the 'Casa de Cortés.' The tiny walled **Ermita del Rosario church**, probably dating from 1523, is considered to be the oldest in the Americas.

Lanchas will motor you along the pleasant Río Antigua for around M$50 to M$100 per person, depending on how many people want to go.

Along the river there's a cluster of seafood restaurants. At the end of the row adjacent to a pedestrian-only suspension bridge, the celebrated **Las Delicias Marinas** (Río Huitzilapan waterfront; mains M$90-200) serves exquisite fresh and saltwater fish that could emulate anything in Veracruz. There's music and dance entertainment here at weekends.

Colectivo taxis charge M$6 to M$10 from the village to the highway 1km away where buses to Veracruz and Cardel pass every 15 minutes or so (flag down the driver just north of the toll booth).

Cardel

TRANSPORTATION HUB

Cardel (or José Cardel) is a busy transit hub which, because of its geographic location, makes a good launch-pad for surrounding attractions, namely: Zempoala, Antigua and Chachalacas. Among bird-watchers it is also a seasonal fly-by for hundreds of thousands of migratory raptors. The bus terminal, banks, restaurants and internet cafes are scattered around the plaza; a lively square which though not as drop-dead-gorgeous as other cities, ignites a musical passion at night. You'll find acceptable accommodations at **Hotel Bienvenido** (296-962-07-77; José Cardel Sur 1; s/d M$250/400; P❄️🛜) which has a handy modern restaurant called **La Palma** (mains M$70-100) on the ground floor

that serves fine international dishes and carrot cake.

From Veracruz bus station, regular 1st-class ADO buses to Cardel cost M$40; more frequent 2nd-class AU buses cost M$31 and leave every 15 minutes. Cardel's bus station is right on the main plaza. Buses to Zempoala leave one block to the west from outside Hotel Cardel.

Xalapa

228 / POP 425,000 / ELEV 1427M

Appearing positively trendy after Veracruz, Xalapa (which is sometimes spelled 'Jalapa' but always pronounced 'ha-*la*-pa') is Mexico in an Afghan coat with a heavy literary tome under its arm. Welcome to the political and cultural capital of Veracruz state, a city as urbane as it is urban where everything seems to be a little 'cooler' than it is on the coast, including the climate. While Veracruz enjoys tropical Miami-like weather, Xalapa – on a wet weekend in January – could pass for Seattle.

Sprawled around the verdant skirts of Cofre de Perote, the city juxtaposes its jungle-like environs with a traffic-asphyxiated urban core punctuated – life-savingly – with a smattering of pleasant parks. The state's most important university resides here, as does a superb anthropological museum that rivals El Tajín as Veracruz state's top sight. The gargantuan pre-Hispanic relics are supplemented by hip bars, weighty bookstores and enough quality coffee bars to make a caffeine-infused Roman jealous. Reminding you that you're still in Mexico are narrow colonial streets clogged with traffic and policed by brave whistle-blowing transit cops.

History

Founded by Totonacs in the early 1200s, Xalapa was part of the Aztec empire when Hernán Cortés and his men passed through in 1519. Because of its appealing climate and location, Spain strategically placed a monastery here to proselytize to the indigenous population. By the 17th century it had evolved into a commercial axis and meeting hub. Today Xalapa is still a commercial center for coffee, tobacco and flowers.

◉ Sights

TOP CHOICE **Museo de Antropología** MUSEUM
(Av Xalapa s/n; adult/student M$50/25, audioguide M$20; ⊙9am-5pm Tue-Sun) Last things

first; the building which encases this remarkable museum (containing Mexico's second-finest archaeological collection) is a work of art in its own right – a series of interconnecting galleries that fall, like a regal staircase, down the side of a lush hill. Viewing archaeological treasures has rarely been this pleasurable.

Now, onto the exhibits themselves, whose scale and breadth rival the museum's intricate lay-out. Three key Gulf coast pre-Hispanic civilizations are represented – namely the Olmecs, the Totonacs and the Huastecs – and the exhibits are presented chronologically within their sections with clearly labeled explanations in Spanish. Laminated English information sheets are attached to the wall at the entrance to each new room. As there's so much to see, allow yourself a good chunk of time to visit. There's a small unexciting cafe on the upper floor and a truly excellent bookstore.

Several spaces concentrate on the Olmec culture from southern Veracruz, from which comes the most celebrated piece, **El Señor de Las Limas**. There's also an array of fine work associated with the pre-Hispanic ball game.

The museum is set in spacious gardens on the west side of Avenida Xalapa, 4km northwest of the center. To get there, take a 'Camacho-Tesorería' bus (M$6) from the corner of Enríquez and Parque Juárez. To return, take a bus marked 'Centro.' A taxi costs M$20 to M$30.

Parque Juárez   PLAZA
The centrally located main square feels like a terrace, with its south side overlooking the valley below and the snowcapped cone of Pico Orizaba beckoning in the distance. Greener than other plazas, you'll find Monkey Puzzle trees and manicured hedges in among the shoe-shiners, balloon sellers and wandering minstrels.

On the plaza's north side is the neoclassical **Palacio Municipal** (1855) and on the east side is the **Palacio de Gobierno**, the seat of Veracruz's state government. The Palacio de Gobierno has a fine mural by Mario Orozco Rivera depicting the history of justice above the stairway near the eastern entrance on Enríquez.

Parque Paseo de los Lagos   PARK
(Zona Universitaria) Xalapans escape the monstrous traffic just south of Parque Juárez in this serendipitous park which has 3km of delightful lakeside paths (most commonly used for jogging and making out). At its northern end is the **Centro Cultural Los Lagos** (Paseo los Lagos s/n), a lovely cultural center where you check out the bulletin board to find out about drop-in dance or yoga classes among other cultural-event announcements.

FREE **Pinacoteca Diego Rivera**   GALLERY
(Herrera 5; 10am-6pm Tue-Sat) Tucked beneath the west side of the plaza, this small gallery houses a modest collection of Rivera's works, as well as pieces from other Mexican artists. It was being renovated at the time of writing.

Catedral Metropolitana   CATHEDRAL
(cnr Enríquez & Revolución) As unfinished as Schubert's Eighth Symphony, Xalapa's cathedral lacks a second tower rather than a grand musical finale but it still impresses with its scale and grandiosity. The architecture, a mélange of neo-Gothic and baroque, is a product of its era, the 1770s, while inside lie the remains of St Rafael Guízar y Valencia, beatified by Pope John Paul II in 1995.

Parque Ecológico Macuiltépetl   PARK
(5am-7pm) Atop a hill north of the city, this 40-hectare park is actually the heavily wooded cap of an extinct volcano called Nevado de Toluca. Spiraling to the top, the park's paths are a treasure for the city's surprisingly robust fraternity of joggers, and provide expansive views of Xalapa and the surrounding area. Waiting at the summit, the small **Museo de la Fauna** (admission M$10; 10am-6pm Tue-Fri) has some shamefully tethered eagles on display, plus snakes and other reptiles.

FREE **Museo Casa de Xalapa**   MUSEUM
(Herrera 7; 9am-7pm) For a quick expose of Xalapan history, head to this new museum in an old colonial house close to Parque Juárez. It's small, but lovingly put together.

Museo Interactivo de Xalapa   MUSEUM
(www.mix.org.mx; Av Murillo Vidal 1735; adult/child M$60/45; 9am-5pm Mon-Fri, 10am-7pm Sat & Sun) In the city's less intriguing suburbs, this new jack-of-all-trades museum works wonders on rainy days with hyperactive kids. There are six themed rooms (science, ecology, art etc), a planetarium and an IMAX cinema. The latter two cost extra.

Xalapa

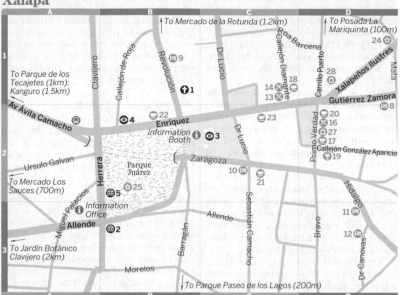

To Mercado de la Rotunda (1.2km)

To Posada La Mariquinta (100m)

To Parque de los Tecajetes (1km); Kanguro (1.5km)

To Mercado Los Sauces (700m)

To Jardín Botánico Clavijero (2km)

To Parque Paseo de los Lagos (200m)

FREE Galería de Arte
Contemporáneo   GALLERY
(Xalapeños Ilustres 135; ☺10am-7pm Tue-Sun)
The town's contemporary art gallery is in
a renovated colonial building 1km east of
the center showing worthwhile, sometimes
edgy, temporary exhibitions, plus some ceramics. There's a small movie theater here
that screens artsy films, mostly for free.

Parroquia de San José   CHURCH
(cnr Xalapeños Ilustres & Arieta) In the learned
San José quarter, this church dates from
1770 and confirms Xalapa's penchant for
asymmetrical one-towered religious edifices.
Architecturally, it displays an unusual blend
of baroque and Mudejar styles including
some horseshoe arches. Directly behind is
the **Mercado Alcalde y García**, a covered
market recently spiced up with some cool
new cafe-restaurants in the lower levels.

Parque de los Tecajetes   PARK
(Av Ávila Camacho & Victoria; ☺6am-6pm) Another dense, jungle-like nature park where
you'll forget you're in the city. It's 1km from
the center on Avenida Ávila Camacho. Joggers and walkers enjoy rustic paths and
stone aqueducts.

Jardín Botánico Clavijero   PARK
(Antigua Carretera a Coatepec Km 2.5; ☺9am-5pm)
Southwest of the town center this attractive
park has an expansive collection of subtropical and cloud-forest plants. The pines are
particularly prolific.

🏃 Activities
Local tour operators offer cultural trips to
outlying towns and archaeological sites, and
also provide easygoing sports-oriented outdoor excursions such as hiking, rafting and
rappelling. See tours, opposite.

Bird-watching   BIRD-WATCHING
(☎818-18-94; tours M$350-750) Local bird-
watching guide Robert Straub, a member of
COAX, a conservation-minded bird-watching club, offers tours in the area. Straub
authored a bird-watching guide to Veracruz,
Guía de Sitios, whose proceeds go to Pronatura, a conservation nonprofit.

🐊 Courses

**Escuela para Estudiantes
Extranjeros**   LANGUAGE
(School for Foreign Students; ☎817-86-87; www.
uv.mx/eee; Gutiérrez Zamora 25; courses per hr
from US$20, for 2 weeks US$220 plus US$100 reg-

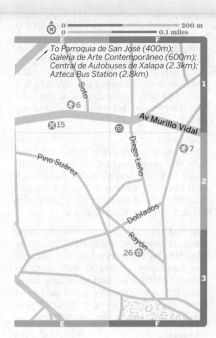

To Parroquia de San José (400m);
Galería de Arte Contemporáneo (600m);
Central de Autobuses de Xalapa (2.3km);
Azteca Bus Station (2.8km)

Xalapa

◉ Sights

◉ Activities, Courses & Tours

🛏 Sleeping

✕ Eating

◉ Drinking

◉ Entertainment

◉ Shopping

istration fee) The Universidad Veracruzana's Escuela para Estudiantes Extranjeros offers short-term, accredited programs on the Spanish and Náhuatl languages and on Mexican culture – including cooking, dancing and guitar classes – and homestays (US$400 for two weeks, US$785 for a month).

☞ Tours

Veraventuras   ADVENTURE
(☎818-95-79; www.veraventuras.com.mx; packages incl lunch from M$780) Offers rafting excursions, among other activities, and trips to a nearby hot springs.

🛏 Sleeping

Posada del Cafeto   HISTORIC HOTEL **$$**
(☎817-00-23; www.pradodelrio.com; Dr Canovas 8; s/d incl breakfast M$450/540; ❀@🛜) Promising moments of dreamy bliss amid Xalapa's traffic chaos, the Cafeto hides the noisy city behind its thick colonial walls. The dual inner patios with their finely sculpted stairways and arches create a kind of 'secret garden' feel, while subtle eco-features (water chillers, shampoo dispensers) add depth to the greenness. Breakfast in a cute onsite cafe is included.

Mesón del Alférez Xalapa   HISTORIC HOTEL **$$**
(☎818-01-13; www.pradodelrio.com; cnr Sebastián Camacho 2 & Zaragoza; s/d M$650/750; ❀🛜) Owned by the same company as the Posada del Cafeto, the Alférez sets the comfort gauge even higher with beautiful split-level rooms (beds upstairs, living room below), flower-filled greenery and – allegedly – the best breakfast in town in its refined La Candela restaurant. A sublime bargain.

Posada La Mariquinta
GUESTHOUSE $$

(📞818-11-58; www.lamariquinta.xalapa.net; Alfaro 12; s/d from M$490/570; 🅿️😊🛜) This homey, plant-filled guesthouse is set in an 18th-century colonial residence with rooms arranged around a lovely garden. The M$200 mini-suite upgrade with a balcony is nice. Extra charges are heavy: M$100 for parking and M$30 per day for wireless.

Posada Casa Regia
HOTEL $

(📞812-05-91; www.posadacasaregia.com; Hidalgo 12; s/d M$385/435; 🅿️🛜) Pleasant and colorful, this small hotel lures you in with its fancy plant- and tile-filled lobby. The inward-facing rooms are quite adequate but less exciting.

Hostal de la Niebla
HOSTEL $

(📞817-21-74; www.delaniebla.com; Gutiérrez Zamora 24; dm incl breakfast M$150, s incl breakfast M$220-330; 🅿️@🛜) Something of a mirage in these climes, this modern Scandinavian-style hostel is no half-baked nod to the backpacker market. Rather it's a spotless, well-organized, community-oriented accommodations that comes with airy rooms with decks and terraces. There's access to lockers and a kitchen.

Hotel Limón
HOTEL $

(📞817-22-04; Revolución 8; s M$155, d M$200-230) The term 'dusty jewel' could have been invented with Hotel Limón in mind. The 'dusty' part is the rooms which are perfectly adequate but crying out for a refurb. The 'jewel' is the lovely blue-tiled courtyard seemingly inherited off richer past owners. The summing up: a good economical option for the unfussy. It's also very central (just steps from the cathedral).

✕ Eating

Stylish cafes and restaurants in Xalapa, many offering ethnic and/or vegetarian choices. Callejón González Aparicio, between Primo Verdad and Mata, is an alley loaded with hip, international eateries and even hipper crowds. Try Cubanías for mojitos, El Callejón for soup and salad, or Shalom for falafels.

One local specialty is *chiles rellenos* (stuffed peppers). Of course, jalapeño chilies are from the region too.

La Fonda
MEXICAN $

(Callejón Diamante 1; dishes M$45-100; ⏱8am-5:30pm Mon-Sat) A microcosm of the Xalapa eating experience, La Fonda invites you to squeeze past the tortilla-making señorita at the door and climb upstairs to where a mural-festooned interior gives onto a narrow plant-adorned balcony overlooking the main street. The menu juxtaposes formidable *mole* with *chileatole de pollo* (chicken soup with little floating corns on the cob). The four-course set meal is a giveaway M$45.

Postodoro
ITALIAN $

(Primo Verdad 11; pasta & pizza M$50-70) The best local take on Italian food inhabits a sinuous space in Primo Verdad with a larger open area out back. Tuscany it isn't, but the pasta's close to al dente, there's a lengthy wine list and service is eager-to-please.

Plazoleta
MEXICAN, CAFE $$

(Gutiérrez Zamora 46; dishes M$40-110; ⏱8am-10pm Mon-Sat, to 6pm Sun) This cool cafeteria has street-view seating as well as tables placed around trees and vines in a courtyard. It has an extensive coffee menu and fresh fruit juices, along with traditional Mexican food and an open-air *tortillería*.

La Sopa
MEXICAN $

(Callejón Diamante 3; set lunch M$50) Another Diamond Alley diamond, which specializes in – wait for it – soup, backed up with tortillas, rice and a meat dish. For what you get, it's dirt cheap.

Mercado de la Rotonda
MARKET $

(Revolución s/n; ⏱7am-6pm) At the north end of Revolución, this untouristed market with numerous, orderly eateries has delicious regional food on the cheap.

🍷 Drinking

Xalapa has two branches of Veracruz' Gran Café de la Parroquia: one on Enríquez opposite Parque Juárez and the other on Zaragoza, though neither can match the original for size and atmosphere. Elsewhere, indie cafes abound.

⭐TOP CHOICE Café Cali
CAFE

(Callejón Diamante 23A; ⏱9am-11pm) A real diamond in Diamond Alley, Café Cali sits next to its eponymous roasting room, meaning delicious coffee smells permeate the whole block. The interior is classic bohemia. Expect earnest bearded types discussing philosophy alongside chic girls with A-line bobs. Less pretentious are the cakes; light, buttery and worth writing home about.

Espresso 58 CAFE
(Primo Verdad 7; coffee M$13-25; ☺8am-11pm; 🛜)
A sleek, modern, student joint that gets an
equal smattering of wi-fi geeks and loqua-
cious student debaters. The in-house Café
Mahal coffee (locally grown, of course) is
muy rico and the baristas are charming.

Jugos California JUICE BAR
(Enríquez 26; juices M$18-30; ☺7am-9:30pm; 🖋)
Besides *antojitos* (typical Mexican snacks),
this place serves fantastic volcano-like fruit
salads, delicious juice combos, smoothies
and even chocolate soy shakes.

Angelo Casa de Té CAFE
(Primo Verdad 21A; ☺8am-9pm) Linger over a
pot of rose tea (one of many tea choices),
while savoring homemade cookies.

Cubanías BAR
(Callejón González Aparicio; ☺5pm-1:30am) Veracruz's Cuban influences rise to the surface
in this boisterous bar that guards the entrance to Callejón González Aparicio with
mojitos, beer and – should you be peckish –
large Cuban sandwiches. Live music rocks
up later on.

☆ Entertainment

Being a university town, Xalapa has a vi-
vacious nightlife. The loudest buzz can be
found in jam-packed Callejón González
Aparicio, the covered alley off Primo Verdad,
filled with trendy bars.

🔺Tierra Luna PERFORMING ARTS
(Rayón 18; ☺9am-10pm Mon-Thu, 9am-2am Fri
& Sat) Provides poetry readings, music and
sanctuary for arty types in a lovely high-
ceilinged space. It serves tasty cafe fare and
wine, and hosts a small bookstore and craft
store.

Centro Recreativo Xalapeño ARTS CENTER
(Xalapeños Ilustres 31; ☺9am-8pm) On bookish
Xalapeños Ilustres, this cultural center is a
font of pretty much everything that passes
for 'art' in Xalapa. Jam sessions, tango
classes, art expos, sculpture competitions
and Cine Francés all kick off here. Keep your
eye on the poster board. The building is an
attractive 19th-century colonial gem with a
courtyard and small cafe (Luna Negra).

El Ágora ARTS CENTER
(Parque Juárez; ☺10am-10pm Tue-Sun, 9am-6pm
Mon) A busy and sleekly modern arts center

with a cinema, theater, gallery, bookstore
and cafe.

**Teatro del Estado Ignacio
de la Llave** THEATER
(cnr Llave & Av Ávila Camacho; ☺from 8pm) The
impressive state theatre hosts both the Orquesta Sinfónica de Xalapa and the Ballet
Folklórico of the Universidad Veracruzana.
It is situated 1.5km northwest of Parque Juárez up Avenida Ávila Camacho.

🛍 Shopping

An epicenter of Xalapa's alternative culture
is Callejón Diamante, an alley lined with
boutiques and street vendors selling cheap
jewelry, incense and paraphernalia. Bookstores line Xalapeños Ilustres.

Popularte HANDICRAFTS
(Xalapeños Ilustres 3) High-quality local handicrafts made by, and supporting, Veracruz's
indigenous communities.

Café Colón COFFEE
(Primo Verdad 15) Old-school coffee roasters
will grind Coatepec's best in front of your
eyes in their aromatic store. It sells for
M$140 per kilo.

ℹ Information

Internet Access
Internet Bravo 8 (Bravo 8; per hr M$12;
☺9am-8pm) Open late.

Laundry
Lavandería Las 4 Estaciones (Pino Suárez
59; per kg M$10; ☺9:30am-2pm & 4-8:30pm
Mon-Fri, to 6:30pm Sat)

Media
Performance Free magazine devoted to the
cultural scene.

Medical Services
Centro de Especialidades Médicas (☎814-
45-00; www.cemev.gob.mx; Ruíz Cortines
2903; ☺8am-6pm) Excellent medical care.

Money
There are banks with 24-hour ATMs along
Enríquez–Gutiérrez Zamora.

Post
Post office (cnr Gutiérrez Zamora & Leño)

Tourist Information
An **information booth** (www.xalapa.gob.mx;
Palacio Municipal; ☺9am-3pm & 4-7pm Mon-
Fri) in the Palacio Municipal has helpful info and

VERACRUZ XALAPA

BUSES FROM XALAPA

DESTINATION	FARE (M$)	DURATION	FREQUENCY (DAILY)
Cardel	64	1hr	18
Mexico City (TAPO)	278	4½hr	6
Papantla	218	4hr	14
Puebla	172	2½hr	15
Tampico	470	9½hr	2
Veracruz	98	2hr	frequent
Veracruz airport	268	1½hr	5
Villahermosa	492	8½hr	7

maps. There's another larger **office** (Palacios 9) nearby (same hours).

Websites
Xalapa Mio (www.xalapamio.com)
Xalapa Tourist Network (www.xalapa.net)

 **Getting There & Away**

Xalapa is a transportation hub with excellent connections throughout the state and beyond.

Bus
Xalapa's modern, well-organized bus station, the **Central de Autobuses de Xalapa** (CAXA; Av 20 de Noviembre), is 2km east of the center and has an ATM, cafes and telephones. Second-class buses for Xico and Coatepec regularly leave from Mercado Los Sauces, about 1km west of the center on Circuito Presidentes. First-class service is offered by ADO and good 2nd-class services by AU. The daily ADO services listed in the table leave from CAXA.

Other places served by ADO include Acayucan, Campeche, Cancún, Catemaco, Córdoba, Mérida, Orizaba and Poza Rica.

Buses to Jalcomulco leave from the **Azteca bus station** (Niños Heroes 85).

Car & Motorcycle
For car rentals, try **Kanguro** (☏817-78-78; Av Ávila Camacho 135; per day from M$545), which offers better prices the more days you rent. Hwy 140 to Puebla is narrow and winding until Perote; the Xalapa–Veracruz highway is very fast and smooth. Going to the northern Gulf coast, it's quickest to go to Cardel, then north on Hwy 180.

Getting Around

For buses from CAXA to the center, follow signs to the taxi stand, then continue downhill to the main Avenida 20 de Noviembre. The bus stop is to the right. Any bus marked 'Centro' will pass within a block or two of Parque Juárez (M$6).

For a taxi to the center, you have to buy a ticket in the bus station (M$30). To return to the bus station, take the 'Camacho-CAXA-SEC' bus from Avenida Ávila Camacho or Hidalgo.

Around Xalapa

The dramatic landscapes around Xalapa, with rivers, gorges and waterfalls, cradle some charming mountain towns and worthwhile places.

HACIENDA EL LENCERO
Almost as old as New Spain itself, this former posada (inn) was initiated in 1525 by Juan Lencero, a soldier loyal to Hernán Cortés, as a resting place for tired travelers toiling between a newly Europeanized Mexico City and the coast. Today it is the **Museo Ex-Hacienda El Lencero** (Carretera Xalapa-Veracruz Km 10; adult/child M$30/25; ☉10am-5pm) incorporating a superbly restored house furnished with antiques, along with some delightful gardens embellished with a lake and a 500-year-old fig tree.

To get to the estate travel 12km southeast of Xalapa on the Veracruz highway, and then turn down a signposted road branching off to the right for a few kilometers. From Xalapa, catch one of the regular 'Miradores' buses (M$9) from the Plaza Cristal shopping center.

COATEPEC
☏228 / POP 54,000 / ELEV 1200M
Waking up and smelling the coffee has rarely been this epiphanic. Cradled in the Sierra Madre foothills, coffee production has long been Coatepec's raison d'être, a fact that will become instantly clear as soon as you step off the bus and inhale. The settlement dates from 1701 and coffee has been

grown in the surrounding cloud forests for almost as long. The crop has brought wealth to the town. Coatepec – which lies a mere 15km south of Xalapa – is adorned with rich colonial buildings and, in 2006, was nominated a *pueblo mágico* by the Mexican government for its cultural, historical and natural relevance. In late September, Coatepec vivaciously celebrates its patron saint, San Jerónimo. Rare orchids light up Coatepec's exceptionally verdant surrounding hills. The streets, unlike Xalapa, are arranged in a grid, but beware: the traffic can be Xalapa-like in its intensity.

◎ Sights

Parque Miguel Hidalgo   PLAZA
Coatepec's main square is green and bereft of the worst of the town's traffic. In its center stands a glorious *glorieta* (bandstand) that doubles up (surprise, surprise!) as a cafe. Set back from the road on the eastern side is the unashamedly baroque **Parroquia de San Jerónimo**, named after the city's patron saint.

Cerro de Culebra   LOOKOUT
Cerro de Culebra or Snake Hill (or Coatepec in the Náhuatl language) is easily accessible from the town center. The walk takes you up cobbled steps to a lookout tower with a white Christ statue on top. From here there are magnificent city and mountain views. To get there, walk three blocks west from the main plaza on Lerdo, then north all the way up Independencia.

FREE **Museo y Jardin de Orquideas**   MUSEUM, GARDEN
(Aldama 20; ☺10am-5pm Wed-Sun) Coatepec's humid cloud forests support numerous species of orchid and an amiable local *señora* has collected many of them in this museum/garden a few blocks from the main square. Displays highlight both cultivation and conservation techniques. Reserve 30 minutes to see the full gamut.

Museo El Cafétal Apan   MUSEUM
(www.elcafe-tal.com; Carretera Coatepec-Las Trancas Km 4; admission M$35; ☺9am-5pm) If you want to learn a bit more about the history of coffee in the region, visit this museum that displays antique tools used to make coffee, conducts hands-on demonstrations on how coffee is produced and also offers coffee tastings. It's a bit out of town. A taxi will cost M$35 to M$40.

Cascada Bola de Oro   WATERFALL
The nearest waterfall to town is in the environs of a well-known Coatepec coffee *finca* (estate) with various trails and a natural swimming pool. To get there follow Calle 5 de Mayo north to a bridge, continue north on Calle Prieto and then turn left into Calle Altamirano. After passing the last shop hang a right, cross a bridge and turn left onto a path. The tourist office dispenses useful maps.

⌂ Sleeping

TOP CHOICE **Casa Real del Café**   HISTORIC HOTEL $$
(☎816-63-17; www.casarealdelcafe.com.mx; Gutiérrez Zamora 58; d/ste M$850/1300; ⓟ❋⊛) Providing healthy competition to the Posada de Coatepec is the equally deluxe Casa Real del Café, a colonial-style hotel owned by local coffee farmers whose aromatic products fortuitously find their way into the onsite Antiguo Beneficio cafe. Split level rooms offer historic luxury with dark woods and gorgeously tiled bathrooms, while the communal courtyard sports reclining chairs, a spa (with massage, hot tub and temascal, ie indigenous sauna) and a reading room with a full set of the Encyclopedia Britannica.

Posada de Coatepec   HISTORIC HOTEL $$
(☎816-05-44; www.posadacoatepec.com.mx; Hidalgo 9; r from M$965; ⓟ◒❋⊛) Coatepec's hallmark hotel is in a resplendent colonial-era building with a nice pool, exhibits from local artists, tranquil gardens and a full-sized antique coach parked in the lobby. The rooms are upscale, if sometimes a little dark.

Ashram Coatepec   HOSTEL, LODGE $
(☎816-10-55; www.ashramdecoatepec.org; Mina 100; dm or campsite M$100; ⓟ◒) On the outskirts of town, this ashram has yoga, meditation and walking trails on its lush grounds. The immaculate treatment of the gorgeous meditation and yoga spaces isn't simulated in the dormitories, but it's a manageable place to hang your hat. Only vegetarian food is served here.

✗ Eating

Casa Coffino   CAFE, INTERNATIONAL $
(www.coffino.com.mx; Jiménez del Campillo 17; snacks M$30-70) An interesting cafe encased in a head-turning art nouveau–style building a block from the plaza, Coffino's specialty is its own rich coffee (called *Café de Altura*), but it also serves light food, cakes

VERACRUZ AROUND XALAPA

VERACRUZ'S MESOAMERICAN CULTURES

Several pre-Hispanic cultures inhabited Mexico's central Gulf coast. Here's a brief who's who.

» **Olmec** Often referred to as the 'mother culture' of the civilizations that followed, the Olmecs invented many of Mesoamerica's cultural hallmarks, including colossal stone heads carved from basalt boulders, the legendary Mesoamerican ball game and the macabre practice of human sacrifice. As early agriculturists, they emerged in southern Veracruz and Tabasco in the regional centers of San Lorenzo (35km southeast of Acayucan), La Venta (in present-day Tabasco) and, later, Tres Zapotes. Their culture flourished from around 1200–900 BC in San Lorenzo and from about 800–400 BC in La Venta.

» **Classic Veracruz** The Classic period (AD 250–900) saw the rise of a number of statelets with a shared culture, together known as the Classic Veracruz civilization. Classic Veracruz was particularly obsessed with the ball game: its most important center, El Tajín, which flourished from about 600 to 900, contains 17 ball courts. The artistic hallmark of Classic Veracruz is a style of abstract carving featuring pairs of curved and interwoven parallel lines.

» **Totonac** The Gulf coast's most colorful culture flowered between AD 800 and 1200 on the thin coastal strip between Zempoala and Papantla. Calling their land Totonacapan, the Totonacs built great cities such as Zempoala and Quiahuiztlán where they practiced weaving and embroidery, and farmed the land for maize, squash, cotton and vanilla. Though big proponents of the Mesoamerican ballgame, the Totonacs also concocted more lasting legacies such as the still surviving *voladores* rite (see boxed text, p230). Despite aiding the Spanish in their quest to defeat the Aztecs, Totonacapan quickly fell to smallpox and Spanish treachery after the 1520s. There are still around 244,000 native Totonac speakers today, mainly in northern Veracruz and the Sierra Norte de Puebla.

» **Huastec** Native to the far north of Veracruz state, the ancient Huastecs spoke a language related to Mayan. Historical evidence suggests that they migrated north from the Yucatán Peninsula around 1000 BC. Industrious cotton farmers and painters of elaborate pottery, the Huastecs were also known for their musical prowess; *huapango* played by a trio of two guitars and a violin has made notable contributions to mariachi music. Huastec culture reached its zenith between AD 800 and 1200. The language has survived into modern times and still lists approximately 145,000 speakers.

and smoothies in a beautiful flower-filled courtyard.

El Caporal　　　　　INTERNATIONAL, SEAFOOD **$$**
(Luís de San José 3B; mains M$105-145; ◷8am-midnight) In colonial digs on the main square, El Caporal has a long wine list – Chilean and Spanish vintages dominate – hefty paella, large prawns and well-seasoned fish filets. Next door in the same blue house is the lighter **La Vereda Cafeteria**.

Drinking & Entertainment

TOP CHOICE El Café de Avelino　　　　CAFE
(Aldama 4; ◷noon-5pm) The best coffee in Coatepec (no mean feat!), comes out of a cafe with one table and two chairs that occupies the lobby of the resplendent Mansión de los Azulejos (House of Tiles). Owner Avelino Hernández – known locally as the

Poeta del Café (coffee poet) – brews minor miracles from his Coatepec, Cosailton, Xico and Teocelo brands, or you can buy the beans for M$200 per kilo.

El Kiosko　　　　　　　　　　　CAFE
(Parque Hidalgo) Small alfresco cafe selling java out of the old *glorieta* in the center of the plaza.

La Pausa　　　　　　　　BAR, LIVE MUSIC
(Jiménez del Campillo 1; ◷4-11pm Tue-Thu & Sun, to late Fri & Sat) Raucous upstairs bar good for a cocktail and live music on the weekend.

Shopping

La Misión　　　　ACCESSORIES, SOUVENIRS
(Aldama 6; ◷9am-7pm) Here you'll find local peace-loving items: organic coffee, essential oils, maguey honey and soymilk.

ℹ Information

There's a helpful **tourist office** (◷10am-5pm Mon-Fri) in the Palacio Municipal on Parque Hidalgo.

ℹ Getting There & Away

Regular buses (M$7.50) arrive from Xalapa's CAXA and Los Sauces terminals, or a taxi is M$80. Buses for Xico (M$7.50) leave from Constitución between Aldama and Juárez. The ADO **bus station** (5 de Mayo s/n) serves Puebla and Mexico City.

XICO

☏228 / POP 19,000 / ELEV 1300M

Eight kilometres south of Coatepec, lies Xico, its quieter but equally beguiling mountain twin, celebrated more for its *mole* than its coffee. Cobbled roads are dotted with colonial architecture; however, the town is best known for its annual Fiesta de Santa Magdalena with sawdust carpets and a running of the bulls à la Pamplona in Spain.

◉ Sights

📷 Café Gourmet Pepe   COFFEE PLANTATION

(Carretera Xico-Coatepec Km 1; tour M$55) This is an almost-organic, shade-grown coffee plantation that offers tours and sells delicious coffee and liquors. Get off at the first bus stop in Xico and walk back 150m to where you'll see signs on the right.

Waterfalls   WATERFALL

It's a pleasant, signposted 3km walk from Xico past an ex-hacienda to the plunging 80m **Cascada de Texolo** and the **Cascada de la Monja** (Waterfall of the Nun), which provides a luxurious place to take a dip. The former cascade featured in (and was integral to the plot of) the movie *Romancing the Stone* (1984); the said 'stone' was hidden behind the waterfall.

Museo del Vestido   MUSEUM

(Parroquia, cnr Av Hidalgo & Juárez; admission M$5; ◷3-7:30pm Tue-Sun) An esoteric niche museum displaying a revolving collection of St María Magdalena's past festival dresses dating from 1910.

FREE Casa-Museo Totomoxtle   MUSEUM

(cnr Aldama & Juárez; ◷10am-4pm) A small museum displaying the town's peculiar artisanal pastime of making intricate and detailed figures from *hojas de maíz* (maize leaves). Only in Xico!

🏃 Activities

Xico Aventuras   ADVENTURE SPORTS

(Venustiano Carranza Sur s/n) An outdoor-adventure outfit, based in Hotel Paraje Coyopolan, offering hiking, zip-lines, four-wheeling and rappelling in the fabulous surrounding mountains and canyons.

🎊 Festivals & Events

Fiesta de Santa Magdalena   RELIGIOUS

The mother of all festivals takes place between July 15 and 24. Gigantic floral arches are raised, and streets are artistically decorated with carpets of colored sawdust in preparation for the saint's procession. The Magdalena statue, in the Parroquia de Santa María Magdalena, located at the end of Avenida Hidalgo, is clothed in a different elaborate dress each day for 30 days around the fiesta. A running of the bulls takes place through the streets on July 22.

🛏 Sleeping & Eating

Hotel Paraje Coyopolan   HOTEL $

(☏813-12-66; www.coyopolan.com; Venustiano Carranza Sur s/n; r incl breakfast M$450; 🅿❄🛜) Just outside Xico, this center enjoys an exquisite location right on the river. The economical rooms here are delightful and vibrant, and the restaurant serves superb regional food.

Posada los Naranjos   HOTEL $

(☏813-12-66; Av Hidalgo 193; d M$300; 🅿) The most central option, steps from the church, feels more like a guesthouse than a hotel. It sports nine rooms overlooking a courtyard, plus a small cafe.

Restaurante Mesón Xiqueño   MEXICAN $$

(Av Hidalgo 148; meals M$90-120; ◷9am-9pm) If you don't like *mole* (or coffee), you may want to reconsider visiting Xico or, at least, eating here. Mesón Xiqueño is where you can sit down to see if all the rumors are true. The *mole,* best served over chicken, is thick, rich and has the faintest chocolaty taste. Caged parrots squawk in the colonial courtyard.

🛍 Shopping

Derivados Acamalin Productos Xiquenial Artesanías   FOOD

(Av Hidalgo 156) Xico's trademark *mole* (a complex mix of chocolate, banana, apple, chili, sucrose and numerous secret ingredients) can be procured at Derivados Acamalin Productos Xiquenial Artesanías. Also sells organic coffee for M$100 per kilo.

JALCOMULCO – RAFTING ADVENTURES

Surrounded by lush ravines, this town, just 30km southeast of Xalapa, hugs the Río Antigua (known as the Río Pescados) and is very picturesque. The area is rich with caves and luscious swimming spots, but it's most famous for its rapids, which accommodate white-water enthusiasts, from beginners through to the more advanced. Trips are more regular during the high seasons, but they may be full, so it's best to plan in advance. Trips can be more expensive if there are just a few people.

Though Jalcomulco is still relatively under the radar, rafting outfits, both sketchy and experienced, are beginning to migrate to this sleepy town.

The well-recommended **Aventuras Sin Límites** (☑279-832-35-80; www.raftingsinlim ite.com; Zaragoza 58; full day per person M$790) is a rafting outfit that has high standards. It's also the only outfit here that's run by locals. The basic but clean accommodations are for guests only. Another quality rafting outfit is **México Verde** (☑279-832-37-34; www.mexicoverde.com; trips from M$660), which has its own resort on the road coming into town from the northwest. **Ignacio Romero Bobillo** (☑279-832-35-80; bobillomx@ hotmail.com; 5 de Mayo 14) is a local kayaker who runs courses, rents out real white-water kayaks and provides transportation.

There are buses (M$27) to Jalcomulco from Xalapa at the Azteca bus terminal, as well as buses from Cardel.

ℹ Information

The small **tourist office** (Av Hidalgo 76; ⊗9am-6pm) is encased in the Casa de la Cultura and is a friendly source of information for the town and its surroundings.

ℹ Getting There & Away

From Xalapa, take a 'Xico' bus (M$15) from Los Sauces terminal. From Coatepec, Xico buses (M$7.50) frequently leave from Constitución, one block southeast of the main plaza.

Córdoba

☑271 / POP 140,000 / ELEV 924M

Mention you're going to Córdoba to a coastal dweller and you might well get a sarcastic eye-roll. *Cordobeses* are often seen as haughtier and less modest than their more down-to-earth *jarocho* brethren, though 'urbane' would be a kinder description.

Not to be confused with its famous namesakes in Spain and Argentina, Córdoba, Veracruz has an illustrious history and a justifiable sense of civic pride. The contract that sealed Mexico's independence was signed here in 1821, though the city itself was founded two centuries earlier by Spanish families in 1618 to inhibit escaped African slaves from attacking travelers between Mexico City and the coast.

As an overnight stop, Córdoba trumps other central Veracruz cities such as Orizaba and Fortín de las Flores on the strength of its main plaza, a 24-hour live 'show' where

theater-goers in high heels dodge hungry pigeons and grandpas moonlight as marimba players. Watching over it all is an impressive baroque cathedral, easily the most resplendent in the state.

◉ Sights

Most of Córdoba's sights ring its main plaza, Parque de 21 de Mayo, which is a sight in itself.

TOP CHOICE **Parque de 21 de Mayo** PLAZA

Not overly endowed with sights per se, Córdoba's main plaza vies with Veracruz's as the region's most entertaining. It's far larger than the port city's plaza, though a seemingly unending line of musicians makes up for any lack of intimacy. Opposite the cathedral on the square's west side is the splendiferous **Palacio Municipal** replete with an interior mural that Diego Rivera would've been hard-pressed to emulate.

Ex-Hotel Zevallos HISTORIC BUILDING

(Parque de 21 de Mayo) The Ex-Hotel Zevallos, built in 1687, is the former home of the *condes* (counts) of Zevallos. It's on the northeast side of the plaza, behind the *portales*. Plaques in the courtyard record that Juan O'Donojú and Agustín de Iturbide met here on August 24, 1821, and agreed on terms for Mexico's independence. They also concurred that a Mexican, not a European, should be head of state. Iturbide went on to briefly reign as Emperor Agustín I. The building is now notable for its cafe-restaurants.

Catedral de la Inmaculada Concepción
CATHEDRAL

(Parque de 21 de Mayo) At the southeast end of the main plaza is the pale blue baroque cathedral which dates from 1688. It has an elaborate facade flanked by twin bell towers. The showy interior is surprisingly ornate for Mexico with gold-leaf detailing and marble floors. The chapel is flanked by candlelit statues with altars, such as a gruesome Jesus on the cross and an eerily despairing Virgen de la Soledad. The mixture of glitz and gore is a visual metaphor for a disturbing historical dichotomy: the richness of the conquistadors and the misery that the indigenous people subsequently endured.

FREE Museo de Antropología
MUSEUM

(Calle 3 s/n; ⊙9am-2pm & 4-8pm) Half a block southwest of the plaza, this museum has a modest but interesting collection of artifacts that aren't especially well cared for. You'll find a fine Aztec ball-court marker, some Olmec figurines and a replica of the magnificent statue of El Señor de Las Limas that resides in Xalapa's Museo de Antropología. The 2nd floor was being renovated at the time of writing.

Parque Ecológico Paso Coyol
PARK

(cnr Calle 6 & Av 19, Bella Vista; admission M$2) This park is a jewel in the urban rough. The neighborhood joined with the government to turn what was once a 4-hectare abandoned lot overrun by 'delinquents' into a park. Now this eco-conscious park is patronized by *cordobeses,* who run and walk trails that snake around gardens punctuated with exercise stations. Your meager entrance fee pays for both *campesinos* (country people) and biologists alike to maintain the place. Follow Calle 3 south from the plaza for 1.5km. The street changes names, weaves through a suburb and bottoms out at the park.

✳✳ Festivals & Events

Good Friday
RELIGIOUS

On the evening of Good Friday, Córdoba marks Jesus' crucifixion with a procession of silence, in which thousands of residents walk through the streets behind an altar of the Virgin. Everyone holds a lit candle, no one utters a word and the church bells are strangely quiet.

🛏 Sleeping

TOP CHOICE Hotel Mansur
HOTEL $$

(☎712-60-00; www.hotelmansur.com.mx; Av 1 No 301; r from M$470; P✳) Claiming five stories of prime viewing space above Córdoba's main plaza, the Mansur with its vast balconies equipped with thick wooden chairs makes you feel as if you're part of the 'show' going on below. The cathedral is so close you could almost touch it and the Pico de Orizaba (when it takes its cloudy hat off) is equally impressive. None of the rooms are particularly flashy, but the Mansur's charms are about genuine Mexican hospitality rather than North American chain-hotel efficiency.

Hotel Layfer
HOTEL $$

(☎714-05-05; www.hoteleslayfer.com; Av 5 No 908; s/d M$750/850; P✳🛜🏊) Definitely Córdoba's fanciest hotel, though not its finest (the Mansur trumps it on atmosphere, friendliness *and* location), the Layfer, nonetheless, has sleek modern rooms arranged around a central swimming pool. Mileage is added with a wide array of extras including complimentary body-care products, a bar, gym, restaurant and games room.

Hotel Bello
HOTEL $$

(☎712-81-22; www.hotelbello.com/cordoba; cnr Av 2 & Calle 5; s/d M$550/650; P✳@🛜) This modern hotel is spotless and smartly decorated. The rooms are fresh and the staff affable. Go for the top-floor balcony rooms.

Hotel Palacio
HOTEL $

(☎712-21-88; www.hotelpalaciocordoba.com.mx; cnr Calle 2 & Av 3; s/d M$390/420; P✳🛜) The best budget option is a rather sickly pink and white building with a sleek cafe-restaurant on the ground floor and slightly darker and more basic rooms (60 of 'em) up above. It's one block from the plaza and has its own underground car park.

🍴 Eating & Drinking

For a cheap meal, try the little eateries on Avenida 5 in between Calles 1 and 2.

TOP CHOICE Calufe Café
CAFE, SANDWICHES $

(Calle 3 No 212; ⊙8am-11pm) If only all cafes could be like this. Calufe occupies the interior of an agreeably peeling colonial mansion with eclectic nooks arranged around a dimly lit plant-filled courtyard. Guitar and

BUSES FROM CÓRDOBA

DESTINATION	FARE (M$)	DURATION	FREQUENCY (DAILY)
Fortín	24	25min	9
Mexico City (TAPO)	302	5hr	frequent
Oaxaca	342	6½hr	4
Orizaba	28	40min	frequent
Puebla	184	3hr	frequent
Veracruz	116	1½hr	hourly
Xalapa	158	3hr	10

vocal duos provide a melancholy musical backdrop in the evenings. Calufe sells its own blend of coffee, along with melt-in-the-mouth coffee cake and other interesting organic snacks.

El Balcón del Zevallos   PARRILLA, MEXICAN $$$
(Av 1 No 101; mains M$100-200) The upper floor of the eerily beautiful former Hotel Zevallos claims the prize for Córdoba's best fine-dining restaurant with a refined inner sanctum and a balcony overlooking the plaza. There's an extensive wine list here (the usual Spanish and Chilean suspects), and good meat dishes cooked *a la parrilla* (on the barbecue). Service is sharp but not overly officious.

Tabachín   MEXICAN $$
(Av 1 No 101; mains M$70-120) Downstairs at Zevallos puts you in among the marimba players and wandering salesmen (fresh potatoes anyone?). But mixing in the street-level melee brings El Balcón's upstairs prices down by a good 20%. Tabachín's specialty dish is the giant *Plato Cordobés* with a raft of meats, easily divided between two, unless you're exceptionally hungry.

Mulata   INTERNATIONAL $$
(Av 1 No 721; dishes M$80-150; ⊙1-10pm Sun-Thu, to 11pm Fri & Sat) Named after a beautiful African slave who, according to legend, escaped from prison through the picture she drew in her cell. Appropriately, you'll find a gorgeous mural here as well as creative, internationally influenced food and bakery items. The breakfast is best.

❶ Information

Banks around the Plaza de Armas have 24-hour ATMs.

Cibermania (Av 2 No 306; per hr M$10; ⊙9:30am-10:15pm Mon-Sat, noon-7pm Sun) Internet access.

Hospital Covadonga (☎714-55-20; www.corporativodehospitales.com.mx; Av 7 No 1610; ⊙24hr) Urgent medical care at all hours.

Tourist office (☎717-17-00 ext 1778; turismo@mpiocordoba.gob.mx; Palacio Municipal; ⊙8am-7pm Mon-Sat) Helpful staff offer maps and information. Volunteers sometimes give tours of the city.

❶ Getting There & Around

Bus

Córdoba's **bus station** (Av Privada 4), which has deluxe, 1st-class and 2nd-class services, is 2.5km southeast of the plaza. To get to the town center from the station, take a local bus marked 'Centro' or buy a taxi ticket (M$25). To Fortín de las Flores and Orizaba, it's more convenient to take a local bus from the corner of Avenida 11 and Calle 3 than to go out to the Córdoba bus station.

Deluxe and 1st-class buses from Córdoba include the ones in the following table.

Car & Motorcycle

Córdoba, Fortín de las Flores and Orizaba are linked by toll Hwy 150D, the route that most buses take, and by the much slower Hwy 150. A scenic back road goes through the hills from Fortín, via Huatusco, to Xalapa.

Fortín de las Flores

☑271 / POP 21,000 / ELEV 970M

The mid-point on the Córdoba–Orizaba urban axis, Fortín de las Flores is where you can briefly come up for air in a tranquil cut-flower cultivation center with nurseries and private gardens. Though it's a peaceful weekend retreat for Mexico City's middle class, those from further afield might find it better day-trip fodder from bases in Córdoba or Orizaba. Fortín's annual **flower festival** runs for a week in late April or early May.

🏃 Activities

📷 Barranca de Metlac
OUTDOORS

Fortín's most striking feature is this deep, bio-diverse ravine carved out by the Río Metlac. Spanning it is the **Puente de Metlac**, the highest rail bridge in North America, measuring 131m high by 90m long. Alongside it sits a slightly older and marginally lower road bridge. The original rail bridge, the **Puente de San Miguel**, sits a couple of kilometers to the north. Built in 1873 it sweeps across the canyon in an unusual curve.

The Barranca hides some excellent hikes. For the quickest access head west from the center of Fortín down Avenida 1 which turns into the Fortín Viejo road. This quiet road bends steeply downhill for about 2km to join another busier road. Pass over the river here, turn immediately right and follow a dirt forest road north alongside the river to **El Corazón** (admission M$15), a basic facility with a weathered swimming pool and a snack-shack. Past the pool and behind an electric plant, you can climb a huge staircase (440 steps) up to the Metlac road bridge for vertiginous and verdant views. To get back to Fortín, cross the bridge and cut back along the path that forks to the right at its eastern side.

Plans are afoot to make the 6km of old railway line to the north of the Puente de Metlac into a **Vía Verde** for walkers and cyclists. This beautiful juxtaposition of nature and 19th-century engineering includes seven tunnels, two stations, a bridge house ruin and the original 1873 bridge.

Cecilia Rábago
CULTURAL TOUR

(📷 cell phone 271-1202030; www.turismorecreativo.com.mx; 1-4 people per day M$900-1000) A well-established, bilingual tour guide in the area and a firecracker of a lady, Cecilia's an expert on history and sites in the Fortín-Córdoba-Orizaba area. She can offer tours of the city and organic coffee plantations, and take you on all-day hiking excursions off the tourist track, and many other things in between.

🛏 Sleeping

📷 Hotel Posada Loma
HOTEL $$

(📷 713-06-58; www.posadaloma.com; Carretera Córdoba-Fortín Km 333; s/d M$650/750, bungalows per month M$13,500; P😊❄🛜🏊) If you're a garden lover, this is your oasis. Its grounds are a marvel of greenhouses, famous orchid collections, gardens with exotic and local flowers, terraces and a pool. The airy accommodations come with fireplaces for winter nights. The renowned breakfast in its restaurant, with exotic fresh-juice blends and spectacular views of Pico de Orizaba, is unbeatable, as is the flora tour by its friendly and knowledgeable owner, Lolis Álvarez. Loma is off Hwy 150, about 1km from central Fortín.

Hotel Suites Magnolias
HOTEL $$

(📷 713-22-98; Av 3 No 105; s/d M$300/500, with Jacuzzi M$700; P❄) Skittles box meets bad cubism at this quirky little hotel right off the main plaza. The bright colors, weird tile schemes and somewhat wacky designs will make for an interesting stay. The sanitary standard isn't rigid.

🍴 Eating & Drinking

A number of eateries surround the main plaza.

Kiosko Café
MEXICAN, CAFE $

(mains M$30-70; ⏰7am-11pm) Smack dab in the middle of the main plaza, this cafe enjoys unmatched real estate. Formerly the library, it now serves coffee, fresh juices and meals. The enchiladas have high acclaim.

El Parián
MEXICAN $$

(Av 1 No 110; mains M$35-100; ⏰8am-10pm) Just off the center, El Parián offers hearty plates with good service and a pleasant atmosphere. Try *sopa Azteca,* a soup of shredded, fried tortillas and avocado chunks.

ℹ Information

Tourist office (Palacio Municipal; ⏰8:30am-3pm Mon-Fri)

ℹ Getting There & Away

In Fortín, local bus services arrive and depart from Calle 1 Oriente, on the northeast corner of the plaza. Frequent 2nd-class buses go to Córdoba and Coscomatepec. The ADO **bus station** (cnr Av 2 & Calle 6) has 1st-class bus departures as listed in the table, p222.

BUSES FROM FORTÍN DE LAS FLORES

DESTINATION	FARE (M$)	DURATION	FREQUENCY (DAILY)
Córdoba	24	25min	8
Mexico City (TAPO)	278	4½hr	3
Orizaba	24	25min	10
Veracruz	108	2hr	6
Xalapa	166	3½hr	4

The 2nd-class bus to Orizaba goes through the gorgeous countryside but is more crowded and slower.

Coscomatepec

📞272 / POP 15,000 / ELEV 1588M

Warning: by the time you work out how to pronounce 'Coscomatepec,' the town will have already spun its seductive magic. Hidden in the mountain foothills 24km north of Fortín, Cosco (as it's usually known) is renowned for its intricate handmade saddles, leather goods, quality cigars and delicious bread. It's also decidedly picturesque.

◉ Sights & Activities

You can take tours through the famous bakery, cigar factory and saddle shops. These are arranged through the **tourist office** (cnr Amez & Argüelles s/n; ⊙9am-4pm Mon-Fri) in the Plaza Municipal. There's also info on a variety of activities, such as hiking, rappelling, horseback riding, zip-lines and possibly rock climbing in the area, which is rich with caves, rivers, old bridges and waterfalls.

If you are a climber (with your own equipment) or a hiker and want someone to show you cool places, call experienced bilingual local climbing and hiking guide **Edson Escamilla** (📱cell phone 273-7370481; x_on56@ hotmail.com; per person per day plus tip M$300). He's awfully nice and shows people around part-time.

A superb and famous **tack store** (www.ta labarteria-proarte.com.mx; Victoria 8) displays incredibly ornate, artisanal saddles and horse tack. More leather gear can be admired in **Proyecciones Artesanales** (Av Guadalupe Victoria 8). For Cosco's famous bread head to **La Fama** (Guerrero 6); it's been baking it since 1924.

🛏 Sleeping & Eating

A new 'historic' hotel, Plaza Real, with hand-painted sinks and huge rooms in old colonial digs a block south of the main plaza, was close to completion at the time of research.

TOP CHOICE **Posada del Emperador** HISTORIC HOTEL, HOSTEL $$
(📞737-15-20; www.laposadadelemperador.com; cnr Av Juárez & Domínguez; r M$870-1300; ❋🛜♨) Competing with a handful of others for the 'best-hotel-in-the-state' title, the Emperador wins all but the most unromantic over with its beautiful historical decor, antique furniture, four-poster beds, exquisite views and plant-filled interior. There's even a small chapel! Fated Habsburg emperor Maximilian apparently stopped here in the 1860s (hence the name) before his date with destiny and a firing squad. The hotel, which is also a nerve center for various outdoor activities in the area, has been adding extra parts of late. New features include an onsite hostel (M$150) with two spotless separate sex dorms plus shared kitchen and bathrooms. Even better, there's an extensive spa with massage, hot tubs, pool and temascal.

Hotel San Antonio HOTEL $
(📞737-03-20; Bravo 35; s/d M$180/250) Cosco's bargain basement option has a fine location right on the plaza, though the unexciting rooms are on the musty side. There's a popular local restaurant on the ground floor.

La Carreta MEXICAN $$
(cnr Av Juárez & Domínguez; meals M$75-200) Easily the best place to eat in town (for the view alone), the perfectly poised La Carreta sits inside the equally exquisite Posada del Emperador. Mexican dishes predominate.

❶ Getting There & Away

From Fortín, Coscomatepec is a one-hour bus ride (M$14); a taxi costs M$60 to M$70. Regular buses also connect to Córdoba. **The bus terminal** (Miguel Lerdo de Tejada btwn Reforma & Gutiérrez Zamora) is five minutes northeast of the main plaza.

Orizaba

📱272 / POP 120,000 / ELEV 1219M

Orizaba is a dark horse city, overshadowed in more ways than one by its eponymous volcano (the highest mountain in Mexico) and characterized by an unconventionally laid-out downtown which, while not drop-dead gorgeous, has enough booty to lure the moderately discerning. The most striking sight is Gustave Eiffel's unique art-nouveau Palacio de Hierro (Iron Palace). The most revealing is the excellent art museum, home to the second-largest Diego Rivera collection in Mexico. Equally improbable (for Mexico) is a rather salubrious urban river walk, amid bridges, greenery and (caged) animals.

Orizaba was founded by the Spanish to guard the Veracruz–Mexico City road. An industrial center in the late 19th century, its factories were early centers of the unrest that led to the unseating of dictator Porfirio Díaz. In 1898, a Scotsman running a local steel factory founded Mexico's first soccer team, called Orizaba Athletic Club. Today the city has a big brewery and is home to cement, textile and chemical industries.

👁 Sights

🔺TOP CHOICE **Palacio de Hierro**   LANDMARK, MUSEUM
(Parque Castillo) The so-called 'Iron Palace' is Orizaba's fanciful art nouveau landmark built entirely from iron and steel. Alexandre Gustave Eiffel, a master of metallurgy who gave his name to the Eiffel Tower and engineered the Statue of Liberty's framework, designed this pavilion, which was built in Paris. Orizaba's mayor, eager to acquire an impressive European-style Palacio Municipal, bought it in 1892. Piece by piece it was shipped, then reassembled in Orizaba.

No longer serving as a government building, the palace's interior has recently been converted into half a dozen small **museums** (admission free; ⊙9am-7pm). Most notable are the **Museo de la Cerveza** (beer), tracking Orizaba's famous beer industry; the **Museo de Fútbol** (soccer); the **Museo de Presidentes** with pics and info on *every* Mexican president, and the **Museo Interactivo** with a small planetarium and

some science exhibits (including a bed of nails you can lie on). Also onsite are the **Museo de Banderas** (flags) and **Museo de las Raíces de Orizaba** (archaeological artifacts).

Museo de Arte del Estado   MUSEUM
(State Art Museum; cnr Av Oriente 4 & Sur 25; admission M$10; ⊙10am-5pm Tue-Sun) Orizaba's wonderful Museo de Arte del Estado is housed in a gorgeously restored colonial building dating from 1776. The museum is divided into rooms that include Mexico's second-most important permanent Diego Rivera collection with 33 of his original works. There are also contemporary works by regional artists. Guides give complimentary tours (in Spanish). The museum is frustratingly situated a good 2km east of Parque Castillo.

Parque Castillo   PLAZA
Smaller than your average Mexican city plaza, Parque Castillo is bereft of the normally standard Palacio Municipal (town hall) which sits several blocks away on Av Colón Poniente. Instead, it is watched over by the eclectic Palacio de Hierro and a 17th-century parish church, the **Catedral de San Miguel Arcángel**. On the south side is the neoclassical and still-functioning **Teatro Ignacio de la Llave** (1875), font of opera, ballet and classical music concerts.

Parque Alameda   PARK
(Av Poniente 2 & Sur 10) About 1km west of the center, Parque Alameda is either a very large plaza or a very small park depending on your expectations. What it doesn't lack is activity. Aside from the obligatory statues of dead heroes, you'll find an outdoor gym, a bandstand, food carts, shoe-shiners and a kid's playground (including a huge jungle of bouncy castles and air-filled slides). Practically the whole city rolls in at weekends after Sunday Mass.

Cerro del Borrego   PARK
This forested hill park looms lusciously over Parque Alameda and offers brilliant views if you get to the top very early before the mist rolls in. However, avoid it in the evening. The entrance is easy to miss. Walk westbound on Avenida Poniente 3 until it bottoms out, and take a left. Look for a very narrow alleyway entrance on the right, which will lead you past the quirky Ermita de la Virgen de Guadalupe and finally to the trail's stairs.

VERACRUZ ORIZABA

♣ Activities

Río Orizaba
OUTDOORS, WALKING

Unusually for a Mexican city, Orizaba has an unbroken collection of pleasant paths bordering its clean eponymous river. There are 13 bridges along the way including a suspension bridge and the arched Puente La Borda dating from 1776. A good starting point is off Poniente 8 about 600m northwest of the Palacio de Hierro. From here you can head north to the Puente Tlachichilico or south to Puente La Borda. The weaving paths are punctuated by various fauna exhibits in an animal reserve. Caged beasts include turtles, crocodiles, llamas, jaguars and foxes.

Adventure Tours
ADVENTURE TOUR

A number of adventure-tour operators are based in Orizaba. They can arrange various outdoor activities in nearby hills, mountains and canyons, including climbs partway up Pico de Orizaba. Highlights of the area include the gorgeous Cañón de la Carbonera near Nogales and the Cascada de Popócatl near Tequila. But, really, exquisite natural places saturate this region. DIY adventures are waiting to be had. Recommended operators include **Alberto Gochicoa** (⌨cell phone 272-1037344) and **Erick Carrera** (⌨cell phone 272-1345571). There's also an outfit associated with one of the only real rock-climbing/outdoor-equipment stores in Veracruz, **Montañas y Cavernas** (⌨728-93-81; www.mcaventura.com; Sur 16 No 365). Servimont (p225) in Tlachichuca provides bona fide hiking and biking guides for areas around the Pico.

🛏 Sleeping

Higher-end options are on the Avenida Oriente 6 traffic strip. Low-end choices are near the center.

Gran Hotel de France
HISTORIC HOTEL $$

(⌨725-23-11; Av Oriente 6 No 186; s/d M$445/545; P❄✳) This historic late-19th-century building has a splendid high-ceilinged patio with azulejos tiles, hanging plants and a fountain. The rooms are pleasantly simple, if a little on the dark side.

Hotel Fiesta Cascada
HOTEL $$

(⌨724-15-96; www.hotelcascada.com.mx; Hwy Puebla-Córdoba Km 275; s/d M$660/790; P✳@≋) The Cascada sits above a gorgeous canyon, has a pool, gardens and forest trails, and is near a fantastic waterfall. The spacious rooms come at a terrific price. It's about 2km east of the center.

Hotel del Río
HOTEL $

(⌨728-92-26; Av Poniente 8 No 315; r from M$400; P✳🛜) A new place next to one of the more pleasant parts of the river, this hotel has simple modern rooms in an old building and a congenial, bilingual owner.

Hotel Aries
HOTEL $

(⌨725-35-20; Av Oriente 6 No 263; r from M$380; P✳🛜) Among the crap-shoot of hotels on busy Oriente 6, the Aries offers all the standard amenities and at a competitive price, too. Drawing you in is the rather alluring Churros y Porras Chocolate Café guarding the entrance.

Hotel Posada del Viajero
HOTEL $

(⌨726-33-20; Madero Norte 242; s/d M$100/200; P) This narrow central hotel doesn't look overly appealing from the outside, but it's clean, safe, cheap and family run within.

🍴 Eating & Drinking

In sedate Orizaba many restaurants close early. Head to the plaza for noteworthy Orizaban snacks including *garnachas* (open tortillas with chicken, onion and tomato salsa) and filled *pambazos* (soft white bread rolls dipped in pepper sauce).

Gran Café de Orizaba
CAFE, INTERNATIONAL $

(Palacio de Hierro, cnr Av Poniente 2 & Madero; snacks M$50-70) Sitting pretty inside the Palacio de Hierro with its polished-wood floors and pictures of old city sights, this cafe has a regal Parisian feel, which is all the more weird considering you're in – Orizaba. Waiters in white jackets serve high-quality tea or coffee.

La Pergola
MEXICAN $

(cnr Av Oriente 8 & Sur 7; mains M$40-90; ⊙7am-10pm) There are actually two Pergolas, both near the Avenida Oriente 6 mean drive-by. Which you choose is a toss-up. Both offer no-nonsense Mexican food and receive a communal 'thumbs-up' from local opinion.

Mariscos Boca del Río
SEAFOOD $$

(Av Poniente 7 s/n; seafood M$50-100; ⊙noon-8pm Tue-Sun) Known as the best seafood restaurant in town, its big portions should not leave you hungry.

El Interior
CAFE $

(Av 4 No 361; snacks M$30-50) A small literary cafe that is connected to a book and craft store, the Interior is handily sandwiched between Parque Castillo and the Museo Arte del Estado.

BUSES FROM ORIZABA

DESTINATION	FARE (M$)	DURATION	FREQUENCY (DAILY)
Córdoba	28	40min	every 30min
Fortín de las Flores	24	25min	10
Mexico City (TAPO)	268	4hr	16
Mexico City (Terminal Norte)	284	4hr	8
Oaxaca	324	5hr	3
Puebla	166	2hr	17
Veracruz	132	2½hr	25
Xalapa	176	4hr	10

ⓘ Information

Banks with ATMs are on Avenida Oriente 2, a block south of the plaza.

Hospital Orizaba (☎725-50-19; www.corporativodehospitales.com.mx; Sur 5 No 398)

Net-plus (2nd fl, Av Colón Oriente s/n; per hr M$10) Internet access.

Tourist office (☎728-91-36; www.orizaba.gob.mx/turismo.htm; Palacio de Hierro; ☺8am-3pm & 4-8pm Mon-Fri, noon-8pm Sat, noon-4pm Sun) Has enthusiastic staff and plenty of brochures. City maps cost M$10.

ⓘ Getting There & Around

Bus

Local buses from Fortín and Córdoba stop four blocks north and six blocks east of the town center, around Avenida Oriente 9 and Norte 14. The AU 2nd-class bus station is at Zaragoza Poniente 425, northwest of the center.

The modern 1st-class **bus station** (cnr Av Oriente 6 & Sur 13) handles all ADO, ADO GL and deluxe UNO services. Daily 1st-class buses are as flisted in the table.

Car & Motorcycle

Toll Hwy 150D, which bypasses central Orizaba, goes east to Córdoba and west, via a spectacular ascent, to Puebla (160km). Toll-free Hwy 150 runs east to Córdoba and Veracruz (150km) and southwest to Tehuacán, 65km away over the hair-raising Cumbres de Acultzingo.

Pico de Orizaba

Mexico's tallest mountain (5611m), called 'Citlaltépetl' (Star Mountain) in the Náhuatl language, is 25km northwest of Orizaba. From the summit of this dormant volcano, one can see the mountains Popocatépetl, Iztaccíhuatl and La Malinche to the west and the Gulf of Mexico to the east. The only higher peaks in North America are Mt McKinley in Alaska and Mt Logan in Canada.

Unless you're an experienced climber with mountaineering equipment, you'll need a guide and a good level of fitness. There are a number of recommendable guide companies from the US, but the only local one is **Servimont** (☎245-451-50-82; www.servimont.com.mx; Ortega 1A, Tlachichuca; packages from M$5040), a climber-owned outfit passed down through the Reyes family. As the longest-running operation in the area, it also acts as a Red Cross rescue facility. It's based in the small town of Tlachichuca (2600m), which is a common starting point for expeditions. Book your expedition with Servimont two to four months in advance and allow four to seven days to acclimatize, summit and return.

Mexico's Volcanoes by RJ Secor offers some good info, and topographical maps can be mail-ordered way ahead of time or bought in person from **Inegi** (www.inegi.gob.mx) offices in Veracruz or Xalapa. The best climbing period is October to March, with the most popular time being December and January.

Hostel accommodations at Servimont's base camp (which is a former soap factory adorned with interesting mountaineering antiques) are included in your package. If you want a private room, **Hotel Coyote** (☎245-451-54-25; 5 de Mayo s/n; s/d M$150/250; P) is right on the plaza, as is **La Casa Blanca** (mains M$30-80), a restaurant with delightful heating.

From Orizaba, catch a bus from the 1st-class terminal to Ciudad Serdán (M$43, two hours), then another to Tlachichuca (M$14, one hour).

HEADING NORTH

If you're heading north from Tuxpan into the state of Tamaulipas and ultimately onto the Mexico–US border at Matamoros-Brownsville, but want to break the 11-hour journey, catch an ADO bus from Tuxpan to Tampico (M$222, 3½ hours, hourly). Here you can bed down for the night at the **Hotel Marsella** (☑833-229-38-14; www.hotelmarsella.com.mx; Altamira 220; r from M$640; P🅿❄@🛜) and connect the next morning with a direct ADO bus to Matamoros (M$452, 7½ hours, nine daily). Travelers on the Tampico–Matamoros highway should be on their guard; the area is a well-known black spot in Mexico's ongoing drug cartel 'war' and car-jackings have occurred.

NORTHERN VERACRUZ

The northern half of Veracruz state, between the coast and southern fringes of the Sierra Madre Oriental, mainly consists of lush rolling pastureland. Laguna de Tamiahua is the region's largest wetland, while the Gulf has some fine isolated (sometimes polluted) beaches. The major archaeological attraction is El Tajín.

At the regular army checkpoints along this coast the soldiers are usually very respectful toward tourists.

Tuxpan

☑783 / POP 85,000

Tuxpan (sometimes spelled Túxpam), 300km north of Veracruz and 190km south of Tampico, is a steamy fishing town and minor oil port. If you have some time here, cross the broad Río Tuxpan to visit a little museum devoted to Cuban-Mexican friendship or join vacationing Mexicans on Playa Norte, the beach 12km to the east.

👁 Sights & Activities

FREE **Museo de la Amistad México-Cuba**   MUSEUM
(Mexican-Cuban Friendship Museum; Obregón s/n; ⏱9am-7pm) On November 25, 1956 a private yacht named *Granma* loaded with 82 poorly equipped soldiers led by errant lawyer turned revolutionary Fidel Castro set sail from the Río Tuxpan to Cuba to start an uprising. The sailing was made possible thanks to an encounter in Mexico City between Castro and Antonio del Conde Pontones (aka 'El Cuate'). On meeting Castro for the first time, Pontones, a legal arms dealer, was immediately taken by the Cuban's strong personality and agreed to help him obtain guns and a boat. To smooth the process he bought a house on the south side of the Río Tuxpan where he moored the boat and allowed Fidel to meet in secret. Today the house is the Museo de la Amistad México-Cuba which has a room filled with displays on José Martí and pictures of Che Guevara and Castro as well as other memorabilia. To get to the museum, take a boat (M$4) across the river from the quay near the ADO bus station, walk several blocks south to Obregón, then turn right – the museum is at the western end of Obregón on the river. Cuban-themed cultural events happen here on Friday nights.

Playa Norte   BEACH
Tuxpan's beach, Playa Norte, 12km east of town, is a wide strip stretching 20km north from the Río Tuxpan's mouth. *Palapa* restaurants make it a chilled-out place to eat cheap seafood and take a break from the city. Flag down the local buses (M$12, 25 minutes) marked 'Playa'; they leave regularly from the south side of Blvd Reyes Heroles by the river quay and drop you at the south end of the beach.

Paseos Turísticos Negretti   BOAT TRIPS, DIVING
(www.turismonegretti.mx) A local tour operator that organizes diving (M$1800 per group), fishing (M$400 per boat per hour), boat trips to nearby mangroves (M$550 for two hours), kayaking (M$100 per person) and water-skiing (M$250 for 30 minutes). It has an office on the south side of the river where the boat/ferry docks.

Aqua Sports   DIVING, FISHING
(☑837-02-59; Carretera Tuxpan-La Barra Km 8.5; 2 dives M$1200) Aqua runs diving and fishing trips out to nearby reefs or the Isla de Lobos. Visibility for diving is best between May and August, and from January to March you can fish for giant tarpon. Its office is around 8km from the center going toward the beach.

🛏 Sleeping

Hotels in Tuxpan fill up quickly during holiday periods, but discounts may be available at other times. Not much of a hot spot on the tourist track, the town lacks top-end lodgings.

Hotel Florida   HOTEL **$$**
(📞834-02-22; www.hotel-florida.com.mx; Av Juárez 23; s/d incl breakfast M$600/700; 🅿🏊❄🛜) The centrally located Florida outshines its main competitors: Hotel Reforma, May Palace and Best Western Riviera, which are all downtown, comparable and in its price range. It has friendly staff, continental breakfast included, spacious rooms with big windows and communal decks that look over bustling (read noisy) Avenida Juárez. Check out your room before, though: the inner rooms have no windows looking outside.

🍴 Eating

The main plaza is flanked by restaurants, and the market has cheap eats. For the best seafood, locals will direct you downriver to a strip of *palapas* in the fishing community of La Mata, 6km east of the center at the mouth of the Laguna de Tampamachoco. There are more *palapas* at Playa Norte.

⎡TOP⎤
⎣CHOICE⎦ **Restaurante Atracadero**   SEAFOOD **$$$**
(Blvd Reyes Heroles 35; mains M$100-180) This barge-turned-restaurant docked by the riverbank, just west of the center, is a fabulous place to splash out, with its open-air, upscale ambience. Drink red wine while enjoying the house specialty: paella (M$300), which can feed three to four people and is made with all sorts of meat, *mariscos* and vegetables.

VERACRUZ TUXPAN

WORTH A TRIP

LAS POZAS

Take a wealthy English eccentric, an idyllic tract of Mexican jungle and an extremely hyperactive imagination, and you'd still struggle to come up with the audacious, bizarre and – frankly – madcap experiment that is **Las Pozas** (The Pools; www.xilitla.org; admission M$50; ⊗9am-6pm).

Situated on the sweeping slopes of the Sierra Madre Oriental near the mountain town of Xilitla (he-*leet*-la), Las Pozas is a monumental sculpture garden built in thick jungle that links a series of concrete temples, pagodas, bridges, pavilions and spiral stairways with a necklace of natural waterfalls. The surreal creation stands as a memorial to the imagination and excessive wealth of Edward James (1907–84), a drop-out English aristocrat and poet who in the late 1930s became a patron of Salvador Dalí and subsequently went on to amass the largest private collection of surrealist art in the world.

In 1945 James' adventures took him to Xilitla where he met Plutarco Gastelum, who helped build Las Pozas. It began with 40 local workers crafting giant, colored, concrete flowers beside an idyllic jungle stream. Then, for 17 years, James and Gastelum created ever larger and stranger structures, many of which were never finished, at an estimated cost of US$5 million.

James died in 1984, leaving no provision to maintain his creation, which, since 2008, has been in the hands of a nonprofit Mexican-run foundation. The extravagant labyrinth of surreal sculptures and edifices with stairways leading nowhere (to heaven?) covers 36 hectares and is worth a significant diversion for anyone with the vaguest creative inclinations. If you're in fairly good shape, you could spend the whole day contemplating the lovely swimming holes and mazelike trails.

The site has a **cafe** (⊗10am-6pm) and you can stay in **Posada El Castillo** (📞365-00-38; www.junglegossip.com; Ocampo 105; r M$800-1500; ❄🏊), the former Gastelum home (and James' lodgings) now transformed into a verdant, Pozas-esque guesthouse run by the family in the town of Xilitla.

To get to Las Pozas you'll need to connect through Tuxpan to Tampico. From here regular connections travel to Xilitla. There are also buses from Xilitla to San Luis Potosí (M$354).

A taxi from Xilitla to the Las Pozas site is M$65. Guided tours are available from M$200 (Spanish) and M$250 (English).

BUSES FROM TUXPAN

DESTINATION	FARE (M$)	DURATION	FREQUENCY (DAILY)
Matamoros	650	11hr	2
Mexico City (Terminal Norte)	270	6hr	hourly
Papantla	60	2hr	hourly
Poza Rica	34	1hr	hourly
Tampico	200	4hr	hourly
Veracruz	262	6hr	hourly
Villahermosa	592	14hr	6
Xalapa	276	6hr	7

Barra de Mariscos　　　　SEAFOOD $$
(Av Juárez 44; seafood M$40-150; ⊗8am-11pm)
An enjoyable, atmospheric place near the
Parque Reforma, where freshness is valued;
try the *pulpo con salsa de ajo* (octopus in
garlic sauce), *camarones a la plancha*
(grilled shrimp) or *empanadas de maris-
cos,* the specialty.

Los Quijotes　　　　　　　　CAFE $
(Av Juárez 23; snacks/cakes M$30-50; ⊗6am-mid-
night) Coffee and cheesecake heaven in the
entrails of the Hotel Florida.

⊙ Information

Tuxpan's simple **tourist booth** (www.foro
tuxpan.com; Palacio Municipal; ⊗9am-7pm
Mon-Fri, 10am-2pm Sat) has a smattering of
maps and tourist brochures. ATMs are on Ave-
nida Juárez and you'll find internet cafes around
the center.

⊙ Getting There & Around

Most 1st-class buses leaving Tuxpan are *de paso*
(passing through). Booking a seat in advance
might be a good idea. There are several bus ter-
minals, but the 1st-class ADO **bus station** (cnr
Rodríguez & Av Juárez) is the most convenient
from the center. First-class departures from the
ADO station are as listed in the table.

Covered launches (M$3) ferry passengers
across the river and depart from a number of
locations along the river, between Guerrero and
Parque Reforma.

Poza Rica

TRANSPORTATION HUB

The modern industrial oil city of Poza Rica
is a big transportation hub, handy if you're
traveling north to Tuxpan, or south to Pa-
pantla and El Tajín.

If you find yourself stranded overnight,
the **Best Western Hotel Poza Rica** (⌂782-
826-04-00; www.bestwestern.com; cnr Calles 2
Norte & 10 Oriente; s/d M$900/1150; P⊕❀🌐)
is a good choice with helpful staff, modern
amenities and a cafe-restaurant.

The main Poza Rica bus station, on Pue-
bla east off Blvd Lázaro Cárdenas, has 2nd-
class and some 1st-class buses. The 2nd-class
bus line Transportes Papantla will take you
to coastal towns. Most 1st-class buses leave
from the adjoining ADO building, including
the departures listed in the table.

For El Tajín take any of the frequent 2nd-
class buses to Coyutla, El Chote, Agua Dulce
or San Andrés (M$18) from the main bus
station.

Papantla

⌂784 / POP 54,000 / ELEV 196M

Getting off the bus in Papantla, it's easy to
feel as if you've decamped to the Andean alti-
plano. Spread across a succession of wooded
hills, this is a solidly indigenous city whose
geography belongs in La Paz, but whose his-
tory, look and feel is distinctly pre-Hispanic
or, more precisely, Totonac. Predating the
Spanish conquest, the city was founded
around AD 1230. Traditionally a launching
pad for people visiting the nearby ruins of
El Tajín, Papantla has carved its own niche
in recent years, stressing its indigenous her-
itage and promoting its central position in
the world's best vanilla-growing region (al-
though these days the bulk of production
has migrated to Madagascar). Art, and in
particular murals, is another of the city's
fortes. Don't be surprised to see Totonacs
wearing traditional clothing here – the men
in loose white shirts and trousers, women

BUSES FROM POZA RICA

DESTINATION	FARE (M$)	DURATION	FREQUENCY (DAILY)
Mexico City (Terminal Norte)	225	5½hr	hourly
Pachuca	150	5hr	2
Papantla	28	40min	frequent
Tampico	278	4½hr	frequent
Tuxpan	34	1hr	frequent
Veracruz	200	5hr	hourly

in embroidered blouses and *quechquémitls* (traditional capes).

Sights

Zócalo
PLAZA

Officially called Parque Téllez, Papantla's *zócalo* is terraced into the hillside below the Iglesia de la Asunción. Wedged beneath the cathedral is a symbolic 50m-long relief **mural** facing the square and depicting Totonac and Veracruz history designed by Papantla artist Teodoro Cano in 1979. A serpent stretches along the mural, bizarrely linking a pre-Hispanic stone carver, El Tajín's Pirámide de los Nichos, and an oil rig.

Iglesia de Nuestra Señora de la Asunción
CHURCH

Overlooking the *zócalo* from its high platform, this church was begun in 1570 by the Franciscans and added to in stages over the subsequent centuries. The bell tower wasn't completed until 1875. The church is notable for its large cedar doors and quartet of indoor canvases by a Jalisco artist. Outside the doors stands a 30m-high *voladores* (fliers) pole (see boxed text, p230). Ritualistic performances normally take place at noon from Thursday to Sunday.

Museo de la Ciudad Teodoro Cano
MUSEUM

(Curti s/n; admission M$40; ⊙10am-7pm Tue-Sun) Teodoro Cano (b 1932), Papantla's legendary, still living artist was once a student of Mexican art giant Diego Rivera. This small museum displays a handful of his fine paintings – an alluring combination of both dark and ebullient scenes that are drawn almost exclusively from Totonac culture. The Totonac theme extends to the museum's other artifacts, including photos and traditional clothing displays. It's small, but immensely

satisfying. A modern onsite auditorium hosts regular cultural events.

Volador Monument
MONUMENT

(Callejón Centenario s/n) At the top of the hill towers Papantla's *volador* monument, a 1988 statue portraying a musician playing his pipe, preparing for the four fliers to launch. To reach the monument, take Calle Centenario heading uphill from the southwest corner of the cathedral yard before turning left into steep Callejón Centenario.

Casa de la Cultura
ARTS CENTER

(Pino Suárez s/n; ⊙10am-2pm Mon-Sat) The Casa de la Cultura hosts art classes and a display of local artwork on the top floor.

Tours

Gaudencio Simbrón
WALKING

(⊙842-01-21; per day M$300-400) Guide Gaudencio Simbrón is more commonly known as *el de la ropa típica* (the guy who wears traditional clothes) because he sports Totonac costume. He works through Hotel Tajín and can guide you through El Tajín, Papantla and its environs.

Festivals & Events

Feria de Corpus Christi
CULTURAL

The fantastic Feria de Corpus Christi, in late May and early June, is the big annual event. As well as the bullfights, parades and *charreadas* (Mexican rodeos) that are usual in Mexico, Papantla celebrates its Totonac cultural heritage with spectacular indigenous dances. The main procession is on the first Sunday when *voladores* fly two or three times a day.

Festival de Vainilla
FOOD

Papantla's other major celebration is the Vanilla Festival on June 18, featuring indigenous dancers, gastronomic delights sold in street stalls and all manner of vanilla products.

🛏 Sleeping

Papantla currently has a fairly limited selection of hotels, though a new place (Las Pirámides) right in the town center with an entry off Mercado Juárez was in the works at the time of writing.

TOP
CHOICE **Hotel Tajín** HOTEL $$

(☑842-01-21; www.hoteltajin.com.mx; cnr Núñez & Domínguez 104; s/d M$400/530; P🚫🤖📶🏊) So what if the interior is a little dated; the Tajín is an intrinsic part of the Papantla experience with a prime edge-of-*zócalo* location and a recently added Italianate pool and onsite cafe (a Parroquia, no less). Tiny private bathrooms aim their shower heads over the wash basin, meaning you can shower and brush your teeth at the same time. Ingenious!

Hotel Familiar La Pasadita HOTEL $

(☑842-56-73; Obispo de las Casas 102; s/d M$300/400; P🚫) Even though the newish Pasadita has updated furnishings, fresh tiling and spacious accommodations near the center, it remains in the shadow of the old-guard strongholds near here. Opt for the window rooms.

Hotel Totonacapán HOTEL $$

(☑842-12-20; cnr 20 de Noviembre & Olivo; s/d M$410/500; 🚫) About 400m downhill from the *zócalo*, the highlight of this hotel is its large Totonac-style mural in the lobby. The rooms, some of which have balconies, are a good decade past their renovation due date and the restaurant downstairs would struggle to pull you away from the *zócalo* stalwarts.

🍴 Eating

Papantla's trio of gregarious, homespun restaurants all occupy view perches overlooking the *zócalo*. **Mercado Juárez**, at the southwest corner of the plaza opposite the cathedral, has stalls that sell cheap, fresh regional food.

TOP
CHOICE **Plaza Pardo** MEXICAN $

(1st fl, Enríquez 105; mains M$35-140) There are far worse things in life than eating enchiladas with a cold beer at a balcony table overlooking the *zócalo* at Plaza Pardo. Indeed, with its cordial staff and authentic Mexican atmosphere, the Pardo could well be Papantla's best restaurant. Try the menu highlight *pollo en pipián verde* (chicken in green pumpkin seed sauce) and make your own judgment.

Restaurante La Hacienda MEXICAN $

(Calle Centenario; mains M$40-130) With a similar menu and location to the Plaza Pardo, plus equally polite service, it's a toss-up where you'll end up. If *tampiqueña* (grilled steak with enchiladas, beans and cheese) is your thing, then the Hacienda wins.

PAPANTLA'S VOLADORES: BUNGEE-JUMPING PIONEERS

The idea of launching yourself head-first from a great height with only a rope tied around your ankles for support is popularly thought to have been conceived by bungee-jumping New Zealanders in the 1980s. But, in truth, Papantla's Totonac *voladores* (fliers) have been flinging themselves off 30m-high wooden poles (with zero safety equipment) for centuries. Indeed, so old is this rather bizarre yet mystic tradition that no one is quite sure how or when it started.

The rite begins with five men in elaborate ceremonial clothing climbing to the top of the pole. Four of them sit on the edges of a small frame at the top and rotate the frame to twist the ropes around the pole. The fifth man dances on the platform above them while playing a *chirimía*, a small drum with a flute attached. When he stops playing, the others fall backward. Arms outstretched, they revolve gracefully around the pole and descend to the ground, upside down, as their ropes unwind.

One interpretation of the ceremony is that it's a fertility rite and the fliers make invocations to the four corners of the universe. It's also noted that each flier circles the pole 13 times, giving a total of 52 revolutions. The number 52 is not only the number of weeks in the modern year but also was an important number in pre-Hispanic Mexico, which had two calendars, one corresponding to the 365-day solar year, the other to a ritual year of 260 days. The calendars coincided every 52 solar years.

Voladores ceremonies are best observed at El Tajín, outside Papantla's cathedral, and occasionally at Zempoala.

BUSES FROM PAPANTLA

DESTINATION	FARE (M$)	DURATION	FREQUENCY (DAILY)
Mexico City (Terminal Norte)	236	5hr	2:05pm
Poza Rica	28	40min	frequent
Tampico	290	5½hr	2
Tuxpan	60	2hr	hourly
Veracruz	150	4hr	2
Xalapa	218	4hr	4

Restaurante Totonaca　　INTERNATIONAL **$$**
(Hotel Tajín, Núñez 104; mains M$80-150; ☺8am-10pm) This air-conditioned hotel bar-restaurant aims to be a step fancier than the Pardo and has an extensive international menu. There's also a short wine list (M$80 to M$100), and it serves cocktails made with locally produced vanilla extract.

Café Catedral　　BAKERY, CAFE **$**
(cnr Domínguez & Curato; ☺8am-10pm) The town's best coffeehouse (ask any local) doubles as a bakery. Grab a cake, muffin or *pan dulce* (sweet bread) from one of the display cases with the provided tongs, sit at a cheap cafe table, and wait for the chief *señora* to come round with an old-fashioned tin jug to fill up your cup. Everyone seems to know everyone else here and local gossip bounces off the walls.

Caffe Gourmet Voladorini　　CAFE, DESSERTS **$**
(Calle Centenario) A kind of plusher antidote to the traditional Café Catedral, the Voladorini is new, cool and minimalist, although the coffee and cakes are no less tempting. It's perched like a theater box above the *zócalo* action.

 Shopping

Here in Mexico's leading vanilla-growing center, you'll find quality vanilla extract, vanilla pods and *figuras* (pods woven into the shapes of flowers, insects or crucifixes). There's a good artisan store on the southwest corner of the *zócalo*. You'll also encounter traditional Totonac clothing and handmade baskets.

 Information

The helpful **tourist office** (☺9am-2pm & 4-6pm) is inside the Palacio Municipal on the *zócalo*. It's a bit hidden. Enter by the main door and ask the security guard for directions. You'll find two banks with ATMs on Enríquez just east of the *zócalo*, and **Internet** (20 de Noviembre 1; per hr M$8; ☺9am-10pm) has – big surprise – internet services. The post office is four blocks northwest of the plaza.

 Getting There & Away

A few long-distance buses leave from Papantla's quaint ADO **bus station** (cnr Juárez & Venustiano Carranza), a short, steep walk from the center. Taxis from the ADO to the center are M$15 to M$20. You can make bus reservations online or at the ticket counter just east of the plaza. At the 2nd-class **bus station** (cnr 20 de Noviembre & Olivo), just off the plaza by the Pemex station, Transportes Papantla (TP) serves the coastal towns to the south and has slightly less expensive buses to Poza Rica and Tuxpan. The table lists 1st-class ADO services.

El Tajín

For an ancient city 'rediscovered' accidently by an officious Spaniard looking for illegal tobacco plantations in 1785, El Tajín paints a bold contemporary picture. Situated on a plain surrounded by low verdant hills 6km west of Papantla, the extensive ruins are the most impressive reminder of Classic Veracruz civilization and the state's most visited tourist site.

Probably founded in AD 100, El Tajín (the name is Totonac for 'thunder,' 'lightning' or 'hurricane') reached its zenith as a city and ceremonial center between AD 600 and 900. Around 1230 the site was abandoned, possibly after a fire and attacks by Chichimecs. Quickly engulfed by the jungle, it lay unknown to the Spaniards until 1785.

Among El Tajín's special features are rows of square niches on the sides of buildings, numerous ball courts and sculptures depicting human sacrifice connected with the ball game. Archaeologist José García

Payón believed that El Tajín's niches and stone mosaics symbolized day and night, light and dark, and life and death in a universe composed of dualities, though many are skeptical of this interpretation.

You can download a map to the El Tajín ruins for free at www.lonelyplanet.com /additional-mexico-maps.

◉ Sights

The **El Tajín site** (admission M$51; ⊗9am-5pm) covers an area of about 10 sq km. To see everything, you'll walk a few kilometers over a couple of hours. There's little shade and it can get blazingly hot, so an early start is recommended. Most buildings and carvings here are labeled in English and Spanish, and some have information panels in German and French as well.

Bordering the parking lot are stalls selling food and handicrafts. The visitor center has a restaurant, left-luggage room, information desk, museum and souvenir shops. Those seeking more information should look for the book *Tajín: Mystery and Beauty*, by Leonardo Zaleta, sometimes available in several languages in the souvenir shops. Multilingual guide service is available for M$200 per hour for one to six people. Self-guide maps are not always available.

Plaza Menor   PLAZA
Beyond the Plaza del Arroyo in the south of the site flanked by pyramids on four sides, is the Plaza Menor (Lesser Plaza), part of El Tajín's main ceremonial center and possible marketplace, with a low platform in the middle. All of the structures around this plaza were probably topped by small temples, some decorated with red or blue paint, traces of which remain.

Juego de Pelota Sur   BALL COURT
Some 17 ball courts have been found at El Tajín. The Juego de Pelota Sur (Southern Ball Court) dates from about 1150 and is the most famous of the courts, owing to the six relief carvings on its walls depicting various aspects of the ball-game ritual.

The panel on the northeast corner is the easiest to make out: in the center, three ballplayers perform a ritual post-game sacrifice with one player ready to plunge a knife into the chest of another, whose arms are held by the third player. Death gods and a presiding figure look on. The other panels depict various scenes of ceremonial drinking of *pulque*

(a milky, low-alcohol brew made from the *maguey* plant).

Pirámide de los Nichos   PYRAMID
El Tajín's most emblematic structure, the beautifully proportioned Pyramid of the Niches, is just off the Plaza Menor. The six lower levels, each surrounded by rows of small square niches, climb to 18m. Archaeologists believe that there were originally 365 niches, suggesting that the building may have been used as a kind of calendar.

El Tajín Chico   STRUCTURES
The path north toward Plaza El Tajín Chico passes the **Juego de Pelota Norte** (Northern Ball Court), which is smaller and older than the southern court and bears fainter carvings on its sides.

Many of the buildings at El Tajín Chico have geometric stone mosaic patterns known as 'Greco' (Greek). **Edificio I**, probably once a palace, has some terrific carvings. **Estructura C**, on the east side, with three levels and a staircase facing the plaza, was initially painted blue. **Estructura A**, on the plaza's north side, has an arch construction known as a corbeled arch, with two sides jutting closer to each other until they are joined at the top by a single slab, which is typical of Maya architecture. Its presence here is yet another oddity in the jigsaw puzzle of pre-Hispanic cultures.

Northwest of Plaza El Tajín Chico is the unreconstructed **Plaza de las Columnas** (Plaza of the Columns), one of the site's most important structures. It originally housed a large open patio and adjoining buildings stretching over the hillside. Some wonderful reassembled carved columns are displayed in the museum.

TOP CHOICE **Voladores**
Performances   INDIGENOUS CULTURE
A 30m high *voladores* pole stands outside the entrance to the ruins. Totonacs carry out the *voladores* rite (which was traditionally carried out only once a year) three times per day beside the visitor center. Before they start, a performer in Totonac regalia requests donations (M$20) from the audience. See also boxed text, p230.

❶ Getting There & Away

Frequent buses come from Poza Rica. From Papantla, buses (M$14) marked 'Pirámides Tajín' leave every 20 minutes or so from Calle 16 de Septiembre directly behind Hotel Tajín. The site is 300m from the highway – buses drop you off near the market, before the entrance to Tajín. Taxis to/from from Papantla cost M$50. There are usually one or two waiting outside the ruins.

South of Papantla

Hwy 180 runs near the coast for most of the 230km between Papantla and Veracruz. Highlights include a turtle conservation project, the sparkling Costa Esmeralda and Quiahuiztlán, a stunning, out-of-the-way Totonac site. The area is bereft of tourists during low season.

TECOLUTLA

*766 / POP 4600

If you've ever wondered how middle-ranking Mexican families enjoy the beach, come to Tecolutla, a lazy seaside town with a pleasant strip of sand where weather-beaten vendors hawk seafood cocktails and turtles come to nest. Cancún this most definitely isn't. Instead, the place is as dead as a doornail midweek when it's not a holiday. High summer and Semana Santa are a different story. There are banks and ATMs on the plaza.

◉ Activities

🔎 Grupo Ecologista
Vida Milenaria   VOLUNTEERING
(*846-04-67; www.vidamilenaria.org.mx; donation required; ⊙7:30-9am) This small turtle conservation center (a short walk from the center where Niños Héroes hits the ocean) is run by Fernando Manzano Cervantes, also known locally as 'Papá Tortuga.' In addition to educating the public, he has been effectively protecting and releasing green and Kemp's ridley turtles here for over 35 years. Visitors are welcome to look at the hatchlings. If you stop by, think about buying a trinket souvenir because this is a privately funded show. Volunteers are especially needed here in April and May, when patrolling the beaches (35km worth) and collecting the turtle eggs is imperative. Most of the patrolling is done at night between 10pm and 6am. The highest volume of turtle releasing is in June. Camping and the use of kitchen and bathroom facilities are free to volunteers.

In late October, you can join hundreds of locals in celebrating the releasing of the baby turtles in the **Festival de Las Tortugas**.

Boat Trips   BOAT TRIPS
(per group M$300-400) Walk toward the Río Tecolutla on Emilio Carranza and you'll hit

the *embarcadero* (pier) where boats will take you fishing or through dense mangrove forests rich with wildlife, including pelicans.

🛏 Sleeping

Hotels abound in this tourist-reliant town. Forget high-end options (there aren't any), but there are cheap hotels near the plaza – the nicer ones tend to be near the ocean.

Real del Mar   HOTEL $$
(*846-03-80; www.hotelrealdelmar.com; cnr Aldama & Galeana; r from M$880; P❀≋) As posh as Tecolutla gets, this aspiring 'resort' has light, colorful rooms, some with ocean-view balconies. Rooms surround an indoor pool and a three-story, sea-themed mural. It's comfortable, if a little bland.

Agua Inn Hotel   HOTEL $$
(*846-03-58; www.tecolutla.com.mx/aguainn; cnr Aldama & Av Obregón; s/d M$400/590; P❀🛜≋) The Agua's a vaguely modern place by Tecolutla standards with clean-as-a-whistle rooms, a rather snazzy little rooftop pool, and a cool cafe and restaurant.

🍴 Eating

Unless you hate fresh, inexpensive seafood, you'll be happy as a clam in Tecolutla. On the beach, all the *palapa* places sell cold beer, while vendors hawk seafood cocktails. There are numerous eateries along the walk from the plaza to the beach on Avenida Obregón.

El Cotarro   SEAFOOD $
(Av Obregón s/n; mains M$25-80) It may not keep up with its neighbors' kitschy sea-themed decor, but El Cotarro's food is delicious, fresh and inexpensive. The *mojarra al ajo* is a fish drenched in date-dooming garlic.

Porteño Café   CAFE, SANDWICHES $
(cnr Aldama & Av Obregón) A slick, newish cafe downstairs at the Agua Inn that serves coffee and panini.

ℹ Getting There & Away

Tecolutla is 41km east of Papantla. There are regular 2nd-class Transportes Papantla buses between Tecolutla and Papantla (M$45) that arrive and depart from outside the church in Avenida Obregón, one block west of the main plaza. There is also a small but swanky 1st-class ADO **bus station** (cnr Abasolo & Ahumada) a few blocks from the main plaza. Many buses to and from Tecolutla have to transfer through Gutiérrez Zamora. ADO offers services to some major cities including Mexico City's Terminal Norte

(M$254), as well as frequent services to Poza Rica (M$50) and Papantla (M$32).

COSTA ESMERALDA & AROUND

The Emerald Coast stretches between roughly La Guadalupe and Nautla, and its waters, more accurately described as semiprecious, are various shades of azure, though not crystalline. It's a raging summer and holiday spot where waves crash on 20km of grayish-blond beaches. The rest of the year, especially midweek, it's tranquil and a good match for the beach lovers and crowd haters. You can throw down cash for upscale digs, or do it on the cheap. Advertised and unadvertised campgrounds proliferate.

At the mouth of the Río Filobobos (known as Río Bobos and famous for its rapids), head southwest of Nautla on Hwy 131 and you'll hit **Tlapacoyan**, where a handful of rafting companies are based and where the waterfall Cascada de Encanto provides a gorgeous swimming spot. **Aventura Extrema** (☑229-178-38-12; www.aventuraextrema.com.mx; rafting packages from M$750) has facilities near Tlapacoyan and offers one- to three-day packages including food, accommodations or camping, and various other adventure activities. A highlight of Bobos rafting are the two riverside archaeological sites, **Caujilote** and **Vega de la Peña**, which most companies stop to visit.

Five kilometers south of Nautla is **Hotel Istirinchá** (☑235-317-42-01; www.hotelistirincha.com; Hwy 180 Km 102; r from M$800; P✳🛜🏊), a hard-to-classify resort/eco-hotel with some genuine green credentials. Once a tract of deforested land used for cattle grazing, the 70-hectare site has been transformed since 1999 when it was bought by a private owner intent on returning it to its natural junglelike habitat. There's a lagoon for kayaking, an isolated driftwood-covered beach, trails through pines and palm trees, and a stash of caged animals such as toucans and crocodiles. The organized activities, including horseback riding and cycling, are a little tame, but it's a lovely place to wander. Rooms are bright and comfortable, if a little overpriced. There's also a restaurant and pool. Turtles nest on the beach from June to August. You'll see signs at the entrance on the highway and it's about a 20-minute walk to the hotel from where the bus leaves you.

To get to any coastal location on Costa Esmeralda, take a nondirect bus on Hwy 180 and tell the driver where you want to stop.

PUNTA VILLA RICA & AROUND

Between Nautla and Veracruz, the coast is remarkably wild and unexplored despite its weighty historical significance. The only blemish is Mexico's sole nuclear power station on **Laguna Verde**, about 80km north of Veracruz port on Hwy 180. It's been in operation since 1989.

◉ Sights & Activities

Villa Rica   VILLAGE

Standing in this tiny dusty fishing village 69km north of modern-day Veracruz, it's hard to believe that you're gazing at the site of the first European-founded settlement north of Panama in mainland America. Never properly consolidated, the 'Veracruz that once was,' founded as Villa Rica de la Vera Cruz in 1519, lasted only until 1524 when it was moved to present-day La Antigua. These days the historic settlement doesn't even merit a label on Google Maps, though there's a smattering of houses here along with a small hotel, a couple of rustic restaurants and the weed-covered foundations of some buildings constructed by Cortés and his men soon after their arrival. The beach is small and beautiful, and you can trace it around past some dunes and across an isthmus to the **Cerro de la Cantera**, a rocky outcrop famed for its plunging *quebraditas* (ravines).

Villa Rica is about 1km east of the main Hwy 180. Ask any bus driver on the Cardel–Nautla run to stop at the entrance road to the Quiahuiztlán ruins. From here it's an easy walk to the village.

TOP CHOICE **Quiahuiztlán**   ARCHAEOLOGICAL SITE

(admission M$31, free Sun; ⊘9am-5pm) The first question most of the sporadic visitors to these amazing Totonac ruins ask is: Why, given its historic importance and stunning setting, is there no one else here? Alas, there's no logical answer. Rather it's best just to relish the tranquility and keep mum. Perched on a plateau beneath a horn-shaped mountain (the Cerro de Metates) like a mini–Machu Picchu, Quiahuiztlán is a pre-Hispanic Totonac town and necropolis that counted 15,000 inhabitants at the time of Cortés' arrival in 1519. Its history before that is sketchy although there was certainly a settlement here by AD 800. Enjoying a commanding view of the Gulf coast, the now-deserted site has two pyramids, more than 70 tombs (each resembling a small temple) and some

THE FOUNDING OF VERACRUZ – MARKS I, II AND III

There is an intriguing murkiness about the first Spanish settlement on mainland America north of Panama.

Popular myth suggests Hernán Cortés was the first European to arrive in the Veracruz area, but, in truth, fellow Spaniard Juan de Grijalva beat him to it by about six months. Grijalva docked on the Isla de los Sacrificios in late 1518 where he found evidence of human sacrifice and spent 10 days trading with Mesoamerican natives.

Cortés' more famous flotilla arrived, via the Yucatán coast, on April 21, 1519 (Good Friday) and quickly set up a temporary camp on a beach opposite the island of San Juan de Ulúa on the site of present-day Veracruz. However, a real city wasn't established here for another 80 years. Instead Cortés and his men quickly abandoned their malaria-ridden camp and trekked 40km north to the Totonac settlement of Zempoala where they were courted by the corpulent chief, Xicomecoatl with whom they made a cynical alliance against the Aztecs. Xicomecoatl sent Cortés' entourage 30km further north to the city of Quiahuiztlán with 400 Zempoala-hired porters where they were met by a population of 15,000 curious citizens. With their ships already docked on the adjacent coast, Cortés, determined to cut legal ties with his overseer, Diego Velázquez, in Cuba, decided to found a town near Quiahuiztlán and declare himself the legal *adelantado* (governor). Christened Villa Rica de la Vera Cruz (Veracruz Mk I) it consisted of little more than a fort, a chapel and some barracks, but, small as it was, it was the first recorded European-founded settlement in North America. Around 1524, due to its limitations as a port, the town was moved south to La Antigua (Veracruz Mk II) and sited several kilometers inland on the banks of the Río Antigua where small ships could be docked. But, as the Spanish empire grew, Antigua's river location made it less practical for larger ships, meaning supplies had to be hauled overland to San Juan de Ulúa where they often fell prey to smugglers. As a result, around 1599, Veracruz was moved for a third time back to the site of the original encampment on the coast opposite San Juan de Ulúa.

carved monuments. Rock climbers revere the precipitous Cerro de Metates (with 5.6 to 5.8 graded routes) that rises behind. It's a pleasant 3km walk up a winding paved road to the part of the site that overlooks the ocean. From here you can experience the sacred Totonac ruins in solitude and amid nature, unlike other, touristed ruins. If you want to arrive by a Hwy 180 bus, have the driver drop you at the Quiahuiztlán turnoff. Fares are M$30 to Cardel and M$45 to Nautla.

EcoGuías La Mancha ECOTOUR
(296-100-11-63; www.ecoturismolamancha.com; La Mancha-Actopan; campsites own/borrowed tent M$60/100, cabañas M$150) All hail this progressive association of locals that has developed a homespun, grass-roots environment education center. The facilities, located 1km from the beach, offer interpretive walks, bird-watching excursions, apiary tours, horseback riding and kayak tours where you can see mangroves and wildlife. Accommodations are rustic (eight-person cabins or rent-a-tents), but it's a great off-the-beaten-path choice that supports the local community. From the La Mancha eastbound turnoff on Hwy 180, it's 1km down the road. Bring repellent.

🛏 Sleeping & Eating
Rustic accommodations are available at EcoGuías La Mancha.

Villas Arcon HOTEL $$
(296-109-66-06; www.villasarcon.com; Carretera Veracruz-Poza Rica Km, Villa Rica; s/d M$600/800; ❄❓📶) This pretty, low-rise hotel situated in the village that no one's ever heard of (but should've) might be a little overpriced, but it does allow you to live in some comfort while getting in touch with Mexico's gritty essence. Perks include digital TVs, a restaurant, two swimming pools and pickups from Veracruz airport (M$500).

Restaurante Totonacapan SEAFOOD $
(Villa Rica; mains M$60-100) The jovial proprietor often calls innocent bystanders over to this alfresco thatched-roof Villa Rica affair, the last structure on the right before you hit the beach. Food is ocean-fresh fish. Drinks are beer or 7-Up.

SOUTHEAST VERACRUZ

Southeast of Veracruz city you'll find flat, fecund coastal plains crossed by rivers, as well as the volcano-dappled rainforest commonly referred to as the Los Tuxtlas region. This area comprises Reserva de la Biosfera Los Tuxtlas and its three attendant towns: Santiago Tuxtla, San Andrés Tuxtla and Catemaco. As part of the former heartland of ancient Olmec culture, the area is laden with archaeological sites. The far southeast of the state contains oil metropolises such as Minatitlán and Coatzacoalcos.

Tlacotalpan

📖 288 / POP 7600

Possibly the finest Unesco World Heritage town that no one's ever heard of, Tlacotalpan is a near-perfect identikit of early-19th-century colonial architecture, completely unblemished by modern interferences, save for a light (by Mexican standards) smattering of traffic. The color palette is extraordinary here, the lucid sunsets over the adjacent Río Papaloapan adding subtle oranges and yellows to the rainbow of colonial houses that stand like diminutive precursors to San Francisco's 'painted ladies.' Once an important river port, Tlacotalpan has changed little since the 1820s. The town, Unesco-listed in 1998, was hit by devastating floods during Mexico's bicentennial celebrations in September 2010 which inundated 500 historic buildings and prompted the evacuation of 8500 people. The recovery, as of late 2011, has been remarkably speedy.

🔘 Sights & Activities

Tlacotalpan's two plazas, Hidalgo and Zaragoza, are directly adjacent to each other. Together they harbor two churches including the **Capilla o Santuario de la Candelaria** dating from 1779 and furnished with local coral stone.

Museo Salvador Ferrando MUSEUM
(Alegre 6; admission M$15; ⊘10:30am-6pm Tue-Sat, noon-5pm Sun) One of the town's handful of mini-museums, the Ferrando, named for a Tlacotalpan artist, displays assorted artifacts with a bias for 19th-century paintings.

Casa Museo Agustín Lara MUSEUM
(Beltrán 6; admission M$20; ⊘10am-5pm Mon-Sat) This museum features memorabilia of *tlacotalpeño* Agustín Lara (1900–70), a legendary musician, composer and Casanova.

Casa de la Cultura Agustín Lara ARTS CENTER
(Av Carranza 43; ⊘9am-5pm) This pink house displays art exhibits, plus holds folkloric dance rehearsals and *jarocho* music lessons. Much imitated, it was the first of its kind in Mexico when it opened in 1974.

Villin Montalio HANDICRAFTS
(5 de Mayo No 53; ⊘9am-6pm Mon-Sat) The city is well known for its locally made cedar furniture and such skills were in demand post the 2010 floods. Drop by this office/workshop to see it being made, and leaf through some brochures.

Mini-Zoológico Museo MUSEUM
(Av Carranza 25; donation M$10; ⊘10am-5pm Mon-Sat) The home of Don Pío Barrán, who keeps several crocodiles and a range of artifacts, including a locally excavated mastodon tooth and a sword that supposedly belonged to Porfirio Díaz.

Boat Rides BOAT TOUR
(split between passengers M$250) If you walk the *malecón* near the restaurants, you're bound to run into a *lanchero* offering to whisk you down the scenic river for an hour-long boat ride to see a nearby lagoon. It's not the Amazon, but it's a lovely way to spend a late afternoon. Or take a stroll by the riverside and down Cházaro, which starts from the Palacio Municipal and has wall-to-wall, whacky-colored, colonial-style houses and buildings with columns, tiles and high arches.

✦ Festivals & Events

Día de la Candelaria RELIGIOUS
In late January and early February, Tlacotalpan's huge Candelaria festival features bull-running in the streets and an image of the Virgin being floated down the river followed by a flotilla of small boats.

🛏 Sleeping

Prices triple or quadruple during the Candelaria holiday.

TOP CHOICE Hotel Posada Doña Lala HISTORIC HOTEL $$
(📞884-25-80; www.hoteldonalala.com; Av Carranza 11; r from M$650-850; 🅿✳@🛜❄) Hotel Posada Doña Lala banks on its famous reputation, but it has neat rooms and a

great location near the river and the town's main plaza. The **restaurant** (mains $135-350; ⊘7am-7pm) – recent recipient of a funky makeover – serves up some ravishing fresh and saltwater fish dishes.

Hotel Tlacotalpan HOTEL **$$**
(☑884-20-63; Beltrán 35; r from M$550; P❋🛜⊛) This bright blue-and-yellow building off the main road has fresh rooms that surround a beautifully tiled courtyard. The lobby has an airy, colonial feel with rocking chairs and high ceilings. Room prices are meant to be subtly haggled over.

Hotel Casa del Río HOTEL **$$**
(☑884-29-47; Cházaro 39; r M$750-850; P❋🛜) Creating super-modern rooms in a traditional historic structure can sometimes be a tough task, but 'del Río' gets it right with nine spacious offerings in a house backing onto the river.

✗ Eating & Drinking

The market by the ADO bus station has cheap fresh juices and regional favorites.

Restaurante Tlacotalpan SEAFOOD **$$**
(Malecón s/n; mains M$80-120; ⊘11am-8pm) For good eats try this place, one of the numerous terrific open-air eateries on the riverfront that whip up fresh, traditional seafood. They're more expensive than eateries in town, but the ambience is worth it.

El K-Fecito CAFE **$**
(Plaza Zaragoza; snacks $35-65; ⊘5pm-1am Mon-Thu, to 2:30am Fri-Sun) On the joining point of the two main plazas and serving great coffee, beer and snacks, El K-Fecito seems to have it all. Now, if it wasn't for those blasted mosquitoes! The staff sometimes provides coils but, if you're sitting alfresco, bring repellent.

☆ Entertainment

Plaza Zaragoza has traditional dancing in its bandstand most Saturday nights. The Casa de la Cultura Agustín Lara has been known to throw a mean *fandango* (Veracruzian music and dance party). More formal gatherings convene in the gorgeous French-style **Teatro Netzahualcoyotl** (Av Carranza).

❶ Information

There's an ATM on Avenida Carranza near the plaza.

Mi Sitio.com (Alacio Pérez s/n) Internet cafe one block north of Plaza Hidalgo.
Tourist office (Alegre & Lerdo de Tejada; ⊘9am-3pm Mon-Fri) Right off Plaza Hidalgo. The office has helpful maps.

❶ Getting There & Around

Hwy 175 runs from Tlacotalpan up the Papaloapan valley to Tuxtepec, then twists and turns over the mountains to Oaxaca (320km). ADO, whose riverside station is situated outside the Mercado Municipal three blocks east of the center, offers service to Mexico City, Puebla, Xalapa and Veracruz, while Transportes Los Tuxtlas (TLT) buses cover local routes. Frequent 2nd-class buses that stop along the riverside strip go to and from Veracruz.

Santiago Tuxtla
☑294 / POP 15,000 / ELEV 180M

More laid-back and a touch more charming than its built-up neighbor San Andrés, Santiago is centered on a lovely, verdant main plaza – one of the state's prettiest – and is surrounded by the rolling green foothills of the volcanic Sierra de los Tuxtlas. The plaza is strewn with ladies arm-in-arm, couples lip-to-lip and shoes getting vigorously shined. It's not on the tourist track per se, but the intriguing little museum, the close proximity (23km) to Tres Zapotes and the possibility of a tranquil stay at Mesón de Santiago merit a visit.

All buses arrive and depart near the junction of Morelos and the highway. To get to the center, continue down Morelos, then turn right into Ayuntamiento, which leads to the main plaza, a few blocks away.

◎ Sights

Olmec head MONUMENT
(Plaza Olmeca) Dominating the main plaza, this stone monolith is known as the 'Cobata head,' after the estate where it was found. Thought to be a very late Olmec production, it's the biggest known Olmec head, weighing in at 40 tons, and is unique in that its eyes are closed.

Museo Tuxteco MUSEUM
(admission M$37; ⊘9am-6pm Mon-Sat, 9am-5pm Sun) This central plaza museum exhibits artifacts such as Olmec stone carvings, including another colossal head, a monkey-faced *hacha* (axe) with obsidian eyes and a Tres Zapotes altar replica. Upstairs are local art exhibits and a Spanish colonial room. Large

BUSES FROM SANTIAGO TUXTLA

DESTINATION	FARE (M$)	DURATION	FREQUENCY (DAILY)
Acayucan	80	2½hr	1
Córdoba	198	3½hr	1
Mexico City	444	8hr	2
Minatitlán	120	3½hr	1
Puebla	336	5½hr	2
San Andrés Tuxtla	24	20min	frequent
Veracruz	124	2½hr	9
Xalapa	208	4½hr	3

paintings of the Cortés conquest adorn the walls on the pleasant veranda.

✿ Festivals & Events

Santiago celebrates the festivals of **San Juan** (June 24) and **Santiago Apóstol** (St James; July 25) with processions and dances, including the Liseres, in which the participants wear jaguar costumes.

The week before Christmas is also a time of huge festivity.

⌂ Sleeping & Eating

TOP CHOICE **Hotel Mesón de Santiago**   HOTEL **$$**
(📞947-16-71; www.mesonsantiago.com.mx; 5 de Mayo 202; r from M$550; P✳🛜🏊) With a freshly renovated interior and the building's preserved colonial exterior, this fantastic place right on the main plaza is a jewel. The peaceful, landscaped courtyard has a small pool and is immaculate. Rooms are tastefully decorated with deeply burnished wood furniture and details, fresh white linens and painted tiles.

**Hotel Gran Santiago
Plaza Confort**   HOTEL **$$**
(📞947-03-00; www.hotelgransantiagoplaza.com. mx; cnr Comonfort & 5 de Mayo; r M$550; P✳🛜🏊) A cylindrical giant on the main plaza that manages not to look too obtuse, the Gran offers a more modern alternative to the Mesón. There's a restaurant and large-ish pool.

La Joya   MEXICAN **$**
(cnr Juárez & 2 de Abril; mains M$20-60; ⊙6am-11pm) The crummy plastic tablecloths, alfresco only chairs and rustic open-to-view kitchen scream 'Montezuma's revenge,' but fear not: La Joya delivers where it matters – good, tasty Mexican food. It's on the main

plaza and one of the only restaurants in town.

ⓘ Information

The post office is on the main plaza, as are two banks (with sometimes-dry ATMs), while a handful of internet places are nearby.

ⓘ Getting There & Around

All local and regional buses and *colectivos taxis* to San Andrés Tuxtla are frequent and stop at the junction of Morales and Hwy 180. A private taxi between the towns is M$60. Frequent 2nd-class buses also go to Catemaco, Veracruz, Acayucan and Tlacotalpan.

While the TLT and AU stops are just down Morelos, there's a tiny ADO office on the highway itself. Second-class buses are slower, more frequent to closer destinations and cost about 10% less. First-class buses are listed in the table.

Tres Zapotes

📞294 / POP 3500

The important late-Olmec center of Tres Zapotes is now just a series of mounds in cornfields. However, interesting artifacts are displayed at the museum in the town of Tres Zapotes, 23km west of Santiago Tuxtla. The trip to this tiny town is not convenient, but might be worth it if archaeology floats your boat.

Tres Zapotes was occupied for over 2000 years, from around 1200 BC to AD 1000. It was probably first inhabited while the great Olmec center of La Venta (Tabasco) still flourished. After the destruction of La Venta (about 400 BC), the city carried on in what archaeologists call an 'epi-Olmec' phase – the period during which the Olmec culture dwindled as other civilizations, notably

Izapa and the Maya, came to the fore. Most finds are from this later period.

The small **Museo de Tres Zapotes** (admission M$30; ⊙9am-5pm) notably has the 1.5m Tres Zapotes head, an Olmec head dating from about 100 BC. The biggest piece, Stela A, depicts three human figures in the mouth of a jaguar. Other pieces include a sculpture of what may have been a captive with hands tied behind his back and the upturned face of a woman carved into a throne or altar. The museum attendant is happy to answer questions in Spanish or give a tour (tipping is appreciated).

The road to Tres Zapotes goes southwest from Santiago Tuxtla; a 'Zona Arqueológica' sign points the way from Hwy 180. Eight kilometers down this road, you fork right onto a paved stretch for the last 15km to Tres Zapotes. It comes out at a T-junction, from where you go left then left again to reach the museum. From Santiago Tuxtla there are 2nd-class buses (M$24) and taxis (M$25/85 colectivo/private). Taxis leave from the Sitio Puente Real, on the far side of the pedestrian bridge at the foot of Zaragoza (the street going downhill beside the Santiago Tuxtla museum).

San Andrés Tuxtla

📞294 / POP 62,000 / ELEV 300M

Like a lot of modern towns, San Andrés puts function before beauty. The busy service center of the Las Tuxtlas region is best used for bus connections and link-ups to its more enticing peripheral sights, including a volcano and a giant waterfall. Cigar aficionados may want to linger. San Andrés is Mexico's cigar capital.

◎ Sights & Activities

TOP CHOICE **Salto de Eyipantla**　　　WATERFALL

(Map p244; admission M$10) Twelve kilometers southeast of San Andrés, a 244-step staircase leads down to the spectacular Salto de Eyipantla, a 50m-high, 40m-wide waterfall. To avoid the steps (and a soaking), you can also enjoy it from a *mirador* (lookout). Part of Mel Gibson's movie *Apocalypto* was filmed here.

Follow Hwy 180 east for 4km to Sihuapan, then turn right to Eyipantla. Frequent TLT buses (M$12) make the trip from San Andrés, leaving from the corner of Cabada and 5 de Mayo, near the market.

FREE **Santa Clara Cigar Factory**　　　CIGAR FACTORY

(Blvd 5 de Febrero 10; ⊙9am-9pm Mon-Sat, from 8am Sun) Watch and inhale as the *puros* are speedily rolled by hand at this cigar factory, on the highway a block or so from the bus station. Cigars of assorted shapes and sizes, including the monstrous Magnum, are available at factory prices, and the 50 *torcedores* employed here (together rolling 10,000 *puros* a day) are happy to demonstrate their technique.

Laguna Encantada　　　LAKE

(Map p244) The 'Enchanted Lagoon' occupies a small volcanic crater 3.5km northeast of San Andrés in jungle-like terrain. A dirt road goes there, but no buses do. Some locals advise not walking by the lake alone, so check with the guides at the nearby Yambigapan (following) for updates.

✍ **Ruíz Cortines**　　　HIKING

(Map p244; ☑cell phone 294-1005035; Ejido Ruíz Cortines; campsites/cabañas M$50/400) Tucked at the base of the volcano, an hour north of San Andrés Tuxtla, this little village has installed very rustic cabañas and offers horseback riding, and hikes to caves. Its highlight is the all-day, breathtaking hike up Volcán San Martín (1748m). A taxi from San Andrés Tuxtla costs M$90; a *pirata* (pickup truck) costs M$25.

✍ **Cerro de Venado**　　　NATURE RESERVE

(Map p244; admission M$5) This new 23-hectare reserve created in 2009 with the planting of thousands of trees is 2.5km from Laguna Encantada on the road to Ruíz Cortines. There are 500 steps up to a 650m hill with fabulous views of the town, lake and mountains, plus some caged animals.

🛏 Sleeping

San Andrés doesn't have a lot of choices, but you'll be comfortable.

✍ **Yambigapan**　　　CABINS, CAMPING $

(Map p244; ☑104-46-39; www.yambigapan.com; campsites/s/d M$25/300/400; P) Three kilometers or so from San Andrés, this family-run rural home-stay is equipped with two very rustic *cabañas* with spectacular views. Not to be missed are the **cooking classes** from the *doña* of the house, Amelia, who will teach you traditional Mexican cooking (in Spanish) and its history in her homely kitchen for

BUSES FROM SAN ANDRÉS TUXTLA

DESTINATION	FARE (M$)	DURATION	FREQUENCY (DAILY)
Acayucan	68	2hr	9
Catemaco	22	25min	10
Córdoba	204	3½hr	noon
Mexico City	456	8hr	3
Orizaba	170 (2nd class)	5hr	1
Puebla	270	6½hr	3
Santiago Tuxtla	24	20min	12
Veracruz	130	3hr	15
Villahermosa	270	5hr	4
Xalapa	220	5hr	6

about M$150 to M$200. There's also swimming in the nearby river, Arroyo Seco, and guided hikes. An all-day summit of Volcán San Martín can also be arranged. Taxi (M$35 to M$40) is the easiest way to arrive. Or ask a *pirata* going to Ruíz Cortines to leave you at the turnoff and follow the signs for Yambigapan that eventually lead you up a long dirt driveway. It should cost about M$10.

Hotel Posada San Martín   HOTEL $$
(☑942-10-36; www.hotelposada-sanmartin.com; Av Juárez 304; s/d M$447/543;) Midway between the bus station and the main plaza, this hacienda-style posada is a fabulous deal. It has a pool set in a peaceful garden and unique touches, such as yellow-and-blue sinks and carved headboards, in its spacious rooms.

Hotel del Parque   HOTEL $$
(☑942-01-98; www.hoteldelparque.com; Madero 5; s/d M$472/542; ❀❂) San Andrés' main central option is clean, modern and – not surprisingly – popular. Kudos are added with the normally busy cafe on the ground floor.

✖ Eating

Restaurante Winni's   BAKERY, INTERNATIONAL $
(Madero 10; set meal M$42; ☺7am-1am) Join the rest of San Andrés on the corner of the main plaza and sip an espresso while munching a pastry or a well-priced meal.

Refugio La Casona   MEXICAN $
(Madero 18; dishes M$40-70; ☺7am-2am) Along restaurant-laden Madero, this bar-restaurant serves traditional Mexican fare in its peaceful, leafy rear garden. There's also live bohemian music (from 9pm) most nights.

ℹ Information

The tiny **tourist office** (Madero 1; ☺8:30am-3:30pm) inside the Palacio Municipal is on the west side of the main plaza. A Banamex (with ATM) is on the south side; the market is three blocks west. A couple of blocks away on Avenida Juárez is a tiny plant-covered shopping center called Plaza Jardín that houses an internet place, **Double Click** (Av Juárez 106; per hr M$10; ☺9am-8pm Mon-Sat, 9am-2pm Sun).

ℹ Getting There & Around

San Andrés is the transportation center for Los Tuxtlas, with fairly good bus services in every direction. First-class buses with ADO and 2nd-class with AU depart from their respective stations on Juárez just off the Santiago Tuxtla–Catemaco highway, and about a 10-minute walk from the center. Rickety but regular 2nd-class TLT buses are often the quickest way of getting to local destinations. They leave from a block north of the market and skirt the north side of town on 5 de Febrero (Hwy 180). Regular TLT destinations include Acayucan, Santiago Tuxtla and Veracruz. Frequent *colectivos taxis* to Catemaco and Santiago also leave from the market – they're speedier than the bus but cost a fraction more. Local taxis abound, and catching one to Catemaco or Santiago Tuxtla will run to M$60.

The services listed in the table run from ADO.

Catemaco

☑294 / POP 28,000 / ELEV 340M

'Bewitching' is an adjective that encapsulates Catemaco in more ways than one. First, there's the town's startlingly bewitching location by a side of a large lake surrounded by luscious green hills. Second,

Catemaco

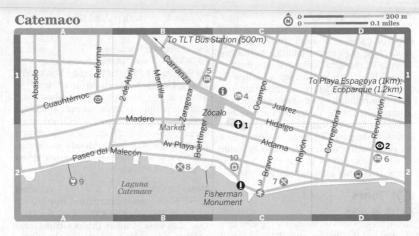

there are the witches (and wizards) themselves; nothing of the fantastical Harry Potter variety, unfortunately; just common everyday working witches who'll tell your fortune and excise you of nasty spirits (see boxed text, p242).

Superstitious witchcraft aside, Catemaco is undoubtedly the best base for ecologically motivated forays into Reserva de la Biosfera Los Tuxtlas. Small, a little scruffy, yet handily positioned right on the lake, it's reminiscent of a dusty backpacker destination from the 1980s, but without a significant number of backpackers – or any other foreigners for that matter. Alluring natural sights branch out in all directions.

◉ Sights & Activities

🏖 Laguna Catemaco   LAKE

Catemaco sits on the shore of the 16km-long Laguna Catemaco, which is ringed by volcanic hills and is actually a lake and not a lagoon. For boat tours on the lake, see p244. East of town are a few modest gray-sand beaches where you can take a dip in cloudy water. Following Hidalgo 1km east of town, the road tees and you'll hit the not too-crowded, if scruffy, **Playa Espagoya**. If you take a left on this waterfront road, you'll find a sign for **Ecoparque** (☎943-04-56; www.ecoparque-lapunta.com; treatments M$250-725), a small, rustic jungle-themed spa, offering mud massage and temascal, among other things. The spa also sells arnica soap and other crunchy items. Treatments are cheaper if you come with a group of people.

El Poder del Tigre
Botánicos y Ciencias Ocultas   SHAMAN

(Power of the Tiger Botanics & Occult Sciences; ☎943-07-46; www.brujogueixpal.com; Hidalgo 2) If you want to visit a local *brujo* (shaman), there's El Poder del Tigre Botánicos y Ciencias Ocultas. The *brujo* might pull up in his Ford Explorer and tell you to check out his website, or he might even be available to see you.

Basílica del Carmen
CHURCH

The intricate interior and haunting stained glass of Catemaco's main church belie its modernity; the current building only dates from 1953, though it looks at least a century older. The church was named a basilica (ie a church with special ceremonial rights) in 1961 due primarily to its position as a pilgrimage site for the Virgen del Carmen who is said to have appeared to a fisherman in a cave by Laguna Catemaco in 1664 in conjunction with a volcanic eruption. A statue of the virgin resides in the church and is venerated on her feast day every July 16.

☞ Tours

Catemacoturs
ADVENTURE

(☎941-58-49; Paseo del Malecón s/n) Based in a *palapa* hut on the *malecón*, these guys rent beat-down adventure gear and offer tours around the lake and to the coast.

Chaneque Tours
ADVENTURE

(☎943-16-14; Carranza 8) Based out of Catemaco Hotel and offering tours to Nanciyaga, Laguna Sontecomapan, Salto de Eyipantla and more.

🛏 Sleeping

Prices fluctuate dramatically according to demand; prices may rise 10% to 35% above those quoted here at high-season weekends, holidays and the March witch-doctor convention.

Catemaco Hotel
HOTEL $$

(☎943-02-03; www.hotelcatemaco.net; Carranza 8; s/d M$400/800; P❋🐾🛜🌊) The Catemaco is on prime *zócalo* real estate, and the restaurant/cafe below is a popular hub with wi-fi freeloaders and spreaders of local gossip.

Its rooms are modern, and there are decent bikes for hire (M$30 per hour).

Hotel Posada Koniapan
HOTEL $$

(☎943-00-63; www.hotelposadakoniapan.com.mx; cnr Revolución & Paseo del Malecón; r from M$550; P❋@🛜🌊🐾) On the easternmost tip of the *malecón*, the Koniapan offers privacy and peace in manicured grounds with a pool and kid's playground. The rooms could do with a creative rethink, but they're bright and spotless and the staff has a friendly demeanor. There's a *brujo* based next door should you need a quick exorcism.

Hotel La Finca
RESORT $$$

(☎947-97-00; www.lafinca.com.mx; Hwy 180 Km 47; r from M$1420; P⊖❋@🛜🌊🐾) Set lakeside 2km west of town, this resortlike hotel has rooms with large, lake-view balconies, and a pool with slides and a hot tub. It's a deal outside peak seasons, if seclusion from town is pleasing to you. It provides *lancha* and spa services.

Hotel Acuario
HOTEL $

(☎943-04-18; cnr Boettinger & Carranza; s/d M$250/350; P) One of several budget places on the *zócalo*; well kept, though plain and fan-cooled. Some rooms have views.

🍴 Eating

The lake provides the specialties here: *tegogolo* (a snail, reputed to be an aphrodisiac, eaten with chili, tomato, onion and lime) sold by street vendors, and *chipalchole* (shrimp or crab-claw soup). Many tourist-aimed restaurants line the *malecón*. Explore the city and you'll find interesting local eateries.

THE WITCHING HOUR

On the first Friday in March each year, hundreds of *brujos* (shamans), witches and healers from all over Mexico descend on Catemaco to perform a mass cleansing ceremony. The event is designed to rid them of the previous year's negative energies, though in recent years the whole occasion has become more commercial than supernatural. Floods of Mexicans also head into town at this time to grab a shamanic consultation or *limpia* (cleansing) and eat, drink and be merry in a bizarre mix of otherworldly fervor and hedonistic indulgence.

Witchcraft traditions in this part of Veracruz go back centuries, mixing ancient indigenous beliefs, Spanish medieval traditions and voodoo practices from West Africa. Many of these *brujos* multitask as medicine men or women (using both traditional herbs and modern pharmaceuticals), shrinks and black magicians (casting evil spells on enemies of their clients). If you're lucky, you could run into a *brujo* on your visit because, really, who couldn't use a little more abracadabra in their life?

BUSES FROM CATEMACO

DESTINATION	FARE (M$)	DURATION	FREQUENCY (DAILY)
Acayucan	60	1½hr	1
Córdoba	236	5hr	1
Mexico City	450	9½hr	3
Puebla	382	7hr	3
Santiago Tuxtla	30	50min	4
Veracruz	136	3½hr	5
Xalapa	234	5½hr	1

La Rioja
SPANISH, BREAKFAST $$

(Carranza 8; dishes M$60-120; ⏰6am-11pm; 🛜) This common meeting hub and wireless hot spot in the Catemaco Hotel is patronized by trendy and business-oriented local crowds as well as a tiny international contingent. The food is Spanish-themed and relatively authentic. Breakfast is a highlight.

La Ola
SEAFOOD, MEXICAN $$

(Paseo del Malecón s/n; dishes M$70-180; ⏰8am-9pm) Vast waterfront restaurant on the *malecón* serving all the seafood you could want including *pargo* (red snapper), *a la veracruzana* (spicy sauce) or *empanizado* (in breadcrumbs).

Il Fiorentino
ITALIAN $$

(Paseo del Malecón 11; mains M$75-90; ⏰6:30-10:30pm Tue-Fri, 3-11:30pm Sat, 1:30-11pm Sun; 🛜) Smarter than your average Italian-abroad restaurant, Il Fiorentino serves handmade pasta, Piedmontese wine, cappuccinos and great cake. It's on the *malecón* and run by an Italian – of course.

Drinking

La Panga
BAR

(Paseo del Malecón s/n; ⏰8am-midnight) This bar-restaurant, literally floating on the lake with its own boardwalk, is an idyllic place to lean back, sip *cerveza* and grab a bite to eat while the sun disappears beyond the lake and the rolling hills.

Shopping

Fractal Naturaleza
HANDICRAFTS

(cnr Paseo del Malecón & Ocampo; ⏰10am-9pm Mon-Fri, 9am-10pm Sat & Sun) Another great place to check out souvenirs made by local Los Tuxtlas artisans is Fractal Naturaleza, a store that does its best to support local art and textiles. It also brews coffee.

Information

Catemaco slopes gently down toward the lake. A **tourist office** (Municipalidad; ⏰9am-3pm Mon-Fri) on the north side of the *zócalo* will impart information, updated or not, about the town and the surrounding region. The **post office** (Cuauhtémoc s/n) is four blocks west of the central plaza.

There are banks and ATMs on the *zócalo*. North of the *zócalo*, **T@xinet** (Boettinger 16; per hr M$8; ⏰8am-10pm) is one of the numerous central internet places.

Getting There & Away

ADO and AU buses operate from a delightful lakeside **bus terminal** (cnr Paseo del Malecón & Revolución). Local 2nd-class TLT buses run from a bus station (Map p244) 700m west of the plaza by the highway junction and are a bit cheaper and more frequent than the 1st-class buses. *Colectivo* taxis arrive and depart from El Cerrito, a small hill about 400m to the west of the plaza on Carranza. A taxi to San Andrés Tuxtla is M$60 to M$70.

ADO's 1st-class bus services include those listed in the table.

To arrive at communities surrounding the lake and toward the coast, take inexpensive *piratas*. They leave from a corner five blocks north of the bus station.

Reserva de la Biosfera Los Tuxtlas

The various nature reserves around Catemaco were conglomerated in 2006 into this biosphere reserve under Unesco protection. This unique volcanic region that rises 1680m above the coastal plains of southern Veracruz lies 160km east of the Cordillera Neovolcánica, making it something of an ecological anomaly. Its complex vegetation is considered the northernmost limit of

Los Tuxtlas

rainforest in America. Being economically depressed, the region has little tourism infrastructure. Nevertheless, what it does have is worthwhile.

LAGUNA CATEMACO

On the lake, one-way *lancha* prices are M$50 *colectivo* or M$350 to M$450 for a private *lancha*. You can take **boat tours** to several islands within the lake. They leave from the Paseo del Malecón in Catemaco town. On the largest, **Isla Tenaspi**, Olmec sculptures have been discovered. **Isla de los Changos** (Monkey Island; Map p244) shelters red-cheeked monkeys, originally from Thailand. They belong to the Universidad Veracruzana, which acquired them for research. *Lancheros,* disturbingly, feed the monkeys for the sake of visitors taking close-up photographs.

On the northeast shore of the lake, the **Reserva Ecológica de Nanciyaga** (☏294-943-01-99; www.nanciyaga.com; Carretera Catemaco-Coyame; ☺9am-2pm & 4-6pm; P) is a kind of reserve within a reserve and pushes an indigenous theme in a small tract of rainforest. The grounds are replete with a temascal (M$250 per person), an ancient planetarium and Olmec-themed decorations and replicas. Day visitors are welcome. One night's lodging (M$900) in solar-powered rustic cabins

includes a mineral mud bath, a massage, a guided walk and the use of kayaks. You have to walk to the bathrooms (torches provided), so it's not for everyone, but it provides an incredible experience for those who want to be very close to nature. Arrive by *pirata* (M$7), taxi (M$80) or boat (M$50 per person; hire in Catemaco).

Follow the lake's eastern shore another 8km and you can earn a bit more luxury at the meditative **Prashanti Tebanca** (☏cell phone 294-1077998; www.prashanti.com.mx; 2-/4-/6-person units M$1000/1200/1400; P✸ ☎☒), a more deluxe version of Nanciyaga with a *nuevo*-Buddhist vibe. Numerous boat and jeep tours can be organized here.

No *colectivo* boats go to **Las Margaritas** (☏294-445-52-71; cabaña per person M$500), a little village on the south shore of the lake, so arrive by private *lancha* (M$350 to M$400) or bumpy *pirata* (M$14). The rural setting by the lake is stunning. Trips are offered to the El Chininal archaeological site and to waterfalls where guides point out birds and medicinal plants.

RAINFOREST

If hidden waterfalls, kayaking, hiking, birdwatching or beautiful beaches are of interest to you, **Ecobiosfera** (☏cell phone 294-103-31-12; www.ecobiosfera.com; Carretera Catemaco-

Sontecomapan Km 10; campsites M$100, cabañas M$400-800) will organize your excursion. Prices vary (about M$400 to M$800 per person), but the owner, Felix, is a biologist and knows the area very well. Felix can take you to the deep-green **Poza Reina** (admission M$25), a swimming hole laden with cascades. The *cabañas* at the Dos Amantes base camp have shared bathrooms and are charming in a Robinson Crusoe kind of way.

LAGUNA DE SONTECOMAPAN

In the town of Sontecomapan, 15km north of Catemaco, there are some lagoon-side restaurants and the idyllic **Pozo de los Enanos** (Well of the Dwarves) swimming hole where local youths launch Tarzanlike from ropes into the water. You can catch a *lancha* (M$20 to M$35) from here to any of the following places on the lake. Taxis from Catemaco cost M$50.

Family-run **Paraíso Real** (☎294-949-59-84; cabañas M$350 & M$600; P), in the tiny town of El Real, has two *cabañas* and a peaceful camping space right on Laguna de Sontecomapan.

✐**Los Amigos** (☎294-943-01-01; www.losamigos.com.mx; dm incl breakfast M$190, cabañas 2 people M$500, 6 people M$1600; P) is a well-run, peaceful retreat close to where the *laguna* enters the ocean. The fantastic *cabañas* tucked into the verdant hillside have lovely balconies sporting hammocks and spectacular views of the bay. There are nature trails to a beautiful lookout, kayak rentals and a restaurant. The boat ride there from Sontecomapan is about 15 to 30 minutes.

THE COAST

The small fishing town of **La Barra**, with its pleasant beaches and seafood restaurants, can be reached by a *lancha* from Sontecomapan (M$400 including a tour of the mangroves on the way) or a side road going east from La Palma, 8km north of Sontecomapan. Do not miss a lunch of *sierra* fish cooked simply in soy sauce, garlic, salt and butter, and enjoyed on the (usually deserted) sea-facing beach.

Northwest of La Barra is the tiny beach town of **Jicacal**. You can access Jicacal from a rough road that forks east from the main road. The family-run restaurant there has delectable, fresh-from-the-line seafood. The dirt road to the left right before you hit Jicacal will lead you 10 minutes down a gorgeous wreck of a road to a moldering relic of

a hotel. From there, you'll find a path leading to a long set of crumbling stairs going to **Playa Escondida** (Hidden Beach), which earns its name. During the work week in the low season, you'll probably have the gorgeous blond sands and turquoise waters to yourself.

North of the junction to Jicacal, you'll soon hit the **Biological Research Station** (☎200-125-54-08; www.ibiologia.unam.mx; ⊙museum 9am-5pm Mon-Fri) and will see a handful of camping opportunities, including at Laguna Escondida and Finca Villa Carino. The ornery biologists have a tiny biology museum and limited patience for tourists. They cobbled the roads through their section of the reserve to limit people, speed and traffic.

Further north in **Montepío** is a picturesque beach at the mouth of the Río Máquina where you can eat seafood on the beach. **Posada San José** (☎294-942-10-10; r M$240, with air-con M$390; P✱) is a reasonably comfortable place to sleep there.

Acayucan

Acayucan is an important and busy commercial center and a passable stopover for those heading south to Villahermosa or inland to Oaxaca and Chiapas. It's at the junction of Hwy 180 and Hwy 185. If you're here in transit, you'll find services are good.

To reach the central plaza from the bus station, walk uphill to Avenida Hidalgo, turn left and walk six blocks. Several banks alongside the plaza have ATMs. There are internet cafes off the pedestrian alley behind the plaza.

🍴 Sleeping & Eating

Hotel Kinaku   HOTEL $$
(☎924-245-04-10; Ocampo Sur 7; s/d M$560/655; P✱🛜🏊) Acayucan's most expensive hotel, equipped with a sort of formal restaurant, is clean and friendly and OK for one night. Upper-floor rooms have sweeping views.

Mercado   MARKET $
(snacks M$10-50) If you're just passing through town or waiting for a bus, you're in luck, *compadre*. Located between the bus stations is a massive labyrinth of little eateries and merchants selling myriad things, including food of all colors, textures and shapes.

BUSES FROM ACAYUCAN

DESTINATION	FARE (M$)	DURATION	FREQUENCY (DAILY)
Catemaco	60	1½hr	1
Mexico City (TAPO)	602	9hr	3
Santiago Tuxtla	80	2¼hr	1
Tuxtla Gutiérrez	348	4hr	3
Veracruz	243	3hr	14
Villahermosa	194	3hr	12

ⓘ Getting There & Away

Local buses (M$6) and taxis (about M$20) run between the **bus station** (Acuña) on the east side of town and downtown. UNO and ADO run 1st-class and deluxe lines; AU provides good 2nd-class service. These companies, and more, operate from the same location flanking the market. Direct 1st-class buses are listed here.

The toll highway, 145D, passes south of town. The tolls are expensive, costing more than M$300 to get to Córdoba.

Yucatán Peninsula

Includes »

Best Places to Eat

» Kinich (p316)
» Hartwood (p282)
» Chaya Maya (p301)
» Eladio's (p315)

Best Places to Stay

» Luz en Yucatán (p299)
» Casa Takywara (p264)
» Hotel Maya Luna (p288)
» Hotel Macan Ché (p316)
» Pickled Onion (p310)
» Hotel El Rey del Caribe (p252)

Why Go?

A better question is why not? With charming colonial cities (both heavily touristed and virtually unheard of), world-famous Maya ruins, thumping nightlife centers, sleepy country villages, talcum-powder beaches leading to crystal turquoise waters and more dive sites than you could ever cram in one vacation, the Yucatán is one sweet destination.

Despite patches of overzealous development, the natural beauty of the Yucatán abides. The coo of the motmot still reverberates overhead, while below the creepy-crawlies continue to writhe. Further down, freshwater rivers gurgle through massive limestone caverns.

Around here, the past is the present and the present is the past: they intertwine like two brawling brothers. You'll witness it in the towering temples of the Maya, Toltecs and Itzáes, in the cobblestone streets of colonial centers and in the culture of the Maya themselves, quietly maintaining their traditions as the centuries tick by.

When to Go

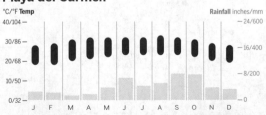

Playa del Carmen

Jun–Aug The summer is hot – the ocean heats up and occasional afternoon rains are very welcome.

Sep & Oct Hurricane season means frequent rain, although temperatures are still warm.

Nov–May Temperatures drop and the rains thin out. The ocean gets warmer and clearer around February.

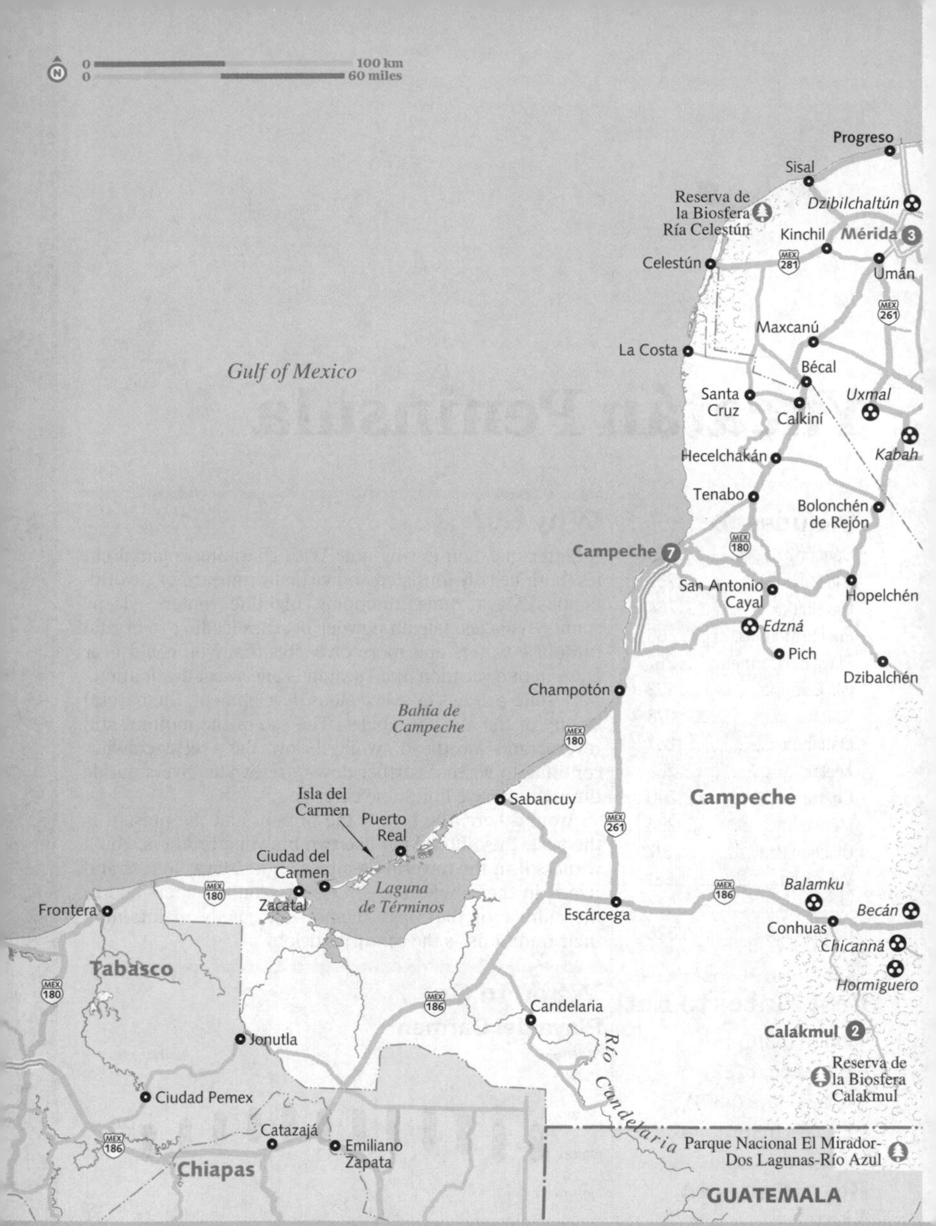

0 ——— 100 km
0 ——— 60 miles

Gulf of Mexico

Progreso
Sisal
Reserva de la Biosfera Ría Celestún
Dzibilchaltún
Kinchil   **Mérida** ❸
Celestún   Umán
MEX 281
Maxcanú
La Costa
Bécal
Santa Cruz   Uxmal
Calkiní
Hecelchakán   Kabah
Tenabo
Bolonchén de Rejón
Campeche ❼
MEX 180
San Antonio Cayal   Hopelchén
Edzná
Pich
Champotón
Dzibalchén

Bahía de Campeche

MEX 180

Isla del Carmen
Puerto Real   Sabancuy   **Campeche**
MEX 261
Ciudad del Carmen
Frontera   Zacatal   *Laguna de Términos*   Balamkú
MEX 180   Escárcega   MEX 186   Becán
Conhuas   Chicanná
Tabasco   Hormiguero
MEX 180   MEX 186   Candelaria   **Calakmul** ❷
Jonutla   Reserva de la Biosfera Calakmul
Ciudad Pemex
Catazajá   Río Candelaria
MEX 186   Emiliano Zapata   Parque Nacional El Mirador-Dos Lagunas-Río Azul
Chiapas
GUATEMALA

Yucatán Peninsula Highlights

❶ Set out for a morning bird-watching mission from the remote Costa Maya beach town of **Xcalak** (p288), then head out for a dive at **Banco Chinchorro** (p288)

❷ Haul yourself up the massive pyramid of **Calakmul** (p335) as heavy-nosed toucans soar past toward their tree-top jungle hideaways

❸ Marvel at the colonial architecture or attend a free concert in **Mérida** (p294)

❹ Find out why they named **Chichén Itzá** (p317) the 'seventh modern wonder of the

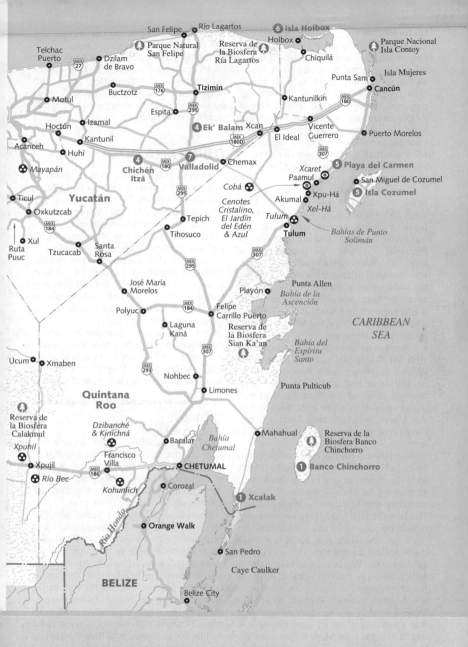

world,' or why **Ek' Balam** (p324) should have made the list

5 Stay out until dawn in one of the happening beachfront clubs in **Playa del Carmen** (p267), before taking the ferry

across to **Isla Cozumel** (p272) the next day for a snorkel and swim

6 Get up close and personal with the whale sharks on **Isla Holbox** (p264)

7 Head away from the crowds to the beautiful colonial cities of **Campeche** (p326) and **Valladolid** (p321)

History

The Maya – accomplished astronomers and mathematicians, and architects of some of the grandest monuments ever known – created their first settlements in what is now Guatemala as early as 2400 BC. Over the centuries, Maya civilization expanded steadily northward, and by AD 550 great Maya city-states were established in southern Yucatán. In the 10th century the great cities of southern Yucatán slowly dissolved, as attention shifted northward to new power centers such as Chichén Itzá.

The last of the great Maya capitals, Mayapán, started to collapse around 1440, when the Xiu Maya and the Cocom Maya began a violent and protracted struggle for power. In 1540, Spanish conquistador Francisco de Montejo the Younger (son of legendary conquistador Francisco de Montejo the Elder) utilized the tensions between the still-feuding Maya sects to conquer the area. The Spaniards allied themselves with the Xiu against the Cocom, finally defeating the Cocom and gaining the Xiu as reluctant converts to Christianity.

Francisco de Montejo the Younger, along with his father and cousin (named...you guessed it, Francisco de Montejo), founded Mérida in 1542 and within four years brought most of the Yucatán Peninsula under Spanish rule. The Spaniards divided the Maya lands into large estates where the natives were put to work as indentured servants.

When Mexico won its independence from Spain in 1821, the new Mexican government used the Yucatecan territory to create huge plantations for the cultivation of tobacco, sugarcane and *henequén* (agave rope fiber). The Maya, though legally free, were enslaved in debt peonage to the rich landowners.

In 1847 the Maya rose up in a massive revolt against the Spanish. This was the beginning of the War of the Castes. Finally, in 1901, after more than 50 years of sporadic, but often intense, violence, a tentative peace was reached; however, it would be another 30 years before the territory of Quintana Roo came under official government control. To this day some Maya do not recognize that sovereignty.

The commercial success of Cancún in the early 1970s led to hundreds of kilometers of beachfront property along the Caribbean coast being sold off to commercial developers, displacing many small fishing communities. While many indigenous people still eke out a living by subsistence agriculture or fishing, large numbers now work in the construction and service industries. Some individuals and communities, often with outside encouragement, are having a go at ecotourism, opening their lands to tourists and/or serving as guides.

QUINTANA ROO

You'd think that as one of Mexico's most visited states, it'd be impossible to find a bit of solitude in Quintana Roo (pronounced 'kin-tah-nah *roh'*). But beyond the open-bar excesses of Cancún and dubiously credentialed 'ecoparks' of the Riviera Maya, you might just find your own quiet slice of paradise.

There are glaring-white beaches stretching all the way from Cancún to the Belizean border, unassuming Caribbean islands protected by the barrier reef, and impressive Maya sites throughout this long-arching sliver of limestone, salt and sea.

The high season for Quintana Roo is basically December to April. Prices (and crowds) peak from mid-December to mid-January, late February to early March (the US spring break) and a week on either side of Easter.

Cancún

✆ 998 / POP 750,000

Like Las Vegas, Ibiza or Dubai, Cancún is a party city that just won't give up. Top that off with a pretty good beach and you have one of the western hemisphere's biggest tourist draws, bringing in as many as 4 million visitors (mostly from the US) each year.

Hurricanes Wilma and Emily whipped into town in 2005, destroying hotels and carrying off tons of Cancún's precious beach sand. The hotels have been rebuilt, and the government invested nearly M$200 million to restore the beaches. But the sand is beginning to wash away again and, to the dismay of many environmentalists, the government has begun excavating sand from around Cozumel and Isla Mujeres (up to 5.6 million cubic meters at a time) to rebuild the area's beaches.

⊙ Sights & Activities

Museo Subacuático de Arte MUSEUM, DIVE SITE (www.musacancun.com) Work began on the Cancún Underwater Museum in late 2009.

It now features over 400 sculptures by Jason de Caires Taylor submerged at various depths in the shallow waters between Cancún and Isla Mujeres. To snorkel or scuba dive it, inquire at tour operators (see p252).

Zona Arqueológica El Rey ARCHAEOLOGICAL SITE (Map p254; admission M$37; ☉8am-5pm) At the southern end of the Zona Hotelera, this small archaeological site features a small temple and several ceremonial platforms. It's worth a look if time permits, but pretty much every other site listed in this chapter is more impressive. You'll find it on the west side of Blvd Kukulcán between Km 17 and Km 18.

Beaches

Under Mexican law, you have the right to walk and swim on every beach in the country, except those within military compounds. In practice, it is difficult to approach many stretches of beach without walking through the lobby of a hotel, particularly in the Zona Hotelera. However, unless you look suspicious or like a local (hotels tend to discriminate against locals, particularly the Maya), you'll usually be able to cross the lobby unnoticed and proceed to the beach.

Starting from Ciudad Cancún in the northwest, all of Isla Cancún's beaches are on the left-hand side of the road (the lagoon is on your right; all appear on Map p254). The following are listed north to south, with their respective Km markers on Blvd Kukulcán:

Playa Las Perlas (Km 2.5) A small beach with a great kids' playground, bathrooms and free *palapa*-topped tables. Free parking. Access from north side of the Holiday Inn.

Playa Langosta (Km 5) One of the prettiest public beaches, with clean white sand, no music, no waves and a few shade trees. There's nothing to eat for miles around, but there are lifeguards on duty.

Playa Pez Volador (Km 5.5) Popular with families for its calm, shallow foreshore. There's free parking (but tip the guys 'minding' your car). Access is from the huge flagpole flying the Mexican flag.

Playa Tortuga (Km 6.3) One of the busiest beaches around, with loud music, cheap restaurants, deck chair and umbrella hire and a bungee jump (US$35). Access from the ferry terminal, where there is free parking if you can find a spot.

Playa Caracol (Km 8.7) Next to the Isla Mujeres ferry dock, this tiny stretch of sand is probably the least inviting, but you can head left when you hit the water to get to the lovely beach 'belonging' to the Hotel Riu. No parking.

Playa Gaviota Azul (Km 8.8) A beautiful little curve at the end of the bay, mostly monopolized by beach clubs. Access is from north side of Cocobongo's where there is extremely limited free parking.

Playa Chac-Mool (Km 9.5) With no parking, this is one of the quieter beaches. Lifeguard on duty and parasailing available. No food but there are stores and restaurants near the access, opposite Señor Frogs.

Playa Marlin (Km 12.5) A long, lovely stretch of sand with lifeguards on duty and deck chairs, umbrellas and tables for rent. There's no food, but there is an Oxxo out on Blvd Kukulcán, north of the Kukulcán Plaza where the beach access is.

Playa Ballenas (Km 14.2) A long, quiet stretch of beach squeezed between luxury hotels. Wave runners (M$70, 30 minutes), bodyboards and parasailing (M$700, 12 minutes) available. Free parking. Access from dirt road on south side of Golden Parnassus hotel.

Playa Delfines (Km 17.5) Gets OK waves (for bodysurfing and bodyboarding – maybe in a hurricane you could surf here), but the sand is darker and coarser than up north. *Palapas* and umbrellas for rent. No food, but fruit vendors walk the beach. Free parking.

Water Sports

Specialized operators (and just about everybody else) offer nearly every water-based activity you could imagine, including PADI open-water certification (M$5277), parasailing (M$615), snorkeling trips (M$492), submarine tours (M$492), speedboat tours (M$492) swimming with dolphins (M$1660) and wave runner hire (M$553).

Aqua World WATER SPORTS (Map p254; ☎848-83-00; www.aquaworld.com.mx; Blvd Kukulcán Km 15.2) Offers all of the above. Also rents sailboats, windsurfers, kayaks and bodyboards.

Scuba Cancún DIVING, SNORKELING (Map p254; ☎849-52-26; www.scubacancun.com.mx; Blvd Kukulcán Km 5.2) A family-owned and

BEACH SAFETY

A system of colored pennants warns beachgoers of potential dangers:

» **Blue** Normal, safe conditions.

» **Yellow** Use caution; changeable conditions.

» **Red** Unsafe conditions; use a swimming pool instead.

PADI-certified dive operation with many years of experience. Offers snorkeling tours, PADI certification and dive trips for certified divers.

Cancún doesn't have great conditions for surfing. But a core group of locals still head out to Playa Chac-Mool and Playa Marlin to hit the little rollers. 'Surf season' runs from October to March.

Koko Dog'z   SURFING
(Map p256; ☑887-36-35; www.kokodogz.com; Av Náder 42-1; ☉noon-8pm Mon-Fri, to 6pm Sat) There's no place in town to rent boards, but you can buy one here. It sells all sorts of boards and arranges wakeboarding on the lagoon for M$2150 an hour per boat.

Courses

Teatro Xbalamqué   THEATER
(Map p256; ☑147-73-22; http://teatroxbalamque.blogspot.com, in Spanish; Av Yaxchilán 31) Has yoga and theater courses.

☞ Tours

Most hotels and travel agencies work with companies that offer tours to surrounding attractions.

Turimex   BOAT, ARCHAEOLOGICAL TOURS
(Map p256; ☑887-40-90; www.turimexcun.com; Av Cobá 5) Offers a variety of reasonably priced packages to popular destinations. As well as boat and archaeology tours, offers ecotours and water sports.

Sleeping

Cancún is actually made up of two very distinct areas: the downtown area, Ciudad Cancún, which is on the mainland, and Isla Cancún, a sandy spit of an island, which is usually referred to as the Zona Hotelera (Hotel Zone).

DOWNTOWN

The downtown area has numerous hostels, budget digs (mostly around Parque Las Palapas) and some charming small hotels. The main north-south thoroughfare is Avenida Tulum, a 1km-long tree-shaded boulevard lined with banks, shopping centers and restaurants. Though the hotels here aren't near the water, the beach is just a taxi or bus ride away.

TOP
CHOICE **Hotel El Rey del Caribe**   HOTEL $$
(Map p256; ☑884-20-28; www.elreydelcaribe.com; cnr Avs Uxmal & Náder; s/d M$1000/1200; ☻❋☎ ☲✦) A surprisingly lush little oasis in the middle of the busy downtown area. Many of the 31 rooms have a fully equipped kitchenette; all have comfortable beds, hairdryers and safes and face onto a jungle-like patio with an inviting swimming pool and casual *palapa*-roofed restaurant.

Moloch Hostel   HOSTEL $
(Map p256; ☑884-69-18; www.moloch.com.mx; Margaritas 54; dm M$180, s/d shared bathroom M$280/420, s/d M$380/480, ste M$400/550; ℗❋☎☲) Sitting pretty between the Parque Las Palapas and the bus terminal, there's a great range of rooms on offer here. They're all fresh and modern and the 'suites' are a very good deal for couples.

Hotel Bonampak   HOTEL $$
(Map p254; ☑884-02-80; www.hotelbonampak.com; Av Bonampak 225 SM4; r M$950; ❋@☎☲) Very much a standard midrange hotel, this is still pretty good value: the pool is sunny, the wide stairways are airy and fresh, the rooms are spotless and many have small balconies. Ask for a room overlooking the pool to avoid the road noise.

Hotel Colonial   HOTEL $$
(Map p256; ☑884-15-35; www.hotelcolonialcancun.com; Tulipanes 22; d with fan/air-con M$750/850; ❋☎) While the best thing about it is the central location, the Colonial has a pleasant central courtyard with tinkling fountain and super-clean rooms with traditional textile

MOVING ON?

For tips, recommendations and reviews, head to shop.lonelyplanet.com to purchase a downloadable PDF of the Guatemala and Belize chapters from Lonely Planet's *Central America on a Shoestring* guide.

bedspreads. Get a room toward the rear – the street noise in this party district can be a bit much.

Hotel Plaza Caribe HOTEL $$
(Map p256; ☑884-13-77; www.hotelplazacaribe. com; cnr Avs Tulum & Uxmal; r M$1050; P❋☎❄) Considering what hotels around the bus terminal are usually like, this is a pretty sweet deal. Rooms are nothing special, but the quiet grounds seem a million miles away from the bustling streets outside.

ZONA HOTELERA
Blvd Kukulcán, a four-lane divided avenue, leaves Ciudad Cancún and goes eastward out onto the narrow island that is home to many restaurants, bars and hotels and is almost universally referred to as the Zona Hotelera.

There aren't many buildings in this area that have numbered addresses. Instead, because the vast majority of them are on Blvd Kukulcán, their location is described in relation to their distance from Km 0, the boulevard's northern terminus in Ciudad Cancún, identified with a roadside 'Km 0' marker. Each kilometer is similarly marked.

Casa Turquesa BOUTIQUE HOTEL $$$
(Map p254; ☑193-22-60; http://home.casaturque sa.com; Blvd Kukulcán Km 13.5; r M$4970-12,434; ❄❋@☎❄) With over 600 works of art distributed through the lobbies, hallways and 35 rooms here, this place is almost more art gallery than hotel. But then there's even more art in the attached gallery. All the amenities are here, including the infinity pool overlooking the ocean, tennis court, gourmet restaurant, a hushed, intimate atmosphere and quietly luxurious rooms.

Hotel Gran Royal Lagoon HOTEL $$
(Map p254; ☑883-27-49; www.grlagoon.com; Quetzal 8A; r M$685; ❄❋@❄) Simple rooms with a couple of stylish touches. Most have lagoon views (it's across the road from the beach) and the property has its own jetty in case you were thinking about bringing the yacht. This is one of the few bargains in the Zona Hotelera – book early.

Me by Melia LUXURY HOTEL $$$
(Map p254; ☑881-25-00; www.me-cancun.com; Blvd Kukulcán Km 12; s/d all-inclusive from M$4886/6731; ❄❋@☎❄) While much of the hotel zone is either going over-the-top baroque or bland 'n' corporate, 'Me' takes its own tack, looking more like a hip Madrid bar than a hotel.

Service is oddly indifferent, but everything is laid on – there's a contemporary art gallery in the lobby area, a range of beachfront bars and restaurants to choose from and the obligatory onsite spa. Book early – this place fills up and the website often has 50%-off promotional deals.

Hostal Mayapan HOSTEL $
(Map p254; ☑883-32-27; www.hostalmayapan. com; Blvd Kukulcán Km 8.5; dm from M$110; ❋@☎) Two remarkable things about this hostel – one, it's set in an ex-shopping mall (sadly, the escalators don't run anymore) and two, it offers cheap sleeps in the Zona Hotelera. There's a nice little hangout spot in the upstairs atrium, but otherwise it's a fairly standard hostel setup.

✖ Eating

Tacos Rigo TAQUERÍA $
(Map p254; Av Playa 50; tacos from M$15; ⊙11am-11:30pm) There's a taco joint on nearly every block in Cancún, but locals drive all the way across town to come to this one. One bite and you'll understand why.

Pescadito's SEAFOOD $
(Map p256; Av Yaxchilán 69; dishes M$30-50; ⊙10am-midnight) Delicious, fresh fish dishes (you'll need a couple to fill you up) done in a variety of classic Mexican and Yucatecan styles. The plastic chairs and hippy-rasta murals may not suit your tastes, but the *chile relleno* (bell pepper stuffed with seafood) can't be argued with.

Perico's MEXICAN $$$
(Map p256; Av Yaxchilán 61; mains M$120-350; ⊙noon-1am) With a lively atmosphere and an attentive staff, Perico's, probably one of the city's longest-running restaurants, sticks to the family recipes, putting out some of the tastiest seafood, steak and Yucatecan food in town. Dinner is accompanied by a show – live marimba, comedy skits and the occasional conga line. Lunch service is much mellower – plan accordingly.

Crab House SEAFOOD $$$
(Map p254; Blvd Kukulcán Km 14.8; dishes M$170-400; ⊙noon-11pm) Completely unaffiliated with the lowbrow chain of a similar name, this refined, casual place does seafood pretty much any way you want it, either in air-con bliss or out on the deck overlooking the lagoon. Crab is (unsurprisingly) the specialty and local ones are reasonably priced, although imported and soft-shell can easily go

Cancún

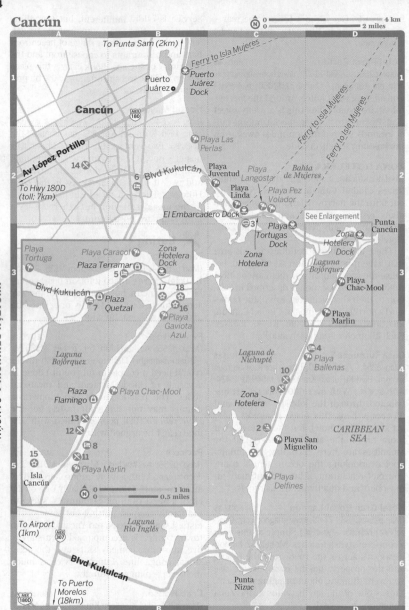

above the M$450 mark. Feeling adventurous? Try the crocodile tail for entrée.

La Distilería
MEXICAN $$$

(Map p254; Blvd Kukulcán Km 12.75; mains M$150-250; ☻1pm-midnight) Serious Mexican food can be hard to come by in the Zona Hotelera, but this place gets the thumbs-up from locals and visitors alike. It's all good, but the chicken dishes – with goat cheese sauce (M$214), or *mole poblano* (in a sauce of chilies, fruits, nuts, spices and choco-

Cancún

late), M$189 – are the standouts. The dining room is dominated by a huge tequila still, but if you're looking for a breeze, head out the back to the deck overlooking the lagoon.

La Habichuela Sunset   FUSION **$$$**
(Map p254; ☎840-62-80; Blvd Kukulcán Km 12.6; mains M$200-360; ◷noon-midnight) Putting a Caribbean twist on Mexican classics with some Italian thrown in may sound like a recipe for disaster, but this regularily recommended restaurant does it in style. Floor-to-ceiling windows with lagoon views and some great Maya artwork and decorations seal the deal.

Lorenzillo's   SEAFOOD **$$$**
(Map p254; ☎883-12-54; Blvd Kukulcán Km 10.5; mains M$300-550; ◷noon-midnight) Live lobster restaurants – they're either outrageously barbaric or luxuriously decadent. Or both. If you're looking, this casual, relaxed restaurant built on a jetty overlooking the lagoon is your best bet. Lobster prices vary according to the market, but at time of research the going rate was M$780 per pound.

Harry's   STEAKHOUSE **$$$**
(Map p254; ☎840-65-50; Blvd Kukulcán Km 14.2; mains M$140-500; ◷noon-1am) For the meat lovers, Harry's serves imported, in-house-dry-aged steaks (you can get them kosher if you want), superfresh fish and even sports a raw bar. The architecture's as much of a draw as anything, with indoor waterfalls, plenty of decking over the lagoon and two bars – one indoors and one out.

Mercados 23 and 28 have a number of tiny eateries, and Parque Las Palapas has food stalls. Most of the best budget restaurants are found in the downtown area.

For groceries, try **Comercial Mexicana** (Map p256; cnr Avs Tulum & Uxmal), a central supermarket close to the bus station.

🍷 Drinking

For a very local night out in the downtown area, check out the bars around the base of the **Plaza de Toros** (Bullring; cnr Avs Bonampak & Sayil). Names and tastes changes quickly here, but **La Chopería** (◷4pm-3am) draws a crowd, as much for the draft beer as the icy air-con. Go for a wander and see where the action is. Don't worry about eating first – the all-night *taquerías* (taco stalls) here are some of the best in town.

If that's a bit raw for you, head across Av Sayil to the Malecón Las Américas, Cancún's mall-of-choice (at time of writing), which is home to the **Black Pub** (◷6pm-3am Tue-Sat) with live music Wednesdays and Saturdays, or the super-chic lounge scene at **Lemon** (◷8pm-3am Wed-Sat) with regular DJs and occasional live music.

☆ Entertainment

Nightclubs

The Zona Hotelera's dance clubs are clustered around Km 9, just south of Punta Cancún. There's not a whole lot to tell them apart – grinding dance music, shouting DJs, people doing things they probably won't be telling their mother about. The cover charge is around M$120, or you can opt for an all-you-can-drink bracelet for M$240. Most people get the bracelet. Some of these places don't open before 10pm, and most don't close until dawn.

Coco Bongo   DANCE
(Map p254; www.cocobongo.com.mx; Blvd Kukulcán Km 9; ◷10:30pm-5am) With an 1800-person capacity, don't come here expecting a quiet drink.

YUCATÁN PENINSULA CANCÚN

Ciudad Cancún

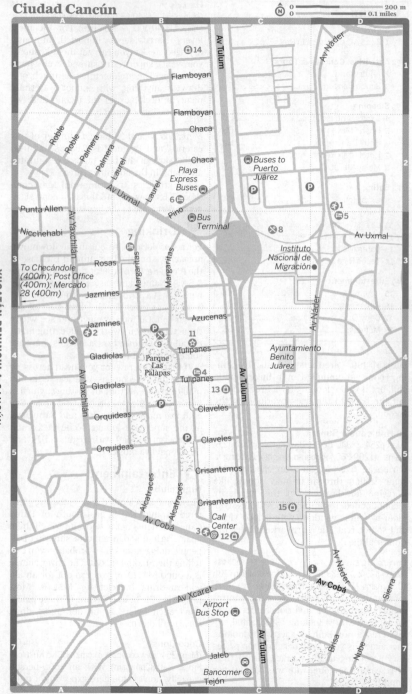

0 200 m
0 0.1 miles

14

Av Tulum

Flamboyan

Flamboyan

Chaca

Chaca

Playa
Express
Buses

6

Pino

Bus
Terminal

Buses to
Puerto
Juárez

P

P

1
5

Av Uxmal

8

Instituto
Nacional de
Migración

Av Náder

Roble

Roble

Palmera

Palmera

Laurel

Laurel

Av Uxmal

Punta Allen

Nicchehabi

Av Yaxchilán

To Checándole
(400m); Post Office
(400m); Mercado
28 (400m)

Rosas

Jazmines

7

Margaritas

Margaritas

Jazmines

2

10

Gladiolas

Gladiolas

Orquideas

Orquideas

Av Yaxchilán

P

9

Azucenas

11

Tulipanes

Parque
Las
Palapas

4

Tulipanes

13

Claveles

P

Claveles

Crisantemos

Ayuntamiento
Benito
Juárez

Av Tulum

Av Náder

Alcatraces

Alcatraces

Av Cobá

Crisantemos

Call
Center

3   12

15

Airport
Bus Stop

Av Xcaret

Jaleb

Bancomer
Tejón

Av Tulum

Av Cobá

Av Náder

Sierra

Brisa

Nube

Ciudad Cancún

Dady'O   DANCE
(Map p254; www.dadyo.com.mx; Blvd Kukulcán Km 9.5; ◷9pm-4:30am) A classic in the area, and a leader in the wet T-shirt competition industry.

Mandala   DANCE
(Map p254; ☑800-234-97-97; Blvd Kukulcán Km 9; ◷10pm-4:30am) At least tries to be a little upscale, with vaguely interesting decor and not-too-mainstream music.

Roots   LIVE MUSIC
(Map p256; ☑884-24-37; Tulipanes 26; cover Fri & Sat M$60; ◷6pm-1am Mon-Sat) Pretty much the hippest downtown bar, Roots features jazz, reggae or rock bands and the occasional flamenco guitarist. It's also a pretty decent restaurant.

Cinemas

Cinemark (Map p254; ☑883-56-03; www.cinemark.com.mx) is in La Isla Shopping Village.

🛒 Shopping

Locals head to either **Mercado 28** (off Map p256; cnr Avs Xel-Há & Sunyaxchén) or **Mercado 23** (Map p256; Av Tulum s/n) for clothes, shoes, inexpensive food stalls, hardware items and so on. Of the two, Mercado 23 is the least frequented by tourists. If you're looking for

a place *without* corny T-shirts, this is where to go.

Mercado Municipal Ki-Huic   MARKET
(Map p256; Av Tulum) This warren of stalls and shops carries a wide variety of souvenirs and handicrafts.

Chedraui Supermarket   SHOPPING CENTER
(Map p256; cnr Avs Tulum & Cobá) Across Avenida Tulum. Its upstairs clothing department sometimes has souvenir-grade items at very affordable prices.

Fama   BOOKS
(Map p256; ☑884-65-41; Av Tulum 105 SM 22 M4 Lotes 27 & 27A) Some English-language titles, a good selection covering the Maya and archaeological topics, and the occasional guidebook.

ℹ Information

Emergency
Cruz Roja (Red Cross; ☑884-16-16)
Fire (☑066)
Police (☑066; Blvd Kukulcán Km 13.5)
Tourist Police (☑885-22-77)

Immigration
Instituto Nacional de Migración (Immigration Office; Map p256; ☑881-35-60; cnr Av Náder 1 & Av Uxmal; ◷9am-1pm Mon-Fri) For visa and tourist permit extensions. Enter the left-hand, southernmost of the two offices.

Internet Access
Internet cafes in central Cancún are plentiful, speedy and cheap, costing M$10 per hour or less.

Laundry
Lavandería Tulum (Av Tulum; per kg M$16)

Left Luggage
Pay-in-advance lockers (per 24hr M$110) At the airport, just outside customs at the international arrivals area.

Medical Services
Centro Médico Caribe Cancún (☑883-92-57; Av Yaxchilán 74A; ◷24hr)

Money
There are several banks with ATMs on Avenida Tulum (Map p256), between Avenidas Cobá and Uxmal.

Post
Main post office (off Map p256; cnr Avs Xel-Há & Sunyaxchén; ◷8am-6pm Mon-Fri, 9am-1pm Sat)

COSTA VS RIVIERA

Traveling through the coastal region of Quintana Roo you're likely to see two phrases bandied about heavily by the tourist industry – the Costa Maya and the Riviera Maya. While they're occasionally used interchangeably, they are in fact two distinct regions. The Costa Maya is about 100km of beachfront stretching from Xcalak in the south to Reserva de la Biosfera Sian Ka'an in the north. The Riviera Maya begins at the northern boundary of the Costa Maya and stretches north to Cancún (or further, depending on which real estate brochure you're reading).

Telephone

Phoning by Voice Over Internet Protocol (VOIP) such as Skype can be done at most internet cafes.

Bancomer (Map p256; Av Tulum 150)

Call Center (Map p256; Soberanis Hostal, Av Cobá 5) Offers good rates on international calls and calls to other parts of Mexico.

Tourist Information

The Cancún Visitors Bureau has an informative website, www.cancun.travel, but it does not have a tourism office open to the general public.

City Tourism Office (Map p256; ☑887-33-79; www.cancun.gob.mx, in Spanish; Av Cobá; ⊕8am-6pm Mon-Fri, 9am-2pm Sat) Near Avenida Tulum; it has tons of printed materials.

Websites

Lonely Planet (www.lonelyplanet.com/mexico/cancun) Planning advice, author recommendations, traveler reviews and insider tips.

 ## Getting There & Away

Air

About 8km south of the city center, **Aeropuerto Internacional de Cancún** (Cancún International Airport; ☑886-00-47; www.cancun-airport.com) is the busiest airport in southeast Mexico. Following is a list of the main airlines servicing Cancún. In addition to the addresses for some shown here, these airlines also have airline counters at the airport unless otherwise stated. A full list can be found at www.cancun-airport.com/airlines-directory.htm.

Air Canada (☑800-719-28-27 www.aeromexico.com; Av Cobá 80)

Air Tran (☑800-965-21-07; www.airtran.com)

American Airlines (☑887-31-87; www.aa.com; Plaza Hollywood, Centro)

Continental Airlines (☑886-01-69; www.continental.com)

Copa (☑886-06-52; www.copaair.com)

Cubana (Map p256; ☑887-72-10; www.cubana.cu; Av Tulum 232) No airport counter.

Delta Airlines (☑800-123-47-10, 886-06-60; www.delta.com)

United Airlines (☑800-003-07-77; www.united.com)

US Airways (☑886-04-99; www.usairways.com)

Boat

There are several points of embarkation to reach Isla Mujeres from Cancún by boat. For fares and details, see table, p264.

Bus

From the **bus terminal** (Map p256; cnr Avs Uxmal & Tulum) services are available in 1st and 2nd class, and in several luxury options. *Colectivos* (set-route minibuses) for Playa del Carmen (M$30) leave every half hour (or when full) from the parking lot north of Comercial Mexicana, across Avenida Tulum from the bus terminal. See the table for major bus daily routes.

Boletotal (☑800-009-90-90; boletotal.mx) is an excellent online source of up-to-date bus schedules.

Car & Motorcycle

Rental-car agencies with facilities at the airport and La Isla Shopping Village in the Zona Hotelera include **Avis** (☑886-02-21 airport, 998-176-80-30 Zona Hotelera) and **Hertz** (☑800-405-70-00 airport, 998-176-80-77 Zona Hotelera). It's worth inquiring about promotions and added costs – the daily rate can vary by as much as M$400 between companies. Hwy 180D, the 238km toll (*cuota*) road running much of the way between Cancún and Mérida, costs M$368 for the distance and has only two exits before the end. The first, at Valladolid, costs M$233 to reach from Cancún, and the second, at Pisté (for Chichén Itzá), is an additional M$57.

 ## Getting Around

To/From the Airport

ADO buses (M$45 to downtown, M$150 to Playa del Carmen), airport shuttles (M$150 per person to downtown) and vans (M$476 per van to downtown) wait outside the departures area of Terminals 2 and 3.

Taxis into town or to the Zona Hotelera will cost around M$500 (up to four people) if you catch them right outside the airport. If you follow the access road out of the airport, however, and past the traffic-monitoring booth (a total

BUSES FROM CANCÚN

DESTINATION	FARE (M$)	DURATION	FREQUENCY (DAILY)
Chetumal	198-284	5½-6½hr	frequent 2nd class
Chichén Itzá	97	3-4hr	hourly Oriente
Chiquilá	80	3½hr	7:50am Mayab
Felipe Carrillo Puerto	120	3½-4hr	hourly Mayab
Mérida	80-322	4-6hr	15 ADO, hourly Oriente
Mexico City (Terminal Norte)	1410-1640	24hr	3 ADO & ADO GL
Mexico City (TAPO)	1350-1640	22-24hr	2 ADO
Palenque	312-478	12-13hr	3 ADO & OCC
Playa del Carmen	30-38	1-1¼hr	every 15min 5am-midnight Riviera, Playa Express & Mayab
Puerto Morelos	18		use Playa del Carmen buses
Ticul	212	6hr	12 Mayab
Tizimín	92	3-4hr	7 Noreste & Mayab
Tulum	68-92	2¼-3hr	frequent ADO & Mayab
Valladolid	136	2-3hr	frequent ADO
Villahermosa	686-826	12hr	9 ADO & ADO GL

trip of about 300m), you can often flag down an empty taxi that is leaving the airport and it will take you into town for much less (you can try for M$100).

Colectivos head to the airport from a stand in front of the Hotel Cancún Handall on Avenida Tulum about a block south of Avenida Cobá. They charge M$25 per person and leave when full. The official rate for private taxis is M$170.

Bus

To reach the Zona Hotelera from downtown, catch any bus with 'R1,' 'Hoteles' or 'Zona Hotelera' displayed on the windshield as it travels along Avenida Tulum toward Avenida Cobá, then eastward on Avenida Cobá. The one-way fare is M$8.50, but since change is often unavailable this varies between M$8 and M$9. The air-conditioned white Bus One also runs between the Zona Hotelera and downtown, charging M$11.

To reach Puerto Juárez and the Isla Mujeres ferries, catch a Ruta 13 ('Pto Juárez' or 'Punta Sam'; M$8.50) bus heading north on Avenida Tulum. Some R1 buses make this trip as well; tickets cost M$9.50.

Taxi

Cancún's taxis don't have meters. Fares are set, but always agree on a price before getting in. From downtown to Punta Cancún is around M$130, to Puerto Juárez M$60. Hourly and daily rates should run about M$200 and M$2000 respectively.

Isla Mujeres

☎998 / POP 16,000

If you are going to visit just one of Quintana Roo's islands, then Isla Mujeres (Island of Women) is probably the place for you. It's not as crowded as Cozumel, yet offers more to do and see than uber-laidback Holbox. Sure, there are quite a few ticky-tacky tourist shops, but folks still get around by golf cart and the crushed-coral beaches are better than those of Cozumel or Holbox. There's not much here, and that's the whole point: come to bask in quiet shallows or stretch out on the sand, to snorkel or scuba dive, or just to put the sunglasses on and open that book you've been dying to finish.

◉ Sights & Activities

Museo Capitán Dulché   MUSEUM
(Map p260; Carretera a Garrafón Km 4.5; admission M$80; ⊙10am-8pm) Detailing the naval history of the island, this museum has some great old photographs including the bizarre US invasion of Veracruz in 1914 and the

Isla Mujeres

Punta Norte

Playa Norte

Playa Pancholo

Car Ferries to Punta Sam (6km)

Ultrafreeze

Ferry to Puerto Juárez (10km)

Ferries to Cancún's Zona Hotelera (13km)

CARIBBEAN SEA

Laguna Makax

Bahía de Mujeres

Salina Grande

Isla Mujeres Turtle Farm

Playa Pescador

Arrecife Manchones

Museo Capitán Dulché

Hacienda Mundaca

Playa Lancheros

Playa Indios

Hotel Garrafón de Castilla

Playa Garrafón Parque Natural

Punta Sur

Maya Ruins

La Bandera

Punta Sur

establishment of the first naval base on the island in 1940.

Beaches

Playa Norte   BEACH, SWIMMING
Once you reach Playa Norte (Map p262), the island's main beach, you won't want to leave. Its warm, shallow waters are the color of blue-raspberry syrup and the beach is crushed coral.

Playa Lancheros   BEACH, SWIMMING
Five kilometers south of town is Playa Lancheros (Map p260), the southernmost point served by local buses. The beach is less attractive than Playa Norte, but it sometimes has free musical festivities on Sunday. A taxi ride from town to Lancheros is M$40.

Playa Garrafón Parque Natural   BEACH, PARK
(Map p260; www.garrafon.com; admission M$739 plus M$38 marine park use fee; ◷10am-5pm) Another 1.5km south of Playa Lancheros is Playa Garrafón Parque Natural, an all-inclusive 'reef park' where the steep admission fee gets you snorkeling, a buffet, bar access and some other things, but the star of the show – the over-the-water zip-line – costs an additional M$65. Nearby and a lot more down to earth, the Hotel Garrafón de Castilla (Map p260; ☎877-01-07; Carretera Punta Sur Km 6; admission M$50; ◷9am-5pm) provides chairs, umbrellas, showers and baths for the entrance fee. Snorkeling gear is M$70 extra and the hotel rents lockers and towels. Taxis from town cost M$78.

Punta Sur   BEACH, VIEWPOINT
At Punta Sur, on the southern tip of the island, you'll find a romantic lighthouse and the severely worn remains of a temple dedicated to Ixchel. You can admire the view for free from the 'Maya Sculpture' Garden at the left of the parking lot. Paying the M$30 admission fee gets you up close to the temple, as well as access to the more interesting contemporary sculpture park located on the point. A stone seaside path winds past small caves and back to the Playa Garrafón park. From Isla Mujeres town, a taxi costs M$85.

Diving & Snorkeling
Within a short boat ride of the island there's a handful of lovely dives, such as **Barracuda**, **La Bandera**, **El Jigueo**, **Ultrafreeze** and **Arrecife Manchones**. You can expect to see sea turtles, rays and barracuda, along with a wide array of hard and soft corals.

Snorkeling with whale sharks (around M$1500) just off Isla Contoy is the latest craze. The season runs from July through September. Folks at the dive shops listed below can arrange your trip.

To protect and preserve the reefs, an M$38 fee is charged for all diving and swimming. At all of the reputable dive centers you need to show your certification card, and you will be expected to have your own gear.

Aqua Adventures   DIVING, SNORKELING
(Map p262; ☎877-16-15; www.diveislamujeres.com; Plaza Almendras 10, Hidalgo) Offers two-tank dives (M$850), a resort course (M$1115) and PADI open-water certification (M$4200).

DREAM GREEN BY VISITING ISLA MUJERES TURTLE FARM

Three species of sea turtle lay eggs in the sand along Isla Mujeres' calm western shore, and they are now being protected – one *tortuguita* (little turtle) at a time.

In the 1980s, efforts by a local fisherman led to the founding of the **Isla Mujeres Turtle Farm** (Isla Mujeres Tortugranja; Map p260; Carretera Sac Bajo Km 5; admission M$30; ⊙9am-5pm), 5km south of town, which protects the turtles' breeding grounds and places wire cages around their eggs to protect against predators. Here you can see turtles in various stages of the growth cycle and other maritime specimens (and it would take a very hardened traveler indeed not to let out a little 'ooh' at the baby seahorses).

If you're driving, cycling or walking from the bus stop, bear right at the 'Y' just beyond Hacienda Mundaca's parking lot (the turn is marked by a tiny sign). The facility is easily reached from town by taxi (M$48).

Sea Hawk Divers DIVING, SNORKELING
(Map p262; ☑877-02-96; www.isla-mujeres.net/seahawkdivers; Carlos Lazo) Offers one-tank dive from M$660, two-tanks from M$825, resort courses (M$1065), PADI open-water certification (M$3850), snorkeling tours from M$315 and fishing tours from M$4340.

The fisherfolk of Isla Mujeres have formed a cooperative to offer snorkeling tours of various sites including the reef off Playa Garrafón, whale shark tours (M$1065) and day trips to Isla Contoy for M$815. You can book through the **Fisherman's Cooperative Booth** (Map p262; Av Rueda Medina) in a small office at the entrance to the dock.

🛏 Sleeping

Poc-Na Hostel HOSTEL $
(Map p262; ☑877-00-90; www.pocna.com; cnr Matamoros & Carlos Lazo; dm with fan/air-con M$105/160, r without bathroom M$270, s/d with air-con & bathroom M$290/350; ❈@🛜) Poc-Na Hostel is only moments away from one of the island's nicest beaches and it is lovingly decorated with shells and hibiscus flowers. It's an example-setting hostel, and once the pool is constructed will be even better.

Hotel Villa Kiin HOTEL $$
(Map p262; ☑877-10-24; www.villakiin.com; Zazil-Ha 129; r with fan/air-con M$620/740, bungalows M$937-1237; 🛜) Great bungalows, ordinary rooms and what would be a superb sea view if not for the monstrous resort hotel built on the island just out front. Rates include continental breakfast and snorkeling gear.

Apartments Trinchan APARTMENT $
(Map p262; ☑877-08-56; atrinchan@prodigy.net.mx; Carlos Lazo 46; r with fan/air-con M$350/450, apt from M$400; ❈🛜) Forget the downtown cheapo hotels with their cramped rooms and musty smells – the spacious digs here are one of the best budget deals on the island.

Hotel Na Balam HOTEL $$$
(Map p262; ☑881-47-70; www.nabalam.com; Zazil-Ha 118; pool front/beachfront M$1250/1500; ❈🛜🏊) Butterflies flit around the beautiful hibiscus and palm garden, and many rooms face Playa Norte. All rooms are decorated with simple elegance and have safes, hammocks, private balconies or patios...and no TVs. The hotel offers yoga and meditation classes (M$120) as well as providing massage services.

Hotel Rocamar HOTEL $$
(Map p262; ☑877-01-01; www.rocamar-hotel.com; cnr Bravo & Guerrero; r from M$600; ❈🛜) Almost achingly modern rooms (the goldfish-bowl bathrooms may not appeal if you're sharing with a casual acquaintance) featuring private balconies with panoramic sea views. Prices drop dramatically in the off-season.

Hotel Belmar HOTEL $$
(Map p262; ☑877-04-30; www.rolandi.com; Hidalgo 110; s/d M$687/741; ❈🛜) Set upstairs above the busy Rolandi's restaurant (making rooms slightly noisy but delicious-smelling), this is a good deal for the price – rooms aren't huge, but they're well decorated and comfortable. Some rooms at the front have balconies.

Hotel Bucanero's HOTEL $$
(Map p262; ☑877-12-28; www.bucaneros.com; Hidalgo 11; r M$585-750; ❈🛜) There are some funky touches to the decor here, and the location's a winner. Cheapest rooms have double beds but are really designed for one person (or two very skinny ones).

Isla Mujeres (Town)

Hotel Playa La Media Luna
HOTEL $$$

(Map p262; ☎877-07-59; www.playamedialuna. com; Sección Rocas, Lotes 9 & 10 Punta Norte; r M$1200-2059, bungalows with kitchen M$3200; ❄@☎≋) This big, beachfront hotel maintains an intimate feel through clever design, driftwood decorations and wooden walkways connecting the rooms. Standard rooms are fine – upgrade to the presidential for an ocean-view Jacuzzi on your private balcony.

✖ Eating

TOP CHOICE Mañana
CAFE $

(Map p262; cnr Matamoros & Guerrero; dishes M$25-80; ☺8am-4pm; ☑) A good-vibe place with colorful hand-painted tables, super-friendly service and some excellent veggie options (the hummus and veggie baguette is the restaurant's signature dish). Mañana is perhaps the best lunch spot on the island. Also sells books.

Viva Cuba Libre
CUBAN $$

(Map p262; Plaza Almendros, Hidalgo; mains M$90-150; ☺5pm-midnight Tue-Sun) Has excellent, authentic Cuban food (with a couple of Mexican faves thrown in) is on offer at this casual streetside diner. The *camarones en mojo criollo* (shrimp in Creole sauce) will keep you coming back.

Como No
FUSION $$

(Map p262; Hidalgo; mains M$80-150; ☺noon-11pm) Features one of the more interesting menus on the island, with influences from Asian, Mediterranean and Mexican cuisine. Live music most nights draws a crowd.

Café del Mar
INTERNATIONAL $$$

(Map p262; Av Rueda Medina; mains M$150-300; ☺10am-midnight) The loungiest and beach-clubbiest place on the island also has some of the best food, with a small but inventive fusion menu focusing on salads, seafood and pastas. The deck chairs and beach beds are

Isla Mujeres (Town)

a great place to finish off that daiquiri (and maybe order another).

For cheap eats, check the **Mercado Municipal** (Town Market; Map p262; Guerrero) during the day and the food stalls on the plaza outside the Iglesia de la Inmaculada Concepción at night.

Drinking & Entertainment

Isla Mujeres' highest concentration of nightlife is along Hidalgo, and hot spots on or near the beach form an arc around the northern edge of town.

Buho's   BAR
(Map p262; Playa Norte; ⊙9am-10pm or later) The quintessential swing-bar experience.

Poc-Na Hostel   BAR
(Map p262; cnr Matamoros & Lazo; ⊙sunset-sunrise) Has a beachfront joint with bonfires, and more hippies than all the magic buses in the world.

La Luna   DANCE
(Map p262; Guerrero; ⊙7pm-3am or later) Starts late, but gets going with the great music.

ℹ Information

Hospital Integral Isla Mujeres (Guerrero) Between Madero and Morelos.

HSBC Bank (Av Rueda Medina)

Ixchel Internet cafe (cnr Matamoros & Guerrero; per hr M$10; ⊙9am-10pm Mon-Sat)

Lavandería Mis Dos Angelitos (cnr Guerrero & Mateos; ⊙8am-11pm Mon-Sat) Two-hour wash and dry for M$10 per kilo.

Police (☏877-04-58)

Post office (Map p262; cnr Guerrero & López Mateos; ⊙9am-4pm Mon-Fri)

Tourist information office (Map p262; ☏877-03-07; Av Rueda Medina; ⊙8am-8pm Mon-Fri, 9am-2pm Sat & Sun)

ℹ Getting There & Away

There are several points of embarkation to reach Isla Mujeres. Punta Sam (off Map p254), about 8km north of Cancún center, is the only one that accepts vehicles. Walk-ons and vehicle passengers pay M$35; drivers are included in the fare for cars (M$256), as are riders in the fare for motorcycles (M$87) and bicycles (M$82). The ride takes about an hour (see also table, p264). To get to Punta Sam or Puerto Juárez (4km north of Cancún), catch any bus (M$8.50) displaying those destinations and/or 'Ruta 13' as it heads north on Avenida Tulum. Some R1 (Zona Hotelera; M$9.50) buses make the trip as well; ask before boarding.

Three docks in the Zona Hotelera have departures for Isla Mujeres:

El Embarcadero (Map p254; Blvd Kukulcán Km 4)

Playa Tortugas (Map p254; Blvd Kukulcán Km 7)

Playa Caracol (Map p254; Blvd Kukulcán Km 9.5)

ℹ Getting Around

Bicycle

Cycling is a great way to get around the island. A number of shops rent bikes for about M$30/120 an hour/day. Some places ask for a deposit of about M$100. **David** (☏cell phone 998-2231365; cnr Matamoros & Guerrero) has a decent selection.

Bus & Taxi

Local buses depart about every 25 minutes (but don't bank on it) from a bus stop next to the Centro de Convenciones (near the back of the market) or from the ferry dock and head along Avenida Rueda Medina, stopping along the way. You can get to the entrance of Hacienda Mundaca, within 300m of the Turtle Farm (Tortugranja), and as far south as Playa Lancheros (1.5km north of Playa Garrafón). Get taxis from the stand at the dock or flag one down. Rates

YUCATÁN PENINSULA ISLA MUJERES

PASSENGER FERRIES FROM CANCÚN TO ISLA MUJERES

DEPARTS FROM	FARE (M$)	DURATION	FREQUENCY
El Embarcadero	125	25min	6 daily between 9am and 4:30pm
Playa Caracol	125	25min	4 daily between 10:10am and 4:50pm
Playa Tortugas	125	25min	hourly 9am-5pm
Puerto Juárez	70	25min	every 30min 5am-8:30pm, then hourly until 11:30pm

are set by the municipal government and posted at the taxi stand just south of the passenger ferry dock. As always, agree on a price before getting in.

Scooter & Golf Cart

Inspect the scooter carefully before renting. Costs vary, and are sometimes jacked up in high season, but generally start at about M$100 per hour, with a two-hour minimum, and M$400 all day (9am to 5pm).

Many people find golf carts a good way to get around the island, and convoys of them can be seen tooling down the roads. They average M$200 per hour and M$600 all day (9am to 5pm). **Gomar** (⌨877-16-86; cnr Av Rueda Medina & Bravo) has a good selection of scooters and golf carts in varying sizes.

Parque Nacional Isla Contoy

Spectacular Isla Contoy is a bird lover's delight: a national park and sanctuary that is an easy day trip from Isla Mujeres. About 800m at its widest point and more than 7km long, it has dense foliage that provides ideal shelter for more than 100 species of birds, including brown pelicans, olive cormorants, turkeys, brown boobies and frigates, and is a good place to see red flamingos, snowy egrets and white herons.

Most of the trips stop for snorkeling both en route to and just off Contoy, which sees about 1500 visitors a month. Bring binoculars, mosquito repellent and sunscreen.

For M$140 per person, a park biologist will take you on a tour of Laguna Puerto Viejo, a prime nesting site; funds go toward park upkeep and research projects. Contact the **park headquarters** (⌨998-877-15-13; cnr Rueda Medina & Madero) on Isla Mujeres. **Amigos de Isla Contoy** (⌨998-884-74-83; www.amigosdeisla contoy.org; Plaza Bonita loc E1) has an office in downtown Cancún, and its website has good information on the island's ecology.

ⓘ Getting There & Away

Daily visits to Contoy are offered by the **Fisherman's Cooperative Booth** (Map p262; ⌨998-877-13-63; Av Rueda Medina) on Isla Mujeres. The trip (M$815 per person) lasts from 9am to 5pm and includes a light breakfast, lunch (with fish caught en route), snorkeling (gear provided), park admission, scientific information on the island, and your choice of purified water, soft drinks or beer.

Isla Holbox

⌨984 / POP 1500

Isn't life great when it's low-fi and low-rise? That's the attitude on friendly Isla Holbox (pronounced 'hol-bosh'), with its sand streets, colorful Caribbean buildings and lazing, sun-drunk dogs. The water is not the translucent turquoise common to Quintana Roo beaches, because here the Caribbean mingles with the darker Gulf of Mexico.

The island is about 30km long and from 500m to 2km wide, with seemingly endless beaches, tranquil waters and a galaxy of shells in various shapes and colors. Lying within the 1541-sq-km Yum Balam reserve, Holbox is home to more than 150 species of bird, including roseate spoonbills, pelicans, herons, ibis and flamingos. In summer, whale sharks congregate relatively nearby in numbers unheard of elsewhere.

🛏 Sleeping

Budget hotels are clustered around the plaza in Holbox town. Upscale accommodations are scattered along the beachfront on the island's northern shore in what locals call the Zona Hotelera.

TOP CHOICE **Casa Takywara**   HOTEL $$

(⌨875-23-52; www.takywara.com; r from M$1050; ❀❂) Out at the quiet, southern end of town, this beautiful hotel features simple, stylishly decorated rooms with kitchenette

A GAME OF DOMINOES – SWIM WITH THE WHALE SHARKS

Between mid-May and mid-September, massive whale sharks congregate around Isla Holbox to feed on plankton. Locals call them dominoes because of their speckled skin.

The best time to swim with these gentle giants is in July. A trip will cost you M$900, plus M$20 to visit the marine reserve.

When swimming with the whale sharks only three swimmers (including your guide) are allowed in the water at a time. You are not allowed to touch the fish, and are required to wear either a life jacket or wetsuit to ensure you do not dive below the shark.

Turística Moguel (☑984-875-20-28; www.holboxislandtours.com; cnr Avs Tiburón Ballena & Banero), operating out of the minimarket on the plaza in Holbox, offers whale shark tours (M$900 per person). Ask to stop for a quick snorkel on the way back from your trip – the guides will normally agree to this.

and sea-view balconies. It's built next to a patch of protected wetlands, which is home to a pet crocodile.

Hostel Tribu   HOSTEL **$**
(☑875-25-07; www.tribuhostel.com; Coldwell 6; dm/r M$130/350; @🛜) The best hostel in town has six-person dorms, a cinema, bar, well-stocked kitchen and fantastic sunset views from the roof terrace.

Casa Sandra   BOUTIQUE HOTEL **$$$**
(☑875-21-71; www.casasandra.com; r incl breakfast M$4000-5550; ✳🛜✲) Holbox's best boutique hotel, this Cuban-owned place has a pleasant, lyrical feel, art-packed walls, sumptuously appointed rooms and individual service. It's on the beachfront, a few hundred meters north of town.

Casa Lupita   HOTEL **$$**
(☑875-20-17; casalupitaholbox@gmail.com; r from M$700; ste from M$700; ✳🛜) An excellent midrange option right on the plaza (and a block and a half from the beach). Rooms here are spacious and catch good breezes, and suites have private balconies overlooking the plaza.

✖ Eating

Ky Waa   BAKERY **$**
(Tiburón Ballena, Plaza El Pueblito; sandwiches M$85-120; ⊘7am-midnight) For a good range of breakfasts, fresh-from-the-oven baked goods and yummy sandwiches, grab a table on the breezy deck outside this Brazilian-run bakery/cafe.

La Guaya   ITALIAN **$$$**
(Tiburón Ballena, Plaza El Pueblito; mains M$160-350; ⊘noon-11pm) The finest dining in town comes from the longtime Holbox-resident Italian couple who run this friendly little place out back of the town's 'mall.' Everything is good – if it looks a little pricey, check out their lasagna restaurant, around the corner.

Raices   SEAFOOD **$$**
(mains M$120-260; ⊘1-9pm) Don't let the humble surrounds of this beachfront eatery put you off – this is some of the best seafood in town. The coconut lobster is definitely worth a look, but the traditional Maya Tikinxic fish is the star of the show.

Pizzería Edelyn   PIZZERIA **$$**
(cnr Palomino & Díaz; pizzas M$80-300; ⊘noon-11pm) Lobster pizza – anywhere else it would be obscene, but on Holbox it just feels right. It seems everybody is serving it, but this simple indoor/outdoor pizza joint on the plaza is always busy, and for a very good reason.

❶ Information

Bancomer has an ATM on the 2nd story of the Alcaldía on the plaza. There's another one in the Hotel Palapa. Sometimes they both run out of money (particularly on weekends), so it's a good idea to bring enough cash to float your trip.

Café Mi Capricio (Tiburón Ballena; per hr M$12; ⊘8am-6pm) Has reasonable-speed internet and offers bike rentals (M$20/120 per hour/day).

Emergency (☑066)

❶ Getting There & Around

A *barco* (boat) ferries passengers (M$70, 25 minutes) to Holbox from the port village of Chiquilá 11 times daily during the week with a couple of extra services on weekends. The last boat leaves Chiquilá at 8pm. Buses departing Chiquilá usually wait for the boat to arrive. Smaller, faster and wetter *lanchas* (motorboats) make the crossing whenever anyone's willing to pay M$350 to

M$400 for the entire boat (up to about six people with gear; the fare is higher after dark).

Buses (all 2nd-class) leave Chiquilá for Cancún (M$80, 3½ hours) at 5:30am and 1:30pm; Tizimín (M$70, 2½ to four hours) at 5:30am and 7:30am; and Valladolid (M$80, 2½ hours) at 5:30am.

If you're driving, you can either park your vehicle in the Chiquilá parking lot for M$50 per day (8am to 6pm or any fraction thereof) or take your chances parking it on the pier (which is crowded in high season).

Rentadora El Brother (✆875-20-18; cart per hr/day/24hr M$100/600/700), on Juárez near the beach, rents golf carts.

Puerto Morelos

✆998 / POP 3200

Halfway between Cancún and Playa del Carmen, Puerto Morelos retains its quiet, small-town feel despite the building boom north and south of town. While the village offers enough restaurants and bars to keep you entertained by night, it's really the shallow Caribbean waters that draw visitors here. Another reason to come is to hit the artisans' market, one block south of the plaza's west corner.

There's an HSBC ATM on the plaza.

◉ Sights & Activities

Jardín Botánico Yaax Che   GARDENS
(adult/child M$100/50; ⊙8am-4pm Mon-Sat) Two kilometers south of the turnoff for Puerto Morelos is this 600,000-sq-meter nature reserve with nearly 3km of trails through several native habitats.

Boca del Puma   PARK
(✆241-28-55; www.bocadelpuma.com) For ziplining, horseback riding and chilling cenote (limestone sinkhole filled with rainwater) action, check out the 'ecopark' Boca del Puma near the village of Vallarta, 16km west of Puerto Morelos.

Dive Puerto Morelos   DIVING
(✆206-90-84; www.divepuertomorelos.com; ⊙8am-7pm) Offers dive trips (from M$510/954 one-/two-tank dive), PADI certification (M$5090), cenote diving and other dive-related services.

☞ Tours

Goyo's   JUNGLE
(✆221-26-79) Offers jungle tours (adult/child under 12 years M$400/200).

☕ Courses

Little Mexican Cooking School   COOKING
(✆251-80-60; www.thelittlemexicancookingschool. com; Quintana Roo 79) Has small-group cooking classes.

Spanish Language Center   LANGUAGE
(✆871-01-62; www.puertomoraleslanguagecenter. com; Av Niños Héroes 41) Offers group and private Spanish classes.

🛏 Sleeping

Posada Amor   HOTEL $
(✆871-00-33; posada.amor@hotmail.com; Av Gómez 3; r with fan/air-con M$300/600; ✱) Cute and fresh little stone rooms about half a block from the plaza. Ask for one at the back as the bar up front can get noisy.

Hacienda Morelos   HOTEL $$
(✆871-04-48; www.haciendamorelos.com; d M$900-1500; ✱❄☎✉) With a fantastic location right on the beach and a short walk from the plaza, the large, rather plain rooms here are a good bet. Those upstairs share a narrow balcony, but downstairs you have the pool and beach right outside your door.

Posada El Moro   HOTEL $$
(✆871-01-59; www.posadaelmoro.com; Av Gómez 17; r with fan/air-con from M$750/875; ☎✉) The biggest hotel in the center is also one of the comfiest, with wonderful jungle-like grounds, an inviting pool area and a good range of rooms a short walk from the plaza.

🍴 Eating

Café d'Amancia   CAFE $
(bagels & croissants M$40-55; ⊙8am-3pm & 6-10pm; ✉) This is a spotlessly clean place with pleasing ambience on the southwest corner of the plaza. It serves bagels, sandwiches, pies, good coffee, and fruit and veggie *licuados* (milkshakes).

El Pirata   MEXICAN $
(mains M$15-30; ⊙7am-midnight) Duck under the *palapa* roof at this plaza-side joint, pull up a plastic chair and enjoy some back-home Mexican cooking.

John Gray's Kitchen   INTERNATIONAL $$
(✆871-06-65; Av Niños Héroes 6; mains M$100-200; ⊙6-10pm Mon-Sat) One block west and two blocks north of the plaza, this eclectic 'kitchen' turns out some truly fabulous food.

THE RIVIERA FUN PARKS

In an area bursting with natural attractions, it may seem odd that 'ecoparks' are such huge business. Or considering the scale of tourism in the region, it may not. The road from Cancún to Tulum is dotted with these places, and while they're a little too Disney for some, the mix of adventure, activities and low-risk interaction with nature make them a pretty fun day out, particularly if you've got the kids along. Following is a list of some of the best.

Selvática (✆998-847-45-81; www.selvatica.com.mx; Ruta de los Cenotes Km 19; adult/child 5-12yr M$1380/685) An award-winning zip-line park about 16km west of Puerto Morales that takes you through the jungle on a circuit of 12 lines, the longest being 350m, the highest 20m. Then cool off in a private cenote.

Hidden Worlds (✆984-877-85-35; www.hiddenworlds.com; Carretera 307 Km 116; basic admission adult/child 5-11yr M$1100/550; ⊗9am-5pm) Zip-lines, sky cycles, rappelling, snorkel tours and various other innovative, cenote-focused options. Good for older kids. It's located 25km south of Playa del Carmen.

Xplor (✆998-251-65-60; www.xplor.travel; Carretera 307 Km 282; basic admission adult/child 6-11yr M$1327/663; ⊗9am-6pm) Six kilometers south of Playa del Carmen, this park features seven circuits take you zip-lining, rafting, driving amphibious jeeps and swimming in an underground river.

Río Secreto (✆984-877-23-77; www.riosecreto.com; Carretera 307 Km 283.5; basic admission adult/child 6-11yr M$960/480; ⊗9am-6pm) Hike and swim through a 600m-long underground cavern 5km south of Playa del Carmen.

Aktun Chen (✆998-881-94-13; www.aktunchen.com; Carretera 307 Km 107; cave, cenote & canopy package adult/child 5-12yr M$1352/675; ⊗9am-5pm Mon-Sat) Forty kilometers south of Playa del Carmen, this smaller park features a 600m-long cave, a 12m-deep cenote, 10 zip-lines and a small zoo.

Xcaret (✆998-883-04-70; www.xcaret.com; Carretera 307 Km 282; basic admission adult/child 5-12yr M$1100/550; ⊗8:30am-9pm) One of the originals in the area, with loads of nature-based activities and stuff for the grown-ups like the Mexican wine cellar and day spa. It's located 6km south of Playa del Carmen.

Xel-Há (✆998-884-71-65; www.xel-ha.com; Carretera 307 Km 240; basic admission adult/child 5-11yr M$1100/550; ⊗9am-6pm) Billing itself as the world's largest outdoor aquarium, built around a natural inlet 13km north of Tulum. There are lots of water-based activities on offer.

Asiaki ASIAN **$$**
(mains M$100-160; ⊗1-10pm Wed-Mon) Longtime visitors were alarmed when local institution Hola Asia changed hands, but it seems the only thing that changed was the name – the eclectic Asian menu is the same and the food is as yummy as ever.

 Shopping

Alma Libre Bookstore BOOKS
(✆871-07-13; www.almalibrebooks.com; ⊗10am-3pm & 6-9pm Tue-Sat, 4-9pm Sun, closed Jul-Sep) Offers a fantastic selection of new and used books, mostly in English but also in other European languages.

 Getting There & Away

Most Playa Express and Riviera buses that travel between Cancún and Playa del Carmen drop you on the highway, from where it's about 2km to the central plaza. Some Mayab buses enter town; the Riviera bus running between Cancún airport and Playa del Carmen will sometimes enter the town on request. The 2nd-class bus fare from Cancún is M$18.

Taxis are usually waiting at the turnoff to shuttle people into town (M$20), or you can wait for a *colectivo* (M$5) to happen past. In town, taxis and *colectivos* hang around the west side of the plaza.

Playa del Carmen
✆984 / POP 68,000

Playa del Carmen is the hippest city in all of the Yucatán Peninsula. Sitting coolly on the lee side of Cozumel, the town's beaches are the place to see and be seen by vacationing Europeans and the occasional American.

YUCATÁN PENINSULA PLAYA DEL CARMEN

The waters aren't as clear as those of Cancún or Cozumel, and the beach sands aren't quite as champagne-powder perfect as they are further north, but still Playa (as it's locally known) grows and grows.

With daily cruise-ship visitors, Playa is starting to feel like a mass-tourism destination, but it retains its European chic, and one need only head two blocks west of haughty Quinta Avenida to catch glimpses of the nontourist side of things.

◉ Sights & Activities

Beaches

Beachgoers will agree that it's pretty darn nice here. If crowds aren't your thing, go north of Calle 38, where a few scrawny palms serve for shade. Many go topless in Playa (though it's not a common practice in most of Mexico and generally frowned upon by locals – except the young bucks, of course); Mamita's Beach, north of Calle 28, is considered the best.

Diving & Snorkeling

Prices are similar at most outfits: resort dives (M$1110), one-tank dive (M$612), two-tank (M$987), cenote dive (M$1360), snorkeling (M$360), whale-shark tours (M$2438) and open-water certification (M$4315).

Dive Mike DIVING, SNORKELING
(✆803-12-28; www.divemike.com; Calle 8 btwn Av 5 & beach) A full-service dive operation.

Scuba Playa DIVING, SNORKELING
(✆803-31-23; www.scubaplaya.com; Calle 10 btwn Avs 1 & 5) Specializes in technical and cenote diving.

🎓 Courses

International House LANGUAGE
(✆803-33-88; www.ihrivieramaya.com; Calle 14 btwn Avs 5 & 10) Has Spanish classes (M$2750 for 20 hours per week) and can arrange accommodations and homestays with local families.

Playa Lingua del Caribe LANGUAGE
(✆873-38-76; www.playalingua.com; Calle 20 btwn Avs 5 & 10) Offers Spanish classes, cooking courses and accommodations half a block off La Quinta.

👉 Tours

Alltournative ADVENTURE
(✆803-99-99; www.alltournative.com; Hwy 307 Km 287; ⊙9am-7pm Mon-Sat) Offers packages that

include zip-lining, rappelling and kayaking, as well as custom-designed trips.

🛏 Sleeping

TOP CHOICE **Hotel Playa del Karma** HOTEL $$
(✆803-02-72; www.hotelplayadelkarma.com; Av 15 btwn Calles 12 & 14; r concrete/palapa roof M$700/800; [P ❄ @ 🖅 ☎]) The closest you're going to get to the jungle in this town, rooms here face a lush courtyard featuring a curly dip pool. More expensive rooms have TV, but the cheaper ones with thatched roofs are more atmospheric. All have sweet little porches with hammocks and sitting areas.

Kinbé Hotel HOTEL $$
(✆873-04-41; www.kinbe.com; Calle 10 btwn Avs 1 & 5; r from M$950; [❄ @ 🖅 ☎]) With a chic, modern design and a great location between the beach and Quinta Avenida, the standard rooms are a good deal here. If you're willing to upgrade, two-bedroom suites with private balconies overlook the pool.

Hotel Hacienda del Caribe HOTEL $$
(✆873-31-32; www.haciendadelcaribe.com; Calle 2 No 130; r from M$650; [❄ @ ☎]) One of the better deals in this price range, rooms here are spacious and brightly decorated and come fitted with room safes and two queen-size beds. The central courtyard is a shady spot to while away an hour in the small pool.

Hostel Río Playa HOSTEL $
(✆803-01-45; www.hostelrioplaya.com; Calle 8 btwn Avs 5 & 10; dm incl breakfast M$180, r without bathroom M$400; [❄ @ 🖅 ☎]) With a great rooftop bar/chillout space (featuring dipping pool), this hostel gets the guernsey for beach proximity, cleanliness and general atmosphere.

Hotel Deseo BOUTIQUE HOTEL $$$
(✆879-36-20; www.hoteldeseo.com; cnr Av 5 & Calle 12; r from M$1800; [❄ @ 🖅 ☎]) Hip and minimal seems to be the way forward for Playa's hotel scene, and this is a classic example – rooms are spacious and almost too white. The best ones have balconies out over Quinta Avenida. An equally hip bar operates in the patio, but rooms are carefully soundproofed in case you don't want to join the party.

Hotel Casa de las Flores HOTEL $$
(✆873-28-98; www.hotelcasadelasflores.com; 20 Av btwn Calles 4 & 6; r from M$900; [❄ 🖅 ☎]) With a good mix of colonial charm and modern comfort, this sizable but intimate hotel

offers big, fresh rooms set around a delightful plant-filled patio.

Posada Marinelly
HOTEL $

(☎873-10-40; Av Juárez 147; s/d with fan M$300/350, with air-con M$400/450) The best of the budget picks around the bus station, this one's clean and newish and set around a little garden. Rooms are big and bare with large windows – get one upstairs for a breeze.

Mosquito Blue
HOTEL $$$

(☎873-12-45; www.mosquitoblue.com; Calle 12; r incl continental breakfast with fan/air-con M$1040/1300; ❋@🖗) A bit more traditional than Playa's other boutique hotels, there's lots of heavy furniture, large artworks and hushed atmosphere here. The gardens – particularly the two pool areas – are well landscaped and guests are invited to use the hotel's private beach club, a few blocks away.

 Eating

Quinta Avenida has the highest concentration of restaurants, especially along its pedestrian stretch (the tourist zone). La Nueva Quinta, its continuation, is the newest pedestrian section. It begins at Calle 22 and stretches north for 10 blocks. Head out of the tourist zone to find cheap, quality eats such as great grilled chicken from **Asadero Olmeca** (Calle 2; mains M$35; ❂7am-6pm), next to the Tulum-bound *colectivos*. There's also a ton of cheap food stands on 10 Avenida between Calles 8 and 10 near the center.

Babe's
ASIAN $$

(Calle 10; mains M$100-180; ❂noon-11:30pm Mon-Sat, 5-11:30pm Sun; ☑) Babe's serves some excellent Thai food, including a really yummy home-style *tom kha gai* (chicken in a coconut-milk soup) brimming with veggies. The cocktail list isn't bad, either.

Yaxché
YUCATECAN $$

(☎803-29-36; cnr Av 5 & Calle 22; mains M$120-250; ❂noon-11pm) Focused on preserving Maya culinary culture, this large but atmospheric restaurant is probably the most original in town. Food isn't exactly out there, but there are some surprising combinations and little-known ingredients in use.

Capriccio Latino
ITALIAN $$

(Av 5 btwn Calle 26 & 28; breakfast M$50-70, mains M$130-180; ❂8am-2am) A cut wa.a.a.y above the rest of the Italian joints along the Riviera, this elegantly casual restaurant serves up a delicious line in the classics with some great contemporary twists. The breakfast menu rocks, as do the sandwiches and the tiramisu.

La Ceiba
CAFE $

(cnr Calle 20 & 30 Av; breakfast M$50-80; ❂7am-10pm Mon-Sat, 7am-2pm Sun) It's a bit of a walk

---

EXPLORE MORE SOUTH OF PLAYA DEL CARMEN

South of Playa del Carmen are several worthwhile coastal villages. These areas tend toward the upscale, and offer spectacular diving, snorkeling and some amazing beaches. Here are a few of our faves:

» **Rancho Punta Venado** (www.puntavenado.com) Five kilometers south of Xcaret, this is a great spot for horseback riding.

» **Paamul** Seventeen kilometers south of Playa del Carmen. The secluded beach makes this area popular with visiting RV travelers, sea turtles and divers alike. **Paamul Hotel** (www.paamul.com.mx) offers lodging and diving services.

» **Xpu-Há** This is a sugar-sweet beach area 38km south of Playa del Carmen.

» **Tankah** A few kilometers south of the Hwy 307 turnoff for Punta Solimán you'll find this cozy beach community. Visit www.tankah.com for info.

» **Xcacel-Xcacelito** Just 3km north of Xel-Há, this is the state's most important turtle-nesting beach. Come to **volunteer** (☎984-871-52-44; www.florafaunaycultura.org) with the turtle conservancy, or just to check out the lovely cenote and snorkeling found here.

» **Dos Ojos** Access this massive cave system with tours from **Cenote Dos Ojos** (www.cenotedosojos.com) or **Hidden Worlds** (www.hiddenworlds.com).

» **Bahías de Punta Solimán** These beautiful bays have basically been privatized, but you can still rent a house here – www.locogringo.com has a good offering.

Playa del Carmen

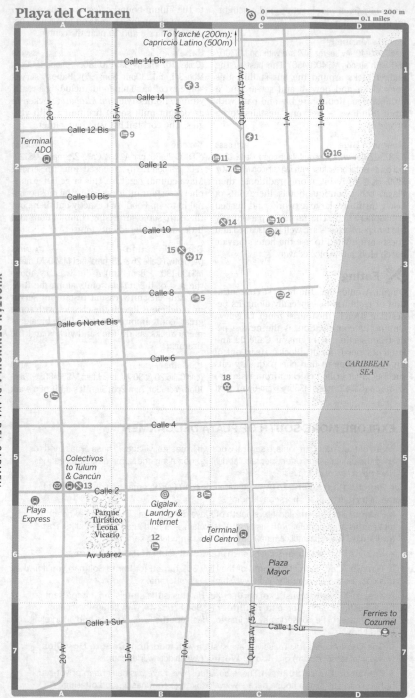

To Yaxché (200m);
Capriccio Latino (500m)

Calle 14 Bis

Calle 14

Calle 12 Bis

Terminal
ADO

Calle 12

Calle 10 Bis

Calle 10

Calle 8

Calle 6 Norte Bis

Calle 6

CARIBBEAN
SEA

Calle 4

Colectivos
to Tulum
& Cancún

Playa
Express

Parque
Turístico
Leona
Vicario

Gigalav
Laundry &
Internet

Terminal
del Centro

Plaza
Mayor

Av Juárez

Calle 1 Sur

Calle 1 Sur

Ferries to
Cozumel

20 Av

15 Av

10 Av

Quinta Av (5 Av)

1 Av

1 Av Bis

YUCATÁN PENINSULA PLAYA DEL CARMEN

Playa del Carmen

to get to this breezy open-air cafe set outside a whole-foods market, but it's well worth the effort. The breakfasts and tortas are delicious, there's a good range of snacks and huge fresh juices including 'energy drinks' made from traditional Maya medicinal plants. To get here, head northeast until you hit Calle 20, then follow it out of town (away from the sea) until 30 Avenida.

☆ Entertainment

The party generally starts on Quinta Avenida then heads down to the beach clubs. Walk along the beach between Calles 6 and 16 to see where the action is. An art walk takes place every Thursday on Quinta Avenida.

Playa 69   GAY
(www.rivieramayagay.com; Callejón off Quinta Av btwn Calles 4 & 6; ⊙to late Tue-Sun) This gay dance club has erratic hours and normally gets going late.

Blue Parrot   DANCE
(www.blueparrot.com; Calle 12 on beach; ⊙to late Tue-Sun) The biggest name among the beach clubs. There are a few in this area, making it easy to find one you like.

Pink Elephant   DANCE
(www.pinkelephantclub.com.mx; Av 10 btwn Calles 8 & 10; ⊙to late Tue-Sun) The most reliable off-beach club has live music on Sundays and big-name DJs on weekends. Check the website for details.

ⓘ Information
Banamex (cnr Calle 12 & 10 Av)
Centro de Salud (☑873-04-93; cnr 15 Av & Av Juárez)
Gigalav Laundry & Internet (Calle 2 No 402; ⊙8am-10pm Mon-Sat) Conveniently has an internet cafe (M$10 per hour) and *lavandería* (M$15 per kg).
Post office (cnr 20 Av & Calle 2; ⊙9am-4pm Mon-Fri)
Tourist information kiosks (cnr Constituyentes & Calle 18; Plaza Mayor) Tons of brochures, the occasional useful answer.

ⓘ Getting There & Away
Boat
Ferries to Cozumel (www.mexicowaterjets.com. mx; M$155 one way) leave hourly between 6am and 11pm. The air-conditioned catamaran takes about a half hour, depending on weather. Buy tickets at the booth on Calle 1 Sur. An open-air boat (same price but running less regularly) takes a bit longer and operates mostly in the summer season.

Bus
Playa has two bus terminals; each sells tickets and provides information for at least some of the other's departures. The newer one, **Terminal ADO** (20 Av), is where most 1st-class bus lines arrive and depart. Riviera's buses (which don't entirely deserve the designation '1st class' anyhow) use the old terminal. A taxi from Terminal ADO to the main plaza will cost about M$25.

All 2nd-class bus lines (including Mayab) are serviced at the old bus station, **Terminal del Centro** (cnr Av Juárez & Quinta Av). Riviera buses to Cancún and its airport have a separate ticket counter on the Avenida Juárez side of the terminal. The table shows some distances, travel times and prices for buses.
Playa Express (Calle 2 Norte) offers quick service to downtown Cancún for M$34.

Colectivo
Colectivos are a great option for cheap travel southward to Tulum (M$35, 45 minutes). They depart from Calle 2 near 20 Avenida as soon as they fill (about every 10 or 15 minutes) from 5am to 10pm. They will stop anywhere along the highway between Playa and Tulum, charging a minimum of M$15. Luggage space is somewhat limited, but they're great for day trips. From the

BUSES FROM PLAYA DEL CARMEN

DESTINATION	FARE (M$)	DURATION	FREQUENCY (DAILY)
Cancún	45	1hr	frequent ADO & Mayab
Cancún airport	150	1hr	frequent ADO
Chetumal	226-270	5-5½hr	frequent ADO & Mayab
Chichén Itzá	256	3-4hr	ADO 8am
Cobá	84	1-1¾hr	2 ADO
Mérida	190-528	5hr	frequent ADO & ADO GL
Palenque	592-706	12-13hr	3 ADO GL & ADO GL
San Cristóbal de Las Casas	792-856	16-18hr	3 ADO GL & ADO GL
Tulum	60	1hr	frequent Riviera & Mayab
Valladolid	96-140	2½-3½hr	frequent ADO & Mayab

same spot, you can grab a *colectivo* to Cancún (M$30) or Akumal (M$30).

Isla Cozumel

✔ 987 / POP 93,000

An immensely popular diving spot since 1961, when Jacques Cousteau, led by local guides, showed its spectacular reefs to the world, Cozumel lies 71km south of Cancún. Measuring 53km by 14km, it is Mexico's third-largest island. Called Ah-Cuzamil-Peten (Island of Swallows) by its earliest inhabitants, Cozumel has become a world-famous diving and cruise-ship destination.

While diving and snorkeling are the main draws around here, the tourist zone offers lots of shopping 'deals' (often not very cheap) and a pleasant town square to spend the afternoon. There are also some small Maya ruins and a few eco-themed parks.

History

Maya settlement here dates from AD 300. During the post-Classic period Cozumel flourished as a trade center and, more importantly, a ceremonial site. Every Maya woman living on the Yucatán Peninsula and beyond was expected to make at least one pilgrimage here to pay tribute to Ixchel (the goddess of fertility and the moon) at a temple erected in her honor. Archaeologists believe this temple was at San Gervasio, a bit north of the island's geographical center.

👁 Sights

After checking out the Museo de la Isla de Cozumel in San Miguel, rent a vehicle or take a taxi to see the rest of the island;

cyclists will need to brave the regular strong winds on the island.

The following travel route starts in San Miguel, and then it takes you in a rough counterclockwise direction around Isla Cozumel.

Museo de la Isla de Cozumel MUSEUM
(Map p276; Av Melgar Sur; admission M$50; ⊗8am-5pm) Exhibits at this fine museum present a clear and detailed picture of Cozumel's flora, fauna, geography and geology and the island's ancient Maya history.

Parque Chankanaab AMUSEMENT PARK
(Map p273; adult/child M$273/182; ⊗8am-5pm) This park is a popular snorkeling spot, especially when cruise ships are in port, though there's not a lot to see in the water beyond some brightly colored fish and deliberately sunken artificial objects. A taxi from town costs M$130 one way.

El Cedral RUIN
(Map p273) This Maya ruin is the oldest on the island. It's the size of a small house and has no ornamentation, but costs nothing to visit and is easy to reach, unlike San Gervasio and other ruins on Cozumel. It's 3.5km down a signed paved road that heads east. Once you hit town, head for the largest *palapa* roof you can see – the ruins are beside the small church. You can also get your photo taken with a donkey here.

Playa Palancar BEACH
(Map p273; ⊗9am-5pm) About 17km south of town, Palancar is a great beach. It has a beach club renting hydro bikes, kayaks, snorkeling gear and sailboats, plus a restaurant

Isla Cozumel

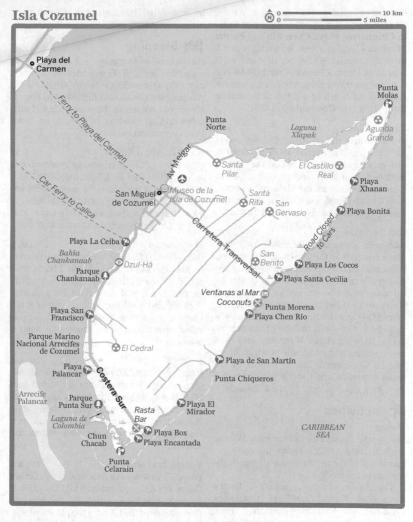

Playa del Carmen

Punta Molas

Ferry to Playa del Carmen

Car Ferry to Calica

Punta Norte

Laguna Xlapak

Aguada Grande

Av Melgar

Santa Pilar

El Castillo Real

San Miguel de Cozumel

Museo de la Isla de Cozumel

Santa Rita

Playa Xhanan

San Gervasio

Playa Bonita

Carretera Transversal

Playa La Ceiba

Road Closed to Cars

Bahía Chankanaab

Dzul-Há

San Benito

Playa Los Cocos

Parque Chankanaab

Playa Santa Cecilia

Ventanas al Mar
Coconuts

Punta Morena

Playa Chen Río

Playa San Francisco

Parque Marino Nacional Arrecifes de Cozumel

El Cedral

Playa de San Martín

Playa Palancar

Punta Chiqueros

Costera Sur

Arrecife Palancar

Parque Punta Sur

Rasta Bar

Playa El Mirador

Laguna de Colombia

CARIBBEAN SEA

Chun Chacab

Playa Box

Playa Encantada

Punta Celarain

and a dive operation. Near the beach, Arrecife Palancar (Palancar Reef) has some very good diving (in Palancar Gardens), as well as fine snorkeling (in Palancar Shallows), though the shallow spots were marked by Hurricane Wilma.

Parque Punta Sur　　　　WILDLIFE RESERVE
(Map p273; adult/child M$144/72; ⏱9am-5pm)
The southern tip of the island has been turned into a rather overpriced 'ecotouristic' park. Visitors board an open vehicle for the 3km ride to visit picturesque Celarain **lighthouse** and the small nautical museum at its

base. Another vehicle carries visitors to **Laguna de Colombia**, part of a three-lagoon system that is the habitat of crocodiles and many resident and migratory waterfowl. Crocs can be seen (when they feel like it) from shore, via a trail through mangroves or a bridge over the lagoon.

East Coast　　　　　　　　BEACH
The eastern shoreline is the wildest part of the island and presents some beautiful seascapes and many small blowholes (there's a bunch around Km 30.5). Swimming is dangerous on most of the east coast

because of riptides and undertows. With a bit of care you can sometimes swim at **Punta Chiqueros**, **Playa Chen Río** and **Punta Morena** – you can rent bodyboards at all three for around M$120 per day, and surfboards at Punta Chiqueros for M$440 per day. As you travel along the coast, consider stopping for lunch or a drink at the **Rasta Bar** (Km 29.5) or **Coconuts** (Km 43.5).

Punta Molas   RUIN
Beyond where the east coast highway meets the Carretera Transversal, intrepid travelers can walk toward Punta Molas, the island's northeast point, accessible only on foot. About 17km up the road are the Maya ruins known as **El Castillo Real**, and a few kilometers further is **Aguada Grande**; see Map p273.

San Gervasio   RUIN
(Map p273; admission M$91; ⏱7am-4pm) This Maya complex is Cozumel's only preserved ruins, and one of the least impressive in the country. You basically pay M$50 to the local government to get access to some gift stores and a ticket booth where you pay an extra M$41 to enter the site. San Gervasio is thought to have been the site of the sanctuary of Ixchel, goddess of fertility, and thus an important pilgrimage site at which Maya women worshipped. But its structures are small and crude, and the clay idols of Ixchel were long ago destroyed by the Spaniards.

🏃 Activities

Diving
Despite the massive hit of Hurricane Wilma, Cozumel, and its 65 surrounding reefs, remains one of the most popular diving destinations in the world.

The top dives in the area include **Santa Rosa Wall**, **Punta Sur Reef**, **Colombia Shallows** and **Palancar Gardens**. Prices vary, but in general expect to pay about M$888 for a two-tank dive, M$910 for an introductory 'resort' course and M$5328 for PADI open-water certification.

Deep Blue   DIVING
(Map p276; ☎872-56-53; www.deepbluecozumel. com; cnr Av 10 Sur & Salas) Has very good gear and fast boats.

Snorkeling
Good snorkeling can be found at Casitas Beach Club, just north of San Miguel de Cozumel, and Dzul-Há to the south. Snorkelers are required to pay M$20 for park admission. The best snorkeling sites are reached

by boat. A half-day boat tour will cost from M$500 to M$650.

🛏 Sleeping

Hacienda San Miguel   HOTEL $$
(Map p276; ☎872-19-86; www.haciendasanmiguel. com; Calle 10 Norte 500; r/ste M$900/1200; ❉🛜) A quiet place, built and furnished to resemble an old hacienda. Niceties such as bathrobes and kitchenettes in every room make this a very good value.

Hotel Colonial Suites   HOTEL $$
(Map p276; ☎872-02-11; www.suitescolonial.com; Av 5 Sur btwn 1 Sur Calle & Salas; r/ste M$810/890; ❉🛜) Just off the plaza, the rooms here are OK, but the suites are a great deal. Decor is so-so, but the well-stocked kitchenettes and comfy lounge areas make them a standout.

El Hostelito   HOSTEL $
(Map p276; ☎869-81-57; www.hostelcozumel.com; Av 10 Norte btwn Av Juárez & Calle 2 Norte; dm/r M$150/450; ❉🛜) Hugely popular and rightly so, this is a hostel done right for a change – clean and well appointed, with a great kitchen, stylish hangout areas and decent-value private rooms for those who need a moment.

Guido's   HOTEL $$$
(Map p276; ☎872-09-46; www.guidoscozumel. com; Av Melgar Sur btwn Calles 6 & 8 Norte; r from M$1120; ❉@🛜) More like luxury apartments than hotel rooms, with full kitchens, chic furnishings, massive lounge areas and private balconies with ocean view. Worth the splurge.

Ventanas al Mar   HOTEL $$$
(Map p273; www.ventanasalmar.biz; Carretera Costera Oriente Km. 43.5; r ground/1st fl M$1200/1330) If you're looking for seclusion, the one hotel on the east side of the island is the place to come. Rooms are big and fresh. All have sea views and tasteful Mexican decoration. Those on the 2nd floor have private balconies.

🍴 Eating

Kinta   FUSION $$$
(Map p276; Av 5 btwn Calles 2 Norte & 4 Norte; mains M$120-200; ⏱5-11pm Tue-Sat) The gourmet take on Mexican classics, superfresh seafood and chic atmosphere (grab a garden table) make this one of the best restaurants in town.

El Coffee Cozumel   CAFE $
(Map p276; cnr Calle 3 Sur & Av Melgar; set lunches M$70; ⏱7am-9pm; 🖉) A tempting array of

RESPONSIBLE DIVING

Please consider the following tips when diving to help preserve the ecology and beauty of reefs:

» Never use anchors on the reef, and take care not to ground boats on coral.

» Avoid touching or standing on living marine organisms, or dragging equipment across the reef. Polyps can be damaged by even the gentlest contact. If you must hold on to the reef, touch only exposed rock or dead coral.

» Be conscious of your fins. Even without contact, the surge from fin strokes near the reef can damage delicate organisms. Take care not to kick up clouds of sand, which can smother organisms.

» Practice and maintain proper buoyancy control. Major damage can be done by divers descending too fast and colliding with the reef.

» Take great care in underwater caves. Spend as little time within them as possible, as your air bubbles may be caught within the roof and thereby leave organisms high and dry. Take turns to inspect the interior of a small cave.

» Resist the temptation to collect or buy corals or shells, or to loot marine archaeological sites (mainly shipwrecks).

» Ensure that you take home all your rubbish and any litter you may find as well. Plastics in particular are a serious threat to marine life.

» Do not feed fish.

» Minimize your disturbance of marine animals. *Never* ride on the backs of turtles.

For important diver safety information, please refer to the boxed text, p850.

baked goods, good-value set lunches and the best coffee on the island make this place popular with locals and visitors alike.

Especias SEAFOOD $$
(Map p276; Calle 3 Sur; mains M$100-140; ☺6-11pm) Intimate and tucked away from the crowds, the balcony is the place to be here. The menu is simple but well done and features yummy empanadas (M$18) and fish any way you want it.

El Foco TAQUERÍA $
(Map p276; Av 5 btwn Salas & 3 Sur; mains M$50-100; ☺5pm-1am) Looking for a late-night taco fix? These folks have got your back, in a very tasty way.

Cheapest of all eating places are the little market *loncherías* (lunch stalls) next to the **Mercado Municipal** on Calle Salas between Avenida 20 Sur and Avenida 25 Sur.

Drinking & Entertainment

Once the cruise-ship passengers get back on board, Cozumel's streets empty out, making it a pretty mellow place by comparison. Many people keep drinking at the touristy

restaurants around the plaza. Other options are scattered along Quinta Avenida.

La Abuelita BAR
(Map p276 cnr Calle 1 Sur & Av 10 Sur) Grab a drink with locals at the 'little grandma.'

Simsons DANCE
(Map p276) This combined disco/bar/karaoke joint/billiard hall thumps out the music, regardless of whether they have customers.

Estadio Javier Rojo Gomez STADIUM
(Map p276 cnr Salas & Av 30 Sur) Hosts rock concerts and *lucha libre* (professional wrestling) matches.

Information

There are ATMs, banks and internet joints on the plaza.

Clínica Médica Hiperbárica (Hyperbaric Chamber; ☎872-14-30; Calle 5 Sur) Between Avenidas Melgar and 5 Sur.

Del Mar Lavandería (Av 20 Sur btwn Av Juárez & Calle 1 Sur) Does a load of laundry for M$70.

Post office (Map p276; cnr Calle 7 Sur & Av Melgar; ☺9am-4:30pm Mon-Sat)

Tourist information office (Map p276; 2nd fl, La Plaza del Sol; ☺8am-3pm Mon-Fri) On the main plaza.

San Miguel de Cozumel

ℹ Getting There & Away

Air

The airport is 2km northeast of San Miguel – follow the signs along Avenida Melgar. Some airlines fly direct from the USA; European flights are usually routed via the USA or Mexico City. International carriers servicing Cozumel include the following: **Continental Airlines** (☎800-900-50-00; www.continental.com) has direct flights from Houston.

Delta Airlines (☎800-123-47-10; www.delta.com) Has a direct flight from Atlanta.

Interjet (☎800-011-23-45; www.interjet.com.mx) Flies direct to Mexico City.

Maya Air (☎872-86-89; www.mayair.com.mx) Flies direct to Cancún and Cleveland.

Boat

Passenger ferries run to Cozumel from Playa del Carmen, and car ferries leave the Calica facility (officially known as the Terminal Marítima Punta Venado) south of Playa del Carmen. The Playa passenger ferries offered by **México Waterjets**

(www.mexicowaterjets.com) or **Ultramar** (www.granpuerto.com.mx) both cost M$155 one way, and there's normally a passenger ferry every hour to and from Cozumel, depending on the season. The ferries run from 6am to midnight.

Schedules are not set in stone, but currently there are four car ferries from Cozumel to **Calica** (www.transcaribe.net) between 6:30am and 8:30pm Tuesday to Saturday and two daily on Sundays and Mondays. Fares are M$683 for cars and M$1068 for a van-sized vehicle (both fares include the driver's passage). You need to line up at least one hour before departure (earlier is better, they say).

ℹ Getting Around

To/From the Airport

The airport is about 2km northeast of town. You can take a *colectivo* from the airport into town for about M$85 (slightly more to the hotels south of town), but you'll have to take a taxi (M$160 from town, up to M$275 from southern hotels) to return to the airport.

San Miguel de Cozumel

Bicycle

A full day's bicycle rental typically costs around M$120 (depending on season) and can be a great way to get to the northern and southern beaches on the west side of flat Cozumel. **Sol y Mar** (☑869-05-45; 2 Calle Norte btwn Avs 5 & 10) has a decent selection. The completely separate bicycle/scooter lane on the Carretera a Chankanaab sees a good deal of car traffic from confused tourists and impatient cab drivers, so be careful.

Car & Motorcycle

All rental contracts should automatically include third-party insurance (*daños a terceros*), which runs about M$130 per day. Collision insurance is usually about M$150 extra with a M$5000 deductible for the cheapest vehicles. Rates start at around M$500 all-inclusive, though you'll pay more during late December and January. There are plenty of agencies around the main plaza, but prices drop about 50% from the dock to the fringes of the tourist zone.

One fairly no-nonsense place, with cars in good shape, is **Rentadora Isis** (☑872-33-67; Av 5 Norte), between Calles 2 Norte and 4 Norte. VW Beetles rent for around M$400 for 24 hours, with little seasonal variation in prices.

Nobody seems to be renting motorbikes these days, with the exception of **Shark Rider** (Av 5 btwn Avs 2 & Juárez), which has a ridiculously large Harley-esque Honda Shadow (M$750 per day). It also has scooters (M$250 per day) as do many other places in town. There is a helmet law, and it is enforced.

Taxi

Fares in and around town are M$40 per ride, to the Zona Hotelera costs M$85 and day trips around the island are M$750 to M$1100; luggage may cost extra.

Akumal

☑984

Famous for its beautiful beach and large, swimmable lagoon, Akumal (Place of the Turtles) does indeed see some sea turtles come ashore to lay their eggs in the summer, although fewer and fewer arrive each year, thanks to resort development. Akumal is one of the Yucatán Peninsula's oldest resort areas and consists primarily of pricey hotels, condominiums and residential developments (occupied mostly by Americans and Canadians) on nearly 5km of wide beach bordering four consecutive bays. All sights and facilities are reached by taking the first turnoff, Playa Akumal, as you come south on the highway.

🏃 Sights & Activities

Although increasing population is taking its toll on the reefs that parallel Akumal, diving remains the area's primary attraction.

Centro Ecológico Akumal MUSEUM
(☑875-90-95; www.ceakumal.org) To learn more about the area's ecology, check out the Centro Ecológico Akumal, on the east side of the road at the town entrance. The center has a few exhibits on reef and turtle ecology. And, for those over 21 years of age, it has six- to 12-week volunteer programs that cost M$2534 to M$19,000 per month, including lodging.

Laguna Yal-Kú LAKE, SWIMMING
(adult/child M$110/70; ⊙8am-5:30pm) At the northern end of Akumal, Laguna Yal-Kú is a beautiful lagoon 2km from the Playa Akumal entrance. The rocky lagoon runs about 500m from its beginning to the sea and makes for an excellent swimming hole. It's home to large schools of brightly colored fish and the occasional visiting turtle and manta ray. There is a tasteful sculpture garden along the shore. Showers, parking and bathrooms are included in the admission price, lockers are an extra M$20, and snorkeling gear and life jackets each cost

WORTH A TRIP

CRISTALINO CENOTE

On the west side of the highway about 38km south of Playa del Carmen is a series of wonderful cenotes. Among these is **Cristalino Cenote** (adult/child M$50/25; ☉6am-5:30pm), just south of the Barceló Maya Resort. It's easily accessible, only about 70m from the entrance gate, which is just off the highway. Two more sinkholes, Cenote Azul and El Jardín del Edén, are just south of Cristalino along the highway. But Cristalino is the best of the three, as you can dive there (or just launch yourself off the rocks into the icy water below).

M$60 to rent. Cabs from the Playa Akumal entrance charge about M$60 to the lagoon. In an effort to protect the lagoon's fragile environment, only chemical-free sun block (also on sale at the ticket office) is allowed.

Akumal Dive Shop　　　DIVING, FISHING
(☎875-90-32; www.akumaldiveshop.com) Dive trips and deep-sea fishing excursions are offered by Akumal, on the east side of the road at the town entrance. It also offers snorkeling trips to the reef and beaches unreachable by car for M$506.

🛏 Sleeping & Eating

You'll find a bunch of houses for rent on www.akumalvacations.com.

Hotel Vista del Mar　　　HOTEL $$
(☎875-901-60; www.akumalinfo.com; r M$1000-1200; ❄) Compact but pleasant rooms, each with beach-view balcony, coffeemaker and minifridge. The two-bedroom condos (from M$1600) are a good deal for families and groups. You can rent bikes here for M$10/60 per hour/day.

El Ultimo Maya　　　HOTEL $
(☎807-72-02; r M$400; ❄) There's not much joy for budget travelers in Akumal, but across the highway in Akumal Pueblo (about a 10-minute walk/M$15 taxi ride from the beach), this family-run place offers rather sparse but clean and comfortable rooms.

Just outside the entrance to Playa Akumal are two minimarkets that stock a good selection of inexpensive food. **Turtle Bay Café** (☉8am-11:30pm), inside and just north of the entrance, has a great range of expat-pleasing breakfasts and seafood dishes. Across the road, **Lonchería Akumalito** (mains M$40-100; ☉8am-11:30pm) is good for simple Mexican eats.

❶ Getting There & Away

Most 2nd-class buses (M$14) and *colectivos* (M$20) traveling between Tulum and Playa del Carmen will drop you on the highway, from where it's about 800m to the entrance to town.

Tulum

📞984 / POP 11,000

Tulum's spectacular coastline – with its sugarlike sands, jade-green water, balmy breezes and bright sun – make it one of the top beaches in Mexico. Where else can you get all that *and* a dramatically situated Maya ruin? There are also fun cenotes, excellent diving, great snorkeling, and a variety of lodgings and restaurants to fit every budget.

There is one big drawback. The town center, where the really cheap eats and sleeps are found, sits right on the highway, making it feel more like a truck stop than a tropical paradise. This said, both Cobá to the west and the massive Reserva de la Biosfera Sian Ka'an to the south make doable day trips.

◉ Sights & Activities

Tulum Ruins　　　ARCHAEOLOGICAL SITE
(admission M$51; ☉8am-4:30pm) The ruins of Tulum preside over a rugged coastline, a strip of brilliant beach and green-and-turquoise waters that will make you want to tear up that return ticket home. It's true the ruins are of a modest scale and the late post-Classic design, workmanship and ornamentation are inferior to those of earlier, more grandiose projects – but wow, those Maya occupants must have felt pretty smug each sunrise. Iguanas are everywhere, and many act as if they own the place.

Tulum is a prime destination for large tour groups. To best enjoy the ruins without feeling like part of the herd, you should visit them either early in the morning or late in the afternoon. Parking costs M$45 for cars and M$90 for vans and pickups. A M$25 train takes you to the ticket booth from the entrance, or just hoof the 300m. Taxi cabs from town charge M$40 and can drop you off at the old entrance road, about an 800m walk from the ticket booth. There's a less-used southerly foot entrance, from the beach road.

History

Most archaeologists believe that Tulum was occupied during the late post-Classic period (AD 1200–1521) and that it was an important port town during its heyday. Remember that the Maya sailed up and down this coast, maintaining trading routes all the way down into Belize. When Juan de Grijalva sailed past in 1518, he was amazed by the sight of the walled city, its buildings painted a gleaming red, blue and yellow and a ceremonial fire flaming atop its seaside watchtower.

The ramparts that surround three sides of Tulum (the fourth side being the sea) leave little question as to its strategic function as a fortress. Several meters thick and 3m to 5m high, the walls protected the city during a period of considerable strife between Maya city-states. Not all of Tulum was situated within the walls. The vast majority of the city's residents lived outside them; the civic-ceremonial buildings and palaces probably housed Tulum's ruling class.

The city was abandoned about 75 years after the Spanish conquest. It was one of the last of the ancient cities to be abandoned; most others had been given back to nature long before the arrival of the Spanish. But Maya pilgrims continued to visit over the years, and indigenous refugees from the War of the Castes took shelter here from time to time.

'Tulum' is Maya for 'wall,' though its residents called it Zama (Dawn). The name Tulum was apparently applied by explorers during the early 20th century.

Exploring the Ruins

From the ticket booth, head along the length of Tulum's enormous **wall**, measuring approximately 380m south to north and 170m along its sides. Rounding the corner and heading toward the beach, you enter the site through a gateway. The **tower** at the corner, once thought to be a guard post, is now believed by some to have been a type of shrine.

Heading east you'll reach the **Casa del Cenote**, named for the small pool at its southern base, where you can sometimes see the glitter of little silvery fish as they turn sideways in the murky water. A small tomb was discovered in the cave. Walking south you'll come across the bluff holding the **Templo del Dios del Viento** (Temple of the Wind God) – roped off at the time

of research – which provides the best views of El Castillo juxtaposed with the sea below.

Below the Wind God's hangout is a lovely little stretch of **beach**. It's quite swimmable when conditions are good, but take note of the lifeguards and the warning flags. After your dip, head west to **Estructura 25**, which has some interesting columns on its raised platform and, above the main doorway (on the south side), a beautiful stucco frieze of the Descending God. Also known as the Diving God, this upside-down, part-human figure appears elsewhere at Tulum, as well as at several other east-coast sites and Cobá. It may be related to the Maya's reverence for bees (and honey), perhaps a stylized representation of a bee sipping nectar from a flower.

South of Estructura 25 is **El Palacio**, notable for its X-figure ornamentation. From here, head east back toward the water and skirt the outside edge of the central temple complex (keeping it to your right). Along the back are some good views of the sea. Heading inland again on the south side, you can enter the complex through a corbeled archway past the restored **Templo de la Estela** (Temple of the Stela), also known as the Temple of the Initial Series. Stela 1, now in the British Museum, was found here. It was inscribed with the Maya date corresponding to AD 564 (the 'initial series' of Maya hieroglyphs in an inscription gives its date). At first this confused archaeologists, who believed Tulum had been settled several hundred years later than this date. It's now thought that Stela 1 was brought to Tulum from Tankah, a settlement 4km to the north dating from the Classic period.

At the heart of the complex you can admire Tulum's tallest building, a watchtower appropriately named **El Castillo** (the Castle) by the Spaniards. Note the Descending God in the middle of its facade and the Toltec-style 'Kukulcanes' (plumed serpents) at the corners, echoing those at Chichén Itzá. To the Castillo's north is the small, lopsided **Templo del Dios Descendente**, named for the relief figure above the door.

Walking west toward the exit will take you to the two-story **Templo de las Pinturas**, constructed in several stages around AD 1400 to 1450. Its decoration was among the most elaborate at Tulum and included relief masks and colored murals on an inner wall. The murals have been partially restored but are nearly impossible to make

Tulum

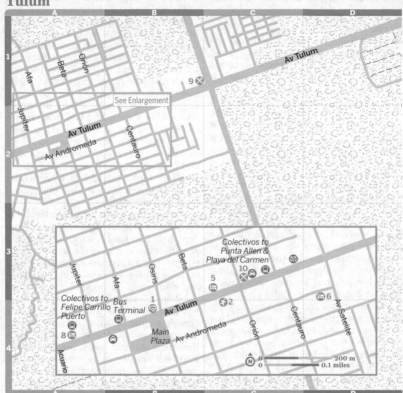

out. This monument might have been the last built by the Maya before the Spanish conquest, and with its columns, carvings and two-story construction, it's probably the most interesting structure at the site.

🏃 Activities

Snorkeling or swimming right from the beach is possible and fun, but be extra careful of boat traffic (a dive flag is a good idea), as the strip between the beach and reef offshore is traveled both by dive boats and fishermen.

Cenote Dive Center   DIVING, SNORKELING
(☑cell phone 984-8763285; www.cenotedive.com; Av Tulum) This recommended outfit specializes in guided cave dives and cenote and cave snorkeling trips. Staff speak English, Spanish, German and Scandinavian languages, and offer trips to the nearby Cenote Angelita.

Zazilkin's   DIVING
(☑cell phone 984-1240082; www.zazilkintulum. com; Carretera Tulum-Punta Allen Km 0.5) The dive shop at Zazilkin's is a PADI, NACD and TDI operation offering low-cost reef dives and renting snorkel gear for M$130 per day.

🎓 Courses

Yoga Shala Tulum   YOGA
(☑cell phone 984-1575101; www.yogashalatulum. com; Carretera Tulum–Punta Allen Km 8.4) About 8km south of the T-junction in the Zona Hotelera, Ocho Tulum offers daily yoga classes (M$180). The weekly pass (M$720) is a good deal for serious stretchers – you can attend any or all of the 19 classes per week.

👉 Tours

Community Tours
Sian Ka'an   ARCHAEOLOGICAL, WILDLIFE
(☑871-22-02; www.siankaantours.org; Av Tulum btwn Beta & Orión) It runs tours to the mag-

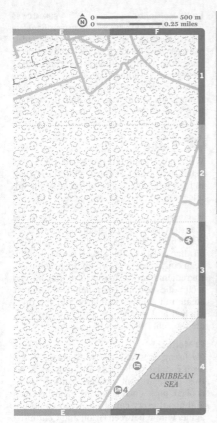

0 — 500 m
0 — 0.25 miles

CARIBBEAN
SEA

YUCATÁN PENINSULA TULUM

nificent Reserva de la Biosfera Sian Ka'an, focusing on Maya sites and wildlife-viewing.

🛏 Sleeping

TULUM PUEBLO

The town center, sometimes referred to as Tulum Pueblo, straddles the highway (called Avenida Tulum through town) south of the Cobá junction. It's at least 3km to the beach from here, but transportation options are plentiful. Still, if you want sand and surf at your doorstep, head for the Zona Hotelera.

El Hotelito
HOTEL **$$**

(☎cell phone 984-1361240; Av Tulum btwn Beta & Orión; r M$615-880; ❋⊛) Wooden boardwalks pass through a jungle-like side patio to generously sized, breezy rooms at this small character-packed hotel. The attached restaurant does good breakfasts, too.

Hotel Posada 06
BOUTIQUE HOTEL **$$$**

(☎cell phone 984-1166757; www.posada06tulum.com; Av Andromeda Oriente 17; r/ste M$1355/1615; ❋⊛⊛) All polished concrete and designer furniture, this is probably the hippest hotel in the pueblo. Rooms are set around a charming little courtyard featuring a curvy swimming pool constructed around a big tree.

Weary Traveler
HOSTEL **$**

(☎871-23-90; www.wearytravelerhostel.com; Av Tulum; dm M$130, r with/without bathroom M$300/375; ❋@⊛) Right by the bus station, this popular hostel offers internet, a shuttle to the beach, and a great central courtyard with hammocks and picnic benches. Private rooms are in a separate building across the highway.

ZONA HOTELERA

Turning south from the highway at the Cobá junction leads about 3km to the north-south road (or T-junction) servicing the Zona Hotelera, the string of waterfront lodgings extending more than 10km south of the ruins. This road eventually enters the Reserva de la Biosfera Sian Ka'an, continuing some 50km past Boca Paila to Punta Allen. The following picks are all found on the beach side of the coastal road.

Diamante K
CABAÑAS **$$**

(☎876-21-15; www.diamantek.com; Carretera Tulum-Punta Allen Km 3.4; cabins with/without bathroom M$1200/600; ⊛) Set on the same rocky stretch of beach as Playa Condessa, cabins here are several steps up in quality and comfort, ranging from budget-rustic to rustic-chic. Those with bathroom vary hugely in size and design – check out a few if you can.

Tulum Ruins

0 ___ 50 m

Tower
Entrance
Gate
Casa del Cenote
To Parking (700m);
Toilets (700m);
Hwy 307 (800m);
Tulum (3km)
Templo del Dios del Viento
Mini-temples
Estructura 25
Beach
Estela 2
El Palacio
Templo del Dios Descendente
Estructura 20
Oratorio
Tickets
Exit
Templo de las Pinturas
El Castillo
Templo de la Estela
Plataforma de la Danza
Archway
(No Public Vehicle Access)
To Punta Allen (60km)
Muralla Fortificada
Guard Tower
Gate
Gate
CARIBBEAN SEA

Shambala Petit Hotel   HOTEL $$

(☎cell phone 984-1256474; www.shambalapetit
hotel.com; Carretera Tulum–Punta Allen Km 7.5;
r M$1000-2000) There's a Zennish starkness
running through this place that you'll either find soothing or terrifying. Rooms vary
in price according to their proximity to the
beach. They could be bigger, but are comfortable nonetheless. Twice-daily yoga sessions cost an additional M$160.

Las Ranitas   HOTEL $$$

(☎871-10-90; www.lasranitas.com; Carretera Tulum-
Punta Allen Km 9; cabins from M$2000, beachfront
M$4000, ste M$5750; P@🛜❄) Way down
the south end of the road, this place's 'eco-
boutique' label is not just marketing; it's all
powered by solar and wind with no gen-
erator. Rooms are what you'd expect for the
price and come in a bewildering range of
configurations. See the website for details.

Cabañas Playa Condesa   CABAÑAS $

(Carretera Tulum – Punta Allen Km 3; cabin with/
without bathroom M$400/300) Just 1km north
of the T-junction, this group of thatched
cabañas are keeping the Old Tulum vibe
alive with very cheap, very basic sleeps right
on the (rocky but swimmable) beach.

La Vita è Bella   BUNGALOW $$

(☎151-47-23; www.lavitaebella-tulum.com; Carretera
Tulum – Punta Allen Km 5.2; bungalows with partial/
full ocean view M$960/1800; 🛜) Offers lovely
bungalows with tiled floors, big, comfy beds,
well-screened sliding doors, good bathrooms
with colorful basins and wide verandas with
hammocks. It's Italian-run, and the restaurant serves delicious handmade pastas and
thin-crust pizza from its wood-fired oven.

✕ Eating

With the exception of Hartwood, the places
listed here are in Tulum Pueblo. Elsewhere
in the Zona Hotelera, head to one of the hotels for good eats.

Hartwood   FUSION $$$

(Carretera Tulum-Punta Allen Km 7.6; mains M$220-
260; ⊙6:30-9:30pm Tue-Sun) Take a break from
all that Italian at this sweet 'n' simple nouveau cuisine eatery down on the beach road.
Ingredients are fresh and local, flavors and
techniques are international. The menu is
small and changes regularly, and the open
kitchen and simple decor serve to accentu-
ate the delicious dishes.

El Mariachi   MEXICAN $

(Av Tulum; tacos M$9, mains M$65-109; ⊙7am-
3am) Popular with locals and tourists alike,
this open-air spot delivers yummy slow-
cooked pork enchiladas, fresh grilled fish
and about every cut of meat you could imagine. Find it between Orión and Centauro.

Da Gigi   ITALIAN $$

(cnr Av Tulum & Hwy 109; mains M$110-210; ⊙3pm-
1am, closed Mon) Serious Italian food is oddly
hard to come by in a place as Italian-packed
as Tulum. This place is the exception, with
great wood-fired pizzas and fresh homemade pasta. You'll find it on the main drag,
at the turnoff to Cobá.

ⓘ Information

Tulum Pueblo has Telmex pay phones, internet
cafes, numerous currency-exchange booths, a
couple of ATMs, two **HSBC banks** (⊙8am-5pm
Mon-Sat) and a **post office** (Av Tulum; ⊙9am-
3:30pm Mon-Fri).

ⓘ Getting There & Away

The bus terminal is toward the southern end of
town. When leaving Tulum, you can also wait at
Crucero Ruinas (on the northern approach to
Tulum on Hwy 307) for intercity buses and the
colectivos to Playa del Carmen. The table shows

BUSES FROM TULUM

DESTINATION	FARE (M$)	DURATION	FREQUENCY (DAILY)
Cancún	68-92	2hr	frequent ADO
Chetumal	212	3½-4hr	frequent ADO & Mayab
Chichén Itzá	105-138	3½hr	2 ADO, 2nd class at 3:30pm
Cobá	38-42	45min	2 ADO & 2 Mayab
Felipe Carrillo Puerto	50-78	1½hr	frequent ADO & Mayab
Mahahual	56	4hr	Mayab 3am
Mérida	154-266	4hr (2nd-class takes much longer)	frequent ADO & Mayab
Playa del Carmen	30-56	1hr	frequent ADO & Mayab
Valladolid	78-82	2hr	frequent ADO & Mayab

some travel times and prices for buses leaving Tulum.

If you're headed for Valladolid, be sure your bus is traveling the short route through Chemax, not via Cancún. *Colectivos* leave from Avenida Tulum for Playa del Carmen (M$35, 45 minutes) and Punta Allen (at 2pm; M$220, four hours). *Colectivos* for Felipe Carrillo Puerto (M$50, one hour) leave from just south of the Weary Traveler hostel.

❶ Getting Around

Except for the shuttles operated from the youth hostels, there are no *colectivos* out to the beach. You'll need to hitch, hire a taxi, rent a bike or walk. And it can be a long, hot walk.

Bicycles can be a good way to get around. Some hotels have them free for guests. **Cabañas Punta Piedra** (Carretera Tulum – Punta Allen Km 5.2) rents bikes (M$100 per day) and scooters (M$400 per day).

Taxi fares are fixed and pretty cheap; from either of the two taxi stands in Tulum Pueblo (one south of the bus terminal, which has fares posted; the other four blocks north on the opposite side of the street) to the ruins is M$40. Fares to most *cabañas* mentioned here are M$50 to M$70.

Around Tulum

There's much to be explored around Tulum. Head inland to visit the ruins at Cobá and the grassroots tourism project at Punta Laguna, or cruise down the coast to Punta Allen and the wild Reserva de la Biosfera Sian Ka'an.

GRAN CENOTE

A little over 3km from Tulum on the road to Cobá is **Gran Cenote** (admission M$100; ⊙8am-6pm), a worthwhile stop on your way between Tulum and the Cobá ruins, especially if it's a hot day. You can snorkel among small fish and see underwater formations in the caverns here if you bring your own gear. A cab from downtown Tulum costs around M$50 one way, or it's an easy bike ride.

COBÁ
📞 984 / POP 300

Imagine a mix between an Amsterdam bike path and the set of *Raiders of the Lost Ark* and you've pretty much got Cobá. It's set deep in the jungle and many of the ruins have yet to be excavated. Walk (or ride) along ancient *sacbé* pathways (stone-paved avenues; *sacbeob* is the plural in Maya), climb up vine-covered mounds, and ascend to the top of Nohoch Mul for a spectacular view of the surrounding jungle.

You can download a map to the Cobá ruin for free at www.lonelyplanet.com/addition al-mexico-maps.

HISTORY

Cobá was settled much earlier than nearby Chichén Itzá and Tulum, and construction reached its peak between AD 800 and 1100. Archaeologists believe that this city once covered an area of 50 sq km and held a population of 40,000 Maya.

Cobá's architecture is a curiosity: its towering pyramids and stelae resemble the architecture of Tikal, which is several hundred kilometers away, rather than the much nearer sites of Chichén Itzá and the northern Yucatán Peninsula.

Some archaeologists theorize that an alliance with Tikal was made through marriage, to facilitate trade between the Guatemalan and Yucatecan Maya. Stelae appear to depict female rulers from Tikal holding ceremonial bars and flaunting their power by standing on captives. These Tikal royal females, when married to Cobá's royalty, may have brought architects and artisans with them.

Archaeologists are also baffled by the extensive network of *sacbeob* in this region, with Cobá as the hub. The longest runs nearly 100km, from the base of Cobá's great pyramid Nohoch Mul to the Maya settlement of Yaxuna. In all, some 40 *sacbeob* passed through Cobá, parts of the huge astronomical 'time machine' that was evident in every Maya city.

◎ Sights

Cobá Ruins   ARCHAEOLOGICAL SITE
(admission M$51; ⊙8am-5pm) The archaeological site has a parking lot that charges M$40 per car. Official guides cost M$450 for 1½ hours. Be prepared to walk (or ride) several kilometers on paths, depending on how much you want to see. If you arrive after 11am, you'll feel a bit like a sheep in a flock. Bring insect repellent and water; the shop next to the ticket booth sells both at reasonable prices.

A short distance inside, at the Grupo Cobá, is a concession renting bicycles at M$35 per day. And where else are you going to cycle around an Mayan site? Pedi-trikes (two people and driver cost M$170 per two-hour tour) are another popular option for those who are tired or have limited mobility.

Grupo Cobá

Walking just under 100m along the main path from the entrance and turning right brings you to the **Templo de las Iglesias** (Temple of the Churches), the most prominent structure in the Cobá Group. It's an enormous pyramid, with views from the top taking in the Nohoch Mul pyramid and surrounding lakes, but climbing it is forbidden.

Back on the main path and 30m further along, you pass through the **juego de pelota**, a well-restored ball court.

Grupo de las Pinturas

Though it's signed to the left at the fork, if you're on foot you can reach the Grupo de las Pinturas (Paintings Group) by heading toward the Grupo Macanxoc a very short distance and turning left. The temple here bears traces of glyphs and frescoes above its door, and remnants of richly colored plaster inside.

You approach the temple from the southeast. Leave by the trail at the northwest (opposite the temple steps) to see several stelae. The first of these is 20m along, beneath a *palapa*. Here a regal figure stands over two others, one of them kneeling with his hands bound behind him. Sacrificial captives lie beneath the feet of a ruler at the base. Continue along the path past another badly weathered stela and a small temple to rejoin the Nohoch Mul path.

Grupo Macanxoc

About 500m beyond the *juego de pelota*, the path forks. Going straight gets you to the Grupo Macanxoc, a group of stelae that bore reliefs of royal women who are thought to have come from Tikal. Most tour groups don't make it down this 'far' (ahem) making it a relatively peaceful spot. The large concentration of stelae (some carved with over 300 glyphs) led scholars to believe this was an important civic-ceremonial site.

Nohoch Mul

A walk of 800m more brings you to Nohoch Mul (Big Mound), also known as the Great Pyramid, which is built on a natural hill. Along the way is another ball court – at the north end of which lie weathered stelae – and the track then bends between piles of stones (a ruined temple) before passing Templo 10 and Stela 20. The exquisitely carved stela bears a picture of a ruler standing imperiously over two captives. Eighty meters beyond stands Nohoch Mul.

At 42m high, Nohoch Mul is the tallest Maya structure on the Yucatán Peninsula. There are two diving gods carved over the doorway of the temple at the top (built in the post-Classic period, AD 1100–1450), similar to the sculptures at Tulum. The view is spectacular! A small kiosk here sells snacks and much-appreciated cold drinks.

🏃 Activities

A 40m-high, 500m-long **zip-line** across the lagoon starts from a tower in the car park and costs M$100 per zip.

About 6km south of town on the road to Chan Chen you'll find a series of three locally administered **cenotes**: Choo-Ha, Tamcach-Ha and Multún-Ha. Prices are M$45 (one cenote), M$70 (two cenotes) and M$100 (all three cenotes).

🛏 Sleeping & Eating

There's no organized campsite, but you can try finding a place along the shore of the lake, which is conveniently located midway between the towns and the ruins. The lake is inhabited by crocodiles, but local children can show you the safe swimming spots.

Hotelito Sac-bé   HOTEL $

(☏206-71-40; r with fan/air-con M$350/450; ❋) Just across from El Bocadito, this one's a little (though not too) rough around the edges, but the king-size beds and new bathrooms are a bonus.

Villas Arqueológicas Cobá   HOTEL $$

(☏206-70-01; www.villasarqueologicas.com.mx; r M$1010; ▣❋🛜🏊) Located next to the lake, this hotel was built to resemble an old hacienda, with red-tiled floors and rooms grouped around a large inner courtyard with an expansive swimming pool. The restaurant is surprisingly affordable and serves good Yucatecan cuisine, but the rooms are too small for the price.

Hotel y Restaurant El Bocadito   HOTEL $

(☏cell phone 985-1069822; r with fan/air-con M$150/350; ❋) A very basic setup – the cheapies are cheap indeed. Air-con rooms have bigger beds, TVs and new bathrooms, but still fall short of what you'd actually call pleasant. The restaurant (mains around M$60) is well run and serves cheap basic food. El Bocadito also serves as Cobá's bus terminal.

Restaurant Ki-Jamal   YUCATECAN $

(mains M$60-150; ◷7:30am-4:30pm) Accessed from the right side of the ruins car park, this large restaurant is owned and operated by the local Maya community and serves up some pretty convincing traditional dishes. Although there's a great view of the lagoon from the upstairs balcony, it's also a tour group favorite, so don't come expecting intimacy.

Several small restaurants on the left side of the archaeological site's parking lot serve inexpensive meals.

❶ Getting There & Away

Most buses serving Cobá swing down almost to the lake to drop off passengers before turning around, but Restaurant El Bocadito serves as the de facto bus station. Buses run six to eight times daily between Tulum and Cobá (M$32 to M$42); four of these also serve Playa del Carmen (M$65 to M$86, one to 1¾ hours). Buses also run to Valladolid (M$30 to M$56, 45 minutes) and Chichén Itzá (M$55 to M$96, 1½ hours).

Day-trippers from Tulum can reach Cobá by forming a group to split the cost of a taxi, which costs about M$700 round-trip, including two hours at the site.

The road from Cobá to Chemax is arrow-straight and in good shape. If you're driving to Valladolid or Chichén Itzá, this is the way to go.

TULUM TO PUNTA ALLEN

Punta Allen sits at the end of a narrow spit of land that stretches south nearly 40km from its start below Tulum. There are some charming beaches along this coast, with plenty of privacy, and most of the spit is within the protected, wildlife-rich Reserva de la Biosfera Sian Ka'an. Hurricane Dean whipped the region in 2007, but the mangrove forest was not substantially damaged.

There's an entrance gate to the reserve about 10km south of Tulum. Entrance is M$23. At the gate, there's a short nature trail taking you to a rather nondescript cenote (Ben Ha). The trail is short, so go ahead and have a gander.

At the time of research, one *colectivo* made the three-hour trip daily, leaving Tulum center at 2pm and arriving in Punta Allen about 5pm and charging foreigners the somewhat painful price of M$240. It returns to Tulum (departing Punta Allen at 5am) the next day. You can also come by boat – talk to Community Tours Sian Ka'an in Tulum (p280).

RESERVA DE LA BIOSFERA SIAN KA'AN

Over 5000 sq km of tropical jungle, marsh, mangroves and islands on Quintana Roo's coast have been set aside by the Mexican government as a large biosphere reserve. In 1987 the UN classified it as a World Heritage site – an irreplaceable natural treasure.

Sian Ka'an (Where the Sky Begins) is home to howler monkeys, anteaters, foxes, ocelots, pumas, crocodiles, eagles, raccoons, tapirs, peccaries, giant land crabs, jaguars and hundreds of bird species, including *chocolateras* (roseate spoonbills) and some flamingos. There are no hiking trails through the reserve; it's best explored with a professional guide.

Entering the reserve by the road to Punta Allen, you pass **Boca Paila Camps** (☏984-871-24-99; www.cesiak.org; Carretera Tulum-Punta Allen Km 21; cabins without bathroom M$960-1080; 🛜). Stay the night in the hotel's pimped-out wall tents or just stop by to see what they do at the turtle rescue operation onsite (M$325) or rent a kayak (M$425). If you'd prefer a guided tour, you can do that, too: kayaking (M$910), boating (M$1000), bird-watching (M$1000) and fly-fishing (M$5000).

YUCATÁN PENINSULA AROUND TULUM

About 1km south of here is the **Centro de Visitantes Reserva de la Biosfera Sian Ka'an** (Carretera Tulum-Punta Allen Km 22.2) where you'll find some natural-history exhibits along with a rather creaky watchtower that provides tremendous bird's-eye views of the lagoon. There's also a two-minute nature trail. Two-hour tours of the lagoon can also be arranged here (M$1500).

Community Tours Sian Ka'an (p280) runs tours out of Tulum that include pickup in Tulum's Zona Hotelera.

If you can get to Punta Allen, the tourism cooperatives there offer a range of tours of the reserve.

Deep in the reserve is the **Sol Caribe** (☑cell phone 984-1393839; www.solcaribe-mexico.com; Carretera Tulum-Punta Allen Km 50; r from M$2400; ☏) featuring almost comically large rooms which all face the sea and get wonderful breezes (no need for air-con). The style is rustic-chic: polished concrete floors with *palapa* roofs. It sits on its own perfect crescent-shaped bay.

PUNTA ALLEN
☑984 / POP 400

The town of Javier Rojo Gómez is more commonly called by the name of the point 2km south. This is truly the end of the road, the 400 or so residents mostly work as fishermen – some residents work in restaurants popular with day-trippers. There's also a healthy reef 400m from shore that offers snorkelers and divers wonderful sights.

The area is known primarily for its catch-and-release bonefishing; tarpon and snook are very popular sport fish as well. The tourism cooperatives in town (inquire at Galletanes, Xo-ken or Vigía Grande eateries), do fishing trips for about M$1780/3560 for a half/full day.

An hour's tour of the lagoon, including turtles, bird-watching and a quick snorkel, costs M$750 per boat. You'll be offered trips by one of the three co-ops. Encourage your captain not to get so close to birdlife that he scares it away. Though very rare, manatee spottings are possible.

There are no ATMs or internet cafes in town. Electricity generally works between 10am and 2pm, and 7pm and midnight.

🛏 Sleeping & Eating

Hotel Costa del Sol HOTEL $$
(☑cell phone 984-1132639; campsites M$250, s/d M$800/1200) At the entrance to town, this beachfront spot sports quaint fan-cooled bungalows and a laid-back feel. The restaurant is pretty decent, and it has karaoke on weekend nights.

Casa de la Sirena HOTEL $
(☑877-85-21; www.casasirena.com; s/d M$400/450, without bathroom M$300/350) The cheapest rooms in town are also the funkiest – owned by an expat American (ask for the shipwreck stories), they're charming, spacious and quirky.

❶ Getting There & Away

The best way to reach Punta Allen by public transportation is by *colectivo* (M$240) out of Tulum: one leaves daily from Tulum center at 2pm and arrives about three hours later. Driving in a rental car is another option, but prepare for 5km/h to 10km/h speeds and more than a few transmission-grinding bumps.

Felipe Carrillo Puerto
☑983 / POP 29,000

Now named for a progressive governor of Yucatán, this crossroads town 95km south of Tulum was once known as Chan Santa Cruz, the rebel headquarters during the War

---

THE TALKING CROSS

In 1849, when the War of the Castes turned against them, the Maya of the northern Yucatán Peninsula made their way to Carrillo Puerto seeking refuge.

Regrouping, they were ready to sally forth again in 1850 when a 'miracle' occurred. A wooden cross erected at a cenote on the western edge of the town began to 'talk,' exhorting the Maya to continue the struggle against the Spanish and promising victory. The talking was actually done by a ventriloquist, but the people looked upon it as the authentic voice of their aspirations.

The oracle guided the Maya in battle for more than eight years, until their great victory, conquering the fortress at Bacalar. Carrillo Puerto today remains a center of Maya pride. The talking cross has been returned to its shrine, and Maya from around the region still come to visit it, especially on May 3, the Day of the Holy Cross.

BUSES FROM FELIPE CARRILLO PUERTO

DESTINATION	FARE (M$)	DURATION	FREQUENCY (DAILY)
Cancún	120	3½-4hr	frequent ADO & Mayab
Chetumal	66-120	2-3hr	frequent ADO & Mayab
Mahahual	86	2hr	2 ADO
Mérida	156-194	5½hr	frequent Oriente
Playa del Carmen	70-124	2½hr	frequent ADO & Mayab
Tulum	50-82	1½hr	frequent ADO & Mayab

of the Castes. Besides its historical and cultural significance and a pretty plaza, Carrillo Puerto has few attractions. The **Dirección de Turismo Municipal** (Municipal Tourist Office; ☑267-14-52; cnr Juárez & Pacheo; ☉7am-2pm) can answer what few questions you may have.

◉ Sights

Santuario de la Cruz Parlante SHRINE
(Sanctuary of the Talking Cross; cnr Calles 60 & 69) Santuario de la Cruz Parlante is five blocks west of the gas station on Hwy 307. It's well signposted and everybody knows it, in case you get lost. The building is set on sloping, parklike grounds and you should remove your hat and shoes before entering. Ask permission before taking photos.

FREE **Centro Cultural Chan Santa Cruz** ARTS CENTER
(☉8am-9:30pm Mon-Fri, 8am-1pm & 6-8pm Sat & Sun) On the plaza, this cultural center hosts art exhibitions, workshops and the occasional exhibit on the War of the Castes.

🛏 Sleeping & Eating

Hotel Chan Santa Cruz HOTEL $$
(☑834-00-21; cnr Calles 67 & 68; d M$440-580; P❄🛜) There's way too much floral fabric going on here. Way too much. But the interi-

or patio is pretty, the rooms are trim and correct and the plaza-side location is a winner.

Hotel San Sebastián HOTEL $
(☑cell phone 983-1333923; Calle 66 btwn Calles 67 & 69; s/d fan M$250/300, air-con M$350/400; ❄🛜) The best budget deal in town is half a block from the plaza and has large, modern rooms with firm beds.

Parrilla Las Galerías MEXICAN $
(Calle 65 btwn Calles 66 & 68; mains M$50-100; ☉6-11:30pm) For atmosphere and people-watching, grab a plaza-side table at this simple restaurant. The menu's limited – fajitas, tortas, burgers and steak, but it's well done and the passing breezes are very welcome.

Hotel El Faisán y el Venado INTERNATIONAL $$
(cnr Juárez & Calle 69; mains M$60-120; ☉7am-11pm) One of the more formal options in town, serving good-value meals and early breakfasts.

❶ Getting There & Away

Most buses serving Carrillo Puerto are *de paso* (they don't originate there). The table shows some of the routes.

Colectivos leave for Playa del Carmen (M$75, two hours) and Tulum (M$55, one hour) from Hwy 307 just south of Calle 73.

ℹ CHECK THE TIME

Unlike the rest of Mexico, Felipe Carrillo Puerto doesn't observe daylight savings time, so if you're there between April and October, it's a good idea to ask people if they're talking about the '*hora local*' (local time) or '*hora nacional*' (national time).

Mahahual
☑983

The arrival of the cruise ships hasn't been as life-altering for Mahahual as many feared – it retains much of its small-town charm, with a pleasant *malecón* (beachfront walkway) packed with tourist services and surrounded by what is still a very laid-back Caribbean village. There's an ATM in the Centro Comercial Maj-Ah-Ual, halfway along the *malecón*.

⊙ Sights & Activities

Malecón
WALKING, BEACH

The beach right off Mahahual's beautiful *malecón* has great sand, plus water so shallow you can walk out a good 100m.

Banco Chinchorro
DIVING, SNORKELING

Divers won't want to miss the reefs and underwater fantasy worlds of the Banco Chinchorro, the largest coral atoll in the northern hemisphere. Some 45km long and up to 14km wide, Chinchorro's western edge lies about 30km off the coast, and dozens of ships have fallen victim to its barely submerged ring of coral. The atoll and its surrounding waters were made a biosphere reserve (the Reserva de la Biosfera Banco Chinchorro) to protect them from depredation. But the reserve lacks the personnel and equipment needed to patrol such a large area, and many abuses go undetected.

There's good snorkeling here as well, including **40 Cannons**, a wooden ship in 5m to 6m of water. Looters have taken all but about 25 of the cannons, and it can only be visited in ideal conditions.

Local tour operators arrange fishing (M$680 per hour for up to four people) and hour-long snorkeling tours (M$270 per person). Look for them beachside along the *malecón*.

Dreamtime Dive Center
DIVING, SNORKELING

(✆cell phone 983-1240235; www.dreamtimediving. com; malecón) Dreamtime Dive Center, 2.5km south of Mahahual, runs trips to stretches of the barrier reef and offers PADI courses.

Las Cabañas del Doctor
CANOEING

(Km 2) Rents out canoes for M$100 an hour.

⟲ Tours

Native Choice
CULTURAL

(✆cell phone 983-1035955; www.thenativechoice. com) Offers guided tours of interesting places inland from here, specializing in little-visited Maya sites.

🛏 Sleeping & Eating

Addresses are given as distances from the military checkpoint at the north entrance to town. There are about a dozen restaurants along the *malecón*, each offering a standard assortment of seafood, Mexican favorites and pub grub.

Quieter, more upscale accommodations are 2km south of the town center – see www. mahahual-southbeach.com for details.

Hotel Maya Luna
HOTEL $$

(✆836-09-05; www.hotelmayaluna.com; Km 5.2; cabañas M$400; @🖵) Four sweet little bungalows on a lovely stretch of beach south of town. Kayaks are available and there's a good restaurant onsite (try the stuffed pineapple, a Mexican/Euro/Indonesian extravaganza; M$150).

Balamkú
HOTEL $$$

(✆732-10-04; www.balamku.com; Km 5.6; r M$1150-1170; 🖵) It has two-storied, circular bungalows that are stringently ecological (composting toilets, 100% solar-powered) and yet hugely comfortable. It's set on another great stretch of beach, about a M$50 cab ride from the *malecón*.

Macho's Hostel
HOSTEL $

(✆cell phone 983-8359336; Km 1.5; dm M$130, r M$320-550) Located about 100m south of the *malecón*, this simple beachfront joint has the cheapest rooms in town. They're basic – and the vibe here seems just a bit odd – but you have beach views and use of the owner's kitchen. The two dorms sleep up to eight people each.

100% Agave
MEXICAN $

(mains M$60-100; ⊙11am-late) Good cheap Mexican food, with the ramshackle ambience adding to the flavor. La Bodeguita across the road is a fun, authentic local drinking spot.

ⓘ Getting There & Around

Mahahual is 127km south of Felipe Carrillo Puerto, and approximately 100km east of Bacalar. A new ADO bus terminal, located next to the Hotel Mahahual, just a block inland from the *malecón*, has made getting here easier than ever, though the buses are infrequent.

Buses depart here for Chetumal (M$106, 2½ hours, 6:30pm), Cancún (M$240, five hours, 5:30pm), Felipe Carrillo Puerto (M$86, two hours, 5:30pm), Laguna Bacalar (M$72, two hours, 6:30pm) and Tulum (M$156, four hours, 5:30pm). There's a Pemex gas station if you need to fill your tank.

Xcalak

The rickety wooden houses, beached fishing launches and lazy gliding pelicans make this tiny town plopped in the middle of nowhere a perfect escape. Blessed by virtue of its remoteness and the Chinchorro atoll (prevent-

YUCATÁN PENINSULA XCALAK

ing the creation of a cruise-ship port), Xcalak may yet escape the development boom.

The mangrove swamps stretching inland from the coastal road hide some large lagoons and form tunnels that invite kayakers to explore. There's a remote Maya ruin on the western side of the lagoon. Your hotelier can tell you how to get there.

Today, there are no signs of Xcalak getting a bank, grocery store or gas station anytime soon, so stock up before you come.

XTC Dive Center (www.xtcdivecenter.com), about 300m north of town on the coast road, offers dive and snorkel trips (from M$300) to the wondrous barrier reef just offshore, and to Banco Chinchorro (three-tank dive M$2580). It also rents diving equipment and offers PADI open-water certificates for M$5655, as well as fishing and bird-watching tours. To visit Chinchorro, you can get your M$50 biosphere reserve wristband here or at the park office in town. Be aware that this is the only dive operator licensed to take boats out to Chinchorro.

🛏 Sleeping

The following hotels are found on the old coastal road leading north from town. Addresses here are expressed in kilometers north along the coast from town.

Hotel Tierra Maya　　　HOTEL $$$
(✆983-839-80-12; www.tierramaya.net; Km 2; r incl continental breakfast M$1100-2015; ☎) A modern beachfront hotel featuring six lovely rooms (three quite large), each tastefully appointed and with many architectural details. Each of the rooms has mahogany furniture and a balcony facing the sea – the bigger rooms even have small refrigerators.

Casa Carolina　　　HOTEL $$
(www.casacarolina.net; Km 2.5; r incl continental breakfast M$1300; ☎) A bright, cheery yellow, the Casa has four guest rooms with large, hammock-equipped balconies facing the sea. Each room has a kitchen with fridge, and the bathrooms try to outdo one another with their beautiful Talavera tiles. All levels of scuba instruction (NAUI) are offered here, as well as recreational dives at the barrier reef.

Caracol Caribe　　　HOTEL $
(Centro; r M$350) Basic, reasonably comfortable rooms a block from the beach. And that's about as 'budget' as this town gets, sorry.

✗ Eating

Leaky Palapa　　　INTERNATIONAL $$$
(mains M$80-200; ☺5-10pm Thu-Sun Nov-May, 5-10pm Fri & Sat rest of year) Chef and owner, Marla and Linda, have turned an old standby into a new sensation, serving wonderful meals such as lobster in caramel ginger sauce. Opinion is unanimous that this is the best place to go to treat your taste buds. It's on the coast road, just north of town.

Toby's　　　SEAFOOD $
(mains M$50-150; ☺noon-10pm) On the main drag in town, this is the preferred expat cheap-eat option. One taste of the coconut shrimp and you'll know why.

ℹ Getting There & Around

Cabs from Limones, on Hwy 307, cost about M$600 (including to the northern hotels). Buses to Chetumal (and Limones) leave at 5am and 2pm and cost M$70. The bus stops by the lighthouse.

Driving from Limones, turn right (south) after 55km and follow the signs to Xcalak (another 60km). Keep an eye out for the diverse wildlife that frequents the forest and mangroves; a lot of it runs out into the road. The coastal road between Mahahual and Xcalak is closed.

You can hire a boat at the XTC Dive Center for M$600 per person (minimum five people) to take you to San Pedro, Belize.

Laguna Bacalar
✆983

A large, clear, turquoise freshwater lake with a bottom of gleaming white sand, Laguna Bacalar comes as a surprise in this region of tortured limestone and scrubby jungle.

The small, sleepy town of Bacalar, just east of the highway, 125km south of Felipe Carrillo Puerto, is the only settlement of any size on the lake. It's noted mostly for its old Spanish fortress and its popular *balnearios* (bathing places).

There's a small **tourist office** (22 Calle btwn Avs 3 & 5) inside the real estate office on the plaza.

◉ Sights

Fortress　　　FORTRESS
(admission M$57; ☺9am-7pm Tue-Thu & Sun, 9am-8pm Fri & Sat) The fortress above the lagoon was built to protect citizens from raids by pirates and the local indigenous population. It also served as an important outpost for the Spanish in the War of the Castes.

Today, with formidable cannons still on its ramparts, the fortress remains an imposing sight. It houses a **museum** exhibiting colonial armaments and uniforms from the 17th and 18th centuries.

Balneario
POOL

(admission M$5; ☺10am-7pm) The *balneario* lies a few hundred meters north along the *costera* (waterfront avenue) below the fort. There are some small restaurants along the avenue and near the *balneario,* which is very busy on weekends.

Cenote Azul
POOL

Just shy of the south end of the *costera* this cenote is a 90m-deep natural pool on the southwest shore of the lake, with a bar and good restaurant (mains M$70 to M$150) onsite. It's 200m east of Hwy 307, so many buses will drop you nearby.

🛏 Sleeping & Eating

Casita Carolina
HOTEL $$

(☎834-23-34; www.casitacarolina.com; s M$300-450, d M$450-600) This is a delightful place about 1½ blocks south of the fort. It has a large lawn leading down to the lake, five fan-cooled rooms and a deluxe *palapa* that sleeps up to four. Guests can explore the lake in the Casita's kayaks.

Casa Corazón
HOTEL $$

(☎834-29-82; www.casacorazonbacalar.com; r M$900; 🛜) The rooms are smallish, but have plenty of character and the private jetty out back is a great place to catch a breeze and go for a splash.

Hostel Ximba Li
HOSTEL $

(☎834-25-16; cnr Av 3 & Calle 30; campsite/hammock/dm M$50/50/70) A rather sparse setup that could be cleaner, but there's a kitchen for use and the water is a short walk away.

Gaia
VEGETARIAN $$

(Av 3 btwn Calles 18 & 20; mains M$80-120; ☺8am-9:30pm) A tranquil little spot half a block south of the plaza serving healthy homemade food and offering yoga, massage, a small health-foods store and book exchange.

Orizaba's
MEXICAN $

(Av 7 btwn Calles 24 & 26; mains M$60-100; ☺8am-2pm) Highly recommended by locals and expats alike, serving fine Mexican favorites in a very casual setting.

ℹ Getting There & Away

Southbound 2nd-class buses go through Bacalar town on Calle 7, passing a block uphill from the central square (*el parque*), which is just above the fortress and has a taxi stand. Northbound 2nd-class buses run along Calle 5, a block downhill from Calle 7. Most 1st-class buses don't enter town, but many will drop you along Hwy 307 at the turnoffs to Hotel Laguna and Cenote Azul; check before you buy your ticket.

If you're driving from the north and want to reach the town and fortress, take the first Bacalar exit and continue several blocks before turning left (east) down the hill. From Chetumal, head west to catch Hwy 307 north; after 25km on the highway you'll reach the signed right turn for Cenote Azul and the *costera*.

Chetumal
📞983 / POP 149,000

The capital city of Quintana Roo, Chetumal has stylish, friendly people, some decent restaurants and a lively music scene.

The bayside esplanade hosts carnivals and events, and the modern Maya museum is impressive (though a bit short on artifacts). Extensive Maya ruins, amazing jungle and the border to neighboring Belize are all close by. Carnaval (late February or early March) is particularly lively in Chetumal.

History

Before the Spanish conquest, Chetumal was a Maya port. After the conquest, the town was not actually settled until 1898, when it was founded to put a stop to the illegal trade in arms and lumber carried on by the descendants of the War of the

Castes rebels. Dubbed Payo Obispo, the town changed its name to Chetumal in 1936. In 1955, Hurricane Janet virtually obliterated it. The rebuilt city is laid out to a grand plan with a grid of wide boulevards along which traffic speeds (be careful at stop signs).

◉ Sights

Museo de la Cultura Maya   MUSEUM
(Av de los Héroes; admission M$57; ⊙9am-7pm Sun-Thu, to 8pm Fri & Sat) Chetumal's Maya Culture Museum is a class act, covering the Maya culture from Mexico, Belize, Guatemala, Honduras and El Salvador with enough scale models and interactive exhibits to keep the kids happy and so much well-presented info (in Spanish and English) that the adults might learn a thing or two as well. The museum's **courtyard**, which you can enter for free, has salons for temporary exhibits of modern artists, paintings reproducing Maya frescoes and a *cinemuseo* giving free film showings.

Museo de la Ciudad   MUSEUM
(Héroes de Chapultepec; admission M$10, free Sun; ⊙9am-7pm Tue-Sat, 9am-2pm Sun) The local history museum is small but neatly done, and worth a 15-minute visit.

Chetumal

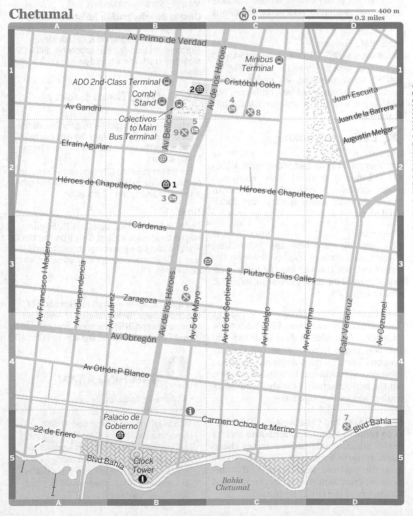

🛏 Sleeping

Hotel Los Cocos HOTEL **$$**
(☎835-04-30; www.hotelloscocos.com.mx; cnr Av
de los Héroes & Héroes de Chapultepec; r M$912,
ste M$1824; ❄@🔊❄) The most conspicuous
hotel in town, taking up almost an entire
block on the main street, is not a bad deal
for the price. Rooms are cool and fresh if
a little lacking in character and the service
and amenities are top-notch.

Hotel Ucum HOTEL **$**
(☎832-07-11, 832-61-86; Av Gandhi 167; s/d with
fan M$200/260, air-con M$300/380; P❄❄🔊❄) A
hulking structure set around a parking lot
and offering pretty decent rooms, a gener-
ously sized swimming pool and a restaurant
serving good, inexpensive food.

Hotel Villa Fontana HOTEL **$$**
(☎cell phone 983-1292004; hotelvillafontana@
hotmail.com; Av de los Héroes 181; s/d M$528/585;
❄@🔊) No surprises at this middle of the
road hotel. Rooms could be a bit bigger, but
they've got touches of style and it's a fair
deal overall.

🍴 Eating & Drinking

La Pantoja YUCATECAN **$**
(cnr Ghandi & Av 16 de Septiembre; mains M$50-
100; ⏱7am-7pm) A sweet little family-run
place serving up regional and Mexican
standards, daily lunch specials and meal-
sized tortas.

Charlotte INTERNATIONAL **$$**
(Blvd Bahía 91; mains M$85-120; ⏱8am-11pm)
There are all sorts of options down on the
waterfront, but this one has the hippest at-
mosphere and the most interesting menu (at
time of writing).

Café-Restaurant Los Milagros CAFE **$**
(Zaragoza btwn Avs de los Héroes & 5 de Mayo; mains
M$30-80; ⏱7:30am-9:30pm Mon-Sat, to 1pm Sun)
The best coffee in town is at this old-guy
hangout. There's a good range of breakfasts,
some decent snacks and light meals on offer,
but the real attraction is the shady outdoors
seating and low-key ambience.

Near the ADO 2nd-Class Terminal, the **Mer-
cado Ignacio Manuel Altamirano** and its
row of small, simple eateries serves cheap
meals. If you're wondering where everybody
is on the weekend, head down to the *ma-
lecón,* where a 3km strip of restaurants and
bars serves as the city's playground.

ℹ Information

There are several banks and ATMs around town,
including an ATM inside the bus terminal.

Arba Internet (Efraín Aguilar; internet per hr
M$10; ⏱8am-1am Mon-Sat, to midnight Sun)

Cruz Roja (☎832-05-71; cnr Avs Independen-
cia & Héroes de Chapultepec)

Fire, Medical, Police (☎066)

Hospital Morelos (☎832-45-95; Av Inde-
pendencia btwn Efraín Aguilar & Héroes de
Chapultepec)

Immigration office Located about 800m north
of the *glorieta* (roundabout; ask for the *oficina
de inmigración*).

Post office (cnr Plutarco Elías Calles & Av 5 de
Mayo; ⏱9am-4pm Mon-Fri)

Oficina de Información Turística Municipal
(Municipal Tourist Office; ☎833-24-65; cnr
Carmen Ochoa de Merino & Av 5 de Mayo;
⏱8am-4pm Mon-Fri) Has brochures and well-
meaning staff. There's also an info kiosk in the
main bus terminal.

ℹ Getting There & Away

Air
Chetumal's small airport is roughly 2km north-
west of the city center along Avenida Obregón.
Plans are in the works to make this an interna-
tional airport.

For flights to Belize City (and on to Flores, to
reach Tikal) or to Belize's cays, cross the border
into Belize and fly from Corozal.

Boat
Boats to San Pedro, Belize (US$35/55 one-
way/return) leave at 3pm, daily from the Muelle
Fiscal. Make sure you complete exit formali-
ties at Chetumal's Immigration office before
departing.

Bus
The main bus terminal is about 2km north of
the center, near the intersection of Avenidas
Insurgentes and Belice. Services are provided by
deluxe Omnitur del Caribe and Maya de Oro; ADO

CATCHING A TAXI

If you're heading for Bacalar and want
to go by taxi, look for the cabs with
'Bacalar' written on the door (they
hang out around the Cruz Roja on Inde-
pendencia). They're the ones who have
come from there and are looking for a
fare back again, so will give you a better
price (sometimes as low as M$30) than
the Chetumal-based ones.

BUSES FROM CHETUMAL

DESTINATION	FARE (M$)	DURATION	FREQUENCY (DAILY)
Bacalar	22-30	45min	frequent Mayab from ADO terminal
Belize City, Belize	150	3-4hr	7am from main terminal, frequent from Nuevo Mercado
Campeche	230-310	6½-9hr	3 ADO
Cancún	198-284	5½-6½hr	frequent ADO
Corozal, Belize	35-40	1hr	frequent 2nd-class from Nuevo Mercado
Escárcega	148-198	4-6hr	frequent ADO
Felipe Carrillo Puerto	66-114	2-3hr	frequent ADO & Mayab
Flores, Guatemala (for Tikal)	400	8hr	7am from main terminal
Mahahual	46-100	4hr	3 ADO
Mérida	246-328	6-8hr	8 Omnitur del Caribe & Super Expresso, 3 Mayab from main terminal
Orange Walk, Belize	35-50	2¼hr	frequent 1st- & 2nd-class Novelos & Northern from Nuevo Mercado
Palenque	354-376	7-8hr	4 OCC, ADO & GL from main terminal
Tulum	132-212	3½-4hr	frequent
Valladolid	156	6hr	2 Mayab from main terminal
Villahermosa	412-432	7-9hr	5 ADO
Xcalak	80	5hr	2 Mayab from ADO terminal
Xpujil	66-100	2-3hr	10 ADO

and OCC (both 1st class); and Mayab and Super Expresso (2nd class). The terminal has lockers (in the store against the east wall, near the pay toilets), a bus information kiosk (open until 3pm), an ATM, a cafeteria and shops.

The **ADO 2nd-Class Terminal** (Av Belice; ⏱6am-10pm), just west of the Museo de la Cultura Maya, is a good place to get info. TRT, Sur and Mayab (a cut above) buses leave from here.

Many local buses and those bound for Belize begin their runs from the Nuevo Mercado Lázaro Cárdenas, on Calzada Veracruz at Confederación Nacional Campesina (also called Segundo Circuito), about 10 blocks north of Avenida Primo de Verdad. From this market, most 1st-class Belize-bound buses continue to the main terminal and depart 15 minutes later from there; the 2nd-class buses don't. Tickets can be purchased on board the buses or (1st class only) at the main terminal.

The **minibus terminal** (cnr Avs Primo de Verdad & Hidalgo) has services to Bacalar (M$25, six daily) and other nearby destinations.

Check your bus details before departure because buses leave from multiple locations and the information in this book is subject to rapid change.

Taxi

Gibson's Tours & Transfers (www.gibsonstours andtransfers.com) costs M$350/700 to the border/Corozal.

Getting Around

From anywhere in town taxis charge a flat fare of M$20. From the traffic circle at Avenida de los Héroes, you can also get a combi (van) for M$3 to the town center on the Santa María or Calderitas lines. To reach the main bus terminal from the center, catch a *colectivo* from Avenida Belice behind the Museo de la Cultura Maya. Ask to be left at the *glorieta* at Avenida Insurgentes. Head west to reach the terminal.

YUCATÁN STATE

A vast expanse of largely undeveloped Gulf coastline, some fantastic nature reserves, a couple of cosmopolitan cities and some world-famous archaeological sites have made Yucatán state a favorite with travelers for decades.

The depth of experience here is almost incomparable – for city lovers, Mérida is big and bustling but wonderfully preserved, with gloriously crumbling, stately buildings on every downtown block. Smaller cities like Valladolid shift down a couple of gears and the pace of life in places like Izamal is downright dreamy.

Archaeology fans are in for various treats, too, from the international-superstar attraction of Chichén Itzá to the lesser-known but equally worthy Uxmal. If you can arrange the transportation, a trip along the Ruta Puuc can take you to four or five ruins in just one day.

Bird-watchers are well catered for, too – the nature reserves protecting the estuaries around Celestún and Río Lagartos are home to eye-popping populations of waterfowl, most notably flamingos.

Mérida

☑ 999 / ELEV 22M / POP 772,000

Since the conquest, Mérida has been the cultural capital of the entire peninsula. At times provincial, at others 'muy cosmopolitano,' it is a town steeped in colonial history, with narrow streets, broad central plazas and the region's best museums. It's also a perfect hub city to kick off your adventure into the rest of Yucatán state. There are cheap eats, good hostels and hotels, thriving markets, and goings-on just about every night somewhere in the downtown area.

Long popular with European travelers looking to go beyond the hubbub of Quintana Roo's resort towns, Mérida is not an 'undiscovered Mexican gem' like some of the tourist brochures claim. Simply put, it's a tourist town, but a tourist town too big to feel like a tourist trap. And as the capital of Yucatán state, Mérida is also the cultural crossroads of the region.

History

Francisco de Montejo the Younger founded a Spanish colony at Campeche, about 160km to the southwest, in 1540. From this base he took advantage of political dissension among the Maya people (see boxed text, p314), conquering T'ho (now Mérida) in 1542. By the decade's end, Yucatán was mostly under Spanish colonial rule.

When Montejo's conquistadors entered T'ho, they found a major Maya settlement of lime-mortared stone that reminded them of the Roman architecture in Mérida, Spain.

They promptly renamed the city and proceeded to build it into the regional capital, dismantling the Maya structures and using the materials to construct a cathedral and other stately buildings. Mérida took its colonial orders directly from Spain, not from Mexico City, and Yucatán has had a distinct cultural and political identity ever since.

During the War of the Castes, only Mérida and Campeche were able to hold out against the rebel forces. On the brink of surrender, the ruling class in Mérida was saved by reinforcements sent from central Mexico in exchange for Mérida's agreement to take orders from Mexico City.

Mérida today is the peninsula's center of commerce, a bustling city that has benefited greatly from the *maquiladoras* (assembly plants) that opened in the 1980s and '90s and the tourism industry that picked up during those decades.

◉ Sights

Plaza Grande   PLAZA

'El Centro' is one of the most attractive plazas in Mexico. Huge laurel trees shade the park's benches and wide sidewalks, and it is surrounded by the bustle of shoppers and by coffee drinkers who sip at the many open-air cafes. It was the religious and social center of ancient T'ho; under the Spanish it was the Plaza de Armas, the parade ground, laid out by Francisco de Montejo the Younger. A ceremony is held daily marking the raising and lowering of the Mexican flag. On Sunday hundreds of *meridanos* take their *paseo* (stroll) here, and there's a cultural exhibit – normally dance or live music on Monday nights.

Catedral de San Ildefonso   CATHEDRAL

(⊙6am-noon & 4-8pm) On the plaza's east side, on the site of a former Maya temple, is Mérida's hulking, severe cathedral, begun in 1561 and completed in 1598. Some of the stone from the Maya temple was used in its construction. The massive crucifix behind the altar is **Cristo de la Unidad** (Christ of Unity), a symbol of reconciliation between those of Spanish and Maya heritage. To the right over the south door is a **painting of Tutul Xiu**, *cacique* (warlord) of the town of Maní, paying his respects to his ally Francisco de Montejo at T'ho (de Montejo and Xiu jointly defeated the Cocomes; Xiu converted to Christianity, and his descendants still live in Mérida).

In the small chapel to the left of the altar is Mérida's most famous religious artifact, a statue called **Cristo de las Ampollas** (Christ of the Blisters). Local legend says the statue was carved from a tree that was hit by lightning and burned for an entire night without charring. It is also said to be the only object to have survived the fiery destruction of the church in the town of Ichmul (though it was blackened and blistered from the heat). The statue was moved to Mérida's cathedral in 1645.

Other than these items, the cathedral's interior is largely plain, its rich decoration having been stripped away by angry peasants at the height of anticlerical fervor during the Mexican Revolution.

FREE Museo de Arte Contemporáneo
ARTS CENTER

(Macay; Calle 60 btwn Calles 61 & 63; ⊘10am-6pm) South of the cathedral, housed in the former archbishop's palace, is the Museo de Arte Contemporáneo. This attractive museum holds permanent exhibits of Yucatán's most famous painters and sculptors, as well as revolving exhibits by local craftspeople.

Casa de Montejo
NOTABLE BUILDING

(Palacio de Montejo, Calle 63; ⊘9am-4pm Mon-Fri, 10am-2pm Sat) The Casa de Montejo is on the south side of the Plaza Grande and dates from 1549. It originally housed soldiers but was soon converted into a mansion that served members of the Montejo family until 1970. These days it houses a bank, and you can enter and look around during bank hours. At other times, content yourself with a close look at the facade, where triumphant conquistadors with halberds hold their feet on the necks of generic barbarians (though they're not Maya, the association is inescapable). Typical of the symbolism in colonial statuary, the vanquished are rendered much smaller than the victors; works on various churches throughout the region feature big priests towering over or in front of little 'Indians.' Also gazing across the plaza from the facade are busts of Montejo the Elder, his wife and his daughter.

Palacio Municipal
HISTORIC BUILDING

Across the square from the cathedral is Mérida's Palacio Municipal (City Hall). Originally built in 1542, it was twice refurbished, in the 1730s and the 1850s. Adjoining it is the **Centro Cultural Olimpio** (cnr Calles 62

& 61), Mérida's municipal cultural center. Attempts to create a modern exterior for the building were halted by government order, to preserve the colonial character of the plaza. The ultramodern interior serves as a venue for films, music and dance performances, and other exhibitions. Schedules for performances and frequent film showings are posted outside.

FREE Palacio de Gobierno
HISTORIC BUILDING

(⊘8am-10pm) On the north side of the plaza, the Palacio de Gobierno houses the state of Yucatán's executive government offices (and one of its tourist information centers). It was built in 1892 on the site of the palace of the colonial governors. Be sure to have a look inside at the murals painted by local artist Fernando Castro Pacheco. Completed in 1978, they were 25 years in the making and portray a symbolic history of the Maya and their interaction with the Spaniards.

FREE Museo de la Ciudad
MUSEUM

(Calle 56 btwn Calles 65 & 67; ⊘9am-8pm Tue-Fri, to noon Sat & Sun) The city museum is housed in the old post office and offers a great reprieve from the hustle, honks and exhaust of this market neighborhood. There are exhibits tracing the city's history back to preconquest days up through the belle époque period, when *henequén* (fibers crafted into ropes from the agave plant) brought riches to the region, and into the 20th century.

Calle 60
STREET

The 17th-century **Iglesia de Jesús**, also called Iglesia de la Tercera Orden, rises a block north of the Plaza Grande, beyond shady Parque Hidalgo. Built by the Jesuits in 1618, it is the sole surviving edifice from a complex of buildings that once filled the entire city block.

North of the church is the enormous bulk of the **Teatro Peón Contreras** (cnr Calles 60 & 57; ⊘visitors 9am-6pm Tue-Sat), built between 1900 and 1908, during Mérida's *henequén* heyday. It boasts a main staircase of Carrara marble, a dome with faded frescoes by Italian artists, and various paintings and murals throughout the building.

Across Calle 60 from the theater is the main building of the **Universidad de Yucatán**. The modern university was established in the 19th century by Governor Felipe Carrillo Puerto and General Manuel Cepeda Peraza.

YUCATÁN PENINSULA MÉRIDA

Mérida

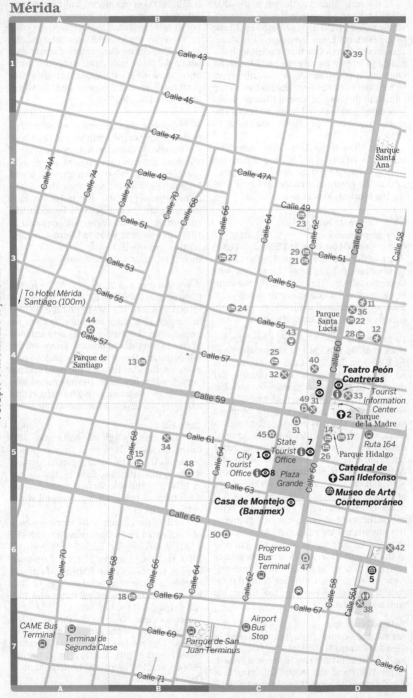

Calle 43

Calle 45

Calle 47

Calle 74A

Calle 74

Calle 72

Calle 49

Calle 47A

Calle 70

Calle 68

Calle 66

Calle 64

Calle 62

Calle 60

Calle 58

Calle 51

Calle 49

Parque Santa Ana

Calle 53

Calle 55

To Hotel Mérida
Santiago (100m)

44

Parque de
Santiago

13

Calle 57

Parque
Santa Lucía

11
36
22
28   12

Calle 59

Teatro Peón
Contreras

Tourist
Information
Center

Parque
de la Madre

Ruta 164

Parque Hidalgo

Catedral de
San Ildefonso

Museo de Arte
Contemporáneo

City
Tourist
Office

State
Tourist
Office

Plaza
Grande

Casa de Montejo
(Banamex)

Calle 65

Calle 68

Calle 66

Calle 64

Calle 62

Progreso
Bus
Terminal

42

5

Calle 70

Calle 67

Airport
Bus
Stop

Calle 58

Calle 56A

38

CAME Bus
Terminal

Terminal de
Segunda Clase

Calle 69

Parque de San
Juan Terminus

Calle 69

Calle 71

A block north of the university is pretty little **Parque Santa Lucía** (cnr Calles 60 & 55), with arcades on the north and west sides. When Mérida was a lot smaller, this was where travelers would get on or off the stagecoaches that linked towns and villages with the provincial capital. The **Bazar de Artesanías**, the local handicrafts market, is held here at 10am on Sunday.

The downtown portion of Calle 60 is closed off to traffic Thursday through Sunday nights, making for a nice stroll.

Paseo de Montejo   STREET

Paseo de Montejo, which runs parallel to Calles 56 and 58, was an attempt by Mérida's 19th-century city planners to create a wide boulevard similar to the Paseo de la Reforma in Mexico City or the Champs-Élysées in Paris.

Europe's architectural and social influence can be seen along the *paseo* in the fine mansions built by wealthy families around the end of the 19th century. The greatest concentrations of surviving mansions are north of Calle 37, and on the first block of Avenida Colón west of Paseo de Montejo.

Museo Regional de Antropología   MUSEUM

(cnr Paseo de Montejo & Calle 43; admission M$41; ⊗8am-5pm Tue-Sun) The massive Palacio Cantón houses Yucatán's regional anthropology museum. Construction of the mansion lasted from 1909 until 1911, and its owner, General Francisco Cantón Rosado (1833–1917), lived here for only six years before his death. The *palacio's* splendor and pretension make it a fitting symbol of the grand aspirations of Mérida's elite during the last years of the Porfiriato, the period from 1876 to 1911 when Porfirio Díaz held despotic sway over Mexico.

The museum covers the peninsula's history since the age of mastodons. Exhibits on Maya culture include explanations (many in Spanish only) of such cosmetic practices as forehead-flattening (done to beautify babies), causing eyes to cross, and sharpening teeth and implanting them with tiny jewels.

FREE **Parque Centenario**   PARK

(⊗6am-6pm Tue-Sun) About 12 blocks west of the Plaza Grande lies this large, verdant park, bordered by Avenida Itzáes, which leads to the airport and becomes the highway to Campeche. The park's **zoo** (admission free; ⊗9am-5pm Tue-Sun) features the fauna of Yucatán, as well as some exotic species.

YUCATÁN PENINSULA MÉRIDA

Mérida

To get there, take a bus west along Calle 61 or 65.

**Museo de Arte Popular
de Yucatán**   ARTS CENTER
(Yucatecan Museum of Popular Art; cnr Calles 50A & 57; donation M$30, Sun free; ⊙9:30am-6pm Tue-Sat, 9am-2pm Sun) This art museum in the Casa Molina is several blocks east of the Plaza Grande in a building built in 1906. There's a small rotating exhibit downstairs that features pop art from around Mexico.

Across the plaza from the museum is **Iglesia La Mejorada**, a large 17th-century church. The building just north of it was a monas-

tery (el Convento de La Mejorada) until the late 19th century. It now houses an architectural school, but visitors are sometimes allowed to view the grounds.

☞ Tours

Many hotels will book the following tours, as will Nómadas Youth Hostel, which also arranges a variety of other tours.

City Tourist Office   WALKING
(☎942-00-00, ext 80119; Plaza Grande, Calle 62) Offers free guided walking tours of the historic center from Monday to Saturday (sometimes in English), focusing on Plaza Grande, departing at 9:30am in front of Pal-

acio Municipal. You can also hire an audio player (in five languages) for a self-guided tour for M$80 from their office.

Turibus BUS
(☏946-24-24; www.turibus.com.mx) Offers hop-on, hop-off tours of Mérida in English and Spanish on its double-decker Circuito Turístico bus (adult/child M$100/50) passing by Plaza Grande, Paseo de Montejo and Parque de las Américas among other places. Buy tickets on board.

Turitransmérida CULTURAL
(☏928-18-71; www.turitransmerida.com.mx; cnr Calles 55 & 58) Offers group tours to sites around Mérida, including Celestún, Chichén Itzá, the Ruta Puuc and Izamal.

Sacred Waters ECOTOUR
(☏928-60-05; www.sacredwaters.com.mx; Calle 53 btwn Calles 58 & 60) Specializes in cenote and ecotourism. Highly trained and experienced in snorkeling, diving and rappelling into some of the region's lesser-known cenotes. Organizes custom tours for people with limited mobility.

🎓 Courses

You can often find a private language tutor through your hostel. Alternatively, **Benjamin Franklin Academy** (☏928-00-97; www.benjaminfranklin.com.mx; cnr Calles 57 & 54) offers Spanish courses.

🎉 Festivals & Events

Universidad de Yucatán Anniversary MUSIC
For most of February the Universidad de Yucatán celebrates its anniversary with free performances by the Ballet Folklórico, concerts of Afro-Cuban music and *son* (Mexican folk music that blends elements of indigenous, Spanish and African musical styles) and other manifestations of Yucatán's cultural roots.

Carnaval CARNIVAL
Prior to Lent, in February or March, Carnaval features colorful costumes and nonstop festivities.

Festival de Trova Yucateca MUSIC
The Festival de Trova Yucateca is held in March. For more on *trova*, see p821.

Semana Santa RELIGIOUS
Semana Santa (Holy Week) is a major celebration in Mérida. The main feature of the celebrations is the city's passion plays.

Cristo de las Ampollas processions RELIGIOUS PARADE
Between September 22 and October 14, *gremios* (guilds or unions) venerate the Cristo de las Ampollas (Christ of the Blisters) statue in the cathedral with processions.

Exposición de Altares de los Muertos RELIGIOUS
Another big religious tradition is the Exposición de Altares de los Muertos (Showing of the Shrines of the Dead) held on the night of November 1. Throughout Mexico families prepare shrines to welcome the spirits of loved ones back to earth. Many Maya prepare elaborate dinners outside their homes, and Mérida observes the occasion with festivities and displays in the center of town from 11am on November 1 until 11am the next day.

🛏 Sleeping

From about December 15 to January 6, and during Semana Santa, many midrange and top-end hotels raise their prices by 10% to 20%. These times and July and August (which also see price increases at some places) tend to be the busiest.

If you're looking for your hotel, remember that odd-numbered streets run east-west; even-numbered streets run north-south. House numbers may increase very slowly, and addresses are usually given in this form: 'Calle 57 No 481 x 56 y 58' (between streets 56 and 58).

TOP CHOICE **Luz en Yucatán** BOUTIQUE HOTEL $$
(☏924-24-00; www.luzenyucatan.com; Calle 55 No 499 btwn Calles 58 & 60; r M$760-830; P❄🐾@🏊) While many much blander hotels are loudly claiming to be 'boutique,' this one is quietly ticking all the boxes – individually decorated rooms, fabulous common areas, a huge staff-to-guest ratio and a wonderful pool/patio area out back. The house they have for rent across the road (US$200/1200 per night/week) is just as good, if not better.

Hotel Piedra de Agua BOUTIQUE HOTEL $$$
(☏924-23-00; www.piedradeagua.com; Calle 60 No 498 btwn Calles 59 & 61; r from M$1600; P❄@🐾🏊) Once a grand old house and now a grand new hotel, this one does it right, with stylish furnishings, good beds, sharp service and a good mix of colonial and modern ambience. The backyard bar is a bonus as is the small gym. Off-season and walk-in discounts go as high as 40%.

Nómadas Youth Hostel HOSTEL **$**

(☑924-52-23; www.nomadastravel.com; Calle 62 No 433 at Calle 51; dm M$129, r with/without bathroom incl breakfast M$358/259; P@🛜🏊) This is Mérida's Backpacker's Central, and the best hostel in the city. There are mixed and women's dorms, as well as private rooms. Guests have use of a fully equipped kitchen with fridge and purified water, 24-hour hot showers, internet and hand-laundry facilities. It even has free salsa classes and an amazing pool out back.

Hotel Marionetas HOTEL **$$$**

(☑928-33-77; www.hotelmarionetas.com; Calle 49 No 516 btwn Calles 62 & 64; r from M$1150; ✳@🛜🏊) Another beautiful colonial hotel set around another inviting patio. The rustic-chic breakfast area overlooking the pool is a nice touch and there are plenty of tastefully selected handicrafts and furnishings serving for decoration. Rooms are everything they should be, but get one upstairs for its ventilation.

Hotel Caribe HOTEL **$$**

(☑924-90-22; www.hotelcaribe.com.mx; Calle 59 No 500 btwn Calles 58 & 60; s/d M$690/750; ✳@🛜🏊) Surrounded by church spires, with a charming fountain tinkling in the courtyard and a fantastic rooftop pool, you can forgive the rooms for being plain here. They're spacious and clean enough – they could be fancier, but then they could be pricier, too.

Rosas y Xocolate BOUTIQUE HOTEL **$$$**

(☑924-29-92; www.rosasandxocolate.com; Paseo de Montejo No 480; r US$215-265, ste US$350-650; P✳@🛜🏊) Built from the remains of two mansions and reusing much of the original materials, this medium-sized boutique hotel goes all-out with custom-made furniture, Bose sound systems in every room and open-air baths. The requisite air-conditioned gym, full-day spa and gourmet restaurant are all onsite.

Hotel Mérida Santiago HOTEL **$$**

(☑cell phone 999-2854447; www.hotelmerida santiago.com; Calle 74 A No 499 btwn Calles 57 & 59 A; s US$65-1100, d US$72-1200; P✳@🛜🏊) With just four rooms, it's a good idea to book ahead here. Rooms are spacious (and bathrooms huge) and stylishly decorated with hand-picked, locally made items. The Dutch/Mexican couple who run it are full of info and tips.

Los Arcos Bed & Breakfast B&B **$$**

(☑928-02-14; www.losarcosmerida.com; Calle 66 btwn Calles 49 & 53; s/d M$1180/1300; P✳@🛜🏊) Certainly not for minimalists – there's art on every wall and in every corner – Los Arcos is a lovely, gay-friendly B&B with two guest rooms at the end of a drop-dead-gorgeous garden and pool area. Book ahead, even in low season.

Hotel Hacienda Mérida HOTEL **$$$**

(☑924-43-63; www.hotelhaciendamerida.com; Calle 62 btwn Calles 51 & 53; r from M$1950; P✳🛜🏊) With a tranquility that belies its great downtown location, the Hacienda is lovely any time but especially at night when illuminated columns lead you past the pool to your classically styled chambers.

Hotel Casa Becil HOTEL **$**

(☑924-67-64; hotelcasabecil@yahoo.com.mx; Calle 67 No 550C btwn Calles 66 & 68; s/d with fan M$270/320, with air-con M$300/350; ✳🛜) Classic budget digs (the spongy mattress, the 'vintage' shower curtain) under the watchful eye of a friendly señora. The kitchen for guest use and plant-filled patio are bonuses.

Hostel Casa Nico HOSTEL **$**

(☑cell phone 999-2868944; www.hostelcasanico. com; Calle 63 No 517 btwn Calles 66A & 68; dm M$80, s/d from M$180/260; @🛜🏊) A simple, family-run hostel that's just far enough off the trail to keep it quiet, but still in a central location. Rooms are big and bare and a little run-down; dorms sleep eight.

Hotel del Peregrino HOTEL **$$**

(☑924-30-07; www.hoteldelperegrino.com; Calle 51 No 488 btwn Calles 54 & 56; r M$700; ✳@🛜) A tranquil little place, offering medium-sized, oddly shaped rooms around a small but pretty patio.

Hotel Montejo HOTEL **$$**

(☑928-03-90; www.hotelmontejo.com; Calle 57 btwn Calles 62 & 64; s/d/tr incl continental breakfast M$550/650/750; ✳🛜) This an eclectic, one-of-a-kind hotel with a central courtyard loaded with 400-year-old stone columns. Its big, clean rooms with classic colonial doors and tiled bathrooms are distributed around the courtyard on two floors.

Casa Mexilio HOTEL **$$**

(☑928-25-05; www.casamexilio.com; Calle 68 No 495 btwn Calles 57 & 59; r incl breakfast M$711-1115; P✳🛜🏊) A charming Colonial hotel with rooms all over the place and antiques by the truckload. The cheapest rooms are small, but the upstairs salon/bar will probably compensate for that.

Hotel Medio Mundo   HOTEL $$
(924-54-72; www.hotelmediomundo.com; Calle 55 No 533 btwn Calles 64 & 66; incl breakfast d with fan M$940, with air-con M$1080-1150; ❄@🛜🏊) Slightly out of the way (but not really) and with a couple of incongruous flaws like patches of peeling paint, the rooms here are generously sized and set around two lovely patios, the back one with a decent-sized swimming pool.

Hotel Maison Lafitte   HOTEL $$
(928-12-43; www.maisonlafitte.com.mx; Calle 60 No 472 btwn Calles 53 & 55; d/tr incl breakfast M$950/1100; P❄🛜🏊) Rooms here are very beige, and the ceilings too low for a colonial house, but with a couple of onsite restaurants, a lovely leafy pool area and a central location, this is a reasonable deal.

Hotel Aragón   HOTEL $$
(924-02-42; Calle 57 No 474 btwn Calles 52 & 54; s/d/ste M$480/580/800; P❄🛜🏊) The common areas of this hotel are great, with a large courtyard and a narrow pool along one side. If only it followed the same theme in the modern, rather stagnant rooms.

Gran Hotel   HOTEL $$
(923-69-63; www.granhoteldemerida.com.mx; Calle 60 No 496 btwn Calles 59 & 61; s/d M$600/800; P❄🛜) With a colorful history (Fidel stayed here), an antique-packed lobby (pieces for sale if something catches your eye) and marble staircase, this classic hotel is all very impressive...until you see the rooms. Drab furniture and seriously worn carpets are the biggest perpetrators. Still, for the price and location it's not a bad deal.

Hotel Dolores Alba   HOTEL $$
(928-56-50; www.doloresalba.com; Calle 63 No 464 btwn Calles 52 & 54; s/d M$650/700; P❄@🛜🏊) Rooms are on three floors (with an elevator) around two large courtyards. Those in the new, modern wing are quite large, with good beds and TV, and face the lovely pool. Those in the older building have a bit more character.

✗ Eating

🔺 Chaya Maya   YUCATECAN $
(cnr Calles 62 & 57; mains M$50-85; ☺7am-11pm; ✍) Extremely popular with locals and visitors alike, this place probably has the best combination of 'authenticity,' atmosphere and value for money of any of the traditional Yucatecan restaurants in town.

Rescoldo's   MEDITERRANEAN $$
(Calle 62 No 366 btwn Calles 41 & 43; mains M$90-1160; ☺6-10pm Tue-Thu, 6-11pm Fri & Sat) Offering up wood-fired pizzas and calzones, yummy pastas and rounding it off with homemade gelato, this highly recommended Mediterranean restaurant is a great place to get a little variety in your diet.

Libertad Café   CAFE $
(Calle 60 btwn Calles 53 & 55; mains M$60-85; ☺7am-11pm; ✍) Soft jazz plays and eclectic art graces the walls at this work-in-progress cafe/bar/restaurant. The food on offer consists of funky twists on classic cafe fare like quiches, salads and sandwiches. Live music Friday and Saturday nights.

La Casa de Frida   MEXICAN $$
(Calle 61 btwn Calles 66 & 68; mains M$115-165; ☺6-11pm) With a leafy courtyard and some original spins on Mexican standards (try the duck in *mole* sauce) this intimate little restaurant makes for a romantic dinner spot.

Slavia   FUSION $$
(cnr Paseo de Montejo & Calle 29; mains M$120-250; ☺7pm-2am) In front of the *monumento a la bandera* (flag monument) this incongruous little place is jam packed with Asian knickknacks and serves up some pretty good fusion food, with an emphasis on carpaccios and fondues. It really works best as a bar, though – the crowd is a bit older and the atmosphere a little more relaxed than many in the downtown area.

Cubaro   CAFE $$
(cnr Paseo de Montejo & Calle 29; mains M$115-240; ☺5pm-2am) Slavia's sister restaurant is a bit more relaxed and has some great outdoor areas, including a terrace with a close-up view of the monument. The menu is a bit more conventional, but everything is carefully prepared and the service is very crisp.

Amaro   MEXICAN $$
(Calle 59 btwn Calles 60 & 62; mains M$80-160; ☺11am-2am; ✍) A romantic dining spot, especially at night, when there's usually a duo performing ballads. It's set in the courtyard of the house in which Andrés Quintana Roo – poet, statesman and drafter of Mexico's Declaration of Independence – was born in 1787. May close at 11pm on slow nights.

YUCATÁN PENINSULA MÉRIDA

Los Almendros

YUCATECAN $$

(cnr Calles 57 & 57A; mains M$85-130; ☺10am-11pm) An institution before they started opening sister restaurants all over the state, Los Almendros is a favorite for traditional Yucatecan food served up in slightly formal surrounds.

Il Caffé Italiano

ITALIAN $$

(Calle 57A btwn Calles 58 & 60; mains M$90-160; ☺8am-midnight Mon-Sat) If you're in need of a pasta fix, this place is about your best bet downtown. Sidewalk tables on the pedestrian thoroughfare add to the appeal.

La Chopería

STEAKHOUSE $$

(Calle 56 No 456 btwn Calles 51 & 53; mains M$80-150; ☺1pm-2am Tue-Sat, 1-7pm Sun) A little bit more of a beer barn than an actual restaurant, La Chopería still serves up some excellent steaks and other meat dishes with a Brazilian slant. It's a bit fancier than most downtown bars and the big outdoor area is the place to be on those balmy Mérida nights.

Restaurante Pórtico del Peregrino

INTERNATIONAL $$

(Calle 57 btwn Calles 60 & 62; mains M$120-180; ☺noon-midnight) Pleasant traditional dining rooms surround a small, pretty patio at this casual but refined eatery offering Yucatecan classics like stuffed cheese as well as a good range of international dishes.

Mercado Municipal Lucas de Gálvez

MARKET $

(cnr Calles 56A & 67) Mérida's least-expensive eateries are in the Mercado Municipal Lucas de Gálvez.

A few blocks east of the Plaza Grande are side-by-side **supermarkets** (Calle 56) as well as a branch of **Super Bodega** (cnr Calles 67 & 54A), a market-department store chain.

🍷 Drinking

Maya Pub

BAR

(Calle 62 btwn Calles 55 & 57; admission free; ☺8pm-late Wed-Sun) Popular with backpackers and *meridano* would-be backpackers, this place keeps it real with a decent pool table and a big beer garden out back. There's live music on weekends and the bar snacks (around M$40) remove the need for an Oxxo run.

☆ Entertainment

Mérida offers many folkloric and musical events in parks and historic buildings, put on by local performers of considerable skill. Admission is free except as noted. Check with one of the tourist information offices to confirm schedules and find out about special events; www.yucatantoday.com offers monthly news and often highlights seasonal events.

Mérida has several cinemas, most of which show first-run Hollywood fare in English, with Spanish subtitles (ask *¿inglés?'* if you need to be sure), as well as other foreign films and Mexican offerings. Cinema tickets cost about M$45 for evening shows, M$25 for matinees. Try **MM Cinemas** (Calle 57 btwn Calles 70 & 72) or **Teatro Mérida** (Calle 62 btwn Calles 59 & 61).

The best combination of drinking and people-watching is to be had at the tables belonging to the restaurants on Calle 60, in front of Parque Hidalgo. Snacks and more serious meals are available at reasonable prices.

Take a cab to the Prolongación de Montejo, where you'll have your choice of bumping discos and uberchic lounges. Most charge a cover. **El Cielo** (☎944-51-27; Prolongación de Montejo btwn Calle 15 & 17) is a local favorite, as is the nearby **La Parranda** (cnr Prolongación de Montejo s/n & Calle 13).

🔒 Shopping

Mérida is a fine place for buying Yucatecan handicrafts. Purchases to consider include hammocks and traditional Maya clothing such as the colorful, embroidered *huipiles* (indigenous woman's sleeveless tunic), panama hats and, of course, the wonderfully comfortable *guayaberas* (thin-fabric shirts with pockets and appliquéd designs worn by Yucatecan men).

During the last days of February or the beginning of March (the dates vary) Kihuic takes place. This is a market that fills the Plaza Grande with handicraft artisans from all over Mexico.

Casa de las Artesanías

HANDICRAFTS

(Calle 63 btwn Calles 64 & 66; ☺9am-8pm Mon-Sat, to 2pm Sun) One place to start looking for handicrafts is this government-supported market for local artisans selling just about everything. Prices are fixed and a bit high.

Artesanías Bazar García Rejón

MARKET

(cnr Calles 65 & 60) Concentrates a wide variety of products into one area of shops.

Guayabera Jack

CLOTHING

(Calle 59 btwn Calles 60 & 62) The *guayabera* is the classic Mérida shirt, but buying the

DON'T MISS

YUCATÁN YUMMIES

One of the great things about traveling in Mexico is the range of regional food on offer. Go a couple of hundred kilometers down the road and the entire menu can change drastically. With strong influences both from Mayan and European cultures, the Yucatán Peninsula is no exception. Here are some dishes you're bound to see on menus and that are well worth checking out:

» **Cochinita pibil** Suckling pig marinated in citrus juices and *achiote* (a spice made from the red seed of the annatto tree) and traditionally buried and roasted in a fire pit.

» **Queso relleno** A ball of Edam cheese, hollowed out, filled with ground pork and smothered with tomato sauce and gravy.

» **Papadzules** Dried, hard-boiled eggs wrapped in tortillas and covered first in a squash sauce, then in a tomato one.

» **Panuchos** Fried tortillas stuffed with black beans, grilled chicken, onion, tomato, lettuce and avocado.

» **Sopa de lima** Soup made from turkey, lime and tortilla pieces.

» **Dulce de papaya** A dessert featuring seasoned green papaya, cooked in a sugary syrup and accompanied by Edam cheese.

wrong one you run the risk of looking like a waiter. Drop into this famous shop to avoid getting asked for the bill.

Hamacas Mérida HANDICRAFTS
(Calle 65 btwn Calles 62 & 64) While everybody in town wants to sell you a hammock, this is a good option – they sell by weight at fixed prices (M$280 to M$350) and can ship worldwide.

Alma Mexicana SOUVENIRS
(Calle 54 btwn Calles 55 & 57) Handicrafts, gifts and souvenirs that you won't see on every street corner.

Librería Dante BOOKS
(☑928-36-74; Calle 59 btwn Calles 60 & 62; ☺8am-9:30pm Mon-Sat, 10am-6pm Sun) An excellent collection focusing on history, culture and travel. Some titles in English, but mostly Spanish.

❶ Information

Emergency
Emergency (☑066)
Fire (☑924-92-42)
Police (☑942-00-70)
Cruz Roja (Red Cross; ☑924-98-13)

Internet Access
Most internet places around town charge M$10 per hour. Most of the plazas in town are wi-fi hot spots.

Laundry
Most upmarket hotels offer overnight laundry service.
Lavandería La Fe (Calle 64 btwn Calles 55 & 57; per 3kg load M$45; ☺8am-6pm Mon-Fri, to 2pm Sat)

Medical Services
Clínica Mérida (☑924-18-00; Av de los Itzáes 242)

Money
Banks and ATMs are scattered throughout the city.

Post
Post office (Calle 53 No 469; ☺9am-4pm Mon-Fri, 9am-1pm Sat)

Tourist Information
City tourist office (☑942-00-00; Plaza Grande, Calle 62; ☺8am-8pm Mon-Sat, to 2pm Sun)
State tourist office (☑930-31-01; Plaza Grande, Calle 61; ☺8am-9pm) In the entrance to the Palacio de Gobierno.
Tourist Information Center (☑924-92-90; cnr Calles 60 & 57A; ☺8am-9pm)
Yucatán Today (www.yucatantoday.com) A Spanish-English magazine devoted to tourism in Yucatán.

Travel Agencies
Nómadas Travel (☑948-11-87; www.nomadas travel.com.mx; Prolongación Paseo de Montejo No 370, Colonia Benito Juárez Norte) Books flights and offers services for student travelers.

Websites

Lonely Planet (www.lonelyplanet.com/
mexico/yucatan-peninsula/merida) Planning
advice, author recommendations, traveler
reviews and insider tips.

Getting There & Away

Air

Mérida's tiny but modern airport is a 10km,
20-minute ride southwest of the Plaza Grande
off Hwy 180 (Avenida de los Itzáes). It has car-
rental desks, an ATM and a currency-exchange
booth, and a **tourist information booth**
(☺9am-5pm) that helps mainly with hotel
reservations.

Most international flights to Mérida are
connections through Mexico City or Cancún.
Nonstop international services are provided
by Continental Airlines (from Houston, several
times weekly). Most domestic flights are operated by small regional airlines, with a few flights
by Aeroméxico. The following airlines are represented in Mérida:

Aeroméxico (☎800-021-40-00; www
.aeromexico.com) Mérida (☎948-14-19) Flies to
Mexico City, Los Angeles and Miami.

Continental Airlines (☎800-900-50-00;
www.continental.com) Mérida (☎946-18-88;
Paseo Montejo No 437 at Calle 29) Flies nonstop between Houston and Mérida.

Bus

Mérida is the bus transportation hub of the
Yucatán Peninsula. Take the usual precautions
with your gear on night buses and those serving
popular tourist destinations (especially 2nd-
class buses) at any time. See the table for prices
and more information.

There are a number of bus terminals, and some
lines operate from (and stop at) more than one
terminal. Tickets for departure from one terminal
can often be bought at another, and destinations
overlap greatly among bus lines. Some lines offer
round-trip tickets to nearby towns that reduce
the fare quite a bit. Check out http://boletotal.
mx. Following are some of the terminals, the bus
lines operating from them and areas served.

CAME bus terminal (☎reservations 924-83-
91; Calle 70 btwn Calles 69 & 71) Sometimes
referred to as the 'Terminal de Primera Clase,'
Mérida's main bus terminal has mostly 1st-class
buses, including ADO, OCC and ADO GL.

Fiesta Americana bus terminal (☎924-08
55; Av Colón near Calle 56A) A small 1st-class
terminal on the west side of the hotel complex.

Noreste bus terminal (Calle 67 btwn Calles 50
& 52) Second-class Noreste, Sur and Oriente
bus lines use this terminal.

Parque de San Juan terminus (Calle 69 btwn
Calles 62 & 64) From all around the square and

church, vans and combis depart for
Dzibilchaltún, Muna, Oxkutzcab, Tekax, Ticul
and other points.

Progreso bus terminal (Calle 62 No 524 btwn
Calles 65 & 67) There's a separate terminal
serving Progreso.

Terminal de Segunda Clase (Calle 69) Also
known as Terminal 69 (Sesenta y Nueve) or
simply Terminal de Autobuses, this terminal is
located just around the corner from the CAME
bus terminal. ADO, Mayab, Oriente and Sur run
mostly 2nd-class buses to points in the state
and around the peninsula.

Car & Motorcycle

The most flexible way to tour the many archaeological sites around Mérida is by rental
car, especially if you have two or more people
to share costs. Assume you will pay a total of
M$550 to M$650 per day (tax, insurance and
gas included) for short-term rental of a cheap
car, although shopping around you might luck
onto one for half that. Getting around Mérida's
sprawling tangle of one-way streets and
careening buses is better done on foot or on a
careening bus.

Several agencies have branches at the airport
as well as on Calle 60 between Calles 55 and 57,
including **National** (☎923-24-93), **Easy Way**
(☎930-90-21) and **Payless** (☎924-14-78). All
rent for about M$350 to M$500 a day. You'll get
the best deal by booking ahead of time over the
internet.

See p258 for details of the pricey toll highway
between Mérida and Cancún.

Getting Around

If you're driving, bear in mind that from 8pm
Saturday to 11pm Sunday, Calles 60 and 62 are
closed to motor vehicles between Plaza Grande
and Calle 55.

To/From the Airport

Bus 69 (Aviación) travels between the airport
and the city center every 15 to 30 minutes until
9pm, with occasional service until 11pm. The
half-hour trip (M$8) is via a roundabout route;
the best place to catch it is on Calle 62, between
Calles 67 and 69.

A taxi from the city center to the airport should
cost about M$90 (but it's hard to get this price
from the airport, so walk out to the main street
and flag one down or else be prepared to pay
M$200).

Bus

Most parts of Mérida that you'll want to visit
are within five or six blocks of the Plaza Grande
and are thus accessible on foot. Given the slow
speed of city traffic, particularly in the market

areas, travel on foot is also the fastest way to get around.

City buses are cheap at M$8, but routes can be confusing. Most start in suburban neighborhoods, skirt the city center and terminate in another distant suburban neighborhood. To travel between the Plaza Grande and the upscale neighborhoods to the north along Paseo de Montejo, catch the Ruta 164 on the corner of Calles 59 and 58, a block north of the Parque Hidalgo. To return to the city center, catch any bus heading south on Paseo de Montejo displaying the same sign and/or 'Centro.'

Taxi

There are more and more *taxímetros* (metered taxis) in town. For regular taxi service, rates should generally be fixed, with a M$30 minimum

BUSES FROM MÉRIDA

DESTINATION	FARE (M$)	DURATION	FREQUENCY (DAILY)
Campeche (short route)	150-180	2½-3½hr	hourly ADO, 3 ADO GL (from CAME, Terminal de Segunda Clase)
Cancún	80-322	4-6hr	2 Oriente, frequent ADO, OCC & ADO GL (from CAME, Terminal de Segunda Clase, Noreste terminal)
Celestún	47	2hr	6 daily Oriente from Noreste terminal
Chetumal	246-300	6-8hr	4 ADO, 5 Mayab from CAME
Chichén Itzá	63	1¾-2½hr	frequent ADO from CAME, Terminal de Segunda Clase
Escárcega	77-202	5-5½hr	5 Sur, 3 ADO (from CAME, Terminal de Segunda Clase)
Felipe Carrillo Puerto	156	5½-6hr	9 Mayab from CAME, Terminal de Segunda Clase
Izamal	22	1½hr	frequent Oriente from Noreste terminal
Mayapán Ruinas	16	1½hr	hourly Sur from Noreste terminal, continuing to Oxkutzcab
Mexico City (Terminal Norte)	1404	19hr	8 ADO from CAME
Palenque	410	8-9hr	4 daily ADO, OCC (from CAME, Terminal de Segunda Clase)
Playa del Carmen	190-528	4½-8hr	frequent Mayab, OCC & ADO (from CAME, Terminal de Segunda Clase)
Río Lagartos	146	3-4hr	1st-class Noreste 5:30pm from Noreste terminal
Ticul	40	1¾hr	3 Mayab from Terminal de Segunda Clase; frequent combis from Parque de San Juan
Tizimín	85-114	2½-4hr	frequent from Noreste terminal
Tulum	154-266	4hr	frequent Mayab & ADO (from CAME, Terminal de Segunda Clase)
Uxmal	44	1-1½hr	5 Oriente from Terminal de Segunda Clase
Valladolid	85-180	2½-3½hr	hourly ADO & 2nd-class Oriente (from CAME, Terminal de Segunda Clase)

fare, which will get you from the bus terminals to all downtown hotels, but be sure to agree on a price beforehand if there's no meter. Most rides within city limits do not exceed M$60. Taxi stands can be found at most of the barrio (neighborhood) parks, or dial ⌨923-13-17 or 920-50-91; service is available 24 hours (dispatch fees cost an extra M$10 to M$20).

South of Mérida

There's a lot to do and see south of Mérida. The major draws are the old *henequén* plantations, some still used for cultivating leaves, and the well-preserved Maya ruins like Uxmal and the lesser-known sites along the Ruta Puuc.

UXMAL

Pronounced 'oosh-mahl,' Uxmal (admission M$166, parking M$20, guides M$450-550; ⊘8am-5pm) is one impressive set of ruins, easily ranking among the top Maya archaeological sites. It is a large site with some fascinating structures in good condition and bearing a riot of ornamentation. Adding to Uxmal's appeal is its setting in the hilly Puuc region, which lent its name to the architectural patterns in this area. *Puuc* means 'hills,' and these, rising up to about 100m, are the first relief from the flatness of the northern and western portions of the peninsula.

The price of admission, if you retain the ticket, includes a 45-minute **sound-and-light show** (⊘8pm summer, 7pm winter). It's in Spanish, but translation devices are available (M$39).

HISTORY

Uxmal was an important city, and its dominance extended to the nearby towns of Sayil, Kabah, Xlapak and Labná. Although Uxmal means 'Thrice Built' in Maya, it was actually constructed five times.

That a sizable population flourished in this dry area is yet more testament to the engineering skills of the Maya, who built a series of reservoirs and *chultunes* (cisterns) lined with lime mortar to catch and hold water during the dry season. First settled in about AD 600, Uxmal was influenced by highland Mexico in its architecture, most likely through contact fostered by trade. This influence is reflected in the town's serpent imagery, phallic symbols and columns. The well-proportioned Puuc architecture, with its intricate, geometric mosaics sweeping across the upper parts of elongated facades, was also strongly influenced by the slightly earlier Río Bec and Chenes styles.

The scarcity of water in the region meant that Chac, the rain god or sky serpent, was supreme in importance. His image is ubiquitous at the site, in the form of stucco masks protruding from facades and cornices. There is much speculation as to why Uxmal was largely abandoned in about AD 900; drought conditions may have reached such proportions that the inhabitants had to relocate. Later, the Xiu dynasty, which had controlled Uxmal for several hundred years, moved their seat of power to near present-day Maní, launching a rebellion against the kingdom of Mayapán, which had usurped much of the power in the region.

Rediscovered by archaeologists in the 19th century, Uxmal was first excavated in 1929 by Frans Blom. Although much of the site has been restored, much has yet to be discovered.

◎ Sights

Casa del Adivino   TEMPLE
This 39m-high temple (the Magician's House) was built on an oval base. The smoothly sloping sides have been restored, and they date from the temple's fifth incarnation. The four earlier temples were covered in the rebuilding, except for the high doorway on the west side, which remains from the fourth incarnation. Decorated in elaborate Chenes style, the doorway proper forms the mouth of a gigantic Chac mask.

Cuadrángulo de las Monjas   PLAZA
The sprawling 74-room Nuns' Quadrangle is west of the Casa del Adivino. Archaeologists guess variously that it was a military academy, royal school or palace complex. The long-nosed face of Chac appears everywhere on the facades of the four separate temples that form the quadrangle. The northern temple, grandest of the four, was built first, followed by the southern, then the eastern and finally the western.

Several decorative elements on the facades show signs of Toltec, Río Bec and Chenes influence. The feathered-serpent (Quetzalcóatl or, in Maya, Kukulcán) motif along the top of the west temple's facade is one of these. Note also the stylized depictions of the *na* (Maya thatched hut) over some of the doorways in the northern and southern buildings.

Passing through the corbeled arch in the middle of the south building of the quadrangle and continuing down the slope takes you through the **Juego de Pelota** (Ball Court). Turn left and head up the steep slope and stairs to the large terrace.

Casa de las Tortugas
TEMPLE

To the right at the top of the stairs is the House of the Turtles, which takes its name from the turtles carved on the cornice. The Maya associated turtles with the rain god, Chac. According to Maya myth, when the people suffered from drought, so did the turtles, and both prayed to Chac to send rain.

The frieze of short columns, or 'rolled mats,' that runs around the temple below

the turtles is characteristic of the Puuc style. On the west side of the building a vault has collapsed, affording a good view of the corbeled arch that supported it.

Palacio del Gobernador
PALACE

The Governor's Palace has a magnificent facade nearly 100m long, which Mayanist Michael D Coe called 'the finest structure at Uxmal and the culmination of the Puuc style.' Buildings in Puuc style have walls filled with rubble, faced with cement and then covered in a thin veneer of limestone squares; the lower part of the facade is plain, the upper part festooned with stylized Chac

Uxmal

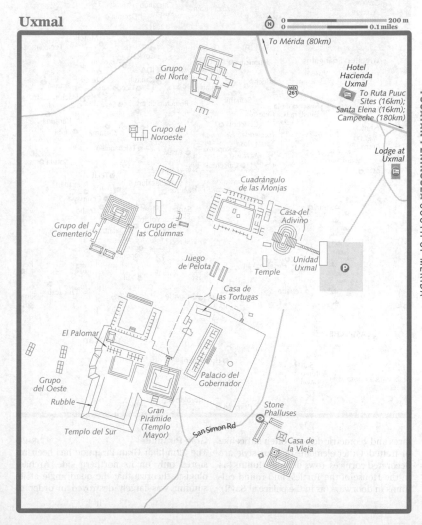

South of Mérida

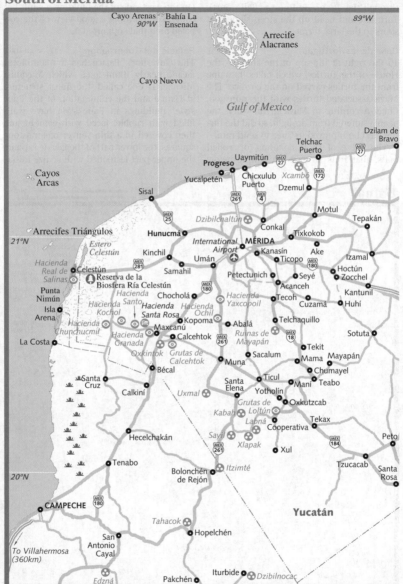

YUCATÁN PENINSULA SOUTH OF MÉRIDA

faces and geometric designs, often latticelike or fretted. Other elements of Puuc style are decorated cornices, rows of half-columns (as in the House of the Turtles) and round columns in doorways (as in the palace at Sayil).

Gran Pirámide   PYRAMID

The 32m-high Gran Pirámide has been restored only on its northern side. Archaeologists theorize that the quadrangle at its summit was largely destroyed in order to

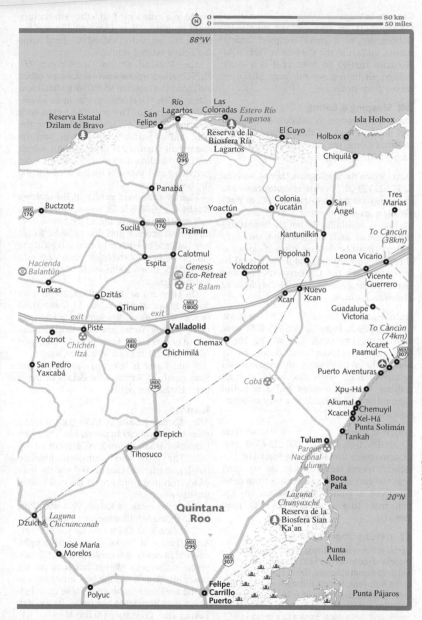

construct a second pyramid above it. Why that work was never completed remains unknown.

El Palomar
BUILDING

West of the Great Pyramid sits a structure whose roofcomb is latticed with a pattern reminiscent of the Moorish pigeon houses built into walls in Spain and northern Africa, hence the building's name, 'The Dovecote.' The nine honeycombed triangular 'belfries' sit on top of a building that was once part of a quadrangle.

Casa de la Vieja
BUILDING

Off the southeast corner of the Palacio del Gobernador is a small complex, largely rubble, known as the Casa de la Vieja (Old Woman's House). In front of it is a small *palapa* sheltering several large phalluses carved from stone.

🛏 Sleeping & Eating

There is no town at Uxmal, only several top-end hotels. Cheaper lodgings can be found in Santa Elena (see p310), 16km away, or in Ticul, 30km to the east.

Hotel Villas Arqueológicas Uxmal
HOTEL $$

(☑222-273-79-00; www.villasarqueologicas.com. mx; r incl continental breakfast M$1030; ✳🛜🛋) This is a good family spot, with a pool, tennis courts and billiards, but the rooms are rather small and the beds are curiously springy (must be the humidity). It's also the cheapest joint around, and it has a good library to check out Catherwood's amazing Uxmal illustrations in the book *Incidents of Travel in Yucatán*.

Hotel Hacienda Uxmal
HOTEL $$$

(☑997-976-20-31, in the US 800-235-4079; www. mayaland.com; r from M$2200; ✳🛋) This Mayaland resort is 500m from the ruins. It housed the archaeologists who explored and restored Uxmal. Wide, tiled verandas, high ceilings, great bathrooms and a beautiful swimming pool make this a very comfortable place to stay.

Lodge at Uxmal
HOTEL $$$

(☑997-976-20-31, in the US 800-235-4079; www. mayaland.com; r from M$1200; ✳🛜🛋) The Hacienda's rooms are a bit nicer, but you can't beat the easy access to the ruins from here. The pool is equally delicious, as are the monstrous tubs – some rooms even have Jacuzzis.

ℹ Getting There & Away

Uxmal is 80km from Mérida. Most buses plying the inland route between Mérida and Campeche will drop you off at Uxmal, Santa Elena, Kabah or the Ruta Puuc turnoff. But when you want to leave, passing buses may be full (especially on Saturday and Monday). Some people avoid the hassle and rent a car or book a tour in Mérida. If you do get stuck, a taxi to nearby Santa Elena shouldn't cost more than M$150.

SANTA ELENA

The nearest town to Uxmal is Santa Elena. There's a small **museum** (admission M$10; ⊙9am-6:30pm Mon-Fri, 9am-7pm Sat & Sun) ded-icated to a gruesome find – the 18th-century child mummies that were found buried beneath the adjoining cathedral – and some *henequén*-related exhibits.

The **Pickled Onion** (☑cell phone 997-1117922; www.thepickledonionyucatan.com; cabins incl continental breakfast M$350; @🛋) hotel and eatery offers the chance to stay in an adobe-walled Maya hut. The primitive rooms keep you cool with a *palapa* roof. We love the pool and its surrounding gardens, and the restaurant (mains M$70 to M$100), which features sizzling fajitas and yummy cold gazpacho and avocado soups, is said to be the best in town.

There's a pleasant garden at **Bungalows Sacbé** (☑997-978-51-58; www.sacbebungalows. com.mx; d from M$350), and all the rooms have fans, good screens and decent beds. To get here, ask the bus driver to drop you off at the *campo de béisbol* (baseball field) *de Santa Elena*. It's about 200m south of the town's southern entrance.

On Hwy 261 at the southern entrance to Santa Elena, **Restaurante El Chac-Mool** (mains M$40-80; ⊙8am-9pm) is a friendly place serving Yucatecan food that includes a hearty vegetarian plate of rice, beans and fried bananas. It has a little store, too.

Santa Elena is 16km east of Uxmal and 8km north of Kabah – for details of buses from Uxmal, see p310.

KABAH

After Uxmal, Kabah (AD 750–950) was the most important city in the region. The **ruins** (admission M$37; ⊙8am-5pm) straddle Hwy 261. The guard-shack–cum–souvenir-shop (selling snacks and cold drinks) and the bulk of the restored ruins are on the east side of the highway.

For a free map of Kabah, visit www.lone lyplanet.com/additional-mexico-maps.

The facade of **El Palacio de los Mascarones** (Palace of Masks) is an amazing sight, covered in nearly 300 masks of Chac, the rain god or sky serpent. Most of their huge curling noses are broken off; the best intact beak is at the building's south end. These curled-up noses may have given the palace its modern Maya name, Codz Poop (Rolled Mat).

Once you're up to your ears in noses, head around the back to check out the two restored **atlantes** (an atlas – plural *atlantes* – is a male figure used as a supporting column). These are especially interesting, as they're among the very few 3D human figures you'll see at a Maya site. One is headless and the other wears a jaguar mask atop his head.

From here be sure to check out **El Palacio** (The Palace), with its groups of decorative *columnillas* (little columns) on the upper part of the facade; these are a distinctive characteristic of Puuc architectural style. A couple of hundred meters through the jungle from here is **Templo de las Columnas**. This building has more rows of impressive decorative columns.

Across the highway from El Palacio, a path leads to the **Gran Pirámide** (Great Pyramid). From here, the path ends at the impressive, restored **El Arco**. It's said that the *sacbé* leading from here goes through the jungle all the way to Uxmal, terminating at a smaller arch; in the other direction it goes to Labná. Once, much of the Yucatán Peninsula was connected by these marvelous 'white roads' of rough limestone.

Kabah is 104km from Mérida, a ride of about two hours. Buses will usually stop if you flag them down at the entrance to the ruins.

RUTA PUUC

Just 5km south of Kabah on Hwy 261, a road branches off to the east and winds past the ruins of Sayil, Xlapak and Labná, ending at the Grutas de Loltún. This is the Ruta Puuc, and its sites offer some marvelous architectural detail and a deeper acquaintance with the Puuc Maya civilization, which flourished between about AD 750 and 950.

Until the Ruta Puuc circuit bus (based in Mérida) is reinstated, the most convenient way to visit the Ruta Puuc sites is by car.

◉ **Sights**

Sayil   RUIN
(admission M$37; ◷8am-5pm) The ruins of Sayil are 4.5km from the junction of the Ruta Puuc with Hwy 261.

Sayil is best known for **El Palacio**, the huge three-tiered building with a facade some 85m long, reminiscent of the Minoan palace on Crete. The distinctive columns of Puuc architecture are used here over and over – as supports for the lintels, as decoration between doorways and as a frieze above them – alternating with huge stylized Chac masks and 'descending gods.'

Taking the path south from the palace for about 400m and bearing left, you come to the temple **El Mirador**, whose roosterlike roofcomb was once painted bright red.

About 100m beyond El Mirador, beneath a protective *palapa*, is a stela bearing the relief of a fertility god with an enormous phallus. About halfway along is a turnoff to the right for the **Templo de las Jambas Jeroglíficas**, with six doorways, one of which features some fine, well-preserved carvings.

FREE **Xlapak**   RUIN
(◷8am-5pm) From the entrance gate at Sayil, it's 6km east to the entrance gate at Xlapak. The name means 'Old Walls' in Maya and was a general term among local people for ancient ruins. The ornate *palacio* at Xlapak (*shla*-pak) is quite a bit smaller than those at Kabah and Sayil, only about 20m in length. It's decorated with the Chac masks, columns and colonnades, and fretted geometric latticework of the Puuc style. The building is interesting and on a bit of a lean. Plenty of motmots (a colorful bird) brighten up the surrounding forests.

Museo de Cacao   MUSEUM
(adult/child M$60/40; ◷9am-6pm) Just off the highway between Xlapak and Labná, this fascinating new museum focuses on the history and use of cacao, a sacred drink of the Maya. Five thematically organized huts take on different aspects of cultivation and preparation as well as traditional Maya architecture, burial rites and clothing. The cafe/gift store here makes for a good lunch stop, too.

Labná   RUIN
(admission M$37; ◷8am-5pm) Archaeologists believe that at one point in the 9th century some 3000 Maya lived at Labná. To support such numbers in these arid hills, water was collected in *chultunes*. At Labná's peak there were some 60 *chultunes* in and around the city. Head over to www.lonelyplanet.com/additional-mexico-maps for a free map of Labná.

El Palacio, the first building you come to at Labná, is one of the longest in the Puuc region, and much of its interesting decorative carving is in good shape. On the west corner of the main structure's facade is a serpent's head with a human face peering out from between its jaws, the symbol of the planet Venus. Toward the hill from this is an impressive Chac mask, and nearby is the lower half of a human figure (possibly a ball player) in loincloth and leggings.

DIY: EXPLORE THE BACK ROADS SOUTH OF MÉRIDA

There are numerous attractions worth seeing as you travel south from Mérida. Here are a few of our favorites.

» **Hacienda Yaxcopoil** A vast estate that grew and processed *henequén;* many of its numerous French Renaissance-style buildings have undergone picturesque restorations.

» **Hacienda Ochil** Provides a fascinating, though basic, look at how *henequén* was grown and processed.

» **Grutas de Calcehtok** These caves are said by some to compose the longest dry-cave system on the Yucatán Peninsula.

» **Oxkintok** Inscriptions found at the site contain some of the oldest known dates in the Yucatán, and indicate that the city was inhabited from the pre-Classic to the post-Classic period (300 BC to AD 1500), reaching its greatest importance between AD 475 and 860.

» **Ruined hacienda route** A fascinating alternative return route if you're driving out of Celestún is to turn south off Hwy 281 where a sign points to Chunchucmil. Here you'll find a series of old haciendas.

» **Ticul to Tihosuco** The route from Ticul to Tihosuco, in Quintana Roo, is seldom traveled by tourists. Part of the route is called the Ruta de los Conventos (Route of the Convents), as each of these tiny villages has a cathedral or church, many in beautiful disrepair.

» **Cuzamá** Three kilometers east of the town of Cuzamá, accessed from the small village of Chunkanan, are the Cenotes de Cuzamá, a series of three amazing limestone sinkholes, accessed by horse-drawn rail cart, in an old *henequén* hacienda.

The lower level has several more well-preserved Chac masks, and the upper level contains a large *chultún* that still holds water. The view from there, of the site and the hills beyond, is impressive.

From the palace a limestone-paved *sacbé* leads to El Arco Labná, which is best known for its magnificent arch, once part of a building that separated two courtyards. The corbeled structure, 3m wide and 6m high, is well preserved, and the reliefs decorating its upper facade are exuberantly Puuc in style.

Standing on the opposite side of the arch and separated from it by the *sacbé* is a pyramid known as El Mirador, which is topped by a temple. The pyramid itself is largely stone rubble. The temple, with its 5m-high roofcomb, is well positioned to be a lookout, hence its name.

GRUTAS DE LOLTÚN

Fifteen kilometers northeast of Labná, a sign points out the left turn to the Grutas de Loltún, 5km further northeast. The road passes through lush orchards and some banana and palm groves, a refreshing sight in this dry region.

These **caverns** (admission M$90; ⊙9am-5pm) are the largest, most interesting cave system on the Yucatán Peninsula, and a treasure trove of data for archaeologists. Carbon dating of artifacts found here reveals that humans used the caves 2200 years ago. Chest-high murals of hands, faces, animals and geometric motifs were apparent as recently as 20 years ago, but so many people have touched them that barely a trace remains. Now, visitors to the illuminated caves see mostly natural limestone formations, some of which are quite lovely.

To explore the labyrinth, you must take a scheduled guided tour at 9:30am, 11am, 12:30pm, 2pm, 3pm or 4pm. The service of the guides is included in the admission price, but since they receive little of that, an additional tip (M$20 to M$50 per person) is appreciated.

❶ Getting There & Away

Renting a car is the best option for reaching the Grutas, and once you're out of Mérida it's easy going on pretty good roads.

There is a bus service to Oxkutzcab (osh-kootz-kahb; M$38, 1½ hours), with departures at 8:30am and 4pm, from the Noreste bus terminal in Mérida. Loltún is 7km southwest of Oxkutzcab, and there is usually some transportation along the road. *Camionetas* (pickups) charge about M$15 for a ride.

A taxi from Oxkutzcab may cost M$120 or so one way.

RUINAS DE MAYAPÁN

These **ruins** (admission M$31; ⊙8am-5pm) are some 50km southeast of Mérida, on Hwy 18. Though far less impressive than many Maya sites, Mayapán is historically significant – it was one of the last major dynasties in the region. The site's main attractions are clustered in a compact core, and visitors usually have the place to themselves.

Among the structures that have been restored is the **Castillo de Kukulcán**, a climbable pyramid with fresco fragments around its base and, at its rear side, friezes depicting decapitated warriors. The reddish color from the original paint job is still faintly visible. The **Templo Redondo** (Round Temple) is vaguely reminiscent of El Caracol at Chichén Itzá. Also notable are the **Sala de los Mascarones**, with well-preserved carvings of Chac and quetzal birds on its south side and the **Templo del Cenote**, built precariously close to a roped-off entrance to a cave system underneath the site.

❶ Getting There & Away

The Ruinas de Mayapán are just off Hwy 18, a few kilometers southwest of the town of Telchaquillo. Sur runs hourly 2nd-class buses between 5:30am and 8pm from the Noreste bus terminal in Mérida (M$16, 1½ hours) that will let you off near the entrance to the ruins and pick you up on your way back. Again, you may want to consider renting a car to get here.

Celestún

☎988 / POP 6400

West of Mérida, Celestún is a sleepy sun-scorched fishing village that moves at a turtle's pace – and that's the way locals like it. There's a pretty little square in the center of this town and you'll encounter some nice beaches (though the water is a bit turbid), but the real draw here is the Reserva de la Biosfera Ría Celestún, a wildlife sanctuary abounding in waterfowl, with flamingos as the star attraction.

◉ Sights & Activities

Reserva de la Biosfera Ría Celestún   WILDLIFE RESERVE

The 591-sq-km Reserva de la Biosfera Ría Celestún is home to a huge variety of animal and birdlife, including a large flamingo colony. The best months to see the flamingos are from March or April to about September, outside the season of the *nortes* (relatively cold storms bringing wind and rain from the north). It's best to visit in the morning or late afternoon.

Bird-watching

North of town, beyond the small navy post, you'll find more secluded stretches of beach. In the same area, inland from the road, lies a large section of scrub stretching east to the estuary that has good bird-watching opportunities. Flamingos, white pelicans, cormorants, anhingas and many other species frequent the shores and waters of the *ría*. South and east of town is the abandoned Hacienda Real de Salinas, another good area for nature observation.

Tours

In Celestún, bird-watchers can hire a motorboat either from the bridge on the highway into town (about 1.5km inland) or from the beach itself. Boats depart from outside Restaurant Celestún, at the foot of Calle 11. The restaurant's beachfront *palapa* is a pleasant place to wait for a group to accumulate, rather than at the tiny *palapa* at the boats themselves. If you prefer, Turitransmérida in Mérida organizes flamingo tours (see p299).

Tours from the bridge are mainly set up for tour groups, and will not allow you to form a group on the spot. If you've got a group of four or more it works out OK – tours (per boat M$750/1350 for one/two hours) take you to see the flamingos, mangrove tunnels and a spring. The longer tour takes in a 'petrified forest' and the spot where the sea and mangroves meet. There's also a M$30 park entrance fee for each passenger. It's not hard to strike a better deal beachside, where the 'long' tour goes for M$200 per person or M$850 per boat.

Manglares de Dzinitún   ECOTOUR

(☎cell phone 988-2358023) About 1km inland from the beach on Calle 11, there are signs to this ecotour operation, where you can kayak, canoe or mountain bike all in one day. A canoe tour runs M$150 per person for two hours, and takes you through a mangrove tunnel and good bird-watching spots, made all the better by the lack of engine noise. You can stay in very basic but OK cabins here for M$300. Camp spaces are also available.

THE RISE OF MAYAPÁN & THE DEATH WARRANT OF MAYA INDEPENDENCE

The rise of Mayapán played an integral role in the ultimate demise of Maya rule in the region. The city was supposedly founded by Kukulcán (Quetzalcóatl) in 1007, shortly after the former ruler of Tula arrived in Yucatán. His dynasty, the Cocom, organized a confederation of city-states that included Uxmal, Chichén Itzá and many other notable cities. Despite their alliance, animosity arose between the Cocomes of Mayapán and the Itzáes of Chichén Itzá during the late 12th century, and the Cocomes stormed Chichén Itzá, forcing the Itzá rulers into exile. The Cocom dynasty emerged supreme in all of northern Yucatán.

Cocom supremacy lasted for almost 250 years, until the ruler of Uxmal, Ah Xupán Xiú led a rebellion of the oppressed city-states and overthrew Cocom hegemony. The capital of Mayapán was utterly destroyed and remained uninhabited ever after.

But struggles for power continued in the region until 1542, when Francisco de Montejo the Younger conquered T'ho and established Mérida. At that point the current lord of Maní and ruler of the Xiú people, Ah Kukum Xiú, proposed to Montejo a military alliance against the Cocomes, his ancient rivals. Montejo accepted, and Xiú was baptized as a Christian, taking the name Francisco de Montejo Xiú (original, no?). The Cocomes were defeated and – too late – the Xiú rulers realized that they had signed the death warrant of Maya independence.

🛏 Sleeping

The hotels are all on the beach road. More upscale accommodations are found heading north out of town.

Hotel Celeste Vida   B&B $$
(☎916-25-36; www.hotelcelestevida.com; Calle 12, 1.5km north of Calle 11; r M$1023, ste M$1366; P🖥) Just out of town, this serene little Canadian-run setup offers comfortably decked out rooms with full kitchen and an apartment that sleeps four, all with water views and the beach at your doorstep. Kayak and bike use are free for guests.

Hotel María del Carmen   HOTEL $
(☎916-21-70; cnr Calles 12 & 15; s/d with fan M$300/350, air-con M$400/450; P❄@) With sweet little private balconies looking right out over the water, these rooms are a good value, even if they are a bit crumbly. Prices drop when things are slow.

Hostel Ría Celestún   HOSTEL $
(☎916-25-97; hostelriacelestun@hotmail.com; cnr Calles 12 & 13; dm M$100, r M$300) This hostel offers a good cheap sleep, with single-sex or mixed fan-cooled dorms (slightly dusty). It also has a kitchen, laundry facilities, a courtyard and TV room for common areas and bicycle rentals (M$20/hour).

🏖 Ecoparaíso Xixim   RESORT $$$
(☎916-21-00; www.ecoparaiso.com; ste M$3300-3960; P🖥🏊) Quietly luxurious beachfront cabins (the view blocked only by the foredune). The 'eco' comes from no air-con, but their design keeps the cross-breezes flowing. Cabins are strung out along a signed nature trail showing over 40 indigenous plants. The restaurant serves reasonably priced meals (which is good because Celestún is 11km away) and the open-air upstairs bar is a good place to while away the hours.

🍴 Eating

Beachfront restaurants close at around 6pm (or earlier) on weeknights – if you're hungry, head for the plaza where there are snack stalls and a decent fast-food place.

La Playita   SEAFOOD $
(Calle 12; mains M$80-120; ⊙10am-6pm) Of all the sandy-floored beachfront joints here, this one gets the thumbs up from the locals. Everywhere basically has the same menu, but the turnover here keeps things fresh.

La Palapa   SEAFOOD $$
(Calle 12; mains M$80-150; ⊙10am-5:30pm) A cut above the other seaside joints, La Palapa has an expansive dining area looking down to the sea, an attentive staff and savory seafood dishes, including a shrimp cocktail served in a coconut shell.

ℹ Information

Don't plan on using high-speed internet here. There's an ATM in the Super Willy's supermarket on the plaza, but bring some cash anyway – it's been known to dry up.

❶ Getting There & Away

Buses from Mérida head for Celestún (M$47, two hours) six times daily between 5:15am and noon from the Oriente bus terminal. The route terminates at Celestún's plaza, a block inland from Calle 12. Returning buses also run from 5am to 8pm.

By car from Mérida, the best route to Celestún is via the new road out of Umán.

Dzibilchaltún

Lying about 17km due north of central Mérida, **Dzibilchaltún** (Place of Inscribed Flat Stones; admission M$107, child under 13yr free, guides M$400; ⊗8am-5pm) was the longest continuously utilized Maya administrative and ceremonial city, serving the Maya from around 1500 BC until the European conquest in the 1540s. At the height of its greatness, Dzibilchaltún covered 15 sq km. Some 8400 structures in the 1960s; few of these have been excavated and restored.

The **Templo de las Siete Muñecas** (Temple of the Seven Dolls), which got its name from seven grotesque dolls discovered here during excavations, is a 1km walk from the central plaza. It would be most unimpressive but for its precise astronomical orientation: the rising and setting sun of the equinoxes lights up the temple's windows and doors, making them blaze like beacons, signaling the year's important turning points.

The **Cenote Xlacah**, now an eminently swimmable public swimming hole (don't forget your swimsuit), is more than 40m deep. In 1958 a National Geographic Society diving expedition recovered more than 30,000 Maya artifacts, many of ritual significance, from the cenote. The most interesting of these are now on display in the site's museum. South of the cenote is **Estructura 44**, which at 130m is one of the longest Maya structures in existence.

Parking costs M$20. Minibuses and *colectivos* depart frequently from Mérida's Parque de San Juan for the village of Dzibilchaltún Ruinas (M$11, 30 minutes), a little over 1km from the museum. Taxis cost around M$200 round-trip.

Progreso

📞969 / POP 50,000

If Mérida's heat has you dying for a quick beach fix, or you want to see the longest wharf (7km) in Mexico, head to Progreso (also known as Puerto Progreso). Winds can hit here full force off the Gulf in the afternoon and can blow well into the night, which means good kiteboarding and windsurfing (check with www.marinasilcer.com to see if they've got their act together with rentals yet). As with other Gulf beaches, the water is murky; visibility even on calm days rarely exceeds 5m.

Even-numbered streets here run east-west; odd ones north-south.

From the plaza on Calle 80, it is six short blocks to the waterfront *malecón* (Calle 19) and *muelle* (wharf); along the way are two Banamex banks, one with an ATM.

East of Progreso, you pass **Laguna Rosada**, a good spot for flamingo sightings, on your way to **Telchac Puerto**, home to many summer houses for Mérida's well-to-do. Along the way, take time to stop at an observation tower in **Uaymitún** and the **Xcambó** Maya ruins.

🛏 Sleeping & Eating

Hotel Yakunah HOTEL $$
(📞935-56-00; www.hotelyakunah.com.mx; Calle 21 btwn Calles 48 & 50; r M$750, apt M$1400; 🅿️❄️🛜🏊) A M$20 cab ride or 1.5km walk from town, this fantastic hotel is set in an old rancher's mansion and offers the best comfort-to-peso ratio around. Rooms are spacious and atmospheric with good fittings and excellent beds, the beach is a short walk away and the outdoor restaurant/bar/garden area is hugely inviting.

Hotel Tropical Suites HOTEL $
(📞935-12-63; cnr malecón & Calle 70; r with fan/air-con M$350/450; ❄️) Slightly better of the beachfront budget joints, rooms here are newish and well maintained, with communal balconies overlooking the water. Off-season bargaining should be a snap.

Eladio's SEAFOOD $$
(cnr malecón & Calle 80; mains M$80-150; ⊗11am-8pm) The local's choice is on the deck, under the *palapa* roof at this casual beachfront eatery. The seafood is superfresh, but don't bother ordering entrées – the five complimentary sampler plates of seafood and salad will keep you going until your food arrives.

THE OTHER BIG BANG

In the small town of Chicxulub, just outside Progreso, is an even smaller plaque dedicated to arguably the most momentous event in planet Earth's history. It's widely believed that around here, 65-odd million years ago, the Chicxulub meteor smashed into the planet. Many scientists believe this event ushered in the ice age, leading to the extinction of the dinosaurs and drastically altering the course of evolution of life on Earth.

There's not much to see here apart from the plaque, but if you're into visiting sites of historical importance, you could hardly find a bigger one than this.

ℹ Getting There & Away

Progreso is 33km north of Mérida along a fast four-lane highway that's basically a continuation of the Paseo de Montejo. The **bus station** (Calle 29 btwn Calles 80 & 82) has numerous Mérida-bound buses from 5:20am to 10pm. For bus information to Progreso from Mérida, see p304.

Izamal

📞988 / POP 16,000

In ancient times, Izamal was a center for the worship of the supreme Maya god, Itzamná, and the sun god, Kinich-Kakmó. A dozen temple pyramids were devoted to these or other gods. It was probably these bold expressions of Maya religiosity that provoked the Spaniards to build the enormous Franciscan monastery that stands today at the heart of this town.

Just under 70km east of Mérida, Izamal is a quiet, colonial gem of a town, nicknamed La Ciudad Amarilla (the Yellow City) for the yellow paint that brightens the walls of practically every building. It is easily explored on foot and makes a great day trip from Mérida.

◉ Sights

FREE **Convento de San Antonio de Padua**   CHURCH

(◎6am-8pm) When the Spaniards conquered Izamal, they destroyed the major Maya temple, the Ppapp-Hol-Chac pyramid, and in 1533 began to build from its stones one of the first monasteries in the New World. Work on Convento de San Antonio de Padua was finished in 1561. Under the monastery's arcades, look for building stones with an unmistakable mazelike design; these were clearly taken from the earlier Maya temple.

The monastery's principal church is the **Santuario de la Virgen de Izamal**. Here the **Atrium**, a huge arcaded courtyard, is where the **Fiesta of the Virgin of Izamal** takes place each August 15, and where a dramatic **sound-and-light show** (M$59) is presented at 8:30pm on Monday to Saturday nights.

Kinich-Kakmó   RUIN

(◎8am-5pm) Three of the town's original 12 Maya pyramids have been partially restored so far. The largest is the enormous Kinich-Kakmó, three blocks north of the monastery. You can climb it for free most of the time. If a guard is there, it's nice to make a M$20 donation.

🛏 Sleeping & Eating

Hotel Macan Ché   HOTEL $$

(📞954-02-87; www.macanche.com; Calle 22 No 305; r with fan/air-con incl breakfast M$500/750; ❄@🛜🏊) Pebbled pathways wind through a lush garden setting to fan-cooled cottage/bungalows and out to the neo-colonial styled building housing the air-conditioned rooms. It's nice.

Posada Flory   HOTEL $

(📞954-05-62; Calle 30 No 267; s with fan M$230; d with air-con M$250; ❄) There's a nice little center patio in this small, uberclean budget hotel on the corner of Calle 22. It's probably the best low-end deal in town.

Kinich   YUCATECAN $$

(Calle 27 btwn Calles 28 & 30; mains M$80-120; ◎8am-10pm) Everything here is delicious, handmade and super-fresh. It's also a great place to try those Yucatecan specialties you've been wondering about.

Several *loncherías* occupy spaces in the market on the monastery's southwest side.

ℹ Getting There & Away

Oriente operates frequent buses between Mérida and Izamal (M$22, 1½ hours) from the Noreste bus terminal. There are buses from Valladolid (M$48, two hours) as well. Coming from Chichén Itzá you must change buses at Hoctún. Izamal's bus terminal is two short blocks west of the monastery.

Chichén Itzá

🎧 985

The most famous and best restored of the Yucatán Maya sites, **Chichén Itzá** (Mouth of the Well of the Itzáes; admission M$166, parking M$22, sound-&-light show M$69, guide M$500-600; ☺8am-6pm summer, to 5:30pm winter), while tremendously overcrowded – every gawker and his or her grandmother is trying to check off the new Seven Wonders of the World – will still impress even the most jaded visitor. Many mysteries of the Maya astronomical calendar are made clear when one understands the design of the 'time temples' here. Other than a few minor passageways, climbing on the structures is not allowed.

At the vernal (spring) and autumnal equinoxes (March 20–21 and September 21–22), the morning and afternoon sun produces a light-and-shadow illusion of the serpent ascending or descending the side of El Castillo's staircase. Chichén is mobbed on these dates, however, making it difficult to get close enough to see. The illusion is almost as good in the week preceding and following each equinox, and is recreated nightly in the sound-and-light show year-round.

History

Most archaeologists agree that the first major settlement at Chichén Itzá, during the late Classic period, was pure Maya. In about the 9th century the city was largely abandoned, for reasons unknown. It was resettled around the late 10th century, and some Mayanists believe that shortly thereafter it was invaded by the Toltecs.

Toltec culture was fused with that of the Maya, incorporating the Toltec cult of Quetzalcóatl (Kukulcán, in Maya). Throughout the city, you will see images of both Chac, the Maya rain god, and Quetzalcóatl, the plumed serpent.

The substantial fusion of highland central Mexican and Puuc architectural styles makes Chichén unique among the Yucatán Peninsula's ruins. The fabulous El Castillo and the Plataforma de Venus are outstanding architectural works, built during the height of Toltec cultural input.

The warlike Toltecs contributed more than their architectural skills to the Maya. They elevated human sacrifice to a near obsession, and there are numerous carvings of the bloody ritual in Chichén demonstrating this. After a Maya leader moved his political capital to Mayapán, while keeping Chichén as his religious capital, Chichén Itzá fell into decline. Why it was subsequently abandoned in the 14th century is a mystery, but the once-great city remained the site of Maya pilgrimages for many years.

◉ Sights

El Castillo

PYRAMID

As you approach the site from the visitors center, El Castillo (also called the Pyramid of Kukulcán) rises before you in all its grandeur. The first temple here was pre-Toltec, built around AD 800, but the present 25m-high structure, built over the old one, has the plumed serpent sculpted along the stairways and Toltec warriors represented in the doorway carvings at the top of the temple. You won't get to see these temple-top carvings, as you are not allowed to ascend the pyramid.

The structure is actually a massive Maya calendar formed in stone. Each of El Castillo's nine levels is divided in two by a staircase, making 18 separate terraces that commemorate the 18 20-day months of the Maya Vague Year. The four stairways have 91 steps each; add the top platform and the total is 365, the number of days in the year. On each facade of the pyramid are 52 flat panels, which are reminders of the 52 years in the Maya Calendar Round. See boxed text, p800 for more on the Maya calendar.

To top it off, during the spring and autumn equinoxes, light and shadow form a series of triangles on the side of the north staircase that mimic the creep of a serpent (note the carved serpents' heads flanking the bottom of the staircase).

The older pyramid *inside* El Castillo boasts a red jaguar throne with inlaid eyes and spots of jade; also lying behind the screen is a chac-mool figure. The entrance to **El Túnel**, the passage up to the throne, is at the base of El Castillo's north side. You can't go in, though.

Gran Juego de Pelota

BALL COURT

The great ball court, the largest and most impressive in Mexico, is only one of the city's eight courts, indicative of the importance of the games held here. The court is flanked by temples and bounded by towering parallel walls with stone rings cemented up high.

There is evidence that the ball game may have changed over the years. Some carvings show players with padding on their elbows and knees, and it is thought that they played

Chichén Itzá

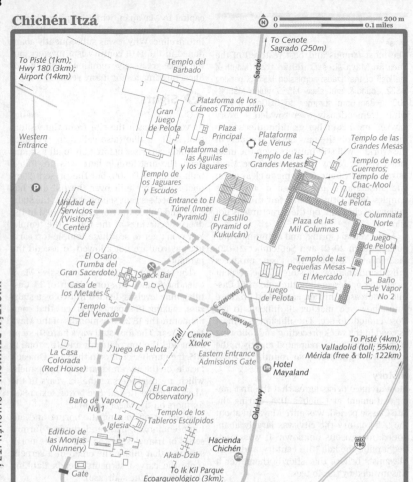

Chichén Itzá

0 ——————— 200 m
0 ——————— 0.1 miles

To Cenote Sagrado (250m)

To Pisté (1km); Hwy 180 (3km); Airport (14km)

Templo del Barbado

Sacbé

Plataforma de los Cráneos (Tzompantli)

Gran Juego de Pelota

Plaza Principal

Plataforma de Venus

Templo de las Grandes Mesas

Western Entrance

Plataforma de las Águilas y los Jaguares

Templo de las Grandes Mesas

Templo de los Guerreros; Templo de Chac-Mool

Templo de os Jaguares y Escudos

Juego de Pelota

Entrance to El Túnel (Inner Pyramid)

El Castillo (Pyramid of Kukulcán)

Plaza de las Mil Columnas

Columnata Norte

Unidad de Servicios (Visitors Center)

Juego de Pelota

El Osario (Tumba del Gran Sacerdote)

Snack Bar

Templo de las Pequeñas Mesas

El Mercado

Baño de Vapor No 2

Casa de los Metates

Juego de Pelota

Templo del Venado

Causeway

Causeway

Trail

Cenote Xtoloc

To Pisté (4km); Valladolid (toll; 55km); Mérida (free & toll; 122km)

La Casa Colorada (Red House)

Juego de Pelota

Eastern Entrance Admissions Gate

Hotel Mayaland

Old Hwy

El Caracol (Observatory)

Baño de Vapor No 1

La Iglesia

Templo de los Tableros Esculpidos

Edificio de las Monjas (Nunnery)

Akab-Dzib

Hacienda Chichén

MEX 180

Gate

To Ik Kil Parque Ecoarqueológico (3km); Grutas de Balankanché (5km); Valladolid (45km); Cancún (free; 205km)

To Chichén Viejo

To Valladolid (45km)

a soccer-like game with a hard rubber ball, the use of hands forbidden. Other carvings show players wielding bats; it appears that if a player hit the ball through one of the stone hoops, his team was declared the winner. It may be that during the Toltec period the losing captain, and perhaps his teammates as well, were sacrificed. Along the walls of the ball court are stone reliefs, including scenes of players being decapitated.

The court's acoustics are amazing – a conversation at one end can be heard 135m away at the other, and a clap produces multiple loud echoes.

Templo del Barbado & Templo de los Jaguares y Escudos   TEMPLE

The structure at the northern end of the ball court, called the Temple of the Bearded Man after a carving inside it, has some finely sculpted pillars and reliefs of flowers, birds and trees.

The Temple of the Jaguars and Shields, built atop the southeast corner of the ball court's wall, has some columns with carved rattlesnakes and tablets with etched jaguars. Inside are faded mural fragments depicting a battle.

Plataforma de los Cráneos   PLATFORM

The Platform of Skulls (*tzompantli* in Náhuatl) is between the Templo de los Jaguares and El Castillo. You can't mistake it, because the T-shaped platform is festooned with carved skulls and eagles tearing open the chests of men to eat their hearts. In ancient days this platform held the heads of sacrificial victims.

Plataforma de las Águilas
y los Jaguares   PLATFORM

Adjacent to the *tzompantli*, the carvings on the Platform of the Eagles and Jaguars depicts those animals gruesomely grabbing human hearts in their claws. It is thought that this platform was part of a temple dedicated to the military legions responsible for capturing sacrificial victims.

Cenote Sagrado   POOL

A 300m pebbled pathway runs north (a five-minute walk) to the huge sunken well that gave this city its name. The Sacred Cenote is an awesome natural well, some 60m in diameter and 35m deep. The walls between the cenote's rim and the water's surface are ensnared in tangled vines and other vegetation.

Plaza de las Mil Columnas   RUIN

Comprising the Templo de los Guerreros (Temple of the Warriors), the Templo de Chac-Mool (Temple of Chac-Mool) and the Baño de Vapor (Sweat House or Steam Bath), this group, behind El Castillo, takes its name (Group of the Thousand Columns) from the forest of pillars stretching south and east.

El Osario   PYRAMID

The Ossuary, otherwise known as the Bonehouse or the Tumba del Gran Sacerdote (High Priest's Grave), is a ruined pyramid southwest of El Castillo. As with most of the buildings in this southern section, the architecture is more Puuc than Toltec. It's notable for the serpent heads at the base of its staircases.

El Caracol   BUILDING

Called El Caracol (the Snail) by the Spaniards for its interior spiral staircase, this observatory is one of the most fascinating and important of all the Chichén Itzá buildings. Its circular design resembles some central highlands structures. In a fusion of architectural styles and religious imagery, there are Maya masks of Chac over four external doors facing the cardinal directions. The windows in the observatory's dome are aligned with the appearance of certain stars at specific dates. From the dome the priests decreed the times for rituals, celebrations, corn planting and harvests.

Edificio de las Monjas & La Iglesia   PALACE

Thought by archaeologists to have been a palace for Maya royalty, the so-called Edificio de las Monjas (Nunnery), with its myriad rooms, resembled a European convent to the conquistadors, hence their name for the building. The building's dimensions are imposing: its base is 60m long, 30m wide and 20m high. The construction is Maya rather than Toltec, although a Toltec sacrificial stone stands in front of the building.

A smaller adjoining building to the east, known as La Iglesia (the Church), is covered almost entirely with carvings.

Akab-Dzib   BUILDING

On the path east of Edificio de las Monjas, the Puuc-style Akab-Dzib is thought by some archaeologists to be the most ancient structure excavated here. The central chambers date from the 2nd century. The name means 'Obscure Writing' in Maya and refers to the south annex door, which has a lintel depicting a priest with a vase that is etched with hieroglyphics that have never been translated.

Cenote Ik Kil   POOL

(adult/child M$50/30; ⊘8am-6pm) A little over 3km southeast of the eastern entrance to the ruins is Ik Kil Parque Ecoarqueológico, where a cenote has been developed into a divine swimming spot. Small cascades of water plunge from the high limestone roof, which is ringed by greenery. It has a good buffet and nice *cabañas* (M$1200) onsite. Get your swim in by no later than 1pm to beat the tour groups.

Grutas de Balankanché   CAVE

(adult/child M$90/5; ⊘ticket booth 9am-5pm) In 1959 a guide to the Chichén ruins was exploring a cave on his day off when he came upon a narrow passageway. He followed the passageway for 300m, meandering through a series of caverns. In each, perched on mounds amid scores of glistening stalactites, were hundreds of ceremonial treasures the Maya had placed there 800 years earlier: ritual *metates* (flattish stones on which corn was ground) and *manos* (grinding stones; basically mortar and pestle), incense burners and pots. In the years following the discovery, the ancient ceremonial objects were removed and studied. Supposedly all the objects here are the originals, returned and placed exactly where they were found.

The Grutas de Balankanché are 5km east of the ruins of Chichén Itzá, on the highway to Cancún. Compulsory 40-minute tours are accompanied by poorly recorded narrations: English (11am, 1pm and 3pm), Spanish (9am, noon, 2pm and 4pm) and French (10am).

🛌 Sleeping

Most of Chichén's lodgings, restaurants and services are ranged along 1km of highway in the village of Pisté, to the western side of the ruins. It's 1.5km from the ruins' main entrance to the first hotel in Pisté. Hwy 180 is known as Calle 15A as it passes through Pisté.

Hotel Chichén Itzá HOTEL $$
(☎851-00-22, in the US 800-235-4079; www.mayaland.com; Calle 15A No 45; r M$800-980, ste M$1200; 🌼✲@🛜🏊🛎) On the west side of Pisté, this is the fanciest place to stay in town. Rooms are OK, but the real draws are the lovely grounds and poolside bar area. Parents may bring two kids under 13 for free.

Posada Olalde HOTEL $
(☎851-00-86; www.chichen.com; Calle 15A No 30; s/d M$250/300; 🛜) There are (slightly) cheaper rooms around, but these ones win in the budget category for being spacious and spotless and set in a shady garden with a barely perceptible wi-fi signal. They're a couple of blocks off the main road – look for the sign leading south across from the Carousel restaurant.

Hacienda Chichén HOTEL $$$
(☎851-00-45, in the US 877-631-4005; www.haciendachichen.com; d M$2100-2771; 🌼🛜🏊) About 300m from the ruins' entrance, this is on the grounds of a 16th-century estate. The hacienda's elegant main house and ruined walls make a great setting, and huge ceiba trees offer welcome shade.

Hotel Mayaland HOTEL $$$
(☎998-887-24-95, in the US 800-235-4079; www.mayaland.com; d/ste M$1800/2345; 🍽✲🛜🏊) Less than 100m from the ruins' entrance – from the lobby and front rooms you can look at El Caracol. The rooms, pools and garden bungalows are nicely built and well appointed.

🍴 Eating

The highway through Pisté is lined with more than 20 eateries, large and small. The cheapest are the market stalls on the main plaza opposite the large tree.

La Casa del Caffe CAFE $
(bagels M$65; ⊙7am-9pm) All things considered, Pisté had to have a coffee shop, and this is a pretty good one. Good coffee, fresh bagels and a shady outside deck to enjoy them.

Restaurant Sayil YUCATECAN $
(mains M$40-80; ⊙7am-9pm) An old standby, with a pleasant garden and simple but tasty regional fare. It's attached to the Felix Inn.

Restaurant Hacienda Xaybe'h d'Camara BUFFET $$
(buffet lunch & dinner M$150; ⊙7:30am-6:30pm; 🅿) Set a block back from the highway opposite Hotel Chichén Itzá, this is a large, rather fancy place with nice grounds. It's popular with tours, but the food is a bit overpriced; the selection of salads makes it a good option for vegetarians.

ℹ Information

The western entrance has a large parking lot and a big visitors center. As at most sites, filming with a video camera costs M$45 extra, and tripods require a special permit from Mexico City. Hold on to your ticket; it gives you in-and-out privileges and admission to that evening's sound-and-light show. Explanatory plaques around the site are in Spanish, English and Maya.

The 45-minute sound-and-light show in Spanish begins at 8pm each evening in summer and 7pm in winter. It costs M$69 if you don't already have a ruins ticket, and it counts toward the admission price the following day. Devices for listening to English, French, German or Italian translations (beamed via infrared) rent for M$39. Specify the language you need or it may not be broadcast.

ℹ Getting There & Away

Oriente has ticket offices near the east and west sides of Pisté, and 2nd-class buses passing through town stop almost anywhere along the way. Many 1st-class buses only hit the ruins and the west side of town, close to the toll highway.

When they're running on schedule, Oriente's 2nd-class buses pass through Pisté bound for Mérida (M$63, 2½ hours) hourly between 8:15am and 4:15pm. Hourly Oriente buses to Valladolid (M$20, 50 minutes) and Cancún (M$97, 4½ hours) pass between 7am and 5:30pm. There's also 2nd-class service to Tulum (M$105, three hours) and Playa del Carmen (M$127, four hours).

First-class buses serve Mérida (M$96 to M$100, 1¾ hours, 2:25pm and 5pm), Cancún (M$120, 2½ hours, 4:30pm) and Tulum (M$115, 2½ hours, 8am and 4:30pm).

Shared vans to Valladolid (M$20, 40 minutes) pass through town regularly.

ℹ Getting Around

During Chichén Itzá's opening hours, 1st- and 2nd-class buses serve the ruins (check with the driver), and they will take passengers from town for about M$6 when there's room. For a bit more, 2nd-class buses will also take you to the Cenote Ik Kil and the Grutas de Balankanché (be sure to specify your destination when buying your ticket). If you plan to see the ruins and then head directly to another city by 1st-class bus, buy your bus ticket at the visitors center before hitting the ruins, for a better chance of getting a seat.

There is a taxi stand near the west end of town; the price to the ruins is around M$25. There are usually taxis at Chichén's parking lot.

Valladolid

📞 985 / POP 42,000

Also known as the Sultaness of the East, Yucatán's third-largest city is known for its quiet streets and sun-splashed, pastel walls. It is certainly a sultry place, and it's worth staying here for a few days or even a week, as this provincial town makes a great hub for visits to Río Lagartos, Chichén Itzá, Ek' Balam and a number of nearby cenotes. The city is poised at that magical point where there's plenty to do, yet it still feels small, manageable and affordable.

History

Valladolid has seen its fair share of turmoil and revolt over the years. The city was first founded in 1543 near the Chouac-Ha lagoon some 50km from the coast, but it was too hot and there were way too many mosquitoes for Francisco de Montejo, nephew of Montejo the Elder, and his merry band of conquerors. So they upped and moved the city to the Maya ceremonial center of Zací (sah-*see*), where they faced heavy resistance from the local Maya. Eventually the Elder's son, Montejo the Younger, took the town. The Spanish conquerors, in typical fashion, ripped down the town and laid out a new city following the classic colonial plan.

During much of the colonial era, Valladolid's physical isolation from Mérida kept it relatively autonomous from royal rule, and the Maya of the area suffered brutal exploitation, which continued after Mexican independence. Barred from entering many areas of the city, the Maya made Valladolid one of their first points of attack following the 1847 outbreak of the War of the Castes in Tepich, not far south on the border with Quintana Roo. After a two-month siege, the city's defenders were finally overcome.

◉ Sights

Templo de San Bernardino & Convento de Sisal   CHURCH

(☉8am-noon & 5-9pm) The church named for San Bernardino de Siena and the Convent of Sisal are about 700m southwest of the plaza. They were constructed between 1552 and 1560 to serve the dual functions of fortress and church.

You may have to knock on the church's left-hand door to gain admittance, or someone may approach and offer you a short tour in exchange for a gratuity. Its charming decoration includes beautiful rose-colored walls, arches, some recently uncovered 16th-century frescoes and a small image of the Virgin on the altar.

The adjacent convent is often closed to the public; your best bets of gaining entrance to it are during the vacation periods of Semana Santa, August and Christmas (December 14 to January 6). It's well worth a visit. The walled grounds hold a cenote with a vaulted dome built over it and a system of channels that once irrigated the large garden.

FREE **Museo de San Roque**   MUSEUM

(Calle 41; ☉9am-9pm) This church-turned-museum, between Calles 38 and 40, has models and exhibits relating the history of the city and the region. Other displays focus on various aspects of traditional Maya life.

Cenotes   POOL

The region has several underground cenotes, one of which is **Cenote Zací** (Calle 36; adult/child M$15/10; ☉8am-6pm), set in a park that also holds traditional stone-walled thatched houses and a small zoo. People swim in Zací, though being mostly open, it has some dust and algae and being in the center of town makes it susceptible to water-table contamination. Enter from Calle 39.

A bit more enticing but less accessible is **Cenote Dzitnup** (Xkekén; adult/child M$52/17; ☉8am-5pm), 7km west of the plaza. It's artificially lit and very swimmable, and a

YUCATÁN PENINSULA VALLADOLID

Valladolid

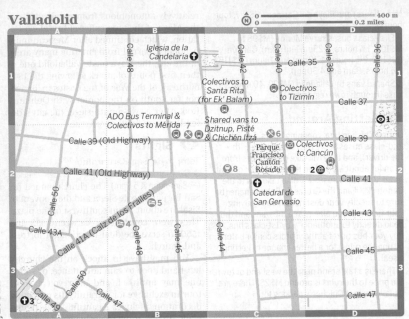

Iglesia de la Candelaria
Calle 48
Calle 42
Calle 40
Calle 35
Calle 38
Calle 36
Calle 37
Colectivos to Santa Rita (for Ek' Balam)
Colectivos to Tizimín
ADO Bus Terminal & Colectivos to Mérida 7
Shared vans to Dzitnup, Pisté & Chichén Itzá 6
Calle 39 (Old Highway)
Calle 39
Parque Francisco Cantón Rosado
Colectivos to Cancún
Calle 41 (Old Highway)
8
2
Calle 41
Calle 50
Catedral de San Gervasio
Calle 41A (Calz de los Frailes) 5
Calle 43
Calle 43A
4
Calle 48
Calle 46
Calle 44
Calle 45
Calle 50
Calle 49
Calle 47
3
Calle 47

massive limestone formation dripping with stalactites hangs from its ceiling.

Across the road approximately 100m closer to town is **Cenote Samulá** (adult/child M$52/free; ⊗8am-6pm), a lovely cavern pool with *álamo* roots stretching down many meters from the middle of the ceiling to drink from it.

Pedaling a rented bicycle (see p324) to the cenotes takes about 20 minutes. If biking from the town center, take Calle 41A (Calzada de los Frailes), a street lined entirely with colonial architecture, which leads past the Templo de San Bernardino and the convent. Keep to the right of the park, then turn right on Calle 49. This opens onto tree-lined Avenida de los Frailes and hits the old highway. Turn left onto the *ciclopista* (bike path) paralleling the road to Mérida. Turn left again at the sign for Dzitnup and continue for just under 2km; Samulá will be off this road to the right and Dzitnup a little further along on the left.

Shared vans from in front of Hotel María Guadalupe (on Calle 44) go to Dzitnup for M$20. Taxis from Valladolid's main plaza charge M$160 for the round-trip excursion to Dzitnup and Samulá, with an hour's wait. You can also try to flag down any westbound bus and ask the driver to let you off at the Dzitnup turnoff, then walk the final 2km (20 to 30 minutes) to the site. Dzitnup has a restaurant and drinks stand. Otherwise, bring a picnic.

Mercado Municipal MARKET
(Calle 32) This is a good, authentic Mexican market where locals come to shop for cheap clothing, homewares, meat, produce and what-have-you, and to eat at inexpensive *taquerías*. You'll fnd it a couple of blocks east of the Cenote Zací.

🛏 Sleeping

Hotel Tunich-Beh HOTEL **$$**
(☎856-22-22; www.tunichbeh.com; Calz de los Frailes btwn Calles 46 & 48; s/d M$450/500; [P][❄][🛜][🏊]) A great old house lovingly converted into accommodations, this features huge rooms with king-size beds, a good-sized swimming pool and a couple of lovely *palapa*-shaded hangout areas.

Hostal Los Frailes HOSTEL **$**
(☎856-58-52; www.hostaldelfraile.com, in Spanish; Calz de los Frailes 212C; dm M$110; r with/without bathroom M$250/290; [❄][@][🛜]) In an old converted *casona* (large mansion), this hostel offers up high-ceilinged rooms, a shared kitchen, a book exchange and a small private hut out back.

Valladolid

◉ Sights
1	Cenote Zací	D1
2	Museo de San Roque	D2
3	Templo de San Bernardino & Convento de Sisal	A3

🛏 Sleeping
4	Hostal Los Frailes	B3
5	Hotel Tunich-Beh	B2

🍴 Eating
6	Hostería del Marqués	C2
7	Squimoz	B2

🍷 Drinking
8	La Chispa de 1910	C2

Casa Quetzal　　　　　　　HOTEL $$
(☏856-47-96; www.casa-quetzal.com; Calle 51 No 218; r M$900; P✶🛜🐾) The spacious rooms here offer a good mix of modern comfort and colonial style. They're set around a lush patio with a decent-sized pool. Get a room upstairs for better ventilation and a private balcony. It's about 200m south of the Convento de Sisal.

🍴 Eating
Squimoz　　　　　　　　　CAFE $
(Calle 39 No 219; mains M$30-80; ⊗7am-10pm Mon-Sat, to 3pm Sun) A delightful little shop just a few doors east of the ADO terminal, Squimoz offers cakes, pastries and good espresso drinks.

Hostería del Marqués　　　YUCATECAN $$
(☏856-20-73; Calle 39 No 203; mains M$90-160; ⊗7am-11pm) Probably the best restaurant in town for lunch and dinner is in Hotel El Mesón del Marqués. You can dine in the tranquil colonial courtyard with its bubbling fountain, or the air-con salon looking onto it. The restaurant also offers some vegetarian choices and steaks priced by weight.

☆ Entertainment
Following a centuries-old tradition, dances are held in the main plaza from 8pm to 9pm Sunday, with music by the municipal band or other local groups.

La Chispa de 1910　　　　　LIVE MUSIC
(Calle 41 No 201; ⊗5pm-1am Mon-Thu, to 2am Fri-Sun) Sparks fly at this bar-restaurant that often features live music.

ℹ Information
The main plaza, also known as Parque Francisco Cantón Rosado, has banks of Telmex card phones in each corner. High-speed internet is available at numerous small cafes in and around the town center for around M$10 per hour.

Hospital Valladolid (☏856-28-83; cnr Calles 49 & 52; ⊗24hr)

Main post office (cnr Calles 40 & 39; ⊗8:30am-3pm Mon-Fri)

Tourist office (cnr Calles 40 & 41; ⊗9am-9pm Mon-Sat, to noon Sun)

ℹ Getting There & Away
Bus
Valladolid's main bus terminal is the convenient **ADO bus terminal** (cnr Calles 39 & 46). The principal services are Oriente, Mayab and Expresso (2nd class), and ADO and Super Expresso (1st class).

Colectivo
Often faster, more reliable and more comfortable than 2nd-class buses are the *colectivos* that

BUSES FROM VALLADOLID

DESTINATION	FARE (M$)	DURATION	FREQUENCY (DAILY)
Cancún	136	2-3hr	frequent ADO
Chichén Itzá/Piste	25-50	45min	frequent Oriente & ADO
Chiquilá (for Isla Holbox)	80	2½hr	Oriente 2:45am
Cobá	30-56	45min	1 ADO, 7 Mayab
Izamal	48	2hr	2 Oriente
Mérida	85-180	2½-3½hr	hourly ADO & 2nd-class Oriente
Playa del Carmen	96-140	2½-3½hr	frequent ADO & Oriente
Tizimín	20	1hr	20 Mayab & Oriente
Tulum	78-82	2hr	10 ADO, 7am Mayab

leave for various points as soon as their seats are filled. Most operate from 7am or 8am to about 7pm. Direct services to Mérida (from the ADO bus terminal; M$105) and Cancún (Calle 38 between Calles 39 and 41; M$125) take a little over two hours – confirm they're nonstop, though. *Colectivos* for Pisté and Chichén Itzá (M$20, 40 minutes) leave from a lot just east of the ADO bus terminal, and for Tizimín (Calle 40 between Calles 35 and 37; M$30, 40 minutes) from a lot north of the plaza. *Colectivos* for Ek' Balam (M$40) leave from the corner of Calles 44 and 37.

❶ Getting Around

Bicycles are a great way to see the town and get out to the cenotes. **Antonio 'Negro' Aguilar** (☎856-21-25; Calle 44 btwn Calles 39 & 41; ☺7am-7pm) rents bikes for about M$10 per hour.

Ek' Balam

The turnoff for this fascinating **archaeological site** (admission M$89, guide M$500-600; ☺8am-4:15pm) is 17km north of Valladolid. Ek' Balam is another 6km east of this. Vegetation still covers much of the area, but excavations and restoration continue to add to the sights, including an interesting ziggurat-like structure near the entrance, as well as a fine arch and a ball court.

Most impressive is the gargantuan **Acrópolis**, whose well-restored base is 160m long and holds a 'gallery' – actually a series of separate chambers. Built atop the base is Ek' Balam's massive main pyramid, reaching a height of 32m and sporting a huge jaguar mouth with 360-degree dentition. Below the mouth are stucco skulls, while above and to the right sits an amazingly expressive figure. On the right side stand unusual winged human figures (some call them Maya angels, although a much more likely explanation is that they are shaman or medicine men).

From the Ek' Balam parking lot you can visit the **X-Canché Cenote** (www.cenotexcanche.com.mx; admission M$30, bike rental M$70, bike, rappel, zip-line & kayak tour M$200; ☺8am-5pm), a 1.5km walk – or get a bicitaxi for M$50 round trip. You can stay here in comfortable cabins (M$450) or camp for M$70.

🛏 Sleeping & Eating

🏠 Genesis Eco-Retreat   HOTEL **$$**
(☎cell phone 985-1010277; www.genesisretreat.com; d M$780, with shared bathroom M$550; ☻@☀) Beautifully simple, truly ecological rooms built around a jungle-like courtyard featuring a cenote-fed swimming pool. A vegetarian restaurant operates for breakfast and dinner (set meals M$145) and the hotel arranges an 'artisans tour' or the local neighborhood, focusing on weaving, hammock-making and traditional village life.

❶ Getting There & Away

It's possible to catch a *colectivo* from Calle 44 between Calles 35 and 37 in Valladolid for Ek' Balam (M$20 to M$40). A round-trip taxi ride from Valladolid with an hour's wait at the ruins will cost around M$400.

Tizimín

📞986 / POP 44,000

Tizimín is dusty, and you won't find much here that's designed with the tourist in mind. Most people find themselves here if they're traveling to Río Lagartos or Holbox. The city fills with people from outlying ranches during its annual fair (January 1 to 15) to celebrate **Día de los Reyes Magos** (Three Kings' Day).

🛏 Sleeping & Eating

Hotel San Carlos   HOTEL **$**
(☎863-20-94; hotelsancarlos@hotmail.com; Calle 54 No 407 btwn Calles 51 & 53; s/d M$400/420;

BUSES FROM TIZIMÍN

DESTINATION	FARE (M$)	DURATION	FREQUENCY (DAILY)
Cancún	92	3-3½hr	6 Mayab & Noreste
Izamal	57	2½hr	Oriente 11am
Mérida	85-205	2½-3½hr	5 ADO, 5 Oriente
Río Lagartos	27-34	1hr	7 ADO, 3 Noreste
Valladolid	20	1hr	16 Oriente

P ❄) The nicest hotel in town has a pleasant '70s exterior and large, standard rooms connected by shady walkways.

Pizzería Cesares PIZZERIA $
(Calles 50 s/n; mains M$50-90; ⊙11am-1am) This friendly little Italian joint, just off the plaza, offers the widest menu in Tizimín.

ℹ Getting There & Away

Oriente and Mayab, both offering 2nd-class services, share a **bus terminal** (Calle 47 btwn Calles 48 & 46) just east of the market. The **Noreste bus terminal** (Calle 46), offering 1st- and 2nd-class services, is just around the corner.

Taxis to Río Lagartos charge about M$220, and leave from outside both bus terminals. The drivers can be asked to wait for you for M$120 per additional hour.

Río Lagartos

✆986 / POP 2100
With the largest and most spectacular flamingo colony in Mexico, Río Lagartos warrants a trip. Situated 103km north of Valladolid and 52km north of Tizimín, this fishing village lies within the **Reserva de la Biosfera Ría Lagartos**. The mangrove-lined estuary is also home to snowy egrets, red egrets, tiger herons, snowy white ibis, hundreds of other bird species and a small number of the crocodiles that gave the town its name (Alligator River).

Spanish explorers mistook the inlet for a river and the crocs for alligators, and the rest is history. The Maya knew the place as Holkobén and used it as a rest stop on their way to the nearby lagoons (Las Coloradas), from which they extracted salt. (Salt continues to be extracted, on a much vaster scale now.)

Intrepid travelers can head east of town past Las Coloradas on a coastal dirt road all the way to the small town of El Cuyo.

Most residents aren't sure of the town's street names, and signs are few. The road into town is the north-south Calle 10, which ends at the waterfront Calle 13. There's no bank or ATM in town, so bring lots of cash.

☞ Tours

Flamingos BIRD-WATCHING
The brilliant orange-red birds can turn the horizon fiery when they take wing. You can generally get within 100m of flamingos before they walk or fly away. Depending on your luck, you'll see either hundreds or thousands of them.

The four primary flamingo haunts, in increasing distance from town, are Punta Garza, Yoluk, Necopal and Nahochín (all flamingo feeding spots are named for nearby mangrove patches). Prices vary by boat, group size (maximum six) and destination. A one-hour trip costs around M$500, and two to three hours is M$600. In addition, the reserve charges visitors a M$24 admission fee.

The best-established tour outfits operate out of the **Restaurante-Bar Isla Contoy** (✆862-00-00; Calle 19) and **Restaurante La Torreja** (✆cell phone 986-1008390; www.riola gartosnaturetours.com; btwn Calles 12 & 14), both on the waterfront. They offer extensive day tours as well as night excursions. Crocodiles are a common nocturnal sight, and from May through September sea turtles are easily spotted.

Alternatively, you can negotiate with one of the eager men in the waterfront kiosks near the entrance to town. They speak English and will connect you with a captain (who usually doesn't speak English).

🛏 Sleeping & Eating

Hotel Villas de Pescadores HOTEL $$
(✆862-00-20; www.riolagartoshotel.com; cnr Calles 14 & 9; s/d M$500/600, ste M$1200; ❄) Near the water's edge, this nice hotel offers nine very clean rooms and three suites, each with good cross-ventilation (all face the estuary). Upstairs rooms have balconies overlooking the water.

Posada Las Gaviotas HOTEL $
(✆862-05-08; Calle 12; d M$350) This simple budget option offers clean, fan-cooled rooms bathed in avocado green right on the riverfront.

Restaurante La Torreja SEAFOOD $
(Calle 9 btwn Calles 12 & 14; mains M$60-150; ⊙8am-9pm) Offers good meals and excellent coffee down on the waterfront near the lighthouse. This is a good place to meet other travelers and form groups for the boat tours.

ℹ Getting There & Away

Several Noreste buses run daily to Río Lagartos from Tizimín (M$25, one hour) and Mérida (M$146, three to four hours). Noreste and Mayab also serve Cancún (M$130, three to four hours) three times daily.

YUCATÁN PENINSULA RÍO LAGARTOS

CAMPECHE STATE

Campeche state is home to vast stretches of tangled jungle, some of the region's least visited and most imposing Maya ruins, forgotten pastoral villages, bird-choked coastal lagoons and an inspiring colonial-era capital city. It's the least touristed of the Yucatán states, and in that lies its provincial, lost-land charm.

The back roads of the northern region bring you to forgotten underground wonderworlds, the massive restored Edzná archaeological site, and a handful of smaller, less-traveled Maya ruins.

This is also the wildest corner of the peninsula, and the Reserva de la Biosfera Calakmul is Mexico's largest. Beyond the cacophonous roar of the howlers and hiccupping frogs rise massive ruined Maya cities, such as Calakmul and Becán. Along the coast, the Laguna de Términos is great for those interested in bird-watching expeditions.

Campeche

☑981 / POP 220,000

Campeche is a colonial fairyland, its walled city center a tight enclave of perfectly restored pastel buildings, narrow cobblestone streets, fortified ramparts and well-preserved mansions. Added to Unesco's list of World Heritage sites in 1999, the state capital has been so painstakingly restored you wonder if it's a real city. Nearly 2000 structures have been renovated. But leave the city's walls and you'll find a Mexican provincial capital complete with a frenetic market, a quiet *malecón* and old fishing docks.

Besides the numerous mansions built by wealthy Spanish families during Campeche's heyday in the 18th and 19th centuries, two segments of the city's famous wall have also survived, as have no fewer than seven of the *baluartes* (bastions or bulwarks) that were built into it.

History

Once a Maya trading village called Ah Kim Pech (Lord Sun Sheep-Tick), Campeche was first briefly approached by the Spaniards in 1517. Resistance by the Maya prevented the Spaniards from fully conquering the region for nearly a quarter of a century. Colonial Campeche was founded in 1531 but later abandoned due to Maya hostility. By 1540,

however, the conquistadors had gained sufficient control, under the leadership of Francisco de Montejo the Younger, to found a permanent settlement. They named the settlement Villa de San Francisco de Campeche.

The settlement soon flourished as the major port of the Yucatán Peninsula, but this made it subject to pirate attacks. After a particularly appalling attack in 1663 left the city in ruins, the king of Spain ordered construction of Campeche's famous bastions, putting an end to the periodic carnage.

Today the economy of the city is largely driven by fishing and, increasingly, tourism, which to some extent have funded the downtown area's renovation.

◉ Sights & Activities

Plaza Principal
PLAZA

Shaded by spreading carob trees, and ringed by tiled benches with broad footpaths radiating from a belle époque kiosk, Campeche's appealingly modest central square started life in 1531 as a military camp. Over the years it became the focus of the town's civic, political and religious activities and remains the core of public life. The plaza is seen at its best on weekend evenings, when it's closed to traffic and concerts are staged (see p332).

The plaza is surrounded by suitably fine buildings. On the northern (seaward) side stands a replica of the old government center, now housing the modern **Biblioteca de Campeche** (State Library; ⊙9am-8pm Mon-Fri, to 1pm Sat). The impressive portico building on the opposite side housed an earlier version of the city hall; it is now occupied by shops and restaurants.

FREE Catedral de Nuestra Señora de la Purísima Concepción
CATHEDRAL

(⊙7am-noon & 4-6pm) Dominating the plaza's east side is the two-towered cathedral. The limestone structure has stood on this spot for more than three centuries. Statues of Sts Peter and Paul occupy niches in the baroque facade; the sober, single-nave interior is lined with colonial-era paintings.

Centro Cultural Casa Número 6
CULTURAL BUILDING

(Calle 57 No 6; admission M$10, audio guide M$15; ⊙9am-9pm) During the prerevolutionary era, when the mansion was occupied by an upper-class *campechano* family, 'Number Six' was a prestigious plaza address. Wandering the premises, you'll get an idea of how the city's high society lived back then.

SACRED WATERS

With over 6000 of them in the region, cenotes (natural sinkholes) are a special feature of the Yucatán Peninsula. While debate continues on exactly why there are so many in the area, many attribute it to the impact of the Chicxulub meteor some 65 million years ago (see boxed text, p316). It's a compelling theory – looking at a map of known cenotes you can see there are none in the near vicinity of the impact site and a huge proliferation beginning at a radius of about 100km. There is at least general agreement that cenotes are formed when the limestone bedrock forming the roof of an underground cavern collapses, exposing the groundwater underneath.

Cenotes are, for the most part, connected to the network of underground rivers that runs beneath the entire peninsula, which of course is every cave diver's dream setup.

An entire industry has grown around cenote diving and, alongside dinosaur and human remains, divers have discovered many valuable items from Maya times. It's believed they were cast into cenotes in rituals to appease the gods (most probably the rain god, Chac). There's also evidence suggesting that cenotes were used for human sacrifice.

That cenotes were sacred to the Maya is no surprise – rivers and lakes are rare in the Yucatán Peninsula and any freshwater source was bound to take on a heightened significance. Caves also had a special meaning as they were believed to be the gateway to Xibalbá, or the underworld.

History and geology aside, cenotes also make for fantastic swimming holes. Many of those close to large population centers are somewhat polluted, but if you can get out of town a bit, there's nothing like slipping into those cool, crystal-clear waters in the middle of the jungle on a steamy Yucatán day.

Baluartes HISTORIC SITE

After a particularly blistering pirate assault in 1663, the remaining inhabitants of Campeche set about erecting protective walls around their city. Built largely by indigenous labor with limestone extracted from nearby caves, the barrier took more than 50 years to complete. Stretching over 2km around the urban core and rising to a height of 8m, the hexagonal wall was linked by eight bulwarks. The seven that remain display a treasure trove of historical paraphernalia, artifacts and indigenous handicrafts. You can climb atop the bulwarks and stroll sections of the wall for sweeping views of the port.

Puerta del Mar

(Sea Gate; cnr Calles 8 & 59) Two main entrances connected the walled compound with the outside world. The Sea Gate provided access from the sea, opening onto a wharf where small craft delivered goods from ships anchored further out. (The shallow waters were later reclaimed, so the gate is now several blocks from the waterfront.)

Puerta de Tierra

(Land Gate; Calle 18; admission free; ⊘9am-9pm) On the eastern side of the town, the Land Gate was opened in 1732 as the principal ingress from the suburbs. It is now the venue for a sound-and-light show (p332).

Baluarte de Nuestra Señora de la Soledad

Designed to protect the Puerta del Mar, this was the largest of the bastions completed in the late 1600s. Appropriately, it was named for the patron saint of sailors. This bulwark contains the fascinating **Museo de la Arquitectura Maya** (Calle 8; admission M$31; ⊘9am-5pm), the one must-see museum in Campeche. It provides an excellent overview of the sites around Campeche state and the key architectural styles associated with them. Five halls display stelae taken from various sites, accompanied by graphic representations of their carved inscriptions with brief commentaries in flawless English.

Baluarte de Santiago

(cnr Calles 8 & 49; admission M$5; ⊘9am-9pm Mon-Sat, to 4pm Sun) Completed in 1704 – the last of the bulwarks to be built – the St James Bulwark houses the **Jardín Botánico Xmuch Haltún**, a botanical garden with numerous endemic plants.

Baluarte de San Carlos

Named after Spain's King Carlos II, this bulwark houses the **Museo de la Ciudad** (Calle 8; admission M$25; ⊘9am-9pm), a small

YUCATÁN PENINSULA CAMPECHE

Campeche

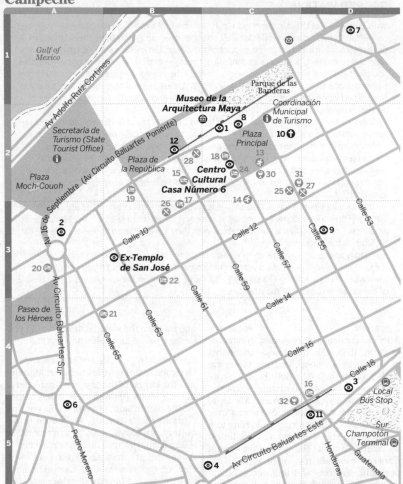

but worthwhile museum chronologically illustrating the city's tempestuous history via well-displayed objects: specimens of dyewood, muskets, a figurehead from a ship's prow and the like. The dungeon downstairs alludes to the building's use as a military prison during the 1700s. The museum was closed during research.

Baluarte de San Pedro
(cnr Avs Circuito Baluartes Este & Circuito Baluartes Norte; admission free; ☉9am-2pm) Directly behind Iglesia de San Juan de Dios, the St Peter Bulwark served a postpiracy defensive

function when it repelled a punitive raid from Mérida in 1824. Carved in stone above the entry is the symbol of San Pedro: two keys to heaven and the papal tiara. Climb the steep ramp to the roof and look between the battlements to see San Juan's cupola. Downstairs, the **Galería y Museo de Arte Popular** (Gallery & Museum of Folk Art; admission free; ☉9am-2pm) displays beautiful indigenous handicrafts.

Baluarte de San Francisco
(Calle 18; entrance to ruins only M$10, entrance to ruins & museum M$40; ☉9am-2pm) Once the

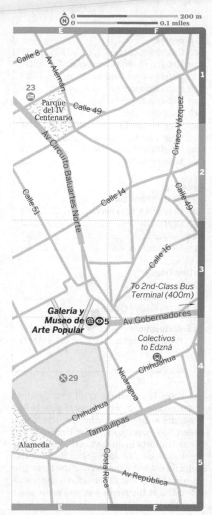

northwest of San Juan, the St Rose Bulwark holds Campeche's art gallery.

Ex-Templo de San José   HISTORIC BUILDING

(former San José church; cnr Calles 10 & 63) Faced with flamboyant blue-and-yellow tiles, the Ex-Templo de San José is a wonder to behold; note the lighthouse, complete with weather vane, atop the right spire. It was built in the early 18th century by Jesuits who ran it as an institute of higher learning until they were booted out of Spanish domains in 1767. It's not open to the public, but you are welcome to admire its lovely exterior.

Museo Arqueológico de Campeche & Fuerte de San Miguel   MUSEUM

(admission M$37; ⊙8am-5pm Tue-Sun) Campeche's largest colonial fort, facing the Gulf of Mexico some 4km southwest of the city center, is now home to the excellent archaeological museum. Here you can admire findings from the sites of Calakmul, Edzná and Jaina, an island north of town once used as a burial site for Maya aristocracy.

Buses marked 'Lerma' or 'Playa' depart from the market and travel counterclockwise around the Circuito before heading down the *malecón*. The access road to the fort is 4km southwest of the Plaza Moch-Couoh. Hike 700m up the hill (bear left at the fork). Otherwise, take a taxi (M$45) or the *tranvía* (trolley; see p330).

Fuerte Museo San José del Alto   FORTRESS

(Av Francisco Morazán; admission M$45; ⊙9am-5pm Tue-Sun) San Miguel's northern counterpart, built in the late 18th century, sits atop the Cerro de Bellavista. From the parapets you can see where the town ends and the mangroves begin. Cross a drawbridge over a moat to enter the neatly restored fortress. Inside, a museum illustrates the port's maritime history through ship models, weaponry and other paraphernalia, including a beautiful ebony rudder carved in the shape of a hound.

To get there, catch a local, green 'Josefa,' 'Bellavista' or 'Morelos' bus from the side of the market.

FREE Casa del Arte   GALLERY

(Calle 55 btwn Calles 12 & 14; ⊙8am-3pm & 5-9pm Mon-Fri) Come to the Casa del Arte for rotating art, photography and painting exhibits by local artists.

primary defensive bastion for the adjacent Puerta de la Tierra, the St Francis Bulwark houses a small arms museum.

Baluarte de San Juan

(Calle 18; admission with San Francisco ticket free; ⊙9am-2pm) Down the street from the San Francisco, the St John Bulwark is the smallest of the seven, containing a permanent exhibition on the history of the bulwarks.

Baluarte de Santa Rosa

(cnr Calles 14 & Av Circuito Baluartes Sur; admission free; ⊙9am-3pm) A couple of blocks to the

YUCATÁN PENINSULA CAMPECHE

Campeche

⊙ Top Sights

Centro Cultural Casa Número 6	C2
Ex-Templo de San José	B3
Galería y Museo de Arte Popular	E4
Museo de la Arquitectura Maya	C2

⊙ Sights

1	Baluarte de Nuestra Señora de la Soledad	C2
2	Baluarte de San Carlos	A3
3	Baluarte de San Francisco	D4
4	Baluarte de San Juan	C5
5	Baluarte de San Pedro	E4
6	Baluarte de Santa Rosa	A5
7	Baluarte de Santiago	D1
8	Biblioteca de Campeche	C2
9	Casa del Arte	D3
10	Catedral de Nuestra Señora de la Purísima Concepción	C2
	Jardín Botánico Xmuch Haltún	(see 7)
	Museo de la Ciudad	(see 2)
11	Puerta de Tierra	D5
12	Puerta del Mar	B2

⊕ Activities, Courses & Tours

13	Tranvía Ticket Booth	C2
14	Xtampak Tours	C2

⊜ Sleeping

15	Casa Don Gustavo	B2
16	Hacienda Puerta Campeche	D4
17	Hotel América Centro	B3
18	Hotel Campeche	C2
19	Hotel Castelmar	B2
20	Hotel del Paseo	A3
21	Hotel Francis Drake	B4
22	Hotel López	B3
23	Hotel Plaza Campeche	E1
24	Monkey Hostel	C2

⊗ Eating

25	Café La Parroquia	C2
26	Cafetería Atrapa Sueño	B3
27	Chef Color	D2
28	Marganzo	B2
29	Mercado Principal	E4

⊙ Drinking

30	La Casa Vieja	C2
31	La Iguana Azul	C2
32	Salón Rincón Colonial	C5

⊙ Entertainment

	Puerta de Tierra	(see 11)

Malecón WALKING

A popular path for joggers, cyclists, strolling friends and cooing sweethearts, the *malecón,* Campeche's waterfront promenade, makes for a breezy sunrise ramble or sunset bike ride.

⇌ Courses

Universidad Autónoma de Campeche Centro de Español y Maya (CEM) LANGUAGE
(http://etzna.uacam.mx/cem/principal.htm; Av Melgar) Universidad Autónoma de Campeche Centro de Español y Maya (CEM), a block east of the *malecón,* offers four- to eight-week summer language courses. Homestays can be arranged. Drop by to sit in on classes or check the noticeboard for Spanish teachers.

⌔ Tours

Check with the hostels if they are arranging tours. If not, try one of these operators.

Tranvía de la Ciudad BUS
(adult/child M$80/25; ⊙hourly 9am-noon & 5-8pm) Three different tours by motorized *tranvía* depart from Calle 10 beside the Plaza Principal daily; all last about 45 minutes and require 10 passengers before leaving. On the same schedule, the trolley called 'El Guapo' goes to the Fuerte de San Miguel or its twin on the north side of town, the Fuerte de San José. (Note that the fort tours do not leave time to visit the museums within them.) Buy tram tickets and check schedules at the booth just inside the plaza from the trolley stop.

Xtampak Tours CITY, ARCHAEOLOGY
(⌕811-64-73; www.xtampak.com; Calle 57 No 14; ⊙8am-4pm & 5:30-8:30pm Mon-Sat, 8:30am-2pm Sun) Offers comprehensive city tours at 9am and 4pm daily (M$250 per person, four hours), as well as archaeological tours to Edzná (M$200), the Chenes sites (M$800) and eastern Campeche.

⌸ Sleeping

The streets in the historic center (which is where you will want to stay) follow a numbered sequence: inland-oriented streets have odd numbers and perpendicular ones even.

Hotel América Centro HOTEL $$

(☑816-45-76; Calle 10 No 252; s/d M$640/700; ❋@🖥) Wide interior balconies overlook a pleasant cafe courtyard at this reasonably priced, semirenovated colonial number. Rooms aren't huge, but those on the east and front sides have little balconies (making them good for people-watching, but a bit noisier).

Monkey Hostel HOSTEL $

(☑811-66-05; www.hostalcampeche.com; cnr Calles 10 & 57; dm M$100, r without bathroom M$250; @🖥) The best hostel in town has a great plaza-side corner location, meaning lots of cross-ventilation and light. Dorms are fine, rooms have little balconies and there are good kitchen and hangout areas.

Casa Don Gustavo BOUTIQUE HOTEL $$$

(☑811-23-50; www.casadongustavo.com; Calle 59 No 4; r from M$3500; P❋🖥🏊) A delightful little hotel, set in a grand old mansion and renovated to colonial perfection. The chic pool area may impress, but the rooftop Jacuzzi is the kicker.

Hotel López HOTEL $$

(☑/fax 816-33-44; www.hotellopezcampeche.com.mx; Calle 12 No 189; r from M$550; ❋🖥🏊) A very good deal for this price range – rooms are a bit cramped and inner-facing windows don't give much privacy, but the charming central patio and medium-sized pool out back make up for that.

Hotel Francis Drake HOTEL $$

(☑811-56-26; www.hotelfrancisdrake.com; Calle 12 No 207; s/d M$750/860; ❋🖥) A somewhat baroque lobby leads on to cool, fresh rooms with a sprinkling of tasteful decoration. Bathrooms and balconies are tiny, but the rooms are huge (other hotels would call them suites) with king-sized beds and separate sitting areas.

Hacienda Puerta Campeche BOUTIQUE HOTEL $$$

(☑816-75-08; www.thehaciendas.com; Calle 59 No 71; r from M$6500; P❋🖥🏊) Features pretty much all you would expect for the price – large, stylish rooms, a good onsite restaurant, bucketloads of atmosphere and an indoor/outdoor pool built to incorporate the old walls of the original house. The same operators have another restored hacienda 26km outside the city in Uayamón.

Hotel del Paseo HOTEL $$

(☑811-01-00; www.hoteldelpaseo.com; Calle 8 No 215; r/ste M$600/800; ❋🖥) Named for its proximity to the pleasant *paseo* (promenade) that connects the historic center with the Barrio San Román, this modern option has an interior promenade too, with street lamps, shops and a bar, all beneath your balcony.

Hotel Campeche HOTEL $

(☑816-51-83; hotelcampeche@hotmail.com; Calle 57 btwn Calles 8 & 10; s/d with fan M$250/290, aircon M$330/390; ❋🖥) Not much in the way of frills here, but the plaza-side location and big rooms in this classically crumbling building are about the best budget bet in town. A couple of rooms have little balconies looking out over the plaza.

Hotel Castelmar HOTEL $$

(☑811-12-04; www.castelmarhotel.com; Calle 61 No 2; r from M$950; ❋🖥🏊) Once an army barracks, the Castelmar has been operating as a hotel for 100 years now. A recent remodeling job upped the casual refinement of this small hotel. Oversized crucifixes and other colonial-era-inspired ornaments add to the charm, as do the amazingly thick walls. Just try to scream – nobody will hear you.

✕ Eating

The emblematic *campechano* dish is *Pan de Cazón* – a tortilla sandwich filled with minced shark meat and beans and smothered in tomato sauce. Wash one down with an *horchata de coco* (rice and coconut drink) and you'll be livin' *la vida local*.

Marganzo YUCATECAN $$

(Calle 8 No 267; mains $80-150; ⊙7am-11pm) Don't let the waitresses in 'traditional dress' fool you – this is no tourist trap. What's on offer is some of the most carefully prepared regional cuisine in town, served up in a dining hall that's just stylish enough, without being fancy.

Chef Color INTERNATIONAL $

(cnr Calles 55 & 12; full/half lunch platter M$55/35; ⊙10am-6pm) This Central American-style eatery serves up large platters of toothsome fare from a steam table. The list of *guisados* (main courses) might include potato croquettes and Cuban-inspired *ropa vieja* ('old clothes,' shredded beef in salsa) accompanied by fried plantains, beans and rice.

Café La Parroquia YUCATECAN $$
(Calle 55 No 8; mains M$85-170; ◷24hr) Any time of day – or night – your table awaits at this classic coffeehouse with a dozen ceiling fans, attentive waiters in white coats and continuous Televisa broadcasts. Not just tourists but local geezers in *guayaberas* hang out here for hours on end.

Cafetería Atrapa Sueño CAFE $
(◪816-50-00; Calle 10 No 260; mains M$25-60; ◷9am-8pm Mon-Sat, 9am-4pm Sun; ◪) This little hippie bistro – complete with a Zen garden out back – features a good selection of vegetarian fare, from sandwiches to refreshing *licuados*. The owners offer yoga courses and meditation sessions.

☕ Drinking

La Casa Vieja BAR
(Calle 10 No 319A; ◷8:30am-12:30am) There's no better setting for an evening cocktail than La Casa Vieja's colonnaded balcony overlooking the Plaza Principal.

La Iguana Azul BAR
(Calle 55 No 11; ◷6pm-2am Mon-Sat) Toward the weekend this casual restaurant across from Café La Parroquia hosts local cover bands and jazz combos in its colonial courtyard.

Salón Rincón Colonial BAR
(Calle 59 No 60; ◷noon-8pm) This Cuban-style drinking establishment served as a location for *Original Sin,* a 2001 movie with Antonio Banderas that was set in Havana. The *botanas* (drinking snacks) are exceptionally fine; you get a different selection with each round. Ladies are welcome to imbibe in the attached, air-conditioned Ladies Salon (we kid you not).

☆ Entertainment

There's invariably someone performing on the Plaza Principal every Saturday and Sunday evening from around 6:30pm. Also, at weekends tables are set up from 6pm to 10pm in front of the cathedral and library for La Lotería (a Mexican version of bingo). For Campeche's hottest bars and clubs, head 1km south from the city center along the *malecón* past the Torres del Cristal skyscraper.

Incidents from Campeche's pirate past are re-enacted several nights a week inside the **Puerta de Tierra** (tickets M$50; ◷8pm Thu-Sun), in a Disney-esque extravaganza with lots of cannon blasts and flashing lights.

The Universidad Autónoma de Campeche (p330) has revolving art exhibits, plays and art-house movies (M$25) at the Cine Teatro Universitario Joaquín Lanz.

ⓘ Information

Internet Access
All of the hotels (and the Plaza Principal) have wi-fi. Internet cafes abound in the Centro.

Laundry
Kler Lavandería (Calle 16 No 305; per kg M$15; ◷8am-6pm Mon-Fri, to 4pm Sat)

Medical Services
Cruz Roja (Red Cross; ◪815-24-11; cnr Av Las Palmas & Ah Kim Pech) Some 3km northeast of downtown.
Emergency (◪066)
Hospital Dr Manuel Campos (◪811-17-09; Av Circuito Baluartes Norte) Between Calles 14 & 16.

Money
Campeche has numerous banks with ATMs, open 8am to 4pm Monday to Friday, 9am to 2pm Saturday.

Post
Central post office (cnr Av 16 de Septiembre & Calle 53; ◷8:30am-3:30pm Mon-Fri)

Tourist Information
Coordinación Municipal de Turismo (◪811-39-89; Calle 55 No 3; ◷9am-9pm)
Secretaría de Turismo (State Tourism Office; ◪811-27-33; www.campeche.travel; Plaza Moch-Couoh; ◷8am-9pm)

ⓘ Getting There & Away

Air
The airport is 6km southeast of the center.
Aeroméxico (◪800-021-40-10) flies to Mexico City at least twice daily.

Bus
Campeche's **main bus terminal** (◪816-28-02; Av Patricio Trueba 237), usually called the ADO or 1st-class terminal, is about 2.5km south of Plaza Principal via Avenida Central. Buses provide 1st-class and deluxe service to major cities as well as 2nd-class service to Sabancuy (M$92), Hecelchakán (M$48), Candelaria (M$149) and points in Tabasco.

The **2nd-class terminal** (◪816-28-02; Av Gobernadores 289), often referred to as the 'old ADO' station, is east of the Mercado Principal. Second-class buses to Hopelchén (M$50), Bolonchén, Xpujil and Bécal (M$45) depart from here.

BUSES FROM CAMPECHE

DESTINATION	FARE (M$)	DURATION	FREQUENCY (DAILY)
Bolonchén de Rejón	68	3hr	6 from 2nd-class terminal
Cancún	430-516	7hr	7 OCC & ADO GL direct
Chetumal	230-326	6hr	ADO noon, 2 from 2nd-class terminal
Hopelchén	50	1½hr	hourly from 2nd-class terminal
Mérida (via Bécal)	160-190	2½hr	half-hourly ADO & ADO GL
Mérida (via Uxmal)	90	4½hr	half-hourly from 2nd-class terminal
Mexico City	1318	17hr	1 ADO, 1 ADO GL
Palenque	282	6hr	9:45pm ADO
San Cristóbal de Las Casas	410	9hr	9:45pm ADO
Villahermosa	265-418	6hr	frequent ADO, Sur & ADO GL
Xpujil	162-230	5hr	ADO 2pm, 3 Sur from 2nd-class terminal

To get to the new terminal, catch any 'Las Flores,' 'Solidaridad' or 'Casa de Justicia' bus by the post office. To the 2nd-class terminal, catch a 'Terminal Sur' or 'Ex-ADO' bus from the same point.

To get to Edzná (M$30, one hour), catch a Valle Edzná *colectivo* from Calle Chihuahua near the corner of Calle Nicaragua, by the market. They leave every half hour from 7am to 7pm.

The destinations in the table are from the 1st-class terminal unless otherwise noted.

Car & Motorcycle

If you're heading for Edzná or taking the long route to Mérida or the fast toll road going south, take Calle 61 to Avenida Central and follow signs for the airport and either Edzná or the *cuota*. For the non-toll route south, just head down the *malecón*. For the short route to Mérida go north on the *malecón*.

Coming to Campeche from the south via the *cuota*, turn left at the roundabout signed for the *universidad,* and follow that road straight to the coast. Turn right up the *malecón* and you will arrive instantly oriented.

In addition to some outlets at the airport, several car-rental agencies can be found downtown. Rates are generally higher than in Mérida or Cancún.

Pirata Rent a Car (✆cell phone 981-1271457; Hotel Castelmar, Calle 61 No 2)

Getting Around

Local buses originate at the market or across Avenida Circuito Baluartes from it and go at least partway around the Circuito before heading to their final destinations. The fare is M$4.50.

Taxis charge a set rate of M$30 (M$40 after dark) for rides within the city; by the hour they're around M$120. Tickets for authorized taxis from the airport to the center (M$85) are sold from a booth in the terminal. To request a taxi, call ✆815-30-36 or 816-11-13.

Consider renting a bicycle for a ride along the *malecón* or through the streets of the Centro Histórico. Monkey Hostel (p331) rents bicycles at reasonable rates (M$100 a day or M$10 per hour).

Drivers should note that even-numbered streets in the Centro Histórico take priority, as indicated by the red (stop) or black (go) arrows at every intersection.

Around Campeche

EDZNÁ

The closest major ruins to Campeche are about 53km to the southeast. Edzná (admission M$41; ⊙8am-4:30pm) once covered more than 17 sq km and was inhabited from approximately 600 BC to the 15th century AD. Most of the visible carvings date from AD 550 to 810. Though it's a long way from such Puuc sites as Uxmal and Kabah, some of the architecture here has elements of the Puuc style. What led to Edzná's decline and gradual abandonment remains a mystery.

Beyond the entrance is a *palapa* protecting carvings and stelae from the elements. A path from here leads about 400m through vegetation to the zone's big draw, the **Plaza Principal** (follow the signs for the Gran

Acrópolis), which is 160m long, 100m wide and surrounded by temples. On your right as you enter from the north is the Nohochná (Big House), a massive, elongated structure that was topped by four long halls probably used for administrative tasks, such as the collection of tributes and the dispensing of justice. The built-in benches facing the main plaza were designed for spectators to view theatrical and ritual events. The spectacles continue in the plaza these days in the form of a sound-and-light show (admission M$71; ☺7pm Nov-Mar, 8pm Apr-Oct).

Across the plaza is the Gran Acrópolis, a raised platform holding several structures, including Edzná's major temple, the 31m-high Edificio de los Cinco Pisos (Five-Story Building). It rises five levels from its vast base to the roofcomb and contains many vaulted rooms. A great central staircase of 65 steps goes right to the top. Some of the weathered carvings of masks, serpents and jaguar heads that formerly adorned each level are now in the *palapa* near the ticket office.

The current structure is the last of four remodels, and was done primarily in the Puuc architectural style. Scholars generally agree that this temple is a hybrid of a pyramid and a palace. The impressive roofcomb is a clear reference to the sacred buildings at Tikal in Guatemala.

In the Pequeña Acrópolis, to the south of the main plaza, is the *palapa*-protected Templo de Mascarones (Temple of Masks), which features carved portrayals of the sun god, Kinich-Ahau. The central motif is the head of a Maya man whose face has been modified to give him the appearance of a jaguar.

You can download a map to the Edzná ruin for free at www.lonelyplanet.com/additional-mexico-maps.

ⓘ Getting There & Away

From Campeche, minibuses (M$30, one hour) leave from Calle Chihuahua every half hour from 7am to 7pm.

Xtampak Tours (see p330) in Campeche provides a shuttle service from Campeche to Edzná (M$200, minimum two passengers) as well as guided tours of the site for an additional M$750.

Leaving the site by car, you can either go north on Hwy 120 to pick up Hwy 261 east to Hopelchén, or alternatively head toward Dzibalchén and the Chenes site of Hochob by going south to Pich, then east to Chencoh, 54km from Edzná over a decent but little-used road.

BOLONCHÉN DE REJÓN & XTACUMBILXUNAAN

Forty kilometers east of San Antonio Cayal is Hopelchén, where Hwy 261 turns north; there's a Pemex gas station on the west side of town. The next town to appear out of the lush countryside, after 34km, is Bolonchén de Rejón. Its local festival of Santa Cruz is held each year on May 3.

Bolonchén de Rejón is near the Grutas de Xtacumbilxunaan (M$50; ☺10am-5pm Tue-Sun), pronounced 'Grutas de *shtaa*-koom-beel-shoo-*nahn*' (go on, give it a shot), about 3km south of town. Lighted steps lead down to a barely visible cenote, beyond which a passage leads 100m further. Be aware that the wooden ladder is for demonstration purposes only, to show how the Maya used to descend to the cave floor. Doing so yourself would be very foolish.

Sur buses traveling between Hopelchén and Mérida will drop you at the cave entrance before Bolonchén (M$15, 25 minutes). In addition, *colectivos* depart for Bolonchén from the north side of Hopelchén's plaza, passing near the caves. Check with the driver for return times.

Hwy 261 continues north into Yucatán state to Uxmal, with a side road leading to the ruins along the Ruta Puuc.

Escárcega to Xpujil

This southern peninsular region – now bordering modern-day Guatemala – was the earliest established, longest inhabited and most densely populated territory in the Maya world. Here you will find the most ancient and most architecturally elaborate archaeological sites on the peninsula. Hwy 186 stretches due east across southern-central Campeche state, from grubby Escárcega through jungle to Xpujil, and on to Chetumal in Quintana Roo – a 273km ride. It passes several fascinating Maya sites and goes through the ecologically diverse and archaeologically rich Reserva de la Biosfera Calakmul. The largest settlement between Escárcega and Chetumal is Xpujil. Situated on Hwy 186 about 2km west of the Campeche–Quintana Roo border, Xpujil is a great place from which to stage your exploration of the region. The only gas station in the same stretch is about 5km east of Xpujil.

The predominant architectural styles of the region's archaeological sites are Río

DIY: EXPLORE MORE OF CAMPECHE

Leave the guidebook behind and head out into the less-explored corners of Campeche. Here are some ideas to get you started.

» **Chenes sites** Northeastern Campeche state is dotted with more than 30 sites in the distinct Chenes style, recognizable by the monster motifs around doorways in the center of long, low buildings of three sections, and by temples atop pyramidal bases.

» **Laguna de Términos** The largest lagoon in the Gulf of Mexico area, the Laguna de Términos comprises a network of estuaries, dunes, swamps and ponds that together form a uniquely important coastal habitat.

» **Bécal** While on the surface Bécal may look like a somnolent *campechano* town, underneath a multitude is laboring away at the traditional craft of hat making.

Bec and Chenes. The former is characterized by long, low buildings that look like they're divided into sections, each with a huge serpent or monster-mouth door. The facades are decorated with smaller masks, geometric designs (with many X forms) and columns. At the corners of the buildings are tall, solid towers with extremely small, steep, nonfunctional steps, topped by small false temples. Many of these towers have roofcombs. The Chenes architectural style shares most of these characteristics, except for the towers.

BALAMKÚ

Discovered in 1990, **Balamkú** (admission M$31; ☺8am-4:30pm) is 60km west of Xpujil (88km east of Escárcega). This small site's attractions are its frescoes and an exquisite, ornate stucco frieze. Amazingly, much original color is still visible on both the frescoes and the frieze. You'll notice toads dominate the designs at Balamkú. These amphibians, not only at home on land and in water, were considered to move easily between this world and the next. The toad was a revered spirit guide who helped humans navigate between earth and the underworld.

The frescoes are open to public viewing, but the frieze is housed in a locked building. The caretaker will open the door – a tip is appreciated.

A taxi from Xpujil to Balamkú costs M$800 (round trip including two hours' waiting time).

CALAKMUL

In 1931 US botanist Cyrus Lundell was the first outsider to 'discover' **Calakmul** (admission M$38; ☺8am-4:30pm), which means 'Adjacent Mounds.' Mayanists consider Calakmul to be a site of vital archaeological significance. The site bears comparison in size and historical significance to Tikal in Guatemala, its chief rival for hegemony over the southern lowlands during the Classic era.

From about AD 250 to 695, Calakmul was the leading city in a vast region known as the Kingdom of the Serpent's Head. Its perpetual rival was Tikal, and its decline began with the power struggles and internal conflicts that followed the defeat by Tikal of Calakmul's king Garra de Jaguar (Jaguar Paw).

As at Tikal, there are indications that construction occurred over a period of more than a millennium. Beneath Edificio VII, archaeologists discovered a burial crypt with some 2000 pieces of jade, and tombs continue to yield spectacular jade burial masks; many of these objects are on display in Campeche city's Museo Arqueológico. Calakmul holds at least 120 carved stelae, though many are eroded.

So far, only a fraction of Calakmul's 100-sq-km expanse has been cleared, and few of its 6500 buildings have been consolidated, let alone restored; however, exploration and restoration are ongoing.

Lying at the heart of the vast Reserva de la Biosfera Calakmul, the ruins are surrounded by rainforest, which is best viewed from the top of one of the several pyramids. There are over 250 bird species living in the reserve, and you are likely to see ocellated turkeys, parrots and toucans. Other wildlife protected by the reserve includes jaguars, spider monkeys, pumas, ocelots and white-lipped peccaries.

Twenty kilometers down the access road is the ultramodern **Museo del Centro de Comunicación y Cultura** (admission free; ☺8am-4pm) which showcases fossil finds from the region and some ceramics from Calakmul, and has a small botanical garden featuring plants traditionally used by the Maya for food and medicine.

ⓘ VISITING CALAKMUL

Calakmul is *big* – you could easily spend a few hours wandering around the site and if you stop to look at details, take photos and climb temples, this could stretch to a couple more. If all that activity is likely to get you peckish, pack some snacks and water – the nearest eats are 40km away.

🛏 Sleeping & Eating

Campamento Yaax'che CAMPGROUND $
(☎983-871-60-64; ciitcalakmul@prodigy.net.mx; campsites per person M$70, with tent from M$200) More than just a campground, Yaax'che, 7km along the access road from Hwy 186 to Calakmul, is the base for tours by Servidores Turísticos Calakmul in Xpujil, a training center for local guides and an experiment in sustainable ecotourism. You can rent a prepitched tent or set up your own under a thatched shelter. Meals cost M$50 to M$75.

Villas Puerta Calakmul CABAÑAS $$$
(☎998-892-26-24; www.puertacalakmul.com.mx; cabañas from M$1950; ✲🗢✱) Luxury/rustic cabins scattered around a woodsy property located just down the turnoff to Calakmul. There's plenty of space between them and the colonial-jungle mix decor could be a nightmare, but they actually pull it off pretty well.

ⓘ Getting There & Away

Xtampak Tours (p330) in Campeche and Río Bec Dreams (p336) near Chicanná run tours to Calakmul.

By car, the turnoff to Calakmul is 56km west of Xpujil, and the site is 60km south of the highway at the end of a decent paved road. A toll of M$56 per car (more for heavier vehicles) and M$20 per person is levied by the *municipio* (township) of Calakmul at the turnoff from Hwy 186. A cab to Calakmul from Xpujil costs M$800.

CHICANNÁ

Aptly named 'House of the Snake's Jaws,' **Chicanná** (admission M$37; ☉8am-4:30pm) is best known for the remarkably well-preserved doorway on Estructura 11, featuring a hideous fanged visage. Buried in the jungle 11km west of Xpujil and 400m south of Hwy 186, Chicanná is a mixture of Chenes and Río Bec architectural styles. The city attained its peak during the late Classic period, from AD 550 to 700, as a sort of elite suburb of Becán.

TOP CHOICE **Río Bec Dreams** (www.riobecdreams.com; Hwy 186 Km 142; cabañas with/without bathroom M$800/420) provides unquestionably the best accommodations in the area. This Canadian-run jungle lodge has thatched-roof 'jungalows' sharing a bathhouse and *cabañas* with private bathrooms in the woods. Environmentally sound facilities include composting toilets, rainwater collection devices and solar electricity.

A taxi from Xpujil to Chicanná costs around M$250 (round trip including one-hour waiting time).

BECÁN

Eight kilometers west of Xpujil, **Becán** (admission M$41; ☉8am-4:30pm) sits atop a rock outcrop and inside a 2km moat that snakes its way around the entire city to protect it from attack. Becán (literally 'path of the snake') is also the Maya word for 'canyon' or 'moat.' Seven causeways crossed the moat, providing access to the city. Becán was occupied from 550 BC until AD 1000.

This is among the largest and most elaborate sites in the area. The first thing you'll come to is a plaza. If you walk while keeping it to your left, you'll pass through a rock-walled passageway and beneath a corbeled arch. You will reach a huge twin-towered temple with cylindrical columns at the top of a flight of stairs. This is **Estructura VIII**, dating from about AD 600 to 730. The view from the top of this temple has become partially obscured by the trees, but on a clear day you can still see structures at the Xpuhil ruins to the east.

Northwest of Estructura VIII is Plaza Central, ringed by 30m-high **Estructura IX** (the tallest building at the site) and the more interesting **Estructura X**. In early 2001, at X's far south side, a stucco mask still bearing some red paint was uncovered. It is enclosed in a wooden shelter with a window for viewing.

In the jungle to the west are more ruins, including the Plaza Oeste, which is surrounded by low buildings and a ball court. Much of this area is still being excavated and restored, so it's open to the public only intermittently.

Loop back east, through the passageway again, to the plaza; cross it diagonally to the right, climbing a stone staircase to the Plaza Sureste. Around this plaza are Estructuras I through IV; a **circular altar** (Estructura IIIA) lies on the east side. **Estructura I** has the two towers typical of the Río Bec style.

To exit, you can go around the plaza counterclockwise and descend the stone staircase on the southeast side, or go down the southwest side and head left.

A taxi from Xpujil to Becán costs around M$250 (round trip including one-hour waiting time).

Xpujil

☑983 / POP 3200

The hamlet of Xpujil (pronounced 'shpu-*heel*') lies at the junction of east-west Hwy 186 and Campeche Hwy 261, which leads north to Hopelchén and eventually Mérida. A good base from which to explore the area's sites, Xpujil is growing rapidly in the anticipation of a tourist boom. However, it still has no bank or laundry, and the nearest gas station is 5km east of town. Several restaurants, a couple of hotels and a taxi stand are near the bus depot.

From the junction, the Xpuhil ruins are less than 1km west, Becán is 8km west, Chicanná is 11.5km west, Balamkú is 60km west and the Calakmul ruins are 120km southwest. **Servidores Turísticos Calakmul** (☑871-60-64; www.ecoturismocalakmul.com; Carretera Escárcega-Chetumal Km 153; ☉9am-2pm & 3-7pm Mon-Sat), around 200m east of the Xpujil junction, provides ecotours led by trained guides from nearby communities.

◎ Sights

Xpuhil RUIN
(admission M$37; ☉8am-4:30pm) Within walking distance of the town, Xpuhil boasts a surreal skyscraper that is a striking example of the Río Bec style. The three towers (rather than the usual two) of Estructura I rise above a dozen vaulted rooms. The central tower, soaring 53m, is the best preserved. With its banded tiers and impractically steep stairways leading up to a temple that displays traces of a zoomorphic mask, it gives a good idea of what the other two must have looked like back in Xpuhil's 8th-century heyday. Go around back to see a fierce jaguar mask embedded in the wall below the temple.

The site's entrance is on the west edge of town on the north side of Hwy 186, at the turnoff for the airport.

⭲ Sleeping & Eating

The nicest and most reasonably priced accommodations are in Zoh-Laguna, 10km north of Xpujil. They are all contactable by dialing ☑200-125-65-87, the village's central phone booth.

ZOH-LAGUNA
Cabañas Mercedes BUNGALOW $
(Calle Zapote; s/d M$200/250; ℙ) The best-value place in the area has 13 thoughtfully designed bungalows with ceiling fans and large, tiled bathrooms. Good home-cooked meals are served in the thatched-roof dining hall. Don Antonio is a gracious and well-informed host, and can take you to the major Maya sites.

XPUJIL
Hotel Calakmul HOTEL $$
(☑871-60-29; calakmul04_06@hotmail.com; s/d M$590/650; ✳☎) If you're looking for midrange, this is pretty much it in this town. The rooms are OK, but the restaurant comes highly recommended.

Cabañas de Don Jorge CABAÑAS $
(☑871-61-28; cabañas M$100-200) Don Jorge's rustic but perfectly acceptable clapboard cabins sit up on a hill behind his store/eatery, Cocina Económica Xpujil, which can be found opposite the entrance to the Xpuhil ruins.

Aside from the hotel restaurants, there are various greasy spoons clustered around the bus station and roadside *taquerías* toward the Xpuhil ruins. Try **Concha del Caribe** (☉7am-10pm), opposite the bus terminal, for a decent range of seafood, meat and snacks, washed down with an ice-cold *agua de jamaica* (hibiscus tea).

❶ Getting There & Around

No buses originate in Xpujil, so you must hope there's a vacant seat on one passing through. The **bus terminal** (☑871-60-27) is just east of the Xpujil junction, on the north side of the highway. You can hire a taxi in town to take you to Zoh-Laguna for around M$40.

For Becán, Hormiguero, Calakmul or other sites you will need to book a tour or hire a cab. The taxi stand is on the north side of the junction.

South of Xpujil

RÍO BEC
Southeast of Xpujil, you can explore the remote Río Bec sites. You're best off hiring a guide with a 4WD truck. It's possible to arrange this in Xpujil or at the Ejido 20 de

Noviembre (a collective farm located roughly 28km southeast of Xpujil); the going rate is M$650 to M$800. A taxi from Xpujil's main junction to the *ejido* will charge M$65 for drop-off service; negotiate waiting time. Alternatively, check with Río Bec Dreams (p336) near Chicanná.

HORMIGUERO

Spanish for 'anthill,' Hormiguero (admission free; ⊙8am-4:30pm) is an old site, with some buildings dating as far back as AD 50; however, the city flourished during the late Classic period. It has one of the most impressive buildings in the region. Entering the site, you will see the 50m-long **Estructura II**, which has a giant Chenes-style monster-mouth doorway with much of its decoration in good condition. Also check out **Estructura V**, 60m to the north.

Hormiguero is reached by heading 14km south from Xpujil junction, then turning right and heading another 8km west on a shoddily paved road. A cab from Xpujil to Hormiguero will cost you around M$250.

East of Xpujil

Continuing east from Xpujil brings you to the archaeological sites of Dzibanché, Kinichná and Kohunlich. About 20km northeast of Dzibanché is the pre-Classic site of Ichkabal. There has been much talk of opening this site to the public, but little action. Ask around for the latest. The following sights are in Quintana Roo and can also be accessed from Chetumal (see p290).

◉ Sights

Dzibanché & Kinichná   ARCHAEOLOGICAL SITE
(combined admission M$41; ⊙8am-5pm) Though a chore to get to, these sites are definitely worth a visit for their secluded, semiwild nature. Dzibanché (meaning 'writing on wood') was a major city extending more than 40 sq km, and on the road to it you pass huge mounds covered in trees. There are a number of excavated palaces and pyramids, but the site itself is not completely excavated.

A little further down the road, Kinichná is a hilltop site whose partially excavated acropolis affords panoramic views of the countryside. The road between the two is poorly signposted. If you're driving, keep

veering left. You'll see the hill – keep moving toward it.

Kohunlich   ARCHAEOLOGICAL SITE
(admission M$49, guide M$250) The archaeological site sits on a carpeted green. The ruins, dating from both the late pre-Classic (AD 100–200) and the early Classic (AD 300–600) periods, are famous for the great **Templo de los Mascarones** (Temple of the Masks), a pyramid-like structure with a central stairway flanked by huge, 3m-high stucco masks of the sun god.

A few hundred meters southwest of Plaza Merwin are the **27 Escalones** (27 Steps), the remains of an extensive residential area.

The hydraulic engineering used at Kohunlich was a great achievement; 90,000 of the site's 210,000 sq meters were cut to channel rainwater into Kohunlich's once enormous reservoir.

🛏 Sleeping

Explorean   LUXURY HOTEL $$$
(☏800-504-50-00; www.explorean.com; Km 5.65; s/d M$5500/6900 all-inclusive; ✻@🛜🕸) Halfway along the entrance road to the site is the super-deluxe Explorean which ticks all the boxes – infinity pool, hushed, sophisticated ambience, staff in flowing white uniforms etc. Cabins (more like small houses) are cool and comfortably furnished. Activities such as tours of the ruins and night kayaking are included in the price.

❶ Getting There & Away

The turnoff for Dzibanché from Hwy 186 is about 44km west of Chetumal and 63km east of Xpujil, just after the Zona Arqueológica sign. From there it's another 24km north and east along a nicely paved road. Just after the tiny town of Morocoy you'll need to turn right again.

Kohunlich's turnoff is 3km west along Hwy 186 from the Dzibanché turnoff, and the site lies at the end of a paved 8.5km road.

There is no public transportation running directly to either of the sites. They're best visited by car, though Kohunlich could conceivably be reached by taking an early bus to the village of Francisco Villa near the turnoff, then either hitchhiking or walking the 8.5km to the site. Flag down a bus from the main highway to get back to Chetumal or Xpujil. Tour operators in Xpujil offer trips to Kohunlich and Dzibanché for M$750.

Chiapas

Includes »

Best Places to Eat

» Don Mucho's (p382)

» Restaurant Los Geranios (p394)

» No Name Quesadillas (p362)

» Las Pichanchas (p345)

» Restaurant Las Tinajas (p382)

Best Places to Stay

» Casa Mexicana (p400)

» Las Guacamayas (p390)

» Boutique Hotel Quinta Chanabnal (p380)

» Madre Sal (p399)

» Casa Felipe Flores (p358)

Why Go?

Chilly pine-forest highlands, sultry rainforest jungles and attractive colonial cities exist side by side within Mexico's southernmost state, a region awash with the legacy of Spanish rule and the remnants of ancient Maya civilization. Palenque and Yaxchilán are evocative vestiges of powerful Maya kingdoms, and the presence of modern Maya is a constant reminder of the region's rich and uninterrupted history. The colonial hubs of San Cristóbal de las Casas and Chiapa de Corzo give way to sandbar beaches and fertile plots of coffee and cacao in the Soconusco, and for outdoor adventurers, excursions to Laguna Miramar and the Cañón del Sumidero are unmissable.

Nature lovers willing to venture off the beaten track will swoon over the frothy cascades and exotic animals of the Lacandón Jungle and the El Triunfo reserve.

When To Go
San Cristóbal de las Casas

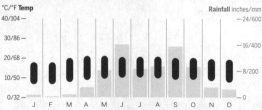

Nov–Apr The driest months statewide, though evenings in high-elevation San Cristóbal are chilly November to February.

Jun–Nov Nesting season for sea turtles along the beaches of the Pacific coast.

Jan Fiesta Grande de Enero in Chiapa de Corzo, and San Juan Chamula's change of cargo-holders.

Chiapas Highlights

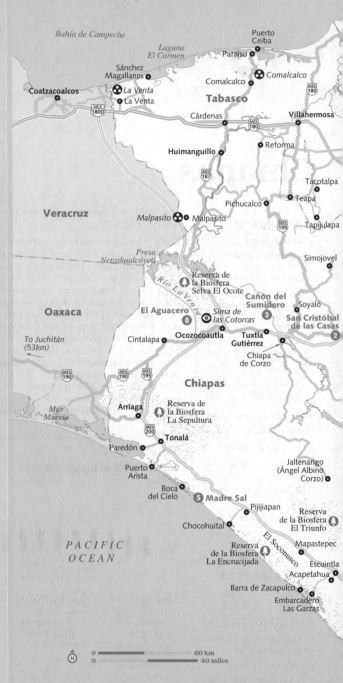

1 Scale the jungly hills and soaring Maya temples of **Palenque** (p373)

2 Stroll the high-altitude cobblestone streets of **San Cristóbal de las Casas** (p350)

3 Cruise through the waterway and sheer high rock cliffs of the spectacular **Cañón del Sumidero** (boxed text p351)

4 Spend a few splendid days hiking and relaxing at pristine mountain-ringed **Laguna Miramar** (p396)

5 Explore the towering mangroves and watch for nesting turtles at **Madre Sal** (p399)

6 Flit between the sapphire and emerald lakes of **Lagos de Montebello** (p395)

7 Wander amid the roar of howler monkeys at the riverside Maya ruins of **Yaxchilán** (p388)

8 Play under the spray of **El Aguacero** (p348) and cool off in a deep river canyon

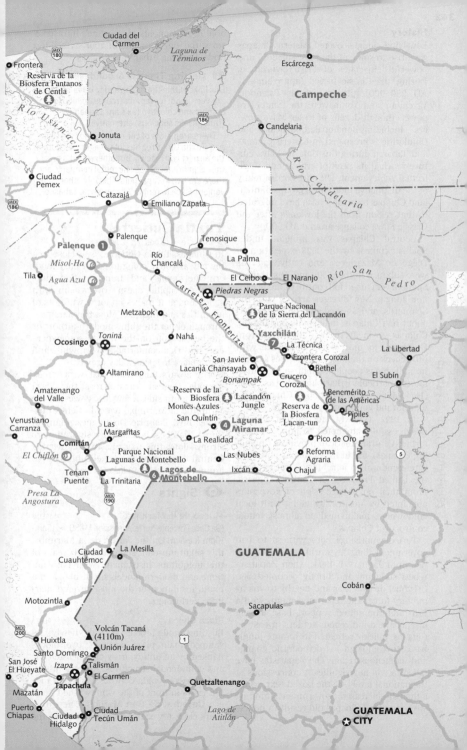

History

Low-lying, jungle-covered eastern Chiapas gave rise to some of the most splendid and powerful city-states of Maya civilization. During the Classic period (approximately AD 250–900), places such as Palenque, Yaxchilán and Tonináwere the centers of power, though dozens of lesser Maya powers – including Bonampak, Comalcalco and Chinkultic – prospered in eastern Chiapas and Tabasco during this time, as Maya culture reached its peak of artistic and intellectual achievement. The ancestors of many of the distinctive indigenous groups of highland Chiapas today appear to have migrated to that region from the lowlands after the Classic Maya collapse around AD 900.

Central Chiapas was brought under Spanish control by the 1528 expedition of Diego de Mazariegos, and outlying areas were subdued in the 1530s and '40s, though Spain never gained full control of the Lacandón Jungle. New diseases arrived with the Spaniards, and an epidemic in 1544 killed about half Chiapas' indigenous population. Chiapas was ineffectively administered from Guatemala for most of the colonial era, with little check on the colonists' excesses against its indigenous people, though some church figures, particularly Bartolomé de Las Casas (1474–1566), the first bishop of Chiapas, did fight for indigenous rights.

In 1822 a newly independent Mexico unsuccessfully attempted to annex Spain's former Central American provinces (including Chiapas), but in 1824 Chiapas opted (by a referendum) to join Mexico, rather than the United Provinces of Central America. From then on, a succession of governors appointed by Mexico City, along with local landowners, maintained an almost feudal control over Chiapas.

Periodic uprisings bore witness to bad government, but the world took little notice until January 1, 1994, when Zapatista rebels suddenly and briefly occupied San Cristóbal de las Casas and nearby towns by military force. The rebel movement, with a firm and committed support base among disenchanted indigenous settlers in eastern Chiapas, quickly retreated to remote jungle bases to campaign for democratic change and indigenous rights. The Zapatistas have failed to win any significant concessions at the national level (see the boxed text, p361), although increased government funding steered toward Chiapas did result in noticeable improvements in the state's infrastructure, the development of tourist facilities and a growing urban middle class.

ℹ️ Getting There & Around

Bus links within the region and to other states are very good; for regional routes, minibuses, combis and *colectivo* taxis are a speedier (though less spacious) alternative.

There aren't lots of car-rental options in Chiapas. Tuxtla Gutiérrez has lots of agencies both at the airport and in town, but otherwise it's pretty thin. San Cristóbal has one rental company, and there are two in Tapachula. The only other convenient place to rent is Villahermosa, Tabasco.

Tuxtla Gutiérrez

📞961 / POP 540,000 / ELEV 530M

In Chiapas, Tuxtla Gutiérrez is as close to a big city as you're going to get. A busy modern metropolis and transportation hub, the state capital doesn't overwhelm with style, though it makes up for it with lots of amenities and nightlife. Most travelers pass through either the shiny modern airport or the bus station on the way to somewhere else, but it's a comfortable, worthwhile and warm place to spend a day or two.

The always busy main east–west street, Avenida Central, runs across the Plaza Cívica's south side. A few blocks west of the Jardín de la Marimba, Avenida Central becomes Blvd Belisario Domínguez; many of the Tuxtla's best hotels and restaurants are strung along this road. Eastward, Avenida Central turns into Blvd Ángel Albino Corzo around 1.5km east of Plaza Cívica.

◎ Sights

Museo de la Marimba   MUSEUM
(9a Calle Poniente Norte; admission M$30; ⊙10am-10pm Tue-Sun) On the Jardín de la Marimba, this small museum showcases 100 years of this ubiquitous instrument, with both antique and modern models on display and a photo exhibition of the most revered marimba performers.

Plaza Cívica   PLAZA
Bustling and broad, Tuxtla's newly revamped main plaza occupies two blocks flanked by an untidy array of concrete civic and commercial structures. At its southern end, across Avenida Central, you'll find nice hill views in front of the whitewashed modern **Catedral de San Marcos**. The cathedral's clock tower tinkles out a tune on the

hour to accompany a kitsch merry-go-round of apostles' images that emerges from its upper levels.

Zoológico Miguel Álvarez del Toro (Zoomat)   ZOO
(www.semahn.chiapas.gob.mx; Calz Cerro Hueco s/n; admission adult/student & child M$60/20, adult before 10am Wed-Sun M$30, free Tue; ☻8:30am-5pm Tue-Sun) Chiapas, with its huge range of natural environments, has the highest concentration of animal species in North America, including several varieties of big cat, 1200 butterfly species and more than 600 birds. About 180 of these species, many of them in danger of extinction, are found in relatively spacious enclosures at Tuxtla's excellent zoo. Beasts you'll see here include ocelots, jaguars, pumas, tapirs, red macaws, toucans, snakes, spider monkeys and three species of crocodile. Most interpretive materials are in both English and Spanish. To get to the zoo take a Ruta 60 'Zoológico' *colectivo* (M$5, 20 minutes) from the corner of 1a Calle Oriente Sur and 7a Avenida Sur Oriente. A taxi from the center is M$40.

Parque Madero   PARK
The park's **Museo Regional de Chiapas** (Calz de los Hombres Ilustres; admission M$41, free Sun; ☻9am-6pm Tue-Sun), an imposing modern building, has a sampling of lesser archaeological pieces from Chiapas' many sites, and a slightly more interesting history section, running from the Spanish conquest to the revolution, all in Spanish only.

Parque Madero also contains the lush oasis of the **Jardín Botánico** (Botanic Garden; admission free; ☻9am-6pm Tue-Sun) – a nice respite from the city heat. There's also a low-key children's theme park.

Take a Ruta 3 or 20 *colectivo* from 6a Av Norte Poniente.

☞ Tours

Viajes Kali   TOUR
(☎611-37-67; www.viajeskali.com.mx; Hotel María Eugenia, Av Central Oriente 507) Organizes trips throughout Chiapas, including a day tour visiting both the Sima de Las Cotorras (p348) and El Aguacero (p348) for M$1400 (up to four people).

🛏 Sleeping

Budget hotels cluster in the city center, while most midrange and luxury hotels are strung out along Avenida Central Poniente and Blvd Belisario Domínguez west of the

---

DON'T MISS

JARDÍN DE LA MARIMBA

To take your *paseo* with the locals, stop by this leafy plaza in the evening. It's located eight blocks west of Plaza Cívica, and the whole city seems to turn out here for the free nightly marimba concerts (6:30pm to 9:30pm), especially at weekends. Couples of all ages dance around the central bandstand, and the scores of sidewalk cafes – which stay open until at least 10pm or 11pm – serve some of the best coffee in town.

center. The larger hotels offer sizeable online and weekend discounts.

Hotel Camino Real   HOTEL $$$
(☎617-77-77, 800-901-23-00; www.caminoreal. com/tuxtla; cnr Blvd Belisario Domínguez & Libramiento Poniente Sur; r M$2336-3898; P☻❄@🛜🏊) Like a feudal castle, the 210-room Camino Real lords over all it surveys from a spectacular hillside perch. A verdant atrium-courtyard features a pool and waterfall, and modern rooms have Mexican craft accents and green marble bathrooms. Amenities include a spa, gym, tennis courts and a 24-hour restaurant. It's 3km west of the Jardín de la Marimba.

Holiday Inn Express   HOTEL $$
(☎618-95-00; www.hiexpress.com/tuxtlamarimba; cnr Av Central Poniente & 12a Calle Poniente Norte; r incl breakfast M$1100; P☻❄@🛜) Conveniently located a quick stroll from the Jardín de la Marimba and on the way to the glitzier Blvd Belisario Domínguez area, the super-modern and brand-new Holiday Inn has free airport transfers, ice machines, a small gym, bath products, flat screen TVs, coffeemaker – everything (sigh) except a pool.

Hilton Garden Inn   HOTEL $$$
(☎617-18-00; www.tuxtlagutierrez.hgi.com; cnr Blvd Belisario Domínguez & Blvd Los Castillos; r Sun-Thu M$1770, Fri & Sat M$1416, ste $2478; P☻❄@🛜🏊) Another newly minted luxury hotel, the 167-room Hilton sits 2.5km west of Plaza Cívica. Gadget-lovers will appreciate the mp3 player/alarm clock, adjustable pillowtop mattresses and internet-ready televisions, and style fans will groove the rainforest showerheads and Herman Miller chairs.

Tuxtla Gutiérrez

Hotel Santa María
HOTEL **$$**

(☎/fax 614-65-77; 8a Calle Poniente Norte 160; r M$450-600, tr M$650; P❄🛜) Situated on the pretty Jardín de la Marimba and near a number of good coffeehouses, this small hotel has rooms featuring folksy decorations and nice bathrooms with mosaic tiling.

Hotel María Eugenia
HOTEL **$$**

(☎613-37-67, 800-716-01-49; www.mariaeugenia.com.mx, in Spanish; Av Central Oriente 507; s/d M$900/1000, d M$650 Fri & Sat; P⊖❄@🛜🅿) All 83 airy, bright and spacious rooms here have either a king-sized or two double beds, and many have great views. It was once the most luxurious option in the center, but some bathroom and room fixtures now show their age.

Hotel Casablanca
HOTEL **$**

(☎611-03-05, 800-560-44-22; fax 961-611-01-42; 2a Av Norte Oriente 251; s M$156, d M$216-294, d/tr/q with air-con M$405/471/555; ⊖❄🛜) Ven-

ture past the drab lobby to where a tranquil open courtyard blooms with palms, and funky-fabulous abstract murals in brilliant lime green, hot pink and electric blue give the rooms a dash of unexpected pizzazz. The upstairs rooms have air-con and more light.

Hotel Catedral
HOTEL **$**

(☎613-08-24; hotelcatredal@hotmail.es; 1a Av Norte Oriente 367; s/d/tr M$350/400/450, with air-con M$450/500/550; P⊖❄🛜) A friendly family-run place, this excellent budget option has neat, super-clean rooms with dark wood furniture and ceiling fans. It also has comfortable hall couches. Pass on the noisier downstairs rooms off the lobby. Free drinking water and morning coffee.

Hotel Regional San Marcos
HOTEL **$$**

(☎/fax 613-19-40; hotelsanmarcos2008@hotmail.com; 2a Calle Oriente Sur 176; s/d/tr M$399/480/519; P⊖❄🛜) Centrally located, with very friendly staff and a good restaurant,

this aging hotel has medium-sized rooms with phones.

✖ Eating

Most upscale and international options are west of the center, along Blvd Belisario Domínguez, and a number of enjoyable places cluster in the center around the Jardín de la Marimba.

Las Pichanchas CHIAPANECO $$
(☎612-53-51; Av Central Oriente 837; www.laspichanchas.com.mx; mains M$80-145; ☺noon-midnight;☻☷) This courtyard restaurant specializes in Chiapas food with live marimba music and, from 9pm to 11pm every night, a show of colorful traditional Chiapas dances that whips up quite a party atmosphere. Try the tasty *tamales* or *pechuga jacuané* (chicken breast stuffed with beans in a *hoja santa* sauce), and leave room for *chimbos*, a dessert made from egg yolks and cinnamon.

Ring the bell over the table to order its signature Pumpo drink.

Restaurante La Casona MEXICAN $
(1a Av Sur Poniente 134; breakfast M$33-60, mains M$43-82; ☺7am-11pm; ☻) Beyond the stately carved wooden doors, high ceilings and columns and interior arches frame a dramatic table-clothed dining room in a century-old building. Dine on regional dishes such as *pollo juchi* (fried chicken with pickled vegetables and potatoes) or *tasajo en salsa de chirmol* (sliced beef in tomato sauce) and listen to marimba performances from 2pm to 6pm.

Cafetería del Parque MEXICAN $$
(8a Calle Poniente Sur 113; breakfast M$50-65, mains M$69-135; ☺8am-10:30pm; ☻) The nice wraparound windows make this one of the better people-watching eateries around the Jardín de la Marimba, and it's elbow to elbow with families on the weekends. With good espresso drinks, consistent food and lots of air-conditioning, it's definitely a blissful place to cool off.

RESERVA DE LA BIOSFERA EL TRIUNFO

The luxuriant cloud forests, high in the remote El Triunfo Biosphere Reserve in the Sierra Madre de Chiapas, are a bird-lover's paradise and a remarkable world of trees and shrubs festooned with epiphytes, ferns, bromeliads, mosses and vines.

The Sierra Madre de Chiapas is home to almost 400 bird species, of which more than 30 are nonexistent or rare elsewhere in Mexico. This is the one place in the country where chances are good of seeing the resplendent quetzal. Visitors see hundreds of butterfly species and, often, jaguar and tapir tracks.

Visits are limited and controlled. Most visitors go in the driest months, January to May; avoid the wettest months, September and October. Make arrangements about six months in advance by contacting **Claudia Virgen** (☑961-125-11-22; cvirgen@ecobiosfera. org.mx; www.fondoeltriunfo.org), the visitor program coordinator. A normal five-day visit from Tuxtla (US$630 to US$795 per person, minimum eight people, maximum 12) starts with one night in a hotel in the nearest town, Jaltenango (also called Ángel Albino Corzo), followed by three nights at the basic Campamento El Triunfo, 1850m high in the reserve. The price includes meals, bilingual guides who are expert bird-spotters, transportation between Jaltenango and the coffee-growing village of Finca Prusia, and mules to carry your baggage on the 14km hike between Finca Prusia and Campamento El Triunfo (three to four hours uphill on the way in). The **Mesoamerican Ecotourism Alliance** (www.travelwithmea.org) has all-inclusive 10-day trips that also visit La Encrucijada (US$3178).

Restaurante Imperial　　　　　MEXICAN $
(Calle Central Norte 263; mains M$50-90, comida corrida M$50; ☺8am-6pm; ☻) This busy, efficient place beside Plaza Cívica offers a wholesome two-course *comida corrida* (set lunch) with plenty of choice. It also offers a full breakfast menu and good drinking chocolate.

🍸 Drinking

Grado Cero　　　　　　　LOUNGE
(1a Av Norte Poniente; ☺6pm-2am) Overlooking the Jardín de la Marimba, this upstairs open-air lounge features karaoke and the occasional *rock en español* band on weekends. It's a chill place with black lights, a friendly atmosphere, and a tasty food selection to accompany the drinks.

Café Biomaya　　　　　　　CAFE
(1a Av Norte Poniente; desserts & coffee M$15-35; ☺9am-midnight Mon-Sat, 6pm-midnight Sun; ☻☎) One of numerous good cafes on the Jardín de la Marimba, this one serves organic indigenous-grown brew and sports low-slung black sofas that may lead to indolent lingering.

☆ Entertainment

There's no shortage of decent bars and raucous dance spots in the 'Zona Dorada,' 2km to 4km west of the center along Blvd Be-

lisario Domínguez. On Friday and Saturday, men must usually pay a M$100 cover. Clubs open and close here at a breakneck pace.

🛍 Shopping

TOP CHOICE Boutique del Café　　　COFFEE
(☑614-78-97; cnr 8a Calle Poniente Norte & 1a Av Norte Poniente; ☺9am-8pm Mon-Fri, 11am-8pm Sat, 4:30-8pm Sun) Java-heads should make a pilgrimage to the Jardín de la Marimba branch of the state crafts store, a friendly coffee exchange selling the aromatic gold of small-scale *chiapaneco* farmers from many different regions. Sit down for a cup in its cafe before scooping up all the bags that will fit in your suitcase.

Casa Chiapas　　　HANDICRAFTS, GIFTS
(☑602-65-65; www.casachiapas.gob.mx, in Spanish; Blvd Belisario Domínguez 2035; ☺9am-8pm Mon-Sat) The Chiapas state crafts shop, 2km west of Plaza Cívica, sells a great range of the state's *artesanías* (handicrafts), from Amatenango 'tigers' and funky Cintalapa ceramic suns to colorful highland textiles.

ℹ Information

Internet Access
Conect@-2 (Av Central Oriente 214; per hr M$5; ☺8am-10pm Mon-Fri, 8am-9:30pm Sat & Sun)

Roqu@cib3r (Av Central Poniente 823; per hr M$5; ⊙9am-9pm)

Money
There's an ATM at the departure level of the airport.

Bancomer (Av Central Poniente 314; ⊙8:30am-4pm Mon-Fri)

Scotiabank (cnr Ave Central Oriente & 4a Calle Oriente; ⊙8:30am-4pm Mon-Fri)

Post
Post office (1a Av Norte Poniente) In the Palacio Federal.

Telephone
Sam Caseta Telefónica (Av Central Poniente 664; ⊙6:30am-10:30pm) Inexpensive phone calls.

Tourist Information
Airport kiosk (⊙9am-7pm) In the arrivals level; closes after the last flight's passengers are in. English assistance sometimes available.

Information kiosk (⊙9am-2pm & 4-8pm) At the Plaza Cívica.

Municipal tourism office (9a Calle Poniente Norte; ⊙9am-2pm & 4-8pm) Very helpful, and some English spoken. Inside the Museo de la Marimba.

Secretaría de Turismo (☎617-05-50, 800-280-35-00; www.turismochiapas.gob.mx; ⊙8am-4pm Mon-Fri) The main state tourism office has a toll-free phone number for Chiapas information; English speakers rarely available.

❶ Getting There & Away

Air
Tuxtla's small and gleaming **Aeropuerto Ángel Albino Corzo** (☎615-50-60) is 35km southeast of the city center and 18km south of Chiapa de Corzo. **Aeroméxico** (www.aeromexico.com), **Interjet** (www.interjet.com.mx) and **VivaAerobus** (www.vivaaerobus.com.mx) have nonstop service to Mexico City. VivaAerobus has the cheapest tickets, but can be somewhat unreliable; it also flies to Guadalajara and Monterrey.

Aerotucán (www.aerotucan.com.mx) Direct flights to Oaxaca.

Continental (www.continental.com) Twice-weekly nonstop flights to and from Houston, Texas.

Bus, Colectivo & Combi
Free wi-fi and a huge contiguous supermarket are bonuses of the modern **OCC terminal** (5a Av Norte Poniente 318). It's about 2.5km northwest of the Jardín de la Marimba and houses all the 1st-class buses (including ADO), and also the deluxe UNO and 2nd-class Rápidos del Sur line. More 2nd-class buses and combis depart from the **Terminal de Transporte Tuxtla** (cnr 9a Av Sur Oriente & 13a Calle Oriente Sur), with frequent destinations including San Cristóbal, Ocosingo and Ocozocoautla. See the boxed text p347 for daily departures from the OCC terminal.

For San Cristóbal de las Casas (M$40, one hour), these are faster and more frequent options (every 10 minutes):

Ómnibus de Chiapas (cnr 15a Calle Oriente Sur & 4a Av Sur Oriente) Comfortable minibuses (called 'sprinters') from 5am to 10pm.

Corazón de María (13a Calle Oriente Sur) Combis from 4am to 9pm depart from storefront near Av Central Oriente; also leave from Terminal de Transporte Tuxtla.

For Chiapa de Corzo (M$10, 45 minutes), combis leave every few minutes between 5am and 10:30pm from 1a Avenida Sur Oriente.

CHIAPAS TUXTLA GUTIÉRREZ

BUSES FROM TUXTLA GUTIÉRREZ

DESTINATION	FARE (M$)	DURATION	FREQUENCY (DAILY)
Cancún	648-1428	17-20hr	6
Comitán	68-83	3hr	20
Mérida	624-1080	13-14hr	5
Mexico City (TAPO & Norte)	450-1310	11½-12hr	24
Oaxaca	351-388	10hr	4
Palenque	192-248	6hr	8
Puerto Escondido	416	11-12hr	3
San Cristóbal de las Casas	36-46	1¼hr	30
Tapachula	257-522	4½-6hr	26
Tonalá	110-156	2-2½hr	24
Villahermosa	237-380	4-5hr	15

Car & Motorcycle

In addition to companies at the airport, in-town rental agencies include the following.

Alamo (www.alamo.com; 5a Av Norte Poniente 2260) Near the OCC bus station.

Europcar (www.europcar.com; Blvd Belisario Domínguez 2075)

Hertz (www.hertz.com; Hotel Camino Real, Blvd Belisario Domínguez 1195)

Getting Around

A brand new biodiesel bus service called **ConejoBus** (M$5; ⏰7am-11pm, to 10pm Sun) plies Blvd Belisario Domínguez–Avenida Central–Blvd Albino Corzo, running as far as the 'Zona Dorada' clubs to the west. Stops, which are frustratingly scarce, are marked by heavily stickered white and orange 'Parada' signs. Taxi rides within the city cost M$30 to M$35.

To/From the Airport

From town, **Monarca Viajes** (☎cell phone 961-1328191; monarcaviajes@hotmail.com) does door-to-door transfers (one to three passengers) for M$200; reserve in advance.

From the airport, pre-pay taxis (one to three passengers) meet all flights and go to central Tuxtla (M$210, 40 minutes), Chiapa de Corzo (M$240, 30 minutes) and San Cristóbal (M$600 private or M$200 shared, one hour). OCC runs minibuses directly from the terminal to San Cristóbal (M$160) at 11:30am, 1pm, 4pm and 6:30pm, though the schedule is subject to change.

Around Tuxtla Gutiérrez

Consider renting a car in Tuxtla to hit both the Sima de las Cotorras and El Aguacero.

SIMA DE LAS COTORRAS

The **Sima de las Cotorras** (Abyss of the Parrots; adult/child over 9yr M$20/10) is a dramatic 160m-wide sinkhole that punches 140m down into the earth. At sunrise, a green cloud of screeching parrots spirals out for the day, trickling back before dusk. With binoculars you can see a series of red pre-Hispanic rock paintings that decorate one side of the cliff face, and you can also hike or rappel down inside this intriguing subterranean hole.

Lodging (☎cell phone 968-6897145, cell phone 968-1061870; campsite M$50, tent rental M$50-100, d/q/6-person cabaña M$300/400/600; 🅿🕙) is available (the spacious six-person, two-room cabañas are well worth the extra cost), as well as a good **restaurant** (mains M$50-70;

⏰8am-7pm) serving scrumptious *tamales* and handmade tortillas.

From Tuxtla's Terminal de Transporte Tuxtla, take a minibus (look for the pineapple on the side) to the last stop in Ocozocoautla (also called Coita; M$13, 30 minutes), located on Hwy 190 right at the signed turnoff for the Sima. From there, take a taxi (M$200 to M$250, 50 minutes) or call the lodging number to arrange a pickup (M$250 per vanload). Three daily Piedra Parada *colectivos* (M$7) also leave from this stop, but let you off 4km before the Sima. Driving from Tuxtla, it's pretty well signed all the way. From the blue turnoff sign in Ocozocoautla, go 3.5km north, then 12km on a good dirt road.

Private tours can be arranged through any Tuxtla tour agency. With a minimum of 10 people, the municipal tourism office organizes group tours (M$350 per person) from Tuxtla's Jardín de la Marimba, leaving at 10am on Sundays. However, tours are infrequent and aren't during prime parrot-watching hours.

EL AGUACERO

Forget the gym – the 724 well-built steps to this cascade will suffice as your workout *du jour*. Plunging into the sheer Río La Venta canyon, **El Aguacero** (☎cell phone 968-1069019; admission M$25; ⏰7am-5pm) is a gorgeous series of frothy stair-steps that tumble and spray. In dryer months (usually December through May), you can stroll along sandy riverbed beaches to the waterfall. When the water's high, it's a half-hour hike from the staircase along a shady jungle trail. Unless the bridge has been repaired along the jungle route, there's a narrow cliff ledge bypass that isn't recommended for children. From December through May, you can also explore an underground river running through the 200m El Encanto cave. An hour-long tour (M$100) includes all equipment (helmet, headlamp etc).

Camping (campsite M$50, campsite & equipment M$250; ⏰Jan-May) and hammock space (with showers) are available in the dry season. When open, a small *comedor* serves quesadillas (M$10).

From Ocozocoautla (Coita), *colectivos* to El Gavilán/Las Cruces (M$10) can drop you off at the highway turnoff, and it's a 3km walk down to the entrance. If the stairs up from the river leave you in a heap, management charges M$40 per vanload to drive you back up. Drivers should look for the turnoff sign about 15km west of Ocozocoautla.

CHIAPA DE CORZO
📞961 / POP 45,000 / ELEV 450M

An overlooked jewel set 12km east of Tuxtla Gutiérrez on the way to San Cristóbal, Chiapa de Corzo is a small and attractive colonial town with an easygoing, provincial air. Set on the north bank of the broad Río Grijalva, it's the main starting point for trips into the Cañón del Sumidero.

Chiapa de Corzo has been occupied almost continuously since about 1200 BC. Before the Spaniards arrived, the warlike Chiapa tribe had their capital, Nandalumí, a couple of kilometers downstream, on the opposite bank of the Grijalva. When Diego de Mazariegos invaded the area in 1528, the Chiapa hurled themselves by the hundreds to their death in the canyon rather than surrender.

Mazariegos founded a settlement called Chiapa de Los Indios here, but quickly shifted his base to San Cristóbal de las Casas, where he found the climate and natives more manageable.

◎ Sights

The *embarcadero* (jetty) for Cañón del Sumidero boat trips is two blocks south of the plaza down 5 de Febrero.

Plaza PLAZA

Impressive arcades frame three sides of the plaza, and a beefy tree called **La Pochota** buckles the sidewalk with its centuries-old roots. Venerated by the indigenous people who founded the town, it's the oldest ceiba tree along the Río Grijalva. But the focal point of the plaza is **La Pila** (also called the Fuente Colonial), a handsome brick fountain completed in 1562 in Mudejar-Gothic style. It's said to resemble the Spanish crown.

FREE **Chiapa de Corzo Archaeological Site** ARCHAEOLOGICAL SITE

(Av Hidalgo, Barrio Benito Juárez; ◎8am-5pm) On a trade route between the Pacific and the Gulf, the sprawling Chiapa de Corzo settlement had close ties to neighboring Maya and Olmec cultures. At its peak, it counted some 200 structures, but was abandoned around 500 AD. After years of excavation, three Zoque pyramid structures are now on view. These visible structures were built between 1600 and 1800 years ago, but sit on mounds dating back as far as 750 BC. Though not open to the public, recent excavation of one nearby mound unearthed the oldest known pyramid tomb in Mesoamerica and new evidence linking it to Olmec centers such as La Venta (see boxed text, p406). Though the guarded ruins receive few visitors, it's worth an hour to climb around the deserted temples and marvel at the big-sky countryside.

The site entrance is 1.5km east of the plaza, near the Nestlé plant and the old highway (on the road that goes to La Topada de la Flor), but the site isn't signed from the road. Taxis charge about M$25 from the plaza; arrange a pickup time.

Templo de Santo Domingo de Guzmán CHURCH, MUSEUM

The large Templo de Santo Domingo de Guzmán, one block south of the plaza, was built in the late 16th century by the Dominican order. Its adjoining convent is now the **Centro Cultural** (Mexicanidad Chiapaneca 10; admission free; ◎10am-5pm Tue-Sun), home to an exposition of the wood and lino prints of talented Chiapa-born Franco Lázaro Gómez (1922–49) as well as the **Museo de la Laca**, which is dedicated to the local craft specialty: lacquered gourds. The museum holds pieces dating back to 1606.

◆ Courses

Dunham Institute LANGUAGE

(📞616-14-98; www.dunhaminstitute.com; Av Urbina 30) Homestay accommodations (no meals) with three hours of individual or small-group weekday Spanish classes for US$650 per month. TOEFL (Test of English as a Foreign Language) certificate program available.

✪ Festivals & Events

Fiesta Grande de Enero TRADITIONAL

Held for a week in mid-January, this is one of Mexico's liveliest and most extraordinary festivals (www.lafiestatradicionaldechiapas.com), including nightly dances involving cross-dressing young men, known as Las Chuntá. Women don the highly colorful, beautifully embroidered *chiapaneca* dress, and blond-wigged, mask-toting *Parachicos* (impersonating conquistadors) parade on a number of days. A canoe battle and fireworks extravaganza follow on the final evening.

⌷ Sleeping

Hotel Los Ángeles HOTEL **$**

(📞616-00-48; www.hotel-chiapas.com, in Spanish; Grajales 2; d/tr/q M$370/385/425, with air-con M$390/450/500; P◎❄✿) This hotel at the southeast corner of the plaza has spotless rooms with hot-water bathroom, cable TV and fan. Upstairs rooms lack air-con, but are bigger and catch more breeze.

Hotel La Ceiba HOTEL $$
(☑616-03-89; www.laceibahotel.com; Av Domingo Ruíz 300; s/d/tr/q M$580/660/720/860; P⊖❋🖝🛋) Also a full-service spa, La Ceiba has an inviting pool, a lush garden and 87 simple but well-kept air-conditioned rooms with cable TV. It's two blocks west of the plaza.

🍴 Eating

Restaurants on the *embarcadero* have near identical, and equally overpriced, menus. The river views are nice, though battling marimba players tend to amp up the noise level. Tascalate (boxed text p391) can be found on most menus, and many shops sell the drink powder.

Restaurant Jardines de Chiapa CHIAPANECO $$
(www.restaurantesjardines.com.mx; Madero 395; mains M$59-110; ⊙9am-7pm summer, 8am-6:30pm fall-spring; ⊜) Not too far from the plaza, this large place is set around a garden patio with atmospheric brick columns. The long menu includes tasty *cochinito al horno* (oven-baked pork).

Restaurant Los Corredores CHIAPANECO $
(Madero 35; mains M$55-105; ⊙9am-6:30pm; ⊜) Facing the southwest corner of the plaza, brightly painted Los Corredores does a bit of everything: good breakfasts, reasonably priced fish plates and a few local specialties including *pepita con tasajo* (beef with a spicy pumpkin-seed sauce). It displays a fascinating collection of historical town photos.

❶ Information

Tourism office (☑616-10-13; 5 de Febrero; ⊙8am-4pm Mon-Fri, 9am-2pm Sat) On the road between the plaza and the *embarcadero*; a kiosk on the northwest corner of the plaza opens in high season.

❶ Getting There & Away

Combis from Tuxtla Gutiérrez (M$10, 45 minutes) leave frequently from 1a Avenida Sur Oriente (between Calles 5a & 7a Oriente Sur) between 5am and 10:30pm. They arrive (and return to Tuxtla) from the north side of the plaza.

There's no direct transportation between San Cristóbal and the center of Chiapa de Corzo. From San Cristóbal, catch a Tuxtla-bound combi and ask to be let off at the Chiapa de Corzo stop on the highway (M$32, 30 minutes). From there, cross the highway and flag down a combi (M$5) to the plaza. From Chiapa de Corzo to San Cristóbal, catch a combi from the plaza back to the highway and then flag down a combi heading to San Cristóbal. You'll rarely wait more than a few minutes for a connecting combi in either direction.

San Cristóbal de las Casas

☑967 / POP 160,000 / ELEV 1940M

Set in a gorgeous highland valley surrounded by pine forest, the colonial city of San Cristóbal (cris-*toh*-bal) has been a popular travelers' destination for decades. It's a pleasure to explore San Cristóbal's cobbled streets and markets, soaking up the unique ambience and the wonderfully clear highland light. This medium-sized city also boasts a comfortable blend of city and countryside, with restored century-old houses giving way to grazing animals and fields of corn.

Surrounded by dozens of traditional Tzotzil and Tzeltal villages, San Cristóbal is at the heart of one of the most deeply rooted indigenous areas in Mexico. A great base for local and regional exploration, it's a place where ancient customs coexist with modern luxuries.

The city is a hot spot for sympathizers (and some opponents) of the Zapatista rebels, and a central location for organizations working with Chiapas' indigenous people. In addition to a solid tourist infrastructure and a dynamic population of artsy and politically progressive foreigners and Mexicans, San Cristóbal also has a great selection of accommodations and a cosmopolitan array of cafes, bars and restaurants.

History

Diego de Mazariegos founded San Cristóbal as the Spanish regional base in 1528. Its Spanish citizens made fortunes from wheat, while the indigenous people lost their lands and suffered diseases, taxes and forced labor. The church afforded some protection against colonist excesses. Dominican monks reached Chiapas in 1545, and made San Cristóbal their main base. The town is now named after one of them, Bartolomé de Las Casas, who was appointed bishop of Chiapas and became the most prominent Spanish defender of indigenous people in colonial times. In modern times Bishop Samuel Ruiz, who passed away in 2011, followed in Las

CAÑÓN DEL SUMIDERO

The Sumidero Canyon is a spectacular fissure in the earth, found north of Tuxtla Gutiérrez. In 1981 the Chicoasén hydroelectric dam was completed at its northern end, damming the Río Grijalva, which flows through the canyon, and creating a 25km-long reservoir. Traveling between Tuxtla and Chiapa de Corzo, the road crosses the Grijalva just south of the canyon mouth.

The most impressive way to see the canyon is from a lancha (return trip M$160; ⊙8:30am-4pm) that speeds between the canyon's towering rock walls. It's about a two-hour return trip, starting at either Chiapa de Corzo or the Embarcadero Cahuaré, 5km north of Chiapa along the road to Tuxtla. You'll rarely have to wait more than half an hour for a boat to fill up. Bring a drink, something to shield you from the sun and, if there's any chance of bad weather, some warm clothing or a waterproof jacket.

It's about 35km from Chiapa de Corzo to the dam. Soon after you pass under Hwy 190, the canyon walls tower an amazing 800m above you. Along the way you'll see a variety of birds – herons, cormorants, vultures, kingfishers – plus probably a crocodile or two. The boat operators will point out a few odd formations of rock and vegetation, including one cliff face covered in thick hanging moss, resembling a giant Christmas tree. *Lanchas* (motorboats) sometimes have to plow through a sheen of floating plastic garbage when wet-season rains wash in trash from Tuxtla Gutiérrez.

Bus tours leave from Tuxtla's Jardín de la Marimba at 9:15am and 1pm daily if a minimum of five people show up. Three tours are available: viewing the canyon from above at five *miradores* (lookout points; adult/child M$100/50, 2½ hours), a *lancha* trip with return transportation (M250, 4½ hours) and an all-day *miradores* and *lancha* trip (M$350, morning departure only).

Casas' footsteps, defending the oppressed indigenous people and earning the hostility of the Chiapas establishment.

San Cristóbal was the state capital of Chiapas from 1824 to 1892, but remained relatively isolated until the 1970s, when tourism began to influence its economy. Recent decades have seen an influx of indigenous villagers into the 'Cinturón de Miseria' (Belt of Misery), a series of impoverished, violence-ridden, makeshift colonies around San Cristóbal's *periférico* (ring road). Many of these people are here because they have been expelled from Chamula and other communities as a result of internal politico-religious conflicts. Most of the craft sellers around Santo Domingo church and the underage hawkers around town come from the Cinturón de Miseria.

San Cristóbal was catapulted into the international limelight on January 1, 1994, when the Zapatista rebels selected it as one of four places from which to launch their revolution, seizing and sacking government offices in the town before being driven out within a few days by the Mexican army. Political and social tensions remain, but San Cristóbal continues to attract travelers, real estate investment and a growing middle class.

San Cristóbal and Los Altos de Chiapas – the state's central highlands, mostly 2000m to 3000m high – have a temperate climate. Daytime temperatures are usually warm, but evenings can get cold between November and February, when you'll want a good jacket to ward off chill.

⊙ Sights

San Cristóbal is very walkable, with straight streets rambling up and down several gentle hills. Heading east from the plaza, Real de Guadalupe has a pedestrian-only section with a concentration of places to stay and eat. Another pedestrian mall, the Andador Turístico (or Andador Eclesiástico), runs up Hidalgo and Avenida 20 de Noviembre.

Plaza 31 de Marzo   PLAZA
The leafy main plaza is a fine place to take in San Cristóbal's unhurried highland atmosphere. Shoe-shiners, newspaper sellers and *ambulantes* (itinerant vendors) gather around the elaborate iron bandstand.

On the north side of the plaza, the **cathedral** was begun in 1528 but wasn't completed until 1815 because of several

San Cristóbal de las Casas

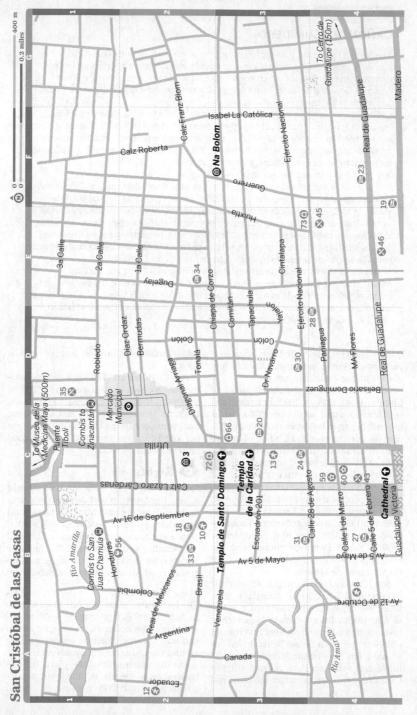

353

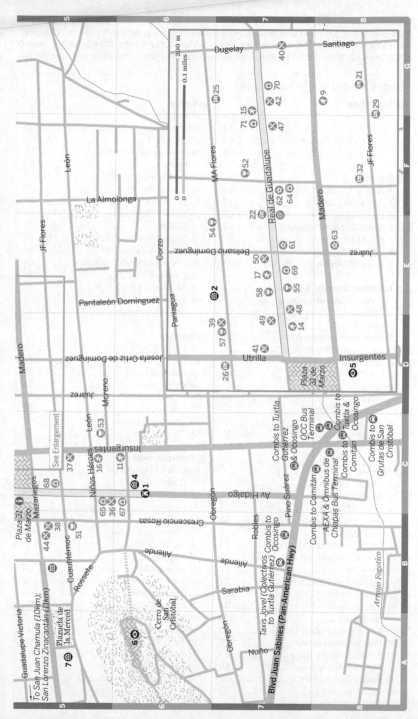

CHIAPAS SAN CRISTÓBAL DE LAS CASAS

natural disasters. Sure enough, new earth-quakes struck in 1816 and also 1847, causing considerable damage, but it was restored again from 1920 to 1922. The gold-leaf in-terior has five gilded altarpieces featuring 18th-century paintings by Miguel Cabrera.

The **Hotel Santa Clara**, on the plaza's southeast corner, was built by Diego de Mazariegos, the Spanish conqueror of Chiapas. His coat of arms is engraved above the main portal. The house is a rare secular example of plateresque style in Mexico.

Cerro de San Cristóbal & Cerro de Guadalupe
CHURCH

Want to take in the best views in town? Well, you'll have to work for them, because at this altitude the stairs up these hills can be punishing. The Cerro de San Cristóbal and Cerro de Guadalupe lord over the town from the west and east, respectively, and churches crown both lookouts. The Iglesia de Guadalupe becomes a hot spot for religious devotees around the Día de la Virgen de Guadalupe (December 12). These areas are not considered safe at night.

FREE Templo & Ex-Convento de Santo Domingo
CHURCH, MUSEUM

(☉6:30am-2pm & 4-8pm) Located just north of the center, the 16th-century Templo de Santo Domingo is San Cristóbal's most beautiful church, especially when its facade catches the late-afternoon sun. This baroque frontage, with its outstanding filigree stucco work, was added in the 17th century and includes the double-headed Hapsburg eagle, symbol of the Spanish monarchy in those days. The interior is lavishly gilded, especially the ornate pulpit.

Around Santo Domingo and the neighboring **Templo de la Caridad** (built in 1712), Chamulan women and bohemian types from around Mexico conduct a colorful daily crafts market. The former monastery attached to Santo Domingo contains two interesting exhibits: one is the weavers' showroom of Sna Jolobil; the other is the **Centro Cultural de los Altos** (Calz Lázaro Cárdenas; admission M$41; ☉10am-5pm Tue-Sun), which boasts a reasonable Spanish-language museum on the history of the San Cristóbal region.

Na Bolom
MUSEUM, LIBRARY

(www.nabolom.org, in Spanish; Guerrero 33; view house only adult/student & senior M$40/25, 1½hr tour in English or Spanish M$50; ☉9am-8pm, tour 4:30pm Tue-Sun) An atmospheric museum-research center, Na Bolom for many years was the home of Swiss anthropologist and photographer Gertrude Duby-Blom (Trudy Blom; 1901–93) and her Danish archaeologist husband Frans Blom (1893–1963).

They bought the 19th-century house in 1950, and while Frans explored and sur-

veyed ancient Maya sites all over Chiapas (including Palenque, Toniná and Chinkultic), Trudy studied, photographed and fought to protect the scattered Lacandón people of eastern Chiapas and their jungle environment. Since Trudy's death, Na Bolom has continued the thrust of the Bloms' work, with the house operating as a museum and research center for the study and support of Chiapas' indigenous cultures and natural environment, and as a center for community and environmental programs in indigenous areas. The library of more than 9000 books and documents here is a major resource on the Maya.

Na Bolom means 'Jaguar House' in the Tzotzil language (as well as being a play on its former owners' name). It's full of photographs, archaeological and anthropological relics and books. The house tour provides a revealing insight into the lives of the Bloms and the Chiapas of half a century and more ago – though the picture presented of the Lacandones does dwell more on their past than their present.

Na Bolom also offers guest rooms and meals made with organic vegetables grown in its garden.

Museo de la Medicina Maya
MUSEUM

(Av Salomón González Blanco 10; admission M$20; ☉10am-6pm Mon-Fri, to 4pm Sat & Sun) This award-winning museum introduces the system of traditional medicine used by many indigenous people in the Chiapas highlands. Traditional Maya medicine is a matter of praying to the spirit of the earth, listening to the voice of the blood and expelling bad spirits from the soul, with the aid of candles, bones, pine needles, herbs and the occasional chicken sacrifice.

This museum, on the northern edge of town, is run by Organización de Médicos Indígenas del Estado de Chíapas (Omiech), a group of 600 indigenous healers, midwives, herbalists and prayer specialists. Exhibits include displays of a ritual scene inside a church and a midwife assisting at a birth, a dated video about the work of traditional midwives and a new display about the issue of native plants and corporate biopiracy. Information is available in English, Spanish, French and German. Also onsite is a medicinal plant garden, a herbal pharmacy and a *casa de curación,* where treatments are done. It's a 20-minute walk north from Real de Guadalupe or M$25 by taxi.

SAN CRISTÓBAL IN...

Two Days

Start the day inhaling the rich aroma of a locally roasted cup of Chiapan **coffee** and then limber up with a **yoga class**. Put on some comfortable walking shoes and explore the colonial churches of **Templo de Santo Domingo** and the **cathedral**, and then get lofty, climbing the twin hills of **Cerro de San Cristóbal** and **Cerro de Guadalupe** to survey the city.

Spend the second day visiting the traditional indigenous villages of **San Lorenzo Zinacantán** and **San Juan Chamula** by horseback or bicycle, and in the evening drop by a **cinema** to catch a movie on local history or current events.

Four Days

With more time, build on the itinerary above and refresh your sagging Spanish with a few days of **language classes**. Dig deeper into the local culture with visits to the **Museo de la Medicina Maya** and the ethno-history landmark of **Na Bolom**.

Browse for the best of local *artesanías* at **women's weaving cooperatives** and the paper- and book-making workshop of **Taller Leñateros**. Jaunt out of town to gawk at the trippy cave formations at the **Grutas de San Cristóbal**. Linger over cocktails and snacks at a convivial bar and groove to the music at **Café Bar Revolution**.

Museo del Ámbar de Chiapas   MUSEUM
(Chiapas Amber Museum; www.museodelambar. com.mx; Plazuela de la Merced; admission M$20; ⊘10am-2pm & 4-8pm Tue-Sun) Chiapas amber – fossilized pine resin, around 30 million years old – is known for its clarity and diverse colors. Most is mined around Simojovel, north of San Cristóbal. The Museo del Ámbar de Chiapas explains all things amber (with information sheets in English, French and Italian) and displays and sells some exquisitely carved items and insect-embedded pieces.

**Arco de El Carmen &
Centro Cultural
El Carmen**   ARCHITECTURE, CULTURAL BUILDING
The Arco de El Carmen, at the southern end of the Andador Turístico on Hidalgo, dates from the late 17th century and was once the city's gateway. The ex-convent just east is a wonderful colonial building, with a large peaceful garden. It's now the **Centro Cultural El Carmen** (Hermanos Domínguez s/n; ⊘9am-6pm Tue-Sun), hosting art and photography exhibitions and the occasional musical event.

Café Museo Café   MUSEUM, CAFE
(MA Flores 10; admission M$30; ⊘8am-10pm Mon-Sat; ☏) This combined cafe and coffee museum is a venture of Coopcafé, a grouping of more than 17,000 small-scale, mainly indigenous, Chiapas coffee growers. The museum covers the history of coffee and its cultivation in Chiapas, from highly exploitative beginnings to the community-based indigenous coffee production that's increasingly well marketed today. The information is translated into English. You can taste some of that flavorful organic coffee in the cafe.

Courses

Several good language schools offer instruction in Spanish, with flexibility to meet most level and schedule requirements. Weekly rates given below are for three hours' tuition five days a week, with seven nights' homestay accommodations and three meals a day, but many variations (classes only, hourly instruction etc) are available. Many hostels offer salsa classes for their guests.

La Casa en el Árbol   LANGUAGE
(☏674-52-72; www.lacasaenelarbol.org; Real de Mexicanos 10; classes only individual/group per week US$328/256, 7 days family accommodations US$136) The 'Tree House' is an enthusiastic, socially committed school that teaches Tzeltal and Tzotzil as well as Spanish. It offers lots of out-of-school activities and is also a base for volunteer programs. Mexican cooking classes and a medical Spanish program are also available.

**El Puente Spanish
Language School**   LANGUAGE
(☏678-37-23; www.elpuenteweb.com; Real de Guadalupe 55; individual/group per week US$230/ 190) Housed in the Centro Cultural El

Puente, which also has a vegetarian cafe, cinema, gallery and an alternative therapy center that gives fabulous massages. Classes are offered for any period, starting from one day.

Instituto de Lenguas Jovel　　LANGUAGE
(☑678-40-69; www.institutojovel.com; Madero 45; individual/group per week US$356/281) Instituto Jovel is professional and friendly, and has a top-class reputation among students. Most tuition is one-to-one, and it has a beautiful location. Classes in Mexican cooking and salsa dancing are offered too.

Shaktipat Yoga　　YOGA
(☑116-09-83; www.casaluz.com.mx; Niños Heroes 2; class M$45) A studio in the healing arts complex of Casa Luz with multilingual Vinyasa, Ashtanga and Hatha yoga classes. Multi-class discounts.

☞ Tours

Many agencies in San Cristóbal offer a variety of tours, often with guides who speak English, French or Italian (for tours of indigenous villages around San Cristóbal, see p379). The following are typical day-trip prices per person (usually with a minimum of four people):

Chiapa de Corzo & Cañón del Sumidero M$200 to M$250, six to seven hours.

Lagos de Montebello & El Chiflón waterfalls M$250 to M$300, nine to 10 hours.

Palenque, Agua Azul & Misol-Ha M$350 to M$400, 14 hours.

Recommended tour agencies (open approximately 8am to 9pm) include the following.

Otisa　　TOUR
(☑678-19-33; www.otisatravel.com; Real de Guadalupe 3C) Its Lagos de Montebello/El Chiflón tours also visit the Grutas de San Cristóbal.

SendaSur　　ECOTOUR
(☑678-39-09; Real de Guadalupe 46B; ☺9am-2pm & 4-7pm Mon-Fri, 11am-2pm Sat) A partner-based ecotourism network in Chiapas, it can help with independent travel and reservations in the Lacandón Jungle.

Trotamundos　　TOUR
(☑/fax 678-70-21; via_chis90@hotmail.com; Real de Guadalupe 26C) Also does trips to Laguna Miramar.

Viajes Chincultik　　TOUR
(☑678-09-57; www.tourshotel.com.mx, in Spanish; Casa Margarita, Real de Guadalupe 34) General tours and regional transfers.

Natutours　　TOUR
(☑cell phone 967-1063170; natutours@hotmail.com) For Lacandón Jungle trips and Laguna Miramar excursions.

The following agencies specialize in more active trips:

Explora　　ADVENTURE TOUR
(☑674-66-60; www.explorachiapas.com; Calle 1 de Marzo 30; ☺9:30am-2pm & 4-8pm Mon-Fri, 9:30am-2pm Sat) Adventure trips to the Lacandón Jungle (four/five days from M$5100/6000, minimum four people) including river kayaking and rafting; also spelunking tours in northwestern Chiapas, and day trips to rappel the Sima de Las Cotorras (M$1500; see p348).

Los Pingüinos　　CYCLING, HIKING
(☑678-02-02; www.bikemexico.com/pinguinos; Ecuador 4B; ☺office 10am-2:30pm & 3:30-7pm Mon-Sat) Operates guided half-day mountain-bike tours of 20km to 25km for M$350 to M$380 per person. Most trips are to little-visited scenic country areas east of San Cristóbal, passing through cloud forests (12km hiking tours M$220 per person). Reserve one day or more ahead; reservations accepted by phone and email on Sundays. Longer tours offered around the Chiapas highlands and beyond. **Bike rental** (4/5/9hr M$130/160/180) also available. English, German and Spanish spoken.

Marco Antonio Morales　　CYCLING, HIKING
(☑967-104-73-09; tonodmar@hotmail.com) Offers tailored hiking tours (M$220) and bike tours visiting San Lorenzo Zinacantán, San Juan Chamula and Rancho Nuevo (M$300 to M$350) or the Cañon del Sumidero (M$550). With advance notice, the operator provides free bikes the third Friday of every month to join the monthly Pedalazo ride (Critical Mass; 6:30pm in front of the cathedral). Speaks English and French. Ask for him at the clothing store at Utrilla 18.

La Pingüina Suiza　　CYCLING
(☑680-91-30; Insurgentes 19; ☺10am-noon & 4:30-7:30pm Mon-Sat) Three- to four-hour bike tours (20km to 25km) cost US$26; minimum two people. Inside Madre Tierra.

✦✦ Festivals & Events

Semana Santa RELIGIOUS
The crucifixion is acted out on Good Friday in the Barrio de Mexicanos in the northwest of town.

Feria de la Primavera y de la Paz CULTURAL
Easter Sunday is the start of the weeklong town fair (Spring and Peace Fair), with parades, musical events and bullfights.

**Festival Internacional
Cervantino Barroco** ARTS
In late October, this free weeklong cultural program (see www.conecultachiapas.gob. mx) keeps things hopping with world-class music, dance and theater.

🛏 Sleeping

San Cristóbal has a wealth of budget accommodations, but also a number of appealing and atmospheric midrange hotels, often set in colonial or 19th-century mansions, along with a smattering of top-end luxury. The high seasons here are during Semana Santa and the following week, and the months of July and August, plus the Día de Muertos and Christmas–New Year holidays. Most prices dip at least 20% outside the high-season prices listed here.

TOP
CHOICE Casa Felipe Flores GUESTHOUSE $$$
(☑678-39-96; www.felipeflores.com; JF Flores 36; r incl full breakfast US$95-125;☺🖥) A dreamy colonial guesthouse decorated with outstanding Mexican and Guatemalan art, crafts and furnishings, this 200-year-old building contains five rooms with fireplace set off two flowery courtyards. The lounge is a wonderful place to have a glass of wine by the fireplace and leaf through the terrific library. Room 5 is a cozy rooftop hideaway, with a private terrace looking out over tiled rooftops and clusters of bougainvillea.

Parador San Juan de Dios BOUTIQUE HOTEL $$$
(☑/fax 678-11-67; www.sanjuandios.com; Calz Roberta 16; ste M$1800-6000; 🅿☺🖥) A stunning boutique hotel on the northern edge of town, the Parador San Juan de Dios offers voluminous and luxurious suites furnished with fascinating antiques and modern art. The hotel occupies the former Rancho Harvard, which dates from the 17th century and has lodged many anthropologists and archaeologists. It has beautiful gardens, vast lawns and a top-class restaurant with an inventive, expensive Chiapas/Mediterranean menu. Herbs and vegetables are grown in its organic garden.

Villas Casa Morada BOUTIQUE HOTEL $$$
(☑678-44-40; www.casamorada.com.mx; Dugelay 45; r & ste M$1586, 2-bedroom villa M$2158; 🅿@🖥)Beautiful murals and tilework adorn these tasteful, modern apartments with kitchen, phone, cable TV, fireplaces and daily cleaning. Rooms face a tranquil fruit-tree garden, and it now has a small restaurant and bar. Note that its two 'studios' are just standard rooms without kitchens – not good value.

Bela's B&B B&B $$
(☑678-92-92; www.belasbandb.com; Dr Navarro 2; s without bathroom US$40, incl breakfast s/d with bathroom US$60/75, ste US$70-85; 🅿☺🖥) A dreamy oasis in the center, this tranquil dog-friendly B&B will seduce you with its lush garden, electric blankets and onsite massages. It's run by a American-Mexican couple. The four comfortable rooms are trimmed in traditional local fabrics and some have lovely mountain views. Discounts available for longer stays.

Na Bolom HOTEL $$
(☑678-14-18; www.nabolom.org; Guerrero 33; s/d/tr/q/ste M$830/1110/1320/1470/1520; 🅿🖥) This famous museum/research institute (p355), about 1km from the plaza, has 16 stylish (though not necessarily luxurious) guest rooms, all loaded with character and all but one with log fires. Meals are served in the house's stately dining room. Room rates include a house tour.

Parador Margarita HOTEL $$
(☑116-01-64; www.paradormargarita.aboutsan cristobal.com; JF Flores 39; incl breakfast s M$750, d M$880-980, tr/q M$1080/1200; 🅿@🖥)Rooms along a pretty courtyard here sport one king- or two queen-sized beds, and some include details like fireplaces, stained-glass windows and bathroom skylights. Other pluses include a pleasant back patio overlooking a large lawn.

Hotel Posada Jovel HOTEL $$
(☑678-17-34; www.hoteljovel.com; Paniagua 27; posada per person without bathroom M$100, posada d/tr/q M$400/550/650, hotel M$650/750/850; 🅿☺🖥) Most rooms in the original 'posada' building have stripped wooden floors, bedside lights and highland blankets, while those in the 'hotel' section across the street, surrounding a pretty garden, are larger and

brightly decorated, with cable TV and a wonderful terrace with views.

Rossco Backpackers
HOSTEL $

(☑674-05-25; www.backpackershostel.com.mx; Real de Mexicanos 16; incl breakfast dm M$150-185, d/tr M$450/600; P☺@☎) Backpackers is a friendly, sociable and well-run hostel with good dorm rooms (one for women only), a guest kitchen and a grassy garden. Private upstairs rooms have nice skylights.

Posada México
HOSTEL $

(☑678-00-14; www.himexico.com/; Josefa Ortiz de Domínguez 12; incl breakfast dm M$150, r with/without bathroom M$420/360, tr with/without bathroom M$630/540; ☺@☎) A large courtyard compound with stunning mountain views, this HI hostel has pretty gardens, good bright rooms and dorms (including one that's women only), a kitchen, a pool table, a library, tons of comfy terraces, patios and lounges and a small bar. A 10% discount is available for HI cardholders.

Hotel El Paraíso
HOTEL $$

(☑678-00-85; www.hotelposadaparaiso.com; Calle 5 de Febrero 19; s/d/tr M$750/950/1150; ☺☎) Combining colonial style with a boutique-hotel feel, El Paraíso has a bright wood-pillared patio, a stunning garden sitting area and loads of character. The high-ceilinged rooms are not huge, but all have natural light, and several are bi-level with an extra bed upstairs. The in-house restaurant, L'Eden, is excellent.

Hotel Diego de Mazariegos
HOTEL $$$

(☑678-08-33; www.diegodemazariegos.com; Calle 5 de Febrero 1; r M$1200, ste M$1600-1800; P☎) This classy, long-established hotel occupies two 18th-century mansions built around beautiful, wide courtyards. The 76 rooms are large and decked out with traditional fabrics and fittings, but also have modern comforts including cable TV. Some have fireplaces, and the suites have spa tubs.

Hotel Casa Mexicana
HOTEL $$$

(☑678-06-98; www.hotelcasamexicana.com; Calle 28 de Agosto 1; d/tr M$1500/1600, ste M$1800-2200; P☺@☎) A gallery as well as a charming colonial hotel, the stylish and inviting Casa Mexicana displays modern art alongside traditional fabrics and solid-wood pillars and furnishings. The main patio is filled with a lush tropical garden, the 54 attractive rooms are equipped with cable TV, and you'll find a restaurant, bar and sauna.

☑ Anthara Hotel
HOTEL $$

(☑674-77-32; www.antharahotel.com; Real de Mexicanos 7; d M$700-900; P☺@☎) Solar-heated hot water and heated floors distinguish this brand new two-floor hotel centered around a small garden courtyard. Rooms have dark wood furniture and large closets, though bathrooms aren't particularly ample. Snag 301 for choice mountain views.

B&B Le Gite del Sol
GUESTHOUSE $

(☑631-60-12; www.legitedelsol.com; Madero 82; incl breakfast s/d/tr/q M$250/320/420/495, without bathroom M$180/220/330/440; P☺@☎) A bountiful breakfast complements simple rooms with floors of radiant sunflower yellow and bathrooms that look a bit like over-sized shower stalls. There are also pleasant rooms with shared facilities in a new location across the street. French and English spoken.

Posada Ganesha
GUESTHOUSE $

(☑678-02-12; http://facebook.com/ganeshaposada.hostal; Calle 28 de Agosto 23; dm/s/d/tr without bathroom incl breakfast M$100/150/250/350; ☎) An incense-infused posada trimmed in Indian fabrics, this is a friendly and vibrant place to rest your head, with a simple guest kitchen, bike rentals and a pleasant lounge area. The free-standing *cabaña* room is especially nice. Yoga sessions twice daily Monday to Friday (by donation).

Hostal Rincón de los Camellos
GUESTHOUSE $

(☑116-00-97; www.loscamellos.over-blog.com; Real de Guadalupe 110; dm M$100, s/d/tr/q M$240/300/380/460, without bathroom M$180/240/320/400; ☺☎) A clean, tranquil little spot run by a welcoming French-Mexican trio. The brightly painted rooms are set around two patios, with a grassy little garden out back. A small kitchen has free drinking water and coffee.

Hotel Casavieja
HOTEL $$$

(☑678-68-68; www.casavieja.com.mx; MA Flores 27; r/tr M$1300/1400, ste M$1650-1800; P@☎) A beautifully renovated 18th-century house with lots of wooden pillars, balustrades and an old-world atmosphere, Casavieja boasts large comfortable rooms with modern amenities arranged around flowery courtyards.

Casa Margarita
HOTEL $

(☑678-09-57; www.margarita.aboutsancristobal.com; Real de Guadalupe 34; s/d/tr/q incl full breakfast M$600/700/850/950; P☺@☎) This popular and well-run travelers' haunt offers tastefully presented, impeccably clean rooms with reading lights.

Posada Corto Maltese
GUESTHOUSE $

(☑674-08-48; www.posadacortomaltese.com; Ejército Nacional 12; dm M$100, s/d/tr without bathroom M$200/250/300; ☺🏠🏠) A simple place, with a large fruit-tree garden, roaming chickens (buy eggs and cook in the guest kitchen) and small kids' play structure. It's a respite for folks who treasure green space in the city.

✗ Eating

The foodie jackpot of Chiapas, San Cristóbal has more tantalizing food options than any other place in the state. If you can verbalize a culinary craving, chances are some restaurant exists here to fulfill it. Vegetarians are embarrassingly spoiled for choice. *¡Provecho!*

REAL DE GUADALUPE AREA

Self-caterers can stock up at the centrally located **Super Más** (Real de Guadalupe 22; ☺8am-10pm) market, plus there's a handy cluster of fruit and vegetable shops on Dugelay between Madero and MA Flores.

TierrAdentro
CHIAPANECO, INTERNATIONAL $

(Real de Guadalupe 24; set menu M$38-110; ☺7:30am-1am; ☺🏠) A popular gathering center for political progressives and coffee-swigging, laptop-toting locals (not that they're mutually exclusive), this large indoor courtyard restaurant and cafe is a comfortable place to while away the hours. It's run by Zapatista supporters, who hold frequent cultural events and conferences on local issues. A simple yet delicious *menú compa* (set menu; M$45) rotates daily, with hearty offerings such as rice and beans with handmade tortillas.

Pizzería El Punto
PIZZERIA $$

(Real de Guadalupe 47; pizzas M$75-125; ☺noon-11pm; ☺) Forget the cardboard crap that passes for pizza in some parts, these crispy pies are the best in town, bar none. The central branch of this excellent pizzeria has a full bar, swanky black and red decor and a lovely balcony overlooking Real de Guadalupe.

Trattoria Italiana
ITALIAN $$

(☑cell phone 967-1016561; Belisario Domínguez 8B; mains M$130-140; ☺1:30-10pm Thu-Mon, 1:30-5:30pm Sun; ☺) This dynamic mother and daughter operation has just a few cloth-covered tables, and no written menu – they recite (in English, Spanish or Italian) what's available based on what was fresh at the market that day.

La Casa del Pan Papalotl
VEGETARIAN $

(Centro Cultural El Puente, Real de Guadalupe 55; mains M$48-105; ☺8am-10:30pm Mon-Sat; ☺🏠🍴) This excellent courtyard vegetarian restaurant does a particularly filling buffet lunch from 1pm to 5pm (M$100). Fresh bread and locally grown organic ingredients are staples here, and its shop sells excellent house-made tofu.

Restaurante Plaza Real
MEXICAN $$

(Real de Guadalupe 5; mains M$70-160; ☺7am-11pm; ☺🏠🍴) The well-prepared meat, poultry and vegetarian dishes at this classy eatery have international appeal, but also authentic Mexican flavor. It's set in the tranquil, wood-pillared and warm courtyard of what was once Chiapas' state congress building. It's shaded by enormous ficus trees.

Pierre Restaurant Francés
FRENCH $$

(☑674-53-18; Real de Guadalupe 73; mains M$80-220; ☺1:30-10pm Fri-Wed; ☺🍴) Everything – including pasta, butter, cheese and bread – is made from scratch at this scrumptious French restaurant with a seasonal menu. A few favorites include duck ravioli with wild mushrooms, *verduras salteadas en hojaldra* (vegetable pastry) and crème brûlée. Vegetarian mains as well.

Horno Mágico
BAKERY, FRENCH $

(Utrilla 7; ☺8:30am-8:30pm) For picnic fixings or a tasty snack, scoop up some crusty French breads (the pecan is divine), a quiche lorraine or a savory pastry.

WEST OF PLAZA 31 DE MARZO

Namandí Café & Crepas
CREPERIE, CAFE $

(Mazariegos 16C; crepes M$60-75; ☺8am-11pm; ☺🏠🍴) Nattily attired waitstaff serve baguette sandwiches, pastas and good coffee at this large modern cafe and restaurant, but the fresh-off-the-griddle crepes are the main draw. Try a savory *crepa azteca* with chicken, corn and peppers drizzled with *salsa poblana*. Kids love the glassed-in modern play space, and frazzled parents can take advantage of *free* childcare while they're on-site (paid babysitting also available).

L'Eden
MEXICAN, INTERNATIONAL $$

(Hotel El Paraíso, Calle 5 de Febrero 19; mains M$63-140; ☺7am-11pm; ☺🍴) This quality restaurant's tempting European and Mexican

THE ZAPATISTAS

On January 1, 1994, the day the North American Free Trade Agreement (Nafta) was implemented, a previously unknown leftist guerrilla army emerged from the forests to occupy San Cristóbal de las Casas and other towns in Chiapas. The Ejército Zapatista de Liberación Nacional (EZLN, Zapatista National Liberation Army) linked antiglobalization rhetoric with Mexican revolutionary slogans, declaring that they aimed to both overturn the oligarchy's centuries-old hold on land, resources and power, and improve the wretched living standards of Mexico's indigenous people.

The Mexican army evicted the Zapatistas within days, and the rebels retreated to the fringes of the Lacandón Jungle to wage a propaganda war, mainly fought via the internet. The Zapatistas' balaclava-clad, pipe-puffing Subcomandante Marcos (a former university professor named Rafael Guillén) rapidly became a cult figure. High-profile conventions against neoliberalism were held, international supporters flocked to Zapatista headquarters at La Realidad, 80km southeast of Comitán, and Zapatista-aligned peasants took over hundreds of farms and ranches in Chiapas.

In 1996 Zapatista and Mexican government negotiators agreed to a set of accords on indigenous rights and autonomy. However, the governing Institutional Revolutionary Party (PRI) never ratified these agreements, and tension and killings escalated in Chiapas through 1997 and 1998. A PRI-linked paramilitary group massacred 45 people in the village of Acteal, north of San Cristóbal, in 1997. By 1999 an estimated 21,000 villagers had fled their homes after the Mexican army, aided and abetted by paramilitaries, launched a campaign of intimidation. Under President Vicente Fox, two attempts to make the necessary constitutional changes failed, and the Zapatistas refused to participate in further talks, concentrating instead on consolidating their revolution and their autonomy in the villages of highland and eastern Chiapas, where they had the most support. In 2003 the Zapatista leadership established five regional 'Juntas de Buen Gobierno' (Committees of Good Government) in villages where they set up schools and clinics. While these frequently rotating committees were set up to democratize governance and teach leadership skills, they are sometimes criticized for lack of continuity and imposing excessive bureaucracy.

By 2005 Zapatista political influence was slight outside their own enclaves, and many former supporters were disillusioned with the EZLN's intransigence. Against this backdrop, Marcos announced a broad new Zapatista political struggle that included all Mexico's exploited and marginalized people, not just the indigenous. He rejected all co-operation or dialogue with mainstream political parties, launching instead La Otra Campaña (The Other Campaign), a movement to run parallel to, but distinct from, Mexico's 2006 presidential election campaign. On January 1, 2006, Marcos, now styling himself Subdelegado Zero, set off by motorcycle from the jungle to do a six-month Zapatista tour of all Mexico's states. The aim was to forge a new leftist political front by making contact with other groups around the country, to develop a new methodology of 'liberation from below' and a new civilian, peaceful, anticapitalist approach to politics. However, many observers saw scant momentum resulting from the campaign, and detractors viewed it as a publicity stunt to jumpstart Marcos' fading celebrity status. Since that time, the EZLN has mostly remained dormant, and some former supporters have grown disillusioned.

The Zapatistas have denounced the concept of ecotourism in Chiapas. They see the improvement and construction of roads in the Montes Azules reserve as being at odds with the government's stated goal of preserving the rainforest. They view the expansion of government tourism infrastructure as a nonmilitary means to make inroads into autonomous EZLN communities.

For more information, you can check in on the Zapatistas online at www.ezln.org.mx (in Spanish). Further background is available in *The Zapatista Reader*, an anthology of writers from Octavio Paz and Gabriel García Márquez to Marcos himself, and Bill Weinberg's *Homage to Chiapas: The New Indigenous Struggles in Mexico*. News updates can be found at SiPaz (www.sipaz.org) and CMI Chiapas (www.chiapas.indymedia.org). Schools for Chiapas (www.schoolsforchiapas.org) organizes educational and volunteer delegations to autonomous Zapatista communities.

CHIAPAS SAN CRISTÓBAL DE LAS CASAS

menu includes *fondue suiza, sopa azteca* and succulent meat dishes. There's a good-sized wine list too, including French and Spanish vintages.

SOUTH OF PLAZA 31 DE MARZO

Anabanana MEXICAN, INTERNATIONAL $
(Hidalgo 9; mains M$22-55; ☻9am-6pm Mon-Sat;☻) With five practically touching tables and a hand-lettered menu colored in with crayons, this long-time *tortas* and juice joint on the *andador* (pedestrian mall) is a cozy choice for typical Mexican food and no-frills international options. It has inexpensive breakfasts too.

Emiliano's Moustache TAQUERÍA $
(Crescencio Rosas 7; breakfasts & snacks M$32-60, mains M$50-90; ☻8:30am-1am; ☎) This large, enjoyable place specializes in tacos filled with combinations of meat, vegetable or cheese. The meat *filetes* are also excellent, and vegetarian possibilities exist.

El Caldero MEXICAN $
(Insurgentes 5; soups M$49; ☻9am-10pm) Simple, friendly little El Caldero specializes in delicious, filling Mexican soups – *pozole* (shredded pork in broth), *mondongo* (tripe), *caldo* (broth) – with avocados, tortillas and various salsas.

NORTH OF PLAZA 31 DE MARZO

TOP CHOICE No Name Quesadillas QUESADILLAS $
(Paniagua 49B; quesadilla M$20; ☻7-10pm Thu-Tue; ✐) After five years of selling gourmet quesadillas from a street stand, this cute couple relocated to a storefront with romantic courtyard seating, but still don't plan to name the place. Only quesadillas and flavored *atoles* are served, and the menu changes daily but follows a schedule: vegetarian Sunday through Tuesday, seafood Thursday, meat on Friday – pretty cheeky in this mostly Catholic country – and a mixed bag on Saturday. Get a gander at ingredients like wild mushrooms, squash flowers and spicy chorizo and line up early before the food sells out.

Falafel FELAFEL $
(MA Flores 4; mains M$50-75; ☻2-10pm Sun-Fri; ☻✐) Has this place stickered its name on every surface in San Cris? A small place with brilliant mural of a mustachioed sun; its filling namesake meal comes wrapped in freshly baked pitas. Hebrew readers should browse the book exchange.

Alebrije MEXICAN $
(Caminero 4; mains M$25-30;☻8am-6pm Mon-Sat) A fun, economical and busy *cocina popular* across from the Mercado Municipal, Alebrije serves freshly prepared food like *enfrijoladas con pollo* (tortillas with bean sauce, cheese and chicken), *chilaquiles* and *pollo con verduras* (chicken and vegetables) to a dedicated local clientele.

La Salsa Verde TAQUERÍA $
(Av 20 de Noviembre 7; 5 tacos M$45-90; ☻8am-midnight; ☻☎) Meat sizzles on the open-air grill and TVs blare at this taco institution (more than 30 years in business), with tables of families and clubgoers packed into its two large dining rooms.

🍷 Drinking

Cafes

The aroma of roasted highland-grown coffee beans wafts through the streets of San Cristóbal, and a strong dose is never far. Along with the Café Museo Café (p356), try **Café La Selva** (Crescencio Rosas 9; ☻8:30am-11pm; ☻☎) or **TierrAdentro** (Real de Guadalupe 24; ☻7:30am-1am; ☻☎) for the good stuff – organic, indigenous-grown and delicious.

For something different, melt into a hot chocolate at the *chocolatería* **Kakao Natura** (Moreno 2A; ☻8am-10pm Mon-Sat; ☎). The dozen or so varieties of artisanal chocolates (M$50 per dozen) make fine gifts – if you can resist eating them yourself.

Bars

TOP CHOICE Cocoliche COCKTAIL BAR, RESTAURANT
(Colón 3; ☻noon-midnight; ☻☎) By day a bohemian international restaurant (mains M$35 to M$75), in the evening its mismatched Chinese lanterns and wall of funky posters set the scene for hanging out with friends over boozy *licuados* (milkshakes). Jostle for a sofa near the fireplace on chilly nights, and check out the cabaret, music and children's theater events Wednesday through Sunday.

La Viña de Bacco WINE BAR
(Real de Guadalupe 7; ☻2pm-midnight Mon-Sat, plus Sun high season) At San Cristóbal's first wine bar, chatty patrons spill out onto the street, a pedestrian block of the main drag. It's a convivial place, pouring a large selection of Mexican options (among others), starting at a reasonable M$18 per glass. A free tapa with every glass of wine.

Mezcalería Gusana Grela　　MEZCALERÍA
(MA Flores 2; ⊘ 6pm-midnight Mon-Sat) Wedge yourself in at one of a handful of tables and try some of the 16 or so artisanal mezcals (M$20 to M$35) from Oaxaca, many which are fruit-infused.

La Sandunga　　COCKTAIL BAR
(MA Flores 16; ⊘6pm-3am Thu-Sat, plus Tue & Wed high season) Small and stylish, La Sandunga has Pop Art on its walls, and loungy music that stays at conversation-friendly levels. Fresh fruit cocktails are divine, made sweeter by the gourmet *botanas* (free snacks) accompanying them.

Los Amigos　　CANTINA
(Honduras 4; ⊘noon-8pm) A popular but reasonably unraucous cantina; the two-for-one beers and tasty *botanas* keep it hopping and fun, as do the wander-in mariachi bands.

☆ Entertainment

The free weekly *MiniGúa* (www.miniguia sancristobal.org, in Spanish) has art and entertainment listings.

Nightclubs & Live Music

Most live-music venues are free, and clubs generally enforce the no-smoking law.

TOP CHOICE **Café Bar Revolution**　　LIVE MUSIC
(cnr Av 20 de Noviembre & Calle 1 de Marzo; ⊘noon-midnight; ⊜) There's always something fun at Revolution, with live music daily from 8pm to 10:30pm and an eclectic lineup of salsa, rock, blues, jazz and reggae. Dance downstairs or order a mojito or *caipirinha* and chat in the quieter upstairs *tapanco* (attic).

La Lupe　　LIVE MUSIC, PERFORMING ARTS
(✆678-12-22; Real De Guadalupe 23; ⊘noon-midnight) A cavernous space with a Mexican/Argentine restaurant; stop by for live-music tango on Friday and Saturday from 9:30pm and fun circus arts for kids earlier Saturday evening. Martinis are the house specialty.

Latino's　　CLUB
(✆678-99-27; Madero 23; admission Fri & Sat M$40; ⊘8pm-3am Mon-Sat) A bright restaurant and dance spot where the city's *salseros* gather to groove. A salsa/*merengue*/*cumbia* band plays nightly, with the crowds getting thick by 10:30pm or so.

Dada Club　　JAZZ, LIVE MUSIC
(✆631-75-61; www.dadaclubjazz.com; Calle 1 de Marzo 6A; ⊘7pm-midnight Thu-Sat) Deep red walls and flickering flame lamps set the backdrop for the best jazz and blues in town. An intimate balcony hovers beside the stage.

Cinema

San Cristóbal is a fine place to immerse yourself in Mexican and Latin American cinema, political documentaries and art-house movies. West of the center, the **Cinépolis multiplex** (www.cinepolis.com; adjacent to the Chedraui) plays first-run flicks for M$50, the cinemas listed here charge M$30.

Kinoki　　CINEMA
(✆678-50-46; www.forokinoki.blogspot.com, in Spanish; Belisario Domínguez 5A; ⊘noon-11:30pm; ⊛) With a beautiful upstairs space and terrace, this art gallery and tea salon screens three films nightly at 6pm, 7pm (on the roof) and 8pm. Private cinema rooms available with over 2000 movies on hand.

Cinema El Puente　　CINEMA
(✆678-37-23; Centro Cultural El Puente, Real de Guadalupe 55; ⊘Mon-Sat) Screenings at 6pm and 8pm.

🔒 Shopping

Real de Guadalupe and the Andador Turístico have some upscale craft shops, but the busy daily crafts market around Santo Domingo and La Caridad churches is also a good place to check out. In addition to textiles, another Chiapas specialty is amber, sold in numerous jewelry shops. When buying amber, beware of plastic imitations: the real thing is never cold and never heavy, and when rubbed should produce static electricity and a resiny smell.

Taller Leñateros　　ARTS & CRAFTS, BOOKS
(✆678-51-74; www.tallerlenateros.com; Paniagua 54; ⊘9am-8pm Mon-Fri, 9am-2pm Sat) A society of Maya artists, the 'Woodlanders' Workshop' crafts exquisite handmade books, posters and fine art prints from recycled paper infused with local plants, using images inspired by traditional folk art. It's an open workshop, so you can watch the art in progress.

Abuelita Books　　BOOKS
(✆631-67-20; www.abuelitabooks.com; Colón 2; ⊘10am-6pm Tue-Fri, 2-6pm Mon & Sat; ⊛) A great place for a leisurely browse over homemade *kombucha* (fermented tea drink), hot coffee or a steamy chai; come here to replenish your reading material from an excellent selection of new and used books in English

INDIGENOUS WOMEN'S WEAVING COOPERATIVES

The outstanding indigenous *artesanías* of the Chiapas highlands are textiles such as *huipiles* (sleeveless tunics), blouses and blankets, and Tzotzil weavers are some of the most skilled and inventive in Mexico. Spanish-speakers should consider visiting these women in their communities to watch them work and support them directly. Most of the weavers are monolingual in Tzotzil, so cooperatives will need to organize a Spanish translator.

A 30-year-old cooperative, **J'pas Joloviletik** (📞678-28-48; Utrilla 43; ⊙9am-2pm Mon-Sat, plus 4-7pm Mon-Fri) – the name means 'those that weave' in Tzotzil – is comprised of 184 women from 12 communities, and they have a spacious shop on the east side of the Templo de Santo Domingo. You can arrange a visit with an artisan weaver in her home – usually in San Andrés Larraínzar – where you can see her work and have a traditional meal, with all the proceeds going directly to the women. Call or stop by a day or two beforehand to schedule a tour (M$350 per person).

On the other side of Santo Domingo, **Sna Jolobil** (📞678-26-46; Calz Lázaro Cárdenas s/n; ⊙9am-2pm & 4-7pm Mon-Sat) – Tzotzil for 'The Weaver's House' – exhibits and sells some of the very best *huipiles*, blouses, skirts, rugs and other woven items, with prices ranging from a few dollars for small items to thousands for the best *huipiles* (the fruit of many months' work). A cooperative of 800 weavers from the Chiapas highlands, it was founded in the 1970s to foster the important indigenous art of backstrap-loom weaving, and has revived many half-forgotten techniques and designs. Its shop can also organize personalized tours with a few days' advance notice.

(other languages also available). Two-for-one trades, plus children's titles too.

Poshería DRINK
(📞631-68-63; Real de Guadalupe 46A; ⊙9am-9pm) Pick up a bottle of artisanal *pox* infused with honey, chocolate or fruits like *nanche* (nance). Definitely not what the common folk are drinking, since bottles sell for M$80 to M$200 and the alcohol content averages only about 14%.

Nemi Zapata HANDICRAFTS, COFFEE
(📞678-74-87; Real de Guadalupe 57A; ⊙9:30am-8pm Mon-Sat) A fair-trade store that sells products made by Zapatista communities: weavings, embroidery, coffee and honey, as well as EZLN cards, posters and books.

Lágrimas de la Selva JEWELRY
(📞674-63-48; Hidalgo 1C; ⊙10am-8pm Mon-Sat, noon-8pm Sun) A lovely jewelry store where you can watch jewelers work with amber.

Casa Chiapas HANDICRAFTS
(📞678-11-80; www.casachiapas.gob.mx, in Spanish; cnr Niños Héroes & Hidalgo; ⊙9am-9pm Mon-Fri, 9am-8pm Sat, 9am-2pm Sun) Sells a good range of Chiapas crafts.

La Pared BOOKS
(📞678-63-67; Hidalgo 13B; ⊙10:30am-8:30pm Tue, Fri & Sat, 4:30-7:30pm Sun, noon-8:30pm Wed & Thu)

New and used books in English and other languages.

Libros Soluna BOOKS
(📞678-68-05; Real de Guadalupe 13B; ⊙9am-9pm Mon-Sat, 10am-9pm Sun) Selection includes maps, plus a central outpost of Taller Leñateros in the back room.

ℹ️ Information

Dangers & Annoyances

Because of incidents of assault on female passengers, women who want to ride alone in taxis at night should take extra precautions, like ordering them through lodgings or restaurants or making sure someone else has the taxi plate number.

Immigration

Instituto Nacional de Migración (Diagonal Hermanos Paniagua; ⊙9am-2pm Mon-Fri) On a corner with the Pan-American Hwy, 1.2km west of the OCC bus station.

Internet Access

San Cristóbal de las Casas has dozens of inexpensive internet cafes, and most cafes have free wi-fi.
Los Faroles (Real de Guadalupe 33; per hr $8)
Fast-Net Cyber Café (Real de Guadalupe 15D; per hr M$10)

Laundry

Lavandería Las Estrellas (Real de Guadalupe 75; per kg M$10; ⊙8:30am-8pm Mon-Sat)

Lavandería Laura (Belisario Domínguez 5; 1-3kg M$45; ☺8am-9pm Mon-Sat)

Medical Services

Hospital de la Mujer (☑678-07-70; Insurgentes 24) General hospital with emergency facilities.

Dr Luis José Sevilla (☑678-16-26, cell phone 967-6775672; Calle del Sol; ☺6am-10pm) Speaks English and Italian; can make house calls. Located west of the center near the Periférico.

Money

Most banks require your passport if you want to change cash or travelers checks, though they only change money Monday through Friday. There are also handy ATMs at the OCC bus station and on the southern side of the Plaza 31 de Marzo.

Banamex (Insurgentes 9; ☺9am-4pm Mon-Sat) Has an ATM; exchanges dollars.

Banco Azteca (Plaza 31 de Marzo; ☺9am-9pm) Hidden in the back of the Elektra furniture store; exchanges dollars and euros whenever open.

Lacantún Money Exchange (Real de Guadalupe 12A; ☺9am-9pm Mon-Sat, 9am-2pm & 4-7pm Sun) Open outside bank hours but rates are worse.

Post

Main post office (Allende 3; ☺7:30am-7pm Mon-Fri, 8:30am-3:30pm Sat)

Telephone

Lada Ahorro (Av 20 de Noviembre btwn 28 de Agosto & Escuadrón 201; ☺9am-9pm) Inexpensive international calls.

Tourist Information

Municipal tourist office (☑678-06-65; Palacio Municipal, Plaza 31 de Marzo; ☺8am-9pm) Staff are generally knowledgeable about the San Cristóbal area; English spoken, plus French and Italian some days.

ⓘ Getting There & Away

A fast toll *autopista* (M$42 for cars) zips here from Chiapa de Corzo. An increased military and police presence has significantly reduced the number of highway holdups on Hwy 199 between Ocosingo and Palenque, but it's still probably best to travel along this winding stretch of road during daylight.

Air

San Cristóbal's airport, about 15km from town on the Palenque road, has no regular passenger flights; the main airport serving town is at Tuxtla Gutiérrez. Three daily direct OCC minibuses (M$160) run to the Tuxtla airport from San Cristóbal's main bus terminal (four in the other direction); book airport-bound tickets in advance. Also, **Taxis Jovel** (☑678-68-99) picks up passengers for the airport, charging M$400 per carload (M$50 *colectivo*); reserve a day beforehand. A number of tour agencies run shuttles to the Tuxtla airport for around M$200 per person, though scheduled service is sometimes at 9am only.

Bus & Colectivo

The Pan-American Hwy (Hwy 190, Blvd Juan Sabines, 'El Bulevar') runs through the southern part of town, and nearly all transportation terminals are on it or nearby. From the OCC bus terminal, it's six blocks north up Insurgentes to the central square, Plaza 31 de Marzo.

The main 1st-class **OCC terminal** (www.ado.com.mx; cnr Pan-American Hwy & Insurgentes) is also used by ADO and UNO 1st-class and deluxe buses, plus some 2nd-class buses. Tickets can also be purchased at **Boletotal** (www.boletotal.mx; Real de Guadalupe 14; ☺7am-10pm) in the center of town.

First-class **AEXA** (☑678-61-78) and 2nd-class Ómnibus de Chiapas share a terminal on the south side of the highway.

Daily departures (from the OCC terminal unless otherwise stated) are listed in the boxed text p366.

All *colectivo* vans (combis) and taxis have depots on the Pan-American Hwy a block or so from the OCC terminal. They generally run from 5am until 9pm and leave when full. *Colectivo* taxis to Tuxtla, Comitán and Ocosingo are available 24 hours; if you don't want to wait for it to fill, you must pay for the empty seats too.

For Tuxtla, comfortable Ómnibus de Chiapas 'sprinter' minibuses (M$40) are the best bet; they leave every ten minutes. For Chiapa de Corzo, see p350.

For Guatemala, most agencies offer daily van service to Quetzaltenango (M$300, eight hours), Panajachel (M$300, 10 hours) and Antigua (M$400, 12 hours); Viajes Chincultik is slightly cheaper, and also has van service to Guatemala City. Otherwise, go to Ciudad Cuauhtémoc and pick up onward transportation from the Guatemala side.

Car & Motorcycle

San Cristóbal's only car-rental company, **Optima** (optimacar1@hotmail.com; Mazariegos 39) rents manual transmission Chevys for M$500 per day and M$3000 per week, including unlimited kilometers, insurance and taxes. Sizeable discounts are given for payment in cash. Drivers must be 25 or older and have a credit card.

BUSES FROM SAN CRISTÓBAL DE LAS CASAS

DESTINATION	FARE (M$)	DURATION	FREQUENCY (DAILY)
Campeche	398	10hr	1
Cancún	300-912	18-19hr	4 OCC, 1 AEXA
Ciudad Cuauhtémoc (Guatemalan border)	90	3½hr	5
Comitán	40-74	1¾hr	Frequent OCC & colectivos
Mérida	566	13hr	1
Mexico City (mostly TAPO)	356-1130	13-14hr	7
Oaxaca	439-522	11hr	3
Ocosingo	36-60	2hr	13 OCC, 4 AEXA, frequent colectivos
Palenque	82-178	5hr	13 OCC, 4 AEXA
Pochutla	424	11-12hr	3
Puerto Escondido	476	12½-13½hr	3
Tuxtla Gutiérrez	36-44	1-1¼hr	Frequent OCC; 4 AEXA; frequent Ómnibus de Chiapas sprinters; frequent colectivos; 24hr Taxis Jovel colectivos taxis
Tuxtla Gutiérrez airport (Ángel Albino Corzo)	160	1¼hr	3
Villahermosa	260	5½-7hr	3

❶ Getting Around

Combis (M$5) go up Crescencio Rosas from the Pan-American Hwy to the town center. Taxis cost M$25 within town and M$30 at night.

Los Pingüinos (p357) rents good-quality mountain bikes with lock and maps and can advise on good and safe routes. You'll need to deposit your passport or credit card.

Croozy Scooters (www.croozyscooterrental. com; Belisario Domínguez 7; per 3hr/additional hr/day motorcycle M$280/50/430, scooter M$190/40/300, bicycle M$60/20/140; ◷9am-6pm Tue-Sun, to 8pm high season) rents well-maintained bicycles, Italika CS 125cc scooters and 150cc motorcycles. The price includes a free tank of fuel, maps, locks and helmets (plus a repair kit and pump for bicycles); passport and deposit required.

Around San Cristóbal

The inhabitants of the beautiful Chiapas highlands are descended from the ancient Maya and maintain some unique customs, costumes and beliefs (see the boxed text p370).

Markets and festivals often give the most interesting insight into indigenous life, and there are lots of them. Weekly markets at the villages are nearly always on Sunday. Proceedings start as early as dawn, and wind down by lunchtime. Occasions like **Carnaval** (late February/early March), for which San Juan Chamula is particularly famous, **Semana Santa**, and **Día de Muertos** (November 2) are celebrated almost everywhere. During Carnaval, groups of minstrels stroll the roads in tall, pointed hats with long, colored tassels, strumming guitars and chanting. Much *pox* (pronounced 'posh'), an alcoholic drink made from sugarcane, is drunk.

During the day, walking or riding by horse or bicycle along the main roads to San Juan Chamula and San Lorenzo Zinacantán should not be risky; however, it's not wise to wander into unfrequented areas or down isolated tracks.

☞ Tours

Exploring the region with a good guide can open up doors and give you a feel for indigenous life and customs you could never gain alone. Most San Cristóbal agencies offer four- or five-hour trips to local villages, usually San Juan Chamula and San Lorenzo Zinacantán, for about M$170 to M$200, or four- or five-hour guided horseback rides to San Juan Chamula for the same price. Don't take anything too valuable with you; thefts have occurred in the past. See p357 for area bicycle tours.

Alex & Raúl Tours   CULTURAL TOUR
(☎967-678-91-41; www.alexyraultours.wordpress. com; per person M$175) Enjoyable and informative minibus tours in English, French or Spanish; Raúl and/or a colleague wait at the wooden cross in front of San Cristóbal's cathedral from 8:45am to 9:30am daily, going to San Juan Chamula and Zinacantán. Trips to Tenejapa, San Andrés Larraínzar or Amatenango del Valle (M$225) can also be arranged for a minimum of four people.

❶ Getting There & Away

Transportation to most villages goes from points around the Mercado Municipal in San Cristóbal. Combis to San Juan Chamula (M$10) leave from Calle Honduras frequently; for Zinacantán, com-

bis (M$15) and *colectivo* taxis (M$20) go at least hourly, from a yard off Robledo. Transportation runs from before daybreak to around dusk.

SAN JUAN CHAMULA
POP 3300 / ELEV 2200M

The Chamulans are a fiercely independent Tzotzil group. Their main village, San Juan Chamula, 10km northwest of San Cristóbal, is the center for some unique religious practices – although conflicts between adherents of traditional Chamulan Catholicism and converts to evangelical, Pentecostal and other branches of Christianity have resulted in the expulsion of many thousands of Chamulans from their villages in the past couple of decades. Here, as in other places in Mexico and Central America, rejection of Catholicism was also in part a political rejection of the longstanding supremacy of the Catholic *mestizo* majority. In San Juan Chamula, evangelicalism is associated with the Zapatista movement. Most of the evangelical

Around San Cristóbal de las Casas

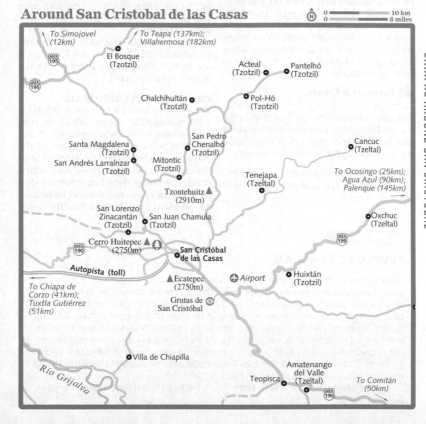

CHIAPAS AROUND SAN CRISTÓBAL

exiles now inhabit the shantytowns around San Cristóbal.

Chamulan men wear loose homespun tunics of white wool (sometimes, in cool weather, thicker black wool), but *cargo-holders* – those with important religious and ceremonial duties – wear a sleeveless black tunic and a white scarf on the head. Chamulan women wear fairly plain white or blue blouses and/or shawls and woolen skirts.

Outsiders can visit San Juan Chamula, but a big sign at the entrance to the village strictly forbids photography inside the village church or at rituals. Do *not* ignore these restrictions; the community takes them very seriously. Nearby, around the shell of an older church, is the village graveyard. Though it's no longer practiced, traditionally black crosses were for people who died old, white for the young, and blue for others.

Sunday is the weekly market, when people from the hills stream into the village to shop, trade and visit the main church. A corresponding number of tourist buses also stream in, so you might prefer to come another day (though avoid Wednesday, when the church is often all but deserted due to local superstitions).

✯ Festivals & Events

Carnaval CARNIVAL
Festivities also mark the five 'lost' days of the ancient Long Count calendar, which divided time into 20-day periods (18 of these make 360 days, leaving five to complete a year).

Fiesta de San Juan Bautista RELIGIOUS
Up to 20,000 people gather to dance and drink on June 24.

Change of Cargo-Holders TRADITIONAL
The annual rotation of the honored (but expensive) community leadership positions known as *cargos;* December 30 to January 1.

SAN LORENZO ZINACANTÁN
POP 3900 / ELEV 2558M

The orderly village of San Lorenzo Zinacantán, about 11km northwest of San Cristóbal, is the main village of the Zinacantán municipality (population 36,000). Zinacantán people, like Chamulans, are Tzotzil. The men wear distinctive pink tunics embroidered with flower motifs and may sport flat, round, ribboned palm hats. Women wear pink or purple shawls over richly embroidered blouses.

A small market is held on Sundays until noon, and during fiesta times. The most important celebrations are for La Virgen de La Candelaria (August 7 to 11) and San Sebastián (January 19 to 22).

The people of Zinacantán are great flower growers. They have a particular love for the geranium, which – along with pine branches – is offered in rituals for a wide range of benefits.

The huge central Iglesia de San Lorenzo (admission M$15) was rebuilt following a fire in 1975. Photography is banned in the church and churchyard.

GRUTAS DE SAN CRISTÓBAL
The entrance to this long cavern (admission M$15, parking M$10; ⊙8am-4:30pm) is situated in pine woods 9km southeast of San Cristóbal, a five-minute walk south of the Pan-American Hwy. The first 350m or so of the cave is lit and open for viewing, with a concrete walkway threading through a dazzling chasm of stalagmites and stalactites. An extensive army base buffers the caves,

---

DON'T MISS

TEMPLO DE SAN JUAN

Standing beside the main plaza, Chamula's main church is a ghostly white, with a vividly painted arch of green and blue. Inside the darkened sanctuary, hundreds of flickering candles, clouds of copal incense, and worshipers kneeling with their faces to the pine-needle-carpeted floor make a powerful impression. Chanting *curanderos* (literally 'curers'; medicine men or women) may be rubbing patients' bodies with eggs or bones, and worshippers often drink soft drinks (burps are believed to expel evil spirits) or copious amounts of *pox*. Images of saints are surrounded with mirrors and dressed in holy garments. Chamulans revere San Juan Bautista (St John the Baptist) above Christ, and his image occupies a more important place in the church.

You must obtain tickets (M$20) at the tourist office (⊙7am-6pm), beside the plaza, before entering the church.

but visitors are still welcome. Horseback riding is available from the parking area, where you'll also find *comedores*.

To get there, take a Teopisca-bound combi from the Pan-American Hwy, about 150m southeast of the OCC bus station in San Cristóbal, and ask for 'Las Grutas' (M$20).

AMATENANGO DEL VALLE
POP 4700 / ELEV 1869M

The women of this Tzeltal village by the Pan-American Hwy, 37km southeast of San Cristóbal, are renowned potters. Pottery here is still fired by a pre-Hispanic method, building a wood fire around the pieces rather than putting them in a kiln. Amatenango children find a ready tourist market with *animalitos* – little pottery animal figures that are inexpensive but fragile. If you visit the village, expect to be surrounded within minutes by young *animalito* sellers.

From San Cristóbal, take a Comitán-bound bus or combi.

Ocosingo
🕿919 / POP 42,000 / ELEV 900M

A respite from both the steamy lowland jungle and the chilly highlands, the bustling regional market town of Ocosingo sits in a gorgeous and broad temperate valley midway between San Cristóbal and Palenque. The impressive Maya ruins of Toniná are just a few kilometers away.

The market area along Avenida 2 Sur Oriente, three to five blocks east (downhill) from the central plaza, is the busiest part of town. The **Tianguis Campesino** (Peasants' Market; cnr Av 2 Sur Oriente & Calle 5 Sur Oriente; ☺6am-5pm) is for the area's small-scale food producers to sell their goods direct; only women are allowed to trade here, and it's

a colorful sight, with most of the traders in traditional dress.

The valleys known as Las Cañadas de Ocosingo, between Ocosingo and the Reserva de la Biosfera Montes Azules to the east, form one of the strongest bastions of support for the Zapatistas, and Ocosingo saw the bloodiest fighting during the 1994 uprising, with about 50 rebels killed here by the Mexican army.

Ocosingo spreads east (downhill) from Hwy 199. Avenida Central runs down from the highway to the broad central plaza, overlooked from its east end by the Templo de San Jacinto. Many hotels, restaurants and services are along Calle Central Norte, running off the north side of the plaza.

🛏 Sleeping

Hospedaje Esmeralda GUESTHOUSE $
(🕿673-00-14; rosi_esmeralda@hotmail.com; Calle Central Norte 14; s/d/tr/q without bathroom M$140/230/270/340; P🕿) The travelers' haunt and de facto tourist office of Ocosingo, this small guesthouse has five adequate rooms, all with bright indigenous bedcovers and fans. A restaurant (mains M$50 to 90), bar and terrace area invites lounging and chatting, and the owner truly enjoys helping people get to know the area. It also offers horseback-riding excursions (M$200, about two hours) in the countryside outside Ocosingo and a book exchange. One room, with bathroom, costs a bit extra.

Hotel Central HOTEL $
(🕿673-00-24; cnr Av Central & Calle Central; s/d/tr/q M$280/330/410/490, air-con extra M$100; P✳🕿) Fronting the plaza, the Hotel Central has clean rooms with cable TV and fan. Ask for one of the upstairs rooms; corner room 12 is especially bright and breezy.

Hotel Margarita HOTEL $
(🕿673-12-15; hotelmargarita@prodigy.net.mx; Calle Central Norte 19; s/d/tr/q M$300/380/450/500, air-con extra M$50; P✳🕿) Next to Hospedaje Esmeralda, the Margarita has clean and comfortable rooms, all with TV, fan, two big double beds and large framed posters of Chiapas attractions.

Eating

Restaurant El Campanario MEXICAN $
(Av Central Oriente 2; mains M$45-90; ☺7am-10pm) Framed by colonial arcades and facing the plaza, El Campanario has tables with

CHIAPAS OCOSINGO

INDIGENOUS PEOPLES OF CHIAPAS

Of the 4.8 million people of Chiapas, approximately a quarter are indigenous, with language being the key ethnic identifier. Each of the eight principal groups has its own language, beliefs and customs, a cultural variety that makes Chiapas one of the most fascinating states in Mexico.

Travelers to the area around San Cristóbal are most likely to encounter the Tzotziles and the Tzeltales. Their traditional religious life is nominally Catholic, but integrates pre-Hispanic elements. Most people live in the hills outside the villages, which are primarily market and ceremonial centers.

Tzotzil and Tzeltal clothing is among the most varied, colorful and elaborately worked in Mexico. It not only identifies wearers' villages but also continues ancient Maya traditions. Many of the seemingly abstract designs on these costumes are in fact stylized snakes, frogs, butterflies, birds, saints and other beings. Some motifs have religious-magical functions: scorpions, for example, can be a symbolic request for rain, since they are believed to attract lightning.

The Lacandones dwelled deep in the Lacandón Jungle and largely avoided contact with the outside world until the 1950s. They now number less than 1000 and mostly live in three main settlements in that same region (Lacanjá Chansayab, Metzabok and Nahá), with low-key tourism being one of their major means of support. Lacandones are readily recognizable in their white tunics and long black hair cut in a fringe. Most Lacandones have now abandoned their traditional animist religion in favor of Presbyterian or evangelical forms of Christianity.

Traditionally treated as second-class citizens, indigenous groups mostly live on the least productive land in the state, with the least amount of government services or infrastructure. Many indigenous communities rely on subsistence farming and have no running water or electricity, and it was frustration over lack of political power and their historical mistreatment that fueled the Zapatista rebellion, putting a spotlight on the region's distinct inequities.

Today, longstanding indigenous ways of life are challenged both by evangelical Christianity – opposed to many traditional animist-Catholic practices and the abuse of alcohol in religious rituals – and by the Zapatista movement, which rejects traditional leadership hierarchies and is raising the rights and profile of women. Many highland indigenous people have emigrated to the Lacandón Jungle to clear new land, or to Mexican and US cities in search of work.

Despite all obstacles, indigenous identities and self-respect survive. They may be suspicious of outsiders, and may resent interference in their religious observances or other aspects of their life, but if treated with due respect they are likely to respond in kind.

bright tablecloths, and serves a typical Chiapas menu of meat, egg and seafood.

Las Delicias MEXICAN, BREAKFAST **$$**
(Av Central 5; mains M$75-110; ⊙7am-11pm; 🛜)
On the plaza-facing veranda of the Hotel Central, this restaurant has big portions and good breakfasts (M$38 to M$65).

Restaurant Los Rosales MEXICAN, BREAKFAST **$**
(Hotel Margarita, Calle Central Norte 19; breakfast M$35-60, mains M$60-90; ⊙7am-11pm; 🛜) With a wall of windows looking out the rooftops to views of never-ending green mountains, this upstairs eatery makes a pleasant place to plot your day.

🛍 **Shopping**

Fábrica de Quesos Santa Rosa CHEESE
(☑673-00-09; 1a Calle Oriente Norte 11; cheese per kg M$75-90; ⊙7am-noon & 4:30-8pm Mon-Sat, 8am-2pm Sun) Ocosingo is known for its *queso amarillo* (yellow cheese). There are six main types sold by this cheesemaker, including 'de bola,' which comes in 1kg balls with an edible wax coating and a crumbly, whole-fat center. Free factory tours available during business hours.

 Information

Santander (cnr Calle Central Norte & Av 1a Norte; ⊙9am-4pm Mon-Fri, 10am-2pm Sat) and the plaza-side **Banamex** (Av Central; ⊙9am-

BUSES FROM OCOSINGO

DESTINATION	FARE (M$)	DURATION	FREQUENCY (DAILY)
Palenque	55-122	2½hr	12 OCC, 3 AEXA; very frequent *colectivos*
San Cristóbal de las Casas	40-64	2¼hr	9 OCC, 4 AEXA; very frequent *colectivos*
Tuxtla Gutiérrez	80-160	3½hr	9 OCC, 4 AEXA

4pm Mon-Fri) both exchange dollars and have ATMs. Santander changes euros and Canadian dollars too. The plaza's a free wi-fi hotspot, and internet cafes there charge M$8 per hour.

ℹ Getting There & Away

See p383 for a safety note concerning the road to Palenque.

For information on getting to Laguna Miramar, see p397.

Ocosingo's **OCC bus terminal** (☎673-04-31) is on Hwy 199, 600m west of the plaza; the 1st-class **AEXA bus terminal** (☎cell phone 919-1140679) is across the road. Buses from the OCC terminal also go to Campeche, Cancún, Mérida and Villahermosa. The main *colectivo* terminal is across the street from AEXA.

Toniná

The towering ceremonial core of **Toniná** (☎cell phone 919-1082239; admission M$41; ⊗8am-5pm), overlooking a pastoral valley 14km east of Ocosingo, comprises one of the Maya world's most imposing temple complexes. This was the city that brought mighty Palenque to its knees.

The year AD 688 saw the inauguration of the Snake Skull–Jaguar Claw dynasty, with ambitious new rulers bent on controlling the region. Palenque was their rival state, and when Toniná captured the Palenque ruler K'an Joy Chitam II in 711, it's likely that he had his head lopped off here.

Toniná became known as the Place of the Celestial Captives, because its chambers held the captured rulers of Palenque and other Maya cities, who were destined to be ransomed for large sums or decapitated. A recurring image in Toniná sculpture is of captives before decapitation, thrown to the ground with their hands tied.

To enter the site, follow the road from the entrance and **site museum** (⊗closed Mon), which details Toniná's history (in Spanish) and contains most of the best artifacts. The road turns into a footpath, crosses a stream and climbs to the broad, flat Gran Plaza. At the south end of the Gran Plaza is the **Templo de la Guerra Cósmica** (Temple of Cosmic War), with five altars in front of it. Off one side of the plaza is a **ball court**, inaugurated around AD 780 under the rule of the female regent Smoking Mirror. A decapitation altar stands cheerfully beside it. In 2011, archaeologists discovered two life-size stone sculptures of captive warriors inscribed as being from Copán (in Honduras), confirming that Maya kingdom's wartime alliance with Palenque.

To the north rises the ceremonial core of Toniná, a hillside terraced into a number of platforms, rising 80m above the Gran Plaza. At the right-hand end of the steps, rising from the first to the second platform, is the entry to a **ritual labyrinth** of passages.

Higher up on the right-hand side is the **Palacio de las Grecas y de la Guerra** (Palace of the Grecas and War). The *grecas* are a band of geometrical decoration forming a zigzag x-shape, possibly representing Quetzalcóatl. To its right is a rambling series of chambers, passages and stairways, believed to have been Toniná's administrative headquarters.

Higher again is Toniná's most remarkable sculpture, the **Mural de las Cuatro Eras** (Mural of the Four Eras). Created between AD 790 and 840, this stucco relief of four panels – the first, from the left end, has been lost – represents the four suns, or four eras of human history. The people of Toniná believed themselves to be living in the fourth sun – that of winter, mirrors, the direction north and the end of human life. At the center of each panel is the upside-down head of a decapitated prisoner. Blood spurting from the prisoner's neck forms a ring of feathers and, at the same time, a sun. In one panel, a dancing skeleton holds a decapitated head.

CHIAPAS TONINÁ

To the left of the head is a lord of the underworld, resembling an enormous rodent.

Up the next set of steps is the seventh level, with remains of four temples. Behind the second temple from the left, more steps descend into the very narrow **Tumba de Treinta Metros** (Thirty-Meter Tomb), an impossibly slim passageway that's definitely not for the claustrophobic!

Above here is the acropolis, the abode of Toniná's rulers and site of its eight most important temples – four on each of the two levels. The right-hand temple on the lower level, the **Templo del Monstruo de la Tierra** (Temple of the Earth Monster), has Toniná's best-preserved roofcomb, built around AD 713.

On the topmost level, the tallest temple, the **Templo del Espejo Humeante** (Temple of the Smoking Mirror), was built by Zots-Choj, who took the throne in AD 842. In that era of the fourth sun and the direction north, Zots-Choj had to raise this, Toniná's northernmost temple, highest of all, which necessitated a large, artificial northeast extension of the hill.

❶ Getting There & Away

Combis to Toniná (M$10) leave from a roofed depot just behind Ocosingo's Tianguis Campesino every 30 minutes. The last one returns around 5:30pm. A taxi costs M$80.

Agua Azul & Misol-Ha

These spectacular water attractions – the thundering cascades of Agua Azul and the 35m jungle waterfall of Misol-Ha – are both short detours off the Ocosingo–Palenque road. During the rainy season, they lose part of their beauty as the water gets murky, though the power of the waterfalls is magnified.

Both are most easily visited on an organized day tour from Palenque, though it's possible, for about the same price, to go independently. One reason to visit on your own is to spend more time at Misol-Ha, which is usually a shorter tour stop.

Agua Azul   WATERFALL
(admission M$32) Agua Azul is a breathtaking sight, with its powerful and dazzling white waterfalls thundering into turquoise (most of the year) pools surrounded by verdant jungle. On holidays and weekends the place is thronged; at other times you'll have few

companions. The temptation to swim is great, but take extreme care, as people do drown here. The current is deceptively fast, the power of the falls obvious, and there are many submerged hazards like rocks and dead trees.

The turnoff for these waterfalls is halfway between Ocosingo and Palenque, some 60km from each. A paved road leads 4.5km down to Agua Azul from Hwy 199. A well-made stone and concrete path with steps runs 700m up beside the falls from the parking area, which is packed with food and souvenir stalls. Basic lodging is also available.

Unfortunately, theft isn't uncommon, so don't bring valuables, keep an eye on your belongings and stick to the main paved trail. Flare-ups have been taking place here between Zapatista communities and the army or anti-Zapatista paramilitaries, so inquire about recent events before heading here on your own.

Misol-Ha   WATERFALL
(total admission M$23) Just 20km south of Palenque, spectacular Misol-Ha cascades approximately 35m into a wonderful wide pool surrounded by lush tropical vegetation. It's a sublime place for a dip when the fall is not excessively pumped up by wet-season rains. A path behind the main fall leads into a cave, which allows you to experience the power of the falls close up. Misol-Ha is 1.5km off Hwy 199 and the turnoff is signposted, and two separate *ejidos* (communcal land-holdings) charge admission.

Centro Turístico Ejidal Cascada de Misol-Ha (⏴in Mexico City 55-5551-3377; www.misol-ha.com, in Spanish; d/tr M$290/400, f with kitchen M$520-630; ℗⊜) has 21 great wooden cabins among the trees near the fall, with fans, hot water bathrooms and mosquito netting, plus a good open-air *restaurant* (mains M$60-120; ⏲7am-7pm, to 10pm high season). Nighttime swims are dreamy.

❶ Getting There & Away

Most Palenque travel agencies offer daily Misol-Ha and Agua Azul trips. Trips cost M$150 to M$180 including admission fees, and last six or seven hours, spending 30 to 60 minutes at Misol-Ha and two to three hours at Agua Azul. Trips can also be organized to deposit you in San Cristóbal (M$300) afterward.

To visit the sites independently from Palenque, hire a taxi (around M$350 to Misol-Ha with a one-hour wait, or M$1000 to Agua Azul with a two-hour wait). Or take an Ocosingo-bound combi from 5a Poniente Sur to the *cruceros* (turnoffs). At Agua Azul (M$30), *camionetas* run down to the entrance. There's no regular transportation from the highway to Misol-Ha (M$25), but it's a pretty 1.5km pastoral walk.

Palenque

🕿 916 / POP 43,000 / ELEV 80M

Deservedly one of the top destinations of Chiapas, the soaring jungle-swathed temples of Palenque are a national treasure and one of the best examples of Maya architecture in Mexico. Modern Palenque town, a few kilometers to the east, is a sweaty, humdrum place without much appeal except as a jumping-off point for the ruins and a place to find internet access, though a makeover has spiffed up the city's main road near the park. Many prefer to base themselves at one of the forest hideouts along the road between the town and the ruins, including the funky travelers' hangout of El Panchán.

History

The name Palenque (Palisade) is Spanish and has no relation to the city's ancient name, which may have been Lakamha (Big Water). Palenque was first occupied around 100 BC, and flourished from around AD 630 to around 740. The city rose to prominence under the ruler Pakal, who reigned from AD 615 to 683. Archaeologists have determined that Pakal is represented by hieroglyphics of sun and shield, and he is also referred to as Escudo Solar (Sun Shield). He lived to the then-incredible age of 80.

During Pakal's reign, many plazas and buildings, including the superlative Templo de las Inscripciones (Pakal's own mausoleum), were constructed in Palenque. The structures were characterized by mansard roofs and very fine stucco bas-reliefs.

Pakal's son Kan B'alam II (684–702), who is represented in hieroglyphics by the jaguar and the serpent (and is also called Jaguar Serpent II), continued Palenque's expansion and artistic development. He presided over the construction of the Grupo de las Cruces temples, placing sizable narrative stone steles within each.

During Kan B'alam II's reign, Palenque extended its zone of control to the Río Usumacinta, but was challenged by the rival Maya city of Toniná, 65km south. Kan B'alam's brother and successor, K'an Joy Chitam II (Precious Peccary), was captured by forces from Toniná in 711, and probably

executed there. Palenque enjoyed a resurgence between 722 and 736, however, under Ahkal Mo' Nahb' III (Turtle Macaw Lake), who added many substantial buildings.

After AD 900, Palenque was largely abandoned. In an area that receives the heaviest rainfall in Mexico, the ruins were soon overgrown, and the city remained unknown to the Western world until 1746, when Maya hunters revealed the existence of a jungle palace to a Spanish priest named Antonio de Solís. Later explorers claimed Palenque was capital of an Atlantis-like civilization. The eccentric Count de Waldeck, who in his 60s lived atop one of the pyramids for two years (1831–33), even published a book with fanciful neoclassical drawings that made the city resemble a great Mediterranean civilization.

It was not until 1837, when John L Stephens, an amateur archaeology enthusiast from New York, reached Palenque with artist Frederick Catherwood, that the site was insightfully investigated. Another century passed before Alberto Ruz Lhuillier, the tireless Mexican archaeologist, uncovered Pakal's hidden crypt in 1952. Today it continues to yield fascinating and beautiful secrets – most recently, a succession of sculptures and frescoes in the Acrópolis del Sur area, which have vastly expanded our knowledge of Palenque's history.

Frans Blom, the mid-20th-century investigator, remarked: 'The first visit to Palenque is immensely impressive. When one has lived there for some time this ruined city becomes an obsession.' It is certainly not hard to understand why.

◉ Sights

Hwy 199 meets Palenque's main street, Avenida Juárez, at the Glorieta de la Cabeza Maya, an intersection with a large statue of a Maya chieftain's head, at the west end of the town. From here Juárez heads 1km east to the central square, El Parque. The main bus stations are on Juárez just east of the Maya head statue.

A few hundred meters south from the Maya head, the paved road to the Palenque ruins, 7.5km away, diverges west off Hwy 199. This road passes the site museum after about 6.5km, then winds on about 1km further uphill to the main entrance to the ruins.

Palenque Ruins ARCHAEOLOGICAL SITE
(admission M$51; ⊙8am-5pm, last entry 4:30pm)
Ancient Palenque stands at the precise point where the first hills rise out of the Gulf

Palenque

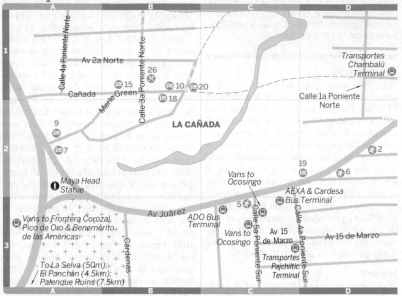

coast plain, and the dense jungle covering these hills forms an evocative backdrop to Palenque's exquisite Maya architecture. Hundreds of ruined buildings are spread over 15 sq km, but only a fairly compact central area has been excavated. Everything you see here was built without metal tools, pack animals or the wheel.

As you explore the ruins, try to picture the gray stone edifices as they would have been at the peak of Palenque's power: painted blood-red with elaborate blue and yellow stucco details. The forest around these temples is still home to howler monkeys, toucans and ocelots. The ruins and surrounding forests form a national park, the Parque Nacional Palenque, for which you must pay a separate M$25 admission fee at Km 4.5 on the road to the ruins.

Palenque sees more than 1000 visitors on an average day, and visitation spikes in the summer holiday season. Opening time is a good time to visit, when it's cooler and not too crowded, and morning mist may still be wrapping the temples in a picturesque haze. Refreshments, hats and souvenirs are available outside the main entrance. Vendors line many of the paths through the ruins.

Official site **guides** (2hr tour for up to 7 people in Spanish/English, French, or Italian

M$600/960) are available by the entrance. Two Maya guide associations offer informative two-hour tours, though French and Italian speakers may have to wait a bit longer as there are fewer guides available.

Most visitors take a combi or taxi to the ruins' main (upper) entrance, see the major structures and then walk downhill to the museum, visiting minor ruins along the way. Note that it's not permitted to exit the site this way before 9am or after 4pm.

Transporte Chambalú (Hidalgo) and **Transportes Palenque** (cnr Allende & Av 20 de Noviembre) run combis to the ruins about every 15 minutes during daylight hours (M$10 each way). They will pick you up or drop you off anywhere along the town-to-ruins road.

Be aware that the mushrooms sold by locals along the road to the ruins from about May to November are the hallucinogenic variety.

Templo de las Inscripciones Group

As you walk in from the entrance, passing to the south of the overgrown Templo XI, the vegetation suddenly peels away to reveal many of Palenque's most magnificent buildings in one sublime vista. A line of temples rises in front of the jungle on your right, culminating in the Templo de las Inscripciones

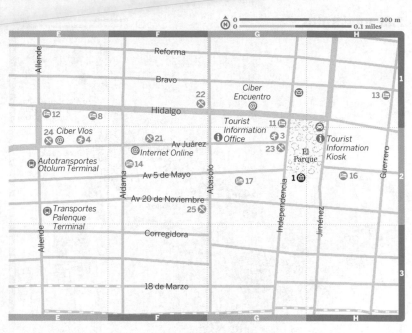

Palenque

⊙ Sights
1 Museo Etnográfico G2

⊙ Activities, Courses & Tours
2 Servicios Turísticos de Palenque D2
3 Transportador Turística
    Scherrer & Barb G2
4 Turística Maya Chiapas E2
5 Viajes Kukulcán C3
6 Viajes Misol-Ha D2

⊙ Sleeping
7 Best Western Maya Palenque
    Hotel A2
8 Hostal San Miguel E1
9 Hotel Cañada Internacional A2
10 Hotel Chablis B1
11 Hotel Chan-Kah Centro G1

12 Hotel Lacandona E1
13 Hotel Lacroix H1
14 Hotel Maya Rue F2
15 Hotel Maya Tulipanes B1
16 Hotel Palenque H2
17 Hotel Posada Tucán G2
18 Hotel Xibalba B1
19 Posada Los Ángeles D2
20 Yaxkin B1

⊙ Eating
21 Aluxes F2
22 Café de Yara F1
23 Mara's G2
24 Pizzería Palenque E2
25 Restaurant Las Tinajas F2
26 Restaurant Maya Cañada B1

about 100m ahead; El Palacio, with its trademark tower, stands to the left of the Templo de las Inscripciones; and the Grupo de las Cruces rises in the distance beneath a thick jungle backdrop.

The first temple on your right is Templo XII, called the **Templo de la Calavera** (Temple of the Skull) for the relief sculpture of a rabbit or deer skull at the foot of one of its pillars. The second temple has little interest. Third is **Templo XIII**, containing a tomb of a female dignitary, whose remains were found colored red (as a result of treatment with cinnabar) when unearthed in 1994. You can enter this Tumba de la Reina Roja (Tomb of the Red Queen) to see her sarcophagus.

Palenque Ruins

Ed Barnhart
2000 ©

With the skeleton were found a malachite mask and about 1000 pieces of jade. Some speculate, from resemblances to Pakal's tomb next door, that the 'queen' buried here was his wife.

The **Templo de las Inscripciones** (Temple of the Inscriptions), perhaps the most celebrated burial monument in the Americas, is the tallest and most stately of Palenque's buildings. Constructed on eight levels, the Templo de las Inscripciones has a central front staircase rising 25m to a series of small rooms. The tall roofcomb that once crowned it is long gone, but between the front doorways are stucco panels with reliefs of noble figures. On the interior rear wall are three panels with the long Maya inscription, recounting the history of Palenque and this building, for which Mexican archaeologist Alberto Ruz Lhuillier named the temple. From the top, interior stairs lead down into the tomb of Pakal (now closed to visitors

indefinitely, to avoid further damage to its murals from the humidity inevitably exuded by visitors). Pakal's jewel-bedecked skeleton and jade mosaic death mask were removed from the tomb to Mexico City, and the tomb was recreated in the Museo Nacional de Antropología. The priceless death mask was stolen in 1985, but the carved stone sarcophagus lid remains in the closed tomb – you can see a replica in the site museum.

The **tomb of Alberto Ruz Lhuillier**, who discovered Pakal's tomb in 1952, lies under the trees in front of Templo XIII.

El Palacio

Diagonally opposite the Templo de las Inscripciones is the **Palace**, a large structure divided into four main courtyards, with a maze of corridors and rooms. Built and modified piecemeal over 400 years from the 5th century on, it probably was the residence of Palenque's rulers. Its tower, built in the 8th century by Ahkal Mo' Nahb' III and

Palenque Ruins

restored in 1955, has remnants of fine stucco reliefs on the walls, but you're not allowed to climb up inside it. Archaeologists believe the tower was constructed so that Maya royalty and priests could observe the sun falling directly into the Templo de las Inscripciones during the winter solstice.

The northeastern courtyard, the **Patio de los Cautivos** (Patio of the Captives), contains a collection of relief sculptures that seem disproportionately large for their setting; the theory is that they represent conquered rulers and were brought from elsewhere.

In the southern part of the complex, the extensive subterranean bathrooms included six toilets and a couple of sweat baths.

Grupo de las Cruces

Pakal's son, Kan B'alam II, was a prolific builder, and soon after the death of his father started designing the temples of the Grupo de las Cruces (Group of the Crosses). All three main pyramid-shaped structures surround a plaza southeast of the Templo de las Inscripciones. They were all dedicated in AD 692 as a spiritual focal point for Palenque's triad of patron deities. The 'cross' carvings in some buildings here symbolize the ceiba tree, which in Maya belief held up the universe.

The **Templo del Sol** (Temple of the Sun), on the west side of the plaza, has the best-preserved roofcomb at Palenque. Carvings inside, commemorating Kan B'alam's birth in AD 635 and accession in 684, show him facing his father. Some view this beautiful building as sure proof that Palenque's ancient architects were inspired by the local

hallucinogenic mushrooms. Make up your own mind!

Steep steps climb to the **Templo de la Cruz** (Temple of the Cross), the largest and most elegantly proportioned in this group. The stone tablet in the central sanctuary shows the lord of the underworld smoking tobacco on the right and Kan B'alam in full royal attire on the left. Behind is a reproduction of a panel depicting Kan B'alam's accession.

On the **Templo de la Cruz Foliada** (Temple of the Foliated Cross), the corbel arches are fully exposed, revealing how Palenque's architects designed these buildings. A well-preserved inscribed tablet shows a king (probably Pakal) with a sun shield emblazoned on his chest, corn growing from his shoulder blades, and the sacred quetzal bird on his head.

Acrópolis Sur

In the jungle south of the Grupo de las Cruces is the **Southern Acropolis**, where archaeologists have made some terrific finds in recent excavations. You may find part of the area roped off. The Acrópolis Sur appears to have been constructed as an extension of the Grupo de las Cruces, with both groups set around what was probably a single long open space.

Templo XVII, between the Cruces group and the Acrópolis Sur, contains a reproduction carved panel depicting Kan B'alam, standing with a spear, with a bound captive kneeling before him (the original is in the site museum).

In 1999, in **Templo XIX**, archaeologists made the most important Palenque find for decades: an 8th-century limestone platform with stunning carvings of seated figures and lengthy hieroglyphic texts that detail Palenque's origins. A reproduction has been placed inside Templo XIX. The central figure on the long south side of the platform is the ruler Ahkal Mo' Nahb' III, who was responsible for several of the buildings of the Acrópolis Sur, just as the Grupo de las Cruces was created by Kan B'alam II. Also on view is a wonderful reproduction of a tall stucco relief of U Pakal, the son of Ahkal Mo' Nahb.'

In **Templo XX**, built in 540, a frescoed tomb of an unknown personage was found in 1999. Ahkal Mo' Nahb' undertook a complete remodeling of this pyramid in the 8th century, but his work was never completed.

In 2002 archaeologists discovered in **Templo XXI** a throne with very fine carvings depicting Ahkal Mo' Nahb,' his ancestor the great Pakal, and his son U Pakal.

Grupo Norte

North of El Palacio is a **ball court** *(juego de pelota)* and the handsome buildings of the Northern Group. Crazy Count de Waldeck (see p373) lived in the so-called **Templo del Conde** (Temple of the Count), constructed in AD 647.

Northeastern Groups

East of the Grupo Norte, the main path crosses Arroyo Otolum. Some 70m beyond the stream, a right fork will take you to **Grupo C**, a set of jungle-covered buildings and plazas thought to have been lived in from about AD 750 to 800.

If you stay on the main path, you'll descend some steep steps to a group of low, elongated buildings, probably occupied residentially from around AD 770 to 850. The path goes alongside the Arroyo Otolum, which here tumbles down a series of small falls forming natural bathing pools known as the **Baño de la Reina** (Queen's Bath). Unfortunately, one can't bathe here anymore.

The path then continues to another residential quarter, the **Grupo de los Murciélagos** (Bat Group), and then crosses the **Puente de los Murciélagos**, a footbridge across Arroyo Otolum.

Across the bridge and a bit further downstream, a path goes west to **Grupos 1 and 2**, a short walk uphill. These ruins, only partly uncovered, are in a beautiful jungle setting. The main path continues downriver to the road, where the museum is a short distance along to the right.

DIGGING DEEPER

» Maya Exploration Center (www.mayaexploration.org) A group of archaeologists, academics and artists who work on Maya sciences such as astronomy and math and offer specialized tours.

» Group of the Cross Project (www.mesoweb.com/palenque) A Palenque archaeologists' site with detailed findings from its landmark 1997–2002 dig.

» INAH (Instituto Nacional de Antropología e Historia; www.inah.gob.mx) The Mexican national antiquities department posts recent news and discoveries, sometimes in English.

Museo de Sitio

(☑345-26-84; Carretera Palenque-Ruinas Km 7; admission free with ruins ticket; ☺9am-4:30pm Tue-Sun) Palenque's site museum is worth a wander, displaying finds from the site and interpreting, in English and Spanish, Palenque's history. Highlights include a blissfully air-conditioned room displaying a copy of the lid of Pakal's sarcophagus (depicting his rebirth as the maize god, encircled by serpents, mythical monsters and glyphs recounting his reign) and recent finds from Templo XXI. Entry permitted every half hour.

El Panchán   LANDMARK

(www.elpanchan.com; Carretera Palenque-Ruinas Km 4.5) Just off the road to the ruins, El Panchán is a legendary travelers' hangout, set in a patch of dense rainforest. It's the epicenter of Palenque's alternative scene and home to a bohemian bunch of Mexican and foreign residents and wanderers, including a number of archaeologists and anthropologists. Once ranchland, the area has been reforested by the remarkable Morales family, some of whom are among the leading archaeological experts on Palenque. El Panchán has several (mostly rustic) places to stay (see p380), a couple of restaurants, a set of sinuous streams rippling their way through every part of the property, nightly entertainment, a meditation temple, a temascal (pre-Hispanic steam bath) and a constant stream of interesting visitors from all over the world.

Museo Etnográfico MUSEUM
(El Parque; M$5 donation requested; ⊙4-9pm Mon-Fri) If you're fascinated by traditional costumes, this small textile museum is an excellent crash course on indigenous clothing in Chiapas. On display are about three dozen ceremonial and everyday outfits, with maps pinpointing their place of origin, language spoken by the community and a description (in Spanish) of the attributes and meaning of each design.

☞ Tours

Numerous travel agencies in Palenque offer transportation packages to Agua Azul and Misol-Ha, to Bonampak, Yaxchilán and Lacanjá, and to Flores, Guatemala (see p384). Agencies, mostly open from around 8am to 9pm daily, include: **Servicios Turísticos de Palenque** (☑345-13-40; www.stpalenque.com; cnr Avs Juárez & 5 de Mayo), **Turística Maya Chiapas** (☑345-07-98; www.tmayachiapas.com. mx; Av Juárez 123), **Viajes Kukulcán** (☑345-15-06; www.kukulcantravel.com; Av Juárez) and **Viajes Misol-Ha** (☑345-22-71; Av Juárez 148).

**Transportador Turística
Scherrer & Barb** TOUR
(☑cell phone 916-1033649; Av Juárez 13) Tours to the remote Lacandón communities of Metzabok and Nahá (day trip M$200, three days M$3000) or Guatemala's Piedras Negras archaeological site (M$2100) with a minimum of four people. English and Italian spoken.

🛏 Sleeping

The first choice to make is whether you want to stay in or out of Palenque town. Most out-of-town places, including El Panchán, are along the road to the ruins. Except for leafy La Cañada, Palenque town is not particularly attractive, but if you stay here you'll have plenty of restaurants and services nearby.

Prices given here are for the high season, which is mid-July to mid-August and mid-December to early January, and Semana Santa. Rates drop by up to 35% at other times.

IN TOWN
Hotel Maya Rue BOUTIQUE HOTEL $$
(☑345-07-43; www.hotelmayaruepalenque.com; Aldama; s/d/tr M$550/600/650; ❂✳🛱) Tree-trunk nightstands and dramatic stairway lighting add unexpected style to this new 12-room offering combining traditional materials and industrial chic. Some rooms have shaded private balconies, and all have cable

TV. A few open architectural details are unsafe for younger children.

Hotel Lacandonia HOTEL $$
(☑345-00-57; www.lacandoniahotel.com; Allende 77; s/d/tr/q M$500/600/700/750; ℗❂✳🛱) A modern hotel with a subtle splash of style. Tasteful, light, airy rooms all have wrought-iron beds, reading lights and cable TV.

Hotel Chan-Kah Centro HOTEL $$
(☑345-03-18; www.chan-kah.com.mx/esp/centro. php; Av Juárez 2; s/d/tr/q M$550/625/695/770; ❂✳🛱) In the center and right on the park, this classy place has 17 air-conditioned and stone-adorned rooms with terraces and a park-view restaurant. The corner rooms are best.

Hotel Cañada Internacional HOTEL $$
(☑345-20-94; www.hotelcanadapalenque.com; Av Juárez, La Cañada; r M$750-850; ℗✳🛱🏊) Bright textiles spiff up four storeys of large, comfortable rooms, all with air-con and two double beds. Vines creep up a small garden courtyard, and there's a petite pool. Rooms in the older section are smaller.

Hotel Xibalba HOTEL $$
(☑345-04-11; www.hotelxibalba.com; Merle Green 9, La Cañada; s/d/tr/q M$650/750/850/950; ℗❂✳@🛱) Preened to perfection by a loving owner, the Xibalba enjoys a tranquil location in two buildings (one with an imitation of the ancient Maya corbel-roof style, the other with a full-sized replica of the lid from Pakal's sarcophagus). All rooms have air-con, cable TV and spotless bathrooms, and the bigger ones boast two double beds and bathtubs.

Hotel Palenque HOTEL $$
(☑345-01-03; www.hotelpalenque.com.mx; Av 5 de Mayo 15; dm/d/tr incl breakfast M$180/850/950; ℗✳@🛱🏊) Traditional Chol weaving patterns spice up the staircases, and all 29 rooms are plain but very clean, with two queen beds. Rooftop dorm dwellers get personal ceiling fans as well as room-wide air-con. The full garden, pretty terrace bar and restaurant are all pleasant spots to relax. Entrance may move to Av 20 de Noviembre.

Hotel Chablis HOTEL $$
(☑345-08-70; www.hotelchablis.com; Merle Green 7, La Cañada; r/tr/q M$920/1020/1120; ℗❂✳@🛱) Opposite the Xibalba, this small hotel offers well-presented, spacious rooms, all with air-con, one king- or two queen-sized

beds and balcony. A new wing will double the hotel's size soon.

Hotel Maya Tulipanes HOTEL $$$

(☎345-02-01, 800-714-47-10; www.mayatulipanes.com.mx; Cañada 6, La Cañada; r/tr M$1290/1390; P🐾✱@🛜🏊) Entered through a muraled foyer, this La Cañada hotel has large, comfortable, air-conditioned rooms with two wrought-iron double beds and minimalist decor. It's designed around a pretty garden with a small pool and restaurant.

Best Western Maya
Palenque Hotel HOTEL $$$

(☎345-07-80; www.bestwestern.com; cnr Av Juárez & Merle Green; r/ste M$1080/1250; P🐾✱@🛜🏊) A comfortable international hotel with good-sized air-conditioned rooms, all with two double beds, cable TV, phone, balcony and plenty of natural light.

Hotel Lacroix HOTEL $$

(☎345-15-35; www.lacroixhotel.wordpress.com; Hidalgo 10; r M$700-800; P🐾✱🛜🏊) New management has remodeled this 16-room hotel near El Parque, and rooms – upper ones with small balconies – sport tasteful sponge-painted peach rooms and attractive murals. There's a large pool with a tinted translucent roof, a casual restaurant and super-friendly service.

Yaxkin HOSTEL $

(☎345-01-02; www.hostalyaxkin.com; Prolongación Hidalgo; hammock M$60, dm M$135-150, r without/with bathroom M$200/300, r with air-con & bathroom M$400-450; ✱🐾@🛜) Channeling laidback El Panchán from pretty La Cañada, this former disco has been revamped into a modern hostel with a guest kitchen, ping-pong table, multiple lounges and a swank restaurant and bar. Rooms without air-con are monastic but funky. The fan-cooled dorms (one for women only) and private rooms with air-con feel more pleasant and comfortable. Shared bathrooms could be cleaner.

Hostal San Miguel HOTEL $

(☎345-01-52; hostalmiguel1@hotmail.com; Hidalgo 43; dm M$120, r with fan/air-com M$400/500; ✱🛜) Who doesn't love a hotel with towel animals? A quiet and clean economical choice; rooms have good light views from the upper floors. Dark two- and four-bed dorms don't have hot water or air-con.

Posada Los Ángeles HOTEL $

(☎345-17-38; Av Juárez s/n; r/tr/q M$250/300/400, s/d/tr/q with air-con M$300/400/500/600; P✱)

This basic option across from the bus terminal has clean good-sized rooms with natural light.

Hotel Posada Tucán HOTEL $

(☎345-18-59; ismahpt@hotmail.com; Av 5 de Mayo 3; r M$250, r/tr/q with air-con M$300/400/450; ✱) Textured walls in primary colors spice up the fair-sized, basic and clean rooms with TV and nicely tiled bathrooms.

OUTSIDE TOWN

While Palenque town hosts traffic and commerce, the surrounding area, especially between town and the ruins, offers some magical spots where howler monkeys romp in the tree canopy and unseen animals chirp after dark. The compound of El Panchán is a travelers' favorite, with low-key budget *cabañas* nestled in the stream-crossed jungle. Frequent combis between town and the ruins will drop you off and pick you up anywhere along this road.

🔝 CHOICE Boutique Hotel Quinta
Chanabnal BOUTIQUE HOTEL $$$

(☎345-53-20; www.quintachanabnal.com; Carretera Palenque-Ruinas Km 2.2; incl breakfast r US$150, ste US$250-350; P🐾✱@🛜🏊) A dramatic jungle hideaway, the Maya temple-inspired architecture and the impeccable service at this luxurious new small hotel will leave you swooning. Enter heavy wood doors carved by local artisans, where spacious stone-floor suites contain majestically draped four-poster beds and cavernous bathrooms. Water features include a creek and small lagoon, a petite pool plus three smaller soaking pools. Massages and a temascal are available. The full restaurant (open to nonguests by reservation) serves international and creative pre-Hispanic dishes (dinner mains US$25). The Italian owner also speaks German, French, English and Spanish.

Margarita & Ed Cabañas GUESTHOUSE $

(☎cell phone 916-3486990, cell phone 916-1119112; El Panchán; cabañas M$250, r/tr M$280/350, r/tr/q with air-con M$400/500/600; ⏱office 7:30am-10pm; P🐾✱) With the most spotless digs in the jungle, Margarita has welcomed travelers to her exceptionally homey place for more than a decade. Bright, clean and cheerful rooms have good mosquito netting, and the more rustic screened *cabañas* are well kept too, with reading lights and private bathrooms. There's free drinking water, a book exchange, and a lovely new building with super-spacious rooms.

Villas Mercedes
LUXURY HOTEL **$$$**

(☑345-52-31; www.hotelesvillamercedes.com; Carretera Palenque-Ruinas Km 2.9; r M$1695, incl breakfast d M$2050, ste M$2950-4650; ⓅⓈ❋🛈⁂) Across the road from the Chan-Kah, this five-star hotel has a dramatic open-air lobby and 92 contemporary rooms bathed in warm colors. Amenities include rainforest showerheads, hair dryers and in-room safes, plus a restaurant, spa and temascal. Deep discounts available outside high season.

Hotel La Aldea del Halach-Huinic
CABAÑAS **$$$**

(☑345-16-93; www.hotellaaldea.net, in Spanish; Carretera Palenque-Ruinas Km 2.8; cabaña M$1200; Ⓟ⊕❋@🛈⁂) Some 3km from town, the Halach-Uinic has 33 *palapa*-roofed *cabañas* in spacious gardens. These air-conditioned accommodations are large and bright, with hammock-draped terraces. They have attractive decorations made from stone, rock and tree branches. It has a small pool and a restaurant.

Nututun Palenque Hotel
HOTEL **$$**

(☑345-01-00; www.nututun.com, in Spanish; Carretera Palenque-Ocosingo Km 3.5; campsites per person M$70, r/tr/ste M$600/700/1500, deluxe r/tr M$800/900; Ⓟ❋@🛈⁂) The Nututun, 3.5km south of town on the road toward San Cristóbal, has spacious, comfortable, air-conditioned rooms in large and exuberant tropical gardens. The new addition is the best value, with stylish modern rooms that trump the more frumpy and pricy 'deluxe' ones. As well as a good pool in the gardens, and a restaurant, there's a wonderful bathing spot (M$25 for nonguests) in the Río Chacamax, which flows through the hotel property.

Chan-Kah Resort Village
RESORT **$$$**

(☑345-11-00; www.chan-kah.com.mx; Carretera Palenque-Ruinas Km 3; r/tr/q M$1770/1890/2010, ste M$2340-4330; ⓅⓈ❋@🛈⁂) Swimmers will go woozy contemplating the Chan-Kah's stupendous 70m stone-lined swimming pool in lush jungle gardens. A quality resort on the road to the ruins, 3km from town, it has handsome well-spaced wood-and-stone cottages with generous bathrooms, ceiling fans, terrace and air-con. It's rarely busy, except when tour groups block-book the place.

Mayabell
CABAÑAS, CAMPGROUND **$**

(☑341-69-77; www.mayabell.com.mx; Carretera Palenque-Ruinas Km 6; hammock shelter or campsite per person M$60, hammock rental M$20, small vehicle without hookups M$30, vehicle site with hookups M$180, treehouse M$120-150, cabaña without bathroom M$300, r with fan/aircon M$750/950; Ⓟ❋🛈⁂) With a sprawling jungle-side pool frequented by monkeys, this spacious grassy campground has tons of clean and comfortable sleeping options – including a crazy ramshackle treehouse – plus an enjoyable restaurant. Rooms with air-con are very homey and comfortable; those with fan are more basic. It's just 400m from Palenque's site museum.

El Jaguar
CABAÑAS **$**

(☑cell phone 916-1192829; www.elpanchan.com; Carretera Palenque-Ruinas Km 4.5; s/d/tr M$220/280/350, s/d cabaña without bathroom M$100/120; Ⓟ) Just across the road from El Panchán, and under the same ownership as Chato's Cabañas, El Jaguar has more open grounds and the same creek running through it. Neat, yellow cabins of wood, plaster and thatch have private bathrooms; simpler ones with mosquito-net windows share clean bathrooms.

Jungle Palace
CABAÑAS **$**

(www.elpanchan.com; El Panchán; s/d/tr M$200/250/300, without bathroom M$100/120/200) A basic option in El Panchán, the Jungle Palace offers rudimentary though well-screened cabins with fans, some of which back onto a stream. The best are freestanding, while others share walls and have less privacy.

Chato's Cabañas
CABAÑAS **$**

(☑cell phone 916-1092829; www.elpanchan.com; El Panchán; s/d M$220/300; Ⓟ) Chato's wood and concrete cabins, dotted around the Panchán jungle, all have screened windows and fans, and some have nice little porches.

Mono Blanco
CABAÑAS **$**

(☑cell phone 916-3484299; El Panchán; dm M$60, r with/without bathroom M$150/120; ⊕) Very basic screened-in cement-and-wood structures barely keep out the insects (rent a net). The shared cold-water bathrooms are dark with barely opaque shower-curtain doors. Has an onsite restaurant with live music.

✖ Eating

Palenque is definitely not the gastronomic capital of Mexico. There's a decent variety of restaurants, though some are laughably overpriced. A number of inexpensive stands and sit-down spots can be found near the ADO and AEXA bus terminals.

TOP CHOICE **Don Mucho's** INTERNATIONAL $$
(El Panchán; mains M$50-120; ⊙7am-11pm) The hot spot of El Panchán, popular Don Mucho's provides great-value meals in a jungly setting, with a candlelit ambience at night. Busy waiters bring pasta, fish, meat, plenty of *antojitos,* and pizzas (cooked in a purpose-built Italian-designed wood-fired oven) that are some of the finest this side of Naples. Live music – usually *andina, cumbia* or Cuban – starts around 8pm, plus there's a rousing fire-dancing show most nights at 11pm.

Restaurant Las Tinajas MEXICAN $$
(cnr Av 20 de Noviembre & Abasolo; mains M$75-110; ⊙7am-11pm; ⊜) It doesn't take long to figure out why this place is always busy. It slings enormous portions of excellent home-style food, and it's enough to keep you (and possibly another person) fueled up for hours. *Pollo a la veracruzana* (chicken in a tomato/olives/onion sauce) and *camarones al guajillo* (shrimp with a not-too-hot type of chili) are both delicious, as is the house salsa.

Café de Yara CAFE, BREAKFAST $
(Hidalgo 66; snacks & breakfasts M$38-70, mains M$64-100; ⊙7am-11pm; ☎) A sunny start to the day, this modern and beautiful corner cafe has great breakfasts and excellent organic Chiapan coffee. On Friday and Saturday evenings in high season, the lights get intimate and diners are serenaded with salsa and other live music.

La Selva MEXICAN $$
(☑345-03-63; www.laselvarestaurante.com.mx, in Spanish; Hwy 199; mains M$65-195; ⊙11:30am-11:30pm; ⊜) Palenque's most upscale restaurant serves up well-prepared steaks, seafood, salads and *antojitos* under an enormous *palapa* roof, with jungle-themed stained-glass panels brightening one wall. Try the *pigua* (freshwater lobster) when it's available in the fall. Reserve ahead in high season.

Restaurant Maya Cañada MEXICAN $$
(Merle Green s/n; breakfast M$60-95, mains M$82-180; ⊙7am-midnight) This relatively upmarket and professionally run restaurant in the shady La Cañada area serves fine steaks and terrific seafood kebabs. It's open to the air and has a cool upstairs terrace.

Aluxes MEXICAN $$
(Av Juárez 49; mains M$80-100; ⊙12:30pm-midnight; ⊜) An upstairs restaurant overlooking the main street, Aluxes offers Angus steaks, pastas and seafood dishes under a thatched *palapa* roof. Drop in for evening cocktails at its cute cafe tables.

Mara's MEXICAN $$
(Av Juárez 1; mains M$90-135; ⊙7am-11pm; ☎) On a corner across from the park, this brightly painted traditional restaurant has a great location. It offers a good range of meat, fish and chicken dishes, and patrons can catch an ever-so-welcome tropical breeze.

Pizzería Palenque PIZZERIA $$
(☑345-03-32; Av Juárez 168; pasta M$57-62, pizzas from M$88; ⊙1-11pm) Light wood tables add some sparkle to this very popular pizza place with tasty pies and pastas. Don't feel like leaving your room? Delivery is available in the center of town.

Drinking & Entertainment

Palenque doesn't have much of a nightlife scene. In the evenings, you'll often spot more travelers waiting for a night bus than out on the town. In town, the Aluxes restaurant serves interesting cocktails, and some options – including a karaoke bar at the Hotel Maya Tulipanes – can be found by poking around La Cañada. Along the ruins road, you can listen to live music at Mayabell, and Don Mucho's has hip-swinging live ensembles plus fire dancers performing nightly. Bars in the center tend toward the unsavory.

Information

Immigration
Instituto Nacional de Migración (⊙24hr) About 6km north of town on Hwy 199; reached by 'Playas' combis from the Autotransportes Otolum terminal on Allende (M$15).

Internet Access
There are loads of internet cafes in town (nothing is available at El Panchán); rates run M$6 to M$10 per hour. The main plaza, El Parque, is a free wi-fi hotspot.
Ciber Encuentro (Hidalgo; ⊙7:30am-10pm)
Ciber Vlos (Av Juárez 133; ⊙8am-10pm)
Internet Online (Av Juárez; ⊙7:30am-10pm)

Medical Services
Clínica Palenque (☑345-02-73; Velasco Suárez 33; ⊙8am-2pm & 5-8pm) Dr Alfonso Martínez speaks English.

BUSES FROM PALENQUE

DESTINATION	FARE (M$)	DURATION	FREQUENCY (DAILY)
Campeche	284	5-5½hr	4 ADO
Cancún	250-652	12-13½hr	4 ADO, 1 AEXA
Mérida	420-506	8hr	5 ADO
Mexico City	870-882	13½hr	2 ADO
Oaxaca	640	15hr	1 ADO
Ocosingo	50-178	2½hr	10 ADO, 6 AEXA, very frequent vans
San Cristóbal de las Casas	90-178	5hr	10 ADO, 6 AEXA
Tenosique	50	2hr	Transportes Palenque vans hourly 5am-7pm
Tulum	550-656	10-11hr	6 ADO
Tuxtla Gutiérrez	125-258	6½hr	5 ADO, 6 AEXA
Villahermosa	60-126	2½hr	17 ADO, 16 AEXA
Villahermosa airport	224	2¼ hr	12 ADO

Money

Both these banks change dollars and euros (bring a copy of your passport) and have ATMs.
Banamex (Av Juárez 62; ⊘9am-4pm Mon-Sat)
Bancomer (Av Juárez 96; ⊘8:30am-4pm Mon-Fri)

Post

Post office (Independencia; ⊘8am-8:30pm Mon-Fri, to noon Sat)

Tourist Information

State tourism office (⊘345-03-56; ⊘8am-4pm Mon-Fri) Located outside the center, but can answer questions by phone.
Tourist information kiosk (El Parque; ⊘9am-2pm & 6-9pm Mon-Fri)
Tourist information office (cnr Av Juárez & Abasolo; ⊘9am-9pm Mon-Sat, 9am-1pm Sun) Has the most reliable town, regional and transportation information, as well as maps.

Websites

Head to **Lonely Planet** (www.lonelyplanet. com/mexico/tabasco-and-chiapas/palenque) for planning advice, author recommendations, traveler reviews and insider tips.

ⓘ Getting There & Away

Though an increased military and police presence has made this route pretty safe, highway holdups still occasionally occur on Hwy 199 between Palenque and San Cristóbal de las Casas. It's not advisable to travel on this road at night.

Air

Palenque's airport has no commercial flights. The closest major airport is Villahermosa; ADO runs direct airport service in comfortable minibuses.

Bus

ADO (Av Juárez) has the main bus terminal, with deluxe and 1st-class services, an ATM and left-luggage facilities; it's also used by OCC (1st class). It's a good idea to buy your outward bus ticket a day in advance.

AEXA (Av Juárez 159), with 1st-class buses, and Cardesa (2nd class) are 1½ blocks east.

Colectivos

Vans to Ocosingo (M$50) wait on Calle 5a Poniente Sur, near the bus stations, and leave when full.

Transportes Pajchiltic (Av 15 de Marzo) vans leave for the isolated Lacandón communities of Metzabok (M$35, three hours) at 9am, 11am and 1pm, and Nahá (M$45, four hours) at 9am and 1pm. Note that the solitary departure back leaves Nahá at 1am and Metzabok at 3am (ouch!), and schedules don't use daylight savings time in either direction.

Transportes Palenque (cnr Allende & Av 20 de Noviembre) runs vans to Tenosique, Tabasco, which has onward connections to Flores, Guatemala via El Ceibo, Mexico.

Combis for destinations along the Carretera Fronteriza (Lacanjá Chansayab, Bonampak, Yaxchilán and other destinations) leave from an outdoor terminal adjacent to the Maya head statue. See p397 for information.

ⓘ Getting Around

Taxis wait at the northeast corner of El Parque and at the ADO bus station; they charge M$50 (up to M$60 at night) to El Panchán or Mayabell, and M$60 to the ruins. Combis (M$10) from the center ply the ruins road til dark. **Radio Taxis Santo Domingo** (☏345-01-26) has an on-call service.

Bonampak, Yaxchilán & the Carretera Fronteriza

The ancient Maya cities of Bonampak and Yaxchilán, southeast of Palenque, are easily accessible thanks to the Carretera Fronteriza, a good paved road running parallel to the Mexico–Guatemala border, all the way from Palenque to the Lagos de Montebello, around the fringe of the Lacandón Jungle. Bonampak, famous for its frescoes, is 152km by road from Palenque; the bigger and more important Yaxchilán, with a peerless jungle setting beside the broad and swift Río Usumacinta, is 173km by road, then about 22km by boat.

The Carretera Fronteriza is the main thoroughfare connecting a number of excellent ecotourism projects including some in the Lacandón village of Lacanjá Chansayab (p386) as well as the wonderful Las Guacamayas ecolodge (boxed text p390) and the gorgeous watery wonderland at Las Nubes (p389). For information on other ecotourism projects in the area, check out www.laselvadechiapas.com. In addition, the Carretera Fronteriza is the main route from Chiapas to Guatemala's northern Petén region (home of several major Maya sites, including mighty Tikal) via the town of Frontera Corozal. Phones in this region usually have satellite service or Guatemala-based numbers.

⚑ Tours

There aren't a lot of private cars traveling this area, and though it's perfectly possible to visit here independently and to travel through to Guatemala, there are also tour options. Many Palenque travel agencies run day tours to Bonampak and Yaxchilán for around M$600 to M$650 per person, usually including entry fees, two meals and transportation in an air-conditioned van. There's also a two-day version for around M$1100 to M$1300, with an overnight stay at Lacanjá Chansayab. Most of the same agencies offer transportation packages from Palenque to Flores, Guatemala – usually via an air-conditioned van to Frontera Corozal, river launch up the Usumacinta to Bethel in Guatemala, and public bus on to Flores. This takes 10 or 11 hours altogether, for around M$300 to M$350. Two-day packages to Flores, visiting Bonampak and Yaxchilán en route, are around M$1100 to M$1300. Always check package inclusions and exclusions, so you can plan your meals and not find yourself digging around to pay for unanticipated park fees.

The **Mesoamerican Ecotourism Alliance** (www.travelwithmea.org) organizes all-inclusive trips to the region, including the Lacandón villages of Nahá and Metzabok, and San Cristóbal–based SendaSur (see p357) can help with reservations for independent travelers.

Dangers & Annoyances

Drug trafficking and illegal immigration are facts of life in this border region, and the Carretera Fronteriza more or less encircles the main area of Zapatista rebel activity and support, so expect numerous military checkpoints along the road and from this area to Palenque and Comitán. These checkpoints generally increase security for travelers, but don't tempt easy theft by leaving money or valuables unattended during stops. For your own security, it's best to be off the Carretera Fronteriza before dusk – especially the most isolated section in the far southeast, between Benemérito de las Américas and the Chajul turnoff. For similar reasons all border crossings with Guatemala are places you should aim to get through early in the day.

Don't forget insect repellent.

ⓘ Getting There & Away

From Palenque, vans run to Frontera Corozal (M$100, 2½ to three hours, hourly), and to Benemérito (M$100, 3½ hours, every 40 minutes from 4am to 5pm), leaving from a small terminal behind the Maya head statue.

Línea Comitán Lagos de Montebello (Velasco Suárez s/n), a few blocks west of Palenque

HORA DE DIOS

This part of Mexico tends to ignore daylight saving time, as do *colectivo* companies that originate in cities like Comitán and Palenque that service the region. From April through October, check your watch against the company's to double-check transportation schedules. If they're using 'God's time,' you'll be departing an hour later than the official 'government time.'

market, also runs hourly vans to Benemérito (M$100) 10 times daily (3:30am to 2:45pm), with the first five continuing round the Carretera Fronteriza to the Lagos de Montebello (M$220, seven hours to Tziscao) and Comitán (M$260, eight hours).

All these services stop at San Javier (M$60, two hours), the turnoff for Lacanjá Chansayab and Bonampak, 140km from Palenque, and at Crucero Corozal (M$70, 2½ hours), the intersection for Frontera Corozal.

There are no gas stations on the Carretera Fronteriza, but plenty of entrepreneurial locals sell reasonably priced gasoline from large plastic containers. Look for homemade 'Se vende gasolina' signs.

BONAMPAK

Bonampak's setting in dense jungle hid it from the outside world until 1946. Stories of how it was revealed are full of mystery and innuendo, but it seems that Charles Frey, a young WWII conscientious objector from the US, and John Bourne, heir to the Singer sewing-machine fortune, were the first outsiders to visit the site when Chan Bor, a Lacandón, took them there in February 1946. Later in 1946 an American photographer, Giles Healey, was also led to the site by Chan Bor and found the Templo de las Pinturas, with its famous murals.

The site of **Bonampak** (admission M$41; ⊙8am-5pm) spreads over 2.4 sq km, but all the main ruins stand around the rectangular Gran Plaza. Never a major city, Bonampak spent most of the Classic period in Yaxchilán's sphere of influence. The most impressive surviving monuments were built under Chan Muwan II, a nephew of Yaxchilán's Itzamnaaj B'alam II, who acceded to Bonampak's throne in AD 776. The 6m-high **Stele 1** in the Gran Plaza depicts Chan Muwan holding a ceremonial staff at the height of his reign. He also features in **Stele 2** and **Stele 3** on the Acrópolis, which rises from the south end of the plaza.

However, it's the vivid frescoes (made even more colorful by recent restoration work) inside the modest-looking **Templo de las Pinturas** (Edificio 1) that have given Bonampak its fame – and its name, which means 'Painted Walls' in Yucatecan Maya.

Diagrams outside the temple help interpret these murals, which are the finest known from pre-Hispanic America, but which have weathered badly since their discovery. (Early visitors even chucked kerosene over the walls in an attempt to bring out the colors!) Room 1, on the left as you

Bonampak

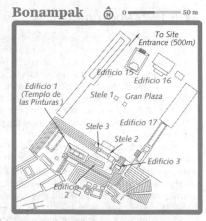

face the temple, shows the consecration of Chan Muwan II's infant son, who is seen held in arms toward the top of the right end of the room's south wall (facing you as you enter). Witnessing the ceremony are 14 jade-toting noblemen. The central Room 2 shows tumultuous battle scenes on its east and south walls and vault, while on the north wall Chan Muwan II, in jaguar-skin battle dress, presides over the torture (by fingernail removal) and sacrifice of prisoners. A severed head lies below him, beside the foot of a sprawling captive. Room 3 shows a celebratory dance on the Acrópolis steps by lords wearing huge headdresses, and on its east wall three white-robed women puncture their tongues in a ritual bloodletting. The sacrifices, the bloodletting and the dance may all have been part of the ceremonies surrounding the new heir.

In reality, the infant prince probably never got to rule Bonampak; the place was abandoned before the murals were finished, as Classic Maya civilization evaporated.

The Bonampak site abuts the Reserva de la Biosfera Montes Azules, and is rich in wildlife. Drinks and snacks are sold at the entrance to the Monumento Natural Bonampak protected zone, 8km before the ruins, and by the archaeological site entrance.

ⓘ Getting There & Away

Bonampak is 12km from San Javier on the Carretera Fronteriza. The first 3km, to the Lacanjá Chansayab turnoff, is paved, and the rest is good gravel/dirt road through the forest. Taxis from San Javier or the Lacanjá turnoff charge an exorbitant M$80 (one person) or M$150 (two people) to the ruins and back. Private vehicles

THE LACANDÓN JUNGLE

Chiapas contains swathes of wild green landscape that have nourished its inhabitants for centuries. But this rich trove of natural resources also makes it a contentious prize in the struggle for its water, lumber and oil and gas reserves.

The Selva Lacandona (Lacandón Jungle), in eastern Chiapas, occupies just one-quarter of 1% of Mexico. Yet it contains more than 4300 plant species (about 17% of the Mexican total), 450 butterfly species (42% of the national total), at least 340 bird species (32% of the total) and 163 mammal species (30% of the Mexican total). Among these are such emblematic creatures as the jaguar, red macaw, white turtle, tapir and harpy eagle.

This great fund of natural resources and genetic diversity is the southwest end of the Selva Maya, a 30,000-sq-km corridor of tropical rainforest stretching from Chiapas across northern Guatemala into Belize and the southern Yucatán. But the Lacandón Jungle is shrinking fast, under pressure from ranchers, loggers, oil prospectors, and farmers desperate for land. From around 15,000 sq km in the 1950s, an estimated 3000 to 4500 sq km of jungle remains today. Waves of land-hungry settlers deforested the northern third of the Lacandón Jungle by about 1960. Also badly deforested are the far eastern Marqués de Comillas area (settled since the 1970s) and Las Cañadas, between Ocosingo and Montes Azules. Most of what's left is in the Reserva de la Biosfera Montes Azules and the neighboring Reserva de la Biosfera Lacan-tun.

The Mexican government deeded a large section of the land to a small number of Lacandón families in the 1970s, creating tensions with other indigenous communities whose claims were put aside. Land within the region remains incredibly contested. Lacandones and their advocates consider themselves to be an environmentally sensitive indigenous group defending their property against invasive settlers. Other communities within the reserve, who provide some of the Zapatista rebels' strongest support, view it as an obfuscated land grab and pretext for eviction under the guise of environmental protection. Zapatista supporters also argue that the settlers are using the forests in sustainable ways, and claim that the government seeks to exploit the forests for bio-prospecting (patenting) traditional plants.

cannot pass the Monumento Natural Bonampak entrance, 1km past the Lacanjá turnoff.

LACANJÁ CHANSAYAB
POP 380 / ELEV 320M

Lacanjá Chansayab, the largest Lacandón Maya village, is 6km from San Javier on the Carretera Fronteriza, and 12km from Bonampak. Its family compounds are scattered around a wide area, many of them with creeks or even the Río Lacanjá flowing past their grassy grounds. Nights here are wonderfully quiet, the sky screaming with stars and the ground twinkling with fireflies. Tourism is now an important income earner, and many families run *'campamentos'* with rooms, camping and hammock space. As you approach the village, you'll cross the Río Lacanjá on a bridge, from which it's about 700m to a central intersection where tracks go left (south), right (north) and straight (west).

The *campamentos* all offer guided walks through the surrounding forests to the 8m-high, 30m-wide **Cascada Ya Toch Kusam** waterfall, some partially unearthed ancient Maya **Lacanjá ruins**, and the 2.5km-long **Laguna Lacanjá**. The waterfall can actually be reached by a self-guiding trail, the 2.5km **Sendero Ya Toch Kusam** (admission M$35), which starts 200m west from the central intersection. To continue from the fall to the ruins (a further 2km or so), you do need a guide. A typical three-hour guided walk to the fall and ruins costs M$250 to M$500 per group, plus the admission fee for the trail.

The Lacandón people are amiable and welcoming, though don't expect to find much evidence of their old way of life: the villagers here are now predominantly Presbyterian and attuned to the modern world, and only some wear the traditional long white Lacandón tunic. Some have developed their traditional crafts into commercial *artesanías,* and you may want to budget some pesos for the pottery, woodcarvings, seed necklaces, arrows and drums that they sell.

📛 Sleeping & Eating

The *campamentos* mentioned here are just a selection from almost a dozen located nearby. Rates dip at least 10% outside the high season.

Campamento Río Lacanjá   CABAÑAS $$
(www.ecochiapas.com/lacanja, in Spanish; dm M$170, d without bathroom M$400, Ya'ax Can s/d/tr/q M$550/650/750/850; P) About 2km south of the central intersection, these rustic semi-open-air wood-framed cabins with mosquito nets stand close to the jungle-shrouded Río Lacanjá and are open to the sounds and sights of the forest and river. A separate group of large rooms with fans, called Cabañas Ya'ax Can, have two solid wooden double beds, tile floors and a hot-water bathroom. There's also a restaurant here serving all meals (M$60 to M$70). As well as guided walks, rafting trips on the Río Lacanjá – which has waterfalls up to 2.5m high but no rapids – are offered for a minimum of four people. A half-day outing including Lacanjá ruins and Cascada Ya Toch Kusam (both reached on foot from the river) costs M$700 per person; an overnight rafting and camping trip also visiting Bonampak ruins is around M$1250 per person. Rafting trips and tours staying at Campamento Río Lacanjá can be reserved through Explora (p357) in San Cristóbal.

Campamento Topche   CABAÑAS $$
(campamento-topche@hotmail.com; r without bathroom M$150, r/tr M$700/800; P🖨@) Fronted by mature papaya trees, this *campamento* about 550m west of the central intersection has three comfortable rooms with terracotta tile floors, hot-water bathrooms and a vaulted and mosquito-proofed *palapa* roof; and four grim barnlike rooms with shared bathroom. There's even internet access, available by satellite, for M$20 per hour. *Topche* is the Lacandón Maya name for a regional wildflower, though the signs to here also say 'Campamento Enrique Paniagua.'

Centro de Alimentos Chankin   MEXICAN $
(meals M$55-70; ⊙7am-9pm) Bordering Enrique Paniagua's *campamento,* this good garden restaurant is run by his daughter. Fragrant walls of flowers attract swarms of hyperactive hummingbirds.

❶ Getting There & Away

From San Javier, a taxi to Lacanjá Chansayab costs M$40 for one person, M$80 for two; combis to Crucero Corozal charge M$30 from San Javier.

FRONTERA COROZAL
POP 5200 / ELEV 200M

This riverside frontier town (formerly Frontera Echeverría) is the stepping-stone to the beautiful ruins of Yaxchilán, and is on the main route between Chiapas and Guatemala's Petén region. Inhabited mainly by Chol Maya, who settled here in the 1970s, Frontera Corozal is 16km by paved road from Crucero Corozal junction on the Carretera Fronteriza. The broad Río Usumacinta, flowing swiftly between jungle-covered banks, forms the Mexico–Guatemala border here.

Long, fast, outboard-powered *lanchas* (motorboats) come and go from the river *embarcadero*. Almost everything you'll need is on the paved street leading back from the river here – including the **immigration office** (⊙8am-4pm), 400m from the *embarcadero,* where you should hand in/obtain a tourist permit if you're leaving for/arriving from Guatemala.

The neat and modern **Museo de la Cuenca del Usumacinta** (Museum of the Usumacinta Basin; admission M$10; ⊙8am-3pm), opposite the immigration office, has good examples of Chol Maya dress, and some information in Spanish on the area's postconquest history, but pride of place goes to two fine and intricately carved steles retrieved from the nearby site of Dos Caobas.

📛 Sleeping & Eating

Nueva Alianza   CABAÑAS, CAMPGROUND $$
(☑in Guatemala 502-4638-2447; www.hotelnuevaalianza.com; campsite per person M$40, s/d without bathroom M$120/240, r M$500-600, f M$700; P@) Friendly, Chol-run Nueva Alianza, among trees 150m along a side road from the museum, has small, plain but cheerful budget rooms with wooden walls that don't reach the ceiling, and newer stand-alone rooms with bathrooms. All have fans, good wooden furniture and hot water. There's a good onsite restaurant (mains M$70, breakfast M$65) and the only internet access in town (M$15 per hour).

Escudo Jaguar   CABAÑAS $$
(☑in Guatemala 502-5353-5637; www.escudojaguarhotel.com; campsite per person M$85; d cabaña without bathroom M$278-345, d cabaña M$512-770, tr cabaña M$937; P) Also run by a local Chol organization, and often used by tour groups, Escudo Jaguar overlooks the river 300m from the *embarcadero.*

Its solidly built thatched *cabañas* are all kept spotless, and come equipped with fan and mosquito net. The best are very spacious and have hot showers and terraces strung with hammocks. The **restaurant** (mains M$33-77, breakfasts M$31-64, ⊙7am-8pm) serves straightforward, but well-prepared Mexican dishes.

Restaurante Imperio Maya   MEXICAN $
(mains M$65-85; ⊙7:30am-3pm) Attached to the museum, this spacious *palapa*-topped restaurant has a lengthy menu and caters to Yaxchilán-bound tourists.

❶ Getting There & Away

If you can't get a bus or combi direct to Frontera Corozal, get one to Crucero Corozal, 16km southeast of San Javier on the Carretera Fronteriza, where taxis (M$20 per person *colectivo*) run to Frontera Corozal. The *ejido* hits up visitors entering or leaving Frontera Corozal for a M$15 per person toll; keep your ticket for exiting unless you're continuing on to Guatemala.

Autotransporte Chamoán vans run hourly from Frontera Corozal *embarcadero* to Palenque (M$100, 2½ to three hours), with the last departure at 4 or 5pm or when full.

Lanchas leave for Bethel (40 minutes upstream) on the Guatemalan bank of the Usumacinta. **Lancha organizations** (boat to Bethel for 1-3/4/5-7/8-10 people M$400/500/600/750) have desks in a thatched building near the embarcadero, and all charge about the same prices. *Colectivo lanchas* (M$50) also go to La Técnica, directly opposite Frontera Corozal, but there are very few onward buses.

Hourly buses depart from Bethel to Flores (4½ hours) from 4am to 5pm. Make sure that the driver stops at the Bethel immigration office.

YAXCHILÁN

Jungle-shrouded **Yaxchilán** (admission M$49; ⊙8am-4:30pm, last entry 3:30pm) has a terrific setting above a horseshoe loop in the Río Usumacinta. The location gave it control over the river commerce, and along with a series of successful alliances and conquests, made Yaxchilán one of the most important Classic Maya cities in the Usumacinta region. Archaeologically, Yaxchilán is famed for its ornamented facades and roofcombs, and its impressive stone lintels carved with conquest and ceremonial scenes. A flashlight is helpful for exploring parts of the site.

Howler monkeys *(saraguates)* inhabit the tall trees here, and are an evocative highlight. You'll almost certainly hear their visceral roars, and you stand a good chance of seeing some. Spider monkeys, and occasionally red macaws, can also be spotted here at times.

Yaxchilán peaked in power and splendor between AD 681 and 800 under the rulers Itzamnaaj B'alam II (Shield Jaguar II,

Yaxchilán

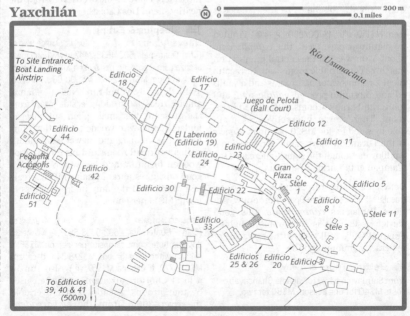

681–742), Pájaro Jaguar IV (Bird Jaguar IV, 752–68) and Itzamnaaj B'alam III (Shield Jaguar III, 769–800). The city was abandoned around AD 810. Inscriptions here tell more about its 'Jaguar' dynasty than is known of almost any other Maya ruling clan. The shield-and-jaguar symbol appears on many Yaxchilán buildings and steles; Pájaro Jaguar IV's hieroglyph is a small jungle cat with feathers on its back and a bird superimposed on its head.

At the site, drinks are sold at a shack near the river landing. Most of the main monuments have information boards in three languages, including English.

◉ **Sights**

As you walk toward the ruins, a signed path to the right leads up to the **Pequeña Acrópolis**, a group of ruins on a small hilltop – you can visit this later. Staying on the main path, you soon reach the mazelike passages of **El Laberinto** (Edificio 19), built between AD 742 and 752, during the interregnum between Itzamnaaj B'alam II and Pájaro Jaguar IV. Dozens of bats shelter under the structure's roof today. From this complicated two-level building you emerge at the northwest end of the extensive **Gran Plaza**.

Though it's difficult to imagine anyone here ever wanting to be any hotter than they already were, **Edificio 17** was apparently a sweat house. About halfway along the plaza, **Stele 1**, flanked by weathered sculptures of a crocodile and a jaguar, shows Pájaro Jaguar IV in a ceremony that took place in AD 761. **Edificio 20**, from the time of Itzamnaaj B'alam III, was the last significant structure built at Yaxchilán; its lintels are now in Mexico City. **Stele 11**, at the northeast corner of the Gran Plaza, was originally found in front of Edificio 40. The bigger of the two figures visible on it is Pájaro Jaguar IV.

An imposing stairway climbs from Stele 1 to **Edificio 33**, the best-preserved temple at Yaxchilán, with about half of its roofcomb intact. The final step in front of the building is carved with ball-game scenes, and splendid relief carvings embellish the undersides of the lintels. Inside is a statue of Pájaro Jaguar IV, minus his head, which he lost to treasure-seeking 19th-century timber cutters.

From the clearing behind Edificio 33, a path leads into the trees. About 20m along this, fork left uphill; go left at another fork after about 80m, and in some 10 minutes, mostly going uphill, you'll reach three buildings on a hilltop: **Edificio 39**, **Edificio 40** and **Edificio 41**.

ℹ️ **Getting There & Away**

Lanchas take 40 minutes running downstream from Frontera Corozal, and one hour to return. The boat companies operate desks in a thatched building near the Frontera Corozal *embarcadero*, all charging about the same prices for trips (return journey with 2½ hours at the ruins for 1-3/4/5-7/8-10 people M$700/800/950/1300). *Lanchas* normally leave frequently until 1:30pm or so; try to hook up with other travelers or a tour group to share costs.

BENEMÉRITO DE LAS AMÉRICAS TO LAGOS DE MONTEBELLO

South of Frontera Corozal is the far eastern corner of Chiapas known as Marqués de Comillas (for its Spanish former landowner). After oil explorers opened tracks into this jungle region in the 1970s, settlers poured in from all over Mexico. Ranching and logging have made some rich, while others profit from smuggling drugs or immigrants. Rough-and-ready Benemérito de las Américas is the region's main town.

Las Nubes
ECOLODGE **$$**

(🖉in Guatemala 502-4972-0204; campsites per person M$40, cabaña M$750; 🅿) A bit of a trek but well worth it, Las Nubes is a heavenly retreat among scores of cascades and rapids on the turquoise Río Santo Domingo. Some of the river pools are great swimming spots – it's M$20 per person to swim here if you're not staying the night. A swinging bridge straddles a fierce section of water-carved canyon, making an excellent vantage point from which to swoon over the grandest waterfalls. There's an adrenaline-pumping zipline (M$75), and you can spelunk and rappel from February through June. A 15-minute hike up to a *mirador* rewards you with blue-green jungle views.

Fifteen well-built *cabañas* have hot water and pleasant porches, and an open restaurant serves meals (breakfast and lunch M$50, dinner M$90), but no alcohol, though you can bring your own.

Las Nubes is 12km off the Carretera Fronteriza, 55km from Tziscao. From Transportes Tzoyol in Comitán, there are four daily combis (M$60, 3½ to four hours) between 7:30am and 4pm, and four daily returns. From Embarcadero Jerusalén, just east of the Las Nubes highway turnoff (and on the combi route), you can raft to the compound for about M$2000 (two to six passengers).

DON'T MISS

LAS GUACAMAYAS

In the small village of Reforma Agraria, 49km southwest of Benemérito, the beautiful ecolodge of **Las Guacamayas** (☎55-5905-4363; www.lasguacamayas.mx; Ejido Reforma Agraria; dm M$264, cabaña M$1320-1620, ste M$1920; 🄿🖳🛜💧) is the heart of an impressive community program to protect the local population of scarlet macaws. This spectacular and endangered member of the parrot family once ranged as far north as Veracruz, but its only Mexican home today is far eastern Chiapas. Numbers at Reforma Agraria have increased to more than 100 pairs since 1991, when the 14.5-sq-km macaw reserve was founded. The birds move in and out of the reserve in seasonal pursuit of food; the best months for observing them are December to June, when they are nesting.

The very friendly and welcoming lodge is right on the bank of the broad Río Lacantún, one of the Usumacinta's major tributaries, with the Reserva de la Biosfera Montes Azules on the opposite bank. Large, superbly comfortable, thatch-roofed *cabañas,* with full mosquito screens, verandas and ample bathrooms with hot showers, are spread around the extensive grounds, linked by wooden walkways. Dorms are shared two-bed rooms with common bathrooms. There's a good restaurant overlooking the river, serving good Mexican meals (mains M$60 to M$130). From March through May, the river level drops and you can swim and take advantage of a sandy beach area.

Two-hour guided macaw-spotting walks cost M$900; they're best in the early morning or at dusk. Boat trips into the Montes Azules reserve cost M$1744/1944 for two/three hours. You should spot crocodiles and howler monkeys, and with luck toucans and white-tailed deer. Villagers in Reforma Agraria also rent out horses for about M$100 per hour, and charge about M$50 per person to camp. In low season, all prices drop around 20% and include breakfast.

Getting There & Away

The road to Reforma Agraria turns west off the Carretera Fronteriza 8km south of Benemérito. It's paved all the way through, rejoining the Carretera Fronteriza 5km south of Chajul, though large (but navigable) potholes, messy rainy-season mudslides and the occasional crumbling of the shoulder pavement will keep your eyes on the road.

From a small terminal near the Maya head statue in Palenque, combis run to Pico de Oro (M$120, four hours) at 8am, 10am, noon and 2pm. Occasional *camionetas* also run between Benemérito and Pico de Oro (M$40, 30 minutes), though you'll often have to hire a taxi (M$40 per person *colectivo* or M$150 private) if it's past early morning. *Camionetas* run from Pico de Oro to Reforma Agraria (M$25, 30 minutes), and vice versa, about hourly from 6am until early afternoon. A taxi from Benemérito to Reforma Agraria costs around M$300.

From Comitán 16 vans a day (see p393) run to Reforma Agraria (M$130, 4½ hours), passing through the Lagos de Montebello en route, though only those from Transportes Tzoyol will drop you off directly in front of Las Guacamayas. Otherwise it's a 1km walk in from the road.

Comitán

☎963 / POP 98,000 / ELEV 1560M

With a pretty plaza of modern sculpture pieces and mature flat-topped trees where birds flock and chirp in the evening, the colonial town of Comitán has a pleasant, artsy atmosphere. Set on a high plain 90km southeast of San Cristóbal, Comitán contains some good places to stay and eat, a few interesting museums, and several natural and archaeological attractions less than an hour away in the surrounding big-sky countryside.

Sights

Iglesia de Santo Domingo　　CHURCH
(◷8am-2pm & 4:30-8pm) On the plaza, the Iglesia de Santo Domingo dates back to the 16th and 17th centuries, and sports unusual and handsome blind arcading on its tower. Its former monastic buildings next door are now the **Centro Cultural Rosario Castellanos** (admission free; ◷9am-8pm Mon-Fri,

10am-6pm Sat, 10am-2pm Sun), which has a pretty wood-pillared patio featuring a mural on local history.

Casa Museo Dr Belisario Domínguez
MUSEUM

(Av Central Sur 35; admission adult/child M$5/2.50; ☺10am-6:45pm Tue-Sat, 9am-12:45pm Sun) Just south of the main plaza is the Casa Museo Dr Belisario Domínguez, the family home of Comitán's biggest hero and the site of his medical practice. It provides (in Spanish) fascinating insights into the state of medicine and the life of the professional classes in early-20th-century Chiapas (with a reconstruction of the onsite pharmacy), as well as the heroic tale of Domínguez' political career, ending in his assassination.

FREE Museo Arqueológico de Comitán
MUSEUM

(1a Calle Sur Oriente; ☺9am-6pm Tue-Sun) This museum, just east of the plaza, displays artifacts from the area's many archaeological sites (Spanish interpretation only). The misshapen pre-Hispanic skulls on display – deliberately 'beautified' by squeezing infants' heads between boards – make you wonder what kind of thoughts would have taken shape inside such distorted brains.

🛏 Sleeping

TOP CHOICE Hotel Posada El Castellano
HOTEL $$

(☎632-33-47; www.posadaelcastellano.com.mx; 3a Calle Norte Poniente 12; s/d/tr M$490/530/570; P❤@🛜) This excellent hotel is colonial in style but modern in build and amenities. Comfy rooms, equipped with fan, cable TV, solid wood furniture and firm beds, are on two floors around wood-pillared patios. The staff are amiable and there's a nice restaurant.

Hotel Hacienda de los Ángeles
LUXURY HOTEL $$

(☎632-00-74; www.hotelhaciendadelosangeles.com; 2a Calle Norte Poniente 6; incl breakfast r M$805-1030, ste M$1380-1720; P❤❄@🛜❄) Comitán's single luxury hotel provides complimentary welcome cocktails, professional service and spacious accommodations with sober, classical-style decor. All rooms have at least two double beds or one king-sized bed, air-con, cable TV, bathtub and quality furnishings, and suites have two levels. There's even a dramatically lit pool with its own bar.

Hotel Internacional
HOTEL $$

(☎963-632-01-10; h_internacional1@hotmail.com; Av Central Sur 16; d M$590-680, tr M$680-750, q M$700-800; P❤🛜) A block south of the plaza, this agreeable midrange offering has remodeled rooms with newly tiled bathrooms and fresh bedspreads, and standard rooms with textured walls, though carpets throughout show some wear. A contemporary lounge and restaurant grace the lobby.

Hotel del Virrey
HOTEL $

(☎632-18-11; hotel_delvirrey@hotmail.com; Av Central Norte 13; d M$380-480, tr M$690; P❤🛜) Resident turtles splash in a fountain at the Virrey, a 19th-century house with rooms of varying sizes radiating from a flower-draped courtyard. All have cable TV, and smaller upstairs rooms enjoy a nice view of nearby El Calvario church.

CHIAPAS COMITÁN

DRINKS OF CHIAPAS

» **Comiteco** A unique variant of *mezcal* made with a mix of *maguey* and *piloncillo* (cooked sugarcane). It's smoother and more syrupy than tequila, with a clear appearance or a greenish tint. Traditionally made in Comitán.

» **Tascalate** A cold sweet concoction prepared from ground cacao, pine nuts, toasted corn, cinnamon and *achiote* (annatto). Very interesting and super delicious!

» **Pox** Inexpensive grain alcohol made from sugarcane, it's pronounced (and sometimes spelled) 'posh.' The undisputed choice for those who want to pass out cold on the street, but not so deadly when mixed with lots of fruit juice.

» **Pozol** A thick, heavy mixture of *masa* (cornmeal dough) in water, it's often mixed with sugar and sometimes has chili or chocolate added. It's the equivalent of an energy drink, and you can see indigenous people everywhere carrying it around in reused plastic 1L bottles. Travelers often take a ball of the *masa* and make some up when there's water available.

Comitán

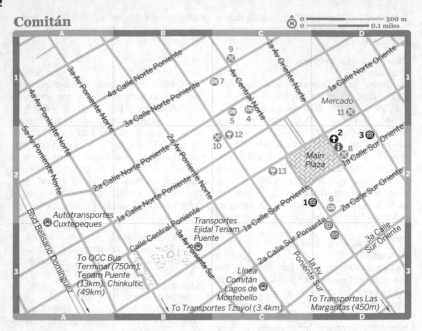

✕ Eating

A handful of good typical restaurants line the west side of the plaza.

TOP CHOICE **Café Quiptic**   CAFE, BREAKFAST **$**
(1a Av Oriente Sur s/n; breakfast M$45-75, mains M$55-85; ☺8am-11pm;☻) A swell spot for coffee on the plaza, the Quiptic is set under an impressive stone colonnade and run by indigenous coffee growers. The menu isn't huge, but it serves tasty and filling breakfasts, plus superb organic coffee, salads, *antojitos,* meat dishes and desserts.

Due Torri   ITALIAN, PIZZERIA **$$**
(Av Central Norte 30; pizza from M$55, mains $75-145; ☺1-11:30pm; ☻) Excellent freshly made pastas and pizzas are served in classy old-world dining rooms of wood-beamed ceilings, stained glass lamps and decorative Italian-style shields. The atmosphere is warm, the service attentive.

Matisse   INTERNATIONAL, ITALIAN **$$**
(1a Av Poniente Norte 16; mains M$90-160, Sunday buffet M$60; ☺11pm Tue-Sat, to 5pm Sun) Stylish Matisse serves inventive and well-presented dishes in contemporary, wood-pillared surroundings. You'll find plenty of wine and cocktails, and a neat patio for al fresco dining when the temperature's right.

Comitán

◎ Sights

1 Casa Museo Dr Belisario Domínguez................................D2
   Centro Cultural Rosario Castellanos..............................(see 8)
2 Iglesia de Santo Domingo...................D2
3 Museo Arqueológico de Comitán...D2

◎ Sleeping

4 Hotel del Virrey.....................................C1
5 Hotel Hacienda de los Ángeles..........C1
6 Hotel Internacional.............................D2
7 Hotel Posada El Castellano................C1

✕ Eating

8 Café Quiptic..D2
9 Due Torri..C1
10 Matisse...C2
11 Yuli Moni Comedor............................D1

◎ Drinking

12 Jarro Café Bar & Grill.........................C2
13 Shangri La...C2

Yuli Moni Comedor   QUESADILLAS **$**
(quesadillas M$12-40; ☺8am-5pm) Come here for an inexpensive meal or snack. This mercado *comedor* has tasty and fill-

ing quesadillas, and the nopales (cactus) and mushrooms are also good options for vegetarians.

Drinking

Shangri La   BAR, CAFE
(Calle Central Poniente 6; ⊘5pm-1am Mon-Sat) Colorful bottles line the entrance, and low lights and open fireplace make this an inviting place for coffee, cocktails and the free snacks that come with them. Cozy up in a futon or beanbag in the toasty attic or inspect the walls plastered with photos of its happy patrons.

Jarro Café Bar & Grill   BAR, LOUNGE
(1a Av Poniente Norte 7; ⊘6pm-3am Tue-Sun; 😊) A semi-futuristic space with a burbling fountain, Jarro is a fun, all-purpose bar with loud music. Depending on the night, it could be showing *fútbol* or hosting patrons crooning karaoke tunes. Pop, electronica or reggaetón DJs some nights after 9pm.

❶ Information

Banco Azteca (1a Calle Sur Poniente 8; ⊘9am-9pm) Changes dollars and euros; no ATM.

BBVA Bancomer (1a Av Oriente Sur 2; ⊘8:30am-4pm Mon-Fri) ATM.

Instituto Nacional de Migración (⊡632-22-00; Carretera Panamericana; ⊘9am-3pm Mon-Fri) The immigration office is on the Pan-American Hwy, just past the turnoff for Tzimol, 5km south of the town center.

Municipal Tourism Office (www.comitan.gob. mx, in Spanish; ⊘8am-8pm) Kiosk next to the Iglesia de Santo Domingo.

Post office (Av Central Sur 45; ⊘9am-4pm Mon-Fri, 9am-2pm Sat)

Santa Lucia (cnr Av Central Sur & 2a Calle Sur Poniente; per hr M$5; ⊘8:30am-8pm Mon-Sat, 10am-2pm Sun) Internet cafe.

State Tourism Office (⊡632-40-47; secturicomitan@gmail.com; ⊘8am-4pm Mon-Fri) Office moves frequently, contact for current

address; English and some French and Italian spoken.

❶ Getting There & Around

The Pan-American Hwy (Hwy 190), named Blvd Belisario Domínguez here but often just called 'El Bulevar,' passes through the west of town.

Comitán's **OCC bus terminal** (Blvd Belisario Domínguez Sur 43) is on the Pan-American Hwy. See the boxed text p393 for destinations.

OCC also serves Oaxaca, Mexico City, Villahermosa, Playa del Carmen and Cancún. Across the road from the OCC terminal, 'centro' combis (M$5) run to the main plaza; a taxi is M$25.

Numerous *colectivos* have terminals on Hwy 190 between 1a & 2a Calles Sur Poniente, about 500m north of the OCC terminal; they depart when full. For San Cristóbal, vans (M$40) and *colectivo* taxis (M$45) are available until 9pm. Vans for Ciudad Cuauhtémoc (M$35, until 8pm), which usually say 'Comalapa,' and Tuxtla Gutiérrez (M$79, until 6pm) are also available.

Línea Comitán Lagos de Montebello (2a Av Poniente Sur 23) runs vans to the Lagos de Montebello and along the Carretera Fronteriza, with departures to Laguna Bosque Azul (M$30, one hour) and Tziscao (M$35, 1¼ hours) every 20 minutes from 3am to 5pm; to Reforma Agraria (M$130, 4½ hours) nine times from 3am until 1:30pm; and to Palenque (M$260, eight hours) seven times daily, 4am to 10am. Schedules don't use daylight-saving time.

Transportes Tzoyol (4a Av Poniente Sur 1039, at 13a Calle Sur Poniente) runs further vans to Reforma Agraria (M$130) seven times daily, 2:30am to 3pm, as well as to Amatitlán and Plan de Río Azul (M$70 to M$73, 3½ hours), the connections for boats to Laguna Miramar, four times a day between 4:30am and 5pm. Returns from Amatitlán five times daily from 6am to 1pm. It doesn't use daylight saving time.

Servicios Aéreos San Cristóbal (serviciosaereos@prodigy.net.mx; Carretera Panamericana Km 1262) runs day trips to Bonampak and Yaxchilán (M$12,500 round trip). The price listed is per plane, not per person. For information on flying to Laguna Miramar, see p397.

CHIAPAS COMITÁN

BUSES FROM COMITÁN

DESTINATION	FARE (M$)	DURATION	FREQUENCY (DAILY)
Ciudad Cuauhtémoc	74	1½hr	5
Palenque	238	7hr	2
San Cristóbal de las Casas	44-76	1¾hr	27
Tapachula	188	6hr via Motozintla	6
Tuxtla Gutiérrez	68-83	3hr	15

PARADOR-MUSEO SANTA MARÍA

Evocative of a past era, this beautiful **hotel-museum** ([☑]/fax 963-632-51-16; www.paradorsantamaria.com.mx, in Spanish; Carretera La Trinitaria-Lagos de Montebello Km 22; r M$2420, 6-8 person tent M$6000; [P][☺][🛜][🐾]), 1.5km off the road to the Lagos de Montebello, is the most luxurious and atmospheric place to stay in the Comitán area. The restored 19th-century hacienda is decorated throughout with period furniture and art; some of the eight rooms have tiled bathtubs and fireplaces, and all look out over expansive grassy lawns to the countryside beyond. An odd but opulent new lodging addition is an enormous Arabian-style tent, furnished with Oriental rugs, a bathroom with a Jacuzzi tub and animal-mouth faucets and lavish room-dividing curtains. Gaze out over green hills from a new solar-heated pool.

The chapel here is a **religious art museum** (admission M$25; [⊙]9am-6pm) with an interesting array of colonial-era work from Europe and the Philippines as well as Mexico and Guatemala. The excellent **Restaurant Los Geranios** (mains M$130-250; [⊙]8am-9pm) serves Chiapan and international dishes prepared with organic ingredients (including coffee) grown onsite. Look for the 22km marker from La Trinitaria on the Montebello road. Prices drop 30% in the low season, but book in advance for high season.

Around Comitán

EL CHIFLÓN

These mighty waterfalls tumble off the edge of an escarpment 41km southwest of Comitán. For an up-close experience of sheer awesome power, El Chiflón is hard to beat. The local *ejido*, **San Cristobalito La Cascada** ([☑]963-596-97-09; www.chiflon.com.mx; admission M$20; [⊙]8am-5pm), has set up a number of attractive amenities on the approach to the falls, including a dozen comfortable, well-built **cabañas** (d/q M$400/750; [☺]), all with river view, bathroom and mosquito nets, and a good open-air restaurant. **Camping** (campsites per person M$25) is permitted as well.

A 1km approach road heads up from Hwy 226 to the parking area, from which a well-made path leads 1.3km up alongside the forest-lined Río San Vicente (which has good swimming spots) to a series of increasingly dramatic and picturesque waterfalls. Finally you reach the 70m Velo de Novia fall: prepare to be drenched by flying spray. You can also fly across the river on a zip-line (M$150).

In the dry season, from roughly February through July, the falls form a foamy line and the blue river water is safe enough to swim in. But during the rainy season, rapid currents turn the river a muddy brown, the falls gush with abandon and swimming is a death wish.

From Comitán, **Autotransportes Cuxtepeques** ([☑]963-632-49-22; Blvd Belisario Domínguez Sur), between Calles 1a and 2a Norte Poniente, runs hourly vans and buses to the El Chiflón turnoff on Hwy 226 (M$25, 45 minutes) from 4am to 8pm. **Mototaxis** (M$5 per person) wait there to ferry passengers up the road. Drivers should take the Tzimol turnoff from the Pan-American Hwy, 5km south of central Comitán.

TENAM PUENTE

These **Maya ruins** (admission M$31; [⊙]9am-4pm) feature three ball courts, a 20m tiered pyramid and other structures rising from a terraced, wooded hillside. Like Chinkultic (see p395), Tenam Puente was one of a set of fringe Classic Maya settlements in this part of Chiapas that (unlike more famed lowland sites such as Palenque and Yaxchilán) seem to have survived in the post-Classic period, possibly as long as AD 1200. It has a pleasant rural setting and good long-distance views.

A 5km-long paved road leads west to the site from Hwy 190, 9km south of Comitán. **Transporte Ejidal Tenam Puente** (3a Av Poniente Sur 8, Comitán) runs combis (M$15) every 45 minutes, 8am to 6pm, to the site (if there are a few tourists) or to the village of Francisco Sarabia, 2km before Tenam Puente. The last combi from the ruins returns at 4pm. A taxi costs about M$250 return (with an hour at the ruins).

CHINKULTIC

Chinkultic was a minor Maya power during the late Classic period and, like Tenam Puente, may have survived into post-Classic times. Of 200 mounds scattered over a wide area of dramatically situated **ruins** (admission M$35; ☺8am-5pm), only a few have been cleared, but the site is worth a visit.

The ruins are in two groups. From the entrance, first take the path to the left, which curves around to the right below one of Chinkultic's biggest structures, E23, covered in vegetation. The path reaches a grassy plaza with several weathered steles, some carved with human figures, and a ball court on the right.

Return to the entrance, from which another path heads to the **Plaza Hundida** (Sunken Plaza), crosses a stream, then climbs steeply up to the **Acrópolis**, a partly restored temple atop a rocky escarpment, with remarkable views over the surrounding lakes and forests and down into a cenote (sinkhole) 50m below – into which the Maya used to toss offerings of pottery, beads, bones and obsidian knives.

Chinkultic is situated about 48km from Comitán, on the road to the Lagos de Montebello. Combis for the lakes can drop you at the intersection (M$30 from Comitán); the site is 2km north via a paved access road. A new tourism project offers lodging and a restaurant just past the ruins.

LAGOS DE MONTEBELLO

The temperate pine and oak forest along the Guatemalan border east of Chinkultic is dotted with more than 50 small lakes of varied hues, known as the Lagos (or Lagunas) de Montebello. The area is very picturesque, refreshing and peaceful. The paved road to Montebello turns east off Hwy 190 just north of La Trinitaria, 16km south of Comitán. It passes Chinkultic after 32km, and enters the Parque Nacional Lagunas de Montebello 5km beyond. A further 800m along is a ticket booth, where you must pay a M$25 park admission fee. Here the road forks – north to the Lagunas de Colores (2km to 3km) and east to the village of Tziscao (9km), beyond which it becomes the Carretera Fronteriza, continuing east to Ixcán and ultimately Palenque.

◉ Sights & Activities

From the park ticket booth, the northward road leads to the Lagunas de Colores, five lakes with vivid hues that range from turquoise to deep green: **Laguna Agua Tinta**, **Laguna Esmeralda**, **Laguna Encantada**, **Laguna Ensueño** and, the biggest, **Laguna Bosque Azul**, on the left where the paved road ends. There's a nice walk from here to the **Grutas San Rafael del Arco**, a group of caves. Follow the track ahead from the parking lot, turn left after 500m at the 'Gruta San Rafael del Arco' sign, then follow the path, mostly downhill, for 500m to 600m to a 'Grutas' sign. To the left here, a river rushes through a natural rock arch. To the right, the path forks after 60m. The left branch leads 100m to a riverside cave downstream from the rock arch; the right branch leads 40m to a more extensive cave that turns out to be the bottom of a sinkhole.

In the Laguna Bosque Azul parking lot, *camiones* (trucks) do shared three- to five-hour lake tours for about M$100 per person,

Lagos de Montebello

though it can be harder to get a group together on weekdays. Local boys offer multi-lake horseback excursions that include **Dos Cenotes** (M$120, two to three hours), a pair of sinkholes in the forest, or to the Laguna de Montebello (about one hour away).

Along the eastward road from the park ticket booth, after 3km a track leads 200m north to the **Laguna de Montebello**, one of the area's larger lakes, with a flat open area along its shore, and more boys offering horseback rides to Dos Cenotes. The local *ejido* charges a M$15 entrance fee to access the lake areas along the Tziscao road; pay once and keep your receipt for the other lakes. About 3km further along the Tziscao road, another track leads left to the **Cinco Lagunas** (Five Lakes). Only four are visible from the road, but the second, **La Cañada**, on the right after about 1.5km, is one of the most beautiful Montebello lakes, nearly cut in half by two rocky outcrops.

About 1km nearer to Tziscao, another track leads 1km north to cobalt-blue **Laguna Pojoj**, which has an island in the middle that you can visit on simple rafts. **Laguna Tziscao**, on the Guatemalan border, comes into view 1km past the Pojoj junction. The turnoff to the Chuj-speaking village of Tziscao, a pretty and spread-out place stretching down to the lakeside, is a little further on.

🛏 Sleeping & Eating

Beside the Laguna Bosque Azul parking lot are several basic **comedores** (dishes M$45; ⏰7am-3pm) that serve drinks and simple plates of *carne asada* (roasted meat) or quesadillas, and food options exist at most other lakes as well.

Hotel Tziscao　　CABAÑAS, CAMPGROUND **$$**
(✆963-110-71-44; www.tziscao.com; campsites per person M$40, 2-/3-bed r or cabaña M$600/800; P♨@🛜) By the lake in Tziscao village (2km from the highway turnoff), this medium-sized lakeside complex is run by an *ejido* co-operative. Extensive, grassy grounds include a sandy beach with terrific views across the lake to the foothills of the Cuchumatanes in Guatemala. You can rent two-person kayaks (M$100 per hour), or bicycles (M$100 for four hours) to go exploring. Rooms in the main hotel building were in the midst of an extensive remodel when we visited, with new beds and bathroom tiling. More rustic wooden *cabañas* are also available, but you might want to skip the shoreside units, as they're partially submerged for weeks during the rainy season. All accommodations have a private bathroom with hot water, and campers can use the kitchen. The hotel also has a restaurant (breakfast M$45, mains M$70).

Cabañas are also available at the Lagunas de Colores for about the same price as those at Hotel Tziscao; contact the hotel to reserve.

❶ Getting There & Away

Public transportation to Chinkultic and the lakes from Comitán is a snap, making it an easy day trip. See p393 for details; vans go to the parking lot at Laguna Bosque Azul and to Tziscao, and will drop you at the turnoffs for Museo Parador Santa María, Chinkultic and the other lakes. The last vehicles back to Comitán leave Tziscao and Laguna Bosque Azul in the early evening.

From San Cristóbal, a number of agencies offer tours that take in the lakes, throw in a visit to El Chiflón and get you back by dinnertime.

Laguna Miramar

ELEV 400M

Ringed by rainforest, pristine Laguna Miramar, 140km southeast of Ocosingo in the **Reserva de la Biosfera Montes Azules** (Montes Azules Biosphere Reserve), is one of Mexico's most remote and exquisite lakes. Frequently echoing with the roars of howler monkeys, the 16-sq-km lake is bathtub-warm and virtually unpolluted. Rock ledges extending from small islands make blissful wading spots, and petroglyphs and a sea-turtle cave are reachable by canoe.

The lake is accessible thanks to a successful ecotourism project in the small Maya community of **Emiliano Zapata** (✆200-124-88-80, 81, 82; www.lagunamiramar.com), near its western shore. If you arrive independently, ask for the Comité de Turismo. Through this representative you must arrange and pay for the services you need – a guide costs M$150 per day (maximum three people), a day-use fee is M$40, and rental of a *cayuco* (traditional canoe) for exploring the lake is M$250. Sleeping bags, hammocks and tents are available to rent and, for groups, local women can be hired to purchase and cook your food at the lake.

The 7km walk from Emiliano Zapata to the lake, through *milpas* (cornfields) and forest that includes *caoba* (mahogany) and the *matapalo* (strangler fig) trees, takes about 1½ hours and can be very muddy – good closed shoes are highly recommended. At the lake, you will hear howler monkeys.

CHIAPAS LAGUNA MIRAMAR

TO/FROM GUATEMALA: CIUDAD CUAUHTÉMOC

Very frequent *colectivos* (M$35) and intermittent buses (M$46) run between Ciudad Cuautémoc and Comitán (1½ hours). From Ciudad Cuautémoc, five daily OCC buses run to San Cristóbal de las Casas (M$94, 3½ hours) and beyond from noon to 10pm, but it's usually quicker to get to Comitán and pick up onward transportation there.

Mexican immigration (⊘6am-10pm) is across the street from the OCC terminal; *colectivos* generally assume that travelers need to be dropped off there. The Guatemalan border post is 4km south at La Mesilla, and taxis (M$10 *colectivo*, M$40 private) ferry people between the two sides. There are banks and moneychangers on both sides of the border, which closes to car traffic from 9pm to 6am.

From La Mesilla, mototaxis (M$5/Q3) can drop you at the 2nd-class bus depot. Second-class buses leave very frequently from 6am to 6pm for Huehuetenango (Q20, two hours) and Quetzaltenango (Q40, four hours), where you can find onward connections to Guatemala City. First-class **Línea Dorada** (www.lineadorada.com.gt) along the main street and about 20m inside the border, has two direct daily departures to Guatemala City (Q170, eight hours) at 12:30pm and 11pm.

For further information, head to shop.lonelyplanet.com to purchase a downloadable PDF of the Guatemala chapter from Lonely Planet's *Central America on a Shoestring* guide.

Other wildlife includes spider monkeys, tapirs, macaws and toucans; butterflies are prolific. Locals fish for *mojarra* (perch), and will assure you that the lake's few crocodiles are not dangerous.

🛏 Sleeping & Eating

At the lakeshore, you can sling a hammock or camp (per person M$40) under a *palapa* shelter. But if you arrive after noon, you'll need to stay in Emiliano Zapata, as the guides want to make it home before dark. The village has a handful of simple *cabañas* (M$150 per person) with river views, all with one queen and one twin bed, a fan and shared bathrooms. A number of *comedores* make meals for about M$25. You can also rent a hammock and mosquito net and string them up in a roofed area next to the *cabañas*.

❶ Getting There & Away

Try to visit outside the rainy seson (late-August to November), when land access is very difficult, and walking the muddy foot trail feels like an aerobics class in quicksand. If you're determined to go then, you can rent a pair of tall rubber boots (M$20) or a hard-working horse (M$300 return). Some agencies in San Cristóbal de las Casas run three- or four-day trips to Miramar from San Cristóbal via the river route, with prices from M$3400 per person.

Air

Servicios Aéreos San Cristóbal (☎963-632-46-62, 800-523-49-54; serviciosaereos@pro

digy.net.mx; 5a Av Norte Poniente s/n, Comitán) has small-plane charter flights (up to four passengers) to San Quintín from Comitán (M$3500) and Ocosingo (M$4000). These one-way prices are per plane, rather than per person.

After you land, follow the dirt road opposite a military complex beside San Quintín's airstrip. It leads to Emiliano Zapata, about a 15- to 20-minute walk; the ecotourism project is at the far end of the village.

Boat

Take a combi to Amatitlán (see p393 for information), a rough 18km from the Carretera Fronteriza Hwy. Cross the bridge to La Democracia, where you can hire a *lancha* (M$925 one way, maximum eight passengers, two hours) to Emiliano Zapata via the Río Jatate until about 3pm. *Lanchas* also leave from Plan de Río Azul, but don't have seating or life jackets. Amatitlán and Plan de Río Azul are located approximately 10km and 15km north, respectively, off the Carretera Fronteriza just east of the Las Nubes turnoff.

Bus & Colectivo

Transportation from Comitán and Ocosingo services San Quintín and Emiliano Zapata. The Comitán route is slightly shorter (the road is paved to Guadalupe Tepeyec, just before La Realidad; the Ocosingo road is paved to La Garrucha) and uses combis instead of tarp-covered trucks. Though San Quintín is technically the last stop, drivers will drop you off five minutes further in Emiliano Zapata if requested. The ecotourism project can usually organize in-town pickups for the return. Schedules are subject to change, and daylight savings time isn't used. Unpaved sections of road can be challenging in rainy season.

FROM COMITÁN

Transportes Las Margaritas (6a Calle Sur Oriente 51) combis service Las Margaritas (M$14, 25 minutes) frequently. From Las Margaritas, **Grupo Monteflor** (cnr Av Central Sur & 1a Calle Sur Poniente), near the plaza, has daily departures (M$75, five to six hours) to San Quintín at 7am, 9am and 11am, and near the market, **Transportes Río Euseba** (3a Av Oriente Sur btwn Calle Central & 1a Calle Oriente Sur) has departures at 8am and 1pm (M$70). Combis return from San Quintín at 1am, 3am, 4am, 5am and 1pm.

FROM OCOSINGO

Stand-up-in-the-back trucks called *tres toneladas* leave for San Quintín (M$70, about six hours in dry season) from a large walled lot at the back of the market. Departures are at 9am, 10:30am, noon and 2pm, or when crammed full. Return trucks at 2am, 5am, 8am and noon.

El Soconusco & Beaches

Chiapas' fertile coastal plain, 15km to 35km wide, is called the Soconusco, and is named for the Aztecs' most distant 15th-century province, called Xoconochco. It's hot and humid year-round, with serious rainfall from mid-May to mid-October. The lushly vegetated Sierra Madre de Chiapas, rising steeply from the plain, provides an excellent environment for coffee, bananas and other crops. Olive ridley and green sea turtles and the occasional leatherback nest along the coastline from June through November, and turtle preservation projects exist in Puerto Arista, Boca del Cielo, La Encrucijada and Chocohuital/Costa Azul.

The endless beach and ocean are wonderfully clean and warm here, but take care where you go in – the surf is often rough, and riptides (known as *canales*) can quickly sweep you out a long way. Bring bug repellant for overnights, as sandflies can be fierce from May through October.

TONALÁ
☏966 / POP 35,000

This sweaty, bustling town on Hwy 200 is the jumping-off point for the northern beaches. You can check your email on the corner facing the plaza at Cyber Cristy (Av Rayon; per hr M$10; ⊙8am-10pm) and the ATM or get dollars changed (weekdays only) at Banamex (Hidalgo 137; ⊙9am-4pm Mon-Sat), a block east of the plaza on the main drag.

A fine central choice fronting the east side of the plaza, the Hotel Galilea (☏663-02-39; Hidalgo 138; s/d/tr M$320/400/450; [P][✳][?]) has

a convenient restaurant and clean medium-sized rooms with dark wooden furniture that give it an old-world feel.

Hotel Grajandra (☏663-01-44; Hidalgo 204; r/tr M$590/800; [P][❄][✳][?][≋]) is a friendly place next to the OCC bus terminal, with bright, large rooms with 1970s-era decor and a breezy upstairs restaurant. You'll find a number of good restaurants on the plaza.

Colectivo taxis for Puerto Arista (M$20, 20 minutes), Boca del Cielo (M$25, 35 minutes) and Madre Sal (M$40) run from Matamoros between 20 de Marzo and Belisario Domínguez, four blocks east of the plaza and one block downhill. Puerto Arista combis (M$14) leave from Juárez at 20 de Marzo, one block further downhill. Taxis and combis run until about 7pm. A private taxi to Puerto Arista is M$100; to Madre Sal is M$350.

From the central plaza, the OCC bus terminal (Hidalgo) is 600m west and the 2nd-class Rápidos del Sur (RS; Hidalgo btwn Belisario Domínguez & Iturbide) is 250m east. Both lines have frequent services to Tapachula (M$96 to M$200, three to four hours) and Tuxtla Gutiérrez (M$76 to M$156, 2½ to three hours).

PUERTO ARISTA
☏994 / POP 900

Most of the time Puerto Arista, 18km southwest of Tonalá, is a small, ultrasleepy fishing town where the most action you'll see is a piglet breaking into a trot because a dog has gathered the energy to bark at it. But at weekends and during August and holidays, *chiapanecos* roll in from the towns and cities inland to take advantage of the state's most developed beach town.

The only real street (called Matamoros in one section) parallels the beach, one block inland. The road from Tonalá hits it at a T-junction by a lighthouse, the midpoint of town. Public transportation terminates here, although *colectivo* taxis will take you to your door for a bit extra. There's an ATM in the tiny Plaza Puerto Arista near the Hotel Arista Bugambilias.

◉ Sights & Activities

FREE **Centro de Protección & Conservación de la Tortuga Marina en Chiapas** WILDLIFE
(Chiapas Marine Turtle Protection & Conservation Center; ⊙10am-5pm) During the nesting season, the state government collects thousands of newly laid olive ridley turtle eggs from 40km of beach, incubating them and releas-

ing the hatchlings when they emerge seven weeks later. At this center located about 3km northwest along the single street from the lighthouse (taxis charge M$25), you can stop in to see the turtle nursery, and sometimes **volunteer** (☎961-618-79-00 ext 225, cell phone 961-6552450; danvs@semahn.chiapas.gob.mx) to help with beach patrols and hatchling release. It's a good idea to inquire beforehand. Volunteers may camp if there's space available.

🛏 Sleeping & Eating
Prices drop significantly outside high season. Scores of almost-identical beachfront *palapa* eateries serve seafood dishes (M$90 to M$120).

Hotel Lucero   HOTEL **$$**
(☎600-90-42; www.hotel-lucero.com, in Spanish; Matamoros 800; s M$600, d M$800-900; P❀ 🛰❄) The Lucero, 800m southeast of the lighthouse and across the street from the beach, has comfortable, pastel-shaded, air-conditioned rooms with up to three double beds. The upper floors have great ocean views. Its open-air restaurant, **Flamingos** (mains M$90-180) and big double pool (nonguests pay M$40 unless they eat at the restaurant) front the beach.

José's Camping Cabañas   CABAÑAS **$**
(☎600-90-48; campsites per person M$50, RV sites M$150-170, dm M$100, s/d/tr M$300/350/400, without bathroom M$170/200/250; P❄) Run by a Canadian who's been living here for three decades, this is a welcoming place to stay and relax. It has a small pool (open in season), serves meals (M$40 to M$100), and the simple brick-and-thatch *cabañas* – all with mosquito nets and screens, fan and shaded sitting areas – are dotted about an extensive coconut and citrus grove. Follow the main street southeast from the lighthouse for 800m, then turn left (inland) by Hotel Lucero.

Hotel Arista Bugambilias   HOTEL **$$**
(☎/fax 600-90-44; www.hotelaristabugambilias. com; r M$1050-1200, 4-person ste M$1350-1500; P❀🛰❄) About 800m northwest of the lighthouse, the Bugambilias has beautiful beachfront grounds, an enticing pool, a restaurant and a bar. Good-sized rooms with white brick walls all have air-con and TV.

MADRE SAL
Drift to sleep pondering the ocean waves at **Madre Sal** (☎cell phone 966-6666147, cell phone 966-1007296; www.madresal.com; Manuel Ávila

Camacho; hammock M$30, campsite M$100, 1-/2-bed cabaña M$400/600; P🛏), a new cooperative-run ecotourism project 25km south of Puerto Arista. Named for a mangrove species, its restaurant (meals M$70) and almost 20 thatched cabañas (with mosquito nets) sit astride a skinny bar of pristine land between the mainland and the Pacific that's reached via *lancha* (M$20 round-trip) through dense mangrove forest.

The ensuite cabañas are solar-powered (guests get candles after the 11pm power shut-off), and crabs skitter along the sand when stars fill the night sky. In season, sea turtles come ashore to lay eggs, and the night watchman can wake you if you want to watch or help collect the eggs for the Boca del Cielo hatchery.

Though the water can be rough, the beach is spotless, and there's excellent birdwatching in the mangroves, including 13 species of herons. Three-hour boat trips are available (M$250 per person, minimum four people), including one for bird-and-crocodile-spotting and another that visits the turtle rescue and hatchery in Boca del Cielo.

From Tonalá, take a taxi (M$50 shared, M$350 private) or combi (M$40) to Manuel Ávila Camacho; it's a 5-minute walk to the *embarcadero*.

RESERVA DE LA BIOSFERA LA ENCRUCIJADA
This large biosphere reserve protects a 1448-sq-km strip of coastal lagoons, sandbars, wetlands, seasonally flooded tropical forest and the country's tallest mangroves (some above 30m). The ecosystem is a vital wintering and breeding ground for migratory birds, and harbors one of Mexico's biggest populations of jaguars, plus spider monkeys, turtles, crocodiles, caimans, boa constrictors, fishing eales and lots of waterfowl – many in danger of extinction. Bird-watching is good any time of year, but best during the November-to-March nesting season. The reserve can be visited via access points from Pijijiapan and Escuintla, and *lancha* rides take you through towering mangroves.

RIBERA COSTA AZUL
A laidback coastal jewel, the beautiful black sandbar of Ribera Costa Azul (also called Playa Azul) is a thin strip of palm-fringed land between ocean and lagoon accessed from the Chocohuital *embarcadero*, 20km southwest of Pijijiapan. There's free camping, though meals (M$80 to M$120) aren't

usually available outside of high season. Ask at the dock about food offerings, as local families can also cook meals by arrangement. *Lanchas* (M$10 one way) ferry passengers to the sandbar, and birding and mangrove trips (M$250 per boat per hour) can also be organized.

If you don't want to camp, the swank beach and pool club of Refugio del Sol (☎962-625-2780; www.refugiodelsol.com.mx; day use Tue-Sun adult/child M$250/150, r Thu-Sat M$1000; P❄❅⊛), 300m north of the Chocohuital dock, has comfortable, though overpriced rooms, available three nights a week by reservation. If you eat at the restaurant (mains M$125 to M$180), day-use swim fees drop by M$100/50.

From Pijijiapan, combis for Chocohuital (M$17, 40 minutes, 5am to 7pm) leave hourly from 1a Av Norte Poniente 27 (between 2a and 3a Poniente Norte); the last one returns at 8pm.

EMBARCADERO LAS GARZAS

Near this dock, the Red de Ecoturismo La Encrucijada (☎cell phone 918-1012161; www.ecoturismolaencrucijada.com), a network of community cooperatives, maintains an office and can arrange tours and lodging. Private *lancha* tours (M$750 to M$1250, up to 10 passengers) can also be organized to local beaches and bird-watching spots. *Lanchas* also serve a number of small communities where you can overnight or camp in simple cabañas. At the settlement of Barra de Zacapulco – which also has a sea-turtle breeding center – you can usually camp or sling a hammock for free if you eat your meals at one of its simple *comedores* (seafood plates M$70). A community cooperative there offers a half dozen basic solar-powered cabañas (☎cell phone 918-5962501; r M$350) with fans, screened windows and cold-water bathrooms.

To get here, take a bus along Hwy 200 to Escuintla, then a *colectivo* taxi to Acapetahua (M$5, 10 minutes). Beside the abandoned railway in Acapetahua, take a combi 18km to Embarcadero Las Garzas (M$13, 20 minutes, every 30 minutes until 5pm). From Embarcadero Las Garzas, *colectivo lanchas* go to communities including Barra de Zacapulco (M$35, 25 minutes). The last boat back from Barra de Zacapulco may be as early as 4pm, and the last combi from Embarcadero Las Garzas to Acapetahua goes at about 5pm.

Tapachula

☑962 / POP 200,000 / ELEV 100M

The 'Pearl of the Soconusco,' Mexico's bustling southernmost city, doesn't quite live up to its nickname, though it does have an interesting combination of urban sophistication and tropical tempo. The city is an important commercial center, not only for the Soconusco but also for cross-border trade with Guatemala.

A hot, humid and busy place year-round, Tapachula's heart is the large, lively Parque Hidalgo, with vistas of the towering 4110m cone of Volcán Tacaná to the north on clear days. Most travelers simply pass through here on their way to or from Guatemala, but it makes a good base for a number of interesting nearby attractions.

◉ Sights

TOP CHOICE/ Museo Arqueológico del Soconusco   MUSEUM

(Av 8a Norte 20; admission M$31; ⊙9am-6pm Tue-Sun) The modernized, well-displayed Museo Arqueológico del Soconusco faces Parque Hidalgo. Steles and ceramics from Izapa (see p404) are prominent. On these steles the top fringe represents the sky and gods, the middle depicts earthly life and the bottom fringe shows the underworld. There are also 5000-year-old stone heads and figurines from the coastal marshes, a collection of pre-Hispanic musical instruments (including scrapers made from human bones), and other items displaying Olmec, Teotihuacán, Maya and Aztec influences. Goths will adore the turquoise-encrusted skull.

◉ Sleeping

TOP CHOICE/ Casa Mexicana   BOUTIQUE HOTEL $$

(☎626-66-05; www.casamexicanachiapas.com; Av 8a Sur 19; r M$692-984, tr/q M$1085/1185; P❁❄❅⊛) An exquisite boutique hotel paying homage to Mexican women in history. Guests can choose from sumptuous rooms named for heroines such as human rights lawyer Digna Ochoa or Zapatista commander Ramona. Antiques, lush plants and all kinds of interesting art create a soothing, creative feel. The 10 rooms on two floors surround a tropical garden-patio that even has a small pool. With a small bar and a restaurant serving excellent homemade meals (breakfast included in room rate outside the high season), this is a fabulous place to stay.

Galerías Hotel y Arts HOTEL $$
(642-75-90; www.galeriashotel.com.mx, in Spanish; Av 4a Norte 21; s M$425-480, d/tr M$595/720; P❀✿❅⚊) Stylish, contemporary and boutique-on-a-budget, Galerías is an excellent small hotel with jazzy art prints and large, comfortable air-conditioned rooms. Double rooms are spacious. Two cozy but comfy singles are a good deal for those going solo.

Hotel Don Miguel HOTEL $$
(626-11-43; www.hoteldonmiguel.com.mx, in Spanish; Calle 1a Poniente 18; s M$600, d M$678-717, ste M$847-960; P❀✿❅) Fastidiously clean rooms, professional service and an excellent restaurant are hallmarks of the Don Miguel, a centrally located option that's popular for conferences. Tasteful green textiles brighten up the rooms, some of which include small terraces. Step-up bathrooms in one-bed rooms will graze the scalp of anyone over 6ft tall. No elevator.

Hotel Fénix HOTEL $$
(628-96-00; www.fenix.com.mx; Av 4a Norte 19; s/d/tr/q M$255/320/380/415, with air-con M$440/550/660/725, remodeled with air-con M$540/675/810/895; P❀✿❅@❅) The labyrinthine Fénix has a selection of rooms, so look before you sleep. The ones at the rear are generally better, though a remodel has upgraded and modernized some of the air-con rooms. Convenient lobby restaurant.

Hotel Diamante HOTEL $
(628-50-32; Calle 7a Poniente 43; r/q M$259/372, with air-con M$474/576; P❀✿❅) A good-value hotel with modern air-conditioning, clean rooms and cable TV. Rooms 12 through 16 have dynamite views of Volcán Tacaná.

🍴 Eating

Scores of clean and popular *comedores* are hidden upstairs at the **Mercado Sebastián Escobar** (Av 10a Norte; mains M$45-60; ⏱6am-5pm), dishing out mammoth plates of cooked-to-order Chinese food. Snag a bench seat at the plastic-tablecloth-covered picnic tables and come hungry!

Los Comales Grill MEXICAN $$
(Av 8a Norte 4; mains M$55-150; ⏱24hr) To feel like you're in the thick of things, dine in this open-air Parque Hidalgo restaurant – it's been here for over half a century. The menu includes good *caldo tlalpeño* (hearty chicken, vegetable and chili soup) and decent steaks. There's marimba music Thursday,

Saturday and Sunday evenings from 8pm to 11pm.

Gramlich Café Terraza CAFE $
(Calle 1a Poniente 14; coffees & snacks M$12-34, mains M$45-70; ⏱9am-9:30pm Mon- Sat) Just across the street from the original, this new branch of the Gramlich Café serves its delectable brew along with an extended menu of breakfasts, sandwiches and Thai salads. Seat yourself on the shaded sidewalk patio or inside with the turbo-charged air conditioning.

La Parrilla Tap PARRILLA $$
(Av 8a Norte 14; tacos & tortas M$25-70, mains $70-120; ⏱7am-11:30pm; ❅) Share a hearty platter of *parrilla*, snack on a quick taco or try the house *pollo con mole* (chicken with *mole* sauce) at this buzzing grill right off the plaza.

Long-Yin CHINESE $
(626-24-67; Av 2a Norte 36; mains $60-110; ⏱9am-8pm; ❅) Just one portion easily feeds two ravenous diners at this excellent red-lantern-festooned place run by a fourth-generation immigrant family. Vegetarians should beeline here for the fabulous tofu dishes. Delivery available, but it's worth seeing the building across the street.

Ristorante Marinni ITALIAN $$
(625-39-97; Av 11a Sur 1; mains M$70-155; ⏱1-11pm Mon-Sat, 1-8pm Sun; ❅) A swanky Italian spot, it has a sophisticated and softly lit indoor dining room and an outdoor patio cloaked in dramatic greenery. Order the *tallarines con camarones* (pasta with shrimp), a thin-crust pizza or the *medallón al balsámico* (beef medallions in red wine and balsamic vinegar). Reserve ahead on weekends.

🍷 Drinking

Nestled in the coffee-growing region of the state, Tapachula has an especially nice coffeehouse culture and lots of evening cafe life.

Gramlich Café CAFE
(Calle 1a Poniente 9; coffees & snacks M$12-34; ⏱8:30am-9:30pm Mon-Fri, 9am-9:30pm Sat, 2-10pm Sun) Serving up organic coffee grown in the mountains north of town, this popular coffeehouse has an old-fashioned feel.

Ángeles Alta Repostería & Café CAFE, BREAKFAST
(Calle 2a Oriente 11; desserts M$35-39, breakfast M$58-70; ⏱8am-11pm) Settle in for a good blood-pumping espresso at this modern

Tapachula

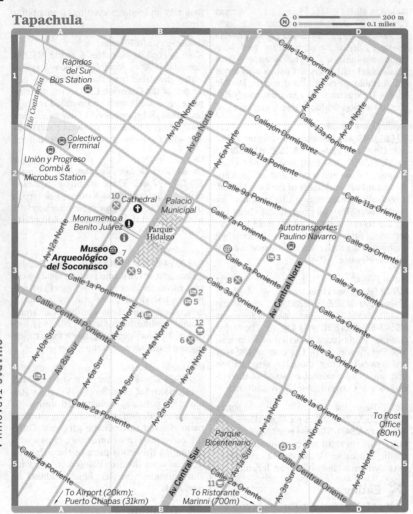

air-conditioned cafe that's good for breakfasts and has a stack of daily newspapers.

🛍 Shopping

Casa Chiapas　　　HANDICRAFTS, GIFTS
(☑118-31-90; www.casachiapas.gob.mx, in Spanish; Calle Central Oriente 18; ◷8am-8pm Mon-Fri, 9am-8pm Sat) Branch of the Chiapas state *artesanías* outlet, with outstanding weaving, toys and locally produced foodstuffs.

ⓘ Information

@ngelitos (Calle 5a Poniente 17; per hr M$10; ◷9am-9pm Mon-Sat) Internet access.

Banorte (cnr Av 2a Norte & Calle Central Poniente; ◷9am-5pm Mon-Fri, 9am-2pm Sat) Changes dollars Monday through Friday; ATM.

Chiapas Divisas (Calle 1a Poniente 13; ◷9:30am-5:30pm Mon-Fri, 9am-2:30pm Sat) Currency exchange.

Instituto Nacional de Migración (☑625-05-59; Vialidad 435, Fracc Las Vegas; ◷9am-3pm) Immigration office.

Post office (Calle 1a Oriente) Next to a plaza where mariachis gather.

Sanatorio Soconusco (☑626-50-74; Av 4a Norte 68) A clinic with 24-hour emergency service; English spoken.

Tapachula

⊙ Top Sights

Museo Arqueológico del
Soconusco...B3

🛏 Sleeping

1 Casa Mexicana....................................A4
2 Galerías Hotel y Arte B3
3 Hotel Diamante...................................C3
4 Hotel Don Miguel B3
5 Hotel Fénix...B3

🍴 Eating

6 Gramlich Café Terraza.........................B4
7 La Parrilla Tap B3
8 Long-Yin...C3
9 Los Comales Grill...............................B3
10 Mercado Sebastián Escobar..............B2

☕ Drinking

11 Ángeles Alta Repostería &
Café..C5
12 Gramlich Café.....................................B4

🛍 Shopping

13 Casa Chiapas......................................C5

Tourist office (☎628-77-25; www.turismotapa
chula.gob.mx, in Spanish; Av 8a Norte; ⊙8am-
7pm Mon-Fri, 9am-2pm Sat & Sun) A helpful
office in the Antiguo Palacio Municipal.

❶ Getting There & Away

Air

Tapachula's modern **airport** (Carretera
Tapachula-Puerto Madero Km 18.5; 📶) is 20km
southwest of the city and has free wi-fi. It's a
drowsy place, with just three daily flights to/
from Mexico City with **Aeroméxico** (☎626-39-
21; Calle Central Oriente 4).

Bus

Deluxe and 1st-class buses go from the **OCC terminal** (Calle 17a Oriente s/n), 1km northeast of
Parque Hidalgo. The main 2nd-class services are
by **Rápidos del Sur** (RS; Calle 9a Poniente 62).
For info on daily departures (from OCC unless
otherwise stated), see the table below.

Other buses from the OCC station go to
Palenque, Puerto Escondido and Villahermosa.
There are also five daily buses from here to Guatemala City (five to six hours), with tickets sold
at the main counter: **Trans Galgos Inter** (www.
transgalgosinter.com.gt, in Spanish) at 6am,
11:30am and 11:45pm (M$280), **Línea Dorada**
(www.lineadorada.com.gt, in Spanish) at 3pm
(M$220) and **Tica Bus** (www.ticabus.com) at
7am (M$220).

Galgos also runs one daily bus to San Salvador,
El Salvador (M$400, nine hours), via Escuintla
in Guatemala. Tica Bus continues all the way to
Panama City, with several long overnight stops
en route.

For destinations in western Guatemala, including Quetzaltenango, it's best to get a bus from
the border (see p405).

Colectivo

A large new *colectivo* terminal now houses many
of the regional taxi and combi companies.

❶ Getting Around

Car & Motorcycle

Tapachula's two rental agencies carry both
automatic and manual transmission cars.

AVC Rente un Auto (☎626-23-16, cell phone
962-6225444; per day M$250) In-town pick-up
service; cash only.

Europcar (Airport; www.europcar.com) Small
fleet but accepts credit cards; best rates
online.

Taxi

Taxis within the central area (including the OCC
terminal) cost M$20.

BUSES FROM TAPACHULA

DESTINATION	FARE (M$)	DURATION	FREQUENCY (DAILY)
Comitán	196	6hr via Motozintla	6
Escuintla	26-73	1½hr	9 OCC, 24 RS
Mexico City	1034-1496	17-18hr	11
Oaxaca	525	12hr	1
San Cristóbal de las Casas	262-340	7½-8hr via Motozintla	7
Tonalá	96-216	3-4hr	24 OCC, 24 RS
Tuxtla Gutiérrez	168-544	4½-6hr	22 OCC, 24 RS

Sociedades Transportes 149 (☑625-12-87) has a booth in the airport arrivals hall, charging M$80 per person for a *colectivo* from the airport to the center, or M$180 for a private taxi (up to three people); it's M$100 door-to-door from the center to the airport.

Around Tapachula

IZAPA

The pre-Hispanic ruins at Izapa are important to archaeologists, and of real interest to archaeology buffs. Izapa flourished from approximately 200 BC to AD 200, and its carving style (mostly seen on tall slabs known as steles, fronted by round altars) shows descendants of Olmec deities with their upper lips unnaturally lengthened. Some Maya monuments in Guatemala are similar, and Izapa is considered an important 'bridge' between the Olmecs and the Maya. Izapa had 91 known stele-and-altar pairings, and you can see some well-preserved examples in the Tapachula museum (p400).

Izapa is around 11km east of Tapachula on the Talismán road. There are three groups of **ruins** (admission to Grupo A & B M$28; ☉10am-5pm Tue-Sun), each looked after by a caretaking family. The northern group is on the left of the road if you're going from Tapachula – watch out for the low pyramid mounds; you'll also see a ball court and several carved steles and altars. For the other groups, go back 700m toward Tapachula and take a signposted dirt road to the left. You'll pass houses with 2000-year-old sculptures lying in their gardens. After 800m you'll reach a fork with signs to Izapa Grupo A and Izapa Grupo B, each about 250m further on. Grupo A has 10 very weathered stele-and-altar pairings around a field. Grupo B is a couple of grass-covered mounds and more stone sculptures, including three curious ball-on-pillar affairs.

To get there from Tapachula, take a **Unión y Progreso** (☑962-626-33-79; Calle 5a Poniente 53) combi or microbús (M$10) or any Talismán-bound bus.

SANTO DOMINGO, UNIÓN JUÁREZ & VOLCÁN TACANÁ

☑962

Volcán Tacaná's dormant cone towers over the countryside north of Tapachula. Even if you're not interested in climbing to its summit, two villages on its gorgeously verdant lower slopes make an attractive day trip, their cooler climate offering welcome relief from the Tapachula steam bath. The scenic road up is winding but well paved.

Santo Domingo lies 34km northeast of Tapachula, amid coffee plantations. The village's gorgeous three-story wooden 1920s *casa grande* has been restored. It belonged to the German immigrants who formerly owned the coffee plantation here, but it's now the **Centro Ecoturístico Santo Domingo** (☑627-00-60; www.centroecoturistico santodomingo.com, in Spanish; ☉7am-8pm; ☎) and has a restaurant (mains M$35 to M$80), a small creaky-floored coffee museum (M$5) and a well-tended tropical garden and pool (M$10; free with a meal).

About 9km beyond Santo Domingo, **Unión Juárez** (population 2600, elevation 1300m) is the starting point for ascents of Tacaná and other, less demanding walks. Tapachula folk like to come up here on weekends and holidays to cool off and feast on *parrillada*, a cholesterol-challenging plate of grilled meat and a few vegetables.

Another local place to head for is **Pico del Loro**, a parrot-beak-shaped overhanging rock that offers fine pánoramas. The rock is 5km up a drivable track that leaves the Santo Domingo–Unión Juárez road about halfway between the two villages. Ask directions to some of the various lookouts over the valley of the Río Suchiate (the international border), or to the **Cascadas Muxbal**, a natural toboggan slope, about one hour's walk from Unión Juárez.

🛏 Sleeping & Eating

There are plenty of *comedores* and restaurants around the plaza in Unión Juárez. Lodging here is nothing extraordinary.

Hotel Colonial Campestre   HOTEL $
(☑647-20-15; Unión Juárez; r M$350-500; P☎) Rambling and Escher-esque, this oddly textured hotel has spacious rooms with bathroom, TV and good views (especially from room number 26). It also has a restaurant (mains M$50 to M$80; *parrillada* for two M$160). Look for the arch a couple of blocks below the plaza.

Hotel Aljoad   HOTEL $
(☑647-21-06; Unión Juárez; s/d/tr M$150/200/250; P☎) Just north of the plaza, the super-basic Aljoad has tidy rooms around a cluttered patio, all with hot-water bathrooms.

SUMMITING TACANÁ

The best months to climb Tacaná are late November to March. There are two routes up the mountain from Unión Juárez. Neither requires any technical climbing, but you need to allow two or three days for either, preferably plus time to acclimatize. Be prepared for extreme cold at the top. The less steep route is via Chiquihuites, 12km from Unión Juárez and reachable by vehicle. From there it's a three-hour walk to Papales, where you can sleep in huts for a donation of about M$20. The ascent from Papales to the summit takes about five hours. The other route is via Talquián (about two hours' walk from Unión Juárez) and Trigales (five hours from Talquián). It takes about six hours to climb from Trigales to the summit. The two routes meet a couple of hours below the summit, and on both you have access to camping areas.

Combis from Unión Juárez will carry you to the small town of Córdoba, about halfway to Talquián, also passing the turnoff for Chiquihuites (about 1½ hours' walk away). It's a good idea to get a guide for Tacaná in Unión Juárez or organize one to meet you. Humberto Ríos at the **Cafetal de la Montaña** (647-20-31; hrios1951@hotmail.com) is a reference for a network of local guides, or ask for the Valera brothers at **Hotel Colonial Campestre** (647-20-15; fernandao772@hotmail.com). Guides charge about M$200 to M$250 per day.

Getting There & Away

From Tapachula, first take a combi from the colectivo terminal to Cacahoatán (M$15, 30 minutes), 20km north. From where these terminate in Cacahoatán, Transportes Tacaná combis travel to Santo Domingo (M$12, 30 minutes) and Unión Juárez (M$15, 45 minutes).

COFFEE FINCAS

The hills north of Tapachula are home to numerous coffee fincas (ranches), many of them set up by German immigrants more than a century ago. Fincas with tours, restaurants and overnight accommodations include: **Finca Argovia** (962-626-61-15; www.argovia.com.mx; s/d/f from M$1205/1415/1530), **Finca Hamburgo** (962-626-64-04; www.fincahamburgo.com; f/ste from M$1200/1662) and **Finca Irlanda** (962-625-92-03; www.fincairlanda.grupopeters.com, in Spanish; r per person M$700).

BORDER TOWNS

It's 20km from Tapachula to the international border at **Talismán**, opposite El Carmen in Guatemala. The border crossing between **Ciudad Hidalgo**, 37km from Tapachula, opposite Ciudad Tecún Umán in Guatemala, is busier and has more onward connections. Both border points have money-changing facilities and are open 24 hours – though you should get through by early afternoon for greater security and to guarantee onward transportation. Watch out for money-changers passing counterfeit bills at both crossings.

Getting There & Away

In Tapachula, you can also catch combis to either border from the street outside the OCC bus station.

From Tapachula, **Autotransportes Paulino Navarro** (Calle 7a Poniente 5) combis head to Ciudad Hidalgo (M$21, 50 minutes) every 10 minutes, 4:30am to 10pm.

Frequent buses leave Ciudad Tecún Umán until about 6pm for Guatemala City (five hours) by the Pacific slope route, through Retalhuleu and Escuintla. Buses to Quetzaltenango (three hours) depart hourly from 5am to 6pm.

Unión y Progreso (Calle 5a Poniente 53, Tapachula) combis leave for Talismán every 10 minutes, between 5am and 9pm (M$15). A taxi from Tapachula to Talismán takes 20 minutes and costs around M$200.

The majority of bus services from El Carmen, which include around 20 a day to Guatemala City (seven hours), go via Ciudad Tecún Umán, and then head along the Pacific slope route. For Quetzaltenango, you can take one of these and change at Coatepeque or Retalhuleu, but it's easier to get a colectivo taxi to Malacatán, on a more direct road to Quetzaltenango via San Marcos, and then look for onward transportation from there.

For Lake Atitlán or Chichicastenango, you need to get to Quetzaltenango first.

TABASCO

They say that Tabasco has more water than land, and looking at all the lagoons, rivers and wetlands on the map you can certainly see why, especially during the rainy season.

It's always hot and sweaty here, but marginally less so when you catch a breeze along the Gulf of Mexico or venture into the southern hills. Travelers to Villahermosa and coastal Tabasco should note the region is subject to seasonal floods, though few travelers linger in Tabasco longer than it takes to see the outstanding Olmec stone sculpture in Villahermosa's Parque-Museo La Venta. The state is the site of extensive onshore and offshore oil exploitation by Mexico's state oil company (Pemex).

Villahermosa

☎993 / POP 640,000

This sprawling, flat, hot and humid city, with more than a quarter of Tabasco's population, was never the 'beautiful town' its

HIGHLIGHTS OF TABASCO

Tabasco has hosted as rich a procession of cultures as anywhere in Mexico. In pre-Hispanic times, Tabasco was the prosperous nexus of a far-reaching trade network extending around the Yucatán coast to Honduras, up the rivers to the jungles and mountains of Guatemala, and westward to highland central Mexico. Olmec religion, art, astronomy and architecture deeply influenced all of Mexico's later civilizations.

To reach Tapijulapa from Villahermosa, take public transportation via Teapa and then Tacotalpa. For the Reserva de la Biosfera Pantanos de Centla, ADO, CAT and Cardesa buses service Frontera, where *colectivos* run to the reserve. For other destinations listed here, see p410.

La Venta

Though most monuments from La Venta are at Villahermosa's Parque-Museo La Venta (p408), this ancient Olmec ceremonial **site** (☎923-232-04-23; admission M$37; ⊗8am-4pm) still fascinates as the largest and most important 'capital' of Mexico's mother culture. La Venta flourished between about 800 and 400 BC on a natural plateau rising about 20m above an area of fertile, seasonally flooded lowlands. Matthew Stirling is credited with discovering, in the early 1940s, four huge Olmec heads sculpted from basalt, the largest more than 2m high.

The museum at the site entrance holds three badly weathered Olmec heads, plus replicas of some of the finest sculptures that are no longer here. The heart of the site is the 30m-high Edificio C-1, a rounded pyramid constructed out of clay and sand. Ceremonial areas and more structures stretch to the north and south.

Comalcalco

The impressive Maya ruins of ancient **Comalcalco** (admission M$41; ⊗8am-5pm), 50km northwest of Villahermosa, are unique because many of their buildings are constructed of bricks and/or mortar made from oyster shells. Comalcalco was at its peak between AD 600 and 1000, when it was ruled by the Chontals. It remained an important center of commerce for several more centuries, trading in a cornucopia of pre-Hispanic luxury goods.

A museum at the entrance has a fine array of sculptures and engravings of human heads, deities, glyphs and animals such as crocodiles and pelicans.

The first building you encounter is the great brick tiered pyramid, **Templo 1**. At its base are the remains of large stucco sculptures, including the feet of a giant winged toad. Further temples line Plaza Norte, in front of Templo I. In the far (southeast) corner of the site rises the **Gran Acrópolis**, which has views from its summit over a canopy of palms to the Gulf of Mexico. The Acrópolis is fronted by **Templo V**, a burial pyramid that was once decorated on all sides with stucco sculptures of people, reptiles, birds and aquatic life. At Templo V's western foot is **Templo IX**, which has a tomb lined by nine stucco sculptures showing a Comalcalco lord with his priests and courtiers. Above Templo V is the crumbling profile of **El Palacio**, with its parallel 80m-long corbel-arched galleries, probably once Comalcalco's royal residence. Information is in both Spanish and English.

name implies. It's settled on the winding Río Grijalva, but Villahermosa's most attractive attribute became its worst enemy when the river burst its banks and engulfed the city in 2007.

Oil money has pumped modernity and commerce into some of the outer districts, where you'll find glitzy malls, imposing public buildings and luxury hotels.

 Sights

The central area of this expansive city is known as the Zona Luz, and extends north–south from Parque Juárez to the Plaza de Armas, and east–west from the Río Grijalva to roughly Calle 5 de Mayo. The main bus stations are between 750m and 1km north of the center.

Teapa

In this bustling town 50km south of Villahermosa, spelunkers should stop by the **Grutas del Coconá** (adult/child M$35/15; ☉10am-5pm), a developed cavern with pools, bats, plenty of stalactites and stalagmites, and a small museum containing pre-Hispanic ritual items found in the cave. Bring a flashlight or be prepared to pay an additional M$50 for a guide to turn on the cavern lights. Guides can also be hired to explore undeveloped caves nearby. Take a 'Grutas' combi from Calle Bastar, beside Teapa's central church.

Tapijulapa

The prettiest village in Tabasco, riverside Tapijulapa sits among the lushly forested hills of far southern Tabasco, 36km from Teapa. It boasts a 17th-century church presiding over beautiful white houses with red-tiled roofs and potted flowers. **Mesón de la Sierra** (🖉932-322-40-27; mesondelasierra@hotmail.com; r M$472; 🅿❷❀📶), located two blocks north of the plaza on the staircase to the church, is a comfortable five-room inn with a light-drenched Mediterranean feel and a prime location for appreciating the spectacular forested hills beyond town.

The beautiful jungle park **Villa Luz** (☉9am-5pm Tue-Sun) is a five-minute boat ride along the Río Oxolotán from the village *embarcadero*. From the landing, it's a 1km walk to the park's **Casa Museo**, the former country villa of Tomás Garrido Canabal, the rabidly anticlerical governor of Tabasco in the 1920s and '30s (he demolished Villahermosa's 18th-century baroque cathedral, banned alcohol and gave women the vote). From here other paths lead 600m to the *cascadas* (beautiful waterfalls tumbling into a river, with pools for a refreshing dip) and 900m to the Cueva de las Sardinas Ciegas (Cave of the Blind Sardines), named for the sightless fish that inhabit the sulfurous river inside the cave.

From Teapa, first take a bus to Tacotalpa.

Reserva de la Biosfera Pantanos de Centla

This 3030-sq-km biosphere reserve protects a good part of the wetlands around the lower reaches of two of Mexico's biggest rivers, the Usumacinta and the Grijalva. These lakes, marshes, rivers, mangroves, savannas and forests are an irreplaceable sanctuary for countless creatures, including the West Indian manatee and Morelet's crocodile (both endangered), six kinds of tortoise, tapir, ocelots, jaguars, howler monkeys, 60 fish species and 255 bird species.

The **Centro de Interpretación Uyotot-Ja** (🖉913-331-09-66; www.tabasco.gob.mx/turismo/rutpantanos.php, in Spanish; Carretera Frontera-Jonuta Km 12.5; admission M$25, reserve fee M$25; ☉9am-6pm Tue-Sun) visitor center, or 'Casa de Agua,' is 13km along the Jonuta road from Frontera, beside the broad, winding Río Grijalva. A 20m-high observation tower overlooks the awesome confluence of the Grijalva, the Usumacinta and a third large river, the San Pedrito – a spot known as Tres Brazos (Three Arms). Boat trips are available into the mangroves, where you should see crocodiles, iguanas, birds and, with luck, howler monkeys. March to May is the best birding season.

From Frontera – near the site of conquistador Hernán Cortés' 1519 first battle against native Mexicans – it's a 15-minute trip.

Parque-Museo La Venta
PARK, MUSEUM

(Av Ruíz Cortines; admission M$40; ⊘8am-4pm)
This fascinating outdoor park and museum
was created in 1958, when petroleum exploration threatened the highly important
ancient Olmec settlement of La Venta in
western Tabasco (boxed text p406). Archaeologists moved the site's most significant
finds, including three colossal stone heads,
to Villahermosa.

Plan two to three hours for your visit,
and take mosquito repellent (the park is
set in humid tropical woodland). Parque-
Museo La Venta lies 2km northwest of the
Zona Luz, beside Avenida Ruíz Cortines, the
main east–west highway crossing the city.
It's M$20 via *colectivo*.

Zoo

Inside, you first come to a zoo devoted to
animals from Tabasco and nearby regions:
cats include jaguars, ocelots and jaguarundi,
and there are white-tailed deer, spider monkeys, crocodiles, boa constrictors, peccaries
and plenty of colorful birds, including scarlet macaws and keel-billed toucans.

Sculpture Trail

There's an informative display in English
and Spanish on Olmec archaeology as you
pass through to the sculpture trail, the
start of which is marked by a giant *ceiba*
(the sacred tree of the Olmec and Maya).
This 1km walk is lined with finds from La
Venta. Among the most impressive, in the
order you come to them, are **Stele 3**, which
depicts a bearded man with a headdress;
Altar 5, depicting a figure carrying a child;
Monument 77, 'El Gobernante,' a very
sour-looking seated ruler; the monkey-
faced **Monument 56**; **Monument 1**, the
colossal head of a helmet-wearing warrior;
and **Stele 1**, showing a young goddess (a
rare Olmec representation of anything female). Animals that pose no danger (such
as coatis, squirrels and black agoutis) roam
freely around the park.

🛏 Sleeping

An oil town, Villahermosa has scores of comfortable midrange and top-end chain hotels,
most of which offer heavily discounted online and weekend rates. Inviting budget options are scarcer.

Hyatt Regency Villahermosa
LUXURY HOTEL $$$

(☑310-12-34; www.villahermosa.regency.hyatt.com;
Av Juárez 106, Colonia Lindavista; r from US$130,

ste from US$180; P☺❄@🅿🛆) Villahermosa's
smartest hotel has amenities that include a
large swimming pool, a smaller kids' pool, a
gym, two restaurants and a wine bar.

Hotel Olmeca Plaza
HOTEL $$$

(☑358-01-02, 800-201-09-09; www.hotelolmeca
plaza.com; Madero 418; r Mon-Thu M$1248, Fri-Sun
M$760; P☺❄@🅿🛆) The classiest down-
town hotel also has an open-air pool and a
well-equipped gym. Rooms are modern and
comfortable, with writing desks and good
large bathrooms, and there's a quality onsite
restaurant.

Hotel Provincia Express
HOTEL $$

(☑314-53-78; www.hotelesprovinciaexpress.infored.
mx, in Spanish; Lerdo de Tejada 303; r incl breakfast
M$450-500; P❄@🅿) An excellent-value
hotel in a central location, with clean and
pleasant rooms and a homey, yellow color
scheme. A bit more scuffed up than the
other midrange options, though it includes
good amenities such as phones, ironing
boards, a simple cafeteria and some in-room
fridges.

Hotel Oriente
HOTEL $

(☑312-01-21; hotel-oriente@hotmail.com; Madero
425; s/d/tr M$240/340/400, with air-con M$340/
420/520; ❄🅿) The friendly Oriente is a well-
run downtown hotel where the comfort-
able rooms are kept spick-and-span, and
the bathrooms even have a little sparkle.
All rooms have TV. Reserve two days in ad-
vance; it's small and fills up quickly.

Hotel Palomino Palace
HOTEL $

(☑314-33-79, reservations 312-84-31; cnr Mina &
Fuentes; r/tr/q M$410/510/610; ❄🅿) A no-frills
but clean option directly across the street
from the ADO bus station. All rooms have
TV, ceiling fans and strong air-con.

🍴 Eating

A large city, Villahermosa has an eclectic
collection of hotel restaurants, chain res-
taurants and eateries specializing in seafood
and international cuisines.

TOP CHOICE Café Punta del Cielo
CAFE $

(Av Ruíz Cortines; coffee M$23-47; ⊘7am-midnight;
☺🅿) A respite from the raging heat and hu-
midity, this small air-conditioned glass box
next to Parque-Museo La Venta is a dream
come true. Primarily a cafe, it serves pre-
mium hot and cold coffee drinks (some or-
ganic), as well as *panini* and light snacks. Go
for brain freeze with an arctic frappé.

CHIAPAS VILLAHERMOSA

BUSES FROM VILLAHERMOSA

DESTINATION	FARE (M$)	DURATION	FREQUENCY (DAILY)
Campeche	348-422	5½-7hr	20 ADO
Cancún	686-1200	12½-14½hr	17 ADO
Comalcalco	20-24	1-1½hr	very frequent Cardesa & CAT
Mérida	496-914	8-9½hr	26 ADO
Mexico City (TAPO)	806-1306	10-12hr	27 ADO
Oaxaca	556	13½hr	2 ADO
Palenque	60-126	2½hr	17 ADO, very frequent CAT & Cardesa
San Cristóbal de las Casas	260	71/2hr	2 ADO
Tenosique	105-166	3½hr	11 ADO, 16 CAT
Tuxtla Gutiérrez	268-330	4-5hr	16 ADO
Veracruz	428-656	6-8½hr	23 ADO

Restaurante Madan MEXICAN $$
(Madero 408; mains M$45-125;) It's not glamorous, but this very reliable and popular hotel restaurant two blocks west of the river has good Mexican dishes and efficient, friendly service.

Rock & Roll Cocktelería SEAFOOD $$
(Reforma 307; seafood cocktails M$95-130; ☺10am-11pm; ☺) A maelstrom of heat, swirling fans, thumping jukebox and garrulous punters. Everyone's here for the *cocteles* (fish or seafood, tomato sauce, lettuce, onions and a lemon squeeze) and the cheap beer.

☆ Entertainment

To find out what's on in town, check out the website of Tabasco's **culture department** (http://iec.tabasco.gob.mx, in Spanish). In the evening, look for bands and marimba musicians playing along the pedestrianized Zona Luz.

ℹ Information

There are plentiful internet cafes charging M$10 per hour. Most banks have ATMs and exchange dollars.

Bancomer (cnr Zaragoza & Juárez; ☺8:30am-4pm Mon-Fri)

Funny Zone (Mina; ☺8am-9pm Mon-Sat) Internet cafe across from ADO bus station.

Oficina de Convenciones y Visitantes de Tabasco (OCV; ☎800-216-08-42; www.visitetabasco.com, in Spanish) Statewide information.

Santander (Madero 504; ☺9am-4pm Mon-Fri) Do your banking here.

State tourism office (www.tabasco.gob.mx/turismo, in Spanish) Maps and some statewide information.

Tourism information kiosk (☺8am-3pm Mon-Fri) At the ADO bus terminal.

ℹ Getting There & Away

Air

Villahermosa's **Aeropuerto Rovirosa** (☎356-01-57) is 13km east of the center, off Hwy 186. Aeroméxico is the major airline, and daily nonstop flights to/from Villahermosa include the following:

Aeroméxico (www.aeromexico.com) Acapulco, Cancún, Guadalajara, Houston, Mérida, Mexico City, Monterrey and Veracruz.

Continental (www.continental.com) Houston.

Interjet (www.interjet.com.mx) Mexico City.

MAYAir (www.mayair.com.mx) Mérida and Veracruz.

VivaAerobus (www.vivaaerobus.com.mx) Mexico City, Monterrey and Guadalajara.

 AIRPORT BUS TO PALENQUE

The Villahermosa airport has a handy counter for **ADO** (www.ado.com.mx, in Spanish), with almost hourly minibuses departing daily to Palenque (M$214, 2¼ hours) between 7:30am and 8:30pm. Check the website for schedules to/from 'Aeropuerto Villahermosa.'

Bus & Colectivo

Deluxe and 1st-class buses depart from the **ADO bus station** (ADO; Mina 297), which has 24-hour left luggage and is located 750m north of the Zona Luz. **La Sultana** (Av Ruíz Cortines 917) has comfortable, very frequent 2nd-class buses to Teapa (M$45, one hour).

Transportation to most destinations within Tabasco leaves from other terminals within walking distance north of ADO, including the 2nd-class **Cardesa bus station** (Cardesa; cnr Hermanos Bastar Zozaya & Castillo) and the main 2nd-class bus station, the **Central de Autobuses de Tabasco** (CAT; cnr Av Ruíz Cortines & Castillo) on the north side of Avenida Ruíz Cortines (use the pedestrian overpass).

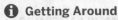 Getting Around

A taxi from the airport to the city costs M$200 (but M$150 to the airport) and takes about 25 minutes. Alternatively, walk 500m past the airport parking lot for a *colectivo* (M$7.50) from the Dos Montes taxi stand. These terminate in the market on Amado Nervo between Piño Suárez and Constitución, about 1km north of the Zona Luz. 'Dos Montes' *colectivos* leave from the same stop going back.

A system of *colectivo* taxis (M$20) provides the backbone of the center's public transit. Join a queue at a stand outside a large store or transportation terminal, where proficient handlers ask for your destination and quickly assign you a shared taxi. There's no fee for the match-up, and no haggling necessary.

Oaxaca

Includes »

Best Places to Eat

» La Biznaga (p428)
» Un Secreto (p467)
» Finca Los Vaqueros (p460)
» El Alquimista (p464)
» La Providencia (p465)

Best Places to Stay

» Casa Oaxaca (p424)
» Casa Pan de Miel (p468)
» Hotel Casa de Dan (p452)
» Las Bugambilias (p424)
» Un Sueño (p466)

Why Go?

The state of Oaxaca (wah-*hah*-kah) has a special magic felt by Mexicans and foreigners alike. A redoubt of indigenous culture, it's home to the country's most vibrant crafts and art scene, some outstandingly colorful and extrovert festivities, a uniquely savory cuisine and varied natural riches. At the center of the state in every way stands beautiful, colonial Oaxaca city, an elegant, fascinating cultural hub. Nearby, the forested Sierra Norte is home to successful community-tourism ventures enabling visitors to hike, bike and ride horses amid delicious green landscapes. To the south, across rugged, remote mountains, is Oaxaca's fabulous coast, with its endless sandy beaches, pumping Pacific surf, seas full of dolphins, turtles and fish, and a string of beach towns and villages that will make any traveler happy: lively Puerto Escondido; planned but relaxed Bahías de Huatulco; and the hedonist's delights of Zipolite, San Agustinillo and Mazunte.

When to Go

Oaxaca City

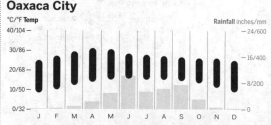

Jan–Mar The driest months: a lively coastal winter-escapee scene, best hiking conditions in the Sierra Norte.

Jul–Aug Guelaguetza festival in Oaxaca city; summer-vacation fun time on the coast.

Late Oct–Nov Día de Muertos celebrations in and around Oaxaca city; Fiestas de Noviembre in Puerto Escondido.

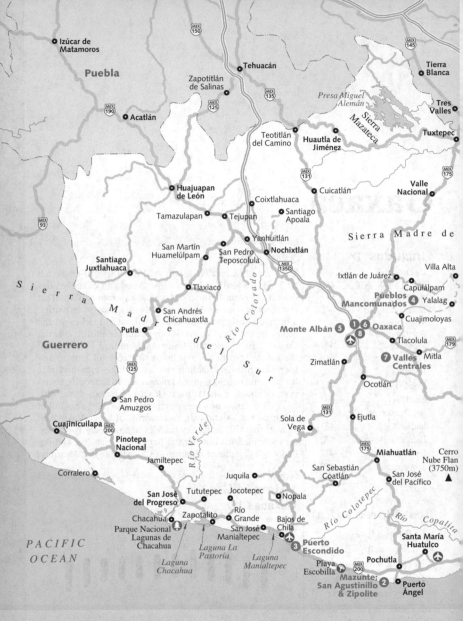

Oaxaca Highlights

① Indulge in the culture, color and culinary delights of festive, colonial **Oaxaca city** (p414)

② Chill out for longer than you planned at the travelers'

hangouts of **Zipolite** (p463), **San Agustinillo** (p465) or **Mazunte** (p467)

③ Ride the surf on the gorgeous beaches of **Puerto Escondido** (p448)

④ Hike through otherworldly cloud forests between the villages of the **Pueblos Mancomunados** (p445)

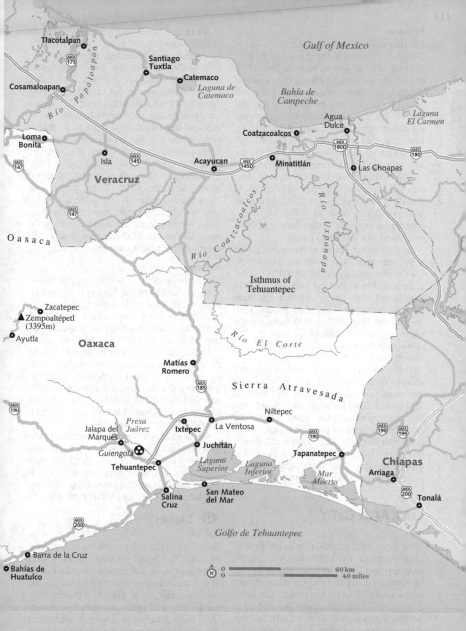

History

Pre-Hispanic cultures in Oaxaca's Valles Centrales (Central Valleys) reached heights rivaling those of central Mexico. The hilltop city of Monte Albán became the center of the Zapotec culture, which conquered much of Oaxaca and peaked between AD 350 and 700. From about 1200 the Zapotecs came under the growing dominance of the Mixtecs from Oaxaca's northwest uplands. Mixtecs and Zapotecs alike were conquered by the Aztecs in the 15th and early 16th centuries.

The Spanish had to send at least four expeditions before they felt safe enough to found the city of Oaxaca in 1529. The indigenous population declined quickly and disastrously: unsuccessful indigenous rebellions continued into the 20th century.

Benito Juárez, the great reforming leader of 19th-century Mexico, was a Zapotec from the Oaxaca mountains. He served as national president from 1861 until his death in 1872 (see boxed text, p425). Another Oaxacan, Porfirio Díaz, rose to control Mexico with an iron fist from 1877 to 1910, bringing the country into the industrial age but fostering corruption, repression and, eventually, the Revolution in 1910.

Today, while tourism thrives in and around Oaxaca city and in some places on the coast, underdevelopment still prevails in the backcountry. Confrontations between the authoritarian state government and opposition organizations in Oaxaca city in 2006 and 2007 highlighted the gulf between the state's rich, largely mestizo (people of mixed ancestry) elite and its poor, disempowered, heavily indigenous majority.

OAXACA CITY

☑951 / POP 260,000 / ELEV 1550M

With a beautiful colonial core of lovely, tree-shaded streets and highly creative artistic, culinary and craft scenes, Oaxaca is one of Mexico's most captivating cities. Artists and artisans alike are inspired by the area's deep-rooted indigenous traditions and by its bright, clear southern light. Oaxaca has top-class museums, charming inns, fascinating markets, a clutch of good language schools and its own exhilarating version of Mexican cuisine. The easygoing pace frequently breaks out into the fireworks of a fiesta, and there's some brightly colored event unfolding in the streets or the Zócalo (Oaxaca's lovely central square) almost every day.

Set at the nexus of three valleys flanked by high mountains, the city is surrounded by fascinating archaeological sites and colorfully traditional villages and small towns with bustling weekly markets. The valley and mountain landscapes provide abundant opportunities for hiking, biking and horseback riding, and good active-tourism operators and successful rural tourism programs make it easy to enjoy these experiences.

Despite its cultural riches, the state of Oaxaca is one of Mexico's poorest, and the city's fringe settlements of migrant villagers, as well as some of the villages themselves, are as impoverished as any in Mexico. There are opportunities for volunteer work among these communities. Yet despite such problems, the people of Oaxaca are among the most warmly hospitable in the country.

History

The Aztec settlement here was called Huaxyácac (meaning 'In the Nose of the Squash'), from which 'Oaxaca' is derived. The Spanish laid out a new town around the existing Zócalo in 1529, and it quickly became the most important place in southern Mexico.

In the 18th century Oaxaca grew rich from the export of cochineal (a red dye made from tiny insects living on the prickly pear cactus) and from the weaving of textiles. By 1796 it was probably the third-biggest city in Nueva España, with about 20,000 people (including 600 clergy) and 800 cotton looms.

Oaxaca's major expansion has come in the past 30 years, with tourism, new businesses and rural poverty all encouraging migration from the countryside. Together with formerly separate villages and towns it now forms a conurbation of perhaps 450,000 people.

⊙ Sights

Zócalo
PLAZA

Traffic-free, shaded by tall trees and surrounded by elegant *portales* (arcades) with numerous cafes and restaurants, the Zócalo is the perfect place to start soaking up the Oaxaca atmosphere. The plaza bustles with life by day and night, as marimba ensembles, brass bands and roving buskers float their melodies among the crowds and lovers parade in slow rounds under the trees, pausing only to share a park bench for a bit of necking. Anyone and everyone sits, drinks and watches from the cafes, and political protesters of some stripe or other are usually ensconced in a makeshift camp in front of the Palacio de Gobierno on the plaza's south side.

The adjoining **Alameda** plaza, also traffic-free but without the cafes, is ripe for people-watching with its trinket-hawking vendors, gawking tourists and an informal clothes market.

Palacio de Gobierno

A 19th-century wonder of marble and murals, the State Government Palace occupies the southern flank of the Zócalo and now houses the very contemporary **Museo del Palacio** (admission M$25, Sun free; ◷10am-7pm Tue-Sat, 10am-5pm Sun & Mon). The main displays, with a primarily educational purpose, are interactive, high-tech and in Spanish only. They range over evolution, the oceans, the pre-Hispanic ball game, geology, biodiversity and more, with a Oaxacan handle on universal themes. Of more interest to the casual foreign visitor is likely to be the large-scale stairway mural (1980) by Arturo García Bustos, which depicts famous Oaxacans and Oaxaca history, including Benito Juárez and his wife, Margarita Maza, and José María Morelos, Porfirio Díaz, Vicente Guerrero (being shot at Cuilapan) and Juana Inés de la Cruz, the 17th-century nun and love poet. The museum also houses what is very probably the world's largest tortilla – a 300kg *tlayuda,* decorated with the history of Mexico by Enrique Ramos.

Catedral

Oaxaca's cathedral, begun in 1553 and finished (after several earthquakes) in the 18th century, stands just north of the Zócalo. Its main facade, facing the Alameda, features fine baroque carving.

Templo de Santo Domingo　　　　CHURCH
(cnr Alcalá & Gurrión; ◷7am-1pm & 4-8pm except during Mass) Five blocks north of the Zócalo, gorgeous Santo Domingo is the most splendid of Oaxaca's churches. It was built mainly between 1570 and 1608 as part of the city's Dominican monastery, with the finest artisans from Puebla and elsewhere helping in its construction. Like other big buildings in this earthquake-prone region, Santo Domingo has immensely thick stone walls.

Amid the fine carving on the baroque facade, the figure holding a church is Santo Domingo de Guzmán (1172–1221), the Spanish monk who founded the Dominican order. The Dominicans observed strict vows of poverty, chastity and obedience, and in Mexico they protected the indigenous people from other colonists' excesses.

Nearly every square inch of the church's interior is decorated in 3-D relief: intricately colored and gilt designs swirl around a profusion of painted figures. An elaborate family tree of Santo Domingo adorns the ceiling immediately inside the main entrance. Most elaborate of all is the decoration in the 18th-century Capilla de la Virgen del Rosario (Rosary Chapel) on the south side of the nave. The whole church takes on a magically warm glow during candlelit evening Masses.

Calle Alcalá　　　　STREET
Alcalá is the dignified, mainly traffic-free street that runs from the Catedral to Santo Domingo, lined by colonial-era stone buildings most of the way. Nearly all its buildings have been cleaned up and renovated into interesting shops, galleries, museums, cafes or bars, making for an always-interesting stroll and a lively nocturnal scene.

Museo Rufino Tamayo　　　　MUSEUM
(Morelos 503; admission M$35; ◷10am-2pm & 4-7pm Mon & Wed-Sat, 10am-3pm Sun) This top-class pre-Hispanic art museum was donated to Oaxaca by its most famous artist, the Zapotec Rufino Tamayo (1899–1991). In a fine 17th-century building, the collection focuses on the aesthetic qualities of ancient artifacts and traces artistic developments in pre-conquest times. It has some truly beautiful pieces and is strong on the pre-Classic era and lesser-known civilizations such as those of Veracruz and western Mexico.

[FREE] **Museo Textil de Oaxaca**　　　　MUSEUM
(Museum of Oaxacan Textiles; www.museotextilde oaxaca.org.mx, in Spanish; Hidalgo 917; ◷10am-8pm Mon-Sat, 10am-6pm Sun) Of Oaxaca's several colonial-era museum renovations, the textile museum, opened in 2009 in an 18th-century mansion, is one of the best. More than just a museum, it aims to promote Oaxaca's traditional textile crafts through exhibitions, workshops, presentations and a library. Themed selections from its stock of around 5000 Oaxacan and international textile pieces, many of them a century or more old, are always on view. Guided visits (M$10) are given at 5pm on Wednesday and Friday – in English as well as in Spanish if three or more people request this. If you're looking to buy fine textiles yourself, this is a good place to ask about weavers who use sustainable methods and natural fibers and dyes.

Oaxaca City

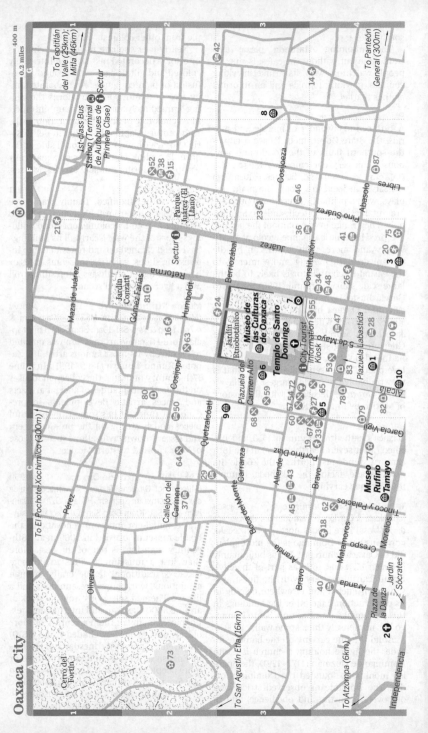

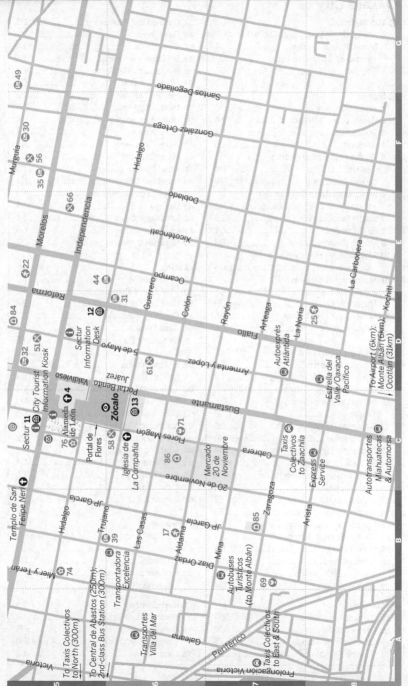

Oaxaca City

Jardín Etnobotánico   GARDENS
(Ethnobotanical Garden; 📞516-79-15; cnr Constitución & Reforma; 2hr tours in English or French M$100, 1hr tours in Spanish M$50; ⊘English tours 11am Tue, Thu & Sat, Spanish tours 10am, noon & 5pm Mon-Sat, French tours 5pm Tue) In former monastic grounds behind the Templo de Santo Domingo, this garden features plants from around the state, including a staggering variety of cacti. Though it has been growing only since the mid-1990s, it's already a fascinating demonstration of Oaxaca's biodiversity. Visits are by guided tour only; for English- or French-language tours it's a good idea to sign up a day or two beforehand.

Museo Casa de Juárez   MUSEUM
(García Vigil 609; admission M$37, Sun free; ⊘10am-6pm Tue-Sun) The simple house of bookbinder Antonio Salanueva, who employed and supported the great Mexican leader of the 19th-century, Benito Juárez during his youth, is now this interesting little museum. The binding workshop is preserved, along with memorabilia of Benito.

Basílica de la Soledad   CHURCH
(Independencia) The image of Oaxaca's patron saint, the Virgen de la Soledad (Virgin of Solitude), resides in the 17th-century Basílica de la Soledad, three-and-a-half blocks west of the Alameda. The church, with a richly carved baroque facade, stands where the image is said to have miraculously appeared in a donkey's pack in 1543. The Virgin lost her 2kg gold crown and several hundred diamonds to thieves in the 1990s.

🏃 **Activities**

🚶 **Tierraventura**   HIKING, TRADITIONAL MEDICINE
(📞501-13-63; www.tierraventura.com; Abasolo 217; ⊘10am-2pm & 4-6pm Mon-Fri) The very well-organized Tierraventura, run by a multi-lingual Swiss and German team, offers a big variety of trips and activities focused on hiking, nature, meeting locals and supporting small, local tourism projects. Local guides accompany travelers wherever possible. Tierraventura can take the logistical work out of visiting the Pueblos Mancomunados (p445) and other enticing areas. It also offers rare opportunities to learn about traditional medicine though a partnership with CECIP-ROC, an NGO working to improve health in indigenous communities. On most overnight trips prices range between M$700 and M$1100 per person per day.

🚶 **Expediciones Sierra Norte**   HIKING, HORSEBACK RIDING, CYCLING
(📞514-82-71; www.sierranorte.org.mx; Bravo 210; ⊘9:30am-7pm Mon-Fri, 9:30am-2pm Sat) Some of the most exhilarating outdoor adventures are to be had among the mountain villages of the Pueblos Mancomunados. Here, community-run Expediciones Sierra Norte maintains a network of good trails, comfortable village accommodations, and horses and bikes for rent. It's a very good idea to visit the Expediciones office in Oaxaca before heading up to the pueblos (villages). The office has English-speaking staff and copious information on trails, villages, accommodations and transportation, and can make reservations for *cabañas* (cabins) and any other services you need. It also sells a useful guide-map for M$50.

Bicicletas Pedro Martínez   CYCLING, HIKING
(📞514-59-35; www.bicicletaspedromartinez.com; Aldama 418; ⊘9am-8pm Mon-Sat, 10am-3pm Sun) Pedro Martínez, an amiable Mexican Olympic cyclist, offers a variety of mostly off-road bike rides amid some of Oaxaca state's most startling scenery. Van support cuts out some of the less interesting bits and hardest climbs. Full-day rides in the Valle de Tlacolula cost M$1210 per person for two people or

M$990 per person for four. The two-day 'Cascadas y Mangos' jaunt runs from Nochixtlán to Santiago Apoala, northwest of Oaxaca, then across part of the Reserva de la Biosfera Tehuacán-Cuicatlán to Cuicatlán on Hwy 135 (M$2200 to M$2570 per person). The three- or four-day Ruta Los Coatlanes (minimum three participants) takes

CONTEMPORARY ART IN OAXACA

Oaxaca state's talented artists continue to produce some of Mexico's most vibrant and pioneering art. A delight in color and light, a dreamlike feeling and references to indigenous mythology have long been trademarks of much Oaxacan art, though the latest generation often rejects such 'folklorism' and may look far beyond Oaxaca to international themes and styles. Any art lover can spend days browsing museums and galleries here and, with luck, attending the odd opening or other art-community event.

The Oaxacan artists who laid the basis for today's flowering of art in their homeland were the great muralist and explorer of color and light Rufino Tamayo (1899–1991), and European-influenced Francisco Gutiérrez (1906–45) who portrayed Oaxacan women rather like Greek goddesses. The next generation was led by three artists. The colorful, dreamlike art of Rodolfo Morales (1925–2001) from Ocotlán, with its characteristic childlike angel figures, has deep local mythical roots. Rodolfo Nieto (1936–85) populated his work with vivid fantasy animals and dream figures. Francisco Toledo (b 1940), from Juchitán, still a prominent figure in Oaxacan life, works in many media; grotesque or imaginary beasts often feature his subject matter.

Workshops for young artists organized by Tamayo in the 1970s encouraged talents such as Abelardo López, Ariel Mendoza, Alejandro Santiago and Felipe de Jesús Morales. Their work is highly varied, but indigenous roots and that persistent dreamlike quality run consistently through much of it. More or less contemporary are Sergio Hernández, whose limitless imagination melds the figurative with the abstract and fantastic, and Marco Bustamante with his haunting hyper-realist images. Today, contemporary artists such as Demián Flores and Soid Pastrana often reject representation in favor of cartoonlike compositions designed to provoke and make us ponder. Following are a number of worthwhile art museums and galleries.

Museo de Arte Contemporáneo de Oaxaca (MACO; www.museomaco.com, in Spanish; Alcalá 202; admission M$20; ⊙10:30am-8pm) Exhibits first-rate contemporary Mexican and international art, in a beautifully revamped colonial house.

Museo de los Pintores Oaxaqueños (Museum of Oaxacan Painters, MUPO; museodelos pintores.blogspot.com, in Spanish; Independencia 607; admission M$20; ⊙10am-8pm Tue-Sun) Changing exhibitions by Oaxaca state's best artists.

Arte de Oaxaca (www.artedeoaxaca.com; Murguía 105; admission free; ⊙11am-3pm & 5-8pm Mon-Fri, 11am-6pm Sat) This commercial gallery presents a wide range of quality art, and includes a room devoted to Rodolfo Morales' work.

Galería Quetzalli (www.galeriaquetzalli.com, in Spanish; Constitución 104; admission free; ⊙10am-2pm & 5-8pm Mon-Sat) Oaxaca's leading serious commercial gallery, handling some of the biggest names, such as Francisco Toledo and Sergio Hernández. It has a second exhibition space, **Bodega Quetzalli** (Murguía 400), a few blocks away.

Centro Fotográfico Álvarez Bravo (www.cfmab.blogspot.com, in Spanish; Bravo 116; admission free; ⊙9:30am-8pm Wed-Mon) With a taste for provocative social commentary, this contemporary photo gallery displays high-quality work by international photographers.

Instituto de Artes Gráficas de Oaxaca (Oaxaca Graphic Arts Institute, IAGO; www.insti tutodeartesgraficasdeoaxaca.blogspot.com, in Spanish; Alcalá 507; admission free; ⊙9:30am-8pm) Offers changing exhibitions of graphic art as well as a superb arts library.

La Curtiduría (lacurtiduria.blogspot.com, in Spanish; 5 de Mayo 307, Barrio Jalatlaco; admission free; ⊙10am-2pm & 4-8pm Mon-Fri) Set in an old tannery, La Curtiduría stages and facilitates contemporary art exhibits, classes and community projects, and runs an artist-in-residence program.

you right down to Puerto Escondido on the Pacific coast, crossing the backcountry of the Sierra Madre del Sur, costing M$5610 including accommodations (one night is camping) and meals. Pedro also offers some great day walks in the Sierra Norte.

Horseback Mexico HORSEBACK RIDING
(☑cell phone 951-1997026; www.horsebackmexico. com; Murguía 403) Based at Rojas de Cuauhtémoc, 15km east of the city, this experienced, enthusiastic Canadian- and North American-run outfit offers a variety of equestrian adventures. Two-hour rides on their Arabian and Mexican cavalry horses in the local valleys and hills cost M$690 (minimum two people). Other options include overnight rides and one-week riding vacations, which might be based at the Rojas ranch (it has comfortable guest accommodations) or riding village to village in the picturesque Sierra Norte. You can make arrangements at the city office (Murguía 403): round-trip transportation is included.

Zona Bici CYCLING
(☑516-09-53; www.bikeoaxaca.com; García Vigil 406; ⊙10am-2:30pm & 4:30-8:30pm Mon-Sat) Zona Bici conducts easy to moderate four-hour mountain-biking trips in the Valles Centrales for M$500 per person (minimum two people). The Italian owner will set a more strenuous pace, if you want. It's also a full-service bike shop and rental outlet.

Centro de Esperanza Infantil VOLUNTEERING
(Oaxaca Streetchildren Grassroots; ☑501-10-69; www.oaxacastreetchildrengrassroots.org; Crespo 308; ⊙9am-3pm Mon-Fri, 9am-2pm Sat) This is a nonpolitical, nonreligious center that sponsors and cares for some 600 kids from poor families who, without assistance, could not attend school. The center has a dining room, library, computers and classrooms, and has helped about 50 kids reach university. The staff does a great job and welcomes donations, sponsors, volunteers and visitors. Volunteers can help with meals, administrative work, the computer lab or projects with the children, and even a half-day of assistance is helpful.

Rancho Buenavista ADVENTURE SPORTS
(www.ranchobuenavista.com.mx) Italian- and Mexican-run Rancho Buenavista focuses on rock climbing, mountaineering, hiking and mountain-biking expeditions. Options range from half a day mountain biking in Oaxaca's Valles Centrales to two-week

climbing expeditions on Mexico's volcanoes. A two-day climbing trip to Apoala is M$1100 to M$1400. Contact them via the website.

Casa Hogar Hijos de la Luna VOLUNTEERING
(☑132-16-87; www.hijosdelaluna-en.org; Cárdenas 212, Colonia Guadalupe Victoria) This hostel for about 30 children of single mothers who work at night depends on volunteers for its day-to-day running. Tasks can include kitchen work, baby care and help with play, activities and studies. It's about 4km northwest of the city center.

Oaxaca Lending Library LIBRARY
(oaxlibrary.org; Pino Suárez 519; ⊙10am-2pm & 4-7pm Mon-Fri, 10am-1pm Sat) This cultural hub for foreign residents and language learners boasts a sizable collection of books and magazines on Oaxaca and Mexico in English and Spanish. Visitor membership (per one/two months M$130/200) allows you to borrow books. Hang out here long enough and you'll likely find an eager English student willing to participate in informal language exchange.

Most of Oaxaca's Spanish-language schools offer volunteer opportunities for their students and in some cases for nonstudents as well.

Courses
Oaxaca is a very popular place for travelers and visitors to learn the Spanish language or take a course in Mexican cooking.

Language Courses
An established language-learning destination, Oaxaca has a clutch of reputable schools, all offering small-group instruction at varied levels and most emphasizing spoken language. At most schools you can start any Monday (at some you can start any day). Most offer individual tuition if wanted, plus volunteer opportunities and optional add-on activities like dance or cooking classes, trips and *intercambios* (meetings with locals for conversation). The schools listed here are among the most frequently and highly recommended. Enrollment/registration fees, textbooks and materials are sometimes hidden costs.

Schools can arrange accommodations with families or in hotels, apartments and in a few cases their own student houses. Family accommodations with a private room

DON'T MISS

MUSEO DE LAS CULTURAS DE OAXACA

The **Museum of Oaxacan Cultures** (cnr Alcalá & Gurrión; admission M$51, video M$45; ◷10am-7pm Tue-Sun), housed in the beautiful monastery buildings adjoining the Templo de Santo Domingo, is one of the best regional museums in Mexico. Displays take you right through the history and cultures of Oaxaca state up to the present day.

A gorgeous green-stone cloister serves as antechamber to the museum proper. The museum emphasizes the direct lineage between Oaxaca's pre-Hispanic and contemporary indigenous cultures, illustrating continuity in such areas as crafts, medicine, food, drink and music. The greatest highlight is the Mixtec treasure from Tomb 7 at Monte Albán, in Room III. This treasure dates from the 14th century, when Mixtecs reused an old Zapotec tomb to bury one of their kings and his sacrificed servants. With the bodies they placed a hoard of beautifully worked silver, turquoise, coral, jade, amber and pearls, finely carved bone, crystal goblets, a skull covered in turquoise and a lot of gold. The treasure was discovered in 1932 by Alfonso Caso.

The museum's first four halls (I to IV) are devoted to the pre-Hispanic period, the next four (V to VIII) to the colonial period (along with nine smaller rooms focusing on colonial-era crafts), the following five (IX to XIII) to Oaxaca in the independence era and after, and the final room (XIV) to Santo Domingo Monastery itself. At the end of one long corridor, glass doors give a view into the beautifully ornate choir of the Templo de Santo Domingo.

Curiously in a city where foreign tourism is an economic mainstay, the museum's explanatory material is in Spanish only, but you can rent decent English-language audio guides for M$50. Also here is a good book and souvenir shop.

typically cost US$18/23/26 a day with one/two/three meals.

Becari Language School SPANISH LANGUAGE
(www.becari.com.mx; 15/20/30hr per week US$150/200/300) Bravo (☎514-60-76; Bravo 210) QR Campus (☎516-46-34; Quintana Roo 209) This highly rated, medium-sized school has two separate branches: you can study at either or both. Maximum class size is five and optional extras include salsa dance, Zapotec language, weaving and woodcarving. The Quintana Roo branch has its own temascal (pre-Hispanic-style steam bath; M$250 per session). It also offers special courses such as medical Spanish and also Spanish for volunteers.

Amigos del Sol SPANISH LANGUAGE
(☎133-60-52, cell phone 951-1968039; www.oaxacanews.com/amigosdelsol.htm; Calzada San Felipe del Agua 322; 15/20/25hr per week US$150/200/250) Professional, good-value school popular with travelers. Maximum class size is three and schedules are flexible. Begin any weekday – contact the school by phone or email beforehand or between 7am and 8:30am the day you want to start. There's no minimum duration and no registration charge. The school is in a residential area in the north of the city, with free transportation for the short drive provided from its meeting point at Pino Suárez 802, facing Parque Juárez (El Llano).

Oaxaca International SPANISH LANGUAGE
(☎503-42-28; www.oaxacainternational.com; Morelos 1003; 10/15/20/30hr per week US$80/120/160/240) Has classes limited to four students and also offers special programs for professionals in several fields. Two weekly cultural activities, from pottery and painting to cooking and dance, are included in the fees.

Ollin Tlahtoalli SPANISH LANGUAGE
(☎514-55-62; www.ollinoaxaca.org.mx; Ocampo 710; group/individual instruction per hr US$8/12) This relatively young operation has earned a reputation for pragmatic language learning and good volunteer opportunities in indigenous empowerment programs. programs include art workshops, film-making projects and English teaching. Oaxacan culture including museum, market and village visits can be integrated into your course. Email the school in advance to discuss your needs. There's no minimum duration and no registration fee. For volunteers, a minimum one-month commitment is preferred.

Oaxaca Spanish Magic SPANISH LANGUAGE
(☎516-73-16; www.oaxacaspanishmagic.com; Berriozábal 200; 15/20hr per week US$120/140) This

small, well-priced school gets good reports for its friendliness and making learning fun.

Instituto Cultural Oaxaca SPANISH LANGUAGE
(ICO; ☎515-34-04; www.icomexico.com; Juárez 909; 15/20/32hr per week US$130/150/170) A larger, long-established school with a professional approach and ample gardens where some of the learning takes place. The 32-hour-a-week main program includes eight hours of cultural workshops (dance, cooking, history and more) and four hours' *intercambio*. You can study for any period from one week up; four weeks is typical. ICO sponsors Fundación en Vía (following), which offers volunteering opportunities.

Cooking Classes

Oaxaca has its own spicy take on Mexican cuisine, based on its famous seven *moles* (sauces based on nuts, chilies and spices; see boxed text, p428), pre-Hispanic culinary traditions and unforgettable flavor combinations. Several of Oaxaca's most expert cooks regularly impart their secrets to visitors, making the city one of the best places in the country to learn Mexican cooking. The following recommended classes are (or can be) held in English, and generally include market visits to buy ingredients, plus a glass or two of good mezcal with your meal.

Seasons of My Heart COOKING
(☎cell phone 951-5080469; www.seasonsofmyheart.com; group day class incl transportation per person US$75, longer courses & tours from US$1495) This cooking school at a ranch at San Lorenzo Cacaotepec in the Valle de Etla is run by North American chef, food writer and Oaxacan food expert Susana Trilling. It offers classes from half-day or one-day group sessions (most Wednesdays) to weeklong courses, plus fascinating culinary tours around Oaxaca state and other Mexican regions.

La Casa de los Sabores COOKING
(☎516-66-68; www.casadelossabores.com; La Olla, Reforma 402; per person US$70) Pilar Cabrera, owner of La Olla restaurant, gives classes on Tuesday and Thursday mornings. Participants (minimum four, maximum 10) prepare and eat one of 16 five-course Mexican or Oaxacan lunch menus on offer. Make inquiries and reservations at La Olla: the classes take place at a house a few blocks away.

Alma de Mi Tierra COOKING
(☎513-92-11; www.almademitierra.net; Aldama 205, Barrio Jalatlaco; per person US$70, if 3 or fewer US$85) Nora Valencia, from a family of celebrated Oaxacan cooks, conducts five-hour classes for a maximum of 10 people at her home in quaint Barrio Jalatlaco; 48 hours' notice is needed. You go to market, prepare a Oaxacan lunch, then sit down to eat it.

Casa Crespo COOKING
(☎516-09-18; www.casacrespo.com; Allende 107; per person US$65) Amiable Óscar Carrizosa gives four-hour classes in Oaxacan cuisine at 10am daily except Sunday, at his restaurant near the Templo de Santo Domingo. You'll prepare two types of tortilla, guacamole, three salsas, an appetizer, a soup, a *mole* dish and a dessert. For any number of participants from one to 12.

☞ Tours

A guided trip can save hassles, be fun and tell you more than you might otherwise learn. A typical four-hour small-group trip to El Tule, Teotitlán del Valle and Mitla costs around M$180 per person, as do guided trips to Monte Albán. Admission fees and meals are usually extra. You can book these tours at many hotels, or direct with an agency such as **Turismo El Convento** (☎516-18-06; www.oaxacaexperts.com; Camino Real Oaxaca, 5 de Mayo 300).

Fundación en Vía VILLAGE LIFE, MICROFINANCE
(☎515-24-24; www.envia.org; Instituto Cultural Oaxaca, Juárez 909) These unique tours give a rare insight into the lives of village women, and your tour fee is used to provide microfinance loans to help them develop small businesses. Nonprofit organization En Vía, staffed largely by volunteers, provides the interest-free loans to groups of three women in the villages of Teotitlán del Valle and Díaz Ordaz, east of Oaxaca. The six-hour tours (US$50 per person, including lunch), starting at 1pm Thursday and 9am Saturday, take you into the women's houses where they explain their businesses and how they use the microfinance. It's a rare chance to understand the reality of village life where a loan of just M$1300 (US$100) can make the difference between business success and failure. You'll also learn about local crafts, foods and the village economy.

Traditions Mexico CULTURAL, CRAFTS
(☎571-36-95; www.traditionsmexico.com) Indefatigable traveler Eric Mindling has been exploring southern Mexico for more than 20 years, and his trips yield insights into

Oaxacan artisanry, festivals and culture that few tours match. They get well off the beaten track and emphasize contact with artisans and village life. Trips range from one day (US$300 for up to four people) to a week or more (up to US$2145 per person for nine-night trips).

Academic Tours in Oaxaca   CULTURAL
(☑518-47-28; academictoursoaxaca.com; Nieve 208A, Lomas del Crestón) Academic Tours offers recommended tours customized to clients' personal interests. Day trips for two to four people in the Valles Centrales around Oaxaca typically cost US$275 to US$330.

★ Festivals & Events

All major national festivals are celebrated here, and local festivals seems to happen every week somewhere in the city. The biggest and most spectacular of Oaxacan festivals is the Guelaguetza (see boxed text, p433).

Día de Muertos   TRADITIONAL
Muertos (Day of the Dead) celebrations in and around Oaxaca are among the most vibrant in Mexico, with concerts, exhibitions, dances and other special goings-on starting several days before in the city and villages. Homes, cemeteries and some public buildings are decorated with fantastically crafted *altares de muertos* (altars of the dead), large *tapetes de arena* (colored sand sculptures) appear in streets and plazas, and *comparsas* (satirical fancy-dress groups) parade through the streets. Oaxaca's main cemetery, the **Panteón General** (cnr Vasconcelos & Calle del Refugio), 1km east of downtown, is the scene of concerts in the evenings of October 31 and November 1, and an official judging of the best *altares* during the afternoon of November 1. Villagers in Santa Cruz Xoxocotlán, a few kilometers south of the city, hold a particularly beautiful candlelit graveyard vigil through the October 31–November 1 night. Many villages and towns stage special events, with some guesthouses and agencies arranging visits.

Oaxaca International Independent Film & Video Festival   FILM
A great program (www.oaxacafilmfest.com) of independent feature films, documentaries and animations from all around the world, at several city venues, during a week in mid-November. Nearly all films have English subtitles or are in English.

Noche de los Rábanos   TRADITIONAL
Amazing figures carved from specially grown giant radishes are displayed in the Zócalo on December 23, the Night of the Radishes.

🛏 Sleeping

Accommodations range from bargain-priced hostels to luxury hotels in historic colonial buildings. There are plenty of charming midrange B&Bs and hotels. Some places (mostly midrange and top-end) raise rates for four peak seasons: Semana Santa, Guelaguetza, Día de Muertos and Christmas–New Year's.

TOP
CHOICE **Casa Oaxaca**   BOUTIQUE HOTEL $$$
(☑514-41-73; www.casaoaxaca.com.mx; García Vigil 407; s M$2150, d M$2850-3890, all incl breakfast; P☕@🛜🏊) The seven large rooms and suites in this converted 18th-century house are in stunning contemporary Oaxacan style with original art and *artesanías* (handicrafts). It has a lovely pool in the rear patio, art exhibits in the beautiful main courtyard and a small restaurant (open to nonguests only by reservation). Mezcal tastings and cooking classes with the chef are on offer, too. No kids under 12.

🗝 **Las Bugambilias**   B&B $$$
(☑516-11-65, in the USA 866-829-6778; www.las bugambilias.com; Reforma 402; s US$70-105, d US$80-115, all incl breakfast; ☕❄@🛜) This delightful B&B has nine rooms decorated with inspired combinations of antiques and folk and contemporary art. Some have air-con and/or a balcony; all have tiled bathrooms and fans. A big treat here is the gourmet two-course Oaxacan breakfast. Further attractions include free international phone calls and an inviting roof terrace with fantastic views. The family also runs two smaller, similarly attractive and similarly priced B&Bs nearby, as well as the adjoining La Olla restaurant and the Casa de los Sabores cooking school.

Hotel Las Golondrinas   HOTEL $$
(☑514-32-98; www.hotellasgolondrinas.com.mx; Tinoco y Palacios 411; s M$550, d M$600-680, tr M$680; ☕@🛜) Lovingly tended by friendly owners and staff, this superb small hotel has about 30 rooms around three beautiful, leafy labyrinthine patios. It's very popular, so try to reserve ahead. None of the rooms is huge, but all are tastefully decorated and immaculately clean. Good breakfasts (dishes M$25

BENITO JUÁREZ

One of the few Mexican national heroes with an unsullied reputation, the great reforming president Benito Juárez (1806–72) was born a humble Zapotec villager in Guelatao, 60km northeast of Oaxaca. His parents died when he was three. At the age of 12, young Benito walked to Oaxaca and found work at the house of Antonio Salanueva, a bookbinder. Salanueva saw the boy's potential and helped pay for an education he otherwise might not have received.

Juárez later started training for the priesthood, but abandoned this to work as a lawyer for poor villagers. He rose to become Oaxaca's state governor from 1848 to 1852, during which term he opened schools and cut bureaucracy. He was made justice minister in Mexico's new liberal government of 1855. His Ley Juárez (Juárez Law), which transferred the trials of soldiers and priests charged with civil crimes to ordinary civil courts, was the first of the Reform Laws, which sought to break the power of the Catholic Church. These laws provoked the War of the Reform of 1858 to 1861, in which the liberals eventually defeated the conservatives.

Juárez was elected Mexico's president in 1861 but had been in office only a few months when France invaded Mexico and forced him into exile. In 1866–67, with US support, Juárez ousted the French and their puppet emperor, Maximilian. One of Juárez' main political achievements was to make primary education free and compulsory. He died in 1872, a year after being elected to his fourth presidential term. Oaxacans are fiercely proud of him and today countless streets, statues, schools, villages, cities, bus companies and even mountain ranges all around Mexico preserve his name and memory. If the world followed his famous maxim '*Entre los individuos, como entre las naciones, el respeto al derecho ajeno es la paz*' ('Between individuals as between nations, respect for the rights of others is peace'), it would be a much more peaceful place.

to M$70) are served on one of the patios. A very good value!

Hotel Azucenas   HOTEL $$
(☎514-79-18, 800-717-25-40, in the USA & Canada 800-882-6089; www.hotelazucenas.com; Aranda 203; s/d M$625/675; ❄@🖥) The Hotel Azucenas is a small, friendly, very well-run, Canadian-owned hotel in a beautifully restored century-old house. The 10 attractive, cool, tile-floored and impeccably clean rooms have ample bathrooms, and a buffet breakfast (M$44) is served on the lovely roof terrace.

La Casa de Mis Recuerdos   B&B $$$
(☎515-56-45, in the USA 877-234-4706; www. misrecuerdos.net; Pino Suárez 508; s US$70-120, d US$95-120, all incl breakfast; ❄✳@🖥) A marvelous decorative aesthetic prevails throughout this welcoming, eight-room guesthouse. Old-style tiles, mirrors, masks and all sorts of other Mexican crafts adorn the walls and halls. The best rooms overlook a fragrant central patio. The large breakfast, a highlight, is served in a beautiful dining room. Host Nora Valencia also offers cooking classes. There's a minimum stay of three nights. The owners also offer B&B at similar prices, with similarly excellent breakfasts, in two

pretty, decorated smaller houses not much further from the center.

Hostal Casa del Sol   HOSTEL $
(☎514-41-40; www.hostalcasadelsol.com.mx; Constitución 301; dm/s/d/tr incl breakfast M$160/ 210/350/450; ❄@) This well-run, friendly spot is as much budget hotel as hostel, and offers an exceptionally good value. There are five large, clean and attractive private rooms with touches of art and crafts, and one spacious eight-person dorm, all set around a leafy courtyard. Beds and bunks are solid and comfortable and the shared bathrooms are good and clean. The guest kitchen opens from 8:30am to 6:30pm.

Casa Ángel   HOSTEL $$
(☎514-22-24; www.casaangelhostel.com; Tinoco y Palacios 610; incl breakfast dm M$130-160, s/d M$400/500, without bathroom M$300/400; ❄@🖥) An excellent hostel run by a friendly and helpful young team and kept scrupulously clean. The good, bright common areas include a good kitchen and a great roof terrace where they cook up a BBQ every Sunday. Most of the dorms hold just three or four people and all the good, solid bunks have their own reading lights – an unusually thoughtful touch.

El Diablo y la Sandía
B&B $$

(☎514-40-95; eldiabloylasandia.com; Libres 205; s M$800-900, d M$900-1100, all incl breakfast; ❄@☎) This B&B is as quirkily stylish as its name ('The Devil and the Watermelon') and has a welcoming, homey atmosphere. The five rooms – four around a light-filled courtyard, the other next to a roof terrace – are spotlessly clean with comfy beds, and adorned with pretty and original Oaxacan *artesanías*. A hearty Oaxacan breakfast emerges from the big kitchen range, which is available for guests' use later in the day, and there's a cozy sitting room, too.

Hotel Casa del Sótano
HOTEL $$

(☎516-24-94; www.hoteldelsotano.net, in Spanish; Tinoco y Palacios 404; s/d/tr/q/ste M$700/850/ 950/1050/1300; P❄✳@☎) Offering a stunning terrace view of Oaxaca's rooftops and church towers, this elegant hotel is an excellent value. The attractive, very clean rooms sport great beds, traditional-style furniture and a spot of antique art.

La Reja
HOTEL $$

(☎514-59-39; www.hospederialareja.com.mx; Absolo 103; s M$850, d M$950-1050; ✳❄) A lovely small hotel with just six tasteful, comfy rooms in orange, yellow and pink tones, around a tranquil patio with tropical plants where breakfast and lunch are available.

Posada Don Mario
GUESTHOUSE $

(☎514-20-12; www.posadadonmario.com; Cosijopí 219; s/d M$350/450, without bathroom M$260/ 360, all incl breakfast; ❄@☎) Cute, cheerful and friendly, this courtyard guesthouse has an intimate feel and is very well priced for what it offers. The rooms are reasonably large and well kept, the four up on the roof terrace being particularly appealing.

Hostal Pochón
HOSTEL $

(☎516-13-22; www.hostalpochon.com; Callejón del Carmen 102; dm M$120-125, d M$285-385, all incl breakfast; ❄@☎) Popular and friendly Pochón, on a quiet street, provides five dorms for no more than six people each (one for women only) and four private rooms with comfortable beds (some with their own bathroom and computer). Well kept and well run, it has a full kitchen and good common areas, and the included breakfast is well worthwhile. It also offers bike rentals, cooking classes and cheap phone calls.

Casa de Sierra Azul
HISTORIC HOTEL $$$

(☎514-84-12; www.hotelcasadesierrazul.com; Hidalgo 1002; r incl breakfast M$1211-1674; P❄@☎) The Sierra Azul is a 200-year-old house converted into a beautiful small hotel, centered on a broad courtyard with a fountain and stone pillars. The good-sized, tasteful rooms have high ceilings, attractive tiled bathrooms and display a mix of old prints and modern art.

Casa de Siete Balcones
BOUTIQUE HOTEL $$$

(☎516-18-56; www.casadesietebalcones.com; Morelos 800; ste incl breakfast M$1400-2700; P❄✳☎) With only seven suites, this softly lit boutique hotel in a colonial house is a lovely option, with a pretty patio, attentive, friendly staff and balconies overlooking the downtown streets.

Hotel Azul
BOUTIQUE HOTEL $$$

(☎501-00-16; www.hotelazuloaxaca.com; Abasolo 313; r US$154-178, ste US$262-595; ✳@☎) A contemporary art experience in every sense, the recently opened Azul has a Francisco Toledo–designed fountain in the cactus-walled rear patio, standard rooms in minimalist black, white and red (with iPod docks), and suites adorned with work by renowned artists and sculptors. The courtyard **restaurant** (mains M$125-185; ⊙7am-11pm), with retractable roof, serves 'postmodern' innovative Oaxacan dishes, and there's a roof terrace with a night bar, a telescope in the library and an audiovisual room where you can screen direct from your laptop.

Casa de la Tía Tere
HOTEL $$

(☎501-18-45; www.casadelatiatere.com; Murguía 612; r incl breakfast M$650-900, bungalow M$1250-1450; P❄✳@☎❄) Tía Tere is one of the few midrange accommodations with a swimming pool. The 20 rooms are large and mostly bright, some with balconies and all boasting good showers. The four 'bungalow' rooms around the rear swimming pool and lawn have their own kitchens, and two of them are two-bedroom with sitting and dining areas. Tía Tere also offers a large, clean kitchen and dining room, plus free coffee.

Hostel Don Nino
HOSTEL $$

(☎518-59-85; www.hosteldonnino.com, in Spanish; Pino Suárez 804; dm M$150-170, s M$500-700, d M$600-800, all incl breakfast; ❄@☎) Part hostel, part hotel, this friendly, family-owned joint in a renovated colonial building offers modern and immaculately clean facilities and amenities (cable TV on plasma screens, leather couches, quality mattresses and bedding, good kitchen, good clean bathrooms). The loads of freebies (wi-fi, filtered water, internet terminals, shampoo, hairdryers, lockers) make it one of Oaxaca's best hostels. There's also a decent onsite **restaurant-bar** (mains M$50-100; ☺8am-5pm).

Casa Vertiz
HOTEL **$$**

(☑516-17-00; www.hotelvertiz.com.mx; Reforma 404; s/d M$950/1000; ✷❄) A pleasant small-ish hotel set around two courtyards, with a restaurant in the front one. The 14 rooms are in a fairly typical tiles-and-wood style and aren't huge, but they're comfy and pleasant and all are equipped with queen-size beds and coffee-makers. The roof terrace has a good view.

La Villada Inn
HOSTEL **$**

(☑518-62-17; www.lavillada.com; Felipe Ángeles 204, Ejido Guadalupe Victoria; dm US$13, s/d/tr US$25/35/45, without bathroom US$19/28/40; P☺@❄▨) Though set on the far northern edge of the city, La Villada offers excellent facilities and friendly, helpful, English-speaking attention on spacious premises. There's no guest kitchen but the public areas include a **restaurant** (dishes M$45-55; ☺8am-8pm), an excellent swimming pool and **Q'Vola** (☺9pm-2am Thu-Sat), a DJ club with pool tables. Rooms boast good wooden furniture and private bathrooms. The hostel will send a taxi to meet you at the bus station if you call on arrival, and will pay for it if you stay two nights. Once you're here, they'll tell you about buses to/from the city center.

Hotel Dainzú
HOTEL **$$**

(☑516-18-21; www.hotelesdeoaxaca.com/hoteldainzu.html; Hidalgo 1013; s/d incl breakfast M$515/645; P❄) A neat little downtown hotel, with spick-and-span, medium-size rooms sporting curly wrought-iron bedheads, along with a pretty patio with a fountain. There's a pleasant little café, too.

Camino Real Oaxaca
HISTORIC HOTEL **$$$**

(☑501-61-00, in the US & Canada 800-722-6466; www.caminoreal.com; 5 de Mayo 300; r from M$3875; ☺✷@▨) Built in the 16th century as a convent, the Camino Real was converted into a very classy hotel in the 1970s. The old chapel is a banquet hall; one of the five attractive courtyards contains an enticing swimming pool; and beautiful thick stone walls help keep the place cool. Though it has a rather formal atmosphere, the 91 rooms are nicely done in colonial styles. Call the hotel or check the website for special rates, which can cut costs heavily.

Hotel Casa Arnel
HOTEL **$$**

(☑515-28-56; www.casaarnel.com.mx; Aldama 404, Barrio Jalatlaco; s US$40-65, d US$45-75; P@❄) A longtime travelers' haunt, this family-run budget hotel is five minutes' walk from the 1st-class bus station. The clean, smallish, well-kept rooms surround a big, leafy courtyard, and the upstairs common areas have some great views.

Hostel Paulina
HOSTEL **$**

(☑516-20-05; www.paulinahostel.com; Trujano 321; dm/s/d/tr/q incl breakfast M$175/325/350/525/700; P☺@❄) Clean and efficient, this 92-bed hostel provides rooms and dorms for four to 11 people and has a rooftop terrace but no cooking facilities. Perks include a made-to-order breakfast and clean shared bathrooms.

Casa Raab
LODGE, HOTEL **$$**

(☑520-40-22; www.casaraab.com; Camino Seminario s/n, San Pablo Etla; r US$85, 4-bedroom Casa Grande US$285, 2-bedroom Casita with kitchen US$100, all incl breakfast; P☺❄▨⊕) Nestled in the foothills of San Pablo Etla, 12km north of the city center, this ranch-cum-small hotel is a great option for families and small groups looking for something beyond the typical hotel experience. Casa Raab offers guests a plunge in its sparkling pool, tailored tours, a menagerie of rescued animals and rowdy weekly jam sessions. When the evenings get cold, communal dinners and crackling fireplaces warm the atmosphere. The houses or rooms can be rented per night or week.

Learning Center
B&B **$$**

(☑515-01-22; www.tolc.org.mx; Murguía 703; s/d incl breakfast US$35/45, apt per day/month US$55/700; ☺@) The Learning Center is a successful, nonprofit tutoring center for young Oaxacans and villagers who need help in continuing their education or developing careers. What guests pay for the two neat B&B rooms and attractive guest apartment here makes a valuable contribution to running costs. All accommodations have fans, phones, good bathrooms and DSL internet connections.

🍴 Eating

From swish restaurants dealing in French-styled fusion to street vendors doling out spicy *tamales* (steamed corn dough with

HOLY MOLE

Oaxaca's multicolored *moles* (nut-, chili- and spice-based sauces), which are served over a cut of poultry or meat, have become the region's inimitable culinary signature. The most famous variety, *mole negro*, is a smoky, savory delight bearing a hint of chocolate. It is the most complex and labor-intensive to create, though its popularity with visitors ensures that it's easy to find. While in Oaxaca, seek out the other colors of the *mole* family:

» *Mole amarillo:* A savory *mole* using a base of tomatillo (a small, husked tomatolike fruit). It is spiced with cumin, clove, cilantro and the herb *hoja santa* and often served over beef.

» *Mole verde:* A lovely, delicate sauce thickened with corn dough and including tomatillos, pumpkin seeds, the herbs *epazote* and *hoja santa*, and different nuts such as walnuts and almonds. Served commonly with chicken.

» *Mole colorado:* A forceful *mole* based on the flavors of *ancho, pasilla* and *cascabel* chilies, black pepper and cinnamon.

» *Mole coloradito* (or *mole rojo*): This sharp, tangy, tomato-based blend might remind gringos of something from their neighborhood Mexican joint back home; it is dumbed down and exported as enchilada sauce.

» *Mancha manteles:* Brick red in color, the deep, woody flavor of this *mole* (whose name translates as 'tablecloth stainer') is often used to complement tropical fruit.

» *Chichilo negro:* Perhaps the rarest of the region's *moles*, the defining ingredients include *chilguacle negro, mulato* and *pasilla* chilies, avocado leaves (which give it a touch of anise flavor), tomatoes and corn dough.

fillings) and *champurrado* (a corn-and-chocolate drink), Oaxaca's food is among the country's most inventive and memorable. Do try to get a good sampling of Oaxaca's *mole* sauces, which come in seven colors covering all manner of meats and vegetable-based mains (see boxed text, above). But the *moles* are just the beginning of Oaxaca's flavors. Other local specialties include *tasajo* (slices of pounded beef), *tlayudas* (big, crisp tortillas with varied toppings, sometimes labeled Oaxacan pizza), *memelas* (thick, smallish tortillas topped with or folded over cheese, beans, chili sauce and sometimes more), *empanadas* (oval corn tortillas usually with a yellow or green *mole*), *tostadas* (small, crisped corn tortillas with assorted toppings), *quesillo* (stringy cheese), *chapulines* (grasshoppers! – usually fried with chili powder, onion and garlic) and steaming hot chocolate (often spiced with cinnamon).

TOP CHOICE **La Biznaga** OAXACAN FUSION **$$**
(www.labiznaga.com.mx; García Vigil 512; mains M$80-160; ⊕1-10pm Mon-Thu, 1-11pm Fri & Sat)
Locals and visitors alike jam the atmospheric courtyard for delicious nouveau-Oaxacan fusion dishes. The choices are written up on blackboards and you could start with the tortilla horns stuffed with seasoned hibiscus, follow up with the *mole* with goat cheese (a beef fillet in *mole coloradito*, with goat cheese and mushrooms), and make sure you leave room for the guava with chocolate mousse dessert. A great range of drinks, too.

La Olla OAXACAN **$$**
(www.laolla.com.mx; Reforma 402; breakfast M$40-90, mains M$80-150; ⊕8am-10pm Mon-Sat; ⊕✓)
This superb little restaurant and cafe produces a spectrum of marvelous Mexican (mainly Oaxacan) specialties from cactus tacos to *camarones a la diabla* (prawns in a hot chili-and-tomato sauce), and good ryebread tortas, juices and salads, all with an emphasis on organic and local ingredients. Terrific breakfasts and a good M$100 set lunch as well.

Comala OAXACAN, INTERNATIONAL **$$**
(Allende 109; dishes M$60-110; ⊕9am-midnight Mon-Sat; ⊕☎) A neat and gently arty cafe, Comala serves up a successful mix of Oaxacan specialties – including a great *botana oaxaqueña* (plate of assorted Oaxacan snacks such as meats, cheeses and, of course, grasshoppers) and a delicious Jell-O-like, corn-based dessert called *nicuatole* –

and more international fare such as salads, baguettes and what are probably the best burgers in town.

Casa Crespo OAXACAN $$$
(www.casacrespo.com; Allende 107; mains M$130-190, 5-/7-/9-dish tasting menu M$400/500/600; ⏱1-11pm Tue-Thu, 1pm-midnight Fri & Sat, 2-9pm Sun; ☎) Casa Crespo offers up delicious dishes from Oaxaca state's seven regions, based on seasonal cycles with market-fresh ingredients. A very tasty three-course meal might comprise *caldo de piedra* ('stone soup' – a shrimp-and-fish soup cooked at your table by a pre-Hispanic method using hot stones inside the bowl), *mole de fiesta* (tender steak in a special *mole*) and home-made chocolate ice cream sprinkled with chili powder. To sample a fuller variety of the superb taste combinations, go for one of the tasting menus.

Casa Oaxaca FUSION $$$
(✑516-85-31; www.casaoaxacaelrestaurante.com; Constitución 104-4; mains M$160-320; ⏱1-11pm; ☺) This restaurant, run by the Casa Oaxaca hotel, works magic combining Oaxacan and European ingredients and flavors: witness the crispy duck tacos with red *mole,* or the Isthmus-style venison in yellow *mole*. There are plenty of seafood and pasta creations, too. Presentation is outstanding, and all is enhanced by the courtyard setting, the bar for pre-dinner drinks and a good wine selection.

La Brújula CAFE $
(www.cafebrujula.com; García Vigil 409D; breakfast, sandwiches & salads M$40-65; ⏱8am-10pm Mon-Sat; ☎) This is a great stop with arguably the best coffee in town (a strong, flavorsome, organic bean from cooperative growers near the Oaxacan coast), not to mention good breakfasts, great fruit smoothies, waffles with fruit and super home-baked banana bread and muffins! It's informal and spacious, with bright, helpful staff.

Café Los Cuiles CAFE $
(www.cuiles.com; Plazuela Labastida 115-1; salads, soups & snacks M$25-65; ⏱8am-10pm; ☺☎✑) Los Cuiles is a lovely spot for breakfast, drinks like mango lassi and good light eats (including organic salads). Popular with visitors and locals alike, it has a handy central location and a spacious lounge-gallery feel.

María Bonita OAXACAN $$
(Alcalá 706B; mains M$85-120; ⏱8:30am-9pm Tue-Sat, 8:30am-5pm Sun; ☺) Come here for economical and tasty traditional Oaxacan food. Precede your fish, steak or *mole* with a good appetizer or soup, such as the *sopa Xóchitl* (squash, squash blossom and sweet corn). There's a good breakfast range, too. The building is on a street corner, but inside the atmosphere is peaceful and intimate.

Zandunga OAXACAN $$
(Carranza 105; mains M$95-110; ⏱2-11pm Mon-Sat; ☎) The Isthmus of Tehuantepec has its own take on Oaxacan cuisine based on the local ingredients of that hot, coastal area including tropical fruits, seafood, and dishes cooked in banana leaves. Festive Zandunga brings those flavors to Oaxaca and the M$280 *botana* (a selection of dishes which easily serves two) is a perfect sampler, just right for whiling away a couple of hours with some of its long list of mezcals (M$35 to M$120 a glass).

1254 Marco Polo BREAKFAST, SEAFOOD $$
(breakfast M$45-70, mains M$100-180) Parque Juárez (Pino Suárez 806; ⏱8am-6pm) Downtown (5 de Mayo 103; ⏱8am-10:30pm Mon-Sat) The popular Pino Suárez branch occupies a long, shady garden patio, and has attentive waiters and good-value food. The large breakfasts come with bottomless cups of coffee; from noon until closing, good seafood including ceviches and oven-baked fish is the specialty. The downtown branch has the same excellent menu and good service.

Manantial Vegetariano VEGETARIAN $
(Tinoco y Palacios 303; mains M$45-60; ⏱9am-9pm Mon-Sat; ✑) Set in a colorfully decked courtyard, the Manantial serves up well-prepared veggie versions of Mexican staples such as enchiladas and *chiles rellenos* (stuffed chilies), as well as fresh salads, crepes and a few meat dishes to keep non-vegetarians content.

El Asador Vasco OAXACAN, SPANISH $$$
(✑514-47-55; www.asadorvasco.com; Portal de Flores 10A; mains M$110-210; ⏱1:30-11:30pm) For a meal, rather than a drink or snack, overlooking the Zócalo, the prime choice is the upstairs Asador Vasco, which provides good Oaxacan, Basque and international food. It's strong on meat, seafood and Oaxacan specialties. For a table with a plaza view on a warm evening, reserve earlier in the day.

Lobo Azul MEXICAN, INTERNATIONAL $
(Armenta y López 120; mains M$60-80; ⏱7:30am-10:30pm; ☺☎✑) A large space decked with

MEZCAL

The king of Oaxacan tipples is mezcal, an agave-based sipping spirit. Mezcal is produced in many parts of Mexico (tequila is one type of it), but Oaxaca's agave fields, especially those around Santiago Matatlán and the Albarradas villages, south and east of Mitla, are widely reckoned to produce the world's finest mezcal. Undiluted white mezcal is the most common variety, but there are also types infused with herbs or fruit. *Reposado* (rested) or *añejo* (aged) mezcal is usually smoother, and discriminating drinkers go for artisanal, small-batch, organic mezcal, the best of which can cost M$100 or more per glass. Some of the cheaper bottles contain a worm – actually a moth caterpillar that feeds on the agave – and while no harm will come from swallowing this, there is definitely no obligation! Mezcal is, however, often served with a little plate of orangey powder that is a mix of salt, chili and ground-up agave worms. Along with slices of orange or lime, this nicely counterpoints the mezcal taste.

international revolutionary posters and attracting a studenty clientele, Lobo Azul serves up a broad range of satisfactory fare from salads and crepes to meats in *mole* and a dish called 'Mahatma Gandhi' – fried rice with chicken, prawns, veggies and ginger. Also there are plenty of breakfast options, exotic teas and Chiapas coffee.

Vieja Lira   ITALIAN $$
(www.viejalira.com; mains M$110-180; ⊘1-11pm Mon-Sat, 1-10pm Sun; ☻) García Vigil (García Vigil 409A) Pino Suárez (Pino Suárez 100) Vieja Lira tops the list of Oaxaca's Italian restaurants for taste, though some portions are small. Choose from 10 types of pasta and 10 sauces, or go for the good lasagna or a pizza. International wines start at M$330 per bottle.

Cenaduría Tlayudas Libres   OAXACAN $
(Libres 212; tlayudas around M$35; ⊘9pm-4am; ☝) Drivers double-park along the entire block to eat here. The filling, tasty *tlayudas* are large, light, crisp, hot tortillas folded over frijoles, *quesillo* and your choice of salsa. Half the fun is taking in the late-night scene as motherly cooks fan the streetside charcoal grills, raising showers of sparks. Sit on benches around the range or at tables in the adjacent building.

Mercado Sánchez Pascuas   OAXACAN $
(btwn Porfirio Díaz & Tinoco y Palacios; dishes M$13-20; ⊘8am-4pm) This excellent indoor food market is just out-of-the-way enough to have a great local feel, and its *comedores* (food stalls) provide a delicious, down-to-earth, local eating experience. Head to the ones with benches just inside the west end of the main building, ask for a *tamal, memela* or *empanada,* and practice your Spanish in deciding what you want on or in it.

Itanoní Antojería y Tortillería   OAXACAN $
(www.itanoni.com.mx, in Spanish; Belisario Domínguez 513, Colonia Reforma; mains M$45-65; ⊘8am-4pm Mon-Sat, 8am-2pm Sun; ☝) This semirustic eatery is dedicated to exploring the unique tastes of native Mexican corn varieties, and takes the craft of tortillas and *antojitos* (light tortilla-based dishes) to new heights. There are plenty of options for vegetarian *tetelas* (a pre-Hispanic tortilla wrap) and a divine 'spiritual egg' dish, which deep-fries a whole egg encased in *hoja santa* leaves. It's in middle-class Colonia Reforma, about 1km north of the 1st-class bus station.

Restaurante Los Danzantes   FUSION $$$
(Alcalá 403; mains M$130-250; ⊘1-11pm; ☻) Excellent Mexican fusion food and a spectacular architect-designed patio setting make Los Danzantes one of Oaxaca's special dining spots. Welcoming staff serve up a small but first-class selection of food: try beef medallions with grasshopper sauce, or a *tlayuda* with shrimp and smoky *chipotle* chili sauce. Servings are not on the generous side, though.

🍷 Drinking

Oaxaca's drinking opportunities come in large number and great variety. Alcalá, García Vigil and nearby streets are quite a party zone on Friday and Saturday nights, full of people moving from one bar to another, many of which have live music of some kind.

Los Amantes   MEZCALERÍA
(mezcalerialosamantes.blogspot.com; Allende 107; ⊘5-11pm Wed-Sat; ☻) Squeeze into this quirky little tasting room near Santo Domingo church for the perfect mezcal primer. Your

amiable host León will happily explain in English all about the three different artisanal mezcals he gets you to taste for M$100.

Café del Jardín
CAFE

(Portal de Flores 10; ☺8am-midnight) The Jardín has a peerless position beneath the arches at the southwest corner of the Zócalo. In the evening you're likely to be serenaded by one of the funkiest marimba ensembles in the country.

Cuish
MEZCALERÍA

(mezcalcuish.blogspot.com, in Spanish; Díaz Ordaz 712; ☺9am-10pm) Narrow Cuish is an *expendio* (drink retailer) rather than a bar, but it has a bar anyway (and an interesting display of old masks on the wall) and will happily let you sample a mezcal before you buy (M$120 for a 0.75L bottle). It's an outlet for small organic producers making mezcal from wild agaves by traditional methods. The product is less refined and more potent (around 50% alc/vol) than regular certified mezcal.

La Casa del Mezcal
CANTINA

(Flores Magón 209; ☺10am-1am) Open since 1935, this is one of Oaxaca's most atmospheric cantinas, and a reasonably respectable one. One room has a large stand-up bar and shelves full of mezcal; the other room has tables where *botanas* (snacks) are served. Most, but not all, customers are men.

El Olivo
COCKTAIL BAR

(2nd fl, Murguía 218; ☺4pm-1am Tue-Sat, 6pm-1am Sun) Serving tasty *pinchos* (skewers) and tapas, this is Oaxaca's most serious cocktail bar, with excellent pours and a good beer. The minimalist decor makes for a refined atmosphere. You might coincide with an occasional flamenco musician.

Several Oaxaca eateries are also fine places for a drink, notably La Brújula (best coffee in town); Comala, which fills up in the evenings with a convivial crowd of studenty/professional young Oaxacans; and the roof terrace at Casa Crespo, where you can sip quality mezcal with a close-up view of Santo Domingo church.

☆ Entertainment

Oaxaca has a pretty vibrant cultural and social life for a city of its size. You'll find what's-on listings (including film showings and concerts) at **Oaxaca Calendar** (www.oaxacacalendar.com) and **El Jolgorio Cultural** (www.eljolgoriocultural.com.mx, in Spanish).

TOP CHOICE Café Central
LIVE MUSIC, CLUB

(www.cafecentraloaxaca.blogspot.com, in Spanish; Hidalgo 302; ☺9pm-approx 2am Wed-Sat) The social hub of Oaxaca's artsy, bohemian, alternative scene, the Central is owned by one of Oaxaca's innovative painters, Guillermo Olguín. It hosts independent films at 9pm Wednesday (free) and a spectrum of rarely seen live music acts at 10pm Thursday and/or Friday (admission from M$40). On Saturday it turns into a packed nightclub (free) with a great house DJ who plays highly danceable music ranging from '60s to Balkan to contemporary electronica and everything in between – 'music you won't hear in your car,' as one regular put it.

Txalaparta
DANCING

(facebook.com/txalapartabar; Matamoros 206; ☺2pm-2am) By day Txalaparta is a colorful bar with hookahs and a tasty set lunch for M$60; around midnight it becomes a place to dance to assorted rhythms from Latin to jazz, world music, trip hop, reggae and more (sometimes with live bands or guest DJs). It gets a good party atmosphere going at weekends, with a mixed local and international crowd.

OAXACA'S FAVORITE HOT DRINK

Chocolate is an ancient Mexican treat and a Oaxacan favorite. A bowl of steaming hot chocolate, with porous sweet bread to dunk, is the perfect warmer when winter sets in 1500m above sea level. The mix, to which hot milk or water is added, typically contains cinnamon, almonds and sugar, as well as ground-up cocoa beans. The area around the southern end of Oaxaca's Mercado 20 de Noviembre has several shops specializing in this time-honored treat – and not just chocolate for drinking but also chocolate for *moles* (dishes with chili-based sauces).

You can sample chocolate with or without cinnamon, light or dark, and with varying quantities of sugar at any of these places. And most of them have vats where you can watch the mixing. If you're feeling adventurous try *champurrado* or *tejate*, which are traditional drinks combining chocolate with corn.

Candela DANCING
(Murguía 413; admission M$50, women free until 11:30pm; ⊘from 10pm Thu-Sat) Candela's writhing salsa, *cumbia* and merengue band and beautiful colonial-house setting have kept it high on the Oaxaca nightlife lists for years. The band starts at 11pm: arrive earlier for a good table. Classes in assorted Latin dances are held here most evenings from 7pm.

Guelaguetza Shows

If you're not in Oaxaca for the Guelaguetza dance festival itself, it's well worth attending one of the regular imitations. The best is at 7pm on Fridays in the classy **Camino Real Oaxaca** (⊘501-61-00; 5 de Mayo 300; incl buffet dinner M$365) – a highly colorful show in what used to be a convent chapel. The **Casa de Cantera** (⊘514-75-85; Ortiz Armengol 104, Colonia Reforma; admission M$200; ⊘8:30pm) does a very bright show nightly, with live music, but is not very conveniently located at about 2km north of the center. Food and drinks are available during the show. **Hotel Monte Albán** (⊘516-27-77; Alameda de León 1; admission M$90; ⊘8:30pm) stages a less exhilarating performance but it's worth 90 minutes of your time if you can't get to one of the others. This show only goes ahead if 10 people make reservations by 7:30pm.

🔒 Shopping

The state of Oaxaca has the richest, most inventive folk-art scene in Mexico, and the city is its chief marketplace. You'll find the highest-quality crafts mostly in smart stores, but prices are lower in the markets. Some artisans have grouped together to market their products directly in their own stores.

Oaxacan artisans' techniques remain fairly traditional – back-strap and pedal looms, hand-turning of pottery – but new products frequently appear in response to the big demand for Oaxacan crafts. The ubiquitous wooden fantasy animals known as *alebrijes* were developed within the last couple of decades from toys that Oaxacans had been carving for their children for centuries.

Other special products to look for include the distinctive black pottery from San Bartolo Coyotepec; blankets, tapestries and rugs from Teotitlán del Valle; creative pottery figures made in Ocotlán and Atzompa; *huipiles* (indigenous women's sleeveless tunics) and other colorful textiles; assorted jewelry; and stamped and colored tin from Oaxaca city itself. Many shops can mail things home for you.

Just as fascinating as the fancy craft stores, in its own way, is Oaxaca's crowded commercial area stretching over several blocks southwest of the Zócalo. Oaxacans flock here, and to the big Central de Abastos market, for all their everyday needs.

Markets

Mercado Juárez MARKET
(btwn Flores Magón & Calle 20 de Noviembre) This indoor daily market, a block south of the Zócalo, peddles a fascinatingly diverse mix of flowers, clothes, hats, shoes, baskets, leather belts and bags and almost every food a Oaxacan could need. Women hawk mounds of grasshoppers outside the Flores Magón entrance.

Mercado de Artesanías HANDICRAFTS
(Crafts Market; cnr JP García & Zaragoza; ⊘9am-9pm) This indoor crafts market is almost entirely devoted to woven and embroidered textiles – tablecloths, bags, blouses, *huipiles*, shawls and more. As you walk through, you're likely to see some of the vendors doing a spot of weaving or embroidering.

Central de Abastos MARKET
(Periférico) The enormous main market, nearly 1km west of the Zócalo, is a hive of activity all week, with Saturday the biggest day. If you look long enough, you can find almost anything here. Each type of product has a section to itself, and you can easily get lost in the profusion of household goods, *artesanías* and the overwhelming quantities of fruit, vegetables, sugarcane, maize and other produce that's grown from the coast to the mountaintops.

El Pochote-Xochimilco FOOD, HANDICRAFTS
(Xochimilco Churchyard, Juárez, Barrio de Xochimilco; ⊘8:30am-3:30pm Fri & Sat) A small but very pleasant and relaxed open-air market dealing in natural products – crafts and food – nearly all sold by their makers. Look for the amazing Yukee pine-needle baskets, and stop for some blue-corn tortillas with fabulous toppings at Guadalupe's food stall under the white awning at the west end.

Labastida Crafts Market HANDICRAFTS
(Plazuela Labastida) This open-air daily market provides a pretty good sampling of Oaxacan crafts, from *alebrijes* to embroidered blouses.

Craft Shops

La Mano Mágica HANDICRAFTS
(Alcalá 203; ⊘10:30am-3pm & 4-8pm Mon-Sat) You'll find some wonderfully original and

GUELAGUETZAS LARGE & SMALL

The Guelaguetza is a brilliant feast of Oaxacan folk dance staged on the first two Mondays after July 16 in the large, semi-open-air Auditorio Guelaguetza on Cerro del Fortín. (The only time the dates vary is when July 18, the anniversary of Benito Juárez' death, falls on a Monday. Guelaguetza then happens on July 25 and August 1.) The event takes place twice on each of the Mondays, at 10am and 5pm, and lasts about three hours. Magnificently costumed dancers from the seven regions of Oaxaca state perform a succession of dignified, lively or comical traditional dances, tossing offerings of produce to the crowd as they finish. Excitement climaxes with the incredibly colorful pineapple dance by women of the Papaloapan region, and the stately Zapotec Danza de las Plumas (Feather Dance), which symbolically re-enacts the Spanish conquest. The auditorium holds about 10,000 people; tickets for the front 3500 seats for each show (M$400) go on sale two or more months ahead through www.ticketmaster.com.mx. The remaining seats are free and first come, first served.

The Guelaguetza period also sees many other colorful celebrations in Oaxaca, including fantastically festive Saturday-afternoon parades along Calle Alcalá. Many thousands of people flock into the city for the festivities (including visiting pickpockets, so stay alert).

The Guelaguetza celebrations have their origins in a colonial-era fusion of indigenous rites with Christian celebrations for the Virgen del Carmen. Smaller Guelaguetzas are held in outlying towns and villages, such as Zaachila, Cuilapan, Tlacochahuaya and Reyes Etla, usually on the same days, and can make a refreshing change from the hubbub of Oaxaca.

sophisticated craft products at this shop and gallery, including extraordinarily fine work by one of its owners, the Teotitlán del Valle weaver Arnulfo Mendoza. Some Mendoza weavings go for tens of thousands of dollars, and when you see them you'll understand why.

Casa de las Artesanías de Oaxaca   HANDICRAFTS
(Matamoros 105; ☺9am-9pm) This large store sells the work of 54 family workshops and craft organizations from around Oaxaca state. Its patio is surrounded by rooms full of rugs, ceramics, silverware, tinware, hammocks, *alebrijes* and other crafts.

Instituto Oaxaqueño de las Artesanías   HANDICRAFTS
(IOA; García Vigil 809; ☺9am-7pm Mon-Fri, 11am-3pm Sat) State-government-run IOA offers a good variety of quality craft items, including ceramics, *alebrijes* and some gorgeous textiles.

MARO   HANDICRAFTS
(5 de Mayo 204; ☺9am-8pm) A rabbit warren of a store offering a big range of good work at good prices, nearly all made by members of the MARO women artisans' cooperative around Oaxaca state. You know your money is going directly to the makers.

Bookstores
Amate Books   BOOKS
(www.amatebooks.com; Alcalá 307; ☺10.30am-7:30pm Mon-Sat, 2-7pm Sun) Probably the best English-language bookstore in Mexico, stocking almost every in-print title related to Mexico, in English.

Mezcal
La Cava   DRINK
(Gómez Farías 212B; ☺10am-3pm & 5-8pm Mon-Fri, 10am-8pm Sat) La Cava sells particularly high-quality mezcal from Santiago Matatlán (over M$600 for the best bottles). It also has a top range of Mexican wines.

Unión de Palenqueros de Oaxaca   DRINK
(Abasolo 510; ☺9am-9pm) This hole-in-the-wall is the outlet for a group of small-scale mezcal producers from Santiago Matatlán. It has smoky *añejo* and fruit-infused varieties that are excellent and very cheap, with prices per liter ranging from M$70 to M$360.

ⓘ Information

Emergency
Ambulance, Fire & Police (☏060, 066)
Ceprotur (Centro de Protección al Turista; ☏502-12-00, ext 1595; Juárez 703; ☺8am-8pm) Ceprotur helps tourists with legal problems, complaints, lost documents and the like.

Internet Access

You can hardly walk a block without passing an internet shop, most offering machines for around M$10 per hour, often with Skype available. There is free wi-fi in some public spaces, including Parque Juárez.

Nred@t (Morelos 600; per hr M$10; ☺8am-8pm Mon-Fri, 8am-2pm Sat; ☻) Upstairs place with amiable staff, good connections, plenty of high-quality headsets for Skype, and scanning and printing.

Medical Services

Clinica 2002 (☑515-72-00; www.medica2002.com.mx; Zapata 316, Colonia Reforma) This private hospital in the north of the city is generally considered to be the best equipped.

Hospital Reforma (☑516-09-89; www.hospitalreforma.com.mx; Reforma 613) Central private hospital, widely considered to have the best doctors.

Money

There are plenty of ATMs around the center, and several banks and *casas de cambio* (exchange houses) will change cash US dollars.

CI Banco (cnr Armenta y López & Hidalgo; ☺8:30am-6pm Mon-Fri, 9am-2pm Sat) Also changes cash euros, yen, pounds sterling, Canadian dollars and Swiss francs.

Post

Main post office (Alameda de León; ☺8am-7:30pm Mon-Fri, 8am-3pm Sat)

Tourist Information

City Tourist Information Kiosks (☺10am-6pm) Santo Domingo (cnr Alcalá & Gurrión) Alameda (Alameda de León) English-speaking staff are keen to help, though students with limited knowledge may be in attendance at weekends.

Sectur (☑516-01-23, 502-12-00, ext 1506; www.oaxaca.travel; Juárez 703; ☺8am-8pm) The Oaxaca state tourism department has a helpful, English-speaking information desk, though on Sundays it's staffed by students. Sectur has further desks (also English-speaking) at the **Museo de los Pintores Oaxaqueños** (☺10am-7pm Tue-Sun), **1st-class bus station** (☺8am-8pm) and **Teatro Macedonio Alcalá** (Independencia 900; ☺9am-8pm).

Websites

Lonely Planet (www.lonelyplanet.com/mexico/oaxaca-state/oaxaca) Planning advice, author recommendations and traveler reviews.

Oaxaca Tu México (www.oaxaca.travel) The official tourism site is a reasonably useful source on what to see, do and buy.

Oaxaca Wiki (oaxaca.wikispaces.com) A goldmine of information and photos on what's happening in and around Oaxaca. Dig around.

Planeta.com (www.planeta.com) This conscientious travel site has tons of good info on Oaxaca, where its webhost, Ron Mader, lives.

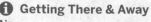 Getting There & Away

Air

Oaxaca Airport (☑511-50-88; www.asur.com.mx) Six kilometers south of the city, 500m west off Hwy 175.

Aeroméxico (www.aeromexico.com; Hidalgo 513) To/from Mexico City three times daily.

Aerotucán (www.aerotucan.com.mx; Amapolas 511A, Colonia Reforma) Thirteen-seat Cessnas make spectacular half-hour hops to Puerto Escondido (M$1465) and Bahías de Huatulco (M$1515), on the Oaxaca coast, both daily. Also flies to Tuxtla Gutiérrez (M$2115) three times weekly.

Continental Airlines (www.continental.com) Direct to/from Houston, Texas, at least five times weekly.

Continental Istmo Tours (Alcalá 201) Downtown travel agency selling all air tickets.

VivaAerobus (www.vivaaerobus.com; Plaza Paseo V, Av Universidad 501, Colonia Ex-Hacienda Candiani) Budget airline flying to/from Mexico City daily except Tuesday.

Volaris (www.volaris.mx) Flights to Tijuana.

Bus & Van

The **1st-class bus station** (Terminal de Autobuses de Primera Clase; Calz Niños Héroes de Chapultepec 1036) is 2km northeast of the Zócalo. Also known as Terminal ADO, it's used by ADO Platino and ADO GL (deluxe service), ADO and OCC (1st class) and Cuenca (2nd class). **Boletotal** (boletotal.mx) has branches in the city center at Valdivieso 2 and 20 de Noviembre 103, selling tickets for these lines throughout Mexico.

For destinations on the Oaxaca coast – Puerto Escondido, Bahías de Huatulco and Pochutla (the jumping-off point for Puerto Ángel, Zipolite, San Agustinillo and Mazunte) – the buses from the 1st-class bus station take a long and expensive route via Salina Cruz. Unless you're prone to travel sickness on winding mountain roads, it's much cheaper and quicker to use one of the comfortable van services that go directly to the coast by Hwy 131 (to Puerto Escondido) or Hwy 175 (to Pochutla and Huatulco). These leave from various terminals south or west of the Zócalo:

Autoexprés Atlántida (cnr Armenta y López & La Noria) To Pochutla.

Autotransportes Miahuatecas (Bustamante 601) To Pochutla.

Express Service (Arista 116) To Puerto Escondido.

Huatulco 2000 (Periférico 408) To Bahías de Huatulco; the terminal is next to Tienda Zetuna,

BUSES & VANS FROM OAXACA CITY

DESTINATION	FARE (M$)	DURATION	FREQUENCY (DAILY)
Bahías de Huatulco	150-342	7-8hr	8 Huatulco 2000, 5 from 1st-class terminal
Mexico City (TAPO)	456-807	6-6½hr	22 from 1st-class terminal
Pochutla	120-298	6-9hr	12 Atlántida, 17 Miahuatecas, 4 from 1st-class terminal
Puebla	342-422	4½hr	9 from 1st-class terminal
Puerto Escondido	165-304	7-10hr	19 Express Service, 15 Villa del Mar, 4 from 1st-class terminal
San Cristóbal de las Casas	456-761	10-11hr	4 from 1st-class terminal
Tapachula	408-532	11-12½hr	2 from 1st-class terminal
Tehuantepec	196	4½hr	16 from 1st-class terminal
Tuxtla Gutiérrez	408-656	9-10hr	5 from 1st-class terminal
Veracruz	450-540	6-7hr	6 from 1st-class terminal

just north of the Periférico's intersection with Trujano.

Transportes Villa del Mar (Galeana 322) To Puerto Escondido.

The **2nd-class bus station** (Terminal de Autobuses de Segunda Clase; Las Casas), 1km west of the Zócalo, is mainly useful for buses to villages around Oaxaca.

Car & Motorcycle

Hwy 135D branches off the Mexico City–Veracruz highway (150D) to make a spectacular traverse of Oaxaca's northern mountains en route to Oaxaca city. Automobile tolls from Mexico City to Oaxaca on these highways total M$343; the trip takes five to six hours. Toll-free alternative Hwy 190, via Huajuapan de León, takes several hours longer.

The roads of Oaxaca state are poorly maintained but away from congested Oaxaca city, traffic is light and the scenery is fantastic to drive through. A car is most useful if you want to visit several places in the Valles Centrales in one outing, or plan some longer-distance touring around the state. Walk-in rental prices in Oaxaca start at around M$500 a day with unlimited mileage. Europcar often has the best rates.

Alamo (alamomexico.com.mx) Airport (Airport); Center (5 de Mayo 203)

Europcar (www.europcar.com.mx, in Spanish) Airport (Airport); Center (Matamoros 101)

Only Rent-A-Car (www.onlyrentacar.com; 5 de Mayo 215A)

ⓘ Getting Around

To/From the Airport

The Transporte Terrestre ticket-taxi desk in the airport terminal charges M$52 per person to anywhere in the city center in a van, or M$220 for a whole cab. You can book a van seat from the city to the airport a day or more ahead at **Transporte Terrestre** (☑514-43-50; Alameda de León 1G; ⊙9am-2pm & 5-8pm Mon-Sat).

Bicycle

Two full-service shops, **Bicicletas Pedro Martínez** (www.bicicletaspedromartinez.com; Aldama 418) and **Zona Bici** (www.bikeoaxaca. com; García Vigil 406), rent out good mountain bikes. Prices are M$250 per day, or M$200 for up to four hours. Both businesses also sell bikes and equipment and offer bike tours.

Bus

City buses cost M$5.50. From outside the 1st-class bus station, a westbound 'Juárez' bus will take you down Juárez and Ocampo, three blocks east of the Zócalo; 'Tinoco y Palacios', 'T Y Palacios' or 'JP García' buses go down Tinoco y Palacios, two blocks west of the Zócalo. To return to the bus station, take an 'ADO' bus north up Pino Suárez or Crespo.

Taxi

A taxi anywhere within the central area, including the bus stations, costs M$35 to M$45.

VALLES CENTRALES

The countryside and villages around Oaxaca are a big part of its appeal. The city stands at the meeting point of three valleys that have been the regional center of civilization since pre-Hispanic times: the Valle de Tlacolula, which stretches 50km east from the city;

the Valle de Zimatlán, which reaches about 100km south; and the Valle de Etla, stretching about 40km north.

These Valles Centrales (Central Valleys), with a population that's mostly indigenous Zapotec, are full of fascinating archaeological sites and traditional villages and small towns that stage bustling weekly markets, produce fine specialty *artesanías* and celebrate their own colorful local fiestas. All are within easy day-trip distance of Oaxaca city.

ⓘ Getting There & Away

Buses from the 2nd-class bus station are one option. *Taxis colectivos* (shared taxis) are another,

a bit quicker and slightly more expensive: they leave from Prolongación Victoria just southeast of the Central de Abastos market (for destinations east and south of Oaxaca), and from Trujano, on the north side of the 2nd-class bus station, for destinations in the Valle de Etla. *Taxis colectivos* depart when they're full (five or six people).

Monte Albán

📷951

The ancient Zapotec capital of **Monte Albán** (📞516-12-15; admission M$51; ⏰8am-5pm) stands on a flattened hilltop 400m above the valley floor, just a few kilometers west

Valles Centrales

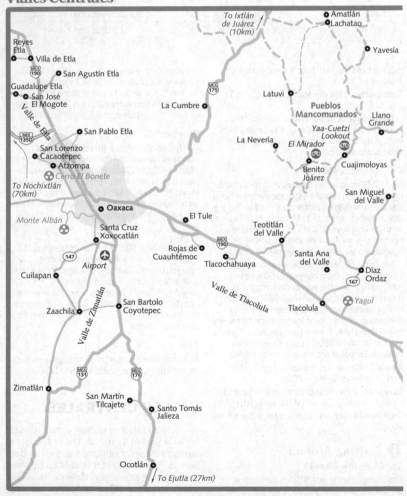

of Oaxaca. It's one of the most impressive ancient sites in Mexico, with spectacular 360-degree views. This strategic position was doubtless one of the reasons why the ancient Zapotecs chose this site for their capital. Its name, Monte Albán, means White Mountain.

At the entrance to the site are a good museum (explanations in Spanish only), a cafe and a bookstore. Official guides offer their services outside the ticket office for tours in Spanish, English, French and Italian (around M$200 for a small group). The heart of the site, the Gran Plaza, is wheelchair accessible, via an elevator and special walkways (ask at the ticket booth for the elevator to be activated). Explanatory signs are in Spanish, English and Zapotec.

History

Monte Albán was first occupied around 500 BC, probably by Zapotecs from the start and with early cultural connections with the Olmecs to the northeast.

The years up to about 200 BC (known as phase Monte Albán I) saw the leveling of the hilltop, the building of temples and probably palaces, and the growth of a town of 10,000 or more people on the hillsides. Hieroglyphs and dates in a dot-and-bar system carved during this era may mean that the elite of Monte Albán were the first people in Mexico to use writing and a written calendar. Between about 200 BC and AD 350 (Monte Albán II) the city came to dominate more and more of the Oaxaca region.

The city was at its peak from about 350 to 700 (Monte Albán III), when the main and surrounding hills were terraced for dwellings, and the population reached about 25,000. Most of what we see now dates from this time. Monte Albán was the center of a highly organized, priest-dominated society, controlling the extensively irrigated Valles Centrales, which held at least 200 other settlements and ceremonial centers. Many buildings here were plastered and painted red, and *talud-tablero* architecture (a stepped building style with alternating vertical and sloping sections) betrays influence from Teotihuacán. Nearly 170 underground tombs from this period have been found, some of them elaborate and decorated with frescoes, though none are open to visitors.

Between about 700 and 950 (Monte Albán IV) the place was abandoned and fell into ruin. Phase Monte Albán V (950–1521) saw minimal activity, except that Mixtecs arriving from northwestern Oaxaca reused some old tombs here to bury their own dignitaries.

◉ Sights

Gran Plaza   PLAZA
About 300m long and 200m wide, the Gran Plaza was and is the center of Monte Albán. Some of its structures were temples, others were elite residential quarters. Many of them are now cordoned off to prevent damage by visitors' feet.

Juego de Pelota
The stone terraces of the deep, I-shaped Ball Court, constructed about 100 BC, were

Sierra Norte

Yalalag

Mitla

Mitla

Xaagá

Santiago Matatlán

Hierve El Agua

San Lorenzo Albarradas

San Juan del Río

179

190

0 — 10 km
0 — 6 miles

Monte Albán

probably part of the playing area, not seats for spectators. It's thought they were covered with a thick coating of lime, meaning the ball would roll down them.

Edificio P

Building P was topped by a small pillared temple and was probably an observatory of some sort. A small opening near the top of the stairway is aligned so that the sun shines directly down a tube inside it at the solar zenith passages (when the sun passes directly overhead at noon on May 5 and August 8). Next door, the **Palacio** (Palace) is topped by a patio surrounded by the remains of typical Monte Albán III residential rooms.

Plataforma Sur

The big South Platform, with its wide staircase, is great for a panorama of the plaza and the surrounding mountains.

Edificio J

The arrowhead-shaped Building J, constructed about 100 BC and riddled with tunnels and staircases (unfortunately you can't go inside), stands at an angle of 45 degrees to the other Gran Plaza structures and was an observatory. Figures and hieroglyphs carved on its walls record Monte Albán's military conquests of other towns.

Edificio L

This is an amalgam of the Monte Albán I building that contained famous carvings known as Danzantes and a later structure built over it. The **Danzantes** (Dancers), some of which are seen around the lower part of the building, are thought to depict sacrificed leaders of conquered neighboring people. Carved between 500 and 100 BC, they generally have open mouths (sometimes down-turned in Olmec style) and closed eyes. Some have blood flowing where their genitals have been cut off. Hieroglyphs

MARKET DAYS

Markets in the towns of the Valles Centrales offer all manner of foodstuffs and produce, as well as handicrafts, domestic goods and sundries of all sorts. The scene is not to be missed; markets draw buyers and sellers from near and far, and bombard the senses with colors, sounds, smells and the sounds of indigenous languages, in a ritual that has been taking place for hundreds, if not thousands, of years. Markets are at their busiest in the morning, and most of them start to wind down in the early afternoon. The region's main markets:

» **Sunday** Tlacolula

» **Tuesday** Atzompa

» **Wednesday** Zimatlán; Ville de Etla

» **Thursday** Zaachila; Ejutla

» **Friday** Ocotlán; San Bartolo Coyotepec

» **Saturday** Mitla

accompanying them are the earliest known examples of true writing in Mexico.

Sistema IV
The twin to Sistema M at the southern end of the plaza, this combines typical Monte Albán II construction with overlays from Monte Albán III.

Plataforma Norte   PLATFORM
The North Platform, on top of a rock outcrop, is almost as big as the Gran Plaza, and offers the best views overall. It was rebuilt several times over the centuries. Chambers on either side of the main staircase contained tombs, and columns at the top of the stairs were part of a roofed hall. On top of the platform is a ceremonial complex created between AD 500 and 800. It includes the **Patio Hundido** (Sunken Patio), which has an altar at its center; **Edificios D, VG** and **E**, which were topped with adobe temples; and the **Templo de Dos Columnas**. **Stela VGE-2**, on the southern side of Edificio E, shows members of Monte Albán's ruling class of around AD 800 – four women and a young man represented by a jaguar.

ⓘ Getting There & Away

A few companies run buses to Monte Albán from Oaxaca for M$40 round trip. **Autobuses Turís-**

ticos (Mina 501) has departures hourly (half-hourly on Saturday and Sunday) from 8:30am to 3:30pm, starting back from the site between noon and 5pm.

East of Oaxaca: Valle de Tlacolula

The Valle de Tlacolula, east of Oaxaca, is home to the major pre-Hispanic sites of Mitla and Yagul as well as the village of Teotitlán del Valle, source of many of the best weavings you'll see in the Oaxaca area. Most of the following places are within walking distance of the Oaxaca–Mitla road, Hwy 190. Transportes Oaxaca-Istmo buses to Mitla, running every 20 minutes (7am to 8pm) from Oaxaca's 2nd-class bus station, will drop you anywhere along this road. Further transportation services are noted in the following sections.

EL TULE
POP 7600 / ELEV 1550M
The village of El Tule, 10km east of Oaxaca along Hwy 190, draws crowds of visitors for one very good reason: **El Árbol del Tule** (Tree of El Tule; admission M$5; ◷9am-5pm), which is claimed to be the largest tree in the world. In trunk thickness (it's about 11m in diameter) this claim is probably true. This vast *ahuehuete* (Montezuma cypress), 42m high, dwarfs the pretty 17th-century village church in whose churchyard it towers. Its age is equally impressive: the tree is at least 1500 years old, which means it was already growing when the ancient city of Monte Albán was at its peak. A park created in the 1990s stretches out in front of the churchyard.

Long revered by Oaxacans, the Árbol del Tule is under threat from local urban growth and irrigated agriculture that tap its water sources. Local campaigners say some of its aquifers must be restored if it is to survive.

Autotransportes Valle del Norte buses go to El Tule (M$5, every 20 minutes) from the 2nd-class bus station in Oaxaca.

TEOTITLÁN DEL VALLE
☑951 / POP 4400 / ELEV 1700M
This famous weaving village is 4km north of Hwy 190, about 25km from Oaxaca. The weaving tradition here goes back to pre-Hispanic times: Teotitlán had to pay tributes of cloth to the Aztecs. Quality today is high, and traditional dyes made from indigo,

cochineal and moss have been revived. The variety of designs is enormous – from Zapotec gods and Mitla-style geometric patterns to imitations of paintings by Rivera and Picasso.

Many tour groups are only taken as far as the larger weaving showrooms on the road approaching the village, which tend to dominate the craft here by buying up weavers' products or employing weavers directly to weave for them, and then taking a nice profit on any sales. They also typically give 30% commission to tour firms or guides whose clients make purchases. For more direct interaction with weavers head on into the village itself, where blankets and rugs wave at you from houses, workshops and showrooms along the streets. Signs point to the central **Mercado de Artesanías**, where yet more are on sale.

Around 150 Teotitlán families specialize in weaving; they are often happy to demonstrate their techniques and methods of obtaining natural dyes. A note of caution: due to the popularity of natural dying methods among foreign buyers, some weavers may falsely claim to use natural dyes. Even though synthetic dyes take a toll on the health of the weavers and the environment, they are much cheaper. For helpful tips about making environmentally responsible purchases, inquire at the Museo Textil de Oaxaca (p415) in the city.

Sights

Museo Comunitario Balaa Xtee Guech Gulal MUSEUM
(☑524-44-63; admission M$10; ⊙10am-6pm Tue-Sun) Facing the Mercado de Artesanías on the central plaza, this is a good community-run museum with local archaeological finds and displays on local crafts and traditions (in English as well as Spanish and Zapotec). Here, with a day's notice, you can organize a two- to three-hour guided walk up **Cerro de Picacho**, a sacred hill just outside the village, costing M$75/100/200 for two/four/10 people.

Templo de la Virgen de la Natividad CHURCH
(⊙6am-6pm) From the plaza, steps rise to this handsome 17th-century church with a fine broad churchyard. The church's altar area and transept are adorned with colorful 18th-century frescoes. It was built atop a Zapotec ceremonial site, many of whose carved stones can be seen in the church walls; look especially in the inner patio.

Eating

Restaurante Tlamanalli OAXACAN $$
(Av Juárez 39; mains M$80-200; ⊙1-4pm Tue-Sun) The Tlamanalli is a great lunch stop, with excellent traditional Oaxacan dishes. Some of them are based on pre-Hispanic recipes, and vegetarian options are offered. Exhibits on weaving add to the interest here.

Getting There & Away

Autotransportes Valle del Norte buses run to Teotitlán (M$10, 45 minutes, hourly 7am to 8pm) from Oaxaca's 2nd-class bus station; the last one back to Oaxaca can leave Teotitlán as early as 6pm. Alternatively, get any Mitla-bound bus to the signposted Teotitlán turnoff on Hwy 190, then a taxi colectivo (M$5) to the village.

TLACOLULA
POP 14,000 / ELEV 1650M

Tlacolula, 31km from Oaxaca, holds one of the Valles Centrales' major **markets** every Sunday, with the area around the church becoming a packed throng. Crafts, foods and plenty of everyday goods are on sale. It's a treat for lovers of market atmosphere. Inside the church, the 16th-century **Capilla del Santo Cristo**, is a riot of golden, indigenous-influenced decoration comparable to the Capilla del Rosario in Oaxaca's Santo Domingo. Among the ceiling ornamentation, spot the plaster martyrs holding their severed heads in their own hands.

YAGUL

The **Yagul ruins** (admission M$37; ⊙8am-5pm) are finely sited on a cactus-covered hill, about 1.5km north of the Oaxaca–Mitla road. The signposted turnoff is 34km from Oaxaca. Unless you have a vehicle you'll have to walk the 1.5km, though caution is advised on this isolated road.

Yagul was a leading Valles Centrales settlement after the decline of Monte Albán. Most of what's visible was built between AD 750 and 950. **Patio 4**, down to the left as you enter the main part of the site from the ticket office, was surrounded by four temples. On its east side is a carved-stone animal, probably a jaguar. Next to the central platform is the entrance to one of several multichambered **underground tombs**.

The beautiful **Juego de Pelota** (Ball Court) is the second biggest in Mesoamerica (after one at Chichén Itzá on the Yucatán Peninsula). To its west, on the edge of the hill, is **Patio 1**, with the narrow **Sala del Consejo** (Council Hall) along its north side. The labyrinthine **Palacio de los Seis**

Patios (Palace of the Six Patios), above the ball court and Patio 1, was probably the leader's residence. Its now creamy-yellow walls were originally plastered and painted red.

It's well worth climbing the Fortaleza (Fortress), the huge rock that towers above the ruins. Several overgrown ruins perch atop the Fortress – and the views are marvelous.

MITLA

🗐951 / POP 8200 / ELEV 1700M

A modern Zapotec town surrounds the unique ruins of Mitla, 46km southeast of Oaxaca. The ruins – a Zapotec religious center dating mostly from the last two or three centuries before the Spanish conquest in the 1520s – are partly covered by a colonial church and tell a vivid tale of the region's past and present. The geometric stone 'mosaics' of Mitla, the site, have no peers in ancient Mexico: the 14 different designs are thought to symbolize the sky and earth, a feathered serpent and other important beings, in highly sophisticated stylized forms. Each little piece of stone was cut to fit the design, then set in mortar on the walls and painted. Many Mitla buildings were also adorned with painted friezes.

◉ Sights

Ancient Mitla   ARCHAEOLOGICAL SITE
(admission Grupo de las Columnas & Grupo del Norte M$37; ⊗8am-5pm) The ruins date mostly from the final two or three centuries before the Spanish conquest. At this time Mitla was probably the most important of the Zapotec religious centers, dominated by high priests who performed heart-wrenching human sacrifices. It's thought that each main group of buildings we see at Mitla was reserved for specific occupants – one for the high priest, one for lesser priests, one for the king and so forth. Visitors usually just visit the two main groups in the town, though the remains of forts, tombs and other structures are scattered for many kilometers around.

If you tell the bus conductor that you're heading for *las ruinas,* you should be dropped at a fork known as *la cuchilla.* From here it's about 1.5km to the ruins, ticket office: go north along Av Morelos, through the plaza and along Calles 5 de Febrero and Reforma toward the three-domed Iglesia de San Pablo. The ticket office is normally behind this church, but was temporarily relocated in front of it at the time of writing. A three-wheeler *moto-taxi* from *la cuchilla* to the ruins costs M$10.

Grupo de las Columnas

The Group of the Columns, the major group of buildings, is just south of the Iglesia de San Pablo. It has two main patios, the Patio Norte and Patio Sur, each lined on three sides by long rooms. Along the north side of the Patio Norte is the **Sala de las Columnas**

PEOPLES OF OAXACA

Much of Oaxaca's special creativity and unique atmosphere is owed to the indigenous population, who may comprise almost half of the state's 3.8 million people. Indigenous peoples are generally at the bottom of the economic and social scale in Oaxaca, as they are throughout Mexico, but they are rich in culture. With their deep-rooted traditions, Oaxaca's 15 indigenous peoples are the driving force behind the state's fine *artesanías* (handicrafts) and unique festivities, and a main inspiration of its booming art scene and amazing output of creative cuisine.

Each of the 15 groups has its own language, customs and colorful traditional costume (though some members now speak only Spanish and many now wear mainstream clothing). The people you will probably have most contact with are the Zapotecs, possibly 800,000 strong, who live mainly in and around the Valles Centrales and on the Isthmus of Tehuantepec. Many of the artisans and market traders in and around Oaxaca city are Zapotec. Up to 750,000 Mixtecs are spread around the mountainous borders of Oaxaca, Guerrero and Puebla states, with more than two-thirds of them in Oaxaca. The state's other large indigenous groups include 300,000 or so Mazatecs and 200,000 Chinantecs in the far north, and some 170,000 Mixes in the mountains northeast of the Valles Centrales.

In Oaxaca city you may well see Triquis; the women wear long, bright red *huipiles* (sleeveless tunics). The Triquis are only about 30,000 strong and have a long history of conflict with mestizos (people of mixed ancestry) and Mixtecs over land rights in their remote home region of western Oaxaca.

(Hall of the Columns), 38m long with six massive columns and unusual, very big, one-piece lintels over the doorways. At one end of this hall, a passage leads into **El Palacio**, which holds some of Mitla's best stonework 'mosaics.' The passage and the *palacio* still bear traces of the original plaster and red paint. The Patio Sur holds two underground tombs.

Grupo del Norte

The North Group is similar to the Grupo de las Columnas but less elaborate. The Spaniards built the Iglesia de San Pablo over one of its patios in 1590.

🛏 Sleeping & Eating

Hotel Don Cenobio   HOTEL **$$**
(📞568-03-30; www.hoteldoncenobio.com, in Spanish; Av Juárez 3; r M$599-799; P🛜🅿) Set on the central plaza, this is easily Mitla's best hotel. The 23 themed rooms are decorated with attractively multicolored, carved headboards and furniture from Guadalajara. They're comfortable and fan-cooled, with good bathrooms and in many cases balconies. The hotel has a grassy central garden with a pool, with its restaurant and bar just off it.

Restaurante Doña Chica   OAXACAN **$$**
(Av Morelos 41; mains M$70-90; ⊙11am-8pm) Less than 100m from *la cuchilla*, spotless, bright and *tranquilo* Doña Chica serves straightforward, delicious Oaxacan dishes like *moles,* enchiladas and *tasajo* from an open kitchen. Good soups, *antojitos* (Mexican light meals) and salads round out the careful menu. The restaurant also makes its own quality mezcal.

🛍 Shopping

Mitla's streets are sprinkled with shops selling local mezcal. Many of them will invite you to taste a couple of varieties – as will some of the small-scale mezcal distilleries along the road toward Oaxaca. Many other shops, and the large **Mercado de Artesanías** near the ruins, sell local textiles including lots of hammocks. Some of the tablecloths are attractive buys.

ℹ Getting There & Away

A *taxi colectivo* from Prolongación Victoria in Oaxaca (one hour) costs M$20. Transportes Oaxaca-Istmo buses to Mitla (M$15, 1¼ hours, every 20 minutes from 7am to 8pm) leave from Oaxaca's 2nd-class bus station. The last one back to Oaxaca leaves Mitla at about 8pm.

HIERVE EL AGUA
ELEV 1800M

At Hierve El Agua, 14km southeast of Mitla, bubbling **mineral springs** (admission M$20; ⊙7am-8pm) run into bathing pools with a spectacular cliff-top location and expansive panoramas. Hierve El Agua means 'the Water Boils,' but the mineral-laden water is actually cold (though just about swimmable). Water dribbling over the cliff edge for millennia has created mineral formations that look like huge frozen waterfalls or outdoor stalactites. Altogether the pools here make for a unique bathing experience: there are changing rooms just above the pools if you fancy braving the waters.

Hierve El Agua is a popular destination for *oaxaqueños* on their days off. Above the pools and cliffs are a number of **comedores** (*antojitos* M$20-35), and **cabañas** (cabins; per person M$100) providing simple rooms with one bathroom per two rooms.

The area is dotted with agave fields: nearby villages such as San Lorenzo Albarradas and San Juan del Río produce some of Oaxaca's finest mezcal.

Hierve El Agua is on the itinerary of some day tours from Oaxaca. Public transportation is only by *camioneta* (pickup truck) from the street outside Mitla bus station (M$25, one hour). These leave when they have six or seven people, and are infrequent except on Saturday and Sunday. Alternatively, take a taxi from Mitla.

If you're driving, take the 'Hierve El Agua' exit from the highway that bypasses Mitla to the south. This passes through the village of Xaagá, from which an unpaved, very scenic road leads 11km to the site.

South of Oaxaca: Valle de Zimatlán

South from Oaxaca, Hwy 175 goes through San Bartolo Coyotepec, famed for its black pottery, and Ocotlán, which has one of the Valles Centrales' busiest weekly markets. Hwy 147 goes to Cuilapan and Zaachila.

SAN BARTOLO COYOTEPEC
📞951 / POP 4000 / ELEV 1550M

All the polished, black, surprisingly light pottery, called *barro negro,* that you find around Oaxaca (in hundreds of shapes and forms – candlesticks, jugs, vases and decorative animal and bird figures) comes from San Bartolo Coyotepec, 11km south of Oaxaca. To head to the pottery's original source, look for the signs to the Alfarería Doña Rosa (Juárez 24; ☺9am-7pm), a short walk east off the highway. It was doña Rosa (Rosa Real Mateo, 1900–80) who invented the method of burnishing the *barro negro* with quartz stones for the distinctive shine. Her family *alfarería* (potters' workshop) is now the biggest in the village, and demonstrations of the process are given whenever a tour group rolls in (usually several times a day). The pieces are hand-molded by an age-old technique that uses two saucers functioning as a rudimentary potter's wheel. They are then fired in pit kilns and turn black from smoke and from the iron oxide in the clay.

There are plenty of other blackware shops and workshops around San Bartolo today. The village is also home to the Museo Estatal de Arte Popular de Oaxaca (www.museo-meapo.com, in Spanish; admission M$20; ☺10am-6pm Tue-Sun), on the south side of the main plaza, which features a collection of fine blackware plus changing exhibitions of quality folk art from around Oaxaca state.

Estrella del Valle/Oaxaca Pacífico (Armenta y López 721, Oaxaca) runs buses to San Bartolo (M$8, 20 minutes) every few minutes.

SAN MARTÍN TILCAJETE
San Martín Tilcajete (population 1600), 1km west of Hwy 175, 24km south of Oaxaca, is the source of many of the bright copalwood *alebrijes* seen in Oaxaca. You can see and buy them in makers' houses, many of which have 'Artesanías de Madera' (Wooden Handicrafts) signs outside. Jacobo & María Ángeles Ojeda (www.tilcajete.org; Olvido 9) make particularly wonderful *alebrijes*. Good pieces are also displayed at the restaurant Azucena Zapoteca (mains M$60-130; ☺8am-7pm), a popular lunch stop serving Oaxacan specialties, beside Hwy 175 opposite the Tilcajete turnoff.

Ocotlán-bound buses from Oaxaca will drop you at the turnoff to San Martín. *Taxis colectivos* run from Ocotlán itself.

OCOTLÁN
POP 21,000 / ELEV 1500M
Ocotlán, 31km south of Oaxaca, was the hometown of the artist Rodolfo Morales (1925–2001), who turned his international success to the area's benefit by setting up the Fundación Cultural Rodolfo Morales (www.fcrom.org.mx, in Spanish; Morales 108), based in his old family home less than a block north of the central plaza. This foundation stages assorted cultural events and works to promote the arts, heritage, environment and social welfare locally. It has done some marvelous restoration work on village churches – including the handsome 16th-century Templo de Santo Domingo just off Ocotlán's main plaza, which now sports beautiful, colorful paintwork inside and out. The foundation also turned the adjoining Ex-Convento de Santo Domingo (admission M$15; ☺9am-6pm), previously a dilapidated jail, into a first-class art museum, which includes several of Morales' own canvases and a room of folk art dominated by Ocotlán's most renowned artisans, the Aguilar sisters. Morales' ashes are interred here, too.

The four Aguilar sisters and their families create whimsical, colorful pottery figures of women with all sorts of unusual motifs. Their houses are together on the west side of the highway as you come into Ocotlán from the north – spot them by the pottery women on the wall, almost opposite the Hotel Real de Ocotlán. Most renowned is the family of Guillermina Aguilar (Morelos 430), who turn out, among other things, miniature 3-D recreations of Frida Kahlo works.

Most visitors come to Ocotlán on Friday, when its big weekly market sprawls around the central plaza. The covered Mercado Morelos, on the west side of the plaza, is worth a look any day of the week, and it contains several *comedores* serving bargain Oaxacan food for M$15 to M$30 per dish. One, La Cocina de Frida, is presided over by a local woman who resembles Frida Kahlo – and dresses for the part.

Estrella del Valle/Oaxaca Pacífico (Armenta y López 721, Oaxaca) runs buses to Ocotlán (one-way/round-trip M$15/20, 45 minutes, every 15 minutes from 5am to 9pm). Automorsa (Bustamante 601, Oaxaca) operates a similar service about every 10 minutes, 6am to 8pm. *Taxis colectivos* to Ocotlán from Prolongación Victoria in Oaxaca cost M$20.

CUILAPAN
POP 12,000 / ELEV 1560M
Cuilapan (Cuilápam), 9km southwest of Oaxaca, is one of the few Mixtec towns in the Valles Centrales. It's the site of a beautiful, historic Dominican monastery, the Ex-Convento Dominicano (admission to cloister M$31; ☺9am-6pm), whose pale stone seems almost to grow out of the land.

In 1831 Mexican independence hero Vicente Guerrero was executed here by soldiers supporting the rebel conservative Anastasio Bustamante, who had ousted the liberal Guerrero from the presidency. Guerrero had fled by ship from Acapulco, but the ship's captain put in at Huatulco and betrayed him to the rebels. Guerrero was then transported to Cuilapan to die.

A long, low, unfinished **church** in front of the monastery has stood roofless since work on it stopped in 1560. It has big, stately arches and some detailed stone carving. Behind is the church that succeeded it, which contains the **tomb of Juana Donají** (daughter of Cosijoeza, the last Zapotec king of Zaachila) and is open only for Mass (usually 7am to 8am and 5pm to 6pm). Around the church's right-hand end is a two-story Renaissance-style **cloister**: some rooms here have faded 16th- and 17th-century murals, and a painting of Guerrero hangs in the small room where he was held. Outside, a **monument** marks the spot where he was shot.

Taxis colectivos to Cuilapan from Prolongación Victoria in Oaxaca cost M$9.50 (20 minutes).

ZAACHILA

📞951 / POP 14,000 / ELEV 1520M

This part-Mixtec, part-Zapotec town, 6km beyond Cuilapan and 4km west of San Bartolo Coyotepec, has a big, busy Thursday market. Zaachila was a Zapotec capital from AD 1400 until the Spanish conquest. Its last Zapotec king, Cosijoeza, died in the 1520s.

Behind the village church overlooking the main plaza, a sign indicates the entrance to Zaachila's **Zona Arqueológica** (Archaeological Zone; admission M$31; ⊙9am-5pm), a small assortment of mounds where you can enter two small tombs used by the ancient Mixtecs. Tumba 1 has sculptures of owls, a turtle-man figure and various long-nosed skull-like masks. Tumba 2 has no decoration, but in it was found a Mixtec treasure hoard that's now in the Museo Nacional de Antropología in Mexico City. When Mexican archaeologists first tried to excavate these tombs in the 1940s and 1950s, they were run off by irate Zaachilans. The tombs were finally excavated under armed guard in 1962. You can see photos of some of the objects that were carted off.

Taxis colectivos from Oaxaca to Zaachila leave from the corner of Bustamante and Zaragoza, and from Prolongación Victoria, costing M$10 (20 minutes).

North of Oaxaca: Valle de Etla

ATZOMPA

POP 22,000 / ELEV 1600M

The potters of Atzompa, 6km northwest of central Oaxaca and now part of the city's urban sprawl, produce attractive, colorful animal figures, pots, plates, lamps and more. Much work is sold at good prices in the village's **Mercado de Artesanías** (Crafts Market; Av Libertad 303; ⊙9am-7pm). Some ceramics bear Atzompa's traditional green glaze; others are in more colorful, innovative styles.

From the village church, a 2.5km road (mostly dirt) leads south up **Cerro El Bonete**. The road ends a few minutes' walk from the hilltop, which is dotted with unrestored pre-Hispanic ruins.

Taxis colectivos to Atzompa (M$6, 20 minutes) leave from Trujano on the north side of Oaxaca's 2nd-class bus station.

SAN JOSÉ EL MOGOTE

POP 800 / ELEV 1600M

Fourteen kilometers northwest of central Oaxaca on Hwy 190, a westward turnoff (signposted 'Nazareno') leads 1.5km to San José El Mogote. Long ago, before even Monte Albán became important, Mogote was the major settlement in Oaxaca. It was at its peak between 650 and 500 BC, and flourished again between 100 BC and AD 150, boasting a main plaza that was almost as big as Monte Albán's. The major surviving structures (partly restored) are a ball court and a sizable pyramid mound behind the primary school in the village center.

The **Museo Comunitario Ex-Hacienda El Cacique** (admission M$10; ⊙variable) is in the former landowner's hacienda next to the primary school. The museum has interesting material on the villagers' 20th-century struggle for land ownership; an archaeological highlight is 'El Diablo Enchilado,' a pre-Hispanic brazier in the form of a bright-red grimacing face. If you find the museum closed, ask anyone for the nearby house of the *encargado* (keeper).

To reach Mogote take a Guadalupe Etla-bound *taxi colectivo* (M$10, 30 minutes) from Trujano on the north side of Oaxaca's 2nd-class bus station.

SAN AGUSTÍN ETLA

📞951 / POP 3700 / ELEV 1800M

Pretty San Agustín sits on the eastern slopes of the Valle de Etla, 18km northwest of Oaxaca. Its large, early-20th-century textile mill has been superbly restored as the **Centro de las Artes de San Agustín** (☑521-30-42; www.casanagustin.org.mx; Independencia s/n, Barrio Vistahermosa; admission free; ☺9am-6pm), a spectacular arts center with two long, large halls, used for concerts, film showings, conferences and often wonderful craft or art exhibitions. The center also hosts many art and crafts courses and workshops.

Balneario Vista Hermosa (☑521-20-49; Hidalgo 16; adult/child M$70/60; ☺10am-6pm) makes a fun day out if you are in Oaxaca with kids. Its six swimming pools, in attractive hillside gardens, include one that's heated, one that's big and shallow, and a couple with waterslides. It also has a modest restaurant (dishes M$30 to M$75).

The turnoff for San Agustín from Hwy 190 is on the east side of the road, 14km from central Oaxaca, opposite the Nazareno turning on the west side. It's 3.5km up to the village center and a further 1.5km to the arts center or Balneario Vista Hermosa. *Taxis colectivos* to San Agustín (M$12, 30 minutes) go from Trujano on the north side of Oaxaca's 2nd-class bus station. For the *balneario* (bathing place) you'll need a further M$15 local taxi on arrival. The arts center provides free round-trip transportation from Oaxaca (Parque Juárez) for events here that finish after 8:30pm.

SIERRA NORTE

The mountains separating the Valles Centrales from low-lying far northern Oaxaca are called the Sierra Juárez, and the more southerly parts of this range, closest to Oaxaca, have become known as the Sierra Norte. These beautiful, well-forested highlands are home to some successful community ecotourism ventures that provide comfortable accommodations and a wonderful opportunity to get out on foot, mountain bike or horseback into some of Mexico's loveliest landscapes. The area's natural diversity is amazing: over 400 bird species, 350 butterflies, all six Mexican wildcats and nearly 4000 plants have been recorded in the Sierra Norte. The variety of wildflowers is astonishing, too. Be prepared for cool temperatures: in the higher, southern villages it can snow in winter. The rainiest season is from late May to September, but there's little rain from January to April.

Scenic Hwy 175 crosses the *sierras* en route to Tuxtepec (population 102,000), the main town in the far north of the state.

Pueblos Mancomunados

The Pueblos Mancomunados (Commonwealth of Villages) are eight remote villages (Amatlán, Benito Juárez, Cuajimoloyas, La Nevería, Lachatao, Latuvi, Llano Grande and Yavesía) in the thickly forested highlands north of the Valle de Tlacolula. The villages offer highly recommended wilderness escapes and an up-close communion with Zapotec village life. It's well worth the time and effort to spend at least one night here, and you can easily enjoy several days walking, mountain biking or horseback riding between villages and exploring around them. Elevations in these hills range from 2200m to over 3200m, and the landscapes, with canyons, caves, waterfalls and panoramic lookouts, are spectacular.

For centuries, these villages have pooled the natural resources of their 290-sq-km territory, sharing the profits from forestry and other enterprises. Connected by more than 100km of scenic tracks and trails, and surrounded by trails to local beauty spots and places of interest, the villages have turned to ecotourism to help stave off economic difficulties and population decline. All offer simple but comfortable, good-value *cabaña* lodging (mostly with hot-water bathrooms and fireplaces), meals, and mountain bikes for rent. Most also have horses.

Although several Oaxaca active-tourism agencies offer trips to the Pueblos Mancomunados, it's not difficult to visit independently. Six of the villages (the exceptions being Lachatao and Yavesía) cooperate in an excellent combined ecotourism program, **Expediciones Sierra Norte** (www.sierranorte.org.mx), which has a helpful office in Oaxaca city (p419). Each participating village also has an information and services office open from 9am to 9pm daily. It's possible just to roll up in a village and organize what you need on the spot, but reservations are a good idea at vacation times and weekends. Horses must be reserved at least one day ahead.

Local guides, knowledgeable about the wildlife, ecology, folklore and history of these *sierras,* are available for excursions. You don't generally need one to follow the main routes between villages, but for smaller trails a guide is recommended. English-speaking

OAXACA PUEBLOS MANCOMUNADOS

guides cost a little extra and should be requested two or three days ahead.

Each village has a camping area as well as *cabañas,* and at least one *comedor* serving good local meals from 8am to 8pm. Prices in the Expediciones Sierra Norte villages are as follows:

» private *cabaña:* M$450 for two people
» shared *cabaña:* M$150 per person
» meals: M$50 to M$55 each
» camping: M$45 per person
» tent rental: M$50 per night
» bicycle: M$100 per three hours
» horse: M$200 per three hours
» guide for up to eight people: M$150/200/240 per 3/5/7 hours
» one-time access fee: adult/child M$50/30

Lachatao village runs a well-organized, separate ecotourism program, **Lachatao Expediciones** ([📞]951-517-60-58; www.lachataoexpediciones.com.mx, in Spanish), with similar services and prices. One of the most attractive and interesting villages, with exceptionally good *cabañas,* Lachatao lies on routes between some of the Expediciones Sierra Norte villages, but any reservations here have to be made separately.

Villages & Routes

The easiest-to-reach and most-visited villages are **Cuajimoloyas, Llano Grande** and **Benito Juárez**, all at the higher, southern end of the Sierra Norte, nearest to Oaxaca. It's possible to base yourself in one village and take local walks or rides from there; Cuajimoloyas and Llano Grande have the most options for this. Some superb lookout points are easily accessible from the southern villages, such as **El Mirador**, a 2.5km walk from Benito Juárez, or the 3200m-high **Yaa-Cuetzi** lookout, 1km from Cuajimoloyas.

Tiny **La Nevería** is less visited but very welcoming and pretty, and additional routes from here take you through the forests to La Cumbre on Hwy 175, or right down to Tlalixtac de Cabrera in the Valle de Tlacolula.

One special highlight walk is the beautiful **Latuvi-Lachatao canyon trail**, along a pre-Hispanic track from the Valles Centrales to the Gulf of Mexico that passes through cloud forests festooned with bromeliads and hanging mosses (keep your eyes peeled for trogons, too).

Lachatao is one of the most atmospheric villages, with a huge 17th-century church (the fruit of nearby colonial gold mines) and an

excellent new community museum focusing on its proud links with some major Mexican historical figures. From Lachatao or nearby **Amatlán** you can visit the old mines and the remains of a colonial textile hacienda.

❶ Getting There & Away

It's a good idea to check with Expediciones Sierra Norte in Oaxaca for current transportation details. Cuajimoloyas and Llano Grande have the best public services from Oaxaca: four daily Flecha del Zempoaltépetl buses (to Cuajimoloyas M$47, two hours; to Llano Grande M$47, 2½ hours) from the 2nd-class bus station, and five daily *taxis colectivos* (to Cuajimoloyas M$60, 1½ hours; to Llano Grande M$65, two hours) from Sitio Yaganiza at Periférico 408, next to Tienda Zetuna, just north of the Periférico intersection with Trujano. For Benito Juárez take a service bound for Cuajimoloyas and get off at the Benito Juárez turnoff (*'desviación de Benito Juárez'*), 3km before Cuajimoloyas, and walk 3.5km west along the unpaved road to Benito Juárez. From Benito Juárez, La Nevería is a 9km walk west, and Latuvi 10km north.

You can reach the northern villages of Amatlán and Lachatao by heading to Ixtlán de Juárez on Hwy 175 (M$55, 1¾ hours, nine daily Cuenca buses from Oaxaca's 1st-class bus station), then taking a *camioneta mixta* (double-cabin pickup) at 7am, noon or 3pm from Ixtlán to Amatlán (M$25, 45 minutes) or Lachatao (M$25, one hour). *Camionetas* start back for Ixtlán from Lachatao at 6am, 9am and 1:30pm.

Note: Unlike Oaxaca, the Pueblos Mancomunados do not observe daylight saving time (see p858), so you should triple-check all departure times, especially for the return trip!

Taxis are also an option for reaching the villages, and Expediciones Sierra Norte can help arrange them.

WESTERN OAXACA

Western Oaxaca is dramatic, mountainous country with a fairly sparse population and some thick forests as well as overfarmed, eroded and deforested areas. Along with adjoining parts of Puebla and Guerrero states, it is known as the Mixteca, for its Mixtec indigenous inhabitants. The region offers a chance to get well off the beaten track, enjoy hiking, biking or climbing in remote areas and see some outstanding colonial architecture. Guided trips are available from Oaxaca with operators such as Tierraventura (p419), Bicicletas Pedro Martínez (p435) and Academic Tours (p424).

In pre-Hispanic times the Mixtecs were famed workers of gold and precious stones, and it's said that Aztec emperor Moctezuma would eat only off fine Mixteca-Puebla ceramics. Today this is one of Oaxaca's poorest regions, with very high emigration rates.

Santiago Apoala

POP 190 / ELEV 2000M

This small, remote village, lying in a green, Shangri La–like valley flanked by cliffs, is a great spot for hiking, biking and climbing. In traditional Mixtec belief, this valley was the birthplace of humanity, and it is easy to see why: the scenery around Apoala is spectacular, with the 60m waterfall **Cascada Cola de la Serpiente**, the 400m-deep **Cañón Morelos** and a number of caves among the highlights.

A community-tourism scheme provides good accommodations, meals and guides. It's easiest to come with an agency from Oaxaca, but cheaper to arrange things independently through the village's **Unidad Ecoturística** (Ecotourism Unit; ☑ 555-151-91-54; cnr Pino Suárez & Independencia; ☉8am-8pm), which runs some of Oaxaca's best village **accommodations** (campsite M$70, 3-/4-person tent rental M$80/100, s/d M$100/200, cabaña for 2 M$350, for 4 M$450-550, meals M$35-40) and offers mountain-bike rental (per three hours/day M$30/150) and guides (per person M$10 to M$30, depending on route). The Oaxaca state tourist department, Sectur (p434), can help you contact Apoala and make any arrangements.

ⓘ Getting There & Away

Santiago Apoala is 40km north of the town of Nochixtlán, by a rough, unpaved road which takes about two hours to drive. Nochixtlán is served by nine daily buses from Oaxaca's 1st-class bus station (M$88 to M$92, one to 1½ hours). Between Nochixtlán and Apoala, take a taxi, camioneta or the bus which normally leaves Apoala for Nochixtlán at 8am on Wednesday, Saturday and Sunday (M$90, three hours), and starts back from Nochixtlán to Apoala at noon or 1pm the same days.

Yanhuitlán, Coixtlahuaca & Teposcolula

The beautiful 16th-century **Dominican monasteries** in the villages of Yanhuitlán, Coixtlahuaca and San Pedro Teposcolula are some of the oldest Christian structures in Oaxaca and rank among Mexico's finest architectural treasures. Their scale – especially the enormous *capilla abierta* (open chapel) spaces used for mass conversions – testifies to the size of indigenous populations when the Spanish arrived. The monasteries' restrained stonework fuses medieval, platteresque, Renaissance and indigenous styles, and all three have ornate interior decoration, including enormous gilded wooden *retablos* (altarpieces). Recent restoration works have restored their grandeur and added interesting museums, which are all open from 9am to 5pm daily except Monday, with admission of M$35. The monastery churches are usually open daily from about 9am to 2pm and 4pm to 6pm. Should you want to stay overnight in the area, Coixtlahuaca and San Pedro Teposcolula have a few acceptable, basic hotels and inns.

The **Templo y Ex-Convento de San Juan Bautista** in **Coixtlahuaca** is 4km east of the Coixtlahuaca tollbooth on Hwy 135D, about 30km north of Nochixtlán. The Renaissance-style, white-stone main facade of the church is magnificent, and the graceful, ruined *capilla abierta* bears Mixtec religious symbols, most notably serpents and eagles.

The **Templo y Ex-Convento de Santo Domingo** at **Yanhuitlán** towers above Hwy 190, some 14km northwest of Nochixtlán. Built atop an important old Mixtec religious site, it has beautiful carving on its north and west facades, and a fine Mudejar ceiling is suspended beneath the choir loft, which contains an impressive pipe organ.

The **Templo y Ex-Convento de San Pedro y San Pablo** dominates the friendly town of **San Pedro Teposcolula**, on Hwy 125 about 30km southwest of Yanhuitlán. The monastery has a particularly stately *capilla abierta* with several beautifully carved arches; the museum in the adjacent monastic buildings contains a sizable collection of early colonial art.

ⓘ Getting There & Away

All three villages can be seen in a longish but not difficult day trip by car from Oaxaca. Public transportation options include **Transportadora Excelencia** (Díaz Ordaz 304, Oaxaca), which runs comfortable large vans to Yanhuitlán (M$50, one hour) and Teposcolula (M$70, 1¾ hours). **Fletes y Pasajes** runs 2nd-class buses to Coixtlahuaca (M$70, 1½ hours, 10 daily) from Oaxaca's 2nd-class bus station.

OAXACA COAST

Oaxaca's spectacular Pacific coast really has everything any traveler needs for a great time by the ocean. With half a dozen relaxed beach destinations each offering their individual take on the coast's manifold attractions, and the near-empty shoreline between them strung with long golden beaches and lagoons full of wildlife, it's hard to go wrong. Offshore, you can sail in search of dolphins, turtles and whales, or go diving, snorkeling or sportfishing – not forgetting some of the best surfing swells in North America and plenty of gentler beaches where beginners can learn to surf.

In this tropical climate, the pace of life is never too hectic and the people are welcoming. In the center of the coast sits the small fishing port and beach town of Puerto Ángel. Just to its west are strung three beach villages – Zipolite, San Agustinillo and Mazunte – that are perfect havens for just taking it easy, with a laid-back traveler vibe and plenty of good-value accommodations and food. Further west lies Puerto Escondido, a larger fishing and market town with a string of great beaches (including Playa Zicatela, home to the pumping surf of the Mexican Pipeline) and appealing sleeping, eating and nightlife options for all budgets. Toward the eastern end of the coast is Bahías de Huatulco, a modern, planned beach resort along a string of beautiful bays that has a pleasantly low-key atmosphere.

This coast is one of the world's most important sea-turtle nesting areas, and the many lagoons behind it are full of bird and aquatic life that will delight nature lovers. The coastal plain is backed everywhere by dramatic, forested mountains – and the trip down to the coast from Oaxaca city is a spectacular experience in itself, whether you go by bus, car or light plane. There are airports at Huatulco and Puerto Escondido, both with daily flights from Oaxaca and Mexico City. Huatulco is the more convenient for the Puerto Ángel–to–Mazunte area and has some direct flights from the USA and Canada, as well as more frequent flights from Mexico City.

Most of the year's rain here falls between June and September, turning everything green. From October the landscape starts to dry out, though conditions can remain humid. May is the hottest month.

Puerto Escondido

📞954 / POP 40,000

Loved by surf bums, water-sports junkies, perma-tan international travelers and Canadian and US snowbirds, this 'Hidden Port' is one of the most enjoyable spots on Mexico's Pacific coast. If you want solitude to commune with nature, you're in the wrong place: Puerto Escondido is a place to catch the legendary Mexican Pipeline, get some sun and party. By day, water sports are popular – you can go surfing, snorkeling, diving, sportfishing or looking for turtles, dolphins and even whales. By night, a busy cafe, restaurant and bar scene brings live music and a freewheeling, unpretentious nightlife. Within easy day-trip distance are the coastal lagoons of Manialtepec and Chacahua, which teem with birdlife. Development here has remained on a human scale, and part of Puerto Escondido's charm is that it remains a fishing port and market town as well as a tourist destination.

The center of town rises above the small Bahía Principal. The Carretera Costera (Hwy 200) runs across the hill above it, dividing the upper town – where buses arrive and most locals live and work – from the lower, more touristic part. The heart of the lower town is Av Pérez Gasga, known as El Adoquín (*adoquín* is Spanish for paving stone). Pérez Gasga winds up the hill to meet the Costera at an intersection known as El Crucero.

Playa Zicatela, hub of the surf and traveler scene, stretches 3km southeast from the east end of Bahía Principal. Most of the action and services are at its northern end, but there's another, smaller cluster of accommodations and eateries down at Punta Zicatela, at the south end of the beach. Rinconada, a quiet residential area above Playa Carrizalillo, west of the center, has further places to stay, restaurants and services.

⊙ Sights & Activities

Beaches

Playa Zicatela BEACH

Long, straight Zicatela (Map p454) is Puerto's happening beach, with enticing cafes, restaurants and accommodations, as well as the waves of the legendary Mexican Pipeline, which test the mettle of experienced surfers from far and wide. Most of the action, including the Pipeline, is at Zicatela's northern end (nearest town). The Punta

Zicatela area at its southern end also has good surfing waves.

Nonsurfers beware: the Zicatela waters have a lethal undertow and are definitely not safe for the boardless. Lifeguards rescue several careless people most months.

Bahía Principal   BEACH
The central beach (Map p450) is long enough to accommodate restaurants at its west end, a fishing fleet in its center (Playa Principal), and sun worshippers and young bodyboarders at its east end (Playa Marinero) where the waters are a little cleaner. Pelicans wing in inches above the waves, boats bob on the swell and a few hawkers wander up and down.

Playa Carrizalillo   BEACH
About 1.5km west of Bahía Principal, small Carrizalillo beach (Map p450) is in a cove reached by a stairway of about 170 steps. It's good for swimming, snorkeling, bodyboarding and surfing, and has a couple of *palapa* (thatch-roofed) beach bars.

Bahía Puerto Angelito   BEACH
The sheltered bay of Puerto Angelito (Map p450), about 1km west of Bahía Principal, has two smallish beaches. The western one, Playa Angelito, has lots of *comedores* and is very busy with Mexican families at weekends and on holidays. Playa Manzanillo, the eastern one, is inaccessible to vehicles but can still get crowded at weekends. Bring a snorkel.

Surfing
Puerto Escondido has surfable waves most days of the year. The **Pipeline** near the north end of Playa Zicatela is a world-class beach break, normally best in the morning and late afternoon, and at its biggest (it can reach 12m or more) between May and July. Even when the Pipeline is flat, the point break down at **Punta Zicatela** works almost day in, day out. **Playa Carrizalillo** has good beginners' waves. **Playa Punta Colorada**, about 4km west of town, is perfect for bodyboarding with its shallow waves and peaks. Surfers and environmentalists are campaigning against construction of a marina here which could kill the wave.

CLASSES
Numerous surf shops, schools and individual local surfers in Zicatela, Punta Zicatela and Rinconada offer surfing lessons. Lessons normally last 1½ to two hours, and the schools will drive you wherever the waves are most suitable (often Carrizalillo). Recommended options include the following.

Oasis Surf Academy   SURFING
(Map p450; ☎582-14-45; www.oasissurffactory .com; Blvd Juárez 6, Rinconada; individual class M$500; ☺9am-6pm Mon-Sat) Based near Playa Carrizalillo, offering classes with experienced, qualified, bilingual teachers. It's run by local pro surfer and board maker Roger Ramírez, and has apartments for rent, too.

Central Surf   SURFING
(Map p454; ☎582-22-85; www.centralsurfshop. com; Calle del Morro s/n, Zicatela; individual/group class per person M$600/350) Classes are given by brothers René and David Salinas, from a well-known local surfing family.

BOARD RENTAL & PURCHASE
Long or shortboard rental is typically M$100/30 per day/hour; bodyboards are normally M$50/20 per day/hour, plus M$20 for fins.

You can buy secondhand surfboards from around M$1000 at places like Cinemar and XXX Surf Shop at Zicatela. Cinemar will buy them back at half price.

COMPETITIONS
Several annual surf contests are held at Zicatela, mostly in August (including a longboard contest organized by Puerto's celebrated masked surfer, Ángel Salinas), with another during the November *fiestas*. An under-18s surf festival at Playa Carrizalillo and a pro bodyboarding event at Punta Colorada also usually happen in August.

Turtle-, Dolphin- & Whale-Watching
Sea turtles and dolphins are common in the seas off Puerto, and from around November to March you have a chance of seeing humpback whales and even whale sharks. Three-hour trips for small groups are usually M$400 per person. Omar Ramírez of **Omar Sportfishing** (Map p450; ☎cell phone 954-5594406; tomzap.com/omar.html; Playa Angelito) specializes in these trips. Dive shops Deep Blue Dive and Aventura Submarina, and travel agency Viajes Dimar, do similar trips. Local fishers will take groups of up to four out for an hour for around M$450 in their *lanchas* (fast, open, outboard boats): contact the **Sociedad Cooperativa Turística Nueva Punta Escondida** (Map p450; ☎582-16-78) at Restaurante El Pescador on Bahía Principal.

Puerto Escondido

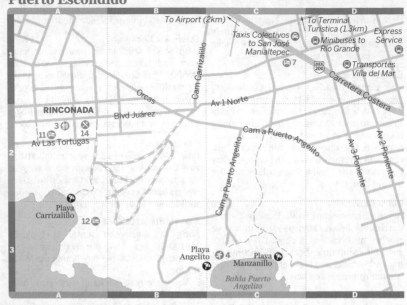

Puerto Escondido

Diving & Snorkeling

You can dive or snorkel year-round here. Typical visibility is around 10m, rising to as much as 30m between May and August, when the seas are warmest. The reefs are of volcanic rock, with lots of marine life, including big schools of fish, spotted eagle rays, stingrays and turtles. Most dive sites are within a 15-minute boat ride of town. Puerto has three dive outfits, all offering snorkeling trips as well as two-tank dives (around M$750) and a variety of courses.

Deep Blue Dive   DIVING, SNORKELING
(Map p454; ☑cell phone 954-1003071; www.deep bluedivemexico.com; Beach Hotel Inés, Calle del Morro s/n, Zicatela) This highly rated, European-run outfit offers one- and two-tank dives, night dives and PADI courses.

Puerto Dive Center   DIVING, SNORKELING
(Map p450; ☑cell phone 954-1027767; www.puerto divecenter.com; Av Pérez Gasga s/n) PDC can cater to various specialties including underwater photography and deep diving, as well as dives for certified divers and beginners, and PADI courses. Owner Sofía Ponce holds the women's world record for saltwater deep diving, having descended to 190m off Puerto in 2010. Snorkel gear rental is M$150 per day.

Aventura Submarina   DIVING, SNORKELING
(Map p450; ☑cell phone 954-5444862; asubma rina@hotmail.com; Av Pérez Gasga 601A) PADI

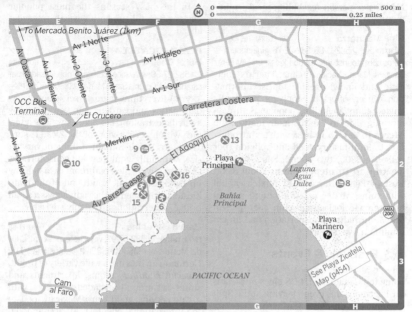

See Playa Zicatela
Map (p454)

instructor Jorge Pérez Bravo has 30 years' experience in local waters.

Fishing

Local fishers will take two to four people fishing for marlin, sailfish, tuna or smaller inshore fish: a three-hour trip costs around M$1200 to M$1500. Contact Sociedad Cooperativa Turística Nueva Punta Escondida or Omar Sportfishing, as for turtle-watching. Catch-and-release is encouraged, but, if you like, boat owners will arrange for some of the catch to be cooked for you at one of the town's seafood restaurants.

🐟 Courses

Learning Spanish is becoming popular here. Schools usually offer homestays or their own accommodations for around US$150 per week.

Experiencia   SPANISH LANGUAGE
(☑588-41-52; www.experienciapuerto.com; cnr Cárdenas & Hidalgo, Punta Zicatela; programs per week US$100-462, registration US$95) Opened in 2010, Experiencia has quickly gained a reputation for a good atmosphere and good organization. Its strategy is linguistic and cultural immersion, combining language learning with educational workshops (helping ecological and social work programs),

and cultural, sports and social activities. Programs range from 10 to 40 classes per week (often a mix of group and private sessions), with all levels catered for. Special programs are available for travelers, children and surfers, and you can join several volunteer work projects.

**Instituto de Lenguajes
Puerto Escondido**   SPANISH LANGUAGE
(Map p454; ☑582-20-55; www.puertoschool.com; Carretera Costera, Zicatela; small-group/private classes per person per hr US$8/12) This small school emphasizes both spoken and written Spanish, with a variety of complementary activities including surfing, cooking and salsa lessons and volunteer opportunities. You can start any day, for as long as you like: packages from one week upwards are also offered.

🧭 Tours

Viajes Dimar   GENERAL
Dimar (p456), a long-established and reliable local travel firm, offers a good range of day and half-day trips to Manialtepec, Chacahua, waterfalls, a coffee plantation and other places of interest in the area, with English-speaking guides, for M$350 to

M$750 per person (excluding meals; minimum two or four people).

Gina Machorro
CULTURAL, HISTORICAL

(Map p450; ☑582-11-86, 582-02-76; ginainpuerto@yahoo.com; tourist information kiosk, cnr Av Pérez Gasga & Marina Nacional) Gina, Puerto's energetic and knowledgeable tourist information officer, offers a variety of personally guided tours including popular Saturday-morning visits to Puerto's main market, the **Mercado Benito Juárez**, with an introduction to local history, food and religion (per person M$300, two hours). She also takes day trips to **Tututepec** village, about 85km west of Puerto, an ancient Mixtec capital with ruins, Mixtec *artesanías* and a good little archaeological museum (per person M$650 including transportation and lunch; minimum five people).

🎉 Festivals & Events

Puerto Music
MUSIC

Some top Canadian and US blues musicians hit Puerto for this event, playing at the Split Coconut bar on Playa Marinero. There are usually two gigs every second week from early January to early March.

Fiestas de Noviembre
CULTURAL

These festivities (www.cdpuertoescondido.com, in Spanish) keep Puerto buzzing throughout November with many varied events, including the three-day Festival Costeño de la Danza (folk dance), concerts by big-name Mexican musical acts, the three-day International Sailfish Tournament (www.pescadeportivaenpuertoescondido.com), a surfing contest, kite-flying, food tastings, crafts exhibits and plenty more.

🛏 Sleeping

The two main accommodations zones are Playa Zicatela and the central Adoquín (Av Pérez Gasga) area. Zicatela has the most appealing surroundings, with great places to eat as well as sleep. The only drawback is that you can't swim here.

Rates given here are those that commonly apply during the main visitor seasons – roughly mid-December to Easter, and July and August. During the Christmas–New Year and Easter vacations, prices can double or even more, but outside the main seasons many places drop their rates dramatically. Discounts are widely available for stays of several days or more.

In the busy seasons the most popular places often fill up, so it's worth reserving ahead.

PLAYA ZICATELA

Hotel Casa de Dan
HOTEL $$

(☑582-27-60; www.facebook.com/hotelcasadan; Jacarandas 14, Colonia Santa María; r M$300-600; P ☺ @ 🛜 🐦) Everything here is set around verdant patios and gardens, and you can enjoy a terrific extra-long lap pool as well as a terrace with a perfect view of the Zicatela surf. There are 15 self-contained units of varying size, with fully equipped kitchens, terraces and attractively tiled bathrooms. Go halfway up Las Brisas at the south end of the main Zicatela strip, then to the right across a small bridge. Reservations are highly advisable.

Beach Hotel Inés
HOTEL $$

(Map p454; ☑582-07-92; www.hotelines.com; Calle del Morro s/n; r M$300-1300; P ✳ @ 🛜 🐦 👣) The German-run Inés has a wide variety of bright, cheerful *cabañas*, rooms, apartments and suites, set around a shaded pool area with a cafe serving good Euro/Mexican food to the international clientele. All accommodations have hot water, good mosquito screens and fans, and some come with kitchens or air-con. You can arrange horseback riding, surf lessons, diving and other outings, and security is particularly good here.

Hotelito Swiss Oasis
HOTEL $$

(Map p454; ☑582-14-96; www.swissoasis.com; Andador Los Adobes; s/d/tr/q M$450/550/650/750; 🛜 🐦 👣) This good small hotel provides a guest kitchen, and a pool in the pretty garden, in addition to eight spotless rooms with good beds and attractive color schemes. The four upstairs rooms are two-level – good for families. The well-traveled Swiss owners speak four languages and are very helpful with local information.

Hotel Buena Vista
HOTEL $

(Map p454; ☑582-14-74; buenavista101@hotmail.com; Calle del Morro s/n; r M$400, with air-con M$500, with kitchen extra M$50; ✳ 🛜) The well-built Buena Vista, reached by its own steps up from Calle del Morro, is an excellent value. Rooms are big, no-frills and spotlessly clean, all with two beds, mosquito screens, hot-water bathroom and breezy balconies looking toward the beach.

Bungalows Puerta del Sol
HOTEL $

(Map p454; ☑582-29-22; bungalowspuertadelsol@hotmail.com; Calle del Morro s/n; r M$450, with air-con M$650; (P❋≋) This friendly, helpful and very clean place has a small pool and a communal kitchen either side of a nice green courtyard, and 16 spacious, solid rooms with cheerful art and, in most cases, balcony and hammock.

Hotel Las Olas   HOTEL $

(Map p454; ☑582-09-19; www.hotel-lasolas.com; Calle del Morro s/n; r M$250-350, with air-con M$400-500; ❋☎) Las Olas has exceptionally clean rooms that are an excellent value. Second-floor choices have ocean-view hammocks, and all have access to a kitchen, small sundeck and outdoor grilling space.

Tabachín del Puerto   BOUTIQUE HOTEL $$

(Map p454; ☑582-11-79; www.tabachininfo.com; s US$55-75, d US$65-90, all incl breakfast; P❋☎) Tabachín's gracious and erudite owner offers six studio-rooms in varying sizes (including enormous) and styles (folksy to Regency) with some fascinating original art and artifacts. All have kitchen, air-con and views. The excellent large breakfasts, served from 8am to 11am, include good vegetarian choices and organically grown coffee and fruit. The breakfasts are open to nonguests, too (M$50 to M$105) and are always sociable occasions. It's behind Hotel Santa Fe in Zicatela.

Hotel Santa Fe   HOTEL $$$

(Map p454; ☑582-01-70; www.hotelsantafe.com.mx; Calle del Morro s/n; r M$1700, ste from M$2150; P❋@☎≋) A well-run, neocolonial-style hotel with over 60 rooms set around two good pools in palm-shaded garden courtyards.

Ananda   GUESTHOUSE $

(☑118-60-70; www.anandahotelpuerto.com; Jacarandas 18, Colonia Santa María; r M$150-350; ☎) Friendly, good-value spot two doors past Casa de Dan.

Also worth checking out is **Bungalows Zicatela** (Map p454; ☑582-07-98; www.bungalowszicatela.com.mx; Calle del Morro s/n; s M$300-700, d M$400-800; P❋☎✈).

EL ADOQUÍN & AROUND
Hotel Mayflower   HOSTEL, HOTEL $

(Map p450; ☑582-03-67; minnemay7@hotmail.com; Andador Libertad s/n; dm/s/d/tr/q M$130/300/400/500/600; @☎) Clean, popular Mayflower has nine fan-cooled dorms holding four to seven people each (in beds and bunks), and 16 quite attractive private rooms with bathrooms and small balconies. Facilities include a decent guest kitchen, semi-open sitting areas, a billiard table, lockers and luggage-storage facilities.

Hotel Flor de María   HOTEL $$

(Map p450; ☑582-05-36; www.mexonline.com/flordemaria.htm; 1a Entrada a Playa Marinero; r US$45-65; P☎☎≋) A popular Canadian-owned hotel with 22 ample rooms sporting good large bathrooms and pretty wall paintings. A highlight is the expansive roof terrace with its fabulous views, bar and small pool.

Hotel Paraíso Escondido   HOTEL $$

(Map p450; ☑582-04-44; www.hotelpe.com; Unión 10; r/ste M$790/925; P❋☎≋) Rambling, neo-colonial place with pretty *artesanías* and 20 smallish rooms with good bathrooms – plus five top-floor suites with shared kitchen and the best bay views. Discounts for cash.

PUNTA ZICATELA

Note that Punta Zicatela is the far southern end of Playa Zicatela, and the following options are separated from the main cluster of accommodations listed in the Playa Zicatela section earlier.

Casamar   SUITES $$$

(☑582-25-93; www.casamarmexico.com; Puebla 407, Brisas de Zicatela; d M$882-2003, q M$1865-2558; ⊙groups only May, Oct & Nov; P❋☎≋) The North American–owned Casamar is a very attractive and comfortable vacation retreat. The 12 spacious, air-conditioned rooms are spotless and all have well-equipped kitchens and tasteful, folksy Mexican art and tilework. At the center of things is a large, verdant garden with a sizable pool. You can hang out in breezy common areas, and join regular yoga and salsa classes (free for guests) onsite.

Cabañas Buena Onda   HOSTEL $

(☑582-16-63; buenaonda.hostei.com; Cárdenas 777, Punta Zicatela; camping/hammock/dm per person M$60/60/100, cabaña M$230; ☎) Popular Buena Onda is set in a shady palm grove, with a beachfront *palapa* hangout area where campers can pitch a tent or sling a hammock. The 10 rustic *cabañas* are very clean and equipped with mosquito nets, fans and hammocks, and there are adequate bathrooms and kitchen.

Also recommended is **Frutas y Verduras** (☑540-17-82; frutasyverdurasmexico.com; Cárdenas s/n, Punta Zicatela; s M$150-300, d M$250-400; ☎).

Playa Zicatela

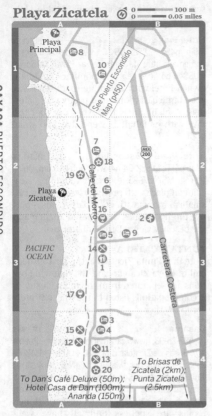

0 —— 100 m
0 —— 0.05 miles

Playa Principal

See Puerto Escondido Map (p450)

Playa Zicatela

Calle del Morro

MEX 200

Carretera Costera

PACIFIC OCEAN

To Brisas de Zicatela (2km); Punta Zicatela (2.5km)

To Dan's Café Deluxe (50m); Hotel Casa de Dan (100m); Ananda (150m)

Playa Zicatela

RINCONADA & CARRIZALILLO

Hotel Villa Mozart y Macondo
BOUTIQUE HOTEL $$

(Map p450; ☎104-22-95; www.hotelmozartyma condo.com, in Spanish; Av Las Tortugas 77, Carrizalillo; r M$350-700; ☀☞) A short walk from Playa Carrizalillo, Villa Mozart has a personal touch both in its individually decorated, comfortable accommodations and in the welcoming attention of its owners. Options range from three medium-sized rooms to two large one-bedroom apartments, a two-bedroom penthouse and a neat bungalow. The aesthetic is a lovely contemporary-folksy blend, with some quality original art. Breakfast is available in the garden, which is another work of art itself.

Villas Carrizalillo
BOUTIQUE HOTEL $$$

(Map p450; ☎582-17-35; www.villascarrizalillo.com; Av Carrizalillo 125, Carrizalillo; apt US$178-244; P☀@☞☒) Sublimely perched on the cliffs above Playa Carrizalillo, Villas Carrizalillo has spacious, stylish, air-conditioned apartments from one to three bedrooms, nearly all with fully equipped kitchens and private terraces. A path goes directly down to the beach, and the hotel has boards, bikes and snorkel gear for rent. There's a good, breezy in-house restaurant, too.

Hostel Losodeli
HOSTEL $

(Map p450; ☎582-42-21; www.hostelpuertoescon dido.com; Prolongación 2 Norte; dm/s/d/tr M$100/ 250/300/400; P☞☒) It's a little out of the way, but Losodeli has clean and colorful accommodations, a good pool and friendly, English-speaking staff.

Eating

Regardless of your palate, you'll have little trouble finding food to your liking. The big selection of eateries ranges from solidly satisfying Mexican/international places to some enticing contemporary fusion eateries.

Seafood is plentiful and usually fresh, and there is also some good vegetarian fare.

PLAYA ZICATELA

El Maná del Jardín   MEXICAN, VEGETARIAN $$
(Map p454; Calle del Morro s/n; mains M$60-120; ☺8am-11pm; 🖉🍴) This friendly beachside restaurant, with a triple deck offering a great view over the Pipeline, serves very good vegetarian dishes, from *gado-gado* (vegetables in peanut sauce) to tempeh and hummus offerings. The menu also includes plenty of fish, chicken, pizzas and pasta. For a great snack try the *torta* Popeye with a mini-spinach-and-cheese omelet inside. The coffee's good, too!

El Cafecito   MEXICAN, INTERNATIONAL $$
(breakfast M$50-60, mains M$50-150; 🖉) Zicatela (Map p454; Calle del Morro s/n; ☺6:30am-11pm; 🍴) Rinconada (Map p450; Blvd Juárez; ☺7am-10pm) It sometimes seems as if the whole town is at the Zicatela Cafecito for breakfast, and with good reason, as the combinations (including a 'Hungry Starving Surfer' offering) are tasty and filling, the service good and the coffee cups bottomless. The Cafecito also serves up plenty of cooling drinks and good-value lunch and dinner dishes.

La Hostería Bananas   ITALIAN, MEXICAN $$
(Map p454; Calle del Morro s/n; mains M$75-155; ☺8:30am-12:30am; 🖉🖉🍴) The Hostería is an Italian labor of love, from its gleaming kitchen (with computerized wood-fired pizza oven) to the Talavera-tiled bathrooms. A broad selection of tasty dishes, including many veggie options, is paired with a great drinks list, good breakfast deals and real coffee. There's a nice pool table, too.

Dan's Café Deluxe   NORTH AMERICAN, MEXICAN $
(www.facebook.com/danscafedeluxe; Jacarandas 14, Colonia Santa María; breakfast M$30-45, light meals M$37-59; ☺7am-4pm Mon-Sat, 7am-2pm Sun; 🖉🖉) Attached to Hotel Casa de Dan, this is a great spot for hearty, inexpensive breakfasts, and healthy lunch options like salads, wholewheat sandwiches and vegetable stir-fry. And there are Baja-style fish tacos on Friday and Saturday.

Mangos   MEXICAN, VEGETARIAN $$
(Map p454; Calle del Morro s/n; breakfast M$29-49, mains M$60-150; ☺7am-11:45pm; 🖉) Palm-roofed Mangos might have the best-value breakfast combinations in town, and its tropical-fruit and vegetable juices (M$22 to M$28) are great thirst-killers. It does some

rare veggie options like tofu burgers, and good fresh salads, plus plenty of pasta options and well-prepared seafood.

Guadua   FUSION $$
(www.guadua.com.mx; Tamaulipas s/n, Brisas de Zicatela; mains M$100-190; ☺5-11pm; 🖉🖉) Guadua's solid wooden deck sits beneath a thick, soaring *palapa* roof toward the far southern end of Playa Zicatela, with quirkily constructed loungers on the sands out front. The delicious, attractively presented food is a global fusion with dishes like shrimp coconut curry, cashew couscous and seared tuna with teriyaki sauce. Guadua is also a hip beach lounge, with a good bar and assorted soundtrack. And it recycles waste water and trash.

Restaurante Los Tíos   SEAFOOD $
(Map p454; Calle del Morro s/n; dishes M$30-100; ☺9am-10pm Wed-Mon) 'The Uncles' serves great *licuados* (milkshakes) and fresh juices to go with its tasty egg dishes, *antojitos* and seafood. It's popular with locals and very relaxed.

EL ADOQUÍN & AROUND

Pascale   MEXICAN, EUROPEAN $$
(Map p450; www.pascale.mx; Playa Principal; mains M$80-170; ☺6-11pm, closed mid-Sep–mid-Oct; 🖉) Romantically candlelit and right under the palms on the Playa Principal sands, Pascale prepares original and delicious seafood, meat and homemade pasta dishes with rare flair. There's a choice of tasty sauces for all pasta dishes, and the seafood is as fresh as can be. Service is professional, and there's occasional live jazz or salsa.

La Langosta   SEAFOOD $$
(Map p450; Marina Nacional; mains M$100-200; ☺7am-10pm) One of the best of the local seafood places. You can have a whole snapper for M$130 to M$200, or a fillet or a whole *mojarra* (bream) for less, and there are good seafood cocktails and tacos for something lighter and cheaper.

Baguettería Vivaldi   CAFE $
(Map p450; light dishes M$40-60; ☺8am-10pm; 🖉) A nice semi-open-air spot for breakfast with your laptop.

OTHER AREAS

Restaurante Las Margaritas   OAXACAN $
(Av 8 Norte; mains M$60-120; ☺8am-6pm) For a dose of well-prepared local fare in a local

atmosphere, head half a block east of the Juárez market in the upper part of town. In a pleasant roofed courtyard with plenty of greenery, Las Margaritas serves a big range of excellent-value seafood and meat dishes, plus cheaper *antojitos,* egg dishes and of course, this being Oaxaca, *chapulines.* 'Mercado' buses and *colectivos* (both M$5) go up Av Oaxaca.

Drinking

If your dream of Mexico is sitting in a palm-roofed bar, enjoying the crash of waves and an ice-cold *cerveza* (beer), you might have to pinch yourself in Puerto Escondido. Numerous establishments are lined up along Playa Zicatela and Bahía Principal for this very purpose (and you can eat well at some of them, too). Zicatela also has a few spots open late with a party scene for its international crowd.

Playa Kabbalah   BAR
(Map p454; www.playakabbalah.com; Calle del Morro s/n, Zicatela; ⊗8:30am-late) A hip beach bar for nocturnal drinks, with a Zicatela crowd clustering at the bar and mostly electronic dance music playing to flashing fluorescent lights. The Tuesday and Thursday Ladies' Nights (free cocktails for women from 10pm to midnight) are especially popular.

Casa Babylon   BAR
(Map p454; Calle del Morro s/n, Zicatela; ⊗10:30am-2pm & 8pm-late; 🖥) This quirky bar has a great Mexican mask collection, a big selection of books to exchange, and live music or a DJ some nights. The owner prides herself on her mojitos.

Guadua   BAR
(www.guadua.com.mx; Tamaulipas s/n, Brisas de Zicatela; ⊗from 11pm Thu & Sun) Guadua's soaring *palapa* is the place to be for the Sunday Mystic Nights and Thursday Funky Nights with DJ Matus. Two-for-one drinks from 11pm to midnight.

☆ Entertainment

Cinemar   CINEMA
(Map p454; www.cinemar.org; Calle del Morro s/n; admission M$40; ⊗films 5pm, 7pm & 9pm) This comfortable, air-conditioned, 30-seat mini-cinema shows films ranging from the best Mexican movies to the latest general releases in English and Spanish. Also here are a cafe with wi-fi and secondhand book and surfboard stores.

Live Music
Puerto has a good music scene combining the talents of locals and expats and playing a wide range of styles. The scene is busiest from around Christmas to March, when you can find half a dozen live shows almost every night around town, from Latin and jazz to blues and rock, at places like Playa Kabbalah, Casa Babylon, Sativa or Guadua on Zicatela (Map p454), or Congo (Map p450) on El Adoquín. Local Latin singer Mayca plays several evenings a week at **La Esmeralda** (Map p454) on the beach at Zicatela.

❶ Information

Dangers & Annoyances
To minimize any risks, avoid isolated or empty places and stick to well-lit areas (or use taxis) at night.

Internet Access
There are a few internet shops on El Adoquín and Calle del Morro (Zicatela), charging M$10 to M$15 per hour.

Medical Services
Dr Omar López Pérez (☎582-36-34; Av Oaxaca 603 Altos) A recommended English-speaking GP.

Money
Banks and *casas de cambio* generally exchange cash US dollars and euros. Playa Zicatela has a couple of *casas de cambio* and two ATMs, but the ATMs have low withdrawal limits and higher-than-usual charges.
Banamex (Av Pérez Gasga s/n; ⊗9am-4pm Mon-Sat) Currency exchange and ATM.
Money Exchange (Av Pérez Gasga 905; ⊗10am-9pm Mon-Sat, 10am-3pm Sun) Changes Canadian dollars, too.

Tourist Information
Tourist Information Kiosk (☎582-11-86; ginainpuerto@yahoo.com; cnr Av Pérez Gasga & Marina Nacional; ⊗9am-2pm & 4-6pm Mon-Fri, 10am-1pm Sat) Gina Machorro, the energetic, dedicated, multilingual information officer here, happily answers your every question, conducts her own interesting tours and can help set up visits to ecotourism projects in the area.

Travel Agencies
Viajes Dimar (www.viajesdimar.com; ⊗9am-9pm Mon-Sat, 9am-3pm Sun) Adoquín (Av Pérez Gasga 905); Zicatela (Calle del Morro s/n) You can buy air and bus tickets, rent cars and book excursions at this reliable, long-established local firm.

Websites

Head to **Lonely Planet** (www.lonelyplanet.com/mexico/oaxaca-state/puerto-escondido) for planning advice, author recommendations, traveler reviews and insider tips.

Getting There & Away

Air

Airport (✆582-04-91) Three kilometers west of the center on the north side of Hwy 200.

Aeromar (www.aeromar.com.mx; airport) Daily flights to/from Mexico City.

Aerotucán (www.aerotucan.com.mx; airport) Flies 13-seat Cessnas daily to/from Oaxaca (M$1387).

VivaAerobus (www.vivaaerobus.com) Budget airline flying to/from Mexico City on Thursdays and Sundays. Flights bought well in advance can cost as little as M$643 (M$743 with check-in baggage).

Bus & Van

OCC bus terminal (Map p450; Carretera Costera btwn Avs Oaxaca & 1 Poniente) Used by OCC 1st-class and Sur 2nd-class services.

Terminal Turística (Central Camionera; cnr Avs Oaxaca & 4 Poniente) In the upper part of town, 2km up from El Crucero; used by other long-distance bus lines, including AltaMar (1st- and 2nd-class) and Turistar (deluxe).

OAXACA

The most convenient way of traveling to Oaxaca is in the comfortable van services via Hwy 131 (seven hours), offered by at least two companies:

Express Service (Map p450; Hotel Luz del Ángel, cnr Avs 1 Norte & Oaxaca) Departs hourly, 4am to 11pm (except 7pm), charging M$165.

Transportes Villa del Mar (Av 1 Norte btwn Avs 2 & 3 Poniente) Goes hourly, 4:30am to 8:30pm, for M$170.

OCC's 1st-class buses (M$284, 11 hours, three daily) take a long route via Salina Cruz and Hwy 190.

OTHER DESTINATIONS

For Mexico City, the AltaMar and Turistar services from the Terminal Turística go via the outskirts of Acapulco and are much quicker than OCC, which takes a longer route via Salina Cruz.

Car & Motorcycle

From Oaxaca city, Hwy 131 traverses the lovely scenery of the Sierra Madre del Sur. Even though it's only 254km, don't underestimate the winding, often potholed route, where you'll contend with hell-bent minibuses, ambling donkeys and plenty of passing on blind corners. Estimate nine hours including a couple of rest stops. Service stations are rare, so keep your tank topped up.

Between Puerto Escondido and Acapulco, figure on about seven hours for the 400km drive along Hwy 200, which is well enough surfaced but has a lot of speed bumps.

Los Tres Reyes (www.lostresreyes.com.mx; Las Brisas 9, Zicatela) Rents out small saloon cars from M$550 per day, and also Honda 125 scooters.

Viajes Dimar Rents out Ford Fiestas for M$650 to M$800 per day (see p456).

ⓘ Getting Around

Ticket taxis from the airport (M$35 per person) will drop you anywhere in town. You might find a whole cab for a similar price on the main road outside the airport. Taxis within town cost M$20 to M$30.

Taxis colectivos and local buses (both M$5) marked 'Zicatela' run frequently to Punta Zicatela from Mercado Benito Juárez up in the north of the town, from sunrise to sunset. To find them from the Terminal Turística bus station, walk a block east, then two blocks south on 3 Poniente. They travel down 3 Poniente then east along the Carretera Costera: for the Adoquín area or Playa

BUSES FROM PUERTO ESCONDIDO

DESTINATION	FARE (M$)	DURATION	FREQUENCY (DAILY)
Acapulco	272-341	8hr	8 AltaMar
Bahías de Huatulco	46-92	2½hr	24 from OCC terminal
Mexico City (various terminals)	712-975	12-18hr	5 from Terminal Turística, 3 OCC
Pochutla	35-62	1¼hr	24 from OCC terminal
San Cristóbal de las Casas	466	13hr	2 OCC
Tehuantepec	202	5½hr	6 OCC
Tuxtla Gutiérrez	408	12hr	2 OCC

Zicatela you can hop off en route and walk down in two minutes.

To reach the Terminal Turística, you can take an 'UMAR' *taxi colectivo* (M$5) from the corner of Avs Oaxaca and Hidalgo.

Around Puerto Escondido

PLAYA ESCOBILLA

This 15km-long beach, beginning about 30km east of Puerto Escondido, is one of the world's major nesting grounds for the olive ridley turtle (*tortuga golfina* to Mexicans). Up to a million female olive ridleys a year arrive at Escobilla to lay their eggs: their numbers have recovered dramatically since Mexico banned the killing of sea turtles in 1990. They come chiefly at night, for three or four days either side of full moons from May to February, a phenomenon known as an *arribada*. The olive ridley is one of the smaller sea turtles (around 70cm long), but still an impressive animal, especially when seen emerging from the surf in its thousands, as happens during Escobilla's biggest *arribadas* from August to December.

There is no general public access to the beach, and this is strictly enforced by the Mexican army. But a community ecotourism program, **Santuario La Escobilla** (cell phone 958-5879882; www.ecoturismoenoaxaca.com; Hwy 200 Km 181; cabañas M$250; P), offers good, clean, solid, tile-floored *cabañas* with hot-water private bathrooms, meals, camping, and guides who will take you to see the *arribadas* (per person M$100) and offer canoe trips (adult/child M$25/15) on a local lagoon. Gina Machorro, the tourist information officer in Puerto Escondido (p456) takes occasional groups to learn about and observe the *arribadas* at night (per person M$400 including transportation). She can also help with arrangements for staying at the *cabañas*.

LAGUNA MANIALTEPEC

This 6km-long lagoon, beginning 14km west of Puerto Escondido along Hwy 200, is a paradise for bird enthusiasts and a fascinating place for anyone interested in nature. Among others, ibises, roseate spoonbills, parrots, pelicans, falcons, ospreys, egrets, herons, kingfishers and several types of hawk and iguana call Manialtepec home for at least part of the year. The best months for seeing birds are December to March, and the best time is soon after dawn. The lagoon is mainly surrounded by mangroves, but tropical flowers and palms accent the ocean side, and the

channel at the west end winds through mangroves to a pristine sandbar beach.

Several operators run two- to three-hour bird-spotting trips, and rents out kayaks for ambitious paddlers. A rare and magical Manialtepec phenomenon is the appearance of phosphorescent plankton for several days three or four times a year. At these times night-boat trips are offered, and you can swim or trail your hand in the water to activate the strange phosphorescent glow.

Tours

Hidden Voyages Ecotours BIRD-WATCHING (www.peleewings.ca; Mon-Wed, Fri & Sat mid-Dec–mid-Mar) Trips are led by knowledgeable Canadian ornithologist Michael Malone, costing M$600 per person including round-trip transportation from your accommodations in Puerto Escondido (departure 7am) and a 45-minute beach break mid-cruise. Guided kayak trips are also available. Book at Viajes Dimar in Puerto Escondido, which itself offers year-round trips (per person M$450) with local bird guides.

Lalo Ecotours BIRD-WATCHING (954-588-91-64, cell phone 954-1189073; www.lalo-ecotours.com) Based at Las Negras Manialtepec, on Hwy 200 halfway along the north side of the lake, and run by an experienced, English-speaking, local bird guide. Boat trips cost M$500 for up to three people, M$600 for four to six people, and M$100 per person for seven or more; one-/two-person kayaks are M$75/150 per hour. Ask for Lalo Ecotours at Restaurante Flor del Pacífico on the lakeside at Las Negras. It also offers boat trips with round-trip transportation from Puerto Escondido for US$40 per person (leaving Puerto at 7am and 3:30pm); telephone for reservations.

La Puesta del Sol BIRD-WATCHING (954-588-38-67) This pleasant lakeside restaurant, just off Hwy 200 about 2.5km from the eastern end of the lake, has good food (breakfasts M$30 to M$50, mains M$50 to M$110), does boat trips for M$700 for up to five people, and rents out two-person kayaks for M$120 per hour. If you want an English-speaking bird guide, call the day before.

Getting There & Away

From Puerto Escondido, take a *taxi colectivo* bound for San José Manialtepec from Av 4 Poniente, just north of the Carretera Costera (M$12, 20 minutes), or a Río Grande–bound minibus (M$15) from the corner of Avs 2 Norte and 3 Poniente, leaving about every 10 minutes from 6am to 7pm.

PARQUE NACIONAL LAGUNAS DE CHACAHUA

Heading west toward Acapulco, Hwy 200 wends its way along a coast studded with lagoons, pristine beaches and prolific bird and plant life. Settlements in this region are home to many Afro-Mexicans, descendants of slaves who escaped from the Spanish.

The area around the coastal lagoons of Chacahua and La Pastoría forms the beautiful Parque Nacional Lagunas de Chacahua, which attracts migratory birds from Alaska and Canada in winter. Mangrove-fringed islands harbor roseate spoonbills, ibises, cormorants, wood storks, herons and egrets, as well as mahogany trees, crocodiles and turtles. El Corral, a mangrove-lined waterway filled with countless birds in winter, connects the two lagoons. The boat trip along the lagoons is fabulous, and at its end Chacahua village sits upon a gorgeous beach curving at least 20km eastward, inviting you to stop for a meal or a night in rustic *cabañas*. The website www.lagunasdechacahua.com gives a useful introduction to visiting the area.

The starting point for boat trips is the small fishing village of Zapotalito, at the eastern end of Laguna La Pastoría, 70km from Puerto Escondido. Two or three boat cooperatives here offer *lancha* service to Chacahua village, charging M$500/800 one way/return for up to eight people. The return option lasts about five hours, including halts at various islands and channels where a Spanish-speaking guide will point out the birds, and a couple of hours on the beach at Chacahua. When there is sufficient traffic, *colectivo* services are operated for M$60 to M$75 per person each way, or M$40 by the *terrestre* route, which means you take a short boat ride from Zapotalito to meet a *camioneta* that then makes a half-hour trip to Chacahua along the spit of land between the lagoons and the ocean. Check return times before you settle in at Chacahua.

CHACAHUA

Chacahua village straddles the channel that connects the west end of Chacahua lagoon to the ocean. The ocean side of the village, fronting a wonderful beach, is a perfect place to bliss out. The waves here (a very long right-hand point break) can be good for surfers, including beginners, but there are some strong currents; check where it's safe to swim. The inland half of the village

WORTH A TRIP

OCHO VENADO

The **Ocho Venado** (☏954-506-41-31, 954-543-82-84; ochovenado.wikispaces. com) community ecotourism scheme offers the chance to experience village life in the forested hills behind the Lagunas de Chacahua. It's a rare opportunity to see a little-visited part of the coastal region, take guided walks or horseback rides, eat home-cooked food and join in whatever the villagers are doing when you visit.

The main base, with well-built *cabañas* (M$300 for two people), is the village of Jocotepec, 700m above sea level, with deer and wild-boar breeding areas, coffee plantations, waterfalls and a hilltop sacred site where locals still go for rain and harvest ceremonies. The Tourist Information Kiosk in Puerto Escondido can help you make contact and tell you about transportation.

contains a **Cocodrilario** (Crocodile Sanctuary; admission free; ⊗erratic), with a sizable collection of large and small crocs kept for protection and breeding; Chacahua's wild croc population has been depleted by hunting. There's also a sea-turtle conservation program here (collecting and protecting eggs and releasing hatchlings). If you're staying overnight, try a sunset boat trip on Laguna Salina, west of the village (around M$300).

The ocean side of the village has a number of simple beach *comedores,* offering egg, pasta and seafood dishes for around M$30 to M$80. Many of them also have basic, often sand-floored *cabañas* costing M$100 to M$150 for two people, with shared bathrooms. You can usually sleep in a hammock or camp for free if you eat at a particular establishment. Theft is a potential risk, though. **Restaurante Siete Mares** (☏954-540-54-90; cabañas M$150-400), at the west end of the beach (nearest the river), prepares excellent seafood meals. It has some of the better *cabañas,* some boasting two double beds, fans, nets, electric light and clean private bathrooms. The señora here will lock up your valuables.

❶ Getting There & Away

To reach Zapotalito from Puerto Escondido, you first have to get to the town of Río Grande,

50km west of Puerto on Hwy 200. Río Grande-bound minibuses (M$25, one hour), mostly marked 'Charquito,' leave from the corner of Avs 2 Norte and 3 Poniente in Puerto, about every 10 minutes from 6am to 7pm. From Río Grande, get a *taxi colectivo* (M$12) to Zapotalito, 13km southwest. The turning to Zapotalito is marked by a military checkpoint on Hwy 200, 8km from Río Grande. For drivers, a dirt road heads 29km south to Chacahua village from San José del Progreso on Hwy 200, but this is often waterlogged between May and November.

Pochutla

☎958 / POP 14,000

Bustling, sweaty Pochutla is the market town, services center and transportation hub for the central part of the Oaxaca coast, which includes the nearby beach spots of Puerto Ángel, Zipolite, San Agustinillo and Mazunte. If you are coming to Pochutla from one of those blissed-out places, welcome back to the real world.

Hwy 175 from Oaxaca runs through Pochutla as Av Lázaro Cárdenas, the narrow, traffic-clogged, north-south main street, and meets the coastal Hwy 200 about 1.5km south of town. The bus and van terminals cluster toward the southern, downhill end of Cárdenas.

🍽 Sleeping & Eating

Pochutla's accommodations are ordinary (get to one of the coastal villages if you can), but one of the best places to eat on the whole Oaxaca coast is just outside town.

Hotel San Pedro   HOTEL **$$**
(☎584-11-23; Av Cárdenas s/n; s/d M$400/500; P❋🤍) The San Pedro, 300m south of the main bus station, has pleasant, spacious, all air-conditioned rooms, with nicely tiled bathrooms.

Hotel Izala   HOTEL **$**
(☎584-01-15; Av Cárdenas 59; d/q M$200/400, with air-con M$300/600; P❋) This will do for a night. It's 450m north of the main bus station.

TOP CHOICE / Finca Los Vaqueros   BARBECUE **$$**
(El Colorado village; meals M$100-150; ⊙10am-9pm) This ranch-style eatery with long tables in a sort of large, open-sided barn is worth an expedition from anywhere on the coast for its superb grilled meats and other Mexican ranchers' fare. Order some *frijoles charros* (a sort of bean soup with bacon bits) and *queso fundido* (melted cheese) to start, followed by some tender *arrachera* (skirt steak) and *chistorra* sausage and maybe a couple of lamb chops for a carnivore's feast you won't quickly forget. And there's excellent mezcal and draft Corona Oscura beer to help it all down. When it's busy, your host Pedro may start to sing some sentimental *ranchera* songs. El Colorado is on the road to Puerto Ángel, 2km beyond the Hwy 200 intersection at the southern end of Pochutla (M$40 by taxi from Pochutla).

ℹ Information

Clínica Hospital San Carlos (☎584-06-03; Zaragoza 14, Sección 4a; ⊙24hr) A fine, clean private hospital with good equipment and good specialist doctors; on the hill behind the municipality building.

HSBC (Av Cárdenas 48; ⊙9am-5pm Mon-Fri) Changes cash US dollars and has an ATM; 400m north of the main bus station.

BUSES FROM POCHUTLA

DESTINATION	FARE (M$)	DURATION	FREQUENCY (DAILY)
Acapulco	402	9hr	4 Futura
Bahías de Huatulco	14-40	1hr	59 TRP, 14 Sur, 8 OCC
Mexico City (Sur) via Acapulco	795-955	13hr	Turistar 5pm, AltaMar 6:20pm
Mexico City (TAPO) via Salina Cruz	730	16½hr	2 OCC
Puerto Escondido	35-62	1¼hr	24 OCC & Sur
San Cristóbal de las Casas	424	11-12hr	3 OCC
Tapachula	470	12hr	OCC 6:50pm
Tehuantepec	158	4½hr	4 OCC
Tuxtla Gutiérrez	366	10-11hr	3 OCC

ℹ CENTRAL COAST TRANSPORTATION

There are three forms of transportation between Pochutla and the nearby beach villages of Puerto Ángel, Zipolite, San Agustinillo and Mazunte: *camioneta* (pickup truck with benches in the back), *taxi colectivo* (shared taxi) and private taxi. One main route heads from Pochutla to Puerto Ángel; the other heads west from Pochutla to San Antonio on Hwy 200, then southeast to Mazunte, San Agustinillo and the west end of Zipolite (Colonia Roca Blanca).

Camionetas and *taxis colectivos* mostly start from various Pochutla side streets then travel south down Cárdenas, picking up passengers as they go. They operate during daylight hours, charging M$10 to M$15 from Pochutla to any of the villages, and a little less for trips between the different villages. A private taxi is around M$80 from Pochutla to Puerto Ángel, M$100 from Pochutla to Zipolite, and M$40 from Zipolite to Puerto Ángel, San Agustinillo or Mazunte. Add M$20 or M$30 after about 9pm.

Coming from Puerto Escondido to Mazunte, San Agustinillo or Zipolite, take a 2nd-class Pochutla-bound Sur bus to San Antonio, and switch to local transportation there.

A taxi to Huatulco airport from any of the villages or towns costs M$400 to M$600; to Puerto Escondido airport it's around M$650 to M$750.

ℹ Getting There & Away

Terminal San Pedro Pochutla (cnr Av Cárdenas & Constitución) The main bus station, entered through a white-grilled doorway toward the south end of Cárdenas. It's used by Turistar (deluxe), OCC, AltaMar and Futura (1st-class) and Sur (2nd-class) services, but OCC and Sur tickets are sold at a separate office about 100m south.

Transportes Rápidos de Pochutla (TRP; Av Cárdenas) About 30m north of the main terminal's street entrance; runs 2nd-class buses to Huatulco.

Oaxaca is 245km away by the curvy Hwy 175 – six hours in the convenient and fairly comfortable air-conditioned van services (M$120) offered by several companies, including these:

Autotransportes Atlántida (☎584-01-16; Hotel Santa Cruz, Av Cárdenas 88) Twelve departures daily; it's 150m north of the main bus terminal and you can call ahead to reserve a seat and pay when you depart.

Autotransportes Miahuatecos (Av Cárdenas 94) Just north of the main bus terminal, across the street, with hourly departures from 4am to 10pm.

Helpfully, drivers will usually stop when you need a bathroom break, or want to take photos (or vomit, as some people do on this route).

OCC runs three daily 1st-class buses to Oaxaca (M$284, 10 hours), but they take a much longer (though less winding) route via Salina Cruz.

Puerto Ángel

☎958 / POP 2600

Thirteen kilometers south of Pochutla, the small fishing port and naval town of Puerto Ángel straggles around a beautiful little bay between two rocky headlands, surrounded by thickly wooded hills. The town itself is a bit drab – many travelers prefer to stay a few kilometers west at Zipolite, San Agustinillo or Mazunte – but the marginally more urban Puerto Ángel also offers some acceptable accommodations, its own little beaches and activities, and easy transportation to Zipolite.

The road from Pochutla emerges at the east end of the small Bahía de Puerto Ángel. The road winds around the bay, passing the fishing pier on the left, opposite Calle Vasconcelos, crossing an often-dry *arroyo* (stream) and then heading uphill. It then forks – right to Zipolite, San Agustinillo and Mazunte, left down to Playa del Panteón. It's called Blvd Uribe as far as the *arroyo*, and then Carretera a Zipolite.

◉ Sights & Activities

Azul Profundo WATER SPORTS
(☎584-31-09; azul_profundomx@hotmail.com; Playa del Panteón) Azul Profundo does an enjoyable four-hour, four-beach snorkeling boat trip, with snorkel gear included, for M$150 per person, at 10am daily. They can pick you up and drop you off in Zipolite, where they have an office and internet cafe. The amiable guide, Chepe, speaks English and German. En route you should see turtles and, with luck, dolphins and even (from December to April) whales. Azul Profundo will also take up to five people sportfishing (per hour two/four rod M$400/600) for marlin, swordfish, tuna or *dorado* (dolphinfish): start at 6am and try the local method of

trawling with handlines for tuna or *dorado*. They do diving too, with one-/two-tank dives costing M$800/1000 including equipment and a dive guide. The drops and canyons out to sea from Puerto Ángel are suitable for very deep dives; they're thick with fish life and there's an 1870 shipwreck.

Playa del Panteón   BEACH
On the west side of the bay, this is a small, shallow and calm beach, with several rather overpriced beachside restaurants, and its waters are cleaner than those near the fishing pier across the bay.

Playa La Boquilla   BEACH
The coast east of Puerto Ángel is dotted with some nice small beaches, none of them very busy. Playa La Boquilla, on a bay about 5km round the coast, is the site of the Bahía de la Luna accommodations. It's nice to go by boat (around M$350 round trip): ask at Puerto Ángel pier or Playa del Panteón. You can also get here by a 3.5km unpaved road from a turnoff 4km out of Puerto Ángel on the Pochutla road: a taxi from either town costs M$120 to M$150 each way.

🛏 Sleeping

Casa de Huéspedes
Gundi y Tomás   GUESTHOUSE $
(☑584-30-68; www.puertoangel-hotel.com; s/d M$250/350, without bathroom M$200/300, r for 6 M$750; 🐕🛜) Relaxed and rambling Gundi's sits above Blvd Uribe near the center of town, with a variety of brightly decorated, basic rooms, all with fans, mosquito nets and/or screens, and some offbeat artistic touches. It also has probably the best restaurant in town. The friendly, helpful family speaks English, German and Spanish, and offers surf lessons at Zipolite or San Agustinillo, Huatulco airport pickups (M$500 for up to four people), a book exchange, laundry service, money exchange, bus reservations and a safe for valuables.

Bahía de la Luna   HOTEL $$$
(☑589-50-20; www.bahiadelaluna.com; Playa La Boquilla; r M$1350-1500, q M$2100, 4-/7-person house with kitchen M$2900/3900, all incl breakfast; ℗) This 'rustic chic' tropical hideaway sits in splendid isolation out at lovely Playa La Boquilla. Its attractive, bright, adobe bungalows, on a tree-covered hillside overlooking the beach, have terracotta-tiled floors and touches of artisanry. Snorkel gear and kayaks are free for guests, and there are trails to

explore and an open-air yoga/art studio. For getting here, see Playa La Boquilla above.

Hotel Cordelia's   HOTEL $$
(☑584-30-21; hotelcordelias@hotmail.com; Playa del Panteón; r M$350-600; ℗✳🛜) Right on Playa del Panteón and run by the same family as Azul Profundo diving/fishing/snorkeling shop, Cordelia's has 17 rooms with nice tiled floors, good wood furniture and some attractive *artesanías*. The best rooms are big and have their own terraces overlooking the bay.

Hotel Puesta del Sol   HOTEL $
(☑584-33-15; www.puertoangel.net; Carretera a Zipolite; r M$280-350, s/d without bathroom M$120/180; 🛜) Trilingual (English, German, Spanish) Puesta del Sol offers sizable, clean rooms with fans and screens. The more expensive ones have their own terraces and hot-water bathroom. A breezy hammock area invites relaxation; breakfast is available; and the touches of art, useful maps, verdant garden and friendly, informative owners make this a decent choice.

🍴 Eating

Casa de Huéspedes
Gundi y Tomás   MEXICAN, INTERNATIONAL $
(dishes M$35-120; ⏱7am-9pm; 🖉) The rooftop dining area here has outstanding views and food to match, including a very good M$85 set dinner, different every night. Salads, pancakes, fish, shrimp, pasta, tacos, sandwiches and satisfying breakfasts are also on offer, including many vegetarian options.

La Costeñita   SEAFOOD $
(Blvd Uribe; mains M$50-90; ⏱9am-10pm) For fresh-as-can-be fish, head to humble little Costeñita right beside the fishing pier. It's run by fishers and a tasty whole fish with trimmings only costs around M$80.

El Almendro   BARBECUE $
(off Blvd Uribe; BBQ dinner M$85; ⏱6pm mid-Dec–Easter) From about mid-December to Easter Almendro holds a 6pm to 7pm happy hour followed by a good-value barbecue dinner of marinated meats or fish or chicken, a salad bar and baked potatoes. It is run by Casa de Huéspedes Gundi y Tomás.

ℹ Information

Banco Azteca (Blvd Uribe; ⏱9am-4pm Mon-Sat) Changes cash US dollars and euros. Some Puerto Ángel accommodations and restaurants will change cash at their own rates.
Bancomer ATM (cnr Blvd Uribe & Vasconcelos)

OAXACA ZIPOLITE

❶ Getting There & Away

A *taxi colectivo* to or from Zipolite costs M$7 (if you can find one). A private cab is M$40 (M$60 to M$70 after about 9pm).

Zipolite

📞 958 / POP 1100

The beautiful 1.5km stretch of pale sand called Zipolite, beginning about 2.5km west of Puerto Ángel, moves at a slow pace, withering in the midday heat. It's the perfect option for budget beach bums in southern Mexico, attracting an international class of sun lovers, shirtless yoga gurus and surfers to its wonderfully elemental surroundings of crashing surf, pounding sun and rocky headlands. Inexpensive places to stay and eat line the beach, many still reassuringly ramshackle and wooden and with tall thatched roofs that help to create the unique Zipolite landscape. There's a certain magic here, and you may postpone departure more than once.

Zipolite has a certain overstated fame as a nudist beach; in fact, total nudity is common only at the western end of the beach and in the small cove called Playa del Amor at the east end, and even there it meets the raised eyebrows of locals.

The eastern end of Zipolite (nearest Puerto Ángel) is called Colonia Playa del Amor, the middle part is Centro, and the area toward the western end (divided from Centro by a narrow lagoon and creek) is Colonia Roca Blanca. The only street with a commonly used name is Av Roca Blanca (also called El Adoquín), a block back from the beach in Colonia Roca Blanca.

🏃 Activities

The essence and glory of Zipolite is that organized activity is very minimal. This is a place for hanging out and doing exactly nothing, if that's what you feel like.

Azul Profundo (p465) provides free round-trip transportation from Zipolite for its snorkeling, diving and fishing trips from Puerto Ángel: you can reserve at its office/internet shop on Av Roca Blanca.

Solstice Yoga Center   YOGA
(solstice-mexico.com; Centro) At Solstice Yoga Center, located within the La Loma retreat, Brigitte Longueville leads 1½-hour hatha yoga classes (US$7) in a large, inviting space most days in the morning and/or afternoon. Five-day retreats and yoga vacations are offered here, too. Drop by for a schedule.

❶ ZIPOLITE PRECAUTIONS

Beware: the Zipolite surf is deadly. It's fraught with riptides, changing currents and a strong undertow. Locals don't swim here, and going in deeper than your knees can be risking your life. Local voluntary lifeguards have rescued many, but they don't maintain a permanent watch, and people drown here yearly. The shore break is one only experienced surfers should attempt.

Theft can be a problem, so it's good to stay where you can lock your valuables in a safe.

Take care when out at night, especially at weekends: in recent years Zipolite, including the Roca Blanca area, has seen a few violent attacks and robberies and at least two murders. A gang of locals in their teens and 20s called Los Ocho Mil is widely blamed.

Piña Palmera   VOLUNTEERING
(📞584-31-47; www.pinapalmera.org; Centro; ⏰9am-3pm Mon-Sat) Piña Palmera, an independently run rehabilitation and social integration center for physically and intellectually disabled people from rural communities, does fantastic work with workshops and therapies at its beautiful palm-grove site and on village visits. Over 5000 disabled kids and adults have participated in Piña Palmera programs since 1984. Piña Palmera can use volunteers who speak reasonable Spanish and are willing to sign on for six months, though volunteer programs are flexible.

🛏 Sleeping

For those who've long had the dream of swaying in a hammock under the stars and listening to the sound of crashing waves, this is the place. Plenty of beach restaurants have hammocks to rent for M$40 or so, and those traveling with their own hammock or tent will find loads of places to sling/pitch it for around M$30. It's a great way to save some money and sleep in the breeze; just mind the sand flies and lock away your valuables.

There's also a good number of more substantial accommodations. Rates given here are for the main season, between January and Easter. From about September to November and May and June, some places slash prices by as much as half. They may also double them during the Christmas–New Year and Semana Santa vacation periods.

El Alquimista
BUNGALOW $$

(☎587-89-61; www.el-alquimista.com; west end Playa Zipolite; bungalows M$800-1500; P❄🐾🛜🏊) Attached to one of Zipolite's best restaurants, this very popular place has 16 fine thatch-roofed bungalows set just off the beach, most with a double bed, fan, four-poster mosquito net, hot-water bathroom and hammocked porch. The three beautiful superior bungalows, in a tower just behind, can accommodate three people, and two of them have air-con. A pool and yoga room are recent additions.

Lo Cósmico
CABAÑAS $

(www.locosmico.com; west end Playa Zipolite; hammock M$50, s M$180, d M$200-400; P🛜) Very relaxed Lo Cósmico has conical-roofed *cabañas* dotted around a tall rock outcrop, and they are among the best value on the beach. Rooms are clean and quite neat, in varying degrees of rusticity. Each has a hammock and mosquito net; the cheaper ones are a bit enclosed, while the pricier ones have two floors, views and private bathroom. You can sleep very cheaply on its hammock terrace (dry season only). A security box is available, and there's a good onsite restaurant.

Posada México
HOTEL $$

(☎584-31-94; www.posadamexicozipolite.com; Av Roca Blanca; s M$250-500, d M$300-600, s/d without bathroom M$200/250; P🐾🛜) This Italian-run joint has the most character among the Roca Blanca beachfront places. The clean wood-and-palm rooms have good beds with four-poster mosquito nets, fans, safes and their own sandy little sitting-out areas with hammocks. Best are the two larger, more expensive, beach-facing rooms. It's on a friendly, personal scale and good breakfasts are served at the beachside cafe.

Las Casitas
BUNGALOW $$

(☎cell phone 958-5878464; www.las-casitas.net; d M$280-600, q M$500-700, house M$1000-1200; P🛜) Set back from the west end of Playa Zipolite on a hill, Italian-owned Las Casitas has seven tasteful rooms in semi-open-air bungalows of wood, adobe and palm-thatch. All have private bathrooms and kitchen use. Most have good views as well, at least in the dry, leafless season, and some have swing-

ing beds. There's also a larger house for up to four people, and an excellent restaurant.

Posada San Cristóbal
HOTEL $$

(☎584-30-20; Av Roca Blanca; r M$500-600; P) The most appealing of a handful of bigger, three-story places toward the west end of the beach, San Cristóbal has 15 good, large, breezy and bright rooms facing the sea, all with balcony or terrace and tiled floors. The eight cheaper rooms are less appealing.

🌿 Shambhala
GUESTHOUSE $$

(Casa de Gloria; ☎cell phone 958-1094359; shambhalavision.tripod.com; west end Playa Zipolite; dm M$100, camping per person M$50, d/tr M$500/800, s/q without bathroom M$150/400; P) This ecologically run, long-established guesthouse climbs a hill and has great views looking right along the beach. In part a spiritual retreat, with its own meditation hill and no alcohol or illegal drugs permitted, it's also a good place for anyone looking for a tranquil and economical place to stay. All the varied accommodations are individually and attractively built. The **restaurant** (mains M$50-70; ⊗6am-10pm; 🌿) serves no red meat: offerings include tabbouleh salad, homemade fruit yogurts, seafood and chicken. Shambhala hosts a big spiritual festival, embracing all beliefs, every New Year's Eve, and is often full over the Christmas–New Year period.

La Havana
CABAÑAS $

(☎cell phone 958-1139951; Centro; cabañas without bathroom M$250; P) A row of colorful little *palapa*-roofed shacks on stilts, with little balconies, just east of the lagoon at the east end of Colonia Roca Blanca. If all you need is a place to lay your head under a mosquito net with the beach at your doorstep, this is a good bet. The shared bathrooms are clean.

🍴 Eating

Eating and drinking in the open air a few steps from the surf is an inimitable Zipolite experience. Most places serve a mix of Mexican and international fare with a maritime slant.

El Alquimista
INTERNATIONAL $$

(west end Playa Zipolite; mains M$90-140; ⊗8am-11pm) The classy Alchemist is delightfully sited in a sandy cove, and atmospherically lit by oil lamps at night. Its wide-ranging fare runs from falafel and hummus to good meat, seafood and pasta dishes and brick-oven pizzas, complemented by a full bar and good espresso.

La Providencia
MEXICAN, FUSION $$

(☑cell phone 958-1009234; www.laprovidencia zipolite.com; Colonia Roca Blanca; mains M$120-150; ☺7-11pm Tue-Sun mid-Nov-late Apr, Jul & Aug) Zipolite's most suave dining option has an open-air lounge area where you can sip a drink while you peruse the menu and place your order. The flavorsome and well-presented food is a contemporary Mexican treat, from cold beetroot and ginger soup to chicken breast in a blue cheese and pumpkin flower sauce. Reservations advised during busy seasons.

Piedra de Fuego
SEAFOOD $

(Colonia Roca Blanca; mains M$60-75; ☺3-11pm) You'll get a generous serving of fresh fish fillet or prawns, accompanied by rice, salad, potatoes and tortillas at this superbly simple, very clean, family-run place. It's a good value and highly popular. Good *aguas de frutas,* too.

El Terrible
FRENCH $$

(Av Roca Blanca; crepes M$35-80, mains M$75-125; ☺3pm-last customer) The French couple who run this neat little corner place make a variety of very good French dishes including crepes (a specialty), *filete mignon* (tenderloin steak) in a choice of sauces (another specialty) and, of course, snails. Plus pasta, chicken and seafood (curried, if you like).

Lo Cósmico
INTERNATIONAL $

(www.locosmico.com; west end Playa Zipolite; dishes M$30-50; ☺8am-4pm Tue-Sun; ☺☑) Mellow out on the rocks above the beach in this open-air restaurant at the accommodations of the same name. Cósmico provides good food from an impeccably clean kitchen – especially tasty are the crepes (sweet and savory) and salads.

Las Casitas
ITALIAN, SEAFOOD $$

(www.las-casitas.net; mains M$100-120; ☺8:30-11:30am & 7:30-10:30pm Wed-Mon, closed evenings Sep-Nov, May & Jun) Sample the great homemade pasta (with fish, seafood or vegetable sauces) and the meat dishes and homemade baked goods at this Italian-run place back from the west end of the beach. For its specialty *pescado al horno de leña* (fish baked in a wood-fired oven; M$120), ask a day before.

Orale! Cafe
BREAKFAST $

(off west end Av Roca Blanca; breakfast dishes M$30-45; ☺8am-3pm) This shady tropical-garden cafe with its soothing music is perfect for a relaxed breakfast.

🍷 Drinking & Entertainment

Zipolite's beachfront restaurant-bars have unbeatable locations for drinks from sunset onward. Those toward the west end of the beach are generally the most popular – especially El Alquimista, which plays cool music and serves cocktails as well as the usual beer and mezcal.

Barracuda
LOUNGE, DANCING

(Av Roca Blanca; ☺8pm-2am) In classic Zipolite style, with *palapa* roof and dim lighting (and hookahs), Barracuda is the place for after-dark drinks and dancing to music ranging from reggae and salsa to blues and jazz. There are live bands some nights; M$30 admission is charged for some special events.

ⓘ Information

The nearest ATM is in Puerto Ángel, but some accommodations may exchange or accept payment in US dollars or euros.

Azul Profundo (☑584-34-37; Av Roca Blanca; internet per hr M$15, wi-fi M$10; ☺8am-10pm) You can Skype and phone from here, too.

ⓘ Getting There & Away

After dark, a non-*colectivo* taxi is your only option for getting to Puerto Ángel, San Agustinillo or Mazunte (about M$40 until around 9pm; more after that).

San Agustinillo
☑958 / POP 290

The tiny, one-street village of San Agustinillo is centered on a small, curved bay – Playa San Agustinillo – 4km west of Zipolite by road. The waves here are perfect for bodyboarding. The swimming is good as well, but avoid the rocks. San Agustinillo's charms have spawned a small bunch of attractive accommodations, good eateries and an eclectic set of aficionados.

🏃 Activities

Ola Verde Expediciones
RAFTING

(☑cell phone 958-1096751; www.olaverdeexpediciones.com.mx) This team of very professional adventure-sports enthusiasts takes recommended rafting trips on the Río San Francisco inland from here (Class 1 to Class 3; August to October; half-day trip adult M$450 to M$500, child M$300) and the Río Copalita near Huatulco (Class 2 to Class 4 depending on season; late July to January; day trip M$900 to M$1000). Ola Verde also does a fun half-day river hike on the San Francisco (July to April; adult/child M$450/300), which includes swimming, floating (with life jacket and helmet) and jumping into pools. Several of its trips are great for children as well as adults, and on all of them you'll enjoy great tropical scenery. The office is opposite Restaurante Paraíso del Pescador: they'll pick you up anywhere from Puerto Ángel to Mazunte. Minimum numbers range from two to four.

Coco Loco Surf Club   SURFING, SNORKELING
(www.cocolocosurfclub.com; México Lindo y qué Rico) Playa San Agustinillo is a very good beach for learning to surf, and Coco Loco's qualified instructor, French David Chouard, gives surfing classes for anyone from five years old upwards (one hour for one/two/four people M$300/550/800). Coco Loco also does an enjoyable three-beach 'discovery trip' combining snorkeling, bodyboarding and a visit to La Ventanilla (p468) for M$280 per person (minimum four people). It rents out surfboards (per hour/half-day/day M$50/150/200), bodyboards and snorkel gear (both M$30/80/120).

Boat Trips   WILDLIFE-WATCHING, FISHING
Local fishers will take you out for three hours' **marine-life spotting** to look for turtles, dolphins, manta rays and (between November and April) whales. The cost is around M$180 per person (usually with a minimum of four) and this often includes a stop for snorkeling. They also do **sportfishing** trips for around M$400 per hour for up to three people, including equipment. Ask at your accommodations.

🛏 Sleeping

Most places are set right on the beach. Rooms have either mosquito-screened windows or mosquito nets.

Un Sueño   CABAÑAS $$
(🖉cell phone 958-1138749; www.unsueno.com; r/q M$750/1000; 🅿🛜🍴) Sueño, toward the east end of the village, is a fine place to stay, with 16 lovely, good-sized rooms, four in freestanding beachfront *cabañas,* the others in two-story units behind. All are decorated with art and crafts from different places around the world, and have a semi-open-air feel with bamboo-slat windows.

Nearly all have their own terraces with hammocks. Also fronting the sands, under *palapa* roofs, are a breezy hammock area and a good **cafe** (🕙8am-6:30pm), with the same excellent menu (and same owners) as nearby Un Secreto.

Punta Placer   CABAÑAS $$$
(www.puntaplacer.com; r US$90; 🅿🛜🍴) Punta Placer's eight beautiful circular rooms and one large apartment have a fresh, open-air feel thanks to their breezy terraces and wood-slat windows. With welcome touches like good reading lights and stone-lined hot showers with good water pressure, they're a cut above other San Agustinillo accommodations. The garden of native plants and stone paving opens directly on to the beach, and there's an excellent restaurant with fresh, home-style international dishes that change daily.

México Lindo y qué Rico!   ROOMS $
(faustojasso@gmail.com; r with/without sea view M$400/350; 🕙closed Sep & Oct; 🅿😊🛜🍴) Near the west end of the beach, México Lindo has friendly owners and staff, and its six large rooms feature slatted windows, fans and some bright touches like tiled bathrooms. Especially good are the two breezy rooms upstairs under the tall *palapa* roof. There's also excellent food here (mains M$60 to M$100), including pizzas from a wood-fired brick oven.

🌿**Rancho Cerro Largo**   CABAÑAS $$
(📞584-30-63; ranchocerrolargomx@yahoo.com.mx; Playa Aragón; s M$650-1050, d M$800-1150, all incl breakfast & dinner; 🅿🖉) With a stunning position above Playa Aragón, which stretches east from Playa San Agustinillo, Cerro Largo offers idyllic, rustic but comfortable accommodations in nine *cabañas,* most constructed of mud and wattle and all with ocean views. Many have open walls overlooking the crashing coast below, and most have private bathrooms. Top-notch, mainly vegetarian meals are taken by all guests together (Cerro Largo makes its own bread, yogurt and granola), and there's a nice yoga room with daily 1½-hour morning sessions (payment by donation). It's a wonderful place to get away from everything, and it's operated with ecologically low-impact practices. You get here by a signed, drivable track from the Zipolite–San Agustinillo road. Rooms fill in high seasons, so book ahead by email.

Bambú
CABAÑAS $$

(www.bambuecocabanas.com; d M$600-850, q M$800-1050; [P][icon]) The half-dozen all-different rooms here, toward the east end of town, are large, attractive, open to as much breeze as possible, and set under high *palapa* roofs. All are cleverly designed and solidly built, mainly from bamboo, with pretty tilework, fans and mosquito nets. On the beach out front is a good hammock and lounging area. There's no cafe but there is an equipped kitchen for guests. It's a good mid-market option, maintained with ecofriendly principles.

Posada La Mora
HOTEL $

([icon]584-64-22; www.lamoraposada.com; r with/without kitchenette M$450/400, apt M$900; [icon]) Friendly, well-kept La Mora makes the most of its little site toward the east end of San Agustinillo. The ground floor is home to a neat **cafe** (light dishes M$30-55; [icon]8am-9pm) serving, among other things, tasty waffles and organic, fair-trade coffee. Upstairs are three nice clean, cheerful rooms in blue, white and yellow, and above them is a bright, spacious apartment that's good for families. All three floors have terraces that enjoy close-up sea views.

La Termita
ROOMS $$

([icon]589-30-46;www.posadalatermita.com;dM$700-1000, q M$1000-1300; [P][icon]) This restaurant has four attractive rooms for rent.

Palapa Jazmín
ROOMS $

([icon]584-32-50; d/q M$250/500) Economical lodgings with private bathroom toward the west end of the beach.

[icon] Eating & Drinking

[TOP CHOICE] Un Secreto
SEAFOOD, FUSION $$

(mains M$75-120; [icon]8am-11pm; [icon]) Run by Julien from Un Sueño along the street, Un Secreto serves up *sabores del Pacífico* (tastes of the Pacific) with a touch of French flair. The short but sweet seafood-based menu runs from a delicious foil-wrapped fish with mint to Thai-style shrimp, and lemon pie to round things off. Excellent breakfasts, *licuados,* salads, pasta and coffee, too.

La Termita
ITALIAN $$

(www.posadalatermita.com; mains M$65-125; [icon]8am-noon & 7-11pm Mon-Sat; [icon][icon]) Roughly in the center of the village, La Termita's moist, flavorsome, wood-oven pizzas are the best anywhere in the area, and there are good salads to go with them.

Restaurante Paraíso del Pescador
SEAFOOD $$

(mains M$65-110; [icon]8am-9pm) This marine-themed spot, sitting right above the beach and open to sea breezes, is a top spot for fresh fish of the day, which you can have *a la plancha* (grilled), *empanizado* (breaded), *al mojo de ajo* (in garlic sauce) or *a la diabla* (deviled, in *chipotle* chilies and tomato). Shrimp, octopus, meats and salads are available as well.

El Sueño de Frida
BREAKFAST, TAPAS $

(dishes M$20-50; [icon]8:30am-1pm & 4-11pm Tue-Sun; [icon]) Frida's tiny kitchen serves brightly colored fruit plates and light breakfasts, plus plates of tapas and cocktails in the evening. It's perched along the main drag, opposite the ocean, just perfect for people-watching and catching a nice breeze.

La Casa Mágica
BAR

(la_casa_magica@yahoo.ca; [icon]4-11pm) A favorite with San Ag's amiable little bunch of expats, this welcoming Irish-run bar offers pool, darts, drinks and light food, a couple of hundred meters up the hill opposite Posada La Mora.

Mazunte
[icon]958 / POP 870

A kilometer west of San Agustinillo, Mazunte has a fine, curving, sandy beach, an interesting turtle center, and a variety of basic and fancier places to stay and eat. The village is well known as a travelers' hangout and has a number of foreign residents, attracted either by the area's beauty or, as one put it, the 'old-time hippie vibe.' The economic mainstays here used to be turtle meat and eggs: after the turtle industry was banned in 1990, attempts were made to turn Mazunte into a kind of model ecotourism village. Many enterprises still maintain an emphasis on sustainability.

The paved road running west from Zipolite and San Agustinillo to Hwy 200 passes through the middle of Mazunte as Paseo del Mazunte. Four lanes run about 500m from the road to the beach: from east to west they are Andador Golfina, Andador Carey, Andador La Barrita and Andador Rinconcito – this last leading down to the western end of Mazunte beach, which is called El Rinconcito.

◉ Sights & Activities

Boat Trips   WILDLIFE-WATCHING, SNORKELING
Local fishermen will take three or more people out for three-hour boat trips to snorkel, look for turtles, dolphins and whales, check out some of the beaches along the coast, and fish, if you like. Departure is usually at 8am and costs around M$180 per person, including snorkel equipment. Organize this through your accommodations or just head out to the beach in the morning to catch a tour before it leaves.

Punta Cometa   LOOKOUT, WALKING
This rocky cape, jutting out from the west end of Mazunte beach, is the southernmost point in the state of Oaxaca and a fabulous place to be at sunset, with great long-distance views in both directions. It's now a community nature reserve. You can walk to the point in 30 minutes over the rocks from the end of Mazunte beach. Or take the lane that heads up to the west off Andador Rinconcito and turn left along a path just after the entrance to the Alta Mira accommodations. A round-trip walking trail (two hours at a gentle pace) runs from here to the end of the cape then back via its western side.

Centro Mexicano de la Tortuga   AQUARIUM
(www.centromexicanodelatortuga.org; Paseo del Mazunte; admission M$25; ⊙10am-4:30pm Wed-Sat, 10am-2:30pm Sun) The much-visited Mexican Turtle Center, at the east end of Mazunte, is an aquarium and research center containing specimens of five of Mexico's seven marine turtle species, plus some freshwater and land varieties. They're on view in fairly large tanks – it's enthralling to get a close-up view of these creatures, some of which are BIG!

⬮ La Ventanilla   WILDLIFE-WATCHING
Some 2.5km along the road west from Mazunte a sign points left to the tiny village of La Ventanilla, 1.2km down a dirt track. **Servicios Ecoturísticos La Ventanilla** (☎cell phone 958-1087288; www.laventanilla.com. mx; 1½hr lagoon tours adult/child M$60/30, under 6yr free; ⊙tours 8:30am-5pm), on the left of the road as you enter the village, is Ventanilla's successful conservation and ecotourism cooperative, whose work includes a crocodile nursery, mangrove reforestation and turtle protection. Its 12-passenger boat trips on a mangrove-fringed lagoon will show you endangered river crocodiles (there are several hundred of these in the local protected area) and lots of water birds (most prolific from April to July). For the best wildlife-spotting, go in the early morning. Servicios Ecoturísticos also offers three-hour horseback rides (M$350), specialized bird-watching tours (per person per hour M$100; best at 6am and arranged the day before), and on certain days the chance to release turtle hatchlings into the ocean (M$30 per hatchling) and to join night patrols (per person M$100) to see turtles laying and help collect their eggs.

Servicios Ecoturísticos has a few clean, well-built *cabañas* with bathroom (per *cabaña* M$300) and dorms for up to four (per room M$300), next to the office. Fairly frequent *camionetas* and *taxis colectivos* on the Pochutla–Mazunte–San Agustinillo–Zipolite route pass the Ventanilla turnoff, leaving you with the 1.2km walk. A taxi from Mazunte should cost M$30.

⬮ Cosméticos Naturales   HANDICRAFTS
(☎587-48-60; www.cosmeticosmazunte.com, in Spanish; Paseo del Mazunte; ⊙9am-4pm Mon-Sat, 10am-3pm Sun) Cosméticos Naturales is toward the west end of the village. A small cooperative making and selling shampoo, cosmetics, mosquito repellents, bath gel and soap from natural sources (like maize, coconut, avocado and sesame seeds), it also sells organic coffee, and you can have a look at the workshop while you are here.

Yoga Classes   YOGA
(1½hr class US$7) Teachers from Zipolite's Solstice Yoga Center give classes most mornings and afternoons at the Posada del Arquitecto.

🎎 Festivals & Events

Encuentro de Jazz y Algo Más   MUSIC
This festival (mazunte.org.mx) brings top-quality jazz and other entertainment to Mazunte for two or three days around November 20.

🛏 Sleeping

Most of the *comedores* along Playa Mazunte have basic rooms or *cabañas,* hammocks to rent and often tent space. Security can be a problem here. Better lodgings are scattered here and there around the village.

⬮TOP CHOICE Casa Pan de Miel   HOTEL $$$
(☎584-35-09; www.casapandemiel.com; Cerrada del Museo de la Tortuga; r US$100-225; P⊛✴

🛜🏊) Up a steep track from the main road just east of the Turtle Center and enjoying wonderful coastal views, this is a place designed for real relaxation. The nine large, bright, elegant, air-conditioned rooms are adorned with varied Mexican art, and all have sea views, kitchen or kitchenette, and terraces with hammocks. There's an inviting large *palapa* area where good breakfasts (US$7 to US$11) are served, and a lovely infinity pool in front of it. Kids are not accepted here for safety reasons (the cliff-top position).

Posada del Arquitecto   CABAÑAS **$$**
(www.posadadelarquitecto.com, in Spanish; El Rinconcito; dm/estrella per person M$70/80, cabañas d M$400-750; 🛜) Built around the natural features of a small hill by the beach, this popular Italian-owned place provides a variety of airy accommodations on several levels. Options range from hilltop open-air hanging beds with mosquito nets, known as *estrellas,* to attractive *cabañas* and casitas (bungalows) built with mostly natural materials, some of which can accommodate six. It has a beachfront cafe, and at the rear of the property **Sahuaro** (mains M$50-100; 🕙11am-11pm) serves up Baja-style shrimp, veg and fish tacos, Argentine *empanadas* and homemade ravioli.

Cabañas Balamjuyuc   CABAÑAS **$**
(📱cell phone 958-1011808; www.balamjuyuc.com.mx; Camino a Punta Cometa; hammock/camping per person M$50/60, tent & bedding rental M$100, cabañas M$300-500; 🅿🛜) Relaxed Balamjuyuc occupies a spacious hilltop site above the west end of the beach, with some superb views. The entrance is about 400m up a road off Andador Rinconcito. It has six *cabaña* rooms, some of which are large and airy; all have mosquito nets, fans and clean shared bathrooms. There's a restaurant with many vegetarian options (mains M$70 to M$100), and also on offer are yoga classes, therapeutic massages and sessions in the onsite temascal (per person including dinner M$200).

Posada Arigalan   HOTEL **$$**
(arigalan.com; Cerrada del Museo de la Tortuga; cabañas M$450, r M$850-1000, ste M$1000-1200; 🅿🌀❄🛜) Behind Casa Pan de Miel and also with commanding coastal views, Arigalan offers nine sizable, tastefully furnished rooms and suites with air-con and terraces, plus three fan-cooled *cabañas*. The suites have plunge pools. Breakfast is available on request. Prices drop considerably from March to October (except Semana Santa).

El Copal   CABAÑAS **$$**
(www.elcopal.com.mx; Playa Mermejita; cabañas M$1050; 🅿🛜) This eco-friendly retreat sits over on Playa Mermejita, a long, little-developed strand stretching west from Punta Cometa, reached by a rough 1km track off Andador Rinconcito. The four *cabañas* of adobe, wood and palm-thatch are spaced around a leafy hillside garden and all contain a double bed on the ground floor and two or three singles above. Their showers are quaint open-air affairs with views. The international fusion **restaurant** (mains M$70-110; 🕙8:30am-10:30pm Thu-Tue, 8:30am-2pm Wed) has beautiful views along the beach. Unfortunately, tricky currents and strong waves make swimming inadvisable on the beach here.

Posada Ziga   HOTEL **$**
(www.posadaziga.com; Andador Golfina; r M$400-500, without bathroom M$300-380; 🅿) Ziga sits just above the east end of Mazunte beach. It has an economical restaurant, a little flower garden and 14 rooms, all with mosquito nets. The doubles are bigger, with tiled private bathrooms and safes, but the best views are from some of the singles above the restaurant.

✕ Eating

Estrella Fugaz   INTERNATIONAL **$**
(El Rinconcito; dishes M$30-70; 🕙8am-11pm; 🛜) This upstairs terrace restaurant, with a beach view through the palm fronds, has a wide selection of good eats as well as vegetable and fruit drinks and coffees, and is also a popular spot for evening drinks and music.

La Vieja Sirena   ITALIAN **$**
(Andador Golfina; medium pizzas M$70-100, pasta M$45-60; 🕙6:30-11pm) Terrific pizzas and pasta and relaxed but efficient service – if you can get a table.

Restaurante Tania   MEXICAN, VEGETARIAN **$**
(Paseo del Mazunte; veg & breakfast dishes M$30-40, fish & seafood M$55-110; 🕙9am-11pm; 🖊) Locally owned Tania's scores high for both good-value food and hospitality. Try a whole snapper or a seafood cocktail. It's at the western end of town, and is prettily lit at night.

Siddhartha
INTERNATIONAL **$$**

(El Rinconcito; dishes M$60-140; ⊗8am-11pm; 📶💷) This joint with a view to the beach from its patio does some tasty vegetarian options (try the falafel wraps) and strong coffee. It also has a pool table, live Latin music on Sunday nights and an excellent bar.

La Empanada
MEXICAN, ASIAN **$**

(Paseo del Mazunte; mains M$45-120; ⊗9am-11pm; 💷) Leafy La Empanada is opposite Restaurante Tania and also locally owned and with a pretty, candlelit atmosphere after dark. Choose from a mix of economical, carefully prepared items, including curries, sushi and pizzas.

La Baguette
BAKERY **$**

(Andador Rinconcito; baked goods M$15; ⊗8am-9pm Wed-Mon) Stop by here for tasty mini-quiches and chocolate or banana cake.

☆ Entertainment

Luna Nueva
BAR, LIVE MUSIC

(Andador La Barrita; ⊗9pm-2am, closed May, Jun, Sep & Oct) Run by indefatigable Carlos from Argentina, barnlike Luna Nueva is Mazunte's nightlife center. Drinks are inexpensive and most nights there is live music of varying kinds or an aerial acrobatics show.

❶ Information

Tourist Information Kiosk (Paseo del Mazunte; ⊗10am-5pm) By the roadside at the west end of the village. Ask here about the new community tourism initiative which is training young villagers to lead kayaking trips around Punta Cometa, mountain biking to La Ventanilla and other activities.

Bahías de Huatulco

📞958 / POP 16,000

Mexico's youngest planned coastal resort lies along a series of beautiful sandy bays, the Bahías de Huatulco (wah-*tool*-koh), 50km east of Pochutla. This stretch of coast had just one small fishing village until the 1980s. The developers have trodden fairly gently here: pockets of construction are separated by tracts of unspoiled shoreline, the maximum building height is six stories and no sewage goes into the sea. For now Huatulco is still a relaxed and relatively uncrowded resort, though between October and May an average of five cruise ships a month dock at the pier in Bahía de Santa Cruz.

The cruise market has helped to spawn all sorts of active pursuits for visitors here, but Huatulco is not a place to stay very long on a tight budget.

The Huatulco bays are strung along the coast about 10km in each direction from the harbor at Santa Cruz Huatulco. The 'downtown' area is La Crucecita, 1km north of Santa Cruz, with a grid of straight streets focused on the leafy Plaza Principal. The other main developments are at Santa Cruz Huatulco, Chahué and Tangolunda.

⊙ Sights & Activities

Beaches

Huatulco's beaches are sandy with clear waters (though boats and jet skis leave an oily film here and there). As in the rest of Mexico, all beaches are under federal control, and anyone can use them, even when hotels appear to treat them as private property. Some have coral offshore and excellent snorkeling.

Some of the western bays and most of the eastern ones are accessible by road, but a boat ride is more fun, if more expensive, than a taxi. *Lanchas* will whisk you out to most beaches from Santa Cruz harbor any time between 8am and 5pm, and they'll return to collect you by dusk. Round-trip *lancha* rates for up to 10 people from Santa Cruz harbor: Playa La Entrega M$300, Bahía Maguey or Bahía El Órgano M$800, Bahía Cacaluta M$1000, Playa La India M$1700, Bahía San Agustín M$2500. There's also a M$5 fee to enter the harbor. For beaches to the west of Bahía de Santa Cruz, there's a M$21 fee for entering the **Parque Nacional Huatulco**, also collected at the harbor. Use of nonbiodegradable suntan lotions or sunscreen is prohibited within the national park.

Several operators offer a **seven-bay tour** in larger boats for around M$250 per person. You can buy tickets in hotels, and at agencies and tour kiosks.

Playa Santa Cruz
BEACH

The small beach at Santa Cruz Huatulco is easily accessible but often crowded, and its looks are somewhat marred by the cruise-ship pier. It has several beach restaurants.

Playa La Entrega
BEACH

La Entrega lies toward the outer edge of Bahía de Santa Cruz, a five-minute *lancha* trip or 2.5km along a paved road from Santa Cruz. This 300m beach, backed by a line of seafood *palapas*, can get crowded, but it has decent snorkeling on a coral plate

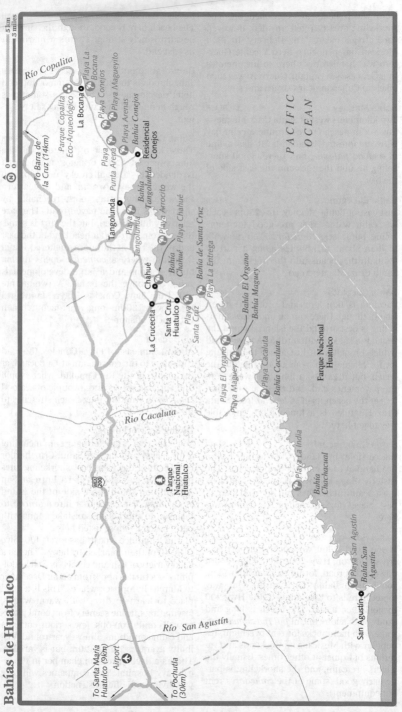

Bahías de Huatulco

Río Copalita

Parque Copalita
Eco-Arqueológico

To Barra de
la Cruz (14km)

La Bocana
Playa La
Bocana
Playa Conejos
Playa Magueyito
Playa Arenas
Bahía Conejos
Residencial
Conejos

Playa
Punta Arena

Tangolunda
Playa
Tangolunda

Bahía
Tangolunda

Playa Arrocito

Playa Chahué

Chahué
Bahía
Chahué

Bahía de Santa Cruz
Playa La Entrega

La Crucecita
Santa Cruz
Huatulco
Playa
Santa Cruz

Bahía El Órgano
Bahía Maguey

Playa El Órgano
Playa Maguey

Playa Cacaluta
Bahía Cacaluta

Parque Nacional
Huatulco

Río Cacaluta

MEX
200

Parque
Nacional
Huatulco

Playa La India

Bahía
Chachacual

Playa San Agustín
Bahía San
Agustín

San Agustín

Río San Agustín

To Santa María
Huatulco (9km)

Airport

To Pochutla
(30km)

PACIFIC
OCEAN

5 km
3 miles

N
0   0

from which boats are cordoned off. The snorkeling area can get crowded, however. 'La Entrega' means 'The Delivery.' In 1831, Mexican independence hero Vicente Guerrero was handed over here to his enemies by a Genoese sea captain. Guerrero was then taken to Cuilapan near Oaxaca and shot.

Bahía Maguey   BEACH
Two kilometers west of Santa Cruz, Maguey's fine 400m beach curves around a calm bay between forested headlands. It has a line of seafood *palapas,* and there's good snorkeling around the rocks on the east side of the bay.

Bahía El Órgano   BEACH
Just east of Bahía Maguey, this 250m beach has calm waters that are good for snorkeling, but it lacks *comedores.* You can walk to it in about 10 minutes along a narrow footpath that heads into the trees from the Santa Cruz–Maguey road.

Bahía Cacaluta   BEACH
Cacaluta is 1km long and protected by an island, though there can be undertow. Snorkeling is best around the island. Behind the beach is a lagoon with birdlife. A paved road (which branches off just above the parking lot for Maguey) ends about 1km before the beach, but it can be a long, hot walk from the pavement's end, and there are no services at the beach itself. A *lancha* from Santa Cruz Huatulco is a much more enjoyable way to get here.

Bahía Chachacual   BEACH
Inaccessible by land, Chachacual has a headland at each end and two beaches. The easterly Playa La India is one of Huatulco's most beautiful beaches and one of the area's best places for snorkeling. No *comedores* here.

Bahía San Agustín   BEACH
If you head 1.7km west of the airport to a crossroads on Hwy 200, then 13km south down a dirt road, fording a river after 9km, you'll reach Bahía San Agustín. One way to get here is to take a bus to the Hwy 200 turnoff, then a taxi. The beach is long and sandy, with a long line of *palapa comedores,* some with hammocks for rent overnight. It's popular with Mexicans on weekends and vacations but quiet at other times. Usually the waters are calm, and the snorkeling is particularly good (some of the *comedores* rent out equipment).

Bahía Chahué   BEACH
The beach here is good, though the surf can be surprisingly strong. There's a marina at its east end.

Bahía Tangolunda   BEACH
Tangolunda is the site of the major top-end hotel developments. The sea is sometimes rough here: heed the colored-flag safety system.

Bahía Conejos   BEACH
Three kilometers east of Tangolunda, the long sweep of Bahía Conejos' main beach is divided by a small rocky outcrop into the western Playa Arenas and the eastern Playa Punta Arenas, both reachable by short walks from the paved road. They are relatively little visited, but the surf is sometimes strong. Around a headland at the east end of the bay is the more sheltered Playa Conejos, where a *comedor* opens during busier seasons and a large development is going on above the beach. A two-minute walk from Playa Conejos, Playa Magueyito is a lovely, 300m-long, east-facing beach with rocks offshore.

La Bocana   BEACH
About 1.5km east of Playa Conejos, the road runs close to the coast again at La Bocana, at the mouth of the Río Copalita, where you'll find surfable waves and a couple of seafood *comedores.* Another long beach stretches to the east.

Diving & Snorkeling
You can rent snorkeling gear, including a life jacket and fins, at Santa Cruz harbor for M$100 a day. The best snorkeling sites include the coral plates at La Entrega, San Agustín and the inshore side of the island at Cacaluta. You can either hire a *lancha* to take you to snorkel sites or take a tour with outfits such as those listed here.

The Huatulco coast has over 100 dive sites, 40 of them marked by buoys. There's a good variety of fish and corals, as well as dolphins, sea turtles and (from about December to March) humpback whales. This is a good place to learn to dive, with warm waters, fascinating marine scenery from coral plates to walls and drop-offs, few serious currents and calm conditions almost year-round. Visibility averages 10m to 20m but is variable. There's a decompression chamber in the local navy hospital. Two companies will take you diving and offer instruction.

Hurricane Divers
DIVING, SNORKELING

(☎587-11-07; www.hurricanedivers.com; Playa Santa Cruz; ☺9am-6pm Mon-Sat, 9am-4pm Sun) This very professional international crew speaks English, French, Spanish, Dutch and German, and offers a variety of courses and dives. It's one of Mexico's few PADI 5-Star Dive Resorts. Options include two-tank dives (US$95), night dives (US$70) and PADI Scuba Diver course (US$275 for two days). Hurricane's most popular outing is a full-day snorkeling excursion for US$120 per person (minimum two people) with about four snorkeling stops and a good beach lunch. Hurricane's website is a very good source of information on Huatulco diving and snorkeling.

Buceo Sotavento
DIVING, SNORKELING

(☎587-21-66; www.tomzap.com/sotavento.html; Local 18, Plaza Oaxaca Mall, Plaza Principal, La Crucecita; ☺9am-2pm & 5-9:30pm) A friendly local company offering a range of options from a four-hour introduction (US$75) to open-water certification (five days, US$380). One-/two-tank dives for qualified divers are US$50/70. Sotavento also does four-hour snorkeling trips for US$30 per person (minimum two people). It is certified by the internationally recognized Federación Mexicana de Actividades Subacuáticas (Mexican Underwater Activities Federation).

Fruit & Coffee Plantations

Hagia Sofia
FARM, GARDENS

(www.hagiasofia.mx; Apanguito; incl round-trip transportation & fruit drinks M$400, with 2 meals M$500) Office (☎587-08-71; Local 7, Mitla 402, Santa Cruz Huatulco; ☺9am-2pm & 4-7pm Mon-Sat) One of Huatulco's loveliest and most interesting day trips, this 'agro-ecotourism' operation is an organic fruit farm 9km northwest of Santa María Huatulco and about 30km from La Crucecita (a 45-minute drive). It includes a gorgeous 500m riverside flower trail with 60 kinds of exotic tropical flowering plants that attract many colorful birds and butterflies. The extensive orchard has around 70 types of fruit tree, including varieties new to the region such as rambutan, mangosteen and noni, which the owners are donating to local small farmers. You can visit any day, but reserve the day before: tours are given in English or Spanish and you can have a swim in the creek while you're there. Most visitors stay several hours. The cost is M$100 less if you have your own transportation.

Finca La Gloria
COFFEE PLANTATION

(☎587-06-97; lagloria@hispavista.com; day trip per person M$350) Another fun trip into the hills is to this coffee plantation near Llano Grande, where you are shown the production process and visit its butterfly enclosure, swim in pools below jungle-clad waterfalls and enjoy an excellent lunch. Reserve through agencies, hotels and tour kiosks.

Rafting

The Ríos Copalita and Zimatán near Huatulco have waters ranging in rafting terms from Class 1 (suitable for beginners and children) to Class 4 (requiring white-water experience). The rivers are at their biggest between about late July and January.

Huatulco Expediciones
RAFTING

(☎587-21-26; www.huatulcoexpediciones.com, in Spanish; Hwy 200 Km 256, Puente Tangolunda, Comunidad La Jabalina) Well-established Huatulco Expediciones does a range of rafting trips, from all-day outings on the Class 3–4 Alemania section of the Copalita (per person M$650, minimum four) to a 2½-hour jaunt down the final 5km of the Río Copalita to the sea at La Bocana – more of a float, really, and suitable for children from five years up (per person M$250 to M$300, minimum two people, available all year). They also offer rappelling and zip-lining. They'll pick you up from your accommodations for all activities.

Aventura Mundo
RAFTING

(☎581-03-71; www.aventuramundo.net; Hotel Plaza Huatulco, Blvd Juárez 23, Tangolunda) Canadian-owned Aventura Mundo offers similar trips to Huatulco Expediciones.

Other Sights & Activities

Parque Eco-Arqueológico Copalita
ARCHAEOLOGICAL SITE

(☎587-15-91; Blvd Copalita-Tangolunda; Mexican/foreigner M$50/100; ☺8am-5pm Tue-Sun) The only pre-Hispanic site on the Oaxaca coast to have been seriously excavated and developed for visitors, Copalita was occupied by different groups between about 900 BC and AD 1000. The main plaza, the ball court and a large pyramidal structure are the chief archaeological features, but the pathways through semitropical forest and a spectacular beach-view lookout add to the appeal. The site only opened to visitors in 2010 and is still being excavated. It takes 1½ to two hours to walk around, including a visit to its interesting museum.

🛏 Sleeping

You'll find all budget and many midrange options in La Crucecita, many of them close to the Plaza Principal. Further midrange possibilities are in Chahué and Santa Cruz. The top-end resort hotels are at Tangolunda. Midrange and top-end places tend to raise their rates dramatically for a couple of weeks around Christmas–New Year and Easter, and from about mid-July to mid-August.

Air-and-lodging package deals are your best bet for a good-value vacation in a top-end Huatulco hotel. Also look for promotions on hotel websites.

Camino Real Zaashila   LUXURY HOTEL **$$$**
(☎583-03-00; www.caminoreal.com/zaashila; Blvd Juárez 5, Tangolunda; r from M$2100, incl breakfast from M$2300; P❄☀@🌐🏊🐾) This attractively landscaped, modern-hacienda-style property has a fabulously enormous pool in lovely gardens. There are 148 rooms, most with sea view; 41 come with their own small pool.

Quinta Real   LUXURY HOTEL **$$$**
(☎581-04-28, 800-500-40-00; www.quintarealhotels.com; Blvd Juárez 2, Tangolunda; ste from US$177; P❄☀@🌐🏊) The utterly gorgeous, Moorish-inspired Quinta Real has just 28 suites, all with Jacuzzis, marble bathrooms and ocean views. Some have fountain-fed private pools that seem to spill down the hillside to the beach and main pool area.

Misión de los Arcos   HOTEL **$$**
(☎587-01-65; www.misiondelosarcos.com; Gardenia 902, La Crucecita; r M$655, ste M$774-893; ☀🌐) This very well-run, welcoming hotel, half a block off the Plaza Principal, is embellished by a touch of colonial style and interior greenery. It has big, bright rooms with air-con and very comfortable beds, and most rooms have a balcony. There's also walk-through access to Terra-Cotta restaurant, under the same ownership.

Agua Azul   B&B **$$**
(☎581-02-65; www.bbaguaazul.com; Lote 18, Las Brisas, Manzana 6, Residencial Conejos; r incl breakfast US$89-109; ❄☀🌐🏊) Designed for couples, this welcoming Canadian-owned B&B sits on a hillside garden site, with pool and sea views, in a residential area a couple of kilometers east of Tangolunda. Its six pleasing rooms are decorated with original Mexican and Guatemalan crafts and are all on different levels with their own hammock-hung terraces. There's a nice airy

dining area, where you can have restaurant meals delivered, if you like. Playa Arenas is a 15-minute walk away; a taxi to La Crucecita or Playa Conejos is M$40.

Hotel Posada Edén Costa   HOTEL **$$**
(☎587-24-80; www.edencosta.com, in Spanish; Zapoteco 26, Chahué; d/tr/q M$600/750/900, ste d/tr/q M$800/950/1100, all incl breakfast; P❄☀🌐🏊🐾) Swiss- and Laotian-owned Edén Costa, 500m inland from Bahía Chahué, has quiet and attractive rooms with nice touches including colorful bird murals. Rooms have two double beds, and most overlook the small central pool. Suites have their own kitchens. The attached restaurant, L'échalote, is a big bonus.

Hotel Villablanca   HOTEL **$$**
(☎587-06-06; www.hotelesvillablanca.com; cnr Blvd Juárez & Zapoteco, Chahué; r from M$880, incl breakfast from M$1080; ☀🌐) In a vaguely colonial style, this hotel, 300m from Chahué beach, has helpful staff and a nice large pool. The 60 attractive, white-and-blue rooms are tile-floored and all have balconies. And there's a good restaurant serving an excellent breakfast.

Hotel María Mixteca   HOTEL **$$**
(☎587-23-36; www.travelbymexico.com/oaxa/mariamixteca; Guamuchil 204, La Crucecita; r M$750; P☀🌐) The María Mixteca offers prettily decorated yellow-and-white rooms on two upper floors around an open patio, with super-comfy beds, air-conditioning, good bathrooms and room safes. It's half a block east of the Plaza Principal.

Hotel Jaroje Centro   HOTEL **$**
(☎583-48-01; www.hotelhuatulco.com.mx; Bugambilia 304, La Crucecita; r M$400-450; ☀🌐) Bright Jaroje, two blocks south of the Plaza Principal, has 14 large, clean, white rooms with mosquito screens, air-con, fine bathrooms and towels folded into cute swan shapes and scattered with flower petals! A very good value.

Hostal Luna Creciente   HOTEL **$**
(☎503-45-94; hostalunacreciente@gmail.com; Guarumbo 15, La Crucecita; d/q M$400/500; ☀🌐) A very clean little budget hotel a block north of the Plaza Principal, with bright rooms in yellows and blues and nice bits of tiling in the bathrooms.

Hotel Arrecife   HOTEL **$$**
(☎587-17-37; www.hotelarrecife.com.mx, in Spanish; Colorín 510, La Crucecita; r with fan/air-con

M$500/560, q with fan M$655; (P❄️📶🏊) In a quiet, leafy neighborhood two blocks south and two west of the Plaza Principal, the Arrecife has a nice little pool with a cafe. Most of the 24 good, clean rooms are sizable, with pleasing decor, white tile floors, balcony and air-con.

Posada Leo　　　　　　　HOTEL $
(✆587-26-01; posadaleo_hux@hotmail.com; Bugambilia 302, La Crucecita; s/d M$300/350, with air-con M$350/400; ❄️📶) A friendly little budget spot just past Hotel Jaroje Centro, with six smallish but neat and well-kept rooms, all with hot-water bathrooms.

🍴 Eating

Terra-Cotta　　　MEXICAN, INTERNATIONAL $$
(Gardenia 902, La Crucecita; breakfast M$40-70, light dishes M$45-85, mains M$50-150; ⏰7:30am-11:30pm; 📶📶) Highly popular Terra-Cotta, half a block north of the Plaza Principal, has sidewalk tables as well as a soothing air-con interior. Good service complements the excellent food: breakfasts, shrimp, steaks, *antojitos,* waffles, baguettes and ice cream all go down easily.

Trattoria Italiana　　　　ITALIAN $$
(✆583-43-24; Palma Real btwn Gardenia & Bugambilia, La Crucecita; pasta M$75-110, baguettes M$50-110; ⏰10am-10pm Tue-Sun) Also called Giordana's after its talented Italian chef, this tiny spot has just three tables, so it's a good idea to reserve. Delicious homemade pasta options include ravioli, fettuccine and meat or vegetarian lasagna. Giordana also makes a great choice of baguettes with Italian cheeses and salamis. If you can't get a table, head next door to the also-Italian Mamma Mia. It's five blocks north of the plaza.

El Sabor de Oaxaca　　　OAXACAN $$
(Guamuchil 204, La Crucecita; mains M$80-160; ⏰7am-11pm) Attached to the Hotel María Mixteca, this is a good spot to sample authentic Oaxacan specialties such as *tlayudas, tasajo, moles* and even *chapulines,* with a few Mexican standards such as seafood cocktails and *chiles rellenos* on offer, too. Folksy *artesanías* add to the regional ambience.

L'échalote　　　INTERNATIONAL $$
(www.edencosta.com, in Spanish; Hotel Posada Edén Costa, Zapoteco 26, Chahué; mains M$80-220; ⏰2-11pm Tue-Sun; 📶) The French-Swiss chef prepares very tasty French, Southeast Asian, Oaxacan and other dishes. The Thai

salad with prawns and bean sprouts is delicious. Main dishes include fish, steaks, the house-specialty fondues, and the desserts aren't too shabby, either.

Azul Profundo　　SEAFOOD, FUSION $$$
(✆583-03-00; Camino Real Zaashila, Blvd Juárez 5, Tangolunda; mains M$150-300; ⏰7pm-midnight) Tangolunda's big hotels offer a choice of expensive bars, coffee shops and restaurants. For a romantic, no-expense-spared dinner you won't go wrong at the Camino Real's Azul Profundo, right over the beach, which combines European and Mexican cuisine with a few Asian touches. One specialty is shrimp sautéed with garlic, wild mushrooms and prosciutto in a red wine sauce. Reservations required.

Restaurante Onix　　MEXICAN, EUROPEAN $$$
(Plaza Principal, La Crucecita; mains M$130-215; ⏰3:30-11:30pm; 📶) This airy upstairs eatery overlooking the plaza offers well-prepared dishes and a reasonable wine list. Try the mussels with ham and cheese or the *sopa de Donají* (shrimp, prickly-pear cactus and chickpea soup), followed by steak or tuna *al chipotle* (in a fermented-chili sauce).

El Patio　　　　　　MEXICAN $
(Flamboyán 214, La Crucecita; breakfast M$30-58, set lunch M$50-150; ⏰7am-10pm) An appealing garden patio half a block east of the plaza, with good-value breakfasts. The rest of the day you're offered the usual range of seafood, chicken dishes and Oaxacan specialties, as well as a full selection of alcoholic drinks.

🍷 Drinking

La Crema　　　　　　　　BAR
(www.lacremahuatulco.com; Gardenia 311, La Crucecita; ⏰7pm-2am) A lively mixed crowd of locals and visitors knocks 'em back at this quirky, dark and spacious rock-themed den overlooking the Plaza Principal. La Crema boasts loud tunes, the best cocktail list in town, and terrific wood-oven pizza (medium size MS$70 to M$125). The entrance is just off the plaza on Gardenia.

Café Dublin　　　　　　PUB
(Carrizal 502, La Crucecita; ⏰6pm-last customer) A friendly little Irish bar proffering darts, good burgers, sports on TV and lots of drinks, including Guinness in cans. It's located one block east and half a block south of the plaza.

Paletería Zamora JUICE BAR
(Plaza Principal, La Crucecita; drinks M$15-50; ⊙9am-11pm) Thirst-zapping Zamora blends up a full range of cooling fresh-fruit juices, *licuados* and *aguas frescas* (fruit blended with water and sweetener).

☆ Entertainment

La Papaya CLUB
(Blvd Juárez, Chahué; ⊙10pm-4am Thu-Sat) Huatulco's hottest club for the 18-to-25 crowd plays reggaeton and electro, with dancing on the bar and an aquarium with bikini-clad humans helping to warm up the atmosphere. **Mango** (tropical music) and **Mandarine** (electronic) are slightly more chilled bars in the same building.

Magic Tropic CLUB
(Mitla, Santa Cruz Huatulco; ⊙from 10pm Thu-Sat) This cavelike basement is the place to go to dance to salsa, *cumbia* and other Latin rhythms. The music is often live.

ℹ Information

Internet Access
Plenty of internet shops, many with options for international phone calls, are around the square in La Crucecita. There are also a few in Tangolunda.

Money
Banamex ATM (cnr Carrizal & Guamuchil, La Crucecita)
Banorte (Guamuchil 604, La Crucecita; ⊙9am-5pm Mon-Fri) Currency exchange and ATM.

Tourist Information
Tourist Information Kiosk (Plaza Principal, La Crucecita; ⊙9am-2pm & 4-7pm Mon-Fri, 9am-1pm Sat)

ℹ Getting There & Away
Air
Huatulco Airport (☎581-90-04; www.asur.com.mx) Located 400m north of Hwy 200, 12km west of the turnoff to La Crucecita.
Aeromar (☎581-91-24; airport) Flies to and from Mexico City daily.
Aeroméxico (www.aeromexico.com) Mexico City daily.
Aerotucán (☎587-24-27; www.aerotucan.com.mx; Plaza Carmelinas, Blvd Chahué 164, Chahué) Flies 13-seat Cessnas daily to/from Oaxaca (M$1515).
Continental Airlines (www.continental.com) Direct to/from Houston, Texas, at least once weekly.
Interjet (☎105-13-36; www.interjet.com.mx; Super Che, cnr Blvd Chahué & Mixteco, Lote 23A, Manzana 2, Chahué) Mexico City at least twice daily.
Magnicharters (www.magnicharters.com.mx; Sabalí 304, La Crucecita) Mexico City daily except Tuesday.
VivaAerobus (www.vivaaerobus.com) Mexico City three or more times weekly; one-way fares can be as low as M$765 (M$865 with check-in baggage).

Cheap charters from main Canadian cities and occasionally from the US or UK are available during the winter season, avoiding the need for an overnight stop in Mexico City.

Bus, Van & Taxi Colectivo
Some buses to Huatulco are marked 'Santa Cruz Huatulco,' but they still terminate in La Crucecita. Make sure your bus is not headed to Santa María Huatulco, which is some way inland.
Estrella Blanca bus station (Carpinteros s/n, Sector V) Located 1.2km northwest of central La Crucecita; used by Turistar (deluxe), AltaMar (1st-class) and Transportes Rápidos de Pochutla (TRP; 2nd-class) buses.
Huatulco 2000 (Guamuchil, La Crucecita) Located 150m east of the Plaza Principal; comfortable passenger vans to Oaxaca.
OCC bus station (Blvd Chahué, La Crucecita) Located 500m north of the Plaza Principal; used by ADO GL (deluxe), OCC (1st-class) and Sur, Ecobús and AU (2nd-class) buses.
Taxis colectivos to Pochutla (M$25, one hour) leave from a stand on Blvd Chahué, 450m north of the Plaza Principal in La Crucecita.

Car & Motorcycle
Auto-Car Rental Oaxaca (oaxacacarrental.com.mx; Centro Comercial Las Conchas, Blvd Juárez, Tangolunda)
Europcar (www.europcar.com.mx, in Spanish) Airport (airport); La Crucecita (☎583-47-51; Plaza Carmelinas, Blvd Chahué 164, Chahué) Reasonable rental rates and efficient service.
Hertz (www.hertz.com; airport)

ℹ Getting Around
To/From the Airport
Authorized Transporte Terrestre vans cost M$101 per person from the airport to La Crucecita, Santa Cruz or Bahía Chahué, and M$118 to Tangolunda. Get tickets at the airport kiosk. A whole cab is M$370 to most places in Bahías de Huatulco, M$730 to Puerto Ángel or M$950 to Mazunte, but you may be able to get one much cheaper just outside the airport gate. Or walk 400m down to Hwy 200 and catch a Transportes Rápidos de Pochutla bus for M$6 to La Crucecita or M$14 to Pochutla (they pass every 15 minutes in both directions from about 6am to 8pm).

BUSES & VANS FROM BAHÍAS DE HUATULCO

DESTINATION	FARE (M$)	DURATION	FREQUENCY (DAILY)
Acapulco	444	10hr	4 AltaMar
Mexico City (Sur) via Acapulco	847-1020	14hr	Turistar 4pm, AltaMar 5:30pm
Mexico City (TAPO) via Salina Cruz	626-864	15hr	7 from OCC terminal
Oaxaca via Pochutla	150	7hr	8 Huatulco 2000
Oaxaca via Salina Cruz	276-326	8hr	4 from OCC terminal
Pochutla	20-40	1hr	22 from OCC terminal, 59 TRP
Puerto Escondido	46-94	2½hr	22 from OCC terminal
San Cristóbal de las Casas	394	10-11hr	2 OCC
Tehuantepec	107-148	3½hr	11 from OCC station
Tuxtla Gutiérrez	332	9-10hr	2 OCC

Taxi

Blue local buses run every few minutes during daylight. To Santa Cruz Huatulco (M$5, five minutes) they go from Plaza El Madero mall on Guamuchil, two blocks east of the plaza in La Crucecita. To the Estrella Blanca bus station (M$3, five minutes) they go from Blvd Chahué, 450m north of the plaza.

Taxis from central La Crucecita cost M$20 to the OCC bus station or Santa Cruz, M$30 to Tangolunda and M$55 to Bahía Maguey. Intermittent *taxis colectivos* from Plaza El Madero charge M$5 per person to Santa Cruz and M$7 to Tangolunda.

Barra de la Cruz

POP 740

This well-tended indigenous Chontal village, about 20km east of Huatulco, offers surfers the chance to catch some amazing waves and everyone the chance to get off the grid and slow right down. The right-hand point break, off the beach 1.5km from the rustic village, gets up to a double overhead and is long and fast. Good swells for experienced surfers are frequent from March to early October and generally at their best in June and July. November to February brings good waves for learners.

There's not much to do except surf and swim, but Barra's beautiful beach has showers, toilets and a good *comedor* with hammocks and shade. The municipality charges M$20 per person to pass along the road to the beach and imposes a 7pm curfew on it (8pm during the daylight saving period).

The fee goes to help maintain the road and keep the beach clean.

You can rent **surfboards** (per day M$100) at El Chontal restaurant, under a large octagonal *palapa* beside the entrance to the beach road. El Chontal's English-speaking owner **Pablo Narváez** (pablo_rafting@yahoo.com), who first brought international surfers to Barra in the 1990s, also gives **surf classes** (3-4hr around M$450), and expertly leads **bird-watching tours** (3 or 4hr per person M$250) around the very varied local habitats. Cabañas Pepe rents out **bicycles** (per day M$25) with surfboard racks.

🛏 Sleeping & Eating

Cabañas Pepe　　　　　　　　CABAÑAS $
(per person M$90; dishes M$40-65) Behind El Chontal, Pepe's has well-built wood-and-palm-thatch cabins with hammocks out front and shared toilets and showers, plus a large *palapa comedor* with couches, table tennis and a good selection of dishes.

El Chontal　　　　　　　　ROOMS $
(pablo_rafting@yahoo.com; per person M$80-90; mains M$65-75) El Chontal has two quite large, bright and breezy upstairs rooms, with shared bathrooms, and serves good chicken, seafood and other Mexican dishes. It also runs nearby Barradise, which has rooms with private bathroom at the same price.

Comedor　　　　　　　　MEXICAN $
(mains M$70-80; ⊙9am-5pm) The community-run beach *comedor* is good for both

breakfast and lunch. Try its specialty *pescado empapelado* (foil-wrapped fish).

ℹ️ Getting There & Around

Barra de la Cruz is reached via a 2.5km road that heads coastward from Hwy 200, 2km east of Puente Zimatán bridge. *Taxis colectivos* run to Barra (M$20, 40 minutes) about every half-hour (less often in the middle of the day), 7am to 5pm, from the Estrella Blanca bus station at Bahías de Huatulco. They charge an additional M$15 to carry a surfboard. A private taxi from central La Crucecita costs around M$150, with or without surfboards.

ISTHMUS OF TEHUANTEPEC

The southern half of the 200km-wide Isthmus of Tehuantepec (teh-wahn-teh-*pek*), Mexico's narrow waist, forms the hot, flat eastern end of Oaxaca state. Indigenous Zapotec culture is strong here, with its own regional twists. In 1496 the isthmus Zapotecs repulsed the Aztecs from the fortress of Guiengola, near Tehuantepec, and the isthmus never became part of the Aztec empire. An independent spirit pervades the region to this day.

If you stay around, you'll encounter a lively, friendly populace, whose open and confident women take leading roles in business and government. Isthmus people let loose their love of music, dancing and partying in numerous annual *velas* (fiestas) lasting several days. If you're here for one of these, you will see women displaying wonderfully worked, highly colorful *huipiles,* gold and silver jewelry, skirts embroidered with fantastic silk flowers, and a variety of odd headgear. Many isthmus fiestas feature the *tirada de frutas,* in which women climb on roofs and throw fruit on the men below!

Of the three main isthmus towns, isthmus culture is stronger in Tehuantepec and Juchitán than in Salina Cruz, which is dominated by its oil refinery. All three towns can be uncomfortable in the heat of the day, but come the evening breeze they take on a more agreeable air.

Tehuantepec

📞971 / POP 42,000

Even though Tehuantepec, some 245km from Oaxaca city, is a friendly town, most travelers blow by here on the way to somewhere else. June and August are the main months for partying in the fiestas of the 15 barrios (neighborhoods), each of which has its own colonial church.

◉ Sights

Ex-Convento Rey Cosijopí   CULTURAL BUILDING
(📞715-01-14; Callejón Rey Cosijopí; admission free; ⊙8am-8pm Mon-Fri, 9am-2pm Sat) A former Dominican monastery, on a short street off Guerrero, is now Tehuantepec's **Casa de la Cultura**, where various arts and crafts workshops and activities are held. It bears traces of old frescoes, and some rooms hold modest exhibits of traditional dress, archaeological finds, historical photos, religious regalia and the like: ask for them to be opened. The last Zapotec king, Cosijopí, paid for the monastery's construction in the 16th century, at the urging of Hernán Cortés. Staff also provide useful tourist information.

Guiengola   RUIN
(admission free; ⊙8am-5pm) This old hillside Zapotec stronghold, where King Cosijoeza rebuffed the Aztecs in 1496, is north of Hwy 190 from a turnoff 11km west of Tehuantepec. A sign just past Puente Las Tejas bridge indicates 'Guiengola 7': the unpaved road is passable in dry weather, though the last kilometer or so (heading uphill) requires a high-clearance vehicle. The road ends at a signed trailhead, from where a sweaty 2km walk uphill through tropical woodland gets you to the remains of two pyramids, a ball court, a 64-room complex and a thick defensive wall. Many more remains lie overgrown by the surrounding forest. You'll also see interesting limestone formations and some fine views over the isthmus. Spanish-speaking guide **Victor Velázquez** (📞cell phone 971-1223966; vicveneno@hotmail.com) leads all-day trips to Guiengola for M$500, plus M$250 for a round-trip taxi. Contact him at least one day ahead: the Casa de la Cultura can help with this.

Market   MARKET
Tehuantepec's dim, almost medieval, indoor market is open daily on the west side of the plaza, and spills out into surrounding streets.

🛏️ Sleeping & Eating

Hostal Emilia   GUESTHOUSE $
(📞715-00-08; Ocampo 8; per person M$150; 📶) A block south of the plaza, Emilia is run by a friendly, English-speaking family and is keen to attract backpackers to its three

BUSES FROM TEHUANTEPEC

DESTINATION	FARE (M$)	DURATION	FREQUENCY (DAILY)
Bahías de Huatulco	88-124	3½hr	10
Mexico City (TAPO or Norte)	580-834	10-11½hr	9
Oaxaca	110-196	4½hr	24
Pochutla	158	4½hr	4
Puerto Escondido	196-206	6hr	4

reasonably comfy rooms, one with its own bathroom. It has a good clean ground-floor restaurant, **Pueblo Mío** (dishes M$40-100; ⊘9am-9pm), serving fare from *antojitos* and seafood cocktails to burgers and pizzas.

Hotel Calli HOTEL $$
(☑715-00-85; www.hotelcalli.com; Carretera Cristóbal Colón, Km 790; r/ste M$1100/1400; P✱@☎☞) Tehuantepec's most comfortable, though not exactly exciting, lodgings are beside Hwy 185 about 700m toward Juchitán from La Terminal. The 100 good-sized, modern, bland rooms, designed for bus-tour groups, boast cable TV, air-con and small balconies. Ample common areas include a reasonable restaurant (mains M$70 to M$180), colorful lobby murals and a pool in grassy gardens.

Restaurante Bar Scarú MEXICAN $$
(Callejón Leona Vicario 4; mains M$70-140; ⊘8am-10:30pm) Scarú occupies an 18th-century house with a courtyard and colorful murals of Tehuantepec life. Sit beneath a fan, quaff a *limonada* and sample one of the many varied dishes on offer. On weekends old-timers plunk out marimba tunes. To find it, go 200m south from the east side of the plaza to the end of Juárez, then one block east, then 40m north.

At night the whole east side of the plaza is lined with tables and chairs beside carts serving cheap tacos and other delights.

ⓘ Information

Bancomer (5 de Mayo; ⊘8:30am-4pm Mon-Fri) A few steps west of the plaza. Has ATMs and changes cash US dollars.

Tourist information office (Hwy 185; ⊘8am-8pm Mon-Fri, 9am-6pm Sat, 9am-2pm Sun) Two blocks west from the plaza along 5 de Mayo, then 70m south on the highway; staff don't see many foreigners here, but they are knowledgeable about the area.

ⓘ Getting There & Around

Tehuantepec's main bus station, known as La Terminal, is by Hwy 185 on the northern edge of town. It's shared by deluxe, 1st-class and 2nd-class services of the ADO/OCC group. Second-class Istmeños buses to Juchitán (M$20, 30 minutes) depart across the street from La Terminal at least every half-hour during daylight.

Taxis from La Terminal to the plaza cost M$15. To walk it, head 600m to the left along Av Héroes until it ends at a T-junction, then turn right along Guerrero. Take the fifth street to the left, Hidalgo, and walk two blocks to the plaza.

Juchitán
☑971 / POP 75,000

Istmeño culture is strong in this friendly town, which is visited by few gringos. About 30 different neighborhood *velas* almost fill the calendar with music, dancing, drinking, eating and fun from mid-April to early September, above all in May. Juchitán is also famed for its *muxes* – the town's openly gay, frequently cross-dressing, men, who are fully accepted in local society and hold their own *vela* in November.

◉ Sights

Jardín Juárez PLAZA
Jardín Juárez is a lively central square. In the busy two-story market on its east side you'll find locally made hammocks, isthmus women's costumes, and maybe iguana on the menus of the *comedores*.

Lidxi Guendabiaani CULTURAL BUILDING
(Casa de la Cultura; ☑711-32-08; Belisario Domínguez; admission free; ⊘9am-2pm & 4-7pm Mon-Fri, 9am-1pm Sat) Beside the San Vicente Ferrer church a block south and west of Jardín Juárez, Lidxi Guendabiaani is set around a big patio that buzzes with children. It has an interesting gallery and a small archaeological museum.

BUSES FROM JUCHITÁN

DESTINATION	FARE (M$)	DURATION	FREQUENCY (DAILY)
Bahías de Huatulco	124-176	3½-4hr	9
Mexico City (Norte or TAPO)	682-1176	11-12hr	11
Oaxaca	202	5hr	18
Pochutla	174-188	4½-5hr	6
San Cristóbal de las Casas	262	5½-6½hr	3
Tapachula	270-378	6-8hr	5
Tonalá	138-168	3-4hr	3

🛏 Sleeping & Eating

Hotel Central   HOTEL **$**
(☎712-20-19; www.hotelcentral.com.mx; Av Efraín
Gómez 30; s/d/tr/q M$300/390/460/510; ☯❄
@🔊) This good-value hotel is 1½ blocks east
of the central plaza, Jardín Juárez. It offers
bare, freshly painted rooms with comfy beds
and good-sized bathrooms, though some
have little natural light.

Casa Grande   MEXICAN, INTERNATIONAL **$$**
(Jardín Juárez; mains M$75-180; ⊘7:30am-10pm
Tue-Sun; 🔊) The choice eatery in town serves
a mix of local specialties and other dishes in
a covered courtyard, with ceiling fans and
hanging plants. The seafood is good, and
for local flavor try the *garnachas juchitecas*
(small corn tortillas with pork and cheese

toppings) as a starter. Enter under the Cin-
ema Casa Grande sign.

In the evening, plenty of economical, open-
air *comedores* set up tables along the north
side of Jardín Juárez.

ℹ Getting There & Around

The main **bus station** (Prolongación 16 de
Septiembre), used by deluxe, 1st-class and 2nd-
class services of the ADO/OCC group, is 100m
south of Hwy 190 on the northern edge of town.
Many buses depart inconveniently between
11pm and 7am. 'Terminal-Centro' buses run
between the bus station and the central Jardín
Juárez. A taxi costs M$25.

Second-class Istmeños buses to Tehuantepec
(M$20, 30 minutes) leave at least every 30
minutes during daylight, from the next corner
south from the main terminal.

Central Pacific Coast

Includes »

Best Places to Eat

» Las Hamacas del Mayor (p531)

» Zihuatanejo Cooking School (p545)

» Molika (p491)

» Red Cabbage Café (p515)

» Rollie's (p506)

Best Places to Stay

» Vallarta Sun Hostel (p511)

» Quinta Erika (p549)

» Casa del Encanto (p548)

» Mar de Jade (p504)

» Hotel Hacienda Flamingos (p500)

Why Go?

Those gigantic aquamarine waves keep rolling in, as they have forever along Mexico's central Pacific coast. It's the primal rhythm that backs any visit to this land of stunning beaches and giant sunsets.

Sit yourself down in the sand and spy humpback whales breaching on the horizon, pelicans flying in formation or a pod of dolphins rising from the waves. Surf the world-class breaks, kayak through mangrove-fringed lagoons, trade stories with expatriates in a ramshackle fishing village, or hang onto the back of a pickup packed with locals roaring inland toward the blue silhouette of the lofty Sierra Madre. Or switch into resort mode, margarita in hand and salsa blaring on the poolside sound system, at a world-class luxury hotel.

Whether you're here for a week of cushy beachfront decadence, or months of down-to-earth exploration on the cheap, the good life on Mexico's central Pacific coast means finding your own rhythm.

When to Go
Puerto Vallarta

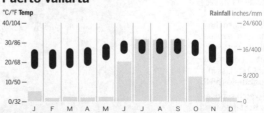

Feb Perfect beach weather reigns everywhere, and Carnaval brings exuberant new life to Mazatlán's historic center.

Jun–Aug Surf's up and prices are down at Pacific Mexico's prime surfing destinations.

Nov–Dec Puerto Vallarta celebrates everything from sportfishing to mariachis, gay pride to the Virgin of Guadalupe.

Central Pacific Coast Highlights

1 Take the pulse of the new **Old Mazatlán** (p490) in its gorgeously renovated historic center

2 Stroll streets pungent with drying shrimp in **Mexcaltitán** (p496), thought by some to be the Aztecs' ancestral homeland

3 People-watch and promenade on the beautiful beachfront *malecón* (oceanfront promenade) in **Puerto Vallarta** (p508)

4 Surf the aggressive barrel swells in **Boca de Pascuales** (p531)

5 Thrill at the fearless finesse of **La Quebrada Clavadistas** (cliff divers, p552) in Acapulco

6 Soak up the mellow party vibe along the surfer-happy sands and the cafe-encircled plaza in **Sayulita** (p505)

7 Shop for ingredients you've never heard of and learn to make the perfect *chile relleno* (chili stuffed with meat or cheese) at a cooking class in **Zihuatanejo** (p545)

8 Watch sunrise over the lagoon and sunset over the Pacific in **Pie de la Cuesta** (p549)

History

Archaeologists view pre-Hispanic Mexico's Pacific coast as a unified region, defined by its tradition of shaft or chamber tombs (underground burial chambers at the base of a deep shaft). The ceremonial centers around the tombs suggest a fairly developed spiritual and religious life.

The Spanish arrived in Mexico in 1519 and soon traveled to Acapulco, Zihuatanejo, Puerto Vallarta and Manzanillo. In 1564 conquistador Miguel López de Legazpi and Father André de Urdaneta first sailed from Barra de Navidad to the Philippines and soon after claimed the area for Spain. Acapulco quickly became an established port link in the trade route between Asia and Europe.

It was not until the middle of the 1950s that tourism really hit the coast, starting in Acapulco and Mazatlán, with Puerto Vallarta soon to follow. In recent years more and more foreigners have bought and developed land along the coast, most noticeably around Puerto Vallarta.

❶ Getting There & Away

There are plenty of direct international flights from the US and Canada to Puerto Vallarta, Mazatlán and Zihuatanejo, with a few to Manzanillo and Acapulco. For those traveling by car, the toll roads between the US border and Tepic make for easy sailing, but they're not cheap. As with elsewhere in Mexico, the free roads oscillate between smooth pavement and shock-busting potholes. High-quality bus services connect the resort centers to inland Mexico.

Away from the resorts, coastal Hwy 200 has had an up-and-down safety record, and you'll see convoys of military trucks patrolling the area, especially in the states of Nayarit, Michoacán and Guerrero, which still have a reputation for being unsafe at night. While this may feel unsettling to tourists, many Mexicans will tell you that the increased army presence makes them feel more secure.

❶ Getting Around

Bus travel in this region is easy and surprisingly comfortable. Second-class buses serve nearly every community, large or small, while nicer buses – with air-con, comfortable seats, cleanish bathrooms, TVs and other classy comforts – serve bigger towns.

If you're driving, note that nearly everything on coastal Hwy 200 – service stations, stores, tire shops – closes around sundown.

Mazatlán

☑669 / POP 380,000

Having outgrown its image as a chintzy mid-20th-century resort town, today's Mazatlán is one of Mexico's most alluring and inviting beach destinations. Over the past decade, the 'Pearl of the Pacific' has breathed new life into its historic center, and the ongoing renewal program continues to bear fruit. The result is something truly unique: a historic city with a resplendent colonial district only a short walk from a 20km-long crescent of sandy beach.

To take the pulse of Mazatlán, don't linger too long in the Zona Dorada (Golden Zone), Mazatlán's traditional tourist playground. There you'll find knickknack shops, pack-'em-in restaurants and resort hotels lined up like dominoes, but few surprises. Instead head straight for the city's gorgeous *pueblo viejo* (old town). Here, against a backdrop of cobbled streets, crumbling edifices and an ever-increasing number of newly restored gems, you'll find a cultural renaissance under way. Catch a performance at the wonderful refurbished Teatro Ángela Peralta and then a late-night bite at the atmospheric Plazuela Machado. Step into one of Mazatlán's excellent small museums or go treasure hunting in one of the many new small boutiques. One big attraction is free for all – the daily spectacle of rocky islands silhouetted against the tropical sunset as the fiery red fades into the sea and another starry night begins.

Old Mazatlán, the city center, is near the southern end of a peninsula, bounded by the Pacific Ocean on the west and the Bahía Dársena channel on the east. The center of the city is the cathedral, on Plaza Principal, which is surrounded by a rectangular street grid. At the southern tip of the peninsula, El Faro (The Lighthouse) stands on a rocky prominence, overlooking Mazatlán's sportfishing fleet and the Baja Ferries terminal.

The beachside boulevard changes names frequently as it runs along the Pacific side of the peninsula north from Playa Olas Altas. It heads around some rocky outcrops, and around the wide arc of Playa Norte to the Zona Dorada, a concentration of hotels, bars and businesses catering mainly to package tourists. Further north are more hotels, two marinas (Marina El Cid and Marina Mazatlán) and some time-share condominium developments.

Greater Mazatlán

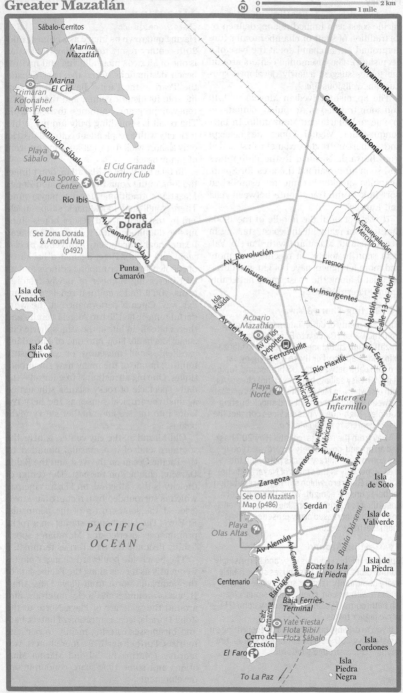

0 — 2 km
0 — 1 mile

Sábalo-Cerritos

Marina Mazatlán

Libramiento

Marina El Cid

Trimaran Kolonahe/ Aries Fleet

Carretera Internacional

Av Camarón Sábalo

Playa Sábalo

El Cid Granada Country Club

Aqua Sports Center

Río Ibis

Zona Dorada

Av Camarón Sábalo

Av Circunvalación Mercurio

See Zona Dorada & Around Map (p492)

Av Revolución

Fresnos

Punta Camarón

Av Av Insurgentes

Av Insurgentes

Isla de Venados

Isla Asada

Av del Mar

Acuario Mazatlán

Agustín Melgar

Calle 13 de Abril

Isla de Chivos

Av de los Deportes

Ferrusquilla

Río Piaxtla

Circ Estero Ote

Playa Norte

Av Ejército Mexicano

Estero el Infiernillo

Carrasco

Av Ejército Mexicano

Av Nájera

Isla de Soto

PACIFIC OCEAN

Zaragoza

Serdán

Caliz Gabriel Leyva

Isla de Valverde

See Old Mazatlán Map (p486)

Playa Olas Altas

Av Alemán

Bahía Dársena

Isla de la Piedra

Centenario

Av Canaval

Boats to Isla de la Piedra

Av Barragán

Baja Ferries Terminal

Catz Camarena

Yate Fiesta/ Flota Bibi/ Flota Sábalo

Isla Cordones

Cerro del Crestón

El Faro

Isla Piedra Negra

To La Paz

History

In pre-Hispanic times Mazatlán (which means 'Place of Deer' in the Náhuatl language) was populated by Totorames, who lived by hunting, gathering, fishing and growing crops. 'Old' Mazatlán, the traditional town center, dates from the 19th century. Tourists started coming in the 1930s, and in the 1950s some hotels appeared along Playa Olas Altas, Mazatlán's first tourist beach. From the 1970s onward, a long strip of hotels and tourist facilities spread north along the coast. More significantly, in the late 1980s restoration efforts began on key downtown buildings, including the theater and other stately edifices facing Plazuela Machado. By 2005 the picturesque plaza had been transformed, and a year later work was concluded on the boardwalk and monuments of Avenida Olas Altas.

◎ Sights

Old Mazatlán   NEIGHBORHOOD

The old town is a forward-thinking place rooted firmly in the past. At its center is the soaring 19th-century **cathedral** (Map p486; cnr Juárez & Calle 21 de Marzo) with its high yellow twin towers and a dramatic interior. Two blocks north, on Juárez and Valle, is the vibrant local **centro mercado** (central market; Map p486), full of clothes, housewares, produce, juice stands and shoppers.

A short southwesterly walk will bring you to the corner of Avenida Carnaval and Constitución, where you'll find the tree-lined **Plazuela Machado**. The plaza and surrounding streets are abuzz with art galleries, cafes and restaurants.

The center of attention is the **Teatro Ángela Peralta** (Map p486), half a block south of the plaza. Constructed between 1869 and 1874, the 1366-seat theater was a thriving center of local cultural life for nearly a century, first as an opera house, then as a cinema. Abandoned in 1964, and battered by Hurricane Olivia in 1975, it fell into decay and was slated for demolition by the city government before a dedicated group of local citizens came to its rescue in the late 1980s. Declared a national heritage site in 1990 and reopened to the public in 1992, the three-level interior has been restored to its former splendor, and all kinds of cultural events are again staged here, including the annual Festival Cultural Mazatlán (see p494).

West of the center is **Playa Olas Altas** (Map p486), a small beach in a cove. The breezy seafront road, Paseo Olas Altas, strongly evokes 1950s-era Mazatlán, with a couple of faded relic hotels.

Nearby is the platform from which the **clavadistas** (cliff divers; Map p486) cast their bodies into the treacherous ocean swells for your enjoyment. Tip accordingly. You're most likely to see the divers perform around lunchtime on Saturday and Sunday (they won't risk their necks until a crowd has assembled).

At the peninsula's southern end, a prominent rocky outcrop is the base for **El Faro** (Map p484), which is 135m above sea level and said to be the second-highest lighthouse in the world (after the one in Gibraltar). You can climb up here for a spectacular view of the city and coast.

Museums   MUSEUM

The small but absorbing **Museo Arqueológico** (Map p486; Sixto Osuna 76; admission M$31, Sun free; ◎9am-5pm Tue-Fri, 9am-3pm Sat & Sun) displays pre-Hispanic archaeological finds accompanied by fascinating wall texts in Spanish and English.

FREE **Museo de Arte** (Map p486; cnr Sixto Osuna & Carranza; ◎10am-2pm & 4-6pm Mon-Sat), opposite, is a small museum which makes a convincing case for the vitality and innovation of contemporary Mexican art with changing exhibitions of digital works, sculpture, prints and paintings.

Also worth a peek is the **Casa Machado** (Map p486; Constitución 77; adult/student M$20/10; ◎10am-6pm), a restored 19th-century house filled with antique French and Austrian furniture, Carnaval costumes, historic photos and other items. Its 2nd-floor terrace affords a panoramic view over Plazuela Machado.

Beaches   BEACH

With over 16km of beaches, it's easy to find a stretch of sand to call your own. The following beaches are listed in geographic order, from south to north.

In Old Mazatlán, the crescent-shaped **Playa Olas Altas** (Map p486) is where tourism first flourished in the 1950s, although the pebbly beach is not ideal for swimming.

Flanked by a broad *malecón* popular with joggers and strollers, the golden sands of **Playa Norte** (Map p484) begin just north of Old Mazatlán. The beach arcs toward **Punta Camarón** (Map p484), a rocky point

Old Mazatlán

Old Mazatlán

dominated by the conspicuous castlelike Fiesta Land nightclub complex.

The most luxurious hotels face the fine, uncrowded Playa Las Gaviotas (Map p492) and Playa Sábalo (Map p484), the latter extending north of the Zona Dorada. Sheltered by picturesque islands, here the waters are generally calm and ideal for swimming and water sports. Further north, past Marina El Cid (Map p484) and the ever-evolving Marina Mazatlán (Map p484), are Playa Brujas (Witch Beach), a once-serene beach that has seen a flood of high-rise development in recent years, and Playa Cerritos. Both have a smattering of excellent seafood restaurants and are surfing destinations. To reach these northern beaches, catch a 'Cerritos Juárez' bus along Avenida Camarón Sábalo in the Zona Dorada.

Islands   ISLAND

Resembling breaching whales in silhouette, the three photogenic land masses jutting from the sea offshore of the Zona Dorada are Mazatlán's signature islands. With secluded beaches and limpid waters ideal for snorkeling – and great multitudes of seals and marine birds – they provide an ideal day-trip destination. On the left is Isla de Chivos (Goat Island); Isla de Pájaros (Bird Island) is on the right. Most visited is the one in the middle, Isla de Venados (Deer Island). The islands are part of a wildlife refuge designated to help protect the local birds and marine fauna. For information on boat tours to the island, see p488.

Isla de la Piedra

Escape artists love Isla de la Piedra (Stone Island; Map p484), located southeast of Old Mazatlán, for its beautiful, long sandy beach bordered by coconut groves. Surfers come for the waves, and on Sunday afternoons its simple *palapa* (thatched-roof shelter) restaurants draw Mexican families. Most other times you'll have the beach to yourself.

It's a simple matter to get to Isla de Piedra on your own. Take a water taxi (round trip M$20, every 10 minutes from 7am to 6pm) from the Playa Sur *embarcadero* (boat dock) near the Baja Ferries terminal. You'll be dropped off at a jetty just a short walk from the Isla de la Piedra beach. 'Playa Sur' buses leave for the *embarcadero* from the corner of Serdán and Escobedo, two blocks southeast of Plaza Principal in Old Mazatlán.

🏃 Activities

Surfing

With a season lasting from late March through November, Mazatlán boasts several noteworthy surfing sites. You can rent equipment or take lessons from Mazatlán Surf Center (Map p492; ☎913-18-21; www.mazatlansurfcenter.com; Av Playa Gaviotas 210; wetsuit/bodyboard/surfboard rental per day US$10/15/25, 2hr lesson incl hotel pickup US$65).

Other Water Sports

The Aqua Sports Center (Map p484; www.aquasportscenter.com; El Cid Mega Resort, Av Camarón Sábalo s/n) is the place to go for other water sports, including scuba diving (one-/two-tank dive US$70/100), banana-boat rides (per person US$8), waterskiing (per two people US$135) and parasailing (US$40). It also rents out sailboats (per hour US$50), kayaks (per day single/double US$35/50), surfboards (US$40) and snorkeling equipment (per day US$15). Watersports equipment can also be hired from the beaches of most other large beachfront hotels.

Horseback Riding

If you dream of cantering beside the sea, check out Ginger's Bi-Lingual Horses (☎988-12-54; www.mazinfo.com/gingershorses; Playa Bruja; 1hr tour US$30; ☉10am, 11:30am, 1pm & 2:30pm Mon-Sat). Hour-long rides lead through coconut plantations to the sands of Playa Bruja. Take a 'Cerritos Juárez' bus from Zona Dorada or a taxi to Playa Bruja.

Sportfishing

Handily located at the confluence of the Sea of Cortez and the Pacific Ocean, Mazatlán is world famous for its sportfishing – especially for marlin, swordfish, sailfish, tuna and *dorado* (dolphinfish). It can be an expensive activity (US$350 to US$675 per boat per day, for boats ranging in size from 8m to 11m with four to nine people fishing); small-game fishing from a 7m *super panga* (fiberglass skiff) is less expensive (around US$275 per day with up to four people fishing).

The spiffiest boats leave from Marina El Cid (Map p484) and Marina Mazatlán; for lower prices, try the operators near El Faro on Calz Camarena or negotiate directly with one of the independent fishermen offering half-day *panga* trips along Paseo Claussen near Playa Norte.

Among the recommended operators there is Aries Fleet (Map p484; ☎916-34-68;

MAZATLÁN FOR CHILDREN

Kids love this town, if only for the many opportunities to get wet.

One economical place to take a dip is at the small, all-natural **saltwater pool** (Map p486) on Playa Olas Altas. Kids and their adults splash around as waves crash over the pool's seaward edge.

Kids go hog wild on the waterslides and wave pool at **MazAgua** (www.mazagua.com, in Spanish; Entronque Habal-Cerritos s/n; admission M$150; ⊙10am-5pm Fri-Sun), a family water park about 5km north of Marina Mazatlán. Take the 'Cerritos-Juárez' bus from anywhere along the coastal road.

One of Mexico's largest aquariums, **Acuario Mazatlán** (Map p484; www.acuariomazatlan.gob.mx; Av de los Deportes 111; adult/child M$85/60; ⊙8am-6pm) has 52 tanks containing 250 freshwater and saltwater species. Sea-lion, diving and bird shows are each presented three times daily.

www.elcid.com/sporting_activities/aries_fleet.cfm; Marina El Cid), which supports catch-and-release practices; **Flota Bibi** (Map p484; ☎913-10-60; www.bibifleet.com; Calz Camarena s/n), which operates four boats accommodating four to eight people each, and gives steep discounts in the low season; and **Flota Sábalo** (Map p484; ☎981-27-61; Calz Camarena s/n), which offers a wide variety of reasonably priced trips in boats holding two to eight people.

Golf

Mazatlán has two renowned championship golf courses. The most striking is the **Estrella del Mar Golf Club** (☎800-727-46-53; www.estrelladelmar.com; green fees 9/18 holes US$75/110), just south of the airport along the coast. **El Cid Granada Country Club** (Map p484; ☎989-69-69; cclub@elcid.com.mx; Av Camarón Sábalo; 9/18 holes US$60/80) offers a challenging alternative north of the Zona Dorada.

☞ Tours

⌇Onca Explorations   ECOTOUR
(☎913-40-50; www.oncaexplorations.com) Wildlife observation and conservation are the focus of these ecotours, led by marine ecolo-

gist Oscar Guzón. Most popular are his Whale Quest (adult/child US$85/65, December to March) and Dolphin Quest (per person US$65, year-round) tours, which offer excellent opportunities to observe marine mammals up close. Other options include an excursion to Las Labradas (US$60), site of the only beachside petroglyphs in the Americas, and custom bird-watching tours to Santa María Bay, Isla Isabel National Park and the Chara Pinta Tufted Jay Preserve.

Trimaran Kolonahe   BOAT TOUR
(Map p484; ☎916-34-68; Marina El Cid; www.elcid.com/marinas/marina_tour_mazatlan.cfm) The speedy *Trimaran Kolonahe* sets sail for Isla de Venados Tuesday through Sunday at 9:30am. The five-hour cruise costs US$55, including use of kayaks, snorkeling equipment, lunch and drinks. There's also a Thursday sunset cruise for US$40.

King David   BOAT TOUR
(Map p492; ☎914-14-44; www.kingdavid.com.mx; Camarón Sábalo 333) Offers a variety of boat tours, including a five-hour bird-watching tour (adult/child including lunch US$50/35) into the mangrove-fringed waterways of the Isla de Piedra wildlife refuge.

Yate Fiesta   BOAT TOUR
(Map p484; ☎982-31-30; www.yatefiesta.com; Calz Camarena 7) Offers 2½-hour sightseeing tours (M$250) and sunset cruises (including open bar M$300), as well as two-hour cruises to Isla de la Piedra (including lunch and open bar M$350).

Kelly's Bicycle Shop & Tours   CYCLING
(☎914-11-87; kellysbikeshop@hotmail.com; Av Canseco 6020; ⊙10am-2pm & 4:30-8pm Mon-Sat) Leads wild and woolly one- to four-hour mountain-bike tours (US$30) into the hills, over scenic paved routes and down challenging single-track trails.

Vista Tours   TOUR
(Map p492; ☎986-86-10; www.vistatours.com.mx; Av Camarón Sábalo 51) Offers a variety of tours in and around Mazatlán, including a colonial tour (US$55) to the foothill towns of Concordia and Copala, and a tequila-factory tour (US$40).

★ Festivals & Events

Carnaval   CARNIVAL
Mazatlán has Mexico's most flamboyant Carnaval celebrations. For the week leading up to Ash Wednesday, the town goes on a non-

DON'T MISS

SIX THINGS NOT TO MISS IN MAZATLÁN

Mazatlán has a split personality. Opportunities for classic beachside fun-in-the-sun are everywhere, but the downtown area also provides an unexpected counterpoint with its artsy cultural life. So mix it up a little – ballet and *ballenas* (whales), sun worship and gallery walks... Who says you can't have it all?

» Take in an evening performance at the beautifully restored **Teatro Ángela Peralta** (p494).

» Rub elbows with local artists while gallery-hopping on Old Mazatlán's **First Friday Artwalk** (p489).

» Browse the artisans' market or dine alfresco on the Pacific Coast's prettiest square, **Plazuela Machado** (p485).

» Accompany professional biologists on a **whale- or dolphin-watching expedition** (p488).

» Settle in at a beachside bar and watch the fiery sunset over Mazatlán's photogenic **offshore islands** (p487).

» Try to catch a fish bigger than yourself, and see why Mazatlán ranks high among the Pacific's sportfishing capitals on a **fishing tour** (p487).

stop partying spree. Reserve a hotel room in advance.

Festival Cultural Mazatlán   ARTS
Culture vultures should plan to visit in November and December for this arts and performance festival centered on the Teatro Peralta.

First Friday Artwalk   ARTS
Get a taste of Mazatlán's arts scene through this art walk (www.artwalkmazatlan.com), held on the first Friday of each month from November through May. Between 3pm and 8pm, studios and galleries open their doors to the public.

**Día de Nuestra
Señora de Guadalupe**   RELIGIOUS
The day of the Virgen de Guadalupe is celebrated on December 12 at the cathedral. Children come in colorful costumes.

🛏 Sleeping

Old Mazatlán Inn   APARTMENT $$
(Map p486; ☑981-43-61, cell phone 669-1220909; www.oldmazatlaninn.com; Pedregoso 18; studio/1-/2-bedroom apt M$875/1000/1500; ✴🛜🛏) Perched on a hillside downtown, this multi-tiered brick structure is a dynamite option, especially for longer stays. A labyrinth of comfy studios and one- and two-bedroom apartments – all with wi-fi, well-equipped kitchenettes and individual water heaters – overlooks a central pool and bar area with lounge chairs, gas and charcoal grills and a

shared 'party kitchen.' The roof terrace has a bird's-eye view of the city and beaches. Book well in advance – snowbirds pack the place from December through April. Rates are slashed in half during the off-season.

Casa de Leyendas   B&B $$$
(Map p486; ☑981-61-80; www.casadeleyendas.com; Carranza 4; r incl breakfast US$89-125; ⊜✴@🛜🛏) Affable expatriates Glenn and Sharon Sorrie play host to one of Old Mazatlán's homiest B&Bs. Six comfy rooms, all with coffeemakers, fridges, hair dryers, safes, wi-fi and other nice touches occupy two floors of a sprawling old house near Plazuela Machado and Playa Olas Altas. Several inviting common areas promote socializing, including a library with plush armchairs and guest computer; a well-stocked, reasonably priced bar; a central 'cocktail pool' with Jacuzzi jets; a fully equipped guest kitchen; and two spacious upstairs patios, one with a partial ocean view. The included full breakfast is icing on the cake.

Playa Mazatlán   HOTEL $$$
(Map p492; ☑989-05-55; www.hotelplayamazatlan.com; Av Playa Gaviotas 202; r US$119-138, ste US$173-211; 🅿⊜✴@🛜🛏) This large resort – the first built in the Zona Dorada – maintains impeccable standards. Half of the rooms have ocean views, and all come equipped with satellite TV, private terrace and the thoughtful touches that mark a classy operation. Manicured tropical gardens and a breezy oceanside restaurant

make this Mazatlán's most stylish large hotel.

El Cid Mega Resort
RESORT $$$

(off Map p492; ☑913-33-33; www.elcid.com; Av Camarón Sábalo s/n; r/ste US$187/213, all-inclusive r/ste US$384/410; P❄❁@🛜❄🚲) A behemoth decked out in 1980s-style luxury. This 1068-room, 2.9-sq-km mini city has it all: seven pools, a water-sports center, shops, restaurants, travel agencies, kids' areas, gyms and more. Online specials often cut the official price in half.

Hotel La Siesta
HOTEL $$

(Map p486; ☑981-26-40; www.lasiesta.com.mx; Paseo Olas Altas 11; interior/ocean-view r M$475/595; ❁@🛜❄) Sitting pretty above Playa Olas Altas, La Siesta is a good option if you can snag one of the choice sea-view rooms. Interior rooms, while spacious and tidy, are less appealing. The pleasant central courtyard and attached restaurant are good places to meet other travelers. Check online for discounts.

Marley Motel
MOTEL $$

(Map p492; ☑913-55-33; travelbymexico.com/sina/marley; Av Playa Gaviotas 226; 1-/2-bedroom apt M$1020/1220; P❁🛜❄) This small Zona Dorada motel offers eight comfortable seafront apartments with well-equipped kitchens, a pool and – best of all – privileged beach access.

Hotel Belmar
HOTEL $

(Map p486; ☑985-11-12; www.hotelbelmar.com.mx, in Spanish; Paseo Olas Altas 166; interior/ocean-view r M$450/550; P❁🛜❄) This totally faded 1950s classic harkens back to Mazatlán's swanky early days as a tourist mecca. The more than 200 rooms run the gamut from threadbare and dingy to perfectly acceptable. The best upstairs rooms – including the one John Wayne favored – have air-con and sea-view balconies with salty breezes and gratifying views over Playa Olas Altas.

Casa Lucila
BOUTIQUE HOTEL $$$

(off Map p486; ☑982-11-00; www.casalucila.com; Paseo Olas Altas 16; r US$125-295; ❁🛜❄) This boutique hotel in a lavishly restored waterfront home dazzles guests with huge walk-in closets and showers, ultracomfy memory foam beds, Bose CD players, flat-screen TVs, European-style bathroom fixtures and state-of-the-art Italian doors and windows. Six of the eight rooms have private Jacuzzis. The spa, infinity pool and in-house restaurant add to the sophisticated appeal.

Hotel Machado
HOTEL $$$

(Map p486; ☑669-27-30; www.hotelmachado.com; Sixto Osuna 510A; d incl breakfast M$1100-1400; ❁@🛜) The only hotel on gorgeous Plazuela Machado is a mixed bag. Despite the funky charm of its checkerboard floors and wrought-iron beds, the rather basic rooms don't live up to the promise of the lovely facade. The hotel's best feature is the high-ceilinged 2nd-floor *salón social* (sitting room), a delightful place to read or simply gaze out over the square.

Azteca Inn
HOTEL $$

(Map p492; ☑913-46-55; www.aztecainn.com.mx; Av Playa Gaviotas 307; r M$800; P❁@🛜❄) Close to the beach and smack-dab in the middle of the Zona Dorada, the Azteca's 74 rooms lack personality but offer firm mattresses and room service from the onsite restaurant.

Apartamentos Fiesta
APARTMENT $$

(Map p492; ☑913-53-55; www.mazatlanapartments.com; Río Ibis 502; studio/1-/2-bedroom apt from US$36/52/64; P❁🛜) Tucked down an alleyway four blocks inland from Playa Las Gaviotas, these 13 apartments of different size and layout all have kitchens and pleasing decor and surround a peaceful tropical garden.

Mar Rosa Trailer & RV Park
TRAILER PARK $

(off Map p492; ☑913-61-87; www.pacificpearl.com/marrosa; Av Camarón Sábalo 702; RV sites M$240-480) Shadeless and not especially attractive for tent camping, this place still gets the thumbs-up for its excellent location overlooking Playa Sábalo, just north of Zona Dorada.

✖ Eating

With all those fishing and shrimping boats heading out to sea every morning, it's no wonder that Mazatlán is famous for fresh seafood. Treat yourself to *pescado zarandeado* – a delicious charcoal-broiled fish stuffed with onion, tomatoes, peppers and spices. A whole kilo, feeding two people well, usually costs around M$150.

OLD MAZATLÁN

Pretty Plazuela Machado is completely surrounded by atmospheric eateries. It's sublime in the evening when music plays, kids frolic and the plaza is softly lit to create a very romantic ambience. Take a five-minute stroll around the perimeter and see what catches your fancy.

TOP CHOICE Molika   BAKERY, SANDWICHES **$$**

(Map p486; Domínguez 1503; mains M$60-120; ☺9am-11pm Mon-Sat) Exquisite sandwiches, salads and homemade breads make this Old Mazatlán's hottest new lunch and dinner hangout. The high-ceilinged old building, redone with clean modern lines and designer colors, is also a great place to grab a morning pastry, including the fabulous M$5 madeleines, bursting with orange flavor.

Topolo   MEXICAN **$$$**

(Map p486; ☎cell phone 669-1360660; www.topolomaz.com; Constitución 629; mains M$130-220; ☺1-11pm Mon-Sat, 4-11pm Sun) For a romantic dinner, step into the softly lit courtyard at this Mexican fusion restaurant and wine bar in a historic building near Plazuela Machado. Waiters prepare salsa fresh at your table while the chefs cook up seafood specialties such as tequila shrimp or fish in lime and cilantro sauce.

La Cueva del León   MEXICAN **$$**

(Map p486; Paseo Olas Altas 166; mains M$60-120; ☺8am-10pm) Bargain prices keep diners happy at this eatery with indoor-outdoor seating and views of the ocean across the street at Playa Olas Altas. Get a shrimp-stuffed chili with rice, beans and tortillas for only M$65, or splurge on the house special, *camarones a la cueva* (brandy-seared shrimp with peppers and mushrooms).

Panamá   BAKERY, MEXICAN **$$**

(Map p486; www.panama.com.mx, in Spanish; cnr Carrizales & Juárez; mains M$80-135; ☺7am-10:30pm) With a zillion different breakfast combos, ranging from North American standards to Mexican treats such as shredded smoked marlin and sweet corn *tamales* (masa mixed with lard, stuffed with stewed meat, fish or vegetables, wrapped and steamed), this old-fashioned bakery and diner is a great place to start the day (though you may also want to pop in for a midafternoon slice of cake).

Mariscos La Puntilla   SEAFOOD, MEXICAN **$$**

(www.lapuntilla.com.mx, in Spanish; Flota Playa Sur s/n; mains M$95-137; ☺8am-7pm) Popular with Mexican families for its Saturday and Sunday breakfast buffet (M$99), this open-air eatery has a relaxed atmosphere and fantastic *pescado zarandeado*. It's near the Isla de la Piedra ferries, on a small point with a view across the water.

La Tramoya   MEXICAN **$$$**

(Map p486; Constitución 509; mains M$120-180; ☺11am-1am) Hearty Mexican meat and seafood dishes are set out on spacious sidewalk tables on Mazatlán's loveliest square. Unconventional choices include *filete azteca* – a steak stuffed with *huitlacoche* (corn fungus).

Super Cocina d'Paulina   MEXICAN **$**

(Map p486; Sixto Osuna 61; mains M$60-90; ☺8:30am-9pm Mon-Sat, 11am-6pm Sun) This family-run place specializes in down-to-earth home cooking, overseen by a local chef with many years' experience in Mazatlán hotels. Daily specials (M$60) include rice, beans, guacamole and *agua fresca* (chilled fruit drink).

Puerto Viejo   SEAFOOD **$$**

(Map p486; Paseo Olas Altas 25; mains M$50-130; ☺10am-11pm) A good-time mix of locals and expats gathers here for sunset drinks and superfresh seafood sent straight from the port. Daily specials (M$50) include swordfish, marlin soup and shrimp tacos.

Machado Fish Taco   MEXICAN **$**

(Map p486; Sixto Osuna 34; tacos M$18, mains from M$49; ☺8am-11pm) For an inexpensive snack with a priceless view of the plaza, order a few of Machado's delicious fish or shrimp tacos, slather on some slaw and salsa, and dig in!

Helarte Sano   ICE CREAM **$**

(Map p486; Carnaval 1129; popsicles M$3-15, ice cream M$15-35; ☺9am-9pm Mon-Fri, 10am-9pm Sat, 11am-8pm Sun) Makes over three dozen flavors of *paletas* (ice lollies), sherbets and Mexican-inspired gelato, including unconventional fruit flavors (lemon-rosemary, kumquat, avocado), diabetic-friendly sugar-free offerings, and small ice lollies (M$3) for kids.

Nieves de Garrafa de con Medrano   ICE CREAM **$**

(Map p486; cnr Flores & Calle 5 de Mayo; ice cream M$20; ☺11am-9pm) A local tradition since 1938, this unpretentious family-run cart opposite Mazatlán's cathedral square dishes out delicious homemade ice cream to devoted crowds. Try the vanilla, prune or mandarin flavors.

ZONA DORADA & AROUND

Carlos & Lucía's   CUBAN, MEXICAN **$$**

(off Map p492; Av Camarón Sábalo 2000; mains M$90-200; ☺8:30am-10:30pm Mon-Sat) What

do you get when you combine the talents of a Mexican named Carlos and a Cuban-born chef named Lucía? A vibrant, colorful little restaurant serving specialties from both countries. Try the *plato Carlos y Lucía*: shrimp or fish cooked in brandy, accompanied by rice, veggies and plantains.

Pancho's Restaurant   MEXICAN $$

(Map p492; Av Playa Gaviotas 408; mains M$91-204; ⊙7am-11pm) Overlooking Playa Las Gaviotas, this is a good spot to catch the sunset, slurp a monster margarita or devour a huge seafood platter including lobster, shrimp, octopus, a whole red snapper and, for good measure, a pair of frog legs.

Casa Loma   INTERNATIONAL $$$

(Map p492; ☑913-53-98; www.restaurantcasaloma .com; Av Las Gaviotas 104; mains M$145-378; ⊙1:30-10:30pm) At this genteel eatery, enjoy roast duck *à l'orange* or poached fish *blanca rosa* (with shrimp, asparagus and

mushrooms), in the swanky dining room or outdoors by the burbling fountain.

Vittore Italian Grill   ITALIAN $$$

(Map p492; ☑986-24-24; vittore.com.mx; Av Playa Gaviotas 100; mains M$114-257; ⊙noon-midnight) This elegant spot with romantic patio seating features delicious calorie-rich pasta and memorable seafood and beef dishes.

Tomates Verdes   MEXICAN $

(Map p492; Laguna 42; mains M$40; ⊙8:30am-5pm Mon-Sat) Cozy and unpretentious, this breakfast and lunch spot serves dishes such as *pechuga rellena* (stuffed chicken breast) and flavorful soups such as *nopales con chipotle* (spicy cactus).

La Cocina de Ana   BUFFET $

(Map p492; Laguna 49; meals from M$35; ⊙noon-4pm Mon-Sat) This homey place offers well-prepared buffet lunch fare including marlin, meatball soup, *chiles rellenos* (chili stuffed with meat or cheese) and *pollo estofado*

Zona Dorada & Around

(stewed chicken). Everything is sold by the kilo, and the menu changes daily.

Pura Vida   MEXICAN $
(Map p492; Bugambilias 18; juices M$28-39, snacks, salads & sandwiches M$33-65; ⊗8am-10:30pm; ☞) Fresh juices, salads, Mexican snacks and vegetarian fare.

🍷 Drinking

EtniKafé   CAFE
(Map p486; Sixto Osuna 50; ⊗8am-7pm Mon-Sat) Adjacent to the Casa Etnika gallery, this little cafe brews a mean cappuccino.

La Tertulia   BAR
(Map p486; cnr Domínguez & Constitución 1406; ⊗3pm-1am Mon-Sat, 5pm-1am Sun) This lively spot, perfect for top-shelf tequila-sipping, is decorated exclusively with bullfighting posters and the stuffed heads of vanquished *toros* (bulls).

Pitypolski   PUB
(Map p486; es-es.facebook.com/pitypolskipub; cnr Constitución & Niños Héroes; ⊗5pm-2am) This atmospheric European-style pub serves a zillion different beers from dozens of countries; grab an official 'beer passport' and start tracking your progress through the list.

Jungle Juice   CANTINA
(Map p492; Av de las Garzas 101; ⊗8pm-2am Tue-Sun) This cantina-style place in the Zona Dorada offers exotic fruit drinks and a breezy nook upstairs. There's live music from Thursday through Sunday.

☆ Entertainment

What could be better than a day on a warm beach followed by a night in a town that really knows how to party? Choose from throbbing discos, a couple of thriving gay venues and a much-loved theater. For entertainment listings check *Pacific Pearl* (www.pacificpearl.com), available in hotel lobbies around town.

Inland from the Zona Dorada traffic circle on Avenida Buelna, Mazatlán's only bullring hosts *corrida de toros* (bullfights) on Sundays from mid-December to Easter.

Nightclubs

Mazatlán has earned its reputation as a nightlife destination with a great selection of high-energy dance clubs. Most charge covers in the M$100 to M$200 range; the price of admission generally includes a free drink. The scene starts percolating around 10pm and boils over after midnight. While some clubs close at 2am, several others remain lively until 5am.

TOP CHOICE Fiesta Land   CLUB
(off Map p492; ☎989-16-00; Av del Mar s/n) That ostentatious white castle on Punta Camarón at the south end of the Zona Dorada is the undisputed epicenter of Mazatlán's nightlife. Inside its walls are a half-dozen clubs, including several of the city's most popular dance spots: **Valentino's** draws a mixed crowd to three dance floors throbbing with hip-hop and Latin music; **Bora Bora** is popular for its open-air dance floor and lax policy on bar-top dancing; **Sumbawa Beach Club** is the perfect after-hours spot for dancing in the sand, lounging on an oversized mattress or cooling off in the pool; and **El Nivel** is a cantina-style bar that sometimes features *banda sinaloense*, a boisterous brass band unique to the state of Sinaloa.

Joe's Oyster Bar   DJ
(Map p492; www.joesoysterbar.com; Av Playa Gaviotas 100; ⊗11am-4am) This popular beachside bar with a never-ending two-for-one happy hour makes a scenic spot for snacks and sunset drinks. At nightfall it morphs into a DJ-fueled disco that goes ballistic after

11pm, when it's packed with college kids dancing on tables, chairs and each other.

Cinemas

Cinemas Gaviotas
CINEMA

(Map p492; www.cinemasgaviotas.com.mx, in Spanish; Av Camarón Sábalo 218; admission Thu-Tue M$25, Wed M$20) Six screens showing recent releases, including some in English.

Theater

TOP CHOICE Teatro Ángela Peralta
THEATER

(Map p486; ☎982-44-47, ext 103; www.culturamaz atlan.com; Av Carnaval 47) To feel the pulse of Mazatlán's burgeoning culture scene, a night at the Peralta is a must. Built in 1860, the theater was lovingly restored over five years to reopen in 1992. It has an intimate auditorium with three narrow, stacked balconies. Events of all kinds are presented – movies, concerts, opera, theater and more. A kiosk on the walkway out front announces current and upcoming events. The schedule is fullest in November and December during the Festival Cultural Mazatlán.

Gay Venues

Pepe Toro
GAY

(Map p492; www.pepetoro.com, in Spanish; Av de las Garzas 18; ☺11pm-5am Thu-Sun) This colorful club attracts a fun-loving, mostly gay crowd. On Saturday night there's a transvestite strip show at 1am.

Vitrolas Bar
GAY

(Map p486; www.vitrolasbar.com, in Spanish; Frias 1608; ☺7pm-2am Thu-Sun) This gracious gay bar in a beautifully restored building is romantically lit and, overall, more button-down than mesh muscle-shirt. It's also a popular spot for karaoke.

🛍 Shopping

The Zona Dorada is replete with tourist-oriented stores that sell clothes, jewelry, pottery and crafts.

Old Mazatlán's Centro Mercado (Central Market; Map p486) offers a classic Mexican market experience, complete with vegetable stands, spice dealers, food stalls and shops selling bargain-priced crafts.

If you're looking for something a little more artsy, head to Plazuela Machado, where artisans display their wares on the square at night and a growing selection of galleries and boutiques gives joy to browsers in the surrounding streets.

Casa Etnika
ARTS & CRAFTS

(Map p486; www.casaetnika.com.mx; Sixto Osuna 50; ☺9am-7pm Mon-Sat) Family-run Casa Etnika offers a small, tasteful inventory of unique objects from Mexico and elsewhere.

Nidart
CERAMICS, HANDICRAFTS

(Map p486; http://nidart.com; Libertad 45; ☺10am-6pm Mon-Fri, 10am-2pm Sat) Sells handmade leather masks and ceramics from its in-house studio and also represents numerous other local artisans.

ℹ Information

Banamex Old Mazatlán (Juárez s/n); Zona Dorada (Av Camarón Sábalo) One of many banks near Plaza Principal and in the Zona Dorada.

Clínica Balboa (☎916-79-33; Av Camarón Sábalo 4480; ☺24hr) Well-regarded, English-speaking walk-in medical clinic.

Cyber Robles (Flores 834; internet per hr M$10; ☺8am-8pm Mon-Sat) Dozens of computers, on the south side of Plaza Principal.

Emergency (☎060)

Fire (☎981-27-69)

Main post office (Map p486; Juárez s/n) On the east side of Plaza Principal.

Secretaría de Turismo (Map p486; ☎981-88-83/87; www.vivesinaloa.com; Paseo Olas Altas 1501; ☺8am-6pm Mon-Sat) Proffers information about Mazatlán and Sinaloa state.

Tourist police (☎914-84-44)

ℹ Getting There & Away

Air

Rafael Buelna International Airport (☎982-23-99; www.oma.aero/es/aeropuertos/mazat lan; Carretera Internacional al Sur s/n) is 27km southeast of the Zona Dorada. Carriers servicing the airport include the following:

Aeroméxico (www.aeromexico.com); Zona Dorada (☎914-11-11; Av Camarón Sábalo 310); Airport (☎982-34-44) Direct service to Guadalajara and Mexico City.

MagniCharters (☎55-1999-1611; www.magni charters.com.mx; Airport) Direct service to Monterrey.

VivaAerobus (☎55-4777-5050; www.vivaaero bus.com; Airport) Direct service to Mexico City and Monterrey.

Volaris (☎800-122-80-00; www.volaris.mx; Airport) Direct service to Tijuana.

Boat

Baja Ferries (off Map p486; www.bajaferries. com; seat adult/child one-way M$978/489; ☺ticket office 8am-4pm Mon-Fri, 8am-3pm Sat, 9am-3pm Sun), with a terminal at the southern end of town, operates ferries

BUSES FROM MAZATLÁN

DESTINATION	FARE (M$)	DURATION	FREQUENCY (DAILY)
Culiacán	152	2½hr	very frequent
Durango	320-476	7-8hr	7
Guadalajara	345-452	7-8hr	very frequent
Los Mochis	320-367	5-6½hr	hourly
Manzanillo	625-693	12-13hr	10:20pm
Mexicali	934-1076	24-25hr	frequent
Mexico City (Terminal Norte)	856-968	13-16hr	frequent
Monterrey	876-1166	14-16hr	2
Puerto Vallarta	400-420	7-8hr	6
Tepic	209-220	4-5hr	frequent
Tijuana	1050-1207	26-28hr	frequent

CENTRAL PACIFIC COAST TEACAPÁN

between Mazatlán and La Paz in Baja California Sur (actually to the port of Pichilingue, 23km from La Paz). The 16-hour ferry to Pichilingue departs at 4pm (you should be there with ticket in hand at 2pm) on Monday, Wednesday and Friday from the terminal. Strong winter winds may cause delays. See p723 for cabin and vehicle prices.

Bus

The full-service **Central de Autobuses** (main bus station; Map p484; Ferrusquilla s/n) is just off Avenida Ejército Mexicano, three blocks inland from the northern end of Playa Norte. All bus lines operate from separate halls in the main terminal.

Local buses to small towns nearby (such as Concordia, Copala and Rosario) operate from a smaller terminal, behind the main terminal.

Car & Motorcycle

Local all-inclusive rental rates begin at around M$600 per day during the high season. Online booking is often cheaper.

Alamo Airport (☑981-22-66); Zona Dorada (☑913-10-10; Av Camarón Sábalo 410)

Budget Airport (☑982-12-20); Zona Dorada (☑913-20-00; Av Camarón Sábalo 413)

Europcar Airport (☑954-81-15); Zona Dorada (☑913-33-68; Av Camarón Sábalo 357)

Hertz Airport (☑985-08-45); Zona Dorada (☑913-60-60; Av Camarón Sábalo 314)

❶ Getting Around

To/From the Airport

Taxis and *colectivos* (minibuses picking up and dropping off passengers along predetermined routes) operate from the airport to town (27km). Tickets (*colectivo*/taxi M$100/310) can be pur-

chased for both at a booth just outside the arrival hall. There is no public bus running between Mazatlán and the airport.

Bus

Local buses run from 6am to 10:30pm. Regular white buses cost M$6; air-con green buses cost M$9.50.

To get into the center of Mazatlán from the bus terminal, go to Avenida Ejército Mexicano and catch any bus going south. Alternatively, walk 300m from the bus station to the beach and take a Sábalo-Centro bus heading south to the center.

Major routes:

Route Playa Sur Travels south along Avenida Ejército Mexicano, near the bus station and through the city center, passing the market, then to the ferry terminal and El Faro.

Route Sábalo-Centro Travels from the Centro Mercado to Playa Norte via Juárez, then north on Avenida del Mar to the Zona Dorada and further north on Avenida Camarón Sábalo.

Taxi

Mazatlán has a special type of taxi called a *pulmonía*, a small open-air vehicle similar to a golf cart. There are also regular red-and-white and green-and-white taxis. Rates for rides within Mazatlán range from M$50 to M$100, depending on your bargaining skills, the time of day and whether or not there is a cruise ship in port.

Teacapán

695 / POP 4300

Surrounded by a rich mangrove ecosystem and several pristine beaches, this small fishing village at the tip of an isolated peninsula,

126km south of Mazatlán, is prime territory for nature buffs.

The surrounding estuaries are replete with egrets, ducks and herons. Local boatsmen offer day trips (M$750 for up to five people) into the mangrove swamps, including visits to local archaeological sites and the Islas de Pájaros, an epic bird-watching spot. Overnight excursions to Parque Nacional Isla Isabel can also be arranged from November to May (M$6000 for up to four people, including fishing and snorkeling gear). The latter trip offers excellent opportunities for whale- and seabird-watching; a recommended guide is **Victor Méndez** (✆951-22-24, cell phone 695-1085044; vmanuel mendez@hotmail.com).

The family-run **Restaurant-Hotel Señor Wayne** (✆954-56-95; r/cabaña M$250/300; ✵✿) has seven clean rooms, two *palapa*-roofed *cabañas* (cabins) and Teacapán's best restaurant (mains M$65 to M$150), serving big breakfasts, steaks and seafood.

Right next door, **Villas María Fernanda** (✆954-53-93; www.villasmariafernanda.com; d M$500-600, q M$750, house M$2000; ✹✵✿✿) is an attractive small hotel offering spacious, comfortable rooms, suites with kitchen, and a house for up to eight people. Kids love the cheerful pool with waterslide.

From Mazatlán, catch one of the frequent 2nd-class buses to Escuinapa (M$50, 1½ hours), then walk three blocks east (past Escuinapa's town hall and cathedral) to the square where Transportes Escuinapa buses depart hourly for Teacapán (M$30, one hour). By car, take Hwy 15 to Escuinapa (86km), then turn off on Hwy Y1-04 to Teacapán (40km).

Mexcaltitán

✎323 / POP 820

This ancient island village, settled some time around the year AD 500, is believed by some experts to be Aztlán, the ancestral homeland that the Aztecs left around AD 1091 to begin their generations-long migration to Tenochtitlán (modern Mexico City). Proponents point to the striking similarities between the cruciform design of Mexcaltitán's streets and the urban layout of early Tenochtitlán. A pre-Hispanic bas-relief in stone found in the area is also provided as evidence – it depicts a heron clutching a snake, an allusion to the sign the Aztecs hoped to find in the promised land.

These days Mexcaltitán is foremost a shrimping town. Men head out into the surrounding wetlands in the early evening in small boats, to return just before dawn with

---

WORTH A TRIP

SINALOA'S COLONIAL GEMS

Several small, picturesque colonial towns in the Sierra Madre foothills make pleasant day trips from Mazatlán.

Concordia, founded in 1565, has an 18th-century church with a baroque facade and elaborately decorated columns. The village is known for its manufacture of high-quality pottery and hand-carved furniture. It's about a 45-minute drive east of Mazatlán; head southeast on Hwy 15 for 20km to Villa Unión, turn inland on Hwy 40 (the highway to Durango) and go another 20km.

Also founded in 1565, **Copala**, 40km past Concordia on Hwy 40, was one of Mexico's first mining towns. It still has its colonial church (1748), colonial houses and cobblestoned streets. It's a 1½-hour drive from Mazatlán.

Rosario, 76km southeast of Mazatlán on Hwy 15, is another colonial mining town. It was founded in 1655 and its most famous feature is the towering gold-leaf altar in its church, the Nuestra Señora del Rosario. You can also visit the home of beloved songstress Lola Beltrán, whose long recording career made *ranchera* (Mexico's urban 'country music') popular in the mid-20th century.

In the mountains north of Mazatlán, **Cosalá** is a beautiful colonial mining village that dates from 1550. It has a 17th-century church, a mining museum in a colonial mansion on the plaza, and two simple but clean hotels. To get here, go north on Hwy 15 for 113km to the turnoff (opposite the turnoff for La Cruz de Alota on the coast) and then climb 45km into the mountains.

You can also take tours to any of these towns (see p488).

their nets bulging. All day long, shrimp are spread out to dry on any available surface in the town, making the prospect of an afternoon stroll a pungent, picturesque proposition.

Tourism has scarcely made a mark here. Mexcaltitán has one hotel, a couple of pleasant waterside restaurants and a small museum, making it a pleasant place to visit for a night.

◉ Sights & Activities

Museo Aztlán del Origen   MUSEUM
(admission M$5; ⊙9am-2pm & 4-7pm Tue-Sun) This small but enchanting museum, on the northern side of the plaza, was closed indefinitely for renovation at the time of research. Among the exhibits are many interesting ancient objects and a reproduction of a fascinating long scroll (the *Códice Ruturini*), telling the story of the Aztec peoples' travels, with notes in Spanish.

Boat Trips   BOAT TOUR
You can arrange boat trips on the lagoon for bird-watching, fishing and sightseeing – every family has one or more boats.

✵ Festivals & Events

Semana Santa   RELIGIOUS
Holy Week is celebrated in a big way here. On Good Friday a statue of Christ is put on a cross in the church, then taken down and carried through the streets.

Fiesta de San Pedro Apóstol   RELIGIOUS
During this raucous late June festival, which celebrates the patron saint of fishing, statues of St Peter and St Paul are taken out into the lagoon in decorated *lanchas* (fast, open outboard boats).

⊨ Sleeping & Eating

Don't leave town without trying the local specialty of *albóndigas de camarón* (battered and fried shrimp balls served with a savory broth) or perhaps a rich *jugo de camarón* (shrimp juice) or *paté de camarón*. The shrimp *tamales* sold in the morning from a wheelbarrow on the streets are another local culinary highlight.

Hotel Ruta Azteca   HOTEL $
(☑235-60-20; Venecia s/n; r per person M$100-175) The town's only hotel. Rooms are simple and marginally clean; ask for one out the back that has a view of the lagoon.

Restaurant Alberca   SEAFOOD $$
(mains M$60-120; ⊙7am-6pm) On the east shore, accessible by a rickety wooden walkway, Alberca has a great lagoon view and a menu completely devoted to shrimp.

Mariscos Kika   SEAFOOD $
(mains M$70-80; ⊙8am-6pm) For fish, shrimp and octopus cooked a dozen ways, hop a boat to this family-run place on a small island just across from Mexcaltitán's main dock.

❶ Getting There & Away

Catch a bus from San Blas (M$45, 1½ hours) or Tepic (M$40, 1½ hours) to the town of Santiago Ixcuintla, 7km west of Hwy 15 and about 70km northwest of Tepic. Once in Santiago, take a *colectivo* (M$25, 40 minutes, four daily) or taxi (M$150) to La Batanga, a small wharf where *lanchas* depart for Mexcaltitán. The arrival and departure times of the *lanchas* are coordinated with the *colectivo* schedule. The boat journey takes 15 minutes and costs M$10 per person. If you miss the *lancha*, you can hire a private one for M$40 per person between 8am and 7pm.

San Blas

☑323 / POP 10,000

The tranquil fishing village of San Blas, 70km northwest of Tepic, has been slated by government tourism officials to become a big resort town for decades. That's not to say it's changed much. It's still the peaceful, drowsy backwater it's always been, and therein lies its charm. Visitors come to enjoy isolated beaches, fine surfing, abundant birdlife, and tropical jungles reached by riverboats, much as they always have. A smattering of entertaining bars and restaurants and an amiable beach scene add to the mix, making for an enjoyable stay.

San Blas was an important Spanish port from the late 16th century to the 19th century. The Spanish built a fortress here to protect their trading galleons from marauding British and French pirates. It was also the port from which Junípero Serra, the 'Father' of the California missions, embarked on his northward peregrination.

◉ Sights & Activities

Life on the water is a recurring theme here, from beaches and offshore islands to boat tours through local estuaries where birds and wildlife abound.

San Blas

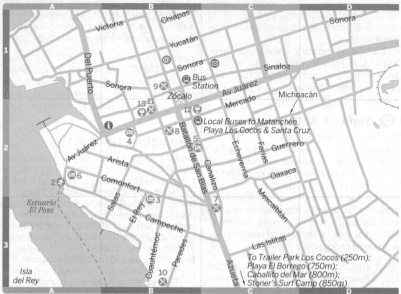

Cerro de la Contaduría

FORTRESS, RUINS

(admission M$10; ⊗8am-7pm) The climb to the top of the Cerro de la Contaduría has a double payoff: a gratifying view and a strong aura of history. Stroll around the ruins of the 18th-century Spanish **La Contaduría Fort**, where colonial riches were once amassed and counted before being shipped off to Mexico City or the Philippines. The place is still guarded by a collection of corroded cannons. Nearby are the gorgeous ruins of the **Templo de la Virgen del Rosario**, built in 1769. You'll find the road up just west of the bridge over Estuario San Cristóbal.

Boat Trips

A boat trip through the jungle to the freshwater spring of **La Tovara** – a federally protected estuary – is a real San Blas highlight. Small boats go from the *embarcadero* at the eastern edge of town, or from the main dock 4.5km further east on the road to Matanchén. The three-hour trips go up Estuario San Cristóbal to the spring, passing thick jungle and mangroves. There's a restaurant at La Tovara, where you can stop for lunch, or you can extend the trip to the **Cocodrilario** (crocodile nursery), where toothy reptiles are reared in captivity for later release in the wild. For a group of up to four people it costs M$440 to go to La Tovara (two hours

round trip) and M$560 to the Cocodrilario (three hours). Each additional person pays M$110 to M$140, depending on destination.

More boat trips depart from a landing on Estuario El Pozo. They include a trip to **Piedra Blanca** (M$400 for up to six people, one hour) to visit a statue of the Virgin, to **Isla del Rey** (M$15 per person, five minutes) just across from San Blas, and to **Playa del Rey**, a 20km beach on the other side of the Isla del Rey peninsula. Here you can also hire boatmen to take you on bird-watching excursions (M$400 first hour for up to six people, M$300 per hour thereafter).

🌿**Isla Isabel** makes for an interesting overnight trip. It's a national park and protected ecological preserve three hours northwest of San Blas by boat. The island is a bird-watcher's paradise, with colonies of many species and a volcanic crater lake. There are no facilities, so be prepared for self-sufficient camping. You can fish for your own dinner, or tour operators will help you negotiate good prices with local fishermen. See listings under Tours and Sportfishing for operators who make this trip.

Beaches

The beach closest to the town is **Playa El Borrego**, at the end of Azueta. Broad waves

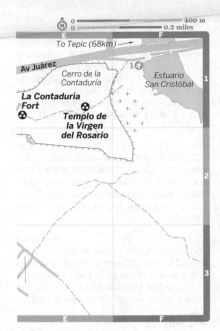

roll in with bravado, and swimming can be treacherous in some conditions – beware of rip currents and heed locals' warnings.

The best beaches are southeast of town around Bahía de Matanchén, starting with **Playa Las Islitas**, 7km from San Blas. To get here, take the main road toward Tepic and turn off to the right after about 4km. This paved road goes east past the village of Matanchén, where a dirt road goes south to Playa Las Islitas and continues on to follow 8km of wonderfully isolated beach. Further down on the paved road, **Playa Los Cocos** and **Playa Miramar**, also popular for surfing, have *palapas* under which you can lounge and drink fresh coconut milk.

Surfing

Beginner and intermediate surfers choose to hone their skills at San Blas because of its many beach and point breaks. The season starts in May, but the waves are fairly mellow until September and October when the south swell brings amazingly long waves curling into Matanchén Bay. Surf spots include El Borrego, Las Islitas, Second Jetty (adjacent to Stoner's Surf Camp), La Puntilla (by a river mouth south of Playa El Borrego), Stoner's (further south, between San Blas and Las Islitas) and El Mosco (west of San Blas on Isla del Rey).

At Playa El Borrego, **Stoner's Surf Camp** (www.stonerssurfcamp.com; board rental per day M$200, lessons per hr M$200) is the nexus of the scene. National longboard champion 'Pompis' Cano gives lessons and holds court under the *palapa*. You can also stay at the camp.

Sportfishing

Numerous operators offer sportfishing excursions from the boat landing on Estuario El Pozo. **Ricardo Murillo Olmeda** (⏧cell phone 323-7297944; pato_murillo@yahoo.com.mx) runs a well-established father/son operation, charging M$2000 for five-hour shallow-water trips, or M$2500 for eight-hour deep-water trips. The maximum capacity is four persons per boat. He also organizes overnight trips to Isla Isabel, charging M$7000 for up to six people, including fishing and snorkeling gear, meals and hikes on the island.

Tours

San Blas Safaris TOURS
(⏧282-88-35; safarisanblas@gmail.com) Local surfers and fishermen serve as guides for the wide range of tours offered by San Blas Safaris, including whale-watching trips (M$300

per person, minimum six people), sportfishing trips (M$2000 to M$3500 per boat, up to six people), excursions to local surf spots (M$200 to M$400 per person, minimum three people), inland safaris to local waterfalls (M$200 per person, minimum three people) and a three-day, two-night tour to the national park of Isla Isabel (M$4500, up to four people). Further information is available at Stoner's Surf Camp.

✦ Festivals & Events

Festival Internacional de Aves
Migratorias   BIRD-WATCHING
Bird-watchers flock to San Blas in late January or early February for the weeklong International Migratory Bird Festival (avessan blas.uan.mx). Highlights include tours with English-speaking ornithologists and nightly entertainment in the plaza.

🛏 Sleeping

San Blas has plenty of very reasonably priced accommodations.

TOP CHOICE Hotel Hacienda Flamingos   HOTEL $$
(☎285-09-30; www.sanblas.com.mx/flamingos; Av Juárez 105; r from M$970, ste M$1230-1610; P✳ 🕾🌊) This superbly restored colonial gem provides the classiest accommodations in town. The spacious rooms and courtyard are evocative of old Mexico without even a whiff of kitsch. There's a lounge serving well-crafted cocktails and *botanas* (snacks).

Casa Roxanna Bungalows   BUNGALOW $$
(☎285-05-73; www.casaroxanna.com; El Rey 1; d M$600-700, q M$700-800; P✳🕾🌊) This refined haven offers eight bungalows of varying sizes; angle for one of the larger upstairs units with full kitchen and screened porch overlooking the pool and manicured grounds. English is spoken and discounts are offered for longer stays.

Stoner's Surf Camp   CABAÑAS, CAMPGROUND $
(☎232-22-25; www.stonerssurfcamp.com; Playa El Borrego; campsites per person M$50, cabins M$150-400; 🕾) Right on the beach are five rustic cabins with electricity, mosquito nets and fans at this friendly traveler hangout and surf center. There's space to camp, a communal kitchen, lots of hammocks, and a restaurant serving well-prepared fare. Guests in the cabins get free use of bikes plus discounts at the surf center.

Hotel Morelos   HOTEL $
(☎285-13-45; Batallón de San Blas 108; r M$200; P🕾) Friendly, homey and family-run, the Morelos has simple fan-cooled rooms and a bare-bones guest kitchen around a central courtyard. An old pelican has made the place home for over a decade, ever since the proprietors nursed him back to health after an injury. He's cute but decidedly not cuddly.

Hotelito Casa de las Cocadas   HOTEL $$
(☎285-09-60; professional_sanblas@hotmail.com; Juárez 145; d/tr/q M$607/766/825; ✳🕾🌊) This newer small hotel down by the boat docks offers clean, bright rooms surrounding a central pool, with low-season rates under M$500.

Trailer Park Los Cocos   CAMPGROUND $
(☎285-00-55; Azueta s/n; tent or RV site for 2 people M$170, plus M$20 each additional person; 🕾) Only a stone's throw from Playa El Borrego, this place has pleasant grassy sites shaded by palm trees; beware the insects at dusk!

✕ Eating

San Blas is a casual town with casual restaurants and beachfront *palapas,* all serving fresh seafood; cheaper eats can be found at the local *mercado* on the corner of Sinaloa and Batallón de San Blas.

Restaurant El Delfín   FUSION $$$
(☎285-01-12; Paredes 106 Sur; mains M$169-239; ⏱8-10am & 1-9pm) Under the direction of internationally renowned chef Betty Vázquez, this restaurant at the Hotel Garza Canela serves an impressive array of rich, gourmet dishes, magnificent desserts and international wines.

La Isla   SEAFOOD $$
(cnr Paredes & Mercado; mains M$80-125; ⏱2-9pm Tue-Sun) With its over-the-top seashell-encrusted interior, this place serves some of the best seafood in San Blas. Indulge yourself with a mix of the *platillos especiales,* a mix of shrimp, octopus and fresh fish cooked however you like it, accompanied by rice, salad and fried banana.

Juan Bananas   BAKERY $
(Batallón 219; banana bread M$40-50; ⏱8am-8pm) For four decades, this little bakery has been cranking out some of the world's best banana bread; with any luck, you'll get a loaf hot from the oven. While you're at it, grab a souvenir T-shirt advertising San Blas'

less-than-enviable status as 'world capital of mosquitoes and no-see-'ems.'

Wala Wala
MEXICAN $$

(Av Juárez 183; mains M$75-140; ⊗7am-10pm Mon-Sat; 🛜) This cheerfully decorated restaurant serves tasty home-style meals, including specialties such as lobster and *pollo con naranja* (chicken with orange). In high season, there's live music three nights a week.

Caballito del Mar
SEAFOOD $$

(Playa El Borrego; mains M$90-115; ⊗noon-6pm) Under the same management as La Isla, this is among the best of the seafood *enramadas* (thatch-covered, open-air restaurants) lined up along Playa El Borrego.

🍸 Drinking & Entertainment

The nightlife in San Blas is unexciting but pleasant enough, with a good selection of low-key watering holes.

TOP CHOICE San Blas Social Club
BAR

(cnr Av Juárez & Canalizo; ⊗9am-midnight; 🛜) Run by the affable Agustín, this cozy, eclectically decorated bar is the hub of San Blas' expatriate nightlife. Jazz records line the wall – you're welcome to pick one out and the bartender (a former matador and actor named Bernardo) will slap it on. Here you can down a mean margarita or one of the bar specialties – ask for a 'Martin Lewis' and see what you get. There's a revolving schedule of evening events (live music, steak night, movie night, guest-chef night), plus good strong coffee every morning and free wi-fi at all hours.

Torino
BAR

(Av Juárez s/n; ⊗9:30am-midnight) Another popular local bar. If you've had one too many, don't venture out back without a flashlight – the 75-year-old crocodile (Fluffy, kept inside an enclosure) is no hallucination.

❶ Information

Free municipal wi-fi is available within a 150m radius of the central plaza.

Banamex ATM (Av Juárez s/n)

Cybernet Web On (Canalizo 155B; per hr M$10; ⊗9am-9pm Mon-Sat, 5-9pm Sun) One of several net cafes north of the plaza.

Health Clinic (☑285-12-07; cnr Azueta & Campeche; ⊗24hr)

Post office (cnr Sonora & Echeverría)

Tourist office (☑285-00-73; Juarez s/n; ⊗9am-3pm Mon-Fri) This basic tourist office,

in the Casa de Cultura, has maps and brochures about the area and the state of Nayarit.

❶ Getting There & Around

The little **bus station** (cnr Sinaloa & Canalizo) is served by Norte de Sonora and Estrella Blanca 2nd-class buses. For many destinations to the south and east, it may be quicker to go to Tepic first. For Mazatlán, transfer in Tepic. Daily departures include the following:

Puerto Vallarta (M$150, 3½ hours, 7:30am, 10am, 1:30pm and 4:30pm)

Tepic (M$50, 1½ hours, hourly 6am to 8pm)

Between 7am and 3pm, hourly buses depart the bus station for Playa Las Islitas (M$12), Playa Los Cocos (M$23) and Playa Miramar (M$25). Second-class buses also depart from the corner of Canalizo and Mercado several times a day, serving all the villages and beaches on Bahía de Matanchén.

Taxis will take you around town and to nearby beaches – a good option with two or more people. Rent bicycles from Wala Wala for M$20/100 per hour/day or Stoner's Surf Camp for M$50 per day.

Tepic

📞311 / POP 330,000 / ELEV 920M

Founded by the nephew of Hernán Cortés in 1524, Tepic is nowadays the capital of Nayarit state, a predominantly middle-class place with a veritable hum of provincial hustle and bustle playing out on its narrow streets. Indigenous Huicholes are often seen here, wearing their colorful traditional clothing, and Huichol artwork is sold on the street and in several shops. Adding interest are an imposing neo-Gothic cathedral and several engrossing museums.

Plaza Principal, with the large cathedral at the eastern end, is the heart of the city. Avenida México, the city's main street, runs south from the cathedral to Plaza Constituyentes, past banks, restaurants, the state museum and other places of interest. The main bus station is on the southeastern side of the city.

In the past couple of years, Tepic has attained unwelcome fame as the site of some grisly drug-related murders. While tourists are unlikely to be affected by the violence, it's wise to remain vigilant and avoid driving after nightfall.

◉ Sights

Historic Buildings

The ornate cathedral on Plaza Principal, dedicated in 1804, casts a regal eye over the plaza. Opposite the cathedral is the Palacio Municipal (city hall), where you'll often find Huicholes under the arches selling handicrafts at very reasonable prices. South of the plaza, look inside the Palacio de Gobierno (Av México; ⊙8am-6pm) to see some impressive and colorful murals painted by José Luis Soto.

Museums

Residing in a palatial 18th-century neoclassical house with a lovely courtyard, the Museo Regional de Nayarit (Av México Norte 91; admission M$37; ⊙9am-6pm Mon-Fri, to 3pm Sat) presents changing exhibitions concerned primarily with pre-Hispanic objects, including ancient pottery and tomb artifacts, as well as colonial painting and Huichol culture. Also on hand are an important pre-Hispanic bas-relief found near Mexcaltitán, and one stupendous stuffed crocodile. It was closed for renovations at the time of research, but scheduled to reopen by the time this edition is in print.

FREE Museo de los Cuatro Pueblos (Museum of the Four Peoples; cnr Zapata Poniente & Av México Norte; ⊙10am-2pm & 4-7pm) displays contemporary popular arts of Nayarit's Huichol, Cora, Nahua and Tepehuano peoples, including clothing, yarn art, weaving, musical instruments, ceramics and beadwork.

FREE Casa y Museo Amado Nervo (Zacatecas Norte 284; ⊙10am-2pm & 5-7pm Tue-Sun) celebrates the life of the preeminent 19th-century Mexican poet Amado Nervo, born here in 1870.

FREE Casa Museo Juan Escutia (Hidalgo Oriente 71; ⊙10am-2pm & 4-7pm Tue-Fri, 10am-2pm Sat & Sun) was the home of Juan Escutia, one of Mexico's illustrious *niños héroes* (child heroes), who died at age 17 defending Mexico City's Castillo de Chapultepec from US forces. Both Casa y Museo Amado Nervo and Casa Museo Juan Escutia are housed in impressive restored colonial residences.

🛏 Sleeping

In its historic center Tepic rewards travelers with a selection of comfortable, good-value independent hotels.

Hotel Real de Don Juan HOTEL $$$
(☎216-18-88; www.realdedonjuan.com, in Spanish; cnr Juárez & Av México Sur; r/ste M$1280/2060; P✳@🅐) This beautifully done-up old hotel overlooking Plaza Constituyentes strikes the right balance between colonial character and urbane style. Two imposing angel warrior statues keep watch over the tranquil lobby, while upstairs the 48 rooms are decked out in appealing pastel colors, with luxurious king beds and marble-accented bathrooms. A good restaurant and classy bar dominate the 1st floor, while the rooftop lounge affords great views.

Hotel Fray Junípero Serra HOTEL $$
(☎212-25-25; www.hotelfrayjunipero.com, in Spanish; Lerdo Poniente 23; s/d M$857/941; P✳🅐) The 98 rooms in this efficient modern hotel are tastefully appointed and come with deluxe amenities; many have a view over the plaza.

🍴 Eating & Drinking

Tepic's local specialties are shrimp-based, but the city also has a good selection of vegetarian restaurants.

Emiliano Comida y Vino MEXICAN $$$
(Zapata Oriente 91; mains M$180-250; ⊙8am-midnight Mon-Sat) Tepic's cuisine scene gets a lift from this chic restaurant and its intimate bar. Staff have a nice way of pulling a cork, and the restaurant stocks a selection of the finest wines produced in Mexico. Still, the best reason to show up is the menu, which features artistically crafted dishes from around the country.

El Trigal VEGETARIAN $
(Veracruz Norte 112; mains M$30-75; 🥗) It has whole-grain quesadillas, soy-based *pozole* (a soup or thin stew of hominy, vegetables and chilies), a full page of juices, *licuados* (milkshakes) and other tropical fruit drinks, and an all-you-can eat vegetarian buffet (M$75).

❶ Information

Banks, internet cafes and *casas de cambio* (money exchanges) line Avenida México between the two plazas.

City tourist office (☎215-30-00/01/02, ext 2000; Plaza Principal; ⊙9am-7pm) On the main square.

Post office (cnr Durango Norte & Morelos Poniente)

BUSES FROM TEPIC

DESTINATION	FARE (M$)	DURATION	FREQUENCY (DAILY)
Guadalajara	189-210	3½hr	frequent
Mazatlán	209-220	4-5hr	hourly
Mexico City	693-770	10-11hr	hourly
Puerto Vallarta	176-196	3½-4hr	hourly

ℹ Getting There & Away

Air

Tepic's **airport** (☑214-18-50; www.asa.gob.mx/wb/webasa/tepic_aeropuertos; Colonia Pantanal) is in Pantanal, 16km from Tepic, going toward Guadalajara. There's no public transportation into town; a taxi costs about M$150. **Aeromar** (☑cell phone 311-1331201; www.aeromar.com.mx; Airport) offers daily flights to Mexico City.

Bus

The main bus station is on the southeastern outskirts of town; local buses marked 'Estación' make frequent trips between the bus station and the city center, stopping at the corner of Amado Nervo and Durango.

TNS operates a small terminal north of the cathedral near the Río Mololoa, with 2nd-class service to San Blas (M$50, 1½ hours, hourly from 5am to 7:15pm).

ℹ Getting Around

Local buses (M$5) operate from around 6am to 9pm. Combis (M$5) operate along Avenida México from 6am to midnight. There are also plenty of taxis, and a taxi stand opposite the cathedral.

Around Tepic

LAGUNA SANTA MARÍA DEL ORO

Surrounded by steep, forested mountains, idyllic Laguna Santa María del Oro fills a volcanic crater 2km around and is thought to be over 100m deep. The clear, clean water takes on colors ranging from turquoise to slate. It's a pleasure to walk around the lake and in the surrounding mountains, spotting numerous birds (some 250 species) and butterflies along the way. You can also climb to an abandoned gold mine, cycle, swim, row on the lake, kayak or fish for black bass and perch. A number of small restaurants serve fresh lake fish and seafood.

Koala Bungalows & RV Park (☑cell phone 311-2643698; www.koalabungalows.com; camp-site per adult/child US$5.50/3, RV site per couple US$12, r/bungalow from US$40/54) is a peaceful park with a restaurant, campsites and well-maintained bungalows sleeping up to 10 people. Turn left at the end of the road that descends to the lake.

The luxurious **Santa María Resort** (☑311-213-26-54; www.santamariaresort.com; 2-person ste M$1499, 4-/6-person bungalow M$2915/3625; ⊞❀☷➘) resembles a stately old hunting lodge with its rustic chic rooms, bungalows and dramatic views. The deluxe amenities, day spa and dramatic pool make for a relaxing stay.

If driving, take the Santa María del Oro turnoff about 40km from Tepic along the Guadalajara road; from the turnoff it's about 10km to Santa María del Oro village, then another 8km to the lake. By bus, catch a 'Santa María del Oro' *colectivo* on Avenida México in Tepic, then change to a *colectivo* marked 'Laguna' at Santa María's town square.

VOLCÁN CEBORUCO

This active volcano consisting of two calderas and three cinder cones last erupted in 1870, so you'll be safe walking the short trails at the top. The 15km cobblestoned road up the volcano passes lava fields, *fumaroles* (steam vents), and lush vegetation growing on the slopes. The road begins at the village of Jala, 7km off the highway from Tepic to Guadalajara; the turnoff is 76km from Tepic, 12km before you reach Ixtlán del Río. You can also visit as part of a tour; several Puerto Vallarta–based companies include a stop at the volcano as part of their 'tequila tour' itineraries.

Chacala

☑327 / POP 320

Like other small towns along this stretch of coast, the tiny coastal fishing village of Chacala is changing fast as its reputation grows as a travelers' destination. For now, it retains its status as a not-quite-so-secret-anymore paradise. Located 96km north of Puerto Vallarta and 10km west of Las Varas on Hwy 200, it sits pretty along a beautiful little cove backed by verdant green slopes and edged by rugged black rock formations at either end. With just one main, sandy thoroughfare and a few cobbled side streets, it's a lovely place to unwind and contemplate the horizon.

There's no ATM; banking and communication services are readily available in Las Varas. Wi-fi is widely available at hotels and cafes in town.

🏃 Activities

Hereabouts, the sea provides most of the action. For **small-boat excursions** ask at the fishing dock, located at the northern tip of the shoreline. **Whale-watching** and **fishing trips** cost around M$250 per person, while a **surfing** expedition to the prime spot La Caleta – where a wicked left-breaking point break tries to dump surfers on the rocky beach – runs M$400 to M$500 per person. You can also **hike** to La Caleta; it's a challenging but rewarding two-hour effort each way.

🛏 Sleeping & Eating

Accommodations here range from the simple to the luxurious. For longer stays with a bit more autonomy, **Chacala Villas** (www.chacalavillas.com) offers a variety of rental housing with full kitchens starting at US$60 per night.

TOP CHOICE Mar de Jade   RESORT $$$

(☎219-40-60, in the US 800-257-0532; www.mardejade.com; r per person incl yoga classes & 3 meals US$130-215; P❋🛜☀) Founded in the 1980s as housing for visiting volunteer doctors, this idyllic beachside getaway at the far south end of Chacala's beachfront has grown into a miniresort that hosts regular yoga, meditation and wellness retreats. Crashing waves are audible everywhere on the property, from the spacious rooms with deep tiled bathtubs, to the sauna, Jacuzzi and spa area to the sprawling poolside patio where vegetarian-friendly meals (M$140 to M$200) are served, incorporating produce from the resort's own organic farm. High-season treats include wood-fired fish and pizza, free yoga classes in the hardwood-floored studios overlooking the palms and ocean, and weekly cultural events including

Latin dancing and temascal (pre-Hispanic steam bath) purification ceremonies.

🏠 Techos de Mexico   HOMESTAY $

(www.techosdemexico.com; r M$150-500) Travelers interested in befriending the locals should consider this unique organization (inspired by Habitat for Humanity) that helps Chacala residents build good homes with adjacent guest units. Five local families offer lodging through this program, including the well-established **Casa Aurora** (☎219-40-27; casaaurora2@hotmail.com; d with kitchenette M$400-500), one block up from the beach. Look for the distinctive Techos signs as you pass through town.

Casa Mirador   BUNGALOW $

(☎219-40-73; www.casamiradorchacala.com, in Spanish; Océano Pacífico 10; r from M$300, bungalows M$500-700; P❋🛜) This clifftop place offers everything from bare-bones, fan-cooled rooms to an upstairs unit with kitchen, air-con and seaview terrace. There are lovely panoramic vistas from the hammocks on the palm-shaded patio downstairs.

Hotel las Brisas   HOTEL $$

(☎219-40-15; www.lasbrisaschacala.com; Av Chacalilla 4; d/tw M$850/950; P❋🛜) This centrally located, family-run hotel shares beachfront space with one of Chacala's better seafood restaurants. Upstairs are nine clean units with satellite TV; downstairs you'll find shrimp and beer. Sweet.

🏠 Majahua   B&B $$$

(☎219-40-53; www.majahua.com; Playa Chacala; d incl breakfast M$1490-1965, 5-person ste incl breakfast M$3275; 🛜) Tucked away in the unspoiled jungle overlooking the edge of the cove, this earthy ecolodge offers five beautifully designed rooms, an outdoor restaurant and spa services.

Chacmool Cafe   CAFE $$

(www.chacmoolcafe.com; Calle Principal; mains M$65-130; ⏰7:30am-5:30pm Mon & Tue, to 10pm Wed-Sun; 🛜) Open year-round, this British-Mexican-run cafe in the village center is an inviting spot for coffee, breakfast, nightly dinner specials and free wi-fi with an ocean view.

Mauna Kea   BREAKFAST $

(www.casapacificachacala.com; mains M$40-60; ⏰8-11am Mon-Sat Dec-Mar) Watch whales over morning coffee at this seasonal rooftop eatery on the bluffs just north of town (or get your breakfast free by staying at the attached B&B!).

Getting There & Away

For Chacala, get off a Puerto Vallarta–Tepic bus at Las Varas and take a *colectivo* (M$15) from there. If you're driving, the Hwy 200 turnoff is 1km south of Las Varas.

Sayulita

♪329 / POP 2300

Once upon a time – OK, it was the late 1990s – Sayulita really *was* a tranquil fishing village. Many of the town's *norteamericano* residents still describe it that way, but the truth is that Sayulita, while still low-key, has definitely been 'discovered.' In peak season the place is swarming with gringos, drawn here by the beautiful sandy beach, amiable surfing scene, great restaurants and tasteful B&Bs.

⊙ Sights & Activities

You can arrange bicycle hire, boat trips, horseback riding, trekking or kayaking from operators on the main street. One popular nearby destination is **Playa Los Muertos**, where picnics and boogie-boarding top the action. It's a 15-minute walk south along the coast road. You can also hire a boat to take your group out to the uninhabited **Islas Marietas** – a protected national park – for picnicking, snorkeling and swimming.

Surfing

Sayulita is a classic 'boarder' town, and it's a simple matter to join in the fun. Medium-sized waves pour dependably from both the left and the right, so you can practice your well-honed moves or even take up the sport for the first time.

Several local surf shops offer rentals and lessons, including the well-established **Lunazul** (www.lunazulsurfing.com; Marlín 4; surfboard/bodyboard rentals per day M$200/150, group/private lessons per 90min M$350/450; ☺8am-5pm).

Sleeping

A good selection of private villas can be browsed on the website **Sayulita Life** (www.sayulitalife.com). The following prices are for the winter high season.

Amazing Hostel Sayulita HOSTEL **$$**
(☎291-36-88; www.theamazinghostelsayulita.com; Pelicanos 102; dm M$195, d M$550-750; ☜✸) Be-

tween the plaza and the Puerto Vallarta bus stop, this great new hostel has three five-bed dorms with en suite bathrooms, along with two air-conditioned private rooms. The big backyard beckons guests with a 6m-high climbing wall, swimming pool and BBQ, as well as hammocks for lounging under the mango, lemon and tangerine trees. Bikes rent for M$50 per day, kayaks and surfboards for M$200. The friendly, well-traveled owners offer a wealth of local info.

Petit Hotel Hafa BOUTIQUE HOTEL **$$**
(☎291-38-06; www.hotelhafasayulita.com; Revolución 55; r US$50-85; ☜) Just steps away from the plaza, this sweet hotel has six fan-cooled rooms with king-sized beds and optional air-con (M$65 extra). The French-Spanish couple who run the place bring considerable creativity and taste to bear in the design and decor, which favors Moorish flourishes, bright colors and welcoming communal spaces. Nighttime noise from the nearby bars is the only downside.

🏄 Playa Escondida RESORT **$$$**
(☎291-31-07; www.playa-escondida.com; Punta Mita; bungalows US$175-400; ℗☜✸) Luxurious and peaceful, this end-of-the-road, jungle-backed ecoresort is only 2km west of Sayulita, but feels like another universe. Don't expect TVs or air-con, just a spa, an infinity pool, a Jacuzzi tastefully tucked under banana trees, a bar and a fancy restaurant all overlooking the resort's private beach, plus free yoga, Pilates and Zumba classes. Trails meander through the jungle to supercomfy bungalows in a variety of natural settings, from the waterfront villas to the Bird Canyon rooms with long views over the treetops.

Rooms include plush bedding, hammocks and mosquito netting, and some have their own kitchens. To get here, see the excellent directions on the resort's website.

La Casona   B&B $$
(☏291-36-29; www.lacasonasayulita.com; Delfín 7; r incl breakfast US$70-140; ☎) Centrally located, cheerful and comfy, La Casona's rooms feature vibrant colors with tile and stucco accents. The breezy open-air lounge upstairs is a lovely place to enjoy the included breakfast.

Bungalows Aurinko   BUNGALOW $$$
(☏291-31-50; www.sayulita-vacations.com; Marlín s/n; 1-/2-bedroom bungalows US$90/150, ste US$120; ✳☎) Smooth river-stone floors, open-air kitchens, exposed raw beams and well-appointed decor are among the attractions at these bungalows near the plaza.

Palmar del Camarón Camping   CAMPGROUND $
(☏291-33-73; www.palmardelcamaron.com; Del Palmar s/n; campsite per person M$90, 2-person palapa with/without bathroom M$400/350, 4-person palapa with/without bathroom M$800/600) This grassy, kick-back beachfront campground offers welcome shade in the heat of the day. The two-story bungalows are extremely rustic, but the location is unbeatable for this price.

Hotel Diamante   HOTEL $$
(☏291-31-91; www.hoteldiamantesayulita.com; Miramar 40; s/d/tr/q with fan from M$395/550/890/950, with air-con M$595/795/1095/1350; ✳☎☒) This well-priced favorite offers a wide variety of basic but bright rooms, a small pool and breezy communal kitchens.

🍴 Eating & Drinking

A foodie paradise, Sayulita has a beguiling selection of small, bistro-style cafes, providing agreeable contrast to the inexpensive *palapas* on the beach and the lively taco and hotdog stands that sprout every evening on the streets surrounding the plaza.

TOP CHOICE Rollie's   BREAKFAST $
(☏291-33-47; Revolución 58; breakfast M$55-80; ☺7:30am-noon Nov-Apr, plus 5:30-9pm Dec-Apr) This is *the* place for North American–style breakfasts with an occasional Mexican twist, well-pulled espresso and morning cocktails. It's also open for paella in the evenings.

Sayulita Café   MEXICAN $$
(☏291-37-58; Revolución 37; mains M$100-180; ☺5pm-midnight Oct-Aug) With an atmospheric

dining room and candlelit sidewalk tables, this old favorite specializes in high quality *chiles rellenos* and other traditional Mexican dishes, along with seafood and steaks.

Mangiafuoco   ITALIAN $$
(Revolución 68; mains M$85-180; ☺6-10pm Sun-Fri) In a banana-shaded courtyard, the Roman-born owner makes wood-oven-fired pizza and fresh pasta with sauces ranging from traditional Italian (pesto, *puttanesca, amatriciana*) to Mexican fusion (shrimp with *guajillo* chili).

Panino's   BAKERY $
(Delfín 1; pastries, salads & sandwiches M$18-79; ☺7am-5pm; ✎) Freshly baked European-style bread, salads, panini (including vegetarian and vegan options), and apple strudel to die for.

Monchis   BURGERS $
(Marlín 12; burgers from M$65; ☺4pm-1am) A popular plaza-side hangout for burgers and stiff drinks.

Tacos El Ivan   TAQUERÍA $
(tacos M$10; ☺6pm-2am) Down by the bridge, Ivan is still cranking out tasty *tacos al pastor* (rotisserie-cooked pork with slices of onion and pineapple) long after everyone else has turned in for the night.

☆ Entertainment

Bar Don Pato's   LIVE MUSIC
(Marlín 10; ☺8pm-4am) At the sign of the rubber duck, this lively club on the main square pumps out live music six nights a week, with an open mic on Tuesdays.

ℹ Information

There are a couple of ATMs in town, including one on the plaza and another at the Oxxo convenience store a block away. The nearest full-service bank is in Bucerías, 12km to the south on Hwy 200.

Lun@net (Mariscal 5; internet per hr M$20; ☺8am-2pm & 4-9pm Mon-Sat) Just off the plaza. Free wi-fi is also available at cafes on the plaza.

ℹ Getting There & Away

Sayulita is about 35km north of Puerto Vallarta, just west of Hwy 200. Buses (M$25, one hour) operate every 15 minutes or so from the stop in front of Puerto Vallarta's Wal-Mart. For a few more pesos, any northbound 2nd-class bus from the Puerto Vallarta bus terminal will drop you at the Sayulita turnoff, leaving you with a 2km walk into town.

Puerto Vallarta

☑322 / POP 200,000

Puerto Vallarta – referred to simply as 'Vallarta' by its many aficionados – is one of Mexico's liveliest and most sophisticated resort destinations. Stretching around the sparkling blue Bahía de Banderas (Bay of Flags) and backed by lush palm-covered mountains, one couldn't ask for a better place to while away a cosmopolitan vacation. Each year millions come to laze on the dazzling sandy beaches, browse in the quirky shops, nosh in the stylish restaurants and wander through the picturesque cobbled streets or along its beautiful *malecón*. If the pretty town beaches aren't enough, you can venture out on cruises, horseback rides, diving trips and day tours – and be back in time for a late dinner and an even later excursion to one of the many sizzling nightspots on offer. Puerto Vallarta is also the gay beach capital of Mexico (see boxed text, p516).

The 'old' town center, called Zona Centro, is the area north of Río Cuale, with the small Isla Cuale in the middle of the river. The city's two principal thoroughfares are Morelos and Juárez, which sandwich the Plaza Principal. Many fine houses, quite a few owned by foreigners, are found further up the Río Cuale valley, also known as Gringo Gulch.

South of the river, the Zona Romántica is another tourist district with smaller hotels, restaurants and bars. It has the only two beaches in the city center – Playa Olas Altas and Playa de los Muertos.

We've concentrated most of our listings in these eminently walkable downtown neighborhoods, which remain the heart and soul of Puerto Vallarta.

North of the city is a strip of giant luxury hotels, the Zona Hotelera; Marina Vallarta, a large yacht marina (9km from the center); the airport (10km); the bus station (12km); and Nuevo Vallarta, a new area of hotel and condominium developments (18km). To the south of the city are a few more large resorts and some of the area's most beautiful beaches.

History

Soon after reaching Mexico in the 16th century, the Spanish recognized the value of

Greater Puerto Vallarta

To Sayulita (32km); Chacala (90km)
Aquaventuras Park
Gustavo Díaz Ordaz International Airport
Long-Distance Bus Station
Las Palmas
Marina Vallarta Golf Club
Marina Vallarta
Playa El Salado
Marigalante
El Pitillal
Banderas Scuba Republic
Zona Hotelera
Río Pitillal
Playa de Oro
Playa Las Palmas
Bahía de Banderas
Playa Los Tules
Playa Las Glorias
Playa Camarones
See Central Puerto Vallarta Map (p512)
Bypass Road Tunnel
Puerto Vallarta
Río Cuale
Playa Conchas Chinas
Blue Chairs/ Diana's Tours
Playa Estacas
Playa Los Venados
Playa Punta Negra
Playa Garza Blanca
Playa Gemelas
To Mismaloya (2km); Boca de Tomatlán (7km); Yelapa (15km)

the vast Bahía de Banderas as a safe harbor where sailors could stock up on fresh water and firewood, and *naos* (galleons) returning from the Philippines could seek refuge from pirates. However, this stretch of coast played second fiddle to the main regional port of San Blas, and it was only in the 1800s that the bay's main settlement, Las Peñas, began to flourish as a supply center for the silver-mining towns further inland.

In 1918, Las Peñas was renamed Puerto Vallarta (in honor of Jalisco governor Ignacio Vallarta) and a new economy grew up around agriculture and also small-scale

CENTRAL PACIFIC COAST PUERTO VALLARTA

PUERTO VALLARTA IN FOUR DAYS

Rise and shine! Take a morning dip in the sparkling Bahía de Banderas and a stroll on one of Vallarta's many **beaches**, scanning the horizon for **whales** as you walk. Stop in at the **Museo del Cuale** or linger beneath the shady rubber trees on the **Isla Río Cuale**. Join the happy throng on the waterfront **malecón** and enjoy the varied public sculptures. Linger over dinner at one of Vallarta's splendid **restaurants** and then hit one of the sizzling late-night **dance clubs**.

On day two, get up early (yeah, right) and continue indulging in the pleasures of the city with some **shopping**, or pick one of the many **outdoor adventures**, such as diving, fishing or horseback riding.

On your third day, visit the beautiful **Vallarta Botanical Gardens**, or hop aboard a boat headed for the far-flung beaches of **Las Ánimas**, **Quimixto** or **Yelapa**.

For the fourth day, catch a bus to the kick-back town of **Sayulita** for a surfing lesson or simply a surf.

tourism. The pace of development accelerated in 1954, when Mexicana planes filled with tourists started landing on the town's dirt airstrip. A decade later John Huston chose the nearby deserted cove of Mismaloya as a location for the film of Tennessee Williams' *The Night of the Iguana*. Hollywood paparazzi descended on the town to report on the tempestuous romance between Richard Burton and Elizabeth Taylor. Vallarta suddenly became world-famous, with an aura of steamy tropical romance. Travelers have been pouring in ever since.

◎ Sights

Puerto Vallarta has amazing natural scenery (perfect beaches remain the biggest draw) as well as a growing number of cultural attractions.

The heart of Zona Centro is the **Plaza Principal** (Map p512), also called Plaza de Armas, just near the sea between Morelos and Juárez. On the sea side of the plaza is an outdoor amphitheater backed by **Los Arcos** (Map p512), a row of arches that has become a symbol of the city. The wide **malecón** stretches about 10 blocks north from the amphitheater and is dotted with bars, restaurants, nightclubs and a grand collection of public sculptures. Uphill from the plaza, the crown-topped steeple of the **Templo de Guadalupe** (Map p512) is another Vallarta icon.

A trip to Vallarta wouldn't be complete without lingering on **Isla Cuale** (Map p512), where the city's earliest residents built their humble homes. Upstream you'll notice two rickety cable suspension bridges, connecting the island to the Zona Romántica.

Beaches BEACH

The beaches of the Bahía de Banderas have many personalities. Some are buzzing with cheerful activity; others are quiet and private. Most beaches mentioned here feature on the Greater Puerto Vallarta map (p507).

Only two beaches, **Playa Olas Altas** (Map p512) and **Playa de los Muertos** (Beach of the Dead; Map p512), are handy to the city center; they're both south of the Río Cuale. On Sundays join the scores of Mexican families who come to while away their day off. At the southern end of Playa de los Muertos is the stretch of sand called **Blue Chairs**: it's one of Mexico's most famous gay beaches.

North of town, in the Zona Hotelera, are **Playa Camarones**, **Playa Las Glorias**, **Playa Los Tules**, **Playa Las Palmas** and **Playa de Oro**. Nuevo Vallarta also has beaches, and there are other, less developed beaches right around to Punta Mita at the bay's northwesternmost edge.

Mismaloya, the location for *The Night of the Iguana*, is about 12km south of town. The tiny scenic cove is dominated by a gargantuan resort. About 4km past Mismaloya, southwest along the coast, is **Boca de Tomatlán**, a seaside village that's less commercialized than Puerto Vallarta. Buses marked 'Boca' stop at both Mismaloya and Boca de Tomatlán; the 'Mismaloya' bus only goes as far as Mismaloya.

Further around the southern side of the bay are the more isolated beaches, from east to west, of Las Ánimas, Quimixto and Yelapa, all accessible only by boat. **Playa de las Ánimas** (Beach of the Spirits) is a lovely beach with a small fishing village and some *palapa* restaurants offering fresh seafood. **Quimixto**, not far from Las Ánimas, has a waterfall accessible by a half-hour hike or by hiring a pony on the beach to take you up.

Yelapa, furthermost from town, is one of Vallarta's most popular cruise destinations. This picturesque cove is crowded with tourists, restaurants and parasailing operators during the day, but empties out when the tourist boats leave in the late afternoon. There are several comfortable places to stay the night.

✏️ **Vallarta Botanical Gardens** GARDENS (www.vbgardens.org; Hwy 200 Km 24; admission M$60; ⊙10am-5pm Tue-Sun) Orchids, bromeliads, agaves and wild palms line the paths of this gorgeous nature park, located 30km south of Puerto Vallarta. Butterflies flit by as you dine at the open-air Hacienda de Oro restaurant. Follow hummingbirds down paths and through fern grottoes, or head down to bask in a chair on the sand and swim amid huge boulders in the river below. Slap on some bug juice and make a day of it. Take the 'El Tuito' bus (M$20) from the corner of Carranza and Aguacate in Puerto Vallarta, or hop in a taxi (about M$300).

FREE **Museo del Cuale** MUSEUM (Map p512; Paseo Isla Cuale s/n; ⊙10am-2pm & 3-6pm Tue-Sun) This tiny museum near the western end of Isla Cuale has a small collection of beautiful pottery, grinding stones, clay figurines and other ancient objects. Text panels are in Spanish and English.

🏃 Activities

Restless souls need not go far to find activities such as swimming with dolphins, bungee jumping, mountain biking and whale-watching. Snorkeling, scuba diving, deep-sea fishing, waterskiing, windsurfing, sailing and parasailing can be arranged on the beaches in front of any of the large hotels or through the tourist office.

Diving & Snorkeling

Below the warm, tranquil waters of Bahía de Banderas is a world of stingrays, tropical fish and garishly colored corals. Vallarta has several diving operators. Most also offer snorkeling trips, which usually means snorkelers tag along with divers. Dives typically include transportation, gear and light meals.

Banderas Scuba Republic DIVING (📞223-41-03; www.bs-republic.com; snorkeling trips US$50-100, 2-tank dive trips US$85-150, PADI Open Water certification US$350; Zona Romántica

(Map p512; Cárdenas 230); Marina Vallarta (cnr Av Marina Sur & Vela) maintains a high degree of professionalism with its small-group excursions to both well-known and lesser-known sites. Private diving tours are also offered.

Deep-Sea Fishing

Deep-sea fishing is popular all year, with a major international fishing tournament held mid-November every year. Prime catches are sailfish, marlin, tuna, red snapper and sea bass. Fishing trips can be arranged dockside at Marina Vallarta or through various agencies around town.

Horseback Riding

Vallarta's jungly mountains are wonderful to explore from the perspective of horseback.

Rancho El Charro HORSEBACK RIDING (📞224-01-14; www.ranchoelcharro.com; horse rides US$62-120), 12km northeast of downtown Puerto Vallarta, is recommended for its healthy horses and scenic three- to eight-hour trots into the Sierra Madre. Some rides are suitable for kids. Setting it apart from competitors are its multiday tours, including the tempting 'Overnight Lost in the Jungle Ride' (US$350). Transportation is offered from the corner of Proa and Hwy 200 near Marina Vallarta.

Golf

Vallarta's golf courses are north of the city. Most highly acclaimed is the Jack Nicklaus-designed **Pacífico Golf Course** (📞291-60-00; www.fourseasons.com/puntamita/golf/pacifico _golf_course; Four Seasons Resort, Punta Mita; green fees 9/18 holes US$135/210), where golfers are blissfully distracted from the challenging terrain by the sweeping ocean vistas. One hole, nicknamed 'Tail of the Whale,' is located on a natural island and requires the use of an amphibious golf cart.

Other clubs include **Vista Vallarta Golf Club** (📞290-00-30; www.vistavallartagolf.com; Circuito Universidad 653; green fees twilight/daylight US$136/196), 9km east of the airport, which has Nicklaus- and Weiskopf-designed courses side by side, and is one of Mexico's premier golf resorts; **Los Flamingos Golf Club** (📞329-296-50-06; www.flamingosgolf.com .mx; Hwy 200 s/n; green fees twilight/daylight US$90/140), recently renovated, and 13km north of town; and **Marina Vallarta Golf Club** (Map p507; 📞221-00-73; www.marinavallarta golf.com; Paseo de la Marina 430; green fees twilight/daylight US$97/129), just north of Marina Vallarta.

Cruises

A host of daytime, sunset and evening cruises are available in Vallarta. The most popular ones are the cruises to Yelapa and Las Ánimas beaches; others go to the Islas Marietas, further out. Prices are generally negotiable, starting at M$400 for sunset cruises and beach trips; longer trips lasting four to six hours with meals and bottomless cocktails will set you back M$750 to M$1000. Leaflets advertising cruises are available throughout town.

On Thursdays Diana's Tours (www.dianas tours.com) offers an all-day gay and lesbian cruise, with plenty of food, drink and snorkeling (M$950). It leaves from Blue Chairs Beach Resort.

Courses

Six-hour classes in traditional Mexican cooking (US$80 to US$100) are held twice monthly from October through April at El Arrayán Cocina Tradicional (p517). The fee includes breakfast, a trip to the market, instruction in the restaurant's kitchen, take-home recipes and a lunch including cocktails.

Centro de Estudios Para Extranjeros   LANGUAGE COURSE
(CEPE; Map p512; ☎223-20-82; www.cepe.udg.mx; Libertad 105-1) Language courses at this Universidad de Guadalajara–affiliated school range from US$151 for a week of basic tourist Spanish to US$498 for 50-hour intensive courses. Private instruction costs US$25 per hour.

Tours

Nature and outdoor tours are one of Puerto Vallarta's strongest suits. The following companies tread lightly and follow ecofriendly business practices.

Ecotours de México   ECOTOUR
(☎209-21-95; www.ecotoursvallarta.com; Proa s/n, Marina Vallarta) Run by a couple of enthusiastic naturalists, this outfit offers whale-watching (adult/child US$80/65), sea kayaking and snorkeling tours (US$75/60), guided hiking tours (US$65/45), bird-watching tours (from US$80/60) and multiday expeditions further afield focusing on sea turtles, Monarch butterflies, whale sharks and more.

Eco Ride   CYCLING
(Map p512; ☎222-79-12; www.ecoridemex.com; Miramar 382; tours M$550-1400) Surrounded

---

PUERTO VALLARTA FOR CHILDREN

If your tot has a pirate fetish, the little lad or lassie won't tolerate missing a cruise on the **Marigalante** (Map p507; ☎800-832-50-99; www.pirateshipvallarta. com), a reproduction Spanish galleon that does pirate-themed daytime cruises (adult/child US$85/43) from 9am to 4pm Monday through Saturday. It departs from the Terminal Maritima in Marina Vallarta, off Blvd Francisco Ascencio opposite Sam's Club.

Kids will also get a kick out of **Aquaventuras Park** (Map p507; www. aquaventuras.com; Carretera Tepic Km 155; adult/child US$25/19; ☺10am-6pm Tue-Sun), which offers 10 waterslides, a lazy river swimming pool, daily dolphin shows and opportunities to play with dolphins and sea lions.

---

by the mountains, jungle and sea, Vallarta offers some truly thrilling mountain biking. This outfit offers guided one-day cycling tours suited for beginners and badasses alike. The most challenging is a 50km expedition from El Tuito (a small town at 1100m) through Chacala and down to the beach in Yelapa. The views along the way are stunning.

Vallarta Adventures   ADVENTURE TOUR
(☎297-12-12; www.vallarta-adventures.com; Av Las Palmas 39, Nuevo Vallarta) Vallarta's largest adventure tours company, based near Marina Vallarta, offers a dizzying array of options, including whale-watching excursions (adult/child US$85/60), snorkeling and kayaking trips to the Islas Marietas (US$69/50), zip-line canopy tours (US$79/56), sailing trips (US$88), visits to the colonial mining town of San Sebastian (US$84/60) and much more.

Festivals & Events

Marlin & Sailfish Tournament   FISHING
This major international tournament (www. fishvallarta.com) is held every November.

Festival Gourmet International   FOOD
Puerto Vallarta's culinary community has hosted this mid-November festival (www. festivalgourmet.com) since 1995.

Día de Santa Cecilia   MUSIC

On November 22 Vallarta's mariachis play and sing their way through the streets, honoring their patron saint with an early evening musical procession to the Templo de Guadalupe.

**Día de Nuestra
Señora de Guadalupe**   RELIGIOUS

Puerto Vallarta honors Mexico's patron saint with two weeks of celebrations, including processions to the cathedral day and night from November 30 until December 12.

🛏 Sleeping

When it comes to accommodations you're spoiled for choice in Puerto Vallarta.

Vallarta's cheapest lodgings are south of the Río Cuale, particularly along Madero. Closer to the ocean, in the Zona Romántica, you'll find several appealing midrange options. Our top-end listings include several special, small and stylish places that offer an intimate alternative to Vallarta's homogenous megaresorts.

The following prices are for the December to April high season; low-season rates can be as much as 20% to 50% less. Negotiate for discounts if you plan on staying a week or more; monthly rates can cut your rent by half.

**TOP
CHOICE Casa Dulce Vida**   SUITES $$$

(Map p512; 📞222-10-08; www.dulcevida.com; Aldama 295; ste US$70-200; 🛜🏊) With the look and feel of an Italian villa, this collection of seven spacious suites offers graceful accommodations and delicious privacy. Most have private terraces, high ceilings and plentiful windows, with sunny living areas, kitchens and extra beds for groups. Even when the place is fully booked, it retains a quiet and intimate atmosphere. It has a well-situated pool and manicured tropical gardens.

Vallarta Sun Hostel   HOSTEL $

(Map p512; 📞223-15-23; www.vallartasunhostel.com; Rodríguez 169; dm/d M$195/500; 🅴@🛜) A very welcome addition to Vallarta's budget accommodations scene, this hostel two blocks from Playa de los Muertos is run by world travelers Kathy and Ricardo, whose affable personalities and love of adventure recently won them a spot on the Latin American edition of *The Amazing Race* TV show. Homey touches such as the table-tennis table, free wi-fi and in-house laundry service (M$50 per load) supplement four clean six-

bed dorms, each with its own bathroom and spacious locker facilities. For those seeking a bit more privacy, there's also one double room with shared bathroom.

Hotel Posada de Roger   HOTEL $$

(Map p512; 📞222-08-36; www.posadaroger.com; Badillo 237; s/d/tr/q US$60/65/70/80; 🅴🛜🏊) Three blocks from the beach, this agreeable travelers' hangout has long been one of Vallarta's most beloved midrange options.

La Casa del Puente   APARTMENT $$$

(Map p512; 📞222-07-49; www.casadelpuente.com; cnr Libertad & Miramar; d/tr/q US$98/104/110; 🛜) Smack in the center, on the banks of the Río Cuale, this unique lodging features two spacious apartments – one sleeping three, the other sleeping five – with tiled bathrooms, fully equipped kitchens and a shared terrace overlooking the river. Reserve ahead.

Quinta María Cortez   B&B $$$

(📞221-53-17; www.quinta-maria.com; Sagitario 132, Playa Conchas Chinas; r US$167-310; 🅴@🛜🏊) This exclusive resort south of town is perhaps Vallarta's most atmospheric and sophisticated lodging. Each of the seven spacious and romantic suites is uniquely furnished in a style the owner calls 'Mexiterranean;' most come with kitchen, fireplace and sea views. Fluffy towels and bathrobes contribute to the luxurious feel, as does the breakfast served on the terrace overlooking Playa Conchas Chinas. There's a five-night minimum stay, and children under 18 are not allowed.

Hotel Galería Belmar   HOTEL $$

(Map p512; 📞223-18-72; www.belmarvallarta.com; Insurgentes 161; s/d M$400/500, with air-con M$490/590; 🅴@🛜) Brightly painted walls hung with original artwork enliven the tidy, comfortable rooms at this hotel in the heart of the Zona Romántica. Some have kitchenettes (M$100 extra) and many have balconies. Nicest are the top-floor rooms, which get natural light and an ocean breeze, especially room 29 with its kitchenette and corner balcony.

Casa de los Cuatro Vientos   HOTEL $$

(Map p512; 📞222-01-61; www.cuatrovientos.com; Matamoros 520; d/q incl continental breakfast US$69/79; 🛜🏊) The cozy, fan-cooled rooms have white brick walls, hand-painted trim and gleaming red-tiled floors. Quality vintage furnishings add style and class. There's also a two-room suite with a large bedroom

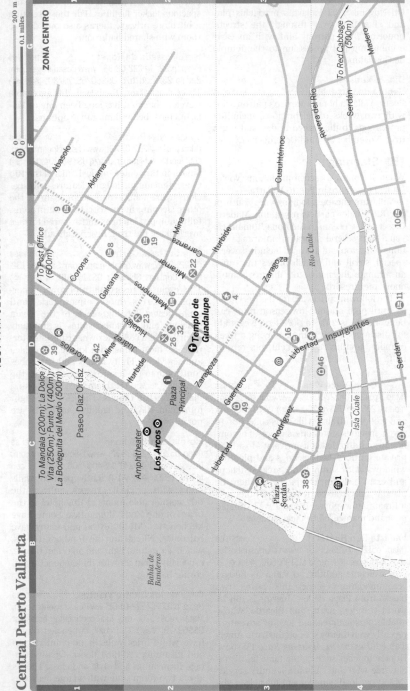

Central Puerto Vallarta

ZONA CENTRO

200 m
0.1 miles

Bahía de
Banderas

Amphitheater

Los Arcos

Paseo Díaz Ordaz

To Mandala (200m); La Dolce
Vita (250m); Punto V (400m);
La Bodeguita del Medio (500m)

Plaza
Principal

Templo de
Guadalupe

To Post Office
(600m)

Abasolo

Aldama

Corona

Galeana

Morelos

Mina

Juárez

Hidalgo

Iturbide

Matamoros

Miramar

Mina

Carranza

Zaragoza

Iturbide

Cuauhtémoc

Zaragoza

Guerrero

Libertad

Rodríguez

Encino

Libertad

Insurgentes

Serdán

Plaza
Serdán

Isla Cuale

Río Cuale

Rivera del Río

Serdán

Madero

To Red Cabbage
(500m)

39

42

23

26

32

6

19

22

8

9

4

16

3

46

49

38

45

1

11

10

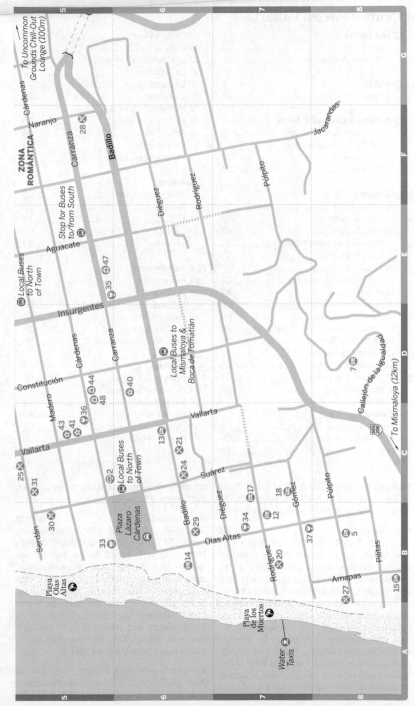

Central Puerto Vallarta

and two day beds. The rooftop bar El Nido is an attraction in itself, affording terrific views of the cathedral and the entire bay.

Casa Amorita B&B $$$
(Map p512; ☎222-49-26, in the US 908-955-0720; www.casaamorita.com; Iturbide 309; r incl breakfast US$160; ☎☀) Located on a quiet street above the din of the *malecón,* this small B&B offers four simple but pleasant rooms, complemented by comfortable common areas including a small pool, a massage area, a rooftop terrace with full-on views of Puerto Vallarta's cathedral, and a fireplace surrounded by couches for reading and lounging. Well-traveled owner Rita Love is a great source of local information and serves a full breakfast featuring fresh fruit and juices, homemade granola and pastries, and ever-changing main courses, from omelets to waffles.

Hotel Posada Lily HOTEL $$
(Map p512; ☎222-00-32; hotel_lily@hotmail.com; Badillo 109; s/d/tr/q M$450/650/750/850; ☀☎) This amazingly priced option just off the beach offers 18 clean and pleasant rooms, most with good natural light. A few rooms have air-con (M$50 extra), free wi-fi and/ or fridges; the largest have three beds and small balconies that overlook the street. Beach chairs and umbrellas are available free to all guests. The only potential downside is noise from the street below.

Vallarta Sun Hotel & Suites HOTEL, SUITES $$
(Map p512; ☎223-15-29; www.vallartasunsuites. com; ☀☎☀); Hotel (Rodríguez 169; d US$79);

Suites (Gómez 169; ste US$99) In the heart of the Zona Romántica, adjacent to the hostel of the same name, these spacious, comfortable and well-equipped hotel rooms share a central pool and lounge area, with distant views of the ocean a couple of blocks downhill. Longer-term visitors can settle in at one of the 15 studio suites a block away, with full kitchens and monthly rates (US$1700). No kids allowed.

Hotel Tropicana HOTEL $$
(Map p512; ✆226-96-96; www.tropicanavallarta.com; Amapas 214; d standard/superior M$1050/1200, ste M$1300; ❄🛜🏊) Catering primarily to package tour groups, this venerable 160-room hotel is showing its age but still offers reasonably priced rooms given its beachside location. The superior rooms are less faded than the standard ones; book ahead for one with an ocean view.

Tacho's Trailer Park TRAILER PARK $
(✆cell phone 322-1462895; www.tachosrv.com; Prisciliano Sánchez s/n; sites per day/week/month M$320/2100/8100; 🛜🏊) Between downtown and the airport, this pleasant RV park offers grassy, shady sites and a swimming pool. From Highway 200 northbound, turn right at Sam's Club and continue 1km east.

Hotel Ana Liz HOTEL $
(Map p512; ✆222-17-57; www.directrents.com; Madero 429; s/d/tr/q M$220/280/340/380; 🛜) For serious peso-pinchers, Ana Liz' no-frills, fan-cooled rooms are among the cheapest in town. The best rooms are those with small balconies upstairs.

✖ Eating

Foodies are pampered in Puerto Vallarta, and return visitors rate its cuisine scene a prime attraction. A goodly number of noteworthy chefs from abroad have put down roots, offering competing menus of tremendous breadth and variety. There's also a great selection of economical, family-run eateries serving mouthwatering traditional Mexican fare.

ISLA RÍO CUALE & SOUTH
Some of the tastiest and cheapest food in town comes from the taco stands along Madero and neighboring Zona Romántica streets in the early evening.

🏆 Red Cabbage Café MEXICAN $$$
(✆223-04-11; www.redcabbagepv.com; Rivera del Río 204A; mains M$120-240; ⏱5-11pm, closed Sep) Though the atmosphere is casual, with eclectic and bohemian artwork, the food is serious and features old recipes and uncommon indigenous sauces. It's a pleasant 10-minute walk from the Zona Romántica; from Cárdenas turn right on Rivero del Río, just before the Río Cuale bridge. No credit cards.

Joe Jack's Fish Shack SEAFOOD $$
(Map p512; http://joejacks-fishshack.com; Badillo 212; mains M$95-180; ⏱noon-11pm) Seafood aficionados flock to this joint for fish and chips, garlic shrimp, whole red snapper and great slabs of mahimahi. Large groups are graciously accommodated on the pleasant rooftop terrace. The service is jovial and quick, and the music classic rock.

Archie's Wok ASIAN $$$
(Map p512; ✆222-04-11; http://archieswok.com; Rodríguez 130; mains M$125-225; ⏱2-11pm Mon-Sat; 🍴) This elegant, urbane restaurant has long showed Puerto Vallarta a thing or two about good eating. The menu changes, but it's always Asian fusion, with savory fish in rich tropical sauces the highlight.

Marisma Fish Taco TAQUERÍA $
(Map p512; www.marismafishtaco.com, in Spanish; Naranjo 320; tacos/quesadillas M$16/24; ⏱10am-5pm) Shrimp and smoked marlin rule the roost at this streetside taquería (taco stand). Pull up a stool and watch as the women behind the counter press fresh tortillas and fry up tasty treats from a simple menu weighted heavily toward seafood tacos and quesadillas.

El Mole de Jovita MEXICAN $
(Map p512; Badillo 220; mains M$60-80; ⏱9am-11pm Mon-Sat) Its tables glowing with colorful Mexican oilcloths in classic fruit and flower designs, this family-run restaurant specializes in chicken with mole (chili sauce), but also serves good breakfasts and reasonably priced Mexican standards.

La Palapa SEAFOOD $$$
(Map p512; www.lapalapapv.com; Púlpito 103; mains M$199-425; ⏱8am-11pm) Elegant beach dining at its best. Tables are positioned to take full advantage of the sea views, making it a particularly marvelous spot for breakfast or sunset. Delicacies include pepper-crusted yellow-fin tuna or sherry-and-soy-marinated snapper with asparagus, chorizo and shrimp beignets.

GAY & LESBIAN PUERTO VALLARTA

Come on out – the rainbow flag flies high over Puerto Vallarta. An ever-increasing stream of visitors descends on Vallarta annually for its formidable selection of gay bars, nightclubs, restaurants and hotels, as well as its busy annual calendar of gay- and lesbian-themed events such as **Vallarta Fever** (www.vallartafever.com) in late November and **Vallarta Girl** (www.vallartagirl.com) in mid-February. The **Gay Guide Vallarta** (www.gayguidevallarta.com) booklet has tons of information and a helpful map for finding gay-friendly businesses.

Clubs & Nightspots

Most dance clubs open from 10pm until at least 4am, and some stay open well past sunrise. For an entertaining introduction to Vallarta's gay nightlife scene, check out the **Old Town Bar Hop** (www.dianastours.com/old_town_bar_hop.php; M$650) offered by Diana's Tours.

Mañana (Map p512; www.manana.mx; Carranza 290) With live entertainment, two dance floors, multiple bars and a swimming pool with a waterfall, this jubilant indoor-outdoor space is at the epicenter of Vallarta's gay club scene.

Paco's Ranch (Map p512; www.pacosranch.com; Vallarta 237) This venerable disco/cantina stages smashing transvestite reviews Friday through Sunday mornings.

Antropology (Map p512; www.antropologypv.com; Morelos 101) It's raining men at this sizzling dance mecca and male-stripper venue with its dark, intimate rooftop patio. Women are unapologetically disallowed.

The Zona Romántica is teeming with atmospheric cocktail bars catering to a gay and lesbian clientele: **La Noche** (Map p512; www.lanochepv.com; Cárdenas 257; ⊗4pm-2am) is well loved for its convivial ambience and buff bartenders; **Sama Bar** (Map p512; Olas Altas 510; ⊗4:30pm-2am) is a likable small place with big martinis; and **Frida** (Map p512; http://barfrida.com; Insurgentes 301A; ⊗1pm-2am) is a cozy and sociable cantina featuring enticing drink specials.

Resorts & Inns

Hotel Mercurio (Map p512; ☑222-47-93, in the US 866-388-2689; www.hotel-mercurio.com; Rodríguez 168; s/d incl breakfast US$98/128; ❄@🗟🗷) Less than two blocks from Muertos

---

La Ciabatta SANDWICHES $
(Map p512; Vallarta 130; mains M$69-89; ⊗8am-6pm Mon-Fri, to 4pm Sat) This is a modern eatery that specializes in excellent homemade European-style bread, sold by the loaf or used in a variety of tempting panini. Other good reasons to visit include the Mexican- and North American–style breakfasts, salads and daily lunch specials including main course, salad and drink for M$69.

Fredy's Tucan BREAKFAST $
(Map p512; www.fredystucan.com; Badillo 245; breakfast M$48-98; ⊗breakfast & lunch) This gringo breakfast paradise serves waffles, omelets and almost anything else you could want in an ample courtyard three blocks from the beach.

Paris Café BAKERY, FRENCH $
(Map p512; Suárez 158; pastries & snacks M$15-40; ⊗8am-8pm Mon-Sat, to 4pm Sun) You could easily miss this hole-in-the-wall bakery, but don't! The flamboyant French owner bakes fabulous sweet and savory goodies, including éclairs, fruit tarts, quiches and chocolate-almond croissants.

Pancho's Takos TAQUERÍA $
(Map p512; Badillo 162; tacos M$10; ⊗6pm-2am Mon-Sat) Drawing a regular nighttime crowd, this taquería serves delicious *tacos al pastor* until the wee hours.

Pie in the Sky BAKERY $
(Map p512; http://pieinthesky.com.mx; Serdán 242; pie slices M$38-45; ⊗8am-10pm; 🗟) Voted Vallarta's best bakery year after year, this little place specializes in pies but also brews a good cup of joe and lets customers linger over the free wi-fi.

NORTH OF THE RÍO CUALE

Café des Artistes INTERNATIONAL $$$
(☑222-32-28; www.cafedesartistes.com; Sánchez 740; mains M$215-430; ⊗6-11:30pm) Many consider this to be Vallarta's finest restaurant.

pier, this three-story hotel features 28 rooms around a pleasant courtyard with a stylish pool and bar. Rooms have fridges, wi-fi, cable TV and double or king-sized beds with fine linens. Gourmet breakfasts, spa packages and free international phone calls are among the other perks on offer.

Blue Chairs Beach Resort (☑222-50-40, from the US 888-302-3662; www.bluechairs resort.com; Almendro 4; r US$112-170, ste US$195-230; ❋❀📶❂) At the south end of Playa de los Muertos – one of Mexico's most famous gay beaches – this resort is a good place to let it all hang out (although officially the beach has a 'no nudity' policy). The attached beach club is Vallarta's most popular, visible gay beach bar, with droves of couples enjoying the sun's ubiquitous rays and cool drinks. There's also a raucous nightspot with live entertainment on the roof. The breezy and attractive rooms have cable TV; suites have kitchenettes.

Casa Cupula (Map p512; ☑223-24-84, from the US 866-352-2511; www.casacupula.com; Callejón de la Igualdad 129; r US$175-295, ste US$365-555; ❋@📶❂) Sophisticated design and luxurious flourishes define this extremely popular resort catering to both gays and lesbians. Each room is uniquely and tastefully decorated, with amenities ranging from home-theater-sized TVs to private Jacuzzis in some suites. The beach is only a few blocks downhill, although the resort's four pools, gym, onsite restaurant and bar may give you enough incentive to linger here all day.

Villa David (Map p512; ☑223-03-15, from the US 877-832-3315; www.villadavidpv.com; Galeana 348; r M$109-139; ❋@📶❂) Reservations are essential and clothing optional at this swanky, male-only gay retreat in a beautiful hacienda-style mansion. It's the only such B&B in Vallarta's historic district. With gorgeously landscaped grounds and tastefully appointed rooms, this is the perfect choice for a romantic getaway with a special Fred.

Abbey Hotel (Map p512; ☑222-84-45; www.abbeyhotelvallarta.com; Púlpito 138; s/d/tr/q US$130/142/165/177, ste US$165-224; ❋@📶❂) This midsized gay-oriented hotel – well known for its large, sociable hot tub – is smack dab in the middle of the Puerto Vallarta action. The 54 bright units are distinguished by the well-equipped bathrooms with big, luxurious showers and the balconies, many with excellent views.

You're sure to enjoy its romantic ambience and exquisite fusion of French and Mexican influences. The service is formal but unobtrusive, and reservations are recommended. It's eight blocks north of the Templo de Guadalupe.

Esquina de los Caprichos   SPANISH $$
(Map p512; Miramar 402; tapas M$40-85, mains M$85-140; ⏰8:30am-10pm Mon-Sat) This classy little place combines an intimate front room with a Gaudi-inspired back patio full of colorfully painted tables and broken tile mosaics. Most of the dishes you'd expect to find at a tapas bar in Barcelona – delicious gazpacho, fried calamari, garlic shrimp and paella (Saturday only) – are served here on charming handmade plates.

La Cigale   FRENCH $$$
(Map p512; www.lacigalebistro.com; Hidalgo 398; mains M$155-220; ⏰5-11:30pm) In the shadow of the cathedral, this casual-chic French bistro with chalkboard menus and checkerboard floors serves everything from quiche Lorraine to steak tartare, accompanied by French, Chilean and Argentine wines.

El Arrayán Cocina Tradicional   MEXICAN $$$
(off Map p512; ☑222-71-95; http://elarrayan.com.mx; Allende 344; mains M$150-245; ⏰5:30-11pm Wed-Mon) Owner Carmen Porras takes special pleasure in rescuing old family recipes from obscurity, with an emphasis on fresh local ingredients. Specialties include crispy duck *carnitas* (braised marinated duck) with orange sauce, and rib-eye steak marinated in Mexican spices and tequila. The restaurant, with its open kitchen and romantic courtyard, also serves as a venue for bimonthly cooking classes (p510). It's 10 blocks northeast of the Templo de Guadalupe.

Gaby's   MEXICAN $$
(Map p512; Mina 252; mains M$80-190; ⏰8:30am-10pm Mon-Sat, 10am-10pm Sun) Since 1989, this

WORTH A TRIP

HACIENDA EL DIVISADERO

Head for the hills and immerse yourself in rural life at **Hacienda El Divisadero** (cell phone 322-1453455; www.haciendaeldivisadero.com; Camino Tuito-Chacala Km 9, Las Guásimas). This vast ranch 90 minutes south of Puerto Vallarta offers a slew of fun activities, including horseback excursions to local petroglyphs, swimming in a gorgeous river, and tours of the distillery where they produce knock-your-socks-off *raicilla* (a tequila-like distillation of wild agave). The onsite restaurant serves delicious meals (mains M$124 to M$189), including steaks, Mexican standards and fabulous *mole poblano* (*mole* from the state of Puebla). If you like, you can even spend the night here (double room M$1350, with meals and horseback-riding tours M$3100).

To get here, drive south of Puerto Vallarta 45km on Hwy 200 to the town of El Tuito, then follow the signs another 10km west to the Hacienda. Alternatively, you can visit the ranch on a tour organized by Vallarta Adventures (p510).

bright and cheerful family-run place with upstairs seating and a tree-shaded back patio has been serving dependably tasty Mexican classics; it's best at lunchtime, when the daily *comida corrida* (prix-fixe menu; including main dish, soup and *agua fresca*) costs only M$59.

La Dolce Vita ITALIAN **$$**
(off Map p512; www.dolcevita.com.mx; Paseo Díaz Ordaz 674; mains M$102-215, pizzas M$115-146; noon-2am Mon-Sat, 6pm-midnight Sun) A cheerful, often-crowded spot for wood-fired pizzas, pastas and people-watching. Request a table upstairs by the window for great views.

Planeta Vegetariano VEGETARIAN **$**
(Map p512; www.planetavegetariano.com; Iturbide 270; buffet breakfast/lunch or dinner M$50/75; 8am-10pm;) This buffet-style place with only 10 tables eschews cheese for fresh, dairy-free dishes such as soy enchiladas, banana lasagna (yes, that's right) and a wide range of creatively conceived salads.

 Drinking

Vallarta has many choice spots for sipping a strong coffee or tipping a tipple. It's ridiculously easy to become inebriated here, where two-for-one happy hours are as reliable as the sunset, and the margarita glasses look like oversized snifters. Coffee shops open about 7am and close around midnight; most bars keep the lime squeezers occupied until well after that.

De Santos BAR
(www.desantos.com.mx; Plaza Peninsula, Blvd Ascensio 2485; 9:30pm-4am Fri & Sat) Candles and strings of vintage light bulbs create a ro-

mantic mood at this terrace bar north of the center, founded by drummer Alex González from the group Maná. On Fridays and Saturdays there's live jazz funk into the wee hours, plus a great drinks list dominated by mezcal, martinis and the infamous house special *pata salada* – an organically grown, agave-derived local firewater.

A Page in the Sun CAFE
(Map p512; Cárdenas 179; 7am-11pm;) This friendly and highly recommended cafe doubles as a bookstore and social hangout, with good espresso drinks, comfy couches, regular conversational language groups, and a play area and Saturday story hour for kids.

Uncommon Grounds
Chill-Out Lounge LOUNGE
(off Map p512; www.uncommon-grounds.com; Cárdenas 625; 4-11pm Wed-Sat) Spacious and homey, this one-of-a-kind bar and restaurant is an agreeable place to settle back on a sofa, sip a cocktail and watch as beautifully presented dishes are trotted out from the kitchen with panache by hosts Lydia and Anne. You can also get a chair massage, shop in the small boutique, or head to the low-lit dance room in back.

La Bodeguita del Medio BAR
(off Map p512; labodeguitadelmedio.com.mx; Paseo Díaz Ordaz 858; 11am-4am) This graffiti-covered Cuban joint has live music Tuesday through Sunday nights, stiff mojitos and a great beach ambience.

Blanco y Negro BAR
(cnr Lucerna & Niza, Zona Hotelera; 10am-10pm Mon-Thu, to 2am Fri & Sat) A pleasant bar and cafe in the Zona Hotelera that attracts mainly locals, this is a great place to hear *trova*

(Latin accoustic pop ballads) on Friday and Saturday evenings.

Andale   BAR
(Map p512; ☏222-10-54; Olas Altas 425; ☺8am-2am) Party hearty with throngs of young vacationers. Very loud classic rock.

☆ Entertainment

Vallarta's main forms of nighttime entertainment revolve around dancing, drinking and dining. At night everyone and their brother strolls the *malecón,* choosing from a fantastic selection of restaurants, bars and hot nightspots. There's often entertainment in the amphitheater by the sea, opposite Plaza Principal. Softly lit Isla Cuale is a quiet haven for a romantic promenade in the early evening.

Bullfights are held at 5pm on Wednesday from November to April in the Plaza de Toros opposite Marina Vallarta.

Nightclubs & Discos

Cover charges are normally waived early in the week; on Friday and Saturday nights they often include one or two drinks.

Roxy Rock House   LIVE MUSIC
(Map p512; www.roxyrockhouse.com.mx; Vallarta 217; ☺8pm-6am) In the heart of the Zona Romántica, this place draws an enthusiastic mixed crowd every Friday and Saturday night with live rock and blues and no cover charge.

J&B Salsa Club   CLUB
(Av Ascencio 2043; ☺8pm-late Mon-Sat) Vallarta's premier Latin dance club (pronounced 'hota-bey') features live bands Friday and Saturday, with DJs the rest of the week. The salsa lessons (M$50, from 8pm to 10pm Tuesday, Thursday and Friday) are a big draw, as are the Monday-night tango lessons. It's about 3.5km north of downtown Vallarta along the main coastal highway.

Hyde   CLUB
(Av Las Garzas s/n; ☺10pm-late Thu-Sat) At the Krystal Puerto Vallarta, this flashy dance club is occasionally explosive, with cutting-edge sound and lighting systems.

Along the *malecón* is a bunch of places where teen and 20-something tourists get trashed and dance on tables. On a good night, they all stay open from 11pm until 5am. You can see from the street which one has the most action. Good bets include **Bebotero** (Map p512; http://bebotero .com.mx; Paseo Díaz Ordaz 522), **Mandala** (off Map p512; http://mandaladisco.com; Paseo Díaz Ordaz 640), **Roo Nightclub** (Map p512; http:// roo-nightclub.com; Morelos 464) and **Punto V** (off Map p512; Paseo Díaz Ordaz 786).

🛍 Shopping

Vallarta is a haven for shoppers, with many shops and boutiques selling fashionable clothing, beachwear and crafts from all over Mexico. Tequila and Cuban cigars are also big business.

Mercado de Artesanías   HANDICRAFTS
(Map p512; A Rodríguez 260) Straddling the north bank of the Río Cuale, this market sells everything from Taxco silver, serapes (blankets with a head opening, worn as a cloak) and huaraches (woven leather sandals) to wool wall-hangings and blown glass.

Huarachería Fabiola   SHOES
(Map p512; Vallarta 145) This Vallarta-style cobbler produces custom-made sandals (M$200 to M$400) in 48 hours.

Olinalá   ARTS & CRAFTS
(Map p512; Cárdenas 274) In business since 1978, this excellent little shop displays authentic Mexican dance masks, folk art and rural antiques.

Mundo de Azulejos   CERAMICS
(Map p512; Carranza 374) This store offers a vast array of brightly colored Talavera tiles and ceramics.

Both **Artesanías Flores** (Map p512; Cárdenas 282) and **Peyote People** (Map p512; Juárez 222) sell Huichol beadwork, thread paintings and jewelry.

A HOLIDAY FOR WHALES

Like many people reading this book, during the winter months humpback whales come to the Bahía de Banderas to mate. They leave their feeding grounds in Alaskan waters and show up in Mexico from around November to the end of March. Once they have arrived, they form courtship groups or bear the calves that were conceived the year before. By the end of March the whales' attention turns to the long journey back to their feeding grounds up north. Whale-watching trips (see p510) operate from December to March.

ℹ Information

Emergency
Ambulance (☎222-15-33)
Fire (☎223-94-76)
Police (☎060, 223-25-00)

Internet Access
Ciber Milenium (Libertad 335; per hr M$10; ☺9am-9:30pm) Just north of the river, with flat screens and fast connections.

Media
A pair of English-language print publications – the weekly *Vallarta Tribune* (www.vallartatribune.com) and the biweekly *Bay Vallarta* (www.bayvallarta.com) – offer useful cultural and shopping listings.

Medical Services
San Javier Marina Hospital (☎226-10-10; Av Ascencio 2760) Vallarta's best-equipped hospital.

Money
Although most businesses in Vallarta accept US dollars as readily as they accept pesos, their exchange rates are generally abysmal. Several banks around Plaza Principal have ATMs.

Vallarta has many *casas de cambio;* their rates differ and are slightly less favorable than the banks. Look for them on Insurgentes, Vallarta and the *malecón.*

Banamex (cnr Juárez & Zaragoza) On the southeast corner of Plaza Principal.

HSBC (cnr Insurgentes & Miramar) Just north of the Río Cuale bridge.

Post
Main post office (Colombia 1014)

Telephone & Fax
Pay phones are plentiful everywhere in town, as are *casetas de teléfono* (public telephone call stations). Many internet cafes offer Skype service.

Tourist Information
Municipal tourist office (Map p512; ☎226-80-80, ext 232; Juárez s/n; ☺8am-8pm Mon-Sat, 10am-6pm Sun) Vallarta's busy but competent office, in the municipal building at the northeast corner of Plaza Principal, has free maps, multilingual tourist literature and bilingual staff.

ℹ Getting There & Away
Air

Gustavo Díaz Ordaz International Airport (Map p507; ☎221-12-98; aeropuertosgap.com.mx/english/airports/puertovallarta-airport; Carretera Tepic Km 7.5) is 10km north of the city and is served by the following carriers.

Aeroméxico (☎221-12-04; www.aeromexico.com; Airport) Direct service to Ciudad Juárez, Guadalajara and Mexico City.

Interjet (☎221-32-06; www.interjet.com.mx; Airport) Direct service to Mexico City and Toluca.

MagniCharters (☎55-1999-1611; www.magnicharters.com.mx; Airport) Direct service to Mexico City and Monterrey.

VivaAerobus (☎55-4777-5050; www.vivaaerobus.com; Airport) Direct service to Monterrey.

Volaris (☎800-122-80-00; www.volaris.mx; Airport) Direct service to Tijuana.

Bus
Vallarta's long-distance bus station (Map p507) is just off Hwy 200, about 10km north of the city center and 2km northeast of the airport.

Primera Plus (Carranza 393) and **ETN** (Cárdenas 268) both have downtown offices south of the Río Cuale where you can buy tickets. If you're heading to Barra de Navidad, Manzanillo or other points south, you can save a trip to the bus terminal by boarding at the corner of Carranza and Aguacate (half a block from the Primera Plus ticket office).

Car & Motorcycle
Starting at about M$500 per day, on-the-spot car rentals are pricey during the high season; you'll often do better booking online. At other times, deep discounts are offered.

A dozen car-rental agencies maintain adjacent counters in the airport arrivals hall, including those listed below.

Alamo (☎221-12-28)
Avis (☎221-16-57)
Budget (☎221-18-88)
Dollar/Thrifty (☎209-10-05)
Europcar (☎209-09-21)
Hertz (☎221-31-59)
National (☎221-12-26)
Sixt (☎209-06-85)

ℹ Getting Around
To/From the Airport
The cheapest way to get to/from the airport is on a local bus for M$6.50. 'Centro' and 'Olas Altas' buses go into town from a stop just outside the arrivals hall. Returning from town, 'Aeropuerto,' 'Juntas' and 'Ixtapa' buses all stop right at the airport entrance.

From the airport to the city, taxis charge fixed rates (posted at the terminal exit) ranging from M$180 to M$310, depending on which neighborhood you're traveling to. You can save money by crossing Hwy 200 via the pedestrian bridge

BUSES FROM PUERTO VALLARTA

DESTINATION	FARE (M$)	DURATION	FREQUENCY (DAILY)
Barra de Navidad	180-218	3½-4hr	frequent
Guadalajara	288-352	5½hr	very frequent
Manzanillo	230-294	5-5½hr	hourly
Mazatlán	400-420	8hr	6
Mexico City (Terminal Norte)	954-1135	12hr	7
San Blas	150	3½hr	4
San Patricio-Melaque	178-215	3½-4hr	frequent
Tepic	176-196	3½-4hr	frequent

outside the arrivals hall and taking a taxi from the opposite side of the street, where drivers are allowed to charge lower fares (M$120 to M$150 per car load). Alternatively, take a *taxi colectivo* (M$75 to M$115 per passenger) from the arrivals hall, available whenever there's an incoming flight. A taxi back to the airport from downtown costs around M$120.

Boat

Vallarta's water taxis serve the beautiful beaches on the southern side of the bay, many of which are accessible only by boat. Departing from the Playa de los Muertos pier (under reconstruction at the time of research), they head south around the bay, making stops at Playa Las Ánimas (25 minutes), Quimixto (30 minutes) and Yelapa (45 minutes); the round-trip fare is M$250 for any destination. Boats depart Puerto Vallarta every hour or two between 10am and 4:30pm, returning from Yelapa (the end of the line) with the same frequency between 7:30am and 3:45pm daily.

Private yachts and *lanchas* can be hired from the southern side of the Playa de los Muertos pier, starting from around M$350 per hour. They'll take you to any secluded beach around the bay; most have gear aboard for snorkeling and fishing.

Bus

Blue and white local buses operate every five minutes from 5am to 11pm on most routes, and cost M$6.50. Plaza Lázaro Cárdenas near Playa Olas Altas is a major departure hub. Northbound local buses also stop on Insurgentes near the corner of Madero.

Northbound buses marked 'Aeropuerto,' 'Ixtapa,' 'Mojoneras' and 'Juntas' pass through the city heading north to the airport and Marina Vallarta; the 'Mojoneras' bus also stops at Puerto Vallarta's long-distance bus terminal.

White and orange 'Boca de Tomatlán' buses (M$7) head south along the coastal highway through Mismaloya (20 minutes) to Boca de Tomatlán (30 minutes). They depart from the corner of Badillo and Constitución every 15 minutes from 5:30am to 11pm.

Taxi

Cab prices are regulated by zones; the cost for a ride is determined by how many zones you cross. A typical trip from downtown to the Zona Hotelera costs M$80; to the airport or the long-distance bus station M$120; and to Mismaloya M$130. Always determine the price of the ride before you get in. Hailing a cab is easy in the city center along Morelos. There are several taxi stands, including one on Morelos between Corona and Galeana, one on Morelos at Rodríguez, and one on Carranza at Plaza Lázaro Cárdenas.

Costalegre Beaches

South of Puerto Vallarta, the stretch of Mexico's Pacific coast from Chamela to Barra de Navidad is blessed with many fine beaches. Tourism promoters and developers refer to this shoreline as the 'Costalegre' (Happy Coast).

Following are the beaches from north to south (with kilometer numbers measured from the junction of Hwys 80 and 200 just outside San Patricio-Melaque).

Playa Pérula (Km 73), a sheltered beach at the northern end of tranquil 11km-long Bahía de Chamela, is great for swimming and extended walks. There are cheap accommodations and a smattering of *palapa* restaurants.

At Bahía de Chamela, **Playa Chamela** (Km 72) and **Playa La Negrita** (Km 64) are isolated, relaxing beaches with a couple of restaurants but no hotels. The nine islands in the expansive bay are beautiful to see in silhouette at sunset.

With the help of local activists, endangered hawksbill sea turtles are making a comeback at **Playa Careyes** (Km 52).

Escape artists love **Playa Tecuán** (Km 33) for its long, deserted white-sand beach and eerie abandoned resort. It's a 10km drive off the highway on a rutted gravel road.

On the palm-fringed Bahía Tenacatita, **Playa Tenacatita** (Km 28) has clear snorkeling waters and a large mangrove lagoon with good bird-watching. Also on this bay are **Playa Boca de Iguanas** (Km 19) and **Playa La Manzanilla** (Km 13). The surf is mild, the sand is hot and wonderful, and the beaches are shallow for a long way out, making them good for a swim. The two latter villages have accommodations and restaurants.

Bahía de Navidad

The tight arc of the Bahía de Navidad is practically ringed by deep, honey-colored sand with two resort towns at either end, waving amiably at each other. Situated 5km apart, Barra de Navidad and San Patricio-Melaque are siblings with distinct personalities. Barra is beloved for its attractive cobbled streets and aura of good living, while San Patricio-Melaque, the scrappier of the two, draws budget-minded travelers seeking to get back to basics in a place that eschews pretension.

SAN PATRICIO-MELAQUE
☎ 315 / POP 7600

Known by most as Melaque (meh-*lah*-keh), this kick-back resort hasn't lost its old Mexico charm. It's a popular vacation destination for Mexican families and a low-key winter hangout for snowbirds (principally Canadians). The main activities are swimming, lazing on the beach, watching pelicans fish at sunrise and sunset, climbing to the *mirador* (lookout point) at the bay's west end, prowling the plaza and public market, or walking the beach to Barra de Navidad.

Tours

Experience Mex-ECO Tours ECOTOURS
(☎355-70-27; www.mex-ecotours.com; Gómez Farías 59-2) Run by zoologist Ruth Hazlewood and marine biologist Daniel Patman, this company operates an impressive array of day trips near Melaque and multiday excursions throughout Mexico, all with a commit-

ment to sustainable tourism. Its new office in Barra de Navidad offers a variety of boat trips and water sports – see p524 for details.

The Only Tours TOURS
(☎355-67-77; raystoursmelaque@yahoo.com; Las Cabañas 26) Runs full-day tours to Tenacatita (M$400) and Colima (M$750), plus bird-watching and all-terrain-vehicle excursions to more remote areas. Also rents out bikes, snorkeling gear and body boards (each M$100 per day).

Festivals & Events

Fiesta de San Patricio TRADITIONAL
Melaque honors its patron saint with a blow-out week of festivities, including all-day parties, rodeos, a carnival, music, dances and nightly fireworks, leading up to St Patrick's Day (March 17).

Sleeping

Rates vary greatly depending on the season; the following prices are for the high season (November through May). Discounts are common for longer stays.

La Paloma Oceanfront Retreat APARTMENT $$$
(☎355-53-45; www.lapalomamexico.com; Las Cabañas 13; 2-/4-person studios per week from US$725/1400; ⓟ❄⊛) Original art abounds at this unique boutique resort. The 14 singular, comfortable studios have kitchens and terraces with rewarding ocean views. Lush gardens, a 25m beachside swimming pool, a well-stocked library, wireless internet access and free breakfast by the poolside in winter make an extended stay here extremely tempting. Drawing, painting and mask-making classes are offered upon request at the owner's art studio next door. From October to April, units rent by the week and advance reservations are essential; per-night rates are sometimes offered during the summer.

Bungalows Villamar BUNGALOW $
(☎355-50-05; bungalowsvillamar@prodigy.net. mx; Hidalgo 1; s/d/tr M$250/350/400; ❄⊛) Yes, the beach access is narrow, but at these prices who's complaining? The six bungalows share a beachfront sitting area and a yard with a porta-pool just back from the waterfront. Smaller bungalows have air-con, while the fan-cooled ones sleep up to 10 people. The owner, Roberto, speaks excellent English.

Hotel Bahía
HOTEL $$

(☎355-68-94; www.melaquehotelbahia.com; Legazpi 5; d/q M$400/500, d/q bungalow M$450/550; ❀🔊☎) Half a block from the beach, this well-maintained family-run place is one of Melaque's best budget options. Six of the 26 units have private kitchens; nine have aircon (M$100 extra).

Villas Camino del Mar
HOTEL $$

(☎355-52-07; www.villascaminodelmar.com.mx; Villa 6; d M$670-1026, ste M$1277-2387, penthouse M$2668; P❀🔊☎) Clean and dazzlingly white, this terrific beach hotel has three pools and accommodations ranging from small rooms to luxurious penthouses. It also handles reservations for other properties in the neighborhood.

Casa Paula
GUESTHOUSE $

(☎355-50-93; Vallarta 6; d/q M$100/150) Around a courtyard in this simple home there are four basic rooms with concrete floors, TV, fridge and shared kitchen. It's very quiet and a pleasant family atmosphere pervades.

Ejidal Campground
CAMPGROUND $

(campsites per night/month M$50/1100) This bare-bones beachfront campground at the west end of town has no hookups, but there are rudimentary shower and bathroom facilities (M$5 per use), and the setting is undeniably beautiful.

✖ Eating & Drinking

From 6pm to midnight, food stands serve inexpensive Mexican fare a block east of the plaza along Juárez. A row of pleasant *palapa* restaurants stretches along the beach at the west end of town.

Concha del Mar
MEXICAN, SEAFOOD $

(Las Palmas 27; mains M$35-105; ◷8am-11pm Dec-Feb, 11am-11pm Mar-Nov) As you stroll 'Palapa Row,' look for the blue archway entrance of this popular beachside eatery, which offers two-for-one drinks all afternoon. From large breakfasts to Mexican combo plates to

shrimp and fish fajitas, the price is right, and the location – with dramatic views of sunset over the rocks offshore – couldn't be better.

Flor Morena
MEXICAN $

(Juárez s/n; mains M$25-50; ◷6-11pm Tue-Sun) Shrimp *pozole* (M$50) is the house specialty at this superfriendly little place on the plaza; peso-pinchers will also appreciate its tasty *sopes* (tortillas with a layer of beans, cheese and salsa), enchiladas, tacos, *tostadas* (tortillas that have been baked or fried until they get crisp and then are cooled) and *tamales* (M$25 to M$35).

Restaurant-Bar Albatroz
BAR

(Cabañas 36; ◷2pm-midnight) Dine on the tiled terrace or dance in the sand at this popular beachfront bar with live music on Friday and Saturday nights.

ℹ Information

Barra de Navidad's tourist office (p525) provides basic information on Melaque, including a street map.

Banamex (Gómez Farías s/n) On Melaque's main street. Has an ATM and will change US and Canadian dollars.

Cyber La Playita (López Mateos; internet per hr M$15; ◷9am-11pm) Half a block south of the plaza.

Post office (Orozco s/n) Three blocks southeast of the plaza.

ℹ Getting There & Away

AIR
For information on flights to nearby Playa de Oro International Airport, see p529.

BUS
Melaque has two bus stations. Transportes Cihuatlán and Primera Plus/Servicios Coordinados are on opposite sides of Carranza at the corner of Gómez Farías. Both have 1st- and 2nd-class buses and ply similar routes for similar fares.

Local buses to Barra de Navidad (M$6, 15 minutes) leave every 15 minutes from a stop at

BUSES FROM SAN PATRICIO-MELAQUE

DESTINATION	FARE (M$)	DURATION	FREQUENCY (DAILY)
Guadalajara	276-326	5½-7hr	hourly
Manzanillo	51-65	1-1½hr	half-hourly
Mexico City (Terminal Norte)	971	13hr	5:15pm & 7:50pm
Puerto Vallarta	178-229	4-5hr	frequent

Juárez and López Mateos, opposite the south-west corner of the plaza.

TAXI

A taxi between Melaque and Barra should cost M$50 to M$60; taxis congregate at the plaza.

BARRA DE NAVIDAD
315 / POP 4300

The charming town of Barra de Navidad (usually simply called Barra) is squeezed onto a sandbar between Bahía de Navidad and the Laguna de Navidad. Barra first came to prominence in 1564 when its shipyards produced the galleons used by conquistador Miguel López de Legazpi and Father André de Urdaneta to deliver the Philippines to King Felipe of Spain. By 1600, however, most of the conquests were being conducted from Acapulco, and Barra slipped into sleepy obscurity (a state from which it has yet to fully emerge).

In October 2011, Hurricane Jova took a big bite out of Barra's beachfront, leaving a couple of landmark businesses tilting at queasy angles into the sand. Rebuilding was underway at the time of research.

Activities

Barra's steep and narrow beach is lovely to behold, but conditions are sometimes too rough for swimming. The gentlest conditions are generally in the mornings.

Boat Trips BOAT TOUR
Trips into the Laguna de Navidad are a Barra highlight. The boatmen's cooperative, **Sociedad Cooperativa de Servicios Turísticos** (Veracruz 40; ⊙7am-sunset), books a variety of boat excursions ranging from half-hour trips around the lagoon ($300 per boat) to all-day jungle trips to Tenacatita (M$3000 per boat). The cooperative also offers fishing, snorkeling and diving trips, plus visits to the tiny village of Colimilla, where there are several welcoming seafood restaurants. Prices are posted at the open-air lagoonside office.

For a short jaunt out on the water you could also catch a water taxi from a nearby dock and head over to the Grand Bay Hotel Wyndham Resort on Isla de Navidad (M$20 round trip).

Fishing FISHING
The waters near Barra are rife with marlin, swordfish, albacore, dorado, snapper and other more rarefied catches. Fishing trips on *lanchas* can be arranged at the boatman's cooperative for M$500 per hour or M$3000

per day, including gear; many trips include snorkeling stops.

Golf GOLF
Grand Bay Golf Course (*337-90-25; Grand Bay Hotel Wyndham Resort, Isla Navidad; green fees 9/18/27 holes US$180/200/220) is a celebrated 27-hole course with excellent vistas and greens carved into ocean dunes against a backdrop of mountains. Caddies and rental clubs are available.

Courses

Amigas LANGUAGE COURSE
(*107-52-80; www.easyspanish.net; Michoacán 58; lessons per hr private/semiprivate/group US$15/11.50/7.50) This small school aims to make language instruction fun and instantly applicable. Many classes are taught in town in real-life situations; along with basic grammar, you'll learn a thing or two about Mexican slang.

Tours

Experience Mex-ECO Tours ECOTOURS
(*355-70-27; www.mex-ecotours.com; Veracruz 204) The new branch of this Melaque-based ecotourism company offers sunset cruises (per person from M$500), fishing charters (per person from M$1250), waterskiing and waverunner excursions (per half-hour M$600), snorkeling excursions (per person M$500), diving trips (one-/two-tank dives M$1000/1500) and day tours to Tenacatita (per person from M$700).

Festivals & Events

Torneo Internacional de Pesca FISHING
This three-day festival, held around the third week in January, is the most noteworthy of several big-money international fishing tournaments held annually for marlin, sailfish, tuna and dorado.

Sleeping

Barra has fewer beachfront rooms than its neighbor Melaque. The prices listed here are for the high season (between November and May).

TOP CHOICE **Grand Bay Hotel Resort** RESORT $$$
(*314-331-05-00; www.wyndham.com; Isla Navidad; d US$199-239, ste US$339-539; P❄@🛜🏊) Across the lagoon from Barra and accessible by a short water-taxi ride, this superluxury resort on Isla de Navidad offers magnificent rooms with marble floors, hand-carved furniture, and bathrooms big enough to herd sheep in. The numerous amenities include

a private marina, three grass tennis courts, golf packages, a 'kids' club' day-care center and big fluffy bathrobes.

Hotel Delfín   HOTEL $$
(☎355-50-68; www.hoteldelfinmx.com; Morelos 23; s/d/tr/q M$495/595/695/795; P🅿🌀❄) The homey Delfín is one of Barra's best deals. It has 24 large and pleasant rooms featuring shared balconies, a grassy pool area and an exercise room. Discounts are available for longer stays, but repeat customers fill the place in winter.

Casa Chips   HOTEL $$
(☎355-55-55; www.casachips.com; Legazpi 198; d M$715-919, ste M$975-1430; ❇❄) One of Barra's few beachfront options, Chips is most appealing for its two big ocean-facing suites with terraces, great views, nice tile and brickwork, and kitchenettes. Less welcoming are the interior and street-facing rooms, which can get a bit claustrophobic.

Hotel Costa Dorada   BUNGALOW $
(☎355-64-10; www.costadorada-hotel.com; Veracruz 174; d/q bungalow M$350/600; P❇❄) Split among three different buildings on Barra's main drag, these bungalows with built-in kitchenettes are attractively tiled with animal designs, and range in size from doubles to units sleeping up to five people. The best rooms are set back from the street, behind the reception area. Larger units across the way are more susceptible to street noise. Six units come with air-con; the rest have fans.

Hotel Posada Pacífico   HOTEL $
(☎355-53-59;   www.hotelposadapacifico.com; Mazatlán 136; s/d/tr/q M$200/300/350/400, bungalow M$600-700; P❄) This friendly, comfortable posada near the bus terminals has 25 large, clean rooms with TV, and an additional four bungalows sleeping up to four people.

🍴 Eating

Simple, inexpensive little indoor-outdoor places line Veracruz in the center of town, while pricier options are found along the Pacific beachfront and the lagoon.

México Lindo   TAQUERÍA $$
(Legazpi 138; tacos & quesadillas M$30-69, mains M$75-120; ⏰8:30am-midnight) With simple plastic tables under a corrugated tin roof, Mexico Lindo's back patio somehow manages to feel romantic and intimate at night. The menu features regional favorites such as savory and sour tortilla soup, quesadil-

las and garlic fish tacos. A good selection of cocktails seals the deal.

Bananas   BREAKFAST $
(Legazpi 250; breakfast mains M$45-66; ⏰8am-noon year-round, plus 6-10pm Dec-Easter) For breakfast with a fine ocean view, nothing beats this 2nd-floor eatery above Hotel Barra de Navidad. Angle for one of the terrace tables overlooking the beach, then sit back and enjoy the menu of Mexican-American favorites, from the trademark banana pancakes to *chilaquiles* (fried tortillas with green or red salsa, eggs and/or chicken).

Restaurant Ramon's   MEXICAN $$
(Legazpi 260; mains M$96-138; ⏰7am-11pm) This casual and friendly restaurant is justifiably popular for its excellent fish tacos, *chiles rellenos,* and local and gringo favorites such as fish and chips.

🍸 Drinking & Entertainment

Towards the pier at the foot of Legazpi, a cluster of bars keeps hopping into the wee hours. **Tres Quince Surf Bar** draws a rowdy crowd to its outdoor patio with margaritas and other mixed drinks, while across the street **Jarro Beach Sports Bar & Disco** has frequent live music.

ℹ Information

Banamex (Veracruz s/n) One of two ATMs just south of Barra's main plaza.

Cyber Spiaggia (Veracruz s/n; internet per hr M$15; ⏰9am-10pm) One of several internet places on Barra's main drag.

Post office (cnr Veracruz & Guanajuato)

Tourist office (☎355-51-00; www.costalegre. com; Jalisco 67; ⏰9am-5pm Mon-Fri) This regional office has maps and information about Barra and the other towns of the Costalegre. It also runs an information kiosk on the jetty during the tourist high season.

ℹ Getting There & Around

AIR

Barra de Navidad is served by nearby **Playa de Oro International Airport** (☎333-11-19; aeropuertosgap.com.mx/english/airports/ manzanillo-airport; Carretera Manzanillo-Barra de Navidad Km 42), 26km southeast of Barra on Hwy 200. To get to town from the airport, take a taxi (M$350, 30 minutes).

BOAT

Water taxis operate on demand 24 hours a day from the dock at the southern end of Veracruz, offering service to the Grand Bay Hotel Resort, the marina, the golf course and Colimilla. Round-trip fare to any destination is M$20.

BUS

The long-distance buses stopping at San Patricio-Melaque (see boxed text, p523) also stop at Barra de Navidad (15 minutes before or after) at the **Transportes Cihuatlán bus station** (Veracruz 228). **Primera Plus** (Veracruz 269) and **ETN** (Veracruz 273) operate from small terminals nearby, on the opposite side of Veracruz.

In addition to the long-distance buses, colorful local buses connect Barra and Melaque (M$6, every 15 minutes, 6am to 9pm), stopping in Barra at the long-distance bus stations (buses stopping on the southbound side of the road loop round Legazpi and back to Melaque).

TAXI

Catch taxis from one of the official stands (corner of Legazpi and Sinaloa, and corner Veracruz and Michoacán) to get the best price. A taxi to San Patricio-Melaque costs M$50 to M$60.

Manzanillo

☎ 314 / POP 190,000

Manzanillo has a bit of an identity crisis. On the one hand, it's Mexico's busiest commercial seaport, servicing cargo ships, pleasure cruises and naval vessels from around the world. On the other hand, it's a tourist destination, attracting beach lovers to its fine golden sands (the famous slow-motion scene of Bo Derek running along the beach in Blake Edwards' *10* was filmed here) and anglers to the self-proclaimed 'Sailfish Capital of the World.'

The personalities don't always match up. The beaches are often streaked with oil that washes up from the busy harbor. And for every ambitious new nightclub or restaurant that opens, another shuts down – a sign that tourism is not keeping up with development.

The government has poured millions of pesos into renovation projects such as the beautiful downtown *malecón* and the seaside main plaza and sculpture gardens to attract visitors, but tourism remains an afterthought in Manzanillo. Still, it's a fine city to chill out in for a few days or to use as a base for exploring the more charming beaches north and south of town.

Manzanillo extends 16km from northwest to southeast. The resort hotels and finest beaches are concentrated about 10km from downtown on Península de Santiago, a rocky outcrop at the far northwestern edge of Bahía de Manzanillo. Just west of the peninsula, Bahía de Santiago is lined with more excellent beaches.

◉ Sights & Activities

Beaches

Playa San Pedrito (Map p527), 1km northeast of the main plaza, is the closest beach to town, and the dirtiest. The next closest stretch of sand, spacious **Playa Las Brisas** (Map p527), caters to a few hotels. **Playa Azul** (Map p527) stretches northwest from Las Brisas and curves around to Las Hadas resort and the best beaches in the area: **La Audiencia, Santiago, Olas Altas** and **Miramar** (all on Map p527). Miramar and Olas Altas have the best surfing and bodysurfing waves in the area; surfboards can be rented at Miramar. Playa La Audiencia, lining a quiet cove on the west side of the Península de Santiago, has more tranquil water and is popular for waterskiing and other motorized water sports. Further west, Playa La Boquita is another beach with calm waters at the mouth of a lagoon; a shipwreck just offshore makes this a popular snorkeling spot.

Water Sports

Snorkeling, diving and surfing are all popular.

The scuba diving in Manzanillo can be spectacular, and there are many sites to explore – either off the beach or out on the bay. The dive center at **Underworld Scuba** (Map p527; ☎333-36-78; www.divemanzanillo.com; Hwy 200 Km 15; ⊗8am-5pm Mon-Sat, 9am-3pm Sun) charges US$95 for two-tank dives, including equipment, or US$350 for PADI certification.

Colima Surfside (Map p527; ☎cell phone 124-08-53; www.colimasurfside.com; Carretera Manzanillo-Cihuatlán Km 15; ⊗9am-2pm & 4-6pm) offers surfboard rentals (US$10/25 per hour/day), 90-minute surfing classes (US$50) and 2½-hour snorkeling excursions (US$30).

Fishing

Sailfish and dorado are found in the waters off Manzanillo year-round, while marlin and tuna are generally in the area from November to March. Supporting Manzanillo's only catch-and-release program, the well-run **Ocean Pacific Adventures** (☎335-06-05; www.gomanzanillo.com/fishing) offers fishing trips on 8m (US$250, five-person maximum) and 12m (US$300, 10-person maximum) cruisers; prices are for the whole boat and

Greater Manzanillo

Map labels:
- N 0 — 4 km / 0 — 2 miles
- Miramar
- Underworld Scuba
- Santiago
- To Barra de Navidad (57km)
- Playa Olas Altas
- Colima Surfside
- Playa Miramar
- Bahía de Santiago
- Playa Santiago
- Salahua
- Playa La Boquita
- Playa La Audiencia
- Península de Juluapan
- Península de Santiago
- Laguna de las Garzas
- To Cuyutlán (42km); Armería (47km)
- Playa Azul
- Playa Las Brisas
- Blvd Miguel de la Madrid
- PACIFIC OCEAN
- Bahía de Manzanillo
- Laguna de San Pedrito
- Playa San Pedrito
- See Central Manzanillo Map (p528)
- Manzanillo

include gear, drinks and having your fish cooked up for dinner.

Festivals & Events

Fiestas de Mayo
TRADITIONAL
These fiestas celebrate the founding of Manzanillo in 1873. Festivities involve sporting competitions and other events over the first 10 days of May.

Sailfish Tournaments
FISHING
(www.torneopescamanzanillo.com) Manzanillo's famous international tournament takes place in November; a smaller national tournament is held in February.

Sleeping

Manzanillo's cheapest hotels are located downtown, in the blocks surrounding the main plaza. Most midrange and top-end places listed here are on the Península de Santiago (Map p527), where the better beaches are located. Prices shown are for high season (December to April) and can drop by 20% outside that period.

Brisas Las Hadas
Golf Resort & Marina
LUXURY HOTEL $$$
(☎331-01-01; www.brisashotelonline.com/manzanillo; Av Vista Hermosa s/n, Playa Audiencia; d incl breakfast from US$205; [P][⊖][✳][@][🛇][🛋]) Manza-

nillo's most exclusive hotel sits above the bay like a Moorish seaside kingdom of white marble, spires and domes. The massive complex contains nearly 300 rooms and suites with marble floors, all-white furnishings and plentiful amenities; some have private pools. The Bo Derek flick *10* was shot here.

Dolphin Cove Inn
HOTEL $$$
(☎334-15-15; www.dolphincoveinn.com; Av Vista Hermosa s/n; r incl breakfast from M$1200, q with kitchenette M$1580, ste M$2250; [P][⊖][✳][@][🛇][🛋]) Offering great value for money, this cliffside hotel adjacent to Las Hadas has killer views and huge white-and-blue rooms cascading down to a pretty bayside swimming pool. Units range from basic doubles to two-room suites sleeping four, with large marble bathrooms and full kitchens. Breakfast is included except on peak holiday weekends.

Hotel Colonial
HOTEL $$
(Map p528; ☎332-10-80; hotelcolonialmanzanillo. com; Bocanegra 28; s/d/tr/q M$560/620/760/810; [P][✳][🛇]) One block from Manzanillo's waterfront plaza, this atmospheric old hotel retains the character of a colonial hacienda, with tiled outdoor hallways and a central courtyard. Big rooms, free wi-fi and a good attached restaurant make it the best deal downtown.

Central Manzanillo

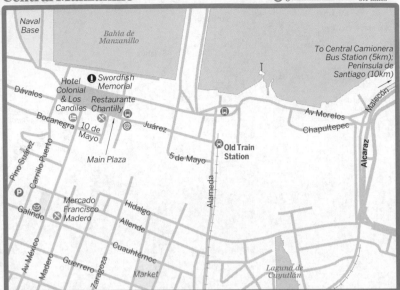

Tesoro Manzanillo HOTEL **$$$**
(☑331-22-00; www.tesororesorts.com; Av de la Audiencia 1, Playa Audiencia; all-inclusive per person from M$1650; 🅿😊✳@🛜🛜✳🛂) With endless activities, a beachfront pool, a swim-up bar and a kids' water park, this white, sterile high-rise above Playa Audiencia caters to families with children and those who enjoy spending their holiday in one place.

Hotel La Posada HOTEL **$$**
(☑333-18-99; www.hotel-la-posada.info; Cárdenas 201; s/d/tr/q incl breakfast US$58/78/98/118; 🅿✳🛜✳) This beachside B&B lures repeat guests with personalized service and amenities including a library, open-air dining room and honor bar. A small pool overlooks the beach, where you can watch ships – and the occasional whale – trawling the harbor. The location – near Manzanillo's busy port but far from everything else – can be challenging for those without a car.

Hotel Playa de Santiago HOTEL **$$**
(☑333-00-55; www.playadesantiago.com; Playa de Santiago; d/tr/q with fan M$982/1182/1382, with air-con M$1157/1357/1557; 🅿✳🛜✳) The nicest hotel on Playa de Santiago has a good family rate, with two children under 10 staying free; all rooms have ocean views.

Hotel Anita HOTEL **$**
(☑333-01-61; Playa de Santiago; s/d M$280/360; ✳) Manzanillo's cheapest beach hotel has 36 large, ultrafaded rooms with cracked plaster. The pluses? Playa Santiago is at your doorstep and the rates, for this location, are unbeatable.

🍴 Eating

Several good down-to-earth options are near the main plaza, while chain and chainlike spots line Hwy 200 around the bay.

CENTRAL MANZANILLO
Restaurante Chantilly CAFETERIA **$**
(Map p528; Juárez 44; mains M$47-100; ⏰7:30am-10:30pm) Adjoining Manzanillo's waterfront plaza, this '50s-era cafeteria and *nevería* (ice-cream parlor) has reasonably priced meals and snacks, plus a generous *comida corrida* (M$65), espresso and good ice cream.

Los Candiles MEXICAN **$$**
(http://hotelcolonialmanzanillo.com/en/restaurant.html; cnr Bocanegra & Av México; mains M$70-130; ⏰8am-10:30pm Mon-Sat) On the ground floor of Hotel Colonial, this restaurant opens onto a pleasant patio, and has a menu of

surf-and-turf fare and a full bar with sports dominating the satellite TV.

Mercado Francisco Madero
MARKET $

(Map p528; cnr Madero & Cuauhtémoc; mains M$30-60; ⊙7am-6pm) Manzanillo's downtown market has a number of inexpensive food stalls to choose from.

OUTSIDE THE CENTER

Juanito's
MEXICAN, NORTH AMERICAN $

(www.juanitos.com; Carretera 200 Km 14; mains M$65-90; ⊙8am-11pm; 🛜) A local tradition since 1976, Juanito's is popular for Mexican and North American comfort food such as pancake breakfasts, hamburgers, tacos, barbecue chicken and milkshakes. It also has satellite TV and free wi-fi.

Café Costeño
CAFE $

(Lázaro Cárdenas 1613, Playa Las Brisas; breakfasts M$30-60; ⊙8am-3pm & 5-10:30pm Mon-Sat) A good start or end to your day: French toast, hotcakes and omelets are cheerfully served along with espresso and cappuccino, while the evening menu features desserts and espresso drinks. Sit in the shady garden out back.

Portofino
ITALIAN $$$

(www.portofinomanzanillo.com; Blvd Miguel de la Madrid 923; mains M$100-198, pizzas from M$138; ⊙2pm-midnight Tue-Sun) This beachfront eatery has checked tablecloths, warm lighting, prime ocean views and a menu packed with pizza, pasta, and Mediterranean-influenced meat and fish dishes.

Tacos Ericka
TAQUERÍA $

(Carretera 200 Km 14.3; tacos & quesadillas M$9-10; ⊙8am-midnight) This popular neighborhood *taquería* specializes in *barbacoa* (savory barbecued beef); eat it on the spot in tacos accompanied by heavenly salsas, or bring home a kilo for M$150!

☆ Entertainment

If you're in town on a Sunday evening, stop by the main plaza (Map p528) where multiple generations come out to enjoy ice cream and the warm evening air. On some nights, bands play traditional music from the gazebo, while swallows and blackbirds perch on overhead wires and fill the air with their songs.

Manzanillo isn't exactly known for its nightlife, but there are a few discos to keep club kids happy.

Teque Night Club
CLUB

(http://es-es.facebook.com/Teque.Night.Club; Carretera 200 Km 12.5; ⊙10pm-late Sat) At the northern end of town, this club at the Gran Festivall resort is a popular Friday and Saturday night dance spot, with DJs spinning everything from disco to *cumbia* (Colombian dance music).

ℹ Information

Caseta Telefónica (Av Morelos 144; ⊙7:30am-9:30pm) Long-distance telephone and fax service.

HSBC (Av México s/n) One block off the plaza. One of several banks with ATMs downtown and along Hwy 200.

Members.com (Juárez 112; internet per hr M$15; ⊙9am-10pm Mon-Fri, noon-9pm Sat & Sun) Fast connections, just off the plaza.

Post office (Map p528; Galindo 30)

State tourism office (📞333-22-77; nicteloim@hotmail.com; Blvd Miguel de la Madrid 875A; ⊙8:30am-7pm Mon-Fri, 9am-2pm Sat) On the main waterfront boulevard, halfway between downtown and Península de Santiago. Dispenses information on Manzanillo and the state of Colima.

Tourist police (📞332-10-04)

ℹ Getting There & Away

Air

Playa de Oro International Airport (📞333-11-19; aeropuertosgap.com.mx/aeropuertos/manzanillo; Hwy 200) lies between a long and secluded white-sand beach and tropical groves of bananas and coconuts, 35km northwest of Manzanillo's Zona Hotelera on Hwy 200. **Aeromar** (📞334-05-32, 334-83-55; www.aeromar.com.mx; Airport) provides a direct service to Mexico City.

Bus

Manzanillo's airportlike **Central Camionera** (Map p527) is northeast of the center near Playa Las Brisas, just off Blvd Miguel de la Madrid (Hwy 200). It's an organized place with tourist information, phones, eateries and left-luggage facilities (M$3 per hour).

Car & Motorcycle

Renting a car is convenient for exploring the Costalegre beaches northwest of Manzanillo's airport. Four car-rental agencies are clustered together in the airport arrivals hall.

Alamo (📞334-01-24)

Budget (📞334-22-70)

Sixt (📞333-31-91)

Thrifty (📞334-32-92)

BUSES FROM MANZANILLO

DESTINATION	FARE (M$)	DURATION	FREQUENCY (DAILY)
Barra de Navidad	47-70	1-1½hr	half-hourly
Colima	66-105	1½-2hr	half-hourly
Guadalajara	252-370	4½-7hr	hourly
Lázaro Cárdenas	250-283	7hr	hourly
Mexico City	798-1080	12hr	7
Puerto Vallarta	230-294	5-6½hr	frequent
San Patricio-Melaque	51-65	1-1½hr	half-hourly

ⓘ Getting Around

There's no bus route to or from the airport, but most resorts have shuttle vans. Fixed-rate taxis from the airport charge M$370 to Península de Santiago or M$430 to downtown Manzanillo. *Colectivo* taxis charge M$155 per passenger to any destination, but only operate when flights are arriving and require a minimum of five passengers. From Manzanillo back to the airport, a taxi costs M$250 to M$350.

Local buses marked 'Santiago,' 'Las Brisas' and 'Miramar' head around the bay to the towns of San Pedrito, Salahua, Santiago, Miramar and beaches along the way. 'Las Hadas' buses take a more circuitous, scenic route down the Península de Santiago. These buses pick up passengers from the corner of Madero and Domínguez; the corner of Juárez and Calle 21 de Marzo near the main plaza; along Avenida Morelos; Avenida Niños Héroes; and from the main bus station every 10 minutes from 6am to 11pm. Fares are M$6 to M$7, depending on how far you're going.

Taxis are plentiful in Manzanillo. From the bus station, a cab fare is around M$40 to the main plaza or Playa Azul, and M$100 to Península de Santiago or Playa Miramar. Always agree on a price before you get into the taxi.

Cuyutlán

📞 313 / POP 1000

With its black-sand beaches, gentle waves and laid-back attitude, the low-key resort of Cuyutlán is a great place to get away from it all. Located at the southeastern end of Laguna de Cuyutlán, 40km southeast of Manzanillo, it's popular with Mexican families but sees few gringos. Bring your flip-flops; the black sand gets very hot!

The town's original tourist boom in the early 1900s, aided by good railway connections from Guadalajara, came to a screeching halt in 1932, when a monster tsunami hit the Colima coast. Tourism resumed in the 1940s and 1950s, but townspeople rejected moves to bring in discos and other resort-style amenities in the 1970s, allowing Cuyutlán to retain its decidedly retro feel.

If visiting in April or May, keep your eyes peeled for Cuyutlán's famous *ola verde,* a giant green wave that appears offshore at dusk. It's supposedly caused by little green phosphorescent critters, but it's the subject of much local debate.

◉ Sights & Activities

🐢 **El Tortugario**   WILDLIFE RESERVE
(tortugacuyutlan@hotmail.com; adult/child M$25/20; ☉10am-5pm Thu-Tue) El Tortugario is a turtle sanctuary located 4km east of Cuyutlán. Since it opened in 1993, conservationists have released more than 500,000 green, black and leatherback turtle hatchlings into the wild here. The center also has small iguana and crocodile sanctuaries, an education center, swimming pools and a picnic area. Don't miss El Tortugario's lagoon trips on the **Palo Verde Estuary**, a nature preserve that's home to more than 100 bird species, including 257 migratory birds. *Lanchas* move through mangrove tunnels and past sunbathing crocodiles. The 45-minute ride costs M$40/20 for adults/children.

Museo de Sal   MUSEUM
(Salt Museum; suggested donation M$10; ☉9am-6pm) This museum, located in an old salt-storage barn a block behind the main plaza, traces the history of the region's sea-salt extraction and economy.

🛏 Sleeping & Eating

Beachfront accommodations here are cheaper than at other coastal resorts. The high seasons are around Christmas and Semana Santa, when hotels are always booked solid. The beaches are lined with dozens of *enramadas* serving fresh, local seafood. At night, Cuyutlán's main plaza comes to life with vendors hawking cheap tacos, hot dogs and other greasy treats.

Hotel Morelos   HOTEL $

(☑326-40-13; alfredoherediaa@live.com.mx; Hidalgo 185; r per person with fan/air-con M$170/270; ✴🐾📶🌊) The bare-bones rooms offer minimal privacy, but this place wins lots of points for its friendly reception, spacious patio restaurant and pool; it's a great place to mingle with Mexican families.

Hotel Fenix   HOTEL $$

(☑326-40-82; www.hotelfenixcuyutlan.com; Hidalgo 201; per person incl breakfast M$280; ✴📶) Modern amenities compensate for the rather gruff reception at this hotel one block in from the beach, run by American Geoff and his Mexican wife Olivia. Remodeled rooms upstairs have air-con, wi-fi and satellite TV.

ℹ️ Information

The town has public telephones, *minisupers* (convenience stores) and beach supply shops. For other basic services such as banks or a post office, you'll have to visit Armería, a regional market town 12km east of Cuyutlán.

ℹ️ Getting There & Away

Cuyutlán is connected to the world through Armería, a dusty but friendly service center on Hwy 200, 46km southeast of Manzanillo and 55km southwest of Colima. From Armería a 12km paved road heads west past coconut plantations to the coast.

Nuevo Horizonte runs two buses daily between Manzanillo's bus terminal and Cuyutlán (M$37, one hour). Alternatively, catch a bus from Manzanillo to Armería (M$42, 45 minutes, every 15 minutes), then walk two blocks north and one block east to Armería's market and transfer to a local bus to Cuyutlán (M$11, 20 minutes, half-hourly). Returning from Cuyutlán, buses leave from the main plaza a few blocks in from the beach.

Buses also run every 20 minutes between Cuyutlán and Tecomán (M$10, 15 minutes), where you can connect with buses heading southeast on Hwy 200 to Lázaro Cárdenas and elsewhere.

Boca de Pascuales

📞313 / POP 100

Boca de Pascuales is a legendary surf spot that attracts the best boarders from around the world. Aggressive barrel swells range from 2m to 5m in the summer season and storm waves occasionally reach 10m. There's a heavy beach break. Pascuales is strictly for experienced surfers; don't tempt fate if you're not up to speed.

🛏️ Sleeping & Eating

Paco's Hotel   HOTEL $$

(☑cell phone 313-1112637; www.pacoshotelpascuales.com, in Spanish; r with/without ocean view M$600/400; ✴) Family-run and plastered with autographed photos of famous surfers, Paco's place offers simple but comfy rooms, each with a different flower theme lovingly painted by his daughter Lulu. The hotel also has a decent restaurant (mains from M$80).

Hotel Real de Pascuales   HOTEL $

(☑cell phone 313-1203549; www.pascualessurf.com; campsites per person M$30, r with fan/air-con M$300/400; ✴) Better known as Edgar's Place, this hotel is the local surfing nexus. Edgar Álvarez welcomes surfers from all over the world and fixes their boards when they get munched. The rooms are spartan to the extreme, but that's the way the dudes seem to like it. Aficionados take note: Edgar also designs his own line of surfboards.

TOP CHOICE Las Hamacas del Mayor   SEAFOOD $$

(☑329-19-50; www.lashamacasdelmayor.com.mx, in Spanish; mains M$80-200; ⊘10:30am-6pm; 👶) A local fixture since 1953, Las Hamacas is one of the most famous eateries in Colima state despite its off-the-beaten-path location. The two-level restaurant seats 1000 people and is open every day of the year. Strolling mariachis entertain the crowd, a swimming pool keeps the kids busy, and there are great views of surfers riding the waves just offshore. Exquisite seafood specialties include fish fillet stuffed with octopus and shrimp, marinated in garlic sauce.

ℹ️ Getting There & Away

To reach Pascuales, first catch a bus from Manzanillo to Tecomán (M$43 to M$53, one hour, every 15 minutes). From here, hourly combis run to Pascuales (M$8, 20 minutes). A taxi from Tecomán is M$70. If driving, follow the sign from downtown Tecomán about 10km to the beach.

Michoacán Coast

Highway 200 hugs the shoreline most of the way along the spectacular 250km coastline of Michoacán, one of Mexico's most

ⓘ MICHOACÁN'S BEACHFRONT PARADORES

Between Km 183 and Km 103 on Hwy 200 you'll see frequent signs for tourist lodgings known as *paradores turísticos* (government-run tourist lodgings); despite mostly wearing the forlorn look of government projects without much local enthusiasm behind them, these offer reasonably priced accommodations right on the beach. For photos of the various *paradores*, see the Spanish-language website paradores ecoturisticos.blogspot.com.

beautiful states. The route passes dozens of untouched beaches – some with wide expanses of golden sand, some tucked into tiny rocky coves, some at river mouths where quiet estuaries harbor multitudes of birds. Several have gentle lapping waves that are good for swimming, while others have big breakers suitable for surfing. Many of the beaches are uninhabited, but some have small communities. Mango, coconut, papaya and banana plantations line the highway, while the green peaks of the Sierra Madre del Sur form a lush backdrop inland. Blue signs along Hwy 200 mark the turnoffs for most beaches. Kilometer markers begin counting down from Km 231 at the state's northern border.

Other beaches of interest beyond those described below are Ixtapilla (Km 180), La Manzanillera (Km 174), Motín de Oro (Km 167), Zapote de Tizupán (Km 103), Pichilinguillo (Km 95) and Huahua (Km 84). It's much easier to explore this stretch of coast, especially the more remote beaches, if you have your own vehicle. However, 2nd-class buses (at least half a dozen daily) along the Manzanillo–Lázaro Cárdenas route will generally drop off and pick up passengers at any town entrance along coastal Hwy 200.

SAN JUAN DE ALIMA

Twenty kilometers south of Boca de Apiza, near where the highway meets the coast, is the cobblestoned town of San Juan de Alima (Km 211). It's popular with surfers due to its creamy medium-sized breakers just off the coast. There are several beachfront restaurants and modern hotels.

Hotel Parador (☏313-327-90-38; r with/without air-con M$600/500; P✻✷) offers a good variety of rooms, some with balconies and views. The hotel's popular restaurant perches directly above the ocean on palm-shaded terraces.

LAS BRISAS

The cliff-hugging road south of San Juan climbs above the coast, offering gorgeous views of desolate sandy beaches below. The tiny white strand of Las Brisas (Km 205) is accented by just a few *palapa* restaurants and the comfortable **Hotel Brisas de Verano** (☏313-327-90-55; hotelbrisasdeverano.com; d/q from M$600/900; P✻✷). If you're a birdwatcher, there is a nice mangrove lagoon about 1km south of town.

PLAYA LA TICLA

Another renowned surfing destination, Playa La Ticla (Km 183) is known for its long, left point break and mostly attracts foreign surfers with their own vehicles. The long beach is divided by a swimmable freshwater river.

On the beachfront, a few *enramadas* serve fresh seafood, and **Parador Turístico La Ticla** (☏424-488-00-25; d/q M$300/600, 7-person cabaña M$1200) offers spartan rooms with minimal privacy in multilevel *cabañas*.

For fine home cooking, head a few blocks inland to **Cabaña de Vicky** (mains M$50-100; ☺8am-11pm Mon-Sat), where daily specials (M$50) are accompanied by good salsa and fresh tortillas made with corn from Vicky's own backyard.

FARO DE BUCERÍAS

Faro de Bucerías (Diver's Lighthouse; Km 173), is a sheltered crescent beach with clear, pale-blue waters and yellow sand that is perfect for sun worshipping, snorkeling or swimming. The local Nahua community operates a long line of *palapa* seafood restaurants offering plentiful, fat lobsters. *Cabañas* and sandy campsites are available at the government-subsidized **Centro Ecoturístico** (cenecoturfaro@hotmail.com; campsite per person M$50; 2-/4-person cabaña M$350/600).

PLAYA COLOLA

An estimated 70% of the world's population of black sea turtles, along with olive ridley and leatherback turtles, lay their eggs on the long flat sands of Playa Colola (Km 160).

✏**Sitio Ramsar Playa de Colola** (an gel-colola@hotmail.es), established in 2008, monitors the beach, protects the eggs and releases hatchlings. For M$35, visitors can accompany local and international volunteers on their nightly rounds, from 8pm to 4am. Turtle viewing is best between September and December. Staff hours are variable; contact the site in advance by email to arrange your visit.

PLAYA MARUATA

With clear turquoise waters and golden sandy beaches, Playa Maruata (Km 150) is the most beautiful beach in Michoacán. The Nahua fishing village has a bit of a hippie reputation, attracting beach bums from all over. It's a tranquil, friendly place to hang out with your sweetie or a large stack of paperbacks. It's also a prime nesting site for black sea turtles (each night from June to December).

Maruata actually has three beaches, each with its own unique character. The left (eastern) is the longest, a 3km pristine crescent- shaped beach with creamy yellow sand and calm waves perfect for swimming and snorkeling. The small middle arc is OK for strong swimmers. It's sheltered by a climbable rocky head riddled with caves, tunnels and blow holes, and marked by the unusual **Dedo de Dios** (God's Finger) formation rising from the sea. The far-right (western) beach is known as **Playa de los Muertos** (Beach of the Dead), and for good reason: it has dangerous currents and ferocious waves. During low tide you can scale the rocks on the far right side of Muertos to reach a secluded cove where discreet nude sunbathing is tolerated. But don't get stuck here when the tide comes in. A crucifix on the rocks serves as a stark memorial to the people who have been swallowed by the sea.

You'll find a small grocery store and a restaurant near the town's bleak plaza. The *enramadas* on the left beach serve delicious fresh seafood and are also your best bet for camping. Most charge M$20 to M$30 per person to pitch a tent or rent a hammock. Those who need four semisolid walls can find a few rustic *cabañas* for M$200 to M$300; alternatively, splurge on one of the 14 tile-floored, *palapa*-roofed units at **Centro Ecoturístico Maruata** (☏cell phone 555-1505110; 2-/4-person cabaña M$500/1000), on a hillside overlooking the far-right beach.

BARRA DE NEXPA
☏753 / POP 100

At Km 55.6, just north of Puente Nexpa bridge and 1km from the highway down a rough cobbled road, lies the small, laid-back community of Nexpa. It's long been a haven for surfers, attracted to the salt-and-pepper sandbar and healthy waves, which build up and curl sharply in the mornings.

Jorge & Helen's Tienda (☺9:30am-9:30pm), to the left as you enter town, is a grocery store offering internet access (M$30 per hour) and surfboard rentals (per hour/day/week M$50/150/600). A newer surf shop in the center of town offers internet and board rentals at similar prices.

🛏 Sleeping & Eating

Several places along the beachfront offer camping from M$30 per person, while a half-dozen *palapas* serve delicious local seafood.

Río Nexpa Rooms   GUESTHOUSE $
(☏cell phone 753-1216501; www.rionexparooms.com; s/d/tr/q M$350/400/450/500) This beautifully crafted Southeast Asian–style *palapa*, about 200m inland along the river, has four comfortable rooms with three full-sized beds and a loft. It has a shared kitchen, a lagoonside garden area and a tranquil communal sitting room.

Mar de Noche   CABAÑAS, HOTEL $$
(☏cell phone 753-1183931; www.nexpasurf.jimdo.com, in Spanish; r or cabaña M$800; ❄) The fan-cooled, two-story *cabañas* here have comfy beds, hammocks, kitchens and private bathrooms. There's also an adjacent six-room hotel with modern amenities including air-con. The attached beachfront restaurant, decorated with hand-carved wood columns, serves three meals a day (mains from M$60). Low-season prices are about 40% below the high-season ones given.

Chicho's   MEXICAN $$
(☏cell phone 753-1309236; meals from M$50) One of several *enramadas* lining the beach, Chicho's is a great choice for breakfast, thanks to gargantuan smoothies (M$35) and inspiring views of wave-riding surfers. It also rents out some very basic two-level beachfront *cabañas* (M$200 to M$300), featuring hammocks strung upstairs above a cement floor, with a fridge, hotplate and hose shower on the lower level.

CALETA DE CAMPOS
☏753 / POP 2600

Caleta (Km 50) is a regional service center with all the essentials, including a gas station, a *caseta de teléfono*, late-night *taquerías*, a pharmacy and several grocery stores. The main part of town is on a bluff overlooking an azure bay. The beach below is not as charming as Nexpa, but it does have a nice selection of seafood *enramadas*, and is more protected and better suited for novice surfers.

The area's best surf shop, **Surf y Espuma** (☏531-52-55; surfyespuma@hotmail.com; surfboard rental per day/week US$10/60; ☺9am-7pm), has two locations, one in town and another (open seasonally) on the beach. The in-town shop washes laundry (M$18 per kilo), and the owners also operate the very nice hostel **Villa Tropical** (www.caletadecampos.com; dm US$15; ▧), with barbecues, hammocks, pools and a whole slew of water sports equipment available to guests.

Parador Turístico (☏531-51-01; www.par tourcaleta.com, in Spanish; Carretera 200 Km 51.25; d/tr M$900/1200, 5-person ste M$1650-1950; ▣▧▧), perched above the beach 1km north of town, has 12 ocean-view units surrounding a circular *palapa*-roofed bar and lounge area. The best suite has a kitchenette, dining room and private terrace with Jacuzzi.

Hourly buses depart Caleta's main plaza for Lázaro Cárdenas (M$54, 1¼ hours) from 5am to 7pm. A taxi between Caleta de Campos and Barra de Nexpa costs about M$50.

Lázaro Cárdenas

☏753 / POP 79,000

As an industrial port city, Lázaro has nothing of real touristic interest – but because it's a hub for buses up and down the coast, travelers regularly pass through. Lázaro is also a regional service center where you'll find banks, a post office, pharmacies and Pemex stations.

🛏 Sleeping & Eating

There are several cheap hotels and restaurants clustered around the bus terminals and along Avenida Lázaro Cárdenas, including **Hotel Reyna Pio** (☏532-06-20; Corregidora 78; s/d/tr/q M$335/405/469/525; ▧), a friendly place with clean, spacious rooms.

❶ Getting There & Away

Lázaro has three bus terminals, all within a few blocks of each other. From the **main terminal** (Lázaro Cárdenas 1810), various operators offer services to Manzanillo, Uruapan, Morelia, Colima, Guadalajara and Mexico City.

From the **Estrella Blanca terminal** (Francisco Villa 65), two blocks west behind the main terminal, buses head southeast to Zihuatanejo and Acapulco; up the coast to Manzanillo and Puerto Vallarta; and inland to Uruapan, Morelia and Mexico City.

The **Estrella de Oro terminal** (Corregidora 318) is one block north and two blocks west of Estrella Blanca and serves Zihuatanejo, Acapulco and Mexico City.

Troncones

☏755 / POP 700

Not long ago, Troncones was a poor, sleepy fishing and farming village. That all changed in the mid-1990s when wealthy North Americans arrived and began building luxury beachfront vacation homes and B&Bs. Tourists followed for the beaches, relaxing atmosphere and world-class surfing.

The expatriate invasion has left an indelible mark: the long strip between Troncones and neighboring Majahua bears more resemblance to a California subdivision than to the traditional Mexican villages at either end, where chickens and burros (donkeys) still roam the streets. For entertainment,

BUSES FROM LÁZARO CÁRDENAS

DESTINATION	FARE (M$)	DURATION	FREQUENCY (DAILY)
Acapulco	210-239	6-7hr	hourly
Guadalajara	495	8hr	4
Manzanillo	250-283	7hr	7
Mexico City	566-635	8-11hr	12
Morelia	285-440	4-5hr	very frequent
Puerto Vallarta	504	12hr	8pm
Uruapan	195-295	3-4hr	frequent
Zihuatanejo	65-91	1½-2hr	hourly

there's precious little to do aside from catching the waves, relaxing in a hammock and soaking up the sun.

Troncones is located about 25km northwest of Ixtapa, at the end of a 3km paved road from Hwy 200. The paved road ends at a T-intersection, from where a dusty beachfront road continues northwest (right) to the communities of Troncones Point, Manzanillo Bay and Majahua. The majority of tourist attractions are along this beachfront road.

Of the four communities, Troncones is the most built up. At the T-intersection you'll find a few small grocery stores, a laundry and several cheap food vendors. The surf in Troncones and Troncones Point is rough and geared to surfers. Manzanillo Bay is a sheltered cove more conducive to swimming and snorkeling, either in the bay or in the lovely tide pools that dot the rocky shore. Majahua is a traditional fishing village with a few *enramadas* and a mellow beach layered with fine shells for beachcombers. From Majahua, another dirt road (rough in the wet season) leads back out to Hwy 200.

🏃 Activities

There's good **snorkeling** and **swimming** in the protected cove off Playa Manzanillo. **Horseback riding** is quite popular; locals stroll the beach with their steeds looking for customers. Other activities that can be arranged through local hotels include **mountain biking, fishing,** and **spelunking** through the limestone cave system near Majahua.

Surfing
SURFING

Troncones has several world-class surf spots. The beach breaks here can be excellent in summer, but the wave to chase is the left at Troncones Point. When it's small, the takeoff is right over the rocks (complete with sea urchins), but when it's big, it's beautiful and beefy and rolls halfway across the bay.

Just north of the T-intersection, surfer Bruce Grimes of **Galería Nuñez** (☏ cell phone 755-1030005; http://primesurfboards.net) offers two-hour lessons (US$60), advanced coaching (US$50 per day) and board repair (from US$30 for a few dings to US$150 for a broken board). He also designs custom boards and rents out boards (M$300 per day) and bikes (M$200 per day).

Near the point, the **Inn at Manzanillo Bay** (www.manzanillobay.com; Playa Manzanillo) rents out an excellent selection of short and long boards (half/full day M$200/320), boogie boards (half/full day M$60/120) and kayaks (half/full day M$350/650). It also offers surf lessons (M$750).

☞ Tours

Costa Nativa Ecotours
ECOTOURS
(☏ 100-74-99; www.tronconesecotours.com) This outfit organizes kayaking, hiking, spelunking, bird-watching and sea-turtle-spotting excursions, ranging in price from M$300 to M$550 per person.

🛏 Sleeping

All businesses listed below are along Troncones' main waterfront road. Reservations are advisable during the high season (November through April), when some places require multiple-night stays. During low season, prices can be 25% to 50% lower, but be aware that many lodging facilities close down for the summer.

Inn at Manzanillo Bay
BUNGALOW **$$$**
(☏ 553-28-84; www.manzanillobay.com; Playa Manzanillo; bungalows US$98-168; P ❄ 🛜 ≋) In a prime setting on Troncones' prettiest beach, this miniresort has eight thatched-roof bungalows with king-sized beds, canopied mosquito netting, ceiling fans and hammocked terraces surrounding a pool. For an extra dose of creature comforts, you can upgrade to one of the newer terrace suites, which feature air-con and HDTV. There's also a popular restaurant and bar, a surf shop and easy access to the primo break at Troncones Point.

🏄 Troncones Point Surf Club & Hostel
HOSTEL **$$**
(☏ 553-28-86; www.tronconespoint.com; dm/d M$300/650, q with kitchenette M$840; 🛜) This great little hostel sits a stone's throw from the dreamy surfing at Troncones Point. Accommodations vary from a pair of four-bed dorms to a spacious upstairs quad with kitchen and outdoor sleeping deck. Composting toilets and a gray water system help reduce your environmental impact; other pluses include board, bike and snorkel rentals, and Play-doh to keep the kids happy. The owners, seasoned travelers who have sailed the globe, can help arrange ecotours in the local area.

Casa Delfín Sonriente
B&B $$

(☎553-28-03; www.casadelfinsonriente.com; bungalow/r/ste incl breakfast US$70/85/119; ❄🛜❄) Guests rave about the peaceful, welcoming atmosphere at this B&B, with its good breakfasts, shared kitchen and barbecue, upstairs lounging area, beachfront massage table and pool, hammocks, games and beach toys available to all. Three rooms have air-con; the rest come with fans. For the budget-minded, there are two very basic bungalows with a shared bathroom; the beach-facing bungalow is considerably more attractive than the darker back unit.

Present Moment Retreat
BUNGALOW $$$

(☎103-00-11; www.presentmomentretreat.com; s/d/tr incl breakfast & 1 class per day US$195/230/315; P❄) This 'conscious living' spa resort is a haven for the body and mind, specializing in yoga, meditation and massage. The 10 minimalist but spacious thatched-roof bungalows all surround a beautiful pool and gardens. The restaurant, on a pretty sea-facing deck, is among the best (and priciest – mains M$125 to M$320) in town, with dishes for vegetarians and carnivores alike.

Casa Ki
BUNGALOW $$$

(☎553-28-15; www.casa-ki.com; bungalows US$95-115, house US$220; P❄🛜) This charming beachside retreat features four colorful freestanding bungalows (one with air-con) with access to a communal kitchen, plus a thoughtfully furnished main house sleeping up to six people.

🍴 Eating & Drinking

Roberto's Bistro
ARGENTINE $$$

(www.robertosbistro.com; mains M$115-250; ⊗8am-10pm) Sizzling steaks and crashing waves create the stereophonic soundtrack at this Argentine-style beachfront grill, 1km south of the T-intersection. From chorizo starters to full-on feasts such as the *parrillada argentina* (T-bone, rib-eye and several zillion other cuts all grilled together with shrimp), this is carnivore paradise.

Jardín del Edén
FUSION $$

(www.jardindeleden.com.mx; mains M$120-180; ⊗8am-10pm Nov-May) At this new place just north of Troncones Point, the French chef's fusion menu ranges from Mediterranean to Pacific Rim to traditional Mexican fare. Nightly specials such as pizza, lasagna and *cochinita pibil* (Yucatán-style slow-roasted pork) are cooked on the grill and in the wood-fired oven. Live jazz and salsa draw crowds on Tuesday and Friday nights.

Café del Sol
CAFE $

(breakfasts & sandwiches M$35-75; ⊗restaurant 8am-4pm, bar 6-10pm Nov-Apr) With its North American breakfasts, smoothies, cappuccinos, book exchange, great pizzas and sandwiches, and Sunday football broadcasts, this cafe just north of the T-intersection is a real gringo magnet.

ℹ Getting There & Away

Driving from Ixtapa or Zihuatanejo, head northwest on Hwy 200 toward Lázaro Cárdenas. Just north of Km 30 you'll see the marked turnoff for Troncones; follow this winding paved road 3km west to the beach.

Second-class buses heading northwest toward Lázaro Cárdenas from Zihuatanejo's long-distance terminals will drop you at the turnoff for Troncones (M$25, 45 minutes), if you ask. For a cheaper ride to the same intersection, catch a La Unión–bound bus (M$18) from the stop a couple of blocks east of Zihuatanejo's market.

White *colectivo* vans shuttle between Hwy 200 and Troncones (M$10) roughly every half-hour; some continue on to Manzanillo Bay (M$16) and Majahua (M$20). Taxis make the same trip for M$50 to M$60.

Taxis de Troncones (☎553-29-11) offers service from Troncones to Zihuatanejo airport (M$500), Zihuatanejo (M$350) and Ixtapa (M$300). A taxi *from* Zihuatanejo's airport will set you back M$750.

Ixtapa

☎755 / POP 9000

Ixtapa was nothing more than a huge coconut plantation until the late 1970s when Fonatur (the Mexican government's tourism development group) decided that the Pacific coast needed a Cancúnlike resort. In came the hotel and golf-course developers and up went the high-rises. The result was a planned city with spotless beaches, luxurious hotels, chain restaurants and not a palm tree or blade of grass out of place.

About 35 years later, Ixtapa continues to offer a high-end, squeaky-clean version of Mexican beach culture that stands in dramatic contrast to the down-to-earth charms of its sister city, Zihuatanejo. Ixtapa's appeal is best appreciated by families seeking a hassle-free all-inclusive beach getaway or those who value modern chain-hotel comforts and nightlife over a full-on cultural immersion experience.

◎ Sights

Beaches
BEACH

Ixtapa's big hotels line **Playa del Palmar**, a long, broad stretch of white sand that's often overrun by parasailing and Jet-skiing outfits. Be very careful if you swim here: the large waves crash straight down and there's a powerful undertow. Just getting onto the beach can be a pain if you're not a hotel guest. There are few public accessways to the beach, and the only other option is to cut through a hotel lobby and hope you don't get hassled by the doormen.

Playa Escolleras, at the west end of Playa del Palmar near the entrance to the marina, has a strong break and is favored by surfers. Further west past Punta Ixtapa, **Playa Quieta** and **Playa Linda** are popular with locals.

Isla Ixtapa
ISLAND

Isla Ixtapa is a beautiful oasis from the concrete jungle of Ixtapa. The turquoise waters are crystal-clear, calm and great for snorkeling (gear rentals cost M$120 per day). Isla Ixtapa has four beaches; **Playa Corales** on the back side of the island is the nicest and quietest, with soft white sand, an offshore coral reef and little tide pools harboring starfish and sea urchins. *Enramada* seafood restaurants and massage providers dot the island. Frequent boats to Isla Ixtapa depart from Playa Linda's pier from 9am to 5pm (M$40 round trip, five minutes). The island gets mobbed by tourists in high season, and you'll likely have to run the attendant gauntlet of hawkers en route to the pier.

Cocodrilario
WILDLIFE RESERVE

Playa Linda has a small *cocodrilario* (crocodile reserve) that is also home to fat iguanas and several bird species. You can watch the crocs from the safety of the well-fenced wooden viewing platform located near the bus stop.

🏃 Activities

Cycling
Cycling is a breeze along a 15km *ciclopista* (cycle path) that stretches from Playa Linda, north of Ixtapa, practically into Zihuatanejo. Mountain bikes can be rented for M$50/250 per hour/day from **Ola Rental** (Centro Comercial Ixpamar; ⊙8am-7pm) and **Bici Rent** (Centro Comercial La Puerta; ⊙7am-8pm).

Surfing
Surfing is good on Playa Linda and Playa Escolleras. You'll find everything you need – rentals, repairs, classes and surfing trips – at **Catcha L'Ola Surf & Stuff** (www.ixtapasurf. com; Centro Comercial Los Patios; board rental per day/week M$200/1000, 3hr lesson M$600; ⊙9am-7pm).

Water Sports
Scuba diving is popular in the warm, clear waters. **Mero Adventure** (✆555-25-00, cell phone 755-1019672; www.meroadventure.com; Hotel Pacifica, Ixtapa; 1-/2-tank dives US$65/90) organizes diving, snorkeling, kayaking and fishing trips, as well as swimming with dolphins.

Golf
The **Ixtapa Club de Golf Palma Real** (✆553-10-62; www.golftourismmexico.com/palma _real.asp; green fee M$1400) and the **Marina Ixtapa Golf Club** (✆553-21-80; www.marina ixtapa.com/golf_courses.htm; green fee M$720) both have 18-hole courses, tennis courts and swimming pools.

Other Activities
Horseback riding (per hour M$200) is available at Playa Linda.

Parque Aventura
ADVENTURE SPORTS

(✆cell phone 755-1151733; www.parque-aventura. com, in Spanish; 90min guided circuit US$45; ⊙8:30am-6:30pm) About 5km north of Ixtapa on Hwy 200 is this outdoor adventure course through the woods, with suspension bridges and zip-lines.

Magic World
WATER PARK

(www.mundomagicoixtapa.com, in Spanish; admission M$100; ⊙10:30am-5:30pm) This aquatic park has rides, waterslides, toboggans and other amusements.

👉 Tours

Adventours
ADVENTURE TOUR

(✆553-35-84; www.ixtapa-adventours.com; Centro Comercial Plaza Ambiente, Blvd Ixtapa s/n; ⊙8am-6pm Mon-Sat, to 2pm Sun) Adventours offers a variety of guided cycling, kayaking, snorkeling and bird-watching tours around Ixtapa and Zihuatanejo.

🛏 Sleeping

With the exception of the campground, Ixtapa's beachfront resorts are all top-end. Prices listed here are rack rates for high season, which runs from mid-December to

Easter. Prices can drop by 25% or more for the rest of the year. Better rates are often available through package deals or from hotel websites.

Las Brisas Ixtapa Resort
RESORT $$$

(☎553-21-21; www.brisashotelonline.com/ixtapa; d incl breakfast from US$205; P⊖❄@🛜🏊🐕) An enormous orange wedge rising from the sands, Brisas sits on an isolated stretch of Playa Vista Hermosa south of Ixtapa's main strip. The recently renovated interior has a contemporary Mexican feel with lots of color and wood throughout. All 416 rooms have extra-large terraces with first-rate ocean views and hammocks. The lobby bar is one of the best in town.

RV Park Ixtapa
CAMPGROUND $

(☎552-02-95; rvparkixtapa@fonatur.gob.mx; per person in campsite M$70, per couple in RV site M$300; 🛜🏊) This is a lovely beachfront campground located in a coconut grove, this large, gated resort has modern amenities including a grocery, showers, clubhouse, restaurant, laundry and wi-fi. It's located 1.7km north of Playa Linda, where the highway from Ixtapa and the *ciclopista* terminate.

Hotel Presidente Inter-Continental
HOTEL $$$

(☎553-00-18, in the US 888-424-6835; www.ixtapa.interconti.com; Blvd Ixtapa s/n; d all-inclusive US$224-312, q US$392; P⊖❄@🛜🏊🐕) This popular beachfront hotel is first-class all the way, with a gym, sauna, tennis courts, seven restaurants and a kids' club with Spanish classes for little ones.

Barceló Ixtapa Beach
RESORT $$$

(☎555-20-00; www.barceloixtapa.com; Blvd Ixtapa s/n; all-inclusive d/q from US$262/307; P⊖❄🛜🏊🐕) This all-inclusive resort with its fine pool and patio area caters to families and groups.

✗ Eating

All the major hotels have their own restaurants. Additional dining options abound in Ixtapa's many shopping centers and at Marina Ixtapa, just northwest of the main hotel strip.

Villa de la Selva
FUSION $$$

(☎553-03-62; www.villadelaselva.com.mx; Paseo de la Roca; mains M$250-470; ⊙6-11:30pm, closed Sep) This elegant contemporary Mediterranean restaurant was once the home of Mexi-can president Luis Echeverría. The cliffside villa has superb sunset and ocean views. Offerings include duck tacos, *chipotle*-glazed salmon with couscous, shrimp in tamarind sauce, lobster and an extensive wine list. Reservations are a must.

Cafeteria Nueva Zelanda
CAFETERIA $$

(Centro Comercial La Puerta; mains M$66-122; ⊙8am-9:30pm) Step back in time at this long-standing institution opposite the downtown hotel strip, where you can order a banana split or chocolate milkshake with your shrimp taco and chicken fajitas. It's also good for breakfast, with fresh-squeezed juice and decent cappuccinos.

🍷 Drinking & Entertainment

All the big hotels have bars and nightclubs. Many also have discos; in the low season most of these charge less and open fewer nights.

Christine
CLUB

(www.krystal-hotels.com/ixtapa/english/restaurants-entertainment; Hotel Krystal, Blvd Ixtapa s/n; admission incl open bar M$350; ⊙11pm-4am Fri & Sat) Christine has the sizzling sound-and-light systems you'd expect from one of the most popular discos in town.

El Faro
JAZZ

(☎555-25-25; www.pacifica.com.mx/pacificaresort/eng/faro.html; Paseo de la Colina s/n; ⊙6-11pm) Located at the top of the Pacifica Resort and accessed by a gondola, El Faro has amazing views and live jazz music Wednesday through Sunday. Reservations required.

Kopado's Music Bar
BAR

(http://es-es.facebook.com/kopados; Centro Comercial La Puerta; ⊙6pm-late) With good drink specials and occasional live music, this local favorite occupies a *palapa*-covered perch in Ixtapa's main shopping center.

ⓘ Information

Listings below are in the *centro commercial* (shopping center) on Blvd Ixtapa. The *centro* also contains banks, ATMs, a movie theater and a 24-hour pharmacy. The nearest post office is in Zihuatanejo.

Kaldhi Café (internet per hr M$30; ⊙8am-11pm) Air-con, good coffee and free wi-fi compensate for the steep internet prices.

Tourist office (☎554-20-01; turismozihixt@hotmail.com; Blvd Ixtapa s/n; ⊙10am-5pm) Provides tourist info from a squat orange building in front of Señor Frog's (directly across from Hotel Presidente Inter-Continental).

❶ Getting There & Around

Private taxis (M$365) and *colectivo* vans (M$120 per person) provide transportation from Ixtapa/Zihuatanejo international airport (see p547) to Ixtapa. A taxi from Ixtapa to the airport costs about M$170.

There are bus ticket offices in the shopping center adjacent to Ixtapa's downtown hotel strip, but very few long-distance buses actually stop here – for most destinations you'll have to go to Zihuatanejo's Central de Autobuses (p547), which services both towns.

Local buses run frequently between Ixtapa and Zihuatanejo from 5:30am to 11pm (15 minutes, M$8). In Ixtapa, buses stop along the main street in front of all hotels. In Zihuatanejo, buses depart from the corner of Juárez and Morelos. Buses marked 'Zihua–Ixtapa–Playa Linda' run from Zihuatanejo through Ixtapa to Playa Linda. The fare to Playa Linda is M$8 from Ixtapa, or M$9 from Zihuatanejo.

A taxi between Zihuatanejo and Ixtapa should be around M$55; always agree on a price before getting into a cab.

Zihuatanejo

♪755 / POP 67,000

The sister cities of Zihuatanejo (see-wah-tah-neh-ho) and Ixtapa could not be more radically different. While Ixtapa is openly a purpose-built, sanitized version of Mexico, Zihuatanejo is the real deal. Zihuatanejo, or Zihua as it's affectionately called, is a Pacific paradise of beautiful beaches, friendly people and an easygoing lifestyle. Until the 1970s, Zihua was a sleepy fishing village best known as a hideaway for pirates and hippies; Tim Robbins and Morgan Freeman escaped here to live out the simple life in *The Shawshank Redemption*. With the construction of Ixtapa next door, Zihua's population and tourism industry boomed practically overnight.

Parts of the city have become quite touristy, especially when cruise ships are in town, and luxury hotels are slowly replacing old family guesthouses. But for the most part, Zihua has retained its lovely, historic charm. The narrow cobblestone streets of downtown hide wonderful local restaurants, bars, boutique shops and artisan studios. Fishermen still meet every morning on the beach by Paseo del Pescador (Fishermen's Passage) to sell their catch of the day. At night, young lovers and families stroll carefree along the romantic waterfront sidewalk. Zihua is the best of both worlds.

While Zihua's suburbs have spread beyond the bay and into the hills, the city's center remains compressed within a few blocks. It's difficult to get lost; there are only a few streets and they're clearly marked.

◉ Sights

Beaches BEACH
Waves are gentle at all of Bahía de Zihuatanejo's beaches. If you want big ocean waves, head west toward Ixtapa.

Playa Municipal, in front of town, is the least appealing beach on the bay. **Playa Madera** (Wood Beach) is a pleasant five-minute walk east from Playa Municipal along a concrete walkway (popular with young couples in the evening) and around a rocky point.

Over a steep hill from Playa Madera (less than 1km) is the gorgeous broad expanse of **Playa La Ropa** (Clothes Beach), named for a Spanish galleon that was wrecked and had its cargo of silks washed ashore. Bordered by palm trees and seafood restaurants, La Ropa is great for swimming, parasailing, waterskiing and sand-soccer. You can also rent sailboards and sailboats. It's an enjoyable 20-minute walk from Playa Madera

---

DON'T MISS

EXPLORING ZIHUATANEJO'S GREAT OUTDOORS

Sure, you can spend your whole vacation basking by the pool, but the Zihuatanejo area offers countless other options for getting outdoors. Here are a few ideas to get you started:

» Swim under a waterfall in the Sierra Madre, learn why the tarantula crossed the road and see how many blue morpho butterflies you can count on an ecotour to **Mesas de Bravo** (p540)

» Cruise across the bay at sunset on a **catamaran sailing tour** (p540)

» Walk barefoot down the entire length of gorgeous **Playa La Ropa** (p539)

» Kayak around the lagoon or explore the spectacular Morros de Potosí rocks at **Barra de Potosí** (p547)

along Carretera Escénica, which follows the clifftops and offers fine views over the water.

Isolated **Playa Las Gatas** (Cat Beach) is named – depending on whose story you believe – for the whiskered nurse sharks that once inhabited the waters or for the wildcats that lurked in the jungles onshore. It's a protected beach, crowded with sunbeds and restaurants. It's good for snorkeling (there's some coral) and as a swimming spot for children, but beware of sea urchins. Beach shacks and restaurants rent out snorkeling gear for around M$100 per day. Boats to Playa Las Gatas depart frequently from the Zihuatanejo pier, from 9am to 5pm. Buy tickets (M$40 round trip) at the **Cooperativa Zihuatan** (☑554-85-81) booth at the foot of the pier; one-way tickets can be bought on board.

About 12km south of Zihuatanejo, just before the airport, **Playa Larga** has big waves, beachfront restaurants and horseback riding. Nearby **Playa Manzanillo**, a secluded white-sand beach reachable by boat from Zihuatanejo, offers the best snorkeling in the area. To reach Playa Larga, take a 'Coacoyul' combi from Juárez near the corner of González and get off at the turnoff to Playa Larga; another combi will take you from the turnoff to the beach.

Museo Arqueológico de la
Costa Grande   MUSEUM
(cnr Plaza Olof Palme & Paseo del Pescador; admission M$10; ☑10am-6pm Tue-Sun) This small archaeology museum houses exhibits on the history, archaeology and culture of the Guerrero coast. Most signs are in Spanish, but gringos can get by with the free English-language handout.

🏃 Activities

Water Sports   WATER SPORTS
Snorkeling is good at Playa Las Gatas and even better at Playa Manzanillo. Marine life is abundant here due to a convergence of currents, and the visibility can be great – up to 35m. Migrating humpback whales pass through from December to February; manta rays can be seen all year, but you're most likely to spot them in summer, when the water is at its most clear, blue and warm.

Carlo Scuba (☑554-60-03; www.carloscuba. com; Playa Las Gatas; 1-/2-tank dives US$65/90), run by a third-generation family operation based at Playa Las Gatas, offers dives, snorkeling trips, instruction and PADI certification. Prices include pick-up and drop-off at Zihuatanejo pier. **Zihua Aquadivers** (☑544-

66-66; www.divezihuatanejo.com; Álvarez 30; 1-/2-tank dives US$55/80) offers a variety of dives and NAUI courses and certification.

Sportfishing
Sportfishing is very popular in Zihuatanejo. Sailfish are caught here year-round; seasonal fish include blue or black marlin (March to May), roosterfish (September and October), wahoo (October), mahimahi (November and December) and Spanish mackerel (December). Deep-sea fishing trips start at around US$180 for a boat holding up to four passengers. Trips run for up to seven hours and usually include equipment.

Two fishing outfits near Zihuatanejo's pier are **Sociedad Cooperativa José Azueta** (☑554-20-56; Muelle Municipal) and **Sociedad de Servicios Turísticos** (☑554-37-58; Paseo del Pescador 38B).

Yoga & Massage
Zihua Yoga Studio   YOGA, MASSAGE
(www.zihuatanejoyoga.com; Playa La Ropa; ☑8-10:45am Mon-Fri, 9-10:15am Sat & Sun) Few yogis can offer the kind of guaranteed enlightenment that comes from gazing through coconut palms into the sun-dappled Pacific from the upstairs terrace of this wonderful studio. Look for it above Paty's Marimar Restaurant on Playa La Ropa. Multilevel classes (US$10) are offered daily in high season; Tuesdays and Thursdays in the off-season. Paty also offers 50-minute massages (US$30), manicures (US$15) and pedicures (US$30).

🧭 Tours

TOP CHOICE **Blue Morpho Ecotours**   ECOTOURS
(www.bluemorphoecotours.com) Run by William Mertz, a US expatriate with a passion for birds, butterflies, reptiles, insects and archaeology, this outfit offers top-notch tours to sites of local interest, with an emphasis on nature and cultural discovery. Destinations include coastal lagoons, the Mesas de Bravo waterfalls in the adjoining Sierra Madre, and the ruins at Soledad de Maciel.

Picante   SAILING TOURS
(☑554-26-94, 554-82-70; www.picantecruises.com; Puerto Mío Marina) This 23m catamaran offers three enjoyable excursions. The 'Sail and Snorkel' trip (US$76 plus US$7 for equipment rental, 10am to 2:30pm) sails south of Zihua to the prime snorkeling of Playa Manzanillo's coral reef. The 'Magical Sunset Cruise' (US$55, 5pm to 7:30pm) heads around the bay and out along the coast

of Ixtapa. The 'Pacific Discovery' cruise (US$60, 9am to 12:15pm, mid-December to mid-April) offers opportunities for whale-, dolphin-, turtle- and bird-watching as you follow the coast towards the dramatic Morros de Potosí rock formations. Prices include food and open bar. Reservations are required.

🛏 Sleeping

Zihuatanejo has a good selection of hotels for all budgets. Prices listed here are rack rates for high season, which generally runs from December through March. Outside high season, prices drop by up to 20%. You can often negotiate lower rates, especially during slow periods or for extended stays.

Villa Casa Luna CABAÑAS $$$
(☎in the US 310-272-9022; www.villa-casa-luna.com; Playa La Ropa s/n; d US$70, cottage US$120, villa from US$350; 🛜🏊) Within this verdant walled compound at the southern end of Playa La Ropa there are three unique living spaces, ranging from the humble 'Cabaña Room' double to a grand villa with multiple bedrooms plus a gorgeously tiled designer kitchen. In the middle of the price range is perhaps the sweetest unit of all, a cozy studio cottage with its own small kitchen, living room and back bedroom. All share a nice swimming pool and the tranquility of the garden setting.

La Casa Que Canta BOUTIQUE HOTEL $$$
(☎555-70-00, 800-710-93-45, from the US 888-523-5050; www.lacasaquecanta.com; Carretera Escénica s/n; r US$395, ste US$475-785; 🅿🌟🛜🏊) Regularly ranked among the finest hotels in the world, La Casa Que Canta – The House that Sings – is the epitome of luxury, exclusivity and customer service. Perched on the cliffs between Playas Madera and La Ropa, the thatched-roof hotel contains exquisitely decorated rooms, a restaurant, a spa, a fitness center and two swimming pools. But perhaps the most valuable amenity is silence; there are no televisions, and children under 16 are banned.

Hotel Brisas del Mar HOTEL $$$
(☎554-21-42; www.hotelbrisasdelmar.com; López Mateos s/n; d incl breakfast from US$140; 🌟@🛜🏊) A cliff-hugging, red adobe village perched above Playa Madera, Brisas del Mar is perfect for a romantic getaway. The spacious rooms and grounds are decorated with traditional Mexican furnishings, tiles

and handicrafts. All have private balconies with exquisite ocean views and a hammock. A steep staircase leads down to the beach and to its Bistro del Mar, one of Zihua's finest restaurants.

Bungalows Madera BUNGALOW $$
(☎554-39-20; www.zihua-hotel.com; López Mateos 25; r with kitchenette US$60-100; 🌟🛜🏊) Run by a pair of bilingual expatriates from Texas, this sprawling place straddles the hillside between Playa Madera and downtown Zihua. The nicest ocean-facing bungalows have two rooms; one for sleeping, one for cooking and dining. Many units have spiffy sea-view terraces, and a couple include outdoor Jacuzzis. In the center there's a pool and patio area with barbecue facilities. The high-rise annex across the street offers several more spacious units overlooking downtown Zihua, along with a rooftop terrace.

Amuleto BOUTIQUE HOTEL $$$
(☎544-62-22, in the US 213-280-1037; www.amuleto.net; Escenica 9; r from US$400; 🅿🌟@🛜🏊) A boutique hotel high in the hills above Playa La Ropa, Amuleto dazzles guests with opulent, earthy rooms decorated in stone, ceramic and wood, plus suites with private swimming pools and scrumptious views. The attached restaurant is equally fabulous. A three-night minimum stay is required.

Hostel Rincón del Viajero HOSTEL $
(☎cell phone 755-1034566; www.rinconviajerozihua.4t.com; Paseo las Salinas 50, La Noria; d/tr M$320/450, campsite/dm/d/tr without bathroom M$80/120/280/380) Housed in a converted, once-derelict *bodega* (storage room) across the bridge from Zihua's pier, this artsy hostel is the brainchild of local artist and surfer Malinalli. The colorful rooms and common areas are decorated with Mali's original artwork and Mexican handicrafts. It also has a communal kitchen, rooftop terrace, hammocks, a laundry area, bike rentals and a cafe featuring fruits from the courtyard orchard. Mali speaks several languages and offers airport pickup in her van, plus surfing trips to local beaches.

Villa Mexicana HOTEL $$$
(☎554-78-88; www.hotelvillamexicana.com.mx; Playa La Ropa s/n; r incl breakfast M$2489; 🅿🌟@🛜🏊) Its chain-hotel sterility won't inspire much enthusiasm, but you can't argue with the choice location right on Playa La Ropa, at a fraction of the price you'd pay

at the luxury resort next door. All 64 tile-and-stucco rooms have cable TV, phone and safe; best of the lot are the 18 front-facing rooms with direct ocean view. There's also a popular pool and beachside bar and restaurant. Wi-fi costs M$100 extra and is only available in some rooms.

Hotel Irma HOTEL $$$

(☎554-84-72; www.hotelirma.com.mx; Adelita s/n; r with garden/ocean view M$1625/1775; P❋🅟🛜🅳) Like a reliable relative, Irma attracts regulars back year after year for the family-like atmosphere and service. Located just above Playa Madera, Irma has renovated

Zihuatanejo

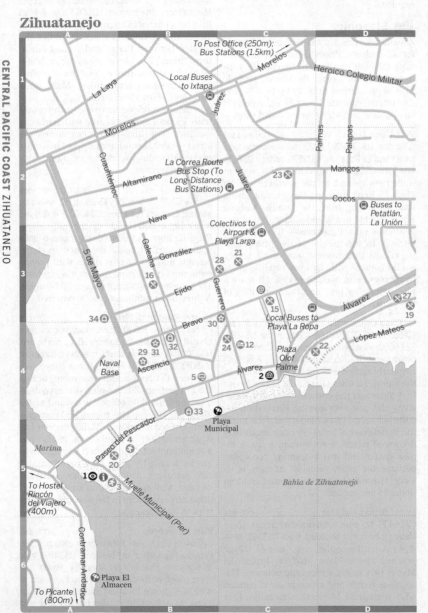

rooms, some with great views of the bay and the huge pool and terrace below. It's a great moderate choice in low season. Wi-fi is available in common areas only, not in rooms.

Arena Suites BUNGALOW $$$
(554-40-87; www.zihuatanejoarenasuites.com; López Mateos s/n; bungalows US$70-125; P❋) Well kept and spacious, with unbeatable

Zihuatanejo

◎ Sights
1 Cooperativa Zihuatan	A5
2 Museo Arqueológico de la Costa Grande	C4

✪ Activities, Courses & Tours
3 Sociedad Cooperativa José Azueta	A5
4 Sociedad de Servicios Turísticos	B5
5 Zihua Aquadivers	B4
Zihuatanejo Cooking School	(see 25)

⊨ Sleeping
6 Arena Suites	E4
7 Bungalows Madera	E4
8 Hotel Brisas del Mar	E4
9 Hotel Irma	F5
10 La Casa Que Canta	F6
11 Mi Casita	F5
12 Posada Citlali	C4
13 Villas Naomi	F3

✗ Eating
14 Bistro del Mar	F4
15 Cenaduría Antelia	C3
16 Chez Leo	B3
17 Doña Licha	E2
18 Il Mare	F6
19 La Gula	D3
20 La Sirena Gorda	A5
21 Los Braseros	C3
22 Mariscos Chendo's	C4
23 Market	C2
24 Panadería Buen Gusto	C4
25 Patio Mexica	E3
26 Restaurant Kau-Kan	F5
Rufo's Grill	(see 25)
27 Salvador's	D3
28 Tamales y Atoles Any	C3

✪ Entertainment
29 Bandido's	B4
30 Black Bull Rodeo	C3
31 Cine Paraíso	B4

⊕ Shopping
32 Alberto's	B4
El Embarcadero	(see 33)
33 El Jumil	B4
34 Mercado Turístico La Marina	A3
Pancho's	(see 31)

N 0 — 200 m
0 — 0.1 miles

To Bus Stations (800m)

Paseo del Palmar

Paseo de la Boquita

17

Plaza Kyoto

N5 de los Remedios

Camino a Playa La Ropa

Adelita

25

13 Ortiz

7 6 López Mateos

8

Playa Madera

14

Adelita

9

Carretera Escénica

26

11

18

To Playa La Ropa (750m);
Villa Mexicana (750m);
Paty's Marimar (800m);
Zihua Yoga Studio (800m);
Villa Casa Luna (1.5km)

10

views and beach access, these bungalows are not fancy, but all have thatched terraces with hammocks, room safes and kitchens or kitchenettes. The newest suite has a Jacuzzi and a terrace overlooking Playa Madera.

Villas Naomi HOTEL, APARTMENT **$$**
(☑544-73-03; www.villasnaomi.com; cnr Adelitas & Ortiz; r/ste with kitchenette M$1000/1300; ❋ ❂ ✆) Built around a lovely old tree, this newer place is conveniently located halfway between downtown and Playa Madera. There are two simple rooms downstairs, plus six pricier suites with kitchenettes.

Mi Casita GUESTHOUSE **$$**
(☑554-45-10; Carretera Escénica s/n; s/d/tr/q M$500/600/700/800; ❋) This humble family-run place perches on the hillside between Playas Madera and La Ropa. The tidy rooms all open onto terraces with hammocks and distant ocean views.

Posada Citlali GUESTHOUSE **$$**
(☑554-20-43; Guerrero 4; s/d M$400/550; ❋ ❂) This pleasant older posada has plain but clean rooms around a dark, leafy central courtyard. One room offers air-con; the rest are fan-cooled.

Eating

Guerrero is famous for its *pozole,* a hearty meat-and-veg soup that's found on most menus in town (especially on Thursday). *Tiritas* (raw fish slivers marinated with red onion, lemon or lime and chili peppers, and served with soda crackers and spicy sauce) are Zihua's specialty, but you won't find them on many menus – look for them at carts near the bus stations, or request them at any beachfront *enramada.*

CENTRAL ZIHUATANEJO
Seafood here is fresh and delicious. Many popular (if touristy) fish restaurants line Paseo del Pescador, parallel to Playa Municipal; however, the quality-to-price ratio tends to improve as you move inland. A hearty and inexpensive breakfast or lunch is available in the **market** (☺7am-6pm), at the corner of Juárez and Gonzalez. Late-night taco stands are ubiquitous around town.

TOP CHOICE **Doña Licha** MEXICAN **$**
(Cocos 8; mains M$35-75; ☺8am-6pm) This place near the market is renowned for its down-home Mexican cooking, casual atmosphere and excellent prices. There are always sev-

eral *comidas corridas* to choose from; all come with rice, beans and handmade tortillas. Breakfasts are huge.

Chez Leo SEAFOOD **$$**
(Galeana 5; mains M$85-155; ☺2-11pm) Chef Lalo takes pride in personally informing guests of what fish has been caught fresh today, then steps back into the kitchen to cook it up however you like, from Parisian style with brandy to Yucatan style with achiote seeds, all accompanied by freshly sautéed vegetables. The menu also features international twists, including sashimi, carpaccio and Cajun tuna, and for dessert there's coconut ice cream with Kahlua.

La Sirena Gorda SEAFOOD **$$**
(The Fat Mermaid; Paseo del Pescador 90; mains M$65-180; ☺8:30am-10pm Thu-Tue) Close to the pier, this place is a casual and popular open-air restaurant that's good for garlic shrimp, curry tuna and fish tacos, as well as burgers and traditional Mexican dishes.

Cenaduría Antelia MEXICAN **$**
(Bravo 14; mains M$20-55; ☺8am-2pm & 5pm-midnight) Antelia's popular and friendly eatery has been dishing out tasty *antojitos mexicanos* (Mexican snacks) and desserts since 1975. Tuck into a *tamal de pollo en salsa verde* (chicken *tamal* in green sauce) or a bursting bowl of daily *pozole,* and top it off with *calabaza con leche* (squash in milk) for dessert.

Los Braseros MEXICAN **$$**
(Ejido 14; mains M$75-189; ☺8am-1am) With 140 dishes on the menu, this is a wonderful place to sample specialties from all over Mexico. For a quick bite on the go, grab a few *tacos al pastor* (M$6 each) from the street-facing counter, or sit down and linger awhile over its trademark *alambres* – tasty mixes of grilled fish, meat, veggies and cheese.

Tamales y Atoles Any MEXICAN **$$**
(☑554-73-73; Ejido 18; tamales M$25-75, mains M$50-120; ☺8am-1am) This friendly, if overpriced, place serves consciously traditional and excellent Mexican cuisine under its big *palapa* roof. Highlights include to-die-for *tamales* and the sweet, corn-based hot drinks known as *atoles.*

Panadería Buen Gusto BAKERY **$**
(Guerrero 11; pastries from M$5; ☺8:30am-9pm) A good traditional Mexican bakery in the heart of downtown Zihua.

ZIHUATANEJO COOKING SCHOOL

Ready for a morning of cultural immersion, good eats and just plain fun? Then make a beeline for the **Zihuatanejo Cooking School** (☎554-39-49, cell phone 755-1167211; www.patiomexica.com; cnr Adelita & NS de los Remedios). Long-time Zihua resident Monica Durán Pérez opens her home kitchen and shares her love of Mexican culinary culture in this wonderful series of classes. Start with a trip to the market to buy ingredients, taste-test fresh cheese, learn about herbs and sample local delicacies that you'd surely miss otherwise. Then return to Monica's backyard, where you grind corn, shape tortillas, pound ingredients in a *molcajete* (traditional mortar and pestle), and cook up one of seven different specialties, depending on the group's interests.

Themes for individual classes include *tamales* (masa mixed with lard, stuffed with stewed meat, fish or vegetables, wrapped and steamed), *pozole* (a soup or thin stew of hominy, meat, vegetables and chilies), ceviche and *tiritas* (raw fish slivers marinated with red onion, lemon or lime and chili peppers, and served with soda crackers and spicy sauce), *mole* (a type of chili sauce), *chiles rellenos* (chili stuffed with meat or cheese) and Mexican desserts.

AROUND THE BAY
Pricey restaurants with panoramic views dominate the hilltops, while casual candlelit beachside eateries are the rule on Playa La Ropa. More affordable fare can be found in the burgeoning 'gastronomic ghetto' along Adelita, just inland from Playa Madera.

Rufo's Grill   PARRILLA $$
(Adelita 1; mains M$90-140; ☺6-10pm Mon-Sat Sep-May) Tucked onto a concrete patio under a bamboo roof fringed with Christmas lights, this unpretentious corner joint serves up fabulous barbecued meat and shrimp marinated in herbs and olive oil. Tasty grilled vegetables – red peppers, carrots, zucchini, eggplant and mushrooms – accompany every main course, a welcome alternative to standard rice and beans fare.

Mariscos Chendo's   SEAFOOD $$
(Adelita s/n; mains M$70-120; ☺noon-8pm Thu-Tue) Fan-cooled and family-run, this sweet little place just in from the waterfront is all about straightforward seafood dishes and reasonably priced beer. Specialties include garlic shrimp, coconut shrimp and dessert crepes.

Paty's Marimar   SEAFOOD $$
(www.patys-marymar.com; Playa La Ropa s/n; mains M$90-180; ☺7am-10pm) Paty does a booming business with expats, who start the day with yoga and breakfast, and return for sunset happy hour (5pm to 7pm) under the coconut palms. Whenever you show up, it's a perfect place to enjoy Mexican seafood while wiggling your toes in the sand and listening to the waves crash a few feet away.

La Gula   FUSION $$$
(http://restaurantelagula.com; Adelita 8; mains M$160-230; ☺5-10:30pm Mon-Sat) This place wins points for its beautifully presented, creative cuisine. Dishes bear names such as *mosaico mexicano* (tequila, peppercorn and dill-marinated fish carpaccio with avocado mousse) and *eclipse de sol* (shrimp medallions with bacon and pasilla chili sauce). The atmosphere, on a breezy upstairs terrace, would be way more pleasant if they'd just turn off the barfy music.

Restaurant Kau-Kan   INTERNATIONAL $$$
(☎554-84-46; www.casakaukan.com; Carretera Escénica 7; mains M$180-380; ☺5pm-midnight) High on the cliffs, this renowned gourmet restaurant enjoys stellar views from its candlelit terrace. Menu choices include stingray in black butter sauce or grilled lamb chops with Dauphinois potatoes and mint sauce.

Patio Mexica   BREAKFAST $
(www.patiomexica.com; cnr Adelita & NS de los Remedios) Squash blossom omelets and other Mexican delicacies get your day off to a sunny start at this informal breakfast place run by Monica Durán Pérez of the Zihuatanejo Cooking School.

Bistro del Mar   FUSION $$$
(☎554-21-42; www.hotelbrisasdelmar.com/res taurant.htm; Playa Madera s/n; mains M$175-280; ☺7am-11pm) With its landmark sail roof over candlelit tables and its fusion of Latin, European and Asian flavors, this beachside bistro is a romantic treat for the heart, soul and stomach.

Il Mare
ITALIAN, SEAFOOD $$$

(554-90-67; Carretera Escénica 105; mains M$145-385; 11am-11pm Mon-Sat, 5-11pm Sun) A romantic Italian restaurant with a bird's-eye perspective on the bay, Il Mare is well regarded for its Mediterranean pasta and seafood specialties.

Salvador's
MEXICAN $

(Adelita s/n; mains M$25-95; 9am-9pm) Friendly owner Salvador serves reasonably priced breakfasts, Mexican snacks, grilled meat, seafood and beer in this tree-shaded spot at the foot of the pedestrian bridge towards Playa Madera.

🍸 Drinking & Entertainment

Downtown Zihua's got the usual slew of bars offering two-for-one beers and margaritas. If it's big-time nightlife you're after, head to Ixtapa; Zihuatanejo is all about being mellow.

Black Bull Rodeo
LIVE MUSIC

(cnr Bravo & Guerrero; from 9pm) This country disco has the best *norteño* band in town, along with *cumbia,* merengue, salsa, electronica and reggae.

Bandido's
LIVE MUSIC

(Calle 5 de Mayo No 8; 10:30pm-late Thu-Sat) On Thursday, Friday and Saturday nights, this Mexican restaurant opens its floor for dancing to live salsa and *cumbia,* interspersed with DJ mixes.

Cine Paraíso
CINEMA

(cnr Cuauhtémoc & Bravo; admission M$40) Shows three films nightly, usually in English with Spanish subtitles.

🛍 Shopping

Zihua offers abundant Mexican handicrafts, including ceramics, clothing, leatherwork, Taxco silver, woodcarvings and masks from around the state of Guerrero.

El Jumil
HANDICRAFTS

(Paseo del Pescador 9; 9am-10pm Mon-Sat) This shop specializes in masks – a well-known traditional handicraft of Guerrero state.

El Embarcadero
CLOTHING

(Paseo del Pescador 9; 9am-10pm Mon-Sat) Embroidery, textiles and hand-woven clothing from Guerrero, Oaxaca, Michoacán and other neighboring states.

Mercado Turístico La Marina
MARKET

(Calle 5 de Mayo; 8am-9pm) Has many stalls selling clothes, bags and knickknacks.

A few shops along Cuauhtémoc sell Taxco silver. **Alberto's** (Cuauhtémoc 12 & 15) and **Pancho's** (Cuauhtémoc 11) have the best selection of quality pieces.

ℹ Information

Emergency

Emergency (060)

Hospital (554-36-50; Av Morelos) Halfway between the post office and the bus station.

Tourist police (554-20-40; Alvarez) Next to the basketball court.

Internet Access

Zihuatanejo is crawling with internet cafes.

Ciber Zihua (Bravo 12; per hr M$10; 8am-10pm) Has 10 computers and air-con; there's another net cafe right across the street.

Money

Zihuatanejo has many banks and *casas de cambio* where you can change US dollars; banks below have ATMs.

Banamex (cnr Ejido & Guerrero)

Bancomer (cnr Juárez & Bravo)

Banorte (cnr Juárez & Ejido)

Post

Post office (8am-6pm Mon-Fri, 8am-noon Sat) Behind the big yellow Coppel department store off Morelos.

Telephone & Fax

Long-distance telephone and fax services are available at several *casetas* along Juárez.

Tourist Information

Tourist office (554-20-01; turismozihixt@hotmail.com; Pier; 10am-6pm Mon-Fri) This convenient office at the foot of Zihua's pier stocks brochures and maps even when unstaffed in the low season.

ℹ Getting There & Away

Air

The **Ixtapa/Zihuatanejo international airport** (554-20-70; www.oma.aero/es/aeropuertos/zihuatanejo; Carretera Nacional) is 13km southeast of Zihuatanejo, a couple of kilometers off Hwy 200 heading toward Acapulco.

The following carriers service the airport.

Aeroméxico (www.aeromexico.com) Airport (554-22-37, 554-26-34); Zihuatanejo (554-20-18, ext 1; Álvarez 42) Service to Mexico City, with many onward connections.

Aeromar (553-70-12; www.aeromar.com.mx; Airport) Direct service to Mexico City.

Interjet (553-70-02; www.interjet.com.mx; Airport) Direct service to Mexico City and Toluca.

BUSES FROM ZIHUATANEJO

DESTINATION	FARE (M$)	DURATION	FREQUENCY (DAILY)
Acapulco	135-170	4-5hr	very frequent EB & EDO
Lázaro Cárdenas	65-84	1½-2hr	hourly EB & EDO
Manzanillo	399	8-9hr	8:40pm EB
Mexico City (Terminal Sur)	630-699	8-10hr	7:20am EDO, noon EB, frequent night buses EB &EDO
Mexico City (Terminal Norte)	562-630	9-10hr	3 EB
Mexico City (Poniente)	625	8-9hr	4 EB
Morelia	400	5hr	8 EB
Puerto Vallarta	787	13hr	8:40pm EB

MagniCharters (☑55-1999-1611; www.magni charters.com.mx; Airport) Direct service to Mexico City.

Bus

Both long-distance bus terminals are on Hwy 200 about 2km northeast of the town center (toward the airport): the **Estrella Blanca terminal** (EB), also known as Central de Autobuses, is a block east of the smaller **Estrella de Oro terminal** (EDO). The former also serves several smaller bus companies including Autovías and Costa Line.

Car & Motorcycle

There are several car-rental companies at the airport, most with branches in Ixtapa.
Alamo Airport (☑554-84-29); Ixtapa (☑553-02-06; Centro Comercial Los Patios)
Dollar Airport (☑553-70-50); Ixtapa (☑553-37-63; Hotel Fontan, Blvd Ixtapa)
Europcar Airport (☑553-71-58); Ixtapa (☑544-82-56; Paseo Ixtapa, Local 2)
Green Motion Airport (☑554-48-37); Ixtapa (☑553-03-97; Blvd Ixtapa s/n, Plaza Ambientes)
Hertz (☑cell phone 755-1090022/23; Airport)
Thrifty Airport (☑553-70-20); Ixtapa (☑553-30-19; Hotel Barceló, Blvd Ixtapa)

ⓘ Getting Around

To/From the Airport

The cheapest way to get to and from the airport is via a public 'Aeropuerto' *colectivo* van (M$8.50) departing from Juárez near González between 6am and 10pm and making many stops before dropping you just outside the airport gate. *Colectivo* taxis are a more direct and convenient option for incoming passengers, whisking you from the arrivals area to Ixtapa or Zihua for M$120 per person. Private taxis from the airport into either town cost M$365, although they charge only $120 or so when returning to the airport.

Bus & Colectivo

To reach downtown Zihua or Ixtapa from Zihua's long-distance bus terminals, cross Hwy 200 using the pedestrian overpass directly opposite the Estrella Blanca terminal, then look for signs. Buses for downtown Zihua stop at the foot of the overpass. The stop for Ixtapa is a little further west along Hwy 200. For more details on buses to/from Ixtapa, see p539.

From downtown Zihua to the bus terminals, catch 'La Correa' route buses (M$5, 10 minutes), which leave regularly from the corner of Juárez and Nava between 5:30am and 9:30pm.

'Playa La Ropa' buses go south on Juárez and out to Playa La Ropa every half-hour from 7am to 8pm (M$5.50).

'Coacoyul' *colectivos* heading toward Playa Larga depart from Juárez, near the corner of González, every five minutes from 5am to 10pm (M$8, 15 minutes).

Taxi

Cabs are plentiful in Zihuatanejo. Always agree on the fare before getting in. Approximate fares from central Zihua include M$55 to Ixtapa, M$40 to Playa La Ropa, M$70 to Playa Larga and M$20 to the Estrella Blanca bus station.

South of Ixtapa & Zihuatanejo

BARRA DE POTOSÍ

☑755 / POP 400

About 26km southeast of Zihuatanejo is the small fishing village of Barra de Potosí at the far tip of an endless, palm-fringed sandy-white beach. The calm green-blue water is great for swimming but too cloudy for snorkeling.

The south side of the beach empties into **Laguna de Potosí**, a saltwater lagoon about 6.5km long brimming with hundreds of species of birds. For M$200 or so, local guides such as **Avi 'Sharkboy' Cadena Bañuelos** (☎cell phone 755-1026509; http://barratours.blogspot.com) can take you on a 90-minute paddling loop through the mangrove-lined channels and the wide-open waters of the lagoon. Along the way, you'll encounter fishermen and a wide variety of birds, including herons, kingfishers, cormorants and pelicans.

Some guides also offer the option of stashing your kayak at the lagoon's edge for the easy 15-minute hike to **Playa Tortuga**, a long, gorgeous stretch of sandy beach where sea turtles come to lay their eggs, backed by a dramatic rocky headland. **Zoe Kayak Tours** (☎553-04-96; www.zoekayaktours.com; tours incl coffee, water & snacks US$90) offers more extensive three- to four-hour guided paddle tours catering to bird-watchers, adventurous kayakers, and those seeking more of a back-country experience. Horseback riding and canoeing are also popular.

If you can gather a few people, it's well worth taking a motorboat tour out to the dramatic **Morros de Potosí**, a cluster of massive guano-covered rocks about 20 minutes offshore. Boats will circle the Morros, affording views of the many seabirds that nest out here. Local guides including **'Cocky' Cabrera Arizmundo** and **Adelaido Martínez** (☎cell phone 755-1217352; www.barradepotosi.jimdo.com) charge about M$800 for the trip, regardless of group size, and for an extra M$400 will also take you snorkeling at nearby **Playa Manzanillo**.

🏄 **El Refugio de Potosí** (☎100-07-43; www.elrefugiodepotosi.org; adult/child M$60/30; ☺10am-5pm daily Dec-Mar, Sun, Mon & Thu Apr-Nov), a recently opened nature center just inland from the beachfront north of town, rehabilitates injured wildlife, breeds butterflies and parrots and offers environmental education programs in local schools. A 30-minute guided tour, with excellent bilingual guides, offers opportunities to pet a porcupine, hold snakes and tarantulas, examine whale and crocodile skeletons and observe a variety of animals, including parrots, hummingbirds, armadillos and a jaguarundi (local wildcat). There's also a 15m observation tower affording dramatic views of lagoons, palm-fringed beaches, the Morros de Potosí and the open ocean beyond.

🛏 Sleeping & Eating

A handful of guesthouses are scattered around town, and seafood *enramadas* line the beach.

TOP
CHOICE Casa del Encanto   B&B **$$**
(☎cell phone 755-1246122; www.lacasadelencanto.com; d incl breakfast US$70-100; ☜) For bohemian charm and an intimate perspective on the local community, nothing beats this magical space of brilliantly colored open-air rooms, hammocks, fountains and candlelit stairways on a residential street about 300m inland from the beach. Crowing roosters serenade you in the morning, and a nice breakfast is served in the central patio area. Expatriate US owner Laura has spent years organizing international volunteers to work with neighborhood schoolchildren, and she's a great resource for getting to know the town, finding local guides, discovering late-night backstreet eateries, and timing your visit to coincide with local festivals and events.

Playa Calli   B&B **$$**
(☎558-84-08; www.playacalli.com; s/d incl breakfast M$1000/1100; ☒) Located on the beachfront about 2km north of the village, this palm-fringed retreat has four spacious rooms with king-sized beds and ceiling fans, a welcoming swimming pool, and beautiful views out to the Morros de Potosí. Friendly host Bernie and son Dani speak English, German, Spanish and French, and exude a tranquility over their home.

La Condesa   SEAFOOD **$$**
(mains M$80; ☺11am-sunset) Northernmost of the beachfront *enramadas*, this is one of the best eateries around. Try its *pescado a la talla* (broiled fish fillets) or *tiritas*, both local specialties, and don't pass up the savory handmade tortillas.

❶ Getting There & Away

By car from Zihuatanejo, drive southeast on Hwy 200 toward Acapulco, take the well-marked turnoff (near Km 225 just south of the Los Achotes bridge) and drive another 9km to Barra de Potosí.

By public transit, catch a Petatlán-bound bus from either of Zihua's main terminals, or from the stop a couple of blocks east of Zihua's market. Tell the driver to let you off at the Barra de Potosí intersection, where you can catch a *camioneta* (pickup truck) the rest of the way. The total trip takes about 90 minutes and costs about M$30.

SOLEDAD DE MACIEL
☑755 / POP 380

Known locally as 'La Chole,' the tiny hamlet of Soledad de Maciel sits atop the largest, most important archaeological ruin in Guerrero state. Since excavations began in earnest in 2007, archaeologists have discovered a plaza, a ball court and three pyramids – one crowned by five temples – all left behind by pre-Hispanic cultures including Tepoztecos, Cuitlatecos and Tomiles.

Just inland from the ruins, a brand-new **museum** (admission free; ◷8am-5pm Tue-Sun) houses three rooms full of Spanish-language displays, which place the local archaeological finds in a broader historical context. The most important local artifact is the Chole King, a 1.5m-tall statue depicting deities of life and death, displayed in the courtyard of the village church. Brothers **Adán and José Guadalupe** (☑103-08-78) offer guided tours of the site for M$200 (any group size), plus an optional 10-minute demonstration on local tobacco processing and cigar-making, which is an economic mainstay of the village.

Soledad de Maciel is 33km southeast of Zihuatanejo off Hwy 200. From the well-marked turnoff near Km 214, a very rugged road leads 5km coastwards to the museum, then continues another kilometer to the archaeological site and village. Any bus heading south to Petatlán or Acapulco will get you here; ask to be dropped at the intersection for 'La Chole,' where you can hop on a *camioneta* into town.

Pie de la Cuesta
☑744 / POP 770

Just 10km – and 100 years – from Acapulco is the tranquil seaside suburb of Pie de la Cuesta, a rustic beach town occupied by some terrific guesthouses and seafood restaurants. But it's the dramatic sunset views from the wide, west-facing beach that have made Pie de la Cuesta famous. The town sits on a narrow, 2km strip of land bordered by the Pacific Ocean and the Laguna de Coyuca (where Sylvester Stallone filmed *Rambo: First Blood Part II*). The large freshwater lagoon contains several islands including Pájaros, a bird sanctuary. Pie de la Cuesta is much quieter, cheaper and closer to nature than Acapulco, but still close enough for those who want to enjoy the city's attractions and nightlife.

🏃 Activities

The surf here can be dangerous due to a riptide and the shape of the waves; the lagoon is better for swimming.

Waterskiing   WATER SPORTS
Waterskiing and wakeboarding on the lagoon are both popular pastimes; there are several waterskiing clubs along the main road, all charging around M$700 per hour, including **Club de Ski Tres Marías** (☑460-00-11) and **Club de Ski Chuy** (☑460-11-04).

Boat Trips   BOATING
Several establishments offer boat trips on the lagoon from M$100 per person; eager captains await your business along the main street and down by the boat launches at the lagoon's southeast corner.

Horseback Riding   HORSEBACK RIDING
Horseback riding on the beach costs about M$200 per hour; book from a hotel or directly from the galloping cowboys on the beach.

🛏 Sleeping

TOP CHOICE **Quinta Erika**   B&B $$
(☑444 41-31; www.quintaerika.com; Carretera Barra de Coyuca Km 8.5; s/d incl breakfast US$50/55, 4-person bungalow US$120; P@🛜❄) For those who just want to get away from it all, Quinta Erika is a hidden, junglelike retreat located 8km northeast of town, 10 minutes on foot from the final bus stop in Playa Luces. The estate sits on 2 hectares of lagoonside property, lovingly landscaped with more than 200 palm and tropical fruit trees. The six colorful rooms and one bungalow are tastefully decorated with handmade furniture and traditional Mexican handicrafts. Other perks include wonderful breakfasts, kayak and horse rentals (M$50 and M$200 per hour, respectively), a whimsically decorated pool and outdoor shower, a dock boasting spectacular lagoon views and an upstairs lounge area with hammocks. Stuttgart-born owner Helmut speaks German, Spanish and English and takes great pride in his hideaway.

Villa Nirvana   HOTEL $$
(☑460-16-31; www.lavillanirvana.com; Av de la Fuerza Aérea 302; r M$400-900; P🛜❄) Villa Nirvana's friendly US owners have lovingly

landscaped this cheerful property. It has a variety of simple, comfortable accommodations surrounding a central garden and pool area. The priciest rooms upstairs include seaview terraces and double hammocks.

Hacienda Vayma Beach Club HOTEL $$$
(☎460-28-82; www.vayma.com.mx; Calz Pie de la Cuesta 378; r M$1050, ste M$2000; P✻🖥️🐕️) This relaxing hotel has an awesome beach with private *cabañas* and double-width lounge chairs, a big pool with swim-up bar, and a choice of room types. 'Rough it' in a smaller budget unit with cold water only, or splurge for a suite with hot water, air-con and Jacuzzi.

Acapulco Trailer Park & Minisuper CAMPGROUND $
(☎460-00-10; acatrailerpark@yahoo.com.mx; Calz Pie de la Cuesta s/n; campsites M$250, RV sites M$350; P🖥️🐕️) The area's nicest campground offers a mix of oceanside and lagoonside spaces, clean bathrooms with showers, a shallow pool, a boat launch and a small grocery store with camping supplies.

Eating

Restaurant Tres Marías SEAFOOD, MEXICAN $$
(Fuerza Aérea s/n; breakfast M$60-80, lunch & dinner M$80-120; ⊗8am-7pm) Facing each other across the main street are these two separate restaurants with identical names and hours, run by a pair of sisters. The one facing the ocean serves fantastic *huachinango al mojo de ajo* (garlicky red snapper) and lets you bring your own drinks if you choose a table on the beach. Its lagoonside counterpart, underneath a huge thatched roof, is popular for its North American–style breakfasts.

Quinta Rosita MEXICAN, SEAFOOD $$
(Playa Pie de la Cuesta; mains M$50-120; ⊗9am-10pm) Treat your taste buds to shrimp cooked six different ways while basking in the ocean breeze at this beachfront eatery. Sunday specials include paella, Veracruz-style fish and homemade stewed pork.

ℹ️ Information

Pie de la Cuesta's long main road (alternately known as Avenida de la Fuerza Aérea Mexicana and Calz Pie de la Cuesta) runs through town, past an Air Force base and on to Playa Luces. Near the arched intersection of the main road and Hwy 200, **Netxcom** (per hr M$15; ⊗10am-9pm) offers fast internet connections. The town also has a pharmacy, telephones and a few

minisuper grocery stores; other services are located in Acapulco.

ℹ️ Getting There & Away

From Acapulco, catch a 'Pie de la Cuesta' bus on La Costera across the street from the post office. Buses go every 15 minutes from 6am until around 8pm; the trip costs M$5 and takes 30 to 90 minutes, depending on traffic – on a bad day, it can be total gridlock leaving Acapulco!

Buses from Acapulco marked 'Pie de la Cuesta–San Isidro' or 'Pie de la Cuesta–Pedregoso' stop at the town's arched entryway on Hwy 200, leaving you with a long walk into town; the more convenient 'Pie de la Cuesta–Playa Luces' buses turn off the main highway and follow Pie de la Cuesta's main street 6km through town to Playa Luces, terminating just before Quinta Erika.

Colectivo taxis to Pie de la Cuesta operate 24 hours along La Costera and elsewhere in Acapulco's old town, and charge M$12. A regular taxi from Acapulco costs between M$100 and M$150 one way, depending on your bartering skills, the time of day and your point of origin.

Acapulco

☎744 / POP 670,000

Before Cancún and Ixtapa, Acapulco was Mexico's original party town. With stunning yellow beaches and a 24-hour nightlife, it was dubbed the 'Pearl of the Pacific.' During its heyday, Acapulco was the playground for the rich and famous including Frank Sinatra, Elvis Presley, Elizabeth Taylor and Judy Garland; John F Kennedy and his wife Jacqueline honeymooned here. It was immortalized in films such as Elvis' *Fun in Acapulco* and TV's *The Love Boat*.

Nowadays, the golden arc of beaches surrounding Bahía de Acapulco remains as gorgeous as ever, but the city's reputation has been severely tarnished by years of violent incidents in Mexico's ongoing drug wars. Many tourists are staying away, and locals have initiated an all-out campaign to bring them back. The city's new slogan, plastered on billboards all over town, is 'Habla bien de ACA,' a play on words that can mean, 'Speak well of this place,' or 'Speak well of Acapulco.' Graffiti on the local buses also makes overt reference to the damage to normal people's livelihoods caused by the drug trade.

Bustling Acapulco does offer pockets of calm: romantic cliffside restaurants, the impressive 17th-century fort, a world-class botanical garden and the old town's charming shady *zócalo* (plaza). And when you tire of the crowds, secluded beaches and seaside villages such as Pie de la Cuesta are just a short drive away.

Acapulco borders the 11km shore of the Bahía de Acapulco (The Bay). Old Acapulco – centered on the cathedral and adjacent *zócalo* – comprises the western part of the city; Acapulco Dorado heads east around the bay from Playa Hornos to Playa Icacos; and Acapulco Diamante is a newer luxury resort area southeast of Acapulco proper, between the Bahía de Acapulco and the airport.

Acapulco's principal bayside avenue, Avenida Costera Miguel Alemán – often called 'La Costera' – hugs the shoreline all the way around the bay. From Playa Caleta on the Península de las Playas, it curves north towards the *zócalo*, then continues east along the beachfront past Parque Papagayo (a large, shady park popular with Mexican families) all the way to Playa Icacos and the naval base at the bay's southeastern edge. Most of Acapulco's hotels, restaurants, discos and points of interest are along or near La Costera, especially near its midpoint at La Diana traffic circle. Past the naval base, La Costera becomes Carretera Escénica, which joins Hwy 200 after 9km at the turnoff to Puerto Marqués. Hwy 200 then leads southeast past ritzy Playa Revolcadero to the airport.

History

The name Acapulco is derived from ancient Náhuatl words meaning 'place of giant reeds.' Archaeological finds show that when the Spanish discovered this bay in 1512, people had already been living here for some 2000 years.

The Spanish, eager to find a commercial route to Asia, built a port and shipbuilding facilities on Acapulco's naturally protected, deepwater harbor. In 1565, Friar Andrés de Urdante discovered Pacific trade winds that allowed ships to quickly and safely reach Asia. For more than 250 years, *naos* (Spanish trading galleons) made the annual voyage from Acapulco to the Philippines and back. Gold, silks and spices were unloaded in Acapulco, carried overland to Veracruz, and then shipped across the Atlantic to Spain. To protect their investment from looting, the Spanish built the Fuerte de San Diego. But it was the Mexican War of Independence (1810–22), not pirates, that abruptly killed the trade route.

For the next century, Acapulco declined and remained relatively isolated until a paved road linked it with Mexico City in 1927. Prosperous Mexicans began vacationing here, and Hollywood came calling. By the '50s, Acapulco was becoming a glitzy, jetset resort. But by the '70s, overdevelopment and overpopulation had taken their toll, and the bay became polluted. Foreign tourists took their cash to the newer resorts of Cancún and Ixtapa. Once again, Acapulco's heyday was over.

In the late 1990s, the city launched ambitious revitalization and bay-cleanup programs. Soon thereafter, US college students, attracted by cheap rooms, began coming to Acapulco in droves, to the extent that it replaced Cancún as Mexico's top springbreak hot spot. Today, Acapulco is investing in developments geared to a more upscale clientele in hope of reclaiming its title as the 'Pearl of the Pacific.'

⊙ Sights

Beaches   BEACH

Acapulco's beaches top the list of must-dos for most visitors. The beaches heading east around the bay from the *zócalo* – **Playa Hornos, Playa Hornitos, Playa Condesa** and **Playa Icacos** (all on Map p554) – are the most popular, though the west end of Hornos sometimes smells of fish from the morning catch. The high-rise hotel district begins on Playa Hornitos, on the east side of Parque Papagayo, and sweeps east. City buses constantly ply La Costera, making it easy to get up and down the long arc of beaches.

Playas Caleta and **Caletilla** (Map p552) are two small, protected beaches blending into each other in a cove on the south side of Península de las Playas. They're both backed by a solid line of seafood *palapa* restaurants. The calm waters here are especially popular with families who have small children. All buses marked 'Caleta' heading down La Costera arrive here. The Mágico Mundo Marino aquarium (p555) sits on an islet just offshore, forming the imaginary line between the two beaches; boats go regularly from the islet to Isla de la Roqueta.

Playa La Angosta (Map p558) is in a tiny, protected cove on the west side of the peninsula. From the *zócalo* it takes about 20 minutes to walk here. Or you can take any 'Caleta' bus and get off near Hotel Avenida, at the corner of Las Palmas and La Costera, just one short block from the beach.

The beaches on **Bahía Puerto Marqués**, about 18km southeast of the *zócalo*, are very

Greater Acapulco

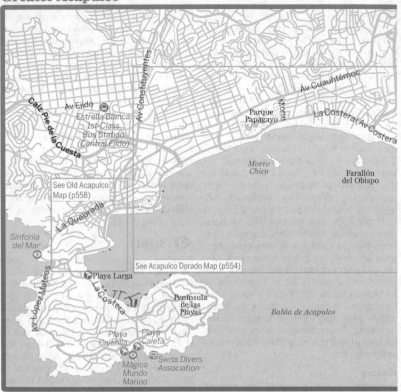

popular, and its calm waters are good for waterskiing and sailing. You get a magnificent view of Bahía de Acapulco as the Carretera Escénica climbs south out of the city. 'Puerto Marqués' buses run here along La Costera every 10 minutes from 5am to 9pm.

Beyond the Puerto Marqués turnoff and before the airport, **Playa Revolcadero** is a long, straight beach that has seen a recent explosion in luxury tourism and residential development. Waves are large and surfing is popular here, especially in summer, but a strong undertow makes swimming dangerous; heed lifeguards' instructions. Horseback riding along the beach is popular.

The two beaches closest to Old Acapulco are **Playa Tlacopanocha**, directly across from the *zócalo*, noteworthy more as a departure point for bay cruises than as a swimming beach; and **Playa Manzanillo**, a small crescent of sand that's popular with locals but not as pristine as the beaches further east.

Isla de la Roqueta   ISLAND
This island offers a popular (crowded) beach, and snorkeling and diving possibilities. You can rent snorkeling gear, kayaks and other water-sports equipment on the beach. From Playas Caleta and Caletilla, boats make the eight-minute trip (M$50 round trip) every 20 minutes or so. Alternatively, glass-bottomed boats make a circuitous trip to the island (M$70), departing from the same beaches but traveling via **La Virgen de los Mares** (Virgin of the Seas), a submerged bronze statue of the Virgen of Guadalupe – visibility varies with water conditions. The trip takes about 45 minutes, depending on how many times floating vendors approach your boat.

La Quebrada Clavadistas   CLIFF DIVERS
(Map p558; Plazoleta La Quebrada; adult/child M$40/5; ⊙shows 12:45pm, 7:30pm, 8:30pm, 9:30pm & 10:30pm) Acapulco's most popular tourist attraction, the famous cliff divers

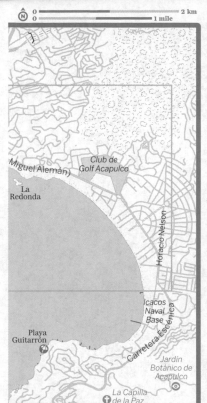

unchanged today. The fort is home to the **Museo Histórico de Acapulco** (Map p554; Hornitos s/n; admission M$43, Sun free; ⊙9am-6pm Tue-Sun), which has fascinating exhibits detailing the city's history, with Spanish and English captions. The fort also puts on regular evening sound-and-light shows, in Spanish and English. Call to confirm times and dates.

Zócalo
PLAZA

(Map p558) Every night, Acapulco's old town *zócalo* comes alive with street performers, mariachis, sidewalk cafes and occasional festivals. It's especially popular on Sunday nights with multiple generations of Mexican families. The **Nuestra Señora de la Soledad cathedral**, built in 1930, dominates the square and is unusual for its blue-domed, neo-Byzantine architecture.

Jardín Botánico de Acapulco
GARDENS

(Map p552; www.acapulcobotanico.org; Av Heróico Colegio Militar s/n; adult/child M$30/free, guided visit per person M$50; ⊙dawn-dusk) Located on the campus of Loyola del Pacífico University, these botanical gardens house an impressive collection of flora and fauna. The well-marked footpath climbs from 204m to 411m above sea level through a shaded tropical forest, with plenty of benches to stop and smell the flowers.

La Capilla de la Paz
CHAPEL

(Chapel of Peace; Map p552; Vientos Galernos s/n; ⊙10am-1pm & 4-6pm) Perched on a hilltop high above Acapulco, La Capilla de la Paz is a quiet spot for reflection and meditation. The minimalist, open-air chapel features cascading water, gardens and benches to savor the beautiful aerial view of Acapulco. The chapel's giant white cross is visible from miles across the bay. Visit in late afternoon, when tourists jockey for positions to capture the sun setting within the sculpture of clasped hands.

🏃 Activities

As one might expect, Acapulco's activities are largely beach-based.

Water Sports

Just about everything that can be done on or below the water is done in Acapulco. Waterskiing, boating, banana-boating and parasailing are all popular. To partake in any of these, walk along the Zona Dorada beaches and look for the kiosks. These charge about M$300 for a five-minute parasailing flight,

of La Quebrada have been dazzling audiences since 1934, diving with fearless finesse from heights of 25m to 35m into the narrow ocean cove below. The last show usually features divers holding torches. Tip the divers when they come through the crowd. La Perla restaurant-bar provides a great but pricey view of the divers from above.

Just south of La Quebrada, you'll find the lovely **Sinfonía del Mar** (Symphony of the Sea; Map p552), an outdoor stepped plaza that occasionally hosts concerts, but mainly serves as an amazing place to view sunsets.

Fuerte de San Diego
FORTRESS

(Map p554; Hornitos s/n) This beautifully restored pentagonal fort was built in 1616 atop a hill east of the *zócalo*. Its mission was to protect the Spanish *naos* conducting trade between the Philippines and Mexico from marauding Dutch and English buccaneers. The fort was destroyed in a 1776 earthquake and rebuilt in 1783. It remains basically

Acapulco Dorado

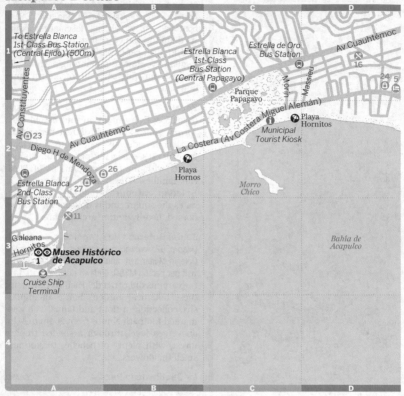

M$400 for a Jet-ski ride and M$800 for one hour of waterskiing. The smaller Playas Caleta and Caletilla have sailboats, fishing boats, motorboats, pedal boats, canoes, snorkeling gear, inner tubes and water bicycles for rent.

Though Acapulco isn't really a scuba destination, there are some decent dive sites nearby. **Acapulco Scuba Center** (Map p558; ☑482-94-74; www.acapulcoscuba.com; Paseo del Pescador 13 & 14; ☺8am-4pm Wed-Mon) and **Swiss Divers Association** (Map p552; ☑482-13-57; www.swissdivers.com; Hotel Caleta, Cerro San Martín 325; ☺9am-5pm) both charge US$70 for a two-tank dive.

The best **snorkeling** is off small Playa Las Palmitas on Isla de la Roqueta. Unless you pony up for an organized snorkeling trip you'll need to scramble over rocks to reach it. You can rent gear on the island or on Playas Caleta and Caletilla, which also have some decent spots. Both scuba operations above take half-day snorkeling trips for around

US$35 per person, including boat, guide, gear, food, drink and hotel transportation.

Sportfishing

Sportfishing is very popular. **Fish-R-Us** (Map p558; ☑482-82-82; www.fish-r-us.com; La Costera 100; ☺9am-6pm) offers half-day fishing trips starting around M$6000 for a six-person boat, including gear and bait. The captain can often combine individuals into a group large enough to cover the cost of the boat, for M$1000 to M$1200 per person.

Golf

For golfers, **Club de Golf Acapulco** (Map p554; ☑484-07-81; La Costera s/n; green fees M$500; ☺7am-6:30pm) has a nine-hole course downtown, while south near Playa Revolcadero you'll find the more exclusive **Tres Vidas** (☑435-08-26; www.tresvidas.com.mx; 9/18 holes US$110/215; ☺7am-7pm) and the newly redesigned **Turtle Dunes Country Club** (☑469-10-00; www.turtledunescc.com; 9/18 holes

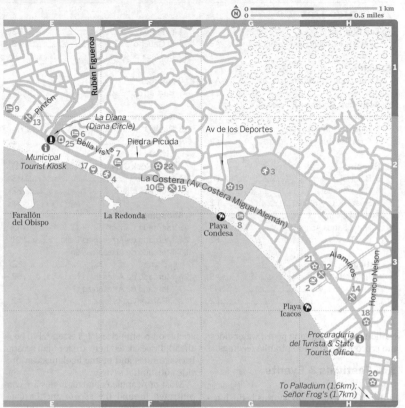

US$100/195; ⊗7:30am-6:30pm), which re-opened to the public in December 2011.

Cruises

Various boats and yachts offer cruises, most of which depart from around Playa Tlaco-panocha or Playa Manzanillo near the *zóca-lo*. Cruises are available day and night. They range from glass-bottomed boats to multi-level craft (with blaring salsa music and open bars) to yachts offering quiet sunset cruises around the bay. **Acarey** (Map p558; ☑482-37-63; La Costera) and **Fiesta/Bonanza** (Map p558; ☑483-15-50; Paseo del Pescador) are two of the more popular operators; make reservations directly with the eager captains at the marina or through travel agencies and most hotels.

Other Activities

Paradise Bungy　　　BUNGEE JUMPING
(Map p554; La Costera 107; ⊗5pm-1am Sun-Thu, 3pm-3am Fri & Sat) This 50m-high bungee tow-er is easy to spot on La Costera. For M$800 you can throw yourself (bungee included) from its platform while crowds cheer you from the street.

CICI　　　WATER PARK
(Map p554; www.cici.com.mx, in Spanish; La Costera 101; adult & child over 2yr M$120, incl dolphin show, tube rental & lunch M$320; ⊗10am-6pm) At this family-oriented water park, there are dolphin shows twice daily, and humans occasionally give diving exhibitions. You can swim with dolphins yourself (M$1350 per hour, M$990 per half-hour) or get your adrenaline rush at the 90m-long waterslide, artificial wave pool or Sky Coaster bungee jump. Any local bus marked 'CICI,' 'Base' or 'Puerto Marqués' will take you here.

Mágico Mundo Marino　　　AQUARIUM
(Map p552; adult/child M$60/30; ⊗9am-6pm) This aquarium stands on a small islet off Pla-yas Caleta and Caletilla. Highlights include a

Acapulco Dorado

sea-lion show; swimming pools; waterslides; and crocodile, turtle and piranha feedings.

★ Festivals & Events

Semana Santa   RELIGIOUS
Running from Palm Sunday, this is the busiest time of year for tourism in Acapulco. There's lots of action in the discos, on the beaches and all over town.

Festival Francés   CULTURAL
The French Festival, held in April or May, celebrates French food, cinema, music and literature.

Acafest   MUSIC
Held for one week in May. Features Mexican and international music stars at venues around town.

🛏 Sleeping

Acapulco has more than 30,000 hotel rooms. Rates vary widely by season; the high season is roughly from mid-December to mid-January, Easter Week and during the July and August school holidays. Given the dramatic drop-off in tourism in recent years, you can often bargain for a better rate, especially in low season for extended stays. During Semana Santa or between Christmas and New Year's Day (at which times all bets

are off on room prices), it's essential to book ahead. Prices listed here are for high season. Package rates and online bookings can provide substantial savings.

Most of Acapulco's budget hotels are concentrated around the *zócalo* and La Quebrada. The original high-rise zone stretches from the eastern end of Parque Papagayo and curves east around the bay; a new luxury 'strip' is springing up on Playa Revolcadero, east of Puerto Marqués.

Banyan Tree Cabo Marqués   LUXURY HOTEL $$$
(☏434-01-00; www.banyantree.com/en/cabo_marques; Blvd Cabo Marqués; r from US$565; 🅿🛏❄@🛜🏊) Jutting into the ocean at the far end of Punta Diamante peninsula, about 32km south of downtown, this gorgeous resort is Acapulco's newest name in luxury, dazzling guests with private villas, ocean-view sundecks, outdoor massage beds and Asian-themed spa treatments. Enjoy gourmet Thai, Mexican, Italian or Spanish cuisine at the hotel's four restaurants, or opt for 'In-Villa' dining – the ultimate romantic room service experience. Check online for early-bird and multiple-night discounts.

Las Brisas   LUXURY HOTEL $$$
(☏469-69-00, in the US 866-221-2961; www.brisashotelonline.com/acapulco; Carretera Escénica

5255; casitas incl breakfast US$303-420; P⊖
❀@🛜≋) Romantic, lovely Las Brisas commands amazing views from its vantage point high above the bay. Built in the late 1950s, the place has great bones, including lovely stonework and tile floors. Each of the 263 casitas has a private terrace or balcony and either a private swimming pool or one shared with, at most, two other casitas. Service gets high ratings. The hotel's beach club, accessed by a regular shuttle service, is nestled far below in a rocky cove.

Hotel Los Flamingos HOTEL $$
(off Map p558; ☑482-06-90; www.hotellosfla mingos.com; Av López Mateos s/n; r from US$65; P❀🛜≋) Once owned by John Wayne, Johnny 'Tarzan' Weissmuller and their pals, Los Flamingos is a living museum to Acapulco's heyday. Perched on a cliff 135m above the ocean, this classic boasts one of the finest sunset views in town and a popular bar and restaurant. Images of Hollywood's golden age grace the walls. The rooms are modest and comfortable. For a retro splurge, rent out Tarzan's Round House (Johnny Weissmuller's former residence), a circular cliffside suite sleeping six.

Hotel Sands Acapulco HOTEL, BUNGALOW $$
(Map p554; ☑435-08-90; www.sands.com.mx; La Costera 178; bungalow/r M$700/1000; P❀🛜≋🚶) An excellent choice for families, Sands is located across the highway from the beach and has a large children's playground, minigolf, pools and a waterslide. Bungalows are small but cozy; the larger rooms sleep up to four people. All have cable TV, air-con and fridge, and there's wi-fi in the common areas. Prices are slashed substantially in the low season.

Hotel Elcano HOTEL $$$
(Map p554; ☑435-15-00; www.hotelelcano. com.mx; La Costera 75; studio/standard/ste M$1500/1800/2000; P❀@🛜≋) Near the center of Acapulco's crescent of beaches, the Elcano is an older high-rise with a nice pool right on the waterfront. Rooms have a spare, clean feel, with white and blue decor; all units except the studios come with terraces, and most boast fine ocean views.

Hostel K3 HOSTEL $
(Map p554; ☑481-31-11; www.k3acapulco.com; La Costera 116; dm/r without bathroom incl Continental breakfast M$210/490; ❀@🛜) The rooms have almost a Japanese capsule-hotel feel, but this hostel has air-con and the terrace, bar

and games room provide ample space for socializing. There's also a tiny shared kitchen. Most importantly, it's right across the highway from the beach.

Bali-Hai MOTEL $$
(Map p554; ☑485-66-22; www.balihai.com.mx, in Spanish; La Costera 186; s/d from M$480/900; P❀🛜≋) This Polynesian-themed motel in the heart of Acapulco Bay and across the street from the beach is a good moderate choice, with long rows of 1960s-vintage rooms flanking a pair of palm-lined pools. Solo business travelers should ask for the M$480 corporate rate prominently advertised out front. Rates jump on long holiday weekends.

Las Torres Gemelas SUITES $$$
(Map p554; ☑481-26-62; www.lastorresgemelas. com, in Spanish; La Costera 93; r M$1200; ❀🛜≋) These 30-story beachfront skyscrapers house 420 virtually identical rooms, all with sea views. Two ocean-facing pools – one for kids and one for grown-ups – are connected by a faux waterfall, and there's a reasonably priced attached restaurant. Most rooms here are booked through agencies, but independent travelers are also welcome; call for current deals. Wi-fi is available in the lobby and pool area only.

Casa Condesa B&B $$
(Map p554; ☑484-16-16; www.casacondesa.com; Bella Vista 125; s/d incl breakfast from M$600/ 1000; ❀🛜≋) This B&B caters to gay men, with homey touches such as kitchen and laundry facilities, an open bar, dinners on the ocean-view terrace and a pool surrounded by tropical plants.

Hotel Etel Suites SUITES $$
(Map p558; ☑482-22-40/1; etelste@yahoo.com.mx; Av Pinzona 92; ste with/without terrace M$800/600; P❀🛜≋🚶) High above Old Acapulco, with views of both the bay and the Pacific Ocean, this place offers family-friendly amenities including full kitchens, a children's play area and three swimming pools.

La Torre Eiffel HOTEL $
(Map p558; ☑482-16-83; http://hoteleconom9 acapulco.es.tl, in Spanish; Pinzona 110; d with fan/air-con M$300/500; P❀🛜≋) Despite the down-on-its-luck atmosphere, this hotel steeply uphill from La Quebrada is still worth a look for its low prices, small pool and shared balconies with spectacular sunset views.

Old Acapulco

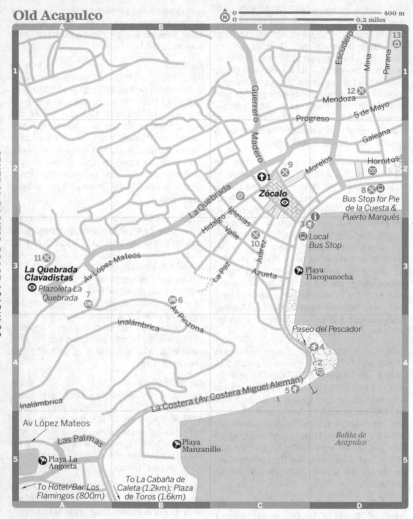

N 0 ____ 400 m
0 ____ 0.2 miles

13

Escudero
Mirna
Parana

Guerrero
Madero

12

Mendoza
5 de Mayo
Progreso

Galeana

Morelos
Hornitos

1

9

Zócalo

La Quebrada

8

Bus Stop for Pie
de la Cuesta &
Puerto Marqués

Hidalgo
Iglesias
Valle
Juárez

3

Local
Bus Stop

11

La Quebrada
Clavadistas

Plazoleta La
Quebrada

Av López Mateos

La Paz

Azueta

Playa
Tlacopanocha

7

6

Av Pinzona

Inalámbrica

Paseo del Pescador

4

2

5

La Costera (Av Costera Miguel Alemán)

Bahía de
Acapulco

Inalámbrica

Av López Mateos

Las Palmas

Playa
Manzanillo

Playa La
Angosta

To Hotel/Bar Los
Flamingos (800m)

To La Cabaña de
Caleta (1.2km); Plaza
de Toros (1.6km)

✗ Eating

OLD ACAPULCO

La Cabaña de Caleta   SEAFOOD **$$**
(off Map p558; www.lacabanadecaleta.com; Playa
La Caleta; dishes M$70-205; ☺8am-11pm) Step
back in time and get a slice of traditional
Mexican beach life, c 1950, at this venerable,
unpretentious seafood shack straddling the
sands of Playa La Caleta. Bask under a blue
umbrella and gaze at the bay while savor-
ing specialties such as *zarzuela de mariscos*
(seafood stew) or *chiles rellenos* stuffed with
shrimp, octopus and fish.

100% Natural   MEXICAN, VEGETARIAN **$$**
(Map p558; http://100natural.com.mx; La Costera
s/n, Old Acapulco; mains M$66-184; ☺7am-11pm;
🛜🖉) This health-conscious chain has a
mellow ambience and good, friendly service. The food is consistently good, eschew-
ing red meat in favor of fish, poultry and
vegetarian fare, plus wholegrain breads and
rolls and a variety of fruit and veggie juices
and shakes. Air-con and free wi-fi make this
a great place to take a break from Acapulco's heat and urban chaos. In addition to
the *zócalo* branch listed above, there are
several others around town. Prettiest is the

Old Acapulco

◉ **Top Sights**
- La Quebrada Clavadistas....................A3
- Zócalo...C2

◉ **Sights**
- 1 Nuestra Señora de la Soledad...........C2

◐ **Activities, Courses & Tours**
- 2 Acapulco Scuba Center......................D4
- 3 Acarey Ticket Booth...........................C3
- 4 Fiesta/Bonanza Ticket Booth............D4
- 5 Fish-R-Us...C4

◉ **Sleeping**
- 6 Hotel Etel Suites................................B3
- 7 La Torre Eiffel....................................A3

◐ **Eating**
- 8 100% Natural......................................D2
- 9 Cafetería Astoria................................C2
- 10 Die Bratwurst.....................................C3
- 11 Restaurant-Bar La Perla....................A3
- 12 Taquería Los Pioneros.......................D1

◉ **Shopping**
- 13 Mercado de Artesanías......................D1

Café del Mar branch (Map p554; La Costera s/n), which features ocean views and outdoor seating on a pier jutting out into the bay near Playa Hornitos.

Restaurant-Bar La Perla   INTERNATIONAL $$$
(Map p558; www.miradoracapulco.com/la-perla. asp; Hotel El Mirador, Plazoleta La Quebrada 74; dishes M$115-325; ◷8am-11pm) Candlelit terraces, sea breezes and first-rate views of the death-defying *clavadistas* almost justify the high price of a meal here; during performances, minimum consumption is M$250 (M$100 at the bar).

Die Bratwurst   GERMAN $
(Map p558; Iglesias s/n; mains M$60-85; ◷2-7:30pm Mon-Sat) When you tire of tacos, head for this traditional German restaurant. Owner Wilde Hilde, from the Bavarian village of Garmisch-Partenkirchen, serves up great sausage with sauerkraut, potatoes, salad and flan.

Taquería Los Pioneros   TAQUERÍA $
(Map p558; cnr Mendoza & Mina; 5 tacos M$25, mains M$35-60; ◷9am-1am) The tacos are tiny but their various fillings are tasty, plus you can load up on accompaniments: jalapeños, pickled carrots, onions, cilantro etc.

Cafetería Astoria   CAFE $
(Map p558; Zócalo; coffee, breakfast & snacks M$18-40) Just steps from the cathedral, this friendly cafe offers prime *zócalo* views from outdoor tables shaded by a lovely ancient tree.

ACAPULCO DORADO

TOP CHOICE El Cabrito   MEXICAN $$
(Map p554; www.elcabrito-acapulco.com; La Costera 1480; M$70-225; ◷2-10pm) Celebrating nearly 50 years in business, this beloved and brightly decorated restaurant has some of the city's finest traditional Mexican food, such as Oaxaca-style black *mole* made from 32 ingredients. For those who like a dare, the house specialty is *cabecita de cabrito* – broiled head of baby goat. The outdoor tables offer prime people-watching.

El Gaucho   ARGENTINE $$$
(Map p554; ☎484-17-00; www.elpresidenteacapul co.com.mx/restaurantes.html; Hotel Presidente, La Costera 8; pasta M$77-99, mains M$185-384; ◷2:30-11:30pm) Upscale but not stuffy, this is one of the top spots in town for a steak. All the meat is grilled in true Argentine style, and less carnivorous or extravagant folk can choose from an assortment of pasta dishes. The short but decent wine list includes selections from Mexico, Chile, Spain and Argentina.

La Casa de Tere   MEXICAN $$
(Map p554; Martín 1721; mains M$70-140; ◷8am-6pm Tue-Sun) This homespun gem near the Estrella de Oro bus station is the place to go for Thursday *pozole* (M$50). Founded on Doña Tere's patio in 1990 using her mother Clarita's traditional recipes, it serves a wide-ranging menu including Thursday and Sunday specials such as *barbacoa de carnero* (barbecued lamb).

Kookaburra   FUSION $$$
(☎446-60-20; Carretera Escénica s/n; mains M$245-350; ◷1pm-midnight) One of Acapulco's most exclusive restaurants, the thatched Kookaburra is memorable as much for its stunning views as for its food. Specialties include spaghetti with caviar, or filet mignon with *chipotle* (a type of chili pepper). It's a perfect place for a romantic dinner. Reservations required.

El Fogón   MEXICAN $$
(Map p554; cnr La Costera & Pinzón; mains M$64-139; ◷24hr) Red-checked tablecloths, an airy dining room facing La Costera and neon

lights blazing out the names of Mexican specialties all create a welcoming atmosphere. If you're hungry, try the house special, *molcajete acapulqueño:* enough steak, pork, ranchero cheese, grilled *nopales* (cactus), avocado slices and freshly made tortillas to feed two people (M$254). There's another **branch** (☑484-50-79; ☺8am-11pm) at the corner of La Costera and Alaminos.

 Drinking

Bar Los Flamingos
BAR

(off Map p558; López Mateos s/n; ☺10am-10pm) The clifftop bar of Hotel Los Flamingos is the hands-down best sunset-viewing/drinking spot in Acapulco. Not a car or hustler in sight, and you can sip one of the famous cocktails invented here – such as *cocos locos* (made with rum, tequila, pineapple juice and coconut crème) – to your heart's content.

Barbarroja
BAR

(Map p554; La Costera s/n; ☺5pm-6am) Ahoy, matey! From a boat-shaped bar to women in sexy pirate costumes dancing on tables, this over-the-top, pirate-themed pub is one of several beachfront bars near the bungee tower. And it's the only one where a 30-year-old can walk in and not feel like the oldest person in the world.

Señor Frog's
BAR

(off Map p554; www.senorfrogs.com; Carretera Escénica 28; ☺1pm-late) Yes, it's cheesy and touristy. But dammit, it's still lots of fun! Zany antics attract families by day, the far-party atmosphere brings in college kids at night and the bay views are unbeatable anytime.

 Entertainment

Bullfights take place at the Plaza de Toros, southeast of La Quebrada and northwest of Playas Caleta and Caletilla, every Sunday at 5:30pm from January to March. The 'Caleta' bus passes near the bullring.

Gay Venues
Acapulco has an active gay scene with several gay bars and clubs, mostly open from 10pm until about 4am.

Demas (Map p554; Av de los Deportes 10A) is open only to men and has shows on Friday and Saturday; **Picante** (Map p554; Piedra Picuda 16) has a minuscule dance floor, the occasional drag or stripper show, and a mostly male clientele. Acapulco's unofficial **gay beach** is the rocky section of Playa Condesa (Map p554) by the Fiesta Americana hotel.

Live Music

Nina's
LIVE MUSIC

(Map p554; www.discotequeninastropicalacapulco. com; La Costera 2909; admission incl open bar M$300; ☺10pm-5am Thu-Sun) Nina's is one of the best places in town for live *música tropical* (salsa, *cumbia,* cha-cha, merengue etc); it has a smokin' dance floor, variety acts and impersonators.

Hard Rock Cafe
LIVE MUSIC

(Map p554; www.hardrock.com/acapulco; La Costera 37; ☺noon-2am) This chain's Acapulco branch has live music with no cover charge from 10:30pm onwards.

Nightclubs

Most clubs don't really get rolling until midnight or later. Cover charges vary by the season, the night and the doorman's mood. Dress to impress; shorts and sneakers are not permitted.

Palladium
CLUB

(off Map p554; www.palladium.com.mx; Carretera Escénica s/n; admission incl open bar women/men M$360/460; ☺10:30pm-late Thu-Sat) Hailed by many as the best disco in town, Palladium attracts a 20- to 30-something crowd with its fabulous bay views from floor-to-ceiling windows. An international cast of DJs pumps out hip-hop, house, trance and techno from an ultraluxe sound system. Around 3am the famous 'Silver Aztec' entertains the screaming crowd with fire and dance. Dress up, and expect to wait in line.

Baby'O
CLUB

(Map p554; www.babyo.com.mx; La Costera 22; admission M$100-380; ☺11pm-5am Thu-Sat) Very popular with the upscale crowd, this cave-like club has a laser light show and Wednesday theme nights, and spins rock, pop, house and 'everything but electronica.'

El Alebrije
CLUB

(Map p554; www.alebrijeacapulco.com; La Costera 3308; women/men M$70/230; ☺11pm-late Fri & Sat) This massive club is usually packed with a young Mexican crowd. The music is a middle-of-the-road mix of mostly Latin rock and pop.

🛍 **Shopping**

Mercado Central
MARKET

(Map p554; Diego H de Mendoza s/n) This sprawling indoor-outdoor bazaar has everything from *atoles* to *zapatos* (shoes), plus produce, hot food and souvenirs. Any eastbound 'Pie de la Cuesta' or 'Pedregoso' bus will drop you here.

Mercado de Artesanías MARKET
(Map p558; cnr Parana & Velásquez de León) Bargaining is the standard at this 400-stall craft market (Acapulco's largest). Here you'll find better deals on everything that you see in the hotel shops including hammocks, jewelry, clothing and T-shirts.

Other handicraft markets include the **Mercados de Artesanías Papagayo, Noa Noa, Dalia** and **La Diana** (all on La Costera, Map p554), and the **Mercado de Artesanías La Caletilla** at the western end of Playa Caletilla.

Information

Dangers & Annoyances
Acapulco has suffered unprecedented levels of violence in the past decade, as rival cartels battle for the area's lucrative drug corridor. Since 2007, when Mexican president Felipe Calderón declared war on the drug cartels, machine-gun-wielding soldiers and police have become a common sight, regularly patrolling the city in Humvees and on foot. While this is understandably unnerving to many visitors, if you stick to the beaches and the tourist strip along La Costera, your chances of being impacted by drug-related violence are probably slimmer than of getting into a car accident back home.

The main annoyances most visitors will experience are relatively mundane: honking taxis, snarled traffic, crowds and aggressive touts. In high season, beaches overflow with a seemingly endless parade of hawkers selling shells, *tamales*, hair braids and temporary tattoos. A simple '*No, gracias'* and smile works wonders.

Less common nuisances include petty crime and scams. Always secure your valuables, and if you do run into problems, contact the Procuraduría del Turista (see following), an agency set up to help tourists in trouble.

Emergency
Ambulance/Fire/Police (☑066)
Locatel (☑481-11-00) A 24-hour hotline for all types of emergencies.
Tourist police (☑440-70-24)

Internet Access
Acapulco has hundreds of cybercafes, most charging M$8 to M$10 per hour.
Vig@net (Hidalgo 8; ☺8am-11pm) One of several surrounding the *zócalo*.

Medical Services
Hospital Magallanes (☑469-02-70; www. hospitalmagallanes.com, in Spanish;

Massieu 2) A well-established private hospital with English-speaking doctors and staff.

Money
Banks and *casas de cambio* cluster around the *zócalo* and line La Costera. Hotels will also change money, but their rates are usually high.

Post
Main post office (Map p558; Palacio Federal, La Costera 125; ☺8am-5pm Mon-Fri, 9am-1pm Sat)

Telephone & Fax
You can make long-distance calls from the many Telmex card and coin phones throughout the city, or from private *casetas* (with signs saying '*larga distancia*').

Tourist Information
Municipal tourist kiosks (☺8:30am-8:30pm) The city government operates four tourist information kiosks, clearly marked 'Secretaría de Turismo Municipal.' Two of these – on the marina across from the *zócalo* (Map p558) and at the flagpole across from Parque Papagayo (Map p554) – are open year-round; two others – at La Diana traffic circle (Map p554) and Playa Caleta – open only in high season.
Procuraduría del Turista (Map p554; ☑435-19-80, ext 3; 2nd fl, La Costera 3221; ☺8am-9pm) This government office, above Santander bank and across from Wal-Mart, assists in mediating tourist complaints against hotels, restaurants and police and can also help resolve problems with lost documents.
State tourist office (Sefotur; Map p554; ☑435-19-80; guerrero.gob.mx/temas/turismo, in Spanish; 2nd fl, La Costera 3221; ☺8am-9pm) This cramped office provides limited information on Guerrero state.

Getting There & Away
Acapulco is accessible via Hwy 200 from the east and west, and by Hwy 95 and Hwy 95D from the north. It's 400km south of Mexico City and 235km southeast of Zihuatanejo.

Air
Acapulco's **Juan Álvarez International Airport** (☑435-20-60; www.oma.aero/es/aeropuertos/acapulco; Blvd de las Naciones s/n) has seen a marked decrease in international non-stop flights, although it's still easy to connect through Mexico City (a short hop from Acapulco). All services listed below are direct; some are seasonal.
Aeroméxico (www.aeromexico.com) Airport (☑466-91-09); La Costera 1632 (☑485-16-00) To Mexico City.

Aeromar (☎466-93-92; www.aeromar.com.
mx; Airport) To Mexico City.

Interjet (www.interjet.com.mx) Airport (☎466-
93-65); La Costera 78 (☎484-37-12) To Mexico
City and Toluca.

VivaAerobus (☎55-4777-5050; www.vivaaero
bus.com; Airport) To Monterrey.

Volaris (☎800-122-80-00; www.volaris.mx;
Airport) To Tijuana.

Bus

Acapulco has two major long-distance bus
companies that offer 1st-class services: Estrella
de Oro and Estrella Blanca. The modern, air-
conditioned **Estrella de Oro bus station** (EDO;
Map p554; www.estrelladeoro.com.mx; Av
Cuauhtémoc 1490), just west of Massieu, has
free toilets, several ATMs and a ticket machine
that accepts bank debit cards; luggage can also
be left for M$5 to M$12 per hour, depending
on size.

Estrella Blanca (EB; www.estrellablanca.com.
mx) has two 1st-class terminals: **Central Papagayo** (Map p554; Av Cuauhtémoc 1605), just
north of Parque Papagayo, and **Central Ejido**
(off Map p554; Av Ejido 47). The **Estrella Blanca
2nd-class bus station** (Map p554; Av Cuauhtémoc 97) sells tickets for all buses, but only has
departures to relatively nearby towns. Estrella
Blanca tickets are also sold at a few agencies
around town, including **Agencia de Viajes
Zócalo** (La Costera 207, Local 18) and **Agencia
Gran Plaza** (Costera 1616).

Both companies offer frequent services to
Mexico City, with various levels of luxury.

Car & Motorcycle

Several car-rental companies have offices at the
airport as well as in town; some offer free delivery to you. Shop around to compare prices.

Alamo Airport (☎466-94-44); La Costera 78
(☎484-33-05)

Budget Airport (☎466-90-03); La Costera 134
(☎481-24-33)

Dollar/Thrifty Airport (☎462-00-04); La
Costera s/n (☎486-19-40)

Europcar (☎466-93-14; Airport)

Hertz (☎466-91-72; Airport)

❶ Getting Around

To/From the Airport

Acapulco's airport is 23km southeast of the
zócalo, beyond the junction for Puerto Marqués.
Arriving by air, you can buy a ticket for transportation into town from the desk at the end of the
domestic terminal. Fares are officially regulated:
colectivo taxis operate whenever there's an incoming flight, charging M$100 per person to any
point within Acapulco city limits; private taxis
from the airport run constantly, ranging in price
from M$150 to M$425, depending on which of
the five designated zones you're traveling to (a
map of the various zones is posted at the taxi
ticket desk).

Leaving Acapulco, phone **Móvil Aca** (☎462-
10-95) 24 hours in advance to reserve transportation back to the airport; the cost varies from a
minimum of M$100 per person in a taxi *colectivo*
to a maximum of M$370 to M$460 – depending
on where your pick-up is – for a private vehicle
holding up to five passengers. Regular taxis from

BUSES FROM ACAPULCO

DESTINATION	FARE (M$)	DURATION	FREQUENCY (DAILY)
Chilpancingo	64-104	1¾-3hr	frequent EDO; frequent EB from Central Ejido & 2nd-class terminal
Cuernavaca	341-358	4-5hr	9 EDO; 5 EB from Central Papagayo
Mexico City (Terminal Norte)	455-600	6hr	frequent EB from Central Papagayo & Central Ejido
Mexico City (Terminal Sur)	425-560	5hr	frequent EDO; frequent EB from Central Papagayo & Central Ejido
Puerto Escondido	341	7-8hr	7 EB from Central Ejido
Puerto Vallarta	1155-1215	17hr	2 EB from Central Ejido, noon from Central Papagayo
Taxco	202	4hr	6 EDO
Zihuatanejo	119-151	4-5hr	very frequent EDO; frequent EB from Central Ejido

the center to the airport cost around M$200 to M$300, depending on the distance and the amount of luggage.

Bus

Acapulco has a good city bus system (especially good when you get a neon-lit beauty with a bumping sound system). Buses operate from 5am to 11pm and cost M$6 with air-con, M$5 without. Numerous stops are located along La Costera, including one directly opposite the *zócalo*. The bus stop opposite the post office, three blocks east of the *zócalo*, is the beginning of several bus routes (including to Pie de la Cuesta), so you can usually get a seat.

Useful city routes:

Base–Caleta From the Icacos naval base at the southeast end of Acapulco, along La Costera, past the *zócalo* to Playa Caleta.

Base–Cine Río–Caleta From the Icacos naval base, cuts inland from La Costera on Avenida Wilfrido Massieu to Avenida Cuauhtémoc, heads down Avenida Cuauhtémoc through the business district, turning back to La Costera just before reaching the *zócalo*, continuing west to Playa Caleta.

Centro–Puerto Marqués From opposite the post office, along La Costera to Puerto Marqués.

Zócalo–Playa Pie de la Cuesta From opposite the post office to Pie de la Cuesta.

Car & Motorcycle

Avoid driving in Acapulco if at all possible. The streets are in poor shape and the anarchic traffic is often horribly snarled.

Taxi

Hundreds of zippy blue-and-white VW cabs scurry around Acapulco like cockroaches, maneuvering with an audacity that borders on the comical. Drivers often quote fares higher than the official ones; whenever possible, ask locals what a fair rate is for your destination, and always agree on a price with the driver before getting in.

Costa Chica

Guerrero's 'Small Coast,' extending southeast from Acapulco to the Oaxacan border, is much less traveled than its bigger brother to the northwest, but it does have at least one spectacular beach.

Afro-Mestizos (people of mixed African, indigenous and European descent) make up a large portion of the population. The region was a safe haven for Africans who escaped slavery, some from the interior, others (it's believed) from a slave ship that sank just off the coast.

From Acapulco, Hwy 200 traverses inland past small villages and farmlands. San Marcos, about 60km east of Acapulco, and Cruz Grande, about 40km further east, are the only two towns of significant size before Cuajinicuilapa near the Oaxaca border. Both provide basic services including banks, gas stations and simple hotels.

PLAYA VENTURA & AROUND
741 / POP 550

Located 131km southeast of Acapulco, Playa Ventura (labeled Juan Álvarez on most maps) is a pristine beach with soft white and gold sands and clear, calm water. A town extends inland for about three blocks and features a small village museum, simple seafood restaurants and a few beachfront hotels.

La Caracola (cell phone 741-1013047; www.playaventura.com; s M$385, d M$500-700; P) is a thatched tree-house-on-stilts, 1.5km north of the church, which has several rooms with basic beds, mosquito netting, hammocks and fans, and a communal kitchen. Tiny adobe pyramids on the beach house cheaper rooms. The open-air architecture doesn't afford a lot of privacy, but lovely Venezuelan-born owner Aura makes everyone feel at home. Pets are welcome; kids under 16 are not.

On the same road as La Caracola, Italian-run **Posada Quintomondo** (cell phone 741-1013018; www.posadaquintomondo.info; campsite per person M$150, d/tr/q M$800/1100/1400; P) offers beachfront camping and rooms sleeping two to four, along with a great restaurant (mains M$90-130) featuring chef Andrea's homemade pizzas, pasta and Mediterranean-influenced seafood recipes.

The positively pink **Hotel Doña Celsa** (cell phone 741-1013069; d/tw with fan M$250/350, r with air-con M$500; P) has 20 simple, clean rooms, a nice pool, a seafood restaurant and a grocery store.

To get here by car, take Hwy 200 to the signposted Playa Ventura turnoff (Km 124), just east of the village of Copala, then continue south 7km to the coast. By bus from Acapulco, take a southeast-bound bus to Copala (M$79, 2¾ hours, 120km). From here, *camionetas* and microbuses depart for Playa Ventura about every half-hour (M$15, 30 minutes, 13km) from just east of the bus stop.

About 13km southeast of the Playa Ventura turnoff on Hwy 200 (Km 137) is the market town of Marquelia. The town offers

WORTH A TRIP

OLINALÁ

The cobblestoned, isolated village of Olinalá, tucked into the mountains between Acapulco and Mexico City, is famous throughout Mexico for its beautiful, hand-painted lacquered boxes, chests and other woodcraft. Traditionally, the pieces were made with fragrant wood from the rare linaloe tree, but pine is now often substituted. Several artisan shops are located along Avenida Ramón Ibarra behind the main plaza; one of the best is **Artesanías Ayala**. The town's two lovely churches – the **Iglesia de San Francisco de Asís** in the main plaza and the magnificent hilltop **Santuario de la Virgen Guadalupe** – are both decorated in traditional Olinalá style with lacquered-wood ornamentation and murals.

To reach Olinalá, first take a bus from Acapulco to Chilpancingo (M$115, 1½ hours), then transfer to a 2nd-class bus headed toward Tlapa, and ask to get off at the crossroads for Olinalá (4½ hours); finally, catch a 3rd-class bus (one hour) to Olinalá. By car, getting here is half the fun on the winding, rollercoaster road from Chilpancingo (3½ hours). Don't attempt this drive in the dark!

access to an immense stretch of beach backed by coconut palms – the beach follows the the contours of the coastline for many kilometers in either direction. From Marquelia's center you can take a *camioneta* to a section of the beach known as **Playa La Bocana**, where the Río Marquelia meets the sea and forms a lagoon. La Bocana has *cabañas,* a small hotel and some *comedores* (food stalls) with hammocks where you can spend the night.

CUAJINICUILAPA

🖉 741 / POP 10,000

About 200km southeast of Acapulco, Cuajinicuilapa, or Cuaji (kwah-hee), is the nucleus of Afro-Mestizo culture on the Costa Chica. The **Museo de las Culturas Afromestizas** (Museum of Afro-Mestizo Cultures; 🖉 414-12-31; cnr Manuel Zárate & Av Cuauhtémoc; admission M$10; ⊙10am-2pm & 4-7pm Mon-Fri) is a tribute to the history of African slaves in Mexico and, specifically, to local Afro-Mestizo culture. Behind the museum are three examples of

casas redondas, the round houses typical of West Africa that were built around Cuaji until as late as the 1960s. The museum is a block inland from the Banamex that's just west of the main plaza.

Buses to Cuajinicuilapa (M$180, 4½ hours) depart Estrella Blanca's Central Ejido bus station in Acapulco hourly from 5am, and Estrella Blanca has several buses daily to Cuaji from Pinotepa Nacional (M$35, one hour) in Oaxaca state.

Punta Maldonado (also known as El Faro) is the last worthwhile beach before the Oaxaca border. The swimming is good and the surfing, on occasion, is excellent; the break is a reef/point favoring lefts. The village (population 670) has some seafood restaurants on the beach and one small, unattractive hotel. To reach Punta Maldonado take a *camioneta* from Cuajinicuilapa (M$25, 45 minutes); they depart half-hourly from just off the main plaza. If driving, turn off the main highway at Km 201 and follow the signs 31km to the coast.

Western Central Highlands

Best Places to Eat

» Birriería las Nueve
Esquinas (p580)

» La Fonda de la Noche
(p580)

» Ajijic Tango (p591)

» Lula Bistro (p581)

» Restaurante Lu (p606)

Best Places to Stay

» La Casa Encantada (p616)

» Casa Rosa (p605)

» Casa de la Real Aduana
(p616)

» Las Sabilas (p577)

» Villa Ganz (p577)

Why Go?

With exquisite colonial architecture, delicious food, butterfly orgies, lonely indigenous pueblos, bustling cities and volcanic calderas, the western central highlands are a wonderland. The climate is wonderfully warm and the natural beauty is as diverse as it is mind-blowing. You'll see layered mountains, expansive lakes, thundering rivers and waterfalls and a tapestry of cornfields, avocado groves, agave plantations and cattle ranches. This is Mexico's beating heart.

Guadalajara sprawls, but it doesn't overwhelm; it's a great walking city, with lovely colonial architecture and some of Mexico's best craft shopping. Morelia boasts a colonial heart unrivalled anywhere in Mexico, a young population and superb eating options. Nearby is the Reserva Mariposa Monarca, a forested butterfly sanctuary you'll remember forever, while Pátzcuaro, an endearing colonial town and the epicenter of the Purépecha culture, is the place to be for the Día de Muertos celebration.

When to Go
Guadalajara

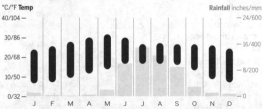

Feb The best time to see the incredible natural canopies of monarch butterflies in the Reserva Mariposa Monarca.

Early Nov Join some of Mexico's most famous celebrations for the Día de Muertos in the indigenous villages around Lake Pátzcuaro.

Mar Come and join the stars of Mexican and world cinema at Guadalajara's excellent Festival Internacional del Cine.

Western Central Highlands Highlights

1 Get to know spectacular **Morelia** (p600), with its glowing cathedral, rooftop bars and clubs nestled in colonial relics

2 Explore charming **Guadalajara** (p568), with its excellent art museums, ancient churches and superb eating possibilities

3 Absorb the beauty of the **Reserva Mariposa Monarca** (Monarch Butterfly Reserve; p610), the winter retreat for millions of butterflies and an incredible natural phenomenon

4 Peer into the mystical soul of the Purépecha people in tranquil **Pátzcuaro** (p612)

5 Bag two volcanic peaks – the snowy and extinct **Volcán Nevado de Colima** (p599) and young, precocious **Volcán Paricutín** (p624)

6 Head to Tlaquepaque, Guadalajara, for some of Mexico's best **crafts shopping** (p585)

7 Travel the Tequila Trail to see Mexico's most famous drink being made in the distilleries of **Tequila** (p592) and other nearby towns

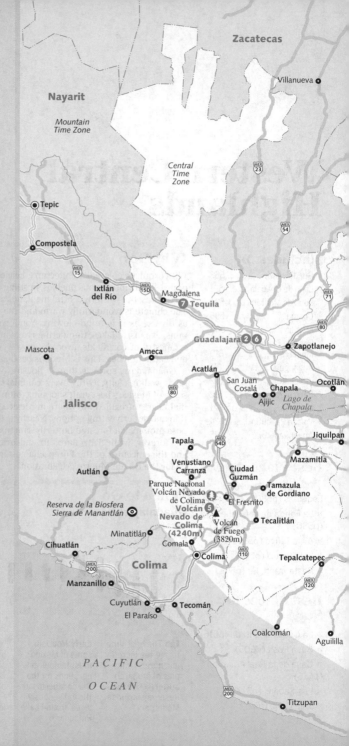

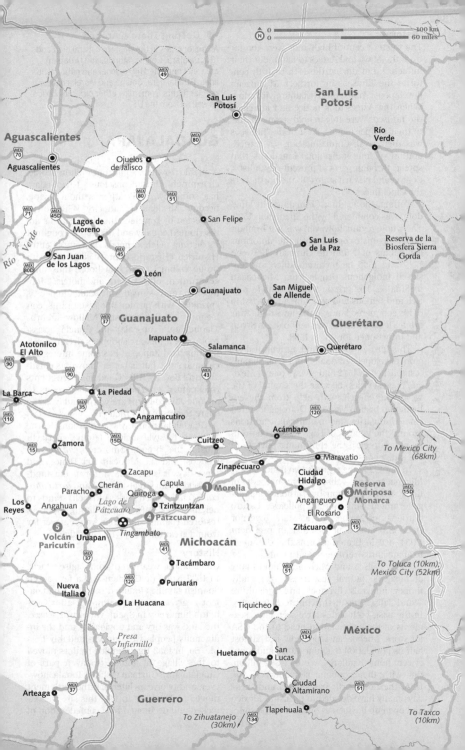

History

The western central highlands were too far from the Maya and Aztecs to fall under their influence, but during the 14th to 16th centuries the Tarascos in northern Michoacán developed a robust pre-Hispanic civilization. When the Aztecs took notice and attacked, the Tarascos were able to hold strong thanks to their copper blades. West of the Tarascos was their rival, Chimalhuacán – a confederation of four indigenous kingdoms that spread through parts of present-day Jalisco, Colima and Nayarit states. To the north were the Chichimecs.

Colima, the leading Chimalhuacán kingdom, was conquered by the Spanish in 1523. The whole region, however, was not brought under Spanish control until the notorious campaigns of Nuño de Guzmán. Between 1529 and 1536 he tortured, killed and enslaved indigenous people from Michoacán to Sinaloa. His grizzly victories made him rich and famous and won him governorship of his conquered lands, until news of his war crimes leaked out. He was sent back to Spain and imprisoned for life in 1538.

This fertile ranching and agricultural region developed gradually and Guadalajara (established in 1542 and always one of Mexico's biggest cities) became the 'capital of the west.' The church, with help from the enlightened bishop Vasco de Quiroga, fostered small industries and handicraft traditions around the villages of Lago de Pátzcuaro in its effort to ease the continuing poverty of the indigenous people.

In the 1920s the region's two major states, Michoacán and Jalisco, were hotbeds of the Cristero rebellion by Catholics against government antichurch policies. Lázaro Cárdenas of Michoacán, as state governor (1928–32) and then as Mexican president (1934–40), instituted reforms that did much to abate antigovernment sentiments.

Today Jalisco and Michoacán hold many of Mexico's natural resources – especially timber, minerals, livestock and agriculture – and Jalisco has a thriving tech industry. In the past, both states have seen large segments of their population head to the USA for work. Michoacán reportedly lost almost half its population to emigrations, and money sent home regularly exceeds US$2 billion. But with the economic slowdown in the USA, the flow north has slowed and these days many have decided to return to Mexico and open up businesses on their home soil.

ℹ Getting There & Around

All major cities in the western central highlands (Guadalajara, Colima, Morelia and Uruapan) are well connected by regional and national bus lines. Guadalajara, Colima and Morelia have regular flights from many other cities in Mexico, as well as from the US.

GUADALAJARA

🎵 33 / POP 4.4 MILLION / ELEV 1550M

A pueblo (town) of some four million people, charmingly unselfconscious Guadalajara has somehow, and rather without trying, become Mexico's second city. While often neglected by travelers, the city's charms are distributed equally and liberally throughout its distinct neighborhoods. The city's Centro Histórico (Historic Center) is dotted with proud colonial relics that house museums, government offices, bars and hotels. More modern and spread out Chapultepec is sprinkled with fashionable restaurants, coffeehouses and nightclubs. Mellow suburbs Tlaquepaque (upscale) and Tonalá (grassroots) are a folk-art shopper's dream destinations; and Zapopan has some interesting colonial sites, but is better known as Guadalajara's Beverly Hills. Guadalajara residents (nicknamed *tapatíos,* which also refers to anyone Jalisco-born) are warm and eager to share the essence of their city.

Guadalajara's many contributions to the Mexican lifestyle include tequila, mariachi music, the broad sombrero, *charreadas* (rodeos) and the Mexican Hat Dance, and these days it is also known for its outstanding food. From streetside taco and *torta ahogada* (chili-soaked pork sandwich) stands to neighborhood cafes to fine dining rooms in restored colonial mansions, you're never far from a great meal in joyful Guadalajara.

History

Guadalajara weathered some false starts. In 1532 Nuño de Guzmán and a few dozen Spanish families founded the first Guadalajara near Nochixtlán, naming it after Guzmán's home city in Spain. Water was scarce, the land was dry and unyielding and the indigenous people were understandably hostile. So, in 1533 the humbled settlers moved to the village of Tonalá (today a part of Guadalajara). Guzmán disliked Tonalá, however, and two years later had the settlement moved to Tlacotán. In 1541 this site was attacked and decimated by a confederation of

GUADALAJARA IN TWO DAYS

Begin your time in Guadalajara with the visceral Orozco murals at the **Instituto Cultural de Cabañas**. Wander through **Plaza de los Mariachis**, explore the labyrinthine **Mercado San Juan de Dios** and stroll the **Plaza Tapatía** to the **Cathedral** and **Plaza de Armas**. Lunch at the wonderful **Birriería las Nueve Esquinas** before heading to the **Museo Regional de Guadalajara** for a taste of Guadalajara's past. In the evening check out Chapultepec's bar scene, and dine out at exceptional **Lula Bistro**.

The next day head to **Tlaquepaque**, where you can stroll the suburb's cobblestone streets, visiting its superb shops and fine galleries. Don't miss the **Museo Pantaleón Panduro**. In the evening head out for a few kitschy, adrenaline-filled rounds of *lucha libre* (free wrestling) at the iconic **Arena Coliseo**. Grab a late bite of *chiles en nogada* (mild green chilies stuffed with meat and fruit, fried in batter and served with a sauce of cream, ground walnuts and cheese) at **La Fonda de la Noche** then head downtown to dance all night to live salsa sounds at **La Mutualista**.

indigenous tribes led by chief Tenamaxtli. The survivors wearily picked a new site in the valley of Atemajac beside San Juan de Dios Creek, which ran where Calzada Independencia is today. That's where today's Guadalajara was founded on February 14, 1542, near where the Teatro Degollado now stands.

Guadalajara finally prospered and in 1560 was declared the capital of Nueva Galicia province. The city, at the heart of a rich agricultural region, quickly grew into one of colonial Mexico's most important population centers. It also became the launch pad for Spanish expeditions and missions to western and northern Nueva España, and others as far away as the Philippines. Miguel Hidalgo, a leader in the fight for Mexican independence, set up a revolutionary government in Guadalajara in 1810, but was defeated near the city in 1811, not long before his capture and execution in Chihuahua. The city was also the object of heavy fighting during the War of the Reform (1858–61) and between Constitutionalist and Villista armies in 1915.

By the late 19th century Guadalajara had overtaken Puebla as Mexico's second-biggest city. Its population has mushroomed since WWII and now the city is a huge commercial, industrial and cultural center, and the hi-tech and communications hub for the northern half of Mexico.

◉ Sights

PLAZA DE ARMAS & AROUND

Cathedral CATHEDRAL
(Map p574; Av 16 de Septiembre btwn Morelos & Av Hidalgo; ☺8am-8pm, closed during Mass) Guadalajara's twin-towered cathedral is the city's most beloved and conspicuous landmark.

Begun in 1558 and consecrated in 1618, it's almost as old as the city itself. And it's magnificent. Time it right and you'll see light filter through stained glass renderings of the Last Supper and hear a working pipe organ rumble sweetly from the rafters. The interior includes Gothic vaults, massive Tuscan-style gold-leaf pillars and 11 richly decorated altars that were given to Guadalajara by King Fernando VII of Spain (1814–33). The glass case nearest the north entrance is an extremely popular reliquary, containing the hands and blood of the martyred Santa Inocencia. In the sacristy, which an attendant can open for you on request, is *La Asunción de la Virgen,* painted by Spanish artist Bartolomé Murillo in 1650. Of course, architectural purists may find flaws. Much like the Palacio de Gobierno, the cathedral is a bit of a stylistic hodgepodge including Churrigueresque, baroque and neoclassical influences. And the towers, reconstructed in 1848, are much higher than the originals, which were destroyed in the 1818 earthquake.

Museo Regional de Guadalajara MUSEUM
(Map p574; Liceo 60; admission M$41, Sun free; ☺9am-5:30pm Tue-Sat, to 4:30pm Sun) North of the cathedral, this excellent museum tells the story of Guadalajara and the surrounding region from prehistory to the revolution. The ground floor houses a natural history collection whose highlight is a mightily impressive woolly mammoth skeleton. There is also a superb collection of pre-Hispanic ceramics dating from 600 BC including figurines, ceramics and silver and gold artifacts. Upstairs are colonial paintings depicting the Spanish conquest as well as more standard

Greater Guadalajara

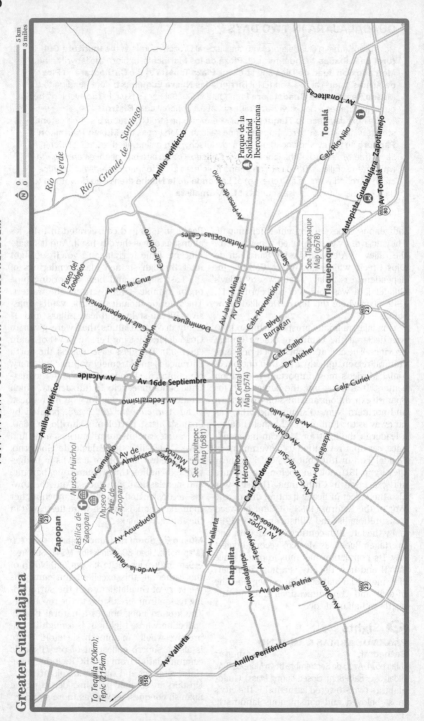

5 km
3 miles

N

Río Verde

Río Grande de Santiago

Anillo Periférico

Parque de la
Solidaridad
Iberoamericana

Av Tonaltecas

Tonalá

Calz Río Nilo

Autopista Guadalajara – Zapotlanejo

Av Tonalá

MEX 80

Av Presa de Osorio

Plutarco Elías Calles

San Jacinto

See Tlaquepaque
Map (p578)

Tlaquepaque

MEX 23

Paseo del
Zoológico

Av de la Cruz

Calz Obrero

Calz Independencia

Domínguez

Av Javier Mina
Av Gigantes

Calz Revolución

Blvd
Barragán

Calz Gallo

Dr Michel

Calz Curiel

Circunvalación

Av Alcalde

Av 16 de Septiembre

See Central Guadalajara
Map (p574)

Av Federalismo

Av 8 de julio

Av Colón

Av de Legazpi

Anillo Periférico

Museo Huichol

Av Camacho

Av de
las Américas

Basílica de
Zapopan

Museo de
Arte de
Zapopan

Zapopan

MEX 23

See Chapultepec
Map (p581)

Av López
Mateos

Av Niños
Héroes

Calz Cárdenas

Av Cruz del Sur

Av Acueducto

Av Vallarta

Av López
Mateos Sur

Av de la Patria

Av de la Patria

Chapalita

Av Guadalupe

Av Tepeyac

Av de la Patria

Av Otero

MEX 23

To Tequila (50km);
Tepic (215km)

Av Vallarta

MEX 15D

Anillo Periférico

religious allegories, an ethnography section with displays about indigenous life in Jalisco and a revolutionary wing where the guns, uniforms and desks of Mexico's great rebels are on display. The building is well worth visiting for itself, with its gorgeous tree-planted courtyard.

FREE Palacio de Gobierno   BUILDING
(Map p574; Av Corona btwn Morelos & Moreno; ⊙9am-8pm) The impressive Palacio de Gobierno, which houses state government offices, was finished in 1774. It's open to the public – just walk in – and it's well worth stopping by, mainly due to two impressive socialist realist murals by local artist José Clemente Orozco (1883–1949). The most impressive is the 1937 mural of Miguel Hidalgo looming over an interior stairway. Hidalgo brandishes a torch in one fist while the masses struggle at his feet against the twin burdens of communism and fascism. Another Orozco mural in the ex-Congreso (former Congress Hall) upstairs depicts Hidalgo, Benito Juárez and other historical luminaries. On the ground floor there's a well-curated **museum** about the history of Jalisco. It's aimed at school groups, but is still worth a look.

Teatro Degollado   CULTURAL BUILDING
(Map p574; Degollado; viewing admission free; ⊙viewing noon-2pm Mon-Fri) Construction on the neoclassical Teatro Degollado, home of the Guadalajara Philharmonic, was begun in 1856 and completed 30 years later. The five-tiered interior is swathed in red velvet and gold and crowned by a Gerardo Suárez mural based on the fourth canto of Dante's *Divine Comedy*. Over the columns on its front is a frieze depicting Apollo and the Nine Muses.

Plaza Guadalajara   PLAZA
(Map p574) Directly west of the cathedral, Plaza Guadalajara is shaded by dozens of laurel trees and has great cathedral views, a few fine cafes and fun people-watching. On its north side is the **Palacio Municipal** (City Hall; admission free; ⊙10am-7pm Mon-Fri), which was built between 1949 and 1952 but looks ancient. Above its interior stairway is a dark mural by Gabriel Flores depicting the founding of Guadalajara.

Rotonda de los Jaliscenses
Ilustres   MONUMENT
(Rotonda of Illustrious Jaliscans; Map p574) Welcome to Jalisco's hall of fame. The plaza on the north side of the cathedral is ringed by 20 bronze sculptures of the state's favorite writers, architects, revolutionaries and a composer. Some of them are actually buried underneath the rotunda, the round-pillared monument in the center. Before the macho city establishment added a woman to the mix, the rotunda was 'de los Hombres Ilustres' ('of Illustrious Men').

Plaza de la Liberación   PLAZA
(Map p574) East of the cathedral, this plaza was a 1980s urban planner's dream project and two whole blocks of colonial buildings were eviscerated to make way for this concrete slab.

On the north side of the plaza, next to the Museo Regional, is the **Palacio Legislativo**. Distinguished by thick stone columns in its interior courtyard, this is where the state congress meets. Across the street to the east is the **Palacio de Justicia** (State Courthouse). It was built in 1588 and began life as Guadalajara's first nunnery. Duck inside to the interior stairwell and check out the 1965 mural by Guillermo Chávez depicting legendary Mexican lawmakers, including Benito Juárez.

FREE Galería Jorge Martínez   ART GALLERY
(Map p574; Belén 120; ⊙10am-7pm) A block north of the northeast corner of the Plaza de la Liberación is this interesting modern and conceptual art gallery. It's adjacent to, and benefiting, Guadalajara's top art school, Artes Plásticas, which is operated by Universidad de Guadalajara.

EAST OF PLAZA DE ARMAS

TOP CHOICE Instituto Cultural
de Cabañas   MUSEUM
(Map p574; Cabañas 8; adult/student M$70/35, Tue free; ⊙10am-6pm) Standing proudly at the east end of the brilliant Plaza Tapatía is another of Guadalajara's architectural gems. Inside its enchanting neoclassical bones, however, is a most unexpected series of modernist murals, which rank among the city's best sights. Founded by Bishop don Juan Cruz Ruiz de Cabañas and designed by Spanish architect Manuel Tolsá, the building was constructed between 1805 and 1810 as an orphanage and home for invalids and remained so for 150 years, housing 500 children at once.

Between 1938 and 1939 José Clemente Orozco, one of the greatest artists of the

COLONIAL CHURCHES

Central Guadalajara has dozens of large and small churches and cathedrals. The following are some of the city's most beautiful and interesting.

The **Santuario de Nuestra Señora del Carmen** (Map p574), facing the small plaza on the corner of Avenida Juárez and Calle 8 de Julio, is lovely with lots of gold leaf, old paintings and murals in the dome. Closer to the city center is the ornate **Templo Nuestra Señora de las Mercedes** (Map p574; cnr Loza & Av Hidalgo), which was built in 1650; inside are several large paintings, crystal chandeliers and more gold leaf. Six blocks further east is the fairly unremarkable **Templo de Santa María de Gracia** (Map p574; cnr Carranza & República), which served as the city's first cathedral (1549–1618). South of the Teatro Degollado is the baroque-style **Templo de San Agustín** (Map p574; Morelos), one of the city's oldest and loveliest churches. The sanctuary at the **Templo Santa Eduviges** (Map p574; Av Javier Mina), built in 1726, is usually packed with worshippers and, during Mass, perfumed with clouds of sandalwood smoke. It's just south of the Mercado San Juan de Dios.

The compact **Templo de Aranzazú** (Map p574; cnr Av 16 de Septiembre & Blanco) is perhaps the city's most beautiful. Built from 1749 to 1752, it has three insanely ornate Churrigueresque golden altars and lovely ceiling detail. Across the road is the larger but less impressive **Templo de San Francisco** (Map p574), built two centuries earlier. Come at dusk and see the stained glass glow.

Mexican muralist movement, channeled the archetypal struggle for freedom into 57 magnificent murals that now decorate the Capilla Mayor at the center of the complex. Widely regarded as Orozco's finest works, they depict pre-Hispanic Jalisco and the conquest and seethe with dark, unnerving and distinctly modern images of fire, armor, broken chains, blood and prayer. Given the issues of Orozco's era, they almost certainly serve as a warning against fascism and any institution that subverts humanity to cultivate power. Free tours of the institute in English and Spanish are available.

Plaza Tapatía   PLAZA
(Map p574) The fabulously wide pedestrian Plaza Tapatía sprawls for more than 500m east from Teatro Degollado. Stroll the plaza on Sundays and you will find yourself in a sea of locals who shop at low-end crafts markets, snack (from both street vendors and cafes), watch street performers and rest on the short walls of gurgling fountains. The plaza dead-ends beautifully at the Instituto Cultural de Cabañas.

Plaza de los Mariachis   STREET
(Map p574) Just south of Av Javier Mina, this is the birthplace of mariachi music. By day it's just a narrow walking street, flanked by charming old buildings and dotted with a few plastic tables and chairs and the odd uniformed mariachi man chatting on a cell phone. At night it can get lively, when patrons swill beer and listen to bands play requests for about M$100 per song.

WEST OF PLAZA DE ARMAS

West of the city center, where Avenidas Juárez and Federalismo meet, is shady **Parque Revolución** (Map p574), which has become a haven for skaters.

Universidad de Guadalajara   UNIVERSITY
(Map p574) Three blocks west of Parque Revolución is the **Paraninfo** (Theater Hall; Av Juárez 975), one of the main buildings of the Universidad de Guadalajara (UDG). Inside, the stage backdrop and dome feature large, powerful murals by Orozco. In the back of the same building is the excellent **Museo de las Artes** (admission free; ☉10am-6pm Tue-Fri, to 4pm Sat & Sun), which houses well-curated temporary exhibitions focusing on contemporary Mexican art.

Templo Expiatorio   TEMPLE
(Madero; ☉7am-11pm) Across the street from Museo de las Artes is this 1897 Gothic temple, accented by enormous stone columns, 15m-high mosaic stained-glass windows and a kaleidoscopic steeple. At 9am, noon and 6pm a door in the clock tower opens and the 12 apostles march right out.

ZAPOPAN

The fashionable, middle-class suburb of Zapopan is about 8km from the city center, on the northwestern edge of Guadalajara. There are a few interesting sights around the main plaza.

To get here from the center of Guadalajara, take any bus marked 'Zapopan' heading north on Avenidas 16 de Septiembre or Alcalde and get off beside the basilica. The trip takes 20 minutes.

Basílica de Zapopan   CATHEDRAL

(Map p570; Eva Briseño 152) Zapopan's pride and joy, the Basílica de Zapopan, built in 1730, is home to *Nuestra Señora de Zapopan*, a petite statue of the Virgin visited by pilgrims year-round. During the Fiestas de Octubre, thousands of kneeling faithful crawl behind as the statue is carried here from Guadalajara's central cathedral. The kneeling pilgrims then make the final trek up the basilica's aisle to pray for favors at her altar. The Virgin receives a new car each year for the procession, but the engine is never turned on (thus remaining 'virginal') – instead it's hauled by men with ropes.

Museo de Arte de Zapopan   MUSEUM

(MAZ; Map p570; www.mazmuseo.com; Andador 20 de Noviembre No 166; admission M$13, Tue free; ⊙10am-6pm Tue-Sun) One block east of the southeast corner of Plaza de las Américas, MAZ is Guadalajara's best modern art museum. Four sleek minimalist galleries hold temporary exhibits, which have included works by Diego Rivera and Frida Kahlo as well as leading contemporary Mexican artists.

Museo Huichol   MUSEUM

(Map p570; Eva Briseño 152; adult/child M$10/5; ⊙10am-2pm & 3-6pm Mon-Sat, 10am-3pm Sun) To the right of the basilica, the Museo Huichol has a worthwhile display of artifacts from the Huichol people, an indigenous group known for their peyote rituals and bright-colored yarn art (see boxed text, p652).

TLAQUEPAQUE

Though just 7km southeast of downtown Guadalajara, Tlaquepaque resembles your typical *pueblo mágico* (magical village): squint and you could well be in a small colonial town miles from anywhere. But its beauty is not its sole draw: artisans live behind the pastel-colored walls of the abandoned old mansions that line Tlaquepaque's narrow cobblestone streets, and their goods, such as wood carvings, sculpture, furniture, ceramics, jewelry, leather items and candles, are sold in smart boutiques that keep the shoppers coming all day long – see boxed text, p585.

The plaza is leafy and blooming with flowers, and the benches around the fountain are always packed. The eating is very good and the strolling is even better, especially at sunset when the sky behind the gorgeous, white-domed basilica burns orange and families take to the streets, enjoying the last ticks of daylight.

The tourist office offers two- to three-hour **walking tours** (by donation) of the area, which include visits to local workshops and museums and can be given in English or Spanish, but you must reserve ahead.

To get to Tlaquepaque from central Guadalajara, take bus 275 Diagonal, 275B or 647 (M$6). The turquoise TUR bus marked 'Tonalá' has air-con and is more comfortable (M$12). All these buses leave central Guadalajara from Avenida 16 de Septiembre between Cotilla and Madero; the trip takes about 20 minutes. As you near Tlaquepaque, watch for the brick arch and then a traffic circle, after which you should get off at the next stop. Up the street on the left is Independencia, which will take you to the heart of Tlaquepaque.

FREE Museo Pantaleón Panduro   MUSEUM

(Map p578; Sánchez 191; ⊙9am-5pm Mon-Sat, 10am-3pm Sun) This superb collection of local folk art is housed in a converted religious mission and includes miniature figurines, as well as enormous, lightly fired urns and other ceramic crafts from all over the country.

FREE Museo Regional de la Cerámica   MUSEUM

(Map p578; Independencia 237; ⊙10am-6pm Tue-Sat, to 4pm Sun) The Museo Regional de la Cerámica is set in a great old adobe building with stone arches and mature trees in the courtyard. It has an impressive collection that exhibits the varied styles and clays used in Jalisco and Michoacán. Explanations are in English and Spanish.

TONALÁ

This dusty, bustling suburb is about 13km southeast of downtown Guadalajara and home to even more artisans. You can feel Tonalá beginning to take Tlaquepaque's lead

Central Guadalajara

with a few airy, inviting showrooms and cafes opening around town, but it remains happily rough around the edges. It's fun to roam through the dark, dusty stores and workshops, browsing glassware, ceramics, furniture, masks, toys, jewelry, handmade soap and more. Anything you can buy in Tlaquepaque you can find here for much less, which is what attracts wholesale buyers from all over the world.

Ask staff at the Tonalá tourist office about two- to three-hour **walking tours** (by donation) of the Tonalá's artisan workshops. They're given in English or Spanish, but need to be reserved a couple of days in advance.

To reach Tonalá, take bus 275 Diagonal or 275D (both M$6). The turquoise TUR bus marked 'Tonalá' has air-con and is more comfortable (M$12). All these buses leave Guadalajara from the corner of Avenida 16 de Septiembre and Madero; the

trip takes about 45 minutes. As you enter Tonalá, get off on the corner of Avenidas Tonalá and Tonaltecas. The Plaza Principal is three blocks east of Avenida Tonaltecas on Juarez.

Street Market   MARKET

On Thursday and Sunday, Tonalá bursts into a huge street market that sprouts on Avenida Tonaltecas and crawls through dozens of streets and alleys and takes hours to explore. With *torta* (sandwich), taco and *michelada* (beer and tomato juice) stands aplenty, the whole area takes on a carnival vibe. The best pieces are usually found at the workshops and warehouses, not on the street.

Courses

Guadalajara is a popular place to study Spanish with classes available to students of all ages. Prices and curricula vary tremendously.

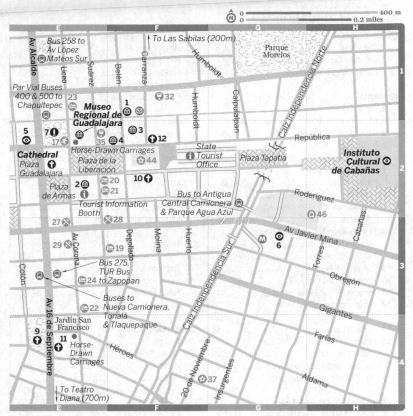

Centro de Estudios para Extranjeros

LANGUAGE COURSE

(CEPE; www.cepe.udg.mx; Gómez 125) Part of the University of Guadalajara, CEPE offers several levels of intensive two- to five-week Spanish-language courses. Day trips, homestays and longer excursions to other parts of Mexico are available.

Instituto Mexicano-Americano de Cultura

LANGUAGE COURSE

(IMAC; Map p574; www.spanish-school.com.mx; Guerra 180) Offers one- to 52-week courses. Study between one and four hours per day. Check its website for course fees and homestay options. Music and dance classes are also available.

👉 Tours

GDL Tours

TOURS

(☎1578-0421; www.gdltours.com) Offers a full menu of English-language guided tours. Op-

tions include walking tours of Guadalajara's main sights (from M$413, four hours), trips to the towns of Lake Chapala (from M$545, six hours), and Tequila Trail tours, which include distillery visits and tastings (from M$413, nine hours). Tour prices drop when there are more participants.

Tapatío Tour

BUS TOURS

(Map p574; ☎3613-0887; www.tapatiotour.com; tours M$90-110) The ubiquitous double-decker buses of Tapatío Tour ply the city's most popular sights on a circuit track. While the prerecorded narration (in English, Spanish, French, Italian, German and Japanese) is less than inspirational, the tours allow you to hop off and on wherever you wish, making sightseeing a breeze. Buses depart from the Rotonda de los Jaliscenses Ilustres and they operate from 10am to 8pm; tickets are M$20 cheaper Monday to Friday.

Central Guadalajara

✨ Festivals & Events

Major festivals celebrated in Guadalajara and its suburbs include the following:

Festival Internacional del Cine   FILM
Mexico's most important film festival (www.ficg.mx) has been drawing top actors and directors to Guadalajara each March for 25 years. Sidle up to stars such as Gael García Bernal and John Malkovich at screenings and parties across the city.

Feria de Tonalá   HANDICRAFTS FAIR
An annual handicrafts fair in Tonalá, specializing in ceramics, is held the weeks before, during and after Semana Santa (Easter week).

Fiestas de Tlaquepaque   HANDICRAFTS FAIR
Tlaquepaque's annual fiesta and handicrafts fair takes place mid-June to the first week of July.

Fiesta Internacional del Mariachi   MUSIC
In late August and early September mariachis come from everywhere to jam, battle and enjoy; check out www.mariachi-jalisco.com.mx for more information.

Fiestas de Octubre   TRADITIONAL
Beginning with a parade on the first Sunday in October, these festivities (www.fiestasdeoctubre.com.mx) last all month long and are Guadalajara's principal annual fair, with free

entertainment, livestock shows, art exhibitions and sporting events.

Feria Internacional del Libro BOOK FAIR

This book fair (www.fil.com.mx) is one of the biggest book promotions in Latin America; held during the last week of November and first week of December, headlined by major Spanish-language authors, such as Gabriel García Márquez.

🛏 Sleeping

During holidays (Christmas and Easter) and festivals you *must* reserve ahead. Ask for discounts if you arrive in the low season or will be staying more than a few days.

CENTRAL GUADALAJARA

Southeast of Mercado San Juan de Dios there's a cluster of budget hotels. This part of town is a bit rough, but you can usually find a cheap room here when other places are full. Budget digs can be found around the Antigua Central Camionera (old bus station) as well. The historic centre is full of midrange options, many of which are housed in charming colonial buildings. Top-end accommodations are generally found in Chapultepec and beyond, and are aimed at guests with their own transportation.

TOP CHOICE Las Sabilas GUESTHOUSE $$

(off Map p574; ☑3613-5544; www.lasabila.com; Carranza 314; r M$635-1270; 🛜) Behind an unmarked door and down a vine-choked passageway, this bohemian guesthouse blooms with hibiscus and pomegranate trees. Many of the guests are repeat visitors and friends of the US owner who love this place, which is in the heart of a working class neighborhood just a short walk from the Plaza de la Liberación. The six rooms range from homey to luxurious – try the hidden garden suite for a splash of romance.

Villa Ganz BOUTIQUE HOTEL $$$

(Map p581; ☑3120-1416; www.villaganz.com; López Cotilla 1739; r incl breakfast from M$3125; �🅿❄@🛜) Undoubtedly the most luxurious and stylish boutique hotel in town, the 10 unique suites in this converted Chapultepec mansion have gorgeous features such as clawfoot tubs, vaulted brick ceilings, rustic wooden furniture and tiled floors throughout. There are also progressive touches such as iPhone docks and a no under-12s rule. The beautiful garden terrace, with an enormous wood-burning fireplace and too many candles to count, oozes romance.

Casa Pedro Loza BOUTIQUE HOTEL $$$

(off Map p574; ☑1202-2423; www.casapedroloza. com.mx; Loza 360; r incl breakfast M$1800; ❄🛜) Housed in an impressive colonial mansion in a charming part of the historic center, this hotel boasts a sometimes dubious 'eclectic concept' that won't appeal to all tastes, though it's certainly been lovingly decorated. The 11 rooms are each wildly different, and while some are gorgeous and stuffed full of beautiful antiques, others are just plain garish, so book ahead! The retractable roof over the courtyard and the superb roof terrace are other points in the hotel's favor.

Hotel Morales HOTEL $$$

(Map p574; ☑3658-5232; www.hotelmorales. com.mx; Av Corona 243; r from M$1360, ste from M$1660; 🅿❄🛜🏊) The towering four-tiered colonial lobby is a suitably impressive entrance to this smart, central hotel. The 94 rooms are spacious; however, due to the nature of the building, some lack light. The pricier rooms in the newly renovated part of the hotel are particularly smart, though many older ones have great views. Staff and service are very professional.

Casa Vilasanta HOTEL $$

(Map p574; ☑3124-1277; www.vilasanta.com; Rayón 170; dm M$200, s/d M$390/450; ❄🛜) This is the best value in Guadalajara. The bright, pastel-colored rooms are scattered around a cool interior courtyard, decorated with pottery and flowers, and there's a sunny 2nd-floor terrace. The singles can feel cramped, but the doubles are large and all rooms have TV. There's a shared kitchen and plenty of chill space on both floors. But with just 17 rooms and English-speaking management, this place books up. Reserve ahead!

Hostel Plaza Liberación HOTEL $

(Map p574; ☑3614-4504; www.hostelplazalibera cion.com.mx; Morelos 247; s/d M$350/400, s without bathroom M$150; 🛜) This brand new place has an unbeatable location right in the heart of the Historic Center, with many of the 17 rooms overlooking Plaza Liberación. It's a bright and pleasantly furnished hotel and great value with all rooms having fans and TV.

Hospedarte Downtown HOSTEL $

(Map p574; ☑3562-7520; www.hostelguadalaja ra.com.mx; Maestranza 147; dm incl breakfast

Tlaquepaque

with/without ISIC card M$160/170, s/d incl breakfast M$350/400; @) One of two Hospedarte hostels now in town, this downtown option is popular with a young crowd looking for a good time. The dorms are spacious four-bed rooms, all with lockers and fans, sharing toilets and showers around a large communal area with a huge kitchen and plenty of activities laid on.

Hotel Francés
HISTORIC HOTEL $$
(Map p574; 3613-1190; www.hotelfrances.com; Maestranza 35; r from M$643; P❋) This living, breathing baroque time capsule has been operating since 1610, and its magnificent three-tiered courtyard lobby is bathed in blue light thanks to an enormous stained glass atrium above. Rooms are a far cry from luxurious, but they are clean. And if you get one on the 3rd floor, you'll have immediate roof access – and insane views of colonial Guadalajara at your fingertips. Magic!

Hospedarte Hostel
HOSTEL $$
(Map p581; 3615-4957; www.hospedartehostel. com; Luna 2075; dm M$170, s/d/tr/q M$400/450/600/750; @) On a residential side street in Chapultepec, this low-key guesthouse attracts a mix of solo travelers and international students. A hammock-filled back garden is great for relaxation, and you can use the communal kitchen for meals or just grab a free bike and explore the neighborhood on two wheels. Unlike its sister hostel downtown, this is not a party zone (there are quiet hours after midnight).

Posada San Pablo
HOTEL $
(Map p574; 3614-2811; www.posadasanpablo .com; Madero 429; s/d M$340/450, s/d without bathroom M$250/370;) This very friendly place comes complete with a grassy garden and sunny terrace. Upstairs rooms with balconies are best. There's a communal kitchen and you can even (hand) wash your clothes

Tlaquepaque

in the old-fashioned *lavandería* (laundry) out back.

Quinta Real Guadalajara   LUXURY HOTEL **$$$**
(⊅1105-1000; www.quintareal.com; Av México 2727; r from M$3500; P🐾⊝❄@≋) There is no denying the beauty of this five-star stay, with its exquisite stone and ivy-covered exterior. The lobby and bar are inviting and stylish, the grounds are impeccably manicured and the service is outstanding. But the rooms are a bit cramped and don't live up to the steep price tag.

Posada Regis   HOTEL **$**
(Map p574; ⊅3614-8633; www.posadaregis.com; Av Corona 171; s/d/tr incl breakfast M$365/430/700; @🔊) High ceilings and ornate gold-and-blue murals make the lobby of this sunny 2nd-floor posada (inn) feel like Marie Antoinette's parlor. The bedrooms are far less splendid, with tiny bare-bones bathrooms and rather worn-out furniture. Rooms on the street are loud but bright, while those at the back are quiet but dark.

La Rotonda   HOTEL **$$**
(Map p574; ⊅3614-1017; www.hoteleselectos.com; Liceo 130; s/d from M$630/750; P🔊) Two sto-

ries of attractively tiled rooms with hardwood furnishings surround a bright colonial stone courtyard, which, frankly could have been made much more of. However, the location is great and the staff friendly.

TLAQUEPAQUE

Just 15 minutes away by bus or taxi from downtown Guadalajara, Tlaquepaque is an excellent option for those who crave small-town charm but still want to visit the sights of the big city. The shopping is superb, and you won't have to lug your purchases too far.

TOP CHOICE Quinta Don José   BOUTIQUE HOTEL **$$$**
(Map p578; ⊅3635-7522; www.quintadonjose.com; Reforma 139; s/d incl breakfast from M$1095/1235, ste incl breakfast from M$1370; ⊝❄@🔊≋🐾) From the cozy sunken lobby to the sunny, flower-filled pool terrace complete with gurgling fountains, this charming hotel is a great place to escape while remaining in the heart of Tlaquepaque. Rooms and suites are rustic chic, with terracotta tile and vaulted brick ceilings. At night the courtyard twinkles with strings of tiny lights while the good in-house Italian restaurant ensures a pleasantly bustling atmosphere.

Casa de las Flores   B&B **$$$**
(Map p578; ⊅3659-3186; www.casadelasflores.com; Santos Degollado 175; r incl breakfast from M$1500; ⊝@🔊) When you enter this impressive courtyard B&B, you will be hit by a swirl of captivating colors. There's an incredible collection of Mexican folk art, including some very rare pre-Hispanic pieces, a blooming garden and patio patrolled by hummingbirds out back, and a stocked bar and fireplace in the living room. Rooms are all spacious and brightly decorated in the same folksy style as the main building, although bathrooms are disappointingly ordinary. Breakfasts verge on the ultragourmet, however, especially when co-owner Stan, a former chef at Berkeley's Chez Panisse, is on breakfast duty.

Casa Campos   GUESTHOUSE **$$**
(Map p578; ⊅3838-5297; www.casacampos.mx; Miranda 30; s/d M$850/1000; ⊝❄@🔊) This pink and orange converted mansion boasts a gorgeous, flower-filled courtyard, stone columns and sleek wood furnishings. The 11 rooms are spacious, tasteful and well equipped (though bathrooms are nothing special) and it's moments from the best shopping on Independencia.

Casa del Retoño
GUESTHOUSE $$

(Map p578; ☑3587-3989; www.lacasadelretono.
com.mx; Matamoros 182; s/d/tr incl breakfast
M$700/850/1000; 🔊) The eight rooms in this
very pleasant traditional house are all color-
fully decorated, share an enormous garden
and boast TVs and good bathrooms. It's a
short walk from the main square and run by
a friendly local family.

Donde el Indio Duerme
HOTEL $

(Map p578; ☑3635-2189; www.indiosleep.com; In-
dependencia 74; r from M$350; 🔊) Right on the
plaza, this hotel has Tlaquepaque's cheapest
rooms as well as a potentially gorgeous roof
terrace. However, the rooms are in a pretty
poor state with flaking paint and small bath-
rooms, but it's adequately clean and decent
value.

✖ Eating

Guadalajara is an ever-improving city for
eating, with many visitors finding that
meals here count among the highlights of
their stay. A few local specialties to look
out for: *birria* (a spicy goat or lamb stew),
carne en su jugo ('meat in its juice,' a type of
beef soup), *tejuino* (a fermented corn drink
often sold by street vendors), and, above
all, the ubiquitous *torta ahogada* (literally
'drowned sandwich'), a chili sauce–soaked
pork roll said to cure everything from hang-
overs to the flu.

CENTRO HISTÓRICO & AROUND
Adventurous stomachs can head to the **Mer-
cado San Juan de Dios** (Map p574), home to
endless food stalls serving the cheapest and
some of the tastiest eats in town. The plaza
in front of the Templo Expiatorio is a good
place to snag late-night tacos, *tortas* and
elote (grilled corn on the cob).

🔺TOP Birriería las
CHOICE Nueve Esquinas
MEXICAN $$

(Map p574; Av Colón 384; mains M$74-97; ⏲8am-
11pm Mon-Sat, to 9pm Sun) The gorgeously
villagelike Nueve Esquinas (Nine Corners)
neighborhood specializes in *birria*, meat
stewed in its own juices until it's so tender
it melts in your mouth. Birriería las Nueve
Esquinas does it best. The two main offerings here are *birria de chivo* (steamed goat)
and *barbacoa de borrego* (baked lamb), although ask the staff and they won't hesitate
to tell you that the *chivo* is the best of the
two, and we can't help but agree. Both come
with a stack of fresh tortillas, pickled onions,

cilantro and two salsas – wrap the meat in
the tortilla, add various flavors and then dip
the tortilla in the meat juice before putting
it in your mouth: heavenly.

La Fonda de la Noche
MEXICAN $$

(Map p574; ☑3827-0917; Jesús 251; mains M$80-
90; ⏲7.30pm-midnight Tue-Sun) This under-
the-radar gem serves food from the owner
Carlos' native Durango in a rambling, art-
filled art nouveau house on a quiet resi-
dential street. Book ahead if you'd like to
eat out under the stars on the terrace. The
menu is simple, and spoken only, so you'll
need to speak some Spanish to enjoy it here,
although Carlos does speak some basic Eng-
lish. Try the *plato combinado* (combined
plate; M$90) – a selection of the four main
dishes served here, or content yourself with
the classic *chiles en nogada* (stuffed poblano
chilies in a walnut-pomegranate sauce). The
door is unmarked – it's on the northwest
corner of Jesús and Reforma.

La Chata
MEXICAN $

(Map p574; Av Corona 126; mains M$50-110; ⏲)
Quality *comida típica* (home-style food), af-
fordable prices and ample portions keep this
family diner packed; indeed, you may have
to wait in line to get in in the late afternoon
when locals finish work. The specialty is the
superb *platillo jaliscense* (fried chicken
with five sides); it also serves a popular *po-
zole* (hominy soup).

Chai
INTERNATIONAL $

(Map p574; mains M$40-100; ⏲8am-midnight;
🔊); Centro Histórico (Av Juárez 200); Chapulte-
pec (Map p581; Av Vallarta 1509) Guadalajara's
young and pretty pack into plush booths to
sip chai lattes and nibble on *panini* at this
casual hippie-chic cafe, home of the city's
best brunches. A second location in a re-
stored mansion in upscale Chapultepec has
a sunny terrace and a very smart feel, popu-
lar with a glam international crowd.

La Fonda de San Miguel
Arcángel
MEXICAN $$

(Map p574; Guerra 25; mains M$100-200; ⏲8:30am-
midnight Tue-Sat, to 9pm Sun & Mon) A sweet
courtyard retreat from the sun where fountains gurgle, an old piano is played and
antique sculpture and bird cages are everywhere. Its specialties are *filete de res oro
negro* – beef with *huitlacoche* (corn fungus)
sauce – and its famously excellent *molcajete*
(a spicy Oaxacan dish served on a sizzlingly
hot stone dish with fajitas).

Chapultepec

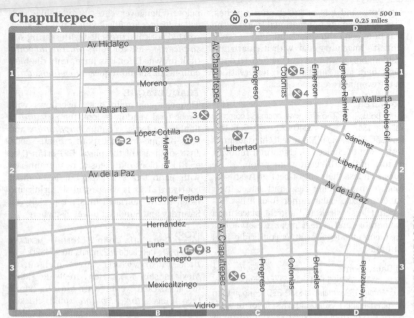

Café Madrid   CAFE **$**
(Map p574; Av Juárez 264; mains M$50-100)
The waiters here are dressed in white dinner jackets and the cash register, espresso
machines and soda fountains are mint-
condition antiques, even though the rest of
the decor is something of an afterthought.
Come for breakfast: the *huevos rancheros*
(fried eggs on a corn tortilla with a tomato,
chili and onion sauce served with refried
beans) and *chilaquiles* (fried tortilla strips
cooked with chili sauce) have been favorites
for 50 years.

CHAPULTEPEC & AROUND
Chapultepec is home to some of Guadalajara's best cuisine and to all its serious culinary experiences. To get here, catch the
westbound Par Vial 400 or 500 bus from
Avenidas Independencia and Alcalde. Taxis
from the city center should cost around
M$50.

Lula Bistro   INTERNATIONAL **$$$**
(☑3647-6432; www.lulabistro.com; San Gabri-
el 3030; mains from M$180; ⏰2-5.30pm &
7.30pm-midnight Tue-Sun) Guadalajara's most
celebrated restaurant is this superchic
Chapultepec establishment, helmed by Irish
chef Darren Walsh, who cut his teeth in
London and New York before opening this

superb venture. Sleek and industrial though
the setting is, it's the food people come
for, and the long, interesting menu, which
is particularly strong on fish and seafood.
Reservations are recommended.

Latina I   INTERNATIONAL **$$**
(☑3647-7774; www.ilatinarest.com; Av Inglaterra
3128; mains M$110-280; ⏰7.30pm-1am Tue-Sat,
1.30-6pm Sun) This eccentrically decorated
place boasts a wall of ceramic pigs, a giant

swordfish and lots of kitsch, fun touches. The Asian-leaning international menu is the reason to come, however, and food is excellent. It's hugely popular with a smart and fashionable crowd, and can be loud, so don't come here for a quiet dinner. Reservations in the evenings are a good idea.

Cocina 88
MEXICAN $$$
(Map p581; ☏3827-5996; www.cocina88.com; Av Vallarta 1342; mains M$140-225; ☺1:30pm-1am Mon-Sat, 2-10pm Sun) Moneyed Guadalajara's restaurant of choice is located in a renovated turn-of-the-20th-century mansion, where guests choose their cut of beef or fresh seafood from a butcher case and select their wine from the cellar rather than a list. It's all effortlessly sleek and a great place for a memorable and stylish meal. Reservations are recommended for dinners on Friday and Saturday.

El Sacromonte
MEXICAN $$$
(Map p574; ☏3825-5447; www.sacromonte.com.mx; Moreno 1398; mains M$130-200; ☺noon-6pm & 7pm-midnight) Guadalajara's favorite *alta cocina* (gourmet Mexican) establishment serves whimsical takes on classic dishes – think quesadillas sprinkled with rose petals, avocado-watermelon soup and giant prawns in lobster sauce with fried spinach. Decor is tastefully arty, with vintage bullfighting posters and folk-art crucifixes. Reservations are recommended.

Karne Garibaldi
MEXICAN $$
(Garibaldi 1306; mains M$60-100; ☺noon-midnight) This large and bright cantina is wildly popular with Mexican family groups and has two specialties: *carne en su jugo* and fast service (so speedy it landed in the *Guinness Book of Records* in 1996). The neighborhood is friendly and buzzes at night, and you're almost guaranteed to be the only traveler.

Tacos Don Luis
MEXICAN $
(Map p574; cnr Chapultepec & Mexicaltzingo; tacos M$7; ☺8pm-4am) At night this Chapultepec parking lot overflows with hungry clubgoers, who crouch on the curb with plastic plates trying not to spill taco fillings on their party dresses and fancy shoes. There are various food stalls, but Don Luis is the oldest and the best.

Tortas Ahogadas César
MEXICAN $
(Map p574; López Cotilla 1449; tortas M$25) This bare-bones cafe traffics in one thing and one thing only: *tortas ahogadas,* Guadalajara's

beloved hangover cure. Baguettelike rolls called *birotes* are filled with chunks of slow-roasted pork and drenched with searing *salsa picante* – ask for yours *'media ahogada'* (half-drowned) for less burn; only die-hard chili-heads should request *'bien ahogada.'*

TLAQUEPAQUE
Tlaquepaque's main plaza overflows with street food vendors – look for *jericalla* (a flanlike custard), coconut *empanadas* and cups of lime-drenched pomegranate seeds. Just southeast of the plaza, El Parián (Map p578) is a block of dozens of restaurant-bars with patio tables crowding a leafy inner courtyard. This is where you sit, drink and listen to live mariachi music, especially on Saturday and Sunday, but eat elsewhere.

TOP CHOICE Cenaduría Doña Victoria
MEXICAN $
(Map p578; Degollado 182; mains from M$20; ☺7-11pm Fri-Wed) Victoria serves high-quality Mexican soul food. Her streetside skillet overflows each evening with *taquitos* (small tacos), tacos, *tortas, pozole,* quail, chicken and potatoes. The *pollo dorado* (fried chicken; M$30) is the best seller. It comes with potatoes, salad, tortillas and three kinds of salsa.

Tortas Ahogadas Chimbombo
MEXICAN $
(Map p578; Madero 74; tortas M$23, steaks M$75; ☺8am-11pm) This streetside grill is where Señor Lopez prepares T-bones and skirt steaks as well as deliciously spicy *tortas ahogadas.* Steaks are rubbed with olive oil, splashed with soy sauce and served with Greek salad and garlic bread. You can eat in, or take your feast to the nearby plaza and enjoy it in the sun.

El Patio
MEXICAN $$$
(Map p578; Independencia 186; mains M$100-250; ☺9am-9pm Mon-Thu, to 11pm Fri-Sun) Popular with Mexican tourists and families, this place nevertheless has plenty of charm, set as it is in an attractive courtyard surrounding a gurgling fountain. The specialty here is the steak, but there's a wide ranging menu of Mexican favorites including a good *birria* and a gourmet *torta ahogada.* Mariachi bands play here between 3pm and 4pm daily.

Casa Fuerte
MEXICAN $$
(Map p578; Independencia 224; mains M$100-200; ☺8am-11pm) This elegant and sprawling place leans toward fine dining, with a full cocktail bar, refreshing garden patio and a rather stately feel. It's very popular with

GAY & LESBIAN GUADALAJARA

Guadalajara is one of the gayest cities in the country – some call it the San Francisco of Mexico. It's not nearly as open as SF, however, and has a far more dual character: despite a conservative president, mayor and local population, somehow Guadalajara becomes very openly gay after dark. In June, everyone gets out and proud when the city hosts one of Latin America's largest gay pride parades.

Guadalajara's so-called 'gay ghetto' radiates out a few blocks from the corner of Ocampo and Sánchez, in the city center, but Avenida Chapultepec, just west of the city center, is starting to see upscale establishments aimed at a gay clientele. The following are some of the busiest bars and clubs in the city. You can read more listings at www. gaymexicomap.com.

Hot spot **California's** (Moreno 652; ⊘8pm-3am Mon-Sat) attracts a diverse and attractive crowd – everything from cowboys to stockbrokers. It gets packed around 10pm, and Friday and Saturday nights are a madhouse, but there's no dancing – this is the place to start your night before heading to a club.

The current hottest club in town is **Babel Club Gay** (Map p574; Morelos 741; admission M$100; ⊘10pm-5am Fri & Sat), a sleek, two-floor disco which is extremely popular and has multiple VIP rooms, go-go dancers, three separate dance floors and a terrace.

La Prisciliana (Map p574; Sánchez 394; ⊘5pm-1:30am Sun-Tue, to 3am Wed-Sat) is laid-back and stylish, with arched windows, burgundy walls, worn tile floors and an antique wood bar in an old colonial building. It can get wild late and there's a drag show from time to time, but usually things stay chill.

Diagonally across from La Prisciliana, **Los Caudillos** (Map p574; Sánchez 407; admission M$50; ⊘5pm-4am daily, after-party 6-10am Sun) is a popular multistory disco, with three dance floors and endless lounges and bars full of gorgeous young things dancing.

Also worth dropping into is **7 Sins** (Map p574; Moreno 532; admission after midnight M$50; ⊘10pm-4am Fri & Sat), the favorite hangout of the younger section of Guadalajara's gay scene. If you're over 30 you'll feel pretty out of place, but this colonial mansion has a cool staircase and ear-bleeding loud music.

Circus (Map p574; Galeana 277; ⊘10pm-4am Fri & Sat) fills up late in the night with hot young hardbodies lounging in heart-shaped chairs and howling at the variety shows. It's also popular with lesbians.

Angels Club (Map p581; López Cotilla 1495B; ⊘9:30pm-5am Wed-Sat, 6pm-11pm Sun) hosts drag shows on Friday and Saturday at midnight and is the most popular club in the city, attracting a mix of gay men, lesbians and a gay-friendly straight crowd.

Tlaquepaque's upper crust, although you can usually get a table with no problem.

Mariscos Progreso SEAFOOD $$
(Map p578; Progreso 80; mains M$100-125; ⊘11am-8pm) On Saturday and Sunday afternoons it feels like all of Guadalajara has packed into this patio seafood restaurant. Dressed-up Mexican families slurp ceviche and pass around platters of pineapple shrimp and *huachinango al estilo Veracruz* (snapper with lime and tomatoes) while mariachis wander from table to table. Oysters are a specialty – you'll recognize the place by the oyster-shucking hut out front.

 Drinking

The Centro Histórico gets fairly quiet at night, though there are several bright spots (if you know where to look) and a thriving gay scene. Chapultepec, however, is always jumping with international-style bars and clubs.

TOP
CHOICE **Café Galería André Breton** BAR
(Map p574; Manuel 175; ⊘10am-3am Tue-Sat, 2-8pm Sun) Tucked away on a side street on the eastern side of the Centro Histórico is this charming bar, cafe and live-music venue. As bohemian as its name suggests, this is one of the city's coolest hangouts. Enjoy the French menu, range of artisan beers from around the world and live music (M$40 cover) each evening from 9pm.

La Fuente BAR
(Map p574; Suárez 78; ⊘8:30am-11pm Mon-Thu, to midnight Fri & Sat) La Fuente, set in the old

Edison boiler room, is an institution – and a rather friendly one. It's been open since 1921 and is mostly peopled by regulars – older men who start drinking too early. But they treat newcomers like family and women like queens. A bass, piano and violin trio sets up and jams from sunset until last call.

Santa   BAR
(Map p581; Luna 2061; ☺8pm-3am Sun & Tue-Thu, to 4am Fri & Sat) Red walls and blinking Señora de Guadalupe pictures sum up the eccentric glam interior at this Chapultepec hot spot. It gets packed on Fridays and Saturdays when DJs take over and get the crowd dancing. During the week well-dressed scenesters sip mezcal (an agave spirit; two for one on Thursday) and listen to lounge music.

Escarabajo Scratch   BAR
(Map p574; Andador Coronilla 28; ☺6pm-2:30am Mon-Thu, from 1pm Fri & Sat) This fun hipster bar in the Centro Histórico has elevated the *michelada* (beer and Bloody Mary's lovechild) to fine art and celebrates the day when grunge rock ruled. It also has 11 labels of good tequila.

Hotel Francés   BAR
(Map p574; Maestranza 35; ☺noon-midnight) The dark marble courtyard bar at this hotel encourages you to relax back into another era, where waiters in bow ties treat you like an old friend, happy hour lasts until 8pm and acoustic troubadours strum gorgeous, weepy ballads.

Candela   BAR
(Mina 183, Zapopan; ☺1:30pm-2:30am Mon-Sat, 5pm-1am Sun) Drink with Zapopan's young, sexy, moneyed bohemia in this converted home with a courtyard lounge, specialty cocktails and a jazz soundtrack. It serves wood-fired pizzas. Friday is the big night.

☆ Entertainment

Guadalajara is a musical place and live performers can be heard any night of the week at one of the city's many venues (including restaurants). Discos and bars are plentiful, but ask around for the newest hot spots – Guadalajarans love to show off their town.

Several popular venues host a range of drama, dance and music performances. The newest and hippest spot is **Teatro Diana** (Map p574; www.teatrodiana.com; Av 16 de Septiembre 710). It stages traveling Broadway shows, concerts with local and international artists and art installations. Other options include the historic **Teatro Degollado** (Map p574; ☎3613-1115; Degollado) and the **Instituto Cultural de Cabañas** (Map p574; ☎3668-1640; Cabañas 8), both downtown cultural centers, as well as the **Ex-Convento del Carmen** (Map p574; ☎3030-1385; Av Juárez 638).

Nightclubs

Most of Guadalajara's hot spots are outside the Centro Histórico. Locals dress up to go out, so try to look the part. Much of the action in the city takes place in its myriad gay clubs, to which straight people are very welcome.

[TOP CHOICE] La Mutualista   DANCING
(Map p574; Madero 553; ☺9pm-2am Mon-Sat) With smoke-yellowed walls and antique chandeliers dangling from high ceilings, this vintage dance hall simmers with the decaying glamour of Old Havana. Thursdays and Saturdays are salsa nights, the real reason to come. A Cuban band kicks off around midnight and the all-ages crowd explodes with eye-popping moves on the dance floor. Prepare to get sweaty.

Angels Club   CLUB
(Map p581; López Cotilla 1495B; ☺9:30pm-5am Wed-Sat, 6pm-11pm Sun) Welcome to Guadalajara's megaclub. Sure, it's a gay venue, but straight guys and gals are just as welcome to join the party. Check out the acrylic tables, cool lounge, throwback beanbag room and the three dance floors blasting (and we mean blasting) house, pop and techno. Saturday nights get wild. Clubbers often leave for breakfast at around 5am and return for sun-drenched fun after hours.

Live Music

You can pay your respects to the mariachi tradition in its home city. The Plaza de los Mariachis (Map p574), just east of the Centro Histórico, is an OK place to sit, drink beer and soak in the serenades of passionate Mexican bands. But you'll be happier at El Parián (Map p578), a garden complex in Tlaquepaque made up of dozens of small cantinas that all share one plaza occupied by droves of mariachis. On Saturdays and Sundays the bands battle and jockey for your ears, applause and cash.

State and municipal bands present free concerts of typical *música tapatía* (Guadalajaran music) in the Plaza de Armas (Map p574) at 6:30pm on most Tuesdays, Thursdays and Sundays and on other days as well

SHOPPING IN TLAQUEPAQUE

Tlaquepaque has legendary shopping. Large home-decor boutiques are stocked with ceramics, exquisite light fixtures and handmade wood furniture. Guadalajara's best interior designers are based here and if you take your time you'll discover some rare and creative pieces.

Gorgeous furniture showpieces, such as benches carved from a single tree, are displayed at **Antigua de México** (Map p578; www.antiguademexico.com; Independencia 255; ⊗10am-2pm & 3-7pm Mon-Fri, 10am-6pm Sat) in expansive, old-world courtyards.

Orígenes (Map p578; Independencia 211; ⊗10am-7pm Mon-Fri, 11am-7pm Sat, 11am-6pm Sun) has a tremendous lighting selection, elegant hammocks and even its own in-house 'Mexican gourmet' restaurant, Casa Luna (mains M$150 to M$250), with tables inside as well as outside in the shade of a tree.

Teté, Arte y Diseño (Map p578; www.tearteydiseno.com; Av Juárez 173; ⊗10am-7:30pm Mon-Sat) offers massive chandeliers, reproduction antique hardware and one-of-a-kind woodcarvings.

A short walk up from the main plaza toward the Museo Pantaléon Panduro is **Paco Padilla** (Map p578; Sánchez 134; ⊗10am-4pm Mon-Sat), a charming ceramics workshop where you can browse a huge range of items on display and watch artisans at work.

If you need something transported, visit **Sebastián Exportaciones** (Map p578; ☑3124-6560; sebastianexp@prodigy.net.mx; Ejército 45; ⊗9am-2pm & 4-6pm Mon-Fri), which ships boxes (minimum 1 cu meter) internationally.

---

during holiday seasons (and especially during the Fiestas de Octubre, p576).

Casa Bariachi   MARIACHIS
(Av Vallarta 2221; ⊗1pm-3am Mon-Sat) This bright barnlike restaurant-bar has romantic lighting and leather chairs, along with piñatas and colorful *papel picado* (cutout paper) hanging from the ceiling. This place may fail the hipster test, but the margaritas are bathtub big and mariachis jam from 4pm to 11pm daily. It's about a 10-minute taxi ride west of the city center.

Sports

Charreadas (rodeos) are held at noon most Sundays in the Lienzo Charros de Jalisco ring behind Parque Agua Azul south of the center. *Charros* (cowboys) come from all over Jalisco and Mexico; *escaramuza* (female stunt riding) teams perform as well.

LUCHA LIBRE (MEXICAN WRESTLING)

TOP
CHOICE **Arena Coliseo**   MEXICAN WRESTLING
(Map p574; ☑3617-3401; Medrano 67; tickets M$30-140; ⊗8.30pm Tue & 6.30pm Sun) Watching masked *luchadores* (wrestlers) with names like El Terrible and Casanova gut-punching each other makes for a memorable night out. Expect scantily clad women, insult-hurling crowds, and screaming doughnut vendors: it's all part of the fun of this classic Mexican pastime. The neighborhood surrounding the beloved coliseum can be a bit dodgy – watch your pockets.

SOCCER

Fútbol flows strongly through Guadalajaran blood. The city has three local teams in Mexico's top league, the *primera división*: **Guadalajara** (Las Chivas; www.chivas.com.mx) – the second most popular team in the country – **Atlas** (Los Zorros; www.atlas.com.mx) and **Universidad Autónoma de Guadalajara** (Los Estudiantes Tecos). The seasons last from July to December and from January to June and teams play at stadiums around the city. You can get an up-to-date season schedule at www.femexfut.org.mx.

Estadio Jalisco   STADIUM
(www.estadiojalisco.net; Siete Colinas 1772; admission M$35-100) Just off Calzada Independencia as you head northeast out of Central Guadalajara, this is the main soccer venue (seating around 60,000) in Guadalajara, and it hosted World Cup matches in 1970 and 1986. Check out the website for schedule information. Big games cost more than regular matches. Trolleybus R600 and buses 60 and 62A heading north on Calzada Independencia can drop you off nearby.

Shopping

Guadalajara's wealthiest like to browse at big shopping centers such as **Centro Magno** (www.magnobowl.com.mx; Av Vallarta 2425),

2km west of the city center, and **Plaza del Sol** (www.plazadelsol.com; Av López Mateos Sur), 7km southwest of the city center. To reach them, take bus 258 going west from the corner of San Felipe and Avenida Alcalde, or TUR 707 going west on Avenida Juárez. The newest, biggest mall, **Galerías Guadalajara** (✆3777-7880; www.galeriasguadalajara. com; Sanzio 150), is 8km west of downtown, served by bus 25. All malls are open from approximately 10am to 9pm.

Far more appealing to travelers will be the excellent handicrafts from Jalisco, Michoacán and other Mexican states that are available in Guadalajara's many markets. Tlaquepaque and Tonalá, two suburbs less than 15km from Guadalajara's center, are both major producers of handicrafts and furniture – anyone with an interior decorating habit should plan to spend some major quality time in each (see boxed text, p585 for Tlaquepaque and p573 for Tonalá). You'll find the best value (read: wholesale prices) in Tonalá.

Mercado San Juan de Dios MARKET
(Mercado Libertad; Map p574; cnr Av Javier Mina & Calz Independencia; ☉10am-9pm) This huge market has three whole floors of stalls offering everything from cowboy boots and DVDs to kitchenware; the salespeople are eager to sell and the food court is outstanding!

Mercado Corona MARKET
(Map p574; cnr Av Hidalgo & Santa Mónica; ☉9am-8pm) Near downtown is this bustling, block-long market with clothes, household items, knickknacks and food.

ℹ Information

Emergency

If you are a victim of crime you may first want to contact your embassy or consulate (p851) and/or the state tourist office (p586).

Ambulance (✆3601-3019, 3614-5252)
Emergency (✆080, 066)
Fire (✆1201-7700)
Police (✆3632-0330)

Internet Access

Internet cafes (M$10 to M$15 per hour) are scattered around the city but tend to change location frequently. Nearly all hotels and many restaurants, cafes and bars offer free wi-fi.

Internet Resources

Gobierno de Jalisco (www.visita.jalisco.gob. mx, in Spanish) Official website of Jalisco.
Gobierno Municipal de Tonalá (www.tonala. gob.mx, in Spanish) Official website of Tonalá.

Gobierno Municipal de Zapopan (www. zapopan.gob.mx, in Spanish) Official website of Zapopan.
Tlaquepaque Gobierno Municipal (www. tlaquepaque.gob.mx, in Spanish) Official website of Tlaquepaque.
Vive Guadalajara (vive.guadalajara.gob.mx, in Spanish) Official website of Guadalajara.

Media

There are several Spanish-language papers competing for business around town: the indie *El Informador* (www.informador.com.mx), and the mainstream *Mural* (www.mural.com). Check out the online *Guadalajara Guadalajara* (www. guadalajaraguadalajara.com) for concert and entertainment listings. The English-language *Guadalajara Reporter* (www.guadalajarareporter. com) caters to local expats.

Medical Services

Farmacia Guadalajara (Moreno 170; ☉8am-10pm) Get your first aid, sundry items and prescribed meds here.
Hospital México Americano (✆3648-3317; www.hma.com.mx; Colomos 2110) About 3km northwest of the city center; English-speaking physicians available.
US Consulate (✆3268-2200; http://guadala jara.usconsulate.gov/medical2.html) Keeps a regularly updated online list of local English-speaking doctors, including specialists and dentists.

Money

Banks are plentiful in Guadalajara and most have ATMs, known as *cajeros*.

You can change cash at competitive prices around the clock at one of the eager *casas de cambio* (money changers) on López Cotilla, between Avenida 16 de Septiembre and Corona. Most will also change traveler's checks.
Amex (✆3630-6680; Av Vallarta 2440) Located in the Plaza Los Arcos shopping center.

Post

Main post office (Map p574; cnr Carranza & Av Independencia, ☉8am-7pm Mon-Fri, 9am-1pm Sat)

Tourist Information

State tourist office (Map p574; ✆3668-1600; Morelos 102; ☉9am-7pm Mon-Fri) Enter from either Morelos or Paseo Degollado. English-speaking staff offers information on Guadalajara, the state of Jalisco and the upcoming week's events.
Tlaquepaque state tourist office (Map p578; ✆3562-7050, ext 2319; www.tlaquepaque.gob. mx; Morelos 88; ☉9am-3pm Mon-Fri) Upstairs in the Casa del Artesano. There is also a helpful

tourist kiosk as you enter the main shopping area of Tlaquepaque on Ejército.

Tonalá tourist office (Map p570; ☑1200-3912; Zapata 244A; ☉9am-3pm Mon-Fri) Three blocks west of Avenida Tonaltecas on Zapata.

Tourist information booth (Map p574; ☉9:30am-2:30pm & 5-7:30pm Mon-Fri, 10am-12:30pm Sat & Sun) In the Palacio de Gobierno, just inside the entrance facing the Plaza de Armas. During cultural events and festivals other information booths pop up around the city center.

Getting There & Away

Air

Guadalajara's **Aeropuerto Internacional Miguel Hidalgo** (☑3688-5504; www.aeropuertosgap.com.mx) is 17km south of downtown, just off the highway to Chapala. Inside are ATMs, money exchange, cafes and car-rental companies. There's also a **tourist office** (☉8am-6pm).

A multitude of airlines offer direct flights to major cities in Mexico, including the following:

Aeroméxico (☑3833-8282; www.aeromexico.com; Ramón Corona 4386-2, Fraccionamiento Jardín Real, Zapopan)

Interjet (☑800-011-23-45; www.interjet.com.mx; Airport)

Volaris (☑800-122-80-00; www.volaris.mx; Airport)

Bus

Guadalajara has two bus terminals. The long-distance bus terminal is the **Nueva Central Camionera** (New Bus Terminal; Map p570; ☑3600-0495), a large, modern V-shaped terminal that is split into seven separate *módulos* (miniterminals). Each *módulo* has ticket desks for a number of bus lines, plus restrooms, web cafes and cafeterias. The Nueva Central Camionera is 9km southeast of Guadalajara city center, past Tlaquepaque, just off the motorway to Mexico City.

BUSES FROM GUADALAJARA

From Nueva Central Camionera

DESTINATION	FARE (M$)	DURATION
Barra de Navidad	420	5½hr
Colima	188	3hr
Guanajuato	350	4hr
Manzanillo	365	4hr
Mexico City (Terminal Norte)	645	7-8hr
Morelia	345	4hr
Pátzcuaro	305	4½hr
Puerto Vallarta	415	5hr
Querétaro	445	5½hr
San Miguel de Allende	460	5hr
Tepic	210	3hr
Uruapan	340	4½hr
Zacatecas	335	5hr
Zamora	205	2¼hr

From Antigua Central Camionera

DESTINATION	FARE (M$)	DURATION
Ajijic	47	1hr
Chapala	45	45min
Ciudad Guzmán	130	2hr
San Juan Cosalá	50	1¼hr
Tapalpa	85	3hr
Tequila	56	1hr

Buses go to and from just about everywhere in western, central and northern Mexico. Destinations are served by multiple companies, based in the different *módulos*, making price comparisons difficult and time-consuming. The good news is that if you're flexible, you won't have to wait long for a bus. For destinations see the boxed table (p587, departures at least once an hour for major destinations, fares are for 1st-class services).

ETN (www.etn.com.mx; Módulo 2) offers a deluxe nonstop ride to many destinations. You'll pay 20% more, but it's more comfortable and faster and its plush waiting room has wi-fi.

Guadalajara's other bus terminal is the **Antigua Central Camionera** (Old Bus Terminal; ☑3619-3312; Dr Michel & Los Angeles), about 1.5km south of the cathedral near Parque Agua Azul. From here 2nd-class buses serve destinations within 75km of Guadalajara. There are two sides to it: Sala A is for destinations to the east and northeast; Sala B is for destinations northwest, southwest and south. There's a M$0.50 charge to enter the terminal, which offers a **left-luggage service** (◷7.30am-8pm) in Sala B. Bus services run between 6am and 9pm, approximately. Buses leave multiple times an hour for nearby locations, and once an hour or so for longer trips.

Car & Motorcycle

Guadalajara is 535km northwest of Mexico City and 344km east of Puerto Vallarta. Highways 15, 15D, 23, 54, 54D, 80, 80D and 90 all converge here, combining temporarily to form the Perférico, a ring road around the city.

Guadalajara has many car-rental agencies. All the large international companies are represented, but you may get a cheaper deal from a local company, so it's worth comparing prices and availability online before you travel. Prices start at around M$350 per day for a four-door sedan. And it will cost you (upwards of M$3000) to leave the car in any city other than the one you rented it from.

Train

The only train serving Guadalajara is the *Tequila Express* – a tourist excursion to the nearby town of Amatitán (see boxed text, p592).

ⓘ Getting Around
To/From the Airport

The airport is about 17km south of the center of Guadalajara, just off the highway to Chapala. To get into town on public transportation, exit the airport and head to the bus stop in front of the Hotel Casa Grande, about 50m to the right. Take any bus marked 'Zapote' (M$6) or 'Atasa' (M$12) – both run every 15 minutes from about 5am to 10pm and take 40 minutes to the Antigua

Central Camionera, where you can hop a bus to the city center.

Taxi prices are M$260 to the city center, M$240 to the Nueva Central Camionera and M$200 to Tlaquepaque. Buy fixed-price tickets inside the airport, but a M$10 tip to the driver is customary.

To get to the airport from Guadalajara's center, take bus 174 to the Antigua Central Camionera (the stop where you get off is in front of the Gran Hotel Canada) and then get on an 'Aeropuerto' bus (every 20 minutes, 6am to 9pm) from this stop. Metered taxis cost roughly M$200.

To/From the Bus Terminals

To reach the city center from the Nueva Central Camionera, take any bus marked 'Centro' (M$6). You can also catch the more comfortable, turquoise-colored TUR bus (M$12). They should be marked 'Zapopan.' Don't take the ones marked 'Tonalá' or you'll be headed away from Guadalajara's center. Taxis to the city center cost around M$200 unless they let the meter tick (some don't use it).

To get to the Nueva Central Camionera from the city center, take any bus marked 'Nueva Central' – these are frequent and leave from the corner of Avenida 16 de Septiembre and Madero.

To reach the city center from the Antigua Central Camionera, take any bus going north on Calzada Independencia. To return to the Antigua Central Camionera from the city center, take bus 174 going south on Calzada Independencia. Taxis cost M$50.

Bus 616 (M$6) runs between the two bus terminals.

Bus

Guadalajara has a comprehensive city bus system, but be ready for crowded, rough rides. On major routes, buses run every five minutes or so from 6am to 10pm daily and cost M$6. Many buses pass through the city center, so for a suburban destination you'll have a few stops to choose from. The routes diverge as they get further from the city center and you'll need to know the bus number for the suburb you want. Some bus route numbers are followed by an additional letter indicating which route they take through the suburbs.

The TUR buses, painted a distinctive turquoise color, are a more comfortable alternative. They have air-con and plush seats (M$12). If they roar past without stopping, they're full; this can happen several times in a row during rush hour and may drive you mad.

The tourist office has a list of the complex bus routes in Guadalajara and can help you reach your destination. Following are some common destinations, the buses that go there and a central stop from where you can catch them.

Antigua Central Camionera Bus 174 going south on Calzada Independencia.

Av López Mateos Sur Bus 258 at the corner of San Felipe and Avenida Alcalde, or TUR 707 going west on Avenida Juárez.

Chapultepec Par Vial buses 400 and 500 at Avenidas (not Calz!) Independencia and Alcalde.

Nueva Central Camionera Bus 275B, 275 Diagonal, TUR marked 'Tonalá' or any bus marked Nueva Central; catch them all at the corner of Avenida 16 de Septiembre and Madero.

Parque Agua Azul Any bus marked 'Agua Azul' going south on Calzada Independencia.

Tlaquepaque Bus 647, 275B, 275 Diagonal or TUR marked 'Tlaquepaque' at Avenida 16 de Septiembre between Calles Cotilla and Madero.

Tonalá Bus 275D, 275 Diagonal or TUR marked 'Tonalá' at Avenida 16 de Septiembre and Madero.

Zapopan Bus 275 or TUR marked 'Zapopan' going north on Avenida 16 de Septiembre or Alcalde.

Horse-Drawn Carriage

If you fancy trotting around the city in a horse-drawn carriage reckon on paying for M$150 per half-hour or M$200 per hour. There's a carriage stand right at Jardín San Francisco and another in front of the Museo Regional de Guadalajara.

Metro

The subway system has two lines that cross the city. Stops are marked with a 'T.' But the metro isn't tourist friendly because most stops are far from the sights. Línea 1 stretches north–south for 15km all the way from the Periférico Norte to the Periférico Sur. It runs below Federalismo (seven blocks west of the city center) and Avenida Colón: catch it at Parque Revolución, on the corner of Avenida Juárez. Línea 2 runs east–west for 10km below Avenidas Juárez and Mina.

Taxi

Taxis are everywhere in the city center. They have meters, but not all drivers use them. Most would rather quote a flat fee for a trip, especially at night. Generally it's cheaper to go by the meter – if you're quoted a flat fee and think it's inflated, feel free to bargain. From 10pm to 6am a 'night meter' is used and fares rise 25%.

AROUND GUADALAJARA

Beyond Guadalajara's sprawling and seemingly endless suburbs, lonely mountain pueblos and lazy lakeshore towns promise an intoxicating shot of old Mexico. Lago de Chapala, just 45km south of Guadalajara, is Mexico's largest natural lake and offers spectacular scenery, traditional lakeside towns and picturesque pueblos full of retired

Around Guadalajara

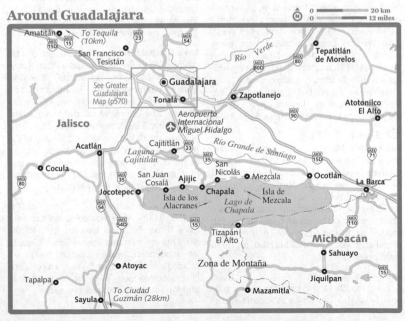

gringos. Further south and west, Jalisco's Zona de Montaña is home to a string of mountain retreats where horses wander free through dusty streets and there's nothing to do but stroll through the pines and sip *rompope* (a local eggnoglike liquor) by the fire.

This region is also a major producer of Tequila: one of the most popular day trips from Guadalajara is to the town of Tequila to see how Mexico's most famous export is made.

Lago de Chapala

Lago de Chapala, Mexico's largest natural lake, lies 45km south of Guadalajara. Surrounded by mountains – some of which tumble dramatically to the shore – its beauty is deep and undeniable, but it's not always healthy. Water levels fluctuate due to Guadalajara's and Mexico City's water needs and on-again, off-again drought. Commercial fertilizers washed into the lake have nourished water hyacinth, an invasive plant that clogs the lake's surface and kills off aquatic life, meaning few people choose to swim here. But beauty and an addictive climate (always warm during the day and pleasantly cool at night) mean that Chapala continues to lure North American retirees to the area.

CHAPALA

📞376 / POP 43.000 / ELEV 1550M

With a commanding location on the shores of its namesake lake, Chapala became a well-known resort destination after president Porfirio Díaz vacationed here every year from 1904 to 1909. DH Lawrence and Tennessee Williams were later visitors, sealing the town's literary pedigree, and today Chapala is a simple but charming working-class Mexican town that makes a popular alternative to the expat community of Ajijic.

⊙ Sights

Isla de Mezcala   ISLAND
The most interesting island to visit on Lake Chapala is Isla de Mezcala. Here you'll find ruins of a fort where Mexican independence fighters held strong from 1812 to 1816, repulsing several Spanish attacks before finally earning the respect of, and a full pardon from, their enemies. A three-hour round-trip boat ride costs M$1500, for up to eight people.

Isla de los Alacranes   ISLAND
A ticket booth at the pier's entrance sells boat tickets to Isla de los Alacranes (Scorpion Island), 6km from Chapala, which has some restaurants and souvenir stalls but is not very captivating. A round trip, with 30 minutes on the island, costs M$450 per boatload; for one hour it's M$500.

Pier   PIER
The pier extends from the end of Avenida Madero, over marshlands and into the sky-blue lake. Relax on one of the white wrought-iron benches and catch an afternoon breeze or some morning sun.

Crafts Market   MARKET
Near the pier is a small crafts market that spills over a network of lawns running parallel to the *malecón* (waterfront walk).

🛏 Sleeping

Quinta Quetzalcóatl   GUESTHOUSE $$$
(📞765-36-53; www.accommodationslakechapala. com; Zaragoza 307; r incl breakfast from M$1125; 🅿😊@🛜🐾) Behind the regal stone walls are a pool, an acre of lush gardens, and plenty of private outdoor space for the nine large rooms. This is where DH Lawrence wrote *The Plumed Serpent* in 1923, and Lawrence fans can even sleep in the room Lawrence himself lived in. Some of the rooms are highly eccentric in style (the riding-themed Carriage House is one thing, while the pink bathroom tower in Lady Chatteley's Lover has to be seen to be believed), but the hotel nevertheless attracts many return visitors. The Australian owners live onsite and are a good source of local information.

Lake Chapala Inn   GUESTHOUSE $$$
(📞765-47-86; www.chapalainn.com; Paseo Ramón Corona 23; r incl breakfast M$1200; 🅿😊🛜🐾) This very imposing white building right on the lakeshore is moments from the center of town and enjoys wonderful views of the mountains. The furnishings here are a little old fashioned, but the views from two of the rooms and the communal terrace are unbeatable. Reductions are available for stays of more than two nights, and the traditional English breakfast is the real deal.

Rincón de los Sueños   GUESTHOUSE $$
(📞765-60-00; www.rincondelossuenos.com.mx; Niños Héroes 59; r incl breakfast from M$625; 🛜) This understated spot offers 17 small-ish, modern and sunny upstairs rooms set around a leafy courtyard. There's a comfortable lobby-lounge, a community kitchen, and long-term discounts are available.

✖ Eating

Seafood joints aimed at tourists can be found all along Paseo Corona (known as the *malecón*); they all have pleasant lake views, although quality can be hit and miss.

La Leña   MEXICAN $

(Madero 236; mains M$40-80; ⊘noon-midnight) Get away from the rather sanitized restaurants around the *malecón* and try a slice of delicious local life at this semi-open-air place on Chapala's main street. With a great selection of meaty dishes, the specialty is the fabulous beef *molcajete* – try it; you won't be disappointed.

Zapote   MEXICAN $

(Morelos 185; mains M$30-60; ⊘2-10.30pm Thu-Tue) There's nothing like a collection of cattle skulls to whet your appetite! This friendly local restaurant could actually be really charming were the TV not always blaring *telenovelas* (soap operas) into the main room. The house specialty is the eponymous *zapote* (chimichanga), but it also does a mean *pozole* and is very popular with locals.

Cozumel   SEAFOOD $$

(Paseo Corona 22A; mains from M$120; ⊘noon-10pm Wed-Mon) The best of the touristy seafront restaurants, Cozumel stands at the end of the waterfront and is very popular with visitors who enjoy the complimentary margaritas served with each meal and who devour the shrimp wrapped in bacon. Service can be rather indifferent, however.

Beer Garden   SEAFOOD $$

(Madero 200; mains from M$100; ⊘noon-9pm Sun-Thu, to 10pm Fri, to 11pm Sat) This Chapala institution has drawn crowds to the lakefront since 1925. Enjoy shrimp, whitefish and, of course, beer on the rambling patio.

❶ Getting There & Away

Buses from Guadalajara (M$45, 45 minutes) to Chapala leave from the Antigua Central Camionera multiple times an hour. Buses connect Chapala to Ajijic (M$9, 15 minutes) and San Juan Cosalá (M$12, 20 minutes) every 20 minutes.

AJIJIC

♪ 376 / POP 15,000 / ELEV 1550M

The wonderfully named Ajijic (ah-hee-*heek*) is an outpost of North American retirees and by far the most sophisticated and energetic of the towns that line the north shore of Lake Chapala. While the gringos may have put Ajijic on the map by opening boutiques, galleries and restaurants galore, much of the town retains its charming, colonial-era vibe, with cobblestone lanes and quiet streets of whitewashed houses. It makes a delightful place to visit, although it's far from the typical Mexico here: English is more commonly heard on the streets than Spanish and prices are relatively high.

🛏 Sleeping

There is no shortage of B&Bs in Ajijic, with many owned by foreign retirees.

Casa Mis Amores   GUESTHOUSE $$

(☎766-46-40; www.misamores.com; Hidalgo 22B; d incl breakfast from M$1000; P❂🐾🛜) Arty without being precious, the town's loveliest guesthouse has a plant-filled courtyard and 12 adobe and tile rooms decorated with local art and Moroccan-style lamps. Bigger rooms are M$200 more each, but all come with gorgeous bathrooms.

La Nueva Posada   GUESTHOUSE $$$

(☎766-14-44; www.hotelnuevaposada.com; Guerra 9; s/d incl breakfast M$1100/1200; P🛜) This rather grand address right by the lakeside offers a taste of genteel, old-world Mexico. The 19 rooms are spacious, with tasteful furnishings, and some have superb lake views. The garden runs right down to the shore, giving you plenty of space to relax (do say hello to Paco the caged parrot). Cash payments get a 10% discount.

Hotel Ajijic   HOTEL $$

(☎766-03-83; www.ajijichotel.com; Colón 33; r Mon-Thu/Fri-Sun M$570/770; P🛜🐾) This low-key hotel is right on the main plaza, with 10 tiled rooms off a beautifully gardened walkway. Rooms are comfy but rather worn. It's one of the best deals in town, though, and the location couldn't be better.

✖ Eating & Drinking

🔺 TOP CHOICE ⟩ Ajijic Tango   ARGENTINE $$

(☎766-24-58; Morelos 5; mains M$75-185; ⊘12:30-10pm Mon & Wed-Sat, to 6:30pm Sun) You'll dine on exceptional Argentine food at unbelievable prices at Tango, Ajijic's most beloved restaurant. The intimately lit indoor-outdoor dining room is always packed with locals and travelers alike, dining on huge, mind-blowingly tender cuts of beef and piles of perfect French fries doused with *chimichurri* (a parsley–olive oil sauce). The wood-fired pizzas look appealing on paper, but don't get distracted: order the steak. Reservations on Friday and Saturday nights are recommended.

THE TEQUILA TRAIL

Tequila, Mexico's most famous firewater and the cause of oh-so-many regrettable late-night decisions, was born nearly half a millennium ago in the state of Jalisco. Today, the highlands and lowlands around Guadalajara are covered in oceans of blue agave – the gorgeous succulent from which tequila is made – and dotted with distilleries ranging from small adobe bunkers to huge haciendas. Many of these welcome visitors, whether or not they have official tours. The Jalisco state tourism department has created its own **Ruta del Tequila** (Tequila Trail; www.rutadeltequila.org.mx) website of suggested tequila-related sights. All are accessible via day trips from Guadalajara.

When imbibing, always remember the wise words of the late comedian George Carlin: 'One tequila, two tequila, three tequila, floor.'

It Begins with Blue Agave

Spanish conquistadors first cultivated the blue agave plant *(Agave tequilana weber)* in Jalisco as early as the mid-1550s. But tequila didn't become popular until after the Mexican Revolution, when José Cuervo introduced the first bottle to the public.

Agave plants are cultivated for eight to 12 years; then the *jimadores* come calling. These tough field hands expertly strip away the spiny foliage until they've found its heart, called a *piña*. The largest, weighing up to 150kg, are hauled from the fields by burros (donkeys), shipped to the distillery by truck and fed into brick or clay ovens where they cook for up to 36 hours. Afterwards the softened pulp is shredded and juiced and the liquid is pumped into fermentation vats where it is usually mixed with yeast.

Five Types of Tequila

Your average cantina tequila is tequila *mixto* (mixed), which can legally contain up to 49% nonagave sugars. The better stuff, which bears the '100% Agave' label, has no additives. Within these two categories, there are five main varieties of tequila.

» *Blanco* or *plata* (white or silver) tequila is relatively unaged, uncolored and has a distinct agave flavor. Best used as a mixer for margaritas or other cocktails.

» *Oro* (gold) tequila is unaged, artificially colored, and best avoided.

» Tequila *reposado* (rested) has been aged from two to nine months in oak barrels and tends to taste sharp and peppery.

» Tequila *añejo* (aged) is aged at least one year in oak barrels. It's sweet and smooth and works best as an after-dinner drink.

» Tequila *extra añejo* (vintage) is aged for at least three years. First sold in 2006, *extra añejo* is the pinnacle of the fast-growing premium tequila market. Sip it neat, of course.

In Mexico you can buy a decent bottle of tequila for M$150, though for something special you'll need to spend over M$300. Treat the good stuff like a bottle of single malt and before you sip it, sniff it a few times to prepare your palate for the heat and it won't taste so harsh.

And don't be looking for a 'special' *gusano* (worm) in each bottle. These are placed in bottles of mezcal (an agave spirit similar to tequila but distilled outside of Jalisco state) as a marketing ploy – and even if you slurp the critter, you won't get any higher.

Number 4 MEDITERRANEAN $$$
([📞]766-13-60; Guerra 4; mains M$100-210; ⊙dinner Thu & Fri, noon-11pm Sat, noon-7pm Sun) This upscale and highly impressive place has been generating buzz all the way to Guadalajara. Chef Greg Couillard's menu borrows flavors from across the globe, from Vietnamese rice noodle salad to an award-winning black-berry and duck confit. The open-air dining room, with a high thatched roof, has a theatrical elegance; the attached bar is the area's hippest. Reservations are recommended.

Yves' Restaurant & Bar INTERNATIONAL $$
(Paseo del Lago 48; mains M$100-200; ⊙8am-8pm; [♿]) Your best bet for a sundowner by

Touring the Distilleries

The town the spirit is named for, Tequila, has the bulk of the tourist attractions, but there are several other worthwhile tequila-producing pueblos within day-trip distance of Guadalajara.

TEQUILA

Designated a *pueblo mágico* (a significant, or charming, village for tourists to visit; literally 'magical village') by the Mexican Secretariat of Tourism, there's nothing particularly enchanting about this sun-baked factory town where tequila got its start. Tequila-barrel-shaped trolleys ply the main road looking to whisk visitors to one of several local distilleries.

Right across from the plaza, **Mundo Cuervo** (www.mundocuervo.com; cnr Corona & José Cuervo; tours M$105-385; ⏰10am-5pm Sun-Fri, to 6pm Sat), a veritable tequila theme park, is the biggest game in town. Hourly tours include tastings and a free plastic cup of margarita.

Five blocks south of Mundo Cuervo, the industrial-looking La Perseverancia distillery **Sauza** (www.sauzatequila.com; Sauza 80; tours M$75; ⏰11am-4pm Mon-Fri, tours 11am & 2pm Sat) has regular factory tours.

The well-done **Museo Nacional del Tequila** (Corona 34; adult/child M$20/10; ⏰9am-4pm) illustrates the history of tequila-making with photos and distillery apparatus.

AMATITÁN

This lowlands town, 39km northwest of Guadalajara, is the biggest tequila-producing pueblo after Tequila itself. The romantic old hacienda of **Herradura** (☎33-3942-3920; Comercio 172; tours M$100; ⏰9am-3pm Mon-Sat, 10am, 11am & 3pm Sun) is Mexico's prettiest distillery, with regularly scheduled English-language tours. Call ahead for Spanish-language tours at the high-end 100% agave distillery **Tres Mujeres** (☎33-3167-9857; Carretera Guadalajara-Nogales Km 39).

ATOTONILCO EL ALTO

Though not on the official Tequila Trail, this highlands town 80km east of Guadalajara is thought by many to produce the sweetest, smoothest tequila due to a high concentration of iron and other nutrients in the red soil.

Call ahead for free tours at **Siete Leguas** (☎391-917-09-96; Independencia 360; ⏰9am-2pm & 4-7pm Mon-Fri, 9am-2pm Sat), a fine tequila distillery located in a large purple building along the main road into town. After your tour, wander along Independencia for great deals on tequila at various distillery warehouse shops.

Organized Tours

Experience Tequila (☎33-3455-1739; www.experiencetequila.com; day trips from M$1325) US tequila aficionado Clayton Szczech offers a variety of individualized private tours departing from Guadalajara, from basic day trips to tequila country to multiday intensive tasting seminars. Book well in advance.

GDL Tours (☎33-1578-0421; www.gdltours.com; per person from M$545) This Guadalajara-based day trip features distillery tours and tastings.

Tequila Express (☎33-3880-9090; www.tequilaexpress.com.mx; adult/child M$1200/800) This popular train-trip/fiesta departs every Saturday from Guadalajara and includes a tour of the Herradura distillery, a mariachi show, lunch and an open bar with *mucho* tequila.

the lake is this popular bar and restaurant right on the beach. The eponymous Yves will make you feel very welcome with anecdotes about seeing the Beatles live as a schoolboy and how he acquired his donkey, Vino Blanco. There's also a full menu and excellent steaks.

Ritchie 88　　　CAFE $
(Colón 41; mains M$30-50; ⏰9am-7pm Tue-Sat, to 4pm Sun; ☎) Just up from the Hotel Ajijic, this friendly little cafe offers a great selection of breakfasts, sandwiches, burgers and burritos. There's a pleasant little back patio for alfresco dining, and local art on the walls for sale.

Café Grano COFFEE SHOP $
(Castellanos 15D; coffee from M$19; ☺9am-9pm Sun-Thu, to 10pm Fri & Sat) The smell of roasting organic coffee will soothe your soul and your conscience, too, because only organic, free-trade beans from Chiapas are roasted and ground here.

ℹ Getting There & Away

Buses from Guadalajara (M$47, one hour) to Ajijic leave from the Antigua Central Camionera multiple times an hour and drop you on the highway at Colón. Buses connect Chapala and Ajijic every 20 minutes (M$9, 15 minutes).

SAN JUAN COSALÁ
📞387 / POP 3000 / ELEV 1560M

At San Juan Cosalá, 10km west of Ajijic, there's a popular **thermal spa** (adult/child M$160/80; ☺9am-7pm) on the lake. It has seven steaming pools, plays loud music and attracts Mexican families on Saturday and Sunday. It's flanked on either side by the hotels below; if you stay at either of these places entry to the spa is free.

Hotel Balneario San Juan Cosalá (📞761-02-22; www.hotelspacosala.com; s/d M$1100/1200; P🅿🛜🏊) has 36 large rooms, all with either patios or balconies: ask for upstairs rooms for lake views. It also features a nicely done new spa and three restaurants.

Villa Bordeaux (📞761-04-94; www.hotelspacosala.com; s/d M$1250/1350; P🛜🏊) is run by the same management as Hotel Balneario, but it's for adults only, which makes a big difference to the atmosphere on a busy Saturday and Sunday. The rooms are more stylish, finished in brick and tiles, but the terraces have a little less privacy.

Autotransportes Guadalajara–Chapala buses depart Sala A of Guadalajara's Nueva Central Camionera every half-hour from 6am to 9pm for San Juan Cosalá (M$50, 1¼ hours). Buses from Ajijic run every 20 minutes (M$9, five minutes).

Zona de Montaña

South of Lago de Chapala, Jalisco's Zona de Montaña – seemingly endless layered mountains – is an increasingly popular weekend retreat for Guadalajarans, who come to enjoy the rangeland, the pines, timeless colonial pueblos, local food and the cooler climes.

TAPALPA
📞343 / POP 16,000 / ELEV 2100M

A labyrinth of adobe walls, red-tiled roofs and cobblestoned streets surround two impressive 16th-century churches. It's no wonder that this old mining town 130km southwest of Guadalajara has become a tourist magnet. Perched on the slopes of the Sierra Tapalpa and ringed by a tapestry of pastureland and pine forests threaded with streams, there is good walking in all directions.

There are two fantastic natural attractions near the town. **Las Piedrotas** are impressive rock formations in cow pastures 5km north of town. It's an easy walk along a country road to these megaliths, past a funky old paper mill. Taxis cost M$60. **El Salto**, a jaw-dropping, 105m-high waterfall, is about 18km south of town (a taxi costs M$120).

Café Molino Rojo (Hidalgo 115; 🛜) rents out mountain bikes for do-it-yourself adventuring (and does the town's best cappuccinos and a mean baguette).

There are dozens of hotels and guesthouses in town, but you should make reservations for Saturday and Sunday and holidays (when Guadalajarans stream in). The pick of the offerings is **Las Margaritas Posada** (📞432-07-99; www.tapalpahotelmargaritas.com; 16 de Septiembre 81; d/q M$600/1200), uphill from the plaza, with well-decorated, rustic rooms with brightly painted furniture. The quads are apartment-style with kitchenettes.

Local street food treats include *tamales de acelga* (chard-filled *tamales*) at the cheap food stalls near the church, *rompope* and *ponche* (pomegranate wine). For something more filling, try **La Troje** (16 de Septiembre 85; mains M$25-115; ☺9am-6pm Wed-Fri, 8am-7pm Sat & Sun), a pleasant upstairs space with a wide menu of local and Asian dishes, an English menu and good breakfasts.

Tapalpa's **tourist office** (📞432-06-50; www.tapalpaturistico.com; plaza; ☺9am-5pm Mon-Fri, 10am-7pm Sat, 10am-3pm Sun) has maps, info and a particularly useful website. There's an ATM on the plaza.

Hourly buses to Tapalpa leave from Guadalajara's Antigua Central Camionera (M$92, three hours); three daily go from the Nueva Central Camionera. There are also four buses a day to/from Ciudad Guzmán (M$66, two hours). Buses in Tapalpa stop at the **Sur de Jalisco bus office** (Ignacio López 10), a block off the plaza.

MAZAMITLA
📞382 / POP 12,000 / ELEV 2200M

Mazamitla, a charming whitewashed mountain town south of Lago de Chapala and 132km by road from Guadalajara, is seldom fully awake. Shops close at 5pm, restaurants open at 6pm and *abuelas* (grandmothers) dressed in black wander haphazardly through the hilly cobbled roads, stopping traffic. Mazamitla sports an interesting take on the Swiss alpine theme and you'll see small storefronts selling fruit preserves, cheeses, *rompope* and *cajeta* (goat's milk and sugar boiled to a paste) around the plaza.

There's a small but lively **market** (⊗8am-9pm) on Juárez. About 5km south of town is the leafy park **Los Cazos** (admission M$12; ⊗9am-5pm), with the 30m waterfall **El Salto**. You can picnic or ride horses here; a taxi costs M$50.

There are a few sleeping options in town; prices rise during holidays. The pick of them is the **Hostal El Leñador** (⊘538-01-85; www.hostalelenador.com.mx; Netzahualcóyotl 4; r M$400-500; P⊗) with modern but large and very comfortable rooms, several of which have balconies with gorgeous views of the town's rooftops and the valleys beyond.

Right on the plaza, **Posada Alpina** (⊘538-01-04; Reforma 8; s/d from M$250/380; P⊗) has a leafy interior courtyard, sweet (if cramped) wooden rooms and outstanding views. It also has a smart restaurant that serves the best *molcajete* (M$85) in town.

Down the hill, **Hotel Cabañas Colina de los Ruiseñores** (⊘538-03-80; Allende 50; r per person M$300; ⊗) is a pleasantly rustic place, with rambling grounds and homey rooms.

The best restaurant in town is **La Troje** (Galeana 53; mains M$70-130; ⊗9am-7pm Mon-Thu, to 8:30pm Fri & Sat), a huge barnlike place decorated with framed tourism posters from around the world. It's famed locally for its excellent seafood, but also for its *trifajitas* (fajitas with chicken, beef and shrimp together).

Mazamitla's **tourist office** (⊘538-02-30; Portal Degollado 4; ⊗9am-3pm Mon-Fri) is by the church. There's a bank on the plaza.

Buses to Colima (M$121, 2¾ hours, five daily), Zamora (M$91, four daily), Querétaro (M$30, one daily) and Morelia (M$218, one daily) leave from in front of the Pemex gas station at Galeana and Guerro.

From Guadalajara's Nueva Central Camionera (M$90, three hours) buses arrive at the small bus station at the corner of 16 de Septiembre and Guerro three blocks north of Mazamitla's plaza.

CIUDAD GUZMÁN
⊘341 / POP 94,000 / ELEV 1500M

Busy Ciudad Guzmán (Zapotlán El Grande) is no tourist attraction, but it is the closest city to Volcán Nevado de Colima, a majestic volcano about 25km to its southwest.

Guzmán's crowded plaza is surrounded by market stalls and shopping arcades set around two churches: the 17th-century **Sagrado Corazón** and a neoclassical **cathedral**. In its center is a stone gazebo with a homage to famous Mexican muralist José Clemente Orozco – called *Man of Fire* – painted on its ceiling. The original is in the Instituto Cultural de Cabañas in Guadalajara. Orozco was born here and some of his original carbon illustrations and lithographs are displayed at the small **Museo Regional de las Culturas de Occidente** (Dr Ángel González 21; admission M$31; ⊗9am-6pm Tue-Sat).

There are numerous hotels surrounding the bustling plaza. The best bet is Colonial-era **Gran Hotel Zapotlán** (⊘412-00-40; Federico del Toro 61; r from M$358; ⊗), set on the main plaza with a pretty tiled atrium full of hanging plants. Rooms at the back are quieter.

The helpful **tourist office** (⊘575-25-27; Colón 63; ⊗8:30am-3pm Mon-Fri) is in the government building on Ciudad Guzmán's main plaza. It can help with planning and booking an ascent of the Volcán Nevado de Colima.

Ciudad Guzmán's modern bus terminal is about 3km west of the plaza near the entrance to the city from the Guadalajara–Colima highway. Hop on Bus 6 (M$5) to get there and back. Destinations include Guadalajara (M$130, two hours), Colima (M$82, one hour to two hours), Tapalpa (M$66, two hours), Mazamitla (M$63, two hours), and Zapotitlán, which passes 2km from El Fresnito (M$12, 15 minutes), the closest village to Volcán Nevado de Colima. An alternative way to reach El Fresnito is taking the 1C *urbano* from the Los Mones crossroad in Ciudad Guzmán (M$6, 20 minutes).

INLAND COLIMA STATE

The tiny but ecologically rich and diverse state of Colima (5191 sq km) connects lofty volcanoes in its arid northern highlands to idyllic turquoise lagoons near the hot and humid Pacific coast. This section deals with the state's inland area; the narrow coastal plain is covered in the Central Pacific Coast chapter (p526).

Inland Colima should become Mexico's next great adventure hub. The famous volcanoes in the north – the active, constantly steaming but inaccessible Volcán de Fuego

(3820m) and the extinct, snowcapped Volcán Nevado de Colima (4240m) – remain the big draws, but the Reserva de la Biosfera Sierra de Manantlán is a jungle-and-limestone playground in waiting, with single-track mountain biking, exceptional hiking and canyons that see a few canyoneers abseiling, leaping into crystalline streams and bathing in the magical El Salto Falls. Tourism infrastructure hasn't caught up to the area's potential yet, so those who like virgin territory should come now.

History

Pre-Hispanic Colima was remote from the major ancient cultures of Mexico. Seaborne contacts with more distant lands might have been more important: legend says one king of Colima, Ix, had regular treasure-bearing visitors from China. Eventually, northern tribes moved in. The Otomí settled here from about AD 250 to 750, followed by the Toltecs, who flourished between 900 and 1154, and the Chichimecs from 1154 to 1428.

All of them left behind exceptional pottery, which has been found in more than 250 sites, mainly tombs, dating from about 200 BC to AD 800. The pottery includes a variety of comical and expressive figures. The most famous are the plump, hairless dogs known as xoloitzcuintles.

Two Spanish expeditions were defeated and turned back by the Chichimecs before Gonzalo de Sandoval, one of Cortés' lieutenants, conquered them in 1523. That year he founded the town of Colima, the third Spanish settlement in Nueva España, after Veracruz and Mexico City. In 1527 the town moved to its present site from its original lowland location near Tecomán.

Colima

📱312 / POP 130,000 / ELEV 550M

Colima is a laid-back city with blooming subtropical gardens, four fine public plazas, a pleasant touch of moisture in the air and the warmest weather in the western central highlands. The city's university attracts students from around the world, while its growing tourism potential derived from nearby canyons, forests and mountains brings in a small but growing number of visitors.

The billowing volcano you see on clear days, Volcán de Fuego – visible 30km to the north – continues to rumble and shake, and the city has been hit by several major quakes over the centuries (the last in January 2003). It's no wonder that Colima has few colonial buildings, despite having been the first Spanish city in western Mexico.

◉ Sights

Cathedral CATHEDRAL
Light floods the cathedral from the dome windows of this would-be relic on the east side of Plaza Principal. It has been rebuilt several times since the Spanish first erected a cathedral here in 1527, most recently after the 1941 earthquake, so it's too new to offer old-world soul, but it remains a focal point of the community.

Palacio de Gobierno BUILDING
Next to the cathedral on Plaza Principal is the Palacio de Gobierno, built between 1884 and 1904. Local artist Jorge Chávez Carrillo painted the stairway mural to celebrate the 200th birthday of independence hero Miguel Hidalgo, who was once parish priest of Colima. The murals honor freedom fighters, the indigenous roots and the beautiful land of Mexico. There's a great collection of pottery in the 1st-floor **museum** (admission free; ⊘10am-6pm Tue-Sun), including some from 1500 BC, and check out the ceramic frogs estimated by UCLA archaeologists to date from AD 600.

**Museo Regional
de Historia de Colima** MUSEUM
(Portal Morelos 1; admission M$41; ⊘9am-6pm Tue-Sat, 5-8pm Sun) This excellent museum has an extensive collection of well-labeled artifacts spanning the region's history, from ancient pottery to conquistadors' armor to a 19th-century horse-drawn carriage. Don't miss the ceramic xoloitzcuintles (Colima dogs) or the walk-through mock tomb excavation.

**Museo Universitario
de Artes Populares** MUSEUM
(University Museum of Popular Arts; cnr Barreda & Gallardo; admission M$10, Sun free; ⊘10am-2pm & 5-8pm Tue-Sat, 10am-1pm Sun) Folk-art lovers will be in heaven at this museum. On display is a stellar collection of masks, *mojigangas* (giant puppets), musical instruments, baskets and wood and ceramic sculpture from every state in Mexico.

**Pinacoteca Universitaria
Alfonso Michel** MUSEUM
(cnr Guerrero & Constitución; admission M$10; ⊘10am-2pm & 5-8pm Tue-Sat, 10am-1pm Sun)

Colima

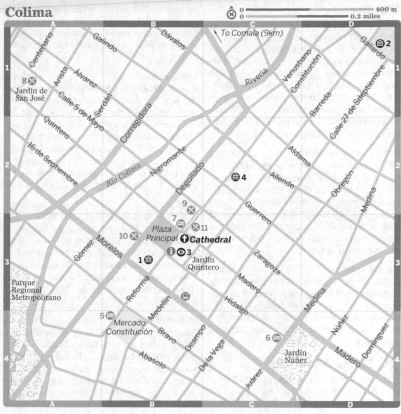

This beautiful museum, in a 19th-century courtyard building, offers four halls filled with surrealist art. Included are a permanent collection of paintings by Colima's Alfonso Michel – whose work has been described as a cross between Picasso and Dalí – and works by other Mexican artists, such as Alfonso Cabrera and Richard Rocha.

La Campana ARCHAEOLOGICAL SITE
(Av Tecnológico; admission M$37; ⊙9am-5pm Tue-Sun) The low, pyramid-like structures at this modest archaeological site date from as early as 1500 BC. They have been excavated and restored, along with a small tomb and a ball court (unusual in western Mexico). The structures are oriented due north toward Volcán de Fuego, which makes an impressive backdrop on clear days. It's about 5km north of Colima city and easily accessible by buses 7 and 22; taxis cost M$30.

🛏 Sleeping

Hotel Ceballos HOTEL $$
(📞316-01-00; www.hotelceballos.com; Portal Mede-
llín 12; r from M$1089; P❋@🛜≋) This Best
Western property has plenty of charm in its
public areas, but its rooms are rather less
characterful and a little overpriced. How-
ever, some of the better rooms have high
ceilings with crown moldings and balconies
that overlook Plaza Principal. There's a small
gym and tiny rooftop plunge pool, too.

Hotel Buena Aventura HOTEL $
(📞136-12-46; www.hotelbuenaaventura.com; Juá-
rez 70; d from M$400; P❋❋🛜) On Jardín
Núñez in the heart of the city, this friendly
hotel is the best value in town. The large
tiled rooms are basic but clean, with queen
beds, air-con (M$50 extra per night) and sat-
ellite TV. There's no food here, but plenty of
options on the doorstep.

Hostal Reforma HOTEL $
(📞330-55-69; Reforma 182; r with/without
bathroom M$270/170; P❋) Near Mercado
Constitución, this sweet budget spot has
friendly management and seven basic but
clean rooms surrounding a tiny Astroturf
courtyard.

🍴 Eating & Drinking

Many small restaurants around Plaza Princi-
pal offer decent fare and are good places for
people-watching on weekends.

TOP CHOICE / Cenaduría Julia MEXICAN $
(Leandro Valle 80, Villa de Álvarez; mains M$25-40;
⊙6pm-midnight Mon & Wed-Fri, 1.30pm-midnight
Sat & Sun; 🍴) Just a M$25 cab ride from the
center of town, this institution is Colima's
best-loved restaurant and wildly popular
any night of the week. The dish to have here
is the *sopitos* (M$30; small circular tortillas
topped with meat, spices and tomato sauce)

as well as the sweet enchiladas (M$24). It
doesn't look like much, but at these prices
for authentic *cocina colimense* (Colima-
style cuisine), it's well worth the short jour-
ney here.

¡Ah Qué Nanishe! MEXICAN $$
(Calle 5 de Mayo 267; mains M$80-95; ⊙noon-11pm
Tue-Sun) The name of this restaurant means
'How delicious!' and the rich, chocolatey, but
not overwhelming *mole* (sauce) is superb.
Other Oaxacan delicacies such as *chiles rellenos* (stuffed chilis) or *chapulines* (crunchy
fried grasshoppers) are also available, and
half orders of many mains are available for
70% of the full price, making for great value.

1800 INTERNATIONAL $
(Calle 5 de Mayo No 15; mains from M$40; ⊙7pm-
2am Tue-Sun) This hip restaurant lounge attracts a late-coming crowd of uni students
for snacks, drinks and, on Thursday nights,
live music from around the globe. The menu
takes in pizza, sushi, burritos and more, but
most people come here to drink and meet
friends.

El Trebol MEXICAN $
(Degollado 59; mains M$25-65; ⊙8am-11pm Sun-
Fri) This long-running family restaurant is a
great spot for breakfast. The scent of freshly
squeezed orange juice perfumes the dining
room, and diners devour *huevos a la mexicana* (eggs scrambled with green pepper,
onion and tomatoes, representing the three
colors of the Mexican flag) and scrambles
with ham, bacon and chorizo.

Pichichi Silvon DOUGHNUTS $
(Constitución; churros M$6; ⊙noon-10pm) Oper-
ating out of a tiny window across the walking street from the Hotel Ceballos, this place
attracts a stream of customers for its addictive *churros rellenos* – hot, sugar-crusted
Mexican doughnuts stuffed with chocolate,
caramel or strawberry sauce.

BUSES FROM COLIMA

DESTINATION	FARE (M$)	DURATION
Ciudad Guzmán	82	1-2hr
Guadalajara	188	3hr
Manzanillo	77	2hr
Mexico City (Terminal Norte)	778	10hr
Morelia	389	2hr
Uruapan	330	6hr

ℹ️ Information

State tourist office (📞312-43-60; www.
visitacolima.com.mx; Palacio de Gobierno;
⊘8am-8pm Mon-Fri, 8am-2pm Sat) Also open
on public holidays.

ℹ️ Getting There & Around

Colima's **airport** (📞314-41-60; www.asa.gob.
mx/wb/webasa/colima_aeropuertos; Av Lic
Carlos de la Madrid Bejar) is near Cuauhtémoc,
12km northeast of the city center off the highway
to Guadalajara (taxis M$120). **Aeromar** (📞313-
13-40; www.aeromar.com.mx; Airport) flies to
Mexico City three times a day.

Colima has two bus terminals. The long-
distance terminal is Terminal Foránea, 2km
east of the city center at the junction of Avenida
Niños Héroes and the city's eastern bypass.
There's a **left-luggage facility** (⊘6am-10pm).
To reach downtown, hop on a Ruta 4 or 5 bus.
For the return trip catch the same buses on
Calle 5 de Mayo or Zaragoza. The destinations
in the boxed table (p598) have multiple daily
departures; nearer destinations such as Ciudad
Guzmán depart hourly.

Colima's second bus terminal (serving local
towns) is Terminal Rojos, about 7km west of
Plaza Principal. Ruta 4 or 6 buses run to Colima's
center from this terminal. To get back here, take
any bus marked 'Rojos' going north on Morelos.

Taxi fares within town are M$10 to M$25.

Around Colima

The outlying villages and countryside
around Colima are gorgeous and demand
exploration. You can visit most worthy destinations on day trips or by public transportation, but a rental car is liberating.

PARQUE NACIONAL VOLCÁN NEVADO DE COLIMA

This national park, straddling the Colima–
Jalisco border, includes two dramatic volcanoes: the still-active Volcán de Fuego and
the inactive Volcán Nevado de Colima. Ciudad Guzmán is the closest city, but Colima
is a more pleasant base. Contact the tourist
office in Colima for a list of operators offering trips to climb Volcán Nevado de Colima.
It can be difficult to find a guide on the fly
if you only have a few days – so it's best to
organize things in advance.

VOLCÁN DE FUEGO

Overlooking Colima, 30km north of the
city, is steaming Volcán de Fuego (3820m),
Mexico's most active volcano. It has erupted
dozens of times in the past four centuries,

with a big eruption about every 70 years. In
June 2005 a large explosion sent ash 4.8km
into the sky, all the way to Colima. Current
information about the volcano is posted on
the website of the **Universidad de Colima**
(www.ucol.mx/volcan).

VOLCÁN NEVADO DE COLIMA

The higher, more northerly peak, Nevado
de Colima (4240m) is accessible on foot for
most of the year. Patches of pine forest cover
Nevado's shoulders, while alpine desert
takes over at the highest altitudes. Area
wildlife includes deer, wild boar, coyote and
even a few pumas.

The best months for climbing are the
dry months of December through May. But
temperatures from December to February
often dip below 0°C (32°F) and snow does
regularly fall on the upper slopes – *nevado*
means 'snow-covered.' Weather changes
fast here and lightning strikes the peak in
stormy weather, so make sure you keep an
eye on the clouds. The park's October to
March hours are 6am to 6pm (no cars up
after 2pm). The summer rainy season is
from July to September, when park hours
are longer.

To get here on your own from Ciudad
Guzmán, take the bus to El Fresnito (M$12),
where you can try to hire a driver to take you
to La Joya/Puerto Las Cruces (3500m); from
there, you can sign in and pay the M$20
park entry fee. Alternatively, you can walk
up, and if so, stay on the bus as it covers
some of the distance beyond the town. If you
plan to hitch up, try coming on a Saturday
or Sunday, when there is a steady stream of
visitors; weekdays can be very quiet.

The *micro-ondas* (radio antennae) are a
strenuous 90-minute hike up from the end
of the road at La Joya/Puerto Las Cruces. If
you want to bag the peak, you'll need another 90 minutes and while the peak is easy to
see, you shouldn't go alone. There are many
trails up and back and it's very easy to get
lost or led to areas with hazardous footing.
Going with a guide or good maps and GPS
(hard to find in Colima) is highly recommended. Bring extra water!

Driving up this volcano on the relatively
good dirt road means that you'll be ascending to a high altitude very quickly. If you feel
lightheaded or dizzy, you may be suffering
from altitude sickness. Descend as quickly
as possible, as this condition can be fatal.
For more on this health problem, see p853.

RESERVA DE LA BIOSFERA SIERRA DE MANANTLÁN

A 1396-sq-km swath of the jungle-clad limestone mountains northwest of the city of Colima is protected by Unesco as critical habitat. It's certainly diverse, ranging in elevation from 400m to 2960m, with eight varieties of forest ecosystem – including tropical, cloud, oak and alpine. This land is rich and alive with nearly 2000 varieties of plants, 160 orchid species, 336 bird species (a third of Mexico's bird species can be found here), 60 types of reptile and the two big cats – puma and jaguar. It's also drop-dead gorgeous with spectacular limestone karsts, narrow canyons and powerful waterfalls.

Adventurers will not be bored. There are canyons to explore, 50km of adrenaline-addled downhill single-track for mountain bikers and an abundance of trekking trails. **Fuego Bike** (☏312-119-95-82; www.fuegobike.com) runs adventure trips to the reserve.

If you choose to go it alone, know that tourist infrastructure is virtually nonexistent. But those who like to break trail will be in heaven.

INLAND MICHOACÁN

Pre-Hispanic traditions and colonial-era architecture meet in Michoacán to dramatic effect. The state is home to three of Mexico's coolest, most under-the-radar cities: the adobe-and-cobblestone town of Pátzcuaro, where Purépecha women sell figs and *tamales* in the shadow of 16th-century churches; the lush agricultural city of Uruapan, gateway to the mythic Paricutín volcano; and the vibrant and cultured colonial city of Morelia, with ancient cathedrals and aqueducts built from rosy pink stone. Michoacán is also gaining renown as a crafts capital – the Purépecha artisans of the state's Cordillera Neovolcánica highlands create wonderful masks, pottery, straw art and stringed instruments – and put on some of the country's best Día de Muertos (Day of the Dead) celebrations. Rich in natural treasures, Michoacán has one of the world's true 'life list'–caliber sights: the annual butterfly migration to the rugged Reserva Mariposa Monarca (Monarch Butterfly Reserve), where millions of mating Monarchs cover the grass and trees in a shimmering Aladdin's carpet.

Morelia

☏443 / POP 600,000 / ELEV 1920M

The state capital of Michoacán and its most dynamic and beautiful city, Morelia is an increasingly popular destination, and rightly so: the colonial heart of the city is so well preserved that it was declared a Unesco World Heritage site in 1991, and its cathedral is not just gorgeous – it's inspirational.

Morelia, founded in 1541, was one of the first Spanish cities in Nueva España. The first viceroy, Antonio de Mendoza, named it Valladolid after the Spanish city and he encouraged Spanish nobility to move here with their families. In 1828, after Nueva España had become the Republic of Mexico, the city was renamed Morelia in honor of local hero José María Morelos y Pavón, a key figure in Mexico's independence.

Sixteenth- and 17th-century stone buildings, baroque facades and archways line the narrow downtown streets, and are home to museums, hotels, restaurants, exquisite bars and rooftop lounges, *chocolaterías* (chocolate shops), sidewalk cafes, a popular university and cheap-and-tasty *taquerías* (taco stalls). There are free public concerts, frequent art installations, and yet so few foreign tourists! Those that do come often extend their stay and enroll in classes to learn how to cook and speak Spanish. Yes, word has started to leak out and more and more internationals are beginning to discover Mexico's best-kept secret. So get here soon.

◉ Sights

Cathedral CATHEDRAL

(Plaza de Armas; ☹8am-10pm) Morelia's beautiful cathedral (unforgettable when it's lit up at night) dominates the plaza. It took more than a century to build (1640–1744), which explains its combination of Herreresque, baroque and neoclassical styles: the twin 70m-high towers, for instance, have classical Herreresque bases, baroque midsections and multicolumned neoclassical tops. Inside, much of the baroque relief work was replaced in the 19th century with neoclassical pieces. Fortunately, one of the cathedral's interior highlights was preserved: a sculpture of the Señor de la Sacristía made from dried corn paste and topped with a gold crown from 16th-century Spanish king Felipe II. It also has a working organ with 4600 pipes.

FREE **Museo del Estado**   MUSEUM
(Prieto 176; ☉9am-8pm Mon-Fri, 10am-6pm Sat & Sun) This museum objectively presents the state's history from prehistoric times to first contact with the conquistadors. Pre-Hispanic arrowheads, ceramic figures, bone jewelry and a shimmering quartz skull can be found downstairs. Upstairs are first-person accounts of how force-fed religion coupled with systematic agricultural and economic development tamed the region's indigenous soul.

Museo Regional Michoacano   MUSEUM
(Allende 305, cnr Abasolo; admission M$37, Sun free; ☉9am-4.30pm Tue-Sun) Located just off the plaza, this museum is housed in a late-18th-century baroque palace where you can view an impressive variety of pre-Hispanic artifacts, colonial art and relics, including one of the carved stone coyotes from Ihuatzio (see p619). There's also an evocative Alfredo Zalce mural, *Cuauhtémoc y la Historia,* on the stairway. It offers a taste of Mexican history with a good-versus-evil twist. Sadly all labeling is in Spanish only.

FREE **Palacio Clavijero**   MUSEUM
(Galeana) From 1660 to 1767 the **Palacio Clavijero**, with its awesome main patio, imposing colonnades and pink stonework, was home to the Jesuit school of St Francis Xavier. After the Jesuits were expelled from Spanish lands, the building became a warehouse, a prison and then in 1970 it was completely renovated, restored and rechristened as state government offices. Today the building houses exhibition spaces showing off high-quality displays of contemporary art, photography and other creative media. It's well worth a visit to see what's happening in the local art scene.

Fuente Las Tarascas   FOUNTAIN
On Plaza Villalongín, this iconic fountain erupts from a fruit tray held by three beautiful, topless Tarascan women. The original vanished mysteriously in 1940 and this reproduction was installed in the 1960s.

El Acueducto   AQUEDUCT
Morelia's impressive aqueduct runs for several kilometers along Avenida Acueducto and bends around Plaza Villalongín. It was built between 1785 and 1788 to meet the city's growing water needs. Its 253 arches are gorgeous when illuminated at night.

Palacio de Justicia   BUILDING
(Plaza de Armas; ☉7am-7pm Mon-Sat) Across from the Museo Regional Michoacano is the Palacio de Justicia, built between 1682 and 1695 to serve as the city hall. Its facade blends French and baroque styles, with stairwell art in the courtyard. An Agustín Cárdenas mural portrays Morelos in action. A small two-room **museum** (admission free; ☉10am-2pm & 5-8pm) shares the history of Michoacán's justice system through old photos and papers (look for the grisly cadaver shots).

Palacio de Gobierno   BUILDING
(Av Madero Oriente) The 17th-century palace, originally a seminary and now state government offices, has a simple baroque facade and impressive historical murals inside. The murals were commissioned in 1961, painted by Alfredo Zalce and are worth a peek.

FREE **Museo Casa Natal de Morelos**   MUSEUM
(Morelos Birthplace Museum; Corregidora 113; ☉9am-8pm Mon-Fri, to 7pm Sat & Sun) José María Morelos y Pavón, one of the most important heroes in Mexico's struggle for independence, is king in Morelia – after all, the entire city is named after him. He was born in this house on the corner of Calles Corregidora and García Obcso, on September 30, 1765. Now home to a museum in his honor, the collection includes old photos and documents. An eternal torch burns next to the projection room.

Museo Casa de Morelos   MUSEUM
(Morelos House Museum; Av Morelos Sur 323; admission M$37, Sun free; ☉9am-7pm) In 1801 Morelos bought the Spanish-style house on the corner of Avenida Morelos and Soto y Saldaña. Today it's another Morelos museum, explaining his role in the independence movement, and has an array of photos, books and antique furniture.

Colegio de San Nicolás   BUILDING
(cnr Av Madero Poniente & Nigromante; ☉8am-8pm Mon-Sat) Morelos studied here, one block west of the plaza. While not another Morelos museum, it has become a foundation for the Universidad Michoacana. Upstairs, the **Sala de Melchor Ocampo** is a memorial to another Mexican hero, a reformer-governor of Michoacán. Preserved here is Ocampo's library and a copy of the document he signed donating it to the

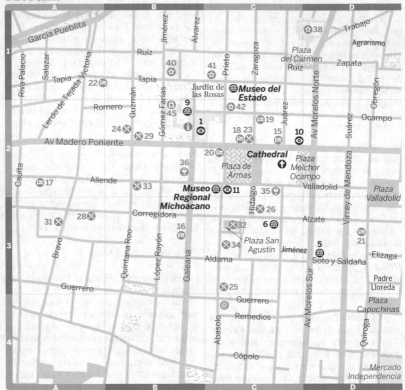

college, just before he was executed by a conservative firing squad on June 3, 1861.

Plaza Morelos PLAZA

This irregular, conspicuously vacant plaza surrounds the **Estatua Ecuestre al Patriota Morelos**, a majestic statue of Morelos on horseback, sculpted by Italian artist Giuseppe Ingillieri between 1910 and 1913. Running from here to the Fuente Las Tarascas is the shaded and cobbled **Calzada Fray Antonio de San Miguel**, a wide, romantic pedestrian promenade framed by exquisite old buildings. Branching off its west end, narrow **Callejón del Romance** (Romance Alley) looks like something out of a vintage postcard, all pink stone and trailing vines. Unsurprisingly, it's a popular smooching spot for young couples.

Santuario de Guadalupe CHURCH

On the northeast edge of the Plaza Morelos, the pink-and-red walls of this baroque church built from 1708 to 1716 bloom with white flowers and glisten with an abundance of gold leaf. There's so much color, the interior (decorated in 1915) feels not unlike a Hindu temple. Beside the church, the much less splashy **Ex-Convento de San Diego** was built in 1761 as a monastery and now houses the law school of the Universidad Michoacana.

Bosque Cuauhtémoc PARK

Morelia's largest park is favored by families because of its shady trees, amusement park and museums, although it arguably is a bit of a let down for a city as majestic as Morelia. On its grounds are two worthwhile museums. Housed in a 19th-century building, the **Museo de Arte Contemporáneo Alfredo Zalce** (Av Acueducto 18; admission free; ⊙10am-8pm Mon-Fri, to 6pm Sat & Sun) has temporary exhibitions of contemporary art. The quirky **Museo de Historia Natural** (Ventura Puente 23; admission free; ⊙9am-6pm), on the east side

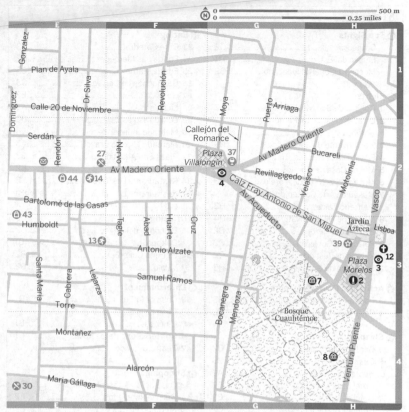

of the park, displays stuffed, dissected and skeletal animals and human fetuses.

🍳 Courses

Few foreigners and plenty of culture make Morelia an exceptional place to learn how to cook, dance and speak Spanish. Ask for a discount if taking a course for more than two weeks.

Baden-Powell Institute LANGUAGE COURSE
(☑312-20-02; www.baden-powell.com; Antonio Alzate 569; private lessons per hr from M$230, group lessons per week from M$2435) The small, well-run and affordable Baden-Powell Institute offers courses in Spanish language, as well as Mexican politics, cooking, culture, guitar and salsa dancing. It books homestays (per day M$380) for students.

Centro Cultural de Lenguas LANGUAGE COURSE
(☑312-05-89; www.ccl.com.mx; Av Madero Oriente 560; group/private lessons per week M$2435/4600) Offers Spanish-language classes running from one hour to four weeks, as well as music, dance and cooking classes. Homestays (per night from M$250, including meals) are available.

👉 Tours

For tours outside the city ask the tourist office for recommendations.

Mex Mich Guías TOURS
(☑340-46-32; www.mmg.com.mx) Provides personalized and small-group tours, including a spooky nighttime Legends of Morelia tour (M$550) and trips to the Reserva Mariposa Monarca (M$550).

Mexico Cooks! CULINARY TOURS
(patalarga@baddog.com, www.mexicocooks.type pad.com) US-born Cristina Potters, a true expert on Mexican cuisine, gives wonderful personalized foodie tours of Morelia, despite now being based in Mexico City.

Morelia

Contact her in advance to arrange a tour of the city.

✯✯ Festivals & Events

In addition to the usual Mexican celebrations, Morelia's many annual festivals include the following.

Feria de Morelia TRADITIONAL
Morelia's biggest fair, running for three weeks in May, hosts exhibits of handicrafts, agriculture and livestock, plus regional dances, bullfights and fiestas. May 18 is the city's founding date (1541) and is celebrated with a fireworks show.

Cumpleaños de Morelos FIREWORKS
Morelos' birthday is celebrated on September 30 with a parade and fireworks show.

**Festival Internacional
de Cine de Morelia** FILM
This major international exhibition (www.moreliafilmfest.com) for Mexico's vibrant film industry brings a week of parties and star sightings each October.

Día de Muertos TRADITIONAL
Michoacán's outlying villages and smaller cities are the top attraction in the week of November 1, but Morelia hosts free flamenco concerts and stunning art installations in and around Plaza de Armas.

Festival Internacional de Música MUSIC
The international classical music festival (www.festivalmorelia.com) occurs for two weeks in mid-November with orchestras, choirs and quartets giving concerts in churches, plazas and theaters around town.

Día de la Virgen de Guadalupe RELIGIOUS
The Day of the Virgin of Guadalupe is celebrated on December 12 at the Ex-Convento de San Diego; in the preceding weeks a carnival erupts on Calzada Fray Antonio de San Miguel.

Feria Navideña TRADITIONAL
The Christmas Fair, with traditional Christmas items, foods and handicrafts from Michoacán, happens during the month of December.

🛏 Sleeping

TOP CHOICE Casa Rosa GUESTHOUSE $$
(☑312-3127, in the US 773-696-5771; www.casadelarosa.info; Galeana 274; r M$745-1300; @🖥🛈) Affable expat Rose and her team have done a great job in converting this old building into an absolutely charming guesthouse, decorated with folk art, bright colors and beautiful furniture right in the heart of colonial Morelia. Weekly rates are available, the communal kitchen and lounging area makes self-catering a cinch and all stays come with the mothering attention of the staff, who you'll almost certainly leave as friends.

Cantera Diez BOUTIQUE HOTEL $$$
(☑312-54-19; www.canteradiezhotel.com; Juárez 63; r from M$2000; P✳🖥) Facing the cathedral is Morelia's slickest boutique hotel. The 11 rooms are all suites, which range from spacious to palatial, all with dark-wood floors, stylish modern furnishings and sumptuous bathrooms you could throw parties in.

Hotel de la Soledad HISTORIC HOTEL $$$
(☑312-18-88; www.hsoledad.com; Zaragoza 90; r incl breakfast M$1500-2000, ste incl breakfast M$2500; P➔🖥) This gorgeous upmarket hotel is housed in an expansive stone hacienda and centered around a courtyard full of palm trees and a burbling fountain. Rooms aren't fabulous but they are spacious and have lovely tile bathrooms.

Tequila Sunset HOSTEL $
(☑313-84-97; www.tequilasunsethostal.com.mx; Tapia 679; dm/r incl breakfast M$180/400; @🖥) This friendly and well-run hostel caters to the young and fun, with spotless dorms featuring skylights and groovy graphic murals, a common room stocked with the latest DVDs, and sparkling, sunny bathrooms. Staff are eager to please, there's a good shared kitchen, and there are laundry facilities and pleasant outdoor areas. It's right in the heart of town.

Hotel Virrey de Mendoza HISTORIC HOTEL $$$
(☑312-00-45; www.hotelvirrey.com; Av Madero Poniente 310; r from M$1800; P✳@🖥) The lobby is drop-dead gorgeous with a spectacular stained-glass atrium, and the rooms have an aging grace with old, wood floors and high ceilings – ask for a room with plenty of windows, as some can be dark. The restaurant does Morelia's swankiest Sunday brunch (mains average M$100), complete with made-to-order omelets, platters of fresh tropical fruits and a dessert table with a flowing chocolate fountain.

Villa Montaña Hotel & Spa LUXURY HOTEL $$$
(☑314-02-31; www.villamontana.com.mx; Patzimba 201; r from M$2850; P➔✳@🖥⛱) Nestled 3km south of the city center is this hacienda-like luxury hotel, with huge elegant suites (think antiques, fireplaces and private stone patios) and breathtaking city and mountain views. The verdant grounds include a heated swimming pool, tennis court, business center and spa. If you don't stay here, come have a drink at the bar.

Hostel Allende HOSTEL $
(☑312-22-46; www.hostelallende.com.mx; Allende 843; dm M$150, r M$250-320; @🖥) A favorite with a mixed-age crowd of international travelers, Hostel Allende has two dorms and 33 private rooms surrounding a leafy courtyard planted with citrus trees. There's also a communal kitchen and a chilled-out vibe. More money will buy you extra space and cable TV.

Hotel Casino HOTEL $$
(☑313-13-28; www.hotelcasino.com.mx; Portal Hidalgo 229; r from M$725; P@🖥) Set front and center on the plaza, this place (until recently a Best Western hotel) has a very chic and inviting lobby area, which contains perhaps Morelia's best restaurant. The rooms themselves are a little less exciting, but its superb location and professional service make it worth considering.

Posada Don Vasco GUESTHOUSE $
(☑312-14-84; Quiroga 232; s/d/tr from M$250/300/420; 🖥) The tiled rooms are small and very bare bones here, but they are also clean: you won't find a better deal for this price and location. Check out the gory crucifix that overlooks the courtyard.

✗ Eating

Morelia enjoys some superb eating options to suit all budgets. Street food can be harder to find, but your searching will be well rewarded.

TOP CHOICE Iglesia La Inmaculada   MEXICAN $

(Tejedores de Aranza 243; items from M$5; ⊙6-11.30pm) Every night for more than 40 years, volunteers have served up local delicacies such as *corundas* (triangular *tamales*), *uchepos* (fresh corn *tamales*), fried quesadillas and *buñuelos* (syrupy doughnuts) in the basement of this huge modern church, with proceeds going to charity. Buy tickets at the counter to redeem for food at the various booths – leftover tickets can be returned for cash. It's definitely one of Morelia's most memorable eating experiences, and you'll be lucky to see another foreigner here! To get to the church, follow the aqueduct out of town along Avenida Acueducto, and Tejedores de Aranza is on your left four blocks after the end of Bosque Cuauhtémoc.

Restaurante Lu   MEXICAN $$

(📞313-13-28; www.lucocinamichoacana.mx; Portal Hidalgo 229; mains M$120-180; ⊙7:30am-10pm Mon-Thu & Sun, to 11pm Fri & Sat) This unassuming restaurant inside Hotel Casino is actually Morelia's most inventive place to dine. Talented young chef Lucero Soto Arriaga turns pre-Hispanic ingredients into exquisite gems of *alta cocina,* all beautifully presented. Her four-course tasting menu (with/without wine M$380/285) is superb, although for something simpler, such as Pátzcuaro-style chicken cooked in orange and chili or fish filet in coconut and avocado salsa, you can order à la carte. Service can be a bit erratic, however; there's no English menu (and the menu is complicated to say the least!), and it's worth reserving a table in the evening.

Los Mirasoles   MEXICAN $$$

(www.losmirasoles.com; Av Madero Poniente 549; mains M$100-300; ⊙1-11pm Mon-Sat, to 6pm Sun) Authentic Michoacán cooking is served up in the sumptuous premises here – try the four-course tasting menu (M$225) for a culinary tour de force. Specialties include Tarascan soup, *jahuácatas* (triangular unfilled *tamales*) with pork and chili and a pork shank in pulque sauce. There's also a huge wine list.

Fonda Las Mercedes   MEXICAN $$$

(Guzmán 47; mains M$150-200; ⊙1:30pm-midnight Mon-Sat, noon-8pm Sun) The bar ceiling at this hip, upscale spot is embedded with 200 clay pots, the intimate courtyard dining room is decorated with old stone columns and spheres and the kitchen serves four cuts of steak 10 different ways.

Pulcinella   ITALIAN $$

(Allende 555; mains M$100-200; ⊙11am-10pm Tue-Sat, 1-5pm Sun) This fantastic new Italian restaurant began life in nearby Pátzcuaro, but has since moved to Morelia along with its growing reputation for fresh and delicious fare. Housed in a converted colonial house and run by a charming family, Pulcinella's specialty is its pizzas, but there's a full range of pastas, salads and meat dishes available, too.

Licha's   MEXICAN $

(Corregidora 669; set meals M$35; ⊙1-5pm) One of Morelia's best deals is this superfriendly place, which serves up what it undersells as *cocina económica* (literally 'economic cuisine') to a crowd of loyal locals. The daily changing set meal includes a choice of delicious starters and main courses as well as a drink.

Restaurante Las Tarascas   MEXICAN $

(Abasolo 313; mains M$25-45; ⊙8am-8pm) This unassuming place is run with great passion and enthusiasm by the young women who staff it. Their specialty is consommé, but they also do a deliciously creamy Tarascan soup and superb enchiladas.

Café Catedral   CAFE $

(Zaragoza 37; mains from M$45; ⊙8am-11:30pm) Packed from breakfast to the wee hours, this is easily the most popular sidewalk cafe beneath the arches across from the cathedral. It has great coffee, hot chocolate, tasty breakfasts (make sure to mix that smoked chipotle salsa with your eggs) and good pizza.

Govinda's   VEGETARIAN $

(Av Madero Oriente 549; mains M$50-70; ⊙10:30am-6pm; 🖈) Despite the Indian name and the Hindu art on the walls, this 2nd-floor vegetarian restaurant is not Indian, but serves an odd, yet tasty, international mishmash of cuisines. Massive combo lunches might include anything from curried broccoli to spaghetti to soy *taquitos* to yogurt.

Fonda Marceva   MEXICAN $

(Abasolo 455; mains M$45-85; ⊙9am-6pm Tue-Sun) Specializing in the cuisine of the *tierra caliente* (hot lands) region of Michoacán's southeast, this lovely courtyard restaurant

TOP MEALS IN MICHOACÁN

» Buying a handful of plastic tickets to exchange for *uchepos* (fresh corn *tamales*), *corundas* (triangular *tamales*) and deep-fried quesadillas in the basement of Morelia's **Iglesia La Inmaculada** (p606). Communal tables mean you're sure to make new friends, and all proceeds go to charity!

» Sampling chef Lucero Soto Arriaga's exquisite pre-Hispanic tasting menus at **Restaurante Lu** (p606) at the Hotel Casino in Morelia. Think miniature *tamales* (masa mixed with lard, stuffed with stewed meat, fish or vegetables, then wrapped and steamed) with dipping sauces and squash-blossom tacos.

» Tucking into so-fresh-it's-practically-swimming trout with macadamia crust at **La Terraza de la Trucha** (p622) overlooking Uruapan's Río Cupatitzio. Wash it down with an avocado shake (way better than it sounds) – you are, after all, in the Avocado Capital of the World.

» Climbing wearily off your horse after the loooong ride up Volcán Paricutín and ambling over to **Maria's** (p624), a rustic food stall at the base of the lava-covered church. María, a local Purépecha woman, will revive your energy with cinnamon-spiked coffee and bubbling cheese-stuffed, blue-corn quesadillas. Simple food never tasted so good.

serves a mind-blowing *aporreadillo* (breakfast stew of eggs, dried beef and chili) and some of the best *frijoles de olla* (beans slow-cooked in a pot) we've ever tasted.

Mercado Independencia　　MARKET $
(cnr Santa Maria & Cárdenas; ⏱7am-5pm) South of downtown, this massive market bustles with vendors hawking everything from DVDs to watermelons, and is a good place to grab fresh bread and steaming bowls of *pozole*.

Gaspachos La Cerrada　　SALAD BAR $
(Hidalgo 67; gaspachos M$23; 🖉) *Gaspacho* – a salad of diced mango, pineapple and jicama, drowned in orange and lime juice and dashed with salt, chili sauce and cheese (optional) – is a local delicacy served all over town. But according to locals, this place is the best.

Mercado Nicolás Bravo　　MARKET $
(Mercado Santo Niño; cnr Bravo & Corregidora; snacks M$20-50; ⏱7am-5pm) Here you'll find great food stalls on the 2nd floor. Try stall 127 for Doña Feli's locally famous *birria*.

Plaza San Agustín　　FAST FOOD $
(cnr Abasolo & Corregidora; ⏱1-11pm) A few cheap food stalls with lots of tables can be found under the covered arches here.

🍸 **Drinking & Entertainment**

Being a university town and the capital of one of Mexico's most interesting states,

Morelia has a thriving cultural life. Stop by the tourist office or the Casa de la Cultura for *Cartelera Cultural*, a free weekly listing of films and cultural events. Nightlife is more genteel than rowdy, though a few clubs keep the music pumping into the wee hours.

Bars
Villaló　　BAR
(☎274-22-31; Jardín Villalongín 42; ⏱7pm-2am Wed-Sat) A gorgeous bar housed in a beautifully converted old villa just by the Fuente Las Tarascas, Villaló gets it all right, with cool live music, superb cocktails, great DJs and friendly, attentive staff. It's best to reserve a table (which is essential on Fridays and Saturdays).

Balcones del Ángel　　BAR
(Valladolid; ⏱5:30pm-midnight Mon-Sat) A hip and beautiful crowd gathers in this open courtyard lounge on the top floor of a 17th-century building just south of the cathedral. The design is seamless, the music bounces between global pop and electronic tunes and the glowing dome of the cathedral is visible through the open roof.

La Peña Colibrí　　BAR
(Galeana 36; ⏱6pm-late) Beyond a heavy wooden door, this intimate courtyard cafe glows with candlelight, illuminating the grinning Day of the Dead skeletons on the walls. Live music starts at 10pm – guitarists pluck weepy ballads, folk singers wail mournfully. Come on Friday or Saturday to

SWEETS IN MORELIA

Dulces morelianos – delicious sweets made with ingredients such as fruit, nuts, milk and sugar – are famous throughout the region. They're showcased at Morelia's Mercado de Dulces (p609) and at **Dulces Morelianos** (Av Madero Oriente 440; sweets from M$5). This old fashioned *chocolatería* is stacked with truffles, preserves, candied nuts and sugary chunks of candied peaches and pumpkin, and patrolled by women in starched green uniforms.

Watch for these tasty treats.

» *Ate de fruta* – jewel-colored squares or strips of fruit leather, commonly made from guava, mango and quince.

» *Cocadas* – chewy-crunchy pyramids of caramelized coconut.

» *Frutas cubiertas* – chunks of candied fruits such as squash, fig and pineapple.

» *Glorias* – cellophane-wrapped rolls of caramel studded with pecans.

» *Jamoncillo* – fudgelike milk sweets sold in rectangles or molded into shapes like walnuts.

» *Limón con coco* – candied lime halves stuffed with sweetened shredded coconut.

» *Obleas con cajeta* – gooey caramel sandwiched between two thin round wafers.

» *Ollitas de tamarindo* – tiny clay pots filled with sweet-salty-tangy tamarind paste.

see a well-known local troupe perform the *danza de los viejitos,* a classic Michoacán folk dance.

Dekopa
BAR

(cnr Gómez Farías & Tapia; ☺5pm-midnight Tue-Thu, to 1am Fri & Sat) This spot on the roof of the Cinépolis building is extremely hip and is a home from home to Morelia's movers and shakers, with commanding cathedral views and great cocktails. During the film festival, producers, directors and stars party here.

Nightclubs

Grand Hotel
CLUB

(Thomas Jefferson 666; men M$100-200, women M$50-100; ☺10pm-4am Fri & Sat) On the hillside 3km south of town, Morelia's hottest club thumps, bumps and grinds to house and pop tunes. Designed to look like an actual hotel, this fun place pulses with pleasure and the VIP room actually *is* a hotel room. With a fabulous view over the city through the huge windows, this place attracts a gorgeous, dressed-up crowd that doesn't stop dancing until sunrise.

Casa de la Salsa
DANCING

(Plaza Morelos 121; admission free; ☺7-9pm Mon-Fri, live salsa music & dancing 9:30pm-2:30am Wed-Sat) Locals converge to shake their collective ass to a rocking four-piece band on a raised stage in this dark, cavernous club. Don't worry, this is not one of those snooty, show-off salsa clubs, so feel free to get loose. Tequila and beer are dirt cheap, which makes the atmosphere lots of fun.

Performing Arts

For international films, dance, music and art exhibitions check what's up at the **Casa de la Cultura** (Av Morelos Norte 485), a hive of creative energy with music and dance classes and a cool coffeehouse set in an old colonial palace.

For theater experiences visit the **Teatro Ocampo** (✆313-16-79; cnr Ocampo & Prieto) or **Teatro Morelos** (✆314-62-02; www.ceconexpo. com; cnr Camelinas & Ventura Puente); the latter is part of the Centro de Convenciones complex, 1.5km south of the city center. **Cinépolis** (www.cinepolis.com; cnr Gómez Farías & Tapia) screens blockbusters in English with subtitles or dubbed Spanish, so make sure you know which show you're seeing.

Conservatorio de las Rosas (✆312-14-69; www.conservatoriodelasrosas.edu.mx; Tapia 334), the oldest music conservatory in the Americas, has frequent concerts inside its ancient stone complex. The **cathedral** (Plaza de Armas) has occasional impressive organ recitals.

Shopping

Casa de las Artesanías
MARKET

(Plaza Valladolid; ☺10am-8pm Mon-Sat, 9am-3pm Sun) If you don't have time to scour the Purépecha pueblos for the perfect folk art piece, come to the House of Handicrafts, a cooperative marketplace launched to benefit indigenous craftspeople. Attached to the renaissance-style Templo de San Francisco, arts and handicrafts from all over Michoacán are displayed and sold here. Prices are high, but so is the quality and all your cash goes directly to the craftspeople. Upstairs, artists demonstrate their craft in small shops that represent specific Michoacán towns. You'll find guitars from Paracho, copper from Santa Clara del Cobre, lacquerware, pottery and much more.

Mercado de Dulces   MARKET
(Sweets Market; Gómez Farías; ☺9am-10pm) This seductive market, on the western side of the Palacio Clavijero, deals in the region's famous sweets, including a rainbow selection of *ate de fruta* (fruit leather) in a variety of exotic flavors.

❶ Information

Dangers & Annoyances
Violent gang warfare has scarred Michoacán for years, most recently following the decline of the La Familia drug cartel, which was quickly replaced by the Caballeros Templarios (Knights Templar), a group of drug-dealing Christian zealots who have killed scores of people around the state. Fortunately, bystanders are very rarely impacted by drug violence in Michoacán. Travelers are unlikely to face anything out of the ordinary except for a higher-than-average army and police presence in some places throughout the state.

Internet Access
La Mancha Internet Cafe (Abasolo 489; per hr M$10; ☺9am-2pm & 4-8pm Mon-Fri)

Medical Services
Hospital Star Médica (☎322-77-00; Virrey de Mendoza 2000)

Money
Banks and ATMs are plentiful around the plaza, particularly on and near Avenida Madero.

Post
Main post office (Av Madero Oriente 369)

Tourist Information
Tourist office (☎317-23-71; www.visitmorelia.com; cnr Av Madero Poniente & Nigromante; ☺9am-7pm)

❶ Getting There & Around

Air
The **Francisco J Mújica Airport** (☎317-67-80; www.aeropuertosgap.com.mx) is 27km north of Morelia, on the Morelia–Zinapécuaro Hwy. There are no public buses, but taxis to the airport cost M$200. Plenty of flights are available to cities in Mexico and limited flights serve destinations elsewhere in North America.

Airlines servicing Morelia include the following:
Aeromar (☎324-67-78; www.aeromar.com.mx; Hotel Fiesta Inn, Pirindas 435)
Volaris (☎800-122-80-00; www.volaris.mx)

Bus & Combi
Morelia's bus terminal is about 4km northwest of the city center. It's separated into three *módulos*, which correspond to 1st-, 2nd- and 3rd-class buses. To get into town from here take a Roja 1 combi (red) from under the pedestrian bridge, or catch a taxi (M$35). First-class buses depart hourly or more frequently for most destinations.

Around town, small combis and buses operate from 6am until 10pm daily (M$5). Combi routes are designated by the color of their stripe: Ruta Roja (red), Ruta Amarilla (yellow), Ruta Rosa (pink), Ruta Azul (blue), Ruta Verde (green), Ruta Cafe (brown) and so on. Ask at the tourist office for help with bus and combi routes.

WESTERN CENTRAL HIGHLANDS MORELIA

BUSES FROM MORELIA

DESTINATION	FARE (M$)	DURATION
Colima	389	2hr
Guadalajara	345	4hr
Mexico City (Terminal Norte)	325	4¾hr
Mexico City (Terminal Poniente)	325	4hr
Pátzcuaro	32	1hr
Uruapan	95	2hr
Zitácuaro	124	3hr

Reserva Mariposa Monarca

In the easternmost corner of Michoacán, straddling the border of México state, lies the incredible 563-sq-km **Monarch Butterfly Reserve** (admission M$35; ⊙6am-6pm mid-Nov–Mar), the site of the butterfly Burning Man. Every autumn, from late October to early November, millions of monarch butterflies flock to these forested Mexican highlands for their winter hibernation, having flown all the way from the Great Lakes region of the US and Canada, some 4500km away. As they close in on their destination they gather in gentle swarms, crossing highways and fluttering up steep mountainsides where they cling together in clusters that weigh down thick branches of the *oyenal* (fir) trees. When the sun rises and warms the forest, they take to the sky in gold and orange flurries, descending to the humid forest floor for the hottest part of the day. By midafternoon they often carpet the ground brilliantly. The best time to see them is on a warm, sunny afternoon in February – they don't fly as much in cool weather.

In the warm spring temperatures of March the butterflies reach their sexual maturity and the real fun begins – mating. When the vernal equinox strikes (March 20 or 21), pregnant females fly north to the southeastern US, where they lay their eggs in milkweed and die fulfilled. Their eggs hatch into caterpillars that feed on the milkweed, then make cocoons and emerge in late May as new butterflies. These young monarchs flutter back to the Great Lakes, where they breed, so that by mid-August yet another generation is ready to start the long trip south. This is one of the most complex animal migrations on earth and scientists still have no idea how or why they do it.

Though monarch butterflies are not in danger of extinction, the migratory behavior of this particular population is threatened by insecticides and habitat destruction. Some organizations are trying to change these patterns by offering local communities incentives to not only protect their remaining forests, but also to restore habitat via tree planting projects. For more information check out www.monarchwatch.org.

The publicly accessible part of the reserve is divided into three areas that are open to visitors from mid-November through March,

🛈 HIGH IS WHERE IT HAPPENS

Monarch butterflies like basking at altitude, so getting to them requires hiking (or horseback riding) up to 3000m. Hike slowly, remember to take plenty of breaks (and water) and be aware of the symptoms of altitude sickness (see p853).

but exact opening dates depend on weather, temperatures and the butterflies' arrival. El Rosario and Sierra Chincua are the most popular reserve areas. Both are accessible from Angangueo. Angangueo is the closest town to Sierra Chincua (just 8km away) and the best base for this end of the reserve. El Rosario is close to the pueblo of the same name and can be reached from Angangueo via Ocampo. Cerro Pelón is the newest reserve area and has the healthiest habitat. It's best reached from Zitácuaro.

At the beginning or end of the season ask for information on butterfly activity at the Morelia or Mexico City tourist offices before visiting the reserve. Some people do day trips or tours from Morelia (p603) or Mexico City to see the butterflies, but this means more than eight hours of travel in one day. It's better to take your time and enjoy this unique and beautiful region.

The reserve areas are spread out, so you'll probably only be able to visit one. But the butterflies all look and behave the same in each spot.

Daily admission for each of the reserve areas costs M$35 and all areas rotate compulsory local guides. Expect to pay around M$150 per horse, if you don't want to hike, plus M$150 for the guide. Note that the length of your hike/horseback ride will be shorter later in the season – the butterflies work their way down as the weather warms up. Parking is M$20.

EL ROSARIO

El Rosario is the most popular area but during the height of butterfly voyeurism (February and March) it gets as many as 8000 visitors a day. It is also the most commercial – souvenir stalls abound on the hillside and the habitat has been severely impacted by illegal logging. El Rosario village and the entrance to the El Rosario reserve area are located about 12km up a good gravel road from the small village of Ocampo. Getting to the butterflies requires a steep hike (or horseback ride) of 2km to 4km from the reserve's parking lot, depending on the time of year. There are a couple of hotels in Ocampo, but it's a far more pleasant experience to stay in the cute village of Angangueo (just 45 minutes on foot from Ocampo).

SIERRA CHINCUA

Sierra Chincua is 8km beyond Angangueo, way up in the mountains. This area has also been damaged by logging, but not as badly as El Rosario. It's a less strenuous hike, so this sanctuary is for those who want an easier walk. To get here from Angangueo take the 'Tlalpujahua' bus (M$1) or a taxi (M$10).

CERRO PELÓN

Cerro Pelón, which is actually located in México state, is the newest reserve area and by far the best choice. The mountains rise high (more than 3000m) here, the forest is in great shape and there is barely a trickle of tourism (on its busiest day it may get 80 visitors; you'll usually find yourself all alone on the mountain). Logging has been eliminated and local guides have replanted trees for years to restore habitat. Expect to see huge, cathedral fir trees, moss-covered trunks, wildflowers and incredible canyon views. Camping in a natural meadow just below Cerro Pelón peak, only an hour's hike from where the butterflies gather in the early season, is a terrific option (talk to Pablo and Lisette at Rancho San Cayetano, p612, outside Zitácuaro for more information). Guides will arrange burros to haul the heavy stuff up the mountain.

This reserve area is about a 40-minute drive southeast of Zitácuaro, Michoacán's third-largest city, where you can buy necessary food, water and supplies. You should bring your own camping gear. There are a couple of access points – Macheros and El Capulín. Both are within 1.5km of each other and can be reached by public transportation from outside Zitácuaro's bus terminal (take a bus marked 'Aputzio,' for M$12, which goes as far as the border to México state, then a taxi, which will cost M$10 to M$20). A taxi straight from Zitácuaro to either of the reserve areas costs M$180 to M$250. The steep hike from the sanctuary entrances to the butterflies can take from 1½ to more than two hours depending upon your fitness.

Angangueo

☑715 / POP 5000 / ELEV 2980M

This sweet, drowsy old mining town is the most popular base for butterfly-watchers, because it's close to both the Sierra Chincua and the El Rosario sanctuaries. The town is layered into the hills, knitted with pine forest, grazing land and cornfields. Most services can be found along a single main drag with two names (Nacional and Morelos). There are two attractive churches on Plaza de la Constitución, the center of town, from which Nacional runs down the hill.

By far the best place to stay in town is **Albergue Don Bruno** (☑156-00-26; Morelos 92; s/d from M$750/895), which offers 30 upscale rooms (some with fireplace) a mile down the hill from the plaza. There's also a decent restaurant on the premises.

Cheap sleeps include the decent **Hotel Real Monarca** (☑156-03-24; Nacional 21; r M$200), with an appealing kitchen; and the less comfortable **Hotel Juárez** (☑156-00-23; Nacional 15; s/d M$150/250), with basic, molding rooms that at least have hot water. Both are a short stroll down the hill from the central plaza.

Restaurants include **Restaurante Los Arcos** (Independencia; mains M$30-50; ⊙10am-8pm) on the main plaza, which serves up tasty *corundas*. Another good bet is the food stalls inside the Mercardo Miguel Hidalgo, just up beyond the plaza on Independencia.

The **tourist office** (☑156-00-44; ⊙8am-8pm Nov-Apr) is just downhill from the plaza.

Frequent buses from Morelia go first to Zitácuaro (M$124, three hours), where you'll hop another bus to Angangueo (M$18, 1¼ hours). From Mexico City's Terminal Poniente you can take Autobuses MTZ (M$140, four hours, every two hours) direct to Angangueo; most of the rest of the bus lines go through Zitácuaro.

To reach the El Rosario sanctuary from Angangueo, first take a combi to Ocampo (M$5, 15 minutes, hourly), then another to El Rosario (M$18, 30 minutes, hourly), from the corner of Independencia and Ocampo. In season there are also *camionetas* (pickup trucks) that leave from the *auditorio* (auditorium) in Angangueo, or from outside hotels; these cost about M$600 for around 10 people and take 45 bumpy minutes (via a back road) to reach the sanctuary.

WESTERN CENTRAL HIGHLANDS ANGANGUEO

Zitácuaro

715 / POP 80,000/ ELEV 1940M

Zitácuaro is Michoacán's third-largest city, but it feels like a provincial working-class town. Known primarily for its baked bread and its trout farms, it is also the best base for visiting the butterflies at Cerro Pelón. Other attractions include the **Iglesia de San Pancho** (☺9am-2pm & 4-7pm) in the village of San Pancho, just south of Zitácuaro. It's the restored 16th-century church that appeared in the great John Huston–Humphrey Bogart film, *The Treasure of the Sierra Madre*. Come at sunset when light streams through the stained glass – take a taxi (M$45).

The best hotel in the entire butterfly region is just a couple of kilometers south of town. **Rancho San Cayetano** (☎153-19-26; www.ranchosancayetano.com; Carretera a Huetamo Km 2.3; s/d incl service charge M$1416/1534; casitas from M$2242; P@☎☎) is owned and run by English- and French-speaking Pablo and Lisette, retirees from Mexico City. Pablo is passionate about butterflies and offers detailed maps and driving directions and shows background videos to interested guests. He can also arrange transportation to and from the sanctuaries. The grounds are huge with stands of pine and fruit trees, and great canyon views. Rooms are rustic chic with exposed stone walls, beamed ceilings and marble bathrooms. And its multicourse, gourmet meals (breakfast/dinner M$196/403) are superb. A taxi here is M$40.

The best downtown restaurant is **La Trucha Alegre** (☎153-98-09; Av Revolución Norte 2; mains M$75-150). There are tablecloths and fresh flowers on the tables and it cooks up local trout 35 different ways. But it's so fresh it doesn't need mushroom sauce or shrimp stuffing. Get it grilled, give it a squeeze of lime and a douse of *salsa verde*. Divine!

Zitácuaro's bus terminal is 1km from the center. There are frequent buses to and from Morelia (M$124, three hours) and Angangueo (M$18, 1¼ hours), among other destinations.

Pátzcuaro

434 / POP 51,000 / ELEV 2175M

This small, well-preserved colonial town in the Michoacán highlands is the beating commercial heart of Purépecha country. Indigenous craftspeople from surrounding villages journey here to sell their wares, and their presence, as well as Pátzcuaro's dramatic history, infuses the town with a palpable mystical energy.

Its center is defined by impressive old churches – including a hillside basilica – dusty, cobbled streets, tiled adobe buildings brushed white and reddish-brown, and two bustling plazas: Plaza Vasco de Quiroga (known as Plaza Grande) and the smaller Plaza Gertrudis Bocanegra (popularly known as Plaza Chica). At night it is so quiet that you can actually hear the wind whisper through the narrow backstreets as you bed down in one of the town's unusual number of charming hotels.

Just 3km to the north lies scenic Lago de Pátzcuaro, ringed by traditional Purépecha villages and sprinkled with a few islands. Isla Janitzio is Mexico's biggest party magnet during early November's Día de Muertos, when Mexican tourists flock to Pátzcuaro, though plenty also come for Christmas, New Year and Semana Santa. Make advance reservations during holidays and bring warm clothes from November to February – you're at altitude here and it gets frigid.

History

Pátzcuaro was the capital of the Tarasco people (now known as the Purépecha) from about AD 1325 to 1400. After the death of King Tariácuri, the Tarascan state became a three-part league. Comprising Pátzcuaro, Tzintzuntzan and Ihuatzio, the league repulsed repeated Aztec attacks, which may explain why they welcomed the Spanish, who first arrived in 1522. Bad idea. The Spanish returned in 1529 under Nuño de Guzmán, a vicious conquistador.

Guzmán's six-year reign over the indigenous people was brutal, even for those times. The colonial government recalled Guzmán to Spain, where he was arrested and locked up for life, and dispatched Bishop Vasco de Quiroga, a respected judge and cleric from Mexico City, to clean up his mess. Quiroga was an impressively enlightened man. When he arrived in 1536, he established village cooperatives based on the humanitarian ideals of Sir Thomas More's *Utopia*.

To avoid dependence on Spanish mining lords and landowners, Quiroga successfully encouraged education and agricultural self-sufficiency in the Purépecha villages around Lago de Pátzcuaro, with all villagers contributing equally to the community. He also helped each village develop its own craft specialty, from masks to pottery to guitars and violins. The utopian communities declined after his death in 1565, but the crafts traditions continue to this day. Not surprisingly, Tata Vascu, as the Tarascos called Quiroga, has not been forgotten. You'll notice that streets, plazas, restaurants and hotels all over Michoacán are named after him.

◉ Sights

Plaza Vasco de Quiroga
(Plaza Grande) PLAZA
Pátzcuaro's leafy main plaza is one of Mexico's best hangout spots. It is framed by the 17th-century facades of old mansions that have since been converted to hotels, shops and restaurants, and watched over by a serene **statue of Vasco de Quiroga** which rises from the central fountain. The arched sides of the plaza are full of food stalls, jewelry and folk-art sellers, and the atmosphere, particularly on the weekend, is wonderful.

Museo de Artes Populares MUSEUM
(cnr Enseñanza & Alcantarillas; admission M$37; ☺9am-6pm Tue-Fri, to 5pm Sat & Sun) This folk-art museum is housed on the former site of the Colegio de San Nicolás, arguably the Americas' first university, founded by Quiroga in 1540. The building was constructed on pre-Hispanic stone foundations, some of which can be seen behind the museum courtyards. Highlights of the impressive permanent collection include a room set up as a typical Michoacán kitchen, cases of gorgeous jewelry, and an entire room filled with *retablos* – crudely rendered devotional paintings offering thanks to God for saving the owner from illness or accident. Some are quite gory. Also don't miss the wooden *troje* (traditional Purépecha house) in the garden.

Plaza Gertrudis Bocanegra
(Plaza Chica) PLAZA
Pátzcuaro's second plaza is named after a local heroine who was shot by firing squad in 1818 for her support of the independence movement. Her statue commands the center of the plaza and she looks like your basic badass.

The local **market** (☺7am-5pm) on the west side of the plaza is where you can find everything from fruit, vegetables and fresh trout to herbal medicines, crafts and clothing – including the region's distinctive striped shawls and sarapes. There's outstanding cheap food, too. A tumbledown **Mercado de Artesanías** (☺8am-6pm) operates on the side street adjacent to the library. Wooden masks and pastel crucifixes are among the crafts sold here. The quality varies but prices are low.

Biblioteca Gertrudis Bocanegra LIBRARY
(cnr Padre Lloreda & Títere; ☺9am-7pm Mon-Fri, 10am-1pm Sat) On the north side of Plaza Chica is one of the coolest libraries of all time, occupying the cavernous interior of the 16th-century San Agustín church. There are oyster-shell skylights and a massive, colorful Juan O'Gorman mural on the rear wall that depicts the history of Michoacán from pre-Hispanic times to the 1910 revolution. On the west side of the library, the **Teatro Emperador Caltzontzin** was a convent until it was converted into a theater in 1936; it hosts occasional films and performances.

Basílica de Nuestra
Señora de la Salud CHURCH
(Plaza de la Basílica) This gorgeous church, built on the hill atop a pre-Hispanic ceremonial site, was intended to be the centerpiece of Vasco de Quiroga's utopia. The building wasn't completed until the 19th century and only the central nave was faithful to his original design. Quiroga's tomb, the Mausoleo de don Vasco, is left of the main doors.

Behind the altar at the east end stands a much revered figure of the Virgin, **Nuestra Señora de la Salud** (Our Lady of Health), which 16th-century Tarascans crafted from a corncob-and-honey paste called *tatzingue*. Soon after, people began to experience miraculous healings and Quiroga had the words 'Salus Infirmorum' (Healer of the Sick) inscribed at the figure's feet. Ever since, pilgrims have come from all over Mexico to pray for miracles. They crawl on their knees across the plaza, into the church and along its nave. Upstairs, behind the image, you'll see many tin impressions of hands, feet and legs that pilgrims have offered the mystical Virgin.

Casa de los Once Patios MARKET
(House of the 11 Courtyards; Madrigal de las Altas Torres) This cool, rambling colonial edifice was built as a Dominican convent in the 1740s. (Before that, the site held one of Mexico's first hospitals, founded by Vasco de Quiroga.) Today it houses small *artesanías* (handicrafts) shops, each specializing in a particular regional craft. Look for copperware from Santa Clara del Cobre and musical instruments from Paracho, as well as lacquerware, hand-painted ceramics and

Pátzcuaro

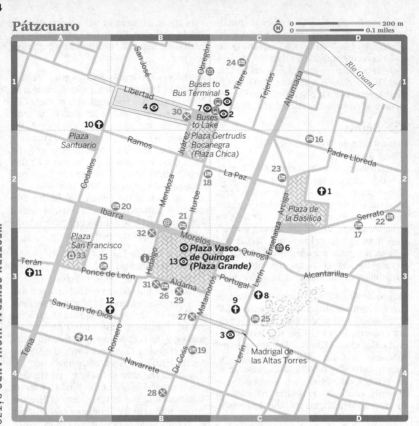

vibrant textiles. You'll likely find privacy on the top floors where you can take in the surrounding natural and architectural beauty.

Most shops are open from 10am to 7pm daily, with a lunch break in the afternoon.

Churches
CHURCH

Built in the 16th century, the **Templo de la Compañía** (cnr Lerín & Portugal) became a Jesuit training college in the 17th century. The church is still in use and houses some Vasco de Quiroga relics. The adjacent college building fell into ruin after the expulsion of the Jesuits. It is now used for community activities and often has free temporary exhibits.

Pátzcuaro has several other old churches of interest, including the creaky **Templo del Sagrario** (cnr Lerín & Portugal), **Templo San Juan de Dios** (cnr Romero & San Juan de Dios), the pink stone **Templo San Francisco** (Tena) and **Templo El Santuario** (cnr Ramos & Codallos).

El Estribo
HILL

This hilltop lookout, 3.5km west of the city center and popular with joggers, walkers and couples, has a great view of Lago de Pátzcuaro. It takes about an hour to traverse the cobbled, cypress-lined road up to the viewing pavilion. Take Ponce de León from the southwest corner of Plaza Grande and follow the signs.

🎓 Courses

Centro de Lenguas y Ecoturismo de Pátzcuaro
LANGUAGE COURSE

(CELEP; ☎342-47-64; www.celep.com.mx; Navarrete 50; 2-week Spanish-language course M$4800, language & culture program M$7400) Courses here involve four to six hours of classes Monday to Friday. Cultural programs include seminars in Mexican literature and excursions to the butterfly sanctuary (in season) and local villages. Homestays, in-

Pátzcuaro

cluding meals with local families, can also
be arranged.

Tours

Several tour guides operate around the
Pátzcuaro area.

Miguel Ángel Núñez   TOUR GUIDE
(cell phone 443-1093516; casadetierra@hotmail.
com) English-speaking Miguel Ángel Núñez,
an anthropologist, offers insider tours of the
Pátzcuaro area and throughout Michoacán.
He covers indigenous culture, archaeology,
colonial history, art and architecture. Tour
prices depend on the destination, but local
tours cost M$350 per person; transportation
is provided. He can also organize cooking
classes and food tours upon request.

Bird Guides of Pátzcuaro   TOUR GUIDE
(112-28-61; http://patzcuarobirder.blogspot.com)
Georgia Conti, a US expat living in Pátzcuaro,
has set up this excellent organization, offering tours with her or her Purépecha col-
league Victor Hugo Valencia. Itineraries are
created based on what bird-watchers want
to see after an initial online chat. Daily rates

are US$50 to US$80 per person, with extras
charged for transportation, meals and other
incidentals. Contact Georgia via her blog to
find out what she proposes for you.

Festivals & Events

The villages around Pátzcuaro, most notably Tzintzuntzan and Isla Janitzio, stage the
most popular (and crowded!) **Día de Muertos** (Day of the Dead) celebrations in Mexico
on November 1 and 2. Parades, crafts markets, dancing, ceremonies, exhibitions and
concerts are held in and around Pátzcuaro
on the days before and after Día de Muertos. Cemeteries are packed with observants
throughout the festivities.

Other interesting events in Pátzcuaro include the following:

Semana Santa   RELIGIOUS
Easter week is full of events in Pátzcuaro
and the lakeside villages, including Palm
Sunday processions; Viacrucis processions
on Good Friday morning, enacting Christ's
journey to Calvary and the crucifixion;
candlelit processions in silence on Good
Friday evening; and, on Easter Sunday

evening, a ceremonial burning of Judas in Plaza Grande.

Nuestra Señora de la Salud RELIGIOUS
On December 8 a colorful procession to the basilica honors Our Lady of Health. Traditional dances are performed, including Los Reboceros, Los Moros, Los Viejitos and Los Panaderos.

Pastorelas RELIGIOUS
These dramatizations of the shepherds' journey to see the infant Jesus are staged in Plaza Grande around Christmas. *Pastorelas indígenas,* on the same theme but including mask dances, enact the struggle of angels against the devils that are trying to hinder the shepherds. These *pastorelas* are held in eight villages around Lago de Pátzcuaro, on different days between December 26 and February 2.

🛏 Sleeping

Pátzcuaro has an excellent range of attractive places to stay and caters to all budgets. Despite this, it's usually worth booking ahead for Friday and Saturday nights, and months ahead for Día de Muertos, when the entire town is booked up well in advance.

TOP CHOICE La Casa Encantada B&B $$$
(☎342-34-92; www.lacasaencantada.com; Dr Coss 15; r incl breakfast from M$1230; ᵽ@🐾) If you are craving for affordable luxury, this intimate Australian- and Canadian-owned B&B offers 12 elegant rooms with local rugs and beautifully tiled bathrooms in a converted 1784 mansion. The friendly owners will happily show you around the place and point out lots of fascinating historical detail. The vegetarian gourmet breakfasts are a real high point and there's a 30% discount between May and September.

Casa de la Real Aduana BOUTIQUE HOTEL $$$
(☎342-02-65; www.realaduana.com; Ponce de León 16; r incl breakfast M$3600; ᵽ🐾) Pátzcuaro's best rooms can be snagged at this converted 16th-century colonial house, run by artists and art collectors who have assembled an amazing selection of art and antiques. The rooms are large and have modern touches such as DVD players and flat-screen TVs, as well as plush linens and gorgeous furnishings, while the stunning courtyard can be hard to leave on a sunny morning. No kids allowed.

Mansión Iturbe BOUTIQUE HOTEL $$$
(☎342-03-68; www.mansioniturbe.com; Portal Morelos 59; r incl breakfast M$2800; 🐾) The rack rates at this very impressive hotel are steep, but in reality there are often big discounts of up to 70% to be had, making it far more affordable. Right on the main square, the rooms here are spacious, furnished in heavy dark woods crammed full of antiques, and feature sumptuous bathrooms. There's a wonderful terrace out the back and the feel is one of luxurious sophistication.

Posada de la Basílica BOUTIQUE HOTEL $$$
(☎342-11-08; www.posadalabasilica.com; Arciga 6; r incl breakfast M$1500, ste incl breakfast M$1800-2200; ᵽ@🐾) For rustic luxury, consider this boutique hotel with a terracotta rooftop and lake views. The surprisingly bright colonial building contains 12 huge rooms with wood floors and open fireplaces. The master suites are truly special, and the entire place exudes elegance, charm and understatement.

La Mansión de los Sueños BOUTIQUE HOTEL $$$
(☎342-11-03; www.mansiondelossuenos.com; Ibarra 15; r/ste incl breakfast M$2445/4271; 🐾) This restored mansion built around three adjacent courtyards offers some of the most luxurious accommodations in town. There is art on every wall, coffee machines and minibars in each room, and even fireplaces and lofts in some. The folk art and decor won't be to everyone's taste, so ask to see a few rooms before deciding which you'd like. There's 50% off the rack rates if you pay in cash (though breakfast is not included), which actually makes for a great deal.

Hotel Portón del Cielo BOUTIQUE HOTEL $$$
(☎342-75-11; www.portondelcielo.com; Camino Real al Estribo 31; r from M$1350; ᵽ🐾) This 10-room place on the Estribo Hill outside of town has breathtaking views towards Lago de Pátzcuaro from each of its very comfortable rooms. Rooms come with fireplaces and, rather unfortunately, modern bathrooms. The entire place is self-contained with a good restaurant and plenty of activities on offer, making it a great place for a romantic getaway. It's best to have a car if you plan to stay here.

Posada San Rafael HOTEL $
(☎342-07-70; Portal Aldama 13; s/d M$300/420; ᵽ🐾) The love child of a colonial mission and a US motel, rooms open onto wide verandas overlooking a driveway and parking area. Service could be friendlier and hot wa-

ter is limited to mornings and evenings, but upstairs rooms are a great deal, with plenty of beautiful details such as columns and beamed ceilings.

Mesón de San Antonio GUESTHOUSE $$
(☑342-25-01; www.mesondesanantonio.com; Serrato 33; s/d M$600/750; @🛜) This old hacienda-style inn is the best of the mid-rangers by far. Rooms border an impressive colonial courtyard, the beamed overhangs are held up by ancient timbers and the extremely cozy rooms are decorated with fine Purépecha pottery and have wood-burning fireplaces and cable TV. There's also a communal kitchen for self-caterers.

Hostal Santa Fe GUESTHOUSE $$
(☑342-05-12; Padre Lloreda 27; s/d/tr incl breakfast M$550/650/750; P🛜) With pottery on the tiled floors and ironwork on the walls, the sunken lobby is as inviting as it is unusual. There's a pleasant back garden and rooms are stuffed full of antiques: the typewriter in room 6 has to be seen to be believed, while room 9 has a romantic terrace.

Posada Mandala GUESTHOUSE $
(☑342-41-76; Lerín 14; r M$300-500, without bathroom M$200; 🛜) Arty international travelers love this low-profile guesthouse, with six simple, whitewashed rooms surrounding a small plant-filled courtyard. The best rooms are those upstairs, with their own facilities and great views over the rooftops of Pátzcuaro.

Posada de los Ángeles GUESTHOUSE $
(☑342-24-40; hposadaangeles@hotmail.com; Títere 17; r M$300; 🛜) One of the town's cheapest options, the rooms here may have tiny bathrooms but they're colorful and there are great views to be had from the upstairs terrace. The friendly owner is delightful and there's even a sunny garden to relax in.

Hotel Posada de la Salud GUESTHOUSE $
(☑342-00-58; www.posadadelasalud.com.mx; Serrato 9; s/d/tr M$200/350/420; 🛜) A lovely, rambling hotel painted in a pastel yellow that just feels like Mexico. There's cable TV, clean rooms, a pleasant lawn out the back and you're in the center of town.

Hotel Rincón de Josefa HOTEL $$
(☑342-55-02; www.hotelrincondejosefa.com.mx; Iturbe 29; s/d M$470/550; P🛜) Well located between the two plazas is this slightly eccentric place. The 60 rooms are all unique, ranging from small and damp in the lower

categories to spacious and comfortable in the higher ones. Some have arced brick ceilings and are furnished with antiques.

✖ Eating

Pátzcuaro has wonderful street food – look out for *corundas* (triangular *tamales* served with and without fillings), bright green *atole de grano* (an anise-flavored local variant of the popular corn-based drink), *nieve de pasta* (almond and cinnamon ice cream) and chunks of candied squash. Some of the best chow can be found at the food stalls in the open-air market on the northwest corner of the Plaza Chica. If it's *corundas* you're after, head to the basilica in the morning and look for the elderly ladies with baskets.

Sadly, decent restaurants are harder to find in Pátzcuaro: many cater to tourists and are fussy and mediocre. Keep your eyes open for *sopa tarasca,* a rich tomato-based soup with cream, dried chili and bits of crisp tortilla.

TOP
CHOICE **Doña Toya** MEXICAN $
(Dr Coss 68; sopes M$8; ⊙7-10:30pm Tue-Sun) At the top of a cobblestone hill and behind an unmarked red door, doña Toya serves up the city's finest *sopes* – disks of fried masa (dough) topped with shredded meat, salsa, squeezed lime and fresh cilantro – at little plastic tables in her home's front room. Look no further for a true local dining experience, not to mention one of the best and cheapest meals in town.

El Patio MEXICAN $
(Portal Aldama 19; mains M$55-80; ⊙8am-10pm) With much coveted seating on the Plaza Grande, this friendly restaurant makes a great spot for breakfast in the sun, or a more formal meal any time of day, with a large menu full of Mexican classics.

Priscilla's MEXICAN $$
(Ibarra 15; mains M$75-140; ⊙noon-10.30pm) This smart restaurant inside posh La Mansión de los Sueños makes for a great meal in its charming courtyard setting. Specialties here include seafood, pasta dishes and Mexican *cocina típica*.

La Surtidora MEXICAN $$
(Portal Hidalgo 71; mains M$65-140; ⊙8am-10pm; 🛜) Waiters are dressed in chef whites and take good care of their clientele at this old-school cafe-cum-deli, which has been in operation on Plaza Grande since 1916. The beamed interior is perfumed with roasting

BUSES FROM PÁTZCUARO

DESTINATION	FARE (M$)	DURATION
Erongarícuaro	11	35min
Guadalajara	305	4½hr
Mexico City (Terminal Norte)	370	5½hr
Mexico City (Terminal Poniente)	370	5½hr
Morelia	32	1hr
Quiroga	15	35min
Tzintzuntzan	13	20min
Uruapan	48	1hr

coffee, it serves all manner of breakfasts, salads, soups and sandwiches, and goodies on sale include cigars and mezcal.

D'La Calle Coss
ARGENTINE $$

(Dr Coss 4; mains M$80-110; ☺noon-9pm Tue-Sun) This attractive enclosed courtyard restaurant serves steak in a variety of ways, such as *milanesa* (pounded thin and breaded) and *chimichurri* (marinated in a garlic, parsley and olive oil sauce). It also has a fantastic Argentine wine list.

La Casa de Arcángeles
MEXICAN $

(Portal Aldama 12; mains M$70-110; ☺8am-10pm) This bright courtyard cafe attached to Hotel Misión San Manuel serves all the typical Mexican favorites. Pátzcuaro's youngest mariachi band performs on Saturday and Sunday, which makes for a lively evening of entertainment.

🛍 Shopping

The Casa de los Once Patios (p613) is a good place to seek Michoacán crafts, but you'll get better deals on similar work in the main market and the Mercado de Artesanías, both next to Plaza Chica. On Friday mornings a ceramics market, with pottery from surrounding villages, is held in Plaza San Francisco. There's also a small crafts market in front of the basilica every day.

There are countless villages within a few hours of Pátzcuaro and they all specialize in different crafts. Shoppers will enjoy the hunt.

ℹ Information

Several banks in the center will change currency; all have ATMs.

Meganet (Portal Morelos 64; internet per hr M$12; ☺9am-10pm)

Municipal tourist office (📞344-34-86; Portal Hidalgo 1; ☺9am-8pm)

Post office (Obregón 13; ☺9am-4pm Mon-Fri, to 1pm Sat)

ℹ Getting There & Around

Pátzcuaro's bus terminal is 1.5km southwest of the city center. It has a cafeteria and left-luggage services.

To catch a bus heading to the center, walk outside the terminal, turn right and at the corner take any bus marked 'Centro' (M$5). Taxis cost M$25 (with a small surcharge after 11pm).

Buses back to the terminal (marked 'Central') leave from the northeast corner of Plaza Chica. Buses to the boat pier (marked 'Lago'; M$5, five minutes) also leave from here and run from about 6am to 10pm daily.

Common destinations that have multiple daily services include those in the boxed table (prices quoted are for 1st-class fares).

Around Pátzcuaro

LAGO DE PÁTZCUARO

About 3km north of central Pátzcuaro you will come over a rise to find a lake so blue that its edge blends seamlessly with the sky. Within it are a few populated islands. It is stream fed and natural, and though pollution is a concern, it's still damn beautiful.

To get to the Muelle General, take a bus marked 'Lago' from Pátzcuaro's Plaza Chica (M$5, five minutes). The dock caters to tourists in a profoundly cheesy way – with cheap fish eateries and souvenir shops. The ticket office is about 50m down on the right-hand side.

Isla Janitzio is a popular weekend and holiday destination. It's heavily devoted to tourism, with lots of low-end souvenir stalls, fish restaurants and drunk college kids on holiday. But it is car-free and threaded with footpaths that eventually wind their way to the top of the island, where you'll find a 40m-high **statue** (admission M$6) of independence hero José María Morelos y Pavón. Inside the statue are murals depicting Morelos' life. Want a stellar panoramic view? Climb up to his see-through wrist.

Hotel Terhunukua (r M$250; 🛜) has small, modest rooms (some with views) and is 50m straight up from the island's dock. Grab a M$10 cup of fried *charoles* (tiny sardinelike fish) before you leave – they're the island's official snack food.

Round-trip boat rides to Janitzio cost M$45 and take 25 minutes each way; they leave when full (about every 30 minutes, quicker on Saturday and Sunday).

LAKESIDE VILLAGES

The villages surrounding Lago de Pátzcuaro make perfect day trips from Pátzcuaro and almost all can be reached by local transportation from Pátzcuaro's bus terminal. Or, to avoid backtracking to the bus station, take a 'Lago' bus from Plaza Chica and get off anywhere between the Posada de don Vasco and Hwy 14; then wait by the roadside for a bus heading to your village. Buses to Ihuatzio run directly from Plaza Chica.

Frequent combis run between the villages, so you can visit several in one day. Transportation between Quiroga and Erongarícuaro is infrequent, however, so travel between the two may be quicker via Pátzcuaro.

IHUATZIO

Ihuatzio, 14km from Pátzcuaro, was capital of the Tarascan kingdom after Pátzcuaro (but before Tzintzuntzan). Today it's just a slow, dusty village where everyone knows everyone else, until *you* walk into town.

Lago de Pátzcuaro

The large and partially restored **Ihuatzio archaeological site** (admission M$31; ⊘9am-5pm) lies just over 1km up a cobbled road from the village's small plaza. The ruins' best attraction is an open ceremonial space. It is 200m long and features two pyramid-like structures at its west end. Climbing the pyramids is forbidden, but it is possible to walk to the top of the restored wall to their left (south) for good views. Two carved stone coyotes were found at the site; one is in the National Anthropology Museum in Mexico City, the other can be found at the Museo Regional Michoacano in Morelia.

To experience a night or two in an indigenous pueblo, head to the rustic-chic, adobe B&B **Casa Santiago** (☑434-344-08-80; www.casasantiagomex.com; r incl breakfast M$1230; 🛜), located 1.5km west of Ihuatzio on the road to Cucuchucho. The owners, a friendly, knowledgeable US-Purépecha couple, run shopping tours and cook delectable local meals upon request.

TZINTZUNTZAN

The tiny town of Tzintzuntzan (tseen-*tsoon*-tsahn), about 15km north of Pátzcuaro, was once the Tarascan capital and served as Vasco de Quiroga's first base in the region. It has a beautiful sprawling cemetery that blooms with flowers and crepe paper during heady Day of the Dead celebrations, crumbling Tarascan ruins and some relics from the early Spanish missionary period. The town's pulse comes from its thriving Saturday and Sunday **crafts market**, saintly Quiroga's beloved olive grove and two old churches.

On the lake side of Avenida Cárdenas lies the **Ex-Convento de San Francisco**, a religious compound built partly with stones from the Tarascan site up the hill which the Spanish demolished. This is where Franciscan monks began the Spanish missionary effort in Michoacán in the 16th century. The gnarled, shady olive trees in the churchyard came from seedlings planted by Vasco de Quiroga; they're believed to be the oldest olive trees in the Americas.

Straight ahead as you enter the churchyard is the crumbling, but still-functioning **Templo de San Francisco**, built exclusively for the monks. Vegetation sprouts from its facade and the lovely cloister, to the left of the *templo*, includes a set of faded murals around the galleries and Mudejar-patterned wooden ceiling ornamentation.

Toward the right rear corner of the complex stands the church built for the Purépecha masses, the **Templo de Nuestra Señora de la Salud**. Inside is El Santo Entierro de Tzintzuntzan, a much-revered image of Christ. For most of the year it lies in a *caja de cristal* (glass coffin). During Day of the Dead celebrations it is festooned with fruit and marigolds. On Good Friday, following an elaborate costumed passion play, the image is removed from its coffin and nailed to the large cross; being a Cristo de Goznes (hinged Christ), his arms can be extended and his legs crossed. Afterwards, the image is paraded through town until dark, when it is returned to the church. Pilgrims descend from all over, some in chains or carrying crosses, some crawling on their knees.

Head out the monastery's front gate, across the highway and up the hill and you'll find the **Tzintzuntzan archaeological site** (Las Yácatas; admission M$41; ⊘10am-5pm), an impressive group of five round, reconstructed temples known as *yácatas*. They are all that remain of the mighty Tarascan empire. The hillside location offers wonderful views of the town, lake and surrounding mountains, and is interesting to see, as it's still being excavated.

QUIROGA

The bustling market town of Quiroga, named for the man responsible for many of its buildings and handicrafts, is 7km northeast of Tzintzuntzan. Every day there's a busy crafts market and there are hundreds of shops selling brightly painted wooden, ceramic and leather goods, as well as colorful woolen sweaters and sarapes. The town is set at the crossroads of Hwys 15 and 120, so there is seldom a dearth of shoppers.

Traffic also stops for Quiroga's famous *carnitas* (chunks of slow-cooked pork) – there are dozens of *carnitas* stands and storefronts to choose from.

On the first Sunday in July the **Fiesta de la Preciosa Sangre de Cristo** (Festival of the Precious Blood of Christ) is celebrated with a long torchlight procession led by a group carrying an image of Christ crafted from a paste made of corncobs and honey.

ERONGARÍCUARO

A pretty 18km trip west from Pátzcuaro, Erongarícuaro (or 'Eronga') is one of the oldest settlements on the lake. French poet André Breton (1896–1966) lived here for a time in the '50s, visited occasionally by Diego Rivera and Frida Kahlo. Breton made the unusual wrought-iron cross in the forecourt of the church. There are gorgeous gardens behind the old seminary attached to the church, and a *troje* (traditional Purépecha house).

A few kilometers south of town, on the circular road around the lake, German-born Rolf Günter Hoppe runs a deliciously retro Bavarian-themed roadhouse, **Campestre Alemán** (☑434-344-00-06; www.campestrealeman.com; Km 14; mains M$80-170; ☉noon-7pm). Carloads of middle-class Mexican families tuck into platters of house-smoked trout, sausages and apple strudel at tables overlooking a pond teeming with fat white ducks. After lunch you can fish, rent a rowboat or buy German jam at the gift shop. Fun.

TÓCUARO

Some of Mexico's finest mask-makers live in this cobblestoned town surrounded by cornfields, 10km west of Pátzcuaro. But there are no traditional shopfronts – just a sign here and there signifying entry into family courtyard compounds with workshops and showrooms.

Prepare to spend. It takes a month or more to produce a fine mask, carved from a single piece of wood. The best ones are wonderfully expressive and surreal and, thanks to a growing legion of global collectors, can cost hundreds of dollars.

Uruapan

☑452 / POP 250,000 / ELEV 1620M

All praise the thundering Río Cupatitzio. This impressive river begins life underground, then rises sensationally to the surface, feeding a subtropical garden of palms, orchids and massive shade trees in urban Uruapan's Parque Nacional Barranca del Cupatitzio. Without the river, the city would not exist. When Spanish monk Fray Juan de San Miguel arrived here in 1533 he was so taken with his surroundings that he gave the area the Purépecha name, Uruapan (oo-roo-*ah*-pahn), which roughly translates into 'Eternal Spring.' Fray Juan designed a large market square – still a hit with area families on weekends – built a hospital and chapel, and arranged streets into an orderly grid that survives today.

Uruapan quickly grew into a productive agricultural center renowned for macadamias and high-quality *aguacates* (avocados) and still holds the title 'Capital Mundial del Aguacate.' The Feria del Aguacate (p622) underlines that point.

Avocados may pay the bills, but the river is king. The city's nicest neighborhoods kiss the riverside. The national park, a 15-minute walk from the city center, is a rush of waterfalls and trickling streams that wind through thick vegetation.

Uruapan is 500m lower than Pátzcuaro and is much warmer. Don't miss the remarkable volcano Paricutín, 35km to the west.

◉ Sights

Parque Nacional Barranca del Cupatitzio PARK
(Independencia; adult/child M$25/10; ☉8am-6pm) This incomparable urban park is just 1km west of the main plaza, but it's another world. Nature is big here. Tropical and subtropical foliage (including burly banana palms) is thick and alive with colorful birds and butterflies. The river boils over boulders, cascades down waterfalls and spreads into wide, crystalline pools. Cobbled paths follow the riverbanks from its source at the **Rodilla del Diablo** pool, near the park's north end. There are a few fruit stands and *taquerías* to choose from, and water from hidden springs peels off the surrounding hillsides before flowing into the great river. There's even a **trout farm** where you can net your own catch.

Museo de los Cuatro Pueblos Indios MUSEUM
(Portal Mercado; admission free; ☉9:30am-1:30pm & 3:30-6pm Tue-Sun) In the Huatápera, an old colonial courtyard building near the northeast corner of the central plaza, is this three-room museum. Built in the 1530s by Fray Juan de San Miguel, this relic once housed the first hospital in the Americas. The decorations around the doors and windows were carved by Purépecha artisans in a Mudejar style. The museum showcases regional *artesanías*, such as ceramics from Capula and lacquerware from Quiroga.

Fábrica San Pedro TEXTILE FACTORY
(☑524-14-63; www.telaresuruapan.com.mx; Treviño s/n; ☉tours 9am-6pm Mon-Sat) This great old textile factory from the 19th century is essentially a living museum. Hand-loomed and hand-dyed bedspreads, tablecloths and curtains are made here from pure cotton and wool, and are available for sale. The original machines are more than 100 years old and are still used. Call ahead for a tour and see the entire weaving process from cotton bale to finished tablecloth.

✷ Festivals & Events

Semana Santa   RELIGIOUS
Palm Sunday is marked by a procession through the city streets. A major crafts competition takes place on this day, and two weeks after Palm Sunday a week-long exhibition of Michoacán handicrafts fills the plaza.

Día de San Francisco   RELIGIOUS
St Francis, the patron saint of Uruapan, is honored with colorful festivities, which are held on October 4.

Festival del Cristo Rey   RELIGIOUS
On the last Sunday of October an evening procession parades an image of Christ along the town's winding streets, which are covered in murals made of flower petals or colored sawdust.

Feria del Aguacate   FOOD
The Avocado Fair erupts for three weeks in November/December and is celebrated with agricultural, industrial and handicraft exhibitions. Previous years have seen record-setting attempts for the world's largest guacamole.

Festival de Coros y Danzas   DANCE
A Purépecha dance and choral contest held December 22.

Día de Muertos   TRADITIONAL
Celebrated across Mexico, the famous Day of the Dead festival happens on November 1 and 2 and brings many visitors to Uruapan for the colorful local celebrations.

🛏 Sleeping

Reserve a room early for the Día de Muertos (November 1 and 2) and Semana Santa (March/April) festivities.

TOP CHOICE Casa Chikita   GUESTHOUSE $$
(✆524-41-74; www.casachikita.com; Carranza 32; s/d incl breakfast M$450/650; P🅿️🛜) This 19th-century house has just four rooms set around a garden decorated with local pottery. The rooms vary quite a bit, but the best are extremely comfortable and decorated with great touches such as granite or wooden counters in the bathroom, tiled floors and local art on the walls. Homemade breakfasts are sumptuous, the friendly artist owners will make you feel right at home and you're also welcome to use the kitchen to make your own meals.

Hotel Mansión del Cupatitzio   HOTEL $$$
(✆523-20-60; www.mansiondelcupatitzio.com; Calz Rodilla del Diablo 20; r from M$1460; P🅿️@🛜 ❄🍴) A beautiful hacienda-style property sitting right next to the entrance of the Parque Nacional Barranca del Cupatitzio, this place has a certain 1940s, California-bungalow charm and the rambling grounds and pool area are absolutely gorgeous. Rooms are also spacious and have some charm, though the hotel can often be overrun with Mexican families and screaming children on the weekend and during holidays.

Mi Solar Bed & Breakfast   BOUTIQUE HOTEL $$
(✆524-09-12; www.hotelmisolar.com; Delgado 10; s/d incl breakfast from M$840/885; P❄@🛜) Uruapan's oldest hotel opened in the 1940s to accommodate tourists flooding in to see the newly erupted Volcán Paricutín. Today it's a wholly remodeled boutique place, with 17 spacious rooms on three floors surrounding an atrium bar. Rooms have luscious king beds, high ceilings and hand-carved wooden furniture. There's a small gym and sauna, and it serves a full breakfast.

Hotel Regis   HOTEL $
(✆523-58-44; www.hotelregis.com.mx; Portal Carrillo 12; s/d/tr M$350/450/550; P🛜) This is the best value among the budget plaza hotels. You'll receive a warm reception in the charming public areas, and while the rooms are totally average and have poky bathrooms, it's very central and there's a degree of eccentric personality here.

Campamento de Área de
Montaña   CAMPGROUND $
(✆524-01-97; Lenin s/n; campsites/cabins per person M$80/140) Camp within a 4.5-sq-km nature reserve located just 5km northeast of downtown. Register at Parque Nacional Barranca del Cupatitzio and ask to see the 'Oficina Área de Montaña' to enter the national park without paying an admission fee. The reserve is best reached by taxi.

✗ Eating & Drinking

TOP CHOICE La Terraza de la Trucha   FISH $$
(Calz Rodilla del Diablo 13; mains M$65-120; ⏱9am-6pm) Irresistibly nestled at the north entrance of the national park, but totally unsigned, you'll find a cozy table with shady cascade views. Order the trout, of course. Get it grilled, crusted in macadamias or *a la tampiqueña* (with guacamole

and beans). It comes with fresh chips and a searing salsa.

La Casa   PIZZERIA **$**
(Revolución 3; mains M$45-100; ☺2-11pm; 🍴) Easily Uruapan's most charming spot with low music, low lighting and folk art scattered within its stone walls. The specialty here is pizza, which, while not particularly great, makes for a welcome change from Mexican fare. Crepes and sandwiches are also on offer and service is friendly. The garden bar is a great place to sit with a cappuccino or a *cerveza* (beer) and groove to the sounds of Mexican indie rock in the background.

Cox-Hanal   MEXICAN **$**
(Independencia 31A; mains M$30-80; ☺11am-9pm) This highly recommended local place serves up delicious *antojitos yucatecos* (dishes from the Yucatán). It's nothing much to look at, but it's normally always busy and the prices are very reasonable for food this good.

Café Tradicional de Uruapan   CAFE **$**
(Carranza 5B; snacks & breakfast M$35-100; ☺8am-11pm) It's got burgers, salads, massive platters of *huevos a la mexicana* and all manner of shakes and cakes. Moreover, you can get good coffee here and enjoy a very pleasant cafe atmosphere full of locals.

La Lucha   CAFE **$**
(Ortiz 20; coffees M$30; ☺9am-9pm) The arched interior of this charming cafe makes for a very pleasant place for a coffee, cake or breakfast, with black-and-white photos on the wall and a great little courtyard out the back.

Mole Orapondiro   MEXICAN **$**
(Independencia 112; mains M$35-60; ☺9am-5pm) This sunny cafe specializes in one thing: a rich, thick and chocolatey *mole* sauce. Local ladies smuggle home bottles of it, so they can pass it off as their own. You can have it ladled over chicken, rice and beans and on *tortas*. Get here early because the chicken always sells out.

Mercado de Antojitos   MARKET **$**
(dishes M$5-25; ☺8am-11pm) The best place for down-home local cooking is the buzzing food court at the center of this labyrinthine market on the north side of the plaza. The *carnitas* are renowned across Michoacán, and the tacos, *pozole* and *cocadas* (haystacks of caramelized coconut) ain't half bad, either.

🛍 Shopping

The **Mercado de Antojitos** (☺8am-11pm), on the north side of the plaza, is ideal if you're in the market for candy, DVDs, strawberries, bras, cowboy boots or a taco.

Fábrica San Pedro (www.telaresuruapan.com.mx; Treviño s/n; ☺9am-6pm) has exquisite handmade textiles.

Opposite the entrance to the Parque Nacional Barranca del Cupatitzio, the **Mercado de Artesanías** (☺9am-6pm) has local crafts, though mostly of a poor quality.

La Macadamia (Carranza 21; ☺9am-2pm & 4-7pm Mon-Sat) sells – you guessed it – products made from local macadamia nuts, from delicious macadamia marzipan to macadamia moisturizer.

ℹ Information

Several banks (with ATMs), along with a few *cambios*, are near the central plaza.

Ciber Marvel (Delgado; per hr M$8; ☺9am-8pm) Internet cafe.

Main post office (Jalisco 81; ☺9am-3pm Mon-Fri, to 1pm Sat)

Secretaría de Turismo (📞524-71-99; Independencia 36; ☺8:30am-3pm & 4-7pm Mon-Fri, 9am-2pm & 4-7pm Sat, 9am-2pm Sun)

WESTERN CENTRAL HIGHLANDS URUAPAN

BUSES FROM URUAPAN

DESTINATION	FARE (M$)	DURATION	FREQUENCY (DAILY)
Angahuan	20	1hr	half-hourly
Colima	325	6hr	4
Guadalajara	340	4½hr	hourly
Mexico City (Terminal Norte)	435	7hr	every 2hr
Morelia	95	2hr	hourly
Paracho	19	1hr	hourly
Pátzcuaro	48	1hr	hourly

❶ Getting There & Around

Uruapan's bus terminal is 2km northeast of central Uruapan on the highway to Pátzcuaro and Morelia. It has a **left-luggage facility** (☺7am-11pm) and an internet cafe. For Tingambato (M$12, 30 minutes) take the same bus as those to Pátzcuaro or Morelia. Frequent destinations include those in the boxed table (p623, prices quoted are for 1st-class buses when available).

Local buses marked 'Centro' run from just outside the bus terminal to the plaza (M$5). For taxis, buy a ticket inside the bus terminal (M$25). For the return trip catch a 'Central Camionera' bus from the south side of the plaza.

Around Uruapan

CASCADA DE TZARÁRACUA

Ten kilometers south of downtown Uruapan, the wild Río Cupatitzio makes its last act count. It pumps hard over the vine-covered, 30m-high red rock cliffs and crashes into a misty turquoise pool. This is the **Tzaráracua waterfall** (admission M$10, car extra M$5; ☺10am-6pm). On the meandering hike down the 557 slippery steps to the falls you'll see that the raging river has been dammed a few kilometers downstream. The tame lake set against rolling green hills is pretty enough, but it's also a sad fate considering the river's furious beauty.

There's also a 20-minute hike upstream from Tzaráracua to the equally beautiful **Tzararacuita**, a smaller waterfall. This trail is not as well maintained, so bring waterproof sandals. To get here, follow the steep muddy track beyond the Tzaráracua bridge and after about 10 minutes turn right at the stone outcropping.

If you don't feel like walking down and back from the dusty parking lot, hire one of the lingering horses. They cost M$100 round trip.

Hourly buses to Tzaráracua depart from in front of the Hotel Regis, on the south side of Uruapan's main plaza (M$6). Taxis cost M$60.

TINGAMBATO

Stroll through luscious avocado groves to the beautiful **ruins** (admission M$37; ☺9am-6pm) of this ceremonial site, which predates the Tarascan empire and thrived from about AD 450 to 900. They are located outside of Tingambato village, about 30km from Uruapan on the road to Pátzcuaro. The ruins, which include two plazas, three altars and a ball court (rare in western Mexico), have a Teotihuacán influence. There's also an 8m-high stepped pyramid and an underground tomb where a skeleton and 32 scattered skulls were found – hinting at beheading or trophy-skull rituals.

Buses to Morelia leave from Uruapan's terminal every 20 minutes and stop in Tingambato (M$12, 30 minutes). The ruins are 1.4km downhill on Juárez, the first street on the right as you enter town.

PARACHO

✆423 / POP 17,000 / ELEV 2220M

Paracho, 40km north of Uruapan on Hwy 37, is a small but lovely Purépecha town famous for its high-quality, handmade stringed instruments. If you're looking for a reasonably priced and well-made guitar, violin, cello or traditional Mexican *guitarrón* (Mexican stand-up bass), you've come to the right pueblo. The liveliest time to come is during the annual **Feria Internacional de la Guitarra** (National Guitar Fair) in early August; it's a week-long splurge of music, dance and exhibitions.

Calle 20 de Noviembre is lined with guitar and woodworking shops. Quality varies – the cliché 'you get what you pay for' certainly holds true. The heir to one of Paracho's most respected family of luthiers, **Filiberto Díaz** (✆525-00-52; Calle 20 de Noviembre No 295; ☺8am-8pm), carves acoustic guitars from mahogany, cedar, cyprus and other valuable woods in a workshop founded by his grandfather in 1945. His best work can sell for thousands of US dollars. Díaz speaks English and is happy to talk about his craft.

Buses for Paracho depart Uruapan's bus terminal every 15 minutes (M$19, 30 minutes).

Volcán Paricutín

On February 20, 1943, Dionisio Pulido, a Purépecha farmer, was plowing his cornfield some 35km west of Uruapan when the ground began to quake and spurt steam, sparks and hot ash. The farmer struggled to cover the blast holes, but he quickly realized his futility and ran. Good thing, because like some Hollywood B-movie, a growling volcano began to rise. Within a year it had reached an elevation of 410m above the rolling farmland and its lava had flooded the Purépecha villages of San Salvador Paricutín and San Juan Parangaricutiro. Thankfully, the lava flowed slowly, giving the villagers plenty of time to escape.

The volcano continued to grow until 1952. Today its large black cone (at 2800m) whispers warm steam in a few places, but otherwise appears dormant. Near the edge of the 20-sq-km lava field, the top of the ruined **Templo San Juan Parangaricutiro**, San Juan's stone church, protrudes eerily from a sea of black lava. Its tower and altar are the only visible traces of the two buried villages. It's a one-hour walk from where the bus lets you off in nearby Angahuan.

Arrive in Angahuan (35km from Uruapan) before 10am if you want to climb Paricutín. Once you step off the bus, guides with horses will offer their services to the ruined church, volcano, or both. Horses and a guide should cost M$500 to M$600 per person per day. The volcano is a 14km round trip that takes up to eight hours – of which you'll spend nearly six in an unforgiving, wooden saddle – so your legs may cramp, your ass will bruise and your spine will tingle when the horse trots. You'll have to scramble the last few hundred meters up to the summit. The view of the massive lava flow is mind-blowing, you'll hear faint announcements from the Angahuan PA system warbling on the wind and feel the steam rising from the earth. It's a rugged hike up, but you'll get to run, jump and slide down the deep volcanic sand on the descent and visit the San Juan church on the way back. The altar is almost always blessed with colorful offerings of candles and flowers and at the entrance you'll see **María's**. María is a Purépecha woman in traditional braids and colorful dress fixing fresh, blue-corn quesadillas on an old, wood-burning, oil-can skillet who will serve you up a well-deserved snack of indigenous treats. Bring enough water, wear decent shoes (trainers will suffice), and perhaps a bum-pad, and you'll have a good time.

If wooden saddles intimidate you, you can walk to the volcano, but you'll still need a guide (M$300) as the trail through the pine forest can be hard to find. The relaxing hike through avocado groves, agave fields and wildflowers takes about eight hours.

Angahuan

📧452 / POP 5700 / ELEV 2693M

Angahuan, the nearest town to Volcán Paricutín, is a typical Purépecha town: there are wooden houses, dusty streets, more horses than cars, women in ankle-length skirts and colorful shawls, and loudspeakers booming announcements in the Purépecha tongue. Greet locals with *'nari eransku'* (good morning) or *'nari chusku'* (good afternoon).

◉ Sights

Iglesia de Santiago Apóstol CHURCH

On the main plaza is the sensational 16th-century Iglesia de Santiago Apóstol. Candles and incense burn, fresh flowers crowd the altar and the detailed doorway was carved by a Moorish stonemason who accompanied the early Spanish missionaries here.

🛏 Sleeping

Cuartos Familiares CABAÑAS $

(📧452-81-84; Camino al Paricutín s/n; s/d M$200/270, 6-person cabin M$650; 🅿) This is the best of the few sleeping options in Angahuan. The rustic cabins have adobe fireplaces and lovely tiled bathrooms, and the saloon-like cafe has a full bar and serves breakfast, lunch and dinner. Look for the orange sign on the road to the ruined church, about 1km from the bus stop.

Centro Turístico de Angahuan CABAÑAS $

(📧128-07-52; www.centroturisticodeangahuan.com .mx; Camino al Paricutín s/n; per person M$130; 🅿) This 'tourist' complex feels like an old elementary school or summer camp. There's a cafeteria that shows a video about the eruption of Volcán Paricutín and terrific views of the lava field, the protruding San Juan church tower and the volcano itself. There's a choice of six- and four-bed cabins; all are basic but brightly decorated.

❶ Getting There & Away

Angahuan is 35km from Uruapan. Buses leave the Uruapan bus terminal for Angahuan every 30 minutes from 5am to 7pm (M$20, one hour).

Buses return to Uruapan every 30 minutes until about 9pm and few cabs are available in town, so unless you have made previous arrangements you may have to hop on a bus back.

Northern Central Highlands

Includes »

Best Places to Eat

» Cafe Rama (p676)

» Las Mercedes (p663)

» Di Vino (p686)

» Los Dorados de Villa (p634)

» El México de Frida (p646)

» San Marcos Merendero (p640)

Best Places to Stay

» Posada Corazón (p674)

» Casa Estrella de la Valenciana (p660)

» Hotel Museo Palacio de San Agustín (p645)

» Hotel Emporio Zacatecas (p633)

» Quinta Real Zacatecas (p633)

Why Go?

From cobbled laneways to pretty plazas, deserts to cloud forest, the northern central highlands region is as varied as its history, cuisine and cultures. It was here that former mineral wealth created colonial cities and revolutionary activity left ghost towns in its wake. Known as the Cuna de la Independencia (Cradle of Independence), the territory is renowned for its part in the country's fight for autonomy.

Particular jewels include silver-ridden Guanajuato and Zacatecas, plaza-filled San Luis Potosí, arty San Miguel de Allende and former activist hot spots Dolores Hidalgo and Querétaro. And as for the cuisine...travel a few kilometers for another take on a trusty tortilla or regional specialty. Culture vultures can feast on pre-Hispanic sites and art museums, concerts, nightlife, festivals and *callejoneadas* (see boxed text, p660) – the northern central highlands continues centuries of pomp and ceremony. It sure knows how to put on a good (if noisy) party.

When to Go

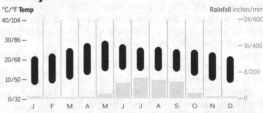

Guanajuato

°C/°F **Temp**	**Rainfall** inches/mm
40/104 —	— 24/600
30/86 —	— 16/400
20/68 —	— 8/200
10/50 —	
0/32 —	— 0

J F M A M J J A S O N D

Jul & Aug Days are mild and wildflowers bloom; it's the perfect time for do-it-yourself explorations.

Nov Villages are abuzz as they prepare for Day of the Dead celebrations (Nov 1 to 2).

Late Mar or Apr Traditional religious festivities abound during Semana Santa.

History

Until the Spanish conquest, the northern central highlands were inhabited by fierce seminomadic tribes known to the Aztecs as Chichimecs. They resisted Spanish expansion longer than other Mexican peoples but were ultimately pacified in the late 16th century. The wealth subsequently amassed by the Spanish was at the cost of many Chichimecs, who were used as slave labor in the mines.

This historically volatile region sparked the criollo fight for independence from Spain, which was plotted in Querétaro and San Miguel de Allende and launched from Dolores Hidalgo in 1810 (see p667). A

NORTHERN CENTRAL HIGHLANDS

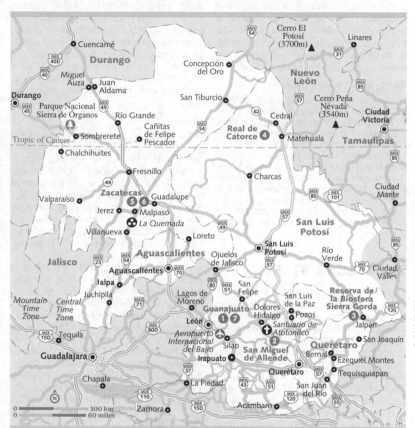

Northern Central Highlands Highlights

❶ Meandering through winding cobbled alleys and marvelous museums in **Guanajuato** (p654)

❷ Feeding your soul with art, food and fiestas in popular **San Miguel de Allende** (p668)

❸ Marveling at the missions and ambling through near-virgin wilderness in the protected jewel, the **Reserva de la Biosfera Sierra Gorda** (see boxed text, p690)

❹ Sensing the spirits of miners in the picturesque, reawakening 'ghost' town of **Real de Catorce** (p648)

❺ Strolling the alleys of **Zacatecas** (p628) to survey this silver city's opulent architecture

❻ Riding high on the *teleférico* (cable car) over the top of **Zacatecas** up to the pinnacle, La Bufa (p629)

❼ Enjoying top-class international performances at the **Festival Internacional Cervantino** in Guanajuato (p660)

century later Francisco Madero released his revolutionary Plan de San Luis Potosí and the 1917 signing of Mexico's constitution in Querétaro cemented the region's leading role in Mexican political affairs.

In more recent times the region flourished economically, due in part to the boom in the motor, manufacturing and agricultural industries, particularly in Querétaro and Guanajuato. This led to the creation of international airports at León (Aeropuerto Internacional del Bajío) and Querétaro, which has helped sustain tourism and provided essential services and links to the region.

ℹ️ Getting There & Around

The Aeropuerto Internacional del Bajío, halfway between León and Guanajuato, is the major hub for the region's southern cities (see p665). Other airports, all with US flights (some via Mexico City), include Aguascalientes, Querétaro, San Luis Potosí and Zacatecas. Buses constantly ply the toll roads between Mexico City, Guadalajara, Querétaro and San Luis Potosí. The larger hubs, including Zacatecas and Aguascalientes, also host connections to northern Mexico, the US border and beyond. Frequent local buses efficiently connect the major cities and all points in between.

ZACATECAS STATE

The state of Zacatecas (za-ka-*te*-kas) is a dry, rugged, cactus-strewn expanse on the fringe of Mexico's northern semideserts. The state is best known for the wealthy silver city of the same name. Visitors can enjoy the region's historical and natural monuments including the mysterious ruins of La Quemada, a testament to centuries of cultures. The state is one of Mexico's largest in area (73,252 sq km) but smallest in population (1.49 million); it is believed that as many people again (1.5 million) who come from the state currently live in the United States.

Zacatecas

📞 492 / POP 130,000 / ELEV 2430M

Set amid arid countryside, the most northern of Mexico's fabled silver cities, fascinating Zacatecas – a Unesco World Heritage site – runs along a narrow valley. The large historic center is jam-packed with opulent colonial buildings, a stupendous cathedral (a useful central landmark), magnificent museums and steep, winding streets and alleys. Excellent restaurants and fine hotels make it a very comfortable location for any traveler.

The city has a legacy of historical highs and lows: it was here that Pancho Villa defeated a stronghold of soldiers (today he is still much feted by the locals). Here, too, thousands of indigenous slaves were forced by the Spanish to toil in the mines under terrible conditions. Today, travelers can have their own lofty experiences in a *teleférico* (cable car) to the Cerro de la Bufa, an impressive rock outcrop; the trip affords great views of a collage of church domes and rooftops. Alternatively, you can drop below the surface to tour the infamous Edén mine, or vibrate to the rhythms of its underground disco.

History

Indigenous Zacatecos – one of the Chichimec tribes – mined local mineral deposits for centuries before the Spanish arrived; it's said that the silver rush here was started when a Chichimec gave a piece of the fabled metal to a conquistador. The Spaniards founded a settlement in 1548 and started mining operations that sent caravan after caravan of silver off to Mexico City, creating fabulously wealthy silver barons in Zacatecas.

By the early 18th century, the mines of Zacatecas were producing 20% of Nueva España's silver and the city became an important base for Catholic missionaries.

In the 19th century political instability diminished the flow of silver. Although silver production later improved under Porfirio Díaz, the Revolution disrupted it. In 1914 in Zacatecas, Pancho Villa defeated a stronghold of 12,000 soldiers loyal to President Victoriano Huerta. After the Revolution, Zacatecas continued to thrive on silver.

◎ Sights

This historic city has much to detain you for several days, from mine visits, to excellent museums and a *teleférico* ride to La Bufa.

Museo Rafael Coronel   MUSEUM
(cnr Abasolo & Matamoros; adult/student M$30/15; ⏰10am-5pm Thu-Tue) The amazing Museo Rafael Coronel is not to be missed. Imaginatively housed in the ruins of the lovely 16th-century Ex-Convento de San Francisco, it houses Mexican folk art collected by the Zacatecan artist Rafael Coronel, brother of Pedro Coronel and son-in-law of Diego Rivera. Take your time to wander through the

various spaces (follow the arrows; it's easy to miss sections). The highlight is the astonishing, colorful display of more than 3000 masks (another 8000 are in storage) used in traditional dances and rituals. Also on display are pottery, puppets, instruments, pre-Hispanic objects and sketches by Rivera. The grounds and garden are a wonderful place to come and relax.

Museo Pedro Coronel   MUSEUM
(Plazuela de Santo Domingo s/n; admission M$30; ☺10am-5pm Tue-Sun) The extraordinary Museo Pedro Coronel is housed in a 17th-century former Jesuit college and is one of provincial Mexico's best art museums. Pedro Coronel (1923–85) was an affluent Zacatecan artist who bequeathed his collection of art and artifacts from all over the world, as well as his own works. The collection includes 20th-century works by Picasso, Rouault, Chagall, Kandinsky and Miró; and pre-Hispanic Mexican artifacts, masks and other ancient pieces.

Teleférico   CABLE CAR
(adult/student M$80/40; ☺10am-6pm, 7pm-midnight Thu-Sat) Zacatecas' most exhilarating ride and the easiest way to Cerro de la Bufa's summit is the Swiss-built cable car that crosses high above the city from Cerro del Grillo. It's a short walk east from Mina El Edén (east entrance) to the teleférico's Cerro del Grillo station. Alternatively, huff up the steep steps of Callejón de García Rojas, which lead straight to the teleférico from Genaro Codina. Cars depart every 15 minutes (except when it's raining or when winds exceed 60km/h) and the trip takes seven minutes.

Cerro de la Bufa   LANDMARK & NEIGHBORHOOD
The most appealing of the many explanations for the name of the hill that dominates Zacatecas is that 'bufa' is an old Basque word for wineskin, which is certainly what the rocky formation looks like. The views from the top are superb and there's an interesting group of monuments, a chapel and a museum. It is also the site of a zip line, **Tirolesa 840** (☎cell phone 492-1031122; www.vivazacatecasadventure.com; rides M$200-250; ☺10am-6pm), a 1km ride (840m of actual flying) across a former open-pit mine.

The small **Museo de la Toma de Zacatecas** (adult/student M$20/10; ☺10am-4:30pm), at the top of the hill, commemorates the 1914 battle fought on the hill's slopes in which the revolutionary División del Norte, led by Pancho Villa and Felipe Ángeles, defeated President Victoriano Huerta's forces. This gave the revolutionaries control of Zacatecas, which was the gateway to Mexico City.

La Capilla de la Virgen del Patrocinio, adjacent to the museum, is named after the patron saint of miners. Above the altar of this 18th-century chapel is an image of the Virgin said to be capable of healing the sick. Thousands of pilgrims flock here each year on September 8, when the image is carried to the cathedral.

Facing the chapel stand three imposing equestrian **statues** of the victors of the battle of Zacatecas – Villa, Ángeles and Pánfilo Natera.

From the right of the statues, a paved path along the foot of the rocky hilltop leads to the **Mausoleo de los Hombres Ilustres de Zacatecas**, with the tombs of Zacatecan heroes from 1841 to the present.

An exciting and convenient way to ascend La Bufa (to the church and museum) is by teleférico. Alternatively, you can walk up, starting at Calle del Ángel from the cathedral's east end. To reach it by car, take Carretera a la Bufa, which begins at Avenida López Velarde, a couple of kilometers east of the center. A taxi costs around M$50. You can return to town by the teleférico or by a footpath leading downhill from the statues.

Mina El Edén   MINE
(☎922-30-02; www.minaeleden.com.mx; tours adult/child M$80/40; ☺tours every 15min 10am-6pm) The Edén Mine, which was once one of Mexico's richest, is a must-see as it provides a dramatic insight into the region's source of wealth and the terrible price paid for it. Digging for fabulous hoards of silver, gold, iron, copper and zinc, the enslaved indigenous people, including many children, worked under horrific conditions. Up to five people a day died from accidents or diseases like tuberculosis and silicosis.

El Edén was worked from 1586 until the 1960s. Today the third and fourth of its seven levels are open to visitors. The lower levels are flooded. An elevator or miniature train takes you deep inside Cerro del Grillo, the hill in which the mine is located. Then guides (some English-speaking) lead you along floodlit walkways past shafts and over subterranean pools.

The mine has two entrances. To reach the higher one (the east entrance), walk 100m southwest from Cerro del Grillo teleférico station; from this entrance, tours start with

Zacatecas

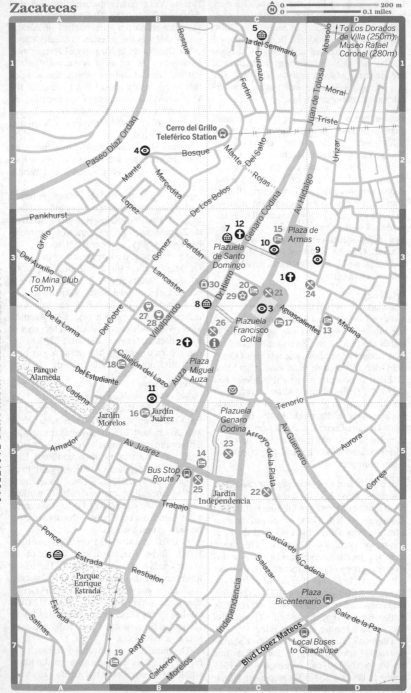

To Los Dorados
de Villa (250m);
Museo Rafael
Coronel (280m)

Zacatecas

Sights

1 Catedral ... C3
2 Ex-Templo de San Agustín ... B4
3 Mercado González Ortega ... C4
4 Mina El Edén (East Entrance) ... B2
5 Museo del Arte Abstracto Manuel Felguérez ... C1
6 Museo Francisco Goita ... A6
7 Museo Pedro Coronel ... C3
8 Museo Zacatecano ... B3
9 Palacio de Gobierno ... D3
10 Palacio de la Mala Noche ... C3
11 Rectoría ... B4
12 Templo de Santo Domingo ... C3

Sleeping

13 Hostal Villa Colonial ... D4
14 Hotel Condesa ... B5
15 Hotel Emporio Zacatecas ... C3
16 Hotel Mesón de Jobito ... B5
17 Hotel Reyna Soledad ... C4
18 La Terrasse ... B4
19 Quinta Real Zacatecas ... B7
20 Santa Rita Hotel ... C3

Eating

21 Acrópolis Café ... C3
22 Mercado Arroyo de la Plata ... C5
23 Mercado El Laberinto ... C5
24 Panificadora Santa Cruz ... D3
25 Restaurant Fonda El Jacalito ... B5
Restaurant La Plaza ... (see 19)
San Patrizio Caffé ... (see 26)
26 Trattoria Il Goloso ... C4

Drinking

27 Cantina 15 Letras ... B4
Dalí Café & Bar ... (see 2)
El Paraíso ... (see 3)
28 Huracán ... B4

Entertainment

29 Teatro Calderón ... C3

Shopping

30 Gallery Centro Platero ... B3

an elevator descent. To reach the west entrance from the town center, walk west along Avenida Juárez and stay on it after its name changes to Avenida Torreón at the Alameda. Turn right immediately after the IMSS hospital (bus 7 from the corner of Avenida Hidalgo goes up Avenida Juárez and past the hospital) and a short walk will bring you to the mine entrance. Tours begin here with a trip on the narrow-gauge railway (540m), after which you walk another 350m or so.

The mine also has a nighttime alter ego, a bar called the Mina Club (see p635).

Museo del Arte Abstracto Manuel Felguérez MUSEUM
(Ex-Seminario de la Purísima Concepción; adult/student M$30/20; 10am-5pm Wed-Mon) This art museum is worth visiting for the building alone; originally a seminary, it was later used as a prison and has been renovated to create some remarkable exhibition spaces, transforming the former dark, depressing cells and steel walkways into a beautiful site.

It has a stunning and varied collection of abstract art, particularly the work of Zacatecan artist Manuel Felguérez.

Catedral CATHEDRAL
(Plaza de Armas) Built between 1729 and 1752, the pink-stone cathedral is an ultimate expression of Mexican baroque.

The stupendous main facade is a wall of detailed carvings; this has been interpreted as a giant symbol of the tabernacle. A tiny figure of an angel holding a tabernacle is in the middle of the design, the keystone atop the round central window. Above this, in the third tier, is Christ and above Christ is God. The 12 Apostles are featured, as well as a smaller Virgin figure above the doorway.

The southern facade's central sculpture is of La Virgen de los Zacatecanos, the city's patroness. The north facade shows Christ crucified, attended by the Virgin Mary and St John.

Unveiled in 2010, the grand altar is the work of Mexico's famous artist, Javier Marín. It features 10 large bronze figures and the figure of Christ, arranged on a backdrop of golden blocks.

Museo Zacatecano MUSEUM
(Dr Hierro 307; adult/student M$30/15; 10am-5pm Wed-Mon) About 100m south of Plazuela de Santo Domingo is the recently renovated **Casa de Moneda**, formerly Zacatecas' mint (Mexico's second-biggest) in the 19th century. Since 2010, it has housed the Museo Zacatecano. Spread over a number of halls and rooms on different levels, this contemporary museum exhibits a weird mix of all things *zacatecano,* from pre-Hispanic objects to the recreated rooms of a popular composer. Unfortunately, the first few *salas* are text-heavy information boards (in Spanish). The highlight – in the last halls – is the

wonderful collection of Huichol art. Videos (all in Spanish) provide each *sala's* context.

Plaza de Armas   PLAZA
The plaza is the open space north of the cathedral. The **Palacio de Gobierno** on the plaza's east side was built in the 18th century for a colonial family. In the turret of its main staircase is a mural of the history of Zacatecas state, painted in 1970 by Antonio Rodríguez.

Across the road, the **Palacio de la Mala Noche** was built in the late 18th century for a mine owner and now houses state-government offices.

Plazuela Francisco Goitia   PLAZA
A block south of the cathedral, a broad flight of stairs descends from Avenida Hidalgo to Tacuba, forming a charming open space. The terraces of the *plazuela* (small plaza) are often used as an informal amphitheater by street performers.

North of the *plazuela,* the **Mercado González Ortega** is an impressive 1880s iron-columned building that used to hold Zacatecas' main market. In the 1980s the upper level was renovated into an upscale shopping center. The lower level was once used as *bodegas* (storage rooms) and now houses several bars and restaurants.

Opposite the *plazuela* on Avenida Hidalgo, the lovely, recently-renovated 1890s Teatro Calderón (p635) dates from the Porfiriato period and holds plays, concerts, films and art exhibitions.

Plazuela de Santo Domingo   PLAZA
A block west of the cathedral, this *plazuela* is dominated by the **Templo de Santo Domingo**. Although the church is done in a more sober baroque style than the cathedral, it has some fine gilded altars and a graceful horseshoe staircase. Built by the Jesuits in the 1740s, the church was taken over by Dominican monks when the Jesuits were expelled in 1767.

Jardín Juárez   PARK
(Jardín Juárez) The street ends at the garden of the same name, a tiny but charming park. The Universidad Autónoma de Zacatecas' administrative headquarters are housed in the neoclassical **Rectoría** building on its west side.

Museo Francisco Goitia   MUSEUM
(Estrada 101; adult/student M$30/15; ⊙10am-4:45pm Tue-Sun) The Museo Francisco Goi-

tia displays work by several 20th-century Zacatecan artists, including some evocative paintings of indigenous people by Goitia (1882–1960) himself. Other artists represented include Pedro Coronel, Rafael Coronel and Manuel Felguérez. The museum is in a former governor's mansion, above Parque Enrique Estrada, and is worth the short walk.

Ex-Templo de San Agustín   NOTABLE BUILDING
Another 100m south in Plaza Miguel Auza, is the Ex-Templo de San Agustín, built for Augustinian monks in the 17th century. During the 19th-century anticlerical movement, the church became a cantina and Masonic lodge. In 1882 it was purchased by American Presbyterian missionaries who destroyed its 'too Catholic' main facade, replacing it with a blank white wall. One surviving feature is the church's plateresque carving of the conversion of St Augustine over the north doorway. In the 20th century the church returned to the government. Today it hosts art exhibitions plus a multimedia light show (⊙8pm Sat winter, 9pm Sat summer). The church's original (and very beautiful) facade is re-created in these extraordinary 3D scenes. The adjoining former monastery is now the seat of the Zacatecas bishopric.

⭐ Festivals & Events

Festival of Santiago de Querétaro   ARTS
A cultural extravaganza held during Semana Santa (Easter; dates change), when both Mexican and international artists perform and exhibit a massive variety of work – from music and dance to painting and literature.

La Morisma   HISTORICAL
Usually held on the last weekend in August. Features a spectacular mock battle commemorating the triumph of the Christians over the Muslims (Moors) in old Spain. Two rival 'armies' – more than 2000 participants – parade through the streets in the mornings, then, accompanied by bands of musicians, enact two battle sequences that take place between Lomas de Bracho and Cerro de la Bufa.

Feria de Zacatecas   TRADITIONAL
Annual fair during the first three weeks in September. Renowned matadors fight famous local bulls. There are also *charreadas* (rodeos), concerts, plays, film festivals and agricultural and craft shows. On September 8 the image of La Virgen del Patrocinio is

carried to the cathedral from its chapel on Cerro de la Bufa.

Festival Internacional de Teatro de Calle   THEATER
In mid-October, drama takes to the streets in this vibrant week-long celebration of street theater.

Festival Internacional Cervantino   ARTS
In the 1950s this arts festival (www.festival cervantino.gob.mx) included merely Miguel Cervantes' *entremeses* performed by students. It has grown to become one of Latin America's foremost arts extravaganzas. Music, dance and theater groups from around the world perform diverse works (mostly non-Cervantes-related) for two weeks in October. Tickets for single events range from M$200 to M$800. Tickets and hotels should be booked in advance at www.ticketmaster.com.mx. In Guanajuato, buy tickets from the temporary ticket office (often on the southeast side of Teatro Juárez).

🛏 Sleeping
Midrange and top-end accommodations tend to hike their rates (on those provided here) up to double during Zacatecas' high seasons – September's festivals, Christmas and Semana Santa (March/April).

Quinta Real Zacatecas   LUXURY HOTEL $$$
(☏922-91-04, 800-500-40-00; www.quintareal.com; Rayón 434; ste from M$2890; P🖶🖸❄@🛜) It's worth seeing red (in terms of your bank balance) to experience this luxury treat. Spectacularly situated around the country's oldest – now retired – bullring and near El Cubo aqueduct, the 49-room hotel is one of Mexico's most contemporary and fetching. The least expensive rooms are spacious, comfortable master suites. An elegant restaurant, La Plaza, (see p634) overlooks the ring, and the bar, Botarell, is in the former holding pens.

🔝 Hotel Emporio Zacatecas   LUXURY HOTEL $$$
(☏925-65-00, 800-800-61-61; www.hotelesempo rio.com; Av Hidalgo 703; s/d/ste M$2714/2242/3717; P🖸❄) Zacatecas' central upmarket choice boasts a superb location, luxurious rooms and delightful terrace areas. The website often promotes special deals.

La Terrasse   BOUTIQUE HOTEL $$
(☏925-53-15; www.terrassehotel.com.mx; Villalpando 209; s/d/tr incl breakfast M$670/780/950;

🖸❄🛜) This small, friendly and centrally located boutique option is run by a proud owner. It has a contemporary and slightly minimalist ambience. Back rooms have internal-facing windows which could be claustrophic for some, quiet for others.

Santa Rita Hotel   BOUTIQUE HOTEL $$$
(☏925-41-41, 800-560-81-15; www.hotelsantarita.com; Av Hidalgo 507A; ste M$1700-2800; P❄@🛜) A stylish, contemporary and cosmopolitan choice. Disappointingly, some of the 41 suites have internal-facing windows. Prices increase up to 30% during high season.

Hotel Mesón de Jobito   HISTORIC HOTEL $$$
(☏924-17-22, 800-021-00-40; www.mesondejobito.com; Jardín Juárez 143; r M$1110-1680, ste M$1200-1755; P🖸❄@🛜) Guests come here to soak up old-fashioned charm, service and a sense of history. This large place has 53 finely decorated rooms; two elegant, if slightly faded, restaurants; a bar and lobby (plus a slanting balcony, a legacy of its construction 200 years ago). Its Sunday buffet breakfast (M$125) is popular with the public. Often offers deals.

Hostal Villa Colonial   HOSTEL $
(☏922-19-80; www.hostalvillacolonial.com; cnr Calle 1 de Mayo & Callejón Mono Prieto; dm/d without bathroom M$100/220, s/d M$250/250; @🛜) At the time this book went to press, the hostel had been sold and was under new management. Based on past experience, it offered a rustic hostel situation: dorms with tiny shared bathrooms and double rooms with bathroom and TV.

Hotel Reyna Soledad   HOTEL $$
(☏922-07-90; www.hostalreynasoledad.com.mx; Tacuba 170; r/ste M$590/690; P🛜) Set in a converted 17th-century convent, the colonial patios of this perfectly located place are tranquil and charming. The rooms are rustic (in a pine-furniture kind of way).

Hotel Condesa   HOTEL $$
(☏922-11-60; www.hotelcondesa.com.mx; Av Juárez 102; s/d/tr M$450/550/580; ❄) The Condesa's 52 '80s-style modern rooms are a good budget option. The nicest have external-facing windows. An attached restaurant serves breakfast (M$45 to M$70) and other meals.

🍴 Eating
There are some excellent Mexican and international restaurants serving a range of fare.

Local specialties feature ingredients such as nopal and pumpkin seeds.

In the morning, look around Avenida Tacuba for burros (donkeys) carrying pottery jugs of *aguamiel* (honey water), a nutritional drink derived from the maguey cactus. The two central produce markets are **Mercado El Laberinto** (Plazuela Genaro Codina) and **Mercado Arroyo de la Plata** (Arroyo de la Plata).

TOP CHOICE **Los Dorados de Villa** MEXICAN $$
(☑922-57-22; Plazuela de García 1314; mains M$70-120; ☺3pm-1am Mon-Sat, 3-11pm Sun; ☻) You may have to fight to get into this popular revolutionary-themed restaurant: knock at the door – it's always locked. It's a blast of color and is chock-a-block with atmosphere and relics. Plus it serves up a delicious array of everything – except Pancho Villa himself. Don't miss the *enchiladas valentinas* (M$80). Oh and for posterity, a flying visit to the toilet may knock you off your perch! (The toilet alcove is filled with birds – you have to walk through the aviary to get to your cubicle.)

Restaurant La Plaza MEXICAN, INTERNATIONAL $$$
(☑922-91-04; Quinta Real Zacatecas, Rayón 434; mains M$100-375; ☻) The elegant hotel dining room at the Quinta Real Zacatecas is especially memorable for its outlook to the aqueduct and bullring, as well as for its refined ambience and superb international and Mexican cuisine from different regions. Charge in for a Sunday brunch (M$225) or an evening cocktail in the bar, opposite the restaurant on the other side of the ring. Tables in the bar area are nestled in niches, former bull-holding pens (6pm to 1am). Reservations are advisable.

Trattoria Il Goloso ITALIAN $$
(Dr Hierro 400; mains M$95-220; ☺2-9:30pm Tue-Sat, 1-7pm Sun; ☻) Trade the tacos for fabulous Italian pasta and other mains in this cozy Sicilian-themed place. It comes complete with checkered tablecloths and an enthusiastic Italian chef (who'd rather be chatting to his clients than cooking up some Italian feasts). It's behind San Patrizio Caffé.

Acrópolis Café MEXICAN $
(cnr Av Hidalgo & Plazuela Candelario Huizar; mains M$40-120; ☻) Near the cathedral, this Greek-owned cafe has a quirky '50s-style diner feel, and is *the* place to meet for locals and visitors – perhaps more for its location than its meals – light snacks and coffees.

San Patrizio Caffé CAFE $
(Av Hidalgo 403C; drinks & snacks M$50-80; ☺10am-10pm Mon-Sat, 3-9pm Sun) Probably does the best cappuccinos in town and has a relaxing courtyard setting, light snacks, and an array of Italian sodas.

Restaurant Fonda El Jacalito MEXICAN $
(Av Juárez 18; mains M$50-110; ☺8am-10:30pm) The place is hardly a 'little shack' (*el jacalito*). It's a very airy eatery that offers hordes of loyal locals breakfasts from M$55 to M$85, good *comidas corridas* (prix-fixe menus; M$70) and tasty versions of traditional favorites.

Panificadora Santa Cruz BAKERY $
(Tacuba 216A; snacks M$5-35; ☺7am-10:30pm) Almost abutting the cathedral, this reliable bakery has sinful treats – *pan dulces* (pastries), *tortas* (sandwiches), *tamales* and frappés.

🍸 Drinking

Zacatecas has a particularly good late-night scene, especially after 9pm.

Cantina 15 Letras BAR
(Mártires de Chicago 309; ☺1pm-3am Mon-Sat; ☻) Stop for a drink at this oft-crowded classic, filled with bohemians, drunks and poets. Photos portray Zacatecas of old; the art showcases some well-known local artists.

El Paraíso BAR
(cnr Av Hidalgo & Plazuela Goitia; ☺1pm-1am Mon-Sat, 1-6pm Sun) This smart bar in the southwest corner of the Mercado González Ortega attracts a friendly, varied, mostly 30s clientele; it's busiest Thursday through Saturday.

Huracán BAR
(Villalpando 406; ☺6pm-3am Wed-Sat) This fun bar is a quirky tribute to both kitsch and Huracán, Mexico's favorite champion of *lucha libre* (wrestling). The walls are covered in funky 1960s-style florals superimposed with Huracán's wrestling mask. You can prop yourself up in a 'boxing ring' surrounded by, um, women's lingerie.

Dalí Café & Bar BAR
(Plaza Miguel Auza 322; ☺noon-1am Mon-Sat, 5pm-midnight Sun) This sprawling cafe-bar in front of Ex-Templo de San Agustín offers a surreal mix of cocktails, hot chocolates and post-drink munchies. On Saturday, reserve a table outside for prime viewing of the multimedia light show (see p632).

Mina Club BAR
(www.minaeleden.com.mx; Dovali s/n; cover M$100; ☺3-10pm Thu-Sat) Strike it lucky in this unique bar – the tunnel of the Mina El Edén. A mix of electronic music and Spanish pop is the soundtrack to the essential Zacatecas experience. Check the opening hours as these tend to change.

Entertainment

Teatro Calderón THEATER
(Av Hidalgo s/n; ☺10am-9pm) This top venue hosts a variety of cultural events including theater, dance and music performances. Check with the tourist office for current events.

Shopping

Zacatecas is known for silver and leather products and colorful *sarapes*. Try along Arroyo de la Plata (and its indoor market) or at the Mercado González Ortega (p632).

Centro Platero JEWELRY
(www.centroplaterodezacatecas.com; ☺9am-6pm Mon-Fri, 10am-5pm Sat) The Zacatecas silversmith industry lives on in workshops at the Centro Platero, a few kilometers east of town on the road to Guadalupe at the converted 18th-century Ex-Hacienda de Bernardez. Here, young artisans produce various designs, from the traditional to the funky contemporary. To get here, it's easiest to take a taxi (around M$50). Alternatively, shop in its **gallery** (☎925-35-50; Villalpando 406; ☺10am-8pm Mon-Sat, 10am-7pm Sun) in town.

❶ Information

Banks in the center have ATMs and change cash and traveler's checks. Public telephones are at Callejón de las Cuevas, off Avenida Hidalgo. Most internet cafes charge around M$15 per hour for internet access.

Hospital Santa Elena (☎924-29-28; Av Guerrero 143)

Post office (Allende 111; ☺8am-4pm Mon-Fri, 8am-2pm Sat)

State Tourist Office (www.zacatecastravel.com; Av Hidalgo 403; ☺9am-9pm) Offers basic maps and brochures (if available; these tend to run out).

❶ Getting There & Away

Air
Zacatecas' airport is 20km north of the city. **Volaris** (www.volaris.com.mx) has budget flights between Zacatecas and Los Angeles.

Bus
Zacatecas' main bus station is on the southwest edge of town, around 3km from the center. Deluxe, 1st- and 2nd-class buses operate to/from here. Deluxe and 1st-class companies include ETN, Ómnibus de México, Futura and Chihuahuenses. Second-class companies include Estrella Blanca and Camiones de los Altos.

Some buses to nearby destinations including Villanueva (for La Quemada) leave from **Plaza del Bicentenario** (Blvd López Mateos).

See the table for daily departures from the main bus terminal. There are also frequent buses to Jerez and Torreón and several a day to Chihuahua, Ciudad Juárez, Saltillo and Nuevo Laredo. For Guanajuato, take a León bus and change there for Guanajuato.

❶ Getting Around

The easiest way to get to/from the airport is by taxi (M$300 to M$350).

Taxis from the bus station to the center cost around M$35 to M$40. Bus 8 from the bus station (M$5) runs directly to the cathedral. Heading out of the center, buses go south on Villalpando.

BUSES FROM ZACATECAS

DESTINATION	FARE (M$)	DURATION	FREQUENCY (DAILY)
Aguascalientes	86-100	2-3hr	hourly
Durango	182-220	4½-7hr	21
Guadalajara	282-320	4-7hr	hourly
León	160-208	3-4hr	4
Mexico City (Terminal Norte)	400-650	6-8hr	hourly
Monterrey	275-314	7-8hr	11
Querétaro	350-380	6-6¼hr	10
San Luis Potosí	125-140	3-3½hr	hourly

Around Zacatecas

GUADALUPE

📞492 / POP 130,000 / ELEV 2272M

About 10km east of Zacatecas, Guadalupe boasts a fascinating historic former monastery featuring one of Mexico's best colonial art collections. The monastery's impressive church attracts pilgrims to honor the country's beloved Virgin. You'll need a couple of hours to wander through the monastery. A quaint plaza, Jardín Juárez, forms a pretty front setting to the convent.

The **Convento de Guadalupe** was established by Franciscan monks in the early 18th century as an apostolic college. It developed a strong academic tradition and was a base for missionary work in northern Nueva España until the 1850s. The convent now houses the **Museo Virreinal de Guadalupe** (📞923-23-86; Jardín Juárez s/n; admission M$41, Sun free; ⊙9am-6pm), with the building's original religious paintings by Miguel Cabrera, Juan Correa, Antonio Torres and Cristóbal Villalpando. Wandering through the building is a delight; note the extraordinary perspective of the paintings in the cloisters from where you stand. Visitors can see part of the library and its 9000 original volumes (the oldest dates to 1529 and thousands are in storage), and step into the stunning choir on the church's upper floor, with its fine carved and painted chairs.

One room to the right of the museum (the former Museo Regional de Historia) now houses vintage cars.

On the church's north side, don't miss the gilded and beautifully decorated 19th-century **Capilla de Nápoles**. It's open for special occasions only but you can see it on the ground floor through the security grille.

The museum hosts the **Festival Barroco**, a cultural festival, at the end of September and the town holds an annual fair during the first two weeks of December, focused on the **Día de la Virgen de Guadalupe** (December 12).

Transportes de Guadalupe buses run between Zacatecas and Guadalupe every few minutes (M$6, 20 minutes); catch one at the bus stop on Blvd López Mateos across from Plaza del Bicentenario. A taxi between Zacatecas and Guadalupe costs around M$50 to M$60.

WORTH A TRIP

JEREZ

The delightful country town of Jerez (pop 43,000), 30km southwest of Zacatecas, is as Mexican as a tortilla. As such, it's is a great place to head for a day to watch the local action. Sundays – market days – are especially fun as you'll see saddle-bound *rancheros* drinking outside the saloons. Jardín Páez, the pretty main plaza, has an old-fashioned gazebo, trees and benches. Here, too, is a **tourist information kiosk** (⊙11am-6pm). Banks (with ATMs) and phones are around the plaza.

Jerez is known for its lively 10-day Easter fair, featuring, among other activities, *charreadas* (Mexican rodeos) and cockfights.

The town also has some fine buildings. The 18th-century Parroquia de la Inmaculada Concepción and the 19th-century Santuario de la Soledad have lovely stone carvings. Go one block south from Jardín Páez's southeast corner, then one block west for the shrine, or one block east for the church. Just past the shrine, on Jardín Hidalgo's north side, is the beautiful 19th-century Teatro Hinojosa.

It's unlikely you'll need to stay here (except, perhaps, during the Easter fair when accommodations prices triple) but if the town captures your heart, try **Posada Santa Cecilia** (📞494-945-24-12; Constitución 4; s/d/tr M$200/250/300), half a block north of the plaza. The great-value rooms feature decor worthy of Marilyn Monroe: spacious rooms, large pieces of mirrored furniture and cable TV.

Good eating options include **Juana Gallo** (📞494-945-51-88; Guanajuato 9; mains M$60-100; ⊙12:30-10pm), which has a great selection of tasty regional and Mexican dishes; and **Hotel Jardín** (📞494-945-20-26; ⊙8am-10pm), on the plaza.

The Jerez turnoff is near Malpaso, 29km south of Zacatecas on the Zacatecas–Guadalajara road. Ómnibus de México and Estrella Blanca/Rojo de los Altos have regular services from Zacatecas's bus station to Jerez (M$50). Jerez's bus station is on the east side of town, 1km from the center along Calzada La Suave Patria. From here, 'Centro' buses (M$6) run to/from the center.

La Quemada

The impressive **ruins** (admission M$50; ☺9am-5pm) of La Quemada stand on a hill overlooking a broad valley 45km south of Zacatecas, 2.5km east of the Zacatecas–Guadalajara road. The remote and scenic setting makes the ruins well worth the day trip from the hustle and bustle of Zacatecas. The area is known to have rattlesnakes; keep an eye – and ear! – out.

The exact history and purpose of the site are extremely vague. Many suppositions surround the area – one theory is that it was where the Aztecs halted during their legendary wanderings toward the Valle de México. What is known for sure is that the constructions were destroyed by fire – and thus they came to be called La Quemada (meaning 'burned city').

The modern **site museum** (adult/student M$20/10; ☺10am-3:30pm) has interesting archaeology exhibits and an excellent video (with English subtitles). It's worth heading here first to contextualize the area and view the museum's miniature site model to get your bearings for your wanderings.

La Quemada was inhabited between about AD 300 and 1200, and it is estimated to have peaked between 500 and 900 with as many as 3000 inhabitants. From around 400 it was part of a regional trade network linked to Teotihuacán (see p801), but fortifications suggest that La Quemada later tried to dominate trade in this region.

Of the main structures, the nearest to the site entrance is the **Salón de las Columnas** (Hall of the Columns), probably a ceremonial hall. Slightly further up the hill are a **ball court**, a steep **offerings pyramid** and an equally steep staircase leading toward the site's upper levels. From the upper levels of the main hill, a path leads westward for about 800m to a spur hilltop (the highest point) with the remains of a cluster of buildings called **La Ciudadela** (the Citadel). To return, follow the defensive wall and path back around to the museum. Take water and a hat; it's mighty exposed out there.

❶ Getting There & Away

From Zacatecas's Plaza del Bicentenario, board a 2nd-class bus for Villanueva (around M$35) and ask beforehand to be let off at *las ruinas*; you'll be deposited at the turnoff, from where it's a 2.5km walk to the site entrance. Returning

to Zacatecas, you may have to wait a while for a bus – don't leave the ruins too late.

AGUASCALIENTES STATE

The state of Aguascalientes (population 1.2 million) is one of Mexico's smallest; its focus is the city of the same name. According to local legend, a kiss planted on the lips of dictator Santa Anna by the wife of a prominent local politician brought about the creation of a separate Aguascalientes state from Zacatecas.

Beyond the museum-rich city formal tourist sites are few, but it's a pleasant enough drive en route to or from Zacatecas, through fertile lands of corn, beans, chilies, fruit and grain.

The state's ranches produce beef cattle as well as bulls, which are sacrificed at bullfights countrywide.

Aguascalientes

⤴449 / POP 720,000 / ELEV 1880M

This prosperous industrial city is home to more than half of the state's population. Despite its messy outer (defined by ring roads), at its heart are a fine plaza and handsome colonial buildings. Museums are its strong point: the Museo de la Muerte well justifies a visit, as do those devoted to José Guadalupe Posada and Saturnino Herrán.

History

Before the Spanish arrived, a labyrinth of catacombs was built here; the first Spaniards called it La Ciudad Perforada (The Perforated City). Archaeologists understand little of the tunnels, which are off-limits to visitors.

Conquistador Pedro de Alvarado arrived in 1522 but was driven back by the Chichimecs. A small garrison was founded here in 1575 to protect Zacatecas–Mexico City silver convoys. Eventually, as the Chichimecs were pacified, the region's hot springs sparked the growth of a town; a large spring beside the Ojo Caliente springs helped irrigate local farms that fed hungry mining districts nearby.

Today, the city's industries include textiles, wine, brandy, leather, preserved fruits and car manufacturing.

◎ Sights & Activities

Museo Nacional de la Muerte   MUSEUM
(www.museonacionaldelamuerte.uaa.mx; Jardín del Estudiante s/n; adult/student M$20/10; Sun

Aguascalientes

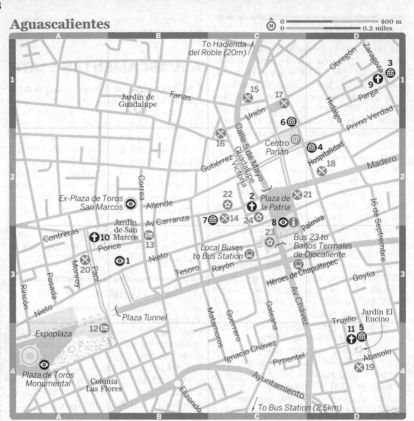

free; ⊗10am-6pm Tue-Sun) This is one 'near death' experience not to be missed. The Museo Nacional de la Muerte exhibits all things relating to Mexico's favorite subject – death – from the skeleton La Catrina to historic artifacts. The contents – over 2500 artifacts, drawings, literature, textiles, toys and miniatures – were donated to the Universidad Autónoma de Aguascalientes by collector and engraver, Octavio Bajonero Gil. Over 1200 are on display. They span several centuries, from Mesoamerican to contemporary artistic interpretations, across seven rooms. In room one, look out for the miniature crystal skull. It's believed to be from Aztec times and there are only two in the world. This wonderful place is far from macabre but a colorful, humorous and insightful encounter.

Museo de Aguascalientes   MUSEUM
(Zaragoza 507; adult/student M$10/5, Sun free; ⊗11am-6pm Tue-Sun) Housed in a handsome neoclassical building, this museum houses a permanent collection of work by the brilliant Aguascalientes artist Saturnino Herrán (1887–1918), and there are also temporary exhibitions. His works are some of the first to honestly depict the Mexican people. The sensual sculpture *Malgretout* on the patio is a fiberglass copy of the marble original by Jesús Contreras.

Plaza de la Patria   PLAZA
The well-restored 18th-century baroque **cathedral**, on the plaza's west side, is more magnificent inside than out. Over the altar at the east end of the south aisle is a painting of the Virgin of Guadalupe by Miguel Cabrera. There are more works by Cabrera, colonial Mexico's finest artist, in the cathedral's *pinacoteca* (picture gallery); ask a priest to let you in.

Facing the cathedral's south side is the **Teatro Morelos**, scene of the 1914 Convention of Aguascalientes, in which revolution-

Aguascalientes

ary factions led by Pancho Villa, Venustiano Carranza and Emiliano Zapata attempted unsuccessfully to mend their differences. Busts of these three, plus one of Álvaro Obregón, stand in the foyer and there are a few exhibits upstairs.

On the plaza's south side, the red-and-pink-stone **Palacio de Gobierno** is Aguascalientes's most noteworthy colonial building. Once the mansion of baron Marqués de Guadalupe, it dates from 1665 and has a striking courtyard with a **mural** of the 1914 convention by the Chilean artist Osvaldo Barra. Barra, whose mentor was Diego Rivera, also painted the mural on the south wall, a compendium of the economic and historic forces that forged Aguascalientes (look for the depiction of the Mexico–US border being drawn).

Jardín El Encino   PLAZA
The fascinating **Museo José Guadalupe Posada** (Jardín El Encino s/n; adult/student M$10/5, Wed free; ⊙11am-6pm Tue-Sun) is on the north side of Jardín El Encino. Aguascalientes native Posada (1852–1913) was in many ways the founder of modern Mexican art. His engravings and satirical cartoons during the Porfiriato dictatorship broadened the audience for art in Mexico, highlighted social problems and were a catalyst in the later mural phase, influencing artists like Diego Rivera, José Clemente Orozco and Alfaro David Siqueiros. Posada's hallmark is the *calavera* (skull or skeleton) and many of his *calavera* engravings have been widely

reproduced. There's also a permanent exhibition of work by Posada's predecessor Manuel Manilla (1830–90).

The **Templo del Encino** (Jardín El Encino; ⊙7am-1pm & 5-7pm), beside the Posada museum, contains a black statue of Jesus that some believe is growing. When it reaches an adjacent column, a worldwide calamity is anticipated. The huge *Way of the Cross* murals are also noteworthy.

Templo de San Antonio   CHURCH
The Templo de San Antonio is a crazy quilt of architectural styles built around 1900 by self-taught architect Refugio Reyes. San Antonio's interior is highly ornate, with huge round paintings and intricate decoration highlighted in gold.

Museo de Arte Contemporáneo   MUSEUM
(cnr Morelos & Primo Verdad; adult/student M$10/5, Sun free; ⊙11am-5:30pm Tue-Sun) A small, modern museum displaying the work of Enrique Guzmán (1952–86) as well as temporary exhibitions, is well worth visiting.

Museo Regional de Historia   MUSEUM
(Av Carranza 118; adult M$37, Sun free; ⊙9am-6pm Tue-Sun) This history museum was designed by Refugio Reyes as a family home and features a small chapel. Its several rooms exhibit items that run all the way from the big bang to the Revolution. Anyone interested in Mexican history will appreciate these displays. For others, the temporary exhibitions can be fascinating; pass by to check what's on.

NORTHERN CENTRAL HIGHLANDS AGUASCALIENTES

Expoplaza & Around
PLAZA

Half a kilometer southwest of Plaza de la Patria via Avenida Carranza, Expoplaza is a modern shopping and restaurant-bar strip. On the mall's south side, the wide and soulless pedestrian promenade comes alive at night and during the annual Feria de San Marcos. At its west end, the mammoth **Plaza de Toros Monumental** is notable for its modern-colonial treatment of traditional bullring architecture.

On Expoplaza's east side the pedestrian street Pani runs two blocks north to the 18th-century **Templo de San Marcos** and the pretty, shady **Jardín de San Marcos**. The **Palenque de Gallos**, in the **Casino de la Feria** building on Pani, is the city's cockfighting arena (only during the *feria*). Near the northeast corner of Jardín de San Marcos is **Ex-Plaza de Toros San Marcos**, the old bullring.

Baños Termales de Ojocaliente
THERMAL BATHS

(☑970-07-21; Tecnológico 102; private baths per hr from M$120; ⊙7am-7pm) Despite the city's name, these charming if slightly shabby thermal baths are the only ones near the center. The restored 1808 architecture truly turns back the clock; the larger baths are more appealing. Take bus 23 or 25 from Mateos.

✥ Festivals & Events

Feria de San Marcos
FAIR

Mid-April sees Mexico's biggest annual month-long state fair, the Feria de San Marcos. It centers on Expoplaza and attracts millions of visitors with exhibitions, bullfights, cockfights, rodeos, concerts and cultural events. The big parade takes place on the saint's day, April 25.

Festival de las Calaveras
TRADITIONAL

During the two-week Festival de las Calaveras (the dates vary but always encompass November 1 and 2), Aguascalientes celebrates **Día de Muertos** (Day of the Dead) with an emphasis on the symbolism of *calavera*.

🛏 Sleeping

Prices skyrocket during the Feria de San Marcos (April) and accommodations are completely booked for the fair's final weekend; residents run a lucrative homestay service at this time.

Fiesta Americana
LUXURY HOTEL **$$$**

(☑910-05-00; www.fiestaamericana.com; Laureles s/n, Colonia Las Flores; r from M$1988; P❂✿🛜🍽) This luxury chain hotel is a pleasant five-star experience; the 192 rooms feature all the amenities and there's a fitness center and an inviting pool. Weekend packages for two cost around M$1500 and include buffet breakfast. Check for discounts.

Hacienda del Roble
HOTEL **$$**

(☑915-39-94; Calle 5 de Mayo 540; r from M$450) This is by far the pick of the midrange choices, with small but modern carpeted rooms, external-facing windows and reasonable bathrooms. The downside is the grittier and noisier location – right on Calle 5 de Mayo – but it's only a 10-minute walk to the plaza.

Hostal Posada
HOSTEL **$**

(☑918-64-36; www.hostalposada.tk; Correa 139; dm/r M$120/260; 🛜) This converted house offers male and female dorms and private rooms. It's not overflowing with toilets and bathrooms, but it's a safe and friendly spot and run by the owners. A kitchen is provided and basic meals are available daily (M$25).

✖ Eating

Four blocks north of the Plaza de la Patria, fresh produce and cheap eats are available in three markets: **Mercado Juárez**, **Mercado Jesús Terán** and **Mercado Morelos**. Avenida Carranza west of the plaza has a wonderful array of trendy cafes, offering snacks and drinks in the evenings.

San Marcos Merendero
MEXICAN **$**

(Andador Pani 144; ⊙noon-3am; mains M$30-100) This bustling, barn-like place is where everyone – young and old – comes to whoop it up. And believe us, it's not-to-be-missed fun. There are performing mixologists who whip up some of the best margaritas around, friendly staff (some of whom have been here longer than the decor) and a blend of traditional Mexican folkloric paraphernalia, from stuffed bulls heads to decaying streamers. Here, the idea is to chat and drink – the more you do of both, the more *botanas* (tasty snacks) are served.

Restaurant Mitla
MEXICAN **$$**

(Madero 220; mains M$60-180; ⊙7am-10pm) This large, pleasant and popular restaurant is caught in a time warp: 1938, the year it started. There are white-shirted waiters and excellent service, plus a grand menu with a choice of Mexican specialties, set breakfasts (from M$75) and buffet lunches (M$85).

Sanborns
MEXICAN $$

(Plaza de la Patria; mains M$65-140) A glorious, old-fashioned salon with good meals (especially breakfast and afternoon teas) and views over the plaza. Located on the 2nd floor of the department store itself.

Rincón Maya
YUCATECAN $$

(Abasolo 113; mains M$90-140; ☺2pm-midnight Mon-Sat, 2-10:30pm Sun) Until lunchtime, this place has service at La Mestiza Yucateca (open 8am till 2pm), its alter ego next door. Both serve delectable Yucatecan specialties.

La Saturnina
MEXICAN

(Av Carranza 110; mains M$60-80; ☺8am-8pm) Set in the courtyard of an 18th-century former mansion, this old-fashioned spot is well known among local diners for its tasty menu. The name is in honor of the tragic heroine, Saturnino Herrán, so beautifully painted.

☆ Entertainment

Pani, the pedestrian street between the Expoplaza and Jardín de San Marcos, is lively most evenings, with a good selection of bars and restaurants.

The trendy nightspots are out in the suburbs; **Centro Comercial Galerías** (☎912-66-12; Independencia 2351) is a shopping mall with several bars and discos, while the main drag for late-night discos is north of town on Avenida Colosio.

In a fine 17th-century building, the **Casa de la Cultura** (Av Carranza 101) hosts art exhibitions, concerts, theater and dance events. The **Teatro Morelos** (Nieto 113, Plaza de la Patria) and the **Teatro de Aguascalientes** (cnr Calles Chávez & Aguascalientes), south of the center, both stage a variety of cultural events.

ℹ Information

Emergency
Police (☎066, 080)

Internet Access
Most places charge around M$12 per hour.
Café Internet 3W (Centro Parián; ☺9am-9pm Mon-Sat, 11am-6pm Sun)

Medical Services
Several pharmacies in the city center are open 24 hours.
Star Médica (☎910-99-00; Universidad 103) Hospital.

Money
Banks with ATMs are common around Plaza de la Patria and Expoplaza. *Casas de cambio* cluster on Hospitalidad, opposite the post office.

Tourist Information
State tourist office (www.aguascalientes.gob. mx; Palacio de Gobierno, Plaza de la Patria; ☺9am-8pm Tue-Sat, 9am-6pm Sun) Free city maps. Ask for *Cartel del Arte*, a what's-on listing.

ℹ Getting There & Away

Air
Aéropuerto Jesús Terán (☎918-28-06) is 26km south of Aguascalientes off the road to Mexico City. **Aeroméxico Connect** (☎918-21-27; Madero 474) has flights to Mexico City, Monterrey plus flights via Mexico City to Los Angeles and New York. **Volaris** (www.volaris.mx) serves Los Angeles and Tijuana. Both Continental and American Airlines have regular flights to Houston, Dallas and Los Angeles.

Bus
The **bus station** (Central Camionera; Av Convención) is 2km south of the center. It has a post office, card phones, a cafeteria and luggage storage.

Deluxe, 1st- and 2nd-class buses operate to/from Aguascalientes. Deluxe and 1st-class companies include ETN, Primera Plus, Futura and

BUSES FROM AGUASCALIENTES

DESTINATION	FARE (M$)	DURATION	FREQUENCY (DAILY)
Guadalajara	200-260	2¾-3hr	25
Guanajuato	161	3hr	7:30pm
León	93-115	2-3½hr	every 30min
Mexico City (Terminal Norte)	460-576	6hr	9
San Luis Potosí	108-140	3-3½hr	5
Zacatecas	85-130	2hr	8

Ómnibus de México. The main 2nd-class line is Coordinados (Flecha Amarilla).

As well as those outlined in the table, frequent services go to Ciudad Juárez, Monterrey, Morelia and Torreón, and two buses daily to San Miguel de Allende.

ℹ Getting Around

Most places of interest are within easy walking distance of each other. Regular city buses (M$6) run from 6am to 10:30pm. Buses display route numbers; check which bus heads to the city center as these change regularly. Disembark at the first stop after you go through the town's one tunnel on Calle 5 de Mayo. This is one block from the plaza. From the city center to the bus station, several buses head to the bus station from the corner Galeana (near Insurgentes).

Taxis charge as per metered fares. Between the bus station and the center the taxi fare is around M$25 to M$30.

SAN LUIS POTOSÍ STATE

The historic state capital city, San Luis Potosí, and the fascinating 'ghost town,' Real de Catorce, are on the high and dry expanses of the state's north and west and are the main reasons visitors come to this region. The pretty tropical, verdant eastern region, the Huasteca, is popular among local tourists.

The state is steeped in history. Before the Spanish conquest, western San Luis Potosí was inhabited by Guachichiles, warlike hunters. In the 18th century the area gained a reputation for maltreatment of indigenous people, partly because the nonmonastic clergy replaced the more compassionate Franciscans.

Today, mining, agriculture, ranching and industry are the economic mainstays of this fairly prosperous state with a population of 2.6 million.

San Luis Potosí

✈ 444 / POP 720,000 / ELEV 1860M

A grand old dame of colonial cities, San Luis Potosí was once a revolutionary hotbed, an important mining town and seat of government to boot. Today the city has maintained its poise as the prosperous state capital, orderly industrial center and university seat.

A great place to wander through, the city's colonial core is made up of numerous beautiful plazas and manicured parks that are linked by attractive pedestrian streets. Although not as striking as Zacatecas or Guanajuato, this lively city's cultural elegance is reflected in its delightful colonial buildings, impressive theater and numerous excellent museums.

History

Founded in 1592, San Luis is 20km west of the silver deposits in Cerro de San Pedro, and was named Potosí after the immensely rich Bolivian silver town, which the Spanish hoped it would rival. The mines began to decline in the 1620s, but the city was established enough as a ranching center to remain the major city of northeastern Mexico until overtaken by Monterrey at the start of the 20th century.

Known in the 19th century for its lavish houses and imported luxury goods, San Luis was twice the seat of President Benito Juárez's government during the 1860s French intervention. In 1910 in San Luis, the dictatorial president Porfirio Díaz jailed Francisco Madero, his liberal opponent, during the presidential campaign. Freed after the election, Madero hatched his Plan de San Luis Potosí (a strategy to depose Díaz), announcing it in San Antonio, Texas, in October 1910; he declared the election illegal, named himself provisional president and designated November 20 as the day for Mexico to rise in revolt – the start of the Mexican Revolution.

◉ Sights

Museo Federico Silva   MUSEUM
(www.museofedericosilva.org; Obregón 80; adult/student M$30/15; ◷10am-6pm Mon-Sat, 10am-2pm Sun) This museum should not be missed. The original 17th-century building on the north side of the Jardín de San Juan del Dios was once a hospital and later a school under *el porfiriato* (the Porfiriato period). It has been exquisitely transformed into a contemporary art museum, ingeniously integrating the building's previous neoclassical finish with the monolithic sculptures of Silva. Temporary exhibitions of internationally known contemporary sculptors.

Museo de Arte Contemporáneo   MUSEUM
(MAC; Morelos 235; adult/child M$20/10; ◷10am-6pm Tue-Sat, 10am-2pm Sun) This museum is housed in the city's former post office; these days, the brilliantly transformed space houses temporary art exhibitions.

San Luis Potosí

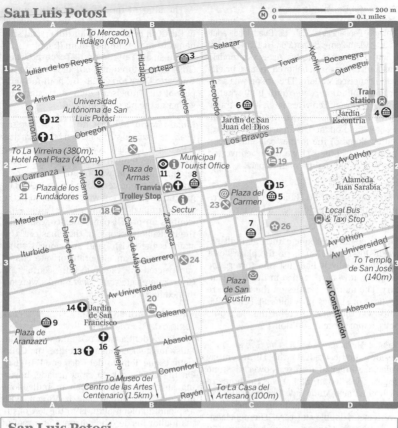

N 0 ——— 200 m
0 ——— 0.1 miles

San Luis Potosí

◉ Sights

1 Capilla de Loreto	A2
2 Cathedral	B2
3 Museo de Arte Contemporaneo (MAC)	B1
4 Museo del Ferrocarril	D1
5 Museo del Virreinato	C2
6 Museo Federico Silva	C1
7 Museo Nacional de la Máscara	C3
8 Museo Othóniano	B2
9 Museo Regional Potosino	A4
10 Palacio de Gobierno	A2
11 Palacio Municipal	B2
12 Templo de la Compañía	A2
13 Templo de la Tercera Orden	A4
14 Templo de San Francisco	A3
15 Templo del Carmen	C2
16 Templo del Sagrado Corazón	B4

⊕ Activities, Courses & Tours

17 Operatour Potosina	C2

⊟ Sleeping

18 Hotel de Gante	B2
19 Hotel María Cristina	C2
20 Hotel Museo Palacio de San Agustín	B3
21 Hotel Panorama	A2

⊗ Eating

22 Antojitos El Pozole	A1
23 Apikus	C2
24 Café Tokio	B3
25 Chaires	B2

⊕ Entertainment

26 Teatro de la Paz	C3

⊙ Shopping

27 Fonart	A3

Museo del Centro de las Artes Centenario
MUSEUM

(Antigua Penitenciaria; Calz de Guadalupe; adult M$5; ⏱10am-2pm & 5-8pm Mon-Fri, 11am-5pm Sat & Sun) The Centro de las Artes Centenario was a former prison, believed to have briefly held Francisco Madero. The prison was a social rehabilitation center until 1999 when it officially closed. Ten years later, it was transformed – without losing its fundamental design – and opened as an arts and cultural center. Some of the former cells have been maintained; others have been converted into offices but maintain an impact.

Plaza de Armas
PLAZA

Also known as Jardín Hidalgo, this pedestrianized plaza is the city's central square.

Cathedral
The three-nave baroque cathedral, built between 1660 and 1730, is on the plaza's east side. Originally it had just one tower; the northern tower was added in the 20th century. The marble apostles on the facade are replicas of statues in Rome's St Peter's Basilica. On the hour, listen for the electronic bells, a more recent addition.

Palacio Municipal & Palacio de Gobierno
Beside the cathedral, the 19th-century Palacio Municipal features powerful stone arches. Finished in 1838, it was the home of Bishop Ignacio Montes de Oca from 1892 to 1915. The city's coat of arms in stained glass overlooks a double staircase. The neoclassical Palacio de Gobierno, built between 1770 and 1816, lines the plaza's west side. Its most illustrious lodger was Benito Juárez – first in 1863 when he was fleeing from invading French forces, then in 1867 when he confirmed the death sentence on the puppet emperor Maximilian.

Museo Othóniano
MUSEUM

(Av Othón 225; admission M$5; ⏱10am-6pm) Behind the cathedral, this museum is the birthplace of much-celebrated Mexican poet, Manuel José Othón (1858–1906). The 19th-century home is furnished in period style and exhibits Othón's manuscripts and personal effects.

Jardín de San Francisco
(Jardín Guerrero) PLAZA

Dominated by the buk of the Templo de San Francisco and convent, and with a lovely fountain gracing its interior, this square is one of the city's most fetching.

The altar of the 17th- and 18th-century Templo de San Francisco was remodeled in the 20th century. A beautiful crystal ship hangs from the church's main dome.

The small Templo de la Tercera Orden (1694 and restored in 1960) and Templo del Sagrado Corazón (1728–31), both formerly part of the Franciscan monastery, stand together at the plaza's south end.

Museo Regional Potosino
MUSEUM

(Plaza de Aranzazú s\n; admission M$37, Sun free; ⏱9am-6pm Tue-Sun) Along Galeana to the west of the Templo de San Francisco, this fetching museum was originally part of a Franciscan monastery founded in 1590. The ground floor – part of which is housed in the small Capilla de San Antonio de Padua – has exhibits on pre-Hispanic Mexico, especially the indigenous people of the Huasteca. Upstairs is the lavish, gold and aqua Capilla de Aranzazú, an elaborate private chapel constructed in the mid-18th century in Churrigueresque style. New monks were ordained here.

Plaza del Carmen
PLAZA

Templo del Carmen
The Plaza del Carmen is dominated by San Luis's most spectacular structure, the Churrigueresque Templo del Carmen (1749–64). On the vividly carved stone facade, hovering angels show the touch of indigenous artisans. The Camarín de la Virgen, with a splendid golden altar, is to the left of the main altar inside. The entrance and roof of this chapel are a riot of small plaster figures.

Teatro de la Paz
Near the church, the neoclassical Teatro de la Paz (1889–94) contains a concert hall and exhibition gallery as well as a theater. Posters announce upcoming events.

Museo del Virreinato
MUSEUM

(www.museodelvirreinato.mx; Villerías 155; admission M$15, Tue free; ⏱10am-7pm Tue-Fri, 10am-9pm Sat, 10am-5pm Sun) Beside the Templo de Carmen, this museum has a large collection of paintings and artifacts from the Spanish vice-regency. More of interest might be its temporary exhibitions – check what's on.

Museo Nacional de la Máscara
MUSEUM

(National Mask Museum; ☎812-30-25; Plaza del Carmen; admission M$15, camera use M$20; ⏱10am-6pm Tue-Fri, to 5pm Sat, 11am-3pm Sun) Displays an interesting collection of ceremonial masks from across Mexico and around the world. There are good descriptions in English and interesting videos of dances performed during festivals in communities.

Plaza de los Fundadores & Around   PLAZA
The least pretty of the plazas, Plaza de los Fundadores (Founders' Plaza) is where the city was born. On the north side is a large building constructed in 1653 as a Jesuit college. Today it houses offices of the Universidad Autónoma de San Luis Potosí. It was probably on this site that Diego de la Magdalena, a Franciscan friar, started a small settlement of Guachichiles around 1585.

To the west of these offices is the **Templo de la Compañía**, built by the Jesuits in 1675 with a baroque facade. A little further west is the **Capilla de Loreto**, a Jesuit chapel from 1700 with unusual, twisted pillars.

Alameda & Around   PARK
The **Alameda Juan Sarabia** marks the eastern boundary of the downtown area. It used to be the vegetable garden of the monastery attached to the Templo del Carmen. Today it's a large, attractive park with shady paths.

Inside the **Templo de San José**, facing the Alameda's south side, lies the image of El Señor de los Trabajos, a Christ figure attracting pilgrims from near and far. Numerous *retablos* (altarpieces) around the statue testify to prayers answered in finding jobs and other miracles.

Museo del Ferrocarril   MUSEUM
(Av Othón; admission M$15; ⊙10am-6pm Tue-Sat, to 4pm Sun) On the north side of the Alameda, this museum is housed in the city's former train station and very cleverly brings to life its past. The existing building was designed by Manuel Ortiz Monasterio and was constructed in 1936. Exhibits include modern installations relating to train travel plus former locomotive parts.

☞ Tours

Tranvía   TRAM
(☏814-22-26; www.tranviasanluis.com; 1hr trip M$50) The Tranvía, an imitation of an antique trolley, does a loop around the historic center starting from in front of the Cathedral on Plaza de Armas. Hours vary seasonally.

Operatour Potosina   CITY, CULTURAL
(☏151-22-01; www.operatourpotosina.com.mx; Sarabia 120) If you want to do a tour, Operatour Potosina is the best outfit to do it with.

This friendly and knowledgeable English-speaking operator offers tours around the city, as well as to haciendas, Real de Catorce and the Huasteca Potosina region. It's located in the Hotel Napoles.

★ Festivals & Events

Semana Santa   RELIGIOUS
Holy Week is celebrated with concerts, exhibitions and other activities; on Good Friday (March/April) at 3pm, Christ's passion is re-enacted in the barrio of San Juan de Guadalupe, followed at 8pm by the Silent Procession through the city center (one of the city's most important events).

Feria Nacional Potosina   FAIR
San Luis' National Fair, normally in the last three weeks of August, includes concerts, bullfights, rodeos, cockfights and agricultural shows.

Día de San Luis Rey de Francia   RELIGIOUS
On August 25 the city's patron saint, St Louis IX (King of France), is honored as the highlight of the Feria Nacional. Events include a parade, concerts and plays.

Festival Internacional de Danza   DANCE
This national festival of contemporary dance is held in September and October.

🛏 Sleeping

San Luis's accommodations can be summed up easily: less comfort means more convenience and, rather unfortunately, more comfort means less convenience. While it's more enjoyable to be in the atmospheric pedestrianized center, midrange and top-end options are limited. Many of the more appealing international chain hotels are located on the main highways (some near the bus station); you'll need to take a taxi.

Hotel Museo Palacio de San Agustín   HISTORIC HOTEL $$$
(☏144-19-00; www.palaciodesanagustin.com; Galeana 240; r M$4800-5300; ⊛) 'Warning': this lush and plush experience comes with a snob rating index. This extraordinary place goes beyond a boutique hotel – it is a 'museum.' Formerly a house belonging to the San Agustín monastery, it has been restored to its original condition (think hand-painted gold-leaf finishes, crystal chandeliers and 700 certified European antiques). The pièce de résistance has to be the hotel's own replica of the San Agustín facade and *capilla*

(we won't spoil the surprise). Advance reservations only.

Hotel Panorama
BUSINESS HOTEL $$

(☑812-17-77, 800-480-01-00; www.hotelpanorama.com.mx; Av Carranza 315; r/ste M$870/1270; P❄✿☎⊠) It's the best of a rather average lot of accommodations options and has position going for it here – opposite Plaza de los Fundadores. Beyond that, it's smart(ish) and all 126 rooms have floor-to-ceiling windows. Those on the south side overlook the pool. A marble-clad lobby and ground-floor restaurant make it popular with business travelers.

Hotel de Gante
PENSION $

(☑812-14-92/93; hotel_degante@hotmail.com; Calle 5 de Mayo 140; s/d/tr M$340/390/450; ☎) In an unbeatable location, near the corner of Plaza de Armas, Gante will please budget travelers – clean, airy rooms with cable TV.

Hotel Real Plaza
HOTEL $$

(☑814-69-69; Carranza 890; s/d M$650/690) This business hotel lacks personality, but it is clean and neat.

Hotel María Cristina
HOTEL $$

(☑812-94-08; www.mariacristina.com.mx; Sarabia 110; s/d/tr M$530/580/640; P@☎) Centrally located, if a little faded.

🍴 Eating

One local specialty is *tacos potosinos* – red, chili-impregnated tacos stuffed with cheese or chicken and topped with chopped potato, carrot, lettuce and loads of *queso blanco* (white cheese).

⭐TOP CHOICE El México de Frida

MEXICAN $$

(☑811-46-03; www.elmexicodefrida.com; Valentín Gama 646; mains M$100-230; ☺1pm-midnight Mon-Sat, 1-6pm Sun) Although it's painted in Kahlo-esque colors, this restaurant is not Frida-kitsch. Rather, the tasteful and tasty menu serves up scrumptious Mexican fare. Try the *chiles ventilla*, chilies with cheese and the most tantalizing creamy sauces. It's 3km along (and just south of) Avenida Carranza.

ℹ️ TOP SPOTS

Head west of the center along Avenida Carranza ('La Avenida') for some good quality cafes and upscale restaurants.

Apikus
MEDITERRANEAN $$

(Escobedo 305; mains M$100-240; ☺1:30-10:30pm Tue-Sat) Sleek and stylish and *a la moda*. Its minimalist setting on the terrace is beautifully offset against the colonial architecture of surrounding buildings. Modern fusion cuisine includes great meat, fish and pasta dishes.

La Virreina
MEXICAN, INTERNATIONAL $$$

(Av Carranza 830; www.lavireeina.com.mx; mains M$180-210; ☺1pm-midnight Tue-Sat, 1-6pm Sun; ☺) A long-established gourmet favorite and the city's oldest surviving restaurant, the charming Virreina has had a recent upmarket overhaul with a twist of contemporary design, but hasn't lost its elegance. The classic menu includes both international and Mexican dishes, delicious desserts and an excellent reputation. A stunning garden terrace is out the back.

Chaires
CAFE $

(Plaza de Armas; snacks M$15-40; ☺8am-10pm) The best ice creamery and cafe for good-quality snacks and surveying the local scene.

Antojitos El Pozole
MEXICAN $

(cnr Calles Carmona & Arista; mains M$30-65; ☺noon-11:30pm Tue-Sun) The place to try the local *enchiladas potosinas* – the tortilla dough is red (from mild chili). This place was started by a woman selling *antojitos* (Mexican snacks) in her home in the 1980s. Demand for her goods was so high she has since opened three restaurants specializing in what she knows best – *tacos rojos, pozole, quesadillas de papa* (potato quesadillas)... Yes, they're that good.

Café Tokio
MEXICAN $

(cnr Calles Zaragoza & Guerrero; mains M$50-80; ☺7:30am-11pm) This bright and sizeable cafe has Japanese owners but Mexican and fast-food standards. Popular for a cheap set lunch and breakfast deals.

☆ Entertainment

San Luis has an active cultural scene. Ask in the tourist office about what's on and keep your eye out for posters. The free monthly *Guiarte* booklet and posters detail cultural attractions. For a night of dancing, San Luis is steeped in Latin rhythms; if you like salsa, then you are in luck. Popular discos, bars and music venues are found west along Avenida Carranza and Jiménez. They change at a beat – it's best to ask the younger crowd.

Teatro de la Paz CONCERT VENUE
(Villerias 2) This neoclassical, 1500-seat venue presents a variety of local and visiting dance, theater and music ensembles.

Orquesta Sinfónica MUSIC
(☎814-36-01; tickets from M$30) Symphony comes to Teatro de la Paz and other venues; check with the tourist office.

🛍 Shopping

The main shopping district is between the Plaza de Armas and the **Mercado Hidalgo**. A few blocks further northeast is the larger, interesting **Mercado República**. Look out for the local specialty, milky sweets.

Fonart HANDICRAFTS
(Aldama 300) Like other shops in the government-run chain, this outlet has a good selection of quality handicrafts from all over Mexico.

La Casa del Artesano HANDICRAFTS
(☎814-89-90; Jardín Colón 23) For more local products, try this shop full of *potosino* pottery, masks, woodwork and canework.

❶ Information

Internet Access
Most places charge around M$15 per hour.
Café Cibernetico (Av Carranza 416)
Fox Ciberkafe (Escobedo 315; ⊙9am-9pm)

Medical Services
Hospital Vivo (☎100-95-00; Arista 735)

Money
Banks with ATMs are scattered around town, including the Plaza de Armas and Plaza de los Fundadores. Several *casas de cambio* are along Morelos.

Banamex (cnr Obregón & Allende) Like other banks, changes cash and traveler's checks.

Post
Post office (Av Universidad 526; ⊙8am-3pm Mon-Fri)

Telephone
Card phones are dotted around the center.

Tourist Information
Municipal tourist office (☎812-27-70; Palacio Municipal; ⊙8am-8pm Mon-Sat, 9am-6pm Sun) On the east side of Plaza de Armas.
Sectur (State tourist office; ☎812-99-39, 800-343-38-87; www.sanluispotosi.gob.mx; Av Othón; ⊙8am-9pm Mon-Fri, 9am-3pm Sat) Has maps of off-the-beaten-track attractions in San Luis Potosí state.

Travel Agencies
2001 Viajes (☎812-29-53; Obregón 604) For air tickets.

❶ Getting There & Away

Air
Aeropuerto Ponciano Arriaga (☎822-00-95) is 10km north of the city off Hwy 57. Aeroméxico Connect offers direct service to/from Mexico City and Monterrey with connecting flights to various US cities.

Bus
The **Terminal Terrestre Potosina** (TTP; ☎816-46-02; Carretera 57), 2.5km east of the center, is a busy transportation hub that has deluxe, 1st-class and some 2nd-class bus services. Its facilities include card phones, 24-hour luggage storage and snack places.

First-class companies include ETN, Primera Plus, Transportes del Norte and Futura. The main 2nd-class companies are Coordinados (Flecha Amarilla) and Estrella Blanca.

BUSES FROM SAN LUIS POTOSÍ

DESTINATION	FARE (M$)	DURATION	FREQUENCY (DAILY)
Guadalajara	340-440	5-6hr	hourly
Guanajuato	200	5hr	7am
Matehuala		2½hr	hourly
Mexico City (Terminal Norte)	255-445	5-6½hr	hourly
Monterrey	385	6hr	3
Querétaro	155-220	2½-4hr	frequent
San Miguel de Allende (via Queretaro)	178	5hr	2
Zacatecas	170	3hr	frequent

In addition to those outlined in the table, daily buses go to Ciudad Juárez, Ciudad Valles, Ciudad Victoria, Chihuahua, Dolores Hidalgo, León, Morelia, Nuevo Laredo, Saltillo and Torreón.

Car & Motorcycle

Car-rental prices range from M$1100 to M$1300 per day. There are also week-long packages available.

Hertz (812-32-29; Obregón 670)

ℹ Getting Around

Taxis charge around M$150 to M$210 for the half-hour trip to/from the airport.

To reach the center from the bus station, take any 'Centro' bus. A convenient place to get off is on the Alameda, outside the former train station. A booth in the bus station sells taxi tickets (M$40 to M$60) to the center.

From the center to the bus station, take any 'Central TTP' bus southbound on Avenida Constitución from the Alameda's west side.

City buses run from 6:30am to 10:30pm (M$7). For places along Avenida Carranza, catch a 'Morales' or 'Carranza' bus in front of the train station.

Matehuala

TRANSPORTATION HUB
☑488 / POP 77,000 / ELEV 1580M

The only town of any size on Hwy 57 between Saltillo and San Luis Potosí, Matehuala is a pleasant but unremarkable place. It is a compulsory changing point for buses to Real de Catorce.

If you do find yourself stuck here, the bus station is just west of the highway, 2km south of the center. To walk to the center, turn left out of the bus station and continue along Avenida 5 de Mayo for 1.5km, then turn left on Insurgentes for a few blocks to reach the Plaza de Armas. Alternatively, take a microbús marked 'Centro'; microbuses marked 'Central' head in the direction of the terminal. A taxi costs M$35.

All essential services (ATMs, phones, internet etc) are around the main plazas – the shady Plaza de Armas and the busy Placita del Rey 300m to its north, which features a neo-Gothic-neoclassical **cathedral**. Cheaper hotels and the town's restaurants are in this area.

Las Palmas Midway Inn (☑882-00-01/02; www.laspalmasmidwayinn.com.mx; Carretera 57, Km 617; RV sites M$285, s/d/tr M$897/996/1025; P❋@☎), out by the highway, is a family-oriented trailer park with nice rooms around landscaped gardens.

To appease grumbling stomachs, try the bustling and longstanding local favorite **Restaurant Santa Fe** (Morelos 709; breakfast M$65-75, mains M$45-85; ☺7am-1am) on Plaza de Armas, where bow-tied waiters will serve you a variety of Mexican standards or breakfast.

From Matehuala, there are daily bus departures to Mexico City Terminal Norte (around M$520, eight hours, seven 1st class direct); to Monterrey (M$300, 4½ hours, hourly 1st class); to Saltillo (M$230, 3¼ hours, nine 1st class); to San Luis Potosí (M$170 to M$215, 2½ hours, hourly 1st class); and Querétaro (M$335, 4½ hours, hourly 1st class). For bus schedules to/from Real de Catorce see p653.

Real de Catorce

☑488 / POP 1300 / ELEV 2730M

Energy – in a spiritual sense – is a word commonly ascribed to the alluring village of Real de Catorce. This stark, compact and functioning 'ghost town' sits high on the fringes of the magical Sierra Madre Oriental. It was a wealthy silver-mining town of 40,000 people until early last century. Not long ago, it was nearly deserted, its streets lined with crumbling buildings, its mint a ruin and a few hundred people eking out an existence from the annual influx of pilgrims and old mine tailings.

Over the last few decades Real has experienced a slight revival; it has attracted several well-to-do Mexicans and foreigners (especially Europeans) who run some of the businesses and smarter hotels in town. Nevertheless, recent economic woes have hit Real hard and although it might never live up to its former 'ghost town' label, doors do creak in the breeze, dusty cobblestone streets end abruptly and many buildings remain in ruins.

To soak up its magic and unique atmosphere, you need to stay a night here, longer if you wish to explore the surrounding hills on foot or horseback.

History

Real de Catorce translates as 'Royal of 14': the '14' may have come from 14 Spanish soldiers killed here by indigenous resistance fighters around 1700. The town was founded in the mid-18th century and the church built between 1790 and 1817.

The town reached its peak in the late 19th century, vying to surpass the famed Valen-

ciana mine of Guanajuato. It had opulent houses, a bullring and shops selling European luxury goods.

Just why Real became a ghost town within three decades is a mystery. Some locals claim (as they do in many ghost towns) that during the Revolution (1910–20) *bandidos* hid out here and scared off other inhabitants. A more plausible explanation is that the price of silver slumped after 1900.

⊙ Sights & Activities

The ambience of the desert setting makes up for the lack of major sights around town. If you're into walking or horseback riding, there's plenty to keep you occupied here for several days.

Templo de la Purísima Concepción CHURCH
(⊙7am-9pm) This charming *parroquia* (parish church) is an impressive neoclassical

building. The attraction for thousands of Mexican pilgrims is the reputedly miraculous image of St Francis of Assisi, recently relocated from a side altar to the front of the church. A cult has grown up around the statue, whose help is sought in solving problems and cleansing sins.

Walk through the door to the left of the altar to find a roomful of *retablos,* small pictures depicting threatening situations from which St Francis has rescued the victim, with a brief description of the incident – car accidents and medical operations, for example – and some words of gratitude. *Retablos* have become much sought after by collectors and are very occasionally seen in antique shops. Sadly, most of those on sale have been stolen from churches.

Just up the street from the Templo de la Purísima Concepción there is a local silver workshop, **Taller de Platería** (Juárez).

Centro Cultural de Real de Catorce
NOTABLE BUILDING

(Casa de la Moneda; admission M$10; ⊙10am-7pm Tue-Sun) Opposite the church's facade, the Centro Cultural de Real de Catorce, the old mint, made coins for 14 months (1,489,405 pesos-worth to be exact) in the mid-1860s. This classic monument has been exquisitely restored over the last few years. It now houses a cultural-center-cum-gallery with several levels of temporary exhibitions, often on loan from museums in Mexico City. The bottom floor has a permanent exhibition depicting photos and machinery from the original mint.

Galería Vega m57
GALLERY

(Zaragoza 3; ⊙11am-4pm Sat, to 3pm Sun) Real's only dedicated art gallery hosts exhibitions and installations of contemporary work in a variety of media in a restored colonial building.

FREE Palenque de Gallos
MONUMENT

(Xicotencatl s/n; ⊙9am-5pm) A block northwest of the plaza lies a monument to the town's heyday – the Palenque de Gallos, a cockfighting ring, built like a Roman amphitheater. It was restored in the 1970s and sometimes hosts theater or dance performances. Then follow Zaragoza-Libertad north to the edge of the town where there are remains of the former bullring **Plaza de Toros**; the **Capilla de Guadalupe** (⊙8am-5pm) and *panteón* (cemetery) across the street are free and worth a look.

Hiking
HIKING

If you prefer to do your own hikes, you can head out from Real in almost any direction. The hike closest to home is that up the hill to the **Pueblo Fantasmo** (Ghost Town), on the hill behind – and clearly visible from – the town center. Head along Lanzagorta and stay left (avoid the road that veers right to the car park). The track you follow was the former entrance to town before the tunnel existed. Allow at least one hour to get to the top – there is another section around 100m further on behind the ruins visible from the town. Beware that there are two large shafts (estimated to be hundreds of meters deep) in the ruins.

To extend this hike, head northwest along the ridge to the antennas and to the cross over the town (make sure you note this from the town before you leave, as it becomes obscured when on the ridge). Follow the path *behind* the cross before you weave your way down to the cemetery (allow three to four hours for the longer hike).

Another shorter hike is to **Socavón de Purísima**, a large chimney of a former mine. Head down Allende and veer right at its end. You are on the road to Estación de Catorce. Follow this road until you reach the chimney (about 45 minutes one way). The road passes through a cut or split rock, the Cerro Trocado. To enter the mine, speak to the caretaker family (a tip is gratefully received). To return, it's a longer and harder slog back up the hill (one hour one way; on weekends you might be able to grab a lift in a 'Jeep Willys'). Caution: be prepared – tell others where you're headed, and take water, a hat and strong footwear; it's dry and unforgiving country.

Horseback Riding
HORSEBACK RIDING

Ride 'em cowboy! Numerous trails lead out into the dry, stark and fascinating desertscapes – hilly and flat – around Real. The most popular guided trail ride is the three-hour trip to **El Quemado**, the sacred mountain of the Huicholes. Here you'll find expansive views of the high-desert plateau and a small shrine to the sun god.

Horse guides now belong to a union, approved by the municipality; if unsure, ask for a guide's credentials. The aim of the union is to standardize prices and safety. Rates are around M$100 per hour. Note that no protective hats are provided; you clomp off at your own risk.

The horses and guides congregate every morning around Plaza Hidalgo. Trips in 'Jeep Willys' can also be arranged to many of the same locations, mainly on weekends. Ask any of the drivers along Lanzagorta or Allende, or at the tourist office. Rates vary according to the trip and numbers.

★ Festivals & Events

Fiesta de San Francisco
RELIGIOUS

Real is quiet during the week and busier on weekends. Semana Santa and Christmas are big events and the Fiesta de San Francisco is huge. Between the end of September to the end of October, 150,000 pilgrims pay homage to the figure of St Francis of Assisi in the town's church. Many of them just come for the day, while thousands stay in the town, filling every rentable room and sleeping rough in the plazas. The streets are lined with stalls selling religious souvenirs and

FIESTA TIME

Tourists who desire the more tranquil 'ghost-town experience' should keep well away from Real de Catorce during the Fiesta de San Francisco; visiting at any other time is ideal.

food, while many of the town's more upmarket restaurants close for a month.

Festival del Desierto   CULTURAL
The Festival del Desierto cultural festival features folkloric music and dance performances in towns all around the region. Dates vary annually; check before you come.

🛏 Sleeping

It can be very cold here in winter in the cheapest digs; bring a sleeping bag or request extra blankets.

Real has seen a recent surge of restoration of old buildings into inviting upmarket accommodations.

TOP CHOICE **Mesón de Abundancia**   HOTEL $$
(📞887-50-44; www.mesonabundancia.com; Lanzagorta 11; d M$650-1000, tr M$1000, ste M$1000-1200, f M$1500; 🛜) Relive the town's bonanza era on the desert plateau in this stone citadel. The 19th-century former *tesorería* (treasury) building has been renovated into a hotel and restaurant. All 11 rooms are simply and tastefully decorated with local crafts (minus TV) and make a cozy retreat on chilly nights. Rates are cheaper Sunday to Thursday, excluding holidays. Ironically, given its cash-oriented past, the hotel accepts some credit cards, except American Express.

Hotel El Real   HOTEL $$
(📞887-50-58; www.hotelreal.com.mx; Morelos 20; r M$520-950; 🛜) Much of the appeal to this comfortable, restored place is the delightful multilingual owners themselves (Cornelia knows all about Real and more, and Humberto has appeared in Hollywood productions, ever since he was an extra in *The Mexican*, filmed in Real and released in 2001). Besides which, there are lovely rooms on three floors around an open courtyard, some with views over the town and the hills. There's a cozy cafe-restaurant and a large terrace. The hotel's tastefully decorated second branch, **Hotel El Real II** (cnr Juaréz &

Iturbide) is along similar lines but with a bar in front called Amor Y Paz (open weekends only). Rates are negotiable according to numbers and nights.

Hostal Alcazaba   APARTMENT $$
(📞887-50-75; www.villaalcazaba.com; Libertad-Zaragoza 33; apt M$750-1000; 🅿) Opposite the cemetery, this option has four bright, light *casitas* (small houses), some with kitchen and all with panoramic views. There's also a house (previously the owners' and great for families). The enormous garden hosts excellent desert flora.

Hotel Shantiniketan   GUESTHOUSE $$
(Morada de Paz; 📞887-50-98; www.shantiniketan.com.mx; cnr Zaragoza & Lerdo; r M$750-1900) There's a definite karma here: the eight rooms are named after Indian spiritual leaders. Each is minimalist and unfussy, although some are a bit dark, and you can't open the windows. They surround a small garden courtyard. Open weekends only.

El Corral del Conde   HOTEL $$
(📞887-50-48; Constitución 17; r M$650-950) The original 11 rustic, stone-walled rooms somehow miss the mark on the boutique hotel front, but it's got character nevertheless. Its second hotel, **El Corral del Conde II** (cnr Morelos & Lanzagorta), just down the hill, has another 13 newer rooms.

Hotel Real de Álamos   PENSION $
(Hospedaje Familiar; 📞887-50-09; Constitución 21; s/d M$150/250) This place has small, basic rooms with concrete walls. The terrace provides excellent views of town.

🍴 Eating & Drinking

Several restaurants compete (with each other and with the better hotels) to do the best Italian and Mexican cuisine. Some close during the week if business is slow.

Mesón de Abundancia   MEXICAN & ITALIAN $$
(www.mesonabundancia.com; Lanzagorta 11; mains M$75-140) There are several cozy eating areas at the restaurant in this hotel, one with a bar and fireplace. The hearty (read massive) servings of Italian and Mexican dishes are *muy rico* (delicious). It's open all day, including breakfast.

Café Azul   CAFE $
(Lanzagorta 27; snacks M$25-60; ⊙8am-5pm Thu-Tue, to midnight Fri & Sat) Open all day, this airy, Swiss-run scene is perfect for breakfasts,

HUICHOL VISIONS

The remote Sierra Madre Occidental, in and around the far north of Jalisco, is the home of the Huicholes, one of Mexico's most distinctive and enduring indigenous groups. Fiercely independent people, they were one of the few indigenous groups not subjugated by the Aztecs. Traditionally, they lived by hunting deer and cultivating scattered fields of corn in the high valleys.

The arrival of the Spanish had little immediate effect on the Huicholes and it wasn't until the 17th century that the first Catholic missionaries reached the Huichol homelands. Rather than convert to Christianity, the Huicholes incorporated various elements of Christian teachings into their traditional animist belief systems. In Huichol mythology, gods become personalized as plants, totem animal species and natural objects, while their supernatural form is explored in religious rituals.

Every year the Huicholes leave their isolated homeland and make a pilgrimage of some 400km across Mexico's central plateau to the Sierra de Catorce, in northern San Luis Potosí state. In this harsh desert region, they seek out the *mescal* cactus (*Lophophora williamsii*), known as peyote cactus. The rounded peyote 'buttons' contain a powerful hallucinogenic drug (whose chief element is mescaline) that is central to the Huicholes' rituals and complex spiritual life. Most of the buttons are collected, dried and carried back to the tribal homelands, but a small piece is eaten on the spot, as a gesture to the plant. Small amounts of peyote help to ward off hunger, cold and fatigue, while larger amounts are taken on ritual occasions, such as the return from the annual pilgrimage. In particular, peyote is used by shamans whose visions inform them about when to plant and harvest corn, where to hunt deer or how to treat illnesses.

Peyote is illegal in Mexico. Under Mexican law, the Huicholes are permitted to use it for their spiritual purposes. For the Huicholes, it has great cultural and spiritual significance; indiscriminate use is regarded as offensive, even sacrilegious.

Traditionally, the main Huichol art forms were telling stories and making masks and detailed geometric embroidery, or 'yarn pictures.' In the last few decades, the Huicholes have been depicting their myths and visions graphically, using brightly colored beads pressed into a beeswax-covered substrate. This exquisite artwork is sold in craft markets, shops and galleries. Prices are usually fixed and the Huicholes don't like to haggle. This art may be expensive compared to some (of the tackier) souvenirs, but each takes a long time to produce and each piece is unique. To see the best work, visit one of the specialist museums or shops in Zapopan (Guadalajara), Tepic, Puerto Vallarta or Zacatecas.

At the time of research, Canadian mining interests had secured mining concessions in the Sierra de Catorce, including in and around sacred areas. Groups of protestors – from Huicholes themselves to famous Mexican actors – were staging protests in Mexico City against both potential mining activities and President Calderón, who seemed to have broken a promise he'd made to the Huichol people. Many viewed it as a potential environmental nightmare – having a detrimental affect on peyote cacti, water springs in the mountains, and age-old Huichol traditions and culture. Local people in Real de Catorce were strangely quiet, if divided, in opinion about the mine. Many saw it as a potential source of employment.

freshly-baked cakes and light meals including excellent crepes. Also has internet.

Cafe El Real
INTERNATIONAL $

(www.hotelreal.com.mx; Morelos 20; mains M$65-80; ⊙9am-6pm) This welcoming spot – with sofas and fire – serves up international cuisine from pastas to meats (including wild goat and rabbit dishes) in a delightfully cozy spot. The generous *comida corrida* (prix-fixe menu) goes for M$130.

TOP CHOICE Amor y Paz
BAR

(www.amorypaz.realde14.net; cnr Juaréz & Iturbide; ⊙6pm-late Fri & Sat) If there's any suggestion that Real is a ghost town it might be because half the town and its visitors 'hides' out here, at this funky bar, hidden behind the walls of Hotel El Real. It's decked out in antiques (note the amazing wooden bar), retro seating, and quirky chandeliers, and serves a range of mezcals, alcoholic tea infusions, live music and lots (read *lots*) of fun.

❶ Information

See www.realdecatorce.net for a good overview of the town. Card phones are located around Plaza Hidalgo. There's one ATM in town, located in the tourist office, but on busy weekends it occasionally runs out of money; best to bring cash.

Mesón de Abundancia (Lanzagorta 11) This hotel changes US dollars, traveler's checks and euros.

Super La Nueva Sorpresa (Lanzagorta 2) Changes US dollars if it has pesos on hand.

Tourist office (☏887-50-71; Palacio Municipal, Constitución s/n; ☺9am-4pm) Opening hours are a little flexible; simple street map available.

❶ Getting There & Away

Sendor runs 1st-class buses from Matehuala's bus station to Real de Catorce (around M$70, two hours) at 7:45am, 11:45am, 1:45pm and 5:45pm (with an extra one on Sundays at 9:45am); the bus can be caught 15 minutes later at the Sendor office in Matehuala, a little east of and across the street from Hotel Álamo on Méndez. However, if you're coming from San Luis Potosí you can buy a one-way (or return; valid for six months) ticket and change in Matehuala (the total cost for two tickets one-way is around M$240).

On arrival in Real, buses park at the east entrance of the Ogarrio tunnel. There, in order to pass through the tunnel, you change to a smaller bus which drops off (or picks up if returning to Matehuala) at the western end of the tunnel, in Real. Confirm the return bus schedule upon arrival. At the time of research, buses from Real to Matehuala (with connections to San Luis Potosí) were at 7:40am, 11:40am, 3:40pm and 5:40pm (M$70, two hours). Tickets are purchased at the Senda ticket office, on the edge of the car park at the tunnel's western entrance in Real; if this is not operating you can buy them on board the bus.

If driving from Hwy 57 north of Matehuala, turn off toward Cedral, 20km west. After Cedral, you turn south to reach Catorce on what must be one of the world's longest cobblestone roads. It's a slow but spectacular zigzag drive up a steep mountainside. The 2.3km-long Ogarrio tunnel (M$20 per vehicle) is only wide enough for one vehicle; workers stationed at each end with telephones control traffic flow between 7am and 11pm. If it's really busy, you'll have to leave your car at the eastern tunnel entrance and continue by pick-up or cart. If you drive through, you must leave your car in the parking area to the left of the market.

Vintage 'Jeep Willys' leave Real around noon (and on demand), downhill from the plaza along Allende, for the rough but spectacular descent to the small hamlet of Estación de Catorce (around M$50 per person, one hour). From there, buses head to San Tiburcio, where there are connections for Saltillo and Zacatecas.

GUANAJUATO STATE

The rocky highland state of Guanajuato (population 5.5 million) is full of riches of every kind. In colonial times, mineral resources attracted Spanish prospectors to mine for silver, gold, iron, lead, zinc and tin. For two centuries the state produced enormous wealth, extracting up to 40% of the world's silver. Silver barons in Guanajuato city enjoyed opulent lives at the expense of indigenous people who worked the mines, first as slave labor and then as wage slaves. Eventually, resenting the dominance of Spanish-born colonists, the well-heeled criollo class of Guanajuato and Querétaro states contributed to plans for rebellion (see boxed text, p667).

These days, the state's treasures are the quaint colonial towns of Guanajuato and San Miguel de Allende. The industrial town of León is important economically as a center of leather production. Visitors to this region can enjoy its precious legacies: stunning colonial architecture, established cultural scenes and a stream of never-ending festivals...not to mention friendly, proud locals and a lively university atmosphere.

Guanajuato

📍473 / POP 72,000 / ELEV 2045M

The extraordinary Unesco World Heritage city of Guanajuato was founded in 1559 due to the region's rich silver and gold deposits. Opulent colonial buildings, stunning tree-filled plazas and brightly colored houses are crammed onto the steep slopes of a ravine. Excellent museums, handsome theaters and a fine marketplace punctuate the cobblestone streets. The city's 'main' roads twist around the hillsides and plunge into tunnels, formerly rivers.

The city is best known internationally for its acclaimed annual international arts festival, the Festival Cervantino. Yet this colorful and lively place holds center stage all year long; much of the youthful vibrancy and prolific cultural activities – *callejoneadas*,

Guanajuato

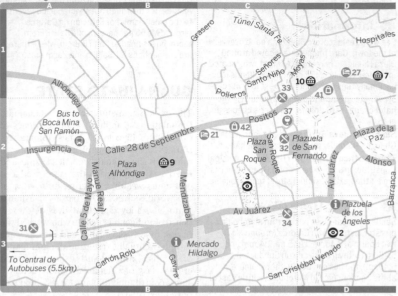

films, theater and orchestras – can be attributed to the 20,000 students of the city's own University of Guanajuato.

The city usually boasts fine weather during the day, but beware of cold and windy nights in the winter.

History

One of the hemisphere's richest silver veins was uncovered in 1558 at La Valenciana mine; for 250 years the mine produced 20% of the world's silver. Colonial barons benefiting from this mineral treasure were infuriated when King Carlos III of Spain slashed their share of the wealth in 1765. The King's 1767 decree banishing the Jesuits from Spanish dominions further alienated both the wealthy barons and the poor miners, who held allegiance to the Jesuits.

This anger was focused in the War of Independence. In 1810 rebel leader Miguel Hidalgo set off the independence movement with his Grito de Independencia (Cry for Independence) in nearby Dolores (see boxed text, p667). Guanajuato citizens joined the independence fighters and defeated the Spanish and loyalists, seizing the city in the rebellion's first military victory. When the Spaniards eventually retook the city they retaliated by conducting the infamous 'lottery of death,' in which names of Guanajuato citizens were drawn at random and the 'winners' were tortured and hanged.

Independence was eventually won, freeing the silver barons to amass further wealth. From this wealth arose many of the mansions, churches and theaters.

In the late 1990s the state prospered under its PAN (National Action Party) governor, Vicente Fox Quesada, with Mexico's lowest unemployment rate and an export rate three times the national average. Fox was chosen as the PAN candidate for the 2000 presidential election and his popularity sealed the victory (his presidential term ended in 2006).

⊙ Sights

Central Plazas   PLAZA
A wander around the beautiful main plazas, the bustling hubs of Guanajuato's social life, is a good introduction to Guanajuato's historic center. Pretty **Jardín de la Unión**, surrounded by restaurants and shaded by Indian laurel trees, is the social heart of the city. Here, tourists and locals congregate in the late afternoon, along with buskers, shoeshiners and Mariachis.

The elegant **Teatro Juárez** sits on its southeast corner. Walk west on Obregón to **Plaza de la Paz**, the small triangle be-

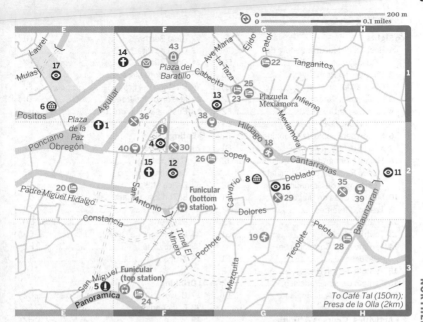

side the basilica, surrounded by the former homes of wealthy silver lords.

Meander west and south along the curving Avenida Juárez to **Plazuela de los Ángeles**, where the steps are popular gathering spots for students. The Callejón del Beso is just a few meters uphill from here.

Continue on Avenida Juárez to three picturesque spaces: the handsome **Jardín de la Reforma**, behind the row of classical columns; **Plaza San Roque**, where *entremeses* (theatrical sketches) are performed in the Cervantino festival; and the pretty, flower-filled **Plazuela de San Fernando** nearby.

Head further west on Avenida Juárez to the bustling area in front of the Mercado Hidalgo. A block north, **Plaza Alhóndiga** has wide steps leading up to the Alhóndiga. From there, wander back east along Calle 28 de Septiembre (which changes names several times), past museums and the university, with a few twists and turns, to **Plaza del Baratillo** with its Florentine fountain. From here you can detour to the tiny **Plazuela Mexiamora** and down again to Baratillo. A right turn and a short block south from there will bring you back to Jardín de la Unión.

Museo y Casa de Diego Rivera　MUSEUM
(Positos 47; adult M$20; ⊙10am-6:30pm Tue-Sat, 10am-2:30pm Sun) Diego Rivera's birthplace

is now an excellent museum honoring the painter (the Marxist Rivera was *persona non grata* here for years); it's worth spending an hour or so at the museum – longer if you're a Rivera fan.

Rivera and a twin brother were born in the house in 1886 (his twin died at the age of two) and lived here until the family moved to Mexico City six years later. The museum's ground floor is the Rivera family home, with 19th-century antiques and fine furniture.

The 1st and 2nd floors feature a permanent collection of his original works and preliminary sketches (completed for some of his famous murals in Mexico City), plus there's a nude of Frida Kahlo. The newer renovated upper floors host temporary exhibitions of work by Mexican and international artists. An intimate theater upstairs has occasional films and features black and white photographs of Kahlo and Rivera.

Funicular　FUNICULAR
(Plaza Constancia s/n; one way/round trip M$15/ 30; ⊙8am-9:45pm Mon-Fri, 9am-9:45pm Sat, 10am-8:45pm Sun) This incline railway inches up (and down) the slope behind the Teatro Juárez to a terminal near the El Pípila monument. Heading up is fun, but to descend, save your pennies and walk down (there are two obvious, well-paved routes).

Guanajuato

Monumento a El Pípila MONUMENT
The monument to El Pípila honors the hero who torched the Alhóndiga gates on September 28, 1810, enabling Hidalgo's forces to win the first victory of the independence movement. The statue shows El Pípila holding his torch high over the city. On the base is the inscription *Aún hay otras Alhóndigas por incendiar* (There are still other Alhóndigas to burn).

Two routes from the center of town go up steep, picturesque lanes. One goes east on Sopeña from Jardín de la Unión, then turns right on Callejón del Calvario (this becomes Pochote; turn right at Subida San Miguel). Another ascent, unmarked, goes uphill from the small plaza on Alonso. Alternatively, the 'Pípila-ISSSTE' bus heading west on Avenida Juárez will let you off right by the statue, or you can ride up in the funicular.

Museo Regional de Guanajuato
Alhóndiga de Granaditas MUSEUM
(Calle 28 de Septiembre; admission M$49, video/camera use M$30/60; ⊙10am-5:45pm Tue-Sat, 10am-2:45pm Sun) The site of the first major rebel victory in Mexico's War of Independence is now a history and art museum. The Alhóndiga was a massive grain-and-seed storehouse built between 1798 and 1808. In 1810 it became a fortress for Spanish troops and loyalist leaders. They barricaded themselves inside when 20,000 rebels led by Miguel Hidalgo attempted to take Guanajuato. It looked as if the outnumbered Spaniards would be able to hold out. Then, on September 28, 1810, a young miner named Juan José de los Reyes Martínez (aka El Pípila), under orders from Hidalgo, tied a stone slab to his back and, thus protected from Spanish bullets, set the main door ablaze. While the Spaniards choked on smoke, the

rebels moved in and took the Alhóndiga, killing all 300 people inside. (El Pípila probably perished in the battle, but some versions of the story have it that he lived to a ripe old age.)

The Alhóndiga was used as an armory, then a school, before it was a prison for 80 years (1864–1948). It became a museum in 1958. Don't miss José Chávez Morado's dramatic murals of Guanajuato's history on the staircases.

Theaters
NOTABLE BUILDING

Don't leave without visiting the magnificent **Teatro Juárez** (▣732-01-83; Sopeña s/n; adult/student M$35/15; ☺9am-1:45pm & 5-7:45pm Tue-Sun). It was built between 1873 and 1903 and inaugurated by the dictator Porfirio Díaz, whose lavish tastes are reflected in the plush red-and-gold interior. The outside is festooned with columns, lampposts and statues; inside, the impression is Moorish, with the bar and lobby gleaming with carved wood, stained glass and precious metals. It's only open when no performances are scheduled; video/camera use is M$60/30.

The **Teatro Principal** (▣732-15-23; Hidalgo s/n) and **Teatro Cervantes** (▣732-11-69; Plaza Allende s/n) are not as spectacular as Teatro Juárez, but they host a full schedule of performances during the Cervantino festival and less-regular shows at other times. Statues of Don Quixote and Sancho Panza grace the small Plaza Allende, in front of Teatro Cervantes.

Ex-Hacienda San Gabriel de Barrera
MUSEUM, GARDEN

(▣732-06-19; Camino Antiguo a Marfil, Km 2.5; adult/student M$22/15; ☺9am-6pm) To escape Guanajuato's bustling streets, head 2.5km west to this magnificent colonial home which is now a museum with stunning gardens. This tranquil retreat is well worth a couple of hours.

Built at the end of the 17th century, this was the grand hacienda of Captain Gabriel de Barrera, whose family was descended from the first Conde de Rul of the famous La Valenciana mine. Opened as a museum in 1979, the hacienda, with its opulent period European furnishings, provides an insight into the lives of the wealthy of the time.

Take one of the frequent 'Marfil' buses heading west in the subterranean tunnel under Avenida Juárez and ask the driver to drop you at Hotel Misión Guanajuato.

Museo Iconográfico del Quijote
MUSEUM

(Doblado 1; adult/student M$30/10; ☺9:30am-6:45pm Tue-Sun) Surprisingly interesting, this museum is worth half an hour of your time. It fronts the tiny plaza in front of the Templo de San Francisco. Every exhibit relates to Don Quixote de la Mancha, the notorious Spanish literary hero, depicted in numerous different media by different artists in different styles. Paintings, statues, tapestries, even chess sets, clocks and postage stamps all feature the quixotic icon and his bumbling companion Sancho Panza.

Templo La Valenciana
CHURCH

On a hill overlooking Guanajuato, 5km north of the center, is the magnificent **Templo La Valenciana** (Iglesia de San Cayetano). Its facade is spectacular and its interior dazzles with ornate golden altars, filigree carvings and giant paintings. One legend says that the Spaniard who started the nearby San Ramón mine promised San Cayetano that if it made him rich, he would build a church to honor the saint. Another says that the silver baron of La Valenciana, Conde de Rul, tried to atone for exploiting the miners by building the ultimate in Churrigueresque churches. Whatever the motive, ground was broken in 1765 and the church was completed in 1788.

Boca Mina San Ramón & Bocamina de San Cayetano
MINES

(admission M$35; ☺10am-6pm) These neighboring mines are part of the famous Valenciana mining district. Silver was discovered here in 1548. **San Ramón** is a bit limited in activities; the most interesting thing is to descend via steps into a mine shaft to a depth of 60m (note: not for claustrophobics). **San Cayetano** has an interesting museum with models of mines and former miners take you on a brief tour – this also includes a visit into a shaft.

To reach the mines, take a regular 'Cristo Rey' or 'Valenciana' bus from the bus stop on the corner of Alhóndiga and Calle 28 de Septiembre. Get off at Templo La Valenciana and follow the signs behind the church.

Museo de las Momias
MUSEUM

(Museum of the Mummies; ▣732-06-39; Explanada del Panteón Municipal s/n; adult/student M$52/35; ☺9am-6pm) This famous museum is one of the most bizarre (some might say grotesque) sights at the *panteón* (cemetery). This popular place is a quintessential example of

HOT-FOOTING IT AROUND GUANAJUATO

Guanajuato's center is quite compact, with a few major streets and lots of tiny *callejones* (alleys). It's ideal for walking but tricky to drive around – leave your car in a car park on the outskirts and catch a taxi or local bus into town. The main street, running roughly east–west, is called Juárez from the Mercado Hidalgo to the basilica on Plaza de la Paz. East of the basilica, it continues as a pedestrian street and changes name several more times.

Roughly parallel to Juárez/Obregón is another long street, running from the Alhóndiga to the university and bearing the names Calle 28 de Septiembre and Positos along the way. Hidalgo (aka Cantarranas) parallels another main access street, Sopeña, and is another important street. Once you know these streets you can't get lost – just walk downhill until you find one of them. You can, however, have a great time getting lost among the maze of crooked *callejones* winding up the hills from the center (beware: muggings have occurred around the alleys near Pípila; don't carry valuables).

Traffic travels east to west on the main arteries. Vehicles (including public buses) going west to east must use the main underground roadway, Subterránea Padre Miguel Hidalgo, a one-way route along the dried-up Río Guanajuato riverbed. (The river was diverted after it flooded the city in 1905.) At least eight other tunnels have been constructed to cope with increasing traffic. No map shows tunnel entry and exits; if on a bus, ask the driver for the nearest exit to your desired landmark.

Surrounding central Guanajuato is the winding Carretera Panorámica, offering great views of the town and surrounding hills.

Mexico's acceptance of, celebration of and obsession with death; visitors come from all over to see disinterred corpses.

While technically these are mummified remains – due to the dry atmosphere in their former crypts – the bodies are not thousands of years old. The first remains were disinterred in 1865 to make room for more bodies in the cemeteries. What the authorities uncovered were not skeletons but flesh mummified (many feature grotesque forms and facial expressions). Today the museum displays more than 100 mummies.

The complex is on the western edge of town, a 10-minute ride from Avenida Juárez on any 'Momias' bus (M$5).

Churches
CHURCH

The **Basílica de Nuestra Señora de Guanajuato** (Plaza de la Paz s/n), a block west of Jardín de la Unión, contains a jewel-covered image of the Virgin, patron of Guanajuato. The wooden statue was supposedly hidden from the Moors in a cave in Spain for 800 years. Felipe II of Spain gave it to Guanajuato in thanks for the wealth it provided to the crown. Next door, the small **Galería Mariana** (Plaza de la Paz s/n; admission M$10; ☺10am-6pm Thu-Mon) is dedicated to images of Mary and other Catholic relics.

Other fine colonial churches include the **Templo de San Diego** (Jardín de la Union s/n), opposite the Jardín de la Unión; the **Templo de San Francisco** (Doblado s/n); and the large **Templo de la Compañía de Jesús** (Lascuraín de Retana s/n), which was completed in 1747 for the Jesuit seminary whose buildings are now occupied by the University of Guanajuato.

Museo del Pueblo de Guanajuato
MUSEUM

(Positos 7; adult/student M$15/5; ☺10am-6:30pm Tue-Sat, 10am-2:30pm Sun) Located beside the university, this fascinating art museum displays an exquisite collection of Mexican miniatures, and 18th- and 19th-century art with works by Guanajuatan painters Hermenegildo Bustos and José Chávez Morado, plus temporary exhibitions. The museum occupies the former mansion of the Marqueses de San Juan de Rayas, who owned the San Juan de Rayas mine. The private church upstairs in the courtyard contains a mural by José Chávez Morado.

Callejón del Beso
NOTABLE BUILDING

Narrowest of the many narrow alleys that climb the hills from Guanajuato's main streets is this *callejón* (the Alley of the Kiss), where the balconies of the houses on either side of the alley practically touch. In a Guanajuato legend, a fine family once lived on this street and their daughter fell in love with a common miner. They were forbidden to see each other, but the miner rented a room opposite and the lovers exchanged furtive *besos* (kisses) from these balconies. Inevitably, the romance was discovered and the couple met a tragic end. From the Plazuela de los Ángeles on Avenida Juárez, walk about 40m up Callejón del Patrocinio to see the tiny alley on your left.

Casa de Arte Olga Costa-José Chávez Morado MUSEUM
(Pastita No. 158, Torre del Arco; adult/student M$20/5; ☉9:30am-4pm Thu-Sat, 10am-3pm Sun) In 1966, artists José Chávez Morado and Olga Costa converted a massive old well into their home and studio; before their deaths, they donated their home and its contents for public use. On display is a small, but fascinating collection of items from the 16th to 18th centuries, including pre-Hispanic and modern ceramics, embroidery, furniture, masks and their own artworks. It's worth heading to the 'suburb' of Pastita to experience a side of Guanajuato you might otherwise miss. The pretty approach follows the former aqueduct which ends at their house. Take any bus marked 'Pastita' from the eastern end of town.

Universidad de Guanajuato NOTABLE BUILDING
(UGTO; ☎732-00-06; www.ugto.mx; Lascuraín de Retana 5) The main building of this university, whose ramparts are visible above much of the city, is one block up the hill from the basilica. The distinctive multistory white-and-blue building with the crenelated pediment dates from the 1950s. The design was (and, some might say, continues to be) controversial as this dominating structure impedes the characteristic, historic cityscape.

Museo del Siglo XIX MUSEUM
(☎734-61-93; www.museodelsiglo19.com.mx; Positos 25; admission M$20; ☉10am-6pm Mon-Sun) Opened in 2010 and housed in a renovated colonial mansion, the seven rooms showcase a private collection of items relating to the history of Guanajuato, from photos and books, paintings and documents of the 19th century, before 1910.

Cristo Rey MONUMENT
Cristo Rey (Christ the King) is a 20m bronze statue of Jesus erected in 1950 on the summit of the Cerro de Cubilete, 15km west of Guanajuato. It is said to be the exact geographical center of Mexico. The statue is a popular attraction for Mexican tourists;

there is a special significance in having Jesus at the heart of their country.

Tour agencies offer 3½-hour trips to the statue, but you can go on your own from the center. Buses marked 'Cubilete' or 'Cristo Rey' depart every hour or so from Alhóndiga (M$17).

Activities

Bike Station Guanajuato CYCLING
(☎732-70-54; Cantarranas 57; bikestationguanajuato@hotmail.com) All cycling enthusiasts shouldn't go past the biking boys at Bike Station. Cycling tours range from a three-hour trip around the Panorámica, to a 10-hour harder and longer route to Dolores Hidalgo via the mountains. Advanced rides cover around 75km. Needless to say, views are stupendous and you get off the beaten track. Prices range from M$585 to M$760 for longer rides, transport and all gear included. Swiss guide Guido speaks English.

Callejoneadas MUSIC, DANCING
The wonderfully fun *callejoneadas* (street parties, or *estudiantinas*) depart nightly from in front of San Diego church on the Jardín de la Unión (see boxed text, p660). It's a unique way to take in Guanajuato by night.

Courses

Guanajuato is a university town and has an excellent atmosphere for studying Spanish. Group classes average around US$150 to US$210 for 20 lessons (one week's worth) and private lessons average US$15 an hour. Schools can arrange homestays with meals for around US$180 per week. Additional costs may include registration and/or placement test fees, excursions and extracurricular activities. Language schools to consider include **Adelita** (☎473-100-49-47; www.la-adelita.org; Agua Fuerte 56), **Don Quijote** (☎923-277-200; www.donquijote.org; Calle Pastita 76, Barrio Pastita), **Plateros Spanish School** (☎732-99-42; www.platerosspanishschool.com; Alonso 14A) and **Escuela Mexicana** (☎732-50-05; www.escuelamexicana.com; Potrero 12).

Mika Matsuishi & Felipe Olmos workshops ART & CRAFT
(☎cell phone 473-1204299; lunamika47@hotmail.com; 5 days from M$800) Hands-on, puppet and fun art workshops for creative souls run by talented artists and *mojiganga* specialists. Materials included; held regularly.

NORTHERN CENTRAL HIGHLANDS GUANAJUATO

CALLEJONEADAS – THE TRADITIONAL WAY TO PARTY, PARTY, PARTY!

The *callejoneada* tradition is said to have come from Spain. A group of professional singers and musicians, dressed in traditional costumes, starts up in a central location such as a plaza, a crowd gathers, then the whole mob winds through the alleyways, streets and plazas playing, dancing and singing heartily. In Guanajuato, they are also called *estudiantinas*. Stories and jokes (in Spanish) are told in between songs, often relating to the legends of the alleys. In Zacatecas, there are no stories, but hired bands called *tamboras* (dressed in uniform, not traditional attire) lead dancing revelers. On special occasions a burro laden with wine is brought along. Often, strangers are just expected to join the party and the crowd swells. Occasionally, the organizers foot the bill, sometimes you pay a small amount for the wine you drink (or you bring your own!). In Guanajuato, the groups themselves or tour companies sell tickets (around M$100; Tuesday through Sunday) for the *callejoneadas* and juice (not alcohol) is provided. It's great fun and a traditional way to party hearty!

Festivals & Events

Baile de las Flores RELIGIOUS
The Flower Dance takes place on the Thursday before Semana Santa. The next day, mines are open to the public for sightseeing and celebrations. Miners decorate altars to La Virgen de los Dolores, a manifestation of the Virgin Mary who looks after miners.

Fiestas de San Juan y Presa de la Olla RELIGIOUS
The festivals of San Juan are celebrated at the Presa de la Olla park in late June. The 24th is the big bash for the saint's day itself, with dances, music, fireworks and picnics. Then on the first Monday in July, everyone comes back to the park for another big party celebrating the opening of the dam's floodgates.

Día de la Cueva RELIGIOUS
Cave Day is a country fair held on July 31, when locals walk to a cave in the nearby hills to honor San Ignacio de Loyola and enjoy a festive picnic.

Fiesta de la Virgen de Guanajuato RELIGIOUS
This festival on August 9 commemorates the date when Felipe II gave the people of Guanajuato the jeweled wooden Virgin that now adorns the basilica.

Festival Internacional Cervantino ARTS
In the 1950s the arts festival was merely *entremeses* from Miguel Cervantes' work performed by students. It has grown to become one of Latin America's foremost arts extravaganzas (www.festivalcervantino.gob.mx). Music, dance and theater groups from around the world perform diverse works (mostly non-Cervantes related) for two weeks in October. Tickets for single events range from M$130 to M$650. Tickets (www.ticketmaster.com.mx) and hotels should be booked in advance. In Guanajuato, buy tickets from the ticket office on the southeast side of Teatro Juárez.

Sleeping

During the Festival Internacional Cervantino in October, Christmas, Semana Santa (and in some cases only, summer holiday periods), prices may be double the regular rates given here.

TOP CHOICE **Casa Estrella de la Valenciana** B&B $$$
(☏732-17-84; www.mexicaninns.com; Callejon Jalisco 10; r M$2000-2700; ☀) This delightful US-owned abode ticks many boxes: eight unique rooms, *boveda* (vaulted) ceilings, private terraces, and stunning, sunny communal areas. Then there's the delightful staff, lavish breakfasts and a swimming pool. Perched high above Guanajuato in La Valenciana (around a M$45 taxi ride or M$5 bus ride), it suits those who don't mind being out of the bustle of the city, but you will have to rely on transport to get you to and 'fro.

Hotel Villa María Cristina BOUTIQUE HOTEL $$$
(☏731-21-82; www.villamariacristina.net; Paseo de la Presa de la Olla 76; ste M$3500-4200; ☻☜☀) This stunning converted mansion is scented with expensive perfume. The decor in the spacious rooms features neoclassical French designer furniture, original paintings by local artist Jesús Gallardo, and beds and bathrooms with all the 'fluffy and puffy'

NORTHERN CENTRAL HIGHLANDS GUANAJUATO

trimmings. Outside, various patios (which are covered in exquisite, original tiles) have everything from fountains and wicker chairs to Jacuzzis plus views of La Bufa. An onsite restaurant is open all day (dinner mains M$195 to M$320). It's in La Presa, a 15-minute walk from the center.

El Zopilote Mojado
GUESTHOUSE $$

(☏732-53-11; www.elzopilotemojado.com; Plazuela Mexiamora 51 & 53; r & apt US$65, 6-person family apt US$220; ⊜ 🛜) Eight pleasant rooms are located above Café Zopilote Mojado and in a house nearby, where they share a spacious communal kitchen, lounge-dining area and outdoor terraces. The lion's head above the fireplace is anomalous; that said, this place should have you purring. Two chic (if dark) apartments and a family apartment are near the plaza. Weekly rates negotiable.

Alonso10 Hotel Boutique & Arte
BOUTIQUE HOTEL $$$

(☏732-76-57; www.hotelalonso10.com.mx; Alonso 10; ste from M$2600; 🌠 🛜) One of Guanajuato's newest additions is this sleek boutique hotel, located a street away from the centralized chaos. White and taupe hues rule, as do smart rooms with all the trimmings. The front two suites have fabulous balconies with quirky views of the basilica and the back of Teatro Juárez. Downstairs is an elegant restaurant (mains M$100 to M$150).

Casa Zuniga
B&B $$

(☏732-85-46; www.casazunigagto.com; Callejón del Pachote 38; r incl breakfast M$800-1000) This sprawling B&B offers various modern rooms and receives rave reviews for its hospitality and breakfasts. It's located at lofty heights – on the hill near El Pípila – to the left of the funicular (as heading uphill), or by car and bus along Panoramica. Rates include a funicular pass throughout your stay.

Antiguo Vapor
HOTEL $$$

(☏732-32-11; www.hotelavapor.com; Galarza 5; r M$1700-2900; 🅿⊜@🛜) For those who want a more personal feel to their accommodations experience, the rooms in this nest (each room has a bird name) are decorated in contemporary Mexican style with brightly colored bedcovers, tiles and *boveda* ceilings. Rooms vary, however – some have a much better outlook and light than others.

Quinta Las Acacias
LUXURY HOTEL $$$

(☏731-15-17, in Mexico 800-710-89-38, in USA 888-497-4129; www.quintalasacacias.com.mx; Paseo de la Presa 168; ste incl breakfast M$2750-5000; 🅿🌠 @🛜) This hideaway combines attentive service and intimate luxury in a former 19th-century French-colonial summer residence. Each of the 17 rooms is uniquely decorated. The elegant, bygone-era style rooms are located in the original house, while newer Mexican-themed suites are located behind the house. The most peaceful and modern suites (all with small patios) are situated around a stunning protected cactus garden. It has a charming, chandeliered restaurant, open for all meals. Head up Paseo de la Presa; the hotel is on the left-hand side opposite the park.

Hostería del Frayle
HOTEL $$

(☏732-11-79; www.hosteriadelfrayle.com; Sopeña 3; r/tr from M$800/900; ⊜🛜) A block from the Jardín, this historic hotel (it was built in 1673 as the Casa de Moneda) has 37 attractive but dark rooms with high, wood-beamed ceilings and satellite TV. The decor is showing a few signs of wear, but the service is friendly and the thick adobe walls keep things quiet.

Mesón de los Poetas
HOTEL $$$

(☏732-07-05; www.mexonline.com/poetas.htm; Positos 35; r incl breakfast M$1265; ⊜🛜) Built against the hillside, this labyrinth of rooms – each named after a poet – offers, on the whole, comfortable, clean lodgings. Some have kitchenettes. You won't wax lyrical about the light (some rooms are dark), but it's worth considering. We like rooms 401, 402 and 403, which share a sunny terrace.

Casa de Pita
PENSION $$

(☏732-15-32; www.casadepita.com; Cabecita 26; r M$450-900, apt M$500; ⊜🛜) A literal maze of atmospheric-cum-quirky guest rooms in a centrally located converted house. They vary in size and facilities – some are apartments and several verge on claustrophic. The terrace provides one of the only 360-degree views in the city.

Casa de Dante
HOSTEL $$

(☏731-09-09; www.casadedante.com; Callejón de Zaragoza 25; dm from M$250, s/d incl breakfast from M$350/700; 🛜) 'My family is your family,' says the owner of this ultrafriendly hostel in greeting. You can opt for a dormitory or for a well-kept room (some with private bathrooms). In addition there's a kitchen, DVD movie lounge, an outdoor barbecue on the terrace and the owners are very hospitable. It's a little out of town and up 156-plus steps. Travelers rave about their experiences here and longer-term deals can be negotiated. Head up the *callejón* next to Hotel Independencia on Paseo de la Presa.

Posada Molino del Rey
HOTEL $

(☑732-22-23; www.molinodelrey.webs.com; cnr Campanero & Belauzaran; s/d/tr M$350/450/575; ☻) An easy stroll from the center, the 'King's Mill' is notable for its dated, brown decor as well as its convenient location. Its 40 rooms are set around a patio, and some rooms are nicer than others.

Casa Bertha
HOSTEL, GUESTHOUSE $

(☑732-13-16; www.paginasprodigy.com/casaber tha; Tamboras 9; r per person with/without bathroom from M$190/160, apt per person M$210-260; ☎) This family-run *casa de huéspedes* (guesthouse) is a labyrinth of various-sized rooms (some with internal-facing windows) and three family-size apartments. Travelers praise the friendly owners for their hospitality and for keeping a homelike place, including kitchen and terrace. Head up beside Teatro Principal to Plazuela Mexiamora and look for the blue 'Casa Bertha' sign.

Eating

Eating in Guanajuato won't blow your culinary world apart. Having said that, there are a few exceptions. For fresh produce and cheap snacks and lunches, head to the **Mercado Hidalgo** (Av Juárez), a five-minute walk west of Jardín de la Unión on Avenida Juárez. Another two blocks further down on the right is **Central Comercio** (Av Juárez), with a large supermarket.

JARDÍN DE LA UNIÓN & AROUND

TOP CHOICE **Casa Valadez**
MEXICAN $$

(www.casavaladez.com; Jardín de la Unión 3; mains M$90-400; ☺9am-11pm; ☻) This classic place is a smart choice in every respect and attracts a loyal crowd of well-dressed locals. Given its fine location – it faces both the Jardín and Teatro Juaréz – it's excellent value. Servings are Mexican (read generous); dishes are a blend of international and Mexican. Especially tasty are the *pollo con enchiladas mineros* (enchiladas with everything) and the beef steak, *filete Valadez*.

El Zopilote Mojado
CAFE $

(Plazuela Mexiamora 51; snacks M$40-50; ☺9am-10pm Mon-Sat; ☻) A stylish and intimate place with rustic wooden decor, overlooking the tranquil Plazuela Mexiamora (the easiest way to get to the cafe is to head up the steps

beside Teatro Principal). Classical music, copies of the local newspaper and good coffee make it a pleasurable experience.

Bagel Cafetín
CAFE $

(Potrero 2; bagels M$40-60; ☺9am-10pm Mon-Sat; ☎) This colorful spot, next to Templo de San Francisco, serves up generous bagels and reasonable coffee. A small bar is upstairs; live jazz on Wednesdays.

Santo Café
CAFE $

(Puente de Campanero; mains M$40-90; ☺10am-midnight Mon-Sat, noon-8pm Sun; ☻☎) Stop by this cozy spot on the quaint Venetian-style bridge and check the latest university vibe. It serves good salads and snacks (the soy burger is great for vegetarians). Some tables overlook the alley below.

Truco 7
MEXICAN $$

(El Truco 7; mains M$26-100; ☺8:30am-11:30pm) This artsy cafe-restaurant featuring folkloric artifacts, paintings and a collection of old radios is fairly reliable. Set lunches are inexpensive (M$45 to M$55).

PLAZUELA DE SAN FERNANDO & AROUND

TOP CHOICE **Delica Mitsu**
JAPANESE $

(Cantaritos 37; mains M$30-100; ☺noon-9pm Mon-Sat) This tiny Japanese-run hole-in-the-wall serves up some of the biggest, freshest and best Japanese flavors around.

Papalotl
MEXICAN $$$

(Galarza 5; www.hotelavapor.com; mains M$100-180; ☺8:30am-9pm Mon-Sat, to 5pm Sun) Surrounded by cantera stone walls, in the renovated bowels of Antiguo Vapor, is this pleasant restaurant. It serves reasonable Mexican fusion dishes and makes an effort with service and contemporary touches. You can head here for a tipple, too.

Meztizo
INTERNATIONAL $$

(Positos 69; mains M$70-100; ☺1-10:30pm Tue-Sat, 1pm-6:30pm Sun) *Meztizo* means 'mix'; this place is so-called because it houses both a restaurant and gallery (run by father-son team Cabelo, a famous local ceramicist and artist, and his son, a trained chef). The menu may be small, but it's big on quality, especially the meat dishes. The downside is the ambience – it still feels like a former (tired) store.

Restaurant La Carreta
GRILL $

(Av Juárez 96; mains M$45-135; ☺11:30am-8pm) Follow your nose to La Carreta, an unpretentious cafe, whose street-front grill spins out a super-scrumptious *pollo asado con leña* (grilled chicken) and *carne asada* (grilled beef), served with large portions of rice and salad.

LA PRESA & AROUND

México Lindo y Sabroso   MEXICAN $$
(Paseo de la Presa 154; mains M$50-130; ⊘9am-10pm; ⊜) Tasty Mexican dishes in tasteful and colorful surrounds, including a delightful outdoor veranda. Head up Paseo de la Presa for about 1.4km and it's on the left-hand side.

Café Tal   CAFE $
(www.cafetal.com.mx; Temezcuitate 4; snacks M$15-30; ⊘7am-midnight Mon-Fri, 8am-midnight Sat & Sun; ⊜⊛) This forever-will-be-grungy coffee spot is the wi-fi-enabled study spot for students. Despite its flaws, it roasts, grinds and serves good coffees. Don't miss the *beso negro* (black kiss), ultra-concentrated Belgian hot chocolate (M$14). If you're lucky, Tal the cat might sit on your lap.

SAN JAVIER

 Las Mercedes   MEXICAN $$$
(☑732-73-75; www.guanajuatoesparati.com/las mercedes; Arriba 6; mains M$140-320; ⊘2-10pm Tue-Sat, 2-6pm Sun) In a residential area overlooking the city from heady heights, is Guanajuato's best restaurant. Popular with government and business officials, plus romantic diners, it serves up Mexican cuisine *á la abuela* – grandmother's cooking that takes hours to prepare, such as *moles* hand ground in *molcajetes*. Dish presentation is contemporary and stylish. Reservations recommended. To get there, take a taxi; you'll head down the valley (in a northwesterly direction as though heading to La Valenciana) but will then turn suddenly to head west up a hill.

🍷 Drinking & Entertainment

Every evening, the Jardín de la Unión comes alive with people crowding the outdoor tables, strolling and listening to the street musicians. International films are screened in several locations, including the Teatro Principal, Teatro Cervantes and Museo y Casa de Diego Rivera.

Bars & Nightclubs

Given the city's student population, bars and nightclubs are the go here. Drinking and dancing establishments in Guanajuato

generally start late and end in the wee hours. For the latest trends, ask the students (Thursday is their big night out).

Zilch   BAR
(El Jardín; ⊘7pm-late Tue-Sat) It's a popular place with a fun, friendly feel and live music from jazz to Indie rock Thursday through Saturday.

Fusilado   MEZCALERÍA
(La Valenciana; ⊘1pm-midnight Tue-Sat, to 8pm Sun) Just below La Valenciana church, nestles this bright blue icon, the cool-crowd, expat hangout. It serves up flavored artesanal mezcals and other drinks in a fun, saloon-style setting (warning: the scorpion mezcal has a sting in the 'tale'). Throw in some board games, crowds and a roof terrace and you're in for the long haul. A taxi to La Valencia costs around M$45.

El Incendio   BAR
(Cantarranas 39; ⊘11am-11pm) A former old-school cantina – whose legacy is swinging doors, an open urinal (as per the old cantinas; no longer used) and mural-covered walls – that caters to a fun and rowdy student crowd.

Whoopees   BAR
(Manuel Doblado 39; ⊘6pm-5am Mon-Sat) This modern, trendy gay bar is hip and Guanajuato's very happening place.

Clave Azul   CANTINA
(☑732-15-61; Segunda de Cantaritos 31; ⊘1:30-10pm Mon-Thu, 1:30pm-midnight Fri & Sat) For an authentic experience of Mexican drinking with accompanying *botanas* (tapas-like snacks served free with drinks, in this case between 2pm and 5:30pm), head to this artifact-filled, atmospheric cantina up a small alley to the left of Bossanova Café.

Performing Arts

A program of events including theater, music, opera and dance runs from March to December. Grab an *Agenda Cultural* from a tourist kiosk.

Guanajuato has three fine centrally located theaters, 100-year-old Teatro Juárez, Teatro Principal and Teatro Cervantes. Check their posters to see what's on.

🛍 Shopping

Donkey Jote   BOOKS
(☑cell phone 473-7340455; Positos 30; ⊘10am-4pm Tue-Sat, noon-3pm Sun) A tiny gem of an English bookstore with a great selection of

BUSES FROM GUANAJUATO

DESTINATION	FARE (M$)	DURATION	FREQUENCY (DAILY)
Dolores Hidalgo	44	1½hr	every 20min 5:30am-10:30pm
Guadalajara	269-325	4hr	16
León	33-55	1-1¼hr	18
Mexico City (Terminal Norte)	314-380	4½hr	20
Querétaro	135	2½hr	5
San Miguel de Allende	68-106	1½-2hr	18

books, plus dual English-Spanish publications and language dictionaries. Look out for cultural events and exhibitions. Sells excellent maps of Guanajuato (M$30).

El Viejo Zaguán   BOOKS
(☎cell phone 473-7323971; Positos 64; ☺10:30am-3pm & 5-8pm Tue-Sat, 11am-3pm Sun) Wonderful bilingual publications, art books, gifts and a relaxing coffee stop.

Xocola-T   FOOD
(Plazuela del Baratillo 15; ☺10am-10pm Mon-Sat, 10am-3pm Sun) This chocoholic's nirvana sells delectable handmade chocolates of pure cocoa with natural flavors and not a trans fat in sight. Quirkier fillings include *chapulines* (grasshoppers from Oaxaca) and mezcal.

ℹ Information

Internet Access
Many internet places line the streets around the university and Plazuela Mexiamora; most charge M$10 per hour.

Medical Services
Hospital General (☎733-15-73/76; Carretera a Silao, Km 6.5)
MIG: Médica Integral Guanajuatense (☎732-00-05; Plaza de la Paz 20)

Money
Banks along Avenida Juárez change cash and traveler's checks (but some only until 2pm) and have ATMs.
Divisas Dimas (Av Juárez 33A; ☺10am-8pm Mon-Sat) Convenient *casa de cambio*.

Post
Post office (☎732-03-85; Ayuntamiento 25; ☺8am-4:30pm Mon-Fri, 8am-noon Sat)

Telephone
Card phones are on Pasaje de los Arcos, an alley off the south side of Obregón.

Tourist Information
Incredibly, currently no formal tourist office functions in Guanajuato. Instead, head to the small **tourist kiosks** (☺10am-5:30pm), located at Jardín de la Unión, Plazuela de los Ángeles and Mercado Hidalgo.

Websites
Head to **Lonely Planet** (www.lonelyplanet.com/mexico/northern-central-highlands/guanajuato) for planning advice, author recommendations, traveler reviews and insider tips.

ℹ Getting There & Away

Air
Guanajuato is served by the Aeropuerto Internacional del Bajío, which is about 30km west of the city, halfway between Léon and Silao.

Bus
Guanajuato's Central de Autobuses is around 5km southwest of town (confusingly, to get there go northwest out of town along Tepetapa). It has card phones and luggage storage (in the cafe). Deluxe and 1st-class bus tickets (ETN and Primera Plus) can be bought in town at **Viajes Frausto** (☎732-35-80; Obregón 10; ☺9am-2pm & 4:30-7:30pm Mon-Fri, 9am-1:30pm Sat).

As well as the services outlined in the table above, hourly 2nd-class buses go to Celaya. For Morelia, catch an Irapuato-bound bus and change there.

ℹ Getting Around

A taxi to Aeropuerto Internacional del Bajío will cost about M$350 to M$400 (there's a set rate of M$400 from the airport; you buy your ticket at a taxi counter inside the airport). A cheaper option from Guanajuato is one of the frequent buses to Silao (M$30; every 20 minutes) and a taxi from there (around M$100). Note: in reverse – from the airport to Silao – the taxi rates are set and cost around 50% more).

Between the bus station and city center, around-the-clock 'Central de Autobuses' buses

(M$5) run constantly. From the center, you can catch them heading west on Avenida Juárez. From the bus terminal, you will enter a tunnel running east under the *centro histórico*. Alight at one of several entry/exit points: Mercado Hidalgo, Plaza de los Ángeles, Jardín de la Unión, Plaza Baratillo/Teatro Principal, Teatro Cervantes or Embajadoras (note: check the destination with the driver). A taxi to/from the bus station costs around M$40.

To get around town keep a look out – local buses display their destination. For the *centro histórico* the rule of thumb is as follows: all buses heading east go via the tunnels *below* Avenida Juárez (for example, if you want to go from the market to the Teatro Principal). Those heading west go *along* Avenida Juárez.

City buses (M$5) run from 7am to 10pm. Taxis are plentiful in the center and charge about M$30 to M$35 for short trips around town (slightly more if heading uphill to El Pípila and the like).

León

TRANSPORTATION HUB

Whether you like it or not, you will probably end up in the industrial city of León, 56km west of Guanajuato, thanks to its importance as a main bus hub within the state of Guanajuato. Also, it's only 20km from Aeropuerto Internacional del Bajío.

It's unlikely you'll need to stay here; bus connections are plentiful. If you want to fill an hour or two before a bus connection, it's worth wandering the streets surrounding the bus terminal, known as the Zona Piel, Leather District. (León has a long history of supplying goods: in the 16th century it was the center of Mexico's ranching district, providing meat for the mining towns and processing hides.)

❶ Getting There & Away

Aeropuerto Internacional del Bajío is 20km southeast of León on the Mexico City road. Many US airlines offer flights between US cities and here (often via Mexico City). Unfortunately, no bus service operates between Bajío airport and

central León or Guanajuato. A taxi between León and the airport costs M$300 to M$415.

The **Central de Autobuses** (Blvd Hilario Medina s/n), just north of Blvd López Mateos 2.5km east of the city center, has a cafeteria, left luggage, money exchange and card phones. There are regular 1st- and 2nd-class services to many places in northern and western Mexico.

Dolores Hidalgo

📲418 / POP 59,000 / ELEV 1920M

Dolores Hidalgo is a compact town with a pretty, tree-filled plaza, a relaxed ambience and an important history. It has acquired pilgrimage status for Mexicans; the Mexican independence movement began in earnest in this small place. At 5am on September 16, 1810, Miguel Hidalgo, the parish priest, rang the bells to summon people to church earlier than usual and issued the Grito de Dolores, also known as the Grito de Independencia. His precise words have been lost to history but their essence was 'Death to bad government and the *gachupines!'* (*Gachupines* was a derisive term for the Spanish-born overlords who ruled Mexico.)

Today, Hidalgo is one of Mexico's most revered heroes. Dolores was renamed in his honor in 1824. Mexicans swarm here for Independence Day (September 16), during which time the price of accommodations can more than double.

The town's *centro histórico* is worth a day visit from San Miguel de Allende, Guanajuato or Querétaro, not only for its interesting independence-themed museums (all of which are within a couple of blocks of the Plaza Principal), but also for its colored Talavera ceramics workshops (several blocks from the plaza) and ice cream (look for the carts on the plaza).

◉ Sights

Plaza Principal & Around   PLAZA

The **Parroquia de Nuestra Señora de Dolores**, the church where Hidalgo issued

BUSES FROM LEÓN

DESTINATION	FARE (M$)	DURATION	FREQUENCY (DAILY)
Guanajuato	52-62	¾hr	9
Mexico City (Terminal Norte)	380-445	5hr	17 (24 hours)
San Miguel de Allende	145-175	2¼hr	5

the Grito, is on the north side of the plaza. It has a fine 18th-century Churrigueresque facade. Legends surround his 'cry'; some say that Hidalgo uttered his famous words from the pulpit, others claim that he spoke at the church door to the people gathered outside.

The plaza contains a **Hidalgo statue** (in Roman garb, on top of a tall column) and also a tree that, according to the plaque beneath it, was a sapling of the tree of the Noche Triste (Sad Night), under which Cortés is said to have wept when his men were driven out of Tenochtitlán in 1520.

The **Casa de Visitas**, on the plaza's west side, was the residence of Don Nicolás Fernández del Rincón and Don Ignacio Díaz de la Cortina, the two representatives of Spanish rule in Dolores. On September 16, 1810, they became the first two prisoners of the independence movement. Today, this is where Mexican presidents and other dignitaries stay when they come to Dolores for ceremonies.

Museo Bicentenario 1810-2010   MUSEUM
(Casa del Capitán Mariano Abasolo; adult/student M$20/10; ☺10am-4.45pm Tue-Sun) Adjacent to the church, this museum (previously the Presidencia Municipal) was inaugurated in 2010 for Mexico's bicentennial celebrations. Despite its name, the majority of its seven rooms provide a cultural and historical context of the first hundred years of independence, including mementos produced for the centenary of 1910. Quirkier items include a stunning silk scarf embroidered with hair (depicting the image of Alejandro Zavala Mangas, an architect from Guanajuato city) and the original painted poster promoting the first century of independence. All explanations are in Spanish.

Museo de la Independencia Nacional   MUSEUM
(National Independence Museum; Zacatecas 6; adult/student M$15/7.50, Sun free; ☺9am-3pm) This museum has few relics but plenty of information on the independence movement. The exhibition spans seven rooms and charts the appalling decline in Nueva España's indigenous population between 1519 (an estimated 25 million) and 1605 (1 million), and identifies 23 indigenous rebellions before 1800 as well as several criollo conspiracies in the years leading up to 1810. There are vivid paintings, quotations and details on the heroic last 10 months of Hidalgo's life.

Museo Casa de Hidalgo   MUSEUM
(cnr Hidalgo & Morelos; admission M$31; ☺10am-5:45pm Tue-Sun) Miguel Hidalgo lived in this house when he was Dolores' parish priest. It was from here, in the early hours of September 16, 1810, that Hidalgo, Ignacio Allende and Juan de Aldama set off to launch the uprising against colonial rule. The house is now something of a national shrine – think memorials, replicas of Hidalgo's furniture and independence-movement documents, including the order for Hidalgo's excommunication.

Museo José Alfredo Jiménez   MUSEUM
(www.museojosealfredojimenez.com; Guanajuato 13, cnr Nuevo León; admission M$35; ☺10am-5pm Tue-Sun) If you don't know of José Alfredo Jiménez before you come to Dolores, you will by the time you leave. (Hint: he's the king of *música ranchera* and beloved by all Mexicans). Housed in a stunning space – the home where he was born – this new, modern museum cleverly depicts his life through paintings, photos, mementos and recordings (there are hi-tech ear-phones). The first room features an extraordinary painting by Octavio Ocampo, in which are hidden many figures and symbols.

✦✦ Festivals & Events

Día de la Independencia   HISTORICAL
Dolores is the scene of major Día de la Independencia (September 16) celebrations, when the Mexican president may officiate – according to tradition – in his fifth year of office.

Fiestas Patrias   CULTURAL
The dates of the Fiestas Patrias festivities change annually; they run for up to two weeks and always encompass September 16.

🛏 Sleeping

Prices can double (even triple) for the independence celebrations in September, and at Easter.

Hotel Posada Hidalgo   HOTEL $
(☏182-04-77; www.hotelposadahidalgo.com; Hidalgo 15; s/d/tr/ste M$352/402/453/808; P❄☺🕾) The reception feels a bit like a doctor's surgery, but this superclean and well-managed place offers a comfortable and '80s-modern' stay. It's conveniently located between the bus stations and the Plaza Principal.

Posada Cocomacán   HOTEL $$
(☏182-60-86; www.posadacocomacan.com.mx; Plaza Principal 4; s/d/tr M$350/470/570; ☺) The

MIGUEL HIDALGO: ¡VIVA MEXICO!

The balding head of the visionary priest Father Miguel Hidalgo y Costilla is familiar to anyone who has ogled Mexican statues or murals. A genuine rebel idealist, Hidalgo sacrificed his career and risked his life on September 16, 1810, when he launched the independence movement.

Born on May 8, 1753, son of a criollo (Mexican-born person of Spanish parentage) hacienda manager in Guanajuato, he earned a bachelor's degree and, in 1778, was ordained a priest. He returned to teach at his alma mater in Morelia and eventually became rector. But he was no orthodox cleric: Hidalgo questioned many Catholic traditions, read banned books, gambled, danced and had a mistress.

In 1800 he was brought before the Inquisition. Nothing was proven, but a few years later, in 1804, he found himself transferred as priest to the hick town of Dolores.

Hidalgo's years in Dolores show his growing interest in the economic and cultural welfare of the people. He started several new industries: silk was cultivated, olive groves were planted and vineyards established, all in defiance of the Spanish colonial authorities. Earthenware building products were the foundation of the ceramics industry that today produces fine glazed pots and tiles.

When Hidalgo met Ignacio Allende from San Miguel, they shared a criollo discontent with the Spanish stranglehold on Mexico. Hidalgo's standing among the *mestizos* and indigenous people of his parish was vital in broadening the base of the rebellion that followed.

Shortly after his Grito de Independencia, Hidalgo was formally excommunicated for 'heresy, apostasy and sedition.' He defended his call for Mexican independence and stated furthermore that the Spanish were not truly Catholic in any religious sense of the word but only for political purposes, specifically to rape, pillage and exploit Mexico. A few days later, on October 19, Hidalgo dictated his first edict calling for the abolition of slavery in Mexico.

Hidalgo led his growing forces from Dolores to San Miguel, Celaya and Guanajuato, north to Zacatecas, south almost to Mexico City and west to Guadalajara. But then, pushed northward, their numbers dwindled and on July 30, 1811, having been captured by the Spanish, Hidalgo was shot by a firing squad in Chihuahua. His head was returned to the city of Guanajuato, where it hung in a cage for 10 years on an outer corner of the Alhóndiga de Granaditas, along with the heads of fellow independence leaders Allende, Aldama and Jiménez. Rather than intimidating the people, this lurid display kept the memory, the goal and the example of the heroic martyrs fresh in everyone's mind. After independence the cages were removed, and the skulls (and bodies) of the heroes are now in the Monumento a la Independencia in Mexico City.

NORTHERN CENTRAL HIGHLANDS DOLORES HIDALGO

centrally located and absolutely apricot Cocomacán is a reliable option. The 37 clean rooms have TV and phones. Rooms on the upper levels, with windows onto the street are the best. There's also a restaurant (open 8am to 10:30pm).

Eating

Don't leave without sampling a hand-turned ice cream (around M$20) from an ice-cream vendor on the plaza or around town. You can test your taste buds on the flavors: *mole* (chili sauce), *chicharrón* (fried pork skin), avocado, corn, cheese, honey, shrimp, beer, tequila and tropical fruits. The busy market on the corner of Chihuahua and Michoacán serves up some satisfying corn-based snacks.

El Carruaje Restaurant   MEXICAN **$$**
(Plaza Principal 8; mains M$60-130; ☺8am-11pm; ☻) This colorful place on the plaza caters to day tripping families with live music from Friday to Sunday and a popular weekend breakfast buffet (M$90) and lunch buffet (M$110).

Restaurant Plaza   MEXICAN **$$**
(Plaza Principal 17B; mains M$60-160; ☺8am-10pm; ☻) A central and OK place serving set breakfasts (from M$70) and lunches (M$75), as well as meat dishes, pasta and *antojitos*.

Shopping

Talavera ceramics have been the signature handicraft of Dolores ever since Padre

BUSES FROM DOLORES HIDALGO

DESTINATION	FARE (M$)	DURATION	FREQUENCY (DAILY)
Guanajuato	53	1¼hr	every 25min
Mexico City (Terminal Norte)	272-273	5-6hr	every 40min
San Miguel de Allende	37	¾hr	frequent

Hidalgo founded the town's first ceramics workshop in the early 19th century. Head to the Zona Artesanal, the workshops along Avenida Jiménez, five blocks west of the plaza, or (by car) to Calzada de los Héroes, the exit road to San Miguel de Allende. Some workshops here make 'antique' colonial-style furniture.

ℹ Information

The **tourist office** (☎182-11-64; ⊙9am-4pm) is on Plaza Principal's southeastern side. The helpful staff provide maps and information. Ask here for the latest internet locations; these change regularly.

Several banks with ATMs are around the plaza. The **post office** (☎182-08-07; ⊙9am-2pm Mon-Sat) is on the corner of Puebla and Veracruz.

ℹ Getting There & Away

The **Primera Plus/Coordinados (Flecha Amarilla) bus station** (Hidalgo) is 2½ blocks south of the plaza, near the **Herradura de Plata/Autovías bus station** (cnr Chiapas & Yucatán).

There are regular 2nd-class connections to Querétaro (M$90), León (M$97) and San Luis Potosí (M$139).

San Miguel de Allende

☎415 / POP 70,000 / ELEV 1900M

Many people say that San Miguel is a bit like a Mexican Disneyland for foreign (mainly American) retirees. Indeed, this is a stunning and neat city, with colonial architecture, enchanting cobblestone streets and striking light. Regular festivals, fireworks and parades dominate the local scene.

The town's cosmopolitan panache is reflected in its excellent restaurants and high-class, colonial-style accommodations. Numerous galleries are stocked with some of the best of Mexican *artesanías* (handicrafts) and cultural activities are on tap for residents and visitors. There are few major sights in the compact *centro histórico*: San Miguel *is* the sight. The city – with El Jardín,

the principal plaza, and the Parroquia, the large church, at its heart – was declared a Unesco World Heritage site in 2008.

Economically speaking, this is no budget destination and is a far cry from the 1940s, when beatniks and artists shacked up here on a shoestring to pursue their creative ventures. Visitors still study at the art institutions – Bellas Artes and the Instituto Allende. While the foreign influence is pervasive (more than 12,000 foreigners are believed to live or have houses here), on the whole the population coexists comfortably.

Beneath the smart B&Bs and fancy shops, another Mexico exists. You only have to laze in the main plaza, visit the food market or interact with the local people to sense a different ambience, color and vibe.

The climate is agreeable: cool and clear in winter and warm and clear in summer, with occasional thunderstorms and heavy rain.

History

The town, so the story goes, owes its founding to a few overheated dogs. These hounds were loved by a Franciscan friar, Juan de San Miguel, who started a mission in 1542 near an often-dry river 5km from the present town. One day the dogs wandered off from the mission; they were found reclining at the spring called El Chorro. The mission was moved to this superior site.

San Miguel was then central Mexico's most northern Spanish settlement. Tarascan and Tlaxcalan allies of the Spanish were brought to help pacify the local Otomí and Chichimecs. San Miguel was barely surviving the fierce Chichimec resistance, until in 1555 a Spanish garrison was established to protect the new road from Mexico City to the silver center of Zacatecas. Spanish ranchers settled in the area and it grew into a thriving commercial center and home to some of Guanajuato's wealthy silver barons.

San Miguel's favorite son, Ignacio Allende, was born here in 1779. He became a fervent believer in the need for Mexican independence and was a leader of a Querétaro-based conspiracy that set December 8, 1810, as the date for an armed uprising. When the plan was discovered by the authorities in Querétaro on September 13, a messenger rushed to San Miguel and gave the news to Juan de Aldama, another conspirator. Aldama sped north to Dolores where, in the early hours of September 16, he found Allende at the house of the priest Miguel Hidalgo, also one of the coterie. A few hours later Hidalgo proclaimed rebellion from his church (see p667). After initial successes Allende, Hidalgo and other rebel leaders were captured in 1811 in Chihuahua. Allende was executed, but on independence in 1821 he was recognized as a martyr and in 1826 the town was renamed San Miguel de Allende.

The Escuela de Bellas Artes was founded in 1938 and the town started to take on its current character when David Alfaro Siqueiros began mural-painting courses that attracted artists of every persuasion. The Instituto Allende opened in 1951, also attracting foreign students. Many were US war veterans (who could settle here under the GI Bill); an influx of artists has continued ever since.

⊙ Sights

Parroquia de San Miguel Arcángel   CHURCH
The parish church's pink 'wedding cake' towers dominate the Jardín. These strange pinnacles were designed by indigenous stonemason Zeferino Gutiérrez in the late 19th century. He reputedly based the design on a postcard of a Belgian church and instructed builders by scratching plans in the sand with a stick. The rest of the church dates from the late 17th century. In the chapel to the left of the main altar is the much-revered image of the *Cristo de la Conquista* (Christ of the Conquest), made in Pátzcuaro from cornstalks and orchid bulbs, probably in the 16th century. The adjacent **Iglesia de San Rafael** was founded in 1742.

**La Esquina: Museo del Juguete
Popular Mexicano**   MUSEUM
(www.museolaesquina.org.mx; Núñez 40; admission M$30; ☉10am-6pm Tue-Sat, 10am-3pm Sun) This new, modern and bright museum is a must-visit for all kids, big and small. To describe it as exhibiting Mexican toys (the 50-year collection of museum owner, Angélica Tijerina) is to do it a disservice. It is much more. It aims to preserve and continue the tradition of toys by showcasing different pieces from the many regions of Mexico. The pieces – divided into three main themed areas – are

made from different materials, from wheat to plastic, wood to fabric. Kids will love the interactive games on the computer. A lovely gift shop is attached.

**Jardín Botánico El Charco
del Ingenio**   BOTANIC GARDEN
(☎154-47-15; www.elcharco.org.mx; off Antiguo Camino Real a Querétaro; admission M$40; ☉dawn-dusk) On the hilltop 1.5km northeast of town is the 88-hectare botanic garden. This wildlife and bird sanctuary, an ongoing project thanks to the efforts of local volunteers, was created by a caring local (who donated the land) to conserve a natural area around the town and to provide a recreational and ceremonial space for the community. Pathways head through magnificent areas of cacti and native plants, through wetlands and above a canyon where lies the eponymous freshwater spring, the **Charco del Ingenio**. A map with the pathways and explanations is provided upon entrance. The route incorporates the **Conservatory of Mexican Plants**, which houses a wonderful array of cacti and succulent species, some of which are endangered species. Excellent two-hour tours (in English) depart every Tuesday and Thursday at 10am (M$80). Monthly **full-moon ceremonies** also take place here.

Getting to the garden can seem a slightly prickly business, thanks to new urban development on the town's outskirts that blocks the original route, but it's worth persevering. Walk uphill from Mercado El Nigromante along Homobono and Cuesta de San José. Fork left up Montitlan past a housing development (known as Los Balcones). Continue for another 15 minutes to the main gate. Be sure to keep the garden boundary fence on your left as much as possible. (Occasionally you may have to head around the new houses on sidewalks, after which you head back to the fence.)

Alternatively, a 2km vehicle track leads north from the Soriana shopping center, 2.5km southeast of the center on the Querétaro road. This can be reached on 'Soriana' buses from the bus stop from Mesones, near Plaza Cívica. A taxi to the gardens from the center costs around M$45. Take a 'Soriana' or 'Placita' bus (10 minutes, M$5).

**Museo Histórico de San
Miguel de Allende**   MUSEUM
(Museo Casa de Allende; Cuna de Allende 1; admission M$37; ☉9:30am-4:30pm Tue-Sun) Near the Parroquia de San Miguel Arcángel is

San Miguel de Allende

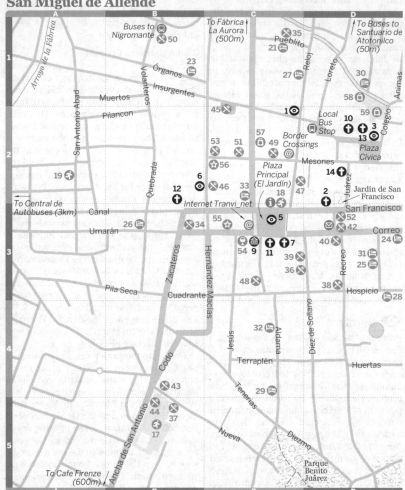

the house where Ignacio Allende was born. These days it is home to the Museo Histórico de San Miguel de Allende. Recently remodeled, the museum relates the interesting history of the San Miguel area. One of the floors is a reproduction of Allende's home. A Latin inscription on the facade reads *Hic natus ubique notus,* which means 'Born here, known everywhere.'

Mirador & Parque Benito Juárez   PARK
One of the best views over the town and surrounding country is from the **mirador** (overlook) southeast of town. Take Callejón del Chorro, the track leading directly downhill from here, and turn left at the bottom to reach **El Chorro**, the spring where San Miguel was founded (note the fountain and public washing tubs). A path – Paseo del Chorro – zigzags down the hill to the shady **Parque Benito Juárez**, a lovely place to relax and meander through.

Other Face of Mexico Gallery   MUSEUM
(www.casadelacuesta.com; Casa de la Cuesta, Cuesta de San José 32; admission M$50) This fascinating private collection of more than 500 masks provides an excellent context of

by David Alfaro Siqueiros (it plays with your mind – we won't spoil the surprise). The rest of the gallery holds temporary exhibitions.

Oratorio de San Felipe Neri CHURCH

(Plaza Cívica) This multi-towered and domed church dating from the 18th century is near the east end of Insurgentes. The pale-pink main facade is baroque with an indigenous influence. A passage to the right of this facade leads to the east wall, where a doorway holds the image of *Nuestra Señora de la Soledad* (Our Lady of Solitude). You can see into the cloister from this side of the church.

Inside the church are 33 oil paintings showing scenes from the life of San Felipe Neri, the 16th-century Florentine who founded the Oratorio Catholic order. In the east transept is a painting of the Virgin of Guadalupe by leading colonial painter Miguel Cabrera. In the west transept is a lavishly decorated 1735 chapel, the **Santa Casa de Loreto**, a replica of a chapel in Loreto, Italy, legendary home of the Virgin Mary. Behind the altar, the *camarín* (chapel behind the main church) has six elaborately gilded baroque altars. In one is a reclining wax figure of San Columbano; it supposedly contains the saint's bones.

Templo de San Francisco CHURCH

(cnr San Francisco & Juárez) This church has an elaborate late-18th-century Churrigueresque facade. An image of St Francis of Assisi is at the top. Opening hours vary.

Capilla de la Tercera Orden CHAPEL

(Chapel of the Third Order; cnr San Francisco & Juárez) Built in the early 18th century, this chapel, like the Templo de San Francisco, was part of a Franciscan monastery complex. The main facade shows St Francis and symbols of the Franciscan order.

Templo de la Salud CHURCH

(Plaza Cívica) This church, with a dome tiled blue and yellow and a big shell carved above its entrance, is just east of San Felipe Neri. The facade is early Churrigueresque. The church's paintings include one of San Javier by Miguel Cabrera. San Javier (St Francis Xavier, 1506–52) was a founding member of the Jesuits. It was once part of the Colegio de Sales.

Templo de la Concepción CHURCH

(Church of the Conception; cnr Zacateros & Canal) This splendid church has a fine altar and several magnificent old oil paintings. Painted

the Mexican mask tradition. It is open by appointment only (call ☑154-43-24). The admission fee goes to charity.

Escuela de Bellas Artes GALLERY

(School of Fine Arts; Centro Cultural Nigromante; ☑152-02-89; Hernández Macías 75) Closed at the time of research for renovations (due to open 2012), this beautiful former monastery of La Concepción church was converted into a fine-arts school in 1938 and still offers courses. Don't miss the murals of Pedro Martínez, plus the Siqueiros Room, which features the extraordinary unfinished mural

San Miguel de Allende

on the interior doorway are a number of wise sayings to give pause to those entering the sanctuary. The church was begun in the mid-18th century; its dome, added in the late 19th century by the versatile Zeferino Gutiérrez, was possibly inspired by pictures of *Les Invalides* in Paris.

Instituto Allende　　　　HISTORIC BUILDING
(Ancha de San Antonio 20 & 22) This large 1736 complex, the original home of the Conde Manuel de la Canal, was used as a Carmelite convent, eventually becoming an art and language school in 1951. These days it's split into two – one area of several patios, gardens and an old chapel is used for functions, the other for courses. Above the main entrance is a carving of the Virgin of Loreto, patroness of the Canal family.

Colegio de Sales　　　　NOTABLE BUILDING
(Plaza Cívica; ◎8am-2pm & 5-8pm) Once a college, founded in the mid-18th century by the San Felipe Neri order, the Colegio de Sales

has regained its educational status; it currently houses part of the University of León. Many of the 1810 revolutionaries were educated here. Spaniards were locked up here when the rebels took San Miguel.

Biblioteca Pública   CULTURAL BUILDING
(☏152-02-93; Insurgentes 25; ⊙10am-7pm Mon-Fri, 10am-2pm Sat) As well as housing one of the largest collections of books and magazines in English in Latin America, this excellent public library functions as a cultural center. Its financial enterprises (*Atención San Miguel* newspaper, tours and an onsite cafe) provide for children's scholarships. The library cafe provides a pleasant spot from which to view the cultural action.

📖 Courses

Several institutions offer Spanish courses, with group or private lessons and optional classes in Mexican culture and history. Most private lessons are around M$210 to M$260 an hour; group and long-term rates are much lower. Homestays with Mexican families – a private room and three meals per day – cost around M$364 per day.

There are also courses in painting, sculpture, ceramics, music and dance. The Escuela de Bellas Artes has courses in art, dance, crafts and music in Spanish and English that cost around M$450 a month, plus materials.

Academia Hispano Americana   SPANISH
(☏152-03-49; www.ahaspeakspanish.com; Mesones 4) This place, housed in a beautiful colonial building, runs quality courses in the Spanish language and Latin American culture.

Instituto Allende   SPANISH
(☏152-01-90; www.instituto-allende.edu.mx; Ancha de San Antonio 22) Offers courses in fine arts, crafts and Spanish. Spanish courses for groups begin every four weeks and range from conversational to intensive.

Warren Hardy Spanish   SPANISH
(☏154-40-17; www.warrenhardy.com; San Rafael 6) Offers Spanish instruction.

👉 Tours

The tourist office has promotional pamphlets of official English-speaking tour guides who offer both walking and driving tours. See *Atención San Miguel* for the weekly list of tours within San Miguel; most of these support local charities.

Bici-Burro   CYCLING
(☏152-15-26; www.bici-burro.com; Hospicio 1; trips M$800-1500) Friendly and professional, English-speaking owner Alberto conducts excellent guided mountain-bike tours for groups of two or more. Popular trips include six- or seven-hour excursions to Atotonilco or Pozos. Bike rental also available (around M$500 per day).

Tranvía Turístico   TRAM
(Tourist Trolley, Transportadora Turística Imperial; ☏154-54-08; www.transtur-imperial.com; Plaza Principal 18, 1st fl; adult/child M$60/40) See the main sights in 1½ hours from the comfort of an original tram. Of the hourly departures, two are bilingual and these depart at 10am and 4pm.

Walking tour   WALKING
This excellent tour takes place every Monday, Wednesday and Friday at 10am, departing from El Jardín (tickets go on sale in El Jardín at 9:45am; M$150). The English-speaking volunteer guides provide a fascinating historical, architectural and cultural commentary on the town's sights.

Horseback riding   HORSEBACK RIDING
Two recommended agencies for half- and full-day guided horseback tours in a nearby canyon are **Xotolar Ranch Adventures** (☏154-62-75; www.xotolarranch.com; rides from USD$85) and **Coyote Canyon Adventures** (☏154-41-93; www.coyotecanyonadventures.com; rides per person from US$90).

✨ Festivals & Events

San Miguel is well endowed with churches and patron saints (it has six) and enjoys a multitude of festivals, many imbued with strong spiritual themes. You'll probably be alerted to a festival event by firework bursts. For programs, ask at the tourist office or check out the website www.visitsanmiguel.travel.

Señor de la Conquista   RELIGIOUS
The image of Christ in the Parroquia de San Miguel Arcángel is feted on the first Friday in March, with scores of dancers in elaborate pre-Hispanic costumes and plumed headdresses.

Semana Santa   RELIGIOUS
A week of religious activities. Two Sundays before Easter, pilgrims carry an image of the Señor de la Columna (Lord of the Column) from Atotonilco, 11km north, to San Miguel's

church of San Juan de Dios, departing at midnight on Saturday. During Semana Santa, the many activities include the solemn Procesión del Santo Entierro on Good Friday and the burning or exploding of Judas effigies on Easter Day.

Fiesta de la Santa Cruz HISTORICAL
This deeply spiritual spring festival has its roots in the 16th century. It happens toward the end of May at Valle del Maíz, 2km from the center of town. Oxen are dressed in lime necklaces and painted tortillas and their yokes festooned with flowers and fruit. A mock battle between 'Indians' and 'Federales' follows. There are *mojigangas* (giant puppets), dancing and musicians, not to mention 96 hours' worth of fireworks.

Fiesta de los Locos RELIGIOUS
Part of the Festividad de San Antonio de Padua in mid-June, the festival of the crazies is a colorful Carnavalesque parade through town with floats, blaring music and costumed dancers throwing out candy to (sometimes at!) the crowd.

Expresión en Corto FILM
Shared with the city of Guanajuato, this short-film festival in July is internationally recognized.

Chamber Music Festival MUSIC
The Escuela de Bellas Artes sponsors an annual festival of chamber music in the first two weeks of August.

Fiestas Patrias CULTURAL
Two months of cultural programs kick off towards the end of August, incorporating Independence Day. Check with the tourist office for a full event schedule.

San Miguel Arcángel RELIGIOUS
Celebrations honoring the town's chief patron saint are held around the weekend following September 29. The party is celebrated with an *alborada,* an artificial dawn created by thousands of fireworks around the cathedral and turns into an all-night festivity with extraordinary pre-Hispanic dances.

Festival of Jazz and Blues MUSIC
February sees national jazz and blues acts hit town, while November is the month for the international jazz and blues festival.

🛏 Sleeping

Accommodations are often full during festivals and high season, so make advance reservations. Budget accommodations hold no surprises, but good-value midrange options are light on; if you can loosen the purse-strings for accommodations, this is the place to do it. Many houses, apartments and rooms are available to rent.

San Miguel is the mecca for luxury B&Bs, boutique hotels and guesthouses. These plush places reek of modern colonial grandeur, with stylish decor and luxuriant gardens or courtyards. With the exception of self-catering Casa Mia, all serve excellent breakfasts.

TOP CHOICE / Posada Corazón B&B $$$
(☎152-01-82; www.posadacorazon.com.mx; Aldama 9; d M$1650-2200; P🐾😊🛜) This gorgeous place has a heart, as the name suggests. It's set behind an inconspicuous wall in a delightfully lush plant and sculpture garden. The home's spacious open-plan living area, complete with library, can be shared by guests, and rooms along a deck are light, simple and stylish. Open daily to the public for full (and very good) breakfast (M$150) and afternoon tea (M$45).

Casa Mia APARTMENTS $$$
(☎152-27-57; www.casamia-sanmiguel.com; Correo 61; apt per night/week from US$95/500) This tastefully renovated spot is a welcome addition to San Miguel – 12 apartments, with comfortable hotel-style bedrooms, cable TV, living areas and kitchens. All suites are unique and all face onto a plant-filled courtyard. It's excellent value if you plan to stay for longer than a night or two.

Casa Misha BOUTIQUE HOTEL $$$
(☎152-20-21; www.casamisha.com; Chiquitos 15; r US$354-500; 😊❄🛜) London meets Mexico in this opulent *casa.* An exclusive factor prevails, but you can still put your feet up. In fact, it's encouraged – there are a range of beautiful personal spaces, from sunny terraces to a library full of giant sofas, puffy cushions, oh, and books. The rooms are private, comfortable and very, *very* nice. (Put another way: try to see some of the city while you're here.)

Antigua Capilla BOUTIQUE HOTEL $$$
(☎152-40-48; www.antiguacapilla.com; Callejon Chepitos 16; r US$149-200; P🐾🛜) Constructed around a tiny 17th-century chapel, this utterly stylish, spick-n-span place is hard to fault; it boasts every mod con and service imaginable plus extraordinary breakfasts

and a gorgeous plant-lined courtyard. The English- and Spanish-speaking owners are delightful. Access is up a hill but the rooftop terrace affords one of the best views in San Miguel.

Casa de la Cuesta
B&B $$$

(☎154-43-24; www.casadelacuesta.com; Cuesta de San José 32; r M$2000; ⊜☎) Perched on a hill behind the Mercado El Nigromante, this ornate, Mexican-themed place has spacious rooms (each unique) in a decorative colonial mansion, lavish breakfasts and friendly, knowledgeable owners.

Casa Calderoni B&B
B&B $$$

(☎154-60-05; www.casacalderoni.com; Callejón del Pueblito 4A; r US$110-140) A very plush, well-managed spot with stylish, puffy-pillow, artistic rooms, each named after a Mexican painter (the owner is a painter, too). We love the Dalí room which is a bit more spacious with good light. Public terraces prevail. It's located in a picturesque *callejón* (small street).

Hotel Hacienda de las Flores
MOTEL $$$

(☎152-18-59; www.haciendadelasflores.com; Hospicio 16; r M$1300-2145, ste M$2275-2405, apt M$2600; ⊜☎☀) This delightful oasis is less pretentious than other upmarket options and is set within an oasis – a lush garden with swimming pool – which offers a pleasant respite from the busy streets. Rooms are bright and modern, in a 'Talavera-tiled' kind of way, and have coffee makers and microwaves. Prices include breakfast.

L'Ôtel
BOUTIQUE HOTEL $$$

(☎154-98-50; www.l-otelgroup.com; Chiquitos 1A; ste US$530-650; ⊜☎) The four extremely stylish and opulent rooms are an interior designer's wet dream – original fabrics, fancy bed heads and quirky touches. The small salon and private roof terraces give it an intimate appeal.

Dos Casas
BOUTIQUE HOTEL $$$

(☎154-40-73; www.doscasas.com.mx; Quebrada 101; d M$3245-4950; ⊜❄) This sleek option oozes contemporary style – there are lots of cream and black hues, plus Jacuzzis and private terraces.

Hotel Matilda
BOUTIQUE HOTEL $$$

(☎152-10-15; www.hotelmatilda.com; Aldama 53; r from US$460; ❄❄☎) Cutting. Edge. Arty. Farty. Spa. Bar. Fashionistas. You get the picture. This contemporary place is so far out of the San Miguel colonial sphere of reference it's hard to know where to start. Think art gallery around rooms (or vice versa) with works by Spencer Tunick to a copy of a Diego Rivera (an image of Matilda, the American hotel owner's mother, who once posed for the artist). The rooms are white and bright and *very* slick. A spa offers wellness experiences and the public can access the bar (⊙4pm to 11pm) and restaurant (⊙7am to 11pm).

Casa de la Noche
GUESTHOUSE $$

(☎152-07-32; www.casadelanoche.com; Organos 19; r US$60-200) A bit like the bordello it once was, the place promises big things, especially at the beginning. The refurbished entry and living areas are superb – spacious, stylish and airy – though some of the rooms (the former bordello spaces) are a bit cramped. To inflate your enthusiasm, numerous fun nooks and crannies are open for the taking and it's a more than satisfying experience for the price. The friendly artist-owner 'Madame' promotes local talent; artworks prevail.

Hotel Quinta Loreto
HOTEL $$

(☎152-00-42; www.quintaloreto.com.mx; Loreto 15; s/d/tr M$480/600/700; ℗☎❄) This dated motel-style place at the back of the artisans' market is spread around large, leafy grounds. Some of the 30 simple rooms have a small private patio. TV costs extra and there's a restaurant (open for breakfast and lunch 8am to 11am and 1pm to 5:30pm).

Posada El Mayorazgo
HOTEL $

(☎152-13-09; posadamayorazgo@hotmail.com; Hidalgo 8; r M$350; ℗⊜) Don't let the unconventional entrance put you off (it resembles an ugly concrete bunker). This centrally located 1980s-style place has plain but modern(ish) and light rooms. Rates are M$50 cheaper Monday through Thursday.

Hostal Alcatraz
HOSTEL $

(☎152-85-43; Reloj 54; dm from M$130, r M$400; @) San Miguel's only HI-affiliated hostel is centrally located, with basic dorms and a shared kitchen. Travelers rave about the friendly staff. The associated **Hostel Inn** (Calzada de La Luz 31A) charges the same prices.

✖ Eating

San Miguel's numerous eateries serve a startling variety of quality Mexican and international fine cuisine. Thrifty travelers enjoy more traditional places catering to loyal crowds of local families. A thriving cafe society prevails, with many serving good local meals at reasonable prices (M$50 to M$150).

TOP CHOICE Cafe Rama
BAR, RESTAURANT $$

(Calle Nueva 7; mains M$60-120; ⊗8:30am-4:30pm Tue – Sat, 7:30-11pm Wed, 5:30pm-midnight Thu-Sat) A largely expat community hangs out here at this appealing, verging on cool cafe-bar-restaurant next to Instituto Allende. It serves among the town's best coffee and excellent international dishes to a changing menu – often with local and organic produce – and tapas from Thursday to Saturday nights. You must reserve for Wednesday night's set menu deal (one sitting).

Cafe Firenze
CAFE

(☑cell phone 415-1210763; Salida a Celaya 3; mains M$140-180; ⊗lunch & dinner Tue-Sat) In a non-descript location, on the continuation of Ancha de San Antonio (past Instituto Allende on the right-hand side), is this tiny, Italian-themed gem. Head upstairs and take your pick from the daily specials – handmade pasta, *osso buco*, great steaks and one of the best chocolate desserts in Mexico. The ultra-friendly and passionate English-speaking owner-chefs are Mexican (but surely Romans in former lives). Reservations recommended as it fills early.

El Manantial
BAR, CANTINA $$

(Barranca 78; mains M$60-150; ⊗1pm-midnight Tue-Sun) Behind the swinging doors of a former saloon, 'The Spring' (whose alter-ego is La Sirena Gorda or 'Fat Mermaid') serves fabulously fresh ceviche snacks and Coronas that would satisfy King Neptune himself. It's got a real buzz, also helped by *jabanero* salsa, the spiciest of chili sauces that will put hair on your chest (warning: we suggest you don't pile it on like the hardy locals here, a little goes a looong way).

Hecho en México
RESTAURANT $$

(Ancha de San Antonio 8; mains M$65-140; ⊗lunch & dinner) This isn't the place to come if you want to tune your ear to Spanish – it's a favorite expat hangout. However, for good reason, it seems. The menu is large, varied and very generous. Grab everything from a veggie burger to Mexican fare (plus great set lunch menus for M$70) and enjoy in a cozy courtyard setting. There's live music every Friday.

Vía Orgánica
CAFE $

(www.viaorganica.org; Margarito Ledesma 2; snacks M$15-30, mains M$50-95; ⊗7:30am-9pm Mon-Sat, 9am-5pm Sun; ☑) This healthy option – a cafe and vegetable shop – is part of the not-for-profit Mexican organization, Vía Orgánica. The organic produce is grown by local farmers. The cafe's menu delights the taste buds; think minestrone soups, salads, and great cakes. Follow your nose north along Hidalgo. Veer right onto Calzada de la Aurora, first left into Talavera and first left again.

Chamonix
INTERNATIONAL $$

(Sollano 17; dishes M$95-200; ⊗1-10pm Tue-Sat; ⊜) The pretty garden atmosphere at this restaurant offers an upmarket, if relaxed, setting and a high-quality international menu and regional specialties. Organic produce is used where possible.

La Posadita
MEXICAN $$

(Cuna de Allende 13; mains M$95-200; ⊗noon-10pm Thu-Tue; ⊜) This enjoyable eatery gets five stars for its excellent service, Mexican fare, and location – near the Parroquia de San Miguel Arcángel. Head up a steep set of stairs to the wonderful rooftop terrace with great vistas. It serves delicious margaritas, enchiladas and meat dishes.

Los Burritos
MEXICAN $

(Mesones 69A; snacks M$5-35; ⊗10:30am-6pm Mon-Sat) The place for cheap *antojitos* and the mouthwatering, made-to-order *guisados* (fillings) from *mole* to *chipotle* (a type of chili) and potato.

Tío Lucas
INTERNATIONAL $$$

(Mesones 103; mains M$120-300; ⊗noon-midnight; ⊜) This stylish place with a silver-star-covered courtyard is known for its beef, especially the fillet steak, and for being 'reliable.' Happy hour runs from 6pm to 8pm Monday to Friday, and there's live jazz nightly.

Berlin
INTERNATIONAL $$

(Umarán 19; mains M$85-190; ⊗noon-1am) Stop in this cool, artsy spot for a tasty blend of German and international food. The bar is very Euro and if you eavesdrop, you may get the scoop on where to find the next hip art opening.

El Pegaso
MEXICAN $$

(Corregidora 6; mains M$70-155; ⊗8:30am-10pm Mon-Sat; ⊜) A friendly, colorful and cozy place, and a reliable option for meals.

Bugambilia
MEXICAN $$

(Sollano 42; mains M$115-180; ⊗9am-10pm; ⊜) Said to be one of the oldest surviving restaurants in San Miguel, it moved to its current location in 2011. It offers traditional cuisine in a bougainvillea-filled patio setting and is famous for *chiles en nogada* (stuffed chilies, fried in batter and served with creamy sauce). Receives mixed reviews.

TOP **San Agustín** CAFE $
CHOICE
(San Francisco 21; snacks M$30-50, mains M$50-140; ⊙8am-11pm; ⊜) A 'don't leave San Miguel without...' experience. This is a sweet tooth's paradise and the best place to go in Mexico for chocolate and *churros* (doughnut-like fritters; M$40).

Petit Four CAFE $
(Mesones 99-1; snacks M$10-45; ⊙8am-8pm Tue-Sat, 8am-3pm Sun; ⊜) A wonderful place to get your sugar hit: French pastries that you can enjoy in a cozy environment.

Buen Día Café CAFE $
(Pueblito 3; mains M$50-70; ⊙8:30am-2pm Wed-Mon) This simple, slightly more than a hole-in-the wall is located in the quaint Callejon Pueblito, opposite Calderoni B&B, and serves up great coffee (complete with coffee art) and excellent breakfasts, as well as other snacks.

Casa de Café CAFE $
(Hospicio 31; snacks M$30-40; ⊙7:30am-8:30pm Thu-Tue, 7:30am-3pm Wed; ⊜⊛) A cute, cozy place with delicious sandwiches, good coffee and freshly baked cakes.

Café Santa Ana CAFE $
(Reloj 50A; breakfast M$60-70; ⊙9am-5pm Mon-Fri, 9am-noon Sun) This relaxing place, in the library annex, is popular with culture vultures.

Self-caterers are best to head to the supermarkets at Soriana shopping center, 2.5km southeast of the center on the Querétaro road.

For budget bites, on the corner of Ancha de San Antonio and tree-shaded Nueva (near Instituto Allende) are several reliable food stands. They alternate in the mornings and evenings, selling great-tasting juice, *gorditas* (small circles of tortilla dough, fried and topped with meat and/or cheese), burritos and tacos. Reliable juice stands front the small plaza off Insurgentes.

Excellent traditional bakeries include **La Buena Vida** (Hernández Macías 72-14; ⊙8am-4pm Mon-Sat) and **La Colmena Bakery** (Reloj 21). Along more contemporary lines serving up excellent French pastries is the trendy panaderia, **Cumpanio** (Correo 29; ⊙8am-9pm).

Mercado El Nigromante (Colegio s/n) has good produce stands and market eateries.

It's centrally located, but light years away from the gringo scene.

🍷 Drinking & Entertainment

In San Miguel, drinking and entertainment are often synonymous. Many bars (and restaurants) host live music. Most of the action is on Thursday to Saturday nights, but some places have live music nightly.

Bars & Nightclubs
Several bars and nightclubs can be found along Umarán.

La Azotea BAR
(Umarán 6) Above the restaurant Pueblo Viejo, this terrace is more of a laid-back lounge and tapas bar, with a smart, gay-friendly crowd and a less touristy vibe.

Mama Mía CLUB
(Umarán 8) This perennially popular place has separate areas with different hours to host its weekly schedule of gigs. Hit Mama's Bar for live rock/funk, or join a more sophisticated crowd in the restaurant patio for live folk music, including South American, salsa and jazz (check the changing schedule). Up front, Bar Leonardo's shows big-screen sports and La Terrazza, the terrace bar, offers a fine view of the town. Some serious nightlife gets going around 11pm.

El Grito CLUB
(Umarán 15; ⊙10pm-4am Fri & Sat) An oversized face above the doorway of this upscale disco shouts out 'high prices' to the young and fashionable Mexican crowd queuing outside.

Mint CLUB
(Mesones 99-1; ⊙10pm-late Fri & Sat) Offers all types of music for an exclusive and exclusively disco-loving crowd. Seems to change ownership and name regularly, however.

Cinemas
Teatro Santa Ana THEATER
(Reloj 50A; tickets M$50-200) This small theater inside the Biblioteca Pública plays host to a good selection of independent and international films, as well as local plays.

Performing Arts
It's one big cultural party in San Miguel; the town seems to host more events than NYC. Check out what's on in *Atención San Miguel*. The Escuela de Bellas Artes and the Biblioteca (in the Sala Quetzal) host a variety of cultural events, many in English; check their notice boards for schedules.

Teatro Ángela Peralta THEATER

(152-22-00; www.teatroangelaperalta.webpin.com; cnr Calles Mesones & Hernández Macías) Built in 1910, this elegant venue often hosts local productions. The **ticket office** (Hernández Macías 62; 8:30am-4pm Mon-Fri) is around the corner; check out its website for productions. Tickets cost up to M$350 depending on the production.

Shopping

Be sure to hit the Tianguis (Tuesday market), the biggest weekly outdoor extravaganza, beside the Soriana shopping center, 2.5km southeast of the center on the Querétaro road. Take a 'Soriana' or 'Placita' bus (10 minutes, M$5) from Mesones, near Plaza Cívica.

The local market **Mercado El Nigromante** (Colegio s/n) sells fruit, vegetables and assorted goods.

Galleries

Part of the joy of wandering around San Miguel is to stumble upon the many galleries tucked away in streets around town; there are more commercial galleries than cafes (and perhaps, real estate agents) in San Miguel. The largest concentration of contemporary art galleries and design studios (mainly expatriates' work) is housed in the trendy **Fábrica La Aurora** (152-13-12; Aurora s/n; 10am-6pm), a remodeled raw-cotton factory on the north end of town. Many galleries are promoted in local papers, but otherwise be guided by your whim.

Craft Shops

San Miguel has a mind-boggling number of craft shops, selling folk art and handicrafts from all over the country. Local crafts include tinware, wrought iron, silver, brass, leather, glassware, pottery and textiles. Many shops are along Canal, San Francisco, Zacateros and Pila Seca. Price and quality varies widely. Places worth considering (if you want to support causes of a different kind) include the following.

FAI HANDICRAFTS

(www.faiguanajuato.rg; Hidalgo 13; 10am-6pm Sun-Wed) Has a great range of handicrafts, many of which are made locally. Proceeds from sales go to the charity.

Mujeres Productoras HANDICRAFTS

(Female Producers; 150-00-25; www.globaljustice center.org/mujeres_productoras; Calzada de la Luz 42) This is a rural women's cooperative from surrounding municipalities. It sells a range of handmade goods, which are the source of income (often the only one) for the family.

Mercado de Artesanías HANDICRAFTS

(Colegio s/n) A collection of handicraft stalls of varying quality in the alleyway between Colegio and Loreto; prices can be on par with the town's shops and the quality varies.

Information

Internet Access

Border Crossings (152-24-97; www.border crossingsma.com; Mesones 57A; per hr M$15; 9am-6:30pm Mon-Fri, to 2pm Sat) Good internet access as well as mail-forwarding, fax, phone-message and shipping services.

Internet Tranvi_net (cnr Umarán & El Jardín, 1st fl; per hr M$10; 9am-9pm) Good internet services with scanning and printing.

Internet Resources

Atención San Miguel (www.atencionsan miguel.org) Weekly bilingual newspaper that runs an excellent website.

Portal San Miguel (www.portalsanmiguel.com) A commercial website with many listings.

Medical Services

Hospital de la Fe (152-22-33; Libramiento a Dolores Hidalgo 43)

Media

Don't contemplate spending time in town without buying the weekly semi-bilingual (English/Spanish) newspaper *Atención San Miguel* (M$10). Published every Friday, it's chock-a-block with what's on for the coming week, including tours, concerts and gallery openings. It also lists yoga, Spanish, art and dance class schedules. You can buy it at the public library and many cafes or from roaming vendors.

Money

Most banks have their own ATMs and are located on, or within two blocks east of, the Jardín. There are also *casas de cambio* on Correo.

Tourist Information

Tourist office (152-09-00; www.visitsan miguel.travel; Plaza Principal 8; 8:30am-8pm Mon-Fri, 10am-8pm Sat, 10am-5:30pm Sun) On the northern side of El Jardín. Good for maps of the town, promotional pamphlets and information on events.

Travel Agencies

Bajio Go (152-19-99; www.bajiogo.com, www.sanmiguelsupershuttle.com; Jésus 11; 8am-8pm Mon-Sat, 10am-3pm Sun) A helpful travel agent with an airport shuttle service.

Viajes Vertiz (152-18-56; www.viajesvertiz. com; Hidalgo 1A; 9am-6:30pm Mon-Fri,

BUSES FROM SAN MIGUEL DE ALLENDE

DESTINATION	FARE (M$)	DURATION	FREQUENCY (DAILY)
Celaya	33	1¾hr	every 15min
Dolores Hidalgo	28	1hr	every 40min 7am-8pm
Guadalajara	367-430	5¼-5½hr	9
Guanajuato	68-196	1-1½hr	19
León	34-160	2¼-2½hr	11
Mexico City (Terminal Norte)	173-285	3½-4¼hr	8
Querétaro	45-80	1-1¼hr	every 40min 7am-8:30pm

10am-2pm Sat) American Express agent (but does not cash traveler's checks); sells domestic and international air tickets.

Websites

Head to **Lonely Planet** (www.lonelyplanet.com/mexico/northern-central-highlands/san-miguel-de-allende) for planning advice, author recommendations, traveler reviews and insider tips.

❶ Getting There & Away

Air

The nearest airpot is the Aeropuerto Internacional del Bajío, between León and Silao, around 1½ hours away by car.

Bus

The Central de Autobuses is on Canal (Calzada de la Estación), 3km west of the center. Tickets can be purchased at the station. First-class tickets for Primera Plus and ETN can also be bought at **Peradora** (☑152-80-11; Cuna de Allende 17).

Second-class services (Coordinados [Flecha Amarilla] and Herradura de Plata) also leave from this station. Other 1st-class buses serve Aguascalientes, Monterrey and San Luis Potosí.

Car & Motorcycle

The only San Miguel–based agency is **San Miguel Rent-a-Car** (☑152-01-98; www.sanmiguelrentacar.com; Codo 9). Prices start at about M$660 per day including insurance.

❶ Getting Around

To/From the Airport

A few agencies provide shuttle transportation to/from Bajío airport. These include **Viajes Vertiz** (☑152-18-56; www.viajesvertiz.com; Hidalgo 1A; ⊙9am-6:30pm Mon-Fri, 10am-2pm Sat), **Viajes San Miguel** (☑152-25-37; www.viajessanmiguel.com; Diez de Sollano 4-Interior 3; ⊙9am-7pm Mon-Fri, 10am-2pm Sat) and **Bajío Go** (☑152-19-99; www.bajiobo.com, www.

sanmiguelsupershuttle.com; Jésus 11; ⊙8am-8pm Mon-Sat, 10am-3pm Sun). Alternatively, take a bus to Silao and get a taxi from there to the airport. For Mexico City airport, get a bus to Querétaro and a bus direct to the airport from there.

If heading from the airport to San Miguel by bus, it's easiest to go to León and take one from there. No bus service operates between Bajío airport and central León. A taxi to León costs M$300 to M$415 and to San Miguel M$1200 (for up to four people).

To/From the Bus Station

Local buses (M$5) run from 7am to 9pm daily. 'Central' buses run regularly between the bus station and the town center. Coming into town these terminate at the eastern end of Insurgentes after winding through the streets. Heading out of the center, you can pick one up on Canal. A taxi between the center and the bus station costs around M$35; trips around town cost around M$30.

Around San Miguel de Allende

CAÑADA DE LA VIRGEN

Opened in 2011 after many years of archaeological excavation and negotiations with the owner (who donated the ruins and surrounds to the government to allow for public access), the **Cañada de la Virgen** (⊙10am-4pm) is an intriguing pre-Hispanic pyramid complex and former ritual and ceremonial site located around 25km southeast of San Miguel, dating from around 300 to 1050AD. Bones, believed to be from sacrificial ceremonies, and remnants were discovered here. The most interesting aspects include the alignment of the planets and the main temple and the design of the site (these reflect the surrounding landscape).

A shuttle bus is the compulsory transportation for visitors. It runs between the site office and the site (several kilometers away); these depart on the hour between 10am and 4pm. The tours are in Spanish, and you'll be walking on cobbled surfaces and steep steps.

Tours in English
TOUR

(☏415-102-55-83; acoffee@live.com.mx; per person, 4 people or more, $40, groups of less than 4 $150) Possibly the easiest and most rewarding visit for non-Spanish speakers is to take a tour with the passionate English-speaking Albert Coffee, an archaeologist who formerly worked on the site. He discusses the site's fascinating cultural and historical context; prices include transport from San Miguel.

SANTUARIO DE ATOTONILCO
The hamlet of Atotonilco, 11km north of San Miguel and 3km west of the Dolores Hidalgo highway, is dominated by an extremely important sanctuary, at least in the eyes of Mexicans. The sanctuary was founded in 1740 as a spiritual retreat, and Ignacio Allende married here in 1802. Eight years later he returned with Miguel Hidalgo and a band of independence rebels en route from Do-

lores to San Miguel to take the shrine's banner of the Virgin of Guadalupe as their flag.

A journey to Atotonilco is the goal of pilgrims and penitents from all over Mexico, and the starting point of an important and solemn procession two weekends before Easter. Participants carry the image of the Señor de la Columna to the church of San Juan de Dios in San Miguel. Inside, the sanctuary has six chapels and is vibrant with statues, folk murals and paintings. Traditional dances are held here on the third Sunday in July.

From San Miguel, taxis charge around M$150 for a one-way trip. Local buses depart from Calzada de La Luz every hour (M$10, 45 minutes).

POZOS
☏412 / POP 2200 / ELEV 2200M

Less than 100 years ago, Mineral de Pozos was a flourishing silver-mining center of 70,000 people, but with the 1910 Revolution and the flooding of the mines, the population dwindled. Empty houses, a large and unfinished church (note the dome!) and discarded mine workings and shafts were the legacy of abandonment. Today, this tiny place is trying valiantly to win a place

---

WORTH A TRIP

HOT SPRINGS

The surrounds of San Miguel are blessed with hot mineral springs. Some of these have been transformed into commercial *balnearios* (swimming pools) in pretty, landscaped gardens and picnic grounds. Most places are crowded with local families on weekends but *muy tranquilo* (very peaceful) during the week.

The *balnearios* are accessed via the highway north of San Miguel and all are clearly signposted. The most convenient transportation is taxis (around M$150 each way; you can ask the driver to return for you at an appointed time). Alternatively, take a Dolores Hidalgo bus from the San Miguel bus station, or a local bus marked 'Santuario' (hourly) from Calzada de la Luz. These buses will stop out front, or at the turnoffs to some of the *balnearios* from where you'll need to walk (check directions and bus connections with the tourist office). To return to town, it's best to pre-arrange a taxi pick-up, or hail a bus heading along the highway.

Taboada (☏152-08-50; admission M$100; ⊗9am-6pm) Olympic-size swimming pool, plus a small pool for children, hot thermal spa and snack kiosk. Hourly 'Nigromante' minibuses, departing from Calzada de la Luz, get you within 1.5km of Taboada.

Balneario Xote (☏155-81-87; www.xoteparqueacuatico.com.mx; adult/child M$100/50; ⊗9am-6pm) A family-oriented water park, 3.5km off the highway down the same cobblestone road as Taboada (without transport this is a long, exposed trek).

Escondido Place (☏185-20-22; www.escondidoplace.com; admission M$100; ⊗8am-5:30pm) Seven small outdoor pools and three connected indoor pools, each progressively hotter. Set in picturesque grounds with snack bar.

La Gruta (admission M$100; ⊗8am-5pm) is one of the easiest to get to – it's on the Dolores highway, just past Parador del Cortijo at Km 9.5. It's justifiably a favorite among visitors and has three small pools, a tunnel and a cave.

on the map. Visitors can explore the crumbling buildings and tour the fascinating surrounds, including several mine ruins, by mountain bike or horse. Warning: many mine shafts are unfenced and, at 150m deep, are extremely dangerous. A number of expat artists run galleries here.

The town's tourism efforts also include an 'art walk,' a tour of the town's main galleries and craft workshops, where community members sell their work. Several workshops make pre-Hispanic musical instruments. For further information on the area, including local guides, see www.mineraldepozos.com.

Sleeping & Eating

El Secreto   B&B $$
(☑293-02-00; www.elsecretomexico.com; Jardín Principal 6; r incl breakfast from M$850; ☎) On the plaza, this is a tasteful gallery-cum-B&B with a lovely garden and elegant rooms. The English-speaking owners know a lot about the area.

Posada de las Minas   BOUTIQUE HOTEL $$
(☑293-02-13; www.posadadelasminas.com; Doblado 1; r from M$1000, apt M$1650; ☎) This restored 19th-century hacienda offers ornate rooms or apartments in a colonial setting. There's a bar, a restaurant with a retractable roof (mains M$80 to M$165) and a small but impressive cactus garden.

For meals, try the three options on the square: **La Pila Seca** (mains M$40-100; ☺9am-9pm) is the smartest place. Other options are tiny, casual **Fonda El Portal** (mains M$440-475; ☺9am-9pm) and **Porfirio Díaz** (mains M$100-130; ☺9am-9pm), which has a full menu.

Getting There & Away

Pozos is 14km south of San Luis de la Paz, a detour east of Hwy 57. To get here by bus from San Miguel (or Querétaro), go first to Dolores Hidalgo, then to San Luis de la Paz and then take a third bus to Pozos. By car it's about 45 minutes from San Miguel. Bici-Burro (see p673) offers fabulous bike tours to the town and mines. Much of the ride is a cross-country trip on tracks across cactus-strewn countryside, via fascinating villages.

QUERÉTARO STATE

Querétaro state (population 1.8 million) is full of surprises. Billed primarily as an agricultural and ranching state – with the handsome Querétaro city as its capital – it is packed with diverse geography, quirky sights and historical gems. Natural phenomena, such as the world's third-largest monolith, La Peña de Bernal, pre-Hispanic ruins and the stunning Sierra Gorda Biosphere Reserve, are located in the state's 11,770 sq km. The reserve protects several mission towns, from where the local people run some excellent, new community-owned tourism activities, a must for the more intrepid traveler.

Querétaro

☑442 / POP 630,000/ ELEV 1800M

As far as the silver cities go, Querétaro is sometimes intimated to be the ugly sibling. Indeed, the rather frantic outskirts with their busy freeways can give a misguided first impression. The city's large, historic heart is characterized by charming *andadores* (pedestrian streets), stunning plazas and interesting churches. The sophisticated restaurants serve up quality cuisine and the museums reflect Querétaro's important role in Mexican history.

History

The Otomí founded a settlement here in the 15th century that was soon absorbed by the Aztecs, then by Spaniards in 1531. Franciscan monks used it as a missionary base not only to Mexico but also to what is now southwestern USA. In the early 19th century, Querétaro became a center of intrigue among disaffected criollos plotting to free Mexico from Spanish rule. Conspirators, including Miguel Hidalgo, met secretly at the house of doña Josefa Ortiz (La Corregidora), who was the wife of Querétaro's former *corregidor* (district administrator).

When the conspiracy was uncovered, the story goes, doña Josefa was locked in her house (now the Palacio de Gobierno) but managed to whisper through a keyhole to a co-conspirator, Ignacio Pérez, that their colleagues were in jeopardy, leading to Padre Hidalgo's call to arms (see boxed text, p667).

In 1917 the Mexican constitution was drawn up by the Constitutionalist faction in Querétaro. The PNR (which later became the PRI, the Institutional Revolutionary Party) was organized in Querétaro in 1929, dominating Mexican politics for the rest of the 20th century.

◉ Sights

Templo de San Francisco   CHURCH
(cnr Av Corregidora & Andador 5 de Mayo; ☺8-10am & 4-9pm) This impressive church fronts

Querétaro

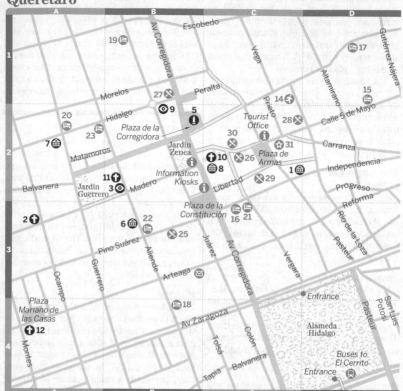

Jardín Zenea. Pretty colored tiles on the dome were brought from Spain in 1540, around the time construction of the church began. Inside are some fine religious paintings from the 17th, 18th and 19th centuries.

Museo Regional   MUSEUM
(cnr Av Corregidora 3 & Jardín Zenea; admission M$30; ⊙10am-6pm Tue-Sun) This museum is beside the Templo de San Francisco. The ground floor holds interesting exhibits on pre-Hispanic Mexico, archaeological sites, Spanish occupation and the state's various indigenous groups.

The upstairs exhibits reveal Querétaro's role in the independence movement and post-independence history (plus religious paintings). The table at which the Treaty of Guadalupe Hidalgo was signed in 1848, ending the Mexican–American War, is on display, as is the desk of the tribunal that sentenced Emperor Maximilian to death.

The museum is housed in part of what was once a huge monastery and seminary. Begun in 1540, the seminary became the seat of the Franciscan province of San Pedro y San Pablo de Michoacán by 1567. Building continued until at least 1727. Thanks to its high tower, in the 1860s the monastery was used as a fort both by imperialists supporting Maximilian and by the forces who defeated him in 1867.

**Templo y Convento
de la Santa Cruz**   NOTABLE BUILDING
(☎212-02-35; Independencia 148 at Felipe Luna; donation requested; ⊙9am-2pm & 4-6pm Tue-Sat, 9am-4pm Sun) Ten minutes' walk east of the center is one of the city's most interesting sights. The convent was built between 1654 and about 1815 on the site of a battle in which a miraculous appearance of Santiago (St James) led the Otomí to surrender to the conquistadors and Christianity. Emperor Maximilian had his headquarters here

Querétaro

while under siege in Querétaro from March to May 1867. After his surrender and subsequent death sentence, he was jailed here while awaiting the firing squad. Today it's used as a religious school.

You can visit with a guide – ask at the entrance – although an English tour will need to be arranged beforehand (donation requested). The site's main legend is the growth of the **Árbol de la Cruz**, an ancient tree in the convent's garden whose thorns are in the shape of crosses. This miracle was the result of a walking stick stuck in the earth by a pious friar in 1697.

Museo de Arte de Querétaro　MUSEUM
(☏212-23-57; www.museodeartequeretaro.com; Allende Sur 14; admission M$30, Tue free; ⊙10am-6pm Tue-Sun) Adjacent to the Templo de San Agustín, Querétaro's art museum occupies a splendid baroque monastery built between 1731 and 1748. It is worth visiting to see the building alone: angels, quirky gargoyles, statues and other ornamental details abound, particularly around the stunning courtyard.

The ground-floor display of 16th- and 17th-century European paintings traces influences from Flemish to Spanish to Mexican art. On the same floor you'll find 19th- and 20th-century Mexican paintings. The top floor has works from 16th-century

Mannerism to 18th-century baroque. The museum has a good bookstore-cum-gift shop.

Museo de la Ciudad   MUSEUM

(☑212-47-02; www.museodelaciudadqro.org; Guerrero Norte 27; admission M$5, students free; ☺11am-7pm Tue-Sat, to 5pm Sun) Inside the ex-convent and old prison that held Maximilian, the 11-room Museo de la Ciudad has some good alternating contemporary-art exhibits.

FREE Museo de la Restauración de la República   MUSEUM

(☑224-30-04; www.queretaro.gob.mx/mrr; Guerrero Norte 23; ☺9am-5pm Tue-Sun) If you can read Spanish or are a real history buff, this museum covers Querétaro's role in Mexico's history, particularly the French occupation and the eventual ousting of Emperor Maximilian.

Teatro de la República   THEATER

(☑212-03-39; cnr Juárez & Peralta; ☺10am-3pm & 5-8pm) This lovely old and functioning theater, complete with impressive chandeliers, was where a tribunal met in 1867 to decide the fate of Emperor Maximilian. Mexico's constitution was also signed here on January 31, 1917. The stage backdrop lists the names of its signatories and the states they represented. In 1929, politicians met in the theater to organize Mexico's long-time ruling party, the PNR (now the PRI).

Acueducto & Mirador   AQUEDUCT, LOOKOUT

Walk east along Independencia past Convento de la Santa Cruz, then fork right along Ejército Republicano, to the mirador. There's a fine view of 'Los Arcos,' Querétaro's emblematic 1.28km-long aqueduct, with 74 towering sandstone arches built between 1726 and 1738. The aqueduct runs along the center of Avenida Zaragoza.

Across the street from the *mirador* is the **Mausoleo de la Corregidora** (Ejército Republicano s/n; ☺9am-6pm), the resting place of doña Josefa Ortiz and her husband, Miguel Domínguez de Alemán.

Casa de la Zacatecana   HOUSE

(☑224-07-58; www.museolazacatecana.com; Independencia 59; admission M$35; ☺10am-6pm Tue-Sun) This is a finely restored 17th-century home with a lovely collection of 18th- and 19th-century furniture and decorations (and its own murder mystery – skeletons were discovered in the basement).

Other Central Sights   NEIGHBORHOOD

Plaza de la Corregidora is dominated by the **Monumento a la Corregidora** (cnr Corregidora & Andador 16 de Septiembre), a 1910 statue of doña Josefa Ortiz bearing the flame of freedom.

A block west of Jardín Zenea is the **Fuente de Neptuno** (Neptune's Fountain; cnr Madero & Allende), designed by noted Mexican neoclassical architect Eduardo Tresguerras in 1797. Next to it, the 17th-century **Templo de Santa Clara** (cnr Madero & Allende) has an ornate baroque interior. Two blocks west of the templo, on Madero, is the rather plain 18th-century **cathedral** (cnr Madero & Ocampo).

At the intersection of Arteaga and Montes is the 18th-century **Templo de Santa Rosa de Viterbos**, Querétaro's most splendid baroque church, with its pagoda-like bell tower, unusual exterior paintwork, curling buttresses and lavishly gilded and marbled interior. The church also boasts what some say is the earliest four-sided clock in the New World.

🍴 Courses

Olé Spanish Language School   SPANISH

(☑214-40-23; www.ole.edu.mx; Escobedo 32) The Olé Spanish Language School offers a range of courses with homestay options and extracurricular programs. Prices start at around US$15 per hour, and week-long courses range from moderate group classes for 15 hours from US$157 to 35 intensive one-hour private classes for US$403.

👉 Tours

Guided Tours   TRAM

(1-/2-hr tours M$80/120) Guided tours of the city center on the Tranvía trolleybus, in Spanish, leave from Plaza Constitución. For details, ask at the tourist office or at the **information kiosk** (☑238-50-67) in Plaza de la Constitución.

Night Tours   WALKING

For Spanish speakers, several different companies run fun night tours. The tours have titles such as Leyendas & Mitos (Myths & Legends), Noche de Leyendas, and actors in period costume dramatically reveal the legends and secrets of the dark lanes and buildings. For details, ask at the **tourist office** (☑238-50-67, 800-715-17-42; www.queretaro.travel; Pasteur Norte 4; ☺9am-8pm). For an additional cost, some can arrange English-speaking guides.

Festivals & Events

Feria Internacional FAIR
Querétaro's Feria Internacional, one of Mexico's biggest state fairs, happens in the first two weeks of December. It focuses on agriculture but also hosts cultural events.

Sleeping

Kuku Rukú HOTEL, HOSTEL $
(☑245-87-77; www.kukuruku.mx; Vergara 12; dm from M$160; d M$600-800) Among Mexico's few green options (solar power, gray water use), this funky spot houses both a hostel and a hotel. The hostel features perky dorms and a communal kitchen. The hotel's decor is cool and hip – public areas feature tongue-in-cheek quotes ('*I don't really think, I just walk,*' attributed to an American celebrity). Plus there are large bunks, white walls with paintings and quirky designer touches. At the time of research Kuku Rukú had just opened; let's hope the premises are well maintained as it's sure to get some traffic.

Doña Urraca Hotel & Spa LUXURY HOTEL $$$
(☑238-54-00, in Mexico 800-021-71-16; www.dona urraca.com.mx; Calle 5 de Mayo 117; ste incl breakfast from M$2965; P❀✳❂✆❄) Perfect for people who prefer to be pampered. The 24 spacious suites are lavished with all the right 'fluffy features': bathrobes and handmade herbal soaps plus sound systems and cable TV. It even boasts a wine cellar. Guests have reported that their Sunday brunch has been 'disrupted' by weekend functions here – from kids' parties to other events.

Home B&B B&B $$
(☑183-91-39; www.queretarobandb.com; Calle 16 de Septiembre 104; r incl breakfast from M$580; ✆) This friendly Canadian-run place is central and very social. Breakfast is an absolute treat: it's prepared by the owner, a former professional chef. Rooms vary in shape and size, all are light and airy and some have private bathroom. Note: by reservation only.

La Casa del Naranjo BOUTIQUE HOTEL $$$
(☑212-76-09; www.lacasadelnaranjo.com; Hidalgo 21; r M$1100-1750; ✆) The six rooms in this boutique hotel are decorated in an eclectic, but stylish, manner. Each room is named after a fruit; the timber from the fruit trees has been incorporated into the design. Downstairs rooms are more cramped than the airier options above, but there are several attractive outdoor lounge areas. Three bikes are available for client use.

La Casa del Atrio B&B $$$
(☑212-63-14; www.lacasadelatrio.com; Allende Sur 15; r incl breakfast M$1450) You are paying for the novelty at this one-of-a-kind conceptual space. Accommodations are incorporated into a gallery-cum-antique-shop (which features the works of famous Mexican artist Julia López). The six rooms offer nearly-there luxury (the bathrooms are small, and there's little natural light in some, but hey, original sculptures are next to your bed). There's a funky lounge area and a pretty back garden.

Hotel Quinta Lucca HOTEL $$
(☑340-44-44; www.hotelquintalucca.com; Juárez Norte 119A; r M$960, ste M$1150-1300; P✆) Mexican-modern interiors in neat, clean rooms. The lighter ones are more pleasant; these surround a luscious green courtyard. A continental breakfast is served here.

Hotel Señorial HOTEL $$
(☑214-37-00; 800-633-2788; www.senorialqro. com; Guerrero Norte 15; r/tr M$600/750; P❀✆) It resembles a prison from the outside, but the inside has clean and neat modern(ish) rooms (being refurbished at the time of research) and extremely friendly staff. It's a US Peace Corps haunt.

Hotel Posada Diamante HOTEL $
(☑212-66 37; www.posadadiamante.com.mx; Allende Sur 45; s M$250-280, d M$380-440, tr M$440; ❀✆) A simple, clean and respectable budget option, with friendly management. Only a short walk to central pedestrian plazas.

El Serafín HOTEL $$$
(☑212-89-99; www.elserafinhotel.mx; Independencia 22; d M$1300-1500; ❀✆) This boutique hotel errs on the try-hard decor but is a comfortable bet. Best to reserve; often offers promotional deals.

Eating

Plaza de Armas has some excellent, more upscale restaurants and cafes with both indoor and outdoor tables.

La Mariposa CAFE $
TOP CHOICE
(Peralta 7; snacks M$20-100; ⊙8am-9:30pm; ❀) Unchanged since 1940 (as the photos will testify), this Querétaro institution is more about the quaint atmosphere than the food. Don't leave without trying the mouthwatering *mantecado* (ice cream made to a special recipe; M$30).

Di Vino ITALIAN $$$
(Andador 5 de Mayo 12; mains M$145-300; ⊘1pm-midnight Mon-Sat) A stylish, sophisticated Italian restaurant with an upmarket ambience, superb cuisine and an impressive wine cellar. A change from the Mexican theme, and a special experience at that.

🖋 **Kuku Rukú** INTERNATIONAL $$
(www.kukuruku.mx; Vergara 12; mains M$60-100; ⊘8am-10pm Mon-Sat) Don't be deceived; this new place may be in the courtyard of a hostel-cum-hotel, but it turns on some of the freshest, most upbeat dishes around. Excellent sandwiches, meat dishes and salads are thrown together by experienced chefs. Organic produce is used when possible. Vegetarians will be well sated here, too. Don't miss the *piloncillo* ice-cream (a 'secret' blend of vanilla, cinnamon, cloves and other delights). A terrace bar is upstairs (6pm to 11pm Monday to Saturday).

Restaurante Bar 1810 MEXICAN $$$
(Libertad 62; mains M$125-235; ⊘8am-11pm Mon-Thu, to midnight Fri & Sat, to 9pm Sun; ⊜) Covered with fairy lights and situated on the pretty plaza, this is *the* eatery for excellent steaks or a variety of pastas and seafood dishes. Live crooners complement (or otherwise) your meal.

Biznarga CAFE $
(Gutiérrez Najera 17; mains M$32-50; ⊘9am-2pm & 6:30-11:30pm Mon-Sat; ⊜) Their friends liked their cooking so much they opened their kitchen to the public. And why not? A fun, slightly Rasta experience with graffiti, artworks and memorabilia. The creativity extends to the dishes – excellent salads, homemade pizzas, juices and more.

🖋 **Neblinas Ecotienda & Café** CAFE $
(Río de la Loza 1; snacks M$45-90; ⊘10am-10pm Mon-Thu, to midnight Fri & Sat; 🖋) This shop, cafe, gallery and cultural center supports communities in the Sierra Gorda. Everything here has an ecofriendly and sustainable message: the shop sells organic produce and the cafe serves everything from hamburgers with handmade animal-shaped rolls to *penca de nopal,* a cactus plate. Cultural performances include live jazz and dance.

San Miguelito MEXICAN $$
(mains M$130-200; ⊘1pm-midnight Tue-Sat, to 6pm Sun; ⊜) This place is popular for its location near the plaza, its ambience and color-ful decor. Popular dishes include *filete de res en salsa de mezquite* (beef fillet with mesquite plant sauce).

La Antojería MEXICAN $
(mains M$20-65; ⊘10am-10pm; ⊜🖋) This family-friendly, fun and Mexican-themed place serves up every style of *antojito* known in Mexico.

Café del Fondo CAFE $
(Pino Suárez 9; everything under M$60; ⊘7am-10pm) This relaxed, rambling alternative hangout is popular with newspaper-reading elder statesmen, chess-heads and chatterboxes. Decent set breakfasts go for only M$35. Snacks and a four-course *comida corrida* (prix-fixe menu) are also available (around M$35).

🍷 **Drinking**

There's a thriving bar scene in Querétaro. Bars and clubs are popping up (and sometimes down) in the historic center and beyond. Calle 5 de Mayo is the fashionable drinking strip in the center; trendy barflies hit these places after 10pm. A slew of trendy bars and nightclubs can be found further out along Avenida Constituyentes and Blvd Bernardo Quintana, the city's eastern and western ring roads – take a taxi. Late-night gay bars line Blvd Bernardo Quintana.

☆ **Entertainment**

Querétaro is action-packed with cultural activities. For the latest on what's happening around town, look out for posters on bulletin boards, or ask at the tourist office. On Sunday, free concerts take place in Plaza de Armas at 1pm and in the evenings in Jardín Zenea.

Casa de la Cultura CULTURAL CENTER
(Calle 5 de Mayo 40; ⊘9am-2pm & 4-5pm Mon-Fri) Sponsors concerts, dance, theater and art events; stop by to view the bulletin board.

Teatro de la República THEATER
(cnr Juárez & Peralta; tickets M$60-180) Has regular symphony concerts most Fridays.

ℹ️ **Information**

There are card phones on Jardín Zenea, Plaza de Armas and elsewhere around the center. A handy no-name internet place is at Libertad 32; it charges around M$10 per hour. There are several banks with ATMs around Jardín Zenea. *Casas de cambio* are along Juárez and Colón.

BUSES FROM QUERÉTARO

DESTINATION	FARE (M$)	DURATION	FREQUENCY (DAILY)
Guadalajara	273-385	4½-5½hr	11
Guanajuato	127-135	2½-3hr	6
Mexico City (Terminal Norte)	110-225	3-4½hr	every 20min 4am-11:30pm
Mexico City Airport	256	3½hr	25
Morelia	150	3-4hr	hourly
San Luis Potosí	152-200	2½-2¾hr	23
San Miguel de Allende	45-80	1-1½hr	every 40min 6am-11pm
Tequisquiapan	34	1hr	every 30min 6:30am-9pm

Hospital Luis Martín (☑214-25-71; Ave Zaragoza Poniente 88)

Post office (☑212-01-12; Arteaga 5)

Tourist office (☑238-50-67, 800-715-17-42; www.queretaro.travel; Pasteur Norte 4; ◷9am-8pm) Has city maps and brochures (in Spanish), although you might need to ask for both. More helpful kiosks are located on the plazas (open 10am to 7pm daily).

Turismo Beverly (☑216-15-00; Tecnológico 118) Travel agent useful for air tickets.

❶ Getting There & Away

Air

The **Aeropuerto Internacional** (☑192-55-00), 8km northeast of the center, is around a M$280 taxi ride. Primera Plus also runs from this terminal to Mexico City airport (M$270, three hours). **Continental Airlines** (www.continental.com) has flights to various US cities from Querétaro.

A useful in-town airline office is **Aeroméxico Connect** (Av Tecnológico 100, San Ángel).

Bus

Querétaro is a hub for buses in all directions; the modern Central Camionera is 5km southeast of the center. There's one building for deluxe and 1st class (labeled A), one for 2nd class (B) and another for local buses (C). Facilities include a cafe, telephone *casetas* (booths), shops and luggage storage.

Primera Plus has regular services to Mexico City airport.

Car & Motorcycle

If you want a car to explore the Sierra Gorda, English-speaking **Express Rent-a-Car** (☑242-90-28; Hotel Real de Minas, Av Constituyentes Poniente 124) has competitive rates. **Budget** (☑213-44-98; Av Constituyentes Oriente 73) is also worth checking.

❶ Getting Around

Once you have reached the city center, you can easily visit most sights on foot. City buses (M$7) run from 6am until 9pm or 10pm. They gather in an area at the end of the bus terminal; turn right from the 2nd-class terminal, or left from the 1st-class side. Several routes go to the center (check as the numbers change). For a taxi, get a ticket first from the bus station booth (M$37 for up to four people).

To get to the bus station from the center, take city bus 19, 25 or 36 from Zaragoza, or any bus labeled 'Terminal de Autobuses' heading south on the east side of the Alameda Hidalgo.

Around Querétaro

EL CERRITO

If you happen to be interested in archaeology, check out **El Cerrito** (Little Hill; admission free; ◷9am-midday Mon-Fri), a 30m-high pyramid-like structure sitting atop a small hill located in El Pueblito, 7km from central Querétaro. Archaeologists, who are still excavating the site, believe it was occupied between AD 600 and 1600 by the Teotihuacán, Toltec, Chichimec, Otomí and Tarasca cultures. Besides the pyramid, there are the remains of a possible ball court and some outlying structures. A later fort-type construction on its top dates from 1876.

Local legend links El Cerrito to the history of the Virgin of El Pueblito, the patron saint of Querétaro.

At the site there are free guides (in Spanish; small tip appreciated) and a small museum. To get there, take a 64 bus (M$7, 25 minutes) from Avenida Constituyentes on the south side of Alameda Hidalgo. It passes through the village and will drop you at the entrance. A taxi costs around M$60.

Check with the tourist office before you go as the site's opening hours are inconsistent and it's sometimes closed due to excavations.

BERNAL
☑441 / POP 4000 / ELEV 2060

The town of Bernal is quaint, if touristy. Its drawcard is the 350m-high rock spire, the **Peña de Bernal**, the third-largest monolith in the world and considered mystical by many Mexicans. During the vernal equinox thousands of pilgrims converge on the rock to take in its positive energy. Visitors can climb to the rock's halfway point (allow one hour both ways); only professional rock climbers can climb to its peak.

Beyond that, you can cover Bernal and its sights in an hour or so. The town has several **churches** and **El Castillo**, a 16th-century viceregal building. For a more in-depth explanation of the area, friendly **La Peña Tours** (☑296-73-98, cell phone 441-1014821; cnr Independencia & Colon) offers an array of tours (M$120 to M$400) plus climbing sessions on the Peña.

La Aurora (Jardín Principal 1; www.bernal magico.com; ☺10am-8pm) is an interesting *artesanías* shop; request permission to see the weavers at work at their looms in the workshop behind the shop.

The town comes to life during the weekends; many things are closed from Monday to Thursday. If you get stuck here, try the basic and friendly **Posada Peña** (☑296-41-49; Iturbide 3; r M$350). A couple of boutique hotels have recently opened in town. Recommended is **Hotel Casa Mateo** (☑296-44-72; www.hotelcasamateo.com.mx; r from M$1300).

There are regular buses from/to Querétaro (M$36, 45 minutes). The last return bus to Querétaro departs from the main road around 5pm. For connections to Tequisquiapan, head to Ezequiel Montes (M$10, 30 minutes).

Tequisquiapan
☑414 / POP 30,000 / ELEV 1870M

This small town (teh-kees-kee-*ap*-an), 70km southeast of Querétaro, is a quaint weekend retreat from Mexico City or Querétaro. Tequisquiapan used to be known for its thermal springs – Mexican presidents came here to ease their aches and tensions. These days, despite the presence of cool water pools in hotel gardens, it's known for its pretty, bougainvillea-lined streets, colorful colonial buildings and excellent markets.

◉ Sights & Activities

Plaza Miguel Hidalgo   PLAZA
The wide and attractive Plaza Miguel Hidalgo is surrounded by *portales* (arcades), overlooked by the 19th-century neoclassical **La Parroquia de Santa María de la Asunción** (☺7:30am-8:30pm) with its pink facade and decorated tower.

Markets   MARKET
Three interesting markets – the **Mercado de Artesanías** (Crafts Market; ☺8am-7pm), **Vara y Mimbre** (household items) and the **Guadalupana** (for food) – are all on Carrizal, a block north and northeast of the plaza. The main wholesale **Mercado Artesania** (☺8am-8pm Sat & Sun) is opposite the bus station.

Parque La Pila   PARK
The large, almost-attractive Parque La Pila is a short distance past the Mercado de Artesanías along Ezequiel Montes.

Horseback Riding   HORSEBACK RIDING
On weekends head off on guided horse trails into the surrounding countryside (M$100 per hour). Guides and their hacks congregate on Fray Junípero, just north of Parque La Pila.

✯ Festivals & Events

Feria Nacional del Queso y del Vino   FOOD
The National Wine & Cheese Fair, from late May to early June, includes tastings and music.

Fiesta de la Asunción   RELIGIOUS
Commemorates the town's patron saint on August 15.

⌂ Sleeping & Eating

The best budget accommodations are the posadas along Moctezuma. Demand is low Monday to Thursday, when you may be able to negotiate a discount. Many restaurants around the plaza offer *comidas corridas* (prix-fixe menus). The Mercado Guadalupana a block east of the plaza has *fondas* (food stalls).

La Granja   BOUTIQUE HOTEL **$$**
(☑273-20-04; Morelos 12; r from M$1800; 🛜❄) Located in a pretty part of town, this colonial building has been renovated into a lovely hotel, with spacious and sleek rooms and a large back garden with a pool.

Posada Tequisquiapan GUESTHOUSE $
(☎273-00-10; Moctezuma 6; s/d M$250/500; P☯☒☗) A kick-back from the fifties, this good-value place offers simple but spacious and clean rooms and cable TV. The sprawling gardens have a grotto-like pool – great for families.

Hotel Hacienda Las Delicias HOTEL $$$
(☎273-00-17; www.hotelhaciendalasdelicias.com; Calle 5 de Mayo 1; s/d M$1200/1500; P☒) A block south of Plaza Principal, this slightly tired but stylish hotel is located around a manicured garden with pool.

K'puchinos MEXICAN $$
(Independencia 7; mains M$60-200) Handily located on the plaza, this reliable place caters to hungry souls for any meal of the day.

❶ Information

The helpful **tourist office** (☎273-08-41; www.vivetequisquiapan.com; Plaza Miguel Hidalgo; ☯9am-7pm) has town maps and information on Querétaro state. On the plaza's southeast side, there's a Bancomer ATM.

❶ Getting There & Around

Tequisquiapan is 20km northeast on Hwy 120 from the larger town of San Juan del Río. The bus terminal is around 2km north of the center in the new part of town. Local buses (M$6) from outside the bus station run to the markets on Carrizal, one block northeast of the Plaza Principal.

Flecha Azul runs half-hourly to/from Querétaro between 6:30am and 8pm (M$42, one hour). Buses also run to Ezequiel Montes (change here for Bernal; M$15, 20 minutes). ETN has deluxe buses to/from Mexico City's Terminal Norte (M$210, three hours, eight daily). Coordinados (Flecha Amarilla) and Flecha Roja have 2nd-class services to the same destination (M$161, three hours, regular departures).

Northeast Querétaro State

Those with a hankering to get off the beaten track – or if you're heading to/from northeast Mexico – shouldn't miss heading to the scenic Sierra Gorda via Hwy 120 northeast from Tequisquiapan. It's possible to get to most places on the way by bus, but it's much easier with your own transportation.

HWY 120

Heading north from Tequisquiapan, you pass the dusty agricultural town of Ezequiel Montes. More interesting is the next stop, around 2km on, the winery **Cavas de Freixenet** (☎441-277-01-47; www.freixenetmexico.com.mx; ☯tours noon, 1:30pm & 3pm), where you can see wine being made by *método champenoise* (champagne method) during free 40-minute tours.

The next big town is Cadereyta, 38km from Tequisquiapan. On the east edge of town, signs point to the **Quinta Fernando Schmoll** (☎441-276-10-71; Colegio Militar 1; M$20; ☯9am-5pm Tue-Sun), a beautiful botanic garden with more than 4000 varieties of plants and cactus.

Continuing another 38km on Hwy 120, there's a turnoff going east to the quaint, if remote, town of **San Joaquín**. If you've got time to spare, follow the good, but extremely winding, road from the turnoff for 32km through the rugged mountains; stay on that road through San Joaquín and continue a few steeply climbing kilometers to the little-visited archaeological site of **Ranas** (☯9am-5pm), with well-built walls and circular steps incorporated into a steep hillside. There are ball courts and a small hilltop pyramid. Dating from as early as the 8th century, the site is appealing for its rugged forest setting. San Joaquín has basic lodgings and eateries.

Jalpan

Within the magnificent Sierra Gorda Biosphere Reserve, Hwy 120 winds up to a height of 2300m at the pretty town of **Pinal de Amoles** and makes dramatic ups and downs (and 860 turns!) before reaching Jalpan at 760m. The attractive town centers on the **mission church**, constructed by Franciscan monks and their indigenous converts in the 1750s. The excellent **Museo de la Sierra Gorda** (☎441-296-01-65; Fray Junípero Serra 1; adult/child M$10/5; ☯10am-3pm & 5-7pm) explores the region's pre-Hispanic cultures and the mission-building period, and has superb reduced-size replicas of the mission churches.

Your best bet for accommodation is to head to the simple **Centro Tierra Sierra Gorda** (☎441-960-700; www.sierragordaeco tours.com; Av La Presa s/n, Barrio El Panteón; per person M$500), a lodging within the grounds of Sierra Gorda Ecotours offices (see p690); this is a 10-minute walk south of the center. This is the perfect place from which to arrange visits to the organization's other community-run ecolodges and programs in its rural destinations.

THE GREEN JEWEL OF CENTRAL MEXICO

Biosphere reserves are a unique conservation strategy seeking to blend sustainable human use with natural area protection (see p843). In the case of the **Reserva de la Biosfera Sierra Gorda**, covering the northeastern third of Querétaro state, more then 90% of its 3836 sq km are privately owned and 95,000 people live in its mission towns and scattered mountain villages.

Despite its mixed land use, this rugged arm of the Sierra Madre Oriental encompasses extensive tracts of wilderness, including old-growth cloud forests covered in orchids; semideserts, with endemic cactuses and wild oregano; and tropical forests home to jaguars and prolific birdlife. With 15 vegetation types, this is the most ecosystem-diverse protected area in Mexico.

Conservation of the Sierra Gorda has always been community based. Grassroots efforts by local citizens led to the reserve's establishment in 1997 and today numerous communities are engaged in sustainable livelihood activities, including developing a locally owned and operated ecotourism infrastructure with cabins, camping areas and guides.

Visitors can enjoy hiking to the **Sótano del Barro**, a 410m-deep vertical cave, to see resident macaws; camping on the ridge of **Cuatro Palos** for expansive views; fording the Río Escanela to **Puente de Dios** waterfall and cavern; and experiencing the traditional way of life in rural mountain communities.

Buffy and Ben Lenth

Tours into Reserva de la Biosfera Sierra Gorda

Travelers with time can experience the above activities in this fascinating area departing from Jalpan or other locations (advance notice required for all) with **Sierra Gorda Ecotours** (☎441-296-02-42; www.sierragorda.net), part of Grupo Ecológico Sierra Gorda, the nonprofit organization which co-manages the reserve. Alternatively, from Querétaro, day trips to the missions plus other longer guided trips can be arranged through the private tour operator **Promo Tur** (Map p682; ☎442-212-89-40; www.promoturqueretaro.com.mx; Río de la Loza 21 Norte, Querétaro). **Operatour Potosina** (Map p643; ☎444-151-22-01; www.operatourpotosina.com.mx; Sarabia 120) in San Luis Potosí runs excellent two- and three-day tours from San Luis Potosí also incorporating visits to Xilitla (see p227). The owner-guide speaks fluent English.

For those who want a more central experience, a block from the plaza is **Hotel Los Ángeles** (☎441-296-16-79; Matamoros 9; r from M$380) with clean, comfortable rooms; but glassless shutter windows face onto a central enclosed courtyard. On the plaza's west side, the **Hotel Misión Jalpan** (☎441-296-04-45; www.hotelesmision.com; Fray Junípero Serra s/n; r from M$860; P❄✿✿) has attractive gardens and a restaurant but rooms are below par for the 'top' spot in town (note: the windows can't be opened, but it suits those who are happy with air-conditioning). It often offers midweek deals. On the main road, **Restaurante Carretas** (☎441-296-03-68; mains M$65-160; ☺8am-10pm Mon-Sat, to 5:30pm Sun) serves up a reasonable feed. Not surprisingly, given its tropical climate, Jalpan specializes in artesanal – and very delicious – ice creams served in many *heladerías* around town.

Sierra Gorda Missions

In the mid-18th century, Franciscans established five beautiful missions in this remote region, including at Jalpan. These were inscribed as a Unesco World Heritage site in 2003. Founder Fray Junípero Serra went on to found the California mission chain. The restored churches are notable for their extraordinary and colorful facades carved with symbolic figures. East from Jalpan on Hwy 120, there are missions at **Landa de Matamoros** (1760–68); **Tilaco** (1754–62), 10km south of the highway; and **Tancoyol** (1753–60), 20km north of the highway. The mission of **Concá** (1754–58) is 35km north of Jalpan on Hwy 69.

Baja California

Includes »

Best Places to Eat

» Café Santa Fe (p733)

» Corazón de Tierra (p699)

» Mi Cocina (p726)

» El Gusto (p734)

» La Fonda (p721)

Best Places to Stay

» Bungalows Breakfast Inn (p729)

» Posada La Poza (p733)

» Casa Natalia (p725)

» La Villa del Valle (p699)

» Palapas Ventana (p724)

Why Go?

Baja is the earth's second-longest peninsula – over 1200km of the mystical, ethereal, majestic and untamed. Those lucky enough to make the full Tijuana to Los Cabos trip will find that the Carretera Transpeninsular (Hwy 1) offers stunning vistas at every turn. The middle of nowhere is more beautiful than you ever imagined, and people are friendly, relaxed and helpful – even in the border towns. Side roads pass through tiny villages and wind drunkenly along the sides of mountains. Condors carve circles into an unblemished blue sky. Some people sip something special (alcoholic) while the sun plunges into the Pacific. Some feel the rush of adrenalin as they surf that perfect wave. Others walk through sherbet-colored canyons or stare up at the night's canopy of scattered-diamond stars. Enjoy it whatever way suits you best and you'll understand what Baja's all about.

When to Go
Cabo San Lucas

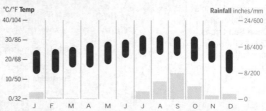

Jan–Mar Flowers bloom, cacti swell, things get green. Whales, whale sharks and big-wave surfing make it a happening time to visit.

Aug–Sep Beaches all but empty, tourists few and far between. You have Baja all to yourself, but it's hot – even in the shade.

Oct–Nov Partygoers, don't miss Sammy Hagar's birthday bash in early October, or the Día de Muertos fiesta at the end of the month.

Baja California Highlights

1 Kayak at **Espíritu Santo** (p719) as the big Baja sun drops into the bay

2 Get good and tipsy tasting the bucolic delights of the **Ruta del Vino** (boxed text p699)

3 Dive or snorkel at mystical **Las Sirenitas** (p724), in Cabo Pulmo National Marine Park, home to the Sea of Cortez's only living coral reef

4 Marvel at mice, deer, hunters and otherworldly creatures in the hundreds of ancient cave paintings at the **Sierra de San Francisco** (p711)

5 Cross the world's most crossed border in **Tijuana** (p693) to gawk, shop or party to your heart's content

6 Assist researchers as you snorkel with whale sharks in the quiet waters of **La Paz Bay** (p719)

7 Take a sunset cruise around Land's End and the Arch in **Cabo San Lucas** (p728) as the sun plunges into the Pacific

History

Before Europeans arrived, an estimated 48,000 mobile hunter-gatherers were living in today's Baja; their mysterious murals grace caves and canyon walls. European settlement failed to reach Baja until the Jesuit missions of the 17th and 18th centuries, and the missions soon collapsed as European-introduced diseases ravaged the indigenous people. Ranchers, miners and fishermen were the next inheritors. During the US prohibition era of the 1920s, Baja became a popular south-of-the-border destination for gamblers, drinkers and other 'sinners,' and the border towns remain popular for those same reasons. Baja continues to grow in economic power, population and popularity, with problematic ecological and environmental consequences.

ⓘ Getting There & Around

There are six official border crossings from the US state of California to Baja. See the boxed text p740 for important information on passports, tourist permits and vehicle permits.

Mexican mainland, US and international flights leave from and arrive at La Paz, Loreto and San José del Cabo. Ferries from Santa Rosalía and Pichilingue, near La Paz, connect Baja California to the mainland by sea.

Air-conditioned, nonsmoking and reasonably priced buses operate daily between towns all along the peninsula, running either north or south three to five times per day. Car travel is often the only way to reach isolated villages, mountains and beaches. You can rent cars in larger cities and major tourist destinations, such as Los Cabos, La Paz, Loreto and the border towns.

Highways are good and there are few toll roads. Drivers using the scenic *(Cuota)* route to Ensenada will need M$84; the Tijuana–Mexicali route costs M$163. Denominations larger than US$20 or M$200 are not accepted.

NORTHERN BAJA

Tijuana, Mexicali and Tecate form the northern border of an area known as La Frontera (not the border line itself), which extends as far south as San Quintín on the west and San Felipe on the east. Recently, the Ruta del Vino (between Ensenada and Tecate) has gained Napa Valley–like fame for its boutique, award-winning wines (boxed text p699). Though northern Baja's border cities and beaches are undeniably hedonistic,

BAJA SAFETY

In Baja California, basic caution and awareness, such as making an effort to keep valuables (including surfboards) out of sight and doors locked, will minimize risk. Most serious crime is not aimed at tourists, and of that, most is crime of opportunity. Border towns such as Tijuana have received awful press due to drug-trade-related killings, but tourists are rarely affected, and Baja California Sur is one of the safest states in all of Mexico.

Sanitation standards in Baja are higher than in other states, and water – even tap water – is usually safe to drink. Discard toilet paper in the trash can; don't flush it.

Tijuana and Mexicali are major manufacturing centers, and the area is a hot retirement spot for both Canadian and US snowbirds.

Tijuana

📞 664 / POP 1.6 MILLION

Tijuana has a bad reputation that it only partly deserves. High-profile murders have made headlines but they are products of the drug trade or retaliations against law officers; tourists are rarely targets, and if you're not looking for trouble (ie drugs or the red-light district) you'll probably have a lot of fun. Tijuana boats the 'most crossed border in the world,' and remains a remarkably friendly jungle; a vibrant cocktail of cultures that's fun for people-watching even if you're not planning on participating in the hedonism or excesses.

South of Calle 1a, La Revo (Avenida Revolución) is the heart of Tijuana's tourist area. Be sure to stroll along it – ubiquitous touts can be answered with a firm, friendly 'no.' The Zona Río upscale commercial center runs alongside the river. Here you'll see crowded discos, restaurants, bars, loud hawkers, brash taxi drivers and souvenir shops.

History

Older locals will confirm that at the beginning of the 20th century, TJ was literally 'just a mud hole.' Prohibition drove US tourists here for booze, gambling, brothels, boxing and cockfights, causing Tijuana's population to balloon to 180,000 by 1960. With continued growth have come severe social and environmental problems. Today the drug and illegal-immigrants trade into the US are the city's biggest concerns.

Sights & Activities

Vinícola LA Cetto
WINERY
(LA Cetto Winery; ☎685-30-31; Cañón Johnson 2108; ⊙10am-6:30pm Mon-Fri, 10am-5pm Sat) This winery, southwest of Avenida Con-

Tijuana

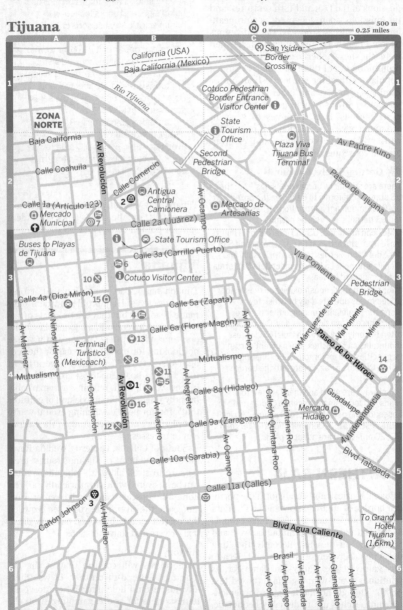

stitución, offers tours and tasting (M$20, M$50 with souvenir glass). LA Cetto produces a range of tasty varietals, as well as sparkling wines and a decent brandy.

Museo de Cera MUSEUM
(Wax Museum; ☑688-24-78; Calle 1a No 8281; admission M$15; ☺10am-6pm Mon-Fri, 10am-7pm Sat & Sun) Most of the motley crew at this wax museum look mildly constipated, but it's fun anyway. Obama is the newest addition, Madonna appears to have had open-heart surgery, Michael Jackson (RIP) looks creepy... and John Lennon, yep, appears appropriately stoned.

⭐ Festivals & Events

As Tijuana's reputation as a cultural center continues to grow, so does its annual calendar of cultural events.

International Craft Beer Festival BEER
In the first week in July, some of the best beers, both new and old, can be chugged down here (www.tjbeerfest.com). Mix with Clamato for the true Mexican experience.

Feria del Platillo Mexicano FOOD
The Mexican Food Festival is held in September; plates are piled high with goodies – and gobbled down.

Festival del Tequila TEQUILA
The Tequila Festival is held in October. Tequila in Tijuana? Fits like a hand in a glove.

Festival Hispano-Americano de Guitarra MUSIC
National guitar graduates and professional players from around the world demonstrate the richness and beauty of the guitar at the Hispanic-American Guitar Festival in November.

🛏 Sleeping

The cheapest rooms in Tijuana are sometimes shared with, ahem, hourly-rate clientele and may be shabbier than most folks are ready for. La Revo can be noisy, so try the side streets if you're keen on getting your Zs.

Hotel Nelson HISTORIC HOTEL $$
(☑685-43-02; www.hotelnelson.com.mx; Av Revolución 721; r Mon-Thu M$452, s/d Fri-Sun M$499/560; ❋❀) The friendly Nelson is a longtime favorite, with high ceilings and 1950s-era touches such as a real live barbershop of old. Tidy, carpeted rooms come with color TV, and some have a view of the (less-than-soothing!) Avenida Revo. Request a room without windows or TV for a discount.

Hotel La Villa de Zaragoza HOTEL $$
(☑685-18-32; www.hotellavilla.biz; Av Madero 1120; s/d M$560/650; P❀❋@❀) Rooms at this modern hotel, directly behind the Palacio Frontón, include TV and telephone, with attractive arched columns outside. There's laundry, a restaurant, a leafy courtyard and room service.

Grand Hotel Tijuana LUXURY HOTEL $$$
(☑681-70-00; www.grandhoteltij.com.mx; Blvd Agua Caliente 4500; r/ste from M$1731/2985; P❋@❀❀) Classical music wafts through the lobby and makes for a soothing check-in. The two 32-story buildings also have offices, restaurants and convention facilities, with a golf course nearby.

Hotel Lafayette HOTEL $
(☑685-39-40; Av Revolución 926; r without/with TV or telephone M$295/380; ❀) Downtown's most popular budget hotel. Rooms overlooking the cacophonous Avenida Revolución are not tranquil havens; request one at the back.

BAJA CALIFORNIA TIJUANA

Hotel Catalina
HOTEL $

(☑685-97-48; cnr Calle 5a & Av Madero 2039; s/d without/with TV M$250/300) This inexpensive, clean and secure hotel, a block away from Avenida Revolución, is comparable to the Lafayette but quieter. Rooms without TVs are even cheaper.

Eating

Avoid the 'free' drink offers and head to the places listed here for great eats or fun surprises.

Chiki Jai
CAFE $$

(☑685-49-55; Av Revolución 1388; dinner mains M$140-170; ⊘11am-10pm Mon-Sat, 11am-9pm Sun) Tiled walls and a painted ceiling make this eatery stand out from other La Revo options. Food is a mix of traditional Mexican favorites, and cocktails are made by hand and sipped by silver-haired grandpas as they watch the soccer game.

Vittorio's
ITALIAN $$

(☑685-17-29; Av Revolución 1691; pizza M$100, pasta M$150; ⊘10am-1am Sun-Thu, 10am-2am Fri & Sat) For years this cozy Italian restaurant has been serving generous portions of reasonably priced pizza and pasta. Head to the back and you'll feel like the Godfather in the plush leather booths with dim lighting. Daily specials cost only M$80.

La Frutería
CAFE $

(☑379-81-12; cnr Calle 8a & Av Madero; mains M$50-80; ⊘8am-7pm Mon-Sat; 🛜@) Latte-lovers can ditch the chain cafes and get their caffeine, juices or smoothies, and sandwiches at this corner stand.

La Petit
TAQUERÍA $

(btwn Calles 3a & 4a; mains M$35-60; ⊘7am-midnight Mon-Sat, 7am-9pm Sun) Hidden in a side alley behind Caliente (a gambling house), La Petit has matrons who will pile your plate with homestyle cheap eats. Grab a plastic fork, squeeze in between the bookie and that guy who bet it all on red and lost, and enjoy.

Restaurant Ricardo's
DINER $$

(☑685-31-46; Av Madero 1410; breakfast M$50-77, mains M$55-140; ⊘24hr) One of Tijuana's best-value places is this bright and cheerful diner-style joint. Excellent breakfasts and *tortas* (sandwiches), among the best in town, are served around the clock. The waterfall adds to the ambience.

Drinking

Drinkers in TJ may feel like hounds let loose in a fire-hydrant factory. The side streets off Avenida Sexta have become popular and the clubs there are often packed on weekends.

La Estrella
BAR

(Av Sexta 215) Just off La Revo, this is a great spot to sip cheap beers, dance salsa with locals or belt out karaoke tunes.

☆ Entertainment

If you're in TJ you owe it to yourself to let loose, if only to pay perfectly good money for a photo of yourself on one of the zebra-painted donkeys. Tourist info will have current events and performances.

Centro Cultural Tijuana
ARTS CENTER

(Cecut; ☑687-96-00; www.cecut.gob.mx; cnr Paseo de los Héroes & Av Independencia; ⊘9am-7pm Mon-Fri, 10am-7pm Sat & Sun) Tijuana's funky Centro Cultural Tijuana is a cultural center of which any comparably sized city north of the border would be proud. It houses an art gallery, the **Museo de las Californias** (admission M$20; ⊘10am-6pm Tue-Sun), a theater and the globular **Cine Omnimax** (tickets from M$45; ⊘1-9pm Tue-Sun).

🔒 Shopping

If you can't find a souvenir in Tijuana you're either hopeless or dead, but be cautious when buying gold and silver – much of it is fake (at those prices it would *have* to be, right?).

Emporium
SOUVENIRS

(☑685-13-24; emporium_tj@yahoo.com; Av Revolución 1025; ⊘9am-7pm) This is one of the few places with fair silver prices that are already marked, and a kind and knowledgeable, English-speaking owner.

Sanborns
DEPARTMENT STORE

(☑688-14-62; Av Revolución 1102) This department store has a decent selection of US and Mexican newspapers and magazines.

ℹ️ Information

Dangers & Annoyances

If you're not here trying to find trouble and you're using basic street smarts then it is unlikely you'll have problems. Touts are sometimes irksome, persistent, brazen, or even funny, but they deserve a respectful 'no' – they are trying to make a living in a place that has seen a huge downturn in tourism. 'Almost free,' 'Cheaper than Wal-

MOVING ON?

For tips, recommendations and reviews, head to shop.lonelyplanet.com to purchase a downloadable PDF of the California chapter from Lonely Planet's *USA* guide.

Mart!' and other invitations are best answered with a polite *no necesito* (I don't need it). But don't be afraid to step in for a peek if something catches your eye.

Don't drink on the streets or carry drugs without a doctor's prescription. As in any big city, being plastered late at night can invite trouble.

Coyotes and *polleros* (both mean 'people smugglers') congregate along the river west of the San Ysidro crossing. After dark, avoid this area and Colonia Libertad, east of the crossing.

Emergency
Tourist Assistance Hotline (☑078)

Internet Access
Internet access is available in many places along Avenida Revolución and its sidestreets.

World Net (☑685-65-14; Calle 2a No 8174; per hr M$10; ☺7am-midnight) Cheap, with lots of computers and English-speaking staff.

Internet Resources
See Tijuana (www.seetijuana.com) A Tijuana tourism site.

Tijuana Online (www.tijuanaonline.org) Run by Cotuco.

Medical Services
Hospital General (☑684-00-78; Av Padre Kino, Zona Río) Northwest of the junction with Avenida Rodríguez.

Money
Use caution when changing money, especially at night. Everyone accepts US dollars. Travelers heading south or east by bus can use the *casa de cambio* at the Central Camionera. Most banks have ATMs, which is often the quickest and easiest way to get cash. Banks in town include Banamex, Banorte and HSBC.

Post
Central post office (cnr Av Negrete & Calle 11a)

Tourist Information
Cotuco (Comité de Turismo y Convenciones, Committee on Tourism & Conventions) Av Revolución visitor center (☑685-31-17; Av Revolución btwn Calle 3a & Calle 4a; ☺9am-6pm); head office (☑684-05-37; ste 201, Paseo de los

Héroes 9365; ☺9am-6pm Mon-Fri); pedestrian border entrance visitor center (☑607-30-97; ☺9am-6pm Mon-Sat, 9am-3pm Sun)

State Tourism Office (Secretaría de Turismo del Estado; ☑682-33-67; Alarcón 1572, Zona Río; ☺8am-8pm Mon-Fri, 9am-1pm Sat) There's also an **info centre** (☑973-04-24; Av Revolución 842; ☺8am-8pm Mon-Fri, 9am-1pm Sat) on Avenida Revolución.

❶ Getting There & Away
Mexican tourist permits are available 24 hours a day at the San Ysidro–Tijuana border in the Mexican **immigration office** (☑683-53-49). They are also available – although less dependably – at a small office in the main bus terminal (Central Camionera, p697). See the boxed text p740 for important details. **Banjército** (☑683-62-44; www.banjercito.com.mx; Calle José María Larroque) is the only bank in town to process vehicle permit payments.

Air
The **Aeropuerto Internacional General Abelardo L Rodríguez** (☑607-82-00) is in Mesa de Otay, east of downtown.

Aeroméxico (☑683-84-44, 684-92-68; Local A 12-1, Plaza Río Tijuana) Serves many mainland Mexican destinations, and has nonstop flights to La Paz and flights to Tucson and Phoenix, both via Hermosillo.

Bus
The main bus terminal, about 5km southeast of downtown, is the **Central Camionera** (☑621-29-82), where **Elite** (☑621-29-58) and **Estrella Blanca** (☑621-29-55; www.estrellablanca. com.mx) offer 1st-class buses with air-con and toilets. Destinations in mainland Mexico include Guadalajara (M$1286, 36 hours) and Mexico City (M$1533, 44 hours). All lines stop at major mainland destinations. Autotransportes del Pacífico, Norte de Sonora and ABC also leave from the Central Camionera and operate mostly 2nd-class buses to mainland Mexico's Pacific coast and around Baja California. See the table p698 for destinations served by **ABC** (☑104-74-00 ext 7471) buses.

Suburbaja (☑688-00-45; ☺5am-9pm) uses the handy downtown **Antigua Central Camionera** (cnr Av Madero & Calle 1a), with buses leaving for Tecate (M$42 to M$55, 1½ hours, every 15 minutes); these are local buses that make many stops.

For border crossings by bus, **Mexicoach** (www.mexicoach.com) runs frequent buses (US$4 one way, US$6 round trip) from its **San Ysidro terminal** (☑619-428-62-00; 4570 Camino de la Plaza) to Tijuana's **Terminal Turístico** (☑685-14-70; Av Revolución 1025) between 8am and 6pm. It also runs Rosarito-bound

BAJA CALIFORNIA TIJUANA

BUSES FROM TIJUANA

DESTINATION	FARE (M$)	DURATION
Ensenada	147	1½hr
Guerrero Negro	964	12hr
La Paz	1580	24hr
Loreto	1526	16hr
Mexicali	314 (deluxe)	2½hr
	275 (1st class)	3hr
Tecate	84	1hr

shuttles (☎619-428-9517; US$100 round trip, minimum of 5 people per ride) from San Ysidro by reservation. Returning shuttles leave from the Rosarito Beach Hotel between 8am and 4pm.

Between 5am and 10:55pm, buses leave from the **San Diego Greyhound terminal** (☎in the US 619-515-1100, 800-231-2222; 120 West Broadway, San Diego) and stop at **San Ysidro** (☎in the US 619-428-1194; 799 East San Ysidro Blvd) en route to Tijuana's Central Camionera bus terminal or the airport. Fares from San Diego/San Ysidro to the Central Camionera or airport are US$15/10.50 one way, US$27/21 round trip.

Car & Motorcycle

The San Ysidro border crossing, which is a 10-minute walk from downtown Tijuana, is open 24 hours, but motorists may find the Mesa de Otay crossing (also open 24 hours) less congested; it's 15km to the east of San Ysidro.

Rental agencies in San Diego are the cheapest option, but most of them only allow journeys as far as Ensenada. Renting a car in Tijuana or taking the bus may be your best option for heading further south.

Trolley

San Diego's popular **trolley** runs from downtown San Diego through to San Ysidro (US$2.50) every 15 minutes from about 5am to midnight. From San Diego's Lindbergh Field airport, city bus 992 (US$2.25) goes to the Plaza America trolley stop in downtown San Diego, across from the Amtrak depot.

❶ Getting Around

For about M$10, local buses go everywhere, but the slightly pricier route taxis are much quicker. To get to the Central Camionera take any 'Buena Vista,' 'Centro' or 'Central Camionera' bus from Calle 2a, east of Avenida Constitución. Alternately, take a gold-and-white 'Mesa de Otay' route taxi from Avenida Madero between Calles

2a and 3a (M$12). Regular taxis will charge about M$75 for rides in and around La Revo or the Zona Río. The airport is about M$150, but always ask the price first.

Playas de Rosarito

☎661 / POP 84,000

Once a deserted, sandy beach and then a Hollywood film location, Playas de Rosarito is finally coming into its own. Developments and condos are everywhere, but despite the construction clamor, Rosarito is a quieter place to party and is an easy day trip (or overnight trip) from Tijuana or San Diego. **Hotel Rosarito** (now the landmark Rosarito Beach Hotel) and its long, sandy beach pioneered local tourism in the late 1920s. **Fox Studios Baja**, built in 1996 for the filming of *Titanic*, has since served as a primary filming location for *Pearl Harbor, James Bond: Tomorrow Never Dies* and, among other films and commericals, the greatly esteemed *Jackass*.

Despite the studio's influence, in many ways Playas de Rosarito remains a one-horse, one-street town, quiet except for during spring break. The amphitheater at the beachfront **Parque Municipal Abelardo L Rodríguez** contains Juan Zuñiga Padilla's impressive 1987 mural *Tierra y Libertad* (Land and Liberty).

Blvd Juárez, Rosarito's only major street (and part of the Transpeninsular) has many restaurants, clubs and hotels where the prices balloon to the outrageous during spring break.

🛏 Sleeping

Hotel del Sol Inn   HOTEL **$$**
(☎612-25-52; Blvd Juárez 32; s/d M$455/585; P⊛) The Sol has clean, carpeted rooms with TV, bottled water and simple furniture.

RUTA DEL VINO & VALLE DE GUADALUPE

You can skip Tijuana's long lines and treat yourself to some beautiful scenery by entering Mexico via Tecate and taking in the beautiful Valle de Guadalupe (Hwy 3). The border crossing (open 6am to 10pm) is far less congested, and south of Tecate lies one of the 'Best Tourist Routes in Mexico': the lovely Ruta del Vino. Maps of the wine route will help you locate the vineyards.

Dedicated drinkers should designate a driver first, as 60-plus wineries and one brewery await. Start at the landmark **Cuauhtémoc Moctezuma Heineken Mexico Brewery** (☑665-654-94-90; cnr Calles Hidalgo & Obregón, Tecate; ◷10am-5pm Mon-Fri, 10am-2pm Sat) which produces Tecate, Dos Equis, Carta Blanca, Indio, Bohemia and Sol, among others, and is now under Heineken's umbrella. Tours run by appointment only from 9am to 5pm Monday to Friday, and 11am to 2pm Saturday. The best-value lodging in Tecate is offered by **Motel La Hacienda** (☑665-654-12-50; Av Juárez 861; s/d M$450/550; P❀❂), which has clean, carpeted rooms with TV and pretty orange trees in the courtyard.

From Tecate, toodle southward, making sure to stop for tours, tastings, lunch and a tipple or two (or 10!) along the way. If time permits, spend a whole day or even a weekend. The vines, planted decades ago, are finally coming into their own and this gorgeous valley is well on its way to being 'Napa Sur.'

If you don't fancy driving, taxis out of Ensenada will take up to four people for a three-hour, three-winery tour for US$100. Note that not all wineries offer free tastings, and that holidays or special events may make offerings change.

Set off from Hwy 3 is the newly built tour center for **Santo Tomás** (☑646-155-31-37; www.santo-tomas.com; tasting/tour & tasting US$10/20; ◷10am-5pm). A 50ft wall of wines backs the sparkling tasting room, where the bar is creatively made from an unused wine press. The tour will show you all you can learn about wine and its making, with unique features like fermenting tanks that double as chalkboards (listing types of grape, their leaf patterns, wine processes, etc), video presentation and even a wine-specific laser show.

Equally unique, the **Vena Cava** (☑646-156-80-07; ◷10am-4pm) winery and tasting room are made out of overturned ships' hulls sunk into the hillside. Despite being a relative newcomer, this is well worth visiting both for the wine and for the views. The award-winning Cabernet was rated 91 points out of 200 top wines in all of Mexico. Nearby, visit **Bibayoff** (☑646-176-10-08; ◷11am-5pm Sat & Sun, later in summer; tasting US$5), a lovely boutique winery set off from the beaten path, with free tastings. It's known for its Cabernet and lovely Moscatel.

Right on the highway, **Liceaga** (☑646-155-32-81; www.vinosliceaga.com; ◷11am-5pm Mon-Sun; tasting M$100) is a well-established winery with a range of wines and even the valley's only true grappa (a strong spirit distilled from grape skins or stems). The tasting fee includes a plate of bread and cheese.

Baron Balche (☑646-155-21-41; www.baronbalche.com; ◷8am-4pm Mon-Fri, 10am-5pm Sat & Sun) and **Emevé** (☑646-684-01-09; ◷noon-5pm) both offer wines worth stopping for. Use these as a starting point for finding your own favorites.

For those ready to turn in for the night but not ready to leave the valley, **La Villa del Valle** (☑646-156-80-07; www.lavilladelvalle.com; d Mon-Thu US$215, Fri-Sun US$240; P❀❂) is a high-end boutique B&B worth splurging for. It makes its own lotions and soaps, has a pool, sauna and yoga studio, all with spectacular views of the valley...and they own both Vena Cava and the **Corazón de Tierra** (☑646-156-80-30; www.corazon detierra.com; breakfast mains US$18, lunch/dinner mains US$55; ◷9:30am-11:30am, 1pm-8:30pm), perhaps the finest dining in the Ensenada area. Brand-new, the restaurant looks out over picturesque rolling vineyards and hillsides, and the juxtaposition of rough-hewn timbers and starched tablecloths fits the rustic vineyard motif to a T. No pets or children under 12.

If you can't make the trip to the valley proper, you can sample many of the local wines in Ensenada at Vimeri (p704).

Some rooms are reserved for nonsmokers. Note that prices triple during the short spring-break holiday.

Festival Plaza Hotel
HOTEL $$

(☑612-29-50; www.hotelfestivalplaza.com; Blvd Juárez 1207; r Sun-Thu M$735, Fri & Sat M$941; P☒) Small, bland rooms with colorful names like 'Rock & Roll Taco' that suit a place within stumbling distance of Papas & Beer (Rosarito's landmark drinking and partying venue). The vibe here is the college party crowd, so bring earplugs if you don't have a case of beer in each hand.

✖ Eating

Tacos El Yaqui
TAQUERÍA $

(cnr Palma & Mar del Norte; tacos M$25; ⊗8am-5pm Mon, Tue & Thu, 8am-9:30pm Fri-Sun) This delicious taco stand is so popular that it often closes early when the ingredients run out. Get in line before 4pm if you don't want to risk missing out.

Los Arcos
MEXICAN $$

(☑612-04-91; Blvd Juárez 29; mains M$65-90; ⊗8am-7pm Mon, Tue, Thu & Fri, 8am-10pm Sat & Sun) For shrimp or fish tacos try this family-owned place, which has tacos and various *antojitos* (typical Mexican snacks), excellent salsa and friendly staff.

Panadería La Espiga
BAKERY $

(☑612-14-59; Blvd Juárez 298; M$8-40; ⊗6:30am-10pm) The scent of fresh-baked rolls, sweets and breads will have your mouth watering long before you enter one of Panadería La Espiga's four locations. Some items are naturally sweetened with Baja honey from La Paz.

❶ Getting There & Around

From downtown Tijuana, *colectivos* (share cars) for Playas de Rosarito (M$15) leave from Avenida Madero between Calles 3a and 4a. Look for a yellow station wagon with a white triangle on the door. You can catch a Mexicoach shuttle (M$113) to Tijuana from the parking lot of the Rosarito Beach Hotel twice daily.

Ensenada

☑646 / POP 280,000

Ensenada, 108km south of the border, is hedonistic Tijuana's cosmopolitan sister. The city has a quirky mix of just-off-the-boat cruise shippers, drive-by tourists from Cali, tourists from mainland Mexico and seen-it-all locals. In case you've forgotten you're in Mexico (what with all those US dollars and the English menus), just look up: a Mexican flag, so large it's probably visible from space, flutters proudly over the tourist zone. Wander Avenida López Mateos (Calle 1a) and you'll find almost anything: ceramics, hammocks, textiles, jewelry...side by side with tasteless T-shirts, raunchy gifts and a host of items you definitely wouldn't give grandma for the holidays. Some of Mexico's best wines come from this region; if you're an oenophile, don't miss the Ruta del Vino and its vineyards and museums.

Outside the tourist zone the prices drop, food gets traditional and hotels become cheap, but Calle 2a – unlit and seedy – is worth avoiding after dark. Singer Jim Morrison, of Doors fame, used to sip tequila and watch surfers 11km to the north at San Miguel.

Ensenada was the capital of Baja territory from 1882 to 1915, but the capital shifted to Mexicali during the revolution. After the revolution the city catered to 'sin' industries until the federal government outlawed gambling in the 1930s...but judging from the strip clubs, peep shows and bars, sin still goes on today as it did in days of old.

⊙ Sights

Riviera del Pacífico
BUILDING

(Blvd Costero) Opened in the early 1930s as Hotel Playa Ensenada, the extravagant Riviera del Pacífico, a Spanish-style former casino, is rumored to have been a regular haunt of Al Capone. It now houses the small **Museo de Historia de Ensenada** (☑177-05-94; admission M$10; ⊗10am-5pm Mon-Sat, noon-5pm Sun) and Bar Andaluz (p704), while the **Casa de Cultura** offers classes, retrospective film screenings and art exhibitions.

FREE Museo del Instituto Nacional de Antropología e Historia
MUSEUM

(Museo del INAH; ☑178-25-31; Av Ryerson 99; ⊗9am-4pm Mon-Fri) Built in 1886 by the US-owned International Company of Mexico, Ensenada's oldest public building, formerly the Aduana Marítima de Ensenada, houses the Museo del Instituto Nacional de Antropología e Historia, a historical and cultural museum. It has a relatively small but comprehensive collection of artifacts, and discusses (mainly in Spanish) the area's history from prehistoric times up to now.

El Mirador
LOOKOUT

Atop the Colinas de Chapultepec, El Mirador offers panoramic views of the city and

Bahía de Todos Santos. Climb or drive (note: there's no off-street parking) to this highest point in town, up Avenida Alemán from the western end of Calle 2a in central Ensenada.

Activities

Surfing

San Miguel　　　　　　　　　SURFING
There's not much here but a few campers, a parking lot, and a wonderful point break just offshore. San Miguel was once a hangout for Doors legend Jim Morrison. Camping (M$130 per car, M$180 per RV, parking M$55) is available. When the waves are big it's an awesome ride.

Isla de Todos Santos　　　　　SURFING
This island off Ensenada's coast (not to be confused with the town near Los Cabos) is where one of the world's top big-wave surfing contests is held each year. **El Martillo** (The Hammer) is legendary, with swells commonly double or triple overhead, even bigger when conditions are right. Boats can be chartered out from the harbor. Prices start at about M$800 per person, four people minimum. Sometimes they can cut you a deal or you could ask to ride with a fisherman.

Fishing & Whale-Watching
Ensenada is known the world over for its excellent sportfishing. Most charter companies also offer whale-watching tours from late December to March. **Sergio's Sportfishing Center & Marina** (☏178-21-85; www.sergiosfishing.com) is well regarded and can be found on the sportfishing pier off El Malecón. Day trips per person start at about M$300 and go up to M$5000 or more for private charter trips, depending on the size of the vessel. You must also have a valid Mexican fishing license.

Courses

The following language schools offer similar immersion programs with homestay opportunities. Accommodations or homestay fees are extra.

**Universidad Autónoma
de Baja California**　　　　　LANGUAGE
(☏175-07-07; http://idiomas.ens.uabc.mx/cursos; cnr Blvd Zertuche & Blvd de los Lagos) Semester-long classes for foreign students.

Spanish School Baja　　　　LANGUAGE
(☏190-60-49; www.spanishschoolbaja.com; Calle 10 btwn Ruiz & Obregón) Costs start at US$300 for a week plus US$30 materials fee.

Festivals & Events
The events listed here constitute a tiny sample of the 70-plus sporting, tourist and cultural happenings that take place each year. Dates change, so contact tourist offices for details.

Carnaval　　　　　　　　　CARNIVAL
A Mardi Gras–type celebration 40 days before Ash Wednesday. Ash Wednesday is February 13 in 2013, and March 5 in 2014. The streets flood with floats and dancers.

Fiesta de la Vendimia　　　　　WINE
Wine harvest, held in the first two weeks of August. Cheers!

International Seafood Fair　　　FOOD
Sample September's scrumptious seafood surprises.

Baja 1000　　　　　　　　　RACING
Baja's biggest off-road race, held in mid-November. See 'truggies' (truck-buggies) tear up the desert to the cheers of just about everyone. The Baja 500 is in June.

Sleeping
Although Ensenada has many hotels, demand can exceed supply at times, particularly on Saturday and Sunday and in summer. Rates vary substantially between weekdays and weekends, and they jump up even more for the Baja 1000 or other big events.

Ritz Hotel　　　　　　　　　HOTEL **$**
(☏174-05-01; explotur@prodigy.net.mx; Calle 4a No 379; s/d/tr M$300/350/460;❋✿) Not at all ritzy, but it is inexpensive. The lobby is newly remodeled, but the carpeted rooms are small and dark. Friendly staff, nice shared balconies, and easy access to the tourist zone, restaurants and bus station make up for it.

America Motel　　　　　　　MOTEL **$**
(☏176-13-33; Av López Mateos 1309; s/d M$350/420;ⓟ) One of the finest budget options, the friendly America motor lodge is quiet, clean and yet only a five-minute walk from the tourist zone. Many rooms have kitchenettes, there's off-street parking, and someone's there in the office looking after things 24 hours.

Ensenada Inn Motel　　　　MOTEL **$$**
(☏176-13-61; www.ensenadainn.com; Sanginés 237; s/d M$815/1000; ⓟ✿) A bit far away from the tourist zone, but clean and quiet, with secure parking and rooms with kitchenettes.

Ensenada

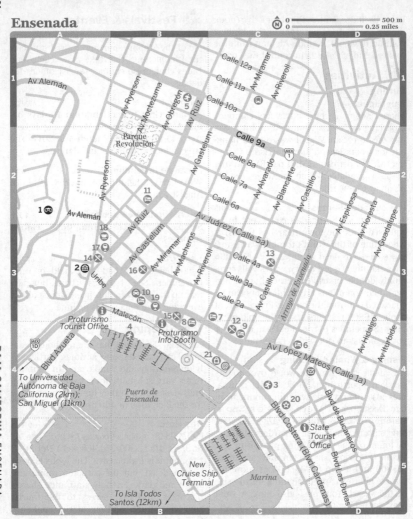

Wait near her cage and Esmerelda the parrot will greet you with a heartfelt '¡Hola!' It's an excellent choice for drivers planning to get an early start for a southward journey. Prices are lower during the week.

Hotel Santo Tomás
HOTEL **$$**

(178-33-11; hst@bajainn.com; Blvd Costero 609; s/d/tr/q M$540/590/615/965; P@*@) It's slick and snazzy, with satellite TV in each room. The quirky lobby has a sweeping Taraesque staircase, an elevator (out of service at the time of research) with disco mirrors and gold trim, and a fishtank that give it charac-ter that other hotels lack. Rates increase on Friday and Saturday.

Hotel Bahía
HOTEL **$$**

(178-21-01; www.hotelbahia.com.mx; Av López Mateos 850; d/q M$650/936; P*) Welcome margaritas, a nice pool and balconies that look out at the port are why folks keep coming here. Psychedelic tiles in the lobby add to the fun.

Hotel Cortez
HOTEL **$$**

(178-23-07; www.bajainn.com; Av López Mateos 1089; r M$1004; P*) This large, family-

Ensenada

friendly hotel has free coffee, a gym, a basketball court and a popular bar and restaurant.

Best Western Hotel El Cid HOTEL $$$
(☎178-24-01; www.hotelelcid.com.mx; Av López Mateos 993; s/d M$989/1369; P❈@🛜🏊) This four-star hotel has unique rooms, a respected restaurant and a lively bar. Prices include continental breakfast with fresh juice. Beds are firm and the bilingual staff are friendly.

Eating

Ensenada has eateries ranging from corner taco stands to places serving excellent Mexican and international cuisine. True gourmets should duck north to Corazón de Tierra (boxed text p699), a restaurant that is several notches above anything in the tourist zone.

Mi Kaza MEXICAN, AMERICAN $$
(☎178-82-11; Av Riveroll 87-2; breakfasts M$40-90, dinner mains M$49-155; ☺7am-10pm; 🛜) Enjoy inexpensive Mexican or American dishes at this not-so-greasy greasy spoon. Free parking and wi-fi make it a nice spot to catch up on email over a hot cup of joe.

El Parián MEXICAN $
(☎128-82-32; cnr Calle 4a & Av Castillo; dinner mains M$40-85; ☺7:30am-11:30pm) Great enchiladas, quesadillas, burritos, *agua de jamaica* (hibiscus water) and friendly service make this perfect for anyone watching their pesos. Flatscreen TVs in every corner mean you (or the wait staff) never have to miss a moment of that cheesy Mexican soap.

La Comadre MEXICAN $
(☎178-85-43; Av Ruiz 37; dinner mains M$45-90; ☺9am-7:30pm Mon-Sat, 10am-7:30 Sun) Enjoy authentic, cheap *antojitos* and friendly service in a family atmosphere. Colorful decorations complement the food.

Churros Rellenos de la Primera SWEETS $
(Av López Mateos 1075; ☺5-9pm Mon-Fri, 3-9pm Sat & Sun) Fresh filled churros (like a donut, but long and skinny) are as sinfully delicious as they are inexpensive. Yum!

La Casa Antigua Café CAFE $
(☎175-73-20; lacasaantiguacafe@hotmail.com; Av Obregón 110; coffee M$15-32, sandwiches M$50; ☺8am-10pm Mon-Sat, 3-10pm Sun;🛜) Vintage photos and clapboards separate this place from the coffee mega-chains. Pastries, pies, bagels, sandwiches and rich coffee are all worth ducking in here for.

Rentería Tortillería TORTILLERÍA $
(☎178-35-79; Calle 2a No 558; ☺6am-5pm) Tiny little grocery store with freshly made flour tortillas for M$12 per kilogram. Enjoy smells and smiles as you watch them being made.

Entertainment

The new **Centro Estatal de las Artes** (☎173-43-07; http://cearte.info; cnr Clubrotario & Blvd Cárdenas; ☺8am-8pm Mon-Sat, noon-7pm Sun, plus event hours in evening) has performances, movies and exhibits throughout the year.

BAJA CALIFORNIA ENSENADA

Drinking

What better place to start that long-awaited bender than the town that claims to have invented the now ubiquitous margarita? On weekends, most bars and cantinas along Avenida Ruiz are packed from noon to early morning. If that's not your scene, head for one of the many quality hotels and fine restaurants where you're likely to find a laid-back spot to sip a top-shelf tequila.

Hussong's Cantina   CANTINA
(☑178-32-10; Av Ruiz 113; ☉11am-2am) The oldest and perhaps liveliest cantina in the Californias has been serving tequila since 1892. A Friday or Saturday night will be packed with locals from all walks of life, all of them having a blast.

Bar Andaluz   BAR
(☑176-43-10; cnr Blvd Costera & Riviera; ☉10am-midnight Mon-Fri, 9am-1am Sat) For a complete change in ambience, visit the cultured bar inside the Riviera del Pacífico, where having a drink is an exercise in nostalgia. It's quiet, perfect for a nightcap with friends.

Vimeri   WINE BAR
(Blvd Costero 1001; ☉Mon-Sun 11am-midnight; glass wine M$50-80, tasting flight M$66) Lovely spot to sip the wines you didn't get to sample on your Ruta del Vino tour (boxed text p699), Vimeri serves local wines only and is a classy spot that seems worlds away from the bump-and-grind scene even though it's just around the corner.

Shopping

Galería Pérez Meillon   HANDICRAFTS
(☑175-78-48; Blvd Costero 1094; ☉9am-5pm) In the Centro Artesanal de Ensenada, this gallery sells authenticated pottery from the Paipai (one of Baja California's indigenous peoples known for fine craftwork, particularly pottery and baskets) and Mata Ortiz (a major pottery center in central north Mexico), and Kumiai weaving.

ⓘ Information

Emergency
Municipal Police (☑066, 176-43-43)
State Police (☑066, 172-35-30)
Tourist Assistance (☑078)

Internet Access
Internet cafes are sprinkled throughout the tourist zone; most charge M$15 to M$25 per hour.
La Web@ (☑175-95-70; Blvd Costero 1094-38; per hr M$12.50; ☉8am-7pm Mon-Fri, 10am-4pm Sat)

Internet Resources
Discover Baja California (www.discoverbaja california.com) The state's tourism site.
Enjoy Ensenada (www.enjoyensenada.com) Ensenada's tourism site.

BAJA'S BEST BITES...

(...and we don't mean restaurant reviews.) Some of Baja's coolest creatures are well worth getting to know, but don't get too close – these critters are sporting nature's meanest defenses and an encounter could send you to hospital.

» **Black Widow Spider** This pea-sized black spider packs a potent (though rarely fatal) punch. Look for the crimson hourglass on the underside of the abdomen for positive ID.

» **Portuguese Man O' War** Also known as *agua mala* (bad water), these jellyfish are stunningly pretty, but their bright-blue tentacles can sting long after the animal is dead. Don't pick one up on the beach, and minimize risk when participating in water sports by wearing a full-body rash guard or wetsuit.

» **Scorpion** Glowing under UV light, Baja's scorpions sting, especially if stepped on. Shake your shoes in the morning, use netting at night and look before you sleep.

» **Stingrays** Painfully common in the shallows of many popular beaches, the stingray usually flicks its tail and stabs heels or ankles with a poisonous barb. Minimize risk at beaches by wearing surf booties and/or dragging your feet until you're in deeper water.

Whether you think they're cool or creepy, these are creatures that will rarely cause you harm if they are left alone. For more information, track down a copy of Roger Tory Peterson's book *A Field Guide to Venomous Animals and Poisonous Plants*.

BUSES FROM ENSENADA

DESTINATION	FARE (M$)	DURATION
Guerrero Negro	817	10hr
La Paz	1466	20hr
Mexicali	441 (1st class)	4hr
	377 (2nd class)	4hr
Rosarito	107	1hr
Tecate	163	2hr
Tijuana	147	1½hr

Medical Services
Sanatorio Del Carmen (178-34-77; cnr Av Obregón & Calle 11a)

Money
Most banks and *casas de cambio* are near the intersection of Avenidas Ruiz and Juárez. There are numerous ATMs throughout Ensenada, and banks can change money or perform the usual transactions during business hours.

Post
Post office (176-10-88; cnr Avs López Mateos & Clubrotario)

Tourist information
Proturismo tourist office (178-24-11; www. proturismoensenada.org.mx; Blvd Costero 540; ☯8am-8pm Mon-Fri, 9am-5pm Sat & Sun) Dispenses maps, brochures and current hotel information. There's an **information booth** (178-30-70; ☯Tue-Sun) in the Plaza Cívica.
State tourist office (172-54-44; Blvd Costero 1477; ☯8am-6pm Mon-Fri, 9am-1pm Sat & Sun) Carries similar information to the Proturismo office.

ⓘ Getting There & Away
The **immigration office** (174-01-64; Blvd Azueta 101; ☯document delivery 8am-6pm Mon-Fri, document pickup 1-3pm Mon-Fri) sells tourist permits for those arriving by boat. If you are not arriving by boat, get your tourist permit in Tijuana or elsewhere, as you will have no way to prove how long you've been in the country and they may not take your word for it.

Car & Motorcycle
The drive from Tijuana to Ensenada on the scenic (*Cuota*) route has three tolls (M$27, M$27, and M$30), and a military checkpoint.

Bus
Ensenada's **Central de Autobuses** (Av Riveroll 1075) is 10 blocks north of Avenida López

Mateos. **Elite** (178-67-70) serves mainland Mexican destinations as far as Guadalajara (M$1400, 36 hours) and Mexico City (M$1800, 48 hours). **ABC** (174-11-77) and its subsidiary Aguíla is the main peninsula carrier; for destinations see the boxed text p705.

ⓘ Getting Around
The main taxi stand is at the corner of Avenidas López Mateos and Miramar; taxis also congregate along Avenida Juárez. Most fares within the city cost from M$50 to M$100.

Surfers can get a trip out to San Miguel and a pickup later in the day for M$100 each way.

Ensenada's main avenues are well served by buses and vans; most routes are designated by street name and charge M$8 for the first 5km.

La Bufadora

La Bufadora is a popular 'blowhole' (really a notch in the rock that sprays waves upwards) 40km south of Ensenada. If conditions are right it sends a jet of water up to 30m into the sky, drenching cheering onlookers. Conditions aren't always right, but if you're up for a gamble you can catch a taxi (M$125 per person round-trip, minimum four persons) or a shuttle tour (M$150), or drive south on the Transpeninsular to the 'Bufadora' sign, then follow the road all the way around to the Pacific side. Parking is M$20.

Parque Nacional Constitución de 1857

At the end of a challenging unpaved 43km road out of Ojos Negros (east of Ensenada at Km 39 on Hwy 3), Parque Nacional Constitución de 1857 has beautiful conifers, fields of wildflowers and a sometimes-dry

PARQUE NACIONAL SIERRA SAN PEDRO MÁRTIR

Bobcats, deer and bighorn sheep await visitors to San Pedro Mártir national park, but its real claim to fame isn't what's on the ground but what's in the air: this park is one of only six places in the world where the almost-extinct California Condor is being reintroduced into the wild. Twenty-six of these majestic birds call this area home, and at the time of writing three chicks had been hatched, showing promise for a future recovery.

Even if one of the world's largest birds won't soar over your head, there are lots of other reasons to make the detour. Conifers scrape the sky, the air is pine-scented and clean, and the (tortuously winding) drive passes through boulder-studded, ethereal landscapes that seem more Martian than something here on Earth.

The **Observatorio Astronómico Nacional** (646-174-45-80; 10am-1pm) is the country's national observatory, from where it's possible to observe both the Pacific Ocean and the Sea of Cortez. On clear days you can see all the way to the Mexican mainland. To reach the park, turn left at the sign at approximately Km 140 on the Transpeninsular, south of Colonet. A 100km paved road climbs to the east through an ever-changing desert landscape, affording satisfying vistas all along the way. Camping is possible (no toilets, bring water) in designated areas, but there are no *cabañas* or other facilities.

lake, **Laguna Hanson** (also known as Laguna Juárez) at an altitude of 1200m. *Cabañas* (cabins; M$700) or campsites (M$130) are available, but the water may be contaminated by livestock so bring your own.

It's a sublime spot for mountain biking, hiking or just getting away from it all, as long as everyone else isn't getting away at the same time – in peak holiday times it can be busy, but it's a beautiful spot any time of year. The park is also accessible by a steeper road east of Km 55.2, 16km southeast of the Ojos Negros junction.

The **Restauran y Hotel Ojos Negros** (646-153-30-06; Entrada principal; d/tr M$250/300) has basic rooms and a nice restaurant. It's a convenient stop for anyone wanting to get to the park early the next morning. Some rooms open onto the sunny courtyard; others face a wall. It's in Ojos Negros, 43km away from the park.

Mexicali

686 / POP 650,000

Mexicali is what Tijuana must have been before the tourist boom – gritty, even scary – and most tourists just head southward. The city offers some decent restaurants and some fun nightlife, but be particularly careful around the border areas after dark.

The Zona Hotelera, far safer at night than the border, is on the east side, along Calzada Juárez from Plaza Azteca to Independencia and beyond. In summer, Mexicali is one of

the hottest places on earth, so hot that residents joke that if you've lived in Mexicali, you'll think hell feels cool.

Sights

Plaza Constitución is a good place to hear *banda* (big-band music) groups rehearse in the late afternoon – hence its nickname, Plaza del Mariachi.

Most of Mexicali's historic buildings are northeast of Calzada López Mateos. The **Catedral de la Virgen de Guadalupe** (cnr Av Reforma & Morelos) is the city's major religious landmark. Now the rectory of the **Universidad Autónoma de Baja California**, the former Palacio de Gobierno, built between 1919 and 1922, interrupts Avenida Obregón just east of Calle E.

Sleeping

If you don't fancy sleeping in a hotel that has iron bars on the reception windows and hourly-rate customers, you're best off in the pricier Zona Hotelera.

Hotel Cosmos Posada　　　　HOTEL $$
(568-97-44; Blvd Juárez 4257, Zona Hotelera; s/d incl breakfast M$450/550; P✳) Rooms here are dark but clean, with decorative columns outside and deep-green tiles. It's nicely located for anyone going south.

Hotel del Norte　　　　HOTEL $$
(552-81-01; hoteldelnorte@hotmail.com; Av Madero 205; s M$515-618, d M$618-721; P✳@⊚)

The most pleasant of the border options, the landmark Hotel del Norte has carpeted rooms, some with color TV, and friendly, English-speaking staff.

Araiza LUXURY HOTEL $$$
(☎564-11-00; www.araizahoteles.com; Calz Juárez 2220, Zona Hotelera; d M$1560; P✳@🀫🏊) This family-friendly deluxe hotel has well-appointed rooms, two excellent restaurants, bar, tennis courts, a fountain and a convention center. There are lobby computers for guests who need them.

✖ Eating & Drinking

La Fratt CAFE $
Avenida Normal 648; pastries/sandwiches M$40-80, coffee M$35-50; ☻8am-midnight Mon-Fri, 4pm-midnight Sun;🀫) Coffee, ice cream and wi-fi mix well with the college crowd and eclectic decor.

Petunia 2 JUICE BAR $
(☎552-69-51; Av Madero 436; breakfast M$50, lunch M$55; ☻7am-8pm Mon-Sat, 8am-4pm Sun) Huge *jugos naturales* (freshly squeezed juices) and delicious quesadillas are a great way to start the day at this cheap eat close to the border.

Los Arcos MEXICAN $$
(☎556-09-03; Av Calafia 454; dinner mains M$126-290) Mexicali's most popular seafood restaurant. The *shrimp culichi* (shrimp in a creamy green chili sauce) is spectacular. Live music brightens the night on Thursday and Friday.

❶ Information

On Avenidas Reforma and Obregón, near the US border, are many health-care providers offering quality services at a fraction of the cost north of the border.

Bancomer (cnr Azueta & Av Madero)
Hospital Hispano-Americano (☎552-23-00; fax 552-29-42; Av Reforma 1000)
Main post office (☎552-25-08; Av Madero; ☻8am-4pm Mon-Sat)
State tourist office (☎566-12-77; Blvd Juárez 1; ☻8am-6pm Mon-Fri, 9am-1pm Sat) Patient, bilingual staff and plenty of information about regional attractions and events.
Tourist Assistance (☎078)

❶ Getting There & Away
Air
The **Aeropuerto Internacional General Rodolfo Sánchez Taboada** (☎552-23-17) is 18km east of town. **Aeroméxico** (☎555-70-47; Calle México 343) flies to La Paz, Mexico City, Mazatlán and other mainland points.

Bus
Long-distance/mainland bus companies leave from the **Central de Autobuses** (☎557-24-15; Calz Independencia; ☻24hr), near Calzada López Mateos, and Baja-bound buses leave from the **Terminal Turística** (☎552-51-00; ☻24hr), closer to the border. Autotransportes del Pacífico, Norte de Sonora and Elite serve mainland-Mexican destinations, while ABC serves the Baja peninsula.

Greyhound (www.greyhound.com; Calexico ☎760-357-18-95; 123 East 1st St; ☻5:30am-11:30pm; Mexicali ☎558-79-95; 1244 Centro Cívico-Comercial) has offices in Mexicali and directly across the border in Calexico. Several departures daily go from Mexicali to Los Angeles (one way/round trip US$42.25/76.50) and four to San Diego (US$34.50/62), as well as other destinations in the US.

BUSES FROM MEXICALI

DESTINATION	FARE (M$)	DURATION
Ensenada	315-441	3½hr
Guadalajara	1459 (1st class)	36hr
	1270 (2nd class)	36hr
Guerrero Negro	1262	15hr
La Paz	1770	24hr
Loreto	1765	20hr
Mazatlán	1706	24hr
Mexico City	1764	42hr
Tijuana	314 (1st class)	2½hr

MISIÓN SAN BORJA

This well-restored mission is between Rosarito and Bahía de los Angeles in pristine, spectacular boojum tree and cardón desert. The bumpy drive alone makes it worth the trip. A family descended from the original preconquest inhabitants is restoring it by hand and will proudly show you the mission, freshwater spring, a secret tunnel (now walled up, shucks!) and the old Jesuit ruins. Heading east from Hwy 1, turn right about 45km after leaving the highway.

Car & Motorcycle

The main Calexico–Mexicali border crossing is open 24 hours. Vehicle permits are available at the border, as are tourist permits for those traveling beyond Ensenada or San Felipe. US and Mexican authorities have opened a second border complex east of downtown to ease congestion. It's open from 6am to 10pm.

❶ Getting Around

Cabs to the airport cost M$160 to M$200 but may be shared. Agree on the price prior to getting in.

Most city buses start from Avenida Reforma, just west of Calzada López Mateos; check the placard for the destination. Local fares are about M$9.

A taxi to the Centro Cívico-Comercial or Zona Hotelera from the border averages about M$60.

SOUTHERN BAJA

Parts of southern Baja look like pages of a Dr Seuss illustration: no plant more than the funky boojum tree *(cirio)*, which looks like a giant inverted parsnip with some yellow fluff at the top. You can't help but smile. Cardón cacti, ocotillo, cholla and other desert marvels thrive in areas that sometimes don't receive any rain for a decade. Crumbling missions, leafy date palms, coconuts and mangrove swamps are all items to look for as you meander southward.

Remember that mountain time (used in Baja California Sur state) is an hour ahead of Baja California's (Norte) Pacific time.

The 25,000-sq-km **Reserva de la Biosfera El Vizcaíno** is one of Latin America's largest single protected areas. It sprawls from the Península Vizcaíno across to the Sea of Cortez and includes the major gray-whale calving areas of Laguna San Ignacio and Laguna Ojo de Liebre, and the Sierra de San Francisco with its stunning pre-Hispanic rock art – more than 60 sites, many of which only archaeologists can view.

The southernmost part of the peninsula contains La Paz, small seaside towns and villages, and the popular resorts of San José del Cabo and Cabo San Lucas, aka 'Los Cabos.' After the quiet isolation of the north, Los Cabos will either be a jarring shock or a welcome relief.

Guerrero Negro

📞 615 / POP 12,000

After the snazziness of the touristy border towns, unassuming Guerrero Negro – a town that sprang up to service the lone salt factory – is a welcome relief. People actually speak Spanish here and nobody's barking out invitations to strip clubs. Though the main tourist draw is the proximity to whales in whale season, there's excellent bird-watching in the shallow marshes, plus friendly hotels and restaurants, and the salt factory's odd white crystalline plains are quite beautiful. The nearby Laguna Ojo de Liebre (known in English as Scammon's Lagoon), which annually becomes the mating and breeding ground of California gray whales, is the prime attraction.

NOTHING LIKE TAKING A GOOD PISMO...

Tiny San Quintín is the pismo clam capital, and these mouthwatering morsels are well worth stopping for. Look for 'Almeja Ahumada' signs as you drive southwards...or if time and itinerary permits, stop in at one of the roadside stalls for a fire-roasted Pismo. **La Ballena** (the one with the whale skeleton) is one of the best. If you're really a do-it-yourselfer, sharpen your clam rake, get a license (M$250 per week) from the Oficina de Pesca (Fisheries Office) and dig them on your own. Yum!

🏃 Activities

Guerrero Negro can surprise you. If whales aren't around, try cave-painting viewing in the Sierra de San Francisco, bird-watching or touring the **salt factory** (one to two hours, M$200 per person). On the east side of the inlet is a mini Sahara of 3m to 6m sand dunes made of powdery white sand.

Bird-watching

Head to the **Old Pier** if you're a bird-watcher, as there is a nice 11km drive through prime territory for ducks, coots, eagles, curlews, terns, herons and other birds.

Whale-watching

Agencies arrange whale-watching trips on the shallow waters of Laguna Ojo de Liebre, where visitors are guaranteed a view of whales in their natural habitat. **Malarrimo Eco Tours** (📞157-01-00; www.malarrimo.com; Blvd Zapata), at the beginning of the strip, offers four-hour tours (adult/child US$45/35). A bit further south *pangueros* (boatmen) from Ejido Benito Juárez take visitors out for whale-watching excursions (adult/child M$500/450).

🛏 Sleeping

The whale-watching season can strain local accommodations; reservations are advisable from January through March.

About 8km south of town, a good graded road leads 25km west to the **Campo de Ballenas** (Whale-Watching Camp) on the edge of the lagoon. Here a M$50 parking fee includes the right to camp, and the *ejido* (communal landholding) runs a simple restaurant (open in the whale season only).

Motel Las Ballenas   MOTEL $

(📞157-01-16; Victoria Sánchez 10; s/d/tr M$300/350/380; P🐕) Clean and comfortable rooms with color TV. Not fancy, but it's one of the few hotels that claims to not raise rates during whale season.

Cabañas Malarrimo   CABAÑAS $$

(📞157-01-00; www.malarrimo.com; Blvd Zapata 42; d M$450-500, campsites M$140, RV sites M$130-200; P🕸@🐕) Hot, strong showers and a lot more ambience than the other options in town. Whale headboards and a general whale theme make it impossible to forget why you've come here. Also offers campsites and RV hookups.

Cowboy Hotel   HOTEL $$

(📞157-27-65; Blvd Zapata; s/d/tr M$400/500/600; P🕸🐕) On the south side of Zapata, this new hotel has an attractive courtyard, clean, tiled floors, TVs and off-street parking.

🍴 Eating

Santo Remedio   MEXICAN $$

(📞157-29-09; www.elsantoremedio.com.mx; Carballo Félix; mains M$70-180; ⊗ 8am-10pm) One of the fancier Guerrero Negro options, with soft lighting and a variety of seafood, meat, vegetable dishes and Chilean wines to choose from.

Caprichos Coffee House   CAFE $

(📞157-14-00; Blvd Zapata; coffee M$28-45; ⊗7am-11pm) Lattes, pies, pastries and occasional impromptu salsa performances make this cafe well worth a stop.

CALIFORNIA GRAY WHALES

The migration of gray whales from Siberian and Alaskan waters to the lagoons of Baja is one amazing animal event. In calving grounds such as Laguna Ojo de Liebre (Scammon's Lagoon), southwest of Guerrero Negro, and Laguna San Ignacio, southwest of San Ignacio, 700kg calves will draw their first breaths and begin learning the lessons of the sea from their ever-watchful mothers. The season is long but varied due to the fact that some whales arrive early in the Pacific lagoons, while others take weeks or months to round Land's End and find their favorite bays in the Sea of Cortez. Peak months to see mothers and calves in the lagoons are February to early April, but the official whale-watching season begins December 15 and lasts until April 15.

If you've got *ballena* (whale) fever, one of these destinations will provide a cure:

» Laguna Ojo de Liebre (Scammon's Lagoon; p709)

» Laguna San Ignacio (p711)

» Puerto López Mateos (p718)

» Puerto San Carlos (p718)

BUSES FROM GUERRERO NEGRO

DESTINATION	FARE (M$)	DURATION
Ensenada	817	9hr
La Paz	1099	12hr
Loreto	592	5-6hr
Mulegé	398	4hr
Tijuana	964	12hr
Mexicali	1262	15hr

ℹ️ Information

Nearly all hotels, restaurants and other services are along Blvd Zapata. Note that places in Guerrero Negro do not have street numbers.

There's a Banamex with an ATM at the far end of the commercial district on Blvd Zapata, just at the start of the company town. Get money here if you'll need it in San Ignacio, as that town has no bank.

Ciber@migos (📞157-26-51; Blvd Leon Amado 2; per hr M$13; ⊙10am-9pm Mon-Fri, noon-9pm Sat) Off Zapata, this place offers internet access just a few streets away from Motel Las Ballenas.

Clínica Hospital IMSS (📞157-03-33; Blvd Zapata) Guerrero Negro's main medical facility is located where the road curves southwest.

ℹ️ Getting There & Away

Guerrero Negro's airport is 2km north of the state border, west of the Transpeninsular.

Aereoservicio Guerrero (📞157-01-32; www.aereoservicioguerrero.com.mx; Blvd Zapata; ⊙7am-7pm Mon-Sat) Runs flights to Hermosillo, Guaymas, Isla Cedros and Ensenada, plus charters.

Aéreo Calafia (📞157-29-99; www.aereocalafia.com.mx; Blvd Zapata; ⊙8am-7pm Mon-Fri, 8am-4pm Sat) Runs flights to Hermosillo and Isla Cedros, and offers charters.

The **bus station** (Blvd Marcello Rubio; ⊙24hr) is served by **ABC** (www.abc.com.mx) and Autotransportes Águila, one of its subsidiaries.

San Ignacio

📞615 / POP 720

Sleepy San Ignacio seems out of place after the endless Desierto de Vizcaíno – the town's lush, leafy date palms and quiet lake are almost shocking. Jesuits located the **Misión San Ignacio de Kadakaamán** here, but Dominicans supervised construction of the striking church (finished in 1786) that still dominates the cool, laurel-shaded

plaza. With lava-block walls nearly 1.2m thick and surrounded by bougainvillea, this is one of Baja's most beautiful churches. A small self-guiding **museum** (admission free; ⊙8am-5pm Mon-Sat) offers a glimpse of the area's natural history.

Most services are around the plaza, including public phones, but there is no bank. International calls can be made from the Hotel La Pinta. Internet access is available at **Fischer Internet** (📞154-04-49; per hr M$20; ⊙9am-11pm), which can also arrange tours.

🛏️ Sleeping & Eating

San Ignacio has excellent accommodations choices tucked away beneath its swaying palms. Many can arrange tours to area attractions.

Despite its tourist attractions, San Ignacio remains a quiet, one-horse town and eats are mainly *antojitos* and *cervezas*. The tiny cafe-restaurants around the plaza are your best best for meals. Dates from the palms cost M$10 to M$30 per bag if you want a quick snack or energy for the road.

TOP CHOICE **Casa Leré**   B&B $$
(📞154-01-58; www.casaleree.com; Morelos 20; r US$90/45/40;📶) Part guesthouse, part museum, this beautiful old building sits around a verdant garden with all kinds of tropical trees. Rooms are small but very tastefully decorated, and the owner is a wealth of information about all aspects of San Ignacio, especially hiking and history.

Ricardo's Hotel & RV Park   MOTEL $$
(📞154-02-83; RV sites M$250, d/tr M$650/1200; 🅿️❄️@) A squeaky-clean hotel offering satellite TV and two queen-sized beds per room. There's a nice restaurant onsite and staff use fresh lime juice in the margaritas. RV sites are spartan but adequate. To get here from

the Transpeninsular, turn right on San Lino, then right again. It is 400m up the street.

❶ Getting There & Away

Buses pick up passengers at the **bus station** (☎154-04-68) near the San Lino junction (2.5km outside of town), arriving about every four hours from 5am to 11pm, both north and southbound to locations such as Tijuana (M$1102), Mexicali (M$1395), La Paz (M$896) and Cabo San Lucas (M$1115).

Around San Ignacio

SIERRA DE SAN FRANCISCO

The sheer quantity of beautiful petroglyphs in this region is impressive, but the ochre, red, black and white paintings remain shrouded in mystery. In recognition of its cultural importance, the Sierra de San Francisco has been declared a Unesco World Heritage site. It is also part of the Reserva de la Biosfera El Vizcaíno.

Cueva del Ratón, a cave named for an image of what inhabitants once thought was a rat (or mouse) but is more likely a deer, is the most easily accessible site. Drivers can get there on their own after registering and paying the park entry (M$37) and guide fee (M$80 for two people) at the office of the **Instituto Nacional de Antropología e Historia** (INAH; ☎615-154-02-22; ◎8am-5pm Mon-Sat Apr-Oct, daily Nov-Mar), adjacent to the Misíon San Ignacio on the plaza in San Ignacio, then picking up their guide in the pueblo closest to the paintings. Bringing a camera costs M$45 per day. INAH fees for guides for other trips start at M$200 per day, and each pack animal adds M$150. These are INAH fees only, and guides themselves charge additional (varying) fees.

Those with time should visit the dramatic **Cañón San Pablo** for sites that are better preserved. At **Cueva Pintada**, Cochimí painters and their predecessors decorated 150m of high rock overhangs with vivid red-and-black representations of human figures, bighorn sheep, pumas and deer, as well as with more abstract designs. **Cueva de las Flechas**, across Cañón San Pablo, has similar paintings, but curiously, some of the figures have arrows through them.

The beautiful mule-back descent of Cañón San Pablo requires at least two days, preferably three, and is best done through a tour operator. **Kuyimá** (☎615-154-00-70; www. kuyima.com; Morelos 23; ◎9am-3pm Mon-Sat),

a cooperative based at the east end of the plaza in San Ignacio, can arrange three-/six-day trips for US$471/927 per person (four-person minimum). Fischer Internet (p710) is another option.

LAGUNA SAN IGNACIO

Along with Laguna Ojo de Liebre and Bahía Magdalena, Laguna San Ignacio is one of the Pacific coast's major winter whale-watching sites, with three-hour excursions costing around M$475 per person. Kuyimá (see above) can arrange both transportation and accommodations.

Santa Rosalía

☎615 / POP 13,000

Southbound travelers will welcome their first sight of the Sea of Cortez after crossing the Desierto de Vizcaíno. Though the town was devastated by flooding in 2009's Hurricane Jimena, it has repaired and rebounded. Brightly painted clapboard-sided houses, the prefab church, a port and *malecón* (seaside promenade), black-sand beaches, lazy pelicans and great views from the surrounding hills are this one-horse town's prime attractions.

◉ Sights

Central Santa Rosalía is a cluster of densely packed houses, restaurants, inns and stores. Plaza Benito Juárez, four blocks west of the highway, is the town center.

Museo Histórico Minero de Santa Rosalía   MUSEUM
(☎152-29-99; Cousteau 1; admission M$20; ◎8am-3pm Mon-Fri, 9am-1pm Sat) Built in 1885 by the French to house the offices of the Boleo Company, this museum watches over the town and the rusting copperworks from its perch on the hill near the Hotel Francés, surrounded by cool abandoned locomotives and other pieces of machinery.

Iglesia Santa Bárbara   CHURCH
Designed and erected for Paris' 1889 World's Fair, then disassembled and stored in Brussels for shipping to West Africa, Gustave Eiffel's (yes, of Eiffel Tower fame) prefabricated Iglesia Santa Bárbara was, instead, shipped here when a Boleo Company director signed for its delivery to the town in 1895. Many travelers agree that the church is interesting more as an example of early prefabricated architecture than for its beauty.

🛌 Sleeping

Of all the towns in central Baja, Santa Rosalía has perhaps the best variety of well-priced accommodations, from the historic to the picturesque.

Hotel Francés   HOTEL $$

(☎152-20-52; Cousteau 15; r M$720; P🖥🛜⊟🏊) Overlooking the Sea of Cortez and curious rusting hulks of mine machinery, the Hotel Francés is charming and historic. Built in 1886 and originally the dormitory for the 'working girls' of a brothel near the mine, the hotel features beautiful rooms with high ceilings, cloth-covered walls and charming stained-wood details. Onsite is a restaurant open Monday to Saturday for breakfast.

Hotel El Morro   HOTEL $$

(☎152-04-14; www.santarosaliaelmorro.com; s/d/t M$450/600/775; P❄🛜🏊) Perched on a cliff 1.5km south of town, the friendly El Morro feels a bit more like Greece than Baja. The view of the Sea of Cortez is enough reason to stay here, but rooms are also spotless, and off-street parking makes for a convenient stay.

🍴 Eating

For cheap eats or fruit for the road, check out the small **fruit market** (Montoya; ⊗6am-6pm) between Hotel del Real and the highway, or hit one of the many taco stands of high quality along Avenida Obregón. Most charge M$8 for a fish taco.

Panadería El Boleo   BAKERY $

(☎152-03-10; Obregón 30; breads M$5-20; ⊗8am-9pm Mon-Sat, 9am-2pm Sun) Since 1901, this has been an obligatory stop for the rare find of good French bread in Baja. The pastries are good too. It's between Calles 3 and 4.

Playas Negras   MEXICAN, SEAFOOD $$

(☎152-06-85; Carretera Sur Km 1; breakfast M$45, dinner mains M$85-135; ⊗8am-11pm) South of downtown and with a gorgeous view and a funky map of Baja done in abalone shell, this waterfront restaurant serves sumptuous seafood as well as steak, chicken and pizza.

El Muelle   MEXICAN $$

(☎152-09-31; cnr Av Constitución & Calle Plaza; mains M$70-225; ⊗8am-11pm) The dock theme fits well with seaside Santa Rosalía. Locals come here for everything from egg breakfasts to the popular red enchiladas.

ℹ Information

Hotel del Real, on the exit road from town, has long-distance *cabinas* (call centers).

Cafe Internet PC Vision (☎152-28-75; cnr Calles 6 & Obregón; per hr M$20; ⊗10am-10pm) Internet access.

Post office (cnr Av Constitución & Calle 2)

ℹ Getting There & Away

Boat

The passenger/auto ferry *Santa Rosalía* sails to Guaymas (boxed text p748) at 9am Tuesday, Wednesday, Friday and Saturday, and 8pm (yes, pm!) on Sunday, arriving ten hours later. Strong winds may cause delays, and the trips may be canceled due to lack of demand. It's best to check the day before whether the ferry will run.

The ticket office is at the **ferry terminal** (☎152-12-46; www.ferrysantarosalia.com; ⊗9am-1pm & 3-6pm Mon-Sat, 9am-1pm & 3-8pm Sun) on the highway; its opening hours may vary with the ferry schedule to open at 7am or 8am. Passenger fares are M$790 for *salón* class (numbered seats), M$700 additional for shared cabins (children's tickets are half-price, and there is a general Sunday discount).

BUSES FROM SANTA ROSALÍA

DESTINATION	FARE (M$)	DURATION
Ensenada	1111	13hr
Guerrero Negro	308	3hr
La Paz	791	8hr
Loreto	284	3hr
Mexicali	1495	16hr
Mulegé	89	1hr
San Ignacio	111	1hr
San José del Cabo	1055	12hr
Tijuana	1197	14hr

Advance reservations are recommended. Vehicle rates vary with vehicle length.

VEHICLE	FARE
car or pickup up to 5m	M$3200, plus M$1040 per extra meter
motorcycle	M$1420
motorhome	varies by length (M$6555 up to 10m)
trailer truck up to 15m	M$11,530

Bus

At least five buses each day in each direction stop at the **bus terminal** (📞152-14-08; ⏱24hr), which is in the same building as the ferry terminal on the highway just south of the entrance to town.

Mulegé

📞615 / POP 3300

The palm- and mangrove-lined Río Mulegé, with its delta, birds, wildlife, snorkeling and diving, makes this a great stop for the outdoorsy or those with kids, but it was pummeled by hurricanes in 2006 and 2009 and, being set down in a narrow *arroyo* (stream), flooding is possible with any major storm. The ancient mission and town square give the town a quiet charm that's fast disappearing in other parts of Baja. Despite the eyesore of a faux rampart at the town entrance and the fact that it now has a bank/ATM, Mulegé still feels in some ways like part of yesteryear.

◉ Sights

Misión Santa Rosalía de Mulegé MISSION
Come to the hilltop Misión Santa Rosalía de Mulegé (founded in 1705, completed in 1766 and abandoned in 1828) for great photos of the mission and river valley.

Museo Mulegé MUSEUM
(Barrio Canenea; admission M$10; ⏱9am-2pm Mon-Sat) The former territorial prison is now the Museo Mulegé. Its eclectic holdings include objects from the Mission de Santa Rosalía and prehistoric artifacts.

🏃 Activities

Diving

Mulegé's best diving spots can be found around the Santa Inés Islands (north of town) and just north of Punta Concepción (south of town).

Cortez Explorers DIVING
(📞153-05-00; www.cortez-explorers.com; Moctezuma 75A; ⏱8:30am-6pm, dives 24hr) Offers all levels of diving instruction and other outdoor sports. One- or two-tank dives cost M$1430 per person, snorkeling M$650.

Kayaking

The beautiful river, the estuary delta and the southern beaches make Mulegé one of the prime spots for kayaking. Baja Outpost (p715) in Loreto is one of the few places for long-term rentals or for those wanting to follow the coastline south over a few days.

🛶NOLS Mexico KAYAKING
(📞in the US 800-710-6657, 307-332-5300; www.nols.edu/courses/locations/mexico/about_mexico.shtml) Runs sea-kayaking courses out of its sustainable, ecofriendly facility on Coyote Bay, south of Mulegé.

🛏 Sleeping

Hotel Las Casitas HOTEL **$**
(📞153-00-19; www.historicolascasitas.com.mx; Madero 50; s/d/tr M$375/425/525; 🅿❄🐾🛜) Beloved Mexican poet Alán Gorosave once inhabited this well-run hotel near Martínez, perhaps inspired by its beautiful courtyard shaded by a well-tended garden of tropical plants. The restaurant serves excellent food and has an open-fire grill. Drew Barrymore is rumored to have stayed here. Prices are higher in peak season.

Hotel Hacienda HOTEL **$**
(📞153-00-21; hotel.hacienda@hotmail.com; Madero 3; r M$400; ❄🐾) The oldest hotel in town was damaged during Jimena's onslaught in 2009 and has now been repaired: the green-and-white, atmospheric Hacienda offers rooms with twin beds and old-time ambience.

Hotel Mulegé HOTEL **$$**
(📞153-00-90; Moctezuma s/n; s/d M$400/460; 🅿❄@🛜) Mulegé's only business hotel has spotless doubles with carpeted floors, bottled water and cable TV. Internet in the lobby is another plus.

Hotel Cuesta Real RV PARK **$$**
(📞153-03-21; http://cuestarealhotel.tripod.com; Transpenínsular Km 132; s/d M$500/600, RV hookups M$250; 🅿❄@🛜🐾) Just on the southward edge of town, this hotel offers a variety of rooms and hookups, plus easy access to Río Mulegé where it empties into the sea. Take in scenic mangrove swamps and pelicans on the way to the town center.

ON A MISSION FROM GOD

Baja's missions have a dubious history – built by Jesuits and Dominicans intent on bringing salvation, they instead brought death through introduced European diseases. Many missions were abandoned as populations dropped below sustainable levels. Today however, these beautiful buildings, whether in use or out in the middle of nowhere, make for great photos and fun day trips, and they're an undeniable part of Baja's checkered past. You should not need a 4WD to visit any of the ones listed here, though the roads can be impressively bad (or impassable) at times.

» **Misión Nuestra Señora de Loreto** (p715) The oldest mission, an impressive monument still in use today.

» **Misión San Borja** (p708) Out in the middle of nowhere but well worth the drive. Its treasures include a hot spring and a secret tunnel (now walled up). One family, descended from the original preconquest inhabitants, is restoring the building rock by rock, by hand.

» **Misión San Francisco Javier de Viggé-Biaundó** (p717) Remote and beautifully preserved; it feels like stepping back in time. The drive here offers awesome vistas and even some cave paintings along the way.

» **Misión Santa Rosalía de Mulegé** (p713) Extremely photogenic. Don't miss the view from behind looking out over the palm-edged river.

Resources for further reading include *Las Misiones Antiguas,* by Edward W Vernon, and www.vivabaja.com/bajamissions; both feature beautiful photos of these interesting ruins.

Casa de Huéspedes Manuelita GUESTHOUSE $
(☑153-01-75; Moctezuma s/n; r M$300; P❋🛜)
Rooms are behind a small grape arbor and, while they're nothing fancy, they are clean and have hot showers.

✖️ Eating & Drinking

The sidewalks are rolled up pretty early in Mulegé, so dine earlier than usual and rest up for that big day tomorrow.

Restaurante Doney MEXICAN $
(☑153-00-95; mulegedoney@hotmail.com; Moctezuma s/n; tacos & mains M$16-155;⊗7:30am-10pm Wed-Mon) There's counter or table seating here, with colorful tablecloths and good *antojitos* and tacos.

Los Equipales MEXICAN, SEAFOOD $$
(☑153-03-30; Moctezuma s/n; mains M$135-275;⊗8am-10pm) Just west of Zaragoza, this restaurant and bar has gargantuan meals and breezy balcony seating that's perfect for an afternoon margarita or an evening chat with friends. Shrimp are snapped up as soon as they are served.

Scott's El Candil BAR $
(Zaragoza s/n; mains M$60-150; ⊗noon-10pm) Nice brick building with open courtyard in the back and arched windows looking onto Zaragoza for those who want to watch the world (or at least Mulegé's portion of it!) pass by. True to its sports-bar core, the day off depends on (American) football season.

ℹ️ Information

Most services are on or near Jardín Corona, the town plaza. Bancomer and the ATM are on Zaragoza between Martínez and Madero. To get online try **Carlos' Place** (per hr M$30; ⊗9am-1pm & 4-8pm Mon-Sat), across from Los Equipales. Hotel Mulegé is another option.

ℹ️ Getting There & Away

Mulegé's **bus terminal** (Transpeninsular Km 132; ⊗8am-11pm) is inconveniently located north of town near the large entry arch. ABC/Águila northbound buses to Santa Rosalía (M$89, one hour) and Tijuana (M$1316, 14 hours) stop six times daily. Southbound buses pass to destinations including Loreto (M$195, 2½ hours) and La Paz (M$702, seven hours).

Around Mulegé

CAÑÓN LA TRINIDAD

Trinity Canyon is great for bird-watchers, with the chance to see vermilion flycatchers, gila woodpeckers and a host of raptors and buteos. The narrow, sherbet-colored canyon walls and shimmering pools of water are stunning, as are the pre-Hispanic cave paintings. Rendered in shades of ochre and rust, the paintings feature shamans, manta rays, whales and the famous Trinity Deer, leaping gracefully from the walls of the cave as arrows pass harmlessly over its head. Dams and climate change have kept the canyon dry for more than a decade. You're not allowed to enter by yourself, but Mulegé native Salvador Castro Drew of **Mulegé Tours** (☎615-161-49-85, 615-153-02-32; day excursions per person M$450) knows just about everything about the site you'd want to know – plants, animals, even how to avoid the two nasty beehives that 'guard' the paintings. He also does taxi runs to other area sites. Call the cell first, as he is often on the road.

BEACHES

As you wind your way south you'll pass some of Baja's most pristine *playas* (beaches). You can string up a hammock, pop the top on something frosty and watch the pelicans dive-bomb for fish. Some beaches have bars, restaurants or *cabañas*. **Bahía Concepción**, with its pelican colonies, funky rock formations and milky, blue-green water, remains a top stop for kayakers, many of whom camp in makeshift RV colonies. **Playa Escondido** (Km 112), **Playa Santispac** (Km 113.5) and **Playa Perla** (Km 91) are just a few of the possible stops along the Transpeninular on the way. Be extremely cautious about weather alerts – the glassy water here and in Loreto can quickly become dangerous in storms.

Loreto

☎613 / POP 12,000

The Loreto area is considered by anthropologists to be the oldest human settlement on the Baja Peninsula. Indigenous cultures thrived here due to plentiful water and food. In 1697 Jesuit Juan María Salvatierra established the peninsula's first permanent mission at this modest port some 135km south of Mulegé. Despite its reputation as Baja's water-sports paradise and the fact that it's nowhere near the border, Loreto has been hit hard by the drop in tourism. Consequently, it's a great time to visit – hotels are open and welcoming, and prices have either dropped or stayed the same. It's home to the Parque Marino Nacional Bahía de Loreto, with shoreline, ocean and offshore islands protected from pollution and uncontrolled fishing; however, the massive development

of the shoreline is already causing irreparable changes to the ecology.

Most hotels and services are near the landmark mission church on Salvatierra, while the attractive *malecón* is ideal for evening strolls. The Plaza Cívica is just north of Salvatierra, between Calles Madero and Davis.

◉ Sights & Activities

Including the 2065-sq-km **Parque Marino Nacional Bahía de Loreto**, Loreto is a world-class destination for all types of outdoor activities; a number of outfitters offer everything from kayaking and diving along the reefs around Islas del Carmen and Coronado to horseback riding, hiking and mountain biking in the Sierra de la Giganta.

Baja Outpost ADVENTURE TOURS
(☎613-135-20-84; www.bajaoutpost.com; Blvd López Mateos) Offers diving, snorkeling, biking and kayaking expeditions in addition to accommodation. Note that its whale-watching tours (M$2035 per person) run a full seven hours on the water, unlike many others (some are as short as 1½ hours), and the owner can offer both blue and gray whale-viewing tours to a variety of locations, such as Guerrero Negro and Puerto López Mateos, or even Loreto when the whales are nearby.

Misión Nuestra Señora de Loreto HISTORIC SITE
The Misión Nuestra Señora de Loreto, dating from 1697, was the first permanent mission in the Californias and the base for the expansion of Jesuit missions up and down the Baja peninsula. Alongside the church, INAH's revamped **Museo de las Misiones** (☎135-04-41; Salvatierra 16; admission M$37; ⊙9am-1pm & 1:45-6pm Tue-Sun) chronicles the settlement of Baja California.

⊨ Sleeping

Most of Loreto's accommodations choices are on or near the picturesque *malecón*.

TOP
CHOICE
Baja Outpost HOTEL, CABAÑAS $$
(☎613-135-20-84; www.bajaoutpost.com; Blvd López Mateos; r incl breakfast US$65, palapa US$86; P❋❀❁) Located off the busy *malecón*, convenient to the town center and the beach, this B&B offers regular rooms, beautiful *palapas* (thatched-roof shelters), great breakfasts made to order and multilingual staff. A swimming pool and restaurant are

in progress. All manner of tours can be done from here as well, and few people know as much about Loreto's natural wonders than Leon.

Iguana Inn
HOTEL $$

(☎135-16-27; www.iguanainn.com; Juarez s/n; bungalows M$715-780; ☻Oct-Aug; ᴾ☻❋☎) Kitchenettes, a video library and clean, comfortable beds make this a great midrange option. It's very close to the town center and still within easy walking distance of the malecón.

Hotel Posada San Martín
HOTEL $

(☎135-11-07; Juárez 4; r with/without kitchenette M$350/450; ❋☻☎) The best value in town, newly remodeled San Martín has large rooms (some with cable TV) and a great location near the plaza, with a covered central courtyard, garden and topiary.

Hotel Junípero
HOTEL $

(☎135-01-22; Av Hidalgo s/n; s/d/tr M$350/400/450; ❋) Overlooking the mission and the town plaza, this family-run hotel has seen better days but rooms at the back have excellent views of the mission. Golf-ball key rings are out of place, but fun.

Motel Salvatierra
MOTEL $

(☎135-00-21; Salvatierra 123; s/d/tr/q M$330/360/420/500; ᴾ❋) Nearish to the bus station, this bright ochre motel offers clean, basic rooms that are some of Loreto's least expensive.

✗ Eating & Drinking

Loreto has a fair selection of restaurants preparing the regional standards: excellent seafood with plenty of tasty lime and cilantro, potent margaritas and fruity aguas frescas (ice drinks). Unfortunately, mistakes in the bill have become commonplace recently, so do the arithmetic after the tab arrives. Plan on eating early on weekdays, since most places close up by 8:30pm to 9pm.

Antojitos McLulu
MEXICAN $

(Hidalgo s/n; mains M$15-30; ☻10am-7pm) Serving nine different types of tacos – and only tacos – on plastic cutlery, the venerable Señora McLulu has been here since the mid 1980s.

Café Olé
CAFE, MEXICAN $

(☎135-04-96; Madero 14; dinner mains M$35-70; ☻7am-9:45pm Mon-Sat, 7am-1pm Sun) The inexpensive Café Olé has good, basic fare: great Mexican breakfasts, lunches and dinners.

Leave a business card in the wicker wall to stake your claim to fame.

México Lindo y Que Rico
MEXICAN, SEAFOOD $$

(☎135-11-75; Hidalgo s/n; mains M$90-200; ☻8am-10:30pm Tue-Sun) Lots of options on the somewhat pricey menu, but the patio setting is pretty and it's open later than many spots. Passing mariachis can be flagged down if you're in the mood for some música romántica.

🔒 Shopping

The pedestrian mall between Madero and Independencia has many shops selling jewelry and souvenirs.

El Alacrán
HANDICRAFTS

(☎/fax 135-00-29; Salvatierra 43; ☻9:30am-1pm & 2:30-7pm Mon-Sat Oct-Aug) This is the place to try for varied handicrafts.

Silver Desert
SILVER

(☎135-06-84; Salvatierra 36; ☻9am-2pm & 3-8pm Mon-Sat, 9am-2pm Sun) Sells Taxco sterling-silver jewelry of good quality. There's an alternate location at Magdalena de Kino 4.

ℹ Information

Bancomer (cnr Calles Salvatierra & Madero) Has an ATM and changes US cash and traveler's checks Monday to Friday.

Hospital General (☎135-01-50; Transpeninsular s/n; ☻24hr) A newly built hospital 300m south of the Loreto turnoff.

Municipal Department of Tourism (☎135-04-11; turismoloreto@hotmail.com; Plaza Cívica; ☻8am-3pm Mon-Fri) On the west side of the Plaza Cívica; has a good selection of brochures.

Parque Nacional Bahía de Loreto (☎135-14-29; ☻8:30am-2pm Mon-Fri, 9am-1pm Sat) Pay the M$25 to M$50 per person entrance fee to the park here in the marina. Staff are a good source of information for all water activities in the area, and the pelican colony is amazing.

PC Express (☎135-02-84; Salvatierra s/n; per hr M$20; ☻8am-2pm & 4-10pm Mon-Sat) Internet, faxes and printing, near the supermarket.

Post office (☎135-06-47; Deportiva; ☻8am-2pm Mon-Fri)

ℹ Getting There & Away

Aeropuerto Internacional de Loreto (☎135-04-99) is now served by several airlines, including Alaska Airlines, Aéreo Calafia and Aereoservicio Guerrero.

Loreto's **bus station** (☻24hr) is near the convergence of Salvatierra, Paseo de Ugarte

BUSES FROM LORETO

DESTINATION	FARE (M$)	DURATION
Guerrero Negro	592	6hr
La Paz	508	5hr
Mexicali	1765	20hr
San José del Cabo	771	8hr
Santa Rosalía	284	3hr
Tijuana	1526	18hr

and Paseo Tamaral, a 15-minute walk from the town center.

❶ Getting Around

Taxis from the airport, 4km south of Loreto, cost M$160 just outside the door, or about M$100 if you walk to the edge of the airport grounds. Groups start at M$70 per person.

The car-rental agency **Fox** (☑135-10-90; Av Hidalgo s/n) has economy models starting at about M$550 per day, including appropriate insurance.

Around Loreto

Whale-watching tours are the biggest tourist draw between Loreto and La Paz, but the wonderful **Misión San Francisco Javier de Viggé-Biaundó** (and the drive to get there!) is well worth a daytime detour. The windy road passes minor cliff paintings and some beautiful *arroyos* before arriving at the mission. Be sure to wander to the back garden to see the 300-year-old olive tree with rope-like bark that looks like something out of a Tolkien fantasy. The mission itself is almost unchanged from its look of three centuries ago. Head south on the Transpeninsular and look for the sign shortly after you leave Loreto, leading you to the right, up into the mountains. All but the last few kilometers has been paved.

CIUDAD CONSTITUCIÓN
☑613 / POP 43,000

Landlocked, and primarily a farming and industrial city, Ciudad Constitución offers little for tourists other than hotels for whale-watching day trips. Transportation to the port cities of López Mateos and San Carlos is infrequent – it's far better to have your own set of wheels. Loreto (p717) or La Paz (p723) have the closest rental agencies.

🛏 Sleeping & Eating

Ciudad Constitución's lodgings are limited; none of them are fancy and prices rise during peak season.

Posadas del Ryal MOTEL $$
(☑132-48-00; Victoria s/n; s/d M$410/470; P ❄) Spotless and sunshiney gold all over, this place just off Olachea has dark rooms with cable TV and there's a cheery fountain in the courtyard.

Hotel Conchit HOTEL $
(☑132-02-66; Olachea 180; s/d M$300/340; ❄ 🕸) Offers basic rooms with blue-green bedspreads, TV and privacy glass that blocks any possible view. Watch your step on that uneven staircase.

Hotel Maribel HOTEL $
(☑132-01-55; Guadalupe Victoria 156; s/d M$300/320; ❄🕸) Rooms are spartan, but small balconies brighten them a bit, and there's a convenient restaurant downstairs. Rooms without cable TV are M$100 cheaper.

Asadero 'Tribi' BARBECUE $
(☑132-73-53; tribimosqueda@hotmail.com; Olachea btwn Madero & Pino Suárez; mains M$90-140; ⊘8am-midnight Mon-Sat) This, the best restaurant in town, serves delicious *arrachera* (marinated) steak and a variety of fish and meat tacos.

❶ Getting There & Away

At the **bus terminal** (☑132-03-76; cnr Juárez & Pino Suárez; ⊘24hr) there are two daily departures for Puerto López Mateos (M$78, 1pm and 8:15pm) and Puerto San Carlos (M$61, 11am and 6pm). Other destinations include La Paz (M$296) and Tijuana (M$1417, six daily from 2am to 11pm).

Taxis, just outside the bus station, charge M$800 for a round-trip ride to Puerto López Mateos or Puerto San Carlos.

PUERTO LÓPEZ MATEOS
☎613 / POP 2200

Shielded by the offshore barrier of Isla Magdalena, Puerto López Mateos is one of Baja's best whale-watching sites. During the season, the narrow waterway that passes by town becomes a veritable *ballena* cruising strip. Curva del Diablo (Devil's Bend), 27km south of town, is reported to be the best viewing spot. Three-hour *panga* (skiff) excursions from Puerto López Mateos (M$700 per hour for six to eight people, from 7am to 6pm in season) are easy to arrange.

Free camping (bring water), with pit toilets only, is possible at tidy **Playa Boca de la Soledad**, which is near Playa El Faro, 1.6km east of town (turn left at the water tower). Accommodations in Puerto López Mateos are at the small but serviceable **El Camarón Feliz** (☎131-50-32; r M$350; ☺whale season only). **Baja Mar** (☎131-51-96; breakfast M$55, mains M$200; ☺8am-8pm; 🛜) offers family-style Mexican dishes of the day, in portions large enough to feed a family of mammoths.

Puerto López Mateos is 34km west of Ciudad Insurgentes. The bus service to Ciudad Constitución (M$97) leaves inconveniently at 6:30am (for Cabo, M$610) and 2:30pm (for La Paz, M$393) from a small ticket office across from the school.

PUERTO SAN CARLOS
☎613 / POP 4700

On Bahía Magdalena, 56km west of Ciudad Constitución, Puerto San Carlos is a deepwater port and fishing town. The *ballenas* arrive in January to calve in the warm lagoon and the town turns its attention to both whales and travelers. From January through March, *pangueros* take passengers for whale-watching excursions (M$750 per hour for six people).

🛌 Sleeping & Eating

With several hotels and restaurants to choose from, San Carlos is a good choice for whale-watching adventures. Accommodations can be tougher to find during the high season, but free camping is possible north of town on the public beach (no toilets). The **Motel Las Brisas** (Puerto Madero; r M$180; 🅿) has dark, spartan rooms.

The green-trimmed **Hotel Brennan** (☎136-02-88; www.hotelbrennan.com.mx; Acapulco s/n; s/d M$650/700; 🅿❄🛜) has clean rooms, friendly staff, and plentiful patio space. With similar amenities, the **Hotel**

Alcatraz (☎136-00-17; www.hotelalcatraz.net; Calle San Jose del Cabo s/n; s/d M$550/780; 🅿❄🛜) offers 25 rooms with satellite TV, parking and laundry service.

At the Hotel Alcatraz, **Restaurant Bar El Patio** (mains M$100-250, lobster M$350) is the town's best eatery. Not to be outdone, **Mariscos Los Arcos** (☎136-03-47; Puerto La Paz 170; 3 tacos M$30, dinner mains M$45-300) has tremendous shrimp tacos and seafood soup, a full breakfast menu and a small bar.

❶ Getting There & Away

From a small house, **Autotransportes Águila** (☎136-04-53; Calle Puerto Morelos; ☺7-7:30am, 11:30am-1:45pm & 6:30-7:30pm) runs buses at 7:30am and 1:45pm daily to Ciudad Constitución (M$71) and La Paz (M$357), Cabo San Lucas (M$547) and San Jose del Cabo (M$566). This is the only public transportation from Puerto San Carlos.

La Paz
☎612 / POP 180,000

Cosmopolitan La Paz is a mix of laid-back, old-world beauty and chichi upscale trend. It's surprisingly international – you're as likely to hear French, Portuguese or Italian here as English or Spanish, and yet paradoxically it's the most 'Mexican' city in all of Baja. Its quirky history includes American occupation and even being temporarily declared its own republic. Hernán Cortés established Baja's first European outpost near La Paz, but permanent settlement waited until 1811. Its rich pearl industry disappeared during the revolution of 1910–20.

The beachside *malecón,* unique restaurants and funky stores make it a great place to meander, and you can shop uninterrupted by touts' invitations. The city is a great hub for day trips to Cabo Pulmo (p724) or even Todos Santos (p732), and there's a lively, laid-back, long-term expat community in and around the marina.

The port of Pichilingue receives ferries from the mainland ports of Topolobampo and Mazatlán, and the airport is served by several US carriers. La Paz' grid pattern makes basic orientation easy, but the center's crooked streets and alleys change names almost every block. *GotBajaMaps* (free and available at most shops' brochure counters) has maps and current events, updated bimonthly.

◉ Sights

Museo Regional de Antropología e Historia
MUSEUM

(☑122-01-62; cnr Calles 5 de Mayo & Altamirano; adult/child M$31/free; ⊘9am-6pm) This is a large, well-organized museum chronicling the peninsula's history from prehistory to the revolution of 1910 and its aftermath.

Biblioteca de la Historia de las Californias
LIBRARY

(cnr Madero & Av Independencia; ⊘8am-3pm Mon-Fri) Across from the Jardín Velasco, La Paz' former Casa de Gobierno is now the Biblioteca de la Historia de las Californias, a history library.

Unidad Cultural Profesor Jesús Castro Agúndez
CULTURAL CENTER

(☑125-02-07; cnr Gómez Farías & Legaspi; ⊘8am-2pm & 4-6pm Mon-Fri) A sprawling concrete edifice, the **Teatro de la Ciudad** is the most conspicuous element of the Unidad Cultural Profesor Jesús Castro Agúndez, a cultural center that takes up most of the area bounded by Altamirano, Navarro, Héroes de la Independencia and Legaspi.

At the periphery of the grounds is the small **Museo Comunitario de la Ballena** (Community Whale Museum; cnr Calles Navarro & Altamirano; admission free; ⊘9am-1pm Tue-Sat).

Santuario de la Virgen de Guadalupe
MONUMENT

(☑122-15-18; cnr Calles 5 de Febrero & Aquiles Serdán; ⊘7am-6pm) The Santuario de la Virgen de Guadalupe is La Paz' biggest religious monument. Its 12m-tall altar is impressive and it's open later on special events or holidays.

Espíritu Santo
ISLAND

A treasure of shallow azure inlets and sorbet-pink cliffs, Espíritu Santo is one of La Paz' gems. It's part of a Unesco World Heritage site comprising 244 Sea of Cortez islands and coastal areas, and a worthy day trip for just about anyone. (It's also part of the Parque Nacional Archipiélago Espíritu Santo and Reserva de la Biosfera Islas del Golfo de California.) A number of operators run activities here.

⚡ Activities

TOP CHOICE Mariana Ledesma
ADVENTURE TOURS

(☑119-32-78; noche_autoexistente@hotmail.com) A one-woman, trilingual (Spanish, English and French) dynamo who can offer amazing stargazing tours, kayaking expeditions, hiking and camping trips and more. She also has a wealth of knowledge about local flora and fauna and ecosocial activism.

◢ Whale Shark Mexico
WILDLIFE-WATCHING

(☑154-9859; www.whalesharkmexico.com) From October to March you can help researchers study juvenile whale sharks, which congregate in the placid waters of La Paz bay. Duties vary each trip: you can assist with tagging and even get a chance to name one. These researchers do not rent or provide any gear, and trips must be arranged in advance when the weather conditions are right. Price is currently M$975 per person, and the fees (minus equipment rental) go directly toward the costs of radio tags and other research expenses.

◢ Baja Paradise
ADVENTURE SPORTS

(☑128-60-97; Madero 23) Offers guided camping tours on Espíritu Santo, plus all other activities. Hostel-type accommodation is available and the owner is a professor in the local university's ecological tourism program who takes care to make the trips as 'green' as possible.

Carey.com
DIVING, SNORKELING

(☑128-40-48; www.buceocarey.com; cnr Topete & Legaspi) A family-run establishment that offers diving and snorkeling day trips to Espíritu Santo, along with other trips and tours.

Mar y Aventuras
KAYAKING

(☑122-70-39; www.kayakbaja.com; Topete 564) Book an eight- or nine-day kayak expedition or outfit a self-guided trip. They also run day trips.

↩ Courses

Se Habla...La Paz
LANGUAGE COURSES

(☑122-7763; http://sehablalapaz.com; Madero 540) Courses cost M$2750 per week plus M$700 registration. All levels of Spanish classes including a medical and legal specialty.

✵ Festivals & Events

Festivals and other seasonal events often take place at the Plaza Constitución, between Revolución and Madero at Calle 5 de Mayo.

La Paz' pre-Lent **Carnaval** is among the country's best. In early May, *paceños* (people from La Paz) celebrate the **Fundación de la Ciudad** (Hernán Cortés' 1535 landing).

BAJA CALIFORNIA LA PAZ

🛏 Sleeping

Accommodation in La Paz runs the gamut from budget digs to big swanky hotels. Mid-range accommodation here is varied and of good quality.

TOP CHOICE **Posada de las Flores** LUXURY HOTEL $$$
(☎125-58-71; www.posadadelasflores.com; Paseo Obregón 440; r/ste incl breakfast M$2308/3847; P➘❄@🛜) Italian-run bed and breakfast. Rooms are beautiful and one couldn't ask

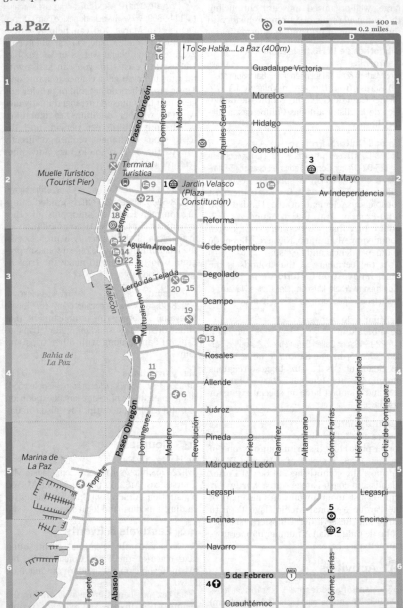

La Paz

To Se Habla...La Paz (400m)

for a nicer view of La Paz bay from the breakfast area.

El Ángel Azul
B&B $$$

(☎125-51-30; Independencia 518; r incl breakfast US$120-200; Ⓟ🗲❄🛜) Possibly the loveliest of La Paz' lodging options, El Ángel Azul offers elegantly appointed rooms and beautifully landscaped grounds in a historic building. The owner speaks English, Spanish and German, and there's tea time and cocktail hour daily.

Pensión California
HOSTEL $

(☎122-28-96; pensioncalifornia@prodigy.net.mx; Degollado 209; s/d M$220/300) The super-low-budget crowd owes it to themselves to seek out this quirky blue and bright-yellow hostel that's so popular it's often full. Cement furniture, icy showers and padlocks give it a meat-locker feel, but the ambience is fun and the plant-filled courtyard and plastic furniture lend themselves to good conversations with newfound friends.

Hotel Mediterrane
HOTEL $$

(☎125-11-95; Allende 36; r M$889-1299; Ⓟ❄@🛜) Greek-inspired hotel that's steps away from the *malecón*, with well-decorated rooms, delicious cafe menu, and a rooftop terrace with nice bay views.

Hotel Quinta Lolita
HOTEL $

(☎125-30-31; Revolución 1551; d M$300;❄) Simple, small, clean – a nice alternative if Pensión California is full. Bring a peso or two and join a cutthroat game of dominos on the front steps.

Hotel Suites Misión
SUITES $$

(☎128-77-67; Paseo Obregón 220; r M$750-850; ❄🛜) Original 1970s pastels make these multilevel suites unique and fun. All have kitchenettes.

Hotel Perla
HOTEL $$

(☎122-07-77; www.hotelperlabaja.com; Paseo Obregón 1570; r incl breakfast M$1048; Ⓟ🗲❄@🛜) Supposedly La Paz' first hotel, this standby offers clean rooms and a popular restaurant and nightclub. Some rooms have nice balconies, so ask. It includes late coffee for night owls.

Baja South Hotel
HOTEL $$

(☎129-42-31; Av Independencia 907; s/d M$550/650; ❄🛜) Clean and inexpensive option that's close to the *malecón*, clubs and bus station. A deposit of M$100 is required.

✖ Eating

La Paz' restaurant scene has become increasingly sophisticated over the past 10 years and now offers much more than the typical *antojitos* and seafood. Do it yourself with a stroll along the *malecón*, or try the spots below.

La Fonda
MEXICAN $$

(☎125-47-00; cnr Bravo & Revolución; dinner mains M$90-150; ⊙7am-11pm) One of La Paz's old standbys for lovely Mexican fare, set menus in the afternoons, and a variety of specials. Dining in the patio area, with its greenery, is delightful.

TOP SPOTS FOR FANTASTIC FISH TACOS

Simple and versatile, the humble fish taco is Baja's comfort food. Done right they're magical. These spots are all worth seeking out for a taste of this drool-creating classic.

» **El Caballero** (Cabo Pulmo; p724) These come with a homemade salsa that's *picante* (spicy) without being smolderingly hot. Great for snacking after a long, invigorating snorkel.

» **Los Arcos** (Playas de Rosarito; p700) Casual family-run place with guacamole, sour cream and *pico de gallo* (fresh chopped salsa).

» **Super Tacos Baja California** (La Paz; p722) Loads of salsas and crispy golden batter make this joint a La Paz institution.

» **Venado** (Cabo San Lucas; p731) Flaky, moist morsels of fish on corn or flour. Shrimp tacos are just as good.

Super Tacos Baja California　　　TAQUERÍA $

(Hermanos Gonsales; Lerdo de Tejada; tacos M$15-20; ⊙8am-5pm) The delicious fish and shrimp tacos at this popular stand are served with freshly made salsas. As with potato chips, it's hard to eat just one. It is conveniently located just outside the Pensión California.

Kiwi　　　MEXICAN, SEAFOOD $$

(✆123-32-82; dinner mains M$90-160, lobster M$350; ⊙8am-midnight Sun-Thu, to 2am Fri & Sat) Touristy, but this is the only restaurant on the ocean side of the *malecón,* between Calle 5 de Mayo and Constitución. It offers great views you can enjoy while eating decent Mexican and American fare.

La Boheme　　　FRENCH, FUSION $$

(✆125-60-80; Esquerro 10; dinner mains M$98-275; ⊙4-11pm) La Boheme's courtyard and historic building make it the perfect spot for a glass of wine or a candlelit dinner.

 Drinking & Entertainment

Many watering holes are within stumbling distance of the *malecón,* where travelers sometimes practice their drunken-sailor routine. La Boheme is a good place for unwinding with a glass of red or maybe a hand-muddled mojito.

Las Varitas　　　NIGHTCLUB

(✆125-20-25; Av Independencia 111; admission M$50-100; ⊙9pm-late Thu-Sat) One of the few spots near the *malecón* with live music and groups that come from all over Mexico. *Banda* – with its 10-person bands dressed in crimson tuxedos – is taken very seriously. Don't plan on coming if you're not prepared to take it seriously, too.

 Shopping

Local stores that cater to tourists have plenty of junk and a smattering of good stuff. **Antigua California** (✆125-52-30; Paseo Obregón 220; ⊙9:30am-8:30pm) features a wide selection of crafts from throughout the country. **Allende Books** (✆125-91-14; http://allendebooks.com; Av Independencia 518; ⊙10am-6pm Mon-Sat) is a lovely English-language bookstore with a good selection of books on Baja California and mainland Mexico.

 Information

Most banks (most with ATMs) and *casas de cambio* are on or around Calle 16 de Septiembre.

Cafe El Callejón (✆125-40-06; Callejón La Paz 51; per hr M$15;☎) Also a restaurant, the Callejón has wi-fi which guests can use for free if they're eating or drinking.

Hospital Salvatierra (✆178-05-01; Av Paseo de los Deportistas 5115; ⊙24hr) The largest hospital in southern Baja and one of the best in Mexico, with some English-speaking staff. Near the Plaza Civica.

Main post office (cnr Calles Constitución & Revolución; ⊙8am-3pm Mon-Fri, 9am-1pm Sat)

State tourist information booth (✆122-59-39; cnr Paseo Obregón & Bravo; ⊙8am-10pm) Brochures and pamphlets are available in English. Some of the staff speak English too.

Tourist police (✆122-59-39, 078; ⊙8am-10pm) Small booth on Paseo Obregón; hours may vary.

Viva La Paz (www.vivalapaz.com) La Paz' official tourism site.

 Getting There & Away

Air

Aeropuerto General Manuel Márquez de León (✆124-63-36; Transpeninsular Km 9) is about 13km southwest of the city. It has an **immigration office** (✆124-63-49; ⊙7am-11pm).

Aeroméxico (☏122-00-91; Paseo Obregón) has flights every day but Sunday between La Paz and Los Angeles, and daily flights to Tijuana and mainland Mexican cities.

The airport is also served by Delta, Alaska and Aéreo Calafia airlines.

Boat

Ferries to Mazatlán and Topolobampo leave the ferry terminal at Pichilingue, 23km north of La Paz. **Baja Ferries** (☏town 123-66-00, port 125-63-24; www.bajaferries.com; Allende 1025; ☉8am-5pm Mon-Fri, 8am-2pm Sat) has a small office at the port and a larger office in town.

Ferries to Mazatlán depart at 6pm Tuesday and Thursday and 5pm at Sunday, arriving 16 to 18 hours later; return ferries leave Mazatlán at 4pm Monday, Wednesday and Friday. Passenger fares are M$978/489 per adult/child in *salón* (numbered seats); cabins with two beds and a bath are M$770 extra.

Topolobampo services depart at 2:30pm Monday to Friday and 11pm on Saturday. The return ferry from Topolobampo to La Paz leaves at 11pm Sunday to Friday, arriving in Pichilingue six to seven hours later. Passenger fares are adult/child M$878/439 in *salón;* cabins for up to four people cost M$770 extra.

Make sure that you arrive at the pier a full two hours before departure in order to ensure passage. Vehicle rates include one operator; any other passengers pay separately. Rates vary with vehicle length and destination.

Before shipping any vehicle to the mainland, officials require a vehicle permit. You can obtain one at **Banjército** (www.banjercito.com.mx; ☉7am-3pm Mon, Wed & Fri-Sun, 7am-7pm Tue & Thu) at the ferry terminal, or from its vehicle permit modules in Mexicali or Tijuana. See p740 and p862 for further important information on vehicle permits.

There's an **immigration office** (☏122-04-29; Paseo Obregón; ☉8am-8pm Mon-Fri, 9am-3pm Sat) near the center of town.

Bus

ABC (☏122-78-98) and **Autotransportes Águila** (☏122-78-98) both leave from the **Terminal Turística** (☏122-78-98; cnr malecón & Av Independencia) along the *malecón*. Buses listed in the boxed text p724 leave hourly around the clock.

Autotransportes Águila also operates five daily buses to Playa Tecolote (M$24, 30 minutes) and six to Playa Pichilingue (M$20, 20 minutes) between 10am and 5pm.

❶ Getting Around

Car-rental rates start around M$600 per day. **Budget** (☏122-60-40; cnr Paseo Obregón & Manuel Pineda) is one of several agencies that all have locations both at the airport and along the *malecón*.

Around La Paz

On Península Pichilingue, the beaches nearest to La Paz are **Playa Palmira** (with the Hotel Palmira and a marina), **Playa Coromuel** and **Playa Caimancito** (both with bar-retaurants, toilets and *palapas*). **Playa Tesoro**, the next beach north, has a restaurant. Some 100m north of the ferry terminal is **Playa Pichilingue**, with camping, restaurants, bar, toilets and shade. **Playa Balandra** is a beautiful enclosed cove with shallow azure water, great for snorkeling. The surrounding hillsides, slated to be developed, have been given a reprieve thanks primarily to students and activists who protested in the streets of La Paz and finally got the government's attention. **Playa Tecolote** has plenty of spots where those with cars could camp, and launches leave from here for Espíritu Santo (p719). It's often called the 'best' beach, but car break-ins are common, so leave valuables out of sight.

BAJA CALIFORNIA AROUND LA PAZ

FERRIES FROM LA PAZ

DESTINATION	VEHICLE	FARE (M$)
Mazatlán	car 5m or less	2088
	motorcycle	1768
	motorhome	13,923
Topolobampo	car 5m or less	1928
	motorcycle	1688
	motorhome	7223

BUSES FROM LA PAZ

DESTINATION	FARE (M$)	DURATION
Cabo San Lucas	216	3hr
Ciudad Constitución	296	3hr
Ensenada	1466	20hr
Guerrero Negro	1099	11hr
Loreto	508	5hr
Mulegé	702	6hr
San Ignacio	896	9hr
San José del Cabo	236	3hr
Tijuana	1580	22hr
Todos Santos	71	2hr

La Ventana

📞612 / POP 180

Come to this strip of seaside to watch whale sharks, sea lions, whales, sea turtles and a myriad of fish – without the crowds. Diving is best in the summer when the water visibility reaches 25m or 30m (80ft or 100ft). The same winds that made Los Barriles (p724) a windsurfing mecca also blow here.

Quiet, *palapa*-style *cabañas* at **Palapas Ventana** (📞114-01-98; www.palapasventana.com; cabañas incl breakfast M$1430-2015; P🐕❄@📶) include hearty, home-style breakfasts that hit the spot. It outfits for diving, snorkeling, windsurfing, kitesurfing, sportfishing, hikes to petroglyphs and just about anything else available...there's even Negra Modelo on tap! Discounts are offered for groups.

Las Palmas (🕐8am-9pm) is a two-story seafood and Mexican spot right on the water.

Los Barriles

📞624 / POP 1100

South of La Paz, the Transpeninsular brushes the gulf at Los Barriles, where brisk winter westerlies, averaging 20 to 25 knots, making this Baja's windsurfing capital. The lack of breaking waves is what makes the entire coastline so spectacular. From April to August the winds die down, making windsurfing impossible.

Vela Windsurf (www.velawindsurf.com) is one of many beachside places that rent gear and offer lessons.

Hotel Los Barriles (📞141-00-24; www.losbarrileshotel.com; 20 de Noviembre s/n; s/d US$60/73; P🐕❄📶🐕) is a laid-back place offering clean, aging rooms. Prices rise during the Christmas/New Year holiday.

Get your morning latte fix at **Caleb's Cafe** (📞141-03-30; Barriles s/n; mains M$60-120; 🕐7am-2pm Tue-Sun). Some travelers say Caleb's gooey, buttery sticky buns are the only thing worth stopping for in Barriles.

El Barrelito (📞124-80-94; 20 de Noviembre 78; 🕐11am-9:30pm Thu-Tue) is a casual spot with bright colors and plastic chairs. The chef worked in Cabo for years prior to opening his own place here.

Fairly good dirt roads follow the coast south to San José del Cabo. Beyond Cabo Pulmo and Bahía Los Frailes, they are sandy but passable for most vehicles, but are impassable for RVs and may be difficult for any vehicles after rainstorms. This road offers awesome glimpses of the coast, Shipwreck Point, and the 'green' desertscape, but see it now before the condos, villas and timeshares block the view.

Cabo Pulmo

📞624 / POP 58

If you're looking for snorkeling or diving without the crowds, slip away from the rowdier southern neighbors and come to Cabo Pulmo, a national marine park that's home to the only Pacific coral reef in the Sea of Cortez. You don't need a 4WD to enjoy the drive out here along the spectacular East Cape (from the south) coastal road or through the Sierra de la Laguna (to the west). Unfortunately, much of the surrounding land is slated for development, which will lead to sedimentary erosion that will likely kill or permanently alter the reef. Visit *pronto*...there's little time to waste.

Cabo Pulmo refers to both the park and the tiny village where the following establishments are located. There is no regular phone service here, or internet, so plan on making most arrangements after you arrive.

Snorkel right from the beach at Los Arbolitos, or follow the shoreline hiking trail to Las Sirenitas, where wind and wave erosion has made the rocks look like melting wax sculptures. Eerie and beautiful, they're accessible by boat as well.

Offshore snorkeling, diving and sea-lion colony trips can be booked either through your hotel or in person when you arrive.

Nancy's B&B (☎in the US 617-524-4440; cabañas with/without bathroom US$60/50; ℗) is simply furnished, quiet and has great mattresses. Nearby is El Caballero (meals M$110-180; ☉7am-10pm Fri-Wed), which has fantastic Mexican meals at very reasonable prices.

Reserva de la Biosfera Sierra de la Laguna

Hardcore backpackers can strap on their hiking boots, fill their water bottles and head into the uninterrupted wilds of the lush and rugged Sierra de la Laguna biosphere reserve, south of the intersection of the Transpeninsular and Hwy 19. This is not a place for inexperienced hikers, or for anyone unfamiliar with the unique challenges presented by desert trails, but the rewards are great: stunning vistas, close encounters with wildlife that just don't happen elsewhere, and a unique meadow that was once a lake bed, from which the area gets its name. Be careful and alert: hikers are sometimes targets of cougar attacks, and medical attention is a long way away should something befall you on the trail. Baja Sierra Adventures (☎624-166-87-06; www.bajasierradventures.com), in a tiny ranch called El Chorro, offers a variety of day and overnight trips, biking and trekking through this unique region. Palapas Ventana (p724) is another option for tours to this region.

San José del Cabo

☎624 / POP 38,000

San José del Cabo is quiet and peaceful, the 'mild' sister of 'wild' Cabo San Lucas. San José offers quiet shopping, an attractive plaza, a beautiful church and excellent dining opportunities.

The Fiesta de San José, on March 19, celebrates the town's patron saint.

◉ Sights & Activities

San José del Cabo consists of San José proper, about 1.5km inland, and a Zona Hotelera with large beachfront hotels, condos and eyesores, er, timeshares. Linking the two areas, just south of shady Plaza Mijares, Blvd Mijares is a tourist zone of restaurants and souvenir shops.

Iglesia San José   CHURCH
The colonial-style Iglesia San José, built to replace the 1730 Misión San José del Cabo, faces the spacious Plaza Mijares.

Arroyo San José   RIVER
Between raids on Spanish galleons, 18th-century pirates are rumored to have taken refuge at the Arroyo San José, now a protected wildlife area replenished by a subterranean spring. A riverside Paseo del Estero (Marshland Trail) runs parallel to Blvd Mijares all the way to the Zona Hotelera.

Beaches   BEACH
The best beaches for swimming are along the road to Cabo San Lucas. Playa Santa María at Km 13 is one of the nicest beaches in Los Cabos.

⊨ Sleeping

During the peak winter months, it's a good idea to make reservations. Free camping is possible at Pueblo La Playa, east of the center.

Casa Natalia   BOUTIQUE HOTEL $$$
(☎146-71-00; www.casanatalia.com; Blvd Mijares 4; d/ste with spa US$186/397; ❄❋🛜🏊) The posh Natalia opens onto San José's plaza and, in addition to the pool, has shuttles to its beachside club. The walk-in bathrooms are big enough to live in. Prices rise during holidays.

Hotel Colli   HOTEL $$
(☎142-07-25; Hidalgo s/n; d/tr M$650/850; ℗❄❋🛜) Friendly and family owned for three generations, the nicely remodeled Colli is clean, cozy, safe, inexpensive, and only steps away from the plaza.

Posada Terranova   HOTEL $$
(☎142-05-34; Degollado s/n; d M$700; ℗❄❋@🛜) There's art on the walls, it's clean and it has views of the pueblo from some rooms. It also

San José del Cabo

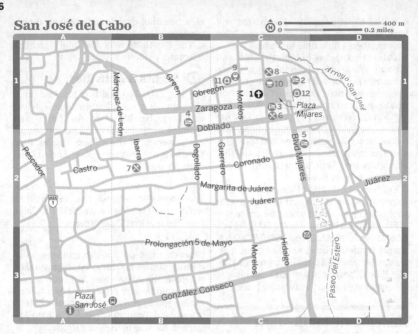

San José del Cabo

has a good restaurant and kind, English-speaking staff.

Tropicana Inn   HOTEL $$$
(☎142-15-80; www.tropicanainn.com.mx; Blvd Mijares 30; d/ste/cabaña M$1584/2112/2232;

❀❄🛋) The spacious rooms here have satellite TV, fridge and a coffeemaker, and the bucolic courtyard has a huge pool and real life parrots. Bring a cracker for Polly. Rates include continental breakfast.

✗ Eating

TOP CHOICE **Mi Cocina**   MEXICAN, FUSION $$$
(☎146-71-00; Blvd Mijares 4; dinner mains M$190-260; ☯3:30-10:30pm Wed-Mon) Set inside the beautiful Casa Natalia hotel, Mi Cocina is as classy a spot to dine as San José gets. The decor is artful, the entrees sublime, and desserts (such as vanilla flan or basil ice cream!) are creative and mouthwatering.

French Riviera   BAKERY, CAFE $$
(☎142-33-50; www.frenchrivieraloscabos.com; cnr Hidalgo & Doblado; pastries M$35, mains M$380; ☯7am-11pm) A delightful French-inspired spot with tasty breads and pastries, *gelati* (ice cream) that hits the spot on a hot day, and excellent dinners. The continental decor is tasteful and romantic.

Salsitas   MEXICAN, BAR $$
(☎142-67-87; Obregón 1732; mains M$65-130) A nice place to beat the heat with a margarita and *antojitos*. Leather-backed chairs lend it additional class.

Mercado Municipal   MARKET $

(Ibarra) Between Calles Coronado and Castro, this clean market has numerous stalls offering simple and inexpensive but good, filling meals.

Drinking

Head to Cabo San Lucas if you're looking for nightlife. San José del Cabo is almost mousey in comparison, but the plaza often has festivals or events; check with your hotel concierge or ask around.

La Dolce   WINE BAR

(☏142-66-21; www.ladolcerestaurant.com; Plaza Mijares; ⏱1-10:30pm Tue-Sun) Right on the plaza, this is a good spot for that evening glass of wine. The owner's wife does the artwork that's on display.

Baja Brewing Co   BREWERY

(☏146-99-95; www.bajabrewingcompany.com; Morelos 1227) A pub-style environment offering local microbrews. The Peyote Pale Ale isn't hallucinogenic, but it's darn good.

🛍 Shopping

Blvd Mijares is a good place to start. the area from Calles Obregón to Degollado is the self-proclaimed art district with numerous galleries, studios and stores. The district has an Art Walk on Thursdays from 5pm to 9pm, with dancing, open studios, wine tasting and more.

Copal   HANDICRAFTS

(☏105-20-17; Plaza Mijares 10; ⏱9am-8pm Mon-Sat, 10am-6pm Sun) On the east side of Plaza Mijares, Copal has an interesting assortment of crafts, jewelry, rugs and masks.

Cochi Art Gallery   GALLERY

(☏127-47-02; cnr Obregón & Morelos;⏱9am-6pm Mon-Sat) One of many nice galleries in the art district, with paintings and sculpture by an Oaxacan artisan.

ℹ Information

Several *casas de cambio* here keep long hours. Banks pay better rates but keep shorter hours.

Bancomer (cnr Calles Zaragoza & Morelos) Cashes traveler's checks and has an ATM.

IMSS Hospital (☏nonemergency 142-00-76, emergency 142-01-80; cnr Calles Hidalgo & Coronado)

Post office (Blvd Mijares 1924; ⏱8am-6pm Mon-Fri)

Secretaria Municipal de Turismo (☏142-29-60 ext 150; Transpeninsular; ⏱8am-5pm Mon-Sat) Has a stock of brochures and maps on hand.

Tourist Aid (☏078)

ℹ Getting There & Away

Air

All airline offices are at **San José del Cabo airport** (☏146-51-11), north of San José del Cabo, which serves both San José del Cabo and Cabo San Lucas. Timeshare touts congregate at the entrance and many offer free transportation to your hotel, but you are best off taking a normal taxi van for M$150 per person.

Aéreo Calafia (☏143-43-02) Flies to Los Mochis, Loreto and Mazatlán.

Aeroméxico (☏146-50-98) Flies daily to and from Los Angeles and to many mainland Mexican destinations, with international connections via Mexico City.

Alaska Airlines (☏146-51-06) Flies to and from Los Angeles, San Diego, San Francisco and San Jose in California, and Phoenix.

American (☏146-53-00) Flies daily to Los Angeles and Dallas.

Continental Airlines (☏146-50-50, in the US 800-900-5000) Flies to and from Houston and, during the high season, Newark.

Bus

Buses depart from the **main bus terminal** (☏130-73-39; González Conseco s/n), east of the Transpeninsular.

BUSES FROM SAN JOSÉ DEL CABO

DESTINATION	FARE (M$)	DURATION
Barriles	77	1½hr
Cabo San Lucas	19	1hr
Ensenada	1664	24hr
La Paz	236	3hr
Tijuana	1778	28hr

Car & Motorcycle

The usual agencies rent from the airport – rates start at about M$600 per day and are cheaper with an internet reservation. Also try **National Car Rental** (142-24-24; Blvd Mijares).

ⓘ Getting Around

Taxi drivers are required by law to display a sanctioned price list. The official government-run company runs bright-yellow taxis and minibuses to the airport for about M$240. Local buses from the main bus terminal to the airport junction cost less than M$25, but taking one means a half-hour walk to the air terminal. The toll road from the Transpeninsular to the airport costs M$27.

Los Cabos Corridor

Nowhere in Baja is the desert disappearing faster than in the Los Cabos 'Corridor,' the strip of coast between San José del Cabo and Cabo San Lucas – in its place, cookie-cutter resorts, American chain stores, aquifer-depleting golf courses and all-inclusive hotels line the once-spectacular coastline.

Experienced surfers claim that summer reef and point breaks at Costa Azul (aka Zippers) match Hawaii's best. The reefs off Playa Chileno are excellent for diving.

Playa Santa María, at Km 13, is one of the nicest for swimming.

Cabo San Lucas

📞 624 / POP 46,000

Come to Cabo expecting to toss your inhibitions to the wind – everyone else does. Where else do clubs round up conga lines so that waiters can pour tequila down dancers' throats? And where else would that seem normal? Those moments of absurdity and abandon notwithstanding, Cabo San Lucas has a curious charm. The beaches are protected by beautiful Land's End, and the activities are endless: Jet-skiing, banana boating, parasailing, snorkeling, kite sailing, diving and horseback riding can all be done just by walking down to the beach. If you rent a car and get outside the city limits you'll be surrounded by majestic cardón cacti, caracara birds and mystical *arroyos* that will impress you just as much as that crazy club ('I did *what* last night?!') you partied at the night before.

◉ Sights

Northwest of Blvd Cárdenas, tourist Cabo has a fairly regular grid; southeast of Blvd Cárdenas, Blvd Marina curves along the Bahía de Cabo San Lucas toward Land's End

Cabo San Lucas

(Finisterra), the tip of the peninsula where the Pacific Ocean and the Sea of Cortez meet.

Land's End
LANDMARK

Land's End is by far the most impressive attraction Cabo has to offer. Get on a *panga* (M$130) and head to **El Arco** (the Arch), a jagged natural feature which partially fills with the tide. Pelicans, sea lions, sea, sky – this is what brought people to Cabo in the first place and it's still magical, despite the mammoth cruise ships towering behind it.

Beaches
BEACH

For sunbathing and calm waters **Playa Medano**, in front of what once was the Hacienda Beach Resort on the Bahía de Cabo San Lucas, is ideal. **Playa Solmar**, on the Pacific, is pretty but has a reputation for dangerous breakers and rip tides. Nearly unspoiled **Playa del Amor** (Lover's Beach) shouldn't be missed; near Land's End, it is accessible by boat (M$130 round trip). Appropriately, **Playa del Divorcio** (Divorce Beach) is nearby, across the point on the Pacific side.

🏃 Activities

The best diving areas are **Roca Pelícano**, the sea-lion colony off Land's End, and the reef off **Playa Chileno**, at Bahía Chileno east of town. Two-tank dives cost around M$1100 and full-certification courses are M$4000 or

higher. **Cabo Acuadeportes** (☑143-01-17; ⊗9am-6pm), at Playa Medano, is the largest water-sports outfitter, but there are numerous alternatives.

Surprisingly good snorkeling can be done right from Playa del Amor, swimming left, toward the marina. A mask, snorkel and fins should run about M$150 per day. *Panga* rides cost about M$120 for a round trip if you bargain directly with a captain. Tipping is expected.

☞ Tours

Ecocat
BOAT

(☑157-46-85; www.caboecotours.com; dock N-12; ⊗6-8:30pm Mon-Sat) Offers two-hour sunset sailing (US$40), snorkeling and whale-watching tours, and also plays host to a variety of other options off its giant catamaran. Check the web for discounts.

La Princesa
BOAT

(☑143-76-76; info@cabosports.com; dock M-O; tours M$400) Located behind Hotel Costa Real, this outfit offers sunset booze trips along with other daytime packages.

✸✸ Festivals & Events

Fishing Tournaments
FISHING

Cabo San Lucas is a popular staging ground for fishing tournaments in October and November. The main events are the **Gold Cup**, **Bisbee's Black & Blue Marlin Jackpot** and the **Cabo Tuna Jackpot**.

Sammy Hagar's Birthday Party
DANCE

Held in early October, this is a major Cabo event with lots of drinking and dancing. Invitations (free) are required – try concierges at the bigger hotels or look out for giveaways. Bring your liver and prepare to punish it.

Día de San Lucas
RELIGIOUS

A local celebration held on October 18, honoring the town's patron saint, with fireworks, food stalls, dancing and (of course) partying.

🛏 Sleeping

Cabo has plenty of accommodation in many price categories, starting at pricey and ending with 'it costs *what* per night?' If you want something on a true backpacker budget, you'll need to sleep in an unlocked car.

[TOP CHOICE] **Bungalows Breakfast Inn**   B&B $$$
(☑143-05-85; www.thebungalowshotel.com; cnr Libertad & Herrera; bungalows incl breakfast

CABO IN...

Two Days

Take a *panga* to **Playa del Amor** and see **El Arco** at the same time. Laze for a while or snorkel, then head back for grub or a margarita. Get tipsy on a gorgeous **sunset tour** and then finish the job at **El Squid Roe**. Then choose between quiet shopping at **San José del Cabo** or something active: surfing at **Los Cerritos** or diving at **Cabo Pulmo**.

Four Days

Four days gives you all of the above. Or you could rent yourself some wheels and do a loop of the southern Cape. Start heading east, through **San José del Cabo** and take in the awesome scenery of the east Cape, one of Baja's best unbeaten paths. Stay in **Cabo Pulmo** for snorkeling and diving, then cruise north on day two to **La Paz**. Hikers will want to see the **Sierra de la Laguna**. Spend day three in the chi-chi galleries and great restaurants of **Todos Santos** or **surfing**. Head back to Cabo San Lucas on day four and end with a fancy meal at **La Fonda** or a relaxing **sunset tour**.

US$95-195, ste incl breakfast US$145-210; P ⊖ ❄ 🛜 🏊) Extremely attentive service, delicious breakfasts, tastefully furnished rooms, fragrant palm-thatched *palapas,* hammocks and an expansive swimming pool set this B&B apart. Fresh-fruit smoothies, fruit juices, excellent coffee and warm, welcoming bilingual staff make the bungalows feel like home. Beautiful handmade soaps are one of the many tiny details that makes this *the* place to splurge. Note that US dollars are preferred here.

Hotel Los Milagros HOTEL $$$
(☎143-45-66, in USA 718-928-6647; www.losmilagros.com.mx; Matamoros 116; d M$1100-1650; P❄🛜🏊) The tranquil courtyard and 12 unique rooms provide a perfect escape from Cabo's excesses. A desert garden (complete with resident iguanas), a beautiful deep-blue pool, and friendly, courteous service make a stay here unforgettable. The place can also be rented in its entirety for groups, such as weddings or birthday parties.

Hotel Olas HOTEL $
(☎143-17-80; cnr Revolución & Farias s/n; r M$400; P❄🛜) The safe, secure, Hotel Olas has clean and simple rooms and is by far the best Cabo deal pricewise. The grandfatherly owner has a wealth of information about Baja and speaks some English. Giant clam shells and other maritime items add to the courtyard decor.

Hotel Oasis HOTEL $
(☎143-20-98; Carretera a Todos Santos s/n; d/q M$430/530; P❄🛜🏊) Only a stone's throw from the bus station (though far from the tourist zone), the shockingly peach Oasis offers clean doubles or quads at rates that are hard to ignore. You can even swim with a 'killer whale' in the oversize pool. Note that there's a M$70 deposit for the TV remote. Only a stone's throw south of the bus station.

Hotel Wilkes HOTEL $$
(☎105-07-11; cnr Cabo San Lucas & 5 de Mayo; s/d/ste M$570/798/1130) The cute and cozy Wilkes has white wrought-iron railings and rooms that are so spacious they feel empty. Verdant potted plants and proximity to Cabo's excesses are additional pluses.

✗ Eating

Cabo's culinary scene features a great variety of eateries, from humble taco stands to gourmet restaurants. As always, avoid the places touting two-for-one freebies or other gimmicks to get you to go there.

La Fonda MEXICAN $$$
(☎143-69-26; cnr Hidalgo & Obregón; dishes M$140-250; ⊙2-10:30pm Mon-Sun) Has superb Mexican cuisine that's worlds away from the typical *antojitos* – try the cream of *poblano* soup with pumpkin flowers or the *huitlacoche* (corn mushroom) stuffed chicken. The Don Julio margarita vies for the title of the best in Baja.

Los Ajos MEXICAN $$
(☎143-77-06; Blvd Cárdenas btwn Vicario & Mendoza; breakfast M$30-140, buffet M$99; ⊙7am-2am Tue-Sun, to 7pm Mon) This casual, clean, family-run place has great breakfasts and an inexpensive lunch and dinner buffet. Look for the large ceramic chef outside the door.

Venado

TAQUERÍA $

(☑147-69-21; Niños Héroes btwn Zaragoza & Morelos; dinner mains M$50-90; ☉11am-7am) Open all night and packed from 3am until dawn, Venado has delicious fish tacos, fresh salsas and other *antojitos*. If it's slow, the friendly waitresses might drop a coin in the jukebox and invite you to dance.

Pancho's

MEXICAN, BAR $$$

(☑143-28-91; www.panchos.com; cnr Hidalgo & Zapata; dinner mains M$220-300, lobster M$420, tequila tasting M$700) Offers 'all you want to know about tequila' in a festive atmosphere. Aromas from the open grill mix with the mariachi band's tunes. The tequila tasting is like an intensive tequila class, with inebriation in place of a graduation certificate.

 ## Drinking

Cabo is a proud party town, and alcoholic revelry is encouraged all day long. The following places are all open well into the wee hours.

Cabo Wabo Cantina

CLUB, LIVE MUSIC, DANCING

(☑143-11-88; cnr Calles Guerrero & Madero) Much like a college frat party, only everyone's older. And drunker.

Slim's Elbow Room

BAR

(Blvd Marina s/n; ☉10am-midnight Mon-Sun) In the shadow of Cabo Wabo, this teeny, easy-to-miss watering hole wallpapered in dollar bills and clients' signatures claims to be the world's smallest bar. With four seats inside and two standing spaces, it's a contender for sure. A shot of the vanilla liqueur is well worth the price tag.

Mango Deck

CLUB

(☑144-49-19; Playa Medano) Great for people-watching and a sunset margarita, and the beach doesn't get any closer. There's even a mechanical bull if you're feeling like a mouthful of sand.

El Squid Roe

CLUB, DANCING

(☑143-12-69; cnr Blvd Cárdenas & Zaragoza) Crazy. Just crazy. Jello shooters, tequila congo lines. Waiters (and drunk clientele) dance on tabletops to cheering crowds.

 ## Shopping

Mercado Mexicano

MARKET

(cnr Madero & Hidalgo) Cabo's most comprehensive shopping area is this sprawling market that contains dozens of stalls with crafts from all around the country.

 ## Information

It's an indication of who calls the shots here that Cabo has no government-sanctioned tourist offices. The 'info' booths you'll see are owned by timeshares, condos and hotels. The staff are friendly and can offer maps and info, but their only pay comes from commissions from selling timeshare visits: expect a firm, sometimes desperate, pitch for you to visit model homes. Be warned – the promised freebies are rarely worth wasting precious vacation time, and touts have gotten more aggressive with the downturn in the economy.

Internet cafes with DSL or broadband now abound and many hotels have lobby computers the public can use. Rates are, not surprisingly, cheaper as you go further away from the water. Banks will cash travelers checks and have ATMs.

All About Cabo (www.allaboutcabo.com) A useful site for visitors.

AmeriMed American Hospital (☑143-96-70; Blvd Cárdenas) Near Paseo de la Marina.

Bancomer (cnr Blvd Cárdenas & Paseo San José)

InternetPuntoCom (☑144-41-90; cnr Vicarío & 20 de Noviembre; per hr M$25)

Post office (Blvd Cárdenas; ☉8am-4pm Mon-Fri) Near Calle 20 de Noviembre.

Tourist Assistance (☑078)

Getting There & Away

There's an **immigration office** (☑143-01-35; cnr Blvd Cárdenas & Farías; ☉9am-1pm Mon-Sat) near the center.

Air

The closest airport is San José del Cabo (p727).

Bus

Bus service to and from Cabo is provided by **Águila** (☑143-78-80; Hwy 19; ☉24hr), located at the Todos Santos crossroad, north of downtown. Be aware that the bus station is about a 40-minute walk northwest from the tourist zone/waterfront.

From a terminal near the Águila station, **Autotransportes de La Paz** (☑105-19-68; cnr Morelos & Ocampo; ☉5am-9pm) has eight daily La Paz buses (M$150, three hours).

Car & Motorcycle

Numerous car-rental agencies have booths along Paseo de la Marina and elsewhere in town. **National** (☑143-14-14; Blvd Cárdenas) offers rentals starting at M$60 per day.

Getting Around

The **airport shuttle bus** (☑146-53-93; per person M$150) leaves every two hours (10am

BUSES FROM CABO SAN LUCAS

DESTINATION	FARE (M$)	DURATION
La Paz	191-216	3hr
Loreto	725	8hr
San José del Cabo	19	1hr
Tijuana	1744	27hr
Todos Santos	88-104	1hr

to 4pm) from Plaza Bonita or Plaza Náutica. Cab van fares within town range from M$70 to M$100, and a taxi to the airport is M$800. The airport shuttle vans (M$150) can drop you off at your hotel. Avoid rides offered by the timeshare touts.

Todos Santos

📞 612 / POP 4700

Todos Santos is one of the most unique towns in all of Baja, maybe even all of Mexico. A quirky mix of locals, fishermen, surfers and New Age spiritualists, the town of 'All Saints' has thus far escaped the rampant tourism of the other Cape towns but still has all kinds of things to see and do. Perhaps it's just that all the 'lines of convergence,' uh, converge here. Think Taos, New Mexico, before Ansel Adams and Georgia O'Keefe brought the world there.

Todos Santos' newfound prosperity does not reflect its history. Founded in 1723, but nearly destroyed by the Pericú rebellion in 1734, Misión Santa Rosa de Todos los Santos limped along until its abandonment in 1840. In the late 19th century Todos Santos became a prosperous sugar town with several brick *trapiches* (mills), but depleted aquifers have nearly eliminated this thirsty industry. The crumbling, photo-worthy brick structures still remain in several parts of town.

Like many other parts of Baja, Todos Santos is changing. A new four-lane highway will make it easier to zip up from Cabo, and local development (even an 18-hole golf course, as if the gazillion in the Cabo Corridor aren't enough) is rampant. So come here now before it changes forever.

👁 Sights & Activities

Trapiches   LANDMARK
Scattered around town are several former *trapiches,* including **Molino El Progreso,**

the ruin of what was formerly El Molino restaurant, and **Molino de los Santana** on Juárez, opposite the hospital. The restored **Teatro Cine General Manuel Márquez de León** is on Legaspi, facing the plaza.

Centro Cultural   MUSEUM
(📞145-00-41; Juárez; admission free, donation encouraged; ⏰8am-8pm Mon-Fri, 9am-4pm Sat & Sun) Housed in a former schoolhouse, the Centro Cultural, near Topete, is home to some interesting nationalist and revolutionary murals dating from 1933. Also on display is an uneven collection of artifacts evoking the history of the region, lots of old photos and a replica ranch house.

Surfing   SURFING
Surfers come here for some of the nicest swells in all of Baja. **San Pedrito** offers Hawaii-like tubes (and Hawaii-like sea urchins if you wipe out). Catch that perfect wave as eagle rays glide below you, or just hang out with the mellow crowd on **Los Cerritos** and watch the coral sun plunge into the Pacific. Boards can be rented for M$150 per day at Pescadero Surf Camp (p733), near the beaches. Mario Beceril's **Mario Surf School** (📞142-61-56; www.mariosurfschool.com) offers excellent lessons for all levels in the Todos Santos and Pescadero area.

Punta Lobos   FISHING, HIKING
This point, named for the sea-lion colony here, is where the fishermen launch *pangas.* It's just a sandy beach and a bit out of the way, but anywhere from 1pm to about 3pm you can come and bargain for just-off-the-boat fish to cook at home. Pelicans joust for scraps, and a nice hiking trail winds up the point to an unparalleled lookout spot.

🎊 Festivals & Events

Todos Santos' two-day **Festival de Artes** is held in early February. At other times it's possible to visit local artists in their home studios, and there are galleries galore.

🛌 Sleeping

TOP CHOICE Posada La Poza SUITES $$$
(☎145-04-00; www.lapoza.com; ste incl breakfast US$210-520; P🐕❄🛜🏊) Boasting 'Mexican hospitality combined with Swiss quality,' this beautiful boutique retreat is right on the Pacific. A saltwater swimming pool, freshwater lagoon, lush garden and superb restaurant with excellent Mexican wines set it apart. A Mexican sweat lodge and saltwater Jacuzzi offer alternate ways to let stress slip away. There are no TVs or phones in the unique, one-of-a-kind rooms, but you will find a pair of binoculars and even a bird book. Rowboat use, bikes and fishing gear are always included. Prices may be lower in the off-season.

Casa Bentley HOTEL $$$
(☎145-02-76; www.casabentleybaja.com; Calle del Pilar 38; r M$1300-2340) A completely unique place built by hand by the owner, Bob Bentley, this castle-like hotel offers beautiful rooms and giant mango trees that seem plucked from a movie set. Bob is a wealth of local knowledge and lore, in part because he moved here when Todos Santos was a one-horse town.

Pescadero Surf Camp CABAÑAS $
(☎130-30-32; www.pescaderosurf.com; casita M$400-550, penthouse M$750, campsites per person M$120) Friendly and helpful, Pescadero Surf Camp has everything a surfer could need – rentals, lessons, advice, a community kitchen and even a BYO swim-up bar. It also sells art supplies.

Hotel California HOTEL $$$
(☎145-05-25; Juárez s/n; r M$1491-2915) Of the three (or more) Hotel Californias in Baja, this one has capitalized on the legendary Eagles song the most. The bar is open later than most spots in Todos Santos, and it is a good spot to meet and mingle.

Motel Guluarte MOTEL $
(☎145-00-06; cnr Juárez & Morelos; s/d M$350/450; P❄) This breezy, whitewashed budget option with laundromat has small rooms with refrigerators and a shared balcony. No pets allowed.

Bungalows Ziranda MOTEL $
(☎130-30-77; elpescaderohotel ziranda@hotmail.com; Pescadero s/n; r M$450; P@) Kitchenettes here are anything but fancy; however, this place is well located for surfers or beachgoers on a budget. It also has a restaurant and internet cafe.

✖ Eating

Taco stands, along Heróico Colegio Militar between Márquez de León and Degollado, offer cheap eats. Beware the places that charge M$90 for a bagel and head instead to these spots.

TOP CHOICE Café Santa Fe ITALIAN $$$
(☎145-03-40; Centenario 4; dinner mains M$180-440; ⊙Wed-Mon) The *insalata Mediterranea* (steamed seafood drizzled in lemon juice and oil) will make even seafood haters change their evil ways. The open-air kitchen,

---

SURF'S UP

Baja is a prime surfer's paradise with swells coming in off the Pacific that, even on bad days, are challenging and fun. Boards can be rented from surf shops (rental costs around M$250), but use extreme care at all times, as rips, undertow and behemoth waves are dangerous even for experienced surfers. If you're looking for good breaks, check out the following:

» **Costa Azul** (p728) Needs southerly swell, but this intermediate break is a whole lot of fun and it's close to either of the Cabos.

» **Los Cerritos** (p732) Beautiful sand, nice waves, mellow vibe – this is a great beginner beach with a powerful Pacific swell...and eagle rays below.

» **San Miguel** (p701) Rocky point break that offers awesome rides when the waves are big. Isla de Todos Santos is another option for the serious.

For more info on surfing, check out the no-nonsense, brown-and-black-covered *Surfer's Guide to Baja* by Mike Parise. For surf lessons, contact Mario Surf School (p732).

designed by the owner himself, allows you to see the food as it's being prepped for your table. Anything on the menu will delight, surprise and tantalize, but if you need suggestions go for the mussels in wine or any one of the various handmade raviolis: lobster, *carne* (meat) or just spinach and ricotta cheese. This is surely one of the best restaurants in Baja and is well worth the splurge.

La Esquina CAFE **$$**
(☎145-08-51; cnr Topete & Horizante; mains M$60-110; ⊙7am-7pm Mon-Sat;☎) The best part about finding La Esquina is that you get to say 'Where is Casa Dracula?' and nobody will look at you strangely (La Esquina is on the opposite corner). A 15-minute walk from the town center will bring you to everything that a coffee shop should be: a community meeting spot and great place to hang out, with free wi-fi, good coffee and food, and friendly service. Get your cup of joe, kick back on the sofas and start making friends.

El Gusto! FUSION, MEXICAN **$$$**
(☎145-04-00; Posada La Poza; mains M$180-240, specials M$350; ⊙lunch & dinner Fri-Wed) Reservations are recommended at this beautiful restaurant, which was recently voted a top place to watch a Pacific sunset – sip a margarita on the terrace or in the beautifully decorated dining area. In season, whales head by as you eat. The extensive wine list is made up of Mexico's finest – selected with care by the owner himself.

Ristorante Tre Galline MEXICAN **$$**
(☎145-02-74; cnr Topete & Juarez; dinner mains M$140-320; ⊙noon-10pm Mon-Sat) Though it's on the pricey side, this attractive, candlelit restaurant has tables arranged on descending terraces giving everyone a little more privacy. Seafood platters are scrumptious.

🔒 Shopping

There are numerous galleries to wander through, especially around the plaza. Do it yourself on this one. The lack of touts is a refreshing change from TJ or Cabo.

Got Baja? SOUVENIRS
(☎178-00-67; www.gotbajamaps.com; Juárez s/n btwn Hidalgo & Topete; ⊙10am-6pm) Created by local artists/entrepreneurs, Got Baja? has cute souvenirs (such as chalkboard piggy banks) and T-shirts with catchy, classy, funky designs.

❶ Information

Banorte (cnr Juárez & Obregón) Exchanges cash and travelers checks and has an ATM.
Cafélix (☎145-05-68; Juárez 4; wi-fi free with purchase; ⊙8am-9pm) Wi-fi, in addition to great coffee and yummy sandwiches.
El Tecolote (☎145-02-95; cnr Juárez & Av Hidalgo) The town lacks an official tourist office, but this English-language bookstore has magazines with town maps and a sketch map of nearby beach areas. Pick up a copy of *GotBaja-Maps* for beach maps and current events.
Post office (Villarino btwn Olachéa & Pedrajo)

❶ Getting There & Away

Hourly between 6:30am and 10:30pm, buses head to La Paz (M$71, two hours) and to Cabo San Lucas (M$88, one hour) from the **bus stop** (☎148-02-89; Heróico Colegio Militar; ⊙7am-10pm) between Zaragoza and Morelos.

Copper Canyon & Northern Mexico

Best Places to Eat

» Bonifacio's (p746)

» Teresitas (p749)

» Cenaduría Döna Lola (p749)

» La Casa de los Milagros (p772)

» Los Equipales (p780)

Best Places to Stay

» Hotel Colonial (p748)

» Hotel Río Vista (p756)

» Hotel Paraíso del Oso (p757)

» Hotel Mansión Tarahumara (p759)

» Hotel San Felipe El Real (p771)

Why Go?

Welcome to ultimate frontier land: Mexico's wild north has, for centuries, been frequented by revolutionaries, bandits, law-makers and law-breakers. Landscapes here suit such types: North America's second-largest desert and some of the world's deepest, most spectacular canyons make this perfect territory to hole up in. This is, indeed, quintessential rough-and-ready Wild West: Hollywood filmmakers used dramatic topography here to shoot many fabled Westerns.

Mexico also scatters its paradoxes most thickly in the north. There is the sensational alpine-to-subtropical switch unfolding in the region's set piece, the Copper Canyon, best traversed via Mexico's greatest train ride. The country's most progressive, culturally rich cities are here, as are some of its most non-Westernized indigenous peoples. It boasts the country's best connections to North America and Europe, but secretes its remotest hiking. It's a place where, like desperados of times past, you'll find yourself lingering.

When to Go
Chihuahua

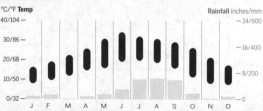

Jun–Jul Heavy rainfall. Key festivals such as Las Jornadas Villistas, commemorating Pancho Villa, in Hidalgo del Parral.

Late Sep–Oct Pleasantly hot during the day. Good time to visit the just-coming-into-bloom Copper Canyon.

Dec–Jan Balmy, dry weather on the Pacific coast makes the region a popular winter escape.

Copper Canyon & Northern Mexico Highlights

1 Wolf down wickedly strong coffee at Café Luz y Sol or enchiladas at Cenaduría Dõna Lola, then walk it off around the colonial streets of the old silver town **Álamos** (p747)

2 Bask in the balmy beach paradise of **Bahía de Kino** (p744)

3 Ride Mexico's last passenger train through mesmerizing canyon scenery

on the **Ferrocarril Chihuahua Pacífico** (p754)

4 Soar on seven zip-lines down the sublimely dramatic Copper Canyon at all-new

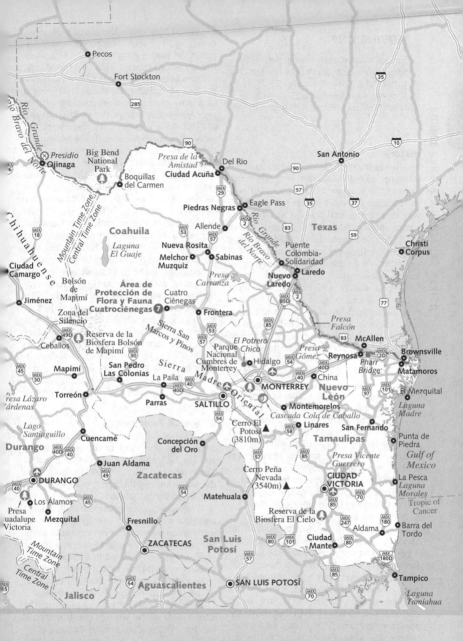

Parque de Aventuras Barrancas del Cobre (p760)

5 Chill in the plunge pool of Mexico's highest full-time waterfall, **Cascada de Basaseachi** (p766)

6 Experience some of Latin America's most masterful ceramics being produced in **Mata Ortiz** (p776)

7 Get up close and personal to the Desierto Chihuahuense

with everything from eclectic ecosystems to *pozas* (natural pools) at **Área de Protección de Flora y Fauna Cuatrociénegas** (p786)

MOVING ON?

For tips, recommendations and reviews, head to shop.lonelyplanet.com to purchase a downloadable PDF of the Arizona, New Mexico and Texas chapters from Lonely Planet's *USA* guide.

History

Pre-Hispanic northern Mexico had more in common with the Anasazi and other cultures of the southwest USA than with central Mexico. The most important town here was Paquimé, a vital trading link between central Mexico and the dry north before its destruction around AD 1340. Outlying Paquimé settlements such as Cuarenta Casas built their dwellings on cliffsides for protection against attack.

Spanish slavers and explorers, arriving chiefly in search of gold in the 16th century, had mixed fortunes in the north. In the northwest they encountered indigenous peoples including the Opata, Seri, Yaqui and Mayo. Rather than the fabled province of Cíbola with its supposed seven cities of gold, the Spanish found silver and, conscripting indigenous people as slave miners, established prosperous mining cities such as Álamos. Spaniards also soon forged the Camino Real de Tierra Adentro (Royal Road of the Interior): a 2560km trade route from Mexico City to Santa Fe, New Mexico, which helped make towns en route such as Durango extremely wealthy. In the northeast, however, harsh conditions and attacks by indigenous Chichimecs and Apaches meant settlement and development came more slowly.

The Spanish never tightened control here sufficiently to quell revolts. In the fight for Mexican Independence (1810), the Mexican–American War of the 1840s and the Mexican Revolution (1910–20) the northern states necessarily played a key role. Frontiers radically changed with Mexico's loss of Texas and New Mexico (1830s–1850s): the Treaty of Guadalupe Hidalgo (1848) that ended the Mexican–American War finally established today's Río Bravo del Norte (Rio Grande) frontier between the two nations.

Glaring inequities of land ownership between the elite – grown wealthy from the mines – and the impoverished majority forced to either mine or farm a barren region for a pittance, contributed to the unrest that made the north a Mexican Revolution hot spot. The revolutionary División del Norte, an army led by legendary Durango-born Pancho Villa (see boxed text, p772), was in the forefront of several major battles. Venustiano Carranza and Álvaro Obregón, other main revolutionary figures, were, respectively, from the northern states of Coahuila and Sonora. All three were initially allies and subsequently enemies in the Revolution, which meant the split of allegiances in the north was acute.

Irrigation programs in the mid-20th century turned Sonora into the granary of Mexico as well as a cattle-ranching center alongside neighboring Chihuahua. Discovery of petroleum, coal and natural gas and the arrival of the railroad also accelerated development from the late 19th century, and the region emerged as an industrial leader.

Today this is the most Americanized part of Mexico, with money and resources surging back-and-forth across the border. The Texan economy is particularly dependent on Mexican workers while US investment was behind most *maquiladoras* (assembly-plant operations) that mushroomed across northern Mexico in the 1990s. Industrial drive in cities here has become the economic focus, at least until tourism recovers from negative publicity as a result of drug cartel violence since 2006.

Dangers & Annoyances

Drug-related violence is worst in Ciudad Juárez, but prevalent in all border towns and (in 2011 and 2012) particularly bad in Monterrey and Tamaulipas. However, with the exception of Monterrey, violence generally occurs far from tourist zones.

While gangs, specifically the Gulf, Sinaloa and Zeta cartels, have been responsible for some gruesome violence in the central north and northeast, most incidents are among Mexicans either involved in the illegal drug trade or in trying to combat it (security/law enforcement). Foreign tourists without such connections are not targeted by assassins.

There is a risk of being caught in the wrong place at the wrong time. However, if you have nothing to do with drugs, stay on the beaten track, take normal precautions against petty crime, don't wander along deserted streets at night and ask about local situations as you travel, you should have a trouble-free trip.

Web resources advising on local security situations exist, although they are updated sporadically, and, as such, can be out of date. The warnings also generally focus on a few specific regions and don't necessarily apply to all of Mexico. The **Trans-border Institute** (http://justiceinmexico.org) provides regular reports on drug violence in Mexico.

If driving, lock up when on the road as well as when parked to guard against car-jackings (which have increased). Care should be taken on roads heading from/to border towns. Other highways with safety concerns are Hwy 49 (Fresnillo–Torreón), 45 (Fresnillo–Durango–Hidalgo del Parral) and 'road of death' (so called because of a spate of car-jackings and violent murders of bus passengers) Hwy 101 in Tamaulipas. Don't drive after dark, especially on these roads.

On top of being a transit zone for US-bound drugs, the region is a cultivation zone for marijuana and (in the Sierra Madre Occidental, which spans parts of Northwest Mexico, the Copper Canyon and parts of Central North Mexico) opium poppies. It is unwise to travel anywhere off-the-beaten-path here without a trusted local guide. See individual sections for region-specific warnings.

ℹ Getting There & Around

Flying into Chihuahua or Hermosillo international airports is currently the safest, most convenient way to enter the region, either via southern Mexico cities or US cities such as Phoenix, Dallas or Los Angeles. Torreón and Monterrey have the other main international airports, and Los Mochis airport has good national connections.

Two ferry crossings link Baja California with northwest Mexico (see boxed text, p748).

Crossing the US–Mexico border overland is easy enough, but comes with associated security risks (see Dangers & Annoyances p738, and for further logistical information, boxed text, p740).

Once inside Mexico, connections are excellent, with good, frequent bus services and good roads heading south. Better roads are usually toll roads, with tolls between Nogales and Los Mochis, for example, totaling almost M$400. It's often remote country, so if you're driving, don't set out beyond major highways without a full tank of gas.

NORTHWEST MEXICO

The magnets for visitors to Mexico's northwest are the picture-perfect beaches beside the Sea of Cortez, and the abundant marine life, including some 40 sea-lion colonies and 27 species of whale and dolphin. Tourism here originates largely from Arizona (some towns are so easily reachable from there

that they're becoming Mexican-American communities) but the region, encompassing Sonora (by far the safest of Mexico's border states) and northern Sinaloa, still bursts with homespun character. The strains of *norteña* (country) music and the inviting smell of the trademark regional snack, *carne asada* (marinated grilled beef), waft past cowboy-hatted ranchers on the streets. The main city hereabouts is Hermosillo, a proud cultural capital with cutting-edge museums, while resplendent colonial towns such as Álamos get you exploring inland. Los Mochis to the south is the jumping-off point for the spectacular train ride that is the Ferrocarril Chihuahua Pacífico.

Puerto Peñasco

☑ 638 / POP 57,000

Until the 1920s, 'Rocky Point' as US citizens affectionately call this Sea of Cortez coastal resort, was just that: a landmark on naval/military maps and no more. Its location alongside one of the driest parts of the Desierto Sonorense (Sonoran Desert) deterred all would-be settlers bar intrepid fishermen until Prohibition gave the fledgling community an unexpected spotlight as a drinking and gambling haven for alcohol-starved North Americans. Peñasco hasn't looked back since. Now this beach town is home to so many non-natives it has become the seaside destination Arizona never had. The historic core hugs the rocky point itself while its main waterfront stretch, Sandy Beach, sports massive condo-hotel resorts which offer luxury rooms with sea views, expensive restaurants and no hint of Mexican culture.

However, Peñasco is still characterful in parts, and there is plenty of fun to be had here.

Travelers without a car, beware: unbelievably for a place this size, there is no reliable local public transportation. Peñasco is also best avoided in March, when margarita-chugging US college students descend for Spring Break.

◉ Sights & Activities

Fishing, snorkeling, diving, kayaking, parasailing and sunset cruises are all popular. Rocky Point has a hectic events calendar: for the low-down, check with the tourist office.

Isla San Jorge   ISLAND
Swimming with sea lions at Isla San Jorge (Bird Island), 40km southeast of Peñasco, is

CROSSING THE BORDER

There are more than 40 official US–Mexico border crossing points, many open 24 hours daily. Opening hours, and estimated waiting times for drivers, are provided by **US Customs & Border Protection** (www.cbp.gov).

Tourists visiting Mexico must carry a passport or similar travel document with, in some cases, a Mexican visa (p859). They must also obtain a Mexican tourist permit (*forma migratoria para turista*, FMT, or *forma migratoria múltiple*, FMM) on arrival, unless they are staying within the border zone and not staying over 72 hours. The border zone generally extends 20km to 30km south from the border but also stretches as far as Puerto Peñasco in Sonora and Ensenada and San Felipe in Baja California. For further information on the tourist permit see p859.

Travelers taking a vehicle into Mexico – except for the Baja California peninsula or (for North Americans) the northwestern half of Sonora state – must obtain Mexican motor insurance (see p862) and a temporary vehicle importation permit (p862).

The Only Sonora program allows North Americans to bring a vehicle into Sonora permit-free, provided they don't stray south of Hwy 2 between Agua Prieta and Imuris, or east of Hwy 15D between Imuris and the checkpoint at Km 98 east of Empalme near Guaymas. To drive beyond these limits but without leaving Sonora state (for example to Álamos), you can get an 'Only Sonora' vehicle permit at the Mexican consulate in Phoenix, Arizona, or through the **Banjército** (www.banjercito.com.mx) website or at Importación e Internación Temporal de Vehículos (IITV) modules at Agua Prieta, Cananea or Hwy 15D Km 98 (Empalme).

If you do need a vehicle permit for beyond Sonora and have not obtained one before arrival, you have to do paperwork at one of Mexico's 46 IITV modules at borders and some locations past the border – including in Sonora at Agua Zarca (21km south of the border at Nogales), in Chihuahua state 30km south of the border past Ciudad Juárez, and in Baja California at Pichilingue (near La Paz) and Ensenada. All IITV locations are given at www.banjercito.com.mx (click on 'Red de Módulos IITV').

If you take a vehicle into Baja California, and then ship it to mainland Mexico by ferry from Pichilingue, you must get a vehicle permit before embarking your vehicle.

The main border crossings (ordered west to east):

Lukeville (Arizona)–Sonoyta (Sonora) (☉6am-midnight) Best for Puerto Peñasco.

Deconcini crossing (☉24hr) From Nogales (Arizona)–Nogales (Sonora). Hwy 15/15D is the main highway south.

Santa Teresa crossing (☉6am-midnight) Some 20km west of Juárez in Chihuahua state; good for avoiding Juárez and the possible security risks.

an outstanding experience. Several boats at the harbor do cruises and offer fishing or Isla San Jorge charters. **Sun n' Fun** (☎383-54-50; www.sunandfundivers.com; Blvd Juárez btwn Calle 13 & Blvd Fremont; ☉9am-5pm Mon-Sat, to 3pm Sun), have Isla San Jorge trips for around M$1400 for divers with two immersions and M$1000 for snorkelers or sightseers; fishing charters start from around M$400.

CEDO WILDLIFE-WATCHING
(Intercultural Center for the Study of Desert & Oceans; ☎382-01-13, in the US 520-320-5473; www.cedointercultural.org; Blvd Las Conchas; admission free; ☉9am-5pm Mon-Sat, 10am-2pm Sun) CEDO, 3km east of the center along Las Conchas, is a wonderful place to learn about Rocky Point's fascinating desert-meets-sea ecosystem. Dedicated to the conservation of the upper Gulf of California and surrounding Desierto Sonorense, CEDO has an 'Earthship' visitor center with a good store, and offers free tours with a natural-history talk in English at 2pm Tuesday and 4pm Saturday. CEDO also runs a fascinating program of nature tours, some in collaboration with local cooperatives. These range from wetland bird-watching walks and kayaking on nearby Morúa estuary to excursions to El Pinacate Biosphere Reserve north of town. Prices for full-day excursions cost up to M$2000. It's best to reserve in advance.

El Paso (Texas)–Ciudad Juárez (Chihuahua) Bridge of the Americas (⊘24hr; free); El Paso St–Av Juárez (⊘24hr; US$0.50); Stanton St–Av Lerdo (⊘24hr; US$0.50) Pedestrian crossings are via the bridges of Stanton St–Avenida Lerdo or El Paso St–Avenida Juárez. To return on foot you must use Avenida Juárez. For vehicles there is Bridge of the Americas (Puente Córdova). Tourist permits are available at the end of Stanton St–Avenida Lerdo bridge and Bridge of the Americas. Hwy 45D from Juárez is the principal southbound route.

Presidio (Texas)–Ojinaga (Chihuahua) (⊘24hr) From Ojinaga it's 225km along Hwy 16 direct to Chihuahua.

Del Rio (Texas)–Ciudad Acuña (Coahuila) (⊘24hr)

Eagle Pass (Texas)–Piedras Negras (Coahuila) (⊘24hr)

Laredo (Texas)–Nuevo Laredo (Tamaulipas) (⊘24hr) Two main crossings: Puente Internacional No 1 and Puente Internacional No 2. Northeast Mexico's best road south is Hwy 85D from Nuevo Laredo to Monterrey, from where there are good connections elsewhere in Mexico.

McAllen (Texas)–Reynosa (Tamaulipas) (⊘24hr)

Brownsville (Texas)–Matamoros (Tamaulipas) Puente Nuevo (⊘24hr); Puente Zaragoza (⊘6am-midnight)

There are plenty of cross-border bus services into the region from US cities, most involving a change of buses in a city on the US or Mexican side of the border. Given the time it can take a bus to get through the border, it is often at least as quick to disembark before the border, make the crossing on foot, and pick up further transportation on the other side.

If you want to avoid staying long in Mexico's border towns, some services will take you direct deeper into Mexico, including Phoenix–Puerto Peñasco via Sonoyta with **Transportes Nena's** (☑in the US 602-442-6802; http://transportesnenas.com; 1426 N 35th Ave, Phoenix) and El Paso–Chihuahua via Juárez with **Autobuses Americanos** (☑in the US 915-532-1748; www.autobusesamericanos.us; 1007 S Santa Fe St, El Paso) who have many offices across Texas. Find other such services at www.greyhound.com.

Most border towns rank among Mexico's most dangerous places; Nuevo Laredo and – worst of all – Juárez see significant violent crime. However, some (such as Matamoros) are quieter. All border cities mentioned in this chapter have good sleeping and eating facilities if you do choose to spend the night.

Tequila Factory DISTILLERY
(www.tequilafactory.mx; cnr Blvd Benito Juárez & Calle 12; admission free; ⊘10am-6pm Wed-Mon) This family-owned factory brews artisan tequilas and offers presentations on tequila production as well as tequila tastings. It has a try-before-you-buy policy in the shop. The oak-aged *Añejo* is recommended. It's downstairs from the tourist office.

🛏 Sleeping

The Old Port has agreeable down-to-earth options (thought it's slim pickings for tight budgets, unless you're in the market for an RV park). All the mega-hotel complexes are at Sandy Beach, to the northwest.

Posada La Roca HISTORIC HOTEL $
(☑383-31-99; www.hotelposadalaroca.blogspot.com; Av Primero de Junio 2; r M$390, without bathroom M$320; P❋🛜) This 1927 inn in the Old Port was constructed as a casino/hotel/brothel for US mobsters, including, by all accounts, Al Capone, during Prohibition. Today it's a quaint stone building with 20 simple but nicely furnished rooms and free coffee.

Hotel Viña del Mar HOTEL $$
(☑383-01-00; www.vinadelmarhotel.com; cnr Av Primero de Junio & Malecón Kino s/n; r M$670-1520; P❋🛜🏊🛗) A decent motel-style option at the Old Port. Basic rooms have nice woodbeam ceilings; the best (with kitchens and/or

Jacuzzis) surround the colorful, mosaic pool area right above the rocky shoreline.

Playa Bonita Hotel
HOTEL $$

(☎800-426-64-82, in the US 888-232-8142; www.playabonitaresort.com; Paseo Balboa 100; r from M$787; P☺☀@❄🐾) This large complex at the east end of Sandy Beach features 124 perfectly OK rooms and suites, plus a beachside restaurant with spectacular sunsets.

Las Palomas Beach & Golf Resort
RESORT $$$

(☎800-681-65-34, in the US 888-642-3495; www.las-palomas-resort.com; Blvd Costero 150, Sandy Beach; 4- to 10-person condos Sun-Thu M$3600-9200, Fri & Sat M$4133-12,000; P☺☀❄🐾) This gargantuan resort and 18-hole golf course is a flashy conglomerate of modern towers, several pools and a lazy river, and more than 200 condos, boasting classy restaurants and Gilchrist & Soames of London toiletries in the rooms.

✗ Eating & Drinking

It takes a little work to find traditional Mexican cuisine between all the sports bars and barbecue joints, but there is some good grub between the cracks.

TOP CHOICE La Casa del Capitán
SEAFOOD $$$

(Cerro de la Ballena; mains M$120-210; ⏰10am-10pm) Up on Cerro de la Ballena (Whale Hill), the *mirador* (lookout) behind the Old Port, the views from this restaurant, wrapped by an open-air terrace, and with some intriguing B&W photographs of the 'old' (pre-mass-development) town, are Peñasco's best. The specialty: gigantic *camarones flameados* (flaming shrimps).

Aqui es Con Flavio
MEXICAN $$

(Malecón Kino; mains M$70-155; ⏰11am-midnight) A great advert for Rocky Point: decent Mexican fare with a seafood bias served up alongside occasionally overexuberant local musicians and by smilingly efficient waiters. A margarita at this seafront-hugging spot around sunset is the way to kick-start your evening in the Old Port.

Manny's Beach Club
BAR

(Coahuila s/n; ⏰7am-11pm Sun-Thu, until 3am Fri & Sat) Manny's is a Peñasco stalwart, going strong almost 30 years on the 'Strip' east of the Cerro de la Ballena*mirador*. Enjoy meals (focusing on steak and seafood) for around M$100, or beers right on the sandy beach with live music in the evenings.

JJ's Cantina
CANTINA

(Cholla Bay; ⏰6pm-2am) Expats patronize this lively cantina in alternative Cholla Bay district west of Sandy Beach: get a taxi here.

ℹ Information

The nearest ATM to the Old Port is **Banamex** (cnr Juárez & Campeche). Other banks are on Blvd Juárez between Calle 13 and Blvd Fremont. Nearly all hotels have internet facilities, including those listed.

Rocky Point Tourism & Visitor Assistance (☎388-66-24, cell phone 638-3869081; www.tourismrockypoint.com; suite 202, cnr Blvd Juárez & Calle 12; ⏰9am-5pm Mon-Fri) offers information, advice and free 24-hour bilingual emergency assistance. It's in the tall blue building on the east side of Juárez.

ℹ Getting There & Around

Puerto Peñasco has a spanking new international airport off the Caborca road east of town, but no commercial flights just yet.

Driving south from Arizona, it's about 100km down Hwy 8 from the no-fuss Lukeville–Sonoyta border crossing to Puerto Peñasco. Drivers from California can use the San Luis Río Colorado crossing, south of Yuma in western Arizona, from where average driving time is three hours.

Several shuttle-van services run to Puerto Peñasco from Arizona, including **Transportes Nena's** (www.transportesnenas.com; cnr Blvd Juárez & Calle 27) behind Coffee Point cafe, which makes the trip to/from Phoenix four times daily (US$45, four hours).

Albatros (Blvd Juárez btwn Calles 29 & 30) runs 12 daily buses to Hermosillo (M$230, 5½ hours) and five to Nogales (M$245, six hours). **ABC** (cnr Calles Constitución & Bravo), one block north of Blvd Juárez, heads to Tijuana (M$463, nine hours) five times daily.

Taxis cost as little as M$20 for rides along and close to Blvd Juárez, but around M$50 to Las Conchas or Sandy Beach resorts – and can be double that or more coming back from resorts.

Hermosillo

☎662 / POP 720,000 / ELEV 238M

Stop by sizzling-hot Hermosillo, Sonora's capital, for some of northern Mexico's coolest museums. It's vexingly spread-out, with the often-unbearable afternoon heat garnering it the moniker of Sun City, but Hermosillo's cultural scene – and, increasingly, its cuisine – may just end up dazzling you. Central Hermosillo fans out around craggy Cerro de la Campana (Hill of the Bell): the city's aerial-mast-festooned viewpoint.

⊙ Sights

Plaza Zaragoza PLAZA
The central orange-tree-shaded main plaza is fronted by the **Catedral de la Asunción** (constructed 1877–1908) and the **Palacio de Gobierno** (admission free; ⊙9am-3pm Mon-Sat), which has murals depicting Sonoran history.

MUSAS MUSEUM
(Museo de Arte de Sonora; www.musas.gob.mx; cnr Blvd Vildósola & Av Cultura; ⊙10am-7pm) New in the city center this spectacular and airy art museum has edgy exhibitions, cultural events, short films and bizarre installations, such as the eye-catching VW with a ladder soaring from its roof into the museum's upper reaches.

Museo de Sonora MUSEUM
(Jesús García s/n; admission M$37, Sun free; ⊙9am-6pm Tue-Sun) On the east side of Cerro de la Campana in a stone-walled, century-old former jail, this museum has comprehensive exhibits (in Spanish) on Sonoran history, from pre-Hispanic times to the 20th century.

Centro Ecológico de Sonora ZOO
(Templo de Tláloc; adult/child M$30/15; ⊙8am-5pm) This lush botanical garden and zoo 7km south of center features an excellent array of plants and wildlife from Sonora's mountains, deserts and prairies, including the endangered, antelope-like Sonoran pronghorn (berrendo): North America's fastest-moving land animal. Take the southbound Línea 11 bus from the west side of Jardín Juárez out into the southern suburbs and get off when the bus turns north off Xolotl on to Templo de Tláloc, then walk 600m south on Templo de Tláloc.

🛏 Sleeping & Eating

Central Hermosillo has adequate budget and midrange accommodations, but most flashy hotels (and restaurants) are in the Zona Hotelera north of center – convenient only if you have your own vehicle.

TOP CHOICE Colonial Hotel MOTEL $$
(☑259-00-00; www.hotelescolonial.com; Vado del Río 9; r/ste incl breakfast M$955/1300; ᴘ⊕✳@ ⍩⛱) The most stylish motel you've ever seen, full of modern art and sleek design touches. To get there, head nine blocks south of center on Rosales: it's near the Paseo Río Sonora ring road.

Hotel Washington HOTEL $
(☑213-11-83; Noriega 68; r M$220-240; ✳@⍩) Rooms appear opium-den musty, but it's a steal at this price. It's just southwest of Jardín Juárez.

Restaurante Mochomos FUSION $$$
(Morelos 701; mains M$160; ⊙1pm-midnight Mon-Thu, until 1am Fri & Sat, until 5pm Sun) In the Zona Hotelera, intimate Mochomos (literally 'shredded beef') serves Sonoran fusion cuisine. With the city in the heart of beef country, meat, for instance cabrera (Sonora's signature T-bone steak fillet), is popular.

Verde Olivo VEGETARIAN $$
(Niños Héroes 75A; mains M$55-118; ⊙7am-10pm Mon-Sat, to 6pm Sun; ⊖⍩⍭) Good downtown option with delicious grain veggie burgers and PETA-friendly versions of Mexican classics.

ⓘ Information

Hospital San José (Blvd Morelos 340; ⊙24hr) Large, modern hospital; has a 24-hour emergency department.

Tourist information kiosk (☑213-55-37, www. gotosonora.com; ⊙9am-9pm Mon-Fri, 10am-9pm Sat) Helpful booth on Plaza Zaragoza.

ⓘ Getting There & Away

Air

Hermosillo Airport (☑261-00-00; www.aero puertosgap.com.mx; Carretera Bahía de Kino Km 9.5) has direct flights to airports including Chihuahua, Guadalajara, Mexico City, Monterrey, San José del Cabo, Tijuana and, internationally, Los Angeles and Phoenix.

Bus

The main bus terminal, with frequent deluxe/1st-class/2nd-class services is the **Central de Autobuses de Hermosillo** (CAH; Blvd Encinas 400), 2km east of the city center. Second-class **Albatros** (Blvd Encinas 354) has another terminal 150m west, and pricier 1st-class **Tufesa** (Blvd Encinas btwn Velázquez & Universidad) is a further 400m west.

Second-class buses to Bahía de Kino (M$77 to M$87, two hours, hourly 5:30am to 6:30pm) depart from **AMH & TCH bus terminal** (Sonora btwn Calles González & García) near Jardín Juárez.

ⓘ Getting Around

City bus 1 (M$7) runs the 2km east to the Blvd Encinas bus terminals from the east side of Jardín Juárez. Bus 9 runs from Elías Calles by the Mercado Municipal to the Zona Hotelera.

BUSES FROM HERMOSILLO

DESTINATION	FARE (M$)	DURATION	FREQUENCY (DAILY)
Guaymas	100-135	2hr	every 30-60min Tufesa, hourly CAH
Los Mochis	330	6-9hr	every 30min CAH
Mexico City (Terminal Norte)	1465	29-33hr	hourly CAH
Nogales	165-225	3-4hr	hourly Tufesa
Phoenix	585	8hr	14 Tufesa
Puerto Peñasco	230	5-6hr	13 Albatros

Taxis cost M$45 to M$60 from the bus terminals to the city center or Zona Hotelera, M$60 between the city center and Zona Hotelera and M$150 from the airport to either zone.

Río de Sonora Valley

North and east of Hermosillo stretches frontier country proper: the mountains and prairies that best convey what life would have been like for Spanish settlers centuries ago. This area is best-known for its well-preserved Jesuit missions, many of which were established by Mexico's famed missionary, Padre Eusebio Kino, and are comparable in grandeur to those in Paraguay and Argentina. Dreamy time-warped colonial towns here also secrete beautiful architecture, thermal baths and interesting accommodations. You'll need your own vehicle: public transportation is scarce.

Following Hwy 14 northwest from Hermosillo, it's 80km up to mellow Ures with its shady Plaza Zaragoza and shops selling the Sonoran version of tequila, *bacanora*. After another 30km Hwy 118 branches north to reach Baviácora, with one of Sonora's finest cathedrals, after 20km. Aconchi, 15km on, has wonderful thermal baths. A further 22km north is the laid-back colonial town of Banámichi where the nearby forests have excellent bird-watching.

🖉 La Posada de Río Sonora (☑623-231-02-59; www.laposadadelriosonora.com; plaza, Banámichi; r M$1000; 🌐❀🐾) in Banámichi is a good base from which bird-watch, and which also provides meals and offers horseback riding.

The landscape becomes increasingly eroded with interesting rock formations as you near Arizpe, once capital of Nueva España's Provincias Internas (including California, New Mexico and Texas) in the 18th and 19th centuries. You can loop back to Hermosillo via Magdalena de Kino. Padre Kino is buried in the town's mission here, and Magdalena is a great base for visiting surrounding missions such as Pitiquito (with outstanding indigenous art on the walls) on the Caborca road, Tubutama and the dramatic ruins of Cocóspera.

Bahía de Kino

📞 662 / POP 6000

Laid-back Bahía de Kino, a dreamy beach paradise 110km west of Hermosillo, is named for Padre Eusebio Kino, who established a small mission here for the indigenous Seri people in the 17th century. The old part of Kino, Kino Viejo, is a typical Mexican fishing village. Beginning 1km west, Kino Nuevo (New Kino) fans out along the lengthy main beach, which is perfect for swimming. It's where you'll likely spend most of your time, and also where you'll find the 'snowbirds' (retired North American citizens who head south for winter). Look out for those hulking RVs. High season is November to March; at other times, you may find yourself blissfully alone in the hotels here.

👁 Sights & Activities

Punta Chueca
& Isla del Tiburón   INDIGENOUS CULTURE
The region's indigenous people, the Seri, mainly live at Punta Chueca, a village 30km north of Bahía de Kino. You'll need a sturdy 4WD with high clearance to make the journey along the dirt road; on arrival, prepare to be pounced upon by Seri women wanting to sell you handicrafts, including their highly regarded baskets. Isla del Tiburón, the large, mountainous, uninhabited island

visible northwest of Kino Nuevo, is owned by the Seri. An intact desert ecosystem, it has good snorkeling and diving around its coast. If you're interested in a boat trip to the island, look for Alfredo López or Ernesto Molina, guides who live in Punta Chueca and can facilitate permits or provide tours. The **Centro de Estudios Culturales y Ecológicos** (www.prescott.edu; Cádiz, Kino Nuevo), a field station of Prescott College, Arizona, one block off Avenida Mar de Cortez near Kino Nuevo's northwestern end, can often advise on arrangements.

Museo de los Seris MUSEUM

(cnr Av Mar de Cortez & Progreso; admission M$10; ⊗9am-5pm Wed-Sun) Near the northwest end of Kino Nuevo, this museums displays an interesting collection of Seri artifacts.

Sleeping & Eating

There are abundant RV parks on the Kino Nuevo strip with little to merit one over another; just ask around.

TOP CHOICE Casa Tortuga APARTMENT $$$

(☎242-01-22; rentcasatortuga@aol.com; Av Mar de Cortez 2645; apartments M$1140-1407; P❄🕸📶🐕) You don't even have to cross the road to reach the beach at Casa Tortuga, where two atmospheric apartments front a beach-side terrace. Pelican (the upper-level digs), with its private balcony is recommended. The owner will happily chat all day about Sonora from the Seri to the steak. Complementary kayaks for guests.

La Playa Hotel HOTEL $$$

(☎242-02-73; www.laplayarvhotel.com; Blvd Mar de Cortez 101; r M$1200; P❄🐕) This whitewashed beachfront hotel's rooms boast postcard-perfect sea views, featuring mini kitchen areas and private front decks with *palapas*. It feels a bit like you're in the Greek Islands. A two-night minimum stay applies during busy periods – from Friday to Sunday, June to September.

Hotel Hacienda HOTEL $$

(☎242-05-90; www.hotelhacienda.info; cnr Blvd Guaymas & Manzanillo; d/ste M$600/750; 🕸❄🏊) This appealing colonial-style hotel is the best option in Kino Viejo, beckoning you in with its rose-pink walls, courtyard swimming pool and sweet-smelling rooms named after Sonoran icons from coyotes to nopales (a cactus species).

Casablanca NORTH AMERICAN $$

(☎242-07-77; casablancainn@aol.com; cnr Cádiz & Av Mar de Cortez; breakfasts M$50-90, mains M$70-150; ⊗8am-10pm, until midnight Fri & Sat) On first appearances, this is an eye-catching restaurant serving tasty Mexican–North American grub specializing in breakfasts, with evening action moving to the upstairs *palapa*-style bar (with pool table). But there are also seven tastefully decorated rooms in the courtyard behind (M$1200 to M$1600 including breakfast). It's at the northwestern end of Nuevo Kino.

La Palapa del Pescador SEAFOOD $$

(cnr Av Mar de Cortez & Wellington; mains M$50-190; ⊗9am-10pm; 🐕) A treasure trove of seafood delights including fried whole lobster. With a *palapa*-covered patio, this joint is also popular for an ice-cold *cerveza* (beer) of an afternoon. It's 2.5km from the southeast end of the Kino Nuevo strip.

ⓘ Information

Email **KBnet News** (kbnetnews@aol.com) for the latest Kino news on everything from new RV sites to travel warnings.

You'll find ATMs at the **Cruz Roja** (Red Cross; ☎242-04-86; cnr Blvr Kino & Av Manzanillo, Kino Viejo), which also provides emergency medical services. **New Space** (cnr Blvr Kino & Topolobampo, Kino Viejo; per hr M$10; ⊗9am-10pm) provides internet access.

The informative **Casa del Mar** (☎242-02-21; cnr Calles Bilbao & Esqueda; admission free; ⊗9am-4pm Wed-Sun) is a visitors center for the 900-island Área de Protección de Flora y Fauna Islas del Golfo de California and issues permits for visiting the islands (M$40 per person per island per day). It's two blocks off Avenida Mar de Cortez near the northwest end of Kino Nuevo.

ⓘ Getting There & Around

Buses from Hermosillo pass through Kino Viejo about 15 minutes past every hour from 7:15am to 8:15pm, except 3:15pm, continuing to the end of the strip via the bus station (6km along) then returning the way they came. Departures from the bus station to Hermosillo (M$78 to M$88, two hours) are about hourly from 5am to 7:45pm. These buses are a good way of getting around the Kinos (local rides cost M$6).

San Carlos

☎622 / POP 2300

Northwest of the gritty port city of Guaymas, San Carlos feels a universe apart with its beautiful desert-and-bay landscape presided over by some dramatic hills – notably the majestic twin peaks of Cerro Tetakawi – that glow an impressive red-earthed hue as the sun descends.

Sonorans flock here at weekends and holidays year-round, and from October to April, the town receives a big influx of *norteamericanos*. But it's beautiful and spread-out enough to provide respite from the sweaty cities at any time. Playa Algodones is the best beach here (famed for its role in the movie Catch-22 which was shot hereabouts); the town also offers a wealth of outdoor activities and ample places to eat, drink and dance.

San Carlos is not pedestrian friendly, spread-eagled over some 8km. Most amenities are on the 2.5km stretch of Blvd Beltrones. Head right at the intersection by the Oxxo store after the Beltrones strip to get out to Playa Algodones (6km), or straight on for Marina San Carlos.

🏃 Activities

For many, sportfishing tops the list here: April to September are best for big fish; there are seven main annual tournaments. There are several beach-lined coves for diving and snorkeling, as well as some wrecks offshore. At **Isla San Pedro Nolasco**, 35km out to sea, you can snorkel or dive with a sea-lion colony.

Catch 22   FISHING
(www.catch22mexicosportfishing.com; suite 1, Marinaterra Hotel, Marina San Carlos; fishing charters per boat per hr M$940-1280; ⊘10am-4pm Tue-Sat) Offers sports-fishing excursions.

Gary's Dive Shop   DIVING
(☑226-00-49; www.garysdiveshop.com; Blvd Beltrones Km 10; ⊘7am-5pm) Specializing in diving, but also snorkeling, gear rental, fishing and trips to Isla San Pedro Nolasco (Seal Island). There's also an office at the Marinaterra Hotel.

Ocean Sports   WATER SPORTS
(www.desertdivers.com; Edificio Marina San Carlos; ⊘8am-5pm Mon, Wed & Thu, 7am-7pm Fri & Sat, 7am-5pm Sun) Diving, fishing, snorkeling and (on-shore) horseback riding.

🛏 Sleeping

🏆 Playa Blanca   APARTMENTS $$$
(☑227-01-00; www.playablancasancarlos.com.mx; Playa Algodones; 4- to 8-person condos M$3165-5958; P❄🛜🏊🐕) This is the big daddy of the accommodations options: in size and style. Rooms could almost be interior design showrooms, and are very well-appointed,

with large kitchens and balconies looking over the enticing pool to the sea. There's a classy gift shop, aqua bar and gym. A two-night minimum stay is required.

Marinaterra Hotel   HOTEL $$$
(☑225-20-20; www.marinaterra.com; Estrada s/n; r M$1260-1496, ste M$2000-2756; P❄🛜🏊) Overlooking Marina San Carlos, Marinaterra is a part-condo resort with bright rooms, most including kitchenette and balcony, plus its own beach club and activities department.

Hotel Creston   MOTEL $$
(☑226-00-20; Blvd Beltrones Km 10; s M$400-500, d M$450-650; P❄🛜🏊🐕) Large, clean, unpretentious rooms (with satellite TV and good air-con) arranged around an OK pool, make this the town's best deal.

🍴 Eating & Drinking

🏆 Bonifacio's   FUSION $$$
(☑227-05-15; www.bonifacios.com; Playa Algodones; mains M$100-350; ⊘11am-11pm Mon-Thu, until 3am Fri & Sat, until 10:30pm Sun; 🐕) This might be poised on the sands of lovely Playa Algodones but don't come here expecting a beach bar (although Bonifacio's has one). The place exudes sophistication, from the spacious chandelier-lit antique-furnished interior to the imaginative Mexican fusion cuisine. Try fat freshwater Río Fuerte prawns or a beef fillet over quesadilla, topped with avocados and guavillo chilies.

Blackie's   INTERNATIONAL $$$
(www.blackies.com.mx; Blvd Beltrones Km 10.3; mains M$110-330; ⊘3:30-10:30pm) A wonderful intimate surprise on Blvd Belatrones, the best dish at this steak and seafood restaurant is the petite chateaubriand, flambéed at your table. It has great wine, too.

Rosa's Cantina   BREAKFAST $$
(Blvd Beltrones Km 9.5; mains M$50-140; ⊘6am-9pm; 🐕) Pancho Villa–themed Rosa's serves up substantial North American and Mexican breakfasts and additional favorites all day.

Hangout/Soggy Peso Bar   BAR
(Playa Algodones; margaritas M$40, snacks M$40-100; ⊘11am-sunset) Great bar at the north end of San Carlos' best beach, serving up some of Mexico's best margaritas.

ℹ Information

Banamex (Blvd Beltrones) Both US dollars and pesos are accepted everywhere. This Banamex, next to the Pemex station on Blvd Beltrones, has two ATMs.

Gary's Dive Shop (☏226-00-49; www.garys diveshop.com; Blvd Beltrones Km 10; ⏰7am-5pm) Has maps and information; there's internet (Mon-Sat; same hours) on the floor above.

❶ Getting There & Around

The buses from Guaymas run as far as Marina San Carlos. Local rides within San Carlos cost M$5. There's a taxi stand at Hotel Marinatierra: trips within San Carlos cost M$50 to M$100.

Long-distance buses will likely drop you at either the **Grupo Estrella Blanca** (Calle 14 No 96, Guaymas) or **Tufesa** (Blvd García López 927, Guaymas) terminals in Guaymas. From Grupo Estrella Blanca, walk north on Calle 14 to Blvd García López and catch the white San Carlos bus (M$12, every 30 minutes). From Tufesa, cross the road to catch the same bus.

The **airport** (☏221-05-11; www.asa.gob.mx/wb/webasa/guaymas_aeropuertos) is about 10km north of Guaymas off the highway to San Carlos, with flights to Phoenix and Baja California destinations. **Aeromexico** (☏222-02-66; Av Serdan 236) has an office in Guaymas.

Álamos & Around

☏647 / POP ÁLAMOS 9300,
LA ADUANA 250 / ELEV 432M

An oasis in the forested foothills of the Sierra Madre Occidental, Álamos, with its hushed cobblestone streets, is layered in a fascinating history, much of it to do with its role as Mexico's northernmost silver town. The silver boom days played out here and in nearby La Aduana, where there are still beautifully preserved mining buildings to see. These days are long gone, but Álamos remains a colonial idyll and the region's culinary capital. The prettily painted buildings, many with an Andalucian slant to the architecture, include some enchanting accommodation possibilities. Little wonder that the town has been declared both a national historical monument and one of Mexico's *pueblos mágicos* (magical towns).

Álamos' charms have proven irresistible to many US retirees and creative types who, since the '50s, have snapped up decaying colonial buildings to renovate into second homes and hotels. The well-heeled expats comprise a small but influential segment of Álamos' population.

The town's lush surroundings, from tropical deciduous forest to mountains covered in pine and oak, also make it a good base for nature-lovers. The 929-sq-km Sierra de Álamos–Río Cuchujaqui Flora & Fauna Protection Area that almost encircles Álamos has great birding and wonderful walks.

More bizarrely, Álamos and vicinity is where most of the world's jumping beans originate (beans sold as a novelty that 'jump' due to the presence of a larvae inside).

The nicest time to come is between mid-October and mid-April, when the air is cool and fresh. The biggest number of Mexican tourists come in the rainy months, July to September; at other times it's far quieter.

History

The area's silver mines were discovered around La Aduana in the 16th century. Álamos itself was founded in the 1680s, probably as a dormitory suburb for La Aduana's wealthy colonists. Despite hostilities from the indigenous Yaqui and Mayo, Álamos boomed into one of Mexico's principal 18th-century mining centers.

During Mexico's 19th-century turmoils, Álamos was attacked repeatedly, by French invaders, by factions seeking its silver wealth and by the fiercely independent Yaqui. The Mexican Revolution took a further toll and by the 1920s most mines were abandoned and Álamos was practically a ghost town.

In 1948 Álamos was reawakened by William Levant Alcorn, a Pennsylvania dairy farmer who bought the Almada mansion on Plaza de Armas and restored it as the Hotel Los Portales. Other *norteamericanos* followed, buying crumbling mansions and restoring them to their former glory. Some of these people still live in Álamos today.

◉ Sights

Mainly, Álamos is for sauntering around, and soaking up one of Mexico's most idyllic colonial centers with perhaps a break at one of the atmospheric restaurants.

The delightful, verdant Plaza de Armas is the setting for **Parroquia de la Purísima Concepción**, built between 1786 and 1804. Much of its original interior was fashioned from silver. The east side of the plaza is abutted by the expansive **Museo Costumbrista de Sonora** (Victoria s/n; admission M$10; ⏰9am-3pm Wed-Fri, to 6pm Sat & Sun), a well-thought museum with exhibits (in Spanish) on the Sonoran history and traditions. Special attention is paid to the influence of mining on Álamos. A shop here sells Mayo crafts.

El Mirador lookout tops a hill on Álamos' southeastern edge, affording sweeping views of the town and its mountainous surroundings. It's accessible by steps from the Arroyo Agua Escondida two blocks down Obregón from Victoria.

Cemetery lovers will salivate over **El Panteón** (cnr Calles las Delicias & Posada; ⊘6am-6pm), Álamos' ancient jumble of above-ground tombs, which began receiving the dead in 1751.

Tours

Emiliano Graseda   CULTURAL TOUR GUIDE
(☑cell phone 647-101-48-75; tourist office, Victoria 5; ⊘8am-8pm) English-speaking Emiliano gives tours of Álamos and the countryside nearby. Half-day historic tours (per person M$220) visit city landmarks, including several local people's houses. They then head out to La Aduana, visiting a brick works, *artesanías* workshops and a mission.

Pronatura   BIRD-WATCHING
(☑428-00-04; Juárez 8; 2hr tour around town per person M$200; ⊘7:30am-7:30pm Mon-Fri) This environmental group is the main contact point for the local guides of bird-watching group **Alas de Álamos** (Wings of Álamos). It charges up to M$650 for day trips further afield for which you must provide the vehicle and a minimum of four participants.

Solipaso   ADVENTURE TOUR
(☑428-15-09; www.solipaso.com; Privada s/n, Barrio el Chalatón) Run by a long-resident US couple, Solipaso offers unique day-long river-float trips (per person M$1430, four to 12 people; November to March) on the remote, wildlife-rich Río Mayo northwest of Álamos. You visit ancient petroglyphs, a historic stone aqueduct and a Mayo village. It also offers bird-watching trips.

Festivals & Events

Festival Alfonso Ortíz Tirado   MUSIC
Álamos' 10-day late-January festival (www.festivalortiztirado.com) of top-class classical music and song, and other less-formal music, dance and art happenings, has grown into one of northern Mexico's main cultural events.

Sleeping

Of all northern Mexico's towns, Álamos has the most unique and attractive accommodations, many in opulent colonial mansions.

TOP CHOICE **Hotel Colonial**   HOTEL $$$
(☑428-13-71; www.alamoshotelcolonial.com; Obregón 4; r incl breakfast M$1285-2300; P✳☺) Stunning and sumptuous, the Colonial feels more like you are stepping into an Edwardian period drama than it does a Mexican hotel. From the stagecoach in the internal courtyard to rooms lined with tapestries and studded with creaking antiques to the vast roof terrace (featuring a dumbwaiter in case you fancy drinking/dining up there) this place is the definition of elegance.

El Pedregal   LODGE $$$
(☑428-15-09; www.elpedregalmexico.com; Privada s/n, Barrio el Chalatón; r incl breakfast M$1200; P✳@☺☷) Five purpose-built, ecofriendly,

---

FERRIES TO BAJA

Two ferry services link mainland northwest Mexico with Baja California. From Topolobampo near Los Mochis, **Baja Ferries** (☑668-862-10-03; www.bajaferries.com; Topolobampo; passengers M$878, cars M$1050, 1- to 4-person cabin M$770; ⊘9am-10pm Sun-Fri) leave at 11pm Sunday to Friday for La Paz in Baja, arriving at 6am. For travel around Semana Santa and Christmas/New Year and in June and July it's recommended to reserve a month ahead: you can do so by telephone and pay on embarkation. See p723 for returning schedules and vehicle fares. You can buy tickets in Los Mochis (see p751) or, on departure day, at the Topolobampo terminal.

The ferry **Santa Rosalía** (www.ferrysantarosalia.com; seating saloon-class M$790, motorcycle/car M$1420/3200) sails from Guaymas, Sonora for Santa Rosalía, Baja California, at 8pm Monday, Tuesday, Thursday and Saturday, arriving the next morning around 7am. From mid-November to mid-March, strong winds may cause delays, and the Monday/Tuesday sailings are occasionally canceled in low season. The **ticket office** (☑622-222-02-04; Recinto Portuario Zona Franca s/n, Terminal de Transbordadores, Colonia Punta Arena; ⊘8am-2pm & 3:30-8pm Mon-Sat) is 2km east of Guaymas city center. Reservations are only necessary if you want a cabin or are taking a vehicle (three days in advance is sufficient). All passengers and vehicles should be at the terminal by 6:30pm. See p712 for information on sailings from Santa Rosalía.

adobe cabins with quality furnishings and attractive *artesanías* (handicrafts) are scattered in 8 hectares of lovely tropical deciduous forest on the edge of Álamos – a perfect natural retreat or base for explorations. The owners also run the adventure-tour company Solipaso and offer yoga classes.

Hacienda de los Santos LUXURY HOTEL **$$$**
(428-02-22; www.haciendadelossantos.com; Molina 8; r incl breakfast M$3840, ste incl breakfast from M$4440;) One of the most beautiful properties in North America, this estate features five restored colonial homes. There are three pools, three restaurants, a theater, a spa, a gym and a 520-strong tequila collection. Rates can be up to M$1300 cheaper outside of the November-to-April period. No children under 12 or pets.

Posada de Don Andrés HOTEL **$$**
(428-11-10; Rosales; s/d M$500/600;) This rambling hotel overlooking Plaza Alameda benefits from large, comfortable rooms and a friendly host whose art is displayed in the welcoming common area.

Casa de María Félix HOTEL **$$**
(428-09-29; www.casademariafelix.com; Galeana 41; r M$650;) A colorful, homey property full of antiques, it also contains a tranquil garden complete with pool and barbecue area and a museum to Mexican golden-age film star María Félix, who was born right here.

Hostal Álamos HOSTEL **$**
(jimtoevs@yahoo.com; Madero 7; dm M$150, r M$450-500) A six-bed dorm and two private rooms, laundry, a book exchange and tours available to visit the region's Mayo people. Book via email as there's no phone.

Eating & Drinking

For a real treat, consider the short trip out to Casa La Aduana.

TOP CHOICE **Cenaduría Dõna Lola** MEXICAN **$**
(Volantín s/n; mains M$40-85; 7am-10pm Mon-Sat, 2-10pm Sun;) With delicious homemade Mexican fare at startlingly low prices, this family-run locals' secret is worth the trip to Álamos alone (the *enchiladas suizas* – Swiss enchiladas – are the best in the world). The place is also known as Koky's.

Teresitas BAKERY **$$**
(Allende 41; meals M$50-110; 8am-7pm Mon-Sat, 8am-4pm Sun;) La Puerta Roja's food survives the sadly closed inn: many of the owner's tasty dishes can now be enjoyed in her tranquil bistro-cum-bakery, Teresitas. Eat either in the fountain-flanked garden or the design-conscious interior. This is the best pit stop for home-baked delights in Álamos.

Café Luz del Sol CAFE **$**
(428-04-66; www.luzdelsolalamos.com; Obregón 3; mains M$55-75; 7:30am-3pm Tue-Sat;) In a region cruelly deprived of decent coffee shops, this colonial cafe is a better find for caffeine-starved travelers than any silver mine. Devour beautifully prepared breakfasts, home-baked cakes, Mexican/North American lunches and, yep, wicked coffee. Did we mention the three atmospheric colonial rooms (M$850) in the attached hotel?

La Casa Aduana MEXICAN **$$$**
(404-34-73; Plaza, La Aduana; meals M$170-280; from 1pm Wed-Sun;) Nine kilometers out in La Aduana in a 1620s customs house, long-resident chef-historian Sam Beardsley makes your evening dinner jaunt worthwhile, turning out New Sonoran cuisine such as butterfly shrimp rolled in tomato-garlic chili marmalade. Reservations are required after 5pm; taxis from Álamos are M$150 to M$175.

La Corregidora BAR
(Juárez 6; evenings) The town's most interesting bar, with historic photos, a pool table and outside tables on the Plaza de Armas.

Information

Banorte (Madero 37; 9am-4pm Mon-Fri) ATM; money exchange.

Ciber Lucas (Callejón del Beso; per hr M$10; 10am-10pm) Internet access.

Hospital General de Álamos (428-02-25; Madero s/n; 24hr) Basic local hospital.

Tourist office (428-04-50; Victoria 5; 8am-8pm) On the Plaza de Armas.

Getting There & Away

Álamos is 53km east of Navojoa, which is 323km southeast of Hermosillo and 156km north of Los Mochis. Second-class buses by **Albatros** (cnr Guerrero & No Reelección, Navojoa) depart Navojoa for Álamos (M$26, one hour) at least hourly from 5am to 10pm. Up to a dozen daily 1st-class Albatros buses connect Navojoa with Guaymas (for San Carlos) and Hermosillo. You can also reach Navojoa from north and south with more frequent **Tufesa** (www.tufesa.com.mx; cnr Hidalgo & No Reelección, Navojoa), one block north from Albatros.

Álamos' **Transportes Baldomero Corral terminal** (Morelos 7) is on Plaza Alameda. Buses leave for Navojoa (M$20, one hour) every half-hour or hour from 5:40am to 9:15pm. Change in Navojoa for services into the US.

The closest commercial airport is at Ciudad Obregón, between Navojoa and Guaymas.

Los Mochis

📞 668 / POP 260,000

Spick-and-span, modern Los Mochis, 488km south of Hermosillo, is a handy, well-appointed stop for travelers in transit between north and south. Great bus links, an airport, a ferry to Baja and its status as terminus for the fabulous Ferrocarril Chihuahua Pacífico train journey all mean Los Mochis milks a lot of tourist traffic.

🛏 Sleeping

The city's good mix of bedding-down options can be invaluable for Copper Canyon information and logistics.

Hotel Fénix HOTEL **$$**
(📞812-26-23; Flores 365 Sur; s/d M$395/465; ❋🛜) The 16 renovated rooms are great value; old rooms for the same price are a bit of a rip-off (all constitute the city's most pleasant lower-end accommodations).

Corintios Hotel HOTEL **$$**
(📞818-22-24; www.hotelcorintios.com; Obregón 580 Poniente; r incl breakfast M$587, ste incl breakfast M$720-989; P❋@🛜) With its airy courtyard and colorful rooms featuring marble-tiled bathtubs, the Corintios is past its best but still good value.

Best Western Los Mochis HOTEL **$$$**
(📞816-30-00; www.bestwestern.com; Obregón 691 Poniente; r M$1566; P🚗❋@🛜🏊🐾) Though the rooms aren't as high-tech and fancy as the lobby and elevators, this all-amenity chain hotel is the most tastefully decorated and comfortable in Mochis. Promotions can bring prices down to under M$1300. It's located in an agreeable spot near the expansive Parque Sinaloa.

🍴 Eating

Enjoy the culinary variety of Los Mochis: out in that canyon, you'll have precious little.

La Cabaña de Doña Chayo TAQUERÍA **$**
(Obregón 99 Poniente; tacos & quesadillas M$23-33; ⊙8am-1am; 🐾) Delectable quesadillas and tacos with *carne asada* or *machaca* (spiced shredded dried beef).

Chics MEXICAN **$$**
(Parque Sinaloa; mains M$58-98; ⊙9am-11pm; 🐾) In that part of the park given over to US

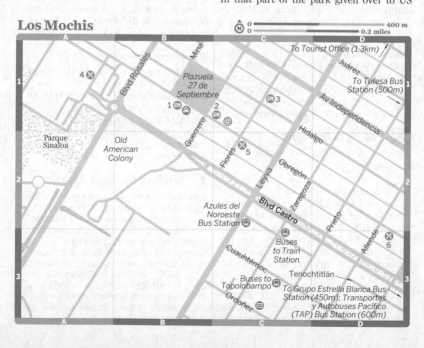

Los Mochis

BUSES FROM LOS MOCHIS

DESTINATION	FARE (M$)	DURATION	FREQUENCY (DAILY)
Guadalajara	720-780	13-15hr	half-hourly TAP, 16 Tufesa
Guaymas	255	6hr	23 Tufesa
Hermosillo	330-355	6-7hr	half-hourly 1st class GEB, hourly Tufesa
Mazatlán	365	6-7hr	frequent GEB/TAP
Navojoa	100-110	2hr	frequent 1st class GEB/Tufesa
Nogales	560	11-12hr	half-hourly Tufesa
Phoenix	950	16hr	13 Tufesa

fast-food chains, this place is a spacious all-Mexican affair, with superb breakfasts (oh, the *omelet sonorense!*), hamburgers, generous salads, *antojitos* (typical Mexican snacks) and beef dishes.

El Farallón   SEAFOOD $$
(Obregón 499 Poniente; mains M$80-160; ☺9am-11pm; ☻) An upscale atmosphere in which to eat excellent ceviche or other varied fish dishes such as *filete zarandeado,* a garlic-and-chili-basted white fish popular in these parts. A roof terrace opened in October 2011.

❶ Information

Online Café Internet (Obregón; per hr M$10; ☺9am-8pm Mon-Sat)
Tourist office (☑812-13-36; Locales 7 & 8, Edificio San Isidro, Zaragoza 444; ☺9am-3pm Mon-Fri) Inconveniently situated away from the center.

❶ Getting There & Away

Air

Los Mochis Airport (☑818-68-70; www.aeropuertosgap.com.mx; Carretera Los Mochis-Topolobampo Km 12.5) has daily flights to Mexico City, Hermosillo, Tijuana, Mazatlán and

Guadalajara by **Aeroméxico Connect** (☑812-02-16; www.aeromexico.com.mx, in Spanish; Obregón 1104 Poniente). Several small airlines fly to Baja California destinations.

Boat

Ferries for Pichilingue, near La Paz in Baja California Sur, leave from Topolobampo, 24km southwest of Los Mochis (see boxed text, p748). In Los Mochis you can buy tickets up to two months ahead at **Baja Ferries** (☑817-37-52; www.bajaferries.com; Local 5, cnr Blvds Rosales & Centenario; ☺8am-6pm Mon-Fri, 9am-3pm Sat).

Bus

The main intercity bus stations all have round-the-clock departures.
Azules del Noroeste (Tenochtitlán 399 Poniente) Second-class. Runs to El Fuerte (M$70, two hours, 16 times daily) from 5:55am to 8:15pm.
Grupo Estrella Blanca/Transportes y Autobuses Pacífico (GEB/TAP; Blvd Castro btwn Constitución & Domínguez) Deluxe and 1st-class buses as far as Mexico City, Nogales and Tijuana. The two company terminals are officially separate but adjacent and interchangeable in the destinations they cover. TAP usually edge it for price.
Tufesa (www.tufesa.com.mx; Zapata 139) First-class service up to Nogales, Phoenix and Los Angeles or down to Guadalajara.

Train

For schedules and more about the train journey between Los Mochis and Chihuahua, see p752. Los Mochis station is 4km southeast of the center at the end of Bienestar. The **ticket office** (☑824-11-51; ☺5am-5:30pm Mon-Fri, 5-8am & 10am-1pm Sat & Sun) sells *primera express* tickets up to a month ahead of travel, and *clase económica* tickets up to three days ahead. Opening hours are notoriously unreliable, however: be warned. In town, **Viajes Flamingo** (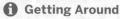812-16-13; www.mexicoscoppercanyon.com; Hotel Santa Anita cnr Calles Leyva & Hidalgo; ⊙8:30am-6:30pm Mon-Fri, 8:30am-2pm Sat) also books *primera express* tickets in advance.

ⓘ Getting Around

Buses 72 'Castro-Chamizal' and 118 'DIF Castro Estación' (M\$5.60) do the 15-minute run to the train station from Blvd Castro, between Zaragoza and Prieto, every 15 minutes (5:30am to 9pm). They drop you one block before the station. You can take the bus for the *clase económica* train, departing at 7am, but to make sure of catching the 6am *primera express* get a taxi.

There are also buses to Topolobampo (M\$17, every 20 minutes until 7:30pm) from the corner of Cauhtémoc and Prieto for the Baja ferry.

Taxis in town cost M\$50, and to the airport/ Topolobampo approximately M\$150 to M\$200. They line up on Obregón, by the Best Western.

THE COPPER CANYON & FERROCARRIL CHIHUAHUA PACÍFICO

When explorer Frederick Schwatka visited the Copper Canyon (Barranca del Cobre) in the 1880s, he was sufficiently wowed by the stunning scenery to predict that, within a century, tourists would be converging here in droves. He was right. Today the Copper Canyon is northern Mexico's tourist magnet. There are two overriding reasons to visit: some of the world's deepest, most diverse canyon country, and the fact that you can ride right through it on Mexico's (and one of Latin America's) last and greatest passenger train rides. Of everything there is to see in the north, none compares in wonder to time spent in this region.

The focal point is a labyrinth of seven main canyons that cover an area four times larger than Arizona's Grand Canyon, and are in several parts considerably deeper (over 1800m). The canyons have been gouged out of the sierra's 25-million-year-old volcanic rock by tectonic movements and the rivers that now flow along their feet. Tropical fruits grow in the depths of some canyons while the high ground above is covered in alpine vegetation and, often, winter snows. Such diversity makes the Copper Canyon area a nature lover's paradise, and it's becoming still more of a buzzword for thrill-seekers too, following the creation of an adventure theme park, the

Parque de Aventuras Barrancas del Cobre, where you can soar over precipitous drops on Mexico's most hair-raising zip-lines or by cable car. The entire region is also home to one of Mexico's largest and most individual indigenous groups, the Tarahumara (see boxed text, p761).

As if this rumbustious rocky topography were not enough, you can also travel up, into and through some of it on the Ferrocarril Chihuahua Pacífico (Chihuahua Pacific Railway, aka the Copper Canyon Railway), which takes passengers on a jaw-dropping rail journey over 656km between Los Mochis near Mexico's Pacific coast and Chihuahua on its central high plains.

You *can* ride the train all the way through, or make an overnight stop then head back the way you came. But the spectacular canyon country deserves much more exploration. Most travelers make Creel their initial base, approximately eight hours from Los Mochis: it's the main base for Copper Canyon tourism and near some fascinatingly scenic spots. For similar cusp-of-the-canyon experiences you can also stay at the smaller Cerocahui, Areponápuchi or Divisadero, all near the railway. To get the real feel of the canyons, venture right down into them and stay at Urique or Batopilas. All manner of natural wonders – canyons, cliffs, towering rock massifs, rivers, waterfalls, lakes, forests – as well as fascinating human culture are accessible from all these places by foot, horse and in many cases mountain bike or motor vehicle.

Good seasons to visit are spring or autumn, when temperatures are not too hot at the bottom of the canyons or too cold at the top. A particularly good time to come is late September and October, when vegetation is green after the summer rains (which fall from around late June to late August). Hiking and riding down in the canyons is only really practicable from mid-October to March. May and June are unbearable at the bottom of the canyons but OK for activities at the top.

It's advisable to load up on cash in Los Mochis or Chihuahua: ATMs en route (in El Fuerte and Creel) should not be depended upon.

The remote recesses of this region harbor marijuana and opium plantations, from which part of the population makes a living and which yield some bloody incidents involving rival groups and/or the Mexican army. The *narcos* do not target tourists, but it's advisable to sound out the situation before venturing to remote areas, and take a trusted local guide if you go anywhere off-the-beaten-track.

The name Copper Canyon, coined by the Spanish when they mistook the greenish glow of lichen for copper, refers specifically to the chasm carved by the upper course of the Río Urique. The canyon's region also

RAILWAY SCHEDULE – FERROCARRIL CHIHUAHUA PACÍFICO

The *primera express* train runs in both directions daily; the *clase económica* runs from Los Mochis to Chihuahua on Tuesday, Friday and Sunday, and from Chihuahua to Los Mochis on Monday, Thursday and Saturday. Schedules change from time to time, and both trains tend to run a little late, so the times given below comprise just a rough guideline. If you are heading to Los Mochis on the *primera express* with hopes of making the Baja ferry from Topolobampo that same day, don't count on it. It almost never works out.

There is no time change between Los Mochis and Chihuahua.

Eastbound – Los Mochis to Chihuahua

STATION	PRIMERA EXPRESS		CLASE ECONÓMICA	
	ARRIVES (DAILY)	FARE FROM LOS MOCHIS (M$)	ARRIVES (TUE, FRI, SUN)	FARE FROM LOS MOCHIS (M$)
Los Mochis	6am (departs Los Mochis)	–	7am (departs Los Mochis)	–
El Fuerte	8:40am	400	9:40am	200
Témoris	11:40am	714	12:50pm	357
Bahuichivo	12:40pm	844	2:16pm	422
San Rafael	1:29pm	951	3:08pm	476
Posada Barrancas (Areponápuchi)	1:58pm	984	3:36pm	492
Divisadero	2:04pm	998	15:42pm	499
Creel	3:38pm	1191	5:22pm	596
Cuauhtémoc	6:30pm	1735	8:13pm	868
Chihuahua	8:56pm	2179	10:42pm	1090

Westbound – Chihuahua to Los Mochis

STATION	PRIMERA EXPRESS		CLASE ECONÓMICA	
	ARRIVES (DAILY)	FARE FROM CHIHUAHUA (M$)	ARRIVES (MON, THU, SAT)	FARE FROM CHIHUAHUA (M$)
Chihuahua	6am (departs Chihuahua)	–	7am (departs Chihuahua)	–
Cuauhtémoc	8:29am	444	9:29am	222
Creel	11:20am	991	12:20pm	496
Divisadero	12:34pm	1184	1:40pm	593
Posada Barrancas (Areponápuchi)	1:01pm	1198	2:11pm	599
San Rafael	1:18pm	1231	2:29pm	616
Bahuichivo	2:15pm	1338	3:30pm	669
Témoris	3:15pm	1468	4:26pm	734
El Fuerte	6pm	1909	7:18pm	955
Los Mochis	8:40pm	2179	9:58pm	1090

forms part of the Sierra Madre Occidental. Apart from the Barranca de Cobre, its other major canyons are the Barrancas de Urique, Sinforosa, Batopilas, Oteros, Chinipas and Candameña. All seven plumb to depths of 1300m or more.

Ferrocarril Chihuahua Pacífico

The stats say everything: 656km of track, 37 bridges, 86 tunnels and more than 60 years in the making. One of the world's most

Copper Canyon

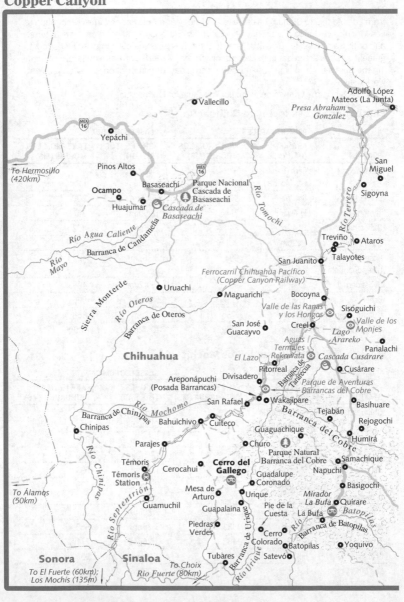

picturesque rail journeys, the **Ferrocarril Chihuahua Pacífico** (Copper Canyon Railway; www.chepe.com.mx), completed in 1961, is as phenomenal in its engineering prowess as in the canyon views it yields. It connects a town 24km shy of the Pacific coast with the mountainous, arid interior of northern

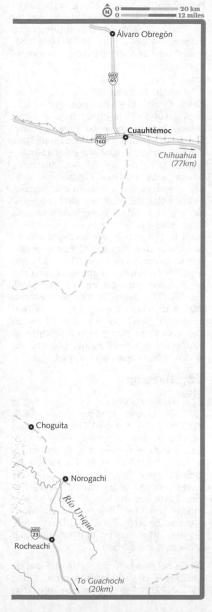

Mexico via tricky canyon gradients which force it to rise up over 2400m. The line is the major link between Chihuahua and the coast, heavily used for freight as well as passengers. The beauty of the landscape it traverses has made it one of Mexico's prime tourist excursions.

Nicknamed 'El Chepe' (using the Spanish initials of 'Chihuahua' and 'Pacífico'), the railway operates two trains. The 1st-class *primera express* runs in both directions daily and has an overpriced restaurant car and bar. The slightly slower and much cheaper *clase económica* runs three times a week in each direction and has a snack bar. Cars on both trains have air-conditioning, heating and comfortable seats with ample leg room. The *clase económica* is certainly nice enough for most travelers, so the choice comes down to your preferred journey time. The *primera express* starts out from Los Mochis and Chihuahua one hour earlier than the *clase económica,* and arrives at the other end of the line a scheduled two hours earlier. If you are stopping off along the way, you can take whichever train fits your schedule better. Buses (see Cerocahui p758, Creel p765 and Chihuahua p774) also cover some sections of the route and generally are a cheaper and quicker alternative.

Heading east (toward Chihuahua) you should be able to see the best views by daylight on either train. In the other direction, consider taking the *primera express,* as the *clase económica* passes much of the best scenery (between Creel and El Fuerte) after dark, especially in winter.

Between Los Mochis and El Fuerte, the train passes through flat farmland, then begins to climb through hills speckled with dark pillars of cacti. It passes over the long Río Fuerte bridge and through the first of 86 tunnels about four hours after leaving Los Mochis. The train hugs the sides of deepening canyons and makes a spectacular zigzag ascent into a tunnel above Témoris, after which pine trees appear on the hillsides. By the next station, Bahuichivo, you are in the Sierra Madre uplands, with flower-dotted meadows bisecting an entrancing alpine landscape. The biggest highlight of the train ride is stopping at Divisadero, where you get your only glimpse of the actual Copper Canyon (Barranca del Cobre). The train circles back over itself in a complete loop to gain height at El Lazo before chugging on to Creel and Chihuahua.

Tickets

At any station you can board the train without a ticket if there are free seats, and buy a ticket from the conductor. Outside the peak seasons (Semana Santa, July/August and Christmas/New Year), you will often be able to do this. However it is never certain and it's advisable to reserve/buy tickets a month or more ahead for peak-season travel, and at least a day ahead at other times.

Tickets are sold at Los Mochis station (p751) and Chihuahua station (p775) for trips starting at any station. *Primera express* tickets are sold up to a month in advance, and *clase económica* tickets a day in advance. **Telephone reservations** (☎614-439-72-12, 800-122-43-73, from the US 888-484-1623), with English speakers available, and **email reservations** (chepe@ferromex.com.mx) can be made up to a year in advance. On the *primera express*, you can make stopovers (usually up to three) at no extra cost, if you specify places and dates when you make the booking.

For same-day tickets, you should be at Los Mochis or Chihuahua station at 5am for the *primera express* train, and 6am for the *clase económica*. Only Los Mochis, Creel, Cuauhtémoc and Chihuahua stations have ticket offices.

Agencies such as Viajes Flamingo (p752) in Los Mochis, and Rojo y Casavantes (p774) in Chihuahua, sell *primera express* tickets at least one day in advance, and any of the area's many **Balderrama Hotels** (www.mexicoscoppercanyon.com) will assist their clients in making reservations.

El Fuerte

☎698 / POP 13,000 / ELEV 180M

Clustered around one of the country's most striking plazas, El Fuerte oozes colonial splendor. For many centuries the most important commercial center in northwestern Mexico due to its proximity to the silver mines in the canyons, this is now a picturesque little town surrounded by one of Latin America's last-standing dry tropical forests. A preferable start or end point for a trip on the Ferrocarril Chihuahua Pacífico, it's worth a stay of more than just a night to take a trip on the Río Fuerte and explore the unique subtropical countryside.

El Fuerte was founded in 1564, and is named for a 17th-century fort built on its distinctive high point of Cerro de las Pilas to protect settlers from indigenous attacks.

◉ Sights & Activities

The riverside *malecón* (waterfront promenade), once completed (the projected date is 2015), should provide engaging strolling.

Museo Mirador El Fuerte　MUSEUM
(admission M$7; ☺9am-7pm Tue-Sun) This museum, built to look like the original fort, but not on the original site, is at the top of Cerro de las Pilas. It has interesting exhibits (mostly in Spanish) on area history, the indigenous Mayo culture and the Bosque Secreto (Secret Forest) – plus marvelous views from its upper walkway.

Bosque Secreto　FOREST
(Secret Forest) Five hundred years ago, over 550,000 sq km of dry tropical forest stretched down the coast from northern Mexico to Panama. Of the remaining 10%, much occupies the land of northern Sinaloa around El Fuerte, an area now known as Bosque Secreto. A local campaign is seeking to protect this area from the rampant deforestation, affecting the 1800 species of native plants and the indigenous Mayo and Yaqui who live in the forest and depend upon it. The campaign encourages visitors to explore this endangered forest ecosystem to increase awareness. The Río Fuerte winds through much of the forest, and can be explored with **Chucho's** (☎cell phone 698-1069590; alfagu7@hotmail.com; Reforma 100), with whom kayak trips are M$400 to M$600. Hotel Río Vista (see following) organizes **tours** (per person M$250) to go bird-watching around Bosque Secreto, and to visit 2000-year-old petroglyphs.

🛏 Sleeping

TOP CHOICE Hotel Río Vista　HOTEL $$
(☎893-04-13; Junto Al Museo Mirador; s/d/tr M$450/600/750; 🅿❄@☀) River views, and astounding ones, are exactly what you get here. The hotel owner, an avid bird-watcher, has lovingly built up his rural multi-tier treasure piece by piece, with expansive rooms boasting bright murals, quirky historical artifacts, airy terraces and a picture-window restaurant. Best is the room which contains the original wall of El Fuerte's fort. He also offers guided bird-watching and petroglyph excursions.

Torres del Fuerte　BOUTIQUE HOTEL $$$
(☎893-19-74; www.hotelestorres.com; Robles 102; r M$1200-1700; 🅿🔄❄☀) Francisco Torres has

turned his family's 400-year-old hacienda into a beautiful boutique hotel: a ménage à trois of colonial relic, rustic elegance and contemporary art, set around gorgeous gardens. All 25 rooms are uniquely themed, many with slate bathrooms and exposed adobe/brick walls. There's also the gourmet (primarily in-house) restaurant **Bonifacio's** (mains M$70-300; ⊙7am-10pm). The associated **Torres Travel** (☑893-19-74; www.coppercanyon explorer.com) can set up most Copper Canyon activities you fancy.

Posada del Hidalgo RESORT $$
(☑893-11-94; www.hotelposadadelhidalgo.com; Hidalgo 101; r/ste M$967/1500; P❋@☎≋) This former hacienda has 54 massive rooms, most with two double beds, and all with bundles of classic colonial charm. Our favorites were those arranged around the inviting internal sunken garden. There is a spa and a beautiful open-air restaurant. It's popular with tour groups.

Hotel Guerrero HOTEL $
(☑893-05-24; Juárez 206; d/tr M$250/350) This welcoming little cheapie is opposite where buses arrive from Los Mochis. The rooms, set around a pillared patio, are basic but colorful.

✗ Eating

The wealth of fresh water around El Fuerte produces must-have local specialties such as *cauques* or *langostinos* (freshwater crayfish) and *lobina* (black bass).

La Canastilla FISH $$
(Juárez 510; mains M$70-188; ⊙9am-9pm) You can't keep a good restaurant down. Burned out by a fire, this secluded riverside spot is back with the same celebrated specialties such as *langostinos rellenos* (stuffed crayfish).

El Mesón del General FISH $$
(Juárez 202; mains M$80-220; ⊙11am-9:30pm; ☻) The most traditional of El Fuerte's options, this institution serves up several styles of *pulpo* (octopus; M$118) and combo plates of various river delicacies.

Restaurante Diligencias MEXICAN $$
(mains M$90-200; ⊙7am-11pm; ☻) Best of several agreeable places on the Plaza de Armas for breakfast, the Hotel La Choza's restaurant does lunch and dinner, too.

ⓘ Information

Banamex (Juárez 212; ⊙9am-4pm Mon-Fri) ATM.
Cafe Internet (Montesclaros; per hr M$10; ⊙8am-11pm Mon-Fri, to midnight Sat & Sun) Also provides tourist information.

ⓘ Getting There & Around

Buses to Los Mochis (M$70, two hours) depart about every half-hour, 5am to 7pm, from Juárez near Calle 16 de Septiembre.

The train station is 6km south of town (M$100 by taxi). Most hotels offer station pickup and drop-off for clients, for which they may or may not charge (up to the taxi rate). If you arrive by train in the evening, you can usually get a ride into town with one of the hotel vans for M$40 or so.

The unpaved back road to Álamos from here requires 4WD and takes five hours.

Cerocahui

☑635 / POP 1500 / ELEV 1600M

The village of Cerocahui is a small *ejido* (communal landholding), dedicated mainly to forestry, in the middle of a verdant, vista-laden valley, and easily reached from Bahuichivo station, 16km away. A stay here gives you the chance to explore canyon country that sees far fewer tourists than places nearer Creel. Cerocahui is also on the road to the enticing canyon-bottom village of Urique.

The village's pretty yellow-domed church, **San Francisco Javier de Cerocahui**, was founded in 1680. Across the street is a much-visited Catholic boarding school for Tarahumara girls.

If you are not going to be continuing to Urique from here, at least take the excursion (offered by all accommodations) to **Cerro del Gallego**, a spectacular lookout over the Barranca de Urique, 25km on along the Urique road.

🛏 Sleeping & Eating

TOP CHOICE **Hotel Paraíso del Oso** HOTEL $$$
(☑in Chihuahua 614-421-33-72, in the US 800-884-3107; www.mexicohorse.com; campsite/dm M$50/100, s/d incl 3 meals & Bahuichivo transfers M$1440/2100; P☻@☎✗) Paraíso del Oso occupies a peaceful and picturesque spot by the road from Bahuichivo, 3km north of Cerocahui. It's a great base for bird-watching, hikes and horseback rides. Rooms are large, simple and comfy, vegetarian meals

are available and there's a great book collection. The best thing about a stay here is the rare chance to mix with and find more about the local Tarahumara. This can be organized through the hotel, which also helps organize the scholarship programs for Tarahumara children. There are horseback treks offered, including down to Urique and beyond.

Hotel Cerocahui
HOTEL $$

(📞456-52-75; www.hotelcerocahui.com; s/d incl Bahuichivo transfers M$300/500; ✱) A lovely, light little place on the main plaza, with four rooms owned by an enthusiastic young couple that run a host of canyon trips. There's a homey attached restaurant. Meals are extra and nonguests are welcome if they reserve in advance. Their excellent guide takes you on beautiful local hikes to waterfalls and viewpoints.

Cabañas San Isidro
CABAÑAS $$$

(📞456-52-57; www.coppercanyonamigos.com; Carretera a Urique Km 24; s/d incl 3 meals & Bahuichivo transfers M$1235/1755; 🅿) Family-run lodge in the forested hills along the Urique road 8km from Cerocahui, with cozy adobe-and-wood cabins on a working ranch and horseback/foot/vehicle trips on offer.

Hotel Misión
HOTEL $$$

(📞456-52-94; www.hotelmision.com; s/d incl 3 meals & Bahuichivo transfers M$1500/2500; 🅿✷) The best-known hotel in Cerocahui and a link in the Balderrama chain of Copper Canyon hotels, this former hacienda opposite the church has rustic rooms complete with wood-burning stoves, and a bar, restaurant, souvenir shop and pool table. The 10 newer rooms overlooking the small vineyard are the better choice.

❶ Getting There & Away

Cerocahui hotels will pick you up at Bahuichivo station if you have reserved. If you haven't, you can often catch a ride with one of their vans anyway, or thumb a lift. A local bus known as La Ruta leaves Bahuichivo station for Cerocahui (M$40, 30 to 45 minutes) and Urique (M$140, 3½ hours or more), daily after the last train of the day arrives. Returning, La Ruta normally leaves Urique about 7:30am or 8am, passes through Cerocahui around 10am to 10:30am, and aims to connect with the bus leaving Bahuichivo for San Rafael (M$80, about one hour). From San Rafael there are buses at 7am, 9am, 11am, 1:30pm and 3:15pm to Areponápuchi (M$15, 15 minutes), Divisadero (M$15, 20 minutes), Creel (M$55, 1½ hours) and Chihuahua (M$270, six to seven hours). A bus back to Bahuichivo leaves San Rafael at 1pm.

Other unpaved roads connect Mesa de Arturo, 12km southeast of Cerocahui off the Urique road, to Choix (from which there's a paved road to El Fuerte); and Bahuichivo to Álamos via Témoris (after which you need to ford the Río Chinipas). These roads have tough 4WD-only stretches and traverse isolated back-country harboring drug plantations. Don't consider driving them without taking very good local advice first, and preferably take a local along with you if you do. For road logs and some maps, see www.mexicohorse.com.

Urique

📞635 / POP 1100 / ELEV 550M

This starry-skied ex-mining village lies at the bottom of the deepest of all the canyons, the spectacular Barranca de Urique (measuring 1870m from rim to river) yet it's by far the easiest canyon-bottom village to access. It's a good base for all kinds of canyon hikes. Getting there is part of the fun: the unpaved road (a 40km trip from Cerocahui) makes a breathtaking 1050m descent to the village. Urique is rural – more Tecates are passed around here than educations – and marijuana fuels the local economy, so be wary about town.

For **day hikes** you can go up the Río Urique (the same river that flows through the Copper Canyon proper) to Guadalupe Coronado village (7km) or downriver to Guapalaina (4km). The two- to three-day trek over to Batopilas is a bigger challenge. Several robberies have occurred on the 'traditional' route via the village of Cerro Colorado, so guides have been taking a more southerly route via Pie de la Cuesta. A good local guide with a pack horse costs M$4000 for this trip; enquire at Entre Amigos.

Urique is also the venue of the **Copper Canyon Ultra Marathon** (www.caballoblanco. com), a 70km-plus run on the first Sunday in March that sees sandaled Tarahumara running with all comers, and is also the excuse for a town party. Its organizer Micah True, alias Caballo Blanco (White Horse), died as this book was going to print, so the future of the event is uncertain.

TOP CHOICE **Entre Amigos** (www.amongamigos. com; campsite per person M$100, dm/r M$170/475; 🅿✉@🛜✷) is a peaceful US-run place 1km north (upriver) from the town center. It has nice stone cabins, dorm rooms, campsites, a big communal kitchen and free fruit and veggies from the garden. Entre Amigos can hook you up with dependable local guides.

Hotels in town include **Hotel Barrancas de Urique** (☑456-60-76; Principal 201; s/d M$250/300; [P][❋]), on the main street with an impressive attached restaurant, and **Hotel Estrella del Río** (☑456-60-03; s/d M$250/500; [❋]), with better rooms. The latter is a block back up the road out of town from Principal, on a dead-end track to the left. **Restaurant Plaza** (Principal; ⊘7am-9pm) has tables in its shady back garden and is known for its *aguachile* (M$80), a soupy shrimp cocktail full of onions and tomatoes and spiced up with *chiltepín* peppers, and served in a *molacajete* (Mexican pestle and mortar).

The town hall on the main street has a small **tourist office** (☑456-60-42; turismo. urique@gmail.com; ⊘8am-3pm).

A local bus known as La Ruta leaves from the Bahuichivo station for Urique (M$140, 3½ hours or more), daily after the last train of the day arrives. Your accommodations may arrange a transfer from Bahuichivo for about M$1000. Cerocahui hotels bring guided trips down here and can also arrange one-way rides.

Areponápuchi (Posada Barrancas)

☑635 / POP 220 / ELEV 2220M

About 4km southwest of Divisadero, Posada Barrancas station is next to Areponápuchi, the only village on the train line right by the rim of the canyon. 'Arepo' – just a couple of dozen houses, a tiny church and a few inns – is where it all comes together for the first time, with spectacular views of the canyon dangling precariously under the patios of a couple of hotels here.

The mega new attraction nearby is the Parque de Aventuras Barrancas del Cobre (Copper Canyon Adventure Park), where activities include formidable zip-lines that whoosh you over precipitous 1500m-plus canyon drops. For more traditional excursions, Arepo accommodations can organize canyon trips from hikes along the rim to horseback rides or overnight camping treks right down to the river.

An easy path with several good viewpoints runs along the canyon rim to the left (north) of Hotel Posada Barrancas Mirador, and several lookouts (as well as the adventure park) lie short distances off the road between here and Divisadero.

🛏 Sleeping & Eating

TOP CHOICE **Hotel Mansión Tarahumara** RESORT $$$

(☑578-30-30, 800-777-46-68; www.hotelmansion tarahumara.com.mx; s incl 3 meals M$1400-1800, d incl 3 meals M$2000-2600; [P][☎][♨]) This quirky resort with its trademark turrets 500m from the station has a variety of attractive rooms. The 17 newest up on the canyon rim (commanding the highest prices) are the showstoppers, with plush beds and balconies that enjoy the same views as those found at Hotel Posada Barrancas Mirador. There's also a brand new rim-poised restaurant (meals M$200; open noon to 4pm and 7 to 9pm).

Cabañas Díaz CABAÑAS $

(☑578-30-08; barrancasdelcobre_mexico@yahoo .com.mx; s/d M$250/500, without bathroom M$200/400; [P]) The Díaz family's guest lodge is known for its hospitable cabins, tasty meals (M$70) and great guided hikes and horseback rides (four-hour outing for two by foot/horse M$300/600). If arriving solo, walk down the main road into the village until you see the sign on the right (900m).

Cabañas Arepo Barrancas CABAÑAS $

(☑578-30-46, cell phone 635-2938411; s/d incl breakfast M$300/400; [P]) This is another good budget option – six cabañas with tiled floors and comfy beds – though it's a bit further from the canyon rim. Look for owner Lolita Mancinas at Divisadero station – she works the middle food stall there, with a 'Renta de Cabañas' sign, and can provide free transportation – or walk through Arepo 750m past the sign for Cabañas Diaz. Meals (damned fine ones) here cost about M$50; there are also van and horseback trips (from M$100 per person per hour).

Hotel Posada Barrancas Mirador HOTEL $$$

(☑578-30-20, 800-816-81-96; www.mexicoscopper canyon.com; s/d incl 3 meals M$1975/2985; [P][⊚]) The main attraction here is drinking in the unbeatable canyon views (from each room's private balcony, or the perfectly perched restaurant), so the fact that this jewel in the Balderrama chain is often swarming with tour groups and doesn't exactly have Michelin-quality food can probably be overlooked.

❶ Getting There & Away

See p758 for information on getting to Posada Barrancas station by train. San Rafael buses en

THE CHANGING FACE OF THE CANYONS

The Parque de Aventuras Barrancas del Cobre is the beginning of the redevelopment project known as Megaproyecto Barrancas del Cobre which, depending on your viewpoint, will either revitalize tourism locally or forever tarnish one of nature's greatest wonders. Overall opinion seems to sway towards the former, and the new canyon attractions are far from the mar on the majestic landscape that was feared. Locals generally welcome the prospect of more money and jobs, though two Tarahumara villages have fought attempts to replace them with hotels. But the next phases of the project have in the pipeline more luxury hotels, an amusement park with canyon-lip roller-coaster, a canyon-top golf course and a new international airport at Creel. Time, perhaps, will be the best gauge of the popularity of the canyon-transforming plans.

route to Creel pass through five times daily at 7.15am, 9.15am, 11.15am, 1.45pm and 3.30pm. Buses drop you at the entrance to the main highway just outside the village. From Creel (M$50, one hour) buses leave for Areponápuchi every two hours from 10:30am to 6:30pm.

Parque de Aventuras Barrancas del Cobre

Opening amid much fanfare in 2011, the ambitious Copper Canyon Adventure Park on the canyon rim between Areponápuchi and Divisadero, including Mexico's longest series of zip-lines, a cable car, and rappelling and rock-climbing opportunities, allows you to experience some of the world's most profound canyon scenery like never before. Once the only way of appreciating the Copper Canyon was via a peep from the rim or a trek down inside. Now, the park's **tirolesas** (zip-lines; ⊙9am-1pm; per person M$600) transport you on a set of seven lines from a height of 2400m to over halfway to the canyon floor. It's Latin America's longest zip-line. Line 4 is the most spine-tingling, with over 1km of cable alone, but Line 7 reveals exquisite views of the Barranca de Urique (Urique Canyon) in addi-

tion to the one you are whooshing through. A couple of heart-in-mouth wobbly bridges help you complete the cross-canyon odyssey. Allow at least an hour to descend to the spectacular viewpoint of Mesón de Bacajípare. It doubles as the lower station for the **teleférico** (cable car; return M$250; ⊙9am-4:30pm), which you will have to take back up. You can skip the zip-lines and head straight down on the cable car (20 minutes each way, plus a 20-minute stop). Tickets and information are available at the souvenir shop inside the **park center** (☑689-589-68-05; Piedra Volada; ⊙9am-5:30pm), built over a gob-smacking fissure in the canyon walls. Rappelling and rock-climbing, both M$450 per person, can be arranged here; there's also a restaurant.

The nearest public transportation is at Arepo or Divisadero, both an easy 1.5km walk away. Direct buses from Chihuahua to Areponápouchi (every two hours) pass the park entrance courtesy of **Autotranspotes Turísticos Noroeste** (www.turisticosnoroeste. com). Returning, it's not always easy to flag a bus down but to Divisadero/Areponápouchi it's a pleasant walk and there's a courtesy mobility vehicle to Divisadero for those who don't want to walk.

Divisadero

ELEV 2240M

Divisadero, a train stop without a village, is your only chance to see into the miraculous canyon without stopping off from the train. All trains halt here for 20 minutes, giving you enough time to jump out, gawk, snap some photos at the viewpoint over the road and hop back on. You can just discern a tiny fragment of the Río Urique at the bottom of the actual Copper Canyon. Ration your time carefully, as the station is also a souvenir market and spectacular food court. *Gorditas* (masa cakes), burritos and *chiles rellenos,* cooked up in makeshift oil-drum stoves, are worth the stop alone. The food at Antojitos Lucy is like edible art. Gobble it up quickly – the conductors aren't supposed to allow food back onto the train.

All this together with the nearby adventure park 1.5km south means a stay of longer than 20 minutes is a great idea. You can check into **Hotel Divisadero Barrancas** (☑in Chihuahua 614-415-11-99, in the US 888-232-4219; s/d incl 3 meals M$1850/2350, r without meals M$1510; ℗❄), right by the canyon viewpoint, which has 52 beautiful rooms (Nos 35 to 52 have the best vistas) and a **restaurant-bar** (mains M$80-160; ☻), with spectacular views guaranteed.

You can also spend more time here without staying the night if you switch from a *primera express* to *clase económica* train, which runs a scheduled 1½ hours behind. You will need two separate tickets to do this. The buses serving Areponápuchi, San Rafael and ultimately Bahuichivo also run through Divisadero, stopping down through the market stalls from the train station – quicker and cheaper than continuing by train.

Creel

🛈 635 / POP 5000 / ELEV 2330M

Creel is a railway and logging town surrounded by pine forests and interesting rock formations, and the center of Copper Canyon tourism. Don't get any visions of teeming megaresorts into your head however: with its wide single main street and log-fuelled architecture, the town has good hotels, just a few restaurants and souvenir shops and an all-pervading, alpine-type serendipity. Tarahumara, in their multihued dress, are commonly seen about town. If you meet other travelers anywhere in northern

THE TARAHUMARA *WITH THE HELP OF DOUG DIEGO RHODES*

A fascinating part of canyon life is the presence of one of Mexico's most distinctive indigenous groups, the Tarahumara, who live in caves and small houses across the countryside here. Most easily identifiable are the women, dressed in colorful skirts and blouses and often carrying infants on their backs. They sell beautiful hand-woven baskets and carved wooden dolls and animals at ridiculously low prices at tourist sites around the sierra. Most men now wear Western jeans instead of the traditional loincloth, but both sexes still often walk in sandals hewn from tire-tread and strips of leather.

The Tarahumara remain largely an enigma. Even their name is debated (Tarahumara, or Rarámuri?). Many believe it was originally 'ralamuli' which was Hispanicized to 'Rarámuri' and evolved to 'Tarahumara,' the term by which they usually refer to themselves. Contrary to popular belief, the Spanish incursion did not force the Tarahumara into the Canyons: they were here when the first Jesuits arrived in 1608. There are two main Tarahumara groups: the Alta (high) and the Baja (low) with whom Western contact was made by Jesuit priests from higher-altitude Hidalgo del Parral and lower-altitude El Fuerte respectively. Culture and language are radically different between the Altas and Bajas, and because of long-term isolation, every community has a slightly different culture and language. No one even knows how many Tarahumara exist. Estimates vary between 50,000 and 120,000.

Rarámuri means 'those who run fast' – and these people are most famous for running long distances swiftly, sometimes up to 20 hours without stopping. They used their aptitude for running to hunt deer by bow and arrow as little as a generation ago. The Copper Canyon area now has its own annual ultramarathon at Urique (p758).

But a better cultural insight into the Tarahumara is their sense of fairness. 'Korima' is a custom where someone who has a good crop is 'blessed' and obliged to share his good fortune with others. Another tradition is the *tesgüinada*, a raucous social gathering at which Tarahumara relax their natural reserve and celebrate communal work and festivals with plenty of *tesgüino,* a potent corn beer.

Even these traditionally isolated people have been influenced by incomers, and many have adopted a type of Catholicism. However, their take on Christianity and Christian festivals is often idiosyncratic – regularly accompanied by drumming and lots of *tesgüino*.

But the Tarahumara have maintained their lifestyle despite incursions of conquistadors, missionaries, railways, drug gangs and tourism. They have one word to refer all non-Tarahumara people: *chabochi,* which means 'with spider-webbing on the face,' a reference to bearded Spanish colonists. The majority continue to live a subsistence life in the remote Sierra Madre Occidental countryside.

The Tarahumara are also generally materially poor, and their communities have some serious health problems: there are high rates of infant mortality, malnutrition and teenage pregnancy, with some of the little relief coming from Catholic missions.

Mexico, it will most probably be here, and while story-swapping in a hostel, hotel or cozy bar is fun, Creel's main value for travelers is as a base for exploring the surrounding canyon country.

Creel can be very cold in winter, even snowy; and it's none too warm at night in autumn. In summer, the cool air and pine-tree aroma from the surrounding forests are a welcome relief from Mexico's coastal lowland and desert heat. Bring a sweater, even if the rest of Mexico is scorching.

⊙ Sights

Museo Casa de las Artesanías del Estado de Chihuahua   MUSEUM
(Av Vías del Ferrocarril 178; admission M$10; ◷9am-6pm Mon-Sat, to 1pm Sun) This museum near the plaza is a great spot to delve deeper into Tarahumara culture. It has excellent exhibits with text in English on local history and Tarahumara culture and crafts. Here you'll see gorgeous woven baskets, traditional clothing, photos and more.

⌲ Tours
These typically divide into either minivan tours which cover different combinations of attractions around Creel, or more themed excursions (by bicycle or horseback). Agencies, understandably, try to offer all the possibilities.

Scenic Minivan Tours   TOUR
Almost all hotels and agencies offer minivan tours to canyons, waterfalls, Tarahumara settlements, hot springs and other places. One popular trip of around five hours covers Cusárare village and waterfall, Lago Arareko and the Valleys of Frogs and Mushrooms (see p765 for more on these places). Other good half- or full-day destinations include Divisadero, the Cascada de Basaseachi and Rekowata hot springs. Typical prices are M$250 per person for half-day trips and up to M$500 for full-day trips. Overnight trips are offered to the wonderful canyon village of Batopilas. You can reach most of these destinations by public transportation but a guided tour is a quicker and, occasionally, more informative way of doing it (although the authenticity of the experience can be greatly diluted). Ascertain what you are getting before committing your cash. Is your guide genuinely knowledgeable and experienced? Will they just drive you there or will they explain it all too, and if so in what language?

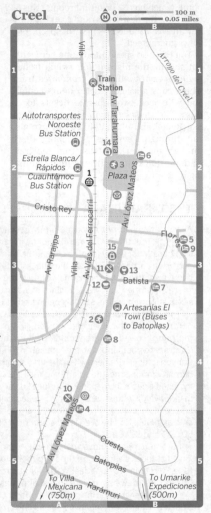

Creel

Cycling & Horseback Riding   TOUR
This is prime riding country, and many attractions near Creel can be enjoyed on horseback, bicycle or scooter. This is particularly attractive as you can cover terrain the minivans can't manage, and with significantly more peace and quiet. The whole area is a mountain-bike playground: you could just rent a bike (several hotels including Casa Margarita have them for around M$100/200 per half/full day), and take in all the area's attractions independently.

Most tours require a minimum number of people, typically four. Casa Margarita or

Creel

Real de Chapultepec Hotel are places where individuals can often find tours to join.

3 Amigos   TOUR
(☑456-00-36; www.amigos3.com, www.amigo trails.com; Av López Mateos 46; ⊘9am-7pm) The 3 Amigos built its reputation on helping you 'be your own guide in the Copper Canyon' through its rentals of quality mountain bikes (per four hours/day M$130/200), scooters (per hour/day including fuel M$100/500) and trucks (double-cab Nissan pickup; per 24 hours M$1300), with free maps, travel information and sometimes lunch. These are great options for independent souls. Affiliated company Amigo Trails also offers self-guided truck tour packages and customized guided canyon trips.

Tarahumara Tours   GUIDED TOUR
(Plaza; ⊘9am-7pm) A group of local driver-guides offering similar trips to the hotels, from two hours to two days, often at better prices. Talk to them at their office on the plaza.

Umarike Expediciones   ADVENTURE TOUR
(☑456-06-32, cell phone 614-4065464; www.uma rike.com.mx) Internet-based mountain-biking specialist offering guided bike and hiking adventure trips from one to eight days. It also rents bikes (M$180 per day), and offers maps and information. Eight-day mountain-bike trips to Batopilas cost M$15,700, including transportation from Chihuahua and most meals. Transportation from the US border can be arranged from M$2700.

🛏 Sleeping

Creel offers every kind of lodging experience, from dorm-style bunks up.

Real de Chapultepec Hotel   HOTEL $
(☑456-08-94; realdechapultepec@hotmail.com; Flores 260; s & d M$150-250; 🐾) Probably Mexico's best bargain: the owner is adding to his property at a rate of knots, but right now there are 10 brand new rooms, many with murals by local artists, plus a common room with free wi-fi. Quad-bikes are for rent.

Casa Margarita   HOSTEL $
(☑456-00-45; www.hoteles-margaritas.com; Av López Mateos 11; dm/s/d inc breakfast & dinner M$150/250/400; ⊖🐾) The long-running Margarita, bang on the plaza, seems to resonate a different vibe every time we visit. This time it felt far quieter, with meals now often served in affiliated Hotel Plaza Mexicana, detracting from the ambience somewhat. Still, it's *the* backpacker classic with a new wing of rooms being added, and the existing ones, while simple, are still as clean. Bathrooms have Creel's hottest, fastest showers.

Hotel Plaza Mexicana   HOTEL $$
(☑456-02-45; www.hoteles-margaritas.com; Batista s/n; s/d/tr/q incl breakfast & dinner M$500/600/700/800; P🐾) If you've outgrown the hostel scene but still want a laid-back base, head for this comfortable hotel, run by the same family as Casa Margarita. Comfy, folksy, recently modernized rooms occupy two floors along a pretty courtyard.

Best Western The Lodge at Creel LODGE $$$
(☑456-00-71, in the US 800-528-1234; www.thelodgeatcreel.com; Av López Mateos 61; s/d M$1310/1330; P⊖@🐾) The classiest spot in town, designed to look like a hunting lodge, has well-heeled log-cabin-style rooms with wood-burning stoves and bathtubs. There's also a fitness center, spa and two of Creel's better eateries, Restaurant Sierra Madre and Pizzeria Artesanal.

Villa Mexicana
LODGE, CAMPGROUND **$$$**

(☏456-06-65; www.vmcoppercanyon.com; Av López Mateos s/n; campsite per person M$100, RV site with full hookups from M$200, 2-/4-person cabin M$1250/1850; P☺@☎🀄) This well-equipped and popular cabin-hotel-cum-RV park at the south end of Creel has very cozy log cabins, as well as a busy restaurant, bar, grocery store, laundry, games room, playground and outdoor barbecues.

Motel Cascada Inn
HOTEL **$$**

(☏456-02-53; www.motelcascadainn.com; Av López Mateos 49; s/d M$500/650; P☺☎🏊) A well-run, main-street spot with good-size, terracotta-floored rooms, an indoor pool, restaurant, bar and plenty of parking.

Casa de Huéspedes Pérez
HOSTEL **$**

(☏456-03-91; Flores 257; dm/d M$100/250; P) This guesthouse has one- to six-person log-walled rooms with wood-stove heating, plus bundles of TLC from the owner.

🍴 Eating & Drinking

Restaurant Verónica
RESTAURANT **$$**

(Av López Mateos 33; mains M$65-120; ☺7:30am-10:30pm; ☺) The must-try dish at this spirited local favorite for steaks and chicken is *el norteño*, a cheesy, beefy mess served in a cast-iron skillet that you eat with tortillas. The salsa's feisty; the value superb.

El Sillón Rojo
MEXICAN **$$**

(Av López s/n; breakfasts M$30-40, mains M$90; ☺8am-9pm; ☑) How do clouds, pygmies and giraffes tie into a dinner menu? Outshining the brightest Tarahumara dress with its decor, this cheerful joint is great for proper Mexican coffee and hotcakes at breakfast or, later, for creative salads and fish and beef dishes. Opposite the Best Western.

Best Western The Lodge at Creel
RESTAURANT **$$$**

(Av López Mateos 61; ☺) It pains us to mention a chain once, let alone twice, per destination but such is Creel's dearth of other decent eats. The main event here is **Restaurant Sierra Madre** (mains M$55-175; ☺noon-9pm) doing steaks and seafood; you can also dine in street-facing **Pizzería Artesanal** (mains M$150-200; ☺2-9pm), with fancy pizza. Expect stone walls, wood beams and plenty of taxidermy.

Luna Creel
CAFE

(Av López Mateos 40 altos; admission evenings M$10; ☺9am-1pm & 4-11pm) The live *trova* ballads and oldies at this upstairs cafe, nightly from 7pm, attract a good crowd. Good light eats are served, including sensational banana or walnut cake. No alcohol, but good hot drinks.

Tío Molcas
BAR

(Av López Mateos 35; ☺6pm-1am Sun-Thu, to 2am Fri & Sat) The cozy, wood-heated bar out back here is the best beer stop.

🛍 Shopping

Shops in Creel sell Tarahumara handicrafts as well as distinctive Mata Ortiz pottery (see p776) amid assorted kitsch. Look for names such as Raweli, where you can pick up locally made jewelry.

Artesanías Misión
HANDICRAFTS

(Parroquia 64, Plaza s/n; ☺9am-1pm & 3-6pm Mon-Sat) Traditional selection of handicrafts: all the store's earnings go to support Creel's Catholic mission hospital, which provides free medical care for the Tarahumara.

LOCAL KNOWLEDGE

VISITING THE COPPER CANYON

Tourists are sometimes staying away from the Copper Canyon at the moment, because it's in the same province as Ciudad Juárez, which is dangerous. But Chihuahua is a province bigger in size than England: people are missing out. The developments going on in the Copper Canyon are some of the Mexico's most radical. These won't spoil the region like some people say. The new adventure park with zip-lines over the canyon; the top-end hotels planned for the canyon bottom; an international airport; a golf course: these are the toys. They're ways to attract people. The real adventures down in the canyons will be the same as ever: even more legendary because of the contrasts they provide with the big tourist developments. Mountain biking down that crazy track into Batopilas; hiking near Urique; driving the back roads by 4WD: these canyons have both amazing adventures and, now, incredible luxury as well.

Ivan Fernández,
Co-owner of 3 Amigos, Creel

ℹ Information

3 Amigos (☎456-00-36; www.amigos3.com; Av López Mateos 46; ☺9am-7pm) A good source for maps and local info.

Clínica Santa Teresita (☎456-01-05; Parroquia; ☺24hr) Behind Casa Margarita.

La Escualita (Av López Mateos s/n; per hr M$15; ☺8am-9pm) Internet access near the Best Western.

Police station (☎456-04-50) Just off the plaza.

Post office (☺8am-4:30pm Mon-Fri, 8am-noon Sat) On the plaza.

Santander (Av López Mateos 17; ☺9am-4pm Mon-Fri) Creel's only (erratic) ATM.

ℹ Getting There & Around

Bus

Travel between Creel and Chihuahua, and between Creel, Divisadero and Areponápuchi, may be more convenient by bus than train: trips are shorter and more frequent. **Autotransportes Noroeste** (Villa) runs buses to Cuauhtémoc (M$160, three hours) and Chihuahua (M$280, 4½ hours) six times daily, and to Divisadero (M$45, one hour), Areponápuchi (M$50, one hour) and San Rafael (M$50, 1¼ hours) every two hours from 10:30am to 6:30pm. The first bus to San Rafael connects with the 1pm departure from there to Bahuichivo.

Estrella Blanca/Rápidos Cuauhtémoc (Villa) has six daily buses to Cuauhtémoc (M$191, three hours) and Chihuahua (M$289, 4½ hours).

Car & Motorcycle

There are paved roads all the way from Chihuahua to Creel and on to Divisadero and San Rafael. From San Rafael, there's an unpaved road to Bahuichivo and beyond. Another road runs southeast to Guachochi, then on to Hidalgo del Parral in southern Chihuahua.

Train

Tickets for the day's *primera express* trains are sold at **Creel station** (☎456-00-15; Av Tarahumara) from one hour before trains depart. *Clase económica* tickets are only available on the train. See boxed text, p753 for schedule information.

Around Creel

The area around Creel is rich in natural wonders, from waterfalls and hot springs to surreal rock formations and expansive parklands, all within a day's hike, ride or drive from town. Local guides offer various tours, or you can go solo on a rented bicycle, scooter or truck. There are some lodging options if you want to stay overnight.

One kilometer southeast of town you enter the Tarahumara *ejido* of San Ignacio (admission M$20), which spreads over some 200 sq km and is home to about 4000 people living in caves and small houses among farmlands, small canyons and pine forests. The road leads into the **Valle de las Ranas y los Hongos** (Valley of the Frogs and Mushrooms), 2km from the edge of town and named for its respectively fat-and-squashed and thin-but-big-headed rocks. Here you'll find the photogenic, 18th-century **San Ignacio Mission Church** and **Cueva de Sebastián**, a cave inhabited by 14 Tarahumara and regularly visited by tourists (donations or craft purchases welcome). Around 7km further east are the **Valle de los Monjes** (Valley of the Monks), whose vertical rock formations inspire its Tarahumara name Bisabírachi, meaning 'Valley of the Erect Penises.' All these make a nice half-day trip on horseback or bike.

Lago Arareko, a twisting, bluish-green lake whose waters reflect the surrounding pines and rocks, sits beside the Cusárare road 8km from Creel. It can be linked with the frogs, mushrooms and monks in a full-day circuit. On the northwestern shore, rowboats can be rented out for M$40.

About 14km on down the road past Arareko is the turning to the Tarahumara village of **Cusárare** (1km), where the 18th-century mission church was restored in the 1970s with striking Tarahumara patterned murals. The **Museo Loyola** (admission M$15; ☺10am-5pm Tue-Sun) here holds an exceptional collection of colonial religious paintings. About 400m past the Cusárare turning on the highway, a right turn marked 'Cascada de Cusárare' and 'Sierra Lodge' leads 400m to the **Sierra Madre Hiking Lodge** (☎635-456-00-36; s/d incl 3 meals M$800/$1600), a tranquil place to hang loose for a while. The comfy rooms have kerosene lamps (there's no electricity), carved pine furniture, fluffy white robes, showers with plenty of hot water, and nice arts and crafts. Full-board rates include margaritas (yes, that's *plural*). A taxi here from Creel costs M$200. From the lodge it's a 2.5km walk beside bubbling Arroyo Cusárare to the lovely 30m waterfall **Cascada Cusárare** (admission M$20), which is free for lodge guests. There are other good walks locally; ask about them at the lodge.

The **Aguas Termales Rekowata** (Rekowata Hot Springs; admission M$20) are also on San Ignacio *ejido* land but approached from the

WORTH A TRIP

CASCADA DE BASASEACHI

Few natural sites in Mexico boast the exquisitely pristine beauty of the country's highest full-time waterfalls, **Cascada de Basaseachi**, where a plume of water tumbles 246m to pools below where you can swim. Basaseachi is 140km northwest of Creel and takes a full day to visit from there (including three hours to walk down to the falls and back). The waterfall is part of the homonymous national park, south of which is the old mining town of Maguarachi, where there are delightful **hot springs**. Both sites are accessible via San Juanito, 35km north of Creel. To visit you'll really need your own wheels or a tour with a Creel agency.

Divisadero road 7km south of Creel. It's 11km southeast, unpaved, from the highway to the parking lot, then a beautiful 3km down a cobblestone road to the warm bathing pools into which the springs are channeled.

Batopilas

📞 649 / POP 1500 / ELEV 460M

Who needs an adventure park? Batopilas citizens could make this argument, as the only road into their splendidly preserved, colonial (former silver-mining) village, deep in canyon country, has more twists, turns and heart-in-mouth vertical drops than any amusement ride. The road, indeed, is a reason to visit in itself, with mountain-biking trips down it a popular activity (see p763). The journey is certainly thrilling – from an altitude of 2330m at Creel to 460m at Batopilas – with dramatic descents and ascents through several canyons, climates and vegetative zones, ending in this stuck-in-time village straggling along the bottom of the Barranca de Batopilas, where the climate is subtropical year-round.

Batopilas, founded in 1708, peaked in prominence in the late 19th century when American Alexander Shepherd owned the mines hereabouts (quirky fact: in 1895 Batopilas became Mexico's second town to receive electricity, after Mexico City).

Like Urique, Batopilas can be slightly rough around the edges. Marijuana fuels the local economy (look out for the state-of-the-art trucks and young men with expensive jewelry) and when the military sporadically destroys a crop, tensions escalate. The area has also experienced some robberies and kidnappings. Foreign tourists aren't usually targeted, but do take local advice about out-of-town excursions.

Things shut up early here, save for some makeshift bars selling Tecates from back rooms. However, there are great excursions locally.

For an overview of this little town's history, visit the **Museo de Batopilas** (admission free; ⊙11am-4pm & 5-7pm Mon-Sat) where proprietor Rafael will embellish proceedings with his own anecdotes. Tourist information on the following hikes and others is available at the museum. Just before you cross the bridge into Batopilas proper are the romantic ruins of the Shepherd's **Hacienda San Miguel** (admission M$10; ⊙8am-5pm).

One of the most popular excursions is to the 18th-century **Satevó Mission Church**, in a remote spot 8km down the canyon. You can hike along the river (the mission suddenly appears, framed in a forested river gorge like something out of a Turner painting) or drive there in 20 minutes. There is also the challenging, spectacular two- to three-day **Urique trek** (2-4 people 3-day hike with/without mule M$4000/2500), probably the region's very best (see p758 for more on this trip and its safety aspects).

🛏 Sleeping & Eating

Casa Real de Minas　　　　HOTEL $$
(📞456-90-45;　batopilashotels@yahoo.com.mx; Guerra 1; r M$750; P🐾❄) A little Sierra Madre oasis with 10 brightly decorated rooms, a lovely courtyard and two reading areas with antiques and historical photos.

Hacienda Batopilas　　　　LUXURY HOTEL $$
(📞in Creel 635-456-02-45; s/d incl breakfast & dinner M$1000/1120; ❄) Top digs is this rebuilt 1760 mining hacienda with enticing features such as stained-glass windows, wood-beam ceilings and cobblestone walls. It's run by the Casa Margarita folks from Creel (best to book ahead through them). The downside: it's 3km north of the town center.

Casa Monse　　　　HOMESTAY $
(Plaza Principal; s/d M$150/200) The basic, clean rooms come with the character of the house, Monse Alcaraz, who will chat your ear off in presentable English, fix you Tarahumara cuisine and help with local guides.

You'll actually meet Tarahumara staying here: Monse does a lot to help local groups.

Hotel Juanita's
HOTEL $

(📞456-90-43; Plaza Principal; s/d M$200/350; 🌐❄️) Charming, well-kept rooms each get their own crucifix plus a shared river-facing courtyard. Juanita says if you don't like Jesus, you can go elsewhere.

Doña Mica
MEXICAN $

(Plaza de la Constitución; meals M$60-80; ⏰7:30am-9pm; 🌐🍴) Locals will point you here for hearty home-cooked Mexican meals. It's an intimate experience – several tables in the proprietor's front room – and there's no menu (just a few choices daily), but the array of business cards testify to doña Mica's long-standing popularity.

❶ Getting There & Away

Ambitiously, they're paving the only road into town: currently, a tarmacked route from Creel follows the highway south towards Guachochi for 72km, then turns off along a panoramic 65km stretch to Batopilas. Paved highway ends just after the Mirador La Bufa, from where an old narrow track skitters hair-raisingly down the side of the Barranca de Batopilas.

The cheapest trip is on the public bus (M$260, five hours), leaving from **Artesanías el Towi** (Av López Mateos) in Creel at 7:30am Tuesday, Thursday and Saturday, and at 9:30am Monday, Wednesday and Friday. On these last three days the 'bus' is actually a suburban van. You'll take a break at La Bufa village, near the bottom of the canyon. Returning, the bus (Monday/Wednesday/Friday) and van (Tuesday, Thursday and Saturday) leave from outside Batopilas church at 5am.

Alternatively, take a two-day van tour from Creel (normally four-person minimum M$4000 to M$5000). Or you can rent a truck from **3 Amigos** (📞456-00-36; www.amigotrails.com; Av López Mateos 46; ⏰9am-7pm) in Creel and drive yourself – though the road is steep and narrow, with precipitous drops.

A back road (high clearance 4WD needed), affording precious canyon-lip views, runs from Batopilas to Urique, fording the Río Urique (passable November–April). Agencies will need advance warning to organize a suitable vehicle.

Cuauhtémoc

📞625 / POP 110,000 / ELEV 2010M

Cuauhtémoc, 103km west of Chihuahua, is chief center for Mexico's Mennonites. Often blonde-haired and blue-eyed, with men wearing baggy overalls and women wearing long dark dresses and headscarves, Mennonites speak in a dialect of Low German and trace their origins to Dutchman Menno Simons who founded the sect in the 16th century. Mennonite beliefs (including an extreme pacifism and a refusal to swear oaths of loyalty other than to God) put them at odds with many governments, and thus communities have from time to time moved en masse from one country to another. In the 1920s around 6000 Mennonites left Canada for northern Mexico and the largest numbers of Mexican Mennonites are today living around Cuauhtémoc.

Indeed, most travelers come to this orderly town, standing in a lush vale of countryside producing most of Mexico's apples, solely to see the Mennonite *campos* (villages). The widely acclaimed movie *Luz silenciosa* (Silent Light), directed by Mexico's Carlos Reygadas – a story of adulterous love in a Mennonite community – was filmed here in 2007. It gave the town unprecedented publicity.

Visiting Mennonite *campos* is best done on a tour, as you will learn far more (and visiting the *campos* independently is not always possible). People principally come on day trips from Creel (about M$400 per person), or Chihuahua. If you haven't prearranged a tour, ask at your accommodation or the Museo y Centro Cultural Menonita. It's best to visit during the week (on Saturdays and Sundays Mennonite businesses are partially or fully closed). You could also independently observe Mennonites in action in Cuauhtémoc itself.

There are banks (with ATMs) around the main plaza.

Museo y Centro Cultural Menonita

(📞583-18-95; Carretera Cuauhtémoc-Álvaro Obregón Km 10.5; adult/child M$25/15; ⏰9am-6pm Mon-Sat) is a large museum out in Mennonite country just north of town holding tools and other paraphernalia from the early years of Mennonite settlement here. A variety of crafts, cheeses and fruit preserves are sold. On the road out, **Campo 2B** (Carretera Cuauhtémoc-Álvaro Obregón Km 7.5) purportedly has the best *quesería* (cheese factory/shop). A taxi to both the museum and cheese factory from downtown will cost you about M$250 with waiting time.

Motel Tarahumara Inn
(📞581-19-19; www.tarahumarainn.com; Av Allende 373; r M$710; 🅿️🌐❄️@🛜) has spacious, comfy rooms and a restaurant and can arrange guides for

out-of-town trips. For good Mexican grub, head to **Rancho Viejo** (Av Guerrero 333; mains M$50-160; ☺) in a homey log cabin with a country-and-western soundtrack. Don't deny yourself the apple pie.

❶ Getting There & Away

The train station, three blocks north and two east of the central square, is last/first stop on the Ferrocarril Chihuahua Pacífico, with daily trains to Chihuahua, and Los Mochis via Creel.

Estrella Blanca (cnr Allende & Calle 13), at the east end of town, has buses to Chihuahua (M$98, 1½ hours) every 45 minutes, 6am to 9pm, several to Creel (M$191, three hours) and seven daily to Madera (M$212, 3½ hours).

CHIHUAHUA & CENTRAL NORTH MEXICO

Alluringly off the tourist radar, and with an affable frontier feel, central north Mexico is barely known except as a start or end point to Copper Canyon excursions (Chihuahua is the eastern terminus for the majestic canyon-traversing train-ride that is the Ferrocarril Chihuahua Pacífico). Yet this region offers in itself some of Mexico's most important historic sights across a triptych of colonial cities (Chihuahua, Hidalgo del Parral and Durango) and pretty damned fantastic scenery. The landscape is classic cowboy flick, typified by the starkly beautiful Desierto Chihuahuense (Chihuahuan Desert), which covers most of Mexico's largest state, Chihuahua – and while it rises in the west into the fertile folds of the Sierra Madre Occidental, you'll be forgiven wherever you go for thinking you've wandered into a B-grade western (Durango, incidentally, is where many famous westerns *were* filmed). Vast cattle ranches and dudes decked out in big sombreros (hats) are the thing here.

Just as Chihuahua state license plates proclaim, this is very much the 'Tierra del Encuentro' (Land of Discovery). History buffs will delight in compelling museums commemorating famous revolutionaries such as Pancho Villa, while in the region's respective corners there are fascinating archaeological sites, some of Latin America's best handicrafts and canyons almost as spectacular as those you'll find in the more-celebrated Copper Canyon area.

Tourism has been ravaged by recent upsurges in drug-gang violence, but most trouble is in and around Ciudad Juárez, along the border and in remoter parts of the Sierra Madre (just do not venture anywhere off-the-beaten-track without a guide). The 'Golden Triangle' area – where southern Chihuahua, northwest Durango and northeast Sinaloa converge – is noted for its opium production and particularly high levels of violence. Danger exists of being caught in the wrong place at the wrong time, but perpetrators have not targeted tourists and there have been few incidents involving tourists.

Chihuahua

📲614 / POP 810,000 / ELEV 1440M

Chihuahua, proud capital of Mexico's biggest state, has more character than any other city in Mexico's north. Many travelers use it only as an overnight stop before or after riding the Ferrocarril Chihuahua Pacífico, but Chihuahua is worth considerably more of your time. Its center combines attractive colonial buildings, several beautiful plazas, good restaurants and bars and brilliant museums (the likes of which few places in Mexico can equal) which bear witness to the key episodes of Mexican history that unfolded here. It's true that certain streets quiver under an incessant tirade of belching traffic and that parts of downtown are swamped with building works and cheap clothes stalls, but this furor is ultimately part of the appeal: a real Mexican city, going about its business.

History

Founded in 1709, Chihuahua soon became the key city of the Nueva España's Provincias Internas (stretching from California to Texas and Sinaloa to Coahuila). The Spanish brought pro-independence rebels including Miguel Hidalgo to be condemned and shot here in 1811, after they captured them in northern Mexico.

The Porfirio Díaz regime brought railways and helped consolidate the wealth of the area's huge cattle fiefdoms. Luis Terrazas, one-time Chihuahua state governor, held lands nearly the size of Belgium: 'I am not *from* Chihuahua, Chihuahua is mine,' he once said.

After Pancho Villa's forces took Chihuahua in 1913 during the Mexican Revolution, Villa established his headquarters here, arranged various civic projects and soon acquired the status of local hero. Today, the city has one of Mexico's highest living standards, with *maquiladora* jobs contributing significantly to this.

Sights

Museo Casa de Villa   MUSEUM
(Calle 10 No 3010; admission M$10; ⊙10am-7pm Tue-Sat, 10am-4pm Sun) Housed in Quinta Luz, the 48-room former mansion and headquarters of Pancho Villa, this museum is a must-see for anyone who appreciates a made-for-Hollywood story of crime, stakeouts and riches.

After his assassination in 1923, 25 of Villa's 'wives' filed claims for his estate. Government investigations determined that Luz Corral de Villa was the *generalísimo's* legal spouse; the mansion was awarded to her and became known as Quinta Luz. She opened the museum and the army acquired it after her death in 1981. You'll see many of Villa's personal effects, plus historical displays on his era, but everyone's favorite stop is the back courtyard where the bullet-riddled black Dodge that Villa was driving when he was murdered in Hidalgo del Parral is on morbid display. Information is in Spanish and English.

It's a pleasant walk from the center if you stay off noisy Avenida Ocampo, or take any bus headed down Avenida Ocampo.

Plaza de Armas   PLAZA
Chihuahua's historic heart, with its mass of pigeons, shoe-shiners and cowboy-hatted characters, is a simple but pretty place. Its majestic baroque **cathedral** (⊙6am-9pm Tue-Sun), built between 1725 and 1826, presides over the bustle, still containing the original organ installed in 1796.

Casa Chihuahua   MUSEUM
(Libertad 901; Museo de Sitio/full admission M$15/40, Sun free; ⊙10am-6pm Wed-Mon) On the edge of the large, monument-studded Plaza Mayor, Chihuahua's former Palacio Federal (built 1908–10), is now a cultural center full of riveting exhibits, with most explanations in English and Spanish. The most famous gallery is the **Calabozo de Hidalgo**, the dungeon where Miguel Hidalgo (see boxed text, p667) was held prior to his execution. The historic dungeon and the church tower above it were preserved within the later buildings erected on the site. A short audiovisual heightens the mournful atmosphere of the dungeon, which contains Hidalgo's bible and crucifix. A plaque outside recalls the verses the revolutionary priest wrote in charcoal on his cell

wall in his final hours thanking his captors for their kindness. The Calabozo and adjoining rooms of historical exhibits comprise the building's **Museo de Sitio**.

Upstairs in the Casa Chihuahua are a space for temporary exhibitions and excellent modern displays on the culture and history of Chihuahua state. You can walk through replicas of ancient cliff dwellings and watch videos of Tarahumara from the Copper Canyon area.

Plaza Mayor is also the setting for the city's oldest church, **Templo San Francisco** (⊙7:30am-1pm & 4:30-8pm) built between 1721 and 1741.

FREE Palacio de Gobierno   HISTORIC BUILDING
(Aldama 901; ⊙8am-8pm) The courtyard of the handsome, 19th-century state government building features fantastic 1950s murals by Aarón Piña Mora showing Chihuahua's highly eventful history: it's an excellent introduction to understanding the city's fabric. Guides wait outside to offer explanatory tours; you can get a free booklet on the murals in the tourist office.

On one side of the courtyard is a small room with a flickering 'eternal flame' marking the spot where Miguel Hidalgo was shot. Further light is shed on Hidalgo and the Mexican independence era in two small museums in the palacio, the **Museo de Hidalgo** (admission free; ⊙9am-5pm Tue-Sun) and the **Galería de Armas** (admission free; ⊙9am-5pm Tue-Sun).

On Plaza Hidalgo's opposite side, Leandro Careon's older murals (1930s), running the gamut of Mexican history from Nahua mythology to Hidalgo, line the **Poliforum de UACH** (Lecture Theatre of Chihuahua University; www.uach.mx; ⊙9am-3pm Mon-Fri).

Museo Casa de Juárez   MUSEUM
(Juárez House Museum; Av Juárez 321; adult/child & student M$10/5; ⊙9am-7pm Tue-Sun) President Benito Juárez' residence in this house during the French occupation made Chihuahua the capital of the Mexican republic from 1864 to 1866. Now a museum with the 1860s feel still intact it includes documents signed by the great reformer, as well as period exhibits including replicas of his furniture and horse-drawn carriage.

FREE Casa Sebastián   GALLERY
(Av Juárez 601; ⊙10am-1pm & 4-6pm Mon-Fri) This restored 1880s gallery's main draws

are the small-scale models of the massive metal sculptures by renowned Chihuahuan artist Sebastián, whose work is seen in cities worldwide. There are several real Sebastiáns around town, including one just above Parque El Palomar northwest of the center.

Quinta Gameros   GALLERY
(Paseo Bolívar 401; adult/child & student M$20/10; ⏱11am-2pm & 4-7pm Tue-Sun) A wealthy mine-owner named Manuel Gameros started building Quinta Gameros in 1907 as a wedding present for his much younger fi-

Chihuahua

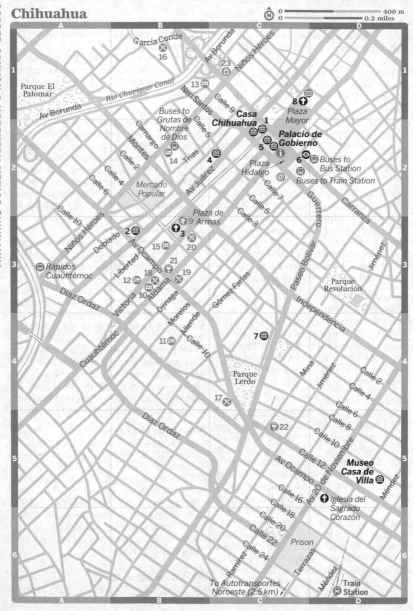

ancée, Elisa Muller. By the time it was finished three years later, she had died, and soon afterwards the Revolution began and the Gameros family fled Mexico. To add yet more color to the story, some guides tell that Elisa fell for Colombian architect Julio Corredor, and ran off with him instead. Today, the house is gorgeously restored and filled with a mix of period furnishings and art from the Universidad de Chihuahua's permanent collection. Every room is unique and the whole place is a sensuous delight of stained glass, carved wood, and floral and bird motifs.

Chihuahua

◉ Top Sights

Casa Chihuahua	C2
Museo Casa de Villa	D5
Palacio de Gobierno	C2

◉ Sights

1	Calabozo de Hidalgo	C2
2	Casa Sebastián	B3
3	Cathedral	B3
	Galería de Armas	(see 5)
4	Museo Casa de Juárez	C2
5	Museo de Hidalgo	C2
6	Poliforum de UACH	C2
7	Quinta Gameros	C4
8	Templo San Francisco	C1

◉ Activities, Courses & Tours

9	Chihuahua Bárbaro	B3

◉ Sleeping

10	Hotel Jardín del Centro	B3
11	Hotel San Felipe El Real	B4
12	Hotel San Juan	B3
13	Motel María Dolores	B1
14	Posada Tierra Blanca	B2
15	Quality Inn	B3

◉ Eating

16	El Papalote	B1
17	Encantado	C4
18	La Casa de los Milagros	B3
19	La Casona	B3
20	Mesón de Catedral	B3

◉ Drinking

21	Café Calicanto	B3
22	La Antigua Paz	C5

◉ Shopping

23	Casa de las Artesanías del Estado de Chihuahua	C1

Grutas de Nombre de Dios CAVE
(Vialidad Sacramento; adult/child M$50/25; ⏰10am-4pm Tue-Fri, 10am-5pm Sat & Sun) These caves on Chihuahua's northeast edge boast impressive stalagmites, stalactites and rock formations, making the one-hour, 17-chamber underground journey fun, especially for kids. To get here take either a taxi (M$80) or a 'Nombre de Dios Ojo' bus (M$6) from outside Posada Tierra Blanca on Niños Héroes. Ask the driver where to get off.

☞ Tours

Chihuahua Bárbaro CITY TOUR
(www.chihuahuabarbaro.com; 2hr city tour adult/child M$100/80) This historic-looking trolley-bus offers different tours of Chihuahua's main historic sights, plus excursions beyond the city limits to caves, archaeological sites and the like (all narrated in Spanish). For city tours it departs from outside the cathedral at 10am, 12:30pm and 4pm daily. Buy tickets at the tourist office or on the Plaza de Armas.

🛏 Sleeping

TOP CHOICE Hotel San Felipe El Real BOUTIQUE HOTEL $$
(☎437-20-37; www.sanfelipeelreal.com; Allende 1005; r/ste incl breakfast M$950/1100; P❀❄@☎) In a gorgeous 1880s house, Chihuahua's sole boutique hotel combines fascinating antiques with modern comforts and oodles of character, centered on a courtyard with a burbling fountain. Rooms are named after old Chihuahua neighborhoods: Nombre de Dios, with its ancient sewing machine and Peck & Hills wardrobe, is our favorite. Breakfast (proper coffee included) is served at one long table in the homely kitchen. It also does airport pickup.

Hotel Jardín del Centro HOTEL $
(☎415-18-32; Victoria 818; r M$380-420; ❀❄) Cozy, modern rooms around a surprisingly quiet plant- and bird-filled courtyard, plus an excellent-value little restaurant, make the Jardín one of Chihuahua's best bargains.

Quality Inn HOTEL $$$
(☎439-90-00; www.qualityinnchihuahua.com; Victoria 409; r/ste incl breakfast M$1357/2065; P❄@☎) This is now the city's plushest option, excellently located just behind the cathedral. It provides ample carpeted rooms brightened by modern art plus a good

PANCHO VILLA: BANDIT TURNED REVOLUTIONARY

Macho womanizer, revolutionary Robin Hood, cattle rustler, lover of children and their need for education, a man of impulsive violence who detested alcohol. No hero in Mexico's history is as colorful or contradictory as Francisco 'Pancho' Villa.

Villa is best known as a leader of the Mexican Revolution but it's a fact that as much of his adulthood was given over to robbing and womanizing as to any noble cause. Born Doroteo Arango to poor hacienda workers in northern Durango state in 1878, he turned to banditry by the age of 16, taking the name Francisco Villa, possibly in honor of his grandfather. The story goes that Villa became an outlaw after shooting one of the hacienda-owning family who tried to rape his sister. Between 1894 and 1910 Villa's life veered between spells of banditry and attempts to lead a legitimate existence.

In 1910, amid intensifying opposition to the dictatorial regime of President Porfirio Díaz, Villa was lobbied for support by Abraham González, leader in Chihuahua state of the revolutionary movement headed by Francisco Madero from neighboring Coahuila. González knew he needed natural fighting leaders such as Villa and encouraged him to return to marauding. Villa soon raised a fighting force to join the Revolution, which began on November 20, 1910.

When Villa's rebels took Ciudad Juárez in May 1911, Díaz resigned. Madero was elected president, but in 1913 he was toppled from power by one of his own commanders, General Victoriano Huerta, and executed. Villa fled across the US border to El Paso, but within a couple of months he was back, one of four revolutionary leaders opposed to Huerta. He quickly raised an army of thousands, the famed División del Norte, and by the end of 1913, with the help of US-supplied guns, he had taken Ciudad Juárez (again) and Chihuahua, installing himself as state governor for the next two years. He expropriated property and money from rich *hacendados* (landowners), lowered prices of basic necessities and established schools, but favored his troops over noncombatants and tolerated no dissent. Villa's Chihuahua house (p769) is today the most evocative of many museums dedicated to him. His victory over a pro-Huerta army at Zacatecas in June 1914 is reckoned to be among his most brilliant, and signaled the end for Huerta. But the four revolutionary forces soon split into

restaurant, the **Degá** (mains M$75-165), and a bar and gym, but lacks character. Check the website for deals, which can reduce the rack rate.

Motel María Dolores　MOTEL $
(☏416-74-20; motelmadol@hotmail.com; Calle 9 No 304; r M$310-360; P✿@◈) Just down from Plaza Mayor, this impeccably run motel's basic but modern rooms are a very good deal.

Posada Tierra Blanca　MOTEL $$
(☏415-00-00; www.posadatierrablanca.com.mx; Niños Héroes 102; s/d M$730/770; P◈✿@◈ 🐾🛏) This large plant-festooned motor-lodge-style place has a good restaurant. Rooms are slightly tired, but large and quiet, despite the downtown bustle outside. Check out the world-cultures mural in the back lounge, even if you aren't staying.

Hotel San Juan　HOTEL $
(☏410-00-35; Victoria 823; s/d M$125/155; ✿) The ever-popular courtyard bar is raucous, but bag one of the back rooms (drab but clean and quiet enough, with TVs and OK

private bathrooms) and at this price you can't complain.

🍴 Eating

TOP CHOICE La Casa de los Milagros　MEXICAN $$
(Victoria 812; dishes M$55-160; ◷4pm-1am; ☻) Legend has it that Pancho Villa and his pals loved this stylish cafe, and you probably will too. In a beautiful, 110-year-old mansion featuring tiled floors and an airy courtyard, the menu here features good coffee drinks, original *antojitos*, steaks and chicken. There's live music, usually ballads and *trova*, from 9pm Wednesday to Sunday.

Encantado　STEAKHOUSE $$
(Av Ocampo 1810; dishes M$35-125; ◷8am-8pm) This colonial house with its courtyard fanning out around a fountain on increasingly happening Parque Lerdo serves decidedly unpretentious food: good old sandwiches and steaks. A Nueva York Vaquero will keep you going for hours.

two camps, with liberal leaders Venustiano Carranza and Álvaro Obregón on one side, and the more radical Villa and Emiliano Zapata on the other. Villa was routed by Obregón in the Battle of Celaya (1915) and never recovered his influence.

After the USA recognized Carranza's government in October 1915, Villa decided to simultaneously discredit Carranza and seek revenge on US president Wilson by launching a series of attacks on North Americans. On March 9, 1916, Villa's men (Villa himself stayed safely several miles behind) sacked the US town of Columbus, New Mexico, which was home to both a US cavalry garrison and Sam Ravel, who had once cheated Villa on an arms deal. Though as many as half of Villa's 500 militiamen may have died that day (there were 18 US deaths), and Ravel wasn't found (he was at the dentist in El Paso), the attack ended up a success for Villa because it drew a US Army punitive expedition into Mexico in pursuit of him, and boosted his legend because they never caught him. Villa carried on fighting the Carranza regime, raiding cities and haciendas, but now had to maintain his fighting force by conscription, and sometimes allowed his men to pillage and slaughter.

In 1920 Carranza was deposed by his former ally Obregón, and Villa signed a peace treaty with provisional president Adolfo de la Huerta. Villa pledged to lay down his arms and retire to a hacienda in Canutillo, 75km south of Hidalgo del Parral, for which the Huerta government paid M$636,000. Villa was given money to cover wages owed to his troops and help the widows and orphans of the División del Norte. He settled 759 of his former troops at Canutillo, setting up a school for them and their children.

For the next three years, Villa led a relatively quiet life. He bought a hotel in Hidalgo del Parral and regularly attended cockfights. He installed one of his many 'wives,' Soledad Seañez, in a Parral apartment, and kept another at Canutillo. Then, one day while he was leaving Parral in his Dodge touring car, a volley of shots rang out (from a house that is now another absorbing Villa museum – Museo Francisco Villa) and the legendary revolutionary was killed. The light prison sentences the eight-man assassin team received led many to conclude that the order for the killing came from President Obregón, though with all the enemies Villa made over the years, there are many suspects.

Mesón de Catedral   INTERNATIONAL $$$

(Plaza de Armas; mains M$95-195; ☉7:30am-midnight Mon-Fri, until 1am Fri & Sat) This fancy new spot, popular with government officials, is the long-awaited restaurant the Plaza de Armas never had. Up a couple of floors with a terrace overlooking the cathedral, it's worth the splurge to eat out here. Bizarrely for a desert city, the house special is a particularly delicious *pulpo* (octopus).

El Papalote   BREAKFAST $

(cnr García Conde & Calle 9; breakfasts M$30-45; mains M$70-90; ☉8am-10pm) Breakfast heartily in this American–style diner among Chihuahua's Mennonite residents. You'll find the city's best choice of egg combinations, and there are abundant *antojitos* too.

La Casona   MEXICAN $$$

(☎410-00-43; cnr Aldama & Av Ocampo; mains M$150-400; ☉noon-midnight Mon-Sat, noon-6pm Sun; ☺☏) Elaborate 19th-century mansion where polished waiters serve up steaks, seafood and pasta alongside an ample wine list. Booking is recommended.

Drinking

TOP CHOICE / La Antigua Paz   CANTINA

(Calle 12 No 2203; ☉until 1am) Probably Mexico's friendliest cantina and one of the few where women are readily accepted. There's revolutionary memorabilia on the walls and a good mix of students, 30-somethings and cowboys. It has live music most nights.

Café Calicanto   BAR

(Aldama 411; ☉4pm-1am) Enjoy live jazz and *trova* (from 8pm Tuesday to Sunday), luscious cocktails, light snacks and a diverse crowd on the tree-lined patio of this intimate cafe.

Mandala   BAR

(☎416-02-66; Urquidi 905; ☉late afternoon-midnight) Chihuahua has never looked prettier than from Mandala's birds-eye terrace atop the city's *mirador*. Opening hours are hit-and-miss: it depends how many customers are about. There are good *artesanías* on sale across the parking lot. It's about 2km southeast of Plaza Hidalgo, down Carranza. It's best to get a taxi here.

Shopping

Cowboy-boot shoppers should make a bee-line to Libertad between Independencia and Avenida Ocampo.

Casa de las Artesanías del Estado de Chihuahua HANDICRAFTS
(Niños Héroes 1101; ⊙9am-5pm Mon-Fri, 10am-5pm Sat) Good selection of *chihuahuense* crafts (including Mata Ortiz pottery) and Mexican foodstuffs such as pecans, sotol and oregano oil.

ⓘ Information

Several banks and ATMs are around the Plaza de Armas. You'll find *casas de cambio* (currency exchange offices) on Aldama, southwest of the cathedral. Call ✆066 for emergency services.

Clínica del Centro (✆439-81-00; www.clinicadelcentro.com.mx; Ojinaga 816) Has a 24-hour emergency department.

Copy & Print Club (cnr Guerrero & Ojinaga; internet per hr M$12; ⊙8am-8pm Mon-Fri, 9am-8pm Sat, 10:30am-5:30pm Sun) Internet access.

Post office (Libertad 1700; ⊙8am-4pm Mon-Fri, 8am-noon Sat)

Rojo y Casavantes (✆439-58-58; www.rojoycasavantes.com; Guerrero 1207; ⊙9am-7pm Mon-Fri, 9am-2pm Sat) Books bus, train and plane tickets.

State Tourist Office (✆429-35-96, 800-508-01-11; www.ah-chihuahua.com, www.chihuahua.gob.mx/turismoweb; Palacio de Gobierno, Aldama; ⊙9am-5pm Mon-Fri, 10am-4pm Sat & Sun) Helpful office that can hook you up with guides for city tours and more.

ⓘ Getting There & Away

Air

Chihuahua's **airport** (✆420-51-04; www.oma.aero; Blvd Juan Pablo II Km 14) has daily flights to Houston (Continental Airlines) and Dallas (American Airlines). **Aeroméxico** (✆201-96-96, 800-262-40-12; www.aeromexico.com; Ortiz Mena 2807, Quinas del Sol, Chihuahua) and **Interjet** (✆430-25-46; www.interjet.com; Centro Commercial Plaza del Sol, Locales 155/156, Periférico de la Juventud) are among the airlines providing diverse domestic services, including to Mexico City.

Bus

Chihuahua's main **bus station** (Blvd Juan Pablo II No 4107) is 6km outside the center, with a myriad bus services including the 1st-class services listed in the boxed table.

Buses to the US also leave from the main bus station. The best company are **Autobuses Americanos** (✆429-02-29) with services to Dallas (M$1210, 16 to 20 hours, one daily), Los Angeles (M$1195, 22 hours, three daily) and Denver (M$1155, 16 to 20 hours, three daily).

For Cuauhtémoc (M$98, 1½ hours) and Creel (M$289, 4½ hours) the most convenient service is by **Rápidos Cuauhtémoc** (Av Borunda), which has buses to Cuauhtémoc every 40 minutes, 6am to 10pm, and to Creel at 5:50am and 1:35pm. **Autotransportes Noroeste** (Av Terrazas 7027) has departures to the same places, plus seven daily departures (M$330) 6am to 6pm to the Copper Canyon hot spots of Divisadero (5½ hours), Areponápuchi (5½ hours) and San Rafael (six hours) via Parque de Aventuras Barrancas del Cobre.

Car & Motorcycle

The easiest way out of central Chihuahua to Hwy 45 is northeast along the canal (Avenida

BUSES FROM CHIHUAHUA

DESTINATION	FARE (M$)	DURATION	FREQUENCY (DAILY)
Ciudad Juárez	355	5-6hr	77
Durango	595	10-13hr	10
Hidalgo del Parral	190	3-5hr	hourly
Madera	290	4½hr	7
Mexico City (Terminal Norte)	1295-1400	19-22hr	15
Monterrey	685	11-12hr	7
Nuevo Casas Grandes	290	4½hr	hourly
Torreón (for Saltillo and Parras)	420	7-8hr	52
Zacatecas	765	12-14hr	46

Borunda). Heading west out of town, take Cuauhtémoc.

Train

Chihuahua is the northeastern terminus for the Ferrocarril Chihuahua Pacífico, with *primera express* departures at 6am daily and *clase económica* departures at 7am on Monday, Thursday and Saturday. The **station** (⏺439-72-12; Méndez s/n; ⏺9am-5:30pm Mon-Fri, 9am-12:30pm Sat) is 1.5km south of the Plaza de Armas. It opens from 5am daily for train departures but don't bank on being able to buy tickets outside of the above hours. For more on the railway, see p754.

ⓘ Getting Around

To get to the bus station, catch a 'Circunvalación Sur' bus (M$6, 30 to 50 minutes) heading northwest on Carranza, almost opposite Plaza Hidalgo. From the bus stop in front of the station, the 'Aeropuerto' bus goes back to the center (it doesn't go to the airport – no public bus does). There's usually someone on hand to tell you which bus to take.

For the train station, take any bus headed south down Avenida Ocampo, or a 'Cerro de la Cruz' bus southeast on Carranza by Plaza Hidalgo, and get off at the Iglesia del Sagrado Corazón. It's a short walk past the medieval-looking prison. Heading toward the center, catch a 'Cerro de la Cruz 23' bus north on Avenida 20 de Noviembre, or any bus north on Avenida Ocampo.

From the center, there are taxis to the train station (M$40), bus station (M$80) and airport (M$150). You'll pay slightly more on the way in.

Nuevo Casas Grandes & Casas Grandes

⏺636 / POP NUEVO CASAS GRANDES 56,000, CASAS GRANDES 5200 / ELEV 1463M

Nuevo Casas Grandes, 320km northwest of Chihuahua, is a prosperous country town with wide streets and a vibe similar to dusty small towns in the US Midwest. Its citizenry is an eclectic mix of working folks, farming families and Mormon and Mennonite settlers. Tourism-wise, its function is as a service center for the prettier village of Casas Grandes by the pre-Hispanic ruins of Paquimé (7km south) and the pottery center of Mata Ortiz (27km south).

⊙ Sights

Paquimé　　　　　ARCHAEOLOGICAL SITE
(⏺692-41-40; admission M$49; ⏺10am-5pm Tue-Sun) The ruins of Paquimé, in a broad valley

with panoramas to distant mountains, give Casas Grandes (Big Houses) its name. The mazelike eroding adobe remnants are from what became, from AD 900, northern Mexico's major trading settlement, connecting the cultures of central Mexico with desert cultures of the north. Paquimé was the center of the Mogollón or Casas Grandes culture, which extended north into New Mexico and Arizona and over most of Chihuahua. It was finally sacked, perhaps by Apaches, around 1340. Excavation and restoration began in the 1950s; Unesco declared it a World Heritage site in 1998. Plaques, in Spanish and English, discuss Paquimé culture: don't miss the clay macaw cages and the distinctive T-shaped door openings. The Paquimé people revered the scarlet macaw, and some structures here represent this beautiful bird – which has never been native to northern Mexico and is evidence of Paquimé's far-reaching trade network.

The site's impressive, meticulously detailed **Museo de las Culturas del Norte** (included in the admission) has displays about Paquimé and the linked indigenous cultures of northern Mexico and the southwest USA.

The Paquimé people were great potters and produced striking cream-colored earthenware with red, brown or black geometric designs; some amazing original examples are on display in the museum. Copying their style has become big business, and you can purchase pottery at the museum, at stores locally and best of all at Mata Ortiz, where the revival began.

🛏 Sleeping & Eating

Bus station pickup can be arranged with Casas Grandes accommodations.

[TOP CHOICE] **Casa de Nopal**　　　GUESTHOUSE $$
(⏺692-44-02; Av Independecia 81, Casas Grandes; r US$45; P✳🛜) The restored adobe buildings around a courtyard are beautiful but the huge rooms are astonishing, finished off in earthy tones and decorated with local handicrafts. Revolution fusion decor wouldn't be an overstatement: the bed in one room was possibly slept in by Pancho Villa himself.

Las Guacamayas B&B　　　　B&B $$
(⏺692-41-44; www.mataortizollas.com; Av 20 de Noviembre, Casas Grandes; s/d incl breakfast M$550/750; P✳🛜) This precious lodge is a stone's throw from the entrance to Paquimé.

WORTH A TRIP

MADERA

In pine-covered foothills, the logging town of Madera with its refreshingly temperate climate couldn't feel more different from the desert settlements of Nuevo Casas Grandes (M$278, 4½ hours, two buses daily at noon and 10pm) and Chihuahua (M$290, five hours, regular buses), and the absorbing nearby archaeological sites, many of which take the form of cliff dwellings, make it a fascinating diversion.

The most impressive cliff dwellings are at **Cuarenta Casas** (admission free; ⊙9am-5pm) where two dozen adobe apartments, probably dating from the 13th century, hug the west cliffside of the dramatic Arroyo Garabato canyon. Cuarenta Casas was an outlying settlement of Paquimé (p775). A round-trip hike takes at least an hour from the small visitor center. The 11:30am bus (M$50, 45 minutes) from Madera's bus station to El Largo goes by the Cuarenta Casas turnoff from where the visitor center is 1.5km. Returning, the bus stops there around 4pm. A great way of getting here, and to the area's other cliff dwellings, is with a local guide. **José Domínguez** (☑652-572-22-11) in Madera is experienced, speaks some English and charges M$500 per person for two or more.

In Madera, **Hotel Parador de la Sierra** (☑572-02-77; cnr Calle 3 & Independencia; s M$250-300, d M$270-320; ✳) near the bus station, is the best deal in town.

The pink building, made mostly of rammed earth (like Paquimé itself), has 15 charming, tile-floored rooms, a lovely garden area with a hammock, and the world's greatest private collection of Mata Ortiz pottery.

Hotel Piñon   HOTEL $$
(☑694-06-55; motelpinon@prodigy.net.mx; Av Juárez 605, Nuevo Casas Grandes; s/d M$440/510; ℗ ☺ ✳ 🛜 ✳) Ultrafriendly lodge, 1½ blocks north of the main square, with a Paquimé-style facade and a decent restaurant, La Vikina.

Pompeii   MEXICAN $$
(☑661-46-03; Av Juárez 2601, Nuevo Casas Grandes; mains M$120-165; ⊙11am-midnight; ☺) Slick spot serving up scrumptious modern Mexican dishes with emphasis on the area's specialty, *pavo* (turkey).

❶ Information

You'll find banks with ATMs on Calle 5 de Mayo in Nuevo Casas Grandes, one block north of Calle 16 de Septiembre.

Agave Lindo Tours (☑692-46-29, cell phone 636-1036004; www.agavelindotours.com; Casa de Nopal, Av Independencia 81, Casas Grandes) Run by knowledgeable Diana Acosta, this godsend of an outfit runs tours to Mata Ortiz (M$400), Cueva de la Olla (10th-century cave houses; M$975) and Hacienda de San Diego, a wonderful 1902 hacienda in the nearby countryside. It's best to email as the office isn't always staffed. She'll also provide tourist information.

Mata Ortiz Calendar (www.mataortizcalendar.com) Comprehensive information on the Casas Grandes area.

❶ Getting There & Away

In Nuevo Casas Grandes, **Ómnibus de México** (Obregón 312) and **Estrella Blanca/Chihuahuenses** (Obregón 308) offer 1st-class bus services including to Chihuahua (M$290, 4½ hours, hourly), Madera (M$278, 4½ hours, 2am & noon daily), the border at Nogales (M$410, seven hours, seven daily) and Juárez (four hours, M$255).

❶ Getting Around

For Paquimé, 'Casas Grandes' buses (M$7.50, 20 minutes) depart every 30 to 45 minutes, northbound from Constitución on the west side of the rail tracks, just north of Calle 16 de Septiembre. Get off in Casas Grandes' plaza and walk 800m south on Constitución to the ruins. A taxi from Nuevo Casas Grandes to Casas Grandes is M$75 to M$90; drivers will happily wait and bring you back for the same fare again.

Mata Ortiz

Twenty-seven kilometers south of Casas Grandes, Mata Ortiz, a tiny town of dusty, unpaved streets, loose chickens and unfinished adobe houses, has become a major pottery center. Artisans here use materials, techniques and decorative styles inspired by those of the ancient Paquimé culture, and their best pieces of work now sell worldwide for over US$10,000 (you can pick up a nice small one for about M$200).

The well-marked workshop-showroom of Juan Quezada, who revived the tradition in the 1970s, is across from the old train station at the village entrance. Strolling through the village, you'll pass numerous other potteries and will be able to see people working.

Mata Ortiz has no bus service. A taxi from Nuevo Casas Grandes, including a one-hour wait, costs about M$400.

Hidalgo del Parral

⌖627 / POP 110,000 / ELEV 1652M

Easy-going Parral has a big place in Mexican history and some good museums. Its chief claim to fame is that it's where Pancho Villa was murdered on July 20, 1923, and buried – with 30,000 attending his funeral at Parral's Panteón de Dolores cemetery. Three years after his burial, his corpse was dug up and beheaded by unknown raiders, and in 1976 his body was moved to Mexico City.

Founded as a mining settlement in 1631, throughout the 17th century enslaved indigenous people mined the rich veins of silver and other minerals from Parral's La Prieta mine, which still provides a dramatic backdrop to the town and makes a fascinating visit.

You've struck it lucky if you like cowboy boots; they're sold by at half of Parral's shops.

◉ Sights

Parral's pretty plazas including Plaza Principal (home of Templo de San José) and Plaza Guillermo Baca (fronting the cathedral), 400m west.

Museo Francisco Villa MUSEUM
(cnr Juárez & Barreda; admission M$10; ⊘10am-5pm Tue-Sun) The building from which Pancho Villa was shot and killed in 1923, toward the west end of town, houses the Museo Francisco Villa. It has two floors of interesting photos of Villa the man (fording a river in his beloved Dodge, posing with his gun in midconflict etc), guns and memorabilia, and guided tours (by donation) available in Spanish and sometimes English. The tale guides tell about Villa's body being switched with a decoy after decapitation, and thus not actually being moved to Mexico City, may have credibility.

Mina La Prieta MINE
(Cerro de la Cruz; adult/child M$25/15; ⊘10am-4pm Tue-Sun) This mine was the basis of Parral's economy from the day it opened in 1629; today it's one of the world's oldest still-worked mines. Once Chihuahua state's richest mine, it produced mainly silver but also gold, copper, zinc and lead. You can drop down 87m in an original elevator to the second of its 25 levels (the 23 below are now flooded) and walk 250m along a tunnel hand-cut around 1820, with historical displays on mining methods used throughout La Prieta's history. The mine is still used for malachite extraction, occasionally meaning it's closed to visitors. On the surface, there is a museum and a *mirador* with a big statue of San José. Tours in Spanish (pay by donation) are given about every hour. The entrance is 200m up Oro and Estaño from García, which runs north off Mercaderes.

Palacio Alvarado PALACE
(Riva Palacio 2; adult/child M$25/15; ⊘10am-5pm) Built a century ago in an eclectic European style for silver tycoon Pedro Alvarado, the beautifully restored Palacio Alvarado has pressed aluminum ceilings and plenty of original furnishings and artifacts including Lady Alvarado's funeral wagon, later used for Pancho Villa. It's a block off Plaza Baca. Alvarado was so rich he once offered to pay off Mexico's entire national debt.

⭐ Festivals & Events

Las Jornadas Villistas HISTORICAL
For a week leading up to the anniversary of Pancho Villa's death (July 20), Parral goes wild. Thousands of bikers show up and horseback riders make a six-day journey from the north, recalling Villa's famous marathons. A reenactment of the assassination itself culminates proceedings. Hotels are booked far in advance.

🛏 Sleeping & Eating

Hotel Acosta HOTEL $
(⌖522-02-21; Barbachano 3; s/d/tr/q M$260/320/380/440; @⌖) From the ancient switchboard in the lobby to the original furniture in the rooms, the extremely friendly, beautifully kept Acosta is a 1950s time warp. It's just off Plaza Principal and has great views from the roof.

Nueva Vizcaya SUITES $$
(⌖525-56-36; Flores Magón 17; r M$526-702; P⊜ ✳@⌖) A modern hotel south of the winding Río Parral, this is far from the most expensive in town, but there's none better. All rooms have kitchens and wi-fi, making it a heck of a bargain.

Al Gusto Restaurante MEXICAN $$
(Calle 20 de Noviembre No 5; dishes M$45-120; ⊘8am-10pm; ⊜) Just across Puente Francisco

Villa from Plaza Principal, this air-con surprise, serves up carefully prepared dishes from burgers and salads to fish and excellent fajitas.

ℹ️ Information

The helpful **tourist office** (☏525-44-00; ⓧ10am-3pm) is at Mina la Prieta. Several banks with ATMs and *casas de cambio* are around Plaza Principal. It's best to get online at your hotel: both hotels listed here provide free access.

ℹ️ Getting There & Around

The **Central de Autobuses** (Calle de Lille 5) is easiest reached by taxi (M$30); it's 2km east from the center along Independencia. Buses run to Chihuahua (M$190, three to four hours, hourly), Torreón (M$265, 4½ hours, two daily) and Durango (M$335, six hours, eight daily) among other destinations. You can also reach better-connected Torreón by bussing it to Jiménez (M$47, 10 daily) from where there are more frequent Torreón-bound departures (M$205, every two hours).

Hwy 45 to Durango is a long, lonely road. Keep a full tank of gas and don't drive it at night. There's also a back road to the Copper Canyon via Guachochi from Hidalgo del Parral.

Durango

☏618 / POP 520,000 / ELEV 1912M

Durango state was the birthplace of Mexico's greatest outlaw (Francisco Villa) while Durango city spawned its first president (General Guadalupe Victoria), and the easygoing capital strikes a happy medium between Wild West backwater and sophisticated metropolis. This is one of Mexico's most isolated cities: it's four hours through the desert or the Sierra Madre mountains from here before you'll hit another significant settlement. Yet isolation has fostered distinctive regional traits, from the cuisine through to Durango's celebrated role in the movie business.

Founded in 1563, Durango's early importance was down to nearby Cerro del Mercado, one of the world's richest iron-ore deposits, along with gold and silver from the Sierra Madre. Industries today also include agriculture and timber. The city has a striking colonial center and plentiful good accommodations and restaurants, yet is also a base for more active tourism in the nearby countryside. Pine-forest-edged canyons and mountainside or desert adventures: the choice is yours.

Note: Durango state is one hour ahead of Chihuahua and Sinaloa.

◉ Sights

Constitución, pedestrianized as of 2012 from Jardín Hidalgo past the Plaza de Armas to Plazuela Baca Ortiz, is among Mexico's most likeable pedestrianized streets.

Plaza de Armas   PLAZA

The wonderful flower- and fountain-filled Plaza de Armas is graced by the handsome baroque **Catedral del Basílica Menor** (ⓧ8am-9pm), constructed between 1695 and 1787. In the plaza's center you can descend to Durango's latest attraction, the **Tunel de Minera** (Tunnel of Mining; admission M$20; ⓧ10am-10pm Sun & Tue-Thu, 10am-11pm Fri & Sat), where Durango's history as one of Mexico's main mining centers is revealed in a specially excavated 300m underground passage with displays and audiovisual presentations.

FREE **Historic Buildings**   HISTORIC BUILDINGS

Two other noteworthy buildings nearby are the late-baroque **Palacio de Gobierno** (Palacio de Zambrano; Av 5 de Febrero 97; ⓧ8am-3pm Mon-Fri), featuring wonderful murals on Mexican history themes; and neoclassical **Teatro Ricardo Castro** (cnr Av 20 de Noviembre & Martínez; ⓧ9am-2pm Mon-Fri), with a large wooden bas-relief of Durango's founding in its lobby.

FREE **Cerro de los Remedios**   LOOKOUT

The city's best *mirador* has cemented its place on the must-see list following completion of the **teleférico** (cable car; return M$20; ⓧ10am-9pm Sun & Tue-Thu, 10am-11pm Fri & Sat), which runs from Cerro del Calvario just west of center. As well as panoramic Durango vistas, Cerro de los Remedios is prettily crowned by the church of **Nuestra Señora de los Remedios**. On Friday and Saturday evenings, open-air films are atmospherically projected onto the church's outer walls.

Museo Regional de Durango   MUSEUM

(Victoria 100 Sur; admission adult/child M$10/2, Sun free; ⓧ9am-4pm Tue-Sat, 10am-2pm Sun) In a palatial, French-style, 19th-century mansion, this museum has thorough displays on Durango state history. Pancho Villa and the area's impressive array of minerals get special attention, and there's a great collection of paintings by Nueva España's best-known painter, Miguel Cabrera. Most explanations are in English and Spanish.

Durango

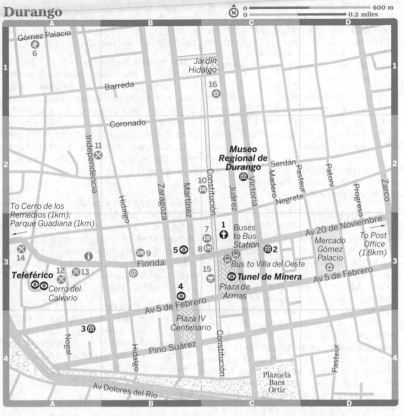

Durango

⊙ Top Sights
Museo Regional de Durango C2
Teleférico A3
Tunel de Minera C3

⊙ Sights
1 Catedral del Basílica Menor C3
2 Durango State Museum C3
3 Museo de las Culturas Populares A4
4 Palacio de Gobierno B3
5 Teatro Ricardo Castro B3

✪ Activities, Courses & Tours
6 Aventura Pantera A1

🛏 Sleeping
7 Hostal de la Monja C3

8 Hotel Plaza Catedral C3
9 Hotel Posada San Agustín B3
10 Hotel Posada San Jorge C2

✕ Eating
11 Cremería Wallander A2
12 Fonda de la Tía Chona A3
13 La Tostada A3
14 Los Equipales A3

🍷 Drinking
15 Da Vinci Café C3

🎭 Entertainment
16 Cineteca Silvestre Revueltas C1

Museo de las Culturas Populares   MUSEUM

(Av 5 de Febrero 1107 Poniente; admission M$5; ⊙9am-6pm Tue-Fri, 10am-6pm Sat, noon-6pm Sun) Exhibits craftwork from Durango state's indigenous Tepehuanes and Huicholes and other artisans, including some hauntingly beautiful masks.

Durango State Museum   MUSEUM

(cnr Av 20 de Noviembre & Victoria) The new predictions for the opening of this much-anticipated museum in the 19th-century Palacio Escárzaga are late 2012.

For greenery and a ton of fun for the little tykes, go to the extensive **Parque Guadiana**, just west of the center.

Tours

TOP CHOICE **Aventura Pantera**   ADVENTURE TOUR

(☎813-98-75; www.aventurapantera.com.mx; Gómez Palacio Poniente 1209; ⊙9am-9pm) This company is run by English-speaking Walter Bishop Velarde, a former Durango rancher who was one of the pioneers of Mexican ecotourism and has vast knowledge and experience of northern Mexico. He masterminds exciting trekking, bird-watching, mountain-biking and camping trips into the Sierra Madre Occidental and the Zona del Silencio. The latter is an eerie desert locale that appears to prevent the propagation of radio waves and is purportedly a UFO-landing site: it's in wildlife-rich Reserva de la Biosfera Bolsón de Mapimí north of Durango. The above trips cost around M$1300 per person per day and require at least eight participants, though guaranteed-date trips (listed on the website) go with any number of people. Walter doesn't have specific opening hours but visiting at any reasonable hour is fine. However, booking is strongly advised.

★彡 Festivals & Events

Feria Nacional   FAIR

For three weeks in late June/early July, Durango's big annual party (www.ferianacional durango.gob.mx) remembers its agricultural roots with *charreada* (Mexican rodeos) plus a *duranguense* music and culture fest.

🛏 Sleeping

TOP CHOICE **Hostal de la Monja**   HOTEL $$$

(☎837-17-19; www.hostaldelamonja.com.mx; Constitución 214 Sur; r incl breakfast M$1335; P❀ ❄@⏾) This 19th-century mansion facing

the cathedral has been converted into an atmospheric 20-room hotel with luxurious rooms, plus its own good restaurant-bar and sidewalk cafe serving delicious coffee.

Hotel Posada San Jorge   HOTEL $$

(☎813-32-57; www.hotelposadasanjorge.com.mx; Constitución 102 Sur; s/d incl breakfast M$590/ 660; P❄@⏾) In a handsome 19th-century ex-convent with rooms upstairs around a courtyard, the San Jorge has larger rooms than the San Agustín, each with two comfy beds and some with sofas and small balconies. The only downside is the occasional noise from the colorful Brazilian restaurant below.

Hotel Posada San Agustín   HOTEL $$

(☎837-20-00; posadasanagustin@terra.com; Av 20 de Noviembre 906 Poniente; s/d M$550/600; P❄ ❀@⏾) Most of the 19 modern and well-appointed rooms/suites face a quiet old colonial courtyard, though the only rooms with windows are on the noisier street side of the building. Has free coffee.

Hotel Plaza Catedral   HOTEL $

(☎813-24-80; Constitución 216 Sur; r M$250; P❀⏾) This labyrinthine, 270-year-old building retains vestiges of bygone splendor, although the large rooms are a bit gloomy: those facing the cathedral, with small balconies, are nicest and brightest.

✖ Eating

Specialties in Durango include *caldillo duranguense* (Durango stew), made with *machaca* (dried shredded meat), and *ate* (pronounced 'ah-tay' – a quince paste enjoyed with cheese).

TOP CHOICE **Los Equipales**   TAQUERÍA $

(Florida 1204; tacos from M$8, mains M$50-105; ⊙1pm-12:30am Sun-Thu, 1pm-1:30am Fri & Sat; ❄) In the increasingly chic old El Calvario neighborhood, Los Equipales serves up satisfying meaty meals, whether they be tacos, a *gringa* (large tortilla topped with cheese and Durango beef) or a steak in one of the most convivial atmospheres in Mexico.

Cremería Wallander   DELI $

(Independencia 128 Norte; tortas M$35-85; ⊙8:30am-9pm Mon-Sat, 9am-3pm Sun; ❄) A wonderful cafe-deli with a courtyard where you can enjoy healthy breakfasts, and extraordinary *tortas* (sandwiches) made with cold cuts and cheese direct from the Wallander family farm on fresh-baked rolls.

BUSES FROM DURANGO

DESTINATION	FARE (M$)	DURATION	FREQUENCY (DAILY)
Chihuahua	595	10-13hr	10
Hidalgo del Parral	335	6hr	8
Mazatlán	360	5-6hr	7
Mexico City (Terminal Norte)	795-860	11-12hr	9
Torreón (for Saltillo)	220	4hr	half-hourly
Zacatecas	250	4-5hr	hourly

La Tostada MEXICAN $$
(Florida 1125; dishes M$75-125; ⊘8am-3pm; ⊜)
With a chirpy blue-and-orange color scheme
and a faithful local following, La Tostada
showcases *comida mexicana* (fajitas, enchi-
ladas and suchlike) at its best, concocted in
an open kitchen.

Fonda de la Tía Chona MEXICAN $$
(Nogal 110; mains M$65-135; ⊘5-11:30pm Mon-Sat,
1-6pm Sun; ⊜) This classy classic fills a gorgeously decorated old building while the
menu is dedicated to *durangueño* cuisine
such as the *caldillo* (a beef and *pasado*-chili
stew).

 Drinking & Entertainment

Bars along Constitución develop a good atmosphere of an evening with a student-and-
20s crowd.

Da Vinci Café CAFE
(Constitución 310 Sur; coffee M$15-25; ⊘10am-
11pm Mon-Sat, 6-11pm Sun) A bohemian upstairs spot with great views of the Plaza de
Armas, and live *trova* or ballads on Tuesday
and Thursday nights. It serves nothing but a
variety of good coffee drinks.

For art-house films, try **Cineteca Silvestre
Revueltas** (Juárez 217 Norte; admission M$15).

ⓘ Information

Durango Turístico (www.durangoturistico.
com) Spanish-language website and free maga-
zine full of interesting Durango-state material.
Hospital General (⌨813-00-11; cnr Av 5 de
Febrero & Fuentes) For emergencies or walk-in
medical care.
HSBC (Constitución s/n; ⊘9am-5pm Mon-Fri)
One of several banks with ATMs around the
Plaza de Armas; cashes traveler's checks.
La Chabela (cnr Av 20 de Noviembre &
Hidalgo; internet per hr M$15; ⊘8:30am-11pm

Mon-Sat, 9am-11pm Sun) Discounts available
when you buy a cup of its organic coffee.
Post office (Av 20 de Noviembre 1016 Oriente;
⊘8am-4pm Mon-Fri, 9am-1pm Sat)
State Tourist Office (⌨811-11-07; www.
durango.gob.mx; www.durangoturismo.com;
Florida 1106; ⊘9am-8pm Mon-Fri, 10am-6pm
Sat & Sun) Friendly and enthusiastic.

ⓘ Getting There & Away

Aeropuerto Guadalupe Victoria (⌨817-88-98;
www.oma.aero; Autopista Gómez Palacios Km
15.5), 15km northeast of town on Hwy 40D, has
three daily Aeroméxico flights to Mexico City. A
taxi here from central Durango is about M$150.

The **Central de Autobuses** (Blvd Villa 101),
4km east of the center, has frequent bus departures, including the 1st-class trips listed in the
boxed table (p781).

ⓘ Getting Around

'ISSSTE' or 'Centro' buses (M$6) from the
Central de Autobuses parking lot get you to the
Plaza de Armas. Metered taxis cost about M$35
to the center.

To reach the Central de Autobuses from downtown, catch 'Camionera' buses along Avenida 20
de Noviembre anywhere near the plaza. Get off
before the major intersection with the Pancho
Villa equestrian monument and a McDonald's,
and walk a short way northeast.

Around Durango

Just outside Durango are the most northerly ancient pyramids in the Americas; **La
Ferrería** (admission free; ⊘9am-5pm), with a
well-kept museum explaining the culture of
the Chalchihuites people who built it, and
the attractive mountainside reservoir **Presa
Guadalupe Victoria**, where there is kayaking, rappelling and zip-lining. Taxis to either
will cost about M$150 one-way.

Movie Locations AMUSEMENT PARKS

From the 1950s to the 1990s, both Hollywood and the Mexican film industry made hundreds of movies in Durango's unspoiled deserts and mountains. John Wayne, Clark Gable and Steve McQueen spent many hours filming here. The decline of the western genre and tax breaks at locations back in the US have largely ended Durango's run as 'La Tierra del Cine' (The Land of Cinema), although *Bandidas* (2006), starring Salma Hayek and Penélope Cruz, was made here.

Many of the big-screen cowboys swaggered through **Villa del Oeste** (Hwy 45; adult/child M$25/15; ⊙11am-7pm), 12km north of Durango. Today, the set is a souvenir-drenched theme park with gunslingers shooting it out at 2pm and 4pm Monday to Friday, and 1:30pm, 3:30pm and 5:30pm on Saturday and Sunday. During the week it's almost deserted. On Saturdays and Sundays, a bus (adult/child M$30/20 including admission) leaves from Durango's Plaza de Armas a half-hour before each show and returns again afterwards. To get there at other times, take a taxi (about M$150 one-way) or any northbound bus (M$10, about every 30 minutes) and remind the driver to drop you there. Returning, flagging down a bus isn't always easy.

The unfazed residents of **Chupaderos** (⊙10am-6pm), 3km north of Villa del Oeste, have moved right into the former set. Big-screen-ready cowboys still ride past the village saloon here, but they aren't actors. Once again, big guns battle it out on Saturdays and Sundays (3pm and 5pm; M$15 entry for the show).

Western Durango State

Western Durango state lies in the Sierra Madre Occidental, replete with forested peaks and deep canyons. Operators such as Aventura Pantera (p780) offer trekking and mountain biking trips here.

Hwy 40 west from Durango to the coast at Mazatlán traverses this fabulous back country. It's best not to drive this route after dark, although there have been no reported holdups involving tourists for some years: the new toll highway, Hwy 40D, paralleling the old road and due for completion in 2012, will make the route far safer.

A series of well-appointed mountain cabins are close to Hwy 40, allowing travelers to experience this mountain scenery close up. Durango's tourist office will make reservations: two-bedroom cabins for up to six people cost M$1000 to M$2000 per night. The only significant settlement is **La Ciudad**, close to cabins such as **Mexiquillo** (⊡675-877-00-48; www.mexiquillodurango.com. mx). Mazatlán-bound buses from Durango's Central de Autobuses will drop you at La Ciudad (around M$130, 2½ hours).

NORTHEAST MEXICO

The northeast gets almost totally shunned by tourists these days, which is a mistake. Close to the US, the foreign visitors are mostly North Americans heading south but the appealing towns and cities here make convenient journey-breakers, and when you do stop, you'll be very glad you did. Colonial centers such as Saltillo; modern, culturally vibrant megalopolises such as Monterrey; and the idyllic wine mecca of Parras make this region a pretty special place to sample. The northeast also does nature like nowhere else. There's the chance to explore unique desert ecosystems at Cuatro Ciénegas, and to hike or watch wildlife in desert scrub or cloud forest at the Reserva de la Biosfera El Cielo, one of Mexico's most biologically diverse corners.

Being close to the US border, the region is not without dangers, and has seen some of Mexico's highest increases in drug violence over the last two years. Monterrey, the border towns (particularly Nuevo 'narco' Laredo), northern Tamaulipas state and Torreón have especially had problems. Outside of Torreón, however, Coahuila state is safer, and Saltillo, Parras and Cuatro Ciénegas are *tranquilo* (safe and relaxed).

Saltillo

⊡844 / POP 710,000 / ELEV 1600M

Set high in the arid Sierra Madre Oriental, Saltillo is large and fast-growing, but the center maintains a relaxed small-town feel. Founded in 1577, it's the northeast's oldest town, boasting fine colonial buildings and cracking cultural surprises (some leading art galleries and museums). Most attractions are conveniently central, and a burgeoning student population adds energy. It's also on the main routes between the northeast border and central Mexico, making it the ideal spot hereabouts to break a journey.

◉ Sights

Alameda Zaragoza, Saltillo's large, leafy central park six blocks northwest of the Plaza de Armas, is great for a picnic.

Plaza de Armas PLAZA

Saltillo's wide, grand plaza has some must-see buildings abutting it, including arguably the north's most beautiful cathedral, the **Catedral de Saltillo** (☺9am-1pm & 4-7:30pm) with elaborately carved Churrigueresque facades and a dome featuring carvings of Quetzalcóatl, the Aztec rain god. Ask at the Módulo de Información in Plaza de Armas about climbing the bell tower. The expansive, neoclassical **Palacio de Gobierno** (admission free; ☺9am-9pm) on the opposite side of the plaza has spectacular murals by Salvador Almaraz López on its 2nd floor, plus a **museum** (admission free; ☺10am-6pm) on Coahuila's eventful past.

Museo del Desierto MUSEUM

(www.museodeldesierto.org; Pérez Treviño 3745; adult/child & student M$75/40; ☺10am-5pm Tue-Sun) Deserts cover about half Mexico's territory, and this excellent no-expense-spared museum will teach you lots about this biome even if you don't speak Spanish. Exhibits reveal why sea currents can create deserts and how sand dunes are formed. Children will enjoy the collection of dinosaur fossils. There's also a reptile house and a botanical garden with more than 400 cactus species. Bus 18, running east down Aldama in the center, will drop you 1km downhill from the entrance.

Museo de las Aves de México MUSEUM

(Museum of Mexican Birds; www.museodelasaves.org; cnr Hidalgo & Bolívar; adult/child & student M$10/5; ☺10am-6pm Tue-Sat, 11am-7pm Sun) Mexico ranks 10th in the world in terms of avian diversity, and this museum, just south of the Plaza de Armas, displays more than 760 stuffed and mounted species, some in convincing dioramas of their natural habitat. There are special sections on feathers, beaks, migration and similar subjects.

FREE **Art Museums** GALLERY

Saltillo's main cultural center, beautiful **Instituto Coahuilense de Cultura** (www.icocult.gob.mx; Juárez 109; ☺10am-7pm Tue-Sun), on the Plaza de Armas' south side, often features good temporary exhibits by artists from Coahuila and beyond. It also hosts concerts and has a bookstore-cafe.

Casa Purcell (Hidalgo 231; ☺10am-7pm Tue-Sun) is located in a wonderful neo-Gothic-style 19th-century mansion and hosts art exhibits, rock concerts and art-house films.

🛌 Sleeping

Hotel Urdiñola HOTEL $$

(☎414-09-40; Victoria 251; s/d M$491/511; P◉@☎) Initial impressions are excellent, what with the stately lobby and sweeping marble stairway. Rooms are less overwhelming, mostly set around a long, narrow courtyard; those on the upper floor enjoy more natural light: good value overall.

Hotel San Jorge HOTEL $$

(☎412-22-22; Acuña 240; s/d M$530/570; ◉✹☎✹) Bland-but-respectable business-style hotel with 120 neutral, generously proportioned rooms. It has a rooftop pool and a 6th-floor open-to-allcomers restaurant with panoramic vistas that's great for hearty breakfasts.

Hotel Colonial Alameda HOTEL $$

(☎410-00-88; www.hotelcolonialalameda.com; Obregón 222; r from M$650; P◉✹@☎) The only fancy digs downtown, this fine Spanish colonial-style hotel has a plush lobby and elegant, tastefully presented rooms, each containing a pair of huge beds and smart furnishings.

🍴 Eating & Drinking

Superb *fondas* (family-run eateries) occupy the 2nd floor of Mercado Juárez, by Plaza Acuña.

TOP CHOICE **Flor y Canela** CAFE $

(Juárez 257; mains M$50-75; ☺8:30am-9:30pm Mon-Fri, 9:30am-4:30pm Sat & Sun; ✐) A stylish cafe with a Bohemian feel ideal for breakfast, a salad or *panini* (M$60), or a fine coffee or tea.

El Tapanco INTERNATIONAL $$$

(Allende 225; dishes M$145-210; ☺noon-11pm) A suave courtyard-facing restaurant serving great cuts of beef, this is one of the city's most upmarket eateries.

Monster Café BAR

(Mario Escobedo 457; dishes M$100; ☺4pm-2:30am Mon-Sat) There are not many bars that are also a monster museum but, somehow, the crossover works. Sit in the lively downstairs or up on the roof terrace. Tasty food (including homemade burgers) is served.

BUSES FROM SALTILLO

DESTINATION	FARE (M$)	DURATION	FREQUENCY (DAILY)
Cuatro Ciénegas	223	5hr	1
Durango	490	7hr	several
Mexico City (Terminal Norte)	795 (deluxe) 735 (1st class)	10hr	frequent
Monterrey	80	1¾hr	frequent
Nuevo Laredo	300	4½-5hr	frequent
Parras	100	2½hr	9
San Luis Potosí	380	5hr	hourly
Torreón	250	3hr	frequent
Zacatecas	320	5hr	hourly

Dublin Irish Pub   BAR
(Zaragoza 246; Guinness M$75; ☻8pm-2am Tue-Sat) New location; same lively spot. Rock bands rock the house on both Fridays and Saturdays.

🛍 Shopping

Saltillo is so famous for its sarapes (blankets with a head opening, worn as a cloak) that the local baseball team is known as the Saraperos.

El Sarape de Saltillo   CLOTHING
(☑414-96-34; Hidalgo 305; ☻9am-1pm & 3-7pm Mon-Sat) This shop sells fine quality, colorful sarapes and other Mexican *artesanías*: see wool being dyed and woven on looms inside.

ℹ Information

Cruz Roja (Red Cross; ☑065)

Cyberbase (Padre Flores 159; per hr M$8; ☻9:30am-9:30pm Mon-Sat) Internet.

Hospital Universitario de Saltillo (☑411-30-00; www.hus.uadec.mx; Madero 1291)

HSBC (Allende 203; ☻8am-7pm Mon-Sat) Changes traveler's checks.

Módulo de Información (☻10am-6pm Mon-Sat, 10am-4pm Sun) Tourist information kiosk in the Plaza de Armas.

Post office (Victoria 203)

ℹ Getting There & Away

Air

Saltillo's **Plan de Guadalupe airport** (☑488-07-70, 488-17-70; Carretera Saltillo-Monterrey Km 13.5) is at Ramos Arizpe 15km northeast from town. **Aeromar** (☑415-01-93, 415-02-67; www.aeromar.com.mx; Europlaza Mall, Carranza 4120) has five daily flights between Mexico City

and Saltillo. Most people fly from Monterrey. There are buses direct between Saltillo's bus station and Monterrey's airport.

Bus

The **bus station** (Periférico Echeverría) is on the south side of town 2.5km from the center (a 10-minute bus ride).

Direct departures to destinations in the boxed table (above) leave at least hourly, except for those to Durango (a change is sometimes required at Torreón) and Cuatro Ciénegas (there's one bus each evening).

Buses also go to Guadalajara (M$655, nine hours), Matamoros (M$375, seven hours) and Mazatlán (M$855, 12 hours). **Autobuses Americanos** (☑417-04-96; www.autobuses americanos.com.mx) has services to Chicago, Dallas (US$63, 14 hours) and Houston (US$55, 13 hours).

Car & Motorcycle

Saltillo is a major road junction. Hwy 40, going northeast to Monterrey, is a good four-lane toll road. Going west to Torreón (262km), Hwy 40D splits off Hwy 40 after 30km, becoming an overpriced toll road. Hwy 40 is free and perfectly good.

The remote Hwy 57 runs north to Monclova (192km) while Hwy 54 crosses high, dry plains south toward Zacatecas (380km).

ℹ Getting Around

Saltillo's airport lies 15km northeast on Hwy 40 and is best reached by taxi (M$100) along Xicoténcatl. To reach the city center from the bus station, take minibus 9 (M$5.50) from in front of the station. To reach the bus station from the center, catch bus 9 on Aldama, between Zaragoza and Hidalgo. Taxis between the center and the bus station cost about M$30.

Parras

📞842 / POP 34,000 / ELEV 1520M

A graceful oasis town in the heart of the Coahuilan desert some 160km west of Saltillo, Parras has a historic center of real colonial character and a delightfully temperate climate, but it's most famous for its wine, with *parras* (grapevines) grown here since the late 16th century. With great places to stay, several enticing bathing pools and all that vino, this is somewhere to soak up and kick back for days – or longer.

◉ Sights & Activities

Parras is renowned for its wine, which accounts for some superb attractions around town including several wineries (see the boxed text below).

Museo de los Monos   MUSEUM
(Madero 37; donations appreciated; ⊙8am-9pm) José Cruz Hernández created this bizarre, low-budget wax museum with not-even-remotely lifelike figures of Freddy Krueger, Barack Obama and the like. It's so bad that it's good.

Iglesia del Santo Madero   CHURCH
(⊙10am-6pm Thu-Tue) The iconic church perched precariously on the rocky outcrop on the south edge of town has, once you've undergone the steep-but-rewarding climb up, some wonderful, expansive views. It's a 30-minute walk from the center, east along Madero then up Benavides.

Estanques   SWIMMING
Parras has three *estanques* (large pools where spring water is stored) that locals use

for swimming. Gorgeous **Estanque La Luz** (adult/child M$15/5; ⊙7am-7am) is on the way to Iglesia del Santo Madero.

🛏 Sleeping & Eating

Parras is packed with *dulcerías* (candy stores) selling the region's famous *queso de higo* (fudgy candy with figs).

Hotel Posada Santa Isabel   HOTEL $$
(📞422-04-00; www.posadasantaisabel.com; Madero 514; s/d M$600/800; ▣☯✳☎🏊) The tidy rooms have some nice touches and are spread out around a fruit-tree-filled courtyard. If public areas aren't quite as atmospheric as El Farol, it's still the better value, especially if you factor in discretionary midweek discounts. The restaurant is decent, as well.

Hostal El Farol   HOTEL $$
(📞422-11-13; www.hostalelfarol.com; Arizpe 301; r M$855-970; ▣☯☎🏊) This excellent colonial-style hotel has spacious rooms with plenty of period character; the best rooms are set off a flower-filled courtyard. The restaurant is good. Rates drop to M$650 Sunday to Thursday.

Restaurante Chávez   MEXICAN $
(Reforma 19; dishes M$40-100; ⊙8am-midnight) This is where the locals eat, and it's obvious why: huge portions of meat-and-fish-focused grub, as well as filling soups and delicious pizza.

ℹ Information

The **tourist office** (📞422-02-59; www.parras coahuila.com.mx; ⊙10am-2pm & 4-6pm Mon-Fri, 10am-2pm Sat) is on the road into town, 3km

---

FINE WINE TIME

Parras claims an important place in the history of Mexican wine. A warm climate together with the region's natural irrigation (underground streams from the sierra which surface hereabouts) meant this part of Coahuila became a principal wine-growing area of Nueva España (New Spain) and a winery here was established in 1597 (the first in all the Americas). Now called **Casa Madero** (www.madero.com.mx; admission free; ⊙8am-5:30pm), it's 7km north of the center on the road to the main highway and is a large-scale operation with free half-hour tours and a shop. All buses heading out of town (M$20) pass the winery, or take a taxi (M$90). In Parras, you can explore the more intimate winery of **El Vesubio** (Madero 36; ⊙9am-1pm & 2-7pm Mon-Fri, 9am-7pm Sat & Sun).

Parras valley wines are mostly Bordeaux-style reds, although Casa Madero produces renowned Chenin Blanc and Chardonnay. These, along with local varieties such as San Lorenzo (a white) are available for trying/buying in Parras restaurants and shops, and there's even a **Feria de la Uva** (Grape Fair) every August with its somewhat cacophonous climax in Casa Madero.

to the north. A tiny tourist **kiosk** (⊗8am-3pm) is in central Plaza de Reloj, by the library.

ℹ Getting There & Away

Only 2nd-class buses serve Parras, but most have 1st-class comfort. There are nine daily to/from Saltillo (M$100, 2½ hours) and five daily to/from Torreón (M$120, three hours). If you want to head to Cuatro Ciénegas without backtracking to Saltillo, catch a bus to San Pedro Las Colonias (M$80, 1½ hours, four daily) and then a bus from there to Cuatro Ciénegas (M$165, two hours, nine daily). Parras is easily reachable by car; turn off the highway at La Paila and drive 27km south.

Cuatro Ciénegas

🖉869 / POP 10,000 / ELEV 747M

The serene town of Cuatro Ciénegas is bespeckled with adobe and colonial buildings and a handful of hotels and restaurants. It's also the perfect base for exploring the Área de Protección de Flora y Fauna Cuatrociénegas.

◉ Sights & Activities

**Área de Protección de
Flora y Fauna Cuatrociénegas**   PARK
With hundreds of shimmering cerulean *pozas* (pools) and streams in the middle of the Desierto Chihuahuense (Chihuahuan Desert), the 843-sq-km Área de Protección de Flora y Fauna Cuatrociénegas is a highlight of any trip to northern Mexico. Fed by a network of more than 500 underground springs, the reserve is a desert habitat of extraordinary biological diversity. It's home to more than 75 endemic species, including three kinds of turtles and 11 kinds of fish, as well as organisms called *estromatolitos* (stromatolites), found in only two other places on earth and similar to the first oxygen-producing life-forms. Some pools and the nearby river have been set aside for recreational spots, including swimming.

Some of the reserve's easily accessible sights are signed off Hwy 30 southwest of town. If you're exploring the area on your own, be aware: desert tracks are not always signposted, and can turn to muck with even a little rain. Summer temperatures can be extreme, so bring plenty of water and avoid midday excursions. Only one pool is currently open to the public for swimming. Sunscreen is prohibited in the pools.

Using the services of a guide is wise. Not only are there fascinating tales to tell about this giant oasis, but many *pozas* and other sites left in a natural state are unmarked. English-speaking biologist **Arturo Contreras** (three-hour tour in Spanish/English M$450/550) knows the local fauna and environment well, and is highly recommended. He charges. He can be contacted through the travel agency on the plaza (cnr Juárez and Carranza); the tourist office can also put you in touch with him and other guides (not all speak English). Hotels recommend guides too, although some are actually taxi drivers who may charge over the odds for tours.

Buses to Torreón will drop you at the entrances to any of the following sites, but usually won't stop to pick people up. Hitchhiking isn't easy because there isn't much traffic on this road, which practically means you'll need your own wheels or a guided tour to explore.

Poza Azul Visitors Center

(admission M$30; ⊗10am-6pm Tue-Sun) Eight kilometers out of town on Hwy 30, this center has illustrated displays about the reserve's ecology in Spanish and English. The little **Poza Las Tortugas**, a good turtle-spotting pool, is right behind here, while 1.5km further back is aptly named **Poza Azul** (Blue Pond), one of the reserve's most photographed sites.

Río Los Mezquites

(admission M$45; ⊗9am-7pm) Just before the visitors center, a rough turn-off on the left leads 2km past *salinas* (salt flats) to a sublime stretch of slow-flowing blue water. Swimming here with the fish and turtles amid the desert landscape is a surreal, revitalizing experience. There's an abundance of *palapas* (thatched shelters) for shade, plus toilets and barbecue spots.

Poza La Becerra

Seven kilometers past the visitors center, Poza La Becerra, where the water temperature is 32°C (90°F), was still closed at the time of writing but it's worth checking to see if it's reopened. There was formerly great swimming here, and good facilities including camping.

Dunas de Yeso

(Las Arenales; admission M$25; ⊗10:30am-6pm) These blinding-white gypsum sand dunes contrast superbly with the six mountain ranges that ring the valley. They can be seen from Hwy 30, but to visit you'll need to stop by the visitor center (where you can learn about the dune ecosystem) to pay and get the key that opens the gate at the beginning of the track out.

Carranza Museums
MUSEUM

Born in Cuatro Ciénagas, Venustiano Carranza was one of the key figures of the revolution before he became president in 1917. His former home is now the **Casa de Cultura** (Hidalgo 401 Poniente; adult/child & student M$10/5; ⊙9am-1pm & 3-7pm Mon-Fri, 10am-6pm Sat & Sun), with a small but interesting archaeological display. For more on Carranza's life, visit **Museo Casa Carranza** (Carranza btwn Juárez & Escobedo; requested donation M$10; ⊙10am-6pm) with audiovisual displays and interesting memorabilia, including the revolutionary's suit and his heartfelt correspondence illustrating his ideals.

Tours

Two- or three-day excursions can be organized with guides such as **Arturo Contreras** for about M$1500 per person. Contact him through the travel agency on the plaza (corner of Juárez and Carranza) or the tourist office. These include trips to Valle Hundidos, a magnificent spot to experience the diverse desert ecosystem; and a candelilla-processing plant at Antiguos Mineros del Norte. Endemic to the Desierto Chihuahuense, the extraction of wax from the candelilla (for everything from gum to shoe polish) is one of the main industries hereabouts.

Sleeping & Eating

Hotel Plaza
HOTEL $$

(696-00-66; www.plazahotel.com.mx; Hidalgo 202 Oriente; s/d incl continental breakfast M$495/680; P❋@🛜🏊) True to its name, this well-run, attractive place is a cowboy's lasso away from the plaza, and built in colonial style. All rooms face a grassy patio and pool and have comfy beds. The plaza-facing restaurant is popular.

Hotel Misión Marielena
HOTEL $$

(696-11-51; Hidalgo 200 Oriente; s/d incl breakfast M$544/696; P❋🛜🏊) This hotel is opposite Hotel Plaza, with larger, wonderfully maintained rooms, all with two double beds. Rooms are set around two rear courtyards, which have a pool and mountain views.

El Doc
MEXICAN $$

(Zaragoza s/n; mains M$45-100; ⊙8am-10pm) Good food (especially steak) comes in a fun

atmosphere on the plaza with lots of chatty desert folks.

Information

You'll find a **bank** (cnr Zaragoza & Escobedo), with an ATM, one block north of the plaza and a **tourist office** (696-09-02; Carranza 100; ⊙9am-5pm Mon-Fri) in the Presidencia Municipal.

Getting There & Away

The bus terminal occupies the southwest corner of the plaza. First-class buses run to Torreón (M$205, 3½ hours, 11 daily), Saltillo (M$223, five hours, one each morning) and the border at Piedras Negras (M$295, six hours, four daily). Monclova (M$77), two hours away via frequent buses, has more services north and south.

Monterrey

81 / POP (METROPOLITAN AREA) 4.1 MILLION/ ELEV 530M

Cosmopolitan Monterrey is Mexico's third-largest city, second-largest industrial center and *número uno* in per-capita income. The economic powerhouse of 'La Sultana del Norte' is justly proud of its entrepreneurial ethos, its humming cultural scene, its vibrant universities (Instituto Tecnológico de Monterrey is one of Latin America's best), its eclectic cuisine and its nightlife.

With sprawling suburbs of gargantuan air-conditioned malls and manicured housing estates, this is also one of Mexico's most Americanized cities. A major transportation hub, it makes a convenient stopover on the road south, with world-class museums and a renowned party scene, while a jagged mountain backdrop harbors outdoor adventure possibilities.

All of this makes Monterrey fiercely independent and very different to any other Mexican metropolis you'll encounter. Sadly, its appeal has recently been overshadowed as the city has become synonymous with some of Mexico's worst drug violence, much of which has been played out even in the city center. Our information on Monterrey was therefore updated by telephone for this edition.

History

Dating from 1596, it wasn't until after Mexican independence that the city began to prosper as proximity to the US gave it advantages in trade and smuggling.

Monterrey

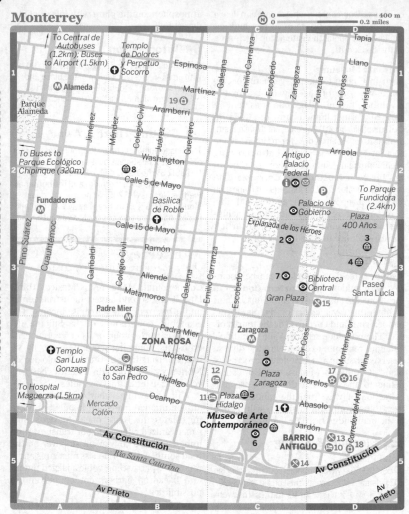

In 1900 the first heavy industry in Latin America, a vast iron and steel works (now the site of the Parque Fundidora), rose to dominate the cityscape. Monterrey soon became dubbed the 'Pittsburgh of Mexico,' and still produces about 25% of Mexico's raw steel. The city also churns out around 60% of the nation's cement and half of its beer.

◉ Sights & Activities

Most major sights are concentrated around the Gran Plaza, to the west of which is glitzy Zona Rosa neighborhood. East of the Gran Plaza is Barrio Antiguo, with colonial buildings and cobbled streets.

Gran Plaza (Macroplaza)   PLAZA
(Ⓜ Zaragoza) A monument to Monterrey's ambition, this city-block-wide series of interconnected squares, also known as the Macroplaza, was controversially created in the 1980s by the demolition of a prime chunk of city-center real estate. This once-naked urban space has been gradually softened by trees, fountains and pools across its several parks and plazas, which include **Plaza Zaragoza** (the largest plaza), the **Parque**

Monterrey

Hundido (Sunken Garden) and **Explanada de los Héroes** (Esplanade of the Heroes).

The modern, concrete **Palacio Municipal** at Plaza Zaragoza's southern end is where the municipal band takes the stage on Sunday (11am to 2pm and 5pm to 9pm) and Thursday (7pm to 9pm), and elderly couples dance away the day. Baroque **Catedral Metropolitano de Monterrey** (⊙7:30am-8pm Mon-Fri, 9am-8pm Sat, 8am-8pm Sun), capped by its neon cross, is nearby.

FREE *Museo Metropolitano de Monterrey* (Zaragoza s/n Sur; ⊙10am-6pm Tue-Sun) Facing the cathedral across the plaza is the 19th-century Palacio Municipal, which now houses the Museo Metropolitano de Monterrey. There's a brief, Spanish-only summary of city history on the ground floor and lovely upstairs galleries featuring works by contemporary painters and sculptors.

Museo de Arte Contemporáneo (Marco; ⌨8262-4500/77; www.marco.org.mx; cnr Zuazua & Jardón; adult/child & student M$60/40, Wed free; ⊙10am-6pm Tue & Thu-Sun, to 8pm Wed) Facing the southeast corner of Plaza Zaragoza is the terrific Museo de Arte Contemporáneo, with its idiosyncratic spaces filled with water and light and major temporary exhibitions. Call in advance to get a tour in English. Marco also has a fine bookstore and restaurant.

Plaza 400 Años & Around   PLAZA
(Ⓜ Zaragoza) Yet another wide-open public space, this plaza just east of the Macroplaza, graced with fountains and pools, forms the grand approach to the sleek, modernist **Museo de Historia Mexicana** (⌨8345-9898; www.museohistoriamexicana.org.mx; adult/child M$40/free, Tue free; ⊙10am-6pm Tue-Fri, until 7pm Sun), which presents an extensive but easily manageable chronology of Mexican history. All explanations are in Spanish, but English tours can be arranged by calling in advance.

Next door is the **Museo del Noreste**, technically a separate institution but practically functioning as a wing of the history museum, with galleries on the culture and history of Nuevo León, Tamaulipas, Coahuila and Texas. One ticket works for both attractions.

Plaza 400 Años is the terminus of recently renovated promenade Paseo Santa Lucía which stretches 2.4km to Parque Fundidora. Take a stroll with the ambling families on this pleasant path, or take a **boat ride** (adult/child round-trip M$40/20) on the (artificial) river.

Parque Fundidora   PARK
(www.parquefundidora.org; ⊙6am-11pm; Ⓜ Parque Fundidora) Formerly a vast steel-factory complex, this once-blighted industrial zone has been transformed into a huge urban park. Designers cleverly retained the iconic smoke stacks and industrial relics to give a surreal and at times apocalyptic feel, but a vibe very much in keeping with Monterrey's heritage. The attractions here are great for children, and a free trolley loops around the park.

Blast Furnace No 3 has been converted into **Horno3** (www.horno3.org; adult/child & student M$90/55; ⊙10am-6pm Tue-Thu, 11am-7pm Fri-Sun), a high-tech, hands-on museum on Mexico's steel industry. Don't miss the overly dramatic furnace show. Ask about nocturnal climbs (M$40; ⊙6-10pm Tue-Thu & Sun, 7-10pm Fri & Sat) of the metal tower. Last tickets are sold one hour before closing.

Three other disemboweled redbrick factories compose the **Centro de las Artes** (www.conarte.org.mx; admission free, film screenings M$40; ⊙10am-9pm Tue-Sun), an arts center with rotating exhibitions that also screens independent/foreign films.

The metro stops near the park, but the best way to get here is along Paseo Santa Lucía from Plaza 400 Años just east of Gran Plaza.

FREE **Pinacoteca de Nuevo León** GALLERY (cnr Washington & Colegio Civil; www.conarte. org.mx; ⊙10am-6pm Tue-Sun; **M**Alameda) This art museum, in the gorgeous Colegio Civil building, displays paintings and sculptures from the state's leading contemporary artists, including Julio Galán (1958–2006), once part of Andy Warhol's circle.

FREE **Cervecería Cuauhtémoc** BREWERY (Reyes 2202 Norte; www.cuamoc.com; **M**General Anaya) Mexico's oldest brewery (established 1890), fills six million bottles of Bohemia, Dos Equis, Tecate and other beers every day. Free **brewery tours** (☑8328-5355; ⊙9am-4pm Mon-Fri) are given about hourly. Reservations are recommended (especially if you'd like a tour in English). Tours start in front of the convivial outdoor **beer garden** (⊙10am-6pm) where you might get a free mug of Carta Blanca. It's 2km north of Gran Plaza; the metro stops nearby.

🎉 Festivals & Events

Festival Internacional de Cine en Monterrey FILM
Mexican and international art-house films. Held during two weeks in August.

Aniversario de Independencia TRADITIONAL
Monterrey's biggest celebrations are held on Mexico's Independence Day, September 16, with fireworks, *musica norteña* (country ballads) and a parade.

🛏 Sleeping

There are just a few choices in the Barrio Antiguo, the best neighborhood to lay your head. The Zona Rosa has several luxury options, including a plethora of international chain hotels. Decent midrange choices are scarce while cheaper hotels congregate around the bus station.

Hostels and budget hotels fill up fast. Reservations are an especially good idea at hostels: if you don't have one, there may be nobody around to check you in.

La Casa del Barrio HOSTEL **$**
(☑8344-1800; www.lacasadelbarrio.com.mx; Montemayor 1221 Sur; dm M$200, r with/without bathroom M$490/410; **M**Zaragoza; ❄@�) This is a decent, friendly, family-run hostel, ideally located in the heart of the Barrio Antiguo. The nine private rooms aren't as good value as the four- to seven-bed dorms.

Santa Rosa Suites APARTMENTS **$$**
(☑8342-4200; Escobedo 930 Sur; ste incl breakfast M$865; **M**Zaragoza; **P**❄✳@�) More intimate than most of Monterrey's pricier hotels, the plush, sizeable suites here each have a separate living area with sofa bed, DVD player and dining space for four. There's a restaurant and piano bar on the 3rd floor.

Radisson Plaza Gran Hotel Ancira HOTEL **$$$**
(☑8150-7000; www.hotel-ancira.com; cnr Hidalgo & Escodeba; r/ste incl breakfast M$1300/2445; **M**Zaragoza; **P**❄✳@�) This stylish Zona Rosa hotel is Monterrey's grand dame with a sweeping staircase, shops, a gym, a small pool, a restaurant-bar and a grand piano. Rooms, however, are standard business class. Promotional rates can reduce rates below M$1000 a night with breakfast included.

🍴 Eating

Monterrey's signature dish is *cabrito al pastor* (roast kid goat), which, according to various legends, was created here. Supposedly there's none better because of the grass the young goats eat in the area. Barrio Antiguo has the best places to eat (and drink). It's wise to book ahead on Friday and Saturday nights.

Mercado Juárez (Av Juárez; ⊙8am-7pm Mon-Sat, to 3pm Sun; **M**Alameda) has *fondas* selling tasty, cheap grub.

TOP CHOICE **Fonda San Francisco** FUSION **$$$**
(☑8336-6706; www.fondasanfrancisco.tumblr.com; Los Aldama 123 Sur, Centro; mains M$60-300; ⊙1-11:30pm Mon-Sat; ✐) Out in the western San Pedro neighborhood, celebrity chef Adrian Herrera's inviting little bistro has recipes inspired by pre-Hispanic cooking. It's located just south of Avenida Vasconcelos; if you take bus 130 get off by the Super Roma. A taxi from the center is M$70.

El Infinito   CAFE $$
(Jardón 904; mains M$70-140; ◎5/6pm-12.30am;
ⓂZaragoza; ✍) Highly enjoyable culture cafe
set inside colonial premises with books to
browse and occasional art-house movies.
There is Friday-night live jazz on the rooftop
terrace. It offers high-priced sandwiches,
cheese plates, pizzas, fruit frappés, mango
martinis and properly made espresso.

Novum   ARGENTINE $$$
(✆8345-4476; Dr Coss 701; M$150-250; ◎1pm-
12:30am Tue-Sat; ⓂZaragoza; ☺) Slick Argentine restaurant with a good wine cellar,
scrumptious pizza and tender hunks of beef.

El Rey del Cabrito   MEXICAN $$$
(✆8345-3352/3292; www.elreydelcabrito.com.mx;
cnr Dr Coss & Av Constitución; mains M$100-250;
◎11am-midnight; ⓂZaragoza) Good for goat-
related dishes.

☆ Entertainment

Monterrey has numerous cinemas and an
active cultural life. The best sources of what
is happening are the daily Gente and Vida
sections of *El Norte* newspaper, and *Agenda
Cultura* which is free from the tourist office
and some museums. For the low-down on
'Montegay' scan www.gaymonterrey.net.

The Barrio Antiguo bars/clubs frequented
by Monterrey's affluent younger set include
fashionable live-music venues such as **Café
Iguana** or **Casa Amarilla** on Montemayor,
the epicenter of the drinking and dancing
scene. However, many venues have closed
down because of drug cartel violence near-
by: sample the city's nightlife with extreme
caution for this reason.

🛍 Shopping

Try the main downtown market, **Mercado
Juárez** (Av Juárez; ◎8am-7pm Mon-Sat, to 3pm
Sun; ⓂAlameda), for everyday items.

Corredor del Arte   CRAFTS MARKET
(Art Corridor; ◎10am-6pm Sun; ⓂZaragoza) Calle
Mina in the Barrio Antiguo becomes the
Corredor del Arte, a combination arts/crafts/
flea market, on Sundays. Bands play too.

ℹ Information

Dangers & Annoyances

Following the killing of 51 people in a casino fire
in the city in August 2011 and 49 mutilated bod-
ies dumped by a roadside in May 2012, Monter-
rey is being called one of Mexico's most danger-
ous cities. Violence is mainly between drug

cartels and the military, and can be anything
from armed robbery to gun battles, but innocent
civilians have got caught in the crossfire and are
occasionally targeted by cartels. The problems
have decimated Monterrey's nightlife and made
the mountains around the city increasingly
unsafe. Exercise extreme caution if out after
dark. The area around the Zona Rosa and Barrio
Antiguo is safest, though not devoid of violence.
Colonia Independencia, just south across the
Río Santa Catarina, should not be ventured into
day or night.

Emergency

Cruz Roja (Red Cross; ✆065)

Internet Access

El Rincón Zapatista (www.rznuevoleon
.ideosferas.org; Tapia 1538; per hr M$7; ◎2-
7pm Tue-Sun; ⓂAlameda) Cool cafe with
internet access and film screenings.

Internet Resources

All About Monterrey (www.allaboutmonterrey.
com) English-language site with an overview of
attractions, restaurants, lodging and activities.

Money

Banks and/or ATMs abound on nearly every
block of the Zona Rosa. The most convenient
ATMs for the Barrio Antiguo are under the Pala-
cio Municipal.

Medical Services

Hospital Muguerza (✆8399-3400; www.chris
tusmuguerza.com.mx; Hidalgo 2525 Poniente;
ⓂHospital)

Post

Post office (Washington 648 Oriente;
ⓂZaragoza)

Tourist Information

Infotur (✆2020-6789, in the US 866-238-
3866; Antiguo Palacio Federal, Washington
648; ◎9am-6:30pm Mon-Fri, to 5pm Sat & Sun;
ⓂZaragoza) Friendly, English-speaking staff at
this info center have plentiful information (much
published in English with some in French) about
sights/events across Nuevo León.

Travel Agencies

Viajes Santa Rosa (✆8344-9202; Galeana
940 Sur; ⓂZaragoza) Travel agency; reliable
for airline tickets.

ℹ Getting There & Away

Air

There are direct flights, usually daily, to all Mexi-
co's major cities, plus direct international flights
to Houston, Dallas, San Antonio, Los Angeles,
Las Vegas, Atlanta, Chicago, Madrid and Barce-
lona. Most other international destinations are

BUSES FROM MONTERREY

Prices are for 1st-class buses unless stated.

DESTINATION	FARE (M$)	DURATION	FREQUENCY (DAILY)
Chihuahua	685-720	11-12hr	7
Dallas, US	715	12hr	5 (changing at Nuevo Laredo)
Durango	570	8hr	15
Houston, US	600-675	11hr	3 direct (plus 6 changing at Nuevo Laredo)
Mazatlán	940	16hr	1
Mexico City (Terminal Norte)	850 (1st class) 920 (deluxe)	11hr	8 deluxe, frequent 1st-class
Nuevo Laredo	245	2¾hr	frequent
Piedras Negras	460	5hr	9
Reynosa	235	3hr	frequent
Saltillo	80	1¾hr	frequent
San Luis Potosí	475	6½hr	frequent
Zacatecas	420	6½hr	frequent

best routed via Mexico City, Houston or Dallas. Airlines include the following:

Aerobus (☑8215-01-50; www.vivaaerobus.com; Av Eugenio Garza Sada 2132)

Aeroméxico (☑800-021-40-00; www.aeromexico.com; Av Eugenio Garza Sada 3551)

Bus

Monterrey's colossal bus station, **Central de Autobuses** (Av Colón; ⓂCuauhtémoc), is 3km north of the center and it's busy 24/7 with departures and arrivals from across Mexico (see boxed table). Taxis to/from the bus station cost around M$30.

ⓘ Getting Around

To/From the Airport

No public transportation serves the airport directly.

Bus

Frequent buses (M$6.50 to M$9) get you most places you can't reach by metro. One noteworthy bus is Ruta 130, which goes from the corner of Juárez and Hidalgo in Zona Rosa through San Pedro, heading west along Avenida Vasconcelos.

Car & Motorcycle

Central parking lots charge around M$15 per hour.

Car rental agencies include the following:

Advantage (☑8345-7334; Ocampo 429 Oriente; ⓂZaragoza) Also has a desk at the airport.

Budget (☑8340-4100; Hidalgo 433 Oriente; ⓂZaragoza) Also has a desk at the airport.

Metro

The **Metrorrey** (metro/metrobus trip M$4.50/8; ⊙5am-midnight), Monterrey's modern, efficient metro system, consists of two lines. Elevated Línea 1 runs from the northwest of the city to the eastern suburbs, passing the Parque Fundidora. Línea 2 begins underground at the Gran Plaza and runs north past Parque Niños Héroes up into the northern suburbs. The two lines cross right by the bus station at Cuauhtémoc station. Several metro stations are connected with metrobuses (specialized buses with set stops) to outlying areas.

Taxi

Taxis (all have meters) are ubiquitous in Monterrey and reasonably priced. From the Zona Rosa to the bus terminal or Parque Fundidora is usually about M$30. Call ☑8372-8800 or ☑8130-0600 for radio-taxi service.

Around Monterrey

Part of Monterrey's charm has always been the awe-inspiring nearby scenery, although the threat of drug violence has made the below less safe: be sure to check the local security situation before embarking on a trip.

Right outside town is a stunning mountainside section of the Parque Nacional Cumbres de Monterrey, **Parque Ecológico**

Chipinque (☑81-8303-5575; www.chipinque. org.mx; pedestrian/cyclist/vehicle M$20/35/35; ☺6am-8pm). It's incredible that such a wild locale can exist so close to such a large city. There are great hiking and mountain-biking opportunities on trails through dense forest, and up to rocky peaks including high point Copete de Águilas (2200m). Maps, snacks, trail advice and permits for those heading into the park are available at the visitor center located near the entrance, a 15-minute drive southwest of central Monterrey via Avenida Gómez Morín in the San Pedro neighborhood.

Free Saturday/Sunday and holiday buses to Chipinque leave from the southwest corner of Parque Alameda at 8am, 10am and noon; be sure to ask when the last bus returns. Alternatively the 135 bus runs along Avenida Cuauhtémoc to the park; taxis are available too.

There are more natural wonders in the vicinity. Six kilometers uphill from El Cercado, a village 35km south of Monterrey on Hwy 85, pretty Cascada Cola de Caballo (Horsetail Falls; ☑8347-1533; adult/child M$35/20; ☺9am-7pm May-Oct, to 6pm Nov-Apr) has Mexico's highest (70m) bungee jump (☑81-8369-6640; www.coladecaballo.com; jump M$360; ☺3-8pm Fri, 11am-8pm Sat & Sun), as well as a 200ft canopy tour in the grounds of Hotel Hacienda Cola de Caballo. Autobuses Amarillos runs frequent 2nd-class buses from Monterrey's bus station to El Cercado (M$30, one hour). Those without wheels beware: taxis are scarce from El Cercado to the falls.

The towering limestone walls of El Potrero Chico (http://potrerochico.org), about 45 minutes northwest of Monterrey near the town of Hidalgo, are home to some of the world's best rock climbing, with more than 600 routes. The El Potrero Chico Climbing School (☑cell phone 81-83626672; www.elpotrerochico.com.mx) charges a whopping M$2025 per day for two people (not including shoe rental, food or water). You can rent climbing gear, or hire mountain bikes, from the same people.

In Monterrey, Autobuses Mina (M$26, 1½ hours) run to Hidalgo. From Hidalgo's central plaza the canyon is a M$60 taxi ride. If you're driving, go to the cement factory in central Hidalgo, then follow signs.

There are decent accommodations at both Cascada Cola de Caballo and El Potrero Chico.

Reserva de la Biosfera El Cielo

The main attraction of Tamaulipas in Mexico's far northeast is the Unesco-listed biosphere reserve of El Cielo, encompassing 1445-sq-km of steep-sided forested mountains ranging from 200m to 2320m. Marking a transition zone between tropical, temperate and semidesert ecosystems, its diversity is incredible. There are 97 species of reptile and amphibian and 430 bird species including the Tamaulipas pygmy owl and yellow-headed parrot. Black bear and jaguar also inhabit the reserve, and there are dozens of orchid varieties (picking them is prohibited), mostly within the cloud-forest zone between 800m and 1400m.

Inside the park there are trails which take you to weird rock formations, caves and waterfalls, and pools where you can swim. In Gómez Farías, the main base for launching park excursions, the fancy Cumbres Inn & Suites (☑832-236-22-18; www.hotelcumbres. com.mx; r/ste from M$1300/1600; ▣✳@☎☒❖) can help arrange kayaking trips within the park. There's a restaurant here with valley views, a rappelling wall, a triple zip-line, and ropey mountain bikes for rent.

❶ Getting There & Away

To reach the reserve, you first need to make it to Ciudad Victoria, accessible by bus from Monterrey (M$280, four hours) and from San Luis Potosí and Mexico City to the south. Aeropuerto Nacional General Pedro Méndez (☑316-46-48; www.asa.gob.mx), which has several daily flights to Mexico City, is 18km east of Ciudad Victoria off the Soto La Marina road. Gómez Farías itself is 11km up a side road off Hwy 85 between Ciudad Victoria and Ciudad Mante. The easiest way to reach Gómez Farías is via taxi from Ciudad Victoria (around M$450). Coming from Ciudad Victoria by bus, get off at the turnoff for Gómez on Hwy 85. From here catch the bus from Mante or the minivan (M$10, about every two hours).

Understand
Mexico

Mexico Today

The Drug War

There's no denying that most of the Mexico news reaching the outside world for the last few years has been bad. Terrible, in fact. Some 50,000 people had been killed by the end of 2011, after President Felipe Calderón declared war on the country's gruesomely vicious drug gangs in late 2006. The Mexican government deployed 50,000 troops as well as naval forces and several police forces against the drug mobs. It's assumed that most of the killers and killed were mobsters themselves, in battles over the multi-billion-dollar trafficking routes for Colombian cocaine and Mexican marijuana and methamphetamines into the US. The 'good' news in 2011 was that the number of killings, while still on the rise, was rising less rapidly. Pessimists argued that any possible respite in the mayhem was simply because the most powerful cartels had effectively wiped out their weaker rivals. Indeed, by 2012 there seemed to be only two major players left – the Sinaloa cartel in the northwest of Mexico and Los Zetas on the eastern side of the country.

The drug-gang violence scared away some tourists and other foreigners from Mexico. Naturally, it had ordinary Mexicans worried too – not just about being caught in the wrong place at the wrong time, but also about the penetration of organized crime in society generally. Minor gangs, squeezed out of the drug trade, were reportedly turning to protection rackets.

But the picture is far from uniform across the country. The great majority of drug-related violence happens in a few specific areas – principally along Mexico's northern border, with the city of Ciudad Juárez notoriously worst hit, and in the states of Sinaloa and Guerrero. Many other areas, including the Yucatán Peninsula (Mexico's major tourist destination), have suffered minimal drug-related violence, and if one takes

» Population: 112 million

» Annual population growth: 1.2%

» Area: 1.9 million sq km

» GDP per capita: US$9200

» US share of Mexican exports: 78%

» Remittances to Mexico by Mexicans living in the US: US$21 billion (2010)

» Adult literacy: 93%

» Number of recognized national languages: 69

Mexico Reading

God's Middle Finger Richard Grant investigates the narco-riddled Sierra Madre Occidental (called *Bandit Roads* in the UK).
Pedro Páramo The ultimate Mexican novel, by Juan Rulfo.
Oh Mexico! Lucy Neville's memoir of a young Australian living in Mexico City.

The Last Narco The hunt for Mexico's most wanted drug baron, by Malcolm Beith.
In the Sierra Madre Jeff Biggers lives with the Tarahumara (Rarámuri).
All the Pretty Horses Cormac McCarthy's tense tale of three latter-day cowboys riding south.

Music Albums

Pecados y milagros (Sins & Miracles) Best-yet from folk-jazz singer Lila Downs.
Avalancha de éxitos (Avalanche of Hits) Café Tacuba's rock/folk/hip-hop classic.

belief systems
(% of population)

85 — Roman Catholic

8 — Protestant & Evangelical

5 — No Religion

2 — Other Biblical

if Mexico were 100 people

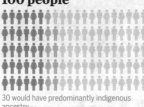

30 would have predominantly indigenous ancestry

9 would have predominantly European ancestry

61 would have mixed ancestry

Note: Figures are estimates; official figures do not use these classifications.

drug-related killings out of the equation for a moment, Mexico actually has a much lower murder rate than it did 10 years ago.

Meanwhile, in Other News...

The Mexican economy sprung back surprisingly well from the recession of 2009, posting 5% growth in 2010 and 4% in 2011, even if nearly half the population was still below the official poverty line of earning about US$167 per month. A little light relief came in 2011 at the sight of two of Mexico's most absurdly rich men, telephone magnate Carlos Slim Helú and TV magnate Emilio Azcárraga, falling out as they tried to move in on each other's patches. There was even a chance that real competition in the telecom business could bring down telephone and pay-TV costs for the public.

The New President

As this book was going to press, Mexico was heading into a new presidential election in which Enrique Peña Nieto was favorite to win the presidency back for the PRI (Institutional Revolutionary Party), which had held a monopoly on power for 80 years until 2000. The right-of-center PAN (National Action Party), which had held the presidency since 2000, was battling to hold on, with its candidate Josefina Vázquez Mota bidding to become Mexico's first woman president. Andrés Manuel López Obrador, who had been narrowly defeated by Felipe Calderón in 2006, was standing again for the left-of-center PRD (Party of the Democratic Revolution) and planned to pull the army out of the drug war.

Mexico telecom magnate Carlos Slim Helú was assessed as the world's richest person (net worth: US$69 billion) by *Forbes* magazine in 2012. Also on the *Forbes* list was Joaquín 'El Chapo' Guzmán, leader of the Sinaloa drug cartel, who ranked as Mexico's 10th richest person with US$1 billion.

Mexican Movies

MTV Unplugged: Los Tigres del Norte & Friends The kings of *norteño* (northern Mexico's equivalent of country music), and friends.

Amores perros (Love's a Bitch; 2000) Gritty groundbreaker that set director Alejandro González Iñárritu and actor Gael García Bernal on the path to stardom.
Rudo y Cursi (2008) Two brothers climb to professional soccer success.

Presunto culpable (Presumed Guilty; 2008) Doco that puts Mexico's justice system to shame.
Y tu mamá también (And Your Mother Too; 2001) Classic 'growing up' road movie about two privileged Mexico City teenagers (Gael García Bernal and Diego Luna).

History

Mexico's story is always extraordinary and at times barely credible. How could a 2700-year tradition of sophisticated indigenous civilization crumble in two short years at the hands of a few hundred adventurers from Spain? How could 19th-century Mexico's 11-year war for independence from Spain lead to three decades of dictatorship by Porfirio Díaz? How could the people's revolution that ended that dictatorship yield 80 years of one-party rule?

From nomadic hunter-gatherer beginnings, the earliest Mexicans developed first agriculture, then villages, then cities with advanced civilizations, then great empires. The 'mother culture' was the Olmecs of the southern Gulf of Mexico lowlands (1200–400 BC). Then came the great central Mexican city of Teotihuacán (AD 0–700), whose tribute-gathering empire stretched down into Central America. Ancient Mexico's most splendid civilization flourished among the Maya of the Yucatán Peninsula and nearby areas between about AD 250 and 900. The bloodthirsty Aztecs ruled a large swath of Mexico from their capital Tenochtitlán (modern Mexico City) from the early 15th to early 16th centuries.

A small Spanish expedition led by Hernán Cortés landed on Mexico's Gulf coast in 1519 and within two years subdued the mighty Aztecs with a combination of ruthlessness, cunning and brilliant tactics. The Spanish pacified most of the rest of Mexico within two decades, and ruled it as a colony for three centuries. Vast wealth from Mexican silver mines flowed back to Spain, some colonists became enormously wealthy, and the indigenous population was decimated by disease and reduced to serf status.

Colonists rebelled against Spanish rule in 1810, and after 11 years of fighting Mexico gained its independence in 1821. The young republic endured half a century of internal strife and several invasions, and lost large parts of its territory to the US. The rule of Porfirio Díaz from 1876

General History Resources

» *A Brief History of Mexico* by Lynn V Foster

» Mexico Online (www.mexonline.com)

» Mexconnect (www.mexconnect.com)

TIMELINE

7000–3000 BC	1200–400 BC	AD 0–150
Agriculture develops in the Tehuacán valley. First, chili seeds and squashes are planted; later, corn and beans are cultivated, enabling people to live semipermanently in villages.	Mexico's 'mother culture' (the Olmecs) flourishes on the Gulf coast at San Lorenzo and La Venta. Jade, a favorite pre-Hispanic material, appears in a tomb at La Venta.	A huge planned city is laid out in a grid arrangement at Teotihuacán in central Mexico, and the 70m-high Pyramid of the Sun is constructed there.

onward brought stability but also political repression and great social injustice.

The Mexican Revolution of 1910 unseated Díaz but plunged the country into 10 years of war between assorted conservative, liberal and revolutionary factions, in which about two million Mexicans died. The outcome was a radical reformist government whose leaders set up a political party that, under the eventual name Partido Revolucionario Institucional (PRI), stayed in power for 80 years, becoming steadily more conservative, corrupt and repressive as the 20th century wore on. Mexico made some economic strides but poverty remained very widespread, exacerbated by explosive population growth until late in the century. The PRI finally lost power in 2000.

The Ancient Civilizations

The political map of ancient Mexico shifted constantly as one city, town or state sought domination over another, and a sequence of powerful states rose and fell through invasion, internal conflict or environmental disaster. But these diverse cultures had much in common, as religion, forms of social organization and economic basics were transmitted from lords to vassals and from one generation to the next. Human sacrifice, to appease ferocious gods, was practiced by many societies; observation of the heavens was developed to predict the future and determine propitious times for important events like harvests; society was heavily stratified and dominated by priestly ruling classes; and women were restricted to domestic and child-bearing roles. Versions of a ritual ball game were played almost everywhere and seems to have always involved two teams trying to keep a rubber ball off the ground by flicking it with various parts of the body. The game sometimes served as an oracle, with the result indicating what course of action should be taken, and could also involve the sacrifice of some players.

There are many ways of analyzing the pre-Hispanic era, but a common framework divides it into three main periods: pre-Classic, before AD 250; Classic, AD 250–900; and post-Classic, AD 900–1521. The most advanced cultures in Mexico emerged chiefly in the center, south and east of the country. Together with Maya lands in what are now Guatemala, Belize and a small part of Honduras, this zone is collectively known to historians and archaeologists as Mesoamerica.

Beginnings

The pre-Hispanic inhabitants of the Americas arrived from Siberia, in several migrations during the last Ice Age, between perhaps 60,000 and 8000 BC, crossing land now submerged beneath the Bering Strait. Early Mexicans hunted big animal herds in the grasslands of the highland

Ancient Cultures

» *Mexico: From the Olmecs to the Aztecs* by Michael D Coe

» *The Aztecs* by Richard F Townsend

» Foundation for Advancement of Mesoamerican Studies (www.famsi.org)

Virtual Visits

» Museo Nacional de Antropología, Mexico City (www.mna.inah.gob.mx, in Spanish)

» Templo Mayor, Mexico City (www.templomayor.inah.gob.mx, in Spanish)

» Museo de Historia Mexicana, Monterrey (www.museohistoriamexicana.org.mx, in Spanish)

HISTORY THE ANCIENT CIVILIZATIONS

250–600	250–900	600–900	750–900
Teotihuacán grows into a city of an estimated 125,000 people, the Pyramid of the Moon is built, and Teotihuacán comes to control the biggest of Mexico's pre-Hispanic empires.	The brilliant Classic Maya civilization flowers in southeast Mexico, Guatemala, Belize and parts of Honduras and El Salvador.	El Tajín, the major center of the Classic Veracruz civilization (a group of small states with a shared culture near the Gulf coast), is at its peak.	Maya civilization in the central Maya heartland – Chiapas (southeast Mexico), El Petén (northern Guatemala) and Belize – collapses, probably because of prolonged severe droughts.

valleys. When temperatures rose at the end of the Ice Age, the valleys became drier, ceasing to support such animal life and forcing the people to derive more food from plants. In central Mexico's Tehuacán Valley, archaeologists have traced the slow beginnings of agriculture between 7000 and 3000 BC.

The Olmecs

Mexico's 'mother culture' was the mysterious Olmec civilization, which appeared in the humid lowlands of Veracruz and Tabasco. The evidence of the masterly stone sculptures they left behind indicates that Olmec civilization was well organized and able to support talented artisans, but

ANCIENT RELIGION & BELIEF

The Maya developed a complex writing system, partly pictorial, partly phonetic, with 300 to 500 symbols. They also refined a calendar used by other pre-Hispanic peoples into a tool for the exact recording and forecasting of earthly and heavenly events. Temples were aligned to enhance observation of the heavens, helping the Maya predict solar eclipses of the sun and movements of the moon and Venus. The Maya measured time in various interlocking cycles, ranging from 13-day 'weeks' to the 1,872,000-day 'Great Cycle.' They believed the current world to be just one of a succession of worlds, and this cyclical nature of things enabled the future to be predicted by looking at the past.

They also believed in predestination and developed a complex astrology. To win the gods' favors they carried out elaborate rituals involving dances, feasts, sacrifices, consumption of the alcoholic drink *balche,* and bloodletting from ears, tongues or penises. The Classic Maya seem to have practiced human sacrifice on a small scale, the later post-Classic Maya on a larger scale.

The Maya inhabited a universe with a center and four directions, each with a color: east was red; north, white; west, black; south, yellow; and the center, green. The heavens had 13 layers, and Xibalbá, the underworld to which the dead descended, had nine. The earth was the back of a giant reptile floating on a pond.

The later Aztecs, similarly, observed the heavens for astrological purposes and also saw the world as having four directions, 13 heavens and nine hells. Those who died by drowning, leprosy, lightning, gout, dropsy or lung disease went to the paradisiacal gardens of Tláloc, the rain god, who had killed them. Warriors who were sacrificed or died in battle, merchants killed while traveling far away, and women who died giving birth to their first child all went to heaven as companions of the sun. Everyone else traveled for four years under the northern deserts in the abode of the death god Mictlantecuhtli, before reaching the ninth hell, where they vanished altogether.

The Aztecs believed they lived in the 'fifth world,' whose four predecessors had each been destroyed by the death of the sun and of humanity. Aztec human sacrifices were designed to keep the sun alive.

c 1000

Chichén Itzá, an abandoned Maya city on the Yucatán Peninsula, is reoccupied, developing into one of Mexico's most magnificent ancient cities, in a fusion of Maya and central Mexican styles.

1325

The Aztecs settle at Tenochtitlán, on the site of present-day Mexico City. Over the next two centuries they come to rule an empire extending over nearly all of central Mexico.

» Chichén Itzá (p317)

lived in thrall to fearsome deities. Its best-known artifacts are the awe-inspiring 'Olmec heads,' stone sculptures up to 3m high with grim, pug-nosed faces and wearing curious helmets.

The Olmecs were involved in trade over long distances: far-flung Olmec sites in central and western Mexico may have been trading posts or garrisons to ensure the supply of jade, obsidian and other luxuries for the Olmec elite.

Olmec art, religion and society had a profound influence on later Mexican civilizations. Olmec gods, such as the feathered serpent, persisted right through the pre-Hispanic era.

Teotihuacán

The first great civilization in central Mexico arose in a valley about 50km northeast of the middle of modern Mexico City. The grid plan of the magnificent city of Teotihuacán was laid out in the 1st century AD. It was the basis for the famous Pyramids of the Sun and Moon as well as avenues, palaces and temples that were added during the next 600 years. The city grew to a population of about 125,000 and became the center of probably the biggest pre-Hispanic Mexican empire, stretching as far south as modern El Salvador. The empire carried Teotihuacán's advanced civilization – including writing, and a calendar system with a 260-day 'sacred year' composed of 13 periods of 20 days – far from its original heartland.

Teotihuacán, probably already weakened by the rise of rival powers in central Mexico, was burned, plundered and abandoned in the 8th century. But many Teotihuacán gods, such as the feathered serpent Quetzalcóatl (an all-important symbol of fertility and life) and Tláloc (the rain and water deity), were still being worshipped by the Aztecs a millennium later.

The Classic Maya

The Classic Maya, in the view of many experts the most brilliant civilization of pre-Hispanic America, flowered in three areas:

» **North** Mexico's low-lying Yucatán Peninsula

» **Central** The Petén forest of northern Guatemala, and the adjacent lowlands in Chiapas and Tabasco in Mexico (to the west) and Belize (to the east)

» **South** Highland Guatemala and a small section of Honduras

It was in the northern and central areas that the Maya blossomed most brilliantly, attaining heights of artistic and architectural expression, and of learning in fields like astronomy, mathematics and astrology, that were not surpassed by any other pre-Hispanic civilization.

The Classic Maya were divided among many independent city-states, often at war with each other. In the first part of the Classic period most

Find out all about Maya time, what your birth day signifies, and what you should do each day of the 20-day week at Mayan Calendar (www.mayan-calendar.com).

Modern Maya

» *The Caste War of Yucatán* by Nelson Reed

» *Time Among the Maya* by Ronald Wright

1487	1519–20	1521	1524
Twenty thousand human captives are sacrificed over a period of four days for the rededication of Tenochtitlán's Great Temple after a major reconstruction.	A Spanish expedition from Cuba, under Hernán Cortés, reaches Tenochtitlán. Initially well received, the Spaniards are attacked and driven out on the 'Noche Triste' (Sad Night), June 30, 1520.	The Spanish, with 100,000 native Mexican allies, capture Tenochtitlán, razing it building by building. They then rename it 'México' and go on to rebuild it as the capital of Nueva España (New Spain).	Virtually all the Aztec empire, plus other Mexican regions such as Colima, the Huasteca and the Isthmus of Tehuantepec, have been brought under Spanish control.

of these appear to have been grouped into two loose military alliances, centered on Tikal (Guatemala) and Calakmul (in the south of the Yucatán Peninsula).

Calakmul lies in a remote area where archaeological investigation is relatively unadvanced but which was one of the four main zones of classic Maya concentration in Mexico. The area is known as the Río Bec zone and is typified by long, low buildings decorated with serpent or monster masks and with towers at their corners. A second main Classic Maya zone was the Chenes area in northeastern Campeche state, with broadly similar architecture, except for the towers. A third area, also on the Yucatán Peninsula, was the Puuc zone, south of Mérida, whose most important city was Uxmal. Puuc ornamentation, which reached its peak on the Governor's Palace at Uxmal, featured intricate stone mosaics, often incorporating faces of the hook-nosed rain god Chac.

The fourth main Classic Maya zone in Mexico was lowland Chiapas, with the cities of Yaxchilán, Toniná and Palenque. For many people the most beautiful of all Maya sites, Palenque rose to prominence under the 7th-century ruler Pakal, whose treasure-loaded tomb inside the fine Templo de las Inscripciones was discovered in 1952.

A typical Maya city functioned as the religious, political and market hub for surrounding farming hamlets. Its ceremonial center focused on plazas surrounded by tall temple pyramids (usually the tombs of rulers, who were believed to be descended from the gods). Stone causeways called *sacbeob*, which were probably for ceremonial use, led out from the plazas.

The Classic Maya Collapse

In the second half of the 8th century, conflict between Maya city-states started to increase, and by the early 10th century, the several million inhabitants of the flourishing central Maya heartland in Chiapas, El Petén and Belize had virtually disappeared. The Classic era was at an end. A series of droughts and population pressure are both thought to have contributed to this cataclysm. Many Maya probably migrated to the Yucatán Peninsula or the highlands of Chiapas, where their descendants live on today. The jungle grew back up around the ancient lowland cities.

The Toltecs

In central Mexico, for centuries after the fall of Teotihuacán, power was divided between varying locally important cities, including: Xochicalco, south of Mexico City; Cacaxtla and Cantona to the east; and Tula to the north. The cult of Quetzalcóatl remained widespread, society in at least some places became more militarized, and mass human sacrifice may have started here in this period. Central Mexico maintained con-

---

1534–92	1540s	1605	1767
The Spanish find huge lodes of silver at Pachuca, Zacatecas, Guanajuato and San Luis Potosí, north of Mexico City.	The Yucatán Peninsula is brought under Spanish control by three (related) conquistadors all named Francisco de Montejo. Nueva España's northern border runs roughly from modern Tampico to Guadalajara.	Mexico's indigenous population has declined from an estimated 25 million at the time of the Spanish conquest to little over a million, mainly because of new diseases.	The Jesuits, important missionaries and educators in Nueva España and many of them criollos, are expelled from all Spanish dominions, fomenting discontent among criollos in the colony.

tact with the southeast: Maya influences are notable at Xochicalco, and the Quetzalcóatl cult and large-scale human sacrifice both reached the Yucatán Peninsula, where they're most evident at the city of Chichén Itzá.

Central Mexican culture in the early post-Classic period is often given the name Toltec (Artificers), a name coined by the later Aztecs, who looked back to the Toltec rulers with awe.

The Aztecs

The Aztecs' legends related that they were the chosen people of their tribal god, the hummingbird deity Huizilopochtli. Originally nomads from somewhere in western or northern Mexico, they were led by their priests to the Valle de México, the site of modern Mexico City, where they settled on islands in the valley's lakes. By the 15th century the Aztecs (also known as the Mexica) had fought their way up to become the most powerful group in the valley, with their capital at Tenochtitlán (where downtown Mexico City stands today). Legend tells that the site was chosen because it was there that the Aztecs witnessed an eagle standing on a cactus and devouring a snake – this was interpreted as a sign they should stop wandering and build a city. Today the eagle-snake-cactus emblem sits in the middle of the Mexican flag. The temple the Aztecs built on the spot, now known as the Templo Mayor, was considered the center of the universe.

The Aztecs formed the Triple Alliance with two other valley states, Texcoco and Tlacopan, to wage war against Tlaxcala and Huejotzingo, east of the valley. The prisoners they took became the diet of sacrificed warriors that voracious Huizilopochtli demanded to keep the sun rising every day.

The Triple Alliance brought most of central Mexico, from the Gulf coast to the Pacific, under its control. This was an empire of 38 provinces and about five million people, geared to extracting tribute (tax in kind) of resources absent from the heartland. Jade, turquoise, cotton, tobacco, rubber, fruits, vegetables, cacao and precious feathers were needed for the glorification of the Aztec elite and to support their war-oriented state.

Economy & Society

Tenochtitlán and the adjoining Aztec city of Tlatelolco grew to house more than 200,000 people. The Valle de México as a whole had more than a million. They were supported by a variety of intensive farming methods based on irrigation, terracing and swamp reclamation.

The Aztec emperor held absolute power but delegated important roles, such as priestly duties or tax collecting, to members of the *pilli*

HISTORY THE ANCIENT CIVILIZATIONS

Maya Websites

» Mesoweb (www.mesoweb.com)

» Maya Exploration Center (www.mayaexploration.org)

» GoMaya (www.gomaya.com)

» Mundo Maya Online (www.mayadiscovery.com)

1810	1810	1811
On September 16 priest Miguel Hidalgo launches Mexico's War of Independence with his Grito de Dolores (Cry of Dolores), a call to rebellion in the town of Dolores.	In October and November, rebels capture Zacatecas, San Luis Potosí and Morelia, and defeat loyalist forces at Las Cruces, but don't attack Mexico City. They are then pushed northward.	Rebel numbers shrink and their leaders, including Hidalgo, are captured and executed in Chihuahua. José María Morelos y Pavón, another priest, assumes the rebel leadership.

WITOLD SKRYPCZAK/LONELY PLANET IMAGES©

MIGUEL HIDALGO

» Statue of Miguel Hidalgo

(nobility). Celibate priests performed cycles of great ceremonies, typically including sacrifices and masked dances or processions enacting myths. Military leaders were usually *tecuhtli* (elite professional soldiers). Another special group was the *pochteca* – militarized merchants who helped extend the empire, brought goods to the capital and organized the large daily markets in big towns. At the bottom of society were pawns (paupers who could sell themselves for a specified period), serfs and slaves.

2012: POST-APOCALYPSE

If you're reading this after December 21, 2012, you'll know that contrary to some predictions, the world didn't end that day. Our author Beth Kohn asked Dr Ed Barnhart, director of the Maya Exploration Center (www.mayaexploration.org), a group of archaeologists studying Maya sciences, to throw some light on the date's meaning.

What's the significance of December 2012? The Maya have a number of different calendrical cycles that they tracked. One, called the 'Long Count,' will get you to the date 2012 with the completion of the 13th *bak'tun* (a *bak'tun* being a roughly 400-year period in time). The Maya believed that there were multiple creations and we're number four, which began on August 11, 3114 BC. We're coming to a point 13 *bak'tuns* later, which is the same amount of time that it took for the entire third creation to begin and end. The ancient texts are very clear that the creation before us only lasted 13 *bak'tun*, and then the Long Count calendar reset.

So why all the doomsday talk? This is primarily a Western phenomenon, brought up by New Agers. Some are making a Western mathematical assumption that, since the third creation lasted 13 *bak'tuns*, this one will also last 13 *bak'tuns*. The Maya actually never say that.

What did the Maya believe happened at the end of cycles? At least one or two of the previous creations in the *Popol Vuh*, the Maya's bible, do end in some sort of cataclysm, but generally the Maya believed that the end of major cycles are signs of transformation and renewal. It would be a great celebration to them, like a super duper anniversary.

What does 2012 signify to modern Maya? Except for very esoteric priestly work, the Maya had mostly dropped the Long Count calendar by the time the Spanish got here 500 years ago. Modern Maya don't use it whatsoever and it has no meaning to them. They continue a calendar tradition, but it's only about their sacred (260-day) and solar (365-day) calendars.

What are people most curious about? I've seen a shift from people asking if the world will end to asking about Maya prophecies. But the Maya brand of prophecy is about identifying cycles of time and the good or bad luck associated with it – prophecies about things that will repeat again and again throughout history.

1813	1821	1821–22	1824
Morelos' forces blockade Mexico City for several months. A congress at Chilpancingo adopts principles for the independence movement, but Morelos is captured and executed two years later.	Rebel leaders Vicente Guerrero and Agustín de Iturbide devise the Plan de Iguala, with guarantees for independence: constitutional monarchy, equality for criollos and *peninsulares*, Catholic religious supremacy.	The Plan de Iguala wins over all influential sections of society, and the incoming Spanish viceroy agrees to Mexican independence. Iturbide takes the new Mexican throne as Emperor Agustín I.	A new constitution establishes a federal Mexican republic of 19 states and four territories. Guadalupe Victoria, a former independence fighter, becomes its first president.

Other Post-Classic Civilizations

On the eve of the Spanish conquest, most Mexican civilizations shared deep similarities. Each was politically centralized and divided into classes, with many people occupied in specialist tasks, including professional priests. Agriculture was productive, despite the lack of draft animals, metal tools and the wheel. Corn tortillas, *pozol* (corn gruel) and beans were staple foods, and many other crops, such as squash, tomatoes, chilies, avocados, peanuts, papayas and pineapples, were grown in various regions. Luxury foods for the elite included turkey, domesticated hairless dog, game and chocolate drinks. War was widespread, and often connected with the need for a supply of prisoners to sacrifice to a variety of gods.

Several important regional cultures arose in the post-Classic period:

» **Michoacán** The Tarascos, who were skilled artisans and jewelers, ruled Michoacán from their base around the Lago de Pátzcuaro, about 200km west of Mexico City. They were one group that managed to avoid conquest by the Aztecs.

» **Oaxaca** After 1200 the Zapotecs were increasingly dominated by the Mixtecs, skilled metalsmiths and potters from the uplands around the Oaxaca–Puebla border. Much of Oaxaca fell to the Aztecs in the 15th and 16th centuries.

» **Yucatán Peninsula** The city of Mayapán dominated most of the Yucatán after the 'Toltec' phase at Chichén Itzá ended around 1200. Mayapán's hold dissolved from about 1440, and the Yucatán became a quarreling ground for many city-states, with a culture much decayed from Classic Maya glories.

The Meso-american Ballgame (www.ballgame.org) is an interesting website about the indigenous ball game, past and present, with video of a modern contest in action.

The Spanish Arrive

Ancient Mexican civilization, nearly 3000 years old, was shattered in two short years by a tiny group of invaders who destroyed the Aztec empire, brought in a new religion and reduced the native people to second-class citizens and slaves. Rarely in history has a thriving society undergone such a transformation so fast. So alien to each other were the newcomers and the indigenous Mexicans that each doubted whether the other was human (Pope Paul III declared indigenous Mexicans to be human in 1537). Yet from their traumatic encounter arose modern Mexico. Most Mexicans today are mestizo, of mixed indigenous and European blood, and thus descendants of both cultures.

The Mel Gibson-directed *Apocalypto* (2006), a violent tale of a young man trying to escape becoming a human sacrifice, gives some idea of what ancient Maya life might sometimes have been like.

The Spanish Background

In 1492, the year Christopher Columbus arrived in the Caribbean, Spain was an aggressively expanding state, fresh from completing the 700-year Reconquista (Reconquest) in which Christian armies had gradually recovered the Spanish mainland from Islamic rule. With a curious mix of brutality and bravery, gold lust and piety, the Spanish conquistadors

HISTORY THE SPANISH ARRIVE

1836	1845–48	1847–48	1858–61
US settlers in the Mexican territory of Texas declare independence. President Santa Anna wipes out the defenders of the Alamo mission, but is routed on the San Jacinto River.	US Congress votes to annex Texas, sparking the Mexican-American War (1846–48). US troops occupy Mexico City. Mexico cedes Texas, California, Utah, Colorado and most of New Mexico and Arizona.	The Maya people of the Yucatán Peninsula rise up against their criollo overlords in the 'War of the Castes' and narrowly fail to drive them off the peninsula.	Liberal government laws requiring the church to sell property precipitate the War of the Reform: Mexico's liberals (with their 'capital' at Veracruz) defeat the conservatives (based in Mexico City).

of the Americas carried the impetus of the Reconquista to a whole new continent.

Seeking new westward trade routes to the spice-rich Orient, Spanish explorers and soldiers landed first in the Caribbean, establishing colonies on the islands of Hispaniola and Cuba. They then began seeking a passage through the land mass to the west, and soon became distracted by tales of gold, silver and a rich empire there.

After the first Spanish expeditions from Cuba had been driven back from Mexico's Gulf coast, Spain's governor of Cuba, Diego Velázquez, asked Hernán Cortés (a colonist there) to lead a new expedition westward. As Cortés gathered ships and men, Velázquez became uneasy about the costs and Cortés' loyalty, and tried to cancel the expedition. But Cortés, sensing a once-in-history opportunity, ignored him and set sail on February 15, 1519, with 11 ships, 550 men and 16 horses.

The Conquest

The Cortés expedition landed first at Cozumel island, then sailed around the coast to Tabasco, defeating inhospitable locals in the Battle of Centla near modern-day Frontera, where the enemy fled in terror from Spanish horsemen, thinking horse and rider to be a single fearsome beast. Afterwards the locals gave Cortés 20 maidens, among them Doña Marina (La Malinche), who became his indispensable interpreter, aide and lover.

Resentful Aztec subject towns on the Gulf coast, such as Zempoala, welcomed the Spaniards. And as the Spaniards moved inland toward Tenochtitlán, they made allies of the Aztecs' long-time enemies, the Tlaxcalans.

Aztec legends and superstitions and the indecisiveness of Emperor Moctezuma II Xocoyotzin also worked to the Spaniards' advantage. According to the Aztec calendar, 1519 would see the legendary Toltec god-king Quetzalcóatl return from banishment in the east. Was Cortés actually Quetzalcóatl? Omens proliferated: lightning struck a temple, a comet sailed through the night skies and a bird 'with a mirror in its head' was brought to Moctezuma, who saw warriors in it.

The Spaniards, with 6000 indigenous allies, were invited to enter Tenochtitlán, a city bigger than any in Spain, on November 8, 1519. Aztec nobles carried Moctezuma out to meet Cortés on a litter with a canopy of feathers and gold, and the Spaniards were lodged, as befitted gods, in the palace of Moctezuma's father, Axayácatl.

Though entertained in luxury, the Spaniards were trapped. Unsure of Moctezuma's intentions, they took him hostage. Believing Cortés a god, Moctezuma told his people he went willingly, but tensions rose in the city. Eventually, after some six or seven months, some of the Spaniards killed about 200 Aztec nobles in an intended pre-emptive strike. Cortés

---

Spanish Conquest: First-Hand Accounts

» *The Broken Spears: Aztec Account of the Conquest of Mexico* by Miguel Leon-Portilla

» *History of the Conquest of New Spain* by Bernal Díaz del Castillo

---

1861–63

Benito Juárez becomes Mexico's first indigenous president, but Mexico suffers the French Intervention: France invades Mexico, taking Mexico City in 1863 despite a defeat at Puebla on May 5, 1862.

1864–67

Napoleon III sends Maximilian of Hapsburg over as emperor in 1864, but starts to withdraw his troops in 1866. Maximilian is executed by Juárez's forces in 1867.

» Benito Juárez monument, Zacatecas (p628)

JOHN ELK III/LONELY PLANET IMAGES©

persuaded Moctezuma to try to pacify his people. According to one version of events, the emperor tried to address the crowds from the roof of Axayácatl's palace, but was killed by missiles; other versions say it was the Spaniards who killed him.

The Spaniards fled, losing several hundred of their own and thousands of indigenous allies, on what's known as the Noche Triste (Sad Night). They retreated to Tlaxcala, where they built boats in sections, then carried them across the mountains for a waterborne assault on Tenochtitlán. When the 900 Spaniards re-entered the Valle de México in May 1521, they were accompanied by some 100,000 native allies. The defenders resisted fiercely, but after three months the city had been razed to the ground and the new emperor, Cuauhtémoc, was captured.

Mexico as a Colony

Spain's policy toward all its conquests in the Americas can be summed up in one word: exploitation. The Spanish crown saw the New World as a silver cow to be milked to finance its endless wars in Europe, a life of luxury for its nobility and a deluge of new churches, palaces and monasteries that were erected around Spain. The crown was entitled to one-fifth (the *quinto real,* or royal fifth) of all bullion sent back from the New World. Conquistadors and colonists saw the American empire as a chance to get rich. Cortés granted his soldiers *encomiendas,* which were rights to the labor or tribute of groups of indigenous people. Spain asserted its authority through viceroys, the crown's personal representatives in Mexico.

The populations of the conquered peoples of Nueva España (New Spain), as the Spanish named their Mexican colony, declined disastrously, mainly from epidemics of new diseases introduced by the invaders. The indigenous peoples' only real allies were some of the monks who started arriving in 1523. The monks' missionary work helped extend Spanish control over Mexico – by 1560 they had converted millions of people and built more than 100 monasteries – but many of them also protected local people from the colonists' worst excesses.

Northern Mexico remained beyond Spanish control until big finds of silver at Zacatecas, Guanajuato and elsewhere spurred efforts to subdue it. The northern borders were slowly extended by missionaries and a few settlers, and by the early 19th century Nueva España included (albeit loosely) most of the modern US states of Texas, New Mexico, Arizona, California, Utah and Colorado.

Colonial Society

A person's place in colonial Mexican society was determined by skin color, parentage and birthplace. At the top of the tree, however humble their origins in Spain, were Spanish-born colonists. Known as

Anna Lanyon's *The New World of Martín Cortés* tells the fascinating and poignant story of the first mestizo, the son of Hernán Cortés and La Malinche.

MESTIZO

1876–1911	1910–11	1913–14	1917
The Porfiriato: Mexico is ruled by conservative Porfirio Díaz, who brings stability but curbs civil liberties and democratic rights, and concentrates wealth in the hands of a small minority.	Mexico rises in revolution against the Díaz regime on November 20, 1910. Díaz resigns in May 1911, and reformist Francisco Madero is elected president in November.	Madero is deposed and executed by conservative rebel Victoriano Huerta. Northern revolutionary leaders unite against Huerta. His troops terrorize the countryside, but Huerta is forced to resign in July 1914.	Reformists emerge victorious over radicals in the revolutionary conflict and a new reformist constitution, still largely in force today, is enacted at Querétaro.

peninsulares, they were a minuscule part of the population, but were considered nobility in Nueva España.

Next on the ladder were the criollos, people of Spanish ancestry born in the colony. As the decades passed, the criollos began to develop a distinct identity, and some of them came to possess enormous estates (haciendas) and amass huge fortunes from mining, commerce or agriculture. Not surprisingly, criollos sought political power commensurate with their wealth and grew to resent Spanish authority.

Below the criollos were the mestizos (people of mixed ancestry), and at the bottom of the pile were the indigenous people and African slaves. Though the poor were paid for their labor by the 18th century, they were paid very little. Many were *peones* (bonded laborers tied by debt to their employers), and indigenous people still had to pay tribute to the crown.

Social stratification follows similar patterns in Mexico today with, broadly speaking, the 'pure-blood' descendants of Spaniards at the top of the tree, the mestizos in the middle, and the indigenous people at the bottom.

SOME WE LOVE, SOME WE LOVE TO HATE

Mexicans have strong opinions about some of their historical characters. Some are held up as shining examples for every Mexican to be proud of, and immortalized by statues and street names all over the country. Others, just as influential, are considered objects of shame and ridicule.

Mexico's Top Heroes

» **Cuauhtémoc** Aztec leader who resisted the Spanish invaders
» **Benito Juárez** Reforming, liberal, indigenous president who fought off French occupiers
» **Miguel Hidalgo** Priest who launched the War for Independence
» **Pancho Villa** Larger-than-life revolutionary

Mexico's Top Villains

» **Hernán Cortés** The original evil Spanish conqueror
» **Carlos Salinas de Gortari** President from 1988 to 1994, blamed for the peso crisis, drugs trade, corruption, Nafta, you name it
» **Santa Anna** Winner at the Alamo, but loser of Texas, California, Arizona, Utah, Colorado and New Mexico
» **La Malinche** Doña Marina, Hernán Cortés' indigenous translator and lover

1920–24	1924–36	1934–40	1940s & '50s
President Álvaro Obregón turns to post-Revolution reconstruction. More than a thousand rural schools are built, some land is redistributed from big landowners to peasants.	President Plutarco Elías Calles closes monasteries and bans religious processions, precipitating the Cristero Rebellion (until 1929). He founds the Partido Nacional Revolucionario, a precursor to PRI, in 1929.	President Lázaro Cárdenas redistributes nearly 200,000 sq km of land and expropriates foreign oil operations in Mexico, forming Petróleos Mexicanos (Pemex). Foreign investors avoid Mexico.	The Mexican economy expands, helped by growth during WWII, major infrastructure projects and the development of tourism. The population almost doubles in two decades, and millions migrate to urban areas.

Mexico as a Republic

Criollo discontent with Spanish rule really began to stir following the expulsion of the Jesuits (many of whom were criollos) from the Spanish empire in 1767. The catalyst for rebellion came in 1808 when Napoleon Bonaparte occupied Spain, and direct Spanish control over Nueva España evaporated. The city of Querétaro, north of Mexico City, became a hotbed of intrigue among disaffected criollos plotting rebellion against Spanish rule. The rebellion was finally launched on September 16, 1810 by Padre Miguel Hidalgo (see boxed text, p667) in his parish of Dolores (now Dolores Hidalgo). The path to independence was a hard one, involving almost 11 years of fighting between rebels and loyalist forces, and the deaths of Hidalgo and several other rebel leaders. But eventually rebel general Agustín de Iturbide sat down with Spanish viceroy Juan O'Donojú in Córdoba in 1821 and agreed on terms for Mexico's independence.

Mexico's first century as a free nation started with a period of chronic political instability and wound up with a period of stability so repressive that it triggered a social revolution. A consistent theme throughout was the opposition between liberals, who favored a measure of social reform, and conservatives, who didn't. Between 1821 and the mid-1860s, the young Mexican nation was invaded by three different countries (Spain, the USA and France), lost large chunks of its territory to the US, and underwent nearly 50 changes of head of state.

Another consistent theme was intervention in politics by ambitious soldiers: Antonio López de Santa Anna first hit the limelight by deposing independent Mexico's first head of state, Emperor Agustín I, in 1823. He overthrew President Anastasio Bustamante in 1831, then was himself elected president in 1833, the first of 11 terms in 22 years. Above all, Santa Anna is remembered for helping to lose large chunks of Mexican territory to the US. After his 1836 defeat in Texas and his disastrous territorial losses in the Mexican-American War in 1848, a Santa Anna government sold Mexico's last remaining areas of New Mexico and Arizona to the US for US$10 million in 1853. This precipitated the Revolution of Ayutla that ousted him for good in 1855.

Amazingly, it was an indigenous Zapotec from Oaxaca who played the lead role in Mexican affairs for two tumultuous decades thereafter. Lawyer Benito Juárez (see boxed text, p425) was a key member of the new liberal government in 1855, which ushered in the era known as the Reform, in which the liberals set about dismantling the conservative state that had developed in Mexico. Juárez became president in 1861. With the French Intervention almost immediately afterwards, his government was forced into exile in provincial Mexico, eventually to regain control

HISTORY MEXICO AS A REPUBLIC

Independence Sites

» Alhóndiga de Granaditas, Guanajuato

» Dolores Hidalgo

» Calabozo de Hidalgo, Casa Chihuahua, Chihuahua

» Ex-Hotel Zevallos, Córdoba

» Museo Casa Natal de Morelos, Morelia

The best movie about the Mexican Revolution is Elia Kazan's *Viva Zapata!* (1952), starring Marlon Brando. John Steinbeck's script is historically sound up to the 1914 meeting between Pancho Villa and Emiliano Zapata in Mexico City. Beyond that point it flounders until Zapata is assassinated.

1953

The only exhibition of Frida Kahlo's art in Mexico during her lifetime is held in Mexico City. The artist arrives on a stretcher due to ill health.

» Museo Frida Kahlo (p89)

1964–70

President Gustavo Díaz Ordaz resists democratizing the PRI. During demonstrations against one-party rule before the 1968 Olympics, an estimated 400 protestors are massacred at Tlatelolco, Mexico City.

1970

In January construction starts on the first hotel at Isla Cancún, a coconut plantation with no permanent inhabitants on the Yucatán Peninsula's Caribbean coast.

in 1866. Juárez set an agenda of economic and social reform. Schooling was made mandatory, a railway was built between Mexico City and Veracruz, and a rural police force, the *rurales*, was organized to secure the transportation of cargo through Mexico. Juárez died in 1872 and remains one of the few Mexican historical figures with a completely unsullied reputation.

A rather different Oaxacan, Porfirio Díaz, ruled as president for 31 of the following 39 years, a period known as the Porfiriato. Díaz brought Mexico into the industrial age, stringing telephone, telegraph and railway lines and launching public works projects. He kept Mexico free of civil wars – but political opposition, free elections and a free press were banned. Peasants were cheated out of their land by new laws, workers suffered appalling conditions, and land and wealth became concentrated in the hands of a small minority. All this led, in 1910, to the Mexican Revolution.

The Mexican Revolution

Revolution Sites

» Museo Casa de Villa, Chihuahua

» Museo Francisco Villa, Hidalgo del Parral

» Cuartel General de Zapata, Tlaltizapán, Morelos

» Museo de la Revolución, Puebla

» Museo Casa Carranza, Cuatro Ciénegas

The Revolution was a tortured 10-year period of shifting conflicts and allegiances between forces and leaders of all political stripes. The conservatives were pushed aside fairly early on, but the reformers and revolutionaries who had lined up against them could not agree among themselves. Successive attempts to create stable governments were wrecked by new outbreaks of devastating fighting. All told, one in eight Mexicans lost their lives.

Francisco Madero, a wealthy liberal from Coahuila, would probably have won the presidential election in 1910 if Porfirio Díaz hadn't jailed him. On his release, Madero called successfully for the nation to revolt, which spread quickly across the country. Díaz resigned in May, 1911, and Madero was elected president six months later. But Madero could not contain the diverse factions that were now fighting for power throughout the country. The basic divide was between liberal reformers like Madero and more radical leaders such as Emiliano Zapata (see boxed text, p171), who was fighting for the transfer of hacienda land to the peasants, with the cry *'¡Tierra y libertad!'* (Land and freedom!).

In 1913 Madero was deposed, executed and replaced as president by one of his own top generals, Victoriano Huerta, who had defected to conservative rebels. The revolutionary forces united (temporarily) in opposition to Huerta. Three main leaders in the north banded together under the Plan de Guadalupe: Venustiano Carranza, a Madero supporter, in Coahuila; Francisco 'Pancho' Villa (see boxed text, p772) in Chihuahua; and Álvaro Obregón in Sonora. Zapata also fought against Huerta.

But fighting then broke out again between the victorious factions, with Carranza and Obregón (the 'Constitutionalists', with their capital at Ver-

1970	1970s	1980s	1985
Mexico stages the soccer World Cup in June. Mexico's team is eliminated in the quarter-finals; Brazil beats Italy in the final with what's reckoned one of the best-ever soccer performances.	Mexico enjoys an economic boom thanks to a jump in world oil prices. On the strength of the country's vast oil reserves, international institutions begin lending Mexico billions of dollars.	Oil prices plunge and Mexico suffers its worst recession in decades. Amid economic helplessness and rampant corruption, dissent and protests increase, even inside the PRI.	On September 19 a massive earthquake, with a magnitude of 8.1 on the Richter scale, strikes Mexico City. At least 10,000 people are killed.

acruz) pitted against the radical Zapata and the populist Villa. The latter pair never formed a serious alliance, and it was Carranza who emerged the victor. He had Zapata assassinated in 1919, only to be liquidated himself the following year on the orders of his former ally Obregón. Pancho Villa was killed in 1923.

Mexico as a One-Party Democracy

From 1920 to 2000, Mexico was ruled by the reformists who emerged victorious from the Revolution and their successors in the political party they set up, which since the 1940s has borne the name Partido Revolucionario Institucional (Institutional Revolutionary Party), or PRI as it's universally known. Starting out with some genuinely radical social policies, these governments became steadily more conservative, more corrupt, more repressive and more self-interested as the 20th century wore on. Mexico ended the century with a bigger middle class but still with a yawning wealth gap between the prosperous few and the many poor.

The problem of land ownership was addressed by the redistribution of more than 400,000 sq km from large estates to peasants and small farmers between the 1920s and '60s. Nearly half the population received land, mainly in the form of *ejidos* (communal landholdings).

At the other end of the economic spectrum, Mexico developed a worrying dependence on its large oil reserves in the Gulf of Mexico. The 1970s and '80s saw the country veer from oil-engendered boom to oil-engendered slump as world oil prices swung rapidly up then just as suddenly down. The huge government-owned oil company Pemex was just one face of a massive state-controlled economic behemoth that developed as the PRI sought control over all important facets of Mexican life.

The PRI was discredited forever in the minds of many Mexicans by the Tlatelolco Massacre of 1968, in which an estimated 400 civil-liberties

In the 1920s, outstanding Mexican artists such as Diego Rivera were commissioned to decorate important public buildings with large, vivid murals on historical and social themes. Many of these can be seen in Mexico City.

POPULATION PRESSURES

Between 1940 and 1980 Mexico's population more than trebled from 20 million to 67 million, and Mexico City's population multiplied tenfold. Many people migrated from the villages to urban areas in search of work, often living in desperate conditions in shanty towns around the edges of cities. Eventually, publicity campaigns, education and family-planning clinics all helped to slow things down. In 1970, the average Mexican woman gave birth seven times in her lifetime. Today the figure is just 2.3. A major economic safety valve is emigration to the US, something very large numbers of Mexicans, especially men from rural areas, do for at least part of their lives. By some estimates, 15 million Mexicans are now (legally or illegally) in the US, where average wages are six times higher than in Mexico.

1988–94	1994	1994–2000	2000
The PRI's Carlos Salinas de Gortari narrowly defeats left-of-center Cuauhtémoc Cárdenas in a disputed presidential election, and reforms Mexico's state-dominated economy toward private enterprise and free trade.	Nafta takes effect. The Zapatista uprising in Chiapas begins. Luis Donaldo Colosio, Salinas' chosen successor as PRI presidential candidate, is assassinated. Days after Salinas leaves office, Mexico's currency collapses.	Under President Ernesto Zedillo, Mexico emerges from a recession triggered by the peso collapse. Crime and emigration to the US increase. Zedillo sets up a more independent, transparent electoral system.	The PRI finally loses power as Vicente Fox of the right-of-center PAN (Partido Acción Nacional) wins the presidential election – the first ever peaceful change of regime in Mexican history.

protestors were shot dead (see p361). The PRI came to depend increasingly on strong-arm tactics and fraud to win elections.

Mexicans' cynicism about their leaders reached a crescendo with the 1988–94 presidency of Carlos Salinas de Gortari, who won the presidential election only after a mysterious computer failure had halted vote-tallying at a crucial stage. During Salinas' term, drug trafficking grew into a huge business in Mexico, and mysterious assassinations proliferated. Salinas did take steps to liberalize the monolithic state-dominated economy. The apex of his program, Nafta (the North American Free Trade Agreement) boosted exports and industry, but was unpopular with food growers and small businesses threatened by imports from the US. The last year of Salinas' presidency, 1994, began with the left-wing Zapatista uprising in Mexico's southernmost state, Chiapas (see boxed text, p361), and shortly before Salinas left office he spent nearly all of Mexico's foreign-exchange reserves in a futile attempt to support the peso, engendering a slump that he left his successor, Ernesto Zedillo, to deal with.

It was also left to Zedillo to respond to the clamor for democratic change in Mexico. He established a new, independently supervised electoral system that opened the way for the country's first-ever peaceful change of regime at the end of his term in 2000, when Vicente Fox of the business-oriented Partido Acción Nacional (PAN) won the presidential election.

Fox's election itself, after 80 years of one-party rule, was really the biggest news about his six-year term. He entered office backed by much goodwill. In the end, his presidency was considered a disappointment by most. He had no magic solutions to the same economic and social problems that previous governments had struggled with. Lacking a majority in Mexico's Congress, Fox was unable to push through the reforms that he believed were key to stirring Mexico's slumbering economy. At least government became more transparent, and Mexicans became a mite less cynical about their political system.

A contingent of 250,000 Mexican and Mexican-American men fought in WWII. One thousand were killed in action, 1500 received purple hearts and 17 received the Congressional Medal of Honor.

2006	2006–11	2009	2012
The PAN's Felipe Calderón narrowly defeats Andrés Manuel López Obrador of the left-of-center PRD in the presidential election, and declares war on Mexico's drug mobs.	In the first five years of Calderón's war on drugs, 50,000 troops are deployed around the country and some 50,000 people are killed, most of them in inter-gang turf wars.	The world swine flu pandemic begins in La Gloria, Veracruz, savaging Mexico's tourism industry. Over 1300 Mexicans die of the virus by 2010.	December 21 is the end of the 13th *bak'tun* (approximately 400-year period) of the fourth creation in the ancient Maya's Long Count calendar. The third creation lasted just 13 *bak'tun*...

The Mexican Way of Life

Life, Death & the Family

One thing you can never do with Mexicans is encapsulate them in simple formulas. They adore fun, music and a fiesta, yet in many ways are deeply serious. They work hard, but enjoy life to the full. They're hospitable, warm and courteous to guests, yet are most truly themselves within their family group. They will laugh at death, but have a profound vein of spirituality. They love the new and modern, while remaining traditional in essence.

Most Mexicans, however contemporary and globalized they may appear, still inhabit a world in which omens, coincidences and curious resemblances take on great importance. When sick, many people still prefer to visit a traditional *curandero* – a kind of cross between a naturopath and a witch doctor – rather than resort to a modern *médico*. The ancient belief in the cyclical, repetitive nature of time persists too, in the Mexican subconscious.

On a more mundane level, most Mexicans are chiefly concerned with earning a crust for themselves and their strongly knit families – but also with enjoying the leisurely side of life, whether partying at clubs or fiestas, or relaxing over an extended-family Sunday lunch at a restaurant. Holidays for religious festivals and patriotic anniversaries are essential to the rhythm of life, ensuring that people get a break every few weeks and bringing them together for the same processions and rituals year after year.

Mexicans may mock their country's failings, but at the same time they are proud of it. Being so close to the US, where millions of them spend years of their lives, Mexicans naturally absorb a certain amount of US culture and consciousness, but they also strongly value what's different about Mexican life – its more humane pace, its strong sense of community and family, its unique food and drinks, and the thriving, multifaceted national culture.

The Great Divides

Fly into Mexico City and you'll get a bird's-eye view of just how little space is not occupied by housing or roads. Around the edges of the city, new streets climb the steep slopes of extinct volcanoes, while shacks on the city's fringes, made from a few concrete blocks or sheets of tin, 'house' the poorest. More affluent neighborhoods have blocks of relatively spacious apartments. In the wealthiest quarters, imposing detached houses with well-tended gardens and satellite dishes sit behind high walls with strong security gates.

One in every two Mexicans now lives in a city or conurbation of more than a million people. A quarter of them live in smaller cities and towns,

Nobel Prize–winning Mexican writer Octavio Paz argues in *The Labyrinth of Solitude* that Mexicans' love of noise, music and crowds is just a temporary escape from personal isolation and gloom. Make your own judgment!

and another quarter in villages. The number of urban dwellers continues to rise as rural folk are sucked into cities.

Out in the villages and small towns, people still work the land and members of an extended family often live in yards with separate small buildings, of adobe, wood or concrete, often with earth floors. Inside these homes are few possessions – beds, a cooking area, a table with a few chairs and a few aging photos of departed relatives. Few villagers own cars.

Mexico's eternal wealth gap yawns as wide as ever. The world's richest man, entrepreneur Carlos Slim Helú, is a Mexican. His net worth was estimated at US$69 billion by *Forbes* magazine in 2012. At the other extreme, the poorest city dwellers barely scrape an existence as street hawkers, buskers or home workers in the 'informal economy,' rarely earning more than M$50 (US$4) a day. Anthropologist Guillermo Bonfil Batalla argues in *México profundo* that Mexico's poor, both indigenous and *mestizo* (of mixed ancestry), constitute a uniquely Mesoamerican civilization quite distinct from the European- and American-influenced middle class.

While rich kids go clubbing in flashy cars and attend private schools (often in the US), and the bohemian urban counterculture enjoys its mezcal bars, state-funded universities and underground dance clubs, poor villagers may dance only at local fiestas and often leave school before they reach the age of 15.

> About one-third of adult Mexicans never completed the basic nine years of primary and secondary schooling. Millions of kids from poorer families do so today only because of government cash handouts that are conditional upon school attendance.

Letting off Steam

Mexicans have many ways of releasing their emotional and physical energy. Artistic expression is key (see p817). So are religion and the countless fiestas (p28); another is sports.

Soccer

No sport ignites Mexicans' passions more than *fútbol*. Games in the 18-team national Primera División (First Division) are watched by crowds averaging 25,000 and followed by millions on TV. Attending a game is fun, and rivalry between opposing fans is generally good-humored. Tickets are sold at the entrance for anything from M$50 to M$600, depending on the stadium, game and seat.

The two most popular teams with large followings everywhere are América, of Mexico City, known as the Águilas (Eagles), and Guadalajara, or the Chivas (Goats). Matches between the two, known as 'Los Clásicos,' are the biggest games of the year. Other leading clubs include Cruz Azul and UNAM ('Pumas') of Mexico City, Monterrey and UANL ('Los Tigres') from Monterrey, Santos Laguna from Torreón, and Toluca.

Games are spread over the weekend from Friday to Sunday. The Primera División season is divided into the Torneo de Apertura (Opening Tournament, July/August to December) and the Torneo de Clausura (Closing Tournament, January to May/June), each ending in play-offs to decide the champion.

> Mexico's national soccer team, known as El Tri (short for Tricolor, the name for the national flag), has reached – and been eliminated in – the last-16 round of every World Cup since 1994.

Bullfights

Bullfighting arouses strong passions in many Mexicans. While a bizarre craze for child bullfights (in which matadors as young as 10 kill bulls in public arenas) has boosted its popularity, there is also an anti-bullfighting movement spearheaded by groups such as AMEDEA (Mexican Animal Rights Association) and AnimaNaturalis.

To aficionados the *corrida de toros* (literally 'running of the bulls') is as much a ritualistic dance as a fight. Usually six bulls are fought in an afternoon, and each is fought in three *suertes* (acts). In the first, the cape-waving *toreros* tire the bull by luring him around the ring, then two *pica-*

dores, on heavily padded horses, jab long lances into the bull's shoulders to weaken him. Next is the *suerte de banderillas,* when the *toreros* stab three pairs of elongated darts into the bull's shoulders. Finally comes the *suerte de muleta,* in which the matador, after some fancy cape work to tire the animal, must deliver the fatal *estocada* (lunge) by plunging a sword into the bull's neck from a position directly in front of the animal.

Bullfights usually take place on Sunday afternoons or during local festivals, chiefly in the larger cities. In northern Mexico the season generally runs from March or April to August or September. In central and southern Mexico, including Mexico City's Monumental Plaza México, one of the world's biggest bullrings, the main season is from October or November to February or March.

Other Sports

The highly popular *lucha libre* (wrestling) is more showbiz than sport. Participants in this pantomime-like activity give themselves names like Último Guerrero (Last Fighter), Místico and Blue Panther, then clown around in Day-Glo tights and lurid masks. For the audience it provides a welcome change from real life because the good guys win. Most bouts pit *rudos* – black-clad rule-breakers who generally get the upper hand initially – against *técnicos* (craftsmen), who finally win out in a stunning reversal of fortune.

Charreadas (rodeos) are held, mainly in the northern half of Mexico, during fiestas and at regular venues often called *lienzos charros.* **Decharros** (www.decharros.com, in Spanish) has plenty of information.

Mexico has produced many world champions in boxing. The legendary Julio César Chávez won five world titles at three different weights, and achieved an amazing 90 consecutive wins after turning pro in 1980.

The Spiritual Dimension

Yoga, the temascal (indigenous cleansing steam-bath) and new-age cosmic energies may mean more to some Mexicans today than traditional Roman Catholicism, but a spiritual dimension of some kind remains important in most Mexicans' lives.

Roman Catholicism

About 85% of Mexicans profess Roman Catholicism, making this the world's second-biggest Catholic country, after Brazil. Almost half of Mexican Catholics attend church weekly. Though church and state have a history of rocky relations, Catholicism remains very much part of the nation's established fabric. Most Mexican fiestas are built around local saints' days, and pilgrimages to important shrines are a big feature of the calendar.

The church's most binding symbol is Nuestra Señora de Guadalupe, the dark-skinned manifestation of the Virgin Mary who appeared to an Aztec potter, Juan Diego, near Mexico City in 1531. A crucial link between Catholic and indigenous spirituality, the Virgin of Guadalupe is now the country's religious patron, an archetypal mother whose blue-cloaked image is ubiquitous and whose name is invoked in political speeches and literature as well as religious ceremonies. December 12, her feast day, sees large-scale celebrations and pilgrimages all over the country, biggest of all in Mexico City.

Though some church figures have supported causes such as indigenous rights, the Mexican Catholic Church is a socially conservative body. It has alienated some sectors of the population by its strong opposition to Mexico City's legalization of abortion and gay marriage.

Soccer Websites

» ESPN Soccernet (soccernet.espn.go.com)

» Femexfut (www.femexfut.org.mx, in Spanish)

» FutMex (www.futmex.com, in Spanish)

The successful 2002 Mexican film *El crimen del Padre Amaro* (The Crime of Father Amaro), starring Gael García Bernal, paints an ugly picture of church corruption in a small Mexican town.

COMMUNING WITH DEPARTED SOULS

Perhaps no other festival reveals more about Mexican spirituality than Día de Muertos (Day of the Dead), the happy-sad remembrance of departed loved ones at the beginning of November. Muertos originated in colonial times, when the Catholic Church fused indigenous rites honoring and communing with the dead with its own celebrations of All Saints' Day (November 1) and All Souls' Day (November 2).

Today Muertos is a national phenomenon, with people everywhere cleaning graves and decorating them with flowers, holding graveyard vigils and building elaborate altars to welcome back their loved ones. For the *mestizo* (mixed-ancestry) majority, it's more of a popular folk festival and family occasion. The Catholic belief is that departed souls are in heaven or in purgatory, not actually back on a visit to Earth. Nevertheless, many find comfort in a sense that lost loved ones are somehow more present at this time. Among many indigenous communities, Muertos is still very much a religious and spiritual event. For them, the observance might more appropriately be called Noche de Muertos (Night of the Dead), because families actually spend whole nights at the graveyard communing with the dead.

Sugar skulls, chocolate coffins and toy skeletons are sold in markets everywhere, both as Muertos gifts for children and graveyard decorations; this tradition derives in great measure from the work of artist José Guadalupe Posada (1852–1913), renowned for his satirical figures of a skeletal Death cheerfully engaging in everyday life, working, dancing, courting, drinking and riding horses into battle.

Indigenous Religion

The Spanish missionaries of the 16th and 17th centuries won indigenous Mexicans over to Catholicism by grafting it onto pre-Hispanic religions. Old gods were renamed as Christian saints, old festivals were melded with Christian feast days. Indigenous Christianity is still fused with ancient beliefs today. Jalisco's Huichol people (see boxed text, p652) have two Christs, but Nakawé, the fertility goddess, is a more important deity. Among peoples such as the Tarahumara (Rarámuri) of the Barranca del Cobre (see boxed text, p761) and many Tzotzil people in highland Chiapas, intoxication is an almost sacred element at festival times. In the Tzotzil church of San Juan Chamula, you may see chanting *curanderos* (healers) carrying out shamanistic rites.

The secrets of physical and spiritual health of a Nahua *curandera* (literally 'curer') are revealed in *Woman Who Glows in the Dark* by Elena Ávila.

In the traditional indigenous world almost everything has a spiritual dimension – trees, rivers, hills, wind, rain and sun have their own gods or spirits. Illness may be seen as a 'loss of soul' resulting from wrongdoing or from the malign influence of someone with magical powers. A soul can be 'regained' if the appropriate ritual is performed by a *brujo* (witch doctor) or *curandero*.

Other Christian Faiths

Around 10% of Mexicans adhere to non-Catholic varieties of Christianity. Some are members of Protestant churches set up by US missionaries in the 19th century. Millions of others, especially among the indigenous rural poor of southeast Mexico, have been converted since the 1970s by a wave of American Pentecostal, Evangelical, Mormon, Seventh-Day Adventist and Jehovah's Witness missionaries.

The Arts

Mexicans are an obsessively creative people. Wherever you go in their country you'll be amazed by the marvelous artistic expression on display. Colorful painting and beautiful crafts are everywhere, Aztec dancers vibrate in the very heart of Mexico City, musicians strike up on the streets and in bars and buses. This is a country that has given the world some of its finest painting, music, movies and writing.

Painting & Sculpture

These art forms may well be the ones best suited to expressing Mexicans' inner and outer beings. Since the earliest times Mexicans have exhibited a love of color and form, and an exciting talent for painting and sculpture. The wealth of art in mural form and in Mexico's many galleries is a highlight of the country.

Pre-Hispanic

Mexico's first civilization, the Olmecs of the Gulf coast, produced remarkable stone sculptures depicting deities, animals and wonderfully lifelike human forms. Most awesome are the huge Olmec heads, which combine the features of human babies and jaguars.

The Classic Maya of southeast Mexico between about AD 250 and 800 were perhaps ancient Mexico's most artistically gifted people. They left countless beautiful stone sculptures, complicated in design but possessing great delicacy of touch. Subjects are typically rulers, deities and ceremonies. The art of the later Aztecs reflects their harsh world view, with many carvings of skulls and complicated symbolic representations of gods.

Colonial Period

Mexican art during Spanish rule was heavily Spanish-influenced and chiefly religious in subject, though portraiture grew in popularity under wealthy patrons. Indigenous artisanry is seen in the elaborately sculpted altarpieces, walls and ceilings – overflowing with tiny detail – of churches and monasteries. Miguel Cabrera (1695–1768), from Oaxaca, was arguably the most talented painter of the era. His scenes and figures, seen in churches and museums all over Mexico, have an exceptional sureness of touch.

Independent Mexico

The landscapes of José María Velasco (1840–1912) capture the magical qualities of the countryside around Mexico City and areas farther afield, such as Oaxaca.

The years before the 1910 Revolution saw a break from European traditions and the beginnings of socially conscious art. Slums, brothels and indigenous poverty began to appear on canvases. José Guadalupe Posada (1852–1913), with his characteristic *calavera* (skull) motif, satirized the

Top Ancient Mural Sites

» Palacio de Tepantitla, Teotihuacán

» Cacaxtla

» Bonampak

Mexico City's annual contemporary art fair, MACO (www. femaco.com), held over five days every March or April, pulls in artists, galleries, dealers and cognoscenti the world over.

injustices of the Porfiriato period, launching a tradition of political and social subversion in Mexican art.

The Muralists

In the 1920s, immediately following the Mexican Revolution, education minister José Vasconcelos commissioned young artists to paint a series of public murals to spread a sense of Mexican history and culture and of the need for social and technological change. The trio of great muralists – all great painters in smaller scales, too – were Diego Rivera (1886–1957), José Clemente Orozco (1883–1949) and David Alfaro Siqueiros (1896–1974).

Rivera's work carried a left-wing message, emphasizing past oppression of indigenous people and peasants. His art, found in many locations in and around Mexico City, pulled Mexico's indigenous and Spanish roots together in colorful, crowded tableaus depicting historical people and events, with a simple moral message.

Siqueiros, who fought in the Revolution on the Constitutionalist (liberal) side, remained a political activist afterward and his murals convey a clear Marxist message through dramatic, symbolic depictions of the oppressed and grotesque caricatures of the oppressors. Some of his best works are at the Palacio de Bellas Artes, Castillo de Chapultepec and Ciudad Universitaria, all in Mexico City.

Orozco, from Jalisco, focused more on the universal human condition than on historical specifics. He conveyed emotion, character and atmosphere. By the 1930s Orozco had grown disillusioned with the Revolution. His work was at its peak in Guadalajara between 1936 and 1939, particularly in the 50-odd frescoes in the Instituto Cultural de Cabañas.

Chief among later muralists, Rufino Tamayo (1899–1991) from Oaxaca was absorbed by abstract and mythological scenes and effects of color. Many of his works are easily identified by his trademark watermelon motif (his father was a fruit seller). Juan O'Gorman (1905–82), a Mexican of Irish ancestry, was even more realistic and detailed than Rivera. His multicolored mosaic interpretation of Mexican culture adorns the Biblioteca Central at Mexico City's Ciudad Universitaria.

Other 20th-Century Artists

Frida Kahlo (1907–54), physically crippled by a road accident and mentally tormented in her tempestuous marriage to Diego Rivera (see boxed text, p93), painted anguished self-portraits and grotesque, surreal images that expressed her left-wing views and externalized her inner tumult. Kahlo's work suddenly seemed to strike an international chord in the 1980s and '90s, becoming as renowned as Rivera's almost overnight. She's now better known worldwide than any other Mexican artist, and her Mexico City home, the Museo Frida Kahlo, is a don't-miss for any art lover.

After WWII, the young Mexican artists of La Ruptura (the Rupture), led by José Luis Cuevas (b 1934), reacted against the muralist movement, which they saw as too obsessed with *mexicanidad* (Mexicanness). They explored their urban selves and opened Mexico up to world trends such as abstract expressionism and pop art.

Other fine artists of the 20th century include María Izquierdo (1902–55), whose paintings have a dreamlike quality for which many later artists strove, and Oaxacans Francisco Toledo (b 1940) and Rodolfo Morales (1925–2001), whose contemporary vision draws on pre-Hispanic roots. Sculptor Sebastián (b 1947), from Chihuahua, is famed for his large, mathematics-inspired sculptures that adorn cities around the world.

Top Art Museums

» Museo Soumaya Plaza Carso, Mexico City

» Museo Nacional de Arte, Mexico City

» Museo Dolores Olmedo Patiño, Mexico City

» Museo de Arte Moderno, Mexico City

» Museo de Arte de Tlaxcala, Tlaxcala

» Museo Pedro Coronel, Zacatecas

» Museo de Arte Contemporáneo, Monterrey

THE GREAT COLLECTORS

One major protagonist of the Mexican art scene is not an artist but a patron: Eugenio López, heir to the Jumex fruit-juice empire, has Latin America's most important contemporary-art collection and is a big force in the globalization of the region's art. His Colección Jumex was due to move into new premises in the wealthy Mexico city district of Polanco in 2012 – right next door to the stunning new Museo Soumaya Plaza Carso with its world-class collection of past masters belonging to Carlos Slim, the world's richest man.

Contemporary Art

Today, thanks to dynamic galleries and patrons and the globalization of the world art scene, new Mexican art is reaching galleries the world over, and art from around the globe is being seen in Mexico. Contemporary artists, galleries and patrons have made Mexico City one of the world's art hot spots, and cities such as Monterrey, Oaxaca, Mazatlán, Guadalajara and Morelia all have thriving art scenes.

Mexican contemporary art attempts to interpret the uncertainties of the 21st century in diverse ways. Frida Kahlo, who inspired many postmodernists, stands as a kind of mother figure amid the maelstrom. The pendulum has swung away from abstraction to hyper-representation, photorealism, installations and video. Rocío Maldonado (b 1951), Rafael Cauduro (b 1950) and Roberto Cortázar (b 1962) all paint classically depicted figures against amorphous, bleak backgrounds. Check out Cauduro's hyperrealist murals on state-sponsored crime in Mexico City's Suprema Corte de Justicia (Supreme Court). Leading contemporary lights such as Miguel Calderón (b 1971) and Gabriel Orozco (b 1962) spread their talents across many media, always challenging the spectator's preconceptions.

Music

Music is everywhere in Mexico. It comes booming out of sound systems in markets and passing automobiles, and live musicians may start up at any time, on plazas, in buses or the Mexico City metro. These performers are playing for a living and range from marimba (wooden xylophone) teams and mariachi bands (trumpeters, violinists, guitarists and a singer, all dressed in smart Wild West–style costumes) to ragged lone buskers with out-of-tune guitars. Mariachi music, perhaps the most 'typical' Mexican music, originated in the Guadalajara area but is played nationwide. Marimbas are particularly popular in the southeast and on the Gulf coast.

Rock & Hip-Hop

So close to the big US Spanish-speaking market, Mexico can claim to be the most important hub of *rock en español*. Talented Mexico City bands such as Café Tacuba and Maldita Vecindad emerged in the 1990s and took the genre to new heights and new audiences (well beyond Mexico), mixing influences from rock, hip-hop and ska to traditional Mexican *son* (folk music) or mariachi. Café Tacuba's exciting handling of so many styles still keeps them at the forefront of Mexican music. Their albums *Re* (1994), *Avalancha de éxitos* (1996), *Tiempo transcurrido* (2001) and *Sino* (2007) are all full of great songs. Also still popular are the Monterrey rap-metal band Molotov, who have upset just about everyone with their expletive-laced lyrics, and Jaguares, mystical rockers who spearheaded Mexican rock's coming of age in the 1980s. The popular, Britpop- and

Modern Art Websites

» Arte México (www.arte-mexico.com)

» Artes Visuales (www.artesvisuales.com.mx, in Spanish)

» Galería Nina Menocal (www.ninamenocal.com)

» Kurimanzutto (www.kurimanzutto.com)

» LatinAmericanArt.com (www.latinamericanart.com)

» Museo Colección Andrés Blaisten (www.museoblaisten.com)

grunge-influenced, alternative-rock band Zoé won a 2011 Latin Grammy with their live album *MTV Unplugged/Música de Fondo*.

Powerful, colorful Alejandra Guzmán is known as La Reina del Rock (Queen of Rock) and has sold 15 million discs in a two-decade career.

The Mexican band most famous outside Mexico is undoubtedly Guadalajara's Maná, an unashamedly commercial outfit reminiscent of The Police. Not to be forgotten are El Tri, the grandfathers of Mexican rock, who are still pumping out energetic rock 'n' roll after more than four decades.

Pop

Paulina Rubio is Mexico's answer to Shakira. She has also starred in several Mexican films and TV series. Natalia Lafourcade, a talented singer-songwriter who mixes pop and bossa nova rhythms, is sometimes compared with Canada's Nelly Furtado. Another versatile singer-songwriter and instrumentalist is Julieta Venegas, from Tijuana, whose 2007 album *Limón y sal* was a huge international hit.

Balladeer Luis Miguel is Mexico's Julio Iglesias and incredibly popular, as is Juan Gabriel, who has sold millions of his own albums and written dozens of hit songs for other singers.

La Jornada newspaper has an excellent cultural section with daily listings of exhibitions and culture of all kinds. The Spanish-language website www. kinetik.tv details upcoming top electronic-music events.

Electronic Music

Almost every weekend there's a big electronica event in or around one of the big cities, with sessions by the country's top DJs and international guests. The most popular Mexican DJs, all spinning various house rhythms, include Jose Spinnin Cortes, Tony Dark Eyes and Giorgio Brindesi.

The Tijuana-based Nortec Collective spent several years melding traditional Mexican music with electronica into a unique, fun genre known as Nortec. Look for *Tijuana Sessions Vol 1* (2001) or *Tijuana Sessions Vol 3* (2005) – there's no Volume 2. Two members of the collective, Bostich and Fussible, released the successful *Tijuana Sound Machine* in 2008.

Regional & Folk Music

The deepest-rooted Mexican folk music is *son* (see boxed text below).

Modern regional music is based on a strong rhythm from several guitars, with the melody coming from voice, accordion, violin or brass. *Ranchera* is Mexico's urban 'country music' – mostly melodramatic stuff with a nostalgia for rural roots, sometimes with a mariachi backing. The hugely popular Vicente Fernández, Juan Gabriel and Alejandro Fernández (Vicente's son) are among the leading *ranchera* artists.

Norteño or *norteña* is country ballad and dance music, originating in northern Mexico but nationwide in popularity. Its roots are in *cor-*

SON – MEXICAN FOLK

Son (literally 'sound') is a broad term covering Mexican country styles that grew out of the fusion of Spanish, indigenous and African music. Guitars or similar instruments (such as the small *jarana*) lay down a strong rhythm, with harp or violin providing the melody. *Son* is often played for a foot-stomping dance audience, and its lyrics tend to be witty and sometimes improvised. There are several regional variants. *Son huasteco* (or *huapango*), from the Huasteca area inland from Tampico, features falsetto vocals between soaring violin passages. Keep an eye open for top group Los Camperos de Valles. In Jalisco, *son jaliscense* originally formed the repertoire of many mariachi bands. The exciting *son jarocho*, from the Veracruz area, is particularly African-influenced: harpist La Negra Graciana is one of its greats, while Grupo Mono Blanco have led a revival of the genre with contemporary lyrics. The famous 'La Bamba' is a *son jarocho*!

MÚSICA TROPICAL

Although their origins lie in the Caribbean and South America, several brands of *música tropical* or *música afroantillana* – percussion-heavy, infectiously rhythmic music – are highly popular in Mexico. Mexico City, in particular, has numerous clubs and large dance halls devoted to this scene, often hosting international bands.

Two kinds of dance music – *danzón,* originally from Cuba, and *cumbia,* from Colombia – both took deeper root in Mexico than in their original homelands. The formal, elegant, old-fashioned *danzón* is strongly associated with the port city of Veracruz (see boxed text, p204) but is currently enjoying quite a revival in Mexico City and elsewhere too. The livelier, more flirtatious *cumbia* has its adopted home in Mexico City. It rests on thumping bass lines with brass, guitars, mandolins and sometimes marimbas. Some *banda* and *norteño* groups throw a lot of *cumbia* into their playlists. *Cumbia sonidera* is *cumbia* as played by some DJs in central Mexico, with their own mixes, speeds and intros.

Almost every town in Mexico has some place where you can dance (and sometimes learn) salsa, which originated in New York when jazz met *son,* cha-cha and rumba from Cuba and Puerto Rico. Musically it boils down to brass (with trumpet solos), piano, percussion, singer and chorus – the dance is a hot one with a lot of exciting turns. *Merengue,* mainly from the Dominican Republic, is a blend of *cumbia* and salsa with a hopping step; the rhythm catches the shoulders, the arms go up and down. The music is strong on maracas, and the musicians go for puffed-up sleeves.

ridos, heroic ballads with the rhythms of European dances such as waltz or polka, which came to southern Texas with 19th-century German and Czech immigrants. Originally the songs were tales of Latino-Anglo strife in the borderlands or themes from the Mexican Revolution. The modern ballads known as *narcocorridos* started out dealing with drug-runners, *coyotes* (people smugglers) and other small-time crooks trying to survive amid big-time corruption and crime, but in recent years some have told of exploits of major Mexican drug gangs. Some gangs even commission *narcocorridos* about themselves.

Norteño groups *(conjuntos)* go for 10-gallon hats, with backing centered on the accordion and the *bajo sexto* (a 12-string guitar), along with bass and drums. The superstars of *norteño* are Los Tigres del Norte, originally from Sinaloa but now based in California. They play to huge audiences on both sides of the frontier, with some *narcocorridos* in their repertoire.

Banda is Mexican big-band music, with large brass sections replacing *norteño's* guitars and accordion. Sinaloa's Banda el Recodo have been at the top of the *banda* tree for decades.

Singer Lila Downs, who has an American father and an Oaxacan Mixtec mother, is a passionate and original reinterpreter of Mexican folk songs, often with a jazz influence. If you saw the 2002 movie *Frida,* you'll have heard Lila on the soundtrack. Her major albums include *La sandunga* (1997), *Border (La línea;* 2001) and *Pecados y milagros* (2011).

Trova

This genre of troubadour-type folk music, typically performed by solo singer-songwriters *(cantautores)* with a guitar, has roots in 1960s and '70s folk and protest songs. Many *trova* singers are strongly inspired by Cuban political musician Silvio Rodríguez. Fernando Delgadillo and Nicho Hinojosa are leading Mexican artists.

Powerful and popular singers like Eugenia León, Tania Libertad and the satirical cabaret artist Astrid Hadad are sometimes categorized under *trova,* but they actually range widely over Mexican song forms and are all well worth hearing.

Art Books

» *The Art of Mesoamerica* by Mary Ellen Miller

» *Mexican Muralists* by Desmond Rochfort

Cinema

The historical golden age of Mexican movie-making was the 1940s, when the country was creating up to 200 films a year – typically epic, melodramatic productions. The four big stars were Dolores del Río, María Félix, Mario Moreno ('Cantinflas') and Pedro Infante. Then Hollywood reasserted itself, and Mexican filmmakers have struggled for funding ever since. Today Mexico has the world's fifth-biggest cinema audience, but more than 90% of box-office takings are for US films.

The 21st century has seen Mexican cinema making a resounding comeback after decades in the doldrums. A clutch of fine, gritty movies by young Mexican directors has won commercial success as well as critical acclaim; government support for the film industry is on the up; the number of Mexican productions has climbed to about 70 a year; and several cities including Guadalajara, Morelia, Oaxaca and Monterrey now stage successful annual film festivals.

The new Mexican films confront the ugly, tragic and absurd in Mexican life as well as the beautiful and comical. The first to really catch the world's eye was *Amores perros* (Love's a Bitch; 2000), directed by Alejandro González Iñárritu and starring Gael García Bernal, who have since both become international celebrities. Set in contemporary Mexico City, with three plots connected by one traffic accident, it's a raw, honest movie with its quota of blood, violence and sex as well as ironic humor.

Y tu mamá también (And Your Mother Too), Alfonso Cuarón's 2001 'growing up' road movie about two privileged Mexico City teenagers (Gael García Bernal and Diego Luna), was at the time the biggest grossing Mexican film ever, netting more than US$25 million.

After *Amores perros*, González Iñárritu moved to Hollywood to direct two more great movies with interconnected multiple plots – *21 Grams* (2003) and *Babel* (2006). The latter, with Brad Pitt, Cate Blanchett and (again) Gael García Bernal, weaves in a sad US–Mexico cross-border tale with other (Moroccan and Japanese) threads. Screenwriter for all three films was Mexican Guillermo Arriaga. In 2010 González Iñárritu returned with the stunning *Biutiful*, a joint Mexican-Spanish production starring Javier Bardem in a harrowing 'down and out in Barcelona' tale with a supernatural twist.

Alfonso Cuarón stepped from *Y tu mamá también* to *Harry Potter and the Prisoner of Azkaban* (2004), then directed the Oscar-nominated *Children of Men* (2006). His 3D science-fiction flick *Gravity* was due for release in late 2012.

Mexican Guillermo del Toro's *Pan's Labyrinth* – another non-Mexican production – won three Oscars in 2006 with a dual plot in which a young girl lives out fairy-tale adventures against a background of the violent realities of 1940s Spain.

Back in Mexico, Francisco Vargas' *El violín* (The Violin; 2005), with a great performance by Ángel Tavira, has a plot set amid Mexico's rural

Arguably the most famous of all Mexican film actors was Zorba the Greek – Anthony Quinn (1915–2001), born Antonio Quiñones in Chihuahua. His family moved to the US when he was four months old.

DOCUMENTARY EVIDENCE

Documentary films have provided some of the most telling cinematic social commentary recently. The year 2010 saw the first screenings of Pedro Ultreras' *La Bestia* (The Beast), a heartbreaking film that follows the danger-fraught freight-train journey of Central Americans through Mexico toward the USA – the best of several recent films about northward migration. *Presunto culpable* (Presumed Guilty), originally released in 2008, is about a young man sentenced to 20 years' jail on flimsy evidence for a murder he didn't commit. Part-directed by one of the lawyers who eventually got him released, Roberto Hernández, the film is a devastating indictment of Mexico's justice system, and its popularity soared when it was briefly banned by a Mexican judge in 2011.

guerrilla struggles of the 1970s. Carlos Reygadas' *Luz silenciosa* (Silent Light; 2007) is a story of adulterous love in a Mexican Mennonite community. Gael García Bernal and Diego Luna renewed their *Y tu mamá también* chemistry in *Rudo y Cursi* (2008), a lovable tale of two rural brothers' rise to professional soccer success, directed by Carlos Cuarón (Alfonso's brother). The same year yielded Amat Escalante's *Los Bastardos,* a grim story of two undocumented Mexican laborers in Los Angeles who turn to violence to improve their pay packets.

The startling 2010 newcomer was the claustrophobic, sexually explicit *Año bisiesto* (Leap Year), directed by Mexico-resident Australian Michael Rowe, with a great performance by Mónica del Carmen. The film won the 2010 Cannes prize for best new director. One of the most talked about Mexican movies of 2011 was *Miss Bala,* a thriller directed by Gerardo Naranjo about a beauty pageant contestant who gets caught up in a drug war.

Literature

Mexicans such as Carlos Fuentes, Juan Rulfo and Octavio Paz produced some of the great Spanish-language writing of the 20th century, and the contemporary literary scene is throwing up some bold talents.

Fuentes (1928–2012), a prolific novelist and commentator, is probably Mexico's best-known writer internationally. His first and one of his best novels, *Where the Air is Clear* (1958), traces the lives of various Mexico City dwellers through Mexico's postrevolutionary decades in a critique of the Revolution's failure. *The Death of Artemio Cruz* (1962) takes another critical look at the postrevolutionary era through the eyes of a dying, corrupted press baron and landowner. *Aura* (1962) is a magical-realist book, with a truly stunning ending.

In Mexico, Juan Rulfo (1918–86) is widely regarded as the supreme novelist. His *Pedro Páramo* (1955), about a young man's search for his lost father among ghostlike villages in western Mexico, is a scary, desolate work with confusing shifts of time – a kind of Mexican *Wuthering Heights* with a spooky, magical-realist twist. Some regard it as the ultimate expression of Latin American existence, and Rulfo never felt the need to write anything else afterward.

Octavio Paz (1914–98), poet, essayist and winner of the 1990 Nobel Prize for Literature, wrote a probing, intellectually acrobatic analysis of Mexico's myths and the national character in *The Labyrinth of Solitude* (1950). Decide for yourself whether you agree with his pessimistic assessments of his fellow Mexicans.

Of a whole school of novels inspired by the Mexican Revolution, the classic is *The Underdogs,* the story of a peasant who becomes a general, by Mariano Azuela (1873–1952). More recent writers have also been inspired by the Revolution: Laura Esquivel (b 1950) made her name with *Like Water for Chocolate* (1989), a Revolution-era rural love story interwoven with both fantasy and recipes.

The 1960s-born novelists of the *movimiento crack* take their name from the sound of a limb falling off a tree, representing their desire to break with Mexico's literary past. Their work tends to adopt global themes and international settings. Best known is Jorge Volpi, whose *In Search of Klingsor* (1999) became an international bestseller. With an exciting plot around efforts to unmask the scientist who led Nazi Germany's atomic weapons program, it also weaves in a good deal of scientific theory to keep your brain cells busy.

In poetry, the great names are Octavio Paz and a reclusive figure from Chiapas, Jaime Sabines (1925–99), who both treated themes of love and death with stark, vivid imagery.

Frida & Diego Books

» *Frida Kahlo and Diego Rivera* by Isabel Alcantara and Sandra Egnolff

» *Dreaming with His Eyes Open* by Patrick Marnham

» *Frida* by Hayden Herrera

MEXICO IN OTHERS' WORDS

Mexico has inspired much fine writing from non-Mexicans. Graham Greene's *The Power and the Glory* (1940) dramatizes the state-church conflict that followed the Mexican Revolution. *Under the Volcano* (1938) by Malcolm Lowry follows a dipsomaniac British diplomat in Mexico who drinks himself to death on the Day of the Dead.

B Traven is best known as the author of the adventure story of gold and greed in northern Mexico, *The Treasure of the Sierra Madre* (1935). But he wrote many other novels set in Mexico, chiefly the six of his Jungle series – among them *The Rebellion of the Hanged* and *General from the Jungle* – which focused on prerevolutionary oppression in Chiapas. The identity of Traven himself is one of literature's great mysteries. Was he really a Bavarian anarchist called Ret Marut, or a Norwegian American living reclusively in Acapulco called Traven Torsvan? Quite possibly he was both.

The Beat generation spent plenty of time in Mexico, too: William Burroughs' early novel *Queer* chronicles the guilt, lust and drug excesses of an American in Mexico City in the 1940s. The city was also the scene of parts of Burroughs' *Junky* and Jack Kerouac's *On the Road* and *Tristessa*, and it was where Kerouac wrote his long work of jazz poetry *Mexico City Blues*.

Cormac McCarthy's marvelous *All the Pretty Horses* (1992) is the laconic, tense, poetic tale of three young latter-day cowboys riding south of the US–Mexico border. *The Crossing* and *Cities of the Plain* completed McCarthy's Border Trilogy.

Folk Art

Mexicans' skill with their hands and their love of color, beauty, fun and tradition find expression everywhere in their appealing *artesanías* (handicrafts). Crafts such as weaving, pottery, leather and copperwork, and shoe-, hat- or basket-making still fulfil key functions in daily life as well as turning out souvenirs and collectibles. Many craft techniques, designs and materials still in use today have pre-Hispanic origins, and it is Mexico's indigenous peoples, the direct inheritors of pre-Hispanic culture, who lead the way in *artesanías* production.

Traditional Textiles

In some of Mexico's indigenous villages you'll be stunned by the variety of colorful, intricately decorated attire, differing from area to area and often from village to village. Traditional costume – more widely worn by women than men – serves as a mark of the community to which a person belongs. Some garments are woven or embroidered with webs of animal, human, plant and mythical shapes that can take months to complete.

Four main types of women's garments have been in use since long before the Spanish conquest:

» *enredo* – a wraparound skirt, almost invisible if worn beneath a long *huipil*
» *faja* – a waist sash that holds the *enredo* in place
» *huipil* – a long, sleeveless tunic, found mainly in the southern half of the country
» *quechquémitl* – a shoulder cape with an opening for the head, found mainly in central and northern Mexico

The 'yarn paintings' of the indigenous Huichol people – created by pressing strands of yarn onto a wax-covered board – depict scenes resembling visions experienced under the influence of the drug *peyote*, which is central to Huichol culture.

Spanish missionaries introduced blouses, now often embroidered with great care and detail, like the more traditional garments. Also dating from Spanish times is the *rebozo*, a long shawl that may cover the shoulders or head or be used for carrying something. The *sarape*, worn by men, is a blanket with an opening for the head.

The basic materials of indigenous weaving are cotton and wool, though synthetic fibers are now common too. Natural dyes have been re vived – deep blues from the indigo plant, reds and browns from various woods, and reds, pinks and purples from the cochineal insect.

The basic indigenous weavers' tool – used only by women – is the *telar de cintura* (back-strap loom) on which the warp (long) threads are stretched between two horizontal bars, one of which is fixed to a post or tree, while the other is attached to a strap that goes around the weaver's lower back; the weft (cross) threads are then woven in. A variety of sophisticated techniques are used to weave amazing patterns into the cloth. *Huipiles* woven this way in the southern states of Oaxaca and Chiapas are among Mexico's most intricate and eye-catching garments.

One textile art that's practiced by men is weaving on a treadle loom, operated by foot pedals. The treadle loom can weave wider cloth than the back-strap loom and tends to be used for blankets, rugs, *rebozos, sarapes* and skirt material. Mexico's most famous rug-weaving village is Teotitlán del Valle, Oaxaca.

Ceramics

Mexico still has many small-scale potters' workshops turning out everything from plain cooking pots to elaborate works of art.

One highly attractive variety of Mexican pottery is Talavera, made chiefly in Puebla and Dolores Hidalgo and characterized by bright colors (blue and yellow are prominent) and floral designs. The Guadalajara suburbs of Tonalá and Tlaquepaque are the country's most renowned pottery centers, producing a wide variety of ceramics. In northern Mexico the villagers of Mata Ortiz make a range of beautiful earthenware, drawing on the techniques and designs of pre-Hispanic Paquimé, similar to some of the native American pottery of the US southwest. Another distinctive Mexican ceramic form is the *árbol de la vida* (tree of life). These elaborate, candelabra-like objects are molded by hand and decorated with numerous tiny figures of people, animals, plants and so on. The Garden of Eden is one common subject. Some of the best are made in the towns of Acatlán de Osorio and Izúcar de Matamoros, in Puebla state, and Metepec, in the state of México. Metepec is also the source of colorful clay suns.

Thanks to a program launched in the 1990s by the government crafts development agency Fonart, many of Mexico's potters have switched from potentially toxic lead-based glazes to a nontoxic boron-based glaze.

Masks

For millennia Mexicans have worn masks in dances, ceremonies and shamanistic rites: the wearer temporarily becomes the creature, person or deity represented by the mask. You can admire mask artistry at museums in cities such as San Luis Potosí, Zacatecas, Morelia and Colima, and at shops and markets around the country. The southern state of Guerrero has probably the broadest range of fine masks.

Wood is the basic material of most masks, but papier-mâché, clay, wax and leather are also used. Mask-makers often paint or embellish their masks with real teeth, hair, feathers or other adornments. 'Tigers,' often looking more like jaguars, are common, as are other animals and birds, and also Christ, devils, and Europeans with comically pale, wide-eyed, mustachioed features.

Today, masks are also made for hanging on walls.

Lacquerware & Woodwork

Gourds, the hard shells of certain squash-type fruits, have been used in Mexico since antiquity as bowls, cups and small storage vessels. The most eye-catching decoration technique is lacquering, in which the gourd is coated with layers of paste or paint, then the final layer is painted with

---

THE ARTS FOLK ART

Crafts Books

» *The Crafts of Mexico* by Margarita de Orellana and Alberto Ruy Sánchez

» *Arts and Crafts of Mexico* by Chloë Sayer

» *Mexican Textiles* by Masako Takahashi

Diamond shapes on some *huipiles* from San Andrés Larráinzar, in Chiapas, represent the universe of the villagers' Maya ancestors, who believed the earth was a cube and the sky had four corners.

HUIPILES

the artisan's chosen design, and varnished. All this makes the gourd non-porous and, to some extent, heat-resistant.

Most lacquerware you'll see in Mexico today is pine, or a sweetly scented wood from remote Olinalá in Guerrero (see boxed text, p519). Olinalá boxes, trays and furniture are lacquered by the *rayado* method, in which designs are created by scraping off part of the top coat of paint to expose a different-colored layer below.

Among Mexico's finest wooden crafts are the polished ironwood carvings of the Seri people of Sonora, who work the hard wood into dramatic human, animal and sea-creature shapes. Also attractive are the *alebrijes* (brightly painted imaginary beasts carved from copal wood) produced by villagers around Oaxaca city.

Mexconnect (www.mexconnect.com) and Mexonline (www.mexonline.com) feature a wealth of articles and links on Mexican arts.

Architecture

Mexico's magnificent architectural heritage is one of its most priceless treasures. While most attention is grabbed by the superb relics of pre-Hispanic civilizations and the beautiful creations of the Spanish colonial era, modern architects have thrown up some spectacular piles too.

Pre-Hispanic

The ancient civilizations built some of the most spectacular, eye-pleasing architecture ever created – all without the aid of metal tools, pack animals or the wheel. At places like Teotihuacán, Monte Albán, Chichén Itzá and Uxmal you can still see fairly intact pre-Hispanic cities. Their spectacular ceremonial centers were designed to impress, with great stone pyramids (topped by shrines), palaces and ritual ball courts.

There were many differences in style between the pre-Hispanic civilizations: while Teotihuacán, Monte Albán and Aztec buildings were intended to awe with their grand scale, Maya architecture paid more attention to aesthetics, with intricately patterned and carved facades, delicate 'combs' (grid-like arrangements of stone with multiple gaps) on temple roofs, and sinuous carvings. Buildings at Maya sites such as Uxmal, Chichén Itzá and Palenque are among the most beautiful human creations in the Americas. Maya buildings are characterized by the corbeled vault, their version of the arch: two stone walls leaning toward one another, nearly meeting at the top and surmounted by a capstone. The hallmark of Teotihuacán architecture is the *talud-tablero* style of stepped buildings, in which height is achieved by alternating upright *(tablero)* sections with sloping *(talud)* ones.

Colonial Period

Architecture changed beyond recognition with the Spanish conquest in the early 16th century. The Spaniards destroyed indigenous temples and built churches in their place, and laid out new towns with grids of streets lined by fine stone edifices. The 300 years of Spanish rule contributed much to Mexico's beauty with their palaces and mansions built around pretty patios, their stately churches and monasteries and their handsome plazas. Colonial architecture is perhaps the most redeeming feature of the often brutal colonial regime.

Building was in Spanish styles, but with some unique local variations. Gothic and Renaissance styles dominated in the 16th and early 17th centuries. Gothic is typified by soaring buttresses and pointed arches, while the Renaissance saw a return to ancient Greek and Roman ideals of harmony and proportion, using shapes such as the square and the circle. A later, more austere Renaissance style was called Herreresque, after the Spanish architect Juan de Herrera. Mérida's cathedral and Casa de Montejo are outstanding Renaissance buildings, while Mexico City and Puebla cathedrals mingle Renaissance and baroque styles.

Baroque style, which reached Mexico from Spain in the early 17th century, layered new dramatic effects – curves, color, contrasts of light and dark,

Mexico's Biggest Pyramids

» Pirámide Tepanapa, Cholula

» Pirámide del Sol (Pyramid of the Sun), Teotihuacán

» Pirámide de la Luna (Pyramid of the Moon), Teotihuacán

FORTRESS-MONASTERIES

Spanish missionary monks played a big part in pacifying indigenous Mexicans by bringing them within the Christian fold. Their missionary work often took them into hostile territory, so it's little wonder that many Mexican monasteries, with their tall, thick, stone walls and strong, solid churches look as much like fortresses as houses of God. Indeed, many were built not just as bases from which to spread the word of God but also as refuges for the colonists when the natives got restless. Monasteries usually had a large church and cloister, and often a *capilla abierta* (open chapel), a characteristically Mexican feature where priests could address large crowds of indigenous people. To see a trio of outstanding 16th-century monasteries, take a trip to Yanhuitlán, Coixtlahuaca and San Pedro Teposcolula in Oaxaca state. All three monasteries have recently been restored to their former grandeur and contain new museums.

increasingly elaborate decoration – onto a Renaissance base. Painting and sculpture were integrated with architecture, notably in ornate, enormous *retablos* (altarpieces). Mexico's finest baroque buildings include Zacatecas cathedral and the churches of Santo Domingo in Mexico City and Oaxaca. Between 1730 and 1780 Mexican baroque reached its final, spectacularly out-of-control Churrigueresque form, with its riotous ornamentation.

Indigenous artisans added profuse sculpture in stone and colored stucco to many baroque buildings, such as the Rosary Chapels in the Templos de Santo Domingo at Puebla and Oaxaca. Spanish Islamic influence showed in the popularity of *azulejos* (colored tiles) on the outside of buildings, notably on Mexico City's Casa de Azulejos and many buildings in and around Puebla.

Neoclassical style, dominant in Mexico from about 1780 to 1830, was another return to sober Greek and Roman ideals. Outstanding examples include the Palacio de Minería in Mexico City and the Alhóndiga de Granaditas in Guanajuato; the most prominent neoclassical architects were Eduardo Tresguerras and Spanish-born Manuel Tolsá.

> **Churri-
> gueresque
> Archi-
> tecture**
>
> » Sagrario
> Metropolitano,
> Mexico City
>
> » Santuario de la
> Virgen de Ocotlán,
> Tlaxcala
>
> » Capilla Domés-
> tica, Tepotzotlán
>
> » Templo de
> Santa Prisca,
> Taxco

19th to 21st Centuries

Independent Mexico in the 19th and early 20th centuries saw revivals of colonial styles and imitations of contemporary French or Italian styles. Mexico City's semi-art-nouveau Palacio de Bellas Artes is one of the most spectacular buildings from this era.

After the 1910–20 Revolution came an effort to return to pre-Hispanic roots in the search for a national identity. This trend was known as Toltecism, and many public buildings exhibit the heaviness of Aztec or Toltec monuments. Toltecism culminated in the 1950s with the Ciudad Universitaria campus in Mexico City, where many buildings are covered with colorful murals.

> Check out the
> good and the bad
> of what's going
> up in Mexico's cit-
> ies (and the rest
> of the world) at
> www.skyscraper
> city.com.

Modern architects have provided some cities with eye-catching, adventurous buildings as well as plenty of dull concrete blocks. The great icon is Luis Barragán (1902–88), a modernist who also exhibited a strong Mexican strain in his use of vivid colors, scale, space and light. His oeuvre includes a set of wacky colored skyscraper sculptures in Ciudad Satélite, a Mexico City suburb. Another modernist, Pedro Ramírez Vázquez (b 1919), designed three vast public buildings in Mexico City: the 1960s Estadio Azteca and Museo Nacional de Antropología and the 1970s Basílica de Guadalupe. But the talk of the town lately has been the capital's new Museo Soumaya Plaza Carso, designed by Fernando Romero for the art collection of his father-in-law Carlos Slim, the world's richest man. It's an ethereal six-story construction that might be described as resembling a giant, twisted blacksmith's anvil covered in 16,000 honeycomb-shaped aluminium plates.

The Mexican Kitchen

By Mauricio Velázquez de León
Mauricio was born in Mexico City where he was given boiled chicken feet and toasted corn tortillas to sooth his teething pains. Mauricio's food writing has been widely published in Mexico and the US. He is the author (under the name Puck) of *My Foodie ABC: A Little Gourmet's Guide* (duopress, 2010). He lives in Maryland with his wife and twin sons, whose teething pains were soothed with toasted corn tortillas.

In Mexico we love food, especially our own. When visiting the country you will soon get a sense of how important food is in our lives. Ask a group of Mexicans where to find, say, the best *carnitas* (braised pork) in Mexico City, or the best *mole* (a type of chili sauce) in Oaxaca, and you are up for a passionate, lengthy and well-informed debate that will fill a notebook with names of places that you *must* go to, and specialties that you *must* try. Interestingly, if you ask who the best cook they know is, they all will be in agreement: *mi madre* (my mother). Another point most Mexicans agree with is that Mexican cuisine has little to do with what is served as Mexican fare in restaurants outside the country. For many visitors their first experience with real Mexican food will be a surprise. There will be no big hats, no flavored margaritas, oversized burritos or cheese nachos on the menu. The food will be fresh, simple and, frequently, locally grown – and, most likely, somebody's mom will be running the kitchen.

During your visit you'll find that the ingredients and methods are far-reaching and varied, closely connected with the history of each of the country's regions and the character of its peoples. Take a look at the history of the Maya and you'll see that corn plays a main role. Should you read about the gargantuan markets in Aztec cities you will share the amazement of the Spanish conquistadors. In Diego Rivera's murals you will discover the vast range of Mexican produce. So if you want to know Mexico and its people, you must try the food.

For information about the price ranges used in this book, tipping and taxes, see the Directory, p852.

What's on the Menu?

A Mexican menu will vary on the region you are visiting, but in most cases you can find food that is made with a few staples: corn, an array of dry and fresh chilies and beans. Contrary to popular belief, not all food in Mexico is spicy, at least not for the regular palate. Chilies are used as flavoring ingredients and to provide intensity in sauces, *moles* and *pipiáns*, and many appreciate their depth over their piquancy. But beware; many dishes indeed have a kick, reaching daredevil levels in some cases. The

Josefina Velázquez de León is considered the mother of Mexican cuisine. She ran a successful culinary school and wrote more than 140 cookbooks, the most ambitious being *Platillos Regionales de la República Mexicana*, considered to be the first book to collect Mexico's regional cuisine in one volume.

habanero chili in the Yucatán is the most spicy pepper in the world, and the *chile de árbol* can be terribly fierce. A good rule of thumb is that when chilies are cooked and incorporated into the dishes as sauces they tend to be on the mild side, but when they are prepared for salsas or relishes, intended for use as condiments, they can be really hot.

There are other staples that give Mexican food its classic flavoring. Among them are spices like cinnamon, clove and cumin, and herbs such as thyme, oregano, and most importantly, cilantro and *epazote*. *Epazote* may be the unsung hero of Mexican cooking. This pungent-smelling herb (called pigweed or Jerusalem oak in the US) is used for flavoring beans, soups, stews and certain *moles*.

Eating as a Whim

An*tojitos* are in the center of Mexican cooking. The problem with the word *antojitos* is that it can encompass everything, as the word *antojo* translates as 'a whim, a sudden craving.' Hence an *antojito* is a little whim, but as any Mexican will quickly point out, it is not just a snack. You can have them as an entire meal, or have a couple as appetizers, or yes, eat one as a *tentempié* (quick bite) before hopping in the subway. American award-winning chef and Mexican food expert Rick Bayless has a great way to define *antojitos* by grouping them according to the one component present in all: corn masa (dough). Using this criterion we can say that there are eight types of *antojitos* (see boxed text opposite).

A Day of Eating: From Sunrise to Sunset & Beyond!

It's easy to find a place to eat in Mexico. From an early *antojito* at a small *puesto* (street or market stall) to a lavish late dinner at a fine restaurant, food seems to always be available. One thing you should know, though, is that mealtimes in Mexico are different from what you might be used to.

» **Desayuno** (breakfast) Usually served in restaurants and *cafeterías* from 8:30am to 11am, and it tends to be on the heavy side. Egg dishes, many of them using fried eggs, are popular morning fare. *Huevos rancheros*, two fried eggs atop lightly fried tortillas with a layer of black beans and topped with a chunky tomato, onion and chili salsa, are widely served. If you are in the Yucatán region, you will find the regional variation called *huevos motuleños*, a similar preparation that also includes diced ham, peas and plantains. Many *cafeterías* offer a bread basket at breakfast with an array of *pan de dulce* (sweet breads). These bakery goods are great company for a cup of coffee or tea, and their names will draw a smile on your face: *bigotes* (mustaches), *conchas* (shells), *besos* (kisses) and *orejas* (ears) are only a few names for these treats.

» **Almuerzo** Those who have a light breakfast or skip it altogether can have an *almuerzo* (a type of brunch) or an *antojito* or other quick bite. *Taquerías* (places specializing in tacos), *torterías* (small establishments selling *tortas*) and *loncherías* (places that serve light meals) are good options for *almuerzo*.

» **Comida** This is the main meal in Mexico. It is usually served from 2pm to 4:30pm in homes, restaurants and cafes. Places called *fondas* are small, family-run eateries that serve *comida corrida*, an inexpensive fixed-price menu that includes soup, rice, a main dish, beverage and dessert. In many big cities it's common to see people enjoying long and relaxed business lunches and friend gatherings where food, conversation and drinks mingle for a couple of hours. Popular *comida* fares are soups, such as *sopa de fideo* (vermicelli noodles in a soupy tomato broth), or *sopa de frijol* (bean soup), while well-liked main dishes include *guisados* (stews) such as slowed-braised meats and vegetables in cooked chipotle, tomatillo or tomato salsas.

Good Mexican cookbooks include *Authentic Mexican, 20th Anniversary Edition: Regional Cooking from the Heart of Mexico* (Rick Bayless), *The Art of Mexican Cooking* (Diana Kennedy) and *The Food and Life of Oaxaca: Traditional Recipes from Mexico's Heart* (Zarela Martínez).

» **Merienda** In some small towns people will have a *merienda,* a light snack between the *comida* and *la cena* (supper), but in most large cities people are too busy working or commuting and don't eat again until dinner time.

» **Cena** Frequently dinner is not served until 9pm and it is usually light when eaten at home. In restaurants, however, dinner is often a social gathering where eaters share a complete meal that can last until midnight.

» **And....** When people go to a bar, a club or a late movie, they often stop off for a quick taco before returning home. Many famous *taquerías* cater to hungry insomniacs and don't close until the wee hours. On Fridays and Saturdays so many customers visit these places that sometimes you have to wait for a table at 3am!

Have You Heard the Word 'Fiesta'?

Food and fiestas go hand-to-hand in Mexico. They can be national holidays, religious festivals, local fiestas or personal celebrations, but chances are you will get caught in one of them during your visit. During national

THE ANTOJITO GUIDE

» **Tacos** The quintessential culinary fare in Mexico can be made of any cooked meat, fish or vegetable wrapped in a tortilla, with a dash of salsa and garnished with onion and cilantro. Soft corn tortillas are used to wrap grilled meats in *tacos al carbón,* an array of stews in *tacos de guisado* or with griddle-cooked meats and vegetables in *tacos a la plancha.* When tacos are lightly fried they are called *tacos dorados.* If you are in northern Mexico, chances are you will find tacos with flour tortilla (*tortilla de harina*) and the fillings will be more meat-based than vegetarian.

» **Quesadillas** Fold a tortilla with cheese, heat it on a griddle and you have a quesadilla. (*Queso* means cheese, hence the name.) But real quesadillas are much more than that. In restaurants and street stalls quesadillas are stuffed pockets made with raw corn masa that is lightly fried or griddled until crisp. They can be stuffed with *chorizo* and cheese, squash blossoms, mushrooms with garlic, *chicharrón* (fried pork fat), beans, stewed chicken or meat.

» **Enchiladas** In Spanish *enchilar* means to put chili over something, therefore enchiladas are a group of three or four lightly fried tortillas filled with chicken, cheese or eggs and covered with a cooked salsa. Enchiladas are usually a main dish, and can also be baked, like the famous *enchiladas suizas* (Swiss-style enchiladas).

» **Tostadas** Tortillas that have been baked or fried until they get crisp and are then cooled. The idea is that in this state they can hold a variety of toppings. *Tostadas de pollo* are a beautiful layering of beans, chicken, cream, shredded lettuce, onion, avocado and *queso fresco* (a fresh cheese).

» **Sopes** Small masa shells, two or three inches in diameter, that are shaped by hand and cooked on a griddle with a thin layer of beans, salsa and cheese. *Chorizo* is also a common topping for *sopes.*

» **Gorditas** Round masa cakes that are baked until they puff. Sometimes *gorditas* are filled with a thin layer of fried black or pinto beans, or even fava beans. In some regions, *gorditas* have an oval shape and are known as *tlacoyos.*

» **Chilaquiles** Typically served as breakfast. Corn tortillas are cut in triangles and fried until crispy. At this point they are indeed tortilla chips, or *totopos.* When cooked in a tomatillo (*chilaquiles verdes*) or tomato salsa (*chilaquiles rojos*) they become soft and then are topped with shredded cheese, sliced onions and Mexican crema.

» **Tamales** Made with masa mixed with lard, stuffed with stewed meat, fish or vegetables, wrapped and steamed. Every region in the country has its own, the most famous being the Oaxacan-style *tamales* with *mole* and wrapped in banana leaves, the Mexico City *tamales* with chicken and green tomatillo sauce wrapped in corn husks, and the Yucatecan style, made with chicken marinated in *achiote* (annatto paste) and wrapped in banana leaves.

holidays food's always present, but toasting with tequila is a prerequisite, especially during Día de la Independencia (September 16), which celebrates independence from Spain. The largest religious festivity is the Día de Nuestra Señora de Guadalupe (December 12), where *tamales, mole* and an array of *antojitos* are traditional fare. During Lent, meatless dishes such as *romeritos* (a wild plant that resembles rosemary served with dried shrimp, potatoes and *mole*) show up on most menus. On Día de los Santos Reyes (January 6), the day when the three wise men arrived bearing their treasured gifts for the baby Jesus, we celebrate by eating *rosca de reyes,* a large oval sweetbread decorated with candied fruit. The *rosca* is served with corn *tamales* and hot chocolate. During Christmas, a traditional Mexican menu includes turkey, *bacalao* (dry codfish cooked with olives, capers, onions and tomatoes) and *romeritos.*

There is no celebration in Mexico with more mystique than Día de Muertos (Day of the Dead), held on the second day of November. Its origins date back to the Aztecs and it celebrates the passing of relatives and loved ones. By celebrating death we salute life and we do it the way we celebrate everything else, with food, drinks and music. An altar to death is set up in a house, or, as some families prefer, in the graveyard. It is decorated with bright *cempasuchil* (marigold) flowers, plates of *tamales,* sugar-shaped skulls and *pan de muerto* (bread of the dead; a loaf made with egg yolks, mezcal and dried fruits), and the favorite foods of the deceased are laid out so that they feel welcomed upon their return.

> *Under the Jaguar Sun* by Italian writer Italo Calvino is a compelling account of a husband and wife discovering Mexico and its cuisine. The couple in the story becomes so enamored of the cuisine that their passion is transferred from the bedroom to the dining table.

¡Salud!
Tequila

In Mexico we love tequila. We drink it on large and small national holidays, at funerals and anniversaries, at casual lunches and at dinner with friends. Legally, tequila is our champagne. All tequila has to come from the state of Jalisco and is protected with a DO (Designation of Origin) by the *Consejo Regulador del Tequila* (Tequila Regulatory Council). This organization ensures that all tequila sold throughout the world comes from this state in central south Mexico. This arid area with highland soil creates the perfect conditions for the blue agave, the plant from which tequila is distilled, to grow. No tequila made in China (or elsewhere), *por favor*. We drink it because we are proud of its Mexican provenance, and because we really like its taste.

Taste is a key word when it comes to tequila. Tequila has become more and more sophisticated and today is considered a refined drink that rivals an imported single-malt whiskey or a quality cognac, and not only in price but in its smooth, warm taste. Today's finest tequilas are meant to be enjoyed in a small glass, with pleasure, in tiny sips.

MARKETS

Markets are perfect places to experience the Mexican way of life and munch on some really good *antojitos*. Markets tend to have a specific section for prepared foods where you can sit around a small counter or at large communal tables. In the gargantuan Mercado de la Merced in Mexico City the best *antojito* may be the *huarache,* a foot-long tortilla shaped like the shoe for which it is named, grilled and topped with salsa, onions, cheese and a choice of *chorizo,* steak, squash blossoms and more. The *huarache* competitor can be found in the markets of Oaxaca City, where large flat tortillas called *tlayudas* are spread with refried beans and topped with Oaxacan string cheese, salsa and pork strips. In the street that separates the Mercado Juárez and Mercado 20 de Noviembre in Oaxaca you may want to try the *chapulines,* or grasshoppers, fried with garlic, two types of chili and lime. No matter where you are in Mexico, a visit to the market is great way to spend some time, take great pictures and discover local and regional specialties.

The process of making tequila starts by removing the *piña* (heart) of the blue agave plant. This *piña* is then steamed for up to 36 hours, a process that softens the fibers and releases the *aguamiel,* or honey water. This liquid is funneled into large tanks where it is fermented. Fermentation determines whether the final product will be 100% agave or *mixto* (mixed). The highest-quality tequila is made from fermenting and then distilling only *aguamiel* mixed with some water. In tequilas *mixtos* the *aguamiel* is mixed with other sugars, usually cane sugar with water. When tequila is 100% agave it will say so on the label. If it doesn't say 100% it is a *mixto*.

The next step in the tequila-making process is to distill the *aguamiel* and store it in barrels for aging. The aging is important, especially for today's fancier tequilas, because it determines the color, taste, quality and price. Silver or *blanco* (white) is clear and is aged for no more than 60 days. Tequila *blanco* is used primarily for mixing and blends particularly well into fruit-based drinks. Tequila *reposado* (rested) is aged from two to nine months. It has a smooth taste and light gold color. Tequila *añejo* (old) is aged in wooden barrels for a minimum of 12 months. The best-quality *añejos* are aged up to four years. Tequila *añejo* has a velvety flavor and a deep dark color. These three kinds of tequilas are equally popular in Mexico, and it is entirely a matter of personal taste that determines which one to drink.

Mezcal

Mezcal is tequila's brother and it is currently experiencing a boom with people who believe tequila has gone too mainstream (and expensive!). Like tequila, mezcal is distilled from the agave plant, but mezcal doesn't have to come from blue agave, or from the tequila-producing areas of Jalisco. In other words, all tequila is mezcal, but not all mezcal is tequila. Since mezcal can be made with any type of agave plant, it can also be produced throughout the country, where it's sometimes known by other names, such as *bacanora* in Sonora state or *sotol* in Chihuahua.

In Oaxaca, the 'Mezcal Capital of the World,' the spirit is traditionally served in small earthenware cups with lime wedges and *sal de gusano,* an orange-colored salt that has been spiced with smoked agave worms. These are the same legendary worms that you find in some bottles of mezcal, and they are actually the larvae of moths that live on the plant. There are many legends about why the worm is added to the bottle, but all of them are too vague to single one out. What is irrefutable is the fact that consuming the worm is completely harmless. Another fact is that high-end mezcals don't include a worm in their bottles.

Pulque

If tequila and mezcal are brothers, then pulque would be the father of Mexican spirits. Two thousand years ago the Aztecs started to extract the juice of the agave plant to produce a milky, slightly alcoholic drink that they called *octli poliqhui*. When the Spanish arrived in Mexico they

English sailors coined the term 'cocktail' upon discovering that their drinks in the Yucatán port of Campeche were stirred with the thin, dried roots of a plant called *cola de gallo,* which translates as 'cock's tail.'

THE MEXICAN KITCHEN

COCKTAIL

THE LADIES BEHIND THE COMAL (GRIDDLE)

The Mexican kitchen is very much a matriarchal place where women have run the show for centuries. Currently, the most visible women cooks are cookbook author and owner of Izote restaurant (p108) Patricia Quintana, chef and owner of El Bajío restaurant (p108) Carmen 'Titita' Ramirez, author and restaurateur Alicia Gironella and British-born bestselling author Diana Kennedy. But it is in the hands and memories of ordinary Mexican women that the food of this country is practiced and preserved every day.

started to call the drink pulque. Early attempts to distill pulque were unsuccessful and the resulting spirit was harsh and unpleasant. It was soon discovered, however, that cooking the agave produced a sweet sap. After fermentation and distillation this juice became what we know today as mezcal.

Even though pulque has a lower alcohol content than tequila or mezcal, it is much harder on the palate. Because it is not distilled, it retains an earthy, vegetal taste and has a thick, foamy consistency that some people find unpleasant. In some places it is mixed with fruit juices such as mango or strawberry to make it more palatable. When pulque is mixed with juices it is called *curado*.

Beer

For many visitors, *'Una cerveza, por favor'* is among the first phrases they learn in Spanish. For some, it is their most commonly used phrase while in Mexico. This makes sense. Mexican *cerveza* is big, and although you don't need to travel to the country to try it (Mexican beers are among the best-selling brands all over the world), drinking beer here makes a big difference because Mexican beer is a great match with, well, Mexican food! Most Mexican brands are light and quench beautifully the spiciness of a plate of enchiladas. Beers are also a great companion for the thousands of *fútbol* (soccer) matches that we follow in this country with religious zeal.

Two major breweries dominate the Mexican market. Grupo Modelo, based in Mexico City and Guadalajara, makes 12 brands, among them Corona, Victoria, Modelo Especial, Pacífico, Montejo and Negra Modelo. Although Corona is the fifth best-selling beer in the world, beer aficionados regard Negra Modelo, a darker beer, as the brewery's jewel. North in the country, in the industrial city of Monterrey, Cervecería Cuauhtémoc Moctezuma produces Sol, Carta Blanca, Dos Equis, Superior, Tecate and Bohemia, among others. With its gold foil wrapping, Bohemia is marketed as the premium Mexican beer. It competes head-to-head with Negra Modelo and is also popular among experts. But the array of Mexican beer allows for drinking them in many different environments. A day on the beach calls for a Corona, a Superior or a Pacífico. Victoria and Montejo are good matches for seafood, and meat goes really well with Modelo Especial and Carta Blanca. A night in a bar feels very Dos Equis to me, and a Bohemia or Negra Modelo would pair perfectly with a very good, decadent dinner.

The practice of serving a beer with a wedge of lime in its mouth is not as common in Mexico as it is in foreign bars, and you will find that places that serve lime with your beer would most likely do it on a small plate. There are many legends around the origin of the practice. Some say that it began as a way of keeping the flies away from the bottles, others maintain that it appeared as a way to clean the rustiness on the mouth of the bottle caused by the old metal caps. In any case some lighter Mexican brands can benefit from the addition of a squeeze of lime, but most Mexican beers don't need anything.

Wine

Now may be the right time to expand your Spanish vocabulary to include *'una copa de vino, por favor.'* Although the wine industry is still much smaller than that of tequila or beer, Mexican wines are leaping forward at a great rate. Since the 1990s, challenged in part by the success of Californian, Chilean and Argentinean wines, Mexican producers began yielding good wines in nine regions, from Querétaro to Sonora, with the best coming from the north of Baja California (for more on Baja's up-and-coming Wine Route, see p699). The two larger wineries in Mexico, Pedro

---

MICHELADAS

Micheladas are prepared chilled beers ranging from simple drinks to complex cocktails. The basic *michelada* is a mix of the juice of one or two key limes on a previously chilled mug, a few ice cubes, a dash of salt and a Mexican cold beer. They are often served with a few drops of hot sauce, Worcestershire sauce and Maggi seasoning.

Domeq and LA Cetto, offer solid table wines and some premium labels like Chateu Domecq and Limited Reserve Nebbiolo. Many 'boutique wineries' with names like Monte Xanic, Casa de Piedra and Casa Valmar are also producing great wine in smaller quantities.

Be aware that wine consumption in Mexico is still pretty much restricted to upper-class establishments, especially outside the larger cities and wine-producing regions. Because most waiters are not much help in recommending wines, the best way to discover new Mexican wines is by conducting your own tasting.

Nonalcoholic Drinks

The great variety of fruits, plants and herbs that grow in this country are a perfect fit for the kind of nonalcoholic drinks Mexicans love. All over the country you will find classic *juguerías,* street stalls or small establishments selling all kinds of fresh-squeezed orange, tangerine, strawberry, papaya or carrot juices. These places also sell *licuados,* a Mexican version of a milkshake that normally includes banana, milk, honey and fruit. Many of these places serve incredibly creative combinations, such as *nopal* (cactus leaves), pineapple, lemon and orange, or vanilla, banana and avocado.

In *taquerías* and *fondas* you will find *aguas frescas,* or fresh waters. Some of them resemble iced teas. In *agua de tamarindo* the tamarind pods are boiled and then mixed with sugar before being chilled, while *agua de jamaica* is made with dried hibiscus leaves. Others like *horchata* are made with melon seeds and/or rice.

Vegetarians & Vegans

In Guadalajara's market there is large sign for an eatery named Restaurante Vegetariano (Vegetarian Restaurant) listing some menu items underneath. It has salads, rice, beans, grilled chicken and fish in garlic sauce. This sign shows one of the problems for vegetarians and vegans in Mexico: the concept is not always fully understood. Many Mexicans think of a vegetarian as a person that doesn't eat meat, and by 'meat' they mean red meat. Many more have never heard the word *veganista,* the Spanish term for vegan. The good news is that almost every city, large or small, has real vegetarian restaurants, and their popularity is increasing. Also, many traditional Mexican dishes are vegetarian: *ensalada de nopales* (cactus-leaf salad); quesadillas made with mushrooms, cheeses and even flowers like zucchini flowers; *chiles rellenos de queso* (cheese-stuffed poblano chilies); and *arroz a la mexicana* (Mexican-style rice). Be warned, however, that many dishes are prepared using chicken or beef broth, or some kind of animal fat, such as *manteca* (lard).

Eating with Kids

In most restaurants in Mexico you'll see entire families with kids eating together, especially on weekends. Waiters are used to accommodating children and will promptly help you with high chairs (*silla para niños*

CHOCOLATE

In Teotihuacán (present-day Mexico City) chocolate was considered the 'drink of the gods' and it was called *tlaquetzalli* or 'precious thing' in the Naúhuatl language. Chocolate was so valued by the Aztecs that the cacao bean, from which chocolate is derived, was also used as a form of currency.

CANTINAS

Cantinas are the traditional Mexican watering holes. Until not long ago, women, military personnel and children were not allowed in cantinas, and some cantinas still have a rusted sign stating this rule. Today everybody is allowed, although the more traditional establishments retain a macho edge. Beer, tequila and *cubas* (rum and coke) are served at square tables where patrons play dominos and watch soccer games on large TV screens. Cantinas are famous for serving *botanas* (appetizers) like *quesadillas de papa con guacamole* (potato quesadillas with guacamole) or escargots in chipotle sauce.

MULLI (MOLE)

Mexican chef and author Zarela Martinez once told me that in *mole* the sauce is the dish. What she meant was that when we eat *mole* we eat it because we want the sauce. The meat – whether it be chicken, turkey or pork – plays a secondary role. The word *mole* comes from the Náhuatl word *molli* or *mulli*. A complex sauce made with nuts, chilies and spices, *mole* defines Mexican cuisine. Although *mole* is often called chocolate sauce, only a very small percentage of *moles* include this ingredient. The confusion is somewhat understandable since the recipe for *mole poblano* (*mole* from the state of Puebla), the most widely known *mole* in the country (and around the world), includes a small amount of chocolate. But most Mexicans would agree that when it comes to *mole*, Oaxaca is the place to go. It's known as 'The Land of Seven *Moles*' (see boxed text, p428 for more on Oaxacan *moles*).

or *silla periquera*) and in some places they will bring crayons or toys to keep them entertained. Across Mexico it is common to see children having dinner in restaurants after 8pm or 9pm.

Cooking Courses

Cooking schools in Mexico can differ greatly depending on their location. A school in Oaxaca would focus on different ingredients and techniques than a school in Monterrey, or Sonora.

Estela Salas Silva has been running the **Mexican Home Cooking School** (www.mexicanhomecooking.com) in Tlaxcala since 1996. Tlaxcala is only a two-hour drive from Mexico City and 45 minutes from Puebla, and visitors will experience hand-on culinary classes based on the cuisine of central Mexico with a focus on Puebla cuisine. See also p160.

Cookbook author Susana Trilling operates **Seasons of My Heart** (www.seasonsofmyheart.com) in Rancho Aurora Oaxaca. Susana offers day and long-weekend classes, weeklong courses and culinary tours of the state of Oaxaca and other regions of Mexico. See p423 for more details.

Food Glossary

a la parrilla	a la pa·*ree*·ya	grilled
a la plancha	a la *plan*·cha	pan-broiled
adobada	a·do·*ba*·da	marinated with *adobo* (chili sauce)
al albañil	al al·ba·*nyeel*	'bricklayer style' – served with a hot chili sauce
al carbón	al kar·*bon*	char-broiled
al mojo de ajo	al *mo*·kho de a·kho	with garlic sauce
al pastor	al pas·*tor*	cooked on a pit, shepherd's style
albóndigas	al·*bon*·dee·gas	meatballs
antojitos	an·to·*khee*·tos	'little Mexican whims,' and tortilla-based snacks like tacos and *gorditas*
arroz mexicana	a·*ros* me·khee·*ka*·na	pilaf-style rice with a tomato base
atole	a·*to*·le	gruel made with ground corn
avena	a·*ve*·na	oatmeal
barbacoa	bar·ba·*ko*·a	pit-smoked barbecue
bolillo	bo·*lee*·yo	French-style roll
brocheta	bro·*che*·ta	shishkabob

buñuelos	boo·*nywe*·los	tortilla-size fritters with a sweet, anise sauce
burrito	boo·*ree*·to	filling in a large flour tortilla
cajeta	ka·*khe*·ta	goat's milk and sugar boiled to a paste
calabacita	ka·la·ba·*see*·ta	squash
carnitas	kar·*nee*·tas	pork simmered in lard
cecina	se·*see*·na	thin cut of meat, flavored with chili and sautéed or grilled
chalupas	cha·*loo*·pas	open-faced, canoe-shaped cooked corn dough, topped with meat and chilies
chicharrones	chee·cha·*ro*·nes	fried pork skins
chilaquiles	chee·la·*kee*·les	fried tortilla strips cooked with a red or green chili sauce, and sometimes meat and eggs
chile relleno	*chee*·le re·*ye*·no	chili stuffed with meat or cheese, usually fried with egg batter
chiles en nogada	*chee*·les en no·*ga*·da	mild green chilies stuffed with meat and fruit, fried in batter and served with a sauce of cream, ground walnuts and cheese
chorizo	cho·*ree*·so	Mexican-style bulk sausage made with chili and vinegar
chuleta de puerco	choo·*le*·ta de *pwer*·ko	pork chop
churros	*choo*·ros	doughnut-like fritters
cochinita pibil	ko·chee·*nee*·ta pee·*beel*	pork, marinated in chilies, wrapped in banana leaves, and pit-cooked or baked
coctel de frutas	kok·*tel* de *froo*·tas	fruit cocktail
costillas de res	kos·*tee*·yas de res	beef ribs
crepas	*kre*·pas	crepes or thin pancakes
empanada	em·pa·*na*·da	pastry turnover filled with meat, cheese or fruits
empanizado	em·pa·nee·*sa*·do	sautéed
enchilada	en·chee·*la*·da	corn tortilla dipped in chili sauce, wrapped around meat or poultry, and garnished with cheese
filete a la tampiqueña	fee·*le*·te a la tam·pee·*ke*·nya	steak, tampico style, a thin tenderloin, grilled and served with chili strips and onion, a quesadilla and *enchilada*
flor de calabaza	flor de ka·la·*ba*·sa	squash blossom
frijoles a la charra	free·*kho*·les a la *cha*·ra	beans cooked with tomatoes, chilies and onions (also called *frijoles rancheros*)
frito	*free*·to	fried
gorditas	gor·*dee*·tas	small circles of tortilla dough, fried and topped with meat and/or cheese
guacamole	gwa·ka·*mo*·le	mashed avocado, often with lime juice, onion, tomato and chili
horchata	hor·*cha*·ta	soft drink made with melon
huachinango veracruzana	wa·chee·*nan*·go ve·ra·kroo·*sa*·na	Veracruz-style red snapper with a sauce of tomatoes, olives, vinegar and capers

huevos motuleños	*we*·vos mo·too·*le*·nyos	fried eggs sandwiched between corn tortillas, and topped with peas, tomato, ham and cheese
huevos rancheros	*we*·vos ran·*che*·ros	fried eggs served on a corn tortilla, topped with a sauce of tomato, chilies, and onions, and served with refried beans
huevos revueltos	*we*·vos re·*vwel*·tos	scrambled eggs
huitlacoche	weet·la·*ko*·che	corn mushrooms – a much esteemed fungus that grows on corn
lomo de cerdo	*lo*·mo de *ser*·do	pork loin
machacado	ma·cha·*ka*·do	pulverized jerky, often scrambled with eggs
menudo	me·*noo*·do	stew of tripe
milanesa	mee·la·*ne*·sa	thin slices of beef or pork, breaded and fried
mixiote	mee·*shyo*·te	chili-seasoned lamb steamed in agave membranes or parchment
mole negro	*mo*·le *ne*·gro	chicken or pork in a very dark sauce of chilies, fruits, nuts, spices and chocolate
mole poblano	*mo*·le po·*bla*·no	chicken or turkey in a sauce of chilies, fruits, nuts, spices and chocolate
mollejas	mo·*ye*·khas	sweetbreads (thymus or pancreas)
nopalitos	no·pa·*lee*·tos	sautéed or grilled, sliced cactus paddles
picadillo	pee·ka·*dee*·yo	ground beef filling that often includes fruit and nuts
pipián verde	pee·*pyan* ver·de	stew of chicken, with ground squash seeds, chilies and *tomatillos*
pozole	po·*so*·le	soup or thin stew of hominy, meat, vegetables and chilies
quesadilla	ke·sa·*dee*·ya	cheese folded between a tortilla and fried or grilled
queso fundido	*ke*·so foon·*dee*·do	cheese melted, often with *chorizo* or mushrooms, and served as an appetizer with tortillas
rajas	*ra*·khas	strips of mild green chili fried with onions
sábana	*sa*·ba·na	filet mignons pounded paper thin and seared
sopa	*so*·pa	soup, either 'wet' or 'dry' – as in rice and pasta
sopa de ajo	*so*·pa de a·kho	garlic soup
sopa de cebolla	*so*·pa de se·*bo*·ya	onion soup
sopa de pollo	*so*·pa de *po*·yo	chicken soup
sope	*so*·pe	type of *gordita*
taco	*ta*·ko	filling of meat, poultry or vegetables wrapped in a tortilla
tinga poblana	*teen*·ga po·*bla*·na	stew of pork, vegetables and chilies

Landscapes & Wildlife

One of the thrills of travel in Mexico is the incredible, ever-changing landscape. From the snowcapped volcanoes of central Mexico and the cactus-strewn northern deserts to the tropical forests and wildlife-rich lagoons of the south, there's rarely a dull moment for the eye. Nature lovers will revel in this country which, straddling temperate and tropical regions, is one of the most biologically diverse on earth.

The Land

Nearly two million sq km in area, Mexico is the world's 14th-biggest country. With 10,000km of coastline and half its land above 1000m in elevation, the country has a spectacularly diverse and rugged topography. Almost anywhere you go except the Yucatán Peninsula, there'll be a range of mountains in sight, close or distant.

Central Volcanic Belt

The Cordillera Neovolcánica, the spectacular volcanic belt running east–west across the middle of Mexico, includes the classic active cones of Popocatépetl (5452m), 70km southeast of Mexico City, and Volcán de Fuego de Colima (3820m), 30km north of Colima. Some 30 million people live within the area that could be directly affected should smoking 'Popo' erupt in a big way. Also in the volcanic belt, but dormant, are Mexico's highest peak, Pico de Orizaba (5611m), and the third-highest peak, Popo's 'sister' Iztaccíhuatl (5220m). Mexico's youngest volcano and the easiest to get to the top of (see p624), Paricutín (2800m) only popped up in 1943 near the Michoacán village of Angahuan.

The upland valleys between the volcanoes have always been among the most habitable areas of Mexico. It's in one of these – the Valle de México (a 60km-wide basin at an elevation of 2200m) – that the country's capital, Mexico City, with its 20 million people, sits ringed by volcanic ranges.

Northern Plains & Sierras

A string of broad plateaus, the Altiplano Central, runs down the middle of the northern half of Mexico, fringed by two long mountain chains – the Sierra Madre Occidental in the west and Sierra Madre Oriental in the east. The altiplano and the two *sierras madre* end where they run into the Cordillera Neovolcánica.

The altiplano is criss-crossed by minor mountain ranges, and rises from an average elevation of about 1000m in the north to more than 2000m toward the center of the country. Most of the northern altiplano is occupied by the sparsely vegetated Desierto Chihuahuense (Chihuahuan Desert), which extends north into Texas and New Mexico. The

Volcano Activity Check

» **Popocatépetl** www.cenapred.gob.mx (in Spanish, with webcam images)

» **Volcán de Fuego de Colima** www.ucol.mx/volcan

landscape here is one of long-distance vistas across dusty brown plains to distant mountains, with eagles and vultures circling the skies. The southern altiplano is mostly rolling hills and broad valleys, and includes some of the best Mexican farming and ranching land in the area known as El Bajío, between the cities of Querétaro, Guanajuato and Morelia.

The extremely rugged Sierra Madre Occidental is fissured by many spectacularly deep canyons, including the famous Barranca del Cobre (Copper Canyon) and its 1870m-deep continuation, the Barranca de Urique.

The Sierra Madre Oriental includes peaks as high as 3700m but has semitropical zones on its lower, eastern slopes.

In all its 1400km length, the Sierra Madre Occidental is crossed by only one railway and two paved roads: the Ferrocarril Chihuahua Pacífico (Copper Canyon Railway) from Los Mochis to Chihuahua, Hwy 16 from Hermosillo to Chihuahua, and the dramatic Espinazo del Diablo (Devil's Backbone) route from Mazatlán to Durango.

Baja California

Baja California, one of the world's longest peninsulas, runs down the northwest coast, separated from 'mainland' Mexico by the Sea of Cortez (Golfo de California). Baja is 1300km of starkly beautiful deserts, plains and beaches with a mountainous spine that reaches up to 3100m at Picacho del Diablo in the Sierra San Pedro Mártir.

Coastal Plains

Coastal plains stretch the whole way down Mexico's Pacific coast and as far as the Tabasco lowlands on the Gulf coast. Both coasts are strung with hundreds of lagoons, estuaries and wetlands, making them important wildlife habitats. On the Pacific side a dry, wide plain stretches south from the US border almost to Tepic, in Nayarit state. As they continue south to the Guatemalan border, the Pacific lowlands narrow to a thin strip and become increasingly tropical.

The Gulf coast plain, an extension of a similar plain in Texas, is crossed by many rivers flowing down from the Sierra Madre Oriental. In the northeast the plain is wide, with some good ranchland, but is semimarshy near the coast. It narrows as it nears Veracruz.

The South

Yet another rugged, complicated mountain chain, the Sierra Madre del Sur stretches across the states of Guerrero and Oaxaca, roughly paralleling the Cordillera Neovolcánica, from which it's divided by the broiling hot Río Balsas basin. The Sierra Madre del Sur ends at the low-lying Isthmus of Tehuantepec, Mexico's narrow 'waist' which is just 220km wide. The north side of the isthmus is a wide, hot, humid plain strewn with wetlands and meandering rivers.

In the southernmost state of Chiapas, the Pacific lowlands are backed by the Sierra Madre de Chiapas. Dormant Volcán Tacaná, whose 4110m cone rises on the Mexico–Guatemala border, is the westernmost of a string of volcanoes that stretch across Guatemala. Behind the Sierra Madre de Chiapas are the Río Grijalva basin and then the Chiapas highlands. Past these highlands, the land sinks to the lowlands of the Lacandón Jungle and the flat, low expanse of the Yucatán Peninsula.

GREAT DIVERSITY

One of the most biologically diverse countries on earth, Mexico is home to over 1000 bird species, more than 500 mammals, nearly 1000 amphibians and reptiles, about 2000 butterflies and about 26,000 plants – for each of these groups, that's about 10% of the total number of species on the planet, on just 1.4% of the earth's land. The southern state of Chiapas alone, thanks largely to its Lacandón Jungle, has some 10,000 plant species, more than 600 bird species (twice as many as the USA) and 1200 species of butterflies.

Wildlife

From the whales, sea lions and giant cacti of Baja California to the big cats, howler monkeys and cloud forests of the southeast, Mexico's fauna and flora are exotic and fascinating. Getting out among it all is becoming steadily easier as growing numbers of local outfits offer trips to see birds, butterflies, whales, dolphins, sea lions and much more.

Those That Walk

The surviving tropical forests of the southeast still harbor five species of large cat (jaguar, puma, ocelot, jaguarundi and margay) in isolated pockets, plus spider and howler monkeys, tapirs, anteaters and some mean reptiles, including a few boa constrictors. Small jaguar populations are scattered as far north as the northern Sierra Madre Occidental, 200km from the US border. You may well see howler monkeys – or at least hear their eerie growls – near the Maya ruins at Palenque and Yaxchilán.

In the north, urban growth, ranching and agriculture have pushed the larger wild beasts – such as the puma (mountain lion), wolf, bobcat, bighorn sheep, pronghorn, coyote and deer – into isolated, often mountainous pockets. Raccoons, armadillos and skunks are still fairly common – the last two in much of the rest of Mexico too.

In all warm parts of Mexico you'll encounter two harmless, though sometimes surprising, reptiles: the iguana, a lizard that can grow a meter or so long and comes in many different colors; and the gecko, a tiny, usually green lizard that may shoot out from behind a curtain or cupboard when disturbed. Geckos might make you jump but they're good news – they eat mosquitoes.

Those That Swim

Baja California is famous for whale-watching in the early months of the year. Gray whales swim 10,000km from the Arctic to calve in its coastal waters (see boxed text, p709). Between Baja and the mainland, the Sea of Cortez hosts more than a third of all the world's marine mammals, including sea lions, fur and elephant seals, and four species of whale. Humpback whales follow plankton-bearing currents right down the Pacific coast between December and March, and, like dolphins and sea turtles, are commonly seen on boat trips from coastal towns.

Mexico's coasts, from Baja to Chiapas and from the northeast to the Yucatán Peninsula, are among the world's chief breeding grounds for sea turtles. Seven of the world's eight species are found in Mexican waters, with some female turtles swimming unbelievable distances (right across the Pacific Ocean in the case of some loggerhead turtles) to lay eggs on the beaches where they were born. Killing sea turtles or taking their eggs is illegal in Mexico, and there are more than 100 protected nesting beaches.

Dolphins play along the Pacific and Gulf coasts, while many coastal wetlands, especially in the south of the country, harbor crocodiles. Underwater life is richest of all on the coral reefs off the Yucatán Peninsula's Caribbean coast, where there's world-class diving and snorkeling. At Isla Holbox, off the peninsula's north coast, you can snorkel with whale sharks, the world's biggest fishes.

Those That Fly

Coastal Mexico is a fantastic bird habitat, especially its estuaries, lagoons and islands. An estimated three billion migrating birds pass by or over the Yucatán Peninsula each year. Inland Mexico abounds with eagles, hawks and buzzards, and innumerable ducks and geese winter in the northern Sierra Madre Occidental. Tropical species such as trogons,

LANDSCAPES & WILDLIFE **WILDLIFE**

ANIMALS

WWF's Wildfinder (www.worldwild life.org/science/ wildfinder) is a database of over 26,000 animal species, searchable by species or place. For each of 23 Mexican ecoregions, it'll give a list of hundreds of species with their names in English and Latin, their threatened status, and often pictures.

Bird Books

» *Mexican Birds* by Roger Tory Peterson and Edward L Chalif

» *Birds of Mexico & Adjacent Areas* by Ernest Preston Edwards

hummingbirds, parrots and tanagers start to appear south of Tampico in the east of the country and from around Mazatlán in the west. The southeastern jungles and cloud forests are home to colorful macaws, toucans, guans and even a few quetzals. Yucatán has spectacular flamingo colonies at Celestún and Río Lagartos.

Mexico's most unforgettable insect marvel is Michoacán's Reserva Mariposa Monarca (p610), where the trees and earth turn orange when millions of monarch butterflies arrive every winter.

Endangered Species

According to WWF Mexico, 222 land, water and amphibious animal species are in danger of disappearing from Mexico. About half of these exist nowhere else. The list includes such wonderful creatures as the jaguar, ocelot, northern tamandua (an anteater), pronghorn, Central American tapir, resplendent quetzal, scarlet macaw, Cozumel curassow, sea otter, Guadalupe fur seal, four types of parrot and both spider and howler monkeys. The Margarita Island kangaroo rat and Oaxacan pocket gopher may be less glamorous, but their disappearance will also forever affect the other plants and animals around them. Additionally, they're endemic to Mexico so once gone from here, they're gone from the universe. A host of factors contribute to these creatures' endangered status, including widespread species trafficking and illegal hunting.

Plants

Northern Mexico's deserts, though sparsely vegetated with cacti, agaves, yucca, scrub and short grasses, are the world's most biodiverse deserts. Most of the planet's 1000 or so cactus species are found in Mexico, including more than 400 in the Desierto Chihuahuense alone. Isolated Baja California has a rather specialized and diverse flora, from the 20m-high cardón (the world's tallest cactus) to the bizarre boojum tree, which looks like an inverted carrot with fluff at the top.

Mexico's great mountain chains have big expanses of pine (with half the world's pine species) and, at lower elevations, oak (135 types). In the southern half of the country, high-altitude pine forests are often covered in clouds, turning them into cloud forests with lush, damp vegetation, many colorful wildflowers, and epiphytes growing on tree branches.

The natural vegetation of the low-lying areas of southeast Mexico is predominantly evergreen tropical forest (rainforest in parts). This is dense and diverse, with ferns, epiphytes, palms, tropical hardwoods such as mahogany, and fruit trees such as the mamey and the chicozapote (sapodilla), which yields chicle (natural chewing gum). Despite ongoing destruction, the Selva Lacandona (Lacandón Jungle) in Chiapas is Mexico's largest remaining tropical forest, containing a large number of Chiapas' 10,000 plant species.

The Yucatán Peninsula changes from rainforest in the south to tropical dry forest and savanna in the north, with thorny bushes and small

---

Spectacular Birds

» **Scarlet macaw** Las Guacamayas, Chiapas

» **Resplendent quetzal** Reserva de la Biosfera El Triunfo, Chiapas

» **California condor** Parque Nacional Sierra San Pedro Mártir, Baja California

---

More Books

» *Animals & Plants of the Ancient Maya* by Victoria Schlesinger

» *Southern Mexico* (Travellers' Wildlife Guides) by Les Beletsky

---

THE 'LITTLE COW' OF THE SEA OF CORTEZ

The most iconic of the endangered Mexican endemics is the vaquita (harbor porpoise), the world's smallest marine mammal, found only in the northern Sea of Cortez and now probably numbering only about 250. It's a beautiful little creature whose name translates as 'little cow'. Many vaquitas die trapped in gillnets set for fish and shrimp. In 2008 Mexico launched a US$18 million bid to save the vaquita by paying fishermen to change their fishing methods or stay away from its waters altogether. Check the website **Vaquita** (http://vaquita.tv) for fascinating information and videos.

trees (including many acacias), resembling the drier parts of the Pacific coastal plain.

Parks & Reserves

Mexico has spectacular national parks and other protected areas – nearly 13% (253,000 sq km) of its territory is under some kind of federal, state or local protection. Governments have never had enough money for effective protection of these areas, but help from conservation organizations is turning increasing numbers of 'paper parks' into real ones.

National Parks

Mexico's 67 *parques nacionales* (national parks) total 14,320 sq km. Many are tiny (smaller than 10 sq km), and around half of them were created in the 1930s, often for their archaeological, historical or recreational value rather than for ecological reasons. Several recently created parks protect coastal areas, offshore islands or coral reefs. Despite illegal logging, hunting and grazing, national parks have succeeded in protecting big tracts of forest, especially the high, coniferous forests of central Mexico.

Biosphere Reserves

Reservas de la biosfera (biosphere reserves) are based on the recognition that it is impracticable to put a complete stop to human exploitation of many ecologically important areas. Instead, these reserves encourage sustainable local economic activities within their territory. Today, Mexico has 57 Unesco-protected and national biosphere reserves, covering some 140,000 sq km. They protect some of Mexico's most beautiful and biologically fascinating areas, focusing on whole ecosystems with genuine biodiversity. Sustainable, community-based tourism is an important source of support for several of them, and successful visitor programs are in place in reserves like Calakmul, Sierra Gorda, Montes Azules, Mariposa Monarca and Sian Ka'an.

Environmental Issues

The Calderón presidency from 2006 to 2012 took important initiatives to tackle some of Mexico's serious environmental problems. It also took a lead in efforts to combat global warning, with President Calderón announcing in 2008 that Mexico would reduce its greenhouse gas emissions by 8% by 2012, and by 50% by 2050. The country is currently responsible for about 1.5% of world emissions.

Calderón launched a US$21 billion program to tackle the country's water problems – crucial in a nation where the south has 70% of the water, but the north and center have 75% of the people. Calderón's target by 2012 was to provide clean drinking water to 10 million more people and drainage systems to another 6.5 million (still leaving around 5 million and 10 million, respectively, without). He also pledged to modernize wasteful irrigation systems and treat at least 60% of sewage (up from 38% in 2008).

Forests were another Calderón priority. Only around 15% of the country (300,000 sq km) is now forested, and the figure has been shrinking by several thousand sq km per year as land is cleared for grazing, logging and farming. But Mexico halved its deforestation rate between 2005 and 2010 and, with the help of ambitious tree-planting programs, aims to achieve zero deforestation by 2020.

Whether all these ambitious targets will be met remains to be seen, but at least the issues have been receiving some overdue attention, and environmental awareness has made big bounds in Mexico. The country

The Nature Conservancy (www.nature.org), Conservation International (www.conservation.org) and WWF (wwf.panda.org) all provide lots of information on the Mexican environment, including on their programs in the country.

LANDSCAPES & WILDLIFE PARKS & RESERVES

Parks & Reserves

» **Comisión Nacional de Áreas Naturales Protegidas** www.conanp.gob.mx/que_hacemos, in Spanish

» **Unesco (biosphere reserves)** www.Unesco.org/new/en/natural-sciences/environment

has no large-scale environmental movement, but it does have plenty of smaller organizations working on local issues. Probably the most influential national group is **Pronatura** (www.pronatura.org.mx), which deploys over M$100 million a year chiefly on climate-change projects, protecting priority species and the conservation of lands and watersheds.

TOP PARKS & RESERVES

PARK/RESERVE	FEATURES	ACTIVITIES	BEST TIME TO VISIT
Parque Marino Nacional Bahía de Loreto (p715)	islands, shores & waters of the Sea of Cortez	snorkeling, kayaking, diving	year-round
Parque Nacional Archipiélago Espíritu Santo (p719)	waters around Espíritu Santo & neighboring islands in Sea of Cortez	kayaking with whale sharks, snorkeling with sea lions, sailing	year-round
Parque Nacional Iztaccíhuatl-Popocatépetl (p157)	live & extinct volcanic giants on rim of Valle de México	hiking, climbing	Nov-Feb
Parque Nacional Lagunas de Chacahua (p459)	Oaxacan coastal lagoons; beach	boat trips, birdwatching, surfing	year-round
Parque Nacional Volcán Nevado de Colima (p599)	live & extinct volcanoes; pumas, coyotes, pine forests	volcano hiking	Dec-May
Reserva de la Biosfera Banco Chinchorro (p288)	largest coral atoll in northern hemisphere	diving, snorkeling	Dec-May
Reserva de la Biosfera Calakmul (p334)	rainforest with major Maya ruins	visiting ruins, wildlife-spotting	year-round
Reserva de la Biosfera El Vizcaíno (p708)	coastal lagoons where gray whales calve; deserts	whale-watching, hikes to ancient rock art	Dec-Apr
Reserva de la Biosfera Mariposa Monarca (p610)	forests festooned with millions of monarch butterflies	butterfly observation, hiking	Nov-Mar
Reserva de la Biosfera Montes Azules (see boxed text, p390)	tropical jungle, lakes, rivers	jungle hikes, canoeing, rafting, bird-watching, boat trips, wildlife-watching	year-round
Reserva de la Biosfera Ría Celestún (p313)	estuary & mangroves with plentiful bird life, incl flamingos	bird-watching, boat trips	Mar-Sep
Reserva de la Biosfera Ría Lagartos (p325)	mangrove-lined estuary full of bird life, incl flamingoes	bird-, crocodile- and turtle-watching	Apr-Jul
Reserva de la Biosfera Sian Ka'an (p285)	Caribbean coastal jungle, wetlands & islands with incredibly diverse wildlife	bird-watching, snorkeling & nature tours, mostly by boat	year-round
Reserva de la Biosfera Sierra Gorda (p690)	transition zone from semidesert to cloud forest	hiking, birdwatching, colonial missions	year-round

Urban Problems

Mexico City is a high-altitude megalopolis surrounded by a ring of mountains that traps polluted air in the city. In an effort to limit pollution levels, many vehicles are banned from the roads one day a week. The capital consumes over half of Mexico's electricity and has to pump up about a quarter of its water needs from outside the Valle de México.

The capital's problems of water supply, sewage treatment, overcrowding and traffic pollution are mirrored on a smaller scale in most of Mexico's faster-growing cities.

Tourism, a key sector of Mexico's economy, can bring its own set of environmental problems when development is on a large scale. Fragile coastal ecosystems are threatened in parts of Baja California and on the Caribbean coast.

After several years of environmental opposition to the planned large-scale Cabo Cortés tourism development near Baja's Cabo Pulmo Marine National Park, Mexico's Senate summoned the country's environment minister for questioning on the issue in February 2012.

On the Caribbean coast's Riviera Maya, organizations such as **Centro Ecológico Akumal** (ceakumal.org) and **Society of Akumal's Vital Ecology** (saverivieramaya.org) campaign to limit damage from reckless tourism development to coral reefs, turtle-nesting beaches, mangrove systems and even the water in the area's famed cenotes (limestone sinkholes). A slowly growing number of hotels and resorts in the region are adopting green policies.

Mexico Sustainable (http://mexico-sustainable.com) includes an emissions calculator which tells you, for example, that a medium-sized car traveling from Mexico City to Cancún emits 0.39 tons of carbon dioxide, while air passengers flying economy class between the same two cities are responsible for 0.26 tons each.

LANDSCAPES & WILDLIFE ENVIRONMENTAL ISSUES

Survival Guide

Directory A–Z

Accommodations

Accommodations in Mexico range from hammocks and huts to hotels of every imaginable standard, including superluxury resorts. In popular destinations at busy times, it's best to reserve a room in advance or go early in the day to secure a room.

Price Categories

Many midrange and top-end establishments in tourist destinations raise their rates during short 'extra' seasons such as the Semana Santa and Christmas–New Year's holiday periods or local festival times, and cut them during low seasons. Budget accommodations are more likely to keep the same rates all year. Information on high- and low-season periods is given in the Need to Know and On The Road chapters.

Budget ($) Every Mexican town has its cheap hotels. There are clean, friendly, secure ones, and there are dark, dirty ones where you may not feel your belongings are safe. Adequate rooms with a private hot shower are available for under M$400 in most of the country. Budget accommodations include campgrounds, hammocks, and most palm-thatched *cabañas,* traveler hostels, guesthouses and economical hotels. Recommended accommodations in this range will be simple and without frills but generally clean. Budget hotel rooms usually have a private bathroom.

Midrange ($$) Mexico specializes in good midrange accommodations. The more you pay, the more facilities, comfort and style the place is likely to have, but in some places even M$500 can get you an attractive room in a friendly small hotel. Many midrange places have a restaurant and a bar and almost all have wi-fi and/or internet-enabled computers. Quite a lot have swimming pools. Many of the country's most appealing and memorable lodgings are in the midrange bracket. Among the most charming lodgings are the many old mansions and inns turned into hotels. These can be wonderfully atmospheric, with fountains gurgling in flower-decked, stone-pillared courtyards or verdant gardens. You'll also find some B&Bs, apartments, bungalows and more comfortable *cabañas* in the midrange bracket.

Top end ($$$) Accommodations in this category offer the expected levels of luxury – pools, gyms, bars, restaurants, design, professional service – at prices that are sometimes agreeably modest, and sometimes not. They range in style from converted haciendas or small, chic boutique hotels to expansive modern resorts. If you like to stay in luxury but also enjoy saving some money, look for deals on hotel websites or phone up and ask how to obtain the best price. Good news for families and other small groups: many hotels have rooms for three, four or five people that cost not much more than a double.

Symbols & Abbreviations

In this book 'single' (abbreviated to 's') means a room for one person, and 'double' ('d') means a room for two people. Mexicans sometimes use the phrase *cuarto sencillo* (single room) to mean a room with one bed, which may be a *cama matrimonial* (double bed); a *cuarto doble* often means a room with

PRICE RANGES

The following price ranges refer to accommodations for two people in high season, including any taxes charged.

$ less than M$460

$$ M$460–1150

$$$ more than M$1150

two beds, which may both be *camas matrimoniales*.

The air-con icon (✲) and nonsmoking icon (☺) mean that the establishment offers at least some air-conditioned and nonsmoking rooms, respectively.

Taxes

The price of accommodations in Mexico is subject to two taxes:

IVA (value-added tax; 16%)
ISH (lodging tax; 2% or 3% depending on the state)

Many of the less expensive establishments only charge you these taxes if you require a receipt, and they quote room rates accordingly (ie not including taxes). Generally, though, IVA and ISH are included in quoted prices. In top-end hotels a price may be given as, say, 'M$1500 *más impuestos*' (M$1500 plus taxes), in which case you must add 18% or 19% to the figure. Prices given in this book are those you are most likely to be charged at each place.

Types of Accommodations

Apartments In some resort towns you can find tourist apartments with fully equipped kitchens. They can be good value for three or four people, especially if you're staying more than a few days. The internet, local ads and tourist offices are good sources of information on these.

B&Bs Mexico's growing number of B&Bs are usually small, comfortable, midrange or top-end guesthouses, often beautifully designed and offering friendly, personal attention. Many of them are effectively boutique hotels.

Cabañas *Cabañas* are usually huts (of wood, brick, adobe or stone) with a palm-thatched roof and are most often found at beach destinations. The most basic have dirt floors and nothing inside but a bed, and you provide the padlock for the door. At the other extreme, some *cabañas* are positively deluxe, with electric lights, mosquito nets, large comfy beds, bathrooms, hammock-strung decks and even air-con and a kitchen – though they'll usually still have an agreeably rustic, close-to-nature ambience. The most expensive *cabañas* are on the Caribbean, where some luxury huts cost well over M$1000.

Campgrounds & Trailer Parks Most organized campgrounds are actually trailer parks set up for RVs (recreational vehicles, campers) and trailers (caravans) that are open to tent campers at lower rates. Some are basic, others quite luxurious. Some restaurants and guesthouses in beach spots or country areas will let you pitch a tent on their patch for around M$50 per person.

Hammocks Hammock space is available in many of the more low-key beach spots. A hammock can be a very comfortable, not to mention cheap, place to sleep in hot areas (keep mosquito repellent handy). Some places have hammocks to rent for anywhere between M$40 and M$100. With your own hammock, the cost comes down a bit.

It's easy to buy hammocks in Mexico, especially in Oaxaca and Chiapas states and on the Yucatán Peninsula.

Hostels There are traveler hostels in most places where budget travelers congregate. They provide dormitory accommodations typically from M$100 to M$200 per person, plus communal kitchens, bathrooms, living space, usually internet access and in many cases economical private rooms too. Some of the best hostels have pools, bars, gardens, sundecks and even design and charm. Cleanliness and security do vary, but popular hostels are great places for meeting fellow travelers. **Hostelworld** (www.hostelworld.com) provides plentiful listings and online reservations. Just 22 hostels are members of Mexico's HI affiliate, **Hostelling International Mexico** (www.himexico. com). Note that establishments named 'Hostal' can be either hostels or budget hotels.

Posadas & Casas de Huéspedes Posadas are inns, meaning anything from basic budget hotels to tastefully designed, small, midrange places. A *casa de huéspedes* is a guesthouse, a home converted into simple, inexpensive guest lodgings, usually family run and often with a relaxed, friendly atmosphere.

Activities

Further information about specific activities can be found in the If You Like chapter (see p23) and via the index.

If you're planning to fly to Mexico with a surfboard, check with the airline first: most of them charge US$50 or more (each way) to carry boards, and some won't carry them at all to some

SAFETY GUIDELINES FOR DIVING

Before embarking on a scuba-diving, skin-diving or snorkeling trip, carefully consider the following points to ensure a safe and enjoyable experience:

» Possess a current diving-certification card from a recognized scuba-diving instruction agency (if scuba diving).

» Be sure you are healthy and feel comfortable diving.

» If you don't have your own equipment, ask to see the dive shop's before you commit. And make sure you feel comfortable with your dive master: after all, it's your life.

» Obtain reliable information about physical and environmental conditions at the dive site from a reputable local dive operation, and ask how local trained divers deal with these considerations.

» Be aware of local laws, regulations and etiquette about marine life and the environment.

» Dive only at sites within your level of experience; if available, engage the services of a competent, professionally trained dive instructor or dive master.

» Find out if your dive shop has up-to-date certification from **PADI** (www.padi.com), **NAUI** (www.naui.com) or the internationally recognized Mexican diving organization **FMAS** (www.fmas.com.mx, in Spanish).

» Know the locations of the nearest decompression chambers and the emergency telephone numbers.

» Avoid diving less than 18 hours before a high-altitude flight.

For further diving tips, see p275.

---

destinations or at some times of year.

RESOURCES
Planeta.com (www.planeta. com) Good resource on active and responsible tourism.
Mexonline.com (www.mex online.com) Includes listings of activities providers.
AMTAVE (www.amtave.org, in Spanish) The Mexican Adventure Tourism & Ecotourism Association, with 79 member organizations.

Business Hours

Standard hours are as follows (exceptions are noted in listings in this book):
Banks 9am-4pm Mon-Fri, 9am-1pm Sat; banks in smaller towns may close earlier and not open Saturday.
Casas de Cambio (currency exchange offices) 9am-7pm daily.
Stores/Shops 9am-8pm

Mon-Sat; in the south, many shops close 2-4pm. Supermarkets and department stores usually open from 9am or 10am to 10pm every day.

Customs Regulations

You may bring the following into Mexico duty-free:
» 2 cameras
» 3 cell phones
» 1 portable computer
» 1 portable CD, DVD or digital music player
» 3 surfboards or windsurfing boards
» 2 musical instruments
» medicine for personal use, with prescription in the case of psychotropic drugs.

See www.aduanas.gob.mx for further details.
    The normal routine when you enter Mexico is to complete a customs declaration form (which lists duty-free allowances), and then place it in a machine. If the machine shows a green light, you pass without inspection. If a red light shows, your baggage will be searched.

Discount Cards

For reduced-price air tickets at student- and youth-oriented travel agencies, the following cards are widely recognized:
» ISIC student card
» IYTC (under 26) card
» ITIC card for teachers

Reduced prices for students and seniors on Mexican buses and at museums and archaeological sites are usually only for those with Mexican residence or education credentials, but the ISIC, IYTC and ITIC will sometimes get you a reduction. The ISIC is the most widely recognized.

Electricity

127V/60Hz

127V/60Hz

Embassies & Consulates

If you're having trouble locating your nearest Mexican embassy or consulate, look at the website of Mexico's foreign ministry, the **Secretaría de Relaciones Exteriores** (www.sre.gob.mx), which links to the websites of all Mexican diplomatic missions including the more than 40 consulates in US cities. Some of these sites have useful information on visas and similar matters.

Mexico City entries in this list are for embassies or their consular sections; other entries are consulates. Embassy websites usually link to consulates' websites (where they exist) and often have much other useful information about Mexico.

Australia (☑55-1101-2200; www.mexico.embassy.gov.au; Rubén Darío 55, Polanco) In Mexico City.

Belize Chetumal (☑983-285-35-11; Génova 369, Colonia Benito Juárez); Mexico City (☑55-5520-1274; www.mfa. gov.bz; Bernardo de Gálvez 215, Lomas de Chapultepec)

Canada (www.canadainternational.gc.ca/mexico-mexique) Acapulco (☑744-484-13-05; Local 23, Centro Comercial Marbella, cnr La Costera & Prolongación Farallón); Cabo San Lucas (☑624-142-43-33; Local 82, Plaza San Lucas, Carretera Transpeninsular Km 0.5, Colonia El Tezal); Cancún (☑998-883-33-60; Oficina E7, Centro Empresarial, Blvd Kukulcán Km 12, Zona Hotelera); Guadalajara (☑33-3671-4740; Piso 8, Torre Pacífico, World Trade Center, Av Otero 1249, Colonia Rinconada del Bosque); Mazatlán (☑669-913-73-20; Office 41, Centro Comercial La Marina Business & Life, Blvd Marina Mazatlán 2302, Colonia Marina Mazatlán); Mexico City (☑55-5724-7900; Schiller 529, Polanco); Monterrey (☑81-8378-0240; Suite 404, Torre Gómez Morín 955, Av Gómez Morín 955, San Pedro Garza García); Oaxaca (☑951-513-37-77; Local 11B, Pino Suárez 700); Puerto Vallarta (☑322-293-00-98; Local Sub F, Plaza Península, Blvd Medina Ascencio 2485, Zona Hotelera Norte); Tijuana (☑664-684-04-61; Condominio del Parque, Gedovius 10411-101, Zona Río)

France Cancún (☑998-147-74-48; Av Huayacán 1000, SM 311, Álamos II); Guadalajara (☑33-3630-3283; Aparto 7, González Luna 2007, Colonia Americana); Mérida (☑999-930-15-00; Calle 60 No 385); Mexico City (☑55-9171-9700; www.ambafrance-mx.org, in Spanish & French; Campos Elíseos 339, Polanco); consulate in Mexico City (☑55-9171-9700; Lafontaine 32, Polanco); Oaxaca (☑951-515-21-84; Planta Baja, 3a Privada de J López Alavez 5, San Felipe del Agua)

Germany Cancún (☑998-884-15-98; Punta Conoco 36, SM24); Guadalajara (☑33-3810-2146; Calle 7 No 319, Colonia Ferrocarril); Mérida (☑999-944-32-52; Calle 49 No 212); Mexico City (☑55-5283-2200; www.mexiko.diplo.de, in Spanish & German; Horacio 1506, Los Morales)

Guatemala Ciudad Hidalgo (☑962-698-01-84; 9a Calle Ote 11, Colonia San José); Comitán (☑963-110-68-16; 1a Calle Sur Pte 35); Mexico City (☑55-5520-6680; http:\\embajada guatemalamx.mex.tl, in Spanish; Av Explanada 1025, Lomas de Chapultepec); Tapachula (☑962-626-12-52; 5a Nte 5)

Ireland Cancún (☑998-112-54-36; Av Coba 15, MZ 8, SM 22); Mexico City (☑55-5520-5803; www.irishembassy. com.mx; Cerrada Blvd Ávila Camacho 76-3, Lomas de Chapultepec)

Italy Guadalajara (☑33-3616-1700; 1st fl, Av López Mateos Nte 790, Fraccionamiento Ladrón de Guevara); Mexico City (☑55-5596-3655; www. ambcittadelmessico.esteri. it, in Spanish & Italian; Paseo de las Palmas 1994, Lomas de Chapultepec); Playa del Carmen (☑984-803-47-14; Av 10 btwn Calles 12 & 14)

Netherlands Cancún (☑998-884-86-72; Pabellón Caribe, Av Nichupté, Lote 22, MZ 2, SM 19); Guadalajara (☑33-1655-0269; Condominio Santa Anita, Paseo de las Jacarandas 243, Tlajomulco de Zuñiga); Mérida (☑999-924-31-22; Calle 64 No 418); Mexico City (☑55-5258-9921; mexico.nlambassade. org, in Spanish & Dutch; 7th fl, Edificio Calakmul, Av Vasco de Quiroga 3000, Santa Fe)

New Zealand (☑55-5283-9460; www.nzembassy.com/mexico; Level 4, Jaime Balmes 8, Los Morales) In Mexico City.

Spain Cancún (☑998-848-99-18; cnr Blvds Kukulcán & Cenzontle, Zona Hotelera); Guadalajara (☑33-3630-0450; Mezzanine izquierdo, Torre Sterling, Quevedo 117, Colonia Arcos Vallarta); Mexico City (☑55-5282-2271; www.maec.es, in Spanish; Galileo 114, Polanco)

UK (ukinmexico.fco.gov.uk) Cancún (☑998-881-01-84; Royal Sands, Blvd Kukulcán Km 13.5, Zona Hotelera); Mexico City (☑55-1670-3200; Río Lerma 71, Colonia Cuauhtémoc); consulate in Mexico City (☑55-1670-3200; Río Usumacinta 30); Tijuana (☑664-686-53-20; Blvd Salinas 1500, Fraccionamiento Aviación Tijuana)

USA Cancún (☑998-883-02-72; Despacho 301, Torre La Europea, Blvd Kukulcán Km 13, Zona Hotelera); Ciudad Juárez (☑656-227-30-00; Paseo de la Victoria 3650, Fraccionamiento Partido Senecú); Guadalajara (☑33-3268-2100; Progreso 175, Colonia Americana); Hermosillo (☑662-289-35-00; Monterrey Pte 141, Colonia Esqueda); Ixtapa (☑755-553-21-00; Hotel Fontán, Blvd Ixtapa); Mazatlán (☑669-916-58-89; Hotel Playa Mazatlán, Av Playa Gaviotas 202, Zona Dorada); Mérida (☑999-942-57-00; Calle 60 No 338K, btwn Calles 29 & 31, Colonia Alcalá Martín); Mexico City (☑55-5080-2000; www.usembassy-mexico.gov; Paseo de la Reforma 305); Monterrey (☑81-8047-3100; Av Constitución 411 Pte); Oaxaca (☑951-514-30-54; Office 20, Plaza Santo Domingo, Alcalá 407); Puerto Vallarta (☑322-222-00-69; Local L7, Paradise Plaza, Paseo de los Cocoteros 85 Sur, Nuevo Vallarta); San José del Cabo (☑624-143-35-66; Local B221, Tiendas de Palmilla, Carretera Transpeninsular Km 27.5); San Miguel de Allende (☑415-152-23-57; Locales 4 & 5, Plaza La Luciérnaga, Libramiento Zavala 164); Tijuana (☑664-977-20-00; Paseo de las Culturas s/n, Mesa de Otay)

PRICE RANGES

The following price ranges refer to prices of typical main dishes, including IVA.

$ less than M$80

$$ M$80–150

$$$ more than M$150

Food

For details about Mexican food, see p829. A mandatory 16% of IVA (or value-added tax) is added to restaurant checks in Mexico, but the *propina* (gratuity) is not. The average tip is 15% to 20%, and although some people argue that the tip should be calculated before IVA, it is just easier to tip the same amount, or a bit more, than the amount marked for the IVA. For instance, in a check that marks IVA M$82, a tip between M$80 and M$100 would be appropriate.

Gay & Lesbian Travelers

Mexico is increasingly broad-minded about sexuality. Gays and lesbians don't generally adopt a high profile, but rarely attract open discrimination or violence. The legalization of gay marriages in Mexico City has energized gay life in the capital, which has a hip, international bar and club scene. Puerto Vallarta is the gay beach capital of Mexico. There are also lively scenes in places like Guadalajara, Veracruz, Cancún, Mazatlán, Mérida and Acapulco. Discrimination based on sexual orientation can be punished with up to three years in prison.

Gay Mexico (www.gaymexico.com.mx) has a clickable map linking to gay guides for many cities. **Gay Mexico Map** (www.gaymexicomap.com) also has listings of accommodations, bars and clubs. Also well worth checking out are the **International Gay & Lesbian Travel Association** (www.iglta.org), with worldwide information on travel providers in the gay sector, and **Out Traveler** (www.outtraveler.com).

Health

Travelers to Mexico need to guard chiefly against food- and mosquito-borne diseases. Besides getting the proper vaccinations, carry a good insect repellent and exercise care in what you eat and drink.

Private hospitals generally provide better care than public ones, but are more expensive: the best are in Mexico City. You should have travel insurance that covers the cost of air evacuation to another country should you develop a life-threatening condition.

Recommended Vaccinations

Make sure all routine vaccinations are up to date and check whether all vaccines are suitable for children and pregnant women.

Hepatitis A All travelers (not recommended for pregnant women or children aged under two: gamma-globulin is the alternative).

Hepatitis B Long-term travelers in close contact with local population (requires three doses over a six-month period).

Rabies For travelers who may have contact with animals and may not have access to medical care.

Internet Resources

MD Travel Health (www.mdtravelhealth.com) Complete travel health recommendations for every country, updated daily.

Centers for Disease Control & Prevention (www.cdc.gov/travel) Official US website

Health Hazards in Mexico

Altitude sickness May develop in travelers who ascend rapidly to altitudes greater than 2500m. Symptoms may include headaches, nausea, vomiting, dizziness, malaise, insomnia and loss of appetite. Severe cases can lead to death. To lessen the chance of altitude sickness, ascend gradually to higher altitudes, avoid overexertion, eat light meals and avoid alcohol. People showing any symptoms of altitude sickness should not ascend higher until the symptoms have cleared. If the symptoms become worse or if someone shows signs of fluid in the lungs (high-altitude pulmonary edema) or swelling of the brain (high-altitude cerebral edema), such as trouble breathing or mental confusion, descend immediately to a lower altitude. A descent of 500m to 1000m is generally adequate except in cases of cerebral edema.

Dengue Fever A viral infection transmitted by aedes mosquitoes, which usually bite during the day. Usually causes flu-like symptoms. There is no vaccine and no treatment except analgesics.

Malaria Transmitted by mosquito bites, usually between dusk and dawn. The main symptom is high spiking fevers. Malaria pills are strongly recommended when visiting rural areas in Oaxaca, Chiapas, Sinaloa, Nayarit, Tabasco and Quintana Roo states, and for parts of Sonora, Chihuahua and Durango states. The first-choice malaria pill is chloroquine. Protecting yourself against mosquito bites is just as important as taking malaria pills.

Snake & Scorpion Bites In the event of a venomous snake bite or scorpion bite, keep the bitten area immobilized, and move the victim immediately to the nearest medical facility. For scorpion stings, immediately apply ice or cold packs.

Precautions

Mosquito Bites Wear long sleeves, long pants, hats and shoes. Don't sleep with the window open unless there is a screen. Use a good insect repellent, preferably one containing DEET, but don't use DEET-containing compounds on children under age two. If sleeping outdoors or in accommodations that allow entry of mosquitoes, use a mosquito coil, or a bed net treated with permethrin.

Sun Stay out of the midday sun, wear sunglasses and a wide-brimmed hat, and apply sunscreen with SPF 15 or higher. Drink plenty of fluids and avoid strenuous exercise when the temperature is high.

Water Tap water in Mexico is generally not safe to drink. Vigorous boiling for one minute is the most effective means of water purification. At altitudes greater than 2000m, boil for three minutes. Another option is to disinfect water with iodine pills or use a **SteriPen** (www.steripen.com), which kills bacteria and viruses with ultraviolet light. Pregnant women and those with a history of thyroid disease should not drink iodinated water.

Insurance

A travel-insurance policy to cover theft, loss and medical problems is a good idea. Some policies specifically exclude dangerous activities such as scuba diving, motorcycling and even trekking.

You may prefer a policy that pays doctors or hospitals directly rather than you having to pay on the spot and claim later. If you have to claim later, ensure that you keep all documentation. Check that the policy covers ambulances or an emergency flight home. For information on motor insurance, see p862.

Worldwide travel insurance is available at www.lonelyplanet.com/travel_services. You can buy, extend and claim online anytime – even if you're already on the road.

Internet Access

Wi-fi ('wee-fee,' internet inalámbrico) is common in Mexican accommodations and also available in some cafes, bars and airports; in this book the wi-fi icon (🛜) means that wi-fi is available to guests in at least some part of the premises. The internet icon (@) means that the establishment has internet-enabled computers for guests to use. These services may or may not be free of charge.

Mexico also has thousands of internet cafes, typically charging M$10 per hour. Many of them are equipped with webcams, headphones, Skype and so on.

Legal Matters

Mexican Law

Mexican law is based on the Roman and Napoleonic codes, presuming an accused person guilty until proven innocent.

As in most other countries, the purchase of controlled medication requires a doctor's prescription. It's against Mexican law to take any firearm or ammunition into the country (even unintentionally).

A new law passed in 2009 determined that possession of small amounts of certain drugs for personal use – including marijuana (up to 5g), cocaine (500mg), heroin (50mg) and methamphetamine (40mg) – would not incur legal proceedings against first-time offenders.

Selling drugs in any quantity remains illegal, and people found in possession of small amounts may still have to appear before a prosecutor for it to be established whether they are for personal use. The easiest way to avoid any problems related to these drugs is certainly to avoid them.

See p862 for information on the legal aspects of road accidents.

Useful warnings on Mexican law are found on the website of the **US State Department** (travel.state.gov).

Getting Legal Help

If a foreigner is arrested in Mexico, the Mexican authorities are required by international law to promptly contact the person's consulate or embassy if asked to do so. Consular officials can tell you your rights, provide lists of lawyers, monitor your case, try to make sure you are treated humanely, and notify your relatives or friends – but they can't get you out of jail. By Mexican law, the longest a person can be detained by police without a specific accusation is 48 hours.

Tourist offices in Mexico, especially those run by state governments, can often help you with legal problems such as complaints and reporting crimes or lost articles. The national tourism ministry, **Sectur** (☏078), has a toll-free number offering 24-hour telephone advice.

If you are the victim of a crime, your embassy or consulate, or Sectur or state tourist offices, can give advice. In some cases, there may be little to gain by going to the police, unless you need a statement to present to your insurance company. If you go to the police, take your passport and tourist permit, if you still have them. If you just want to report a theft for the purposes of an insurance claim, say you want to '*poner una acta de un robo*' (make a record of a robbery). This should make it clear that you merely want a piece of paper, and you should get it without too much trouble.

Maps

GeoCenter, Nelles, ITM and the AAA (American Automobile Association) all produce good country maps of Mexico that are suitable for travel planning and available internationally for between US$6 and US$15. ITM also publishes good 1:1,000,000 (1cm:10km) maps of many Mexican regions.

Tourist offices in Mexico provide free city, town and regional maps of varying quality. Bookstores and newsstands sell commercially published ones, including Guía Roji's *Por Las Carreteras de México* (M$200), a road atlas.

Inegi (Instituto Nacional de Estadística, Geografía e Informática; www.inegi.org.mx, in Spanish) Sells large-scale 1:50,000 and 1:250,000 topographical maps at its Centros de Comercialización in every Mexican state capital (listed on the website), subject to availability. Most cost M$50 to M$100.

Money

Mexico's currency is the peso, usually denoted by the 'M$' sign. Any prices quoted in US dollars will normally be written 'US$5' or '5 USD' to avoid misunderstanding. The peso is divided into 100 centavos. Coins come in denominations of 10, 20 and 50 centavos and one, two, five, 10 and 20 pesos. There are bills of 20, 50, 100, 200, 500 and 1000 pesos.

For information on costs and exchange rates, see p18.

The most convenient form of money in Mexico is a major international credit or debit card – preferably two cards. With these you can obtain cash easily from ATMs. Visa, MasterCard and American Express are accepted for payment by most airlines and car-rental companies, plus many upper midrange and top-end hotels, and some restaurants and stores. Occasionally there's a surcharge for paying by card, or a discount for paying cash. Buying by credit card normally gives you a similar exchange rate to ATM withdrawals. In both cases you'll normally have to pay your card issuer a foreign-exchange transaction fee of around 2.5%.

As a backup to cards, it's a good idea to take a little cash – best in US dollars, which are easily the most exchangeable foreign currency in Mexico. In tourist resorts and many Mexican cities along the US border, you can make some purchases in US dollars, though the exchange rate will probably not be in your favor. Many banks and *casas de cambio* (exchange houses) will also exchange euros, British pounds and Canadian dollars. Traveler's checks are another option, though they can be time-consuming to cash and some Mexican *casas de cambio* and banks will no longer accept them.

ATMs

ATMs (*caja permanente* or *cajero automático*) are plentiful in Mexico, and are the easiest source of cash. You can use major credit cards and some bank cards, such as those on the Maestro, Cirrus and Plus systems, to withdraw pesos from ATMs. The exchange rate you'll get is normally better than the 'tourist rate' for currency exchange at banks and *casas de cambio*, though that advantage may be negated by the M$25 to M$45 fee the ATM company charges and any foreign-transaction fees levied by your card company.

For maximum security, use ATMs during daylight hours and in secure indoor locations, not those in stand-alone booths or on the street.

Banks & Casas de Cambio

You can exchange cash at *casas de cambio* and some banks. *Casas de cambio* exist in just about every large town and in many smaller ones. They are quick and often open evenings or weekends, and usually offer similar exchange rates to banks. Banks go through more time-consuming procedures, and usually have shorter exchange hours (typically 9am to 4pm Monday to Friday and 9am to 1pm Saturday).

International Transfers

Should you need money wired to you in Mexico, an easy method is **Western Union** (www.westernunion.com). It's offered by thousands of bank branches and other businesses around Mexico, identified by black-and-yellow Western Union signs. Your sender pays the money online, by phone or at a Western Union branch, along with a fee, and gives the details on who is to receive it and where. When you pick it up, take photo identification. Western Union has offices worldwide.

US post offices (www.usps.com) offer reasonably cheap money transfers to branches of Bancomer bank in Mexico. The service is called SureMoney (Dinero-Seguro in Mexico).

Taxes

Mexico's *impuesto al valor agregado* (IVA, value-added tax) is levied at 16%. By law the tax must be included in virtually any price quoted to you, and should not be added afterward. Notices in stores and on restaurant menus often state *'IVA incluido.'*

Hotel rooms are also subject to the *impuesto sobre hospedaje* (ISH, lodging tax) of 2% or 3%, depending on which Mexican state they're in.

Tipping & Bargaining

Workers in the tourism and hospitality industries often depend on tips to supplement miserable basic wages. Normal tips:

Restaurants About 15%, unless service is included in the check.

Hotels From 5% to 10% of your room costs for the staff, especially if you stay a few days.

Taxis No tip expected unless some special, extra service is provided.

Airport & hotel porters From M$50 to M$100.

Gas-station & car-parking attendants Tip M$5 or M$10.

Room rates are pretty firm, though it can be worth asking if any discounts are available, especially if it's low season or you are going to stay a few nights. In markets bargaining is the rule. You should also bargain with drivers of unmetered taxis.

Photography

Normal courtesies apply: it's polite to ask before taking photos of people. Some indigenous people can be especially sensitive about this.

Lonely Planet's *Travel Photography* is a comprehensive, jargon-free guide to getting the best shots from your travels.

Post

An airmail letter or postcard weighing up to 20g costs M$11.50 to the US or Canada, M$13.50 to Europe or South America, and M$15 to the rest of the world. Mail to the US or Canada typically takes between four and 10 days to arrive. Mail to Europe averages one to two weeks.

If you're sending a package internationally from Mexico, be prepared to open it for customs inspection at the post office; it's better to take packing materials with you, or not seal it until you get there. For assured and speedy delivery, you can use one of the more expensive international courier services, such as **UPS** (www.ups.com), **FedEx** (www.fedex.com) or Mexico's **Estafeta** (www.estafeta.com). A 1kg package typically costs about M$550 to the US or Canada, or M$750 to Europe.

Public Holidays

On national holidays banks, post offices, government offices and many other offices and shops close throughout Mexico.

Año Nuevo (New Year's Day) January 1

Día de la Constitución (Constitution Day) February 5

Día de Nacimiento de Benito Juárez (anniversary of Benito Juárez's birth) March 21

Día del Trabajo (Labor Day) May 1

Día de la Independencia (Independence Day) September 16

Día de la Revolución (Revolution Day) November 20

Día de Navidad (Christmas Day) December 25

National holidays that fall on Saturday or Sunday are often switched to the nearest Friday or Monday.

In addition, many offices and businesses close on the following optional holidays:

Día de los Santos Reyes (Three Kings' Day, Epiphany) January 6

Día de la Bandera (Day of the National Flag) February 24

Viernes Santo (Good Friday) Two days before Easter Sunday; March or April

Cinco de Mayo (anniversary of Mexico's victory over the French at Puebla) May 5

Día de la Raza (commemoration of Columbus's

PRACTICALITIES

» Mexicans use the metric system for weights and measures.

» If buying DVDs, look for the numbered globe motif indicating world regions. Region 1 is the US and Canada; Europe and Japan are in region 2; Australia and New Zealand join Mexico in region 4.

» Mexico's only English-language daily newspaper (actually, Monday to Friday) is the *News* (www.thenews.com.mx). Distribution is very patchy outside Mexico City. The best and most independent-minded Spanish-language national newspapers include *Reforma* and the left-wing *La Jornada*.

» For links to all types of Mexican media, visit www.zonalatina.com or mexiconews.wikispaces.com.

» Mexican law does not allow smoking in indoor public spaces, except in specially designated smoking areas. It also requires at least 75% of a hotel's rooms to be non-smoking. However, enforcement is extremely patchy.

discovery of the New World) October 12

Día de Muertos (Day of the Dead) November 2

Día de Nuestra Señora de Guadalupe (Day of Our Lady of Guadalupe) December 12

Safe Travel

The news stories of Mexico's drug war are undeniably alarming, but the violence is almost exclusively an internal matter between the drug gangs, or between them and the Mexican security forces. Tourists and other people not involved in the drugs business have very rarely been victims, and then only through extremely bad luck. Additionally, the great majority of the violence takes place in a relatively small number of areas. At the time of writing the worst-hit states were the northern ones of Chihuahua (where Ciudad Juárez has seen the highest number of drugs-related killings in Mexico), Sinaloa, Nuevo León, Durango and Tamaulipas, and, further south, Guerrero (where Acapulco has been badly hit) and Jalisco.

Within each of these states, there are specific areas where most of the violence occurs. Two of Mexico's most visited regions, the Yucatán Peninsula and Baja California Sur, have seen minimal drug-related violence, as have other attractive areas such as Chiapas, Guanajuato and Querétaro.

You can obtain information on drug-violence blackspots from government foreign affairs departments (see boxed text, p857) and from websites of embassies and consulates in Mexico. Such advice is not always kept fully up to date, however, and the drugs war is a changing phenomenon that can break out in new areas while previously badly-hit areas become quieter. So it's a good idea to keep an eye on the media and ask local advice as you travel.

Drug-related violence aside, Mexico's crime rate has fallen considerably over the past 10 to 15 years. Mexico City has a significantly lower murder rate than Miami, Chicago or Washington DC.

Mexico's main visitor destinations are by and large pretty safe places, and your main security precautions should just be those you would take in any unfamiliar place. Enjoy yourself along the coasts, but beware of undertows and riptides on ocean beaches, and don't leave your belongings unattended while you swim.

Theft & Robbery

Pocket-picking and purse- or bag-snatching are risks on crowded buses and subway trains, at bus stops, bus stations, airports, markets and in packed streets and plazas, especially in large cities. Pickpockets often work in teams, crowding their victims and trying to distract them, for example by grabbing hold of your bag or camera while an accomplice picks your pocket. If any valuables you are carrying are underneath your clothing, the chances of losing them are greatly reduced.

Mugging is less common than pocket-picking and purse-snatching, but more serious: these robbers may force you to remove your money belt, watch, rings etc. Do not resist, as resistance may be met with violence, and assailants may be armed.

The following precautions will minimize risks:

» Avoid places where there are few other people, such as empty streets and empty metro cars at night, little-used pedestrian underpasses and isolated beaches.

» Use taxis instead of walking in potentially dodgy areas. In Mexico City, make sure you take the right kind of cab (see p130).

» Be alert to the people around you.

» Leave all valuables in a safe at your accommodations unless you have immediate need of them. If no safe is available, divide valuables into different stashes secreted in your room or a hostel locker.

» Carry just enough cash for your immediate needs

in a pocket. Avoid bulging pockets. If you have to carry valuables, use a money belt, shoulder wallet or pouch *underneath* your clothing.

» Don't keep cash, credit cards, purses, cameras and electronic gadgets in open view any longer than necessary. At ticket counters in bus stations and airports, keep your bag between your feet.

» Go easy on alcohol – drunkenness makes you an easier victim.

» Use ATMs in secure indoor locations, preferably during daylight.

If you do become a crime victim, report the incident to a tourist office, the police or your country's nearest consulate, which should be able to offer useful advice.

ON THE ROAD
When driving, especially in the north of the country where there have been a number of carjackings and illegal roadblocks, stick to major highways (preferably toll highways) wherever possible, and drive only by day. Drive through cities with your doors locked and windows rolled up, and if you do become a victim, don't resist. If you're traveling by bus, take 1st-class or deluxe buses: these normally use toll highways, where they exist.

Telephone
Call Offices
Locutorios & *casetas de teléfono* are call offices where an on-the-spot operator connects your call and you talk inside a booth. Costs are often lower than for public card phones.

Cell Phones
Roaming with your own cell phone from home in Mexico is possible if you have a GSM or 3G phone, but can be extremely expensive unless you organize a travel plan with your phone company. Roaming Zone (www.roamingzone.com) is a useful source on roaming arrangements.

An alternative to roaming is to put a Mexican SIM card ('chip') into your phone, but your phone needs to be unlocked for international use. If it isn't already unlocked, many Mexican cell-phone stores can unlock it for M$200 to M$300.

For the same kind of money you can buy a new Mexican cell phone (*teléfono celular*) with some call credit included. Mexico has three main cell-phone companies – **Telcel** (www.telcel.com), **IUSACell** (www.iusacell.com.mx, in Spanish) and **Movistar** (www.movistar.com.mx, in Spanish). Telcel has the most widespread network, with ubiquitous sales outlets and coverage almost everywhere there are people. Telcel top-up cards are widely available from newsstands and mini-marts. Topping up in larger amounts (M$200-plus) often brings extra free credit.

Like Mexican landlines, every Mexican SIM card has an area code (usually the code of the city it was bought in). The area code and the phone's number total 10 digits.

» From cell phone to cell phone, just dial the 10-digit number.

» From cell phone to landline, dial the landline's area code and number (also a total of 10 digits).

» From landline to cell phone, dial 044 before the 10 digits if the cell phone's area code is the same as the area code you are dialing from, or 045 if the cell phone has a different area code.

» From another country to a Mexican cell phone, dial your international access code, then the Mexican country code (52), then 1, then the 10-digit number.

Credit of M$100 on a Mexican cell phone or SIM card normally gives you about 20 minutes of calls within the card's area code (on these calls, the caller pays the full cost), but once you are outside that area code, it's more expensive to make calls and you'll also pay to receive calls – as do people you call.

Collect Calls
A *llamada por cobrar* (collect call) can cost the receiving party much more than if they call you, so you may prefer to arrange for the other party to call you. You can make collect calls from public card phones without a card. Call an operator on 020 for domestic calls, or 090 for international calls.

Some call offices and hotels will make collect calls for you, but they usually charge for the service.

Landlines
Mexican landlines (*teléfonos fijos*) have two- or three-digit area codes, which are listed

under city and town headings throughout this book.

» From a landline to another landline in the same town, just dial the local number (seven or eight digits).

» From a landline to a landline in a different Mexican town, dial the long-distance prefix ✆01, then the area code, then the local number.

» To make an international call, dial the international prefix ✆00, then the country code (✆1 for the US or Canada, ✆44 for the UK, etc), area code and local number.

» To call a Mexican landline from another country, dial your international access code, then the Mexico country code ✆52, then the area code and number.

Long-Distance Discount Cards

Available from kiosks and some mini-marts, usually in denominations of M$100, M$200 and M$500, *tarjetas telefónicas de descuento* (discount phone cards) offer substantial savings on long-distance and international calls from landlines. You can use them from most public card phones.

Operator & Toll-Free Numbers

Domestic operator ✆020
Emergency ✆066
International operator ✆090
Mexican directory information ✆040
Mexican toll-free numbers ✆800 followed by seven digits; always require the ✆01 long-distance prefix

Public Card Phones

These are common in towns and cities, and you'll usually find some at airports and bus stations. The most abundant are those of the country's main phone company, **Telmex** (www.telmex.com). To use a Telmex card phone you

need a phone card known as a *tarjeta Ladatel*. These are sold at kiosks and shops everywhere in denominations of M$30, M$50 and M$100. You insert the card into the phone while you make the call. Calls cost M$3 for unlimited time for local calls (M$2.76 per minute to cell phones); M$4 per minute long distance within Mexico (M$5.78 to cells); M$5 per minute to the US (except Alaska and Hawaii), Canada and Central America; and M$10 per minute to anywhere else.

VoIP

Thanks to widespread wi-fi, Voice over Internet Protocol services such as **Skype** (www.skype.com) are a very economical option for those with suitable hardware. You can also use Skype at internet cafes with high-speed internet (that's most of them).

Time

Time Zones

Hora del Centro The same as CST (US Central Time; GMT minus six hours in winter, and GMT minus five hours during daylight saving), this time zone applies to most of Mexico.

Hora de las Montañas The same as MST (US Mountain Time; GMT minus seven hours in winter, GMT minus six hours during daylight saving), this time zone applies to five northern and western states – Chihuahua, Nayarit, Sinaloa, Sonora and Baja California Sur.

Hora del Pacífico The same as PST (US Pacific Time; GMT minus eight hours in winter, GMT minus seven hours during daylight saving), this time zone applies to Baja California (Norte).

Daylight Saving

Daylight saving time ('*horario de verano*,' summer

time) in nearly all of Mexico runs from the first Sunday in April to the last Sunday in October. Clocks go forward one hour in April and back one hour in October. Mexico's dates are slightly different from those of many other countries including the US, Canada and European countries. Exceptions to the general rule:

» The northwestern state of Sonora ignores daylight saving (like its US neighbor Arizona), so remains on MST all year.

» Daylight saving is also ignored by a few remote rural zones elsewhere.

» Ten cities on or near the US border – Ciudad Acuña, Ciudad Anahuac, Ciudad Juárez, Matamoros, Mexicali, Nuevo Laredo, Ojinaga, Piedras Negras, Reynosa and Tijuana – change their clocks on the second Sunday in March and the first Sunday in November to synchronize with the US.

Tourist Information

Just about every town of interest to tourists in Mexico has a state or municipal tourist office. These are generally helpful with maps, brochures and questions, and usually some staff members speak English.

You can call the Mexico City office of the national tourism secretariat **Sectur** (✆078, 800-006-88-39, from the US & Canada 866-640-0597, from Europe 00-52-55-5089-7500; www.visitmexico.com) at any time – 24 hours a day, seven days a week – for information or help in English or Spanish. The website of the **Mexico Tourism Board** (www.cptm.com.mx) is also useful. You'll find links to tourism websites of each Mexican state at www.sectur.gob.mx.

Travelers with Disabilities

Mexico is not yet very disabled-friendly, though a gradually growing number of hotels, restaurants, public buildings and archaeological sites provide wheelchair access. Sidewalks with wheelchair ramps are uncommon. Mobility is easiest in major tourist resorts and the more expensive hotels. Bus transportation can be difficult; flying or taking a taxi is easier. The absence of formal facilities is partly compensated by Mexicans' helpful attitudes, and special arrangements are gladly improvised. The following websites have useful information for disabled travelers:

Access-able Travel Source (www.access-able. com)

Disability Travel and Recreation Resources (www. makoa.org/travel.htm)

Mobility International USA (www.miusa.org)

MossRehab ResourceNet (www.mossresourcenet.org)

Visas

Every tourist must have a Mexican-government tourist permit, which is easy to obtain on arrival. Some nationalities also need to obtain visas. Citizens of the US, Canada, EU countries, Argentina, Australia, New Zealand, Israel, Japan, Norway and Switzerland are among those who do not need visas to enter Mexico as tourists. Brazilians, Chinese, Indians, Russians and South Africans are among those who do need a visa. But Mexican visas are not required for people of any nationality who hold a valid visa for the USA, or are arriving in Mexico on a flight from the USA.

If the purpose of your visit is to work (even as a volunteer), report, study or participate in humanitarian aid or human-rights observation, you may well need a visa whatever your nationality. Visa procedures might take a few weeks and you may be required to apply in your country of residence or citizenship.

US citizens traveling by land or sea can enter Mexico and return to the US with a passport card, but if traveling by air will need a passport. Non-US citizens passing (even in transit) through the US on the way to or from Mexico should check well in advance on the US's complicated visa rules. Consult a US consulate or the **US State Department** (travel. state.gov) or **Customs and Border Protection** (www. cbp.gov) websites.

The regulations sometimes change: it's wise to confirm them with a Mexican embassy or consulate. The websites of some Mexican consulates, including the **London consulate** (consul mex.sre.gob.mx/reinounido) and **Washington consulate** (consulmex.sre.gob.mx/wash ington) give useful information on visas and similar matters. The rules are also summarized on the website of Mexico's **Instituto Nacional de Migración** (INM, National Migration Institute; www.inm.gob.mx).

Tourist Permit & Fee

The Mexican tourist permit (tourist card; officially the *forma migratoria múltiple* or FMM) is a brief paper document that you must fill out and get stamped by Mexican immigration when you enter Mexico, and keep till you leave. It's available at official border crossings, international airports and ports, and often from airlines, travel agencies and Mexican consulates. At land borders you won't usually be given one automatically – you have to ask for it.

One section on the back of the card covers the length of your stay in Mexico, and this section is filled out by the immigration officer. The maximum is 180 days, but immigration officers may sometimes put a lower number (even as little as 15 or 30 days) unless you tell them specifically what you need.

The fee for the tourist permit, called the *derecho para no inmigrante* (DNI, nonimmigrant fee), is M$294 (subject to fluctuation with exchange rates), but it's free for people entering by land who stay less than seven days. If you enter Mexico by air, the fee is included in your airfare. If you enter by Mexico land, you must pay the fee at a bank in Mexico at any time before you reenter the border zone to leave Mexico (or before you check in at an airport to fly out of Mexico). The border zone is the territory between the border itself and the INM's control points on highways leading into the Mexican interior (usually 20km to 30km from the border).

Most Mexican border posts have on-the-spot bank offices where you can pay the DNI fee immediately on arrival in Mexico – it's a good idea to do this to avoid having to find a bank later. Your tourist permit will be stamped to prove that you have paid.

Look after your tourist permit because it may be checked when you leave the country. You can be fined for not having it.

Tourist permits (and fees) are not necessary for visits shorter than 72 hours within the border zones.

EXTENSIONS & LOST PERMITS

If the number of days given on your tourist permit is fewer than 180, its validity may be extended, one or more times, up to this maximum. To get a permit extended, you have to apply to the INM, which has offices in many towns and cities: they're listed on the **INM website** (www.inm.gob.mx) under 'Contact Us.' The procedure costs around M$200 and should only take half an hour or so. You'll need your passport, tourist permit, photocopies of them and, at some offices, evidence of 'sufficient funds.' A major credit card is usually OK for the latter. Most INM offices will not extend a permit until a few days before it is due to expire.

If you lose your permit, contact your nearest tourist office, or the **Sectur tourist office** (✆078) in Mexico City, or your embassy or consulate. Any of these should be able to give you an official note to take to your local INM office, which will issue a replacement for about M$450.

Volunteering

A great way to engage with Mexican communities and contribute something other than tourist dollars is to do some volunteer work. Many organizations can use your services for periods from a few hours to a year or more. Work ranges from protecting sea turtles to helping disadvantaged children. Some organizations are looking for people with relevant experience and/or Spanish language skills; others can use almost any willing hand. Longer-term volunteers will often be offered some kind of accommodations. If you arrange volunteer work in Mexico through an organization that specializes in bringing people from other countries, you will often have to pay a significant sum of money for the opportunity. If you make direct contact with a project on the ground in Mexico, your costs are likely to be lower, though you may still be asked to contribute to running costs.

Many language schools (p38) offer part-time local volunteering opportunities to complement the classes you take.

Volunteer Directories

Go Abroad (www.goabroad. com)

Go Overseas (www.go overseas.com)

Go Voluntouring (www. govoluntouring.com)

Idealist.org (www.idealist. org)

The Mexico Report (themexicoreport.com/non -profits-in-mexico)

Transitions Abroad (www. transitionsabroad.com)

Mexico-Based Programs

SOCIAL PROGRAMS

Casa Hogar Hijos de la Luna (www.hijosdelaluna-en. org) Hostel for children of single mothers in Oaxaca (p421).

Centro de Esperanza Infantil (www.oaxacastreet childrengrassroots.org) Center for street kids in Oaxaca (see p421).

En Vía (www.envia.org) Oaxaca-based nonprofit organization providing microfinance loans to help village women develop small businesses (p423).

Junax (www.junax.org.mx) Work with indigenous communities in Chiapas; volunteers must speak Spanish.

Nataté (www.natate.org) Projects in community-based construction, education and the environment, in Chiapas and elsewhere.

Piña Palmera (www. pinapalmera.org) Work with physically and intellectually disabled people at Zipolite on the Oaxaca coast (p463).

ENVIRONMENTAL PROGRAMS

Centro Ecológico Akumal (www.ceakumal.org) Environmental work including turtle protection (see p277).

Grupo Ecologista Vida Milenaria (www.vidamile naria.org.mx) Excellent turtle project at Tecolutla (p233).

Pronatura (www.pronatura. org.mx) This environmental NGO seeks volunteers to work at various projects around the country.

Sitio Ramsar Playa de Colola Turtle conservation on Michoacán coast (p532).

Xcacel-Xcacelito (www. florafaunaycultura.org) Turtle conservation on the Caribbean coast (p269).

Organizations Based Outside Mexico

Global Vision International (www.gviusa.com)

Los Médicos Voladores (www.flyingdocs.org)

Projects Abroad (www. projects-abroad.org)

Proworld (proworldvolun teers.org)

Women Travelers

Women usually have a great time in Mexico whether traveling with companions or solo. Gender equality has come a long way, and Mexicans are generally a very polite people, but lone women may still be subject to some whistles, loud comments and attempts to chat them up.

Don't put yourself in peril by doing things that Mexican women would not do, such as drinking alone in a cantina, hitchhiking, walking alone through empty streets at night, or going alone to isolated places. Keep a clear head. Excessive alcohol will make you vulnerable. For moral support, head for accommodations such as hostels and popular hotels where you're likely to meet other travelers, or join group excursions and activities.

On the streets of cities and towns and local transportation you'll notice that women cover up and don't display too much leg, midriff or even arm. This also makes it easier to keep valuables out of sight.

Transportation

GETTING THERE & AWAY

As well as flying in, you can enter Mexico by car or bus from the USA, Guatemala or Belize. Flights, tours and rail tickets can be booked online at www.lonelyplanet.com/bookings.

Entering the Country

US citizens traveling by land or sea can enter Mexico and return to the US with a passport card, but if traveling by air will need a passport. Citizens of other countries need their passport to enter Mexico. Some nationalities also need a visa (see p859).

Air

More than 30 Mexican airports receive direct flights from the USA (some from several US cities, some from just a couple), and some of them also have direct flights from Canada. Mexico City, Cancún, Guadalajara and Monterrey are Mexico's busiest international airports. Puerto Vallarta also has a good number of direct services from the US and Canada. Toluca, 60km west of Mexico City, is virtually a second airport for the capital and has numerous direct links with the US, including some on low-cost airlines. Only Mexico City and Cancún receive direct scheduled flights from European, Caribbean and Central and South American countries.

Mexico's flag airline is **Aeroméxico** (www.aeromexico.com), formerly government-controlled but now privately owned. Its safety record is comparable to major US and European airlines. The country's other formerly state-owned airline, Mexicana, folded in 2010.

Low-cost airlines providing international flights to Mexico include the USA's **AirTran Airways** (www.airtran.com), **Southwest Airlines** (www.southwest.com), **Spirit Airlines** (www.spiritair.com) and **Sun Country Airlines** (www.suncountry.com), Canada's **WestJet** (www.westjet.com), and Mexico's **Interjet** (www.interjet.com.mx), **VivaAerobus** (www.vivaaerobus.com) and **Volaris** (www.volaris.mx). The three Mexican airlines all fly to several US cities. Interjet also flies to Havana, Cuba, and Guatemala City.

Land

Border Crossings

There are over 40 official crossing points on the US-Mexico border (see the boxed text, p740), about 10 between Guatemala and Mexico, and two between Belize and Mexico. Mexican border towns are not generally places to linger in.

CLIMATE CHANGE & TRAVEL

Every form of transport that relies on carbon-based fuel generates CO_2, the main cause of human-induced climate change. Modern travel is dependent on airplanes, which might use less fuel per kilometer per person than most cars but travel much greater distances. The altitude at which aircraft emit gases (including CO_2) and particles also contributes to their climate change impact. Many websites offer 'carbon calculators' that allow people to estimate the carbon emissions generated by their journey and, for those who wish to do so, to offset the impact of the greenhouse gases emitted with contributions to portfolios of climate-friendly initiatives throughout the world. Lonely Planet offsets the carbon footprint of all staff and author travel.

Car & Motorcycle

The rules for taking a vehicle into Mexico change from time to time. You can check with a Mexican consulate, **Sanborn's** (www.sanborns insurance.com) or, in the US and Canada, the free **Mexican tourist information number** (☎866-640-0597).

You may not find gasoline or mechanics available at all Mexico's road borders: before crossing the border, make sure you have enough fuel to get to the next sizable town inside Mexico. For information on driving and motorcycling once you're inside Mexico, see p865.

VEHICLE PERMIT

You will need a *permiso de importación temporal de vehículos* (temporary vehicle import permit) if you want to take a vehicle into Mexico beyond the border zone that extends 20km to 30km into Mexico along the US frontier and up to 70km from the Guatemalan and Belizean frontiers. The only exceptions to this are the Baja California peninsula, and Sonora state as far south as Guaymas, but you will need a permit if you embark a vehicle at Pichilingue (La Paz) in Baja California, on a ferry to 'mainland' Mexico. See p740 for information on the Sonora regulations.

The permits are issued by offices at border crossings or (in some cases) at posts a few kilometers into Mexico, and also at Ensenada port and Pichilingue ferry terminal in Baja California. Details of all these locations are given in Spanish on the website of **Banjército** (www.banjercito. com.mx), the bank that deals with vehicle-import procedures, – click on 'Red de Módulos IITV.' You can also apply for the permit online at www.banjercito.com.mx ('Application for Temporary Import Permit for Vehicles'), in which case it will be delivered to you by courier. You can pre-register online, which speeds up the process of obtaining the permit on arrival in Mexico. The fee for the permit is US$51 (including IVA tax).

The person importing the vehicle will need to carry the original and one or two photocopies of each of the following documents, which as a rule must all be in his/her own name (except that you can bring in your spouse's, parent's or child's vehicle if you can show a marriage or birth certificate proving your relationship):

» tourist permit (FMM): at the border go to *migración* before you process your vehicle permit
» certificate of title or registration certificate for the vehicle (note that you should have both of these if you plan to drive through Mexico into either Guatemala or Belize)
» a Visa or MasterCard credit or debit card, or a cash deposit of between US$200 and US$400 (depending on how old the car is); your card details or deposit serve as a guarantee that you'll take the car out of Mexico before your FMT expires
» proof of citizenship or residency, such as a passport, birth certificate or voter's registration card
» driver's license
» if the vehicle is not fully paid for, a credit contract, or invoice letter not more than three months old, from the financing institution
» for a leased or rented vehicle, the contract, in the name of the person importing the vehicle, and a letter from the rental company authorizing you to take it out of the US
» for a company car, proof of employment by the company as well as proof of the company's ownership of the vehicle

With the permit you will be given a hologram sticker for you to display on your windshield.

When you leave Mexico, you must have the import permit canceled by the Mexican authorities. An official may do this as you enter the border zone, usually 20km to 30km before the border itself. If not, you'll have to find the right official at the border crossing. If you leave Mexico without having the permit canceled, the authorities may assume you've left the vehicle in the country illegally and decide to keep your deposit, charge a fine to your credit card, or deny you permission to bring a vehicle into the country next time.

Only the owner may take the vehicle out of Mexico. If the vehicle is wrecked completely, contact your consulate or a Mexican customs office to make arrangements for you to leave without it.

INSURANCE

It is essential to have Mexican liability insurance. If you are involved in an accident in Mexico, you can be jailed and have your vehicle impounded while responsibility is assessed. If you are to blame for an accident causing injury or death, you may be detained until you guarantee restitution to the victims and

DEPARTURE TAX

The airport departure tax TUA (Tarifa de Uso de Aeropuerto) is almost always included in your ticket cost, but if it isn't, you must pay in cash during airport check-in. It varies from airport to airport and costs between US$18 to US$29 for international flights and a little less for domestic flights. This tax is separate from the fee for your tourist permit (p859), which is also included in airfares.

payment of any fines. This could take weeks or months. Adequate Mexican insurance coverage is the only real protection: it is regarded as a guarantee that restitution will be paid, and will expedite release of the driver.

Mexican law recognizes only Mexican motor insurance (seguro), so a US or Canadian policy, even if it provides coverage, is not acceptable to Mexican officialdom. You can buy Mexican motor insurance online through the long-established **Sanborn's** (www.sanborns insurance.com) and other companies. Mexican insurance is also sold in border towns in the US and at some border points. At the busiest border crossings there are insurance offices open 24 hours a day. Some deals are better than others.

Short-term insurance is about US$15 a day for full coverage on a car worth under US$10,000; for periods longer than two weeks, it's often cheaper to get a semi-annual or annual policy. Liability-only insurance costs around half the full coverage cost.

Belize

Frequent buses run between Chetumal and Belize City (M$150, three to four hours), via the Belizean towns of Corozal (M$35 to M$40, one hour) and Orange Walk (M$35 to M$50, 2¼ hours). See p292 for further information.

Guatemala

The road borders at La Mesilla/Ciudad Cuauhtémoc, Ciudad Tecún Umán/Ciudad Hidalgo and El Carmen/Talismán are all linked to Guatemala City, and nearby cities within Guatemala and Mexico, by plentiful buses and/or combis.

These companies run a few daily buses the whole way between Guatemala City and Tapachula, Chiapas (five to six hours):

Línea Dorada (www.linea dorada.com.gt, in Spanish; fare M$220)

Tica Bus (www.ticabus.com; fare M$220)

Trans Galgos Inter (www.transgalgosinter.com.gt, in Spanish; fare M$280)

Between Flores and Chetumal, Línea Dorada runs one daily bus each way (M$400 or Q225, eight hours), via Belize City.

For the Río Usumacinta route between Flores and Palenque, Mexico, several daily 2nd-class buses run from Flores to Bethel (4½ hours); from there it's a 40-minute boat trip to Frontera Corozal, Mexico (M$75 to M$400 per person depending on numbers). Vans run between Frontera Corozal and Palenque (M$100, 2½ to three hours). See p388 for information on taking this route in the opposite direction.

Travel agencies in Palenque and Flores offer bus/boat/bus packages between the two places for M$300 to M$350, but if you're traveling this route it's well worth taking the time to visit the outstanding Maya ruins at Yaxchilán, near Frontera Corozal.

Travelers with their own vehicles can travel by road between Flores and Tenosique, Tabasco, via the border at El Ceibo. There are also vans between Flores and the border, and vans, buses and taxis between El Ceibo and Tenosique – about a six-hour trip all up.

USA

Cross-border bus services link many US and Mexican cities. On most trips you will transfer between a US and a Mexican bus on the US or Mexican side of the border, although you can usually buy a ticket right through to your final destination thanks to affiliations between different bus lines.

Autobuses Americanos (www.autobusesamericanos.com.mx, in Spanish) From Chicago and cities across the southern half of the USA

to northeast, central north and central Mexico.

Greyhound (www.greyhound.com) and **Crucero** (www.crucero-usa.com) From California, Arizona and Texas to border cities, with onward transfers into northwest Mexico. The Greyhound website is good for route planning, as it gives full detail on transfers, companies used and journey times.

Ómnibus Mexicanos (www.omnibusmexicanos.com.mx) From Texas and the southeastern USA to northeast, central north and central Mexico.

Transportes Baldomero Corral (www.tbcconexion phoenix.com) Arizona to northwest Mexico.

Transportes Nena's (www.transportesnenas.com) Shuttle-van service between Phoenix and Puerto Peñasco.

Tufesa (www.tufesa.com.mx) From many cities in the US southwest and California to northwest Mexico, Mazatlán and Guadalajara.

Turimex Internacional (www.gruposenda.com, in Spanish) From Texas and southeastern USA to northeast, central north and central Mexico.

ROUTE	FARE (US$)	DURATION (HR)
Dallas–Monterrey	53	12
Houston–Mexico City	128	25
LA–Guadalajara	174	39-43
Phoenix–Guaymas	68	10

Most routes are covered by several buses daily. Above are some typical fares and journey times.

You can (often as quickly) go to the border on one bus (or train – see www.amtrak.com), cross it on foot or by local bus, then catch an onward bus on the other side. Greyhound serves many US border cities.

MEXICAN DOMESTIC AIRLINES

AIRLINE	WEBSITE	AREAS SERVED
Aéreo Calafia	www.aereocalafia.com.mx	Baja California & northwest
Aeromar	www.aeromar.com.mx	central Mexico, west, northeast, Gulf coast, Oaxaca coast
Aeroméxico	www.aeromexico.com	over 40 cities nationwide
Aeroméxico Connect (Aerolitoral)	www.aeromexico.com	40 cities nationwide
Aeropacífico	www.aeropacifico.com, in Spanish	northwest
Interjet	www.interjet.com.mx	Toluca, Mexico City & 22 other cities nationwide
Magnicharters	www.magnicharters.com.mx, in Spanish	Mexico City, Guadalajara, Mérida, coastal resorts
VivaAerobus	www.vivaaerobus.com	26 cities nationwide
Volaris	www.volaris.mx	24 cities nationwide

Sea

Daily boats sail between San Pedro, Belize, and Chetumal (one way/return US$35/55).

GETTING AROUND

Air

Over 60 Mexican cities have airports with scheduled passenger services. Depending on the fare you get, flying can be good value on longer journeys, especially considering the long bus trip that is probably the alternative.

Aeroméxico and its subsidiary Aeroméxico Connect have the biggest networks, but the low-cost airlines Interjet, VivaAerobus and Volaris also serve many cities. VivaAerobus offer some particularly low fares but doesn't have the best reputation for dependability.

Bicycle

Cycling is not a common way to tour Mexico. The size of the country, poor road surfaces, careless motorists and other road hazards (see p866) are deterrents. If you're up for the challenge, take the mountainous topography and hot climate into account when planning your route. All cities have bicycle stores: a decent mountain bike suitable for a few weeks' touring costs around M$5000.

Consider the bring-your-own-bike tours of southern Mexico offered by the fun and friendly ¡El Tour (www.bikemexico.com).

Boat

Vehicle and passenger ferries connecting Baja California with the Mexican mainland sail between Santa Rosalía and Guaymas; La Paz and Mazatlán; and La Paz and Topolobampo. One-way passenger seat fares are from M$790 to M$978 depending on the route; a car up to 5m in length costs between M$1928 and M$3200.

Bus

Mexico has a good road and bus network, and comfortable, frequent, reasonably priced bus services connect all cities. Most cities and towns have one main bus terminal where all long-distance buses arrive and depart. It may be called the Terminal de Autobuses, Central de Autobuses, Central Camionera or simply La Central (not to be confused with el centro, the city center!).

Companies

Many of Mexico's major bus companies belong to large groups that dominate bus transportation in different parts of the country. Their websites have schedule information.

Grupo ADO (www.ado.com.mx, in Spanish) Connects Mexico City and the east, south and southeast of the country; companies include ADO Plátino (deluxe), ADO GL (deluxe/1st class) and ADO and OCC (1st class).

Grupo Estrella Blanca (www.estrellablanca.com.mx, in Spanish) Focuses on Mexico City and the center, north and west of Mexico; includes Futura Plus (deluxe), and Futura, Elite, Oriente and Transportes Chihuahuenses (1st class).

Grupo Flecha Amarilla Includes executive-class

PRACTICAL TIPS

Baggage is safe if stowed in the bus' baggage hold: get a receipt for it when you hand it over. Keep your most valuable documents (passport, money etc) in the cabin with you.

Air-conditioned buses can get cold, so wear long pants or skirt and take a sweater or jacket and maybe a blanket on board. Eyepads can be handy if you don't want to watch videos the entire trip!

ETN (www.etn.com.mx, in Spanish) and **Turistar** (www.turistar.com.mx, in Spanish), and 1st-class **Primera Plus** (www.primeraplus.com.mx), **TAP** (www.com.mx, in Spanish), **Pullman de Morelos** (www.pullman.com.mx) and **Ómnibus de México** (www.odm.com.mx, in Spanish), covering most of the country except the southeast and Baja California.

Classes

Deluxe & Executive *De lujo* services, and the even more comfortable *ejecutivo* (executive) buses, run mainly on the busier intercity routes. They are swift, modern and comfortable, with reclining seats, plenty of legroom, air-conditioning, movies on video screens, few or no stops, toilets on board, and sometimes drinks or snacks. They use toll roads wherever available.

1st Class *Primera (1a) clase* buses have a comfortable numbered seat for each passenger. All sizable towns are served by 1st-class buses. Standards of comfort are adequate at the very least. The buses have air-conditioning and a toilet and they stop infrequently. They show movies on video on TV screens. They also use toll roads where possible.

2nd Class *Segunda (2a) clase* or 'económico' buses serve small towns and villages, and provide cheaper, slower travel on some intercity routes. A few are almost as quick, comfortable and direct as 1st-class buses. Others are old, slow and shabby. These buses tend to take non-toll roads and will stop anywhere to pick up passengers: if you board midroute you might make some of the trip standing. In remoter areas, they are often the only buses available.

Costs

First-class buses typically cost around M$60 to M$70 per hour of travel (70km to 80km). Deluxe buses cost about 10% or 20% more than 1st class; executive services can be as much as 50% more. Second-class buses cost about 20% less than 1st class.

Reservations

For 1st-class, deluxe and executive buses, you buy your ticket in the bus station before the trip. For trips of up to four or five hours on routes with frequent service, you can usually just go to the bus terminal, buy a ticket and head out without much delay. For longer trips, or routes with infrequent service, or for any trip at busy holiday times, it's best to buy a ticket a day or more in advance. Deluxe and 1st-class bus companies have computerized ticket systems that allow you to select your seat when you buy your ticket. Try to avoid the back of the bus, which is where the toilets are and also tends to give a bumpier ride.

Boletotal (boletotal.mx, in Spanish) provides schedule information and online reservations for Grupo ADO bus companies. It also has dozens of ticket offices in around 20 cities.

Many 2nd-class services have no ticket office; you just pay your fare to the conductor.

Car & Motorcycle

Driving in Mexico is not as easy as it is north of the border, and rentals are more

---

HOW MANY STOPS?

It's useful to understand the difference between the types of bus service on offer:

» **Sin escalas** Nonstop

» **Directo** Very few stops

» **Semi-directo** A few more stops than *directo*

» **Ordinario** Stops wherever passengers want to get on or off the bus; deluxe and 1st-class buses are never *ordinario*

» **Express** Nonstop on short to medium-length trips; very few stops on long trips

» **Local** Bus that starts its journey at the bus station you're in and usually leaves on time; *local* service is preferable to *de paso*

» **De paso** Bus that started its journey somewhere else; you may have to wait until it arrives before any tickets are sold, and if it's full you have to wait for the next one

» **Vía corta** Short route

» **Vía cuota** By toll road

» **Viaje redondo** Round trip

expensive, but having a vehicle gives you a whole lot of flexibility and freedom.

Bringing Your Own Vehicle

Bringing a car to Mexico is most useful for travelers who have plenty of time; like independence; have surfboards, diving equipment or other cumbersome luggage; and/or will be traveling with at least one companion.

Drivers should know at least a little Spanish and have basic mechanical knowledge, reserves of patience and access to extra cash for emergencies on the road. Good makes of car to take to Mexico include Volkswagen, Nissan, General Motors (Chevrolet, Opel) and Ford, which have dealers in most big towns. A sedan with a trunk (boot) provides safer storage than a station wagon or hatchback.

Mexican mechanics are resourceful, and most repairs can be done quickly and inexpensively, but it still pays to take as many spare parts as you can manage (spare fuel filters are very useful). Tires (including spare), shock absorbers and suspension should be in good condition. For security, have something to immobilize the steering wheel, and consider getting a kill switch installed.

Motorcycling in Mexico is not for the fainthearted. Roads and traffic can be rough, and parts and mechanics hard to come by. The parts you'll most easily find will be for Kawasaki, Honda and Suzuki bikes.

See p862 for important information on the paperwork for bringing a vehicle into Mexico.

Driver's License

To drive a motor vehicle in Mexico, you need a valid driver's license from your home country.

Fuel

All *gasolina* (gasoline) and diesel fuel in Mexico is sold by the government's monopoly, Pemex (Petróleos Mexicanos). Most towns, even small ones, have a Pemex station, and the stations are pretty common on most major roads. In remote areas, fill up whenever you can. Gasoline is all *sin plomo* (unleaded). There are two varieties:

Magna Sin (87 octane) Roughly equivalent to US regular unleaded, costing about M$9.50 per liter (US$2.60 per US gallon).

Premium (91 octane and lower in sulfur content) Roughly equivalent to US super unleaded, costing about M$10.50.

Diesel fuel is widely available at around M$10 per liter. Regular Mexican diesel has a higher sulfur content than US diesel, but a *bajo azufre* (low sulfur) variety has started to become available in Mexico City and some nearby areas. Gas stations have pump attendants (who appreciate a tip of around M$5).

Maps

Mexican signposting can be poor, and decent road maps are extremely useful. A Mexican road atlas such as Guía Roji's *Por Las Carreteras de México* (M$200) is a good investment. It's sold at bookstores and some newsstands in Mexico, and is available from online booksellers for a little more. A new edition is published annually.

Rental

Auto rental in Mexico is expensive by US or European standards but is not hard to organize. Many major international rental firms have offices throughout the country.

Renters must provide a valid driver's license (your home license is OK), passport and major credit card, and are usually required to be at least 21 (sometimes 25, or if you're aged 21 to 24 you may have to pay a surcharge). Read the small print of the rental agreement. In addition to the basic rental rate, there will be tax and insurance costs. Comprehensive insurance can more than double the basic cost quoted in some online bookings: you'll usually have the option of taking liability-only insurance at a lower rate. Ask exactly what the insurance options cover: theft and damage insurance may only cover a percentage of costs, or the insurance might not be valid for travel on rough country tracks. It's best to have plenty of liability coverage.

In most places the cheapest car available costs around M$500 a day including unlimited kilometers, comprehensive insurance and tax. If you rent by the week or month, per-day cost can come down by 20% to 40%. The extra charge for drop-off in another city, when available, is usually about M$4 per kilometer.

Motorbikes or scooters can be rented in a few tourist centers. You're usually required to have a driver's license and a credit card. Look carefully into insurance arrangements here: some renters do not offer any insurance at all. Keep in mind that a locally acquired motorcycle license is not valid under some travel-insurance policies.

Road Conditions & Hazards

» Mexico's highways are serviceable and fairly fast when traffic is not heavy. There are more than 6000km of toll highways *(autopistas)*, which are generally very good, four-lane roads: tolls can vary from M$0.50 to M$1.50 per kilometer.

» Some hijackings, holdups and illegal roadblocks connected with drug-gang activities have occurred in the north of Mexico. In this part of the country especially, it is best to stick to toll highways and drive only by day. Driving at night is best avoided in any case, since unlit vehicles, hard-to-see speed bumps, rocks, pedestrians and animals on the roads are common.

» Mexicans on the whole drive as cautiously and sensibly as people anywhere. Traffic density, poor surfaces, speed bumps, animals, bicycles and pedestrians all help to keep speeds down.

» There are also some perfectly genuine military or police roadblocks, which are generally looking for illegal weapons, drugs, migrants or contraband. They are unlikely to give tourists a hard time, and are no cause for alarm.

» Be wary of Alto (Stop) signs, *topes* (speed bumps) and holes in the road. They are often not where you'd expect, and missing one can cost you in traffic fines or car damage. 'Tope' or 'Vibradores' signs warn you of many speed bumps: the deadly ones are the ones with no warning signs!

» There is always the chance that you will be pulled over by Mexican traffic police. If this happens, stay calm and polite. If you don't think you have committed an infraction, you don't have to pay a bribe, and acting dumb may eventually make the cop give up. You can also ask to see the officer's identification and documentation about the law you have supposedly broken, ask to speak to a superior, and note the officer's name, badge number, vehicle number and department (federal, state or municipal). Make clear that you want to pay any fines at a police station and get a receipt, then if you wish to make a complaint head for a state tourist office.

Road Rules

» Drive on the right-hand side of the road.

» Speed limits range between 80km and 120km per hour on open highways (less when highways pass through built-up areas), and between

30km and 50km per hour in towns and cities.

» One-way streets are the rule in cities.

» Seat belts are obligatory for all occupants of a car, and children under five must be strapped into safety seats in the rear.

» Antipollution rules in Mexico City ban most vehicles from the city's roads on one day each week (see p129).

Colectivos, Combis & Other Vehicles

In some areas a variety of small vehicles provide alternatives to buses. *Taxis colectivos* (collective taxis, usually carrying four passengers who each pay a quarter of the full cab fare), Volkswagen minibuses (combis) and more comfortable passenger-carrying vans, such as Chevrolet Suburbans or Nissan Urvans, operate services between some towns. Fares are typically a little less than 1st-class buses. *Microbuses* or *'micros'* are small, usually fairly new, 2nd-class buses with around 25 seats, usually running short routes between nearby towns. More primitive are passenger-carrying *camionetas* (pickups) and *camiones* (trucks), with fares similar to 2nd-class bus fares. Standing in the back of a lurching truck full of *campesinos* (land workers) and their machetes

and animals is always an experience to remember!

Local Transportation

Bicycle

Bicycle culture is on the up in Mexican cities. Most of them are flat enough to make cycling an option and some city authorities are starting to accommodate cyclists. Mexico City offers free bike rental and at least three dedicated bike routes; see p129. You can rent bikes in several other towns for M$100 to M$250 per day. Seek out the less traffic-infested routes and you should enjoy it. Mass Sunday rides are a growing phenomenon.

Bus

Generally known as *camiones*, local buses are usually the cheapest way to get around cities and out to nearby towns and villages. They run frequently and fares in cities are just a few pesos. In many cities, fleets of small, modern *microbuses* have replaced the noisy, dirty older buses.

Buses usually halt only at fixed *paradas* (bus stops), though in some places you can hold your hand out to stop one at any street corner.

Colectivo, Combi, Minibus & Pesero

These are all names for vehicles that function as something between a taxi

---

THE GREEN ANGELS

The Mexican tourism secretariat, Sectur, maintains a network of *Ángeles Verdes* (Green Angels) – bilingual mechanics in green uniforms and green trucks who patrol 60,000km of major highways throughout the country daily from 8am to 6pm looking for tourists in trouble. They can give you directions, make minor repairs, change tires, provide fuel and oil, and arrange towing and other assistance if necessary. Service is free; parts, gasoline and oil are provided at cost. If you have access to a telephone, you can call the **hotline** (☎078).

and a bus, running along fixed urban routes usually displayed on the windshield. They're cheaper than taxis and quicker than buses. They will pick you up or drop you off on any corner along their route: to stop one, go to the curb and wave your hand. Tell the driver where you want to go. Usually, you pay at the end of the trip and the fare (a little higher than a bus fare) depends on how far you go.

Metro

Mexico City, Guadalajara and Monterrey all have metro (subway, underground railway) systems. Mexico City's, in particular, is a quick, cheap and useful way of getting around. With 175 stations and over four million passengers every weekday, it's the world's third-busiest subway.

Taxi

Taxis are common in towns and cities, and surprisingly economical. City rides cost around M$10 to M$15 per kilometer. If a taxi has a meter, you can ask the driver if it's working (*'¿Funciona el taxímetro?'*). If the taxi doesn't have a functioning meter, establish the price of the ride before getting in (this may involve a bit of haggling).

Many airports and some big bus terminals have a system of authorized ticket-taxis: you buy a fixed-price ticket to your destination from a special *taquilla* (ticket window) and then hand it to the driver instead of paying cash. This saves haggling and major rip-offs, but fares are usually higher than you could get on the street.

Renting a taxi for a day-long out-of-town jaunt generally costs something similar to a cheap rental car – M$500 or M$600.

Train

The spectacular Ferrocarril Chihuahua Pacífico (Copper Canyon Railway), running between Los Mochis and Chihuahua (p754), is one of the highlights of travel in Mexico. All the rest of Mexico's regular passenger-train system died after the railroads were privatized in the 1990s.

WANT MORE?

For in-depth language information and handy phrases, check out Lonely Planet's *Mexican Spanish Phrasebook*. You'll find it at **shop.lonelyplanet.com**, or you can buy Lonely Planet's iPhone phrasebooks at the Apple App Store.

Language

Mexican Spanish pronunciation is easy, as most sounds have equivalents in English. Also, Spanish spelling is phonetically consistent, meaning that there's a clear and consistent relationship between what you see in writing and how it's pronounced. Note that kh is a throaty sound (like the 'ch' in the Scottish *loch*), v and b are like a soft English 'v' (between a 'v' and a 'b'), and r is strongly rolled. There are also some variations in spoken Spanish across Latin America, the most notable being the pronunciation of the letters *ll* and *y*. In some parts of Mexico they are pronounced like the 'll' in 'million', but in most areas they are pronounced like the 'y' in 'yes', and this is how they are represented in our pronunciation guides. In other Latin American countries you might also hear them pronounced like the 's' in 'measure', the 'sh' in 'shut' or the 'dg' in 'judge'. The stressed syllables are indicated with italics in our pronunciation guides. Bearing these few things in mind and reading our coloured pronunciation guides as if they were English, you should be understood just fine.

The polite form is used in this chapter; where both polite and informal options are given, they are indicated by the abbreviations 'pol' and 'inf'. Where necessary, both masculine and feminine forms of words are included, separated by a slash and with the masculine form first, eg *perdido/a* (m/f).

BASICS

Hello.	*Hola.*	o·la
Goodbye.	*Adiós.*	a·dyos
How are you?	*¿Qué tal?*	ke tal
Fine, thanks.	*Bien, gracias.*	byen gra·syas

Excuse me.	*Perdón.*	per·don
Sorry.	*Lo siento.*	lo syen·to
Please.	*Por favor.*	por fa·vor
Thank you.	*Gracias.*	gra·syas
You're welcome.	*De nada.*	de na·da
Yes.	*Sí.*	see
No.	*No.*	no

My name is ...
Me llamo ...   me ya·mo ...

What's your name?
¿Cómo se llama Usted?	ko·mo se ya·ma oo·ste (pol)
¿Cómo te llamas?	ko·mo te ya·mas (inf)

Do you speak English?
¿Habla inglés?	a·bla een·gles (pol)
¿Hablas inglés?	a·blas een·gles (inf)

I don't understand.
Yo no entiendo.   yo no en·tyen·do

ACCOMMODATIONS

I'd like a ... room.	*Quisiera una habitación ...*	kee·sye·ra oo·na a·bee·ta·syon ...
single	*individual*	een·dee·vee·dwal
double	*doble*	do·ble

How much is it per night/person?
¿Cuánto cuesta por noche/persona?	kwan·to kwes·ta por no·che/per·so·na

Does it include breakfast?
¿Incluye el desayuno?	een·kloo·ye el de·sa·yoo·no

KEY PATTERNS

To get by in Spanish, mix and match these simple patterns with words of your choice:

When's (the next flight)?
¿Cuándo sale   kwan·do sa·le
(el próximo vuelo)?   (el prok·see·mo vwe·lo)

Where's (the station)?
¿Dónde está   don·de es·ta
(la estación)?   (la es·ta·syon)

Where can I (buy a ticket)?
¿Dónde puedo   don·de pwe·do
(comprar un billete)?   (kom·prar oon bee·ye·te)

Do you have (a map)?
¿Tiene (un mapa)?   tye·ne (oon ma·pa)

Is there (a toilet)?
¿Hay (servicios)?   ai (ser·vee·syos)

I'd like (a coffee).
Quisiera (un café).   kee·sye·ra (oon ka·fe)

I'd like (to hire a car).
Quisiera (alquilar   kee·sye·ra (al·kee·lar
un coche).   oon ko·che)

Can I (enter)?
¿Se puede (entrar)?   se pwe·de (en·trar)

Could you please (help me)?
¿Puede (ayudarme),   pwe·de (a·yoo·dar·me)
por favor?   por fa·vor

Do I have to (get a visa)?
¿Necesito   ne·se·see·to
(obtener   (ob·te·ner
un visado)?   oon vee·sa·do)

campsite	terreno de camping	te·re·no de kam·peeng
hotel	hotel	o·tel
guesthouse	pensión	pen·syon
youth hostel	albergue juvenil	al·ber·ge khoo·ve·neel
air-con	aire acondicionado	ai·re a·kon·dee·syo·na·do
bathroom	baño	ba·nyo
bed	cama	ka·ma
window	ventana	ven·ta·na

DIRECTIONS

Where's ...?
¿Dónde está ...?   don·de es·ta ...

What's the address?
¿Cuál es la dirección?   kwal es la dee·rek·syon

Could you please write it down?
¿Puede escribirlo,   pwe·de es·kree·beer·lo
por favor?   por fa·vor

Can you show me (on the map)?
¿Me lo puede indicar   me lo pwe·de een·dee·kar
(en el mapa)?   (en el ma·pa)

at the corner	en la esquina	en la es·kee·na
at the traffic lights	en el semáforo	en el se·ma·fo·ro
behind ...	detrás de ...	de·tras de ...
far	lejos	le·khos
in front of ...	enfrente de ...	en·fren·te de ...
left	izquierda	ees·kyer·da
near	cerca	ser·ka
next to ...	al lado de ...	al la·do de ...
opposite ...	frente a ...	fren·te a ...
right	derecha	de·re·cha
straight ahead	todo recto	to·do rek·to

EATING & DRINKING

Can I see the menu, please?
¿Puedo ver el menú,   pwe·do ver el me·noo
por favor?   por fa·vor

What would you recommend?
¿Qué recomienda?   ke re·ko·myen·da

Do you have vegetarian food?
¿Tienen comida   tye·nen ko·mee·da
vegetariana?   ve·khe·ta·rya·na

I don't eat (meat).
No como (carne).   no ko·mo (kar·ne)

That was delicious!
¡Estaba buenísimo!   es·ta·ba bwe·nee·see·mo

Cheers!
¡Salud!   sa·loo

The bill, please.
La cuenta, por favor.   la kwen·ta por fa·vor

I'd like a table for ...	Quisiera una mesa para ...	kee·sye·ra oo·na me·sa pa·ra ...
(eight) o'clock	las (ocho)	las (o·cho)
(two) people	(dos) personas	(dos) per·so·nas

Key Words

bottle	botella	bo·te·ya
breakfast	desayuno	de·sa·yoo·no
cold	frío	free·o
dessert	postre	pos·tre
dinner	cena	se·na
fork	tenedor	te·ne·dor
glass	vaso	va·so
hot (warm)	caliente	kal·yen·te
knife	cuchillo	koo·chee·yo

lunch	*comida*	ko·*mee*·da
plate	*plato*	*pla*·to
restaurant	*restaurante*	res·tow·*ran*·te
spoon	*cuchara*	koo·*cha*·ra

Meat & Fish

bacon	*tocino*	to·*see*·no
beef	*carne de vaca*	*kar*·ne de *va*·ka
chicken	*pollo*	*po*·yo
crab	*cangrejo*	kan·*gre*·kho
duck	*pato*	*pa*·to
goat	*cabra*	*ka*·bra
ham	*jamón*	kha·*mon*
lamb	*cordero*	kor·*de*·ro
lobster	*langosta*	lan·*gos*·ta
mutton	*carnero*	kar·*ne*·ro
octopus	*pulpo*	*pool*·po
oysters	*ostras*	*os*·tras
pork	*cerdo*	*ser*·do
shrimp	*camarones*	ka·ma·*ro*·nes
squid	*calamar*	ka·la·*mar*
turkey	*pavo*	*pa*·vo
veal	*ternera*	ter·*ne*·ra
venison	*venado*	ve·*na*·do

Fruit & Vegetables

apple	*manzana*	man·*sa*·na
apricot	*albaricoque*	al·ba·ree·*ko*·ke
banana	*plátano*	*pla*·ta·no
beans	*frijoles*	free·*kho*·les
cabbage	*col*	kol
cactus fruit	*tuna*	*too*·na
capsicum	*pimiento*	pee·*myen*·to
carrot	*zanahoria*	sa·na·o·rya
cherry	*cereza*	se·*re*·sa
corn	*maíz*	ma·*ees*
corn (fresh)	*elote*	e·*lo*·te
cucumber	*pepino*	pe·*pee*·no
grape	*uvas*	*oo*·vas
grapefruit	*toronja*	to·*ron*·kha
lentils	*lentejas*	len·*te*·khas
lettuce	*lechuga*	le·*choo*·ga
mushroom	*champiñón*	cham·pee·*nyon*
nuts	*nueces*	*nwe*·ses
onion	*cebolla*	se·*bo*·ya
orange	*naranja*	na·*ran*·kha
peach	*melocotón*	me·lo·ko·*ton*

peas	*guisantes*	gee·*san*·tes
pineapple	*piña*	*pee*·nya
plantain	*plátano macho*	*pla*·ta·no *ma*·cho
plum	*ciruela*	seer·*we*·la
potato	*patata*	pa·*ta*·ta
pumpkin	*calabaza*	ka·la·*ba*·sa
spinach	*espinacas*	es·pee·*na*·kas
strawberry	*fresa*	*fre*·sa
(red) tomato	*(ji)tomate*	(khee·)to·*ma*·te
watermelon	*sandía*	san·*dee*·a

Other

bread	*pan*	pan
butter	*mantequilla*	man·te·*kee*·ya
cake	*pastel*	pas·*tel*
cheese	*queso*	*ke*·so
cookie	*galleta*	ga·*ye*·ta
(fried) eggs	*huevos (fritos)*	*we*·vos (*free*·tos)
French fries	*papas fritas*	*pa*·pas *free*·tas
honey	*miel*	myel
ice cream	*helado*	e·*la*·do
jam	*mermelada*	mer·me·*la*·da
pepper	*pimienta*	pee·*myen*·ta
rice	*arroz*	a·*ros*
salad	*ensalada*	en·sa·*la*·da
salt	*sal*	sal
soup	*caldo/sopa*	*kal*·do/*so*·pa
sugar	*azúcar*	a·*soo*·kar

Drinks

beer	*cerveza*	ser·*ve*·sa
coffee	*café*	ka·*fe*
juice	*zumo*	*soo*·mo
milk	*leche*	*le*·che
smoothie	*licuado*	lee·*kwa*·do
sorbet	*nieve*	*nye*·ve
(black) tea	*té (negro)*	te (*ne*·gro)

Signs

Abierto	Open
Cerrado	Closed
Entrada	Entrance
Hombres/Varones	Men
Mujeres/Damas	Women
Prohibido	Prohibited
Salida	Exit
Servicios/Baños	Toilets

(mineral) water	*agua (mineral)*	*a·gwa (mee·ne·ral)*
(red/white) wine	*vino (tinto/ blanco)*	*vee·no (teen·to/ blan·ko)*

EMERGENCIES

Help!	*¡Socorro!*	*so·ko·ro*
Go away!	*¡Vete!*	*ve·te*

Call ...!	*¡Llame a ...!*	*ya·me a ...*
a doctor	*un médico*	*oon me·dee·ko*
the police	*la policía*	*la po·lee·see·a*

I'm lost.
Estoy perdido/a.   *es·toy per·dee·do/a* (m/f)

I'm ill.
Estoy enfermo/a.   *es·toy en·fer·mo/a* (m/f)

It hurts here.
Me duele aquí.   *me dwe·le a·kee*

I'm allergic to (antibiotics).
Soy alérgico/a a   *soy a·ler·khee·ko/a a*
(los antibióticos).   *(los an·tee·byo·tee·kos)* (m/f)

Where are the toilets?
¿Dónde están los   *don·de es·tan los*
baños?   *ba·nyos*

SHOPPING & SERVICES

I'd like to buy ...
Quisiera comprar ...   *kee·sye·ra kom·prar ...*

I'm just looking.
Sólo estoy mirando.   *so·lo es·toy mee·ran·do*

Can I look at it?
¿Puedo verlo?   *pwe·do ver·lo*

I don't like it.
No me gusta.   *no me goos·ta*

How much is it?
¿Cuánto cuesta?   *kwan·to kwes·ta*

That's too expensive.
Es muy caro.   *es mooy ka·ro*

Can you lower the price?
¿Podría bajar un   *po·dree·a ba·khar oon*
poco el precio?   *po·ko el pre·syo*

There's a mistake in the bill.
Hay un error   *ai oon e·ror*
en la cuenta.   *en la kwen·ta*

Question Words

How?	*¿Cómo?*	*ko·mo*
What?	*¿Qué?*	*ke*
When?	*¿Cuándo?*	*kwan·do*
Where?	*¿Dónde?*	*don·de*
Who?	*¿Quién?*	*kyen*
Why?	*¿Por qué?*	*por ke*

ATM	*cajero automático*	*ka·khe·ro ow·to·ma·tee·ko*
credit card	*tarjeta de crédito*	*tar·khe·ta de kre·dee·to*
internet cafe	*cibercafé*	*see·ber·ka·fe*
market	*mercado*	*mer·ka·do*
post office	*correos*	*ko·re·os*
tourist office	*oficina de turismo*	*o·fee·see·na de too·rees·mo*

TIME & DATES

What time is it?	*¿Qué hora es?*	*ke o·ra es*
It's (10) o'clock.	*Son (las diez).*	*son (las dyes)*
It's half past (one).	*Es (la una) y media.*	*es (la oo·na) ee me·dya*

morning	*mañana*	*ma·nya·na*
afternoon	*tarde*	*tar·de*
evening	*noche*	*no·che*
yesterday	*ayer*	*a·yer*
today	*hoy*	*oy*
tomorrow	*mañana*	*ma·nya·na*

Monday	*lunes*	*loo·nes*
Tuesday	*martes*	*mar·tes*
Wednesday	*miércoles*	*myer·ko·les*
Thursday	*jueves*	*khwe·ves*
Friday	*viernes*	*vyer·nes*
Saturday	*sábado*	*sa·ba·do*
Sunday	*domingo*	*do·meen·go*

January	*enero*	*e·ne·ro*
February	*febrero*	*fe·bre·ro*
March	*marzo*	*mar·so*
April	*abril*	*a·breel*
May	*mayo*	*ma·yo*
June	*junio*	*khoon·yo*
July	*julio*	*khool·yo*
August	*agosto*	*a·gos·to*
September	*septiembre*	*sep·tyem·bre*
October	*octubre*	*ok·too·bre*
November	*noviembre*	*no·vyem·bre*
December	*diciembre*	*dee·syem·bre*

TRANSPORTATION

boat	*barco*	*bar·ko*
bus	*autobús*	*ow·to·boos*
plane	*avión*	*a·vyon*
train	*tren*	*tren*

first	primero	pree·*me*·ro
last	último	*ool*·tee·mo
next	próximo	*prok*·see·mo

A ... ticket, please.	Un billete de ..., por favor.	oon bee·*ye*·te de ... por fa·*vor*
1st-class	primera clase	pree·*me*·ra *kla*·se
2nd-class	segunda clase	se·*goon*·da *kla*·se
one-way	ida	*ee*·da
return	ida y vuelta	*ee*·da ee *vwel*·ta

I want to go to ...
Quisiera ir a ...   kee·*sye*·ra eer a ...

Does it stop at ...?
¿Para en ...?   *pa*·ra en ...

What stop is this?
¿Cuál es esta parada?   kwal es *es*·ta pa·*ra*·da

What time does it arrive/leave?
¿A qué hora llega/ sale?   a ke o·ra ye·ga/ *sa*·le

Please tell me when we get to ...
¿Puede avisarme cuando lleguemos a ...?   pwe·de a·vee·*sar*·me *kwan*·do ye·*ge*·mos a ...

I want to get off here.
Quiero bajarme aquí.   *kye*·ro ba·*khar*·me a·*kee*

airport	aeropuerto	a·e·ro·*pwer*·to
aisle seat	asiento de pasillo	a·*syen*·to de pa·*see*·yo
bus stop	parada de autobuses	pa·*ra*·da de ow·to·*boo*·ses
cancelled	cancelado	kan·se·*la*·do
delayed	retrasado	re·tra·*sa*·do
platform	plataforma	pla·ta·*for*·ma
ticket office	taquilla	ta·*kee*·ya
timetable	horario	o·*ra*·ryo
train station	estación de trenes	es·ta·*syon* de *tre*·nes
window seat	asiento junto a la ventana	a·*syen*·to *khoon*·to a la ven·*ta*·na

I'd like to hire a ...	Quisiera alquilar ...	kee·*sye*·ra al·kee·*lar* ...
4WD	un todo-terreno	oon to·do-te·*re*·no
bicycle	una bicicleta	*oo*·na bee·see·*kle*·ta
car	un coche	oon *ko*·che
motorcycle	una moto	*oo*·na *mo*·to

Numbers		
1	uno	*oo*·no
2	dos	dos
3	tres	tres
4	cuatro	*kwa*·tro
5	cinco	*seen*·ko
6	seis	seys
7	siete	*sye*·te
8	ocho	*o*·cho
9	nueve	*nwe*·ve
10	diez	dyes
20	veinte	*veyn*·te
30	treinta	*treyn*·ta
40	cuarenta	kwa·*ren*·ta
50	cincuenta	seen·*kwen*·ta
60	sesenta	se·*sen*·ta
70	setenta	se·*ten*·ta
80	ochenta	o·*chen*·ta
90	noventa	no·*ven*·ta
100	cien	syen
1000	mil	meel

child seat	asiento de seguridad para niños	a·*syen*·to de se·goo·ree·*da* pa·ra *nee*·nyos
diesel	petróleo	pet·*ro*·le·o
helmet	casco	*kas*·ko
hitchhike	hacer botella	a·*ser* bo·*te*·ya
mechanic	mecánico	me·*ka*·nee·ko
petrol/gas	gasolina	ga·so·*lee*·na
service station	gasolinera	ga·so·lee·*ne*·ra
truck	camion	ka·*myon*

Is this the road to ...?
¿Se va a ... por esta carretera?   se va a ... por *es*·ta ka·re·*te*·ra

(How long) Can I park here?
¿(Cuánto tiempo) Puedo aparcar aquí?   (*kwan*·to *tyem*·po) pwe·do a·par·*kar* a·*kee*

The car has broken down (at ...).
El coche se ha averiado (en ...).   el *ko*·che se a a·ve·*rya*·do (en ...)

I had an accident.
He tenido un accidente.   e te·*nee*·do oon ak·see·*den*·te

I've run out of petrol.
Me he quedado sin gasolina.   me e ke·*da*·do seen ga·so·*lee*·na

I have a flat tyre.
Tengo un pinchazo.   *ten*·go oon peen·*cha*·so

MEXICAN SLANG

Pepper your conversations with a few slang expressions! You'll hear many of the following expressions all around Mexico, but some are particular to Mexico City.

¿Qué onda?
What's up?/What's happening?

¿Qué pasión? (Mexico City)
What's up?/What's going on?

¡Qué padre!
How cool!

fregón
really good at something/way cool/awesome

Este club está fregón.
This club is way cool.

El cantante es un fregón.
The singer is really awesome.

ser muy buena onda
to be really cool/nice

Mi novio es muy buena onda.
My boyfriend is really cool.

Eres muy buena onda.
You're really cool.

pisto (in the north)
booze

alipús
booze

echarse un alipús/trago
to go get a drink

Echamos un alipús/trago.
Let's go have a drink.

tirar la onda
try to pick someone up/flirt

ligar
to flirt

irse de reventón
go partying

¡Vámonos de reventón!
Let's go party!

reven
a 'rave' (huge party with loud music and a wild atmosphere)

un desmadre
a mess

Simón.
Yes.

Nel.
No.

No hay tos.
No problem. (literally: 'there's no cough')

¡Órale! (positive)
Sounds great! (when responding to an invitation)

¡Órale! (negative)
What the ...? (taunting exclamation)

¡Caray!
Shit!

¿Te cae?
Are you serious?

Me late.
Sounds really good to me.

Me vale.
I don't care./Whatever.

Sale y vale.
I agree./Sounds good.

¡Paso sin ver!
I can't stand it!/No, thank you!

¡Guácatelas!/¡Guácala!
How gross!/That's disgusting!

¡Bájale!
Don't exaggerate!/Come on!

¡¿Chale?! (Mexico City)
No way!?

¡Te pasas!
That's it! You've gone too far!

¡No manches!
Get outta here!/You must be kidding!

un resto
a lot

lana
money/dough

carnal
brother

cuate/cuaderno
buddy

chavo
guy/dude

chava
girl/gal

jefe
father

jefa
mother

la tira/julia
the police

la chota (Mexico City)
the police

GLOSSARY

(m) indicates masculine gender, (f) feminine gender, (sg) singular and (pl) plural

adobe – sun-dried mud brick used for building

agave – family of plants with thick, fleshy, usually pointed leaves, from which tequila, mezcal and *pulque* are produced (see also *maguey*)

Alameda – name of formal parks in some Mexican cities

alebrije – colorful wooden animal figure

Ángeles Verdes – Green Angels; government-funded mechanics who patrol Mexico's major highways in green vehicles; they help stranded motorists with fuel and spare parts

arroyo – brook, stream

artesanías – handicrafts, folk arts

atlas (sg), atlantes (pl) – sculpted male figure(s) used instead of a pillar to support a roof or frieze; a *telamon*

autopista – expressway, dual carriageway

azulejo – painted ceramic tile

bahía – bay

balneario – bathing place; often a natural hot spring

baluarte – bulwark, defensive wall

barrio – neighborhood (often poor) of a town or city

boleto – ticket

brujo/a (m/f) – witch doctor, shaman; similar to *curandero/a*

burro – donkey

cabaña – cabin, simple shelter

cabina – Baja Californian term for a public telephone call station

cacique – regional warlord; political strongman

calle – street

callejón – alley

calzada – grand boulevard or avenue

camioneta – pickup truck

campesino/a (m/f) – country person, peasant

capilla abierta – open chapel; used in early Mexican monasteries for preaching to large crowds of indigenous people

casa de cambio – exchange house; place where currency is exchanged; faster to use than a bank

casa de huéspedes – cheap and congenial accommodations; often a home converted into simple guest lodgings

caseta de teléfono, caseta telefónica – public telephone call station

cenote – a limestone sinkhole filled with rainwater; often used in Yucatán as a reservoir

central camionera – bus terminal

cerro – hill

Chac – Maya rain god

chac-mool – pre-Hispanic stone sculpture of a hunched-up figure; the stomach may have been used as a sacrificial altar

charreada – Mexican rodeo

charro – Mexican cowboy

chilango/a (m/f) – person from Mexico City

chinampa – Aztec garden built from lake mud and vegetation; versions still exist at Xochimilco, Mexico City

chultún – cistern found in the Chenes region in the Puuc hills south of Mérida

Churrigueresque – Spanish late-baroque architectural style; found on many Mexican churches

clavadistas – cliff divers of Acapulco and Mazatlán

colectivo – minibus or car that picks up and drops off passengers along a predetermined route; can also refer to other types of transportation, such as boats, where passengers share the total fare

colonia – neighborhood of a city, often a wealthy residential area

combi – minibus

comedor – food stall

comida corrida – set lunch

completo – no vacancy (literally 'full up'); a sign you may see at hotel desks

conde – count (nobleman)

conquistador – early Spanish explorer-conqueror

cordillera – mountain range

criollo – Mexican-born person of Spanish parentage; in colonial times considered inferior by *peninsulares*

cuota – toll; a *vía cuota* is a toll road

curandero/a (m/f) – literally 'curer'; a medicine man or woman who uses herbal and/or magical methods and often emphasizes spiritual aspects of disease

de paso – a bus that began its route somewhere else, but stops to let passengers on or off at various points

DF – Distrito Federal (Federal District); about half of Mexico City lies in the DF

edificio – building

ejido – communal landholding

embarcadero – jetty, boat landing

entremeses – hors d'oeuvres; also theatrical sketches such as those performed during the Cervantino festival in Guanajuato

escuela – school

esq – abbreviation of *esquina* (corner) in addresses

ex-convento – former convent or monastery

feria – fair or carnival, typically occurring during a religious holiday

ferrocarril – railway

fonda – inn; small, family-run eatery

fraccionamiento – subdivision, housing development; similar to a *colonia*, often modern

gringo/a (m/f) – US or Canadian (or other Western) visitor to Latin America; can be used derogatorily

grito – literally 'shout'; the Grito de Dolores was the 1810 call to independence by priest Miguel Hidalgo, sparking the struggle for independence from Spain

gruta – cave, grotto

guayabera – man's shirt with pockets and appliquéd designs up the front, over the shoulders and down the back; worn in place of a jacket and tie in hot regions

hacha – ax; in archaeological contexts, a flat, carved-stone object connected with the ritual ball game

hacienda – estate; Hacienda (capitalized) is the Treasury Department

henequén – *agave* fiber used to make sisal rope; grown particularly around Mérida

hostal – small hotel or budget hostel

huarache – woven leather sandal, often with tire tread as the sole

huevos – eggs; also slang for testicles

huipil (sg), huipiles (pl) – indigenous woman's sleeveless tunic(s), usually highly decorated; can be thigh-length or reach the ankles

Huizilopochtli – Aztec tribal god

iglesia – church

INAH – Instituto Nacional de Antropología e Historia; the body in charge of most ancient sites and some museums

indígena – indigenous, pertaining to the original inhabitants of Latin America; can also refer to the people themselves

isla – island

IVA – *impuesto de valor agregado*, or 'ee-bah'; a sales tax added to the price of many items (16% on hotel rooms)

jai alai – the Basque game *pelota*, brought to Mexico by the Spanish; a bit like squash, played on a long court with curved baskets attached to the arm

jardín – garden

Kukulcán – Maya name for the plumed serpent god *Quetzalcóatl*

lancha – fast, open, outboard boat

larga distancia – long-distance; usually refers to telephones

local – refers to premises, such as a numbered shop or office; a *local* bus is one whose route starts from the bus station you are in

maguey – *agave;* sometimes refers specifically to *Agave americana*, from which *pulque* is made

malecón – waterfront boulevard or promenade

maquiladora – assembly-plant operation importing equipment, raw materials and parts for assembly or processing in Mexico, then exporting the products

mariachi – small ensemble of street musicians playing traditional ballads on guitars and trumpets

marimba – wooden xylophone-like instrument popular in southeastern Mexico

mercado – market; often a building near the center of a town, with shops and open-air stalls in the surrounding streets

Mesoamerica – historical and archaeological name for central, southern, eastern and southeastern Mexico, Guatemala, Belize and the small ancient Maya area in Honduras

mestizo – person of mixed (usually indigenous and Spanish) ancestry

Mexican Revolution – 1910 revolution that ended the *Porfiriato*

milpa – peasant's small cornfield, often cultivated using the slash-and-burn method

mirador (sg), miradores (pl) – lookout point(s)

Mudejar – Moorish architectural style imported to Mexico by the Spanish

municipio – small local government area; Mexico is divided into 2394 of them

Nafta – North American Free Trade Agreement

Náhuatl – language of the Nahua people, descendants of the Aztecs

nao – Spanish trading galleon

norteamericano – North American; someone from north of the US–Mexican border

Nte – abbreviation for *norte* (north); used in street names

Ote – abbreviation for *oriente* (east); used in street names

palacio de gobierno – state capitol, state government headquarters

palacio municipal – town or city hall, headquarters of the municipal corporation

palapa – thatched-roof shelter, usually on a beach

PAN – Partido Acción Nacional (National Action Party); the political party of Felipe Calderón and his predecessor Vicente Fox

panga – fiberglass skiff for fishing or whale-watching in Baja California

parada – bus stop, usually for city buses

parque nacional – national park; an environmentally protected area in which human exploitation is banned or restricted

parroquia – parish church

paseo – boulevard, walkway or pedestrian street; the tradition of strolling around the plaza in the evening, men and women moving in opposite directions

Pemex – government-owned petroleum extraction, refining and retailing monopoly

peninsulares – those born in Spain and sent by the Spanish government to rule the colony in Mexico

periférico – ring road

pesero – Mexico City's word for *colectivo;* can mean 'bus' in the northeast

peyote – a hallucinogenic cactus

pinacoteca – art gallery

piñata – clay pot or papier-mâché mold decorated to resemble an animal, pineapple, star, etc and filled with sweets and gifts, then smashed open at fiestas

pirata – literally 'pirate'; used to describe passenger-carrying pickup trucks in some parts of Mexico

playa – beach

plaza de toros – bullring

plazuela – small plaza

poblano/a (m/f) – person from Puebla; something in the style of Puebla

Porfiriato – reign of Porfirio Díaz as president-dictator of Mexico for 30 years until the 1910 *Mexican Revolution*

portales – arcades

posada – inn

PRI – Partido Revolucionario Institucional (Institutional Revolutionary Party); the political party that ruled Mexico for most of the 20th century

Pte – abbreviation for *poniente* (west), used in street names

puerto – port

pulque – milky, low-alcohol brew made from the *maguey* plant

quetzal – crested bird with brilliant green, red and white plumage native to southern Mexico, Central America and northern South America; quetzal feathers were highly prized in pre-Hispanic Mexico

Quetzalcóatl – plumed serpent god of pre-Hispanic Mexico

rebozo – long woolen or linen shawl covering the head or shoulders

refugio – a very basic cabin for shelter in the mountains

reserva de la biosfera – biosphere reserve; an environmentally protected area where human exploitation is steered toward sustainable activities

retablo – altarpiece, or small painting placed in a church as thanks for miracles, answered prayers etc

río – river

s/n – *sin número* (without number); used in addresses

sacbé (sg), sacbeob (pl) – ceremonial avenue(s) between great Maya cities

sanatorio – hospital, particularly a small private one

sarape – blanket with opening for the head; worn as a cloak

Semana Santa – Holy Week – the week from Palm Sunday to Easter Sunday; Mexico's major holiday period when accommodations and transportation get very busy

sierra – mountain range

sitio – taxi service

stela/stele (sg), stelae/steles (pl) – standing stone monument, usually carved

sur – south; often seen in street names

taller – shop or workshop; a *taller mecánico* is a mechanic's shop, usually for cars; a *taller de llantas* is a tire-repair shop

talud-tablero – stepped building style typical of Teotihuacán, with alternating vertical (*tablero*) and sloping (*talud*) sections

taquilla – ticket window

telamon – statue of a male figure, used instead of a pillar to hold up the roof of a temple; an *atlas*

teleférico – cable car

teléfono (celular) – (cell/mobile) telephone

temascal – pre-Hispanic–style steam bath, often used for curative purposes; sometimes spelt *temazcal*

templo – church; anything from a chapel to a cathedral

teocalli – Aztec sacred precinct

Tezcatlipoca – multifaceted pre-Hispanic god; lord of life and death and protector of warriors; as a smoking mirror he could see into hearts; as the sun god he needed the blood of sacrificed warriors to ensure he would rise again

tezontle – light red, porous volcanic rock used for buildings by the Aztecs and *conquistadores*

tianguis – indigenous people's market

tienda – store

típico/a (m/f) – characteristic of a region; used to describe food in particular

Tláloc – pre-Hispanic rain and water god

tope – speed bump; found on the outskirts of towns and villages; they are only sometimes marked by signs

trapiche – mill; in Baja California usually a sugar mill

UNAM – Universidad Nacional Autónoma de México (National Autonomous University of Mexico)

universidad – university

voladores – literally 'fliers'; Totonac ritual in which men, suspended by their ankles, whirl around a tall pole

War of Independence – war for Mexican independence from Spain (from 1810 to 1821), ending three centuries of Spanish rule

War of the Castes – 19th-century Maya uprising in the Yucatán Peninsula

zócalo – literally 'plinth'; used in some Mexican towns for the main plaza or square

behind the scenes

SEND US YOUR FEEDBACK

We love to hear from travelers – your comments keep us on our toes and help make our books better. Our well-traveled team reads every word on what you loved or loathed about this book. Although we cannot reply individually to postal submissions, we always guarantee that your feedback goes straight to the appropriate authors, in time for the next edition. Each person who sends us information is thanked in the next edition – the most useful submissions are rewarded with a selection of digital PDF chapters.

Visit **lonelyplanet.com/contact** to submit your updates and suggestions or to ask for help. Our award-winning website also features inspirational travel stories, news and discussions.

Note: We may edit, reproduce and incorporate your comments in Lonely Planet products such as guidebooks, websites and digital products, so let us know if you don't want your comments reproduced or your name acknowledged. For a copy of our privacy policy visit lonelyplanet.com/privacy.

OUR READERS

Many thanks to the travelers who used the last edition and wrote to us with helpful hints, useful advice and interesting anecdotes:

Mick Adams, Jennie Antonsen, Manuela Arigoni, Win Armstrong, Claire Arthur, Valerie Beaumont, Jack Benjamin, Marinus Bosters, John Brotherton, Robert Broughton, Mark Buitendach, Pavel Cerny, Richard Clair, Geraldine Claessens, Ursula Conrad, Marco Cristofanelli, Richard Crosby, Armando Cuentas, Ake Dahllof, Linda Daneel, Arpan Dasgupta, Set Domínguez, Deborah Duboulay Rubio, Tyler B Evans, Todd Gallagher, Pedro Gerson, Emily Golan, Sami Greenbury, James Henry, Sonja Heuscher, Dilek Iusuf, Hannah Jacobs, Hanna Jakobson, Julia Jander, Giles Kent, Rashi Kesarwani, Alexander Kjaerum, Lowell Klessig, Francisco Ladron de Guevara, Martjan Lammertink, Sky Lantz-Wagner, Louise Lavallière, Margriet Lenkens, Yihan Li, Adrian Limon, Dan Lyons, Kate Maffei, Tom Maffei, Susanne Majcug, Ed Martin, Loredana Stefania Manzo, Linda Maxwell, Annie McDermott, Dorothy Merriott, Curtis Miller, David Moss, Roseanna Mueller, Martin Nizet, Thomas Notz, Matt Oliver, Aristea Parissi, Andrew Pfeifer, Don Plimer, Alexandru Vladimir Popescu, Juan Ramos Muniz, Steph Rowe, Mirko Saam, Aaron Schur, Wanda Serkowska, Sarah Sharkey, Kim Sherman, Rebecca Shorrock, Kevin Simpson, Stacey Skurnik, Jim Smith, Rebecca Smith, Matteo Sorgato, Jon Stevenson, Nathan R Strening, Bart Van Hoof, John Venator, Dominique Vera, Benny Verbercht, Claus Virmer, Bernard Wasow, Tal Wasser, Dave Wells, Evan Wilson, Diana Zamora, Joanna Zuckerman Bernstein, Yael Zur Nieden

AUTHOR THANKS

John Noble

Special thanks for hospitality, help and fun to Ron Mader, Gina Machorro, Leyla and Fausto, Paul Lye, Julien Pardinilla, John and María Taylor, Gundi Ley, Daniel Schechter and Connie McKeand. And, as ever, thanks to all the author team and in-house team for your enthusiasm, professionalism and being a pleasure to work with.

Kate Armstrong

My warmest thanks (again) to Alfonso, Teresa, Teresita, Nuria and Cristina for their generosity of spirit and for helping me in every way. Similarly Rache in Zacatecas, thank you for your support during my Mexican drama – this couldn't have been done without you. A massive *gracias* to Tom and Leticia and friends in Guanajuato. *Muchísimas gracias:* Cat

Craddock, Bruce Evans, Alison Lyall and John Noble (and fellow scribes) for their ongoing passion. Finally, to the kindness of strangers...

Ray Bartlett

Thanks first and foremost to my family, especially my mother-in-law and brother-in-law who came from so far away to help at home while I was so far away, and my mom, who helped before, during and after. Thanks to all the great people who made the trip so memorable and fun: Scott and Aimee in particular, and all the other folks whom I don't have room to name. You know who you are.

Gregor Clark

Thanks to the countless warm-hearted folks who shared their love and knowledge of Mexico with me, especially Monica in Zihuatanejo, Ricardo and Kathy in Puerto Vallarta, William, Belem and Roberto in Troncones, Laura and Paula in Chacala and Falco in Barra de Potosí. Back home, *besos y abrazos* to Gaen, Meigan and Chloe, whose love and support sustained me over many bumpy roads and late-night research jaunts.

John Hecht

Many thanks to all the good folks in Mexico City who helped shape this chapter. My special gratitude goes out to archaeologist Raul Barrera, Mexico City nomad Feike de Jong, food guru Ruth Alegria, the all-knowing John Dickie and the previous and present authors of this book. Last and certainly not least, a big hug for my wife Laura for making it an exceptionally memorable journey.

Beth Kohn

Love and cartwheels to my amazing San Cris crew of Michael, Lulú and Lucio! Other helpful in-country folks included the Comitán state and San Cristóbal municipal tourism offices, Hospedaje Esmeralda in Ocosingo, the *lanchero* and tour guide who let me hitch rides with them near the border, and everyone who let me cook soup. In Lonely Planet land, big cheers to the awesome Cat Craddock and John Noble. As always, homefront hugs to Claudio.

Tom Masters

In Mexico my gratitude particularly to the staff and owners of Las Sabilas in Guadalajara and Casa Rosa in Morelia for kindness that always went beyond the call of duty. Thanks also to the fun staff at Casa Chikita in Uruapan and to Fernando in Colima, Mario in Guadalajara and María in Pátzcuaro. As ever, thanks too to my fellow writers on the book and to all the in-house team at Lonely Planet.

Freda Moon

Every adventurer needs a safe harbor. To Tim, you're my favorite fellow traveler and my home port, thank you for always being the steady hand on the tiller. To the coolest sailor I know, you're my hero, Fred Evans. Thanks for letting me take over your shed with all my worldly possessions. To Robin Whitley, *muchas gracias* for making that old house feel like home. Don't forget to check your mailbox, Marco Moon, there's a postcard from Mexico with your name on it.

Brendan Sainsbury

Thanks to all the untold bus drivers, tourist info volunteers, restaurateurs, marimba players, weather forecasters, tortilla makers and innocent bystanders who helped me during my research, particularly to Catherine Craddock for offering me the gig in the first place and John Noble for being a supportive coordinating author. Special thanks to my wife Liz and six-year-old son Kieran for their company on the road.

Lucas Vidgen

Thanks first and foremost to the Mexicans in general for making a country that's such a joy to travel and work in. Vanessa Hines was a huge help in Playa del Carmen and all along the coast, and Tom Williams was a fantastic source of information for Mérida and surrounds, as was Conner Gorry. As always, thanks to América, Sofía and Teresa for being there, and for being there when I got back.

Luke Waterson

Rangel Palafox in Hermosillo, Puerto Peñasco's Rosie Glover, Francisco Iorres in San Carlos, Walter Bishop Velarde in Durango and Ivan Fernandez across the entire Copper Canyon: *gracias por todo*. *Saludos también* to all the bus drivers, tourist information workers and hotdog vendors who kept me going en route. Thanks to editor Cat Craddock, coordinating author John Noble and everyone who made this book happen: it was a privilege to work with such an experienced team for this edition of *Mexico*. The biggest thanks, as always, goes to my girlfriend Poppy: for tolerating a travel writer's somewhat erratic life.

ACKNOWLEDGMENTS

Climate map data adapted from Peel MC, Finlayson BL & McMahon TA (2007) 'Updated World Map of the Köppen-Geiger Climate Classification', *Hydrology and Earth System Sciences*, 11, 163344.

Cover photograph: Templo de las Inscripciones in Palenque, Chiapas; Stock Connection Blue/Alamy.

Palenque Ruins map : Ed Barnhart, 2011.

Many of the images in this guide are available for licensing from Lonely Planet Images: www.lonelyplanetimages.com.

THIS BOOK

This 13th edition of Lonely Planet's *Mexico* guidebook was researched and written by John Noble (coordinating author), Kate Armstrong, Ray Bartlett, Gregor Clark, John Hecht, Beth Kohn, Tom Masters, Freda Moon, Brendan Sainsbury, Lucas Vidgen and Luke Waterson. The essay 'The Mexican Kitchen' was written by Mauricio Velázquez de León. The previous edition was written by John Noble (coordinating author), Kate Armstrong, Ray Bartlett, Greg Benchwick, Nate Cavalieri, Gregor Clark, John Hecht, Beth Kohn, Emily Matchar, Freda Moon and Ellee Thalheimer. This guidebook was commissioned in Lonely Planet's Oakland office, and produced by the following:

Commissioning Editor
Catherine Craddock-Carrillo

Coordinating Editor
Branislava Vladisavljevic

Coordinating Cartographers Anita Banh, Eve Kelly

Coordinating Layout Designer Carol Jackson

Managing Editors Bruce Evans, Annelies Mertens, Dianne Schallmeiner

Managing Cartographers Shahara Ahmed, Adrian Persoglia

Managing Layout Designer Chris Girdler

Assisting Editors Kate Evans, Beth Hall, Carly Hall, Kate James, Evan Jones, Kate Kiely, Lucy Monie Hall, Anne Mulvaney, Joanne Newell, Sophie Splatt

Assisting Cartographers
Enes Basic, Jane Chapman, Xavier Di Toro, Julie Dodkins, Rachel Imeson, Joelene Kowalski, Valentina Kremenchutskaya, Sophie Reed, Cameron Romeril, Julie Sheridan

Assisting Layout Designers Paul Iacono, Jacqui Saunders

Cover Research
Naomi Parker

Internal Image Research
Nicholas Colicchia

Thanks to Lucy Birchley, Ryan Evans, Sandra Helou, Yvonne Kirk, Susan Paterson, Trent Paton, Kirsten Rawlings, Gerard Walker

index

000 Map pages
000 Photo pages

000 Map pages
000 Photo pages

000 Map pages
000 Photo pages

how to use this book

These symbols will help you find the listings you want:

◉ Sights	☞ Tours	☕ Drinking
🐾 Beaches	🎊 Festivals & Events	☆ Entertainment
🏃 Activities	🛏 Sleeping	🛍 Shopping
🍃 Courses	✗ Eating	ⓘ Information/Transport

Look out for these icons:

TOP CHOICE	Our author's recommendation
FREE	No payment required
🍃	A green or sustainable option

Our authors have nominated these places as demonstrating a strong commitment to sustainability – for example by supporting local communities and producers, operating in an environmentally friendly way, or supporting conservation projects.

These symbols give you the vital information for each listing:

📞 Telephone Numbers	📶 Wi-Fi Access	🚌 Bus
☉ Opening Hours	🏊 Swimming Pool	⛴ Ferry
P Parking	🥗 Vegetarian Selection	Ⓜ Metro
⊖ Nonsmoking	📖 English-Language Menu	Ⓢ Subway
✳ Air-Conditioning	👪 Family-Friendly	🚊 Tram
@ Internet Access	🐾 Pet-Friendly	🚆 Train

Reviews are organised by author preference.

Map Legend

Sights
- Beach
- Buddhist
- Castle
- Christian
- Hindu
- Islamic
- Jewish
- Monument
- Museum/Gallery
- Ruin
- Winery/Vineyard
- Zoo
- Other Sight

Activities, Courses & Tours
- Diving/Snorkelling
- Canoeing/Kayaking
- Skiing
- Surfing
- Swimming/Pool
- Walking
- Windsurfing
- Other Activity/Course/Tour

Sleeping
- Sleeping
- Camping

Eating
- Eating

Drinking
- Drinking
- Cafe

Entertainment
- Entertainment

Shopping
- Shopping

Information
- Post Office
- Tourist Information

Transport
- Airport
- Border Crossing
- Bus
- Cable Car/Funicular
- Cycling
- Ferry
- Metro
- Monorail
- Parking
- S-Bahn
- Taxi
- Train/Railway
- Tram
- Tube Station
- U-Bahn
- Other Transport

Routes
- Tollway
- Freeway
- Primary
- Secondary
- Tertiary
- Lane
- Unsealed Road
- Plaza/Mall
- Steps
- Tunnel
- Pedestrian Overpass
- Walking Tour
- Walking Tour Detour
- Path

Boundaries
- International
- State/Province
- Disputed
- Regional/Suburb
- Marine Park
- Cliff
- Wall

Population
- Capital (National)
- Capital (State/Province)
- City/Large Town
- Town/Village

Geographic
- Hut/Shelter
- Lighthouse
- Lookout
- Mountain/Volcano
- Oasis
- Park
- Pass
- Picnic Area
- Waterfall

Hydrography
- River/Creek
- Intermittent River
- Swamp/Mangrove
- Reef
- Canal
- Water
- Dry/Salt/Intermittent Lake
- Glacier

Areas
- Beach/Desert
- Cemetery (Christian)
- Cemetery (Other)
- Park/Forest
- Sportsground
- Sight (Building)
- Top Sight (Building)

John Hecht

Mexico City John's passion for Mexico began two decades ago when he moved from San Francisco to Guadalajara to study Spanish. Three years later, he said *adiós* to the mariachi capital and moved to Mexico City, where he currently resides. Working on the Mexico City chapter reminded him of everything he loves about his adopted city, from its convivial cantinas and finger-lickin' street eats to its endless cultural offerings. He has previously contributed to Lonely Planet's *Mexico* and *Puerto Vallarta & Pacific Mexico* guidebooks.

Beth Kohn

Chiapas Beth has been sojourning in Mexico for almost 30 years, and this was her third whirl through Chiapas for the Mexico guide. This time around, she sloshed up muddy waterfalls, contemplated the predawn call-and-response of rowdy howler monkeys and sacrificed her feet to invisible sandflies. A thankful resident of San Francisco, she's co-authored Lonely Planet's *California, Puerto Rico* and *Yosemite, Sequoia & Kings Canyon National Parks* guides. You can see more of her writing and photography at www.bethkohn.com.

Tom Masters

Western Central Highlands Tom is a travel writer based in Berlin. His first experience of Mexico was in the jungles of Chiapas filming at Palenque, which led to repeat visits and a stint of living in Mexico City. Having previously authored the Around Mexico City chapter for Lonely Planet, this time Tom covered the western central highlands and loved every minute of getting to know this much-underrated region. Find more of Tom's work online at www.tommasters.net.

Freda Moon

Around Mexico City Freda first fell in love with Mexico while sailing the Sea of Cortez with her father as a semi-amphibious three-year-old. Later, she revisited the country on a wild multimonth honeymoon with her fellow traveler and partner in adventure, Tim Stelloh. Although she's found herself sick and stranded in the deserts of Baja and stared down by *federales*, she's never grown weary of this, her favorite country. A regular contributor to the *New York Times* travel section, Freda's work as a travel writer and journalist can be seen at www.fredamoon.com.

Brendan Sainsbury

Veracruz An expat Brit now living in Vancouver, Canada, Brendan first visited Mexico in the early 1990s when he foolishly cycled from Veracruz to Mexico City and – miraculously – lived to tell the tale. He has returned numerous times since to get married, to honeymoon and to initiate his two-month-old son, Kieran, to the joys of global travel. Brendan has authored more than 25 guidebooks for Lonely Planet including the current guides to Cuba, Italy, Spain, the USA and Canada.

Lucas Vidgen

Yucatán Peninsula Lucas first visited the Yucatán in 2002, breezing through long enough to be captivated by the lush scenery, irresistible beaches and delicious food. He now lives in Guatemala and makes it a point to pop over the border whenever he can to munch down on *pibil* and splash around in cenotes. Lucas has contributed to a variety of Lonely Planet's Latin American titles. Back home he publishes – and occasionally works on – Quetzaltenango's leading nightlife and culture magazine, *XelaWho* (www.xelawho.com).

Luke Waterson

Copper Canyon & Northern Mexico Returning to Northern Mexico for this edition didn't faze Luke: after all, Juárez (fish tacos, actually) was his first Mexican experience. Why? Because he knew the shallow reporting condemning the entire north as dangerous was inaccurate, and that for those who arrive taking the media hype with a well-deserved pinch of salt, incredible experiences await. Luke has been exploring Mexico since 2004: this is his third book for Lonely Planet. He's also a force behind relaunched UK travel magazine *Real Travel*. Peruse his travel writing at www.lukewaterson.co.uk and find him on Twitter (@lukewaterson1) ranting about Latin America, from border conflicts to Chávez and steak.

OUR STORY

A beat-up old car, a few dollars in the pocket and a sense of adventure. In 1972 that's all Tony and Maureen Wheeler needed for the trip of a lifetime – across Europe and Asia overland to Australia. It took several months, and at the end – broke but inspired – they sat at their kitchen table writing and stapling together their first travel guide, *Across Asia on the Cheap*. Within a week they'd sold 1500 copies. Lonely Planet was born.

Today, Lonely Planet has offices in Melbourne, London and Oakland, with more than 600 staff and writers. We share Tony's belief that 'a great guidebook should do three things: inform, educate and amuse'.

OUR WRITERS

John Noble

Coordinating Author, Oaxaca John has felt Mexico's pull ever since reading the unlikely story of Cortés and the Aztecs as a teenager in his native England. An early backpacking trip took him from Ciudad Juárez to Ciudad Cuauhtémoc and he has since returned for numerous extended visits. Coordinating author of every edition of this guide since 1994, John has explored almost every part of Mexico. On many editions he was joined as an author by his late wife Susan Forsyth. John loves Mexico's art, archaeology, music, food, drinks, languages, traditions, beaches, landscapes, and most of all its charming people. He lives in Spain.

Kate Armstrong

Northern Central Highlands An Australian by birth but a Latina (she believes) in a former life, Kate visits Mexico regularly. She struck gold when asked to cover the silver cities for the third time for Lonely Planet. She cycled among cacti-strewn deserts, attended every festival possible (many – this is Mexico!), consumed kilos of *gorditas* (baked corn-dough cakes) – until she became a bit *gordita* (plump) herself – and talked and danced her way through the magic of Mexico. At other times, she is a freelance writer, based in Australia. Kate's freelance writing adventures appear at www.katearmstrong.com.au.

Ray Bartlett

Baja California Ray first fell in love with Mexico in college, and now divides his time between a casita in Baja California Sur and a house on Cape Cod. He has written about Mexico for more than a decade, and his other Lonely Planet titles include *Japan, Yucatán, New England Trips* and *Korea*. When not traveling, he surfs, writes fiction, drinks way too much coffee and burns way too much midnight oil. For more about Ray visit his website, www.kaisora.com.

Gregor Clark

Central Pacific Coast Gregor's love affair with Mexico began three decades ago, on a multiday bus ride from San Francisco to a summer volunteer project in Oaxaca, eating homemade *tamales* under a sky full of incomparably brilliant Sonoran Desert stars. His travels since then have focused on Mexico's Pacific coast. Favorite memories from this trip include butterfly-spotting in the Sierra Madre, releasing baby turtles into the Pacific and cooking *chiles rellenos* in Zihuatanejo. Gregor has authored more than 20 titles for Lonely Planet since 2000.

OVER PAGE MORE WRITERS

Published by Lonely Planet Publications Pty Ltd
ABN 36 005 607 983
13th edition – Sep 2012
ISBN 978 1 74220 016 3
© Lonely Planet 2012   Photographs © as indicated 2012
10 9 8 7 6 5 4 3 2 1
Printed in Singapore

Bestselling guide to Mexico – source: Nielsen BookScan, Australia, UK and USA, April 2011 to March 2012